Berlin Transit

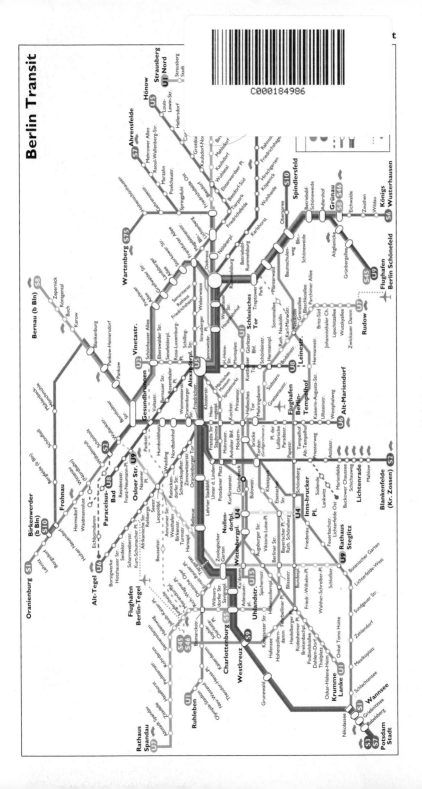

Munich Transit

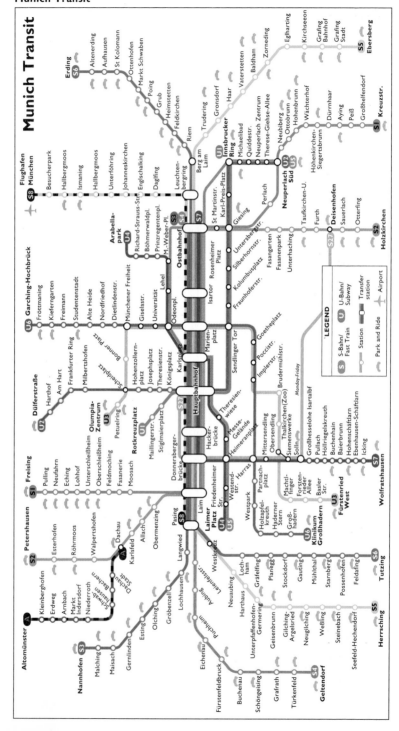

Hamburg Transit

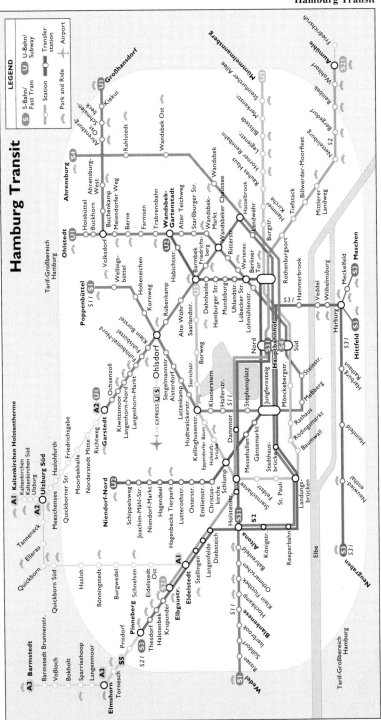

Frankfurt Transit

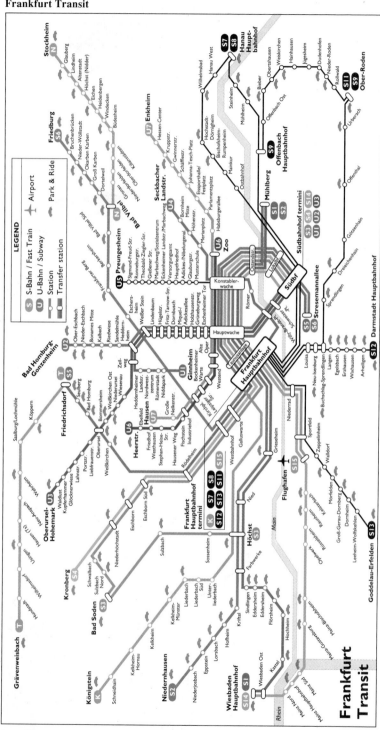

LET'S GO:
Germany

"Lighthearted and sophisticated, informative and fun to read. *[Let's Go]* helps the novice traveler navigate like a knowledgeable old hand."
—*Atlanta Journal-Constitution*

"The guides are aimed not only at young budget travelers but at the independent traveler, a sort of streetwise cookbook for traveling alone."
—*The New York Times*

■ Let's Go writers travel on your budget.

"Retains the spirit of the student-written publication it is: candid, opinionated, resourceful, amusing info for the traveler of limited means but broad curiosity."
—*Mademoiselle*

"The writers seem to have experienced every rooster-packed bus and lunar-surfaced mattress about which they write."
—*The New York Times*

"All the dirt, dirt cheap."
—*People*

■ Great for independent travelers.

"A world-wise traveling companion—always ready with friendly advice and helpful hints, all sprinkled with a bit of wit."
—*The Philadelphia Inquirer*

"Lots of valuable information for any independent traveler."
—*The Chicago Tribune*

■ Let's Go is completely revised each year.

"Unbeatable: good sight-seeing advice; up-to-date info on restaurants, hotels, and inns; a commitment to money-saving travel; and a wry style that brightens nearly every page."
—*The Washington Post*

"Its yearly revision by a new crop of Harvard students makes it as valuable as ever."
—*The New York Times*

■ All the important information you need.

"Enough information to satisfy even the most demanding of budget travelers...*Let's Go* follows the creed that you don't have to toss your life's savings to the wind to travel—unless you want to."
—*The Salt Lake Tribune*

"Value-packed, unbeatable, accurate, and comprehensive."
—*The Los Angeles Times*

Let's Go Publications

Let's Go: Alaska & the Pacific Northwest 1998
Let's Go: Australia 1998 **New title!**
Let's Go: Austria & Switzerland 1998
Let's Go: Britain & Ireland 1998
Let's Go: California 1998
Let's Go: Central America 1998
Let's Go: Eastern Europe 1998
Let's Go: Ecuador & the Galápagos Islands 1998
Let's Go: Europe 1998
Let's Go: France 1998
Let's Go: Germany 1998
Let's Go: Greece & Turkey 1998
Let's Go: India & Nepal 1998
Let's Go: Ireland 1998
Let's Go: Israel & Egypt 1998
Let's Go: Italy 1998
Let's Go: London 1998
Let's Go: Mexico 1998
Let's Go: New York City 1998
Let's Go: New Zealand 1998 **New title!**
Let's Go: Paris 1998
Let's Go: Rome 1998
Let's Go: Southeast Asia 1998
Let's Go: Spain & Portugal 1998
Let's Go: USA 1998
Let's Go: Washington, D.C. 1998

Let's Go Map Guides

Berlin	New Orleans
Boston	New York City
Chicago	Paris
London	Rome
Los Angeles	San Francisco
Madrid	Washington, D.C.

Coming Soon: Amsterdam, Florence

**Let's Go
Publications**

LET'S GO
Germany
1998

Måns O. Larsson
Editor

Alexander Z. Speier
Associate Editor

Jennifer R. Weiss
Assistant Editor

Macmillan

HELPING LET'S GO

If you want to share your discoveries, suggestions, or corrections, please drop us a line. We read every piece of correspondence, whether a postcard, a 10-page email, or a coconut. Please note that mail received after May 1998 may be too late for the 1999 book, but will be kept for future editions. **Address mail to:**

> **Let's Go: Germany**
> **67 Mount Auburn Street**
> **Cambridge, MA 02138**
> **USA**

Visit Let's Go at **http://www.letsgo.com,** or send email to:

> **fanmail@letsgo.com**
> **Subject: "Let's Go: Germany"**

In addition to the invaluable travel advice our readers share with us, many are kind enough to offer their services as researchers or editors. Unfortunately, our charter enables us to employ only currently enrolled Harvard-Radcliffe students.

Published in Great Britain 1998 by Macmillan, an imprint of Macmillan General Books, 25 Eccleston Place, London SW1W 9NF and Basingstoke.

Maps by David Lindroth copyright © 1998, 1997, 1996, 1995, 1994, 1993, 1992, 1991, 1990, 1989, 1988 by St. Martin's Press, Inc.

Map revisions pp. xii, xiii, xiv, xv, 89, 92, 93, 95, 135, 147, 173, 181, 183, 199, 207, 227, 247, 249, 271, 317, 339, 357, 359, 383, 389, 411, 413, 425, 441, 447, 455, 465, 468, 469, 517, 541 by Let's Go, Inc.

Published in the United States of America by St. Martin's Press, Inc.

ISBN: 0 333 71179 3

First edition
10 9 8 7 6 5 4 3 2 1

Let's Go: Germany is written by Let's Go Publications, 67 Mount Auburn Street, Cambridge, MA 02138, USA.

Let's Go® and the thumb logo are trademarks of Let's Go, Inc.
Printed in the USA on recycled paper with biodegradable soy ink.

ADVERTISING DISCLAIMER

Contents

About Let's Go

Back in 1960, a few students at Harvard University banded together to produce a 20-page pamphlet offering a collection of tips on budget travel in Europe. This modest, mimeographed packet, offered as an extra to passengers on student charter flights to Europe, met with instant popularity. The following year, students traveling to Europe researched the first, full-fledged edition of *Let's Go: Europe*, a pocket-sized book featuring honest, irreverent writing and a decidedly youthful outlook on the world. Throughout the 60s, our guides reflected the times; the 1969 guide to America led off by inviting travelers to "dig the scene" at San Francisco's Haight-Ashbury. During the 70s and 80s, we gradually added regional guides and expanded coverage into the Middle East and Central America. With the addition of our in-depth city guides, handy map guides, and extensive coverage of Asia and Australia, the 90s are also proving to be a time of explosive growth for Let's Go, and there's certainly no end in sight. The first editions of *Let's Go: Australia* and *Let's Go: New Zealand* hit the shelves this year, expanding our coverage to six continents, and research for next year's series has already begun.

We've seen a lot in 38 years. *Let's Go: Europe* is now the world's bestselling international guide, translated into seven languages. And our new guides bring Let's Go's total number of titles, with their spirit of adventure and their reputation for honesty, accuracy, and editorial integrity, to 40. But some things never change: our guides are still researched, written, and produced entirely by students who know first-hand how to see the world on the cheap.

HOW WE DO IT

Each guide is completely revised and thoroughly updated every year by a well-traveled set of over 200 students. Every winter, we recruit over 140 researchers and 60 editors to write the books anew. After several months of training, Researcher-Writers hit the road for seven weeks of exploration, from Anchorage to Adelaide, Estonia to El Salvador, Iceland to Indonesia. Hired for their rare combination of budget travel sense, writing ability, stamina, and courage, these adventurous travelers know that train strikes, stolen luggage, food poisoning, and marriage proposals are all part of a day's work. Back at our offices, editors work from spring to fall, massaging copy written on Himalayan bus rides into witty yet informative prose. A student staff of typesetters, cartographers, publicists, and managers keeps our lively team together. In September, the collected efforts of the summer are delivered to our printer, who turns them into books in record time, so that you have the most up-to-date information available for your vacation. And even as you read this, work on next year's editions is well underway.

WHY WE DO IT

We don't think of budget travel as the last recourse of the destitute; we believe that it's the only way to travel. Living cheaply and simply brings you closer to the people and places you've been saving up to visit. Our books will ease your anxieties and answer your questions about the basics—so you can get off the beaten track and explore. Once you learn the ropes, we encourage you to put *Let's Go* down now and then to strike out on your own. As any seasoned traveler will tell you, the best discoveries are often those you make yourself. When you find something worth sharing, drop us a line. We're Let's Go Publications, 67 Mount Auburn St., Cambridge, MA 02138, USA (email: fanmail@letsgo.com).

HAPPY TRAVELS!

Maps

Color Maps

Researcher-Writers

Megan Brenn-White   *Sachsen, Sachsen-Anhalt, Thüringen*

Megan emerged from nowhere to save this book from the treacherous Lorelei beckoning it towards disaster. Armed with a remarkable knowledge of German culture and exhilarating enthusiasm, she wandered through regions both mystic and sublime with a fantastic eye for the bizarre. She majestically swooped through the Harz Mountains before toppling the intellectual houses of cards upon which Thüringen rests. From the heavens, Megan fearlessly dove underground to bring us the subterranean pleasures of Freiberg's silver mines. Never weary, she went on to bring us the majesty of Dresden and its astounding surroundings in detail so vivid it left us crying for more. Good luck in London next year! Cheers. Megan thanks Scott Richardson.

Eric Kurlander   *Hessen, Niedersachsen, Nordrhein-Westfalen*

You can take the boy out of Chicago, but you can't take the Bulls out of the boy. With the smoothness of Scottie Pippen (but less dyed hair than Dennis Rodman), Eric kicked it old school as he informed us of German historical nuances left and right. After casting aspersions upon the bankruptcy of consumerism in the Frisian Duty Free Dash, Eric slammed home the skinny on the Peace of Westphalia and its impending 350th anniversary before exposing the ennui of modernity at documenta X. Leaving no stones unturned (except for the *Externsteine*), Eric found nightlife where there was none to be found, and reinvented it in places where it did exist. For his ventures and the piece of Americana which he infused into Deutschland, a mighty *Prost!*

Kate McCarthy   *Bayern, Frankfurt, Sächsische Schweiz, Zittauer Gebirge*

The eagerly anticipated departure of Kate did not disappoint, as our goddess of the seas alighted from the shores, pen in hand, to attack southern Germany with unflagging aim. While hypertraveling to the extravagant *Königschlösser,* she impressed with her incisive wit and poignant prose, leaving Mad King Ludwig crazier than ever before. Kate's magnificent demeanor helped her to swiftly recuperate after falling sick in Munich, as new-found friends treated her like a queen. She was soon back on the road, winding through the Romantische Straße. Leaving Bayern with a stamp of her own, she sported her *Lederhosen* in Sächsische Schweiz, enlightening us with her stories about the Sorbs and their funky traditions. Top o' thy world ma!

Douglas S. Muller   *Baden-Württemberg, Rheinland-Pfalz*

We hit the jackpot with Doug, whose rich and lively prose never crapped out. After being treated like a New York rock star in the Rhine Gorge by German *Schulkinder,* he showed us what's new (pussycat) on his 1997 World Tour (including the spas and casinos of Baden-Baden and Karlsruhe), in the process becoming more popular than Tom Jones. His pen sang the melodies of the Schwarzwald, incorporating the mystique and fantasy of the region, outplaying the Brothers Grimm in a literary game of Black Jack. Never short of energy, Doug fought off the dragons of Castle Drachenfels, challenged his palate with vintage Moseltal and a diet of Worms, and showed the world it's possible to party like it's 1999 in Bonn. We can't wait for the reunion tour.

Stu Shapley   *Berlin, Mecklenburg-Vorpommern, Schleswig-Holstein*

Our own Hunter S. Thompson, Stu shocked the world when he exploded onto the German landscape with frantic energy. Stu's fearless journey began with a refined detail of Hamburg erotica before he let it all hang out in Sylt. He shivered through the rainy streets of Lübeck, never batting an eye in confrontations with the Brothers Mann and Ernst-isn't-there-anything-else-to-do-here-Barlach. Giving a big *Stinkefinger* to Mecklenburg-Vorpommern, Stu took the soul to the hole in Berlin, offering a sophisticated account of the city's metamorphosis. By night, he was the bomb, blowing up the city's nightlife and the Love Parade, leaving *Schläger* in shambles. After Stu, the Little Pony shall ride no more. He thanks Mike for keeping pace.

Acknowledgments

Gemütlich thanks to: Jake, who kept everything afloat; Andrew, our fearless leader who rocked our collective world; the receptionists (esp. Creek!) for runnin' the lines; #Prod, for resolving the dilemmas of our epileptic computers; Anne, for keeping Jake afloat; the maps team, for indulging us in cartographical delight; and the whole damn office, for making this a fantabulous summer, daily, 24hr.—**GER**

Mighty thanks to Alex, who never failed to both inspire and surprise me with incisive Simpsonesque bons mots and insights into the paradox that is Germany. Jenny's enthusiasm and diligence kept us goin' at all hours. Thanks! Honored be Sir Nieland, whose invaluable guidance and crazy wisdom kept me on track…most of the time. Love to Robyn for always being there; Miss Gates for many dizzying days of dreamin'. Maciej, A4 and M&M never die…Taimur, Genius corner bathroom perseveres! Habyarimana, thanks for past encouragement. D&B you are not forgotten. Mamma, Pappa, Hanna, Elisabet ("keep jazzin'") thanks for your love and support.—**MOL**

Thanks and praised be to Måns, whose wit kept me going and whose name showed me the value of a hat to keep one's vowels warm. *Prost!* to Jenny, whose enthusiasm kept us boomin'. To Andrew, infinite gratitude for putting up with myriad Simpsons refs and for representin', not frontin'. *Danke*s to: Young Spacey, Aaron, Matt, Chuck, and Drew for makin' Homer Sq. the place to be; DF, without whom I'd be jobless; Jake for bein' the bomb; Smitty for bein' the Firestarter; Chunky just cuz; Lucy, Mai, and Ilsa. Love to Mom, Dad, Grampa, Bobie, and Suze.—**AZS**

Danke, Måns; your levelheaded direction kept it all together; and Alex, so mellow, so knowledgable, so vastly funky. Jake and Andrew, thanks for impeccable leadership and unstoppable kindness. Taya and Adam of I&E, thanks for being my home and promised land. Thanks to Alan and FAP for food and company (esp. Helen), and to the FDO for housing. Mom and Dad, I love you very much. To my man in Seattle and Japan, Lonne Allen Jaffe, thanks for making me feel a little crazy.—**JRW**

Editor	Måns O. Larsson
Associate Editor	Alexander Z. Speier
Assitant Editor	Jennifer R. Weiss
Managing Editor	Andrew E. Nieland
Publishing Director	John R. Brooks
Production Manager	Melanie Quintana Kansil
Associate Production Manager	David Collins
Cartography Manager	Sara K. Smith
Editorial Manager	Melissa M. Reyen
Editorial Manager	Emily J. Stebbins
Financial Manager	Krzysztof Owerkowicz
Personnel Manager	Andrew E. Nieland
Publicity Manager	Nicholas Corman
Publicity Manager	Kate Galbraith
New Media Manager	Daniel O. Williams
Associate Cartographer	Joseph E. Reagan
Associate Cartographer	Luke Z. Fenchel
Office Coordinators	Emily Bowen, Charles Kapelke
	Laurie Santos
Director of Advertising Sales	Todd L. Glaskin
Senior Sales Executives	Matthew R. Hillery, Joseph W. Lind
	Peter J. Zakowich, Jr.
President	Amit Tiwari
General Manager	Richard Olken
Assistant General Manager	Anne E. Chisholm

Let's Go Picks

After a summer of wandering and wishing, we at *Let's Go: Germany* have come up with our list of the best of the best. We tracked celestial movements, consulted our in-house research team, and flew in experts from abroad. You've been dreaming this moment would come. So now, without further ado, the winners are …

Best Cathedral: Any heathens who set their eyes on the **Köln Cathedral** (p. 320) immediately drop to the ground and repent for their evil deeds. The *Dom* is a singularly spectacular, titanic, and awe-inspiring phenomenon. The result of centuries of hard work have paid off in spades. In **1998** Köln will celebrate the **750th anniversary** of the laying of the *Dom*'s foundation with its typical verve for *Karnevals*.

Best Clubs: Astoundingly, Munich comes up big with nightlife beyond its beer culture. **Kunstpark Ost** (p. 488) packs the entire city into 27 different venues in one giant, teeming complex. Take that, Berlin! Berlin responds to the challenge, however, snorting indignantly and proclaiming that on **Love Parade** (p. 127) weekend, any of its clubs make Munich's *Biergartens* look like *Kindergarten*. Try as it may, Munich just can't match the superfly hipster vibe of **Insel der Jugend** (p. 129).

Best Liqueur: A delectable, 100-proof, blackberry *Schnapps* **Black Haus** (p. 84) beats both *Jägermeister* and *Kirschwasser*. Say no more!

Best Gardens: The magnificently manicured gardens of the island of **Mainau** (p. 458) enchant with colorful, gargantuan animals made out of flowers, exotic butterflies, and a tropical climate not found elsewhere in Germany. The palm-trees planted around the island's palace add to the magical feel of the place, offering a delicious respite from the glass and steel of modernity.

Best Hostel: Jugendherberge Stahleck (p. 388) in Bacharach, indulges your most lush regal fantasies. Situated in a castle, the hostel amply satisfies its guests with a wine-sampling bar, almost as intoxicating as the panorama of the Rhine Gorge.

Best Laundromat: Groove Station, in Dresden (p. 148). Come for the wash 'n' dry. Stay to see in-house tattoo-ings and body-piercings. (Dirty) dance into it.

Best Monarchs: Bavaria's **Mad King Ludwig** built bombastic castles that became the stuff of legend. **Neuschwanstein** and **Hohenschwangau** make Disneyland look like *Bauhaus* (p. 498). Still, everyone and their Ma knows about the Crazy one; a defenestration is in order. **Elector August the Strong** (p. 152) of Sachsen laced Dresden and his empire with fantastic castles, and he didn't have to bankrupt his kingdom to do so. So many castles did the Elector build, in fact, that travelers can now **buy some of them** for DM1 (p. 169).

Best Spas: Baden-Baden may seem the exclusive playground of the rich and famous, but you'll thank yourself for making a small investment and de-vestment at the **Caracalla-Thermen** (p. 439). Lounge in the aqua-salons of this marble palace while getting whirlpooled and steamed into therapeutic bliss. Thousands of dead (but happy) Romans couldn't all be wrong.

Best Travel Services: Alan Wissenberg's **EurAide** office in the Munich *Hauptbahnhof* is a godsend (p. 467). Wissenberg, an American emigré, knows anything and everything there is to know about travel in Germany. The folks at **DERTravel Services** (p. 43) also comes through big time in helping you to ride the rails of Deutsche Bahn. Finally, the **German National Tourist Office** (p. 1) provides infinite resources and a hefty dose of patience for folks gearing up for departure.

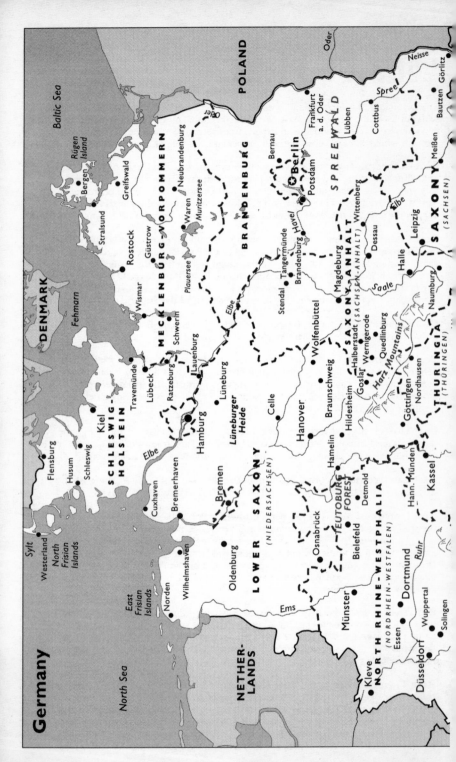

Germany

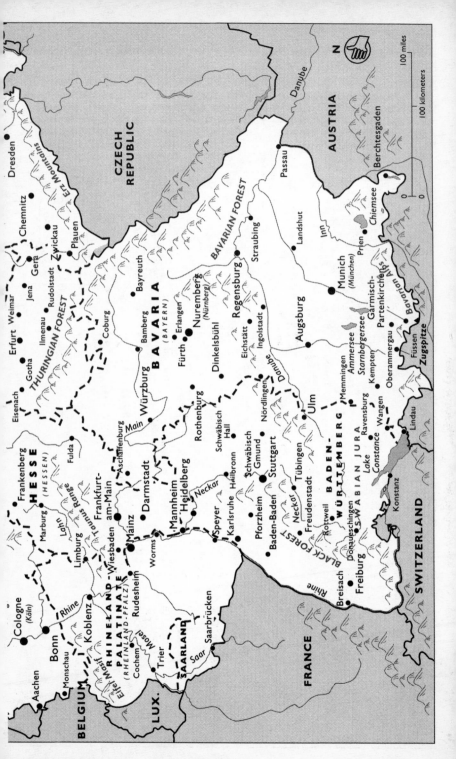

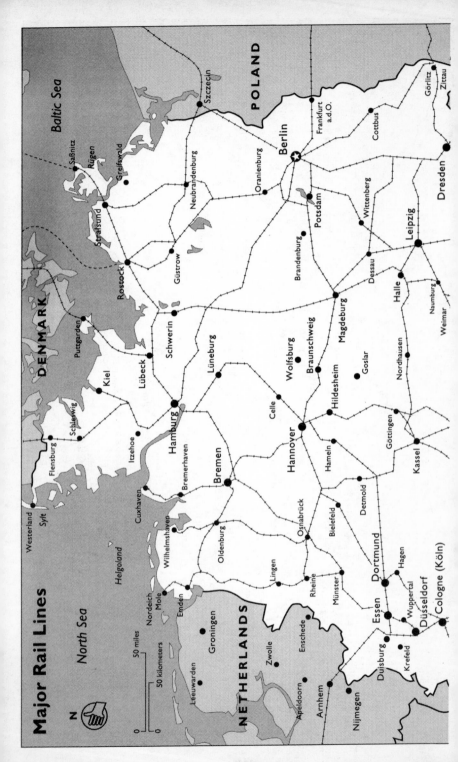

Major Rail Lines

North Sea

Baltic Sea

DENMARK

NETHERLANDS

POLAND

50 miles
50 kilometers

Westerland
Sylt
Nordeich Mole
Emden
Groningen
Leeuwarden
Apeldoorn
Enschede
Zwolle
Arnhem
Nijmegen
Krefeld
Duisburg
Essen
Dortmund
Hagen
Wuppertal
Düsseldorf
Cologne (Köln)
Münster
Rheine
Lingen
Osnabrück
Bielefeld
Detmold
Hameln
Kassel
Göttingen
Nordhausen
Weimar
Naumburg
Halle
Leipzig
Dresden
Görlitz
Zittau
Cottbus
Frankfurt a.d.O.
Berlin
Oranienburg
Neubrandenburg
Szczecin
Greifswald
Rügen
Saßnitz
Stralsund
Rostock
Güstrow
Schwerin
Lübeck
Putgarden
Kiel
Schleswig
Flensburg
Izehoe
Cuxhaven
Wilhelmshaven
Oldenburg
Bremerhaven
Bremen
Hamburg
Lüneburg
Celle
Hannover
Hildesheim
Goslar
Braunschweig
Wolfsburg
Magdeburg
Brandenburg
Potsdam
Dessau
Wittenberg
Helgoland

XIV

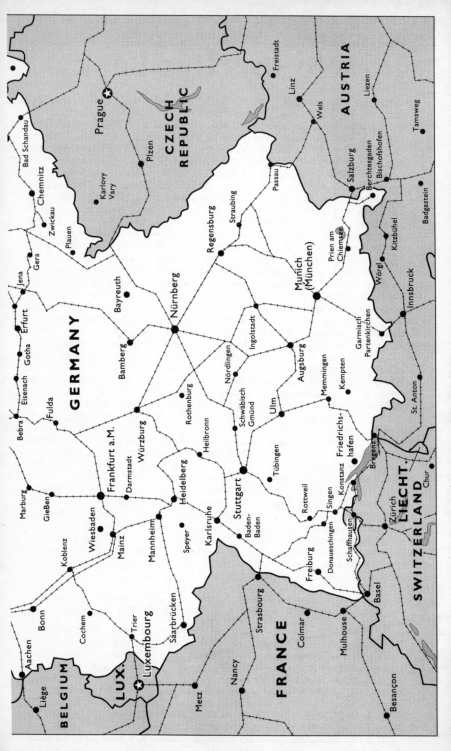

How to Use This Book

Singing the mantra of crazy, hectic travel in big cities, as well as the lullaby of relaxing moments on the beach and in the wilderness, *Let's Go: Germany* is a great companion as you zigzag across Germany. We cover the full spectrum—while this guide provides you with some juicy insights into Berlin's diverse (at times outright bizarre) nightlife, it also ventures into the lovely, serene hiking-paths of the Schwarzwald (the Black Forest). For your convenience, the book is divided into several sections.

The **Essentials** section helps to prepare you *before* the journey begins, giving you the skinny on how to plan a trip, how to get to Germany cheaply, and how to tackle the everyday aspects of life upon arrival. We also list important addresses of embassies, consulates, and budget travel agencies while discussing health and safety concerns. We also provide insight into some great ways to save a few Marks for both whirlwind travelers and folks thinking about settling down in Germany for a while.

In the **History and Culture** section, we trace German history from the Neanderthal era to the fall of the Berlin Wall and the subsequent reunification of East and West. We discuss the German literary, artistic, and philosophical traditions, elucidating the highlights of Goethe, the *Bauhaus* school, and Karl Marx. For the latest happenings in Germany check out This Year in Germany, and to find out more about Beethoven, Bach, and Kraftwerk, read the Music section. The Food and Drink section initiates you to the German beer culture, lays bare the nuances of sausage consumption, and lets you in on the delectable secret known as *Black Haus*. We also have a section on German social life, which guides you through customs and etiquette.

The **main part** of the book, the actual information about the cities, tiny towns, and lakes that you may visit, is roughly divided into Germany's *Länder* (Federal States), starting with Berlin and ending with Bayern. Each city/town is divided into sub-sections. **Orientation and Practical Information** directs you to resources, facilities, and transportation, while the **Food** and **Accommodations** sections list specific establishments by type, location, and quality. **Sights** sections, ranging from Romanesque cathedrals to nonsensical postmodern sculptures, help navigate the rich historical and contemporary offerings of Germany. **Entertainment** details the fantastic wealth of cultural events, while **Nightlife** covers anything from traditional beer gardens to electrifying techno clubs. We also provide listings for **Bisexual, Gay, and Lesbian** information centers, restaurants, and clubs.

The **Let's Go Picks** are our favorite establishments and other funk—you don't want to miss them. The **Appendix** informs you about festivals, climate, telephone codes, German pronunciation, and more. And don't forget to utilize our **Index**—so extensive, you might even track down the elusive Thomas Pynchon there.

Finally, a note **how not to use this book.** Use information and coverage as a guide, not a finalized itinerary. May your travels be delightful and exciting, and please don't hesitate to write to us, telling us about your adventures. Who knows? Perhaps you'll find a gem that we can include next year!

A NOTE TO OUR READERS

The information for this book is gathered by *Let's Go*'s researchers from late May through August. Each listing is derived from the assigned researcher's opinion based upon his or her visit at a particular time. The opinions are expressed in a candid and forthright manner. Other travelers might disagree. Those traveling at a different time may have different experiences since prices, dates, hours, and conditions are always subject to change. You are urged to check beforehand to avoid inconvenience and surprises. Travel always involves a certain degree of risk, especially in low-cost areas. When traveling, especially on a budget, always take particular care to ensure your safety.

ESSENTIALS

PLANNING YOUR TRIP

A fun and inexpensive trip to Germany requires preparation. For better or for worse, there is a big industry designed to help you and other travelers. The many organizations listed below, especially national tourist offices, will send you daunting mounds of literature. Dive in and plan a trip tailored to your specific interests. You can design an historical, hiking, even a beer tour of Germany. The possibilities are endless. Resist the urge to see everything, as a madcap schedule will detract from your enjoyment. If you try to see Berlin, Munich, and Köln in a week, you'll come away with only vague memories of train stations and youth hostels. Similarly, choose your traveling companions carefully—traveling with a group of friends may effectively insulate you from genuine intimacy with local culture. On the other hand, they will share food and lodging costs, provide extra safety in numbers, and often serve as invaluable sources of energy and comfort. Along your journey, you are certain to meet many fascinating folks; a lone traveler is never truly alone. Make sure to use the information provided by *Let's Go* and other sources to assemble your "support system," both in terms of what you bring and the arrangements you make. It's been said that all you really need are time and money, but on a budget voyage you don't want to waste either due to lack of planning.

■ When To Go

In July and August, temperatures, airfares, and tempers rise right along with the number of tourists. In winter months, some hostels hibernate and museum hours may be abbreviated. The cloudy, temperate months of May, June, and September are perhaps your best bet. But bear in mind that many school field trips to historic sites take place in June, and that youth hostels may be inundated with schoolchildren. Winter sports gear up in November and continue through April; high season for skiing hits in mid-December to mid-January and February to March. Germans head to vacation spots en masse with the onset of school vacations; airports and train stations become jammed and the traffic on the *Autobahn* can be measured in meters per hour. The staggering of vacation periods among the federal states has alleviated the crunch a tad, but you should still avoid trekking across Germany the day after school lets out, or risk being buried by throngs. See the **Appendix** for further holiday and weather information.

■ Useful Information

GOVERNMENT INFORMATION OFFICES

These official German outposts in your native country can be a great help in planning your trip; have them send you information and brochures before you leave. The **German National Tourist Offices** distribute useful publications such as *Travel Tips, Camping in Germany,* and *Youth Hostels.*

Australia: German-Australian Chamber of Industry and Commerce, PO Box A 980, Sydney South, NSW 1235 (tel. (02) 9267 8148; fax 9267 9035).
Canada: 175 Bloor St. East, North Tower, Suite 604, Toronto, Ont. M4W 3R8 (tel. (416) 968-1570; fax 968-1986; email germanto@idirect.com).
South Africa: 22 Girton Road, Parktown, PO Box 10883, Johannesburg 2000 (tel. (27 11) 643 16 15; fax 484 27 50).

U.K.: 34 Belgrave Square, London SW1X 8QB (tel. (0171) 824 1300; fax 824 1566; email@infoctr; http://www.german-embassy.org.uk).

U.S.: New York, 122 East 42nd St., 52nd Fl., 10168-0072 (tel. (212) 661-7200; fax 661-7174; email gntony@aol.com); **Los Angeles,** 11766 Wilshire Blvd., Ste. 750, 90025 (tel. (310) 575-9799; fax 575-1565; email gntolax@aol.com). The **German Information Center,** 950 Third Ave., New York, NY 10022 (tel. (212) 888-9840; fax 752-6691; email gic1@ix.netcom.com). Publishes *This Week in Germany,* a free newspaper for Americans.

TRAVEL ORGANIZATIONS

Council on International Educational Exchange (CIEE), 205 East 42nd St., New York, NY 10017-5706 (tel. (888) COUNCIL (268-6245); fax (212) 822-2699; http://www.ciee.org). A private, nonprofit organization, Council administers work, volunteer, academic, internship, and professional programs worldwide. They also offer identity cards (including the ISIC and the GO25) and a range of publications, among them the free magazine *Student Travels.* Call or write for more info.

Federation of International Youth Travel Organizations (FIYTO), Bredgade 25H, DK-1260 Copenhagen K, Denmark (tel. (45) 33 33 96 00; fax 33 93 96 76; email mailbox@fiyto.org; http://www.fiyto.org), is an international organization promoting educational, cultural, and social travel for young people. Member organizations include language schools, educational travel companies, national tourist boards, accommodation centers, and other suppliers of travel services to youth and students. FIYTO sponsors the GO25 Card (http://www.go25.org).

International Student Travel Confederation, Herengracht 479, 1017 BS Amsterdam, The Netherlands (tel. (31) 20 421 2800; fax 20 421 2810; email istcinfo@istc.org; http://www.istc.org). The ISTC is a nonprofit confederation of student travel organizations whose focus is to develop, promote, and facilitate travel among young people and students. Member organizations include International Student Surface Travel Association (ISSA), Student Air Travel Association (SATA), IASIS Travel Insurance, the International Association for Educational and Work Exchange Programs (IAEWEP), and the International Student Identity Card Association (ISIC).

USEFUL PUBLICATIONS

The publications we list here should be useful in preparation for your trip. If you're interested in books on culture or history, see **Further Reading,** p. 74.

Atlantik-Brücke, Adenauerallee 131, 53113 Bonn (tel. (0228) 21 41 60; fax 21 46 59). Devoted to promoting mutual understanding (hence "Atlantic Bridge"), it publishes *These Strange German Ways*—a must for any American planning on living in Germany—as well as *Meet United Germany, German Holidays and Folk Customs,* and *Speaking Out: Jewish Voices from United Germany.*

Blue Guides, published in Britain by A&C Black Limited, 35 Bedford Row, London WC1R 4JH, in the U.S. by W.W. Norton & Co. Inc., 500 Fifth Ave., New York, NY 10110, and in Canada by Penguin Books Canada Ltd., 10 Alcorn Ave. #300, Toronto, Ont. N4V 3B2. Blue Guides provide invaluable and unmatched historical and cultural information as well as sight-seeing routes, maps, tourist information, and listings of pricey hotels.

Bon Voyage!, 2069 W. Bullard Ave., Fresno, CA 93711-1200 (tel. (800) 995-9716, from abroad (209) 447-8441; fax 266-6460; email 70754.3511@compuserve.com). Annual mail order catalogue offers a range of products. Books, travel accessories, luggage, electrical converters, maps, and videos. All merchandise may be returned for exchange or refund within 30 days of purchase, and prices are guaranteed (lower advertised prices will be matched and merchandise shipped free).

The College Connection, Inc., 1295 Prospect St. Ste. B, La Jolla, CA 92037 (tel. (619) 551-9770; fax 551-9987; email eurailnow@aol.com; http://www.eurailpass.com). Publishes *The Passport,* a booklet listing hints about every aspect of traveling and studying abroad. This booklet is free to *Let's Go* readers; send your request by email or fax only.

Forsyth Travel Library, Inc., 1750 East 131st Street, P.O. Box 480800, Kansas City, MO 64148 (tel. (800) 367-7984; fax (816) 942-6969; email forsyth@avi.net; http://www.forsyth.com). A mail-order service that stocks a wide range of maps and guides for rail and ferry travel in Europe; also sells rail tickets and passes, and offers reservation services. Sells the *Thomas Cook European Timetable* for trains, a complete guide to European train departures and arrivals (US$28, with full map of European train routes $39, postage for priority shipping $4.50). Call or write for a free catalogue, or visit their web site.

Hunter Publishing, P.O. Box 7816, Edison, NJ 08818 (tel. (908) 225-1900; fax 417-0482; email hunterpub@emi.net; http://www.hunterpublishing.com). Has an extensive catalogue of travel books, guides, language learning tapes, and quality maps, among them *Charming Small Hotel Guides* for Germany (US$15).

Transitions Abroad, P.O. Box 1300, 18 Hulst Rd., Amherst, MA 01004-1300 (tel. (800) 293-0373; fax 256-0373; email trabroad@aol.com; http://transabroad.com). Invaluable magazine lists publications and resources for overseas study, work, and volunteering (single copy US$6.25, 6 issues $25). Also publishes *The Alternative Travel Directory,* a comprehensive guide to living, learning, and working overseas (US$20, postage $4).

INTERNET RESOURCES

Along with everything else in the 90s, budget travel is moving rapidly into the information age, with the **Internet** as a leading travel resource. Today, people can make their own airline, hotel, hostel, or car rental reservations on the Internet, and connect personally with others abroad, allowing people to become their own budget travel planners. **NetTravel: How Travelers Use the Internet,** by Michael Shapiro, is a very thorough and informative guide which describes the different uses of the Internet and how they are most useful for travelers (US$25).

There are a number of ways to access the **Internet.** Most popular are commercial Internet services, such as **America Online** (tel. (800) 827-6364) and **CompuServe** (tel. (800) 433-0389). Many employers and schools also offer gateways to the Internet, often at no cost (unlike the corporate gateways above). The hardware and software you need to access the Internet should be readily available at a local computer store or through mail-order. The forms of the Internet most useful to budget travelers are the World Wide Web and Usenet newsgroups.

The World Wide Web

Increasingly the Internet forum of choice, the **World Wide Web** provides its users with text, graphics and sound. This and the huge proliferation of web pages (individual sites within the World Wide Web) have made the Web the most active and exciting toy on the Internet, though it has also made it the newest path from corporate advertisers to the minds of the masses. The Web's lack of hierarchy makes it difficult to distinguish between good information, bad information, and marketing. **Search engines** (services that search for web pages under specific subjects) can significantly aid the search process. **Lycos** (http://a2z.lycos.com), **Infoseek** (http://guide.infoseek.com), and **HOTBOT** (http://www.hotbot.com) are among the most popular. **Yahoo!** is a slightly more organized search engine; check out its travel links at http://www.yahoo.com/Recreation/Travel. Another good way to explore is to find a good site and go from there, through links from one web page to another. A search tool for Germany is the suffix web.de. Check out **Let's Go's web site** (http://www.letsgo.com) and find our newsletter, information about our books, an always-current list of links, and more. Or, you can try some of our favorites sites directly:

Big World Magazine (http://www.paonline.com/bigworld), a budget travel 'zine, has a web page with a great collection of links to travel pages.

Camping Site Guide of Germany (http://www.campingweb.com) is an invaluable resource for planning camping trips through Germany, with info about camping sites and the cities in which they are located in five languages.

City.Net (http://city.net/countries/germany) links into tourist information servers in numerous cities. Information on sights, entertainment, and accommodations.

German Information Office (http://germany-info.org/sites/travel.htm) in New York has great links to other sites pertaining to Germany, including detailed overviews and contact references for many cities.

German Tourist Board (http://www.germany-tourism.de) offers the low-down on major festivals and cultural events, tourist tips, and some great photography.

Internet Resources for Germany (http://www.eline.com/Goethe/Net-Sources.html), produced by the Goethe-Institut, explores every nook and cranny of the *Infoautobahn* in Germany, including newspapers, fellowships and academic pursuits, cultural information, and insights into travel and accommodations.

Oskar's Magazine (http://www.oskars.de) is an e-zine for youth and travelers in Germany. It offers the skinny on travel bargains in English and German.

Shoestring Travel (http://www.stratpub.com) is a budget travel e-zine, with feature articles, links, user exchange, and accommodations information.

The Student and Budget Travel Guide (http://asa.ugl.lib.umich.edu/chdocs/travel/travel-guide.html) gives info on accommodations, transportation, packing, and more.

TravelHUB (http://www.travelhub.com) is a great site for cheap travel deals.

The Cybercafes of Europe (http://www.xs4all.nl/~bertb/cybercaf.html) has links to a wide array of cybercafes in Europe and Germany.

Web sites are ephemeral, and a site that's slammin' one week might disappear the next, and a new one might quickly replace it. Thus, as with normal travel, it is important for you to head out on your own in cyber-travel as well.

Usenet Newsgroups

Another popular source of information are **newsgroups,** which are forums for discussion of specific topics. There are thousands of different newsgroups and more crop up every day, so information is available on almost every imaginable topic. In some cases this proliferation has become over-extension; the quality of discussion is often poor, and you often have to wade through nonsense to find useful information. Despite this, there are still a number of useful newsgroups for the traveler.

Usenet, the name for the family of newsgroups, can be accessed easily from most Internet gateways. In UNIX systems, a good newsreader is "tin" (just type "tin" at the prompt). Most commercial providers offer access to Usenet, and often have their own version of Usenet, limited to the members of the provider, which has similar information. "Clari-net" posts AP news wires for many different topics, such as **clari.world.europe.germany.**

■ Documents & Formalities

All applications should be filed several weeks or months in advance of your planned departure date. Remember that you are relying on government agencies to complete these transactions. Demand for passports is highest between January and August, so try to apply as early as possible. A backlog in processing can spoil your plans.

When you travel, always carry on your person two or more forms of identification, including at least one photo ID. A passport combined with a driver's license or birth certificate usually serves as adequate proof of your identity and citizenship. Many establishments, especially banks, require several IDs before cashing traveler's checks. Never carry all your forms of ID together, however—you risk being left entirely without ID or funds in case of theft or loss. Also carry several extra passport-size photos that you can attach to the sundry IDs or railpasses you will eventually acquire. If you are planning an extended stay, register your passport with the nearest embassy or consulate.

GERMAN EMBASSIES AND CONSULATES

The German embassy or consulate in your home country can supply you with legal information concerning your trip, arrange for visas, and direct you to a wealth of other information about tourism, education, and employment in Germany.

Australian Embassy, 119 Empire Circuit, Yarralumla, ACT 2600 (tel. (02) 6270 1911; fax 6270 1951); **Consulates, South Yarra, Vic.,** 480 Punt Rd., 3141 (tel. (03) 9828 6888; fax 9820 2414); another consulate in Wollahra, NSW.

Canadian Embassy, 1 Waverly St., Ottawa, Ont. K2P OT8 (tel. (613) 232-1101; fax 594-9330; email 100566.2620@compuserve.com). **Consulates, Montréal** 1250 René-Lévesque Ouest, Edifice Marathon, Etage 43, H3B 4X1 (tel. (514) 931-2277; fax 931-7239); other consulates in Toronto, Winnipeg, Calgary, and Vancouver.

Irish Embassy, 31 Trimleston Ave., Booterstown, Blackrock, Co. Dublin (tel. (01) 269 30 11 or 269 31 23; fax 269 39 46).

New Zealander Embassy, 90-92 Hobson St., Thorndon, Wellington (tel. (04) 473 6063; fax 473 6069).

South African Embassy, 180 Blackwood St., Arcadia, Pretoria 0083 (tel. (2712) 344 3854 59; fax 343 9401). **Consulate, Cape Town** 825 St. Martini Gardens, Queen Victoria St., 8001 (tel. (021) 24 24 10; fax 24 94 03).

U.K. Embassy, 23 Belgrave Sq., London SW1X 8PZ (tel. (0171) 824 1300; fax 824 1435; email mail@german-embassy.org.uk). **Consulates, Manchester** Westminster House, 11 Portlant St., M60 1HY (tel. (0161) 237 5255; fax 237 5244); **Edinburgh,** 16 Eglinton Crescent, EH12 5DG, Scotland (tel. (0131) 337 2323; fax 346 1578).

U.S. Embassy, 4645 Reservoir Rd. NW, Washington, DC 20007-1998 (tel. (202) 298-8140; fax 298-4249; http://www.germany-info.org). **Consulates, New York,** 460 Park Ave., 10022 (tel. (212) 308-8700; fax 308-3422); **Los Angeles,** 6222 Wilshire Blvd., Ste. 500, 90048 (tel. (213) 930-2703; fax 930-2805); other consulates in Atlanta, Boston, Chicago, Detroit, Houston, San Francisco, and Seattle.

PASSPORTS

Before you leave, photocopy the page of your passport that contains your photograph, passport number, and other identifying information. Carry one photocopy in a safe place apart from your passport, and leave another copy at home. These measures will help prove your citizenship and facilitate the issuing of a new passport if you lose the original document. Consulates also recommend that you carry an expired passport or an official copy of your birth certificate in a part of your baggage separate from other documents.

If you do lose your passport, immediately notify the local police and the nearest embassy or consulate of your home government. To expedite its replacement, you will need to know all information previously recorded and show identification and proof of citizenship. A replacement may take weeks to process, and it may be valid only for a limited time. Some consulates can issue new passports within 24 hours if you give them proof of citizenship. Any visas stamped in your old passport will be irretrievably lost. In an emergency, ask for immediate temporary traveling papers that will permit you to reenter your home country.

Your passport is a public document belonging to your nation's government. You may have to surrender it to a foreign government official, but if you don't get it back in a reasonable amount of time, inform the nearest mission of your home country.

Australia: Citizens must apply for a passport in person at a post office, a passport office, or an Australian diplomatic mission overseas. An appointment may be necessary. Passport offices are located in Adelaide, Brisbane, Canberra City, Darwin, Hobart, Melbourne, Newcastle, Perth, and Sydney. A parent may file an application for unmarried children under 18. Adult 10-year passports cost AUS\$126 (for a 32 page passport) or AUS\$188 (64 page), and a child's 5-year passport is AUS\$63 (32 page) or AUS\$94 (64 page). For more info, call toll-free (in Australia) 13 12 32.

Canada: Application forms in English and French are available at all passport offices, Canadian missions, many travel agencies, and Northern Stores in northern communities. Citizens may apply in person at any 1 of 28 regional Passport Offices across Canada. Canadian citizens residing abroad should contact the nearest Canadian embassy or consulate. Children under 16 may be included on a parent's passport. Passports cost CDN$60, are valid for 5 years, and are not renewable. Processing takes approximately 5 business days for applications in person; 10 days if by mail. For additional info, contact the **Canadian Passport Office,** Department of Foreign Affairs and International Trade, Ottawa, ON, K1A 0G3 (tel. (613) 994-3500; http://www.dfait-maeci.gc.ca/passport). Travelers may also call (800) 567-6868 (24hr.); in Toronto (416) 973-3251; in Vancouver (604) 775-6250; in Montréal (514) 283-2152. Refer to the booklet *Bon Voyage, But...*, free at any passport office or by calling **InfoCentre** at (800) 267-8376, for further help and a list of Canadian embassies and consulates abroad. You may also find entry and background information for various countries by contacting the **Consular Affairs Bureau** in Ottawa (tel. (800) 267-6788 (24hr.) or (613) 944-6788).

Ireland: Citizens can apply for a passport by mail to either the **Department of Foreign Affairs,** Passport Office, Setanta Centre, Molesworth St., Dublin 2 (tel. (01) 671 1633), or the Passport Office, **Irish Life Building,** 1A South Mall, Cork (tel. (021) 272 525). Obtain an application at a local Garda station or request one from a passport office. The new Passport Express Service, available through post offices, allows citizens to get a passport in 2 weeks for an extra IR£3. Passports cost IR£45 and are valid for 10 years. Citizens under 18 or over 65 can request a 3-year passport that costs IR£10.

New Zealand: Application forms for passports are available in New Zealand from travel agents and Department of Internal Affairs Link Centres in the main cities and towns. Overseas, forms and passport services are provided by New Zealand embassies, high commissions, and consulates. Applications may also be forwarded to the Passport Office, P.O. Box 10526, Wellington, New Zealand. Standard processing time in New Zealand is 10 working days for correct applications. The fee for adults is NZ$80, children NZ$40. An urgent passport service is also available for an extra NZ$80. Different fees apply at overseas post: nine posts including London, Sydney, and Los Angeles offer both standard and **urgent services** (adults NZ$130, children NZ$65, plus NZ$130 if urgent). The fee at other posts is adult NZ$260, child NZ$195, and a passport will be issued within three working days. Children's names can no longer be endorsed on a parent's passport—they must apply for their own, which are valid for up to 5 years. An adult's passport is valid for up to 10 years.

South Africa: Citizens can apply for a passport at any **Home Affairs Office** or **South African Mission.** Tourist passports, valid for 10 years, cost SAR80. Children under 16 must be issued their own passports, valid for 5 years, which cost SAR60. If a passport is needed in a hurry, an **emergency passport** may be issued for SAR50. An application for a permanent passport must accompany the emergency passport application. Time for the completion of an application is normally 3 months or more from the time of submission. Current passports less than 10 years old (counting from date of issuance) may be **renewed** until December 31, 1999; every citizen whose passport's validity does not extend far beyond this date is urged to renew it as soon as possible, to avoid the expected glut of applications as 2000 approaches. Renewal is free, and turnaround time is usually 2 weeks. For further information, contact the nearest Department of Home Affairs Office.

U.K.: British citizens, British Dependent Territories citizens, British Nationals (overseas), and British Overseas citizens may apply for a **full passport,** valid for 10 years (5 years if under 16). Application forms are available at passport offices, main post offices, many travel agents, and branches of Lloyds Bank and Artac World Choice. Apply in person or by mail to one of the passport offices, located in London, Liverpool, Newport, Peterborough, Glasgow, or Belfast. The fee is UK£18. Children under 16 may be included on a parent's passport. Processing by mail usually takes 4-6 weeks. The London office offers same-day, walk-in rush service; arrive early. The formerly available **British Visitor's Passport** (valid in some western European countries and Bermuda only) has been abolished; every traveler over 16 now needs a 10yr., standard passport. The U.K. Passport Agency can be reached by phone at (0990) 21 04 10, and information is available on the Internet at http://www.open.gov.uk/ukpass.

U.S.: Citizens may apply for a passport at any federal or state **courthouse** or **post office** authorized to accept passport applications, or at a **U.S. Passport Agency,** located in Boston, Chicago, Honolulu, Houston, Los Angeles, Miami, New Orleans, New York, Philadelphia, San Francisco, Seattle, Stamford, or Washington D.C. Refer to the "U.S. Government, State Department" section of the telephone directory or the local post office for addresses. Parents must apply in person for children under age 13. You must apply in person if this is your first passport, if you're under age 18, or if your current passport is more than 12 years old or was issued before your 18th birthday. Passports are valid for 10 years, under 18 5 years, and cost US$65, under 18 US$40. Passports may be **renewed** by mail or in person for US$55. Processing takes 3-4 weeks. **Rush service** is available for a surcharge of US$30 with proof of departure within 10 working days (e.g., an airplane ticket or itinerary), or for travelers leaving in 2-3 weeks who require visas. Given proof of citizenship, a U.S. embassy or consulate abroad can usually issue a new passport. Report a **passport lost or stolen** in the U.S. in writing to Passport Services, 1425 K St. NW, U.S. Department of State, Washington D.C., 20524 or to the nearest passport agency. For more info, contact the U.S. Passport Information's **24-hour recorded message** (tel. (202) 647-0518). U.S. citizens may receive consular information sheets, travel warnings, and public announcements at any passport agency, U.S. embassy, or consulate, or by sending a self-addressed stamped envelope to: **Overseas Citizens Services,** Room 4811, Department of State, Washington, D.C. 20520-4818 (tel. (202) 647-5225; fax 647-3000). Additional information (including publications) about documents, formalities and travel abroad is available through the **Bureau of Consular Affairs** homepage at http://travel.state.gov, or through the **State Department** site at http://www.state.gov.

ENTRANCE REQUIREMENTS AND VISAS

Citizens of **Australia, Canada, Ireland, New Zealand, the U.K., and the U.S.** do not need to obtain a visa ahead of time to enter Germany. These citizens need to carry only a valid passport in order to remain for up to three months. **Citizens of the EU** don't need visas. **South African citizens** require a visa. Contact the nearest German Consulate General for more information. If your travels extend beyond Germany, remember that some other countries in Europe require a visa. Carry proof of your **financial independence,** such as a visa to the next country on your itinerary, a return air ticket, enough money to cover the cost of your living expenses, etc.

If you wish to stay longer, apply for a visa at the German embassy or consulate in your home country well before your departure. You may also apply for an extended-stay visa at a local aliens' authority after entry. You must obtain a work permit before seeking temporary employment in Germany, presuming you have already obtained a residence permit from a local immigration office (see **Work and Volunteer,** p. 21). You should apply for these permits at least 8 weeks in advance.

CUSTOMS: ENTERING GERMANY

> *Don't mention the war!*
>
> —Basil Fawlty (John Cleese)

Unless you plan to import a BMW or a barnyard beast, you will probably pass right over the customs barrier with minimal ado. Germany prohibits or restricts the importation of firearms, explosives, ammunition, fireworks, controlled substances, many plants and animals, lottery tickets, and obscene literature or films. To prevent problems with transporting **prescription drugs,** ensure that the bottles are clearly marked, and carry a copy of your prescription to show customs officials. When dealing with customs officers, do your utmost to be polite and look responsible; whether or not they give you a difficult time is ultimately a personal decision on their part.

Citizens of European Union (EU) countries can bring up to 800 **cigarettes** into Germany; travelers from outside the EU can bring 200. Germany allows 10 liters of **alcoholic beverages** above 44 proof for EU members, 1 liter for travelers from outside the EU. No one under age 17 is entitled to these allowances. There are no regulations on the import or export of currency. **Gifts** and commodities for personal use are allowed into Germany with the following regulations: the total value of goods imported from the EU cannot exceed DM780, while goods from outside the EU cannot exceed DM115. You can obtain more details from the German Consulate General in your own country. Generally, a budget traveler need not worry about these regulations; you'll want to bring only the bare necessities (see **Packing**, p. 28).

CUSTOMS: GOING HOME

When going home, you must declare all articles you acquired abroad and pay a duty on the value of those articles that exceed the allowance established by your country's customs service. Goods and gifts purchased at duty-free shops abroad are not exempt from duty or sales tax at your point of return; you must declare these items as well. "Duty-free" only means that you need not pay a tax in the country of purchase.

Australia: Citizens may import AUS$400, under 18 AUS$200, of goods duty-free, in addition to 1.125L alcohol and 250 cigarettes or 250g tobacco. You must be over 18 to import alcohol or tobacco. There is no limit to the amount of Australian and/ or foreign cash that may be brought into or taken out of the country, but amounts of AUS$10,000 or more, or the equivalent in foreign currency, must be reported. All foodstuffs and animal products must be declared on arrival. For information, contact the Regional Director, **Australian Customs Service,** GPO Box 8, Sydney NSW 2001 (tel. (02) 9213 2000; fax 9213 4000).

Canada: Citizens who remain abroad for at least 1 week may bring back up to CDN$500 worth of goods duty-free. Citizens or residents who travel for a period between 48 hours and 6 days can bring back up to CDN$200. Both of these exemptions may include tobacco and alcohol. You are permitted to ship goods except tobacco and alcohol home under the CDN$500 exemption if you declare them upon arrival. Goods under the CDN$200 exemption, alcohol, and tobacco must be in your hand or checked luggage. Citizens of legal age (which varies by province) may import up to 200 cigarettes, 50 cigars or cigarillos, 400g loose tobacco, 400 tobacco sticks, 1.14L wine or alcohol, and 24 355mL cans/bottles of beer; the value of these products is included in the CDN$200 or CDN$500. For more information, write to **Canadian Customs,** 2265 St. Laurent Blvd., Ottawa, Ont. K1G 4K3 (tel. (613) 993-0534), phone the **24hr. Automated Customs Information Service** at (800) 461-9999, or visit **Revenue Canada** at http://www.revcan.ca.

Ireland: Citizens must declare everything in excess of IR£142 (IR£73 per traveler under 15 years of age) obtained outside the EU or duty- and tax-free in the EU above the following allowances: 200 cigarettes, 100 cigarillos, 50 cigars, or 250g tobacco; 1L liquor or 2L wine; 2L still wine; 50g perfume; and 250mL toilet water. Goods obtained duty and tax paid in another EU country up to a value of IR£460 (IR£115 per traveler under 15) will not be subject to additional customs duties. Travelers under 17 may not import tobacco or alcohol. For more information, contact the **Revenue Commissioners,** Dublin Castle (tel. (01) 679 27 77; fax 671 20 21; email taxes@iol.ie; http://www.revenue.ie) or the **Collector of Customs and Excise,** The Custom House, Dublin 1.

New Zealand: Citizens may import up to NZ$700 worth of goods duty-free if they are intended for personal use or are unsolicited gifts. The concession is 200 cigarettes, 250g tobacco, 50 cigars or a combination of all 3 not to exceed 250g. You may also bring in 4.5L of beer or wine and 1.125L of liquor. Only travelers over 17 may import tobacco or alcohol. For more information, contact **New Zealand Customs,** 50 Anzac Ave., Box 29, Auckland (tel. (09) 377 35 20; fax 309 29 78).

South Africa: Citizens may import duty-free: 400 cigarettes, 50 cigars, 250g tobacco, 2L wine, 1L of spirits, 250mL toilet water, and 50mL perfume, and other consumable items up to a value of SAR500. Goods up to a value of SAR10,000 over and above this duty-free allowance are dutiable at 20%; such goods are also exempted from payment of VAT. Items acquired abroad and sent to the Republic as unaccompanied baggage do not qualify for any allowances. You may not export or import South African bank notes in excess of SAR2000. For more information, consult the **free pamphlet** South African Customs Information, available in airports or from the **Commissioner for Customs and Excise,** Private Bag X47, Pretoria 0001 (tel. (12) 314 99 11; fax 328 64 78).

U.K.: Citizens must be over 17 to import liquor or tobacco. These allowances also apply to duty-free purchases within the EU, except for the last category, other goods, which then has an allowance of UK£71. Goods obtained duty and tax paid for personal use within the EU do not require any further customs duty. For more information, contact **Her Majesty's Customs and Excise,** Custom House, Nettleton Road, Heathrow Airport, Hounslow, Middlesex TW6 2LA (tel. (0181) 910 3744; fax 910 3765).

U.S.: Citizens may import US$400 worth of accompanying goods duty-free and must pay a 10% tax on the next US$1000. You must declare all purchases, so have sales slips ready. The US$400 personal exemption covers goods purchased for personal or household use (this includes gifts) and cannot include more than 100 cigars, 200 cigarettes (1 carton), and 1L of wine or liquor. You must be over 21 to bring liquor into the U.S. If you mail home personal goods of U.S. origin, you can avoid duty charges by marking the package "American goods returned." For more information, consult the brochure **Know Before You Go,** available from the **U.S. Customs Service,** Box 7407, Washington D.C. 20044 (tel. (202) 927-6724).

YOUTH, STUDENT, AND TEACHER IDENTIFICATION

The **International Student Identity Card (ISIC)** is the most widely accepted form of student identification. Flashing this card can procure you discounts for sights, theaters, museums, accommodations, meals, train, ferry, bus, and airplane transportation, and other services. Present the card wherever you go, and ask about discounts even when none are advertised. It also provides insurance benefits, including US$100 per day off in hospital sickness for a maximum of 60 days, and US$3000 accident-related medical reimbursement for each accident (see **Insurance,** p. 19). In addition, cardholders have access to a toll-free **24hr. ISIC helpline** whose multilingual staff can provide assistance in medical, legal, and financial emergencies overseas.

Many student travel agencies around the world issue ISICs, including STA Travel in Australia and New Zealand; Travel CUTS in Canada; USIT in Ireland and Northern Ireland; SASTS in South Africa; Campus Travel and STA Travel in the U.K.; Council Travel, Let's Go Travel, and STA Travel in the U.S.; and any of the other organizations under the auspices of the International Student Travel Confederation (ISTC). When you apply for the card, request a copy of the *International Student Identity Card Handbook,* which lists by country some of the available discounts. You can also write to Council for a copy. The card is valid from September to December of the following year and costs US$19 or CDN$15. Applicants must be at least 12 years old and degree-seeking students of a secondary or post-secondary school. Because of the proliferation of phony ISICs, many airlines and some other services require other proof of student identity, such as a signed letter from the registrar attesting to your student status and stamped with the school seal or your school ID card. The US$20 **International Teacher Identity Card (ITIC)** offers the same insurance coverage, and similar but limited discounts. For more information on these cards, consult the organization's **web site** (email isicinfo@istc.org; http://www.istc.org).

Federation of International Youth Travel Organizations (FIYTO) issues a discount card to travelers who are under 26 but not students. Known as the **GO25 Card,** this one-year card offers many of the same benefits as the ISIC, and most organizations that sell the ISIC also sell the GO25 Card. A brochure that lists discounts is free when you purchase the card. To apply, you will need a passport, valid driver's license, or copy of a birth certificate; and a passport-sized photo with your name printed on the back. The fee is US$19, CDN$15, or UK£5. Information is available on the web at http://www.fiyto.org or http://www.go25.org, or by contacting **Travel CUTS** in Canada, **STA Travel** in the U.K., **Council Travel** in the U.S., or **FIYTO** headquarters in Denmark (see **Travel Organizations,** p. 2).

DRIVING PERMITS AND CAR INSURANCE

If you plan to drive a car while abroad, you must have an **International Driving Permit (IDP),** though Germany allows travelers to drive with a valid American or Canadian licenses for one year, with certain stipulations (see **By Car,** p. 44). Most car rental agencies don't require the permit. It may be a good idea to get one anyway, in case you're in a position (such as an accident or stranded in a smaller town) where the police may not read or speak English.

Your IDP, valid for one year, must be issued in your own country before you depart. A valid driver's license from your home country must always accompany the IDP. An application for an IDP usually needs to include one or two photos, a current local license, an additional form of identification, and a fee. Australians can obtain an IDP by contacting their local **Royal Automobile Club (RAC),** or the **National Royal Motorist Association (NRMA)** if in NSW or the ACT, where a permit can be obtained for AUS$12. Canadian license holders can obtain an IDP (CDN$10) through any **Canadian Automobile Association (CAA)** branch office in Canada, or by writing to CAA Central Ont., 60 Commerce Valley Drive East, Thornhill, Ont. L3T 7P9 (tel. (416) 221-4300). Citizens of Ireland should drop into their nearest **Automobile Association (AA)** office where an IDP can be picked up for IR£4, or call (1) 283 3555 for a postal application form. In New Zealand, contact your local **Automobile Association (AA),** or their main office at 99 Albert Street, PO Box 5, Auckland (tel. (09) 377 4660; fax 309 4564), IDPs cost NZ$8 and NZ$2 for return postage. In South Africa visit your local **Automobile Association of South Africa** office, where IDPs can be picked up for SAR25, or for more information phone (011) 466 6641, or write to P.O. Box 596, 2000 Johannesburg. In the U.K. IDPs are UK£4 and you can either visit your local **AA Shop,** or call (01256) 49 39 32 and order a postal application form (allow 2-3 weeks). U.S. license holders can obtain an IDP (US$10) at any **American Automobile Association (AAA)** office or by writing to AAA Florida, Travel Agency Services Department, 1000 AAA Drive (mail stop 28), Heathrow, FL 32746-5080 (tel. (407) 444-4245; fax 444-4247).

If you rent, lease, or borrow a car, you will need a **green card,** or **International Insurance Certificate,** to prove that you have liability insurance, which is required by law in Germany. Obtain it through the car rental agency; most of them include coverage in their prices. If you lease a car, you can obtain a green card from the dealer. Some travel agents offer the card, which is also available at the border. Verify whether your auto insurance applies abroad; even if it does, you will still need a green card to certify this to foreign officials. Rental agencies may require you to purchase theft insurance; ask your agency. If you have a collision abroad, the accident will show up on your domestic records if you report it to your insurance company.

■ Money Matters

US$1 = 1.84 Deutschmark (DM)	1DM= US$0.54
CDN$1 = 1.32DM	1DM = CDN$0.76
AUS$1 = 1.36DM	1DM = AUS$0.73
IR£ = 2.70DM	1DM = IR£0.37
NZ$1 = 1.19DM	1DM = NZ$0.84
SAR1 = 0.39DM	1DM = SAR2.55
SEK1 = 0.22	1DM = SEK4.39
UK£1 = 2.95DM	1DM = UK£0.33

The above exchange rates are from August 1997. The *Deutsche Mark* or *Deutschmark* (abbreviated DM, occasionally M) is the unit of currency in Germany. It is one of the most stable and respected currencies in the world; indeed, in most markets in Eastern Europe, "hard currency" means U.S. Dollars and DM exclusively. One DM equals 100 *Pfennig* (Pf). Coins come in 1, 2, 5, 10, and 50Pf, and DM1, 2, and 5 amounts. Bills come in DM5, 10, 20, 50, 100, 200, 500, and 1000 denominations.

Though some (especially Americans) may think of minted metal disks as inconsequential pieces of aluminum, remember that a DM5 coin can easily buy you a meal. A new barrage of bills was unleashed recently upon the people of Germany. The old bills are *no longer valid currency,* although banks will exchange them for new bills. Accept only new bills (they have an embedded silver stripe). Old East German currency lost all but sentimental value in July 1990.

CURRENCY AND EXCHANGE

If you stay in hostels and prepare your own food, expect to spend anywhere from US$15-30 per person daily in Germany. Transportation will increase these figures. Don't sacrifice your health or safety for a cheaper tab. If you plan to travel for more than a couple of days, you will need to keep handy a larger amount of cash than usual. Carrying money around with you, even in a money belt, is risky but necessary. Personal checks from home will probably not be acceptable no matter how many forms of identification you have, and even traveler's checks may not be acceptable in some locations. However, you can cash personal checks at AmEx offices worldwide (if you are a member).

It is cheaper to buy domestic currency than to buy foreign, so as a rule you should convert money after arriving in Germany. However, converting some money before you go will allow you to zip through the airport while others languish in exchange lines. It's a good idea to carry enough *Deutschmarks* to last for the first 24 to 72 hours of a trip to avoid getting stuck with no money after banking hours or on a holiday. Travelers living in the U.S. can get foreign currency from the comfort of home; contact **Capital Foreign Exchange** on the East Coast (toll-free (888) 842-0880; fax (202) 842-8008), or on the West Coast, **International Currency Express** (toll-free (888) 278-6628; fax (310) 278-6410). They will deliver foreign currency (for over 120 countries) or traveler's checks (see **Traveler's Checks,** below) overnight (US$12) or second-day (US$10) at competitive exchange rates.

Watch out for commission rates and check newspapers to get the standard rate of exchange. Banks generally have the best rates, although sometimes tourist offices or exchange kiosks have better rates. Stick to banks or bureaux de change which have only a 5% margin between their buy and sell prices. Anything more and they are making too much profit. Be sure that both prices are listed. Since you lose money with every transaction, convert in large sums, but don't convert more than you need since it also costs money to change it back to your home currency, or to a new one.

If you are using traveler's checks or bills, be sure to carry some in small denominations (US$50 or less), especially for times when you are forced to exchange money at disadvantageous rates. However, it is a good idea to carry a range of denominations since charges may be levied per check cashed, depending on location.

TRAVELER'S CHECKS

Traveler's checks are one of the safest and least troublesome means of carrying funds, as they can be refunded if stolen. Several agencies and many banks sell them, usually for face value plus a small percentage commission. (Members of the American Automobile Association, and some banks and credit unions, can get American Express checks commission-free; see **Driving Permits and Car Insurance,** p. 10.) **American Express** and **Visa** are the most widely recognized, though other major checks are sold, exchanged, cashed, and refunded with almost equal ease. Keep in mind that in small towns, traveler's checks are less readily accepted than in cities with large tourist industries. Nonetheless, there will probably be at least one place in every town where you can exchange them for local currency. If you're ordering your checks, do so well in advance, especially if large sums are being requested.

Each agency provides refunds if your checks are **lost or stolen,** and many provide other services. (Note that you may need a police report verifying the loss or theft.) Inquire about toll-free refund hotlines (in the countries you're visiting), emergency message relay services, and stolen credit card assistance when you purchase checks.

You should expect a fair amount of red tape and delay in the event of theft or loss of traveler's checks. To expedite the refund process, keep your check receipts separate from your checks, store them in a safe place, record check numbers when you cash them, leave a list of check numbers with someone at home, and ask for a list of refund centers when you buy your checks (American Express and Bank of America have over 40,000 centers worldwide). Keep a separate supply of cash or traveler's checks for emergencies. Never countersign your checks until you're prepared to cash them, and always bring your passport when you plan to use the checks.

American Express: In Australia call (800) 25 19 02; New Zealand (0800) 44 10 68; the U.K. (0800) 52 13 13; the U.S. and Canada (800) 221-7282; elsewhere, call U.S. collect (801) 964-6665. American Express traveler's checks are available in German currencies. They are the most widely recognized worldwide and the easiest to replace if lost or stolen. Checks can be purchased for a small fee (1-4%) at American Express Travel Service Offices, banks, and American Automobile Association offices (AAA members can buy the checks commission-free). Cardmembers can also purchase checks at American Express Dispensers at airport Travel Service Offices and by phone (tel. (800) ORDER-TC (673-3782)). American Express offices cash their checks commission-free (except where prohibited by national governments), although they often offer slightly worse rates than banks. You can also buy *Cheques for Two* which can be signed by either of two people traveling together. Request the American Express booklet "Traveler's Companion," which lists travel office addresses and stolen check hotlines for each European country. Visit their online travel offices (http://www.aexp.com).

Citicorp: In the U.S. and Canada call (800) 645-6556; Europe, the Middle East, or Africa (44) 171 508 7007; elsewhere call U.S. collect (813) 623-1709. Sells both Citicorp and Citicorp Visa traveler's checks in German *Marks*. Commission is 1-2% on check purchases. Checkholders are automatically enrolled for 45 days in the Travel Assist Program (hotline (800) 250-4377 or collect (202) 296-8728) which provides travelers with English-speaking doctor, lawyer, and interpreter referrals as well as check refund assistance and general travel information.

Thomas Cook MasterCard: For 24hr. cashing or refund assistance in the U.S. and Canada call (800) 223-9920; from the U.K. call (0800) 622 101 toll free or (1733) 502 995 collect or (1733) 318 950 collect; elsewhere call U.S. collect (609) 987-7300. Offers checks in German *Marks* and ECUs. Commission 1-2% for purchases. Thomas Cook offices may sell checks for lower commissions and will cash checks commission-free. Thomas Cook MasterCard Traveler's Checks are also available from **Capital Foreign Exchange** (see **Currency and Exchange,** above).

Visa: In the U.S. call (800) 227-6811; the U.K. (0800) 895 492; elsewhere call (01733) 318 949 and reverse the charges. Any of the above numbers can tell you the location of their nearest office. Any type of Visa traveler's checks can be reported lost at the Visa number.

CREDIT CARDS

Credit cards are not always useful to the budget traveler in Germany, as many establishments will not accept them, although pricey establishments accept them all too willingly. Still, major credit cards—**MasterCard** and **Visa** are the most welcomed—can be used to extract *Deutschmarks* from associated banks and teller machines throughout Germany. Credit card companies get the wholesale exchange rate, which is generally 5% better than the retail rate used by banks and even better than that used by other currency exchange establishments. However, you will be charged ruinous interest rates if you don't pay off the bill quickly, so be careful when using this service. **American Express** cards also work in some ATMs and at AmEx offices and major airports. All such machines require a **Personal Identification Number (PIN),** which credit cards in the United States do not usually carry. You must ask your credit card company to assign you a PIN before you leave; without it, you will be unable to withdraw cash with your credit card outside the U.S. Keep in mind that MasterCard and Visa have different names elsewhere ("EuroCard" or "Access" for MasterCard and "Carte Bleue" or "Barclaycard" for Visa).

Credit cards are also invaluable in an emergency—an unexpected hospital bill or ticket home or the loss of traveler's checks—which may leave you temporarily without other resources. Furthermore, credit cards offer an array of other services, from insurance to emergency assistance, which depend completely on the issuer.

American Express (tel. (800) 843-2273) has a hefty annual fee (US$55) but offers a number of services. AmEx cardholders can cash personal checks at AmEx offices outside the U.S., and U.S. Assist, a **24hr. hotline** offering medical and legal assistance in emergencies, is also available in U.S. and Canada (tel. (800) 554-2639); from abroad call U.S. collect (301) 214-8228. Cardholders can take advantage of the American Express Travel Service—benefits include assistance in changing airline, hotel, and car rental reservations, baggage loss and flight insurance, sending mailgrams and international cables, and holding your mail at one of the more than 1700 AmEx offices around the world.

MasterCard (tel. (800) 999-0454) and **Visa** (tel. (800) 336-8472) are issued in cooperation with individual banks and some other organizations; ask the issuer about services which go along with the cards.

CASH CARDS

Cash cards—popularly called **ATM** (Automated Teller Machine) cards—are widespread in Germany (including Eastern Germany). Depending on the system that your bank at home uses, you will probably be able to access your own personal bank account whenever you're in need of funds. (Be careful, however, and keep all receipts—even if an ATM won't give you your cash, it may register a withdrawal on your next statement). Happily, ATMs get the same wholesale exchange rate as credit cards. Despite these perks, do some research before relying too heavily on automation. There is often a limit on the amount of money you can withdraw per day (usually about US$500, depending on the type of card and account), and computer network failures are not uncommon. Be sure to memorize your PIN code in numeral form since machines outside the U.S. and Canada often don't have letters on the keys. Many ATMs are outdoors, so be cautious and aware of your surroundings.

The two major international money networks are **Cirrus** (U.S. tel. (800) 4-CIRRUS (424-7787)) and **PLUS** (U.S. tel. (800) 843-7587). Both have international cash machines in numerous countries and territories. Cirrus charges US$3-5 to withdraw non-domestically depending on your bank. If you can do it, carry two cards, one linked to each network.

GETTING MONEY FROM HOME

One of the easiest ways to get money from home is to bring an **American Express** card. AmEx allows green-card holders to draw cash from their checking accounts at any of its major offices and many of its representatives' offices, up to US$1000 every 21 days (no service charge, no interest). AmEx also offers Express Cash, with over 100,000 ATMs located in airports, hotels, banks, office complexes, and shopping areas around the world. Express Cash withdrawals are automatically debited from the Cardmember's checking account or line of credit. Green card holders may withdraw up to US$1000 in a seven day period. There is a 2% transaction fee for each cash withdrawal, with a US$2.50 minimum/$20 maximum. To enroll in Express Cash, Cardmembers may call (800) CASH NOW (227-4669). Outside the U.S. call collect (904) 565-7875. Unless using the AmEx service, avoid cashing checks in foreign currencies; they usually take weeks and a US$30 fee to clear.

Money can also be wired abroad through international money transfer services operated by **Western Union** (tel. (800) 325-6000). The rates for sending cash are generally US$10 cheaper than with a credit card, and the money is usually available in the country you're sending it to within an hour, although this may vary.

Some people also choose to send money abroad in cash via **Federal Express** to avoid transmission fees and taxes. FedEx is reasonably reliable; however, this method may be illegal, it involves an element of risk, and it requires that you remain at a legitimate address for a day or two to wait for the money's arrival. In general, it may be safer to swallow the cost of wire transmission and preserve your peace of mind.

In emergencies, U.S. citizens can have money sent via the State Department's **Overseas Citizens Service, American Citizens Services,** Consular Affairs, Room 4811, U.S. Department of State, Washington, D.C. 20520 (tel. (202) 647-5225; nights, Sundays, and holidays (202) 647-4000; fax (on demand only) (202) 647-3000; http://travel.state.gov). For a fee of US$15, the State Department will send money within hours to the nearest consular office, which will then disburse it according to instructions. The office serves only Americans in the direst of straits abroad; non-American travelers should contact their embassies for information. The quickest way to have the money sent is usually to cable the State Department through Western Union.

TAXES

For large purchases, you may be eligible for a refund of **VAT** (Germany's 15% Value-Added Tax). Acquire a Tax Free Shopping Check at the time of purchase and consult German customs when leaving the country (and before checking the goods). You may also obtain a stamp on your VAT refund form at a German embassy or consulate in your home country—you must present the items, sales slips, and your passport. Upon returning home, you must declare all articles you acquired abroad and pay a duty on the value of those articles that exceed the allowance established by your country's customs service. Goods and gifts purchased at duty-free shops abroad are not exempt from duty or sales tax at your point of return; you must declare these items. "Duty-free" means that you need not pay a tax in the country of purchase.

TIPPING AND BARGAINING

Germans generally round up to the nearest *Mark* when tipping. However, tipping is not practiced as liberally as it is elsewhere—most Germans only tip in restaurants and beer halls, or when they are the beneficiary of a service, such as a taxi ride. It is common to tip as much as 5-10% in fancier restaurants, especially if the service is exceptional. As a rule, Germans never bargain, and posted prices are not negotiable.

■ Safety And Security

PERSONAL SAFETY

Tourists are particularly vulnerable to crime for two reasons: they often carry large amounts of cash and they are not as street savvy as locals. To avoid unwanted attention, try to **blend in** as much as possible. Respecting local customs (in many cases, dressing more conservatively) may placate would-be hecklers. The gawking camera-toter is a more obvious target than the low-profile traveler. Walking directly into a cafe or shop to check a map beats checking it on a street corner. Better yet, look over your map before setting out. Nervous, over-the-shoulder glances can be a tip that you have something valuable to protect.

Safety Warning! Violent crime is less common in Germany than in most countries, but it exists, especially in big cities like Frankfurt and Berlin, as well as economically depressed regions of the eastern parts. Most of Germany's neo-Nazis and skinheads subscribe to the traditional skinhead uniform of flight jackets worn over white shortsleeve shirts and tight jeans rolled up high to reveal high-cut combat boots. Skinheads also tend to follow a **shoelace code,** with white supremacists and neo-Nazis wearing white laces while anti-gay skinheads wear pink laces. Left-wing, anti-Nazi "S.H.A.R.P.s" (Skinheads Against Racial Prejudice) also exist; they favor red laces.

When exploring a new **city,** extra vigilance is wise, but no city should force you to turn precautions into panic. Find out about unsafe areas from tourist information, from the manager of your hotel or hostel, or from a local whom you trust. Especially if you travel alone, be sure that someone at home knows your itinerary. Never say that you're traveling alone. You may want to carry a small **whistle** to scare off attackers or attract attention. Memorize the emergency number of the city or area—the number to contact the **police** in Germany is generally **110.**

When walking at night, stick to busy, well-lit streets and avoid dark alleyways. Do not attempt to cross through parks or large, deserted areas. Whenever possible, *Let's Go* warns of unsafe neighborhoods and areas, but you should exercise your own judgment about the safety of your environs; buildings in disrepair, vacant lots, and unpopulated areas are all bad signs. If you feel uncomfortable, leave as quickly and directly as you can, but don't allow fear of the unknown to turn you into a hermit. Careful, persistent exploration will build confidence and make your stay in an area that much more rewarding.

If you travel by **car,** learn local driving signals. Motor vehicle crashes are a leading cause of travel deaths in many parts of the world. Be sure to park your vehicle in a garage or well-traveled area. Wearing a seatbelt is law in Germany. Children under 40 lb. should ride only in a specially-designed carseat, available for a small fee from most car rental agencies. If you plan on spending a lot of time on the road, you may want to bring spare parts. Study route maps before you hit the road; some roads have poor (or nonexistent) shoulders, few gas stations, and roaming animals.

Sleeping in your car is one of the most **dangerous** (and often illegal) ways to get your rest. If your car breaks down, wait for the police to assist you. If you must sleep in your car, do so as close to a police station or a 24-hour service station as possible. Sleeping out in the open can be even more dangerous—camping is recommended only in official, supervised campsites or in wilderness backcountry.

Let's Go does not recommend **hitchhiking,** particularly for women (for more on hitchhiking see **Getting There,** p. 47). Exercise extreme caution when using pools or beaches without lifeguards. Hidden rocks and shallow depths may cause serious injury or even death. Heed warning signs about dangerous undertows. If you rent scuba-diving equipment, make sure that it is up to par before taking the plunge.

There is no sure-fire set of precautions that will protect you from all of the situations you might encounter when you travel. A good self-defense course will give you more concrete ways to react to different types of aggression, but it often carries a steep price tag. **Impact, Prepare,** and **Model Mugging** can refer you to local self-defense courses in the United States (tel. (800) 345-KICK/5425). Course prices vary from $50-400. Women's and men's courses offered. Community colleges frequently offer inexpensive self-defense courses.

The **Canadian Department of Foreign Affairs and International Trade (DFAIT)** offers advisories and travel warnings at its web address (http://www.dfait-maeci.gc.ca) and is accessible by phone (tel. in Ottawa (613) 944-6788, elsewhere in Canada (800) 267-6788). Official warnings from the **United Kingdom Foreign and Commonwealth Office** are on-line at http://www.fco.gov.uk; you can also call the office at (0171) 238-4503. For official **United States Department of State** travel advisories, call their 24-hour hotline at (202) 647-5225 or check their website (http://travel.state.gov), which provides travel information and publications. Alternatively, order publications, including a free pamphlet entitled *A Safe Trip Abroad,* by writing to Superintendent of Documents, U.S. Government Printing Office, Washington, DC 20402, or by calling them at (202) 512-1800.

FINANCIAL SECURITY

Among the more colorful aspects of large cities are **con artists.** Con artists and hustlers often work in groups, and children are among the most effective. Hucksters possess an innumerable range of ruses. Be aware of certain classics: sob stories that require money, rolls of bills "found" on the street, mustard spilled (or saliva spit) onto your shoulder distracting you for enough time to snatch your bag. Be especially alert in these situations. Do not respond or make eye contact, walk quickly away, and keep a solid grip on your belongings. Contact the police if a hustler is particularly insistent or aggressive.

Don't put a wallet with money in your back pocket. Never count your money in public and carry as little as possible. If you carry a purse, buy a sturdy one with a secure clasp, and carry it crosswise on the side, away from the street with the clasp against you. Secure packs with small combination padlocks which slip through the two zippers. (Even these precautions do not always suffice: moped riders who snatch purses and backpacks sometimes tote knives to cut the straps). A **money belt** is the best way to carry cash; you can buy one at most camping supply stores or through the Forsyth Travel Library (see **Useful Publications,** p. 2). A nylon, zippered pouch with belt that sits inside the waist of your pants or skirt combines convenience and security. A **neck pouch** is equally safe, although far less accessible. Refrain from pulling out your neck pouch in public; if you must, be very discreet. Avoid keeping anything precious in a fanny-pack (even if it's worn on your stomach)—your valuables will be highly visible and easy to steal.

In city crowds and especially on public transportation, pick-pockets are amazingly deft at their craft. Rush hour is no excuse for strangers to press up against you on the metro. If someone stands uncomfortably close, move to another car and hold your bags tightly. Also, be alert in public telephone booths. If you must say your calling-card number, do so very quietly; if you punch it in, make sure no one can look over your shoulder. **Photocopies** of important documents allow you to recover them in case they are lost or filched. Carry one copy separate from the documents and leave another copy at home. Keep some money separate from the rest to use in an emergency or in case of theft. Label every piece of luggage both inside and out.

Be particularly careful on **buses** (for example, carry your backpack in front of you where you can see it), don't check baggage on trains, and don't trust anyone to "watch your bag for a second." Thieves thrive on **trains;** professionals wait for tourists to fall asleep and then carry off everything they can. When traveling in pairs, sleep in alternating shifts. When alone, use good judgement in selecting a train compartment: never stay in an empty one, and use a lock to secure your pack to the luggage rack. Keep important documents and other valuables on your person and try to sleep on top bunks with your luggage stored above you (if not in bed with you).

Let's Go lists locker availability in hostels and train stations, but you'll need your own padlock. Lockers are useful if you plan on sleeping outdoors or don't want to lug everything with you, but don't store valuables in them. Never leave your belongings unattended; crime occurs in even the most demure-looking hostel or hotel. If you feel unsafe, look for places with either a curfew or a night attendant. When possible, keep valuables or anything you couldn't bear to lose at home.

If you travel by **car,** avoid leaving valuable possessions, such as radios or luggage, in it while you're off rambling. If your tape deck or radio is removable, hide it in the trunk or take it with you. If it isn't, at least conceal it under a lot of junk. Similarly, hide baggage in the trunk—although savvy thieves can tell if a car is heavily loaded by the way it sits on its tires.

Travel Assistance International by Worldwide Assistance Services, Inc. offers year-long frequent traveler packages (see **Insurance,** p. 19). The **American Society of Travel Agents** provides helpful tips at their web-site (http://www.astanet.com) and in their free brochure, *Travel Safety.* You can obtain a copy by sending a request and self-addressed, stamped envelope to 1101 King St., Alexandria, VA 22313.

DRUGS AND ALCOHOL

Needless to say, **illegal drugs** are best avoided altogether; the average sentence for possession outside the U.S. is about seven years. Buying or selling narcotics may lead to anything from a prison sentence to the death penalty. Remember that you are subject to the laws of the country in which you travel, not to those of your home country, and it is your responsibility to familiarize yourself with these laws. In 1994, the German High Court ruled that, while possession of marijuana/hashish was still illegal, possession of "small quantities for personal consumption" was not prosecutable. Each *Land* has interpreted the quantities involved in "personal consumption" differently, with possession of 3 to 30 grams *de facto* decriminalized at the time at which this book was written. The more liberal states, notably Berlin and Hamburg, tend towards the higher end of this spectrum, while the more conservative states of Bayern and the former East afford less leniency. Be sure to find out what the latest law is, including what quantities of possession are acceptable in the regions which you visit, before filling a backpack with hash bricks.

Avoid **public drunkenness**; it is against the law in many countries. It can also jeopardize your safety and earn the disdain of locals. The drinking age in Germany is 16 for beer and wine and 18 for spirits, although it is skimpily enforced. The maximum permissible blood alcohol level while driving in Germany is 0.08%. The worst thing you can possibly do is carry drugs across an international border; not only could you end up in prison, you could be blessed with a "Drug Trafficker" stamp on your passport for the rest of your life. If arrested, call your country's consulate. Embassies may not be willing to help those arrested on drug charges. Make sure you get a statement and prescription from your doctor if you'll be carrying insulin, syringes, or any other **prescription drugs.** Refuse to carry even an apparent nun's excess luggage onto a plane; you're more likely to wind up in jail for possession of drugs than in heaven.

■ Health

Common sense is the simplest prescription for good health while you travel: eat well, drink and sleep enough, and don't overexert yourself. To minimize the effects of jet lag, "reset" your body's clock by adopting the time of your destination immediately upon arrival. Most travelers adjust to a new time zone after two or three days.

BEFORE YOU GO

Though no amount of planning can guarantee an accident-free trip, preparation can help minimize the likelihood of contracting a disease and maximize the chances of receiving effective health-care in the event of an emergency.

For minor health problems, bring a compact first-aid kit, including bandages, aspirin or other pain killers, antibiotic cream, a thermometer, a Swiss Army knife with tweezers, cold decongestants, motion sickness remedy, medicine for diarrhea or stomach problems, sunscreen, insect repellent, and burn ointment.

In your passport, write the names of any people you wish to be contacted in case of a medical emergency, and list any allergies or medical conditions you would want doctors to be aware of. If you wear glasses or contact lenses, carry an extra prescription and pair of glasses or arrange to have your doctor or a family member send a replacement pair in an emergency. Allergy sufferers should find out if their conditions are likely to be aggravated in the regions they plan to visit, and obtain a full supply of any necessary medication before the trip, since matching a prescription to a foreign equivalent is not always easy. To get a prescription filled in Germany you must go to an *Apotheke;* a *Drogerie* sells only toilet articles. Most German cities have a rotating all-night pharmacy schedule to ensure that services are available 24 hours per day. Check the **Practical Information** section for each particular city for the location of the major pharmacy. Carry up-to-date, legible prescriptions or a statement from your doctor, especially if you use insulin, a syringe, or a narcotic. While traveling, be sure to keep all medication with you in carry-on luggage.

If you are concerned about being able to access medical support while traveling, the **International Association for Medical Assistance to Travelers (IAMAT)** offers a membership ID card, a directory of English-speaking doctors around the world who treat members for a set fee schedule, and detailed charts on immunization requirements, various tropical diseases, climate, and sanitation. Membership is free, though donations are appreciated and used for further research. Contact chapters in **Canada,** 40 Regal Road, Guelph, Ont., N1K 1B5 (tel. (519) 836-0102) or 1287 St. Clair Avenue

West, Toronto, M6E 1B8 (tel. (416) 652-0137; fax (519) 836-3412), **New Zealand,** P.O. Box 5049, Christchurch 5, or the **U.S.,** 417 Center St., Lewiston, NY 14092 (tel. (716) 754-4883; fax (519) 836-3412; email iamat@sentex.net; http://www.sentex.net/~iamat)

HOT AND COLD

Common sense goes a long way toward preventing **heat exhaustion:** relax in hot weather, drink lots of non-alcoholic fluids, and lie down inside if you feel awful. Continuous heat stress can eventually lead to **heatstroke,** characterized by rising body temperature, severe headache, and cessation of sweating. Wear a hat, sunglasses, and a lightweight longsleeve shirt to avoid heatstroke. Victims must be cooled off with wet towels and taken to a doctor as soon as possible.

Always drink enough liquids to keep your urine clear. Alcoholic beverages are dehydrating, as are coffee, strong tea, and caffeinated sodas. If you'll be sweating a lot, eat enough salty food to prevent electrolyte depletion, which causes severe headaches. Less debilitating, but still dangerous, is **sunburn.** If you're prone to sunburn, bring sunscreen with you. If you get sunburned, drink more fluids than usual.

Travelers to **high altitudes** must allow their bodies a couple of days to adjust to lower oxygen levels in the air before exerting themselves. Also be careful about alcohol, especially if you're used to U.S. standards for beer—German brews and liquors tend to pack more punch than a smooth, cold Colt 45, and at high altitudes where the air has less oxygen, any alcohol will do you in quickly.

BIRTH CONTROL AND ABORTION

Reliable contraceptive devices may be difficult to find while traveling. Women on the pill should bring enough to allow for possible loss or extended stays. Bring a prescription, since forms of the pill vary a good deal. The sponge is probably too bulky to be worthwhile on the road. Women who use a diaphragm should have enough contraceptive jelly on hand. Though condoms are increasingly available, you might want to bring your favorite national brand before you go; availability and quality vary. Condoms *(Kondom)* are widely available in Germany.

Women overseas who want an **abortion** should contact the **National Abortion Federation Hotline** (tel. (800) 772-9100; Mon.-Fri. 9:30am-12:30pm and 1:30-5:30pm), 1775 Massachusetts Ave. NW, Washington, D.C. 20036. **Abortion** is a complicated legal issue in Germany. It is only available within the first trimester, and not on demand; a woman must indicate a reason, and only certain reasons are accepted. In practice, the restrictions simply necessitate a search for a willing doctor. In 1995, new legislation considerably eased legal barriers to abortion in most of the country. Still, if you find yourself with an unwanted pregnancy in Germany and choose to seek an abortion, be aware of the bureaucracy involved, which is stricter in certain states (notably Bayern) than in others (notably the northwestern *Länder*). The German word for abortion is *Abtreibung;* the word for abortion rights is *Abtreibungsrecht.* The "morning after" pill is available in Germany, but the *Abtreibungspille* (RU486; the French "abortion pill") is not.

AIDS, HIV, STDS

The easiest mode of HIV transmission is through direct blood to blood contact with an HIV positive person; *never* share intravenous drug, tattooing, or other needles. The most common mode of transmission is sexual intercourse. Health professionals recommend the use of latex condoms; follow the instructions on the packet. Since it isn't always convenient to buy condoms when traveling, take a supply with you. **Bayern** requires foreigners seeking a residency permit for more than six months to be HIV-negative, and they do not accept the results of tests taken abroad.

Sexually transmitted diseases (STDs) such as gonorrhea, chlamydia, genital warts, syphilis, and herpes are a lot easier to catch than HIV, and can be just as deadly. It's wise to *look* at your partner's genitals before you have sex. Warning signs for

STDs include: swelling, sores, bumps, or blisters on sex organs, rectum, or mouth; burning and pain during urination and bowel movements; itching around sex organs; swelling or redness in the throat, flu-like symptoms with fever, chills, and aches. If these symptoms develop, see a doctor immediately. When having sex, condoms may protect you from certain STDs, but oral or even tactile contact can lead to transmission.

■ Insurance

Beware of buying unnecessary travel coverage—your regular insurance policies (especially university policies) may well extend to travel-related accidents incurred abroad. **Medicare's** "foreign travel" coverage is valid only in Canada and Mexico. Canadians are protected by their home province's health insurance plan for up to 90 days after leaving the country; check with the provincial Ministry of Health or Health Plan Headquarters for details. Australia has Reciprocal Health Care Agreements (RHCAs) with several countries; when traveling in these nations Australians are entitled to many of the services that they would receive at home. The Commonwealth Department of Human Services and Health can provide more information. Your **homeowners' insurance** (or your family's coverage) often covers theft during travel. Homeowners are generally covered against loss of travel documents (passport, plane ticket, railpass, etc.) up to US$500.

ISIC and **ITIC** provide basic insurance benefits, including US$100 per day of in-hospital sickness for a maximum of 60 days, and US$3000 of accident-related medical reimbursement (see **Youth, Student, and Teacher Identification,** p. 9). Cardholders have access to a toll-free 24-hour helpline whose multilingual staff can provide assistance in medical, legal, and financial emergencies overseas (in the U.S. and Canada call (800) 626-2427; elsewhere call the U.S. collect (713) 267-2525). **Council** and **STA** offer a range of plans that can supplement your basic insurance coverage, with options covering medical treatment and hospitalization, accidents, baggage loss, and even charter flights missed due to illness. Most **American Express** cardholders receive automatic car rental (collision and theft, but not liability) insurance and travel accident coverage (US$100,000 in life insurance) on flight purchases made with the card. Customer Service (tel. (800) 528-4800).

Remember that insurance companies usually require a copy of the police report for thefts, or evidence of having paid medical expenses (doctors' statements, receipts) before they will honor a claim and may have time limits on filing for reimbursement. Always carry policy numbers and proof of insurance. Check with each insurance carrier for specific restrictions and policies. Most of the carriers listed below have 24-hour hotlines.

Avi International, 90 Rue de la Victoire, 75009 Paris, France (tel. (1) 44 63 51 07; fax 40 82 90 35). Primarily for the international youth traveler, covering emergency travel expenses, medical/accident, dental, and baggage loss. 24hr. hotline.

Globalcare Travel Insurance, 220 Broadway, Lynnfield, MA 01940 (tel. (800) 821-2488; fax (617) 592-7720; email global@nebc.mv.com; http://www.nebc.mv.com/globalcare). Complete medical, legal, emergency, and travel-related services. On-the-spot payments and special student programs, including benefits for trip cancellation and interruption. GTI waives pre-existing medical conditions, and provides coverage for the bankruptcy or default of cruise lines, airlines, or tour operators. Also included at no extra charge is a Worldwide Collision Damage Provision.

Travel Assistance International, by Worldwide Assistance Services, Inc., 1133 15th St. NW, #400, Washington, D.C. 20005-2710 (tel. (800) 821-2828 or (202) 828-5894; fax (202) 828-5896; email wassist@aol.com). TAI provides its members with a 24hr. free hotline for travel emergencies and referrals in over 200 countries. Their Per-Trip (starting at US$65) and Frequent Traveler (from US$235) plans include medical, travel, and communication assistance services.

■ Alternatives to Tourism

STUDY

Foreign study programs vary tremendously in expense, quality, living conditions, degree of contact with local students, and exposure to local culture and language. There are numerous exchange programs for high school students. Most American undergraduates enroll in programs sponsored by U.S. universities, and many colleges have offices that give advice and information on study abroad. Ask for the names of recent participants in these programs, and get in touch with them in order to judge which program is best for you. Even basic language skills might be sufficient to allow direct enrollment in German universities, which are far cheaper than those in North America (and vastly less expensive than a study abroad program).

Council on International Education Exchange, 205 E. 42nd St., New York, NY 10017 (tel. (888) COUNCIL (268-6245); fax (212) 822-2699; email info@ciee.org; http://www.ciee.org), sponsors study abroad programs throughout the world.

Deutscher Akademischer Austauschdienst (DAAD), 950 3rd Ave., 19th Fl., New York NY 10022 (tel. (212) 758-3223; email daadny@daad.org; http://www.daad.org); in Germany, Kennedyallee 50, 53175 Bonn. Information on language instruction, exchanges, and the wealth of scholarships for study in Germany. The place to contact if you want to enroll in a German university; distributes applications and the valuable *Academic Study in the Federal Republic of Germany*.

Experiment in International Living, Summer Programs, Kipling Rd., P.O. Box 676, Brattleboro, VT 05302 (tel. (800) 345-2929; fax (802) 258-3428; email eil@worldlearning.org; http://www.worldlearning.org). Founded in 1932, it offers cross-cultural, educational homestays, community service, ecological adventure, and language training in Europe. Programs are 3-5 weeks long. Positions as group leaders are available world-wide if you are over 24, have previous in-country experience, are fluent in the language, and have experience with high school students.

Goethe-Institut, Postfach 190419, 80404 München (tel. (089) 15 92 10; fax 15 92 14 50; email zentralverwaltung@goethe.de; http://www.goethe.de/uk/ney/enindex.htm), runs numerous language programs in Germany and abroad; it also orchestrates high school exchange programs in Germany. For information on these and on their many cultural offerings, contact your local branch (**Australia,** Canberra City, Melbourne, Sydney; **Canada,** Montreal, Toronto, Vancouver; **Ireland,** Dublin; **New Zealand,** Wellington; **U.K.,** Glasgow, London, Manchester, York; **U.S.,** New York, Washington, D.C., Boston, Atlanta, San Francisco, Los Angeles, and Seattle) or write to the main office.

Peterson's Guides, P.O. Box 2123, Princeton, NJ 08543-2123 (tel. (800) 338-3282; fax (609) 243-9150; http://www.petersons.com). Their comprehensive *Study Abroad* (US$30) guide lists programs in countries all over the world and provides essential information on the study abroad experience in general. Their new *Learning Adventures Around the World* (US$25) annual guide to "learning vacations" lists volunteer, museum-hopping, study, and travel programs all over the world. Purchase a copy at your local bookstore or call their toll-free number in the U.S.

WORK AND VOLUNTEER

There's no better way to immerse yourself in a foreign culture than to become part of its economy. It's easy to find a **temporary job,** but it will rarely be glamorous and may not even pay for your plane fare, let alone your accommodation. Officially, you can hold a job in most countries only with a **work permit.** Getting permission to work in Germany is a challenge. If you hold EU citizenship, you may work in Germany without special permission, though you must register with local police to take up residence. The organizations and publications listed below can help point you toward employment abroad; you should speak with former clients before paying any registration fees. If your parents were born in an EU country, you may be able to claim dual citizenship or at least the right to a work permit. (Beware of countries where citizenship obligates you to do military service.) There are, however, ways to make it easier. Friends in your destination country can help expedite work permits or arrange work-for-accommodations swaps. Students can check with their universities' foreign language departments, which may have connections to job openings abroad. Call the Consulate or Embassy of the country in which you wish to work to get more information about work permits.

If you are a **U.S. citizen** and a full-time student at a U.S. university, the simplest way to get a job abroad is through work permit programs run by **Council on International Educational Exchange (Council)** and its member organizations. For a US$225 application fee, Council can procure three- to six-month work permits (and a handbook to help you find work and housing) for Germany. Positions require evidence of language skill. Contact Council for more information (see **Study,** p. 21). Vacation Work Publications publishes *Work Your Way Around the World* (UK£11, UK£ 2.50 postage, UK£1.50 within U.K) to help you (see below). With unemployment rising, Germany's days as a mecca for unskilled foreign workers are over. The German government maintains a series of federally run employment offices, the **Bundesanstalt für Arbeit,** throughout the country. Foreign applications are directed to the central office at Feuerbachstr. 42-6, 60325 Frankfurt am Main. The office tends to treat EU citizens with specific skills more favorably than those from other countries. The youth division is a bit more welcoming for foreign students ages 18-30 seeking summer employment; jobs frequently involve manual labor.

The best tips on jobs for foreigners often come from other travelers, so be alert and inquisitive. Some follow the grape harvest in the fall—mostly in France, but also in Germany's Mosel Valley. Menial jobs can be found anywhere in Europe; ski resorts leave much of the gruntwork to foreigners. Ask at pubs, cafes, restaurants, and hotels. Be sure to be aware of your rights as an employee; should a crafty national try to refuse payment at the end of the season, it'll help if you have a written confirmation of your agreement. Youth hostels often provide room and board to travelers willing to stay a while and help run the place. Consider a job **teaching English.** Post a sign in markets or learning centers stating that you are a native speaker, and scan the classifieds of local newspapers. It may be your only option in eastern Germany. Organizations in the U.S. will place you in a (low-paying) teaching job; professional positions are harder to get. Most European schools require at least a bachelor's degree and training in teaching English as a foreign language.

Surrey Books, 230 E. Ohio St. #120, Chicago, IL 60611 (tel. (800) 326-4430; fax (312) 751-7330; email surreybks@aol.com) publishes *How to Get a Job in Europe: The Insider's Guide* (1995 edition US$18).

Transitions Abroad Publishing, Inc., 18 Hulst Rd., P.O. Box 1300, Amherst, MA 01004-1300 (tel. (800) 293-0373; fax (413) 256-0373; email trabroad@aol.com; http://www.transabroad.com). Publishes *Transitions Abroad,* a bi-monthly magazine listing opportunities and printed resources for those seeking to study, work, or travel abroad. They also publish *The Alternative Travel Directory,* an exhaustive list of information for globetrotters. For subscriptions (6 issues in the U.S. US$25, Canada US$30, other countries US$38), contact them at *Transitions Abroad,* Dept. TRA, Box 3000, Denville, NJ 07834 or call (800) 293-0373.

Uniworld Business Publications, Inc., 257 Central Park West, 10A, New York, NY 10024-4110 (tel. (212) 496-2448; fax 769-0413; email uniworld@aol.com; http://www.uniworldbp.com). Check your local library for their *The Directory of American Firms Operating in Foreign Countries* (1996; US$220) and *The Directory of Foreign Firms Operating in the United States* (1995; US$200). They also publish regional and country editions of the two Directories (US$29 and up).

Vacation Work Publications, 9 Park End St., Oxford OX1 1HJ, U.K. (tel. (01865) 24 19 78; fax 79 08 85). Publishes a variety of guides and directories with job listings and info for working travelers, including *Teaching English Abroad* (UK£10, £2.50 postage, within UK £2.50 and £1.50 postage) and *The Au Pair and Nanny's Guide to Working Abroad* (UK£9, £2.50 and £1.50 postage). Options for summer or full-time work in many countries. Write for a catalogue of their publications.

The following **au pair** agencies can help you find work as a nanny in Germany.

Childcare International, Ltd., Trafalgar House, Grenville Place, London NW7 3SA, U.K. (tel. (0181) 959 36 11 or 906 31 16; fax 906 34 61; email office@child-int.demon.co.uk; http://www.childint.demon.co.uk). Offers au pair positions in Germany and elsewhere. Placements are 6-12 months with some available summer positions. Member of the International Au Pair Association. UK£80 placement fee.

InterExchange, 161 Sixth Ave., New York, NY 10013 (tel. (212) 924-0446; fax 924-0575; email interex@earthlink.net; http://www.interexchange.org) offers au pair and teaching opportunities. Places au pairs for 2-18 month placements in Germany and Europe (US$250-450 placement fee).

Volunteer jobs are readily available almost everywhere. You may receive room and board in exchange for your labor; the work can be fascinating (or tedious). You can sometimes avoid the high application fees charged by the organizations that arrange placement by contacting individual work programs directly; check with the organizations. Listings in Vacation Work Publications's *International Directory of Voluntary Work* (UK£10; postage UK£2.50, £1.50 within U.K.) can be helpful (see above).

Council has a Voluntary Services Dept., 205 E. 42nd St., New York, NY 10017 (tel. (888) COUNCIL (268-6245); fax (212) 822-2699; email info@ciee.org; http://www.ciee.org) which offers 2-4 week environmental or community services projects in over 30 countries. Participants must be at least 18 years old. Minimum US$295 placement fee; additional fees may also apply for various countries.

Service Civil International Voluntary Service (SCI-VS), 5474 Walnut Level Rd., Crozet, VA 22932 (tel. (804) 823-1826; fax 823-5027; email sciivsusa@igc.apc.org; http://wworks_com/~sciivs/). Arranges placement in work programs in Europe (ages 18 and over). Local organizations sponsor groups for physical or social work. Registration fees US$50-250, depending on the camp location.

Volunteers for Peace, 43 Tiffany Rd., Belmont, VT 05730 (tel. (802) 259-2759; fax 259-2922; email vfp@vfp.org; http://www.vfp.org). A nonprofit organization that arranges speedy placement in 2-3 week programs of 10-15 people. VFP offers over 1000 programs in 70 countries. Most complete and up-to-date listings provided in the annual *International Workcamp Directory* (US$15). Registration fee US$200. Some programs are open to 16 and 17 year olds for US$225. Free newsletter.

Willing Workers on Organic Farms (WWOOF), Postfach 59, CH-8124, Maur, Switzerland (email wwoof@dataway.ch), and 50 Hans Crescent, London SW1X ONA, England (tel. (0171) 823-9937) distributes a list of names of organic farmers who offer room and board in exchange for help on the farm. Include 2 international postal reply coupon with your request or contact them by email.

■ Specific Concerns

WOMEN TRAVELERS

Women exploring on their own inevitably face additional safety concerns, but these warnings and suggestions should not discourage women from traveling alone. Trust your instincts: if you'd feel better somewhere else, move on. Always carry extra money for a phone call, bus, or taxi. You might consider staying in hostels which offer single rooms that lock from the inside or in religious organizations that offer rooms for women only. Communal showers in some hostels are safer than others. Stick to centrally located accommodations and avoid solitary late excursions. **Hitchhiking** is never safe for lone women, or even for two women traveling together. Choose train compartments occupied by other women or couples; ask the conductor to put together a women-only compartment if he or she doesn't offer to do so first.

When in a foreign country, the less you look like a tourist, the better off you'll be. Look as if you know where you're going (even when you don't) and consider approaching women or couples for directions if you're lost or feel uncomfortable. In general, dress conservatively, especially in rural areas. You must be over 18 to purchase and use various pocket-sized containers of mace (DM12-18), available in many knife and scissor stores. Yes, knife and scissor stores.

Memorize the emergency numbers in Germany: **police: 110** and **ambulance: 115.** If you spend time in cities, you may be harassed no matter how you're dressed. Your best answer to verbal harassment is no answer at all (a reaction is what the harasser wants). In crowds, you may be pinched or squeezed by oversexed slimeballs. Wearing a conspicuous **wedding band** may help prevent such incidents. If need be, turn to an older woman for help in an uncomfortable situation; her stern rebukes will usually be enough to embarrass the most persistent jerks. Unlike in some parts of southern Europe, catcalls and whistling are not acceptable behavior in Germany—you can feel comfortable rebuking your harasser. Loudly saying *"Laß mich in Ruhe!"* ("Leave me alone!"; pronounced LAHSS MEEKH EEN ROOH-eh) should suffice. German standards of public behavior are fairly reserved, and you can often rebuff a harasser by calling the attention of passersby to his behavior. A **Model Mugging** course will not only prepare you for a potential mugging, but will also raise your level of awareness of your surroundings as well as your confidence (see **Safety and Security,** p. 14). The following books provide advice on female traveler safety:

Handbook For Women travelers by Maggie and Gemma Moss (UK£9). Encyclopedic and well-written. Available from Piatkus Books, 5 Windmill St., London W1P 1HF (tel. (0171) 631 0710).

A Journey of One's Own, by Thalia Zepatos, (US$17). Interesting and full of good advice, with a bibliography of books and resources. **Adventures in Good Company,** on group travel by the same author, costs US$17. Available from The Eighth Mountain Press, 624 Southeast 29th Ave., Portland, OR 97214 (tel. (503) 233-3936; fax 233-0774; email eightmt@aol.com).

Women Travel: Adventures, Advice & Experience by Miranda Davies and Natania Jansz (Penguin, US$13). Info on several foreign countries plus a decent bibliography and resource index. The sequel, *More Women Travel,* costs US$15. Both from Rough Guides, 375 Hudson St. 3rd Fl., New York, NY 10014.

A Foxy Old Woman's Guide to Traveling Alone, by Jay Ben-Lesser (Crossing Press, US $11). Info, informal advice, and a resource list on solo travel on a low-to-medium budget.

OLDER TRAVELERS

Senior citizens are eligible for a wide range of discounts on transportation, museums, movies, theaters, concerts, restaurants, and accommodations. If you don't see a senior citizen price listed, ask, and you may be delightfully surprised. Agencies for senior group travel, like **Eldertreks,** 597 Markham St., Toronto, Ont., CANADA, M6G 2L7 (tel. (416) 588-5000; fax 588-9839; email passages@inforamp.net), and **Walking the World,** P.O. Box 1186, Fort Collins, CO 80522 (tel. (970) 225-0500; fax 225-9100; email walktworld@aol.com), are growing in enrollment and popularity.

Gateway Books, 2023 Clemens Rd., Oakland, CA 94602 (tel. (510) 530-0299; credit card orders (800) 669-0773; fax (510) 530-0497; email donmerwin@aol.co; http://www.discoverypress.com/gateway.html). Publishes *Europe the European Way: A Traveler's Guide to Living Affordably in the World's Great Cities* (US $14), which offers hints for budget-conscious seniors considering a long stay or retiring abroad.

Pilot Books, 127 Sterling Ave., P.O. Box 2102, Greenport, NY 11944 (tel. (516) 477-1094 or (800) 79PILOT (797-4568); fax (516) 477-0978; email feedback@pilot-books.com; http://www.pilotbooks.com). Publishes a large number of helpful guides including *Doctor's Guide to Protecting Your Health Before, During, and After International Travel* (US$10, postage US$2) and *Senior Citizens' Guide to Budget Travel in Europe* (US$6, postage US$2, new edition next year). Call or write for a complete list of titles.

No Problem! Worldwise Tips for Mature Adventurers, by Janice Kenyon. Advice and info on insurance, finances, security, health, packing. Useful appendices. US$16 from Orca Book Publishers, P.O. Box 468, Custer, WA 98240-0468.

BISEXUAL, GAY, AND LESBIAN TRAVELERS

Germany is fairly tolerant of homosexuality. The German word for gay is *Schwul,* for lesbian *Lesben*. *Let's Go* provides information on local bisexual, gay, and lesbian culture in **Practical Information** listings and **Entertainment** sections of city descriptions. In general, the larger the city and the farther north you travel, the more tolerant the attitudes towards bisexual, gay, and lesbian travelers. The major centers of gay life are Berlin, Hamburg, Frankfurt, and Munich; there is also a scene in Köln. Women should look for *Frauencafes* and *Frauenkneipen*. It should be stressed that while such cafes are for women only, they are *not* for lesbians only. The local *Frauenbuchladen* (women's bookstores) are a good resource. Local **AIDS-Hilfe** offices tend to be an excellent means of finding bisexual, gay, and lesbian resources and nightlife.

Are You Two...Together? A Gay and Lesbian Travel Guide to Europe. A travel guide with anecdotes and tips for gays and lesbians traveling in Europe. Includes overviews of regional laws relating to gays and lesbians, lists of gay/lesbian organizations, and establishments catering to, friendly to, or indifferent to gays and lesbians. Available in bookstores. Random House, US$18.

Gay Europe. A gay guide providing a quick look at gay life in countries throughout Europe, including restaurants, clubs, and beaches. Introductions to each country cover laws and gay-friendliness. Available in bookstores. Perigee Books, US$14.

Giovanni's Room, 345 S. 12th St., Philadelphia, PA 19107 (tel. (215) 923-2960; fax 923-0813; email giolphilp@netaxs.com). An international feminist, lesbian, and gay bookstore with mail-order service carrying many of the publications listed here.

International Gay and Lesbian Travel Association, P.O. Box 4974, Key West, FL 33041 (tel. (800) 448-8550; fax (305) 296-6633; email IGTA@aol.com; http://www.rainbow-mall.com/igta). Call for lists of travel agents, accommodations, and events serving gay and lesbian travelers worldwide.

Spartacus International Gay Guides (US$33), published by **Bruno Gmunder,** Postfach 61 01 04, D-10921 Berlin, Germany (tel. (030) 615 00 3-42; fax 615 91 34). Lists bars, restaurants, hotels, and bookstores around the world catering to gays. Also lists hotlines for gays in various countries and homosexuality laws for each country. Available in bookstores and in the U.S. by mail from Lambda Rising, 1625 Connecticut Ave. NW, Washington D.C., 20009-1013 (tel. (202) 462-6969). Bruno Gmunder also publishes travel guides to Berlin, Stuttgart, Hamburg, Munich, Köln, Düsseldorf, and Frankfurt for gay men.

MINORITY TRAVELERS

Germany has a significant minority population composed mainly of ethnic Turks. In addition, there are refugees from Eastern and Southern Europe and, facing increasing hostility, a number of Romany-Sinti people (also known as Gypsies). Eastern Germany also has a number of Vietnamese residents. All the same, conspicuously non-German foreigners may stand out.

In certain regions, tourists of color or members of certain religious groups may feel threatened by local residents. Neo-Nazi skinheads in the large cities of former East Germany, as well as in Western Germany, have been known to attack foreigners, especially non-whites. In these areas, common sense will serve you best. Either historical or newly developed discrimination against established minority residents may surface against travelers who are members of those minority groups. *Let's Go* researchers are instructed not to include within our guides establishments that are known to discriminate.

DISABLED TRAVELERS

By and large, Germany is one of the more accessible countries for travelers with disabilities (*Behinderte* or *Schwerbehinderte*). Germany's excellent public transportation systems make most places easily accessible for both older travelers and for travelers with disabilities; many public transport systems are wheelchair-accessible. The international **wheelchair** icon or a large letter "B" indicates access. Major cities have audible crossing signals for the blind. Trains have a few seats or an integrated compartment reserved for passengers with disabilities. Almost all EuroCity (EC) trains in and out of Germany have wheelchair facilities. Many platforms can be hard to reach; alternative ones sometimes exist. For more info, contact **Deutsche Bahn** (see **Getting Around: By Train,** p. 39). Those traveling with guide dogs should be aware that Germany requires evidence from a licensed veterinarian of vaccination for rabies at least 30 days but not more than 12 months before entering the country for all dogs and cats. A notarized German translation of this certificate is required.

Information for disabled travelers:

Facts on File, 11 Penn Plaza, 15th Fl., New York, NY 10001 (tel. (212) 967-8800). Publishers of *Disability Resource,* a reference guide for travelers with disabilities (US$45 plus shipping). Available at bookstores or by mail order.

Graphic Language Press, P.O. Box 270, Cardiff by the Sea, CA 92007 (tel. (760) 944-9594; email niteowl@cts.com; http://www.geocities.com/Paris/1502). Comprehensive advice for wheelchair travelers including accessible accommodations, transportation, and sight-seeing for various European cities. Their web site features worldwide trip reports from disabled travelers, tips, resources, and networking.

Mobility International, USA (MIUSA), P.O. Box 10767, Eugene, OR 97440 (tel. (514) 343-1284 voice and TDD; fax 343-6812; email info@miusa.org; http://miusa.org). International Headquarters in Brussels, rue de Manchester 25 Brussels, Belgium, B-1070 (tel. (322) 410-6297; fax 410 6874). Contacts in 30 countries. Information on travel programs, international work camps, accommodations, access guides, and organized tours for those with physical disabilities. Membership US$30 per year. Sells the 3rd Edition of *A World of Options: A Guide to International Educational Exchange, Community Service, and Travel for Persons with Disabilities* (US$30, nonmembers US$35, organizations US$40).

Moss Rehab Hospital Travel Information Service, (tel. (215) 456-9600; TDD (215) 456-9602). A telephone information resource center on international travel accessibility and other travel-related concerns for those with disabilities.

Society for the Advancement of Travel for the Handicapped (SATH), 347 Fifth Ave. #610, New York, NY 10016 (tel. (212) 447-1928; fax 725-8253; email sath-travel@aol.com; http://www.sath.org). Publishes a quarterly travel magazine *OPEN WORLD* (free for members or on subscription, US$13 for nonmembers). Also publishes a wide range of information sheets on disability travel facilitation and accessible destinations. Annual membership US$45, students and seniors US$30.

Tours or trips for disabled travelers:

Directions Unlimited, 720 N. Bedford Rd., Bedford Hills, NY 10507 (tel. (800) 533-5343; in NY (914) 241-1700; fax 241-0243). Specializes in arranging individual and group vacations, tours, and cruises for the physically disabled. Group tours for blind travelers.

Flying Wheels Travel Service, 143 W. Bridge St., Owatonne, MN 55060 (tel. (800) 535-6790; fax 451-1685). Arranges trips in the U.S. and abroad for groups and individuals in wheelchairs or with other sorts of limited mobility.

The Guided Tour Inc., Elkins Park House, 114B, 7900 Old York Rd., Elkins Park, PA 19027-2339 (tel. (800) 783-5841 or (215) 782-1370; fax 635-2637). Organizes travel programs for persons with developmental and physical challenges and those requiring renal dialysis. Call, fax, or write for a free brochure.

DIETARY CONCERNS

For historic and political reasons, few Jews live in Germany, and the **kosher** offerings are correspondingly small. *Let's Go* makes every attempt to identify kosher restaurants, which lie mostly in large urban areas. Your own synagogue or college Hillel should have access to lists of Jewish institutions across the nation. If you are strict in your observance, consider preparing your own food on the road.

Although Germany is unapologetically carnivorous, **vegetarian** restaurants have proliferated along with the blooming "alternative scene" in larger cities. *Let's Go* makes an effort to identify restaurants that offer vegetarian choices. Dairy products are excellent, and fish is widely available on the North Sea coast and in lakeside towns. Tourist offices often publish lists of kosher and vegetarian restaurants.

The International Vegetarian Travel Guide (UK£2) was last published in 1991. Order back copies from the Vegetarian Society of the U.K. (VSUK), Parkdale, Dunham Rd., Altringham, Cheshire WA14 4QG (tel. (0161) 928 0793). VSUK also publishes other titles, including *The European Vegetarian Guide to Hotels and Restaurants*. Call or send a self-addressed, stamped envelope for a listing.

The Jewish Travel Guide lists synagogues, kosher restaurants, and Jewish institutions in over 80 countries. Available from Ballantine-Mitchell Publishers, Newbury House 890-900, Eastern Ave., Newbury Park, Ilford, Essex, U.K. IG2 7HH (tel. (0181) 599 88 66; fax 599 09 84). It is available in the U.S. from Sepher-Hermon Press, 1265 46th St., Brooklyn, NY 11219 (tel. (718) 972-9010; US$15 plus US$2.50 shipping).

RELIGIOUS TRAVELERS

It is impossible to discuss religion in contemporary Germany without hearing the many voices of past and present: the voices of Holocaust survivors, the voices of neo-Nazis, the voices of the courageous East German pastors who led the peaceful resistance against the communists, and the voice of the modern Basic Law which states that "freedom of faith and conscience as well as freedom of religious or other belief shall be inviolable. The undisturbed practice of religion shall be guaranteed" (paragraph 4). Despite having had until recently Europe's most liberal immigration policies for asylum-seekers, some of these policies have been rescinded in the recent anti-foreigner climate. The total Jewish population in Germany today is approximately 40-50,000. The largest Jewish congregations are in Berlin and Frankfurt am Main, which together are home to over 10,000 Jews. An influx of foreign workers has brought along with it a strong Islamic population; today, almost two million Muslims, mostly from Turkey, live in Germany. For information, contact the following organizations.

Protestant: Kirchenamt der Evangelischen Kirche in Deutschland, Herrenhäuserstr. 12, 30419 Hannover (tel. (0511) 279 60; fax 279 67 07; email ekd@ekd.de).

Catholic: Katholisches Auslandssekretariat der Deutschen Bischofskonferenz Tourismus und Urlauberselsorge, Kaiser-Friedrich-Str. 9 53113 Bonn (tel. (0228) 91 14 30; fax 911 43 33).

Muslim: Islamische Gemeinschaft. **Berlin,** Einemstr. 8 10787, Berlin-Schöneberg (tel./fax (030) 262 54 69).

Jewish: There are Jewish community centers in each of the following cities. **Berlin,** Fasanenstr. 79-80 (tel. (030) 884 20 30); **Bonn,** Tempelstr. 2-4 (tel. (0228) 21 35 60); **Düsseldorf,** Zietenstr. 50 (tel. (0211) 48 03 13); **Frankfurt,** Westendstr. 43, 60325 (tel. (069) 740 72 15; **Köln,** Roonstr. 50 (tel. (0221) 23 56 26 or 23 56 27); **Munich,** Reichenbachstr. 27, 80469 (tel. (089) 202 40 00).

TRAVELERS WITH CHILDREN

Family vacations are recipes for disaster unless you slow your pace and plan ahead. When deciding where to stay, remember the special needs of young children; if you pick a B&B, call ahead and make sure it's child-friendly. If you rent a car, make sure the rental company provides a car seat for younger children. Consider using a papoose-style device to carry your baby on walking trips. Be sure that your child carries ID in case of an emergency; if it gets lost, and arrange a reunion spot in case of separation when sight-seeing (e.g., Cinderella's castle at Disneyland).

Restaurants often have children's menus and discounts. Virtually all museums and tourist attractions also have a children's rate. Children under two generally fly for 10% of the adult airfare on international flights (this does not necessarily include a seat). International fares are usually discounted 25% for children from two to 11. Breast-feeding is often a problem while traveling due to lack of private space; pack accordingly or search for mother-friendly spots wherever you end up.

The following publications offer tips for adults traveling with children or distractions for the kids themselves. You can also contact the publishers to see if they have other related publications that you might find useful.

Backpacking with Babies and Small Children (US$10). Published by Wilderness Press, 2440 Bancroft Way, Berkeley, CA 94704 (tel. (800) 443-7227 or (510) 843-8080; fax 548-1355; email wpress@ix.netcom.com).

Take Your Kids to Europe, by Cynthia W. Harriman (US$17). A budget travel guide geared towards families. Published by Globe-Pequot Press, 6 Business Park Rd., Old Saybrook, CT 06475 (tel. (800) 285-4078; fax (860) 395-1418; email charriman@masongrant.com).

Travel with Children, by Maureen Wheeler (US$12, postage US$1.50). Published by Lonely Planet Publications, Embarcadero West, 155 Filbert St. #251, Oakland, CA 94607 (tel. (800) 275-8555 or (510) 893-8555; fax 893-8563; email info@lonelyplanet.com; http://www.lonelyplanet.com). Also at P.O. Box 617, Hawthorn, Victoria 3122, Australia.

■ Packing

Plan your packing according to the type of travel you'll be doing (multi-city backpacking tour, week-long stay in one place, etc.) and the area's high and low temperatures. If you don't pack lightly, your back and wallet will suffer. The more things you have, the more you have to lose. The larger your pack, the more cumbersome it is to store safely. Before you leave, pack your bag, strap it on, and imagine yourself walking uphill on hot asphalt for the next three hours. A good rule is to lay out only what you absolutely need, then take half the clothes and twice the money.

LUGGAGE

If you plan to cover most of your itinerary by foot, or anticipate frequent moves between and around cities, a sturdy **backpack** is unbeatable. Many packs are designed specifically for travelers, while others are for hikers. In any case, get a pack with a strong, padded hip belt to transfer weight from your shoulders to your hips. Be wary of excessively low-end prices, and don't sacrifice quality. Good packs cost anywhere from US$150 to US$420. A **suitcase or trunk** is fine if you plan to live in 1 or 2 cities and explore from there, but a bad idea if you're going to be moving around a lot. Make sure it has wheels and consider how much it weighs even when empty. Hard-sided luggage is more durable and doesn't wrinkle your clothes, but is also heavier. Soft-sided luggage should have a PVC frame, a strong lining to resist bad weather and rough handling, and triple-stitched seams for durability. If you are not backpacking, an empty, lightweight **duffel bag** packed inside your luggage will be useful: once abroad you can fill your luggage with purchases and keep your dirty clothes in the duffel. Bringing a smaller bag, such as a **backpack** or **rucksack,** in addition to your pack or suitcase lets you leave your big bag behind while sight-seeing. It can be used as an airplane carry-on to keep essentials with you.

A **moneybelt** or **neck pouch,** available at any good camping store, guards your money, passport, railpass, and other important articles. Keep it with you *at all times.* The moneybelt should tuck inside the waist of your pants or skirt; you want to hide your valuables, not announce them with a colorful fanny- or butt-pack. (For more information on protecting you and your valuables see **Safety and Security,** p. 14.)

CLOTHING AND FOOTWEAR

When choosing your travel wardrobe, aim for versatility and comfort, and avoid fabrics that wrinkle easily (to test a fabric, hold it tightly in your fist for 20 seconds). Solid colors match and mix best. In certain clubs, stricter dress codes call for something besides the basic shorts, T-shirts, and jeans. Always bring a jacket or wool sweater. Well-cushioned **sneakers** are good for walking, though you may want to consider a good water-proofed pair of **hiking boots.** A double pair of socks—light silk or polypropylene inside and thick wool outside—will cushion feet, keep them dry, and help prevent blisters. Bring a pair of flip-flops for protection in the shower. **Rain gear** is a must in Germany. A waterproof jacket and a backpack cover will take care of you and your stuff at a moment's notice. Gore-Tex® is a miracle fabric that's both waterproof and breathable; it's all but mandatory if you plan on hiking. Avoid cotton as outer-wear, especially if you will be outdoors a lot.

MISCELLANEOUS

If you plan to stay in **youth hostels,** don't pay the linen charge; make the requisite **sleepsack** yourself. Fold a full size sheet in half the long way, then sew it closed along the open long side and one of the short sides. For those less textilely inclined, sleepsacks can be bought at any HI outlet store. *Let's Go* attempts to provide information on **laundromats** in the **Practical Information** listings for each city, but sometimes it may be easiest to use a sink to get rid of your stink. Bring a small bar or tube of detergent soap, a rubber squash ball to stop up the sink, and a travel clothes line.

Machines which heat-disinfect **contact lenses** will require a small converter (about US$20) if you are visiting an area with a different current. Consider switching temporarily to a chemical disinfection system, but check with your lens dispenser to see if it's safe to switch. Your preferred brand of contact lens supplies are sometimes rare or expensive. Bring enough saline and cleaner for your entire vacation, or wear glasses. In Germany, **electricity** is 220 volts AC, enough to fry any 110V North American appliance. 220V Electrical appliances don't like 110V current, either. Visit a hardware store for an **adapter** (which changes the shape of the plug) and a **converter** (which changes the voltage). Don't make the mistake of using only an adapter (unless appliance instructions explicitly state otherwise), or you'll melt your radio.

Film is expensive just about everywhere. Bring film from home and, if you will be seriously upset if the pictures are ruined, develop it at home. If you're not a serious photographer, you might want to consider bringing a **disposable camera** or two rather than an expensive permanent one. Despite disclaimers, airport security X-rays *can* fog film, so either buy a lead-lined pouch, sold at camera stores, or ask the security to hand inspect it. Always pack it in your carry-on luggage.

Other useful items: first-aid kit; umbrella; sealable plastic bags (for damp clothes, soap, food, shampoo, and other spillables); alarm clock; waterproof matches; hat; moleskin (for blisters); needle and thread; safety pins; sunglasses; a personal stereo (Walkman) with headphones; pocketknife; plastic water bottle; compass; towel; padlock; whistle; rubber bands; toilet paper; flashlight; cold-water soap; earplugs; insect repellent; electrical tape (for patching tears); clothespins; maps and phrasebooks; tweezers; garbage bags; sunscreen; vitamins. Don't forget your travel guide!

DRESS FOR SUCCESS

If you will encounter situations which require more than the jeans and T-shirt uniform, remember that elegance is understated. Black is ideal because it is always in fashion and you can't tell if it's been worn five times. If you have the inclination and the room, you might decide to bring an extra pair of shoes so you don't ruin that snazzy outfit, although some say that hiking boots go with everything.

GETTING THERE

■ Budget Travel Agencies

Students and people under 26 ("youth") with proper ID qualify for discounted air-fares. These are rarely available from airlines or travel agents, but instead from student travel agencies which negotiate special reduced-rate bulk purchase with the airlines, then resell them to the youth market. Return-date change fees also tend to be low (around US$35 per segment through Council or Let's Go Travel). Most flights are on major airlines, though in peak season some agencies may sell seats on less reliable chartered aircraft. Student travel agencies can also help non-students and people over 26, but probably won't be able to get the same low fares.

TRAVEL AGENCIES

Campus Travel, 52 Grosvenor Gardens, London SW1W 0AG (http://www.campus-travel.co.uk). 46 branches in the U.K. Student and youth fares on plane, train, boat, and bus travel. Discount and ID cards for students and youths, travel insurance for students and those under 35, and maps and guides. Puts out travel suggestion booklets. Telephone booking service: in Europe call (0171) 730 34 02; in North America call (0171) 730 21 01; in Manchester call (0161) 273 17 21; in Scotland (0131) 668 33 03; worldwide call (0171) 730 81 11.

Council Travel (http://www.ciee.org/travel/index.htm), the travel division of Council, is a full-service travel agency specializing in youth and budget travel. They offer discount airfares on scheduled airlines, railpasses, hosteling cards, low-cost accommodations, guidebooks, budget tours, travel gear, and international student (ISIC), youth (GO25), and teacher (ITIC) identity cards. U.S. offices include: Emory Village, 1561 N. Decatur Rd., **Atlanta,** GA 30307 (tel. (404) 377-9997); 2000 Guadalupe, **Austin,** TX 78705 (tel. (512) 472-4931); 273 Newbury St., **Boston,** MA 02116 (tel. (617) 266-1926); 1138 13th St., **Boulder,** CO 80302 (tel. (303) 447-8101); 1153 N. Dearborn, **Chicago,** IL 60610 (tel. (312) 951-0585); 10904 Lindbrook Dr., **Los Angeles,** CA 90024 (tel. (310) 208-3551); 1501 University Ave. SE #300, **Minneapolis,** MN 55414 (tel. (612) 379-2323); 205 E. 42nd St., **New York,** NY 10017 (tel. (212) 822-2700); 953 Garnet Ave., **San Diego,** CA 92109 (tel. (619) 270-6401); 530 Bush St., **San Francisco,** CA 94108 (tel. (415) 421-3473); 1314 NE 43rd St. #210, **Seattle,** WA 98105 (tel. (206) 632-2448); 3300 M St. NW, **Washington, D.C.** 20007 (tel. (202) 337-6464). **For U.S. cities not listed,** call 800-2-COUNCIL (226-8624). Also 28A Poland St. (Oxford Circus), **London,** W1V 3DB **U.K.** (tel. (0171) 287 3337), **Paris** (tel. 146 55 55 65), and **Munich Germany** (tel. 089 39 50 22).

Council Charter, 205 E. 42nd St., New York, NY 10017 (tel. (212) 661-0311; fax 972-0194). Offers a combination of inexpensive charter and scheduled airfares from a variety of U.S. gateways to most major European destinations. One-way fares and open jaws (fly into one city and out of another) are available.

CTS Travel, 220 Kensington High St., W8 (tel. (0171) 937 33 66 for travel in Europe, for travel world-wide 937 33 88; fax 937 90 27). Tube: High St. Kensington. Also at 44 Goodge St., W1. Tube: Goodge St. Specializes in student/youth travel and discount flights.

Let's Go Travel, Harvard Student Agencies, 17 Holyoke St., Cambridge, MA 02138 (tel. (617) 495-9649; fax 496-8015; email travel@hsa.net; http://hsa.net/travel). Railpasses, HI-AYH memberships, ISICs, ITICs, FIYTO cards, guidebooks (including every *Let's Go* at a substantial discount), maps, bargain flights, and a complete line of budget travel gear. All items available by mail; call or write for a catalogue.

Rail Europe Inc., 226 Westchester Ave., White Plains, NY 10604 (tel. (800) 438-7245; fax 432-1329; http://www.raileurope.com). Sells all Eurail products and passes, German Rail passes, and point-to-point tickets.

STA Travel, 6560 Scottsdale Rd. #F100, Scottsdale, AZ 85253 (tel. (800) 777-0112 nationwide; fax (602) 922-0793; http://sta-travel.com). A student and youth travel organization with over 150 offices worldwide offering discount airfares for young travelers, railpasses, accommodations, tours, insurance, and ISICs. Sixteen offices in the U.S. including: 297 Newbury Street, **Boston,** MA 02115 (tel. (617) 266-6014); 429 S. Dearborn St., **Chicago,** IL 60605 (tel. (312) 786-9050; 7202 Melrose Ave., **Los Angeles,** CA 90046 (tel. (213) 934-8722); 10 Downing St., Ste. G, **New York,** NY 10003 (tel. (212) 627-3111); 4341 University Way NE, **Seattle,** WA 98105 (tel. (206) 633-5000); 2401 Pennsylvania Ave., **Washington, D.C.** 20037 (tel. (202) 887-0912); 51 Grant Ave., **San Francisco,** CA 94108 (tel. (415) 391-8407), **Miami,** FL 33133 (tel. (305) 285-1044). In the U.K., 6 Wrights Ln., **London** W8 6TA (tel. (0171) 938 4711 for North American travel). In New Zealand, 10 High St., **Auckland** (tel. (09) 309 97 23). In Australia, 222 Faraday St., **Melbourne** VIC 3050 (tel. (03) 9349 6911).

Travel CUTS (Canadian Universities Travel Services Limited), 187 College St., Toronto, Ont. M5T 1P7 (tel. (416) 979-2406; fax 979-8167; email mail@travelcuts.com). Canada's national student travel bureau and equivalent of Council, with 40 offices across Canada. Also in the U.K., 295-A Regent St., **London** W1R 7YA (tel. (0171) 637 3161). Discounted domestic and international airfares open to all; special student fares to all destinations with valid ISIC. Issues ISIC, FIYTO, GO25, and HI hostel cards, as well as railpasses. Offers free *Student Traveler* magazine, as well as information on the Student Work Abroad Program (SWAP).

Unitravel, 117 North Warson Rd., St. Louis, MO 63132 (tel. (800) 325 2222; fax (314) 569 2503). Offers discounted airfares on major scheduled airlines from the U.S. to Europe.

USIT Youth and Student Travel, 19-21 Aston Quay, O'Connell Bridge, Dublin 2 (tel. (01) 677-8117; fax 679-8833). In the U.S.: New York Student Center, 895 Amsterdam Ave., New York, NY 10025 (tel. (212) 663-5435; email usitny@aol.com). Additional offices in Cork, Galway, Limerick, Waterford, Maynooth, Coleraine, Derry, Athlone, Jordanstown, Belfast, and Greece. Specializes in youth and student travel. Offers low-cost tickets and flexible travel arrangements all over the world. Supplies ISIC and FIYTO-GO25 cards in Ireland only.

■ By Plane

The **airline industry** attempts to squeeze every dollar from customers; finding a cheap airfare will be easier if you understand the airlines' systems. The national airline of Germany—**Deutsche Lufthansa** (tel. (800) 645-3880 in the U.S.; (800) 563-5954 in Canada)—serves the most cities, but fares tend to be high. Call every toll-free number and don't be afraid to ask about discounts; if you don't ask, it's unlikely they'll be volunteered. Have knowledgeable **travel agents** guide you; better yet, have an agent who specializes in the region(s) you will be traveling to guide you. An agent whose clients fly mostly to Miami will not be the best person to hunt down a bargain flight to Berlin. Travel agents may not want to spend time finding the cheapest fares (for which they receive the lowest commissions), but if you travel often, you should definitely find an agent who will cater to you and your needs.

Students and others under 26 should not have to pay full price for a ticket. Seniors can also get great deals; many airlines offer senior traveler clubs or airline passes with few restrictions and discounts for their companions as well. Sunday newspapers often have travel sections that list bargain fares from the local airport. Australians should consult the Saturday travel section of the *Sydney Morning Herald.* Outsmart airline reps with the phone-book-sized *Official Airline Guide* (check your local library; at US$359 per yr. the tome costs as much as some flights), a monthly guide listing nearly every scheduled flight in the world (with fares, US$479) and toll-free phone numbers for all the airlines which allow you to call in reservations directly. More affordable is Michael McColl's incredibly useful *The Worldwide Guide to Cheap Airfare* (US$15).

There is also a steadily increasing amount of travel information to be found on the Internet. The *Official Airline Guide* has a website (http://www.oag.com) which allows access to flight schedules. (One-time hook-up fee US$25 and a user's fee (US$0.17-0.47 per min.). The site also provides information on hotels and cruises, as well as rail and ferry schedules. **TravelHUB** (http://www.travelhub.com) will help you search for travel agencies on the web. The **Air Traveler's Handbook** (http://www.cis.ohio-state.edu/hypertext/faq/usenet/travel/air/handbook/top.html) is an excellent source of general information on air travel. Marc-David Seidel's **Airlines of the Web** (http://www.itn.net/airlines) provides links to pages and 800 numbers for most of the world's airlines. The newsgroup **rec.travel.air** is a good source of tips on current bargains. And a few airlines have begun holding auctions on their websites, including **Icelandair** (http://www.centrum.is/icelandair).

Most airfares peak between mid-June and early September. Midweek (Mon.-Thurs. morning) round-trip flights run about US$40-50 cheaper than on weekends; weekend flights, however, are generally less crowded. Traveling from hub to hub (for example, New York to Frankfurt) will win a more competitive fare than from smaller cities. Return-date flexibility is usually not an option for the budget traveler; traveling with an "open return" ticket can be pricier than fixing a return date and paying to change it. Whenever flying internationally, pick up your ticket well in advance of the departure date, have the flight **confirmed** within 72 hours of departure, and arrive at the airport at least three hours before your flight.

COMMERCIAL AIRLINES

The commercial airlines' lowest regular offer is the **Advance Purchase Excursion Fare** (APEX); specials advertised in newspapers may be cheaper, but have more restrictions and fewer available seats. APEX fares provide you with confirmed reservations and allow "open-jaw" tickets (landing in and returning from different cities). Generally, reservations must be made seven to 21 days in advance, with seven- to 14-day minimum and up to 90-day maximum stay limits, as well as hefty cancellation and change penalties (fees rise in summer). Book APEX fares early during peak season; by May you will have a hard time getting the departure date you want.

Look into flights to less-popular destinations or on smaller carriers. **Icelandair** (tel. (800) 223-5500) has last-minute offers and a stand-by fare from New York to Luxembourg (April-June 1 and Sept.-Oct. US$410; June 1-Aug. US$610). Reservations must be made within three days of departure.

Even if you pay an airline's lowest published fare, you may waste hundreds of dollars. For the adventurous or the bargain-hungry, there are other, perhaps less convenient and efficient options, but before shopping around it is a good idea to find out the average commercial price in order to measure just how great a "bargain" you are being offered.

TICKET CONSOLIDATORS

Ticket consolidators resell unsold tickets on commercial and charter airlines at unpublished fares. The consolidator market is by and large international. Consolidator flights are the best deals if you are traveling on short notice to bypass advance purchase requirements on a high-priced trip, to an offbeat destination, or in the peak season, when published fares are jacked way up to jack you. Fares sold by consolidators are generally much cheaper; a 30-40% price reduction is not uncommon. There are rarely age constraints or stay limitations, but unlike tickets bought through an airline, you won't be able to use your tickets on another flight if you miss yours, and you will have to go back to the consolidator to get a refund. Keep in mind that these tickets are often for coach seats on connecting (not direct) flights on foreign airlines, and that frequent-flyer miles may not be credited.

Not all consolidators deal with the public; many sell tickets through travel agents only. **Bucket shops** are retail agencies that specialize in getting cheap tickets. Although ticket prices are marked up slightly, bucket shops generally have access to a larger market than would be available to the public and can also get tickets from wholesale consolidators. Look for bucket shops' tiny ads in the travel section of weekend papers; in the U.S., the *Sunday New York Times* is a good source. In London, a call to the **Air Travel Advisory Bureau** (tel. (0171) 636 5000) can provide names of reliable consolidators and discount flight specialists. Kelly Monaghan's *Consolidators: Air Travel's Bargain Basement* (US$7, shipping US$2) from the Intrepid Traveler, P.O. Box 438, New York, NY 10034 (email intreptrav@aol.com), is an great source for more info and lists of consolidators by location and destination.

Among the many reputable and trustworthy companies are some shady wheeler-dealers. Contact the local Better Business Bureau to find out how long the company has been in business and its track record. It is preferable, although not necessary, to deal with consolidators close to home so you can visit in person. Ask to receive your tickets as quickly as possible so you have time to fix any problems. Get the company's policy in writing: insist on a **receipt** that gives full details about the tickets, refunds, and restrictions, and record who you talked to and when. It may be worth paying with a credit card (despite the 2-5% fee) so you can stop payment if you never receive your tickets. Beware the "bait and switch" gag: shyster firms will advertise a super-low fare and then tell a caller that it has been sold. If they can't offer you a price near the advertised fare on *any* date, it is a scam. Also ask about accommodations and car rental discounts; some consolidators have fingers in many pies. Mmmm, pie.

Try **Airfare Busters** with offices in D.C. (tel. (202) 776-0478), Boca Raton, FL (tel. (561) 994-9590), and Houston (tel. (800) 232-8783); **Cheap Tickets,** with offices in Los Angeles, San Francisco, Honolulu, Seattle, and New York (tel. (800) 377-1000); or **Discount Travel International,** New York (tel. (212) 362-3636; fax 362-3236). For a processing fee, depending on the number of travelers and the itinerary, **Travel Avenue,** Chicago (tel. (800) 333-3335; fax (312) 876-1254; http://www.travelavenue.com), will search for the lowest international airfare available, including consolidated prices, and will even give you a rebate on fares over US$300. To **Europe,** try **Rebel,** Valencia, CA (tel. (800) 227-3235; fax (805) 294-0981; email travel@rebeltours.com; http://www.rebeltours.com) or Orlando, FL (tel. (800) 732-3588). A number of consolidators sell tickets over the Internet; among them are **NOW Voyager** (email info@nowvoyagertravel.com; http://www.nowvoyager-travel.com) and **Travel Avenue** (http://www.travelavenue.com).

STAND-BY FLIGHTS

Airhitch, 2641 Broadway, 3rd Fl., New York, NY 10025 (tel. (800) 326-2009 or (212) 864-2000; fax 864-5489) and Los Angeles, CA (tel. (310) 726-5000), will add a certain thrill to the prospects of when you will leave and where exactly you will end up. Complete flexibility on both sides of the Atlantic is necessary; flights cost US$175 each way when departing from the Northeast, $269 from the West Coast or Northwest, $229 from the Midwest, and $209 from the Southeast. Travel within Europe is also possible, with rates ranging from $79-$129. The snag is that you don't buy a ticket; instead, you purchase the promise that you will get to a destination near where you're intending to go within a window of time (usually 5 days) from a location in a region you've specified. You call in before your date-range to hear all of your flight options for the next seven days and your probability of boarding. You then decide which flights you want to try to make and present a voucher at the airport which grants you the right to board a flight on a space-available basis. This procedure must be followed again for the return trip. Be aware that you may only receive a monetary refund if all available flights which departed within your date-range from the specified region are full, but future travel credit is always available. There are several offices in Europe, so you can wait to register for your return; the main one is in Paris (tel. (01) 47 00 16 30).

Air-Tech, Ltd., 588 Broadway #204, New York, NY 10012 (tel. (212) 219-7000; fax 219-0066), offers a very similar service. Their Travel Window is one to four days. Rates to and from Europe (continually updated; call and verify) are: Northeast US$169; West Coast US$239; Midwest/Southeast US$199. Upon registration and payment, Air-Tech sends you a FlightPass with a contact date falling soon before your Travel Window, when you are to call them for flight instructions. You must repeat the procedure to return—and no refunds are granted unless the company fails to get you a seat before your Travel Window expires. Air-Tech also arranges courier flights and regular confirmed-reserved flights at discount rates.

Be sure to read all the fine print in your agreements with either company—a call to The **Better Business Bureau of New York City** may be worthwhile. Be warned that it is difficult to receive refunds, and that clients' vouchers will not be honored if an airline fails to receive payment in time.

Better Safe than Sorry

Everyone who flies should be concerned with airline safety. The type and age of the aircraft used often indicate the airline's safety level—aircraft not produced by any of the main companies, such as Boeing, Airbus, McDonnell Douglas, or Fokker sometimes fall below acceptable standards (as can these large, more renown companies), and aircraft over 20-years-old require increased levels of maintenance. Travel agencies can tell you the type and age of aircraft on a particular route, as can the *Official Airline Guide* (http://www.oag.com). The **Federal Aviation Administration** (http://www.faa.gov) reviews the airline authorities for countries whose airlines enter the U.S. and divides the countries into three categories: stick with carriers in category 1. Call the **U.S. State Department** (tel. (202) 647-5225; http://travel.state.gov/travel_warnings.html) to check for posted travel advisories which sometimes note foreign carriers.

CHARTER FLIGHTS

Charters are flights a tour operator contracts with an airline (usually one specializing in charters) to fly extra loads of passengers to peak-season destinations. Charters are often cheaper than flights on scheduled airlines, especially during peak seasons, although fare wars, consolidator tickets, and small airlines can beat charter prices. Some charters operate nonstop, and restrictions on minimum advance-purchase and minimum stay are more lenient. However, charter flights fly less frequently than major airlines, make refunds particularly difficult, and are almost always fully booked.

Schedules and itineraries may also change or be cancelled at the last moment (as late as 48 hours before the trip, and without a full refund), and check-in, boarding, and baggage claim are often much slower. As always, pay with a credit card if you can; consider traveler's insurance against trip interruption.

Try **Interworld** (tel. (305) 443-4929; fax 443-0351), **Travac** (tel. (800) 872-8800; fax (212) 714-9063; email mail@travac.com; http://www.travac.com), or **Rebel,** Valencia, CA (tel. (800) 227-3235; fax (805) 294-0981; http://rebeltours.com; email travel@rebeltours.com) or Orlando, FL (tel. (800) 732-3588). Don't be afraid to call every number and hunt for the best deal.

Eleventh-hour **discount clubs** and **fare brokers** offer members savings on European travel, including charter flights and tour packages. Research your options carefully. **Last Minute Travel Club,** 100 Sylvan Rd., Woburn, MA 01801 (tel. (800) 527-8646 or (617) 267-9800), and **Discount Travel International** New York (tel. (212) 362-3636; fax 362-3236; see **Ticket Consolidators** above) are among the few travel clubs that don't charge a membership fee. Others include **Moment's Notice,** New York (tel. (718) 234-6295; fax 234 6450; http://www.moments-notice.com): air tickets, tours, and hotels; US$25 annual fee and **Travelers Advantage,** Stamford, CT (tel. (800) 548-1116; http://www.travelersadvantage.com; US$49 annual fee); and **Travel Avenue** (tel. (800) 333-3335; see **Ticket Consolidators** above). Study these organizations' contracts closely; you don't want to end up with an unwanted overnight layover.

COURIER COMPANIES AND FREIGHTERS

Those who travel light should consider flying internationally as a **courier.** The company hiring you will use your checked luggage space for freight; you're only allowed to bring carry-ons. You are responsible for the safe delivery of the baggage claim slips (given to you by a courier company representative) to the representative waiting for you when you arrive—don't screw up or you will be blacklisted as a courier. You will probably never see the cargo you are transporting—the company handles it all—and airport officials know that couriers are not responsible for the baggage checked for them. Restrictions to watch for: you must be over 21 (18 in some cases), have a valid passport, and procure your own visa if necessary; most flights are round-trip only with short fixed-length stays (usually one week); only single tickets are issued (but a companion may be able to get a next-day flight); and most flights are from New York. Round-trip fares to Western Europe from the U.S. range from US$250-400 (during the off-season) to US$400-550 (in summer). For an annual fee of $45, the **International Association of Air Travel Couriers,** 8 South J St., P.O. Box 1349, Lake Worth, Florida 33460 (tel. (561) 582-8320) informs travelers of courier opportunities worldwide via computer, fax, and mailings. Steve Lantos publishes a monthly update of courier options in **Travel Unlimited** as well as general information on budget travel (write P.O. Box 1058A, Allston, MA, 02134 for a free sample newsletter; subscription runs US$25 per year). Most flights to Europe originate from New York or London. **NOW Voyager,** 74 Varick St. #307, New York, NY 10013 (tel. (212) 431-1616; fax 334-5243); email info@nowvoyagertravel.com; http://www.nowvoyagertravel.com), acts as an agent for many courier flights worldwide primarily from New York and offers special last-minute deals to such cities as London, Paris, Rome, and Frankfurt for as little as US$200 round-trip plus a US$50 registration fee. (They also act as a consolidator; see **Ticket Consolidators** above.) Other agents to try are **Halbart Express,** 147-05 176th St., Jamaica, NY 11434 (tel. (718) 656-5000; fax 917-0708; offices in Chicago, Los Angeles, and London) and **Discount Travel International** (tel. (212) 362-3636; see **Ticket Consolidators,** p. 34).

You can also go directly through courier companies in New York, or check your bookstore or library for handbooks such as *Air Courier Bargains* (US$15 plus $2.50 shipping from the Intrepid Traveler, P.O. Box 438, New York, NY 10034; email intreptrav@aol.com). *The Courier Air Travel Handbook* (US$10 plus $3.50 shipping) explains how to travel as an air courier and contains names, phone numbers, and contact points of courier companies. It can be ordered directly from Bookmasters, Inc., P.O. Box 2039, Mansfield, OH 44905 (tel. (800) 507-2665).

■ By Train

European trains retain the charm and romance their North American counterparts lost long ago, but don't forget you're in the modern world. Bring food and a water bottle to fill at your hostel and take with you on train trips; the on-board cafe can be pricey, and train water is often undrinkable. Trains are not theft-proof; lock your compartment door if you can, and keep your valuables on your person at all times.

Many train stations have different counters for domestic and international tickets, seat reservations, and info—check before lining up. On major lines, reservations are always advisable, and often required, even with a railpass; make them at least a few hours in advance at the train station (US$3-10). Use of many of Europe's high speed or quality trains (such as EuroCity and InterCity) requires a supplementary expenditure for those traveling with German rail passes.

A sleeping berth in a couchette car is an affordable luxury (about US$20; reserve at the station at least several days in advance). Germany offers both youth ticket discounts and youth rail passes. (For more info, see **Getting Around,** p. 38.)

■ By Ferry

Travel by boat is a bewitching alternative favored by Europeans but often overlooked by foreigners. Most European ferries are comfortable and well-equipped. You should check in at least two hours early for a prime spot and allow plenty of time for late trains and getting to the port. Fares jump sharply in July and August. Ask for discounts; ISIC holders can often get student fares, and Eurail passholders get many reductions and free trips (check the brochure that comes with your railpass). You'll occasionally have to pay a small port tax (under US$10).

Ferries in the **North** and **Baltic Seas** are reliable and go everywhere. Ferries run from Rostock, Kiel, Lübeck, Hamburg, and Rügen Island to Scandinavia, Russia, and England. Those content with deck passage rarely need to book ahead. If you really have time to spare, **Ford's Travel Guides,** 19448 Londelius St., Northridge, CA 91324 (tel. (818) 701-7414; fax 701-7415) lists **freighter companies** that sail passengers worldwide in their *Freighter Travel Guide and Waterways of the World* (US$16, plus $2.50 postage if mailed outside the U.S.; for more details, see **By Boat,** p. 46.)

ONCE THERE

■ Tourist Offices

Every German town of any touristic importance is served by a local tourist office. These go by a bewildering variety of names—*Verkehrsamt, Fremdenverkehrsbüro, Verkehrsverein, Fremdenverkehrsverein, Tourist-Information, Gemeindeamt,* and (in spa towns) *Kurverwaltung* or *Kurverein.* To simplify things, all are marked by a standard thick lowercase **"i"** sign. Tourist offices are usually located in the town square or by the main train station—sometimes both. Exploit these offices for city maps (often free), cycling routes and rental options, information on sights and museums, and accommodations lists. Many offices will track down a vacant room for you and make a reservation, sometimes for free, otherwise for DM2–5. While Western German tourist personnel can be relied upon to speak fluent English, their comrades in Eastern Germany seldom possess anything more than a rudimentary knowledge of English. *Let's Go* lists tourist offices in the **Practical Information** sections.

■ Embassies and Consulates

If you're seriously ill or in trouble, your embassy can provide a list of doctors or pertinent legal advice, and can also contact your relatives. In *extreme* cases, they can offer emergency financial assistance. Embassies are located in Bonn; consulates can be found in other major cities. For the addresses of consulates not listed here, check the **Practical Information** sections of individual cities.

Australia: Embassy, Bonn, Godesberger Allee 105-107, 53175 (tel. (0228) 810 30; fax 37 62 68). **Consulates, Berlin,** Uhlandstr. 181-3 (tel. (030) 880 08 80). **Frankfurt am Main,** Gutleutstr. 85, 60329 (tel. (069) 273 90 90).

Canada: Embassy, Bonn, Friedrich-Wilhelm-Str. 18, 53133 (tel. (0228) 96 80; fax 968 39 00). **Consulates, Berlin,** Friedrichstr. 95, 10117 (tel. (030) 261 11 61). **Düsseldorf,** Prinz-Georg-Str. 126, 40476 (tel. (0211) 172170). **Hamburg,** ABC-Str. 45, 20354 (tel. (040) 35 55 62 90; fax 35 55 62 94). **Munich,** Tal 29, 80331 (tel. (089) 219 95 70).

Ireland: Embassy, Bonn, Godesberger Allee 119, 53175 (tel. (0228) 95 92 90). **Consulates, Berlin,** Ernst-Reuter-Platz 10, 10587 (tel. (030) 34 80 08 22). **Hamburg** Feldbrunnerstr. 43 (tel. (040) 44 18 62 13). **Munich,** Mauerkircherstr. 1a, 81679 (tel. (089) 98 57 23).

New Zealand: Embassy, Bonn, Bundeskanzlerpl. 2-10, 53113 (tel. (0228) 22 80 70; fax 22 16 87). **Consulates, Frankfurt,** Friedrichstr. 10-12, 60323 (tel. (069) 971 21 10). **Hamburg,** Heimhuderstr. 56, 20148 (tel. (040) 442 55 50).

South Africa: Embassy, Bonn, Auf der Hostert 3 (tel. (0228) 820 10). **Consulates, Berlin,** Douglasstr. 9, 14171 (tel. (030) 82 50 11; fax 20 18 41 58). **Munich,** Sendlinger-Tor-Platz 5, 80366 (tel. (089) 231 16 30).

U.K.: Embassy, Berlin, Unter Den Linden 32-34 10117 (tel. (030) 20 18 40; fax 20 18 41 58). **Consulates, Düsseldorf,** Yorckstr. 19, 40476 (tel. (0211) 944 80). **Frankfurt Am Main,** Generalkonsulat, Bockenheimer Landstr. 42, 60323 (tel. (069) 170 00 20). **Hamburg,** Harvestehuferweg 8a, 20148 (tel. (040) 448 03 20). **Munich,** Bürkheinstr. 10, 4th Fl. (tel. (089) 21 10 90). **Stuttgart,** Breitestr. 2, 70173 (tel. (0711) 16 26 90). The **Bonn** embassy has no consular services.

United States: Embassies, Bonn, Deichmanns Aue 29, 53170 (tel. (0228) 33 91; fax 339 26 63). **Berlin,** Neustädtische Kirchstr. 425, 10017 (tel. (030) 238 51 74; fax 238 62 90; consular section tel. (030) 832 92 33). **Düsseldorf,** Kennedydamm 15-7, 40476 (tel. (0211) 470 61 23). **Frankfurt Am Main,** Siesmayerstr. 21, 60323 (tel. (069) 753 50). **Hamburg,** Alsterufer 27-28, 20354 (tel. (040) 41 17 10). **Leipzig,** Wilhelm-Seyfferth-Str. 4, 04107 (tel. (0341) 21 38 40). **Munich,** Königinstr. 5, 80539 (tel. (089) 288 80).

■ Getting Around

BY PLANE

More than 100 international airlines serve Germany, but flying across the country is generally expensive and unnecessary. Nearly all airlines cater to business travelers and set prices accordingly. The headquarters for **Lufthansa German Airlines,** the national carrier (tel. (0221) 82 60), is at Deutsche Lufthansa AG, Von-Gablenz-Str. 2-6, 50679 Köln. Its air hub is located in Frankfurt am Main; from there, all its destinations can be reached in an average of 50 minutes. To US residents, Lufthansa (tel. (800) 645-3880) offers "Discover Europe," a package of three flight coupons which cost US$125-200 each, depending on season and destination; up to six additional tickets cost US$105-175 each. *Let's Go* lists airports and flight information telephone numbers in the **Practical Information** sections of major cities. Usually, S-Bahns or buses run between the airport and the nearest city's main train station.

BY TRAIN

"The trains run on time." It's a cliché, almost a joke, and not infallibly true. At the same time, it brings up an important truth about getting around in Germany—if the trains aren't perfect, they do go almost everywhere a traveler would want to go, with the exception of some very rural areas. In fact, the train system's obligation to run lines to inaccessible areas, even at a loss, is written into Germany's Basic Law. The **Deutsche Bahn** sprung from the integration of the western **Deutsche Bundesbahn (DB)** and old eastern **Deutsche Reichsbahn (DR)**. Integration is still taking place; many connections are as yet incomplete. Moving from west to east, there are significant differences in quality and service. One problem in Eastern Germany is connections; on an indirect route, allow about twice as much time as you would in the western parts. Averaging over 120kph, including stops, and connecting some 7000 locations, the DB network is probably Europe's best, and also one of its most expensive, although many discount opportunities exist.

Commuter trains, marked "City-Bahn" (CB), are fairly slow. "S-Bahn" trains are commuter rail lines that run from a city's center out to its suburbs; they are frequently integrated with the local subway or streetcar system. "D" trains are slightly faster. "RE" or "RB" trains include a number of rail networks between neighboring cities. "InterRegio" (IR) trains, covering larger networks between cities, are speedy and comfortable. "IC" (InterCity) trains zoom along between major cities every hour. You must purchase a supplementary "IC Zuschlag" to ride an "IC" or "EC" train (DM6 when bought in the station, DM8 on the train). Even the IC yields to the futuristic-looking InterCity Express (ICE) trains, which approach the luxury and speed of an airplane: they run at speeds up to 174mph. For these, railpass users usually do not pay a *Zuschlag,* unless the train requires a mandatory seat reservation fee.

Most German cities have a main train station; in German, *der Hauptbahnhof.* (This is the point referred to when *Let's Go* gives directions "from the station.") In train stations, yellow signs indicate departures *(Abfahrt),* white signs indicate arrivals *(Ankunft).* The number next to *"Gleis"* is the track number.

Second-class travel is pleasant, and compartments are excellent places to meet friendly folks of all ages and nationalities. Many train stations have different counters for domestic tickets, international tickets, seat reservations, and information; check before lining up. On major lines, reservations are always advisable even if you have a railpass; make them at least a few hours in advance at the train station.

Railpasses

Buying a railpass is both a popular and sensible option under many circumstances. Ideally, a railpass allows you to jump on any train in Europe, go wherever you want whenever you want, and change your plans at will. The handbook that comes with your railpass tells you everything you need to know and includes a timetable for major routes and a map, as well as possible ferry, steamer, bus, car rental, hotel, and **Eurostar** (the high speed train linking London to Paris and Brussels) discounts. In practice, it's not so simple. You still must stand in line to pay for seat reservations, supplements, and couchette reservations, as well as to have your pass validated when you first use it. More importantly, railpasses don't always pay off. For ballpark estimates, consult Rick Steve's *Europe Through the Back Door* newsletter or the **DER-Travel** or **RailEurope** railpass brochure for prices of point-to-point tickets. Add them up and compare with railpass prices. If you're under age 26, the BIJ tickets are probably a viable option.

Eurailpass, P.O. Box 10383, Stamford, CT 06904, remains the best option for non-EU travelers. Eurailpasses are valid in most of Western Europe (not in Britain, however). Eurailpasses and Europasses are designed by the EU itself, and are purchasable only by non-Europeans almost exclusively from non-European distributors. The EU sets the prices, so no one travel agent is better than any other for buying a Eurailpass.

The first class Eurailpass rarely pays off; it is offered for 15 days (US$522), 21 days (US$678), one month (US$838), two months (US$1188), or three months (US$1468).

ESSENTIALS

If you are traveling in a group you might prefer the **Eurail Saverpass,** which allows unlimited first-class travel for 15 days (US$444), 21 days (US$576), one month (US$712), two months (US$1010), or three months (US$1248) per person in groups of two or more. Travelers under age 26 can buy a **Eurail Youthpass,** good for 15 days (US$365), 21 days (US $475), one month (US$587), two months (US$832), or three months (US $1028) of second-class travel. The two-month pass is the most economical. **Eurail Flexipasses** allow limited first-class travel within a two-month period: 10 days (US$616); 15 days (US$812). **Youth Flexipasses,** for those under 26 who wish to travel second-class, are available for US$431 or US$568, respectively.

The **Europass** combines France, Germany, Italy, Spain, and Switzerland in one plan. With a Europass you can travel in any of these five countries from five to 15 days within a window of two months. First-class adult prices begin at US$316 and increase incrementally by US$42 for each extra day of travel. With purchase of a first-class ticket you can buy an identical ticket for your traveling partner for 40% off. Second-class youth tickets begin at US$210 and increase incrementally by $29 for each extra day of travel. Those between the ages of 4-11 travel for half the price of a first-class ticket. You can also add associate countries (Austria/Hungary, Belgium/Luxembourg/Netherlands, Greece, and Portugal) for a nominal fee.The Europass introduces planning complications; you must plan your routes so that they only make use of countries you've "purchased." They're serious about this: if you cut through a country you haven't purchased you will be fined.

You should plan your itinerary before buying a Europass. It will save you money if your travels are confined to between three and five adjacent Western European countries, or if you know that you want to go only to large cities. Europasses are not appropriate if you like to take lots of side trips—you'll waste rail days. If you're tempted to add lots of rail days and associate countries, consider the Eurailpass.

You'll find it easiest to buy a Eurailpass before you arrive in Europe; contact Council Travel, Travel CUTS, Let's Go Travel, or several other travel agents (see p. 31). If you're stuck in Europe and unable to find someone to sell you a Eurailpass, call an American railpass agent, who can send a pass by express mail. Eurailpasses are not refundable once validated; you can get a replacement for a lost pass only if you have purchased insurance on it under the Pass Protection Plan (US$10). All Eurailpasses can be purchased from a travel agent or from **Rail Europe, Inc.,** 226-230 Westchester Ave., White Plains, NY 10604 (tel. (800) 438-7245; fax (800) 432-1329 in the U.S.; and tel. (800) 361-7245; fax (905) 602-4198 in Canada; http://www.raileurope.com), which also sells point-to-point tickets. They offer special rates for groups of six or more traveling together. **DERTravel Services,** 9501 W. Devon Ave. #400, Rosemont IL 60018 (tel. (800) 421-2929; fax (800) 282-7474; http://www.dertravel.com), also deals in rail passes and point-to-point tickets.

For EU citizens, there are **InterRail Passes,** for which six months' residence in Europe makes you eligible. The Under 26 InterRail Card (from UK£189) allows either 15 days or one month of unlimited travel within one, two, three or all of the seven zones into which InterRail divides Europe; the cost is determined by the number of zones the pass covers. The Over 26 InterRail Card offers unlimited second-class travel in 19 countries in Europe for 15 days or one month for UK£215 and UK£275, respectively. For information and ticket sales in Europe contact **Student Travel Center,** 24 Rupert St. 1st Fl., London, W1V7FN (tel. (0171) 437 0121, 437 6370, or 434 1306; fax 734 3836; http://www.hols.com/studentt/). Tickets are also available from travel agents or main train stations throughout Europe.

In addition to simple railpasses, many countries (and Europass and Eurail) offer rail-and-drive passes, which combine car rental with rail travel—a good option for travelers who wish both to visit cities accessible by rail and make side trips into the surrounding areas. Several national and regional passes offer companion fares, allowing two adults traveling together 50% off the price of one pass. Some of these passes can be bought only in Europe, some only outside of Europe, and for some it doesn't matter; check with a railpass agent or with national tourist offices.

German Railpasses

Non-Europeans can purchase the tourist-oriented **German Railpass** in their home countries. The pass allows five, 10, or 15 days of rail travel within a four-week period on all DB trains (for info on types of trains, see p. 39). The first-class version costs US$276 for five days, US$434 for 10 days, and US$562 for 15 days in a month. The second-class version costs US$188 for five days, US$304 for 10 days, and US$410 for 15 days. There is also a **German Rail Youth Pass** version, available to non-Europeans age 12-25, which comes only in a second-class version. It costs US$146 for five days, US$200 for 10 days, and US$252 for 15. Travelers ages 4-11 can purchase the railpasses for half the adult prices, while those under four travel free.

There are also several "internal" national railpasses, which can *only* be purchased once you've arrived. For anyone under age 27, a decent deal is the **Tramper-Ticket,** which allows you to pick 10 days of unlimited second-class rail travel in a month on all DB trains (including the ICE), the railroad-run buses *(Bahnbusse),* and the local S-Bahns in cities, all for DM369. The pass is only available between June 15 and October 31.

The **BahnCard** is a great option for those making frequent and extensive use of German trains. It is valid for one year, and gets you a 50% discount on all rail tickets, including the ICE. A second-class BahnCard is a great deal for young travelers: students 26 and under and anyone ages 18 to 22 can get one for DM120; first-class cards are DM240. Seniors over 60 can get BahnCards at the same discounts. Those between ages four and 17 can purchase a second-class BahnCard for DM60, first-class DM120. Normal rates are DM240 second-class; DM480 first-class. Crazier still: since 1995, BahnCards have been used as Visa **credit cards** for some purchases in Germany. (See a DB brochure for details.) Passes are only available at major train stations throughout Germany, and all require a small photo. You may contact **Deutsche Bahn** by making a local call from any city (tel. 194 19; http://www.bahn.de). In the U.S., contact **DER Travel Services** at 9501 W. Devon Ave. Rosemont, IL 60018-4832 (tel. (800) 782-2424; fax (800) 282-7474). The DER branch in Canada is located at 904 The East Mall Etobicoke, Ont. M9B 6K2 (tel. (800) 463-8767; fax (416) 695-41453). Deutsche Bahn's fantastic **website** details the great deals that they concoct, as well as information on connections between cities.

Youth, Student, and Discount Fares

Travelers under 26 can purchase **TwenTickets,** which knock 25% off of fares over DM10. A **Schönes Wochenende** ticket offers a fantastic deal for weekend trips. For DM35, up to five people receive unlimited travel on any of the slower trains (**not** ICE, IC, EC, D, or IR) from 12:01am Saturday until 2am on Monday. Single travelers often find larger groups who are amenable to sharing their ticket, either free or for a fraction of the purchase cost. The **Guten-Abend-Ticket** provides an excellent deal for long-distance night travel. It entitles its holders to travel anywhere (**not** on InterCity Night or CityNight Lines) in Germany between 7pm and 2am. Second-class tickets are DM59, with ICE surcharge DM69; first-class DM99, with ICE surcharge DM109; Friday and Sunday DM15 extra.

Useful Resources

The ultimate reference for planning rail trips is the **Thomas Cook European Timetable** (US$28, with a map of Europe with all main train and ferry routes US$39, postage US$4.50). This timetable, updated regularly, covers all major and most minor train routes in Europe. In the U.S. and Canada, order it from **Forsyth Travel Library** (see **Useful Publications,** p. 2). In Europe, find it at any **Thomas Cook Money Exchange Center.** Also from Forsyth is **Traveling Europe's Trains** (US$15) by Jay Burnoose, which includes maps and sightseeing suggestions. Available in most bookstores or from **Houghton Mifflin Co.,** 222 Berkeley St., Boston, MA 02116 (tel. (800) 225-3362; fax (800) 634-7568), is the annual **Eurail Guide to Train Travel in the New Europe**

(US$15), giving timetables, instructions, and prices for international train trips, day trips, and excursions in Europe. The annual railpass special edition of the free Rick Steves' **Europe Through the Back Door** travel newsletter and catalogue, 120 Fourth Ave. N., P.O. Box 2009, Edmonds, WA 98020 (tel. (425) 771-8303; fax 771-0833; email ricksteves@aol.com; http://www.ricksteves.com) provides comparative analysis of European railpasses with national or regional passes and point-to-point tickets. **Hunter Publishing,** P.O. Box 7816, Edison, NJ 08818 (tel. (908) 225-1900; fax 417-0482; email hunterpub@emi.net; http://www.hunterpublishing.com), offers a catalogue of rail atlases and travel guides.

BY BUS

Germany does have a few regions inaccessible by train, and some bus lines fill the gaps. Bus services between cities and to small, outlying towns usually run from the *Zentral Omnibus Bahnhof (ZOB),* usually close to the main train station. Buses are often slightly more expensive than the train for comparable distances. Check the bulletin boards in university buildings or the classified pages of local magazines for occasional deals. Railpasses are not valid on any buses other than those (relatively few) run by the national rail company (DB).

 Eurolines, 4 Cardiff Rd., Luton LU1 1PP (tel. (01582) 40 45 11; fax 40 06 94; in London, 52 Grosvenor Gardens, Victoria; tel.(0171) 730 8235), is Europe's largest operator of Europe-wide coach services, including Eastern Europe and Russia. A Eurolines Pass offers unlimited 30-day (under 26 and over 60 UK£159; 26-60 UK £199) or 60-day (under 26 and over 60, UK£199, 26-60 UK£249) travel between 20 major tourist destinations. Eurolines also offers **Euro Explorers,** eight complete travel loops throughout Europe with set fares and itineraries. **Eurobus,** P.O. Box 3016 Workingham Berkshire RG40 2YP (tel. (0118) 936 2321; fax 936 2322; http://www.eurobus.uk.com), offers cheap bus trips in 25 major cities in 10 major European countries for those between ages 16 and 38. The buses, with English speaking guides and drivers, stop door-to-door at one hostel or budget hotel per city, and let you hop on and off. Tickets are sold by zone; for any one zone US$225, for any two zones US$400, for all three zones US$525.

BY CAR

Cars offer speed, freedom, access to the countryside, and an escape from the town-to-town mentality of trains. Unfortunately, they also insulate you from the *esprit de corps* of rail travel. Although a single traveler won't save by renting a car, four usually will. If you can't decide between train and car travel, you may benefit from combining the two; Rail Europe and other railpass vendors offer rail-and-drive packages for both individual countries and all of Europe. Travel agents may have other packages.

 You can **rent** a car from a U.S.-based firm (Alamo, Avis, Budget, or Hertz) with European offices, from a European-based company with local representatives (Europcar), or from a tour operator (Auto Europe, Bon Voyage By Car, Europe By Car, and Kemwel Holiday Autos), which will arrange a rental for you from a European company at its own rates. Multinationals offer greater flexibility, but tour operators often strike better deals. Rentals vary by company, season, and pick-up point; picking up your car and purchasing insurance in Belgium, Germany or Holland is usually cheaper than renting in Paris. Expect to pay US$80-400 per week, plus tax (5-25%), for a teensy car. Reserve well before leaving for Europe and pay in advance if you can. It is always significantly less expensive to reserve a car from the U.S. than from Europe. Always check if prices quoted include tax and collision insurance; some credit card companies will cover this automatically. Ask about discounts and check the terms of insurance, particularly the size of the deductible. Ask your airline about special packages; you may get up to a week of free rental. Minimum age varies by country, but is usually 21-25. At most agencies, all that's needed to rent a car is a U.S. license and proof that you've had it for a year.

Try **Alamo** (tel. (800) 522-9696; http://www.goalamo.com); **Auto Europe,** 39 Commercial St., P.O. Box 7006, Portland, ME (tel. (800) 223-5555; fax (800) 235-6321; http://www.auto-europe.com); **Avis Rent a Car** (tel. (800) 331-1084; http://www.avis.com); **Bon Voyage By Car** (tel. (800) 272-3299; in Canada (800) 253-3876); **Budget Rent a Car** (tel. (800) 472-3325); **Europe by Car,** One Rockefeller Plaza, New York, NY 10020 (tel. (800) 223-1516, (212) 581-3040; in California, (800) 252-9401; fax (212) 246-1458; http://www.europebycar.com); **Europcar,** 145 Avenue Malekoff, 75016 Paris (tel. (800) 227-3876; (800) 227-7368 in Canada; (1) 45 00 08 06 in France); **Hertz Rent a Car** (tel. (800) 654-3001; http://www.hertz.com); **Kemwel Holiday Autos** (tel. (800) 678-0678; http://www.kemwel.com); or **Payless Car Rental** (tel. (800) 729-5377). Travel agents may have other rail-and-drive packages, including the Deutsche Bahn's **Rail 'n' Drive Pass.**

For longer than 17 days, **leasing** can be cheaper than renting and it is sometimes the only option for those ages 18-21. The cheapest leases are agreements to buy the car and then sell it back to the manufacturer at a prearranged price. As far as you're concerned, though, it's a lease and doesn't entail enormous financial transactions. Leases include insurance coverage and are not taxed. Expect to pay at least US$1200 for 60 days. Contact **Bon Voyage By Car, Europe by Car,** or **Auto Europe.** You will need to make arrangements in advance.

If you're brave and know what you're doing, **buying** a used car or van in Europe and selling it just before you leave can provide the cheapest wheels for longer trips. Check with consulates for import-export laws concerning used vehicles, registration, and safety and emission standards. Camper-vans and motor homes give the advantages of a car without the hassle and expense of finding lodgings. Most of these vehicles are diesel-powered and deliver roughly 24 to 30 miles per gallon of diesel fuel, which is cheaper than gas. David Shore and Patty Campbell's **Europe by Van and Motorhome** (US$14; postage US$2, overseas US$6) guides you through the entire process of renting, leasing, buying, and selling vehicles on the Continent, including buy-back options, registration, insurance, and dealer listings. To order, write or call Shore/Campbell Publications, 1842 Santa Margarita Dr., Fallbrook, CA 92028 (tel./fax (800) 659-5222 or (760) 723-6184).

Moto-Europa, by Eric Bredesen (US$16; shipping US$3, overseas US$7), available from Seren Publishing, 2935 Saint Anne Dr., Dubuque, IA 52001 (tel. (800) 387-6728; fax (319) 583-7853), is a comprehensive guide to all of these options, and includes itinerary suggestions, a motorists' phrasebook, and chapters on leasing and buying vehicles. More general info is available from the **American Automobile Association (AAA),** Travel Agency Services Dept., 1000 AAA Dr., Heathrow, FL 32746-5080 (tel. (800) 222-4357 or (417) 444-7380; http://www.aaa.com); and the **Canadian Automobile Association (CAA);** for regional numbers call (800) 222-4357.

Before setting off, know the laws of the countries in which you'll be driving. The **Association for Safe International Road Travel (ASIRT)** can provide more specific information about driving conditions. They are located at 5413 West Cedar Ln. #103C, Bethesda, MD 20814 (tel. (301) 983-5252; fax 983-3663; http://www.horizon-web.com/asirt). Western Europeans use unleaded gas almost exclusively, but it's not available in many gas stations in Eastern Europe.

Americans and Canadians may drive for one year in Germany with a valid national or international license (see **Driving Permits and Car Insurance,** p. 10). The national license must be officially translated by a German diplomatic office, an international motor vehicle office in the country where the license was issued, or a German automobile club (see ADAC below). If you are planning to stay in Germany for more than one year, you must obtain a German driver's license, available upon presentation of your national license. Vehicle liability insurance is required by law in Germany. Foreign motorists must present the green international insurance card or purchase temporary insurance at the point of entry.

Yes, Virginia, there really is no speed limit on the **Autobahn.** Germans drive *fast;* before venturing on the road, be *very* familiar with traffic rules and especially signs and symbols. Germans drive on the right side of the road. It is dreadfully **illegal to**

pass on the right, *even on superhighways.* When not otherwise indicated, the speed limit in Western Germany is 100kph (62mph) for passenger cars, 50kph (31 mph) in cities and towns. The recommended speed on the *Autobahn* is 130kph (81 mph), but if you drive that slowly in the left lane, cars will loom in your rear-view mirror with lights flashing. Passenger cars with trailers are limited to 80kph (50 mph). Drivers might want to know that dotting the *Autobahn* along its 10,000 toll-free kilometers are 170 restaurants and 270 service stations open 24 hours.

German law requires that both front and back seat passengers wear **seat belts;** motorcycle drivers and riders must wear **helmets** if traveling over 24kph. Children under 12 may not sit in the front seat unless special seats have been installed. Studded snow tires are also *verboten.* The maximum permissible **blood alcohol** content is 0.08%, lower than the limit in the United States, and even lower amounts are illegal if you're involved in a violation—basically, if you even *think* of alcohol, you're probably over the limit. Other rules and regulations apply; for more information, contact **Allgemeiner Deutscher Automobil Club e.v. (ADAC)** by mail at: Redaktion ADAC Motorwelt, 81373 München, or visit the office once in Germany at Am Westpark 8, Munich-Sendling (tel. (089) 767 60, emergency tel. 22 22 22; fax 76 76 25 00). Or contact **Automobil Club von Deutschland (AvD),** Lyoner-Str. 16, 60528 Frankfurt-Neiderrad (tel. (069) 660 60, emergency 660 66 00). ADAC maintains **Straßenwachthilfe** units which patrol the roads and assist disabled vehicles. ADAC will provide **road assistance** free of charge if the damage can be repaired within half an hour; if not, you'll pay repair and towing fees. Orange emergency telephones indicated by blue *Notruf* (emergency call) signs summon the free service. A critically important word is **Stau,** meaning "traffic jam"—Germany has plenty. Tune in to local radio stations for traffic reports.

BY BOAT

River boat and motor boat services abound on many inland waters in Germany. In addition to connecting towns within Germany, many passenger and car ferries make connections to offshore islands (the Frisian Islands, for example) in the North and Baltic Seas. On the Danube, Elbe, Main, Mosel, Neckar, Rhine, Oder, Saale, and Weser rivers you can hop a ferry and enjoy seeing Germany from a new perspective. The Mosel, Rhine and Danube steamers have been overrun by tourists; less commercial-looking lines can be more alluring. *Let's Go* details schedules in many towns. Be sure to ask about discounts if you're holding any kind of railpass or ISIC. The German Rail Youth Pass qualifies you for this special bonus: free travel on the KD River Day Steamer on the Rhine, Main, and Mosel between selected major cities.

BY BICYCLE

Today, biking is one of the key elements of the classic budget Eurovoyage. With the proliferation of mountain bikes, you can do some serious natural sight-seeing. Remember that touring involves pedaling both yourself and whatever you store in the **panniers** (bags which strap to your bike). Take some reasonably challenging rides at home to prepare yourself before you leave, and have your bike tuned up by a reputable shop. Wear visible clothing, drink plenty of water (even if you're not thirsty), and ride on the same side as the traffic. Learn the international signals for turns and use them. Know how to fix a modern derailleur-equipped mount and change a tire, and practice on your own bike. A few simple tools and a good bike manual will be invaluable. For info about touring routes, consult national tourist offices or any of the numerous books available. **The Mountaineers Books,** 1001 S.W. Klickitat Way #201, Seattle, WA 98134 (tel. (800) 553-4453 or (206) 223-6303; fax 223-6306; mbooks@mountaineers.org) offers Germany-specific tour books, as well as **Europe By Bike,** by Karen and Terry Whitehill, a great source of tours in 11 countries. Send for a catalogue (US$15, shipping $3). **Cycling Europe: Budget Bike Touring in the Old World** (US$13), by N. Slavinski and available from National Book Network, 15200 NBN Way, PO Box 190, Blue Ridge Summit, PA 17214-0190 (tel. (800) 462-

6420), may also be a helpful addition to your library. **Michelin road maps** are clear and detailed.

If you are nervous about striking out on your own, **Blue Marble Travel** (in U.S. tel. (800) 258-8689 or (201) 326-9533; fax 326-8939; in Paris (01) 42 36 02 34; fax 42 21 14 77; http://www.blumarbl.com) offers bike tours designed for folks age 20-50. **CBT Bicycle Tours** offers one- to seven-week tours, priced around US$95 per day, including all lodging and breakfasts, one-third of all dinners, complete van support, airport transfers, three staff, and extensive route notes and maps each day. Tours run May through August, with departures every seven to 10 days. In 1998, CBT will visit Germany and other European countries. Contact CBT Bicycle Tours, 415 W. Fullerton, #1003, Chicago, IL 60614 (tel. (800) 736-BIKE (2453) or (773) 404-1710; fax 404-1833).

Many airlines will count your bike as your second free piece of luggage; a few charge. The additional or automatic fee runs about US$60-110 each way. Bikes must be packed in a cardboard box with the pedals and front wheel detached; airlines sell bike boxes at the airport (US$10). Most ferries let you take your bike for free or a nominal fee. You can always ship your bike on trains, though the cost varies widely.

Riding a bike with a frame pack strapped on it or your back is about as safe as pedaling blindfolded over a sheet of ice; panniers are essential. The first thing to buy, however, is a suitable **bike helmet.** At about US$25-50, they're a better buy than injury or death. U-shaped **Citadel** or **Kryptonite locks** are expensive (from US$30), but the companies insure their locks against theft of your bike for one to two years. **Bike Nashbar,** 4111 Simon Rd., Youngstown, OH 44512 (tel. (800) 627-4227; fax (800) 456-1223; http://www.nashbar.com), has excellent prices and cheerfully beats advertised competitors' offers by US$.05. They ship anywhere in the U.S. or Canada.

Renting a bike beats bringing your own if your touring will be confined to one or two regions. *Let's Go* lists bike rental shops for most larger cities and towns. A sturdy if unexciting one-speed model will cost US$6-15 per day; be prepared to lay down a sizable deposit. Some youth hostels rent bicycles for low prices. Bike rentals are also available at approximately 250 train stations throughout the country where German Rail's **Fahrrad am Bahnhof** ("Bikes at the Station") program rents for DM6-10 per day. Usually bikes can be rented from one station and returned at another with a deposit of some kind; ask for details at the station.

Germany makes biking easy with its wealth of trails and bike tours, including some organized through hostels and through the rail system. In urban areas, a bicycle can be one of the most efficient ways to get around. German cities and towns usually have designated bike lanes, sometimes in the street, and sometimes laid out in the sidewalk itself. Pedestrians should look out for tell-tale bike icons or changes in pavement color; it may look like those bikers are on the sidewalk, but they move fast, have right-of-way, and with all the conviction of self-righteous biking zeal, expect you to be the one to get out of the way—quickly.

For information about bike routes, regulations, and maps, contact **Allgemeiner Deutscher Fahrrad-Club,** Postfach 10 77 47, 28077 Bremen. The ADFC is the biggest bicycle club for commuters and touring cyclists and an invaluable source of information and support. Ask for the Fahrradtourismus Info-übersicht pamphlet (in German) by sending a self-addressed envelope along with one IRC (international reply coupon). A bike tour guidebook, including extensive maps, is available from Deutsches Jugendherbergswerk (DJH); see its address under **Accommodations: Hostels, p.** 53.

BY THUMB

> *Let's Go* strongly urges you to consider seriously the risks before you choose to hitch. We do not recommend hitching as a safe means of transportation, and none of the information presented here is intended to do so.

No one should hitch without careful consideration of the risks involved. Not everyone can be an airplane pilot, but any bozo can drive a car. Hitching means entrusting your life to a random person who happens to pick you up on the road and risks theft, assault, sexual harassment, and unsafe driving. In spite of this, there are gains to hitching. Favorable hitching experiences allow you to meet local people and get where you're going, especially in northern Europe and Ireland, where public transportation is sketchy. The choice, however, remains yours.

Depending on the circumstances and the norms of the country, men and women traveling in groups and men traveling alone might consider hitching (called "autostop" in much of Europe) beyond the range of bus or train routes. If you're a woman traveling alone, don't hitch. It's just too dangerous. A man and a woman are a safer combination, two men will have a harder time, and three will go nowhere. Success will depend on your appearance. Successful hitchers travel light and stack their belongings in a compact but visible cluster. Most Europeans signal with an open hand, rather than a thumb; many write their destination on a sign in large, bold letters and draw a smiley-face under it. Drivers prefer hitchers who are neat and wholesome. No one stops for hep-cats wearing sunglasses.

Safety issues are always imperative, even for those who are not hitching alone. Safety-minded hitchers avoid getting in the back of a two-door car and never let go of their backpacks. They will not get into a car that they can't get out of again in a hurry. If they ever feel threatened, they insist on being let off, regardless of where they are. Acting as if they are going to open the car door or vomit on the upholstery will usually get a driver to stop. Hitchhiking at night can be particularly dangerous; experienced hitchers stand in well-lit places, and expect drivers to be leery of nocturnal thumbers (or open-handers). Hitching remains common in Eastern Europe, though Westerners are a definite target for theft.

In the **Practical Information** section of many cities, we list the tram or bus lines that take travelers to strategic points for hitching out. It is illegal to hitch on the *Autobahnen* (expressways). Hitchers must stand in front of the *"Autobahn"* signs at on-ramps, or at **Raststätten** (rest stops) and **Tankstellen** (gas stations). *Autobahn* hitchers will need a good map to navigate the tangled interchanges in the Rhine-Ruhr area, and should pay attention to license plates: B=Berlin, M=Munich, F=Frankfurt, HH=Hamburg. There's also plentiful hitching on the heavily traveled *Bundesstraßen*, scenic secondary roads marked by signs with a yellow diamond. **Mitfahrzentralen** (ride-share centers) pair drivers with riders, with a fee to agency (about US$20) and driver (per km). Some belong to nation-wide chains (**CityNetz Mitfahrzentrale** have computerized listings); others are local store-front operations. *Let's Go* lists *Mitfahrzentralen* under the **Practical Information** sections each city; check the white and yellow pages under *"Mitfahrzentrale."*

BY FOOT

Germany's grandest scenery can often be seen only by foot. *Let's Go* describes many daytrips for those who want to hoof it, but native inhabitants (Europeans are fervent, almost obsessive hikers), hostel proprietors, and fellow travelers are the best source of tips. Many European countries have hiking and mountaineering organizations; alpine clubs in Germany provide inexpensive, simple accommodations in splendid settings. **Walking Europe from Top to Bottom** by S. Margolis and G. Harmon details one of Europe's most popular trails (US$11); check your local bookstore for others.

BY PUBLIC TRANSPORTATION

Urban public transit is excellent in the west and fairly good in the east. You'll see four types in German cities: **Straßenbahn** (streetcars), **S-Bahn** (commuter rail), **U-Bahn** (subways), and regular **buses.** Eurailpass holders get free passage *only* on the S-Bahn, which, in large cities, doesn't usually go everywhere one needs to go. Berlin, Bonn, Düsseldorf, Frankfurt, Hamburg, Köln, München, and Stuttgart have U-Bahn systems; Hanover has partially underground streetcar lines. Consider purchasing a day card *(Tageskarte, Tagesnetzkarte)* or multiple-ride ticket *(Mehrfahrkarte or Sammelkarte)*, which usually pay for themselves by the third ride. German subways and

If you're stuck for cash on your travels, don't panic. Western Union can transfer money in minutes. We've 37,000 outlets in over 140 countries. And our record of safety and reliability is second to none. Call Western Union: wherever you are, you're never far from home.

WESTERN UNION | MONEY TRANSFER®

The fastest way to send money worldwide.

Get the MCI Card.
The Smart and Easy Card.

The MCI Card with WorldPhone Service is designed specifically to keep you in touch with people that matter the most to you. We make international calling as easy as possible.

The MCI Card with WorldPhone Service....

- Provides access to the US from over 125 countries and places worldwide.
- Country to country calling from over 70 countries
- Gives you customer service 24 hours a day
- Connects you to operators who speak your language
- Provides you with MCI's low rates with no sign-up or monthly fees
- Even if you don't have an MCI Card, you can still reach a WorldPhone Operator and place collect calls to the U.S. Simply dial the access code of the country you are calling from and hold for a WorldPhone operator.

For more information or to apply for a Card call:
1-800-444-1616

Outside the U.S., call MCI collect (reverse charge) at:
1-916-567-5151

Pick Up The Phone.
Pick Up The Miles.

Please cut out and save this reference guide for convenient U.S. and worldwide calling with the MCI Card with WorldPhone Service.

Your MCI Worldphone Access Numbers

MCI

COUNTRY	WORLDPHONE TOLL-FREE ACCESS #
#South Africa (CC)	0800-99-0011
#Spain (CC)	900-99-0014
#Sri Lanka	440100
#St. Lucia ⁘	(Outside of Colombo, dial 01 first)
#St. Vincent (CC)	1-800-888-8000
#Sweden (CC) ♦	020-795-922
#Switzerland (CC) ♦	0800-89-0222
#Syria	0800
#Taiwan (CC) ♦	0080-13-4567
#Thailand ★	001-999-1-2001
#Trinidad & Tobago ⁘	1-800-888-8000
#Turkey (CC) ♦	00-8001-1177
#Turks and Caicos ⁘	1-800-888-8000
#Ukraine (CC) ⁘	8▼10-013
#United Arab Emirates ♦	800-111
#United Kingdom (CC) To call using BT ▪	0800-89-0222
#United Kingdom (CC) To call using MERCURY ▪	0500-89-0222
#United States (CC)	000-412
#Uruguay	1-800-888-8000
#U.S. Virgin Islands (CC)	172-1022
#Vatican City (CC)	800-1114-0
#Venezuela (CC) ⁘ ♦	1201-1022
Yemen	008-00-102

Automation available from most locations.
(CC) Country-to-country calling available to/from most international locations.
⁘ Limited availability.
▼ Wait for second dial tone.
◄ When calling from public phones, use phones marked LADATEL.
▪ International communications carrier.
✦ Not available from public pay phones.
● Public phones may require deposit of coin or phone card for dial tone.
▲ Local service fee in U.S. currency required to complete call.
◆ Regulation does not permit intra-Japan calls.
❖ Available from most major cities

And, it's simple to call home.

1. Dial the WorldPhone toll-free access number of the country you're calling from (listed inside).

2. Follow the voice instructions in your language of choice or hold for a WorldPhone operator.
   - Enter or give the operator your MCI Card number or call collect.

3. Enter or give the WorldPhone operator your home number.

4. Share your adventures with your family!

✂

The MCI Card with WorldPhone Service...
The easy way to call when traveling worldwide.

MCI Calling Card
415 555 1234 2244
J.D. SMITH
WorldPhone

For more information or to apply for a Card call:
1-800-444-1616

Outside the U.S., call MCI collect (reverse charge) at:
1-916-567-5151

Please cut out and save this reference guide for convenient U.S. and worldwide calling with the MCI Card with WorldPhone Service.

COUNTRY	WORLDPHONE TOLL-FREE ACCESS #
#American Samoa	633-2MCI (633-2624)
#Antigua (Available from public card phones only)	#2
#Argentina (CC)	0800-5-1002
#Aruba ÷	800-888-8
#Australia (CC) To call using OPTUS ■	1-800-551-111
To call using TELSTRA ■	1-800-881-100
#Austria (CC) ◆	022-903-012
#Bahamas	1-800-888-8000
#Bahrain	800-002
#Barbados	1-800-888-8000
#Belarus (CC) From Brest, Vitebsk, Grodno, Minsk	8-800-103
From Gomel and Mogilev regions	8-10-800-103
#Belgium (CC) ◆	0800-10012
#Belize From Hotels	815
From Payphones	557
#Bermuda ÷	1-800-888-8000
#Bolivia ◆	0-800-2222
#Brazil (CC)	000-8012
#British Virgin Islands ÷	1-800-888-8000
#Brunei	800-011
#Bulgaria	00800-0001
#Canada (CC)	1-800-888-8000
#Cayman Islands	1-800-888-8000
#Chile (CC) To call using CTC ■	800-207-300
To call using ENTEL ■	800-360-180
#China (CC) (Available from most major cities)	108-12
For a Mandarin-speaking Operator	108-17
#Colombia (CC) Colombia IIIC Access in Spanish	980-16-0001
	980-16-1000
#Costa Rica ◆	0800-012-2222
#Cote D'Ivoire	0800-012-2222
#Croatia (CC) ★	1001
#Cyprus ◆	0800-90000
#Czech Republic (CC) ◆	00-42-000112
#Denmark (CC) ◆	8001-0022
#Dominica	1-800-888-8000
#Dominican Republic (CC) ÷	1-800-888-8000
Dominican Republic IIIC Access in Spanish	1121
#Ecuador (CC) ÷	999-170
#Egypt ◆ (Outside of Cairo, dial 02 first)	355-5770
El Salvador ◆	800-1767
#Federated States of Micronesia	624

FOLD

COUNTRY	WORLDPHONE TOLL-FREE ACCESS #
#Fiji	004-890-1002
#Finland (CC) ◆	08001-102-80
#France (CC) ◆	0800-99-0019
#French Antilles (CC) (includes Martinique, Guadeloupe)	0800-99-0019
#French Guiana (CC)	0-800-99-0019
#Gabon	00-005
#Gambia ◆	00-1-99
#Germany (CC)	0130-0012
#Greece (CC) ◆	00-800-1211
#Grenada ÷	1-800-888-8000
#Guam (CC) ◆	950-1022
#Guatemala (CC) ◆	99-99-189
#Guyana	177
#Haiti ÷ Haiti IIIC Access in French/Creole	193
	190
#Honduras ÷	800-0122
#Hong Kong (CC)	800-96-1121
#Hungary (CC) ◆	00▼800-01411
#Iceland (CC) ◆	800-9002
#India (CC) ÷ (Available from most major cities)	000-127
#Indonesia (CC) ◆	001-801-11
#Iran ÷ (SPECIAL PHONES ONLY)	172-1022
#Ireland (CC)	1-800-55-1001
#Israel (CC)	177-150-2727
#Italy (CC) ◆	172-1022
#Jamaica ÷	1-800-888-8000
(From Special Hotels only)	873
Jamaica IIIC Access (From public phones)	#2
#Japan (CC) ◆ To call using KDD ■	0039-121▶
To call using IDC ■	0066-55-121
To call using ITJ ■	0044-11-121
#Jordan	18-800-001
#Kazakhstan (CC)	8-800-131-4321
#Kenya ÷ (Available from most major cities)	080011
#Korea (CC) To call using KT ■	009-14
To call using DACOM ■	009-16
Phone Booths÷ Press red button, 03, then ★	
Military Bases	550-2255
#Kuwait	800-MCI (800-624)
Lebanon ÷	600-MCI (600-624)
#Liechtenstein (CC) ◆	0800-89-0222
#Luxembourg	0800-0112

FOLD

COUNTRY	WORLDPHONE TOLL-FREE ACCESS #
#Macao	0800-131
#Macedonia (CC) ◆	99800-4266
#Malaysia (CC) ◆	1-800-80-0012
#Malta	0800-89-0120
#Marshall Islands	1-800-888-8000
#Mexico (CC) Avantel (CC)	91-800-021-8000
Telmex ▲	1-800-888-8000
Mexico IIIC Access	91-800-674-7000
#Micronesia	624
#Monaco (CC) ◆	800-99-019
#Montserrat	1-800-888-8000
#Morocco	00-211-0012
#Netherlands (CC) ◆	0800-022-9122
#Netherlands Antilles (CC) ÷	001-800-888-8000
#New Zealand (CC)	000-912
#Nicaragua (CC) (Outside of Managua, dial 02 first)	166
Nicaragua IIIC Access in Spanish *2 from any public payphone	
#Norway (CC) ◆	800-19912
#Pakistan	00-800-12-001
#Panama	108
Military Bases	2810-108
#Papua New Guinea (CC)	05-07-19140
#Paraguay ÷	008-112-800
#Peru	0-800-500-10
#Philippines (CC) ◆ To call using PLDT ■	105-14
To call using PHILCOM ■	105-15
Philippines IIIC via PLDT in Tagalog	1026-12
Philippines IIIC via PhilCom in Tagalog	1026-15
#Poland (CC) ÷	00-800-111-21-22
#Portugal (CC) ÷	05-017-1234
#Puerto Rico (CC)	1-800-888-8000
#Qatar ★	0800-012-77
#Romania (CC) ÷	01-800-1800
#Russia (CC) ÷ To call using ROSTELCOM ■	747-3322
(For Russian speaking operator)	747-3320
To call using SOVINTEL ■	960-2222
#Saipan (CC) ÷	1-800-888-8000
#San Marino (CC) ◆	172-1022
#Saudi Arabia (CC)	1-800-11
#Singapore	8000-112-112
#Slovak Republic (CC)	0042-000112
#Slovenia	080-8808

FOLD

MCI

commuter rails (and many streetcar and bus systems) operate on an "honor system." The usual procedure is to buy your ticket from a kiosk or automat and then **validate** it by inserting the indicated edge into a little upright box marked with an **"E"** *(Entwerten)*. The ticket is then "clicked" and marked with the time at which you validated it. On subways, you must do this *before* getting in the car or, if the box is inside the car, *as soon as* you enter and before the subway starts moving. Once the doors close and the train gets underway, plainclothes inspectors may appear and thrust an orange badge in your face that says *"Kontrolle."* (The adjectival description of this experience is "being controlled.") If you cannot produce a valid ticket that has been properly cancelled, you will be subject to large fines (DM60 is typical) and immense humiliation. The inspectors don't take excuses and they don't take American Express; if you can't pay up on the spot, a police officer will meet you at the next stop to take you to jail. English-speaking backpackers have a very bad reputation for *Schwarzfahren* ("black riding," or riding without a ticket), so don't expect any sympathy. If you try the "I didn't understand, I don't speak German" excuse, the inspector will brusquely point out the explanatory signs in English. "I thought my Eurailpass was valid," never works, either. Don't assume that folks ride illegally because you don't see them canceling tickets; when the inspector appears, you'll discover that they're all carrying monthly passes.

■ Accommodations

Most local tourist offices distribute extensive listings free of charge and will also reserve a room for a small fee. German National Tourist Offices supply more complete lists of campsites and hotels (see **Government Information Offices,** p. 1)

HOSTELS

In 1908, a German named Richard Schirmann, believing that life in industrial cities was harmful to the physical and moral development of youth, built the world's first **youth hostel** in Altena—a budget dormitory that would bring travel within the means of poor youth. Germany has been a leader in hosteling ever since, and Schirmann is something of a mythical figure. Fees range from US$8-20 per night and hostels affiliated with one of the associations often have lower rates for members. Some hostels are set in strikingly beautiful castles, others in run-down barracks far from the town center. The most common disadvantage is an early curfew—fine if you're climbing a mountain the next morning, but a distinct cramp in your style if you plan to rage in Berlin or the larger cities. Hostels generally feature dorm-style accommodations with large rooms and bunk beds; some allow families and couples to have private rooms. Some have kitchens and utensils for your use, storage areas, laundry facilities, and even bike, moped, or other rentals. There can be drawbacks: some hostels close during certain daytime "lock-out" hours, impose a maximum stay, or, less frequently, require that you do chores. There's often little privacy, rooms are usually segregated by sex, and you may run into more screaming pre-teen groups than you care to remember.

Many hostels require sheet sleeping sacks. Sleeping bags are usually prohibited (for sanitary reasons), but some hostels provide free blankets. You can make your own sheet sack by folding a sheet and sewing it shut on two sides, or order one (about US$14) from Let's Go Travel or AYH (see **Budget Travel Agencies,** p. 31).

A **one-year membership** permits you to stay at youth hostels all over Germany at unbeatable prices. Despite the name, you need not be a youth. Most guests are ages 14 to 26, but hostels are rapidly becoming a resource for all ages (except in Bayern; see below); travelers over 26 pay only a bit more. Many German hostels are open to families. It's best to procure a membership card before you leave home; some hostels do not sell them on the spot. Membership cards are available from some travel agencies and from Hostelling International affiliates:

ESSENTIALS

The **Internet Guide to Hostelling** (http://hostels.com) includes hostels from around the world and oodles of information about hostelling and backpacking. **Eurotrip** (http://www.eurotrip.com/accommodation/accommodation.html) also has information on budget hostels and several international hostel associations. Reservations for over 300 **Hostelling International (HI)** hostels (see listing below) may be made via the International Booking Network (IBN), a computerized system which allows you make hostels reservations months in advance for a nominal fee (tel. (202) 783-6161). If you plan to stay in hostels, consider joining one of these associations:

Hosteling Membership

Australian Youth Hostels Association (AYHA), 10 Mallett St. Level 3, Camperdown NSW 2050 (tel. (02) 9565 1699; fax 9565 1325; email YHA@zeta.org.au). Memberships AUS$44, renewal AUS$27; under 18 AUS$13.

Hostelling International-Canada (HI-C), 400-205 Catherine St., Ottawa, Ont. K2P 1C3, Canada ((613) 237-7884; fax 237-7868). IBN booking centers in Edmonton, Montreal, Ottawa, and Vancouver. Membership packages: 1yr, under 18 CDN$12; 1yr., over 18 CDN$25; 2yr., over 18 CDN$35; lifetime CDN$175.

An Óige (Irish Youth Hostel Association), 61 Mountjoy St., Dublin 7 (tel. (01) 830 4555; fax 830 5808; anoige@iol.ie). One-year membership is IR£7.50, under 18 IR£4, family IR£7.50 for each adult with children under 16 free.

Youth Hostels Association of New Zealand (YHANZ), P.O. Box 436, 173 Gloucester St., Christchurch 1 (tel. (03) 379 9970; fax 365 4476; email info@yha.org.nz; http://www.yha.org.nz). Annual membership fee NZ$24.

Youth Hostels Association of Northern Ireland (YHANI), 22 Donegall Rd., Belfast BT12 5JN, Northern Ireland (tel. (01232) 324733 or 315435; fax 439699). Annual memberships UK£7, under 18 UK£3, family UK£14 for up to 6 children.

Scottish Youth Hostels Association (SYHA), 7 Glebe Crescent, Stirling FK8 2JA (tel. (01786) 891400; fax 891333; email syha@syha.org.uk; http://www.syha.org.uk). Membership UK£6, under 18 UK£2.50.

Hostel Association of South Africa, P.O. Box 4402, Cape Town 8000 (tel. (021) 24 2511; fax 24 4119; email hisa@gem.co.za; http://www.gen.com/hisa). Membership SAR45, group SAR120, family SAR90, lifetime SAR250.

Youth Hostels Association of England and Wales (YHA), Trevelyan House, 8 St. Stephen's Hill, St. Albans, Hertfordshire AL1 2DY, England (tel. (01727) 855215; fax 844126). Enrollment fees are: UK£9.50; under 18 UK£3.50; UK£19 for both parents with children under 18 enrolled free; UK£9.50 for one parent with children under 18 enrolled free; UK£130 for lifetime membership.

Hostelling International-American Youth Hostels (HI-AYH), 733 15th St. NW Ste. 840, Washington, D.C. 20005 ((202) 783-6161; fax 783-6171; email hiayhserv@hiayh.org; http://www.hiayh.org). Memberships can be purchased at many travel agencies (p. 31) or the national office in D.C. One year membership US$25, under 18 US$10, over 54 US$15, family cards US$35; includes *Hostelling North America: The Official Guide to Hostels in Canada and the United States.*

Hosteling in Germany is overseen by **Deutsches Jugendherbergswerk (DJH)** (tel. (05231) 740 10; fax 74 01 49). The DJH has, in recent years, initiated a growing number of *Jugendgästehäuser* (youth guest-houses), the more adult face of the HI system. These are generally more expensive, have more facilities, and attract slightly older guests. All German hostels are rated according to a six-category scale. The most basic fall in category I, the modern *Jugendgästehäuser* in category VI. Prices correspond roughly to these categories. The nightly charge builds from the odd category I hostel in eastern Germany asking DM14 per night, to the demand for DM32 for a bed in a four-person room from a brand-new *Jugendgästehaus*. However, because the prices are set locally rather than nationally, this system is not uniform; a category III hostel might be less expensive than a category II spot elsewhere. The DJH has absorbed hundreds of hostels in Eastern Germany with remarkable efficiency, although somewhere in the process of unification, prices edged upwards. Many of the better eastern hostels have been converted into costly hotels, or closed outright while bureaucrats try to decipher ownership, since new laws allow the owners of property nationalized by the GDR to re-claim their assets. Still, Germany currently has about **600 hostels**—more than any other nation on Earth—and the state hostel associations comprise the well-maintained infrastructure of a youth culture that has no equal anywhere.

DJH publishes *Deutsches Jugendherbergsverzeichnis* (DM14.80), a guide to all federated German hostels, available at German bookstores and major train station newsstands; or write to DJH-Hauptverband, Postfach 1455, 32704 Detmold, Germany.

> HI-affiliated hostels in **Bayern** generally do not admit guests over age 26, although families with young children are usually allowed even if parents are over 26.

HOTELS AND PRIVATE ROOMS

The cheapest hotel-style accommodations are places with *Gasthof, Gästehaus,* or *Hotel-Garni* in the name. Breakfast *(Frühstück),* almost always included, consists of rolls, butter, jam, coffee or tea, and some sausage and cheese slices. Rooms in private homes *(Privatzimmer)* or guest houses are widely available and less expensive than hotels or *Pensionen,* though most require a minimum stay of two or more nights. Local tourist offices usually handle bookings, either for free or for a DM2-5 fee; in less urban areas, look for signs saying *Zimmer frei* (room available) and just knock. Finding affordable hotel rooms in the New Federal States of the east is generally a challenge. Still, Eastern Germany is increasingly developing its own tourist industry, and the prices of its *Pensionen* and hotels are often cheaper than in the west.

Hotels are quite expensive in Germany: rock bottom for singles is US$17-20, for doubles US$22-24, and the price is never subject to haggling. Budget European hotels might come as a rude shock to pampered North American travelers. A bathroom of your own is a rarity and costs extra when provided. Hot showers may also cost extra. *Pension* (guesthouse) owners run smaller establishments and will often direct you to points of interest in the town and countryside. Unmarried couples will generally have no trouble getting a room together, although couples under 21 may occasionally

---

encounter resistance. If you wish to make reservations (at hotels or hostels), you can ensure a prompt reply by enclosing two International Postal Reply Coupons (available at any post office; see **Sending Mail From Germany,** p. 56). Indicate your night of arrival and the number of nights you plan to stay. The hotel will send you a confirmation and may request payment for the first night. Not all hotels accept reservations, and few accept checks in U.S. currency. The **Deutscher Hotel-und Gaststättenverband e.V.** (German Hotel Association or DEHOGA) is located at Kronprinzenstr. 46, Postfach 20 04 55, 53173 Bonn (tel. (0228) 82 00 80; fax 820 08 46).

The best bet in the east is often a **private room** *(Privatzimmer)* in a home. Costs generally run DM20-40 per person, less than for comparable *Privatzimmer* in the west. This option works best if you have a rudimentary knowledge of German, since room owners prefer to lay down a few household rules before handing over the keys for the night. Simply apprise the local tourist office of your language abilities (if any) when you ask for a room reference. Travelers over 26 who would otherwise pay senior prices at youth hostels will find these rooms well within budget range.

ALTERNATIVE ACCOMMODATIONS

Many **colleges and universities** open their residence halls to travelers when school is not in session—some do so during term-time. These dorms are often close to student areas—good sources for information on things to do, places to stay, and possible rides out of town—and are usually very clean. No one policy covers all these institutions. Getting a room may be difficult, but rates tend to be low, and many offer free local calls. *Let's Go* lists colleges which rent dorm rooms among the accommodations for appropriate cities. College dorms are popular with many travelers, especially those looking for long-term lodging, so reserve ahead. **Mitwohnzentralen** in most German cities match people who want to lease apartments from a few days to a couple of months. A number of host networks will help you find accommodations with families throughout Europe. Also see Willing Workers on Organic Farms, p. 23.

CAMPING AND THE OUTDOORS

There are about 2600 campsites in Germany, most of which are accessible by public transportation and about 400 of which are open in the winter. If you're prepared to go rustic, camping is the best option. Often however, campgrounds resemble battlegrounds, with weary travelers and screaming children stacked next to each other. The money and time expended in getting to the site may eat away at your budget and patience. Showers, bathrooms, and a restaurant or store are common. Camping costs US$1-10 per person with additional charge for tents and vehicles.

Blue signs with a black tent on a white background indicate official sites. **Deutscher Camping-Club e.v. (DCC),** Mandlstr. 28, 80802 München (tel. (089) 33 40 21), and **Allgemeiner Deutscher Automobil-Club (ADAC)** (see **Getting Around: By Car,** p. 44) have specific info on campgrounds, and the National Tourist Office distributes a free map, *Camping in Germany,* with a full list of campgrounds. Also check out **Camping Site Guide of Germany** (see **Internet Resources,** p. 3).

A number of hiking guidebooks meet the needs of the novice or expert:

Automobile Association, AA Publishing. Orders and enquiries to P.O. Box 194, Rochester, Kent, ME2 4QG, U.K. (tel. (01634) 29 71 23; fax 29 80 00 or 29 80 02). Publishes a wide range of maps, atlases, and travel guides, including *Camping and Caravanning: Europe* (UK£8).

The Caravan Club, East Grinstead House, East Grinstead, West Sussex, RH19 1UA, U.K. (tel. (0342) 32 69 44; fax 41 02 58). Produces one of the most detailed English-language guides to campsites in Europe and the U.K.

Family Campers and RVers/National Campers and Hikers Association, Inc., 4804 Transit Rd. Bldg. #2, Depew, NY 14043 (tel. or fax (716) 668-6242). Membership fee (US$25) includes their publication *Camping Today.* For US$35, you can also get the International Camping Carnet, which is required by some European campgrounds but can usually be bought on the spot.

Recreational Equipment, Inc. (REI), P.O. Box 1700, Sumner, WA 98352–0001 (tel. (800) 426-4840), publishes *Europa Camping and Caravanning* (US$20), an annually updated catalogue of European campsites.

At the core of your necessary equipment is the **sleeping bag.** Most of the better sleeping bags are rated according to the lowest outdoor temperature at which they will still keep you warm. If you're using a sleeping bag for serious camping, you should also have either a foam **pad** or an air mattress. Just as with selecting a mate, your major considerations in selecting a **tent** should be shape and size. The best tents are free-standing, with their own frames and suspension systems; they set up quickly and require no staking. Low-profile dome tents are the best all-around. Good two-person tents start at about $150, and four-person tents at $400. You can, however, often find last year's version for half the price. If you intend to do a lot of hiking, you should have a **frame backpack.** External-frame packs are more comfortable for long hikes over even terrain. Buy a backpack with an internal frame, however, if you'll be hiking on difficult trails that require a lot of bending and maneuvering. Sturdy backpacks cost anywhere from US$125 to 400. Other necessities include: **battery-operated lantern, plastic groundcloth** for the floor of your tent, **nylon tarp** for general purposes, **"stuff sack"** or plastic bag to keep your sleeping bag dry; rain gear; synthetic tops, socks, and underwear; a canteen or water bottle; a camp stove; waterproof matches; Swiss Army knife; insect repellent. The following outfits can provide you with advice and a wide selection of **camping paraphenalia:**

Campmor, P.O. Box 700, Saddle River, NJ 07458-0700 (tel. (800) CAMPMOR (526-4784), outside the U.S. call (201) 825-8300; email customer-service@campmor.com; http://www.campmor.com), has a wide selection of name brand equipment at low prices. One-year guarantee for unused or defective merchandise.

Discount Camping, 880 Main North Rd., Pooraka, South Australia 5095, Australia (tel. (08) 8262 3399; fax 8260 6240), specializes in tents but also carries other equipment.

Recreational Equipment, Inc. (REI), 1700 45th St. E, Sumner, WA 98390 (tel. (800) 426-4840; http://www.rei.com), stocks a wide range of the latest in camping gear and holds great seasonal sales. Many items are guaranteed for life.

YHA Adventure Shop, 14 Southampton St., London, WC2E 7HA, U.K. (tel. (01718) 36 85 41). The main branch of one of Britain's largest outdoor equipment dealers.

■ Longer Stays

Those planning to remain in Germany for an extended period of time should contact the local **Mitwohnzentrale,** an accommodation-finding office, in the city where they plan to stay. Throughout Germany, *Mitwohnzentralen* match apartments with apartment seekers. The stay can last anywhere from a few days to eternity, depending on the availablity of apartments and the price you are willing to pay. Look under the **Practical Information** or **Accommodations** listings for each individual city to find the address and phone number of individual *Mitwohnzentrale.* Also check postings in universities, where student housing can offer lodging and utilities for DM200-300 per month. Those seeking employment will frequently need a work permit (see **Alternatives to Tourism,** p. 21).

Those looking to **furnish** an abode would do well to capitalize on the German **"Sperrmull"** phenomenon. Cities around Germany have appointed days on which residents dispose of their larger garbage in a designated *Platz,* thus producing a goldmine of free couches, tables, TVs, and more. The local *Stadthaus* has a schedule of these days. Bring a shopping cart to carry larger booty, and show up early (6pm the day **before** the official event generally yields successful plundering), as rabid German *Schulkinder* tend to loot the goods on the actual *Sperrmull* day, destroying those treasured free furnishings.

Those who wish to open a **bank account** should be careful in selecting a bank; the speed with which German banks provide their customers with **ATM cards** varies widely, as do charges for ATM withdrawals. **Dresdner Bank** and **Deutsche Bank** tend to provide their customers with the best ATM deals; both are national banks, meaning that account holders can withdraw money without any charge throughout Germany. These banks are also networked for withdrawals in most European countries. Sparkasse has been known to take longer in providing clients with ATM cards.

▓ Sports

Germany enjoys a long tradition of sports and outdoor recreation and outstanding facilities to boot. The *Vereine* (club) culture, encompassing most sports as well as hiking and crafts, produces almost religious fervor and devotion among many of its members. Nearly every city and town in Germany—especially resort towns—have swimming pools and spas. The North and Baltic Sea coasts, as well as the Frisian Islands and Rügen, offer attractive beaches in the warm months. In winter, the German Alps, Harz Mountains, Schwarzwald, and Bayerischer Wald are host to all sorts of snow sports, including skiing, ski-jumping, tobogganing, skating, hockey, and bobsledding. Garmisch-Partenkirchen, in the Bayerische Alpen, sports high-caliber winter Olympics facilities. The following organizations can provide valuable information:

German Sports Association, Haus des Sportes, Otto-Fleck Schneise 12, 60528 Frankfurt am Main (tel. (069) 670 00; fax 67 49 06).

German Hiking and Climbing Association, Reichsstr. 4, 66111 Saarbrücken (tel. (0681) 39 00 70; fax 390 46 50). This organization provides information about trails, shelters, and huts.

German Alpine Association, Von-Kahr-Str. 2-4, 80997 München (tel. (089) 14 00 30; fax 140 03 11). The association maintains over 9000mi. of trails in the Alps and 252 huts open to all mountaineers. They also offer courses and guided expeditions.

German Sailing Association, Grundgenstr. 18, 22309 Hamburg (tel. (040) 632 00 90; fax 63 20 09 28). The association can provide you with a list of more than 180 schools operating on the North and Baltic sea coasts.

German Aero Club, Rudolf-Braas-Str. 20, 63150 Heusenstamm (tel. (06104) 699 60; fax 69 96 11). Serves over 50 flying schools and 1000 gliding clubs.

German Fishing Association, Siemensstr. 11-13, 63071 Offenbach (tel. (069) 85 50 06; fax 87 37 70). Fishers must obtain a license *(Fischereischein)* from local or municipal authorities for a small fee and a second permit *(Fischereierlaubnisschein)* from the leaseholder or owner of the fishing waters.

German Golf Association, Friedrichstr. 12, 65185 Wiesbaden (tel. (06121) 99 02 00; fax 990 20 40). Foreign visitors are always welcome! Step up to the tee and try to knock down *"ein Birdie"* for about DM30 Mon.-Fri. and DM30-60 on weekends.

▓ Keeping in Touch

MAIL

Germany's postal code system is similar to the one in the United States; codes are based on geographic zones and most cities are divided into many postal code zones. Large companies and industries even have their own postal codes. The codes are all five digits long and should precede the German name of the town.

Sending Mail To Germany

Mail can be sent to Germany through **Poste Restante** (the international phrase for General Delivery; *Postlagernde Briefe* in German) to any city or town; it's worth using and generally reliable. Mark the envelope "BITTE HALTEN" (hold) and address it, for example, "Mick SWEET, *Postlagernde Briefe*, 50668 Köln, Germany." The last name should be capitalized and underlined. The mail goes to a special desk in the central post office unless you specify a post office by street address or postal code. As a rule, it is best to use the largest post office in the area. When possible, it is usually safer and quicker to send mail express or registered.

When picking up your mail, bring your passport or other ID. If the clerks insist that there is nothing for you, have them check under your first name as well. *Let's Go* lists post offices in the **Practical Information** section for each city and most towns.

American Express travel offices throughout the world will act as a mail service for cardholders if you contact them in advance. Under this free **Client Letter Service,** they hold mail for 30 days, forward upon request, and accept telegrams. Just like *Poste Restante,* the last name of the person to whom the mail is addressed should be capitalized and underlined. Some offices will offer these services to non-cardholders (especially those who have purchased AmEx Travelers' Cheques), but call ahead to make sure. Check the **Practical Information** section of the cities you plan to visit; *Let's Go* lists AmEx office locations for most large cities. A complete list is available free from AmEx (tel. (800) 528-4800) in the booklet *Traveler's Companion* or online at http://www.americanexpress.com (follow the travel links to the country index).

Airmail between North America and Germany takes 7 to 10 days. Allow at least two weeks for Australia and New Zealand. Postcards and letters cost 50¢ and 60¢ respectively. It is *vital* to distinguish your airmail from surface mail by labeling it "air mail" in the appropriate language (in German, *"Mit Luftpost"*).

Sending Mail from Germany

Surface mail is by far the cheapest and slowest way to send mail. It takes one to three months to cross the Atlantic, appropriate for sending large quantities of items you won't need to see for a while. Once again, distinguish your airmail from surface mail by explicitly labeling "airmail" *("Mit Luftpost").* When ordering books and materials from abroad, always include one or two **International Postal Reply Coupons (IRCs)**—a way of providing the postage to cover delivery. IRCs should be available from your local post office (US$1.05).

Aerogrammes, printed sheets that fold into envelopes and travel via airmail, are available at post offices. It helps to mark to *"Mit Luftpost,"* though *Par Avion* is universally understood. Most post offices will charge exorbitant fees or simply refuse to send Aerogrammes with enclosures. Airmail between Germany and the U.S. averages 7 to 10 days. Allow *at least* two weeks for Australia, New Zealand, and most of Africa.

Mail moves significantly faster within Western Germany than within the East, and crossovers are slower than either. Still, you can generally get a piece of regular mail from one city in Germany to another overnight. **Postcards** within Germany cost DM0.80, to any international destination DM2. **Letters** (up to 20g) cost DM1 within Germany, DM3 (airmail) beyond. Despite postal unity, it's still slower to mail letters from Eastern Germany. **Mailboxes** are distinguished by their bright yellow color.

TELEPHONES

You can always be sure of finding a **public phone** in a post office. Additionally, phones can be found in the *Hauptbahnhof* in just about every German city.

> ## EMERGENCY
>
> **Police:** tel. 110. **Fire:** tel. 112. **Ambulance:** tel. 115.

Collect calls are not possible from public phones. If you spend a week or more in Germany, invest in a **Telefonkarte** (telephone card), the most sensible way to make calls from public phones. The cards come in DM3, DM6, and, more commonly, DM12, DM20, and DM50 denominations. The two German phone systems merged in 1993, although the availability of private phone lines is still a problem in the east (many businesses get by with mobile phones). Still, except in some very small towns, you should have no trouble finding a public card phone at a post office. Without a card, you must insert 20-30Pf and then feed the meter while talking. The earpiece will usually emit a beep to alert you to add more money.

To **call Germany,** first dial the international access code (in the US, 011), then the **country code (49),** then the city code minus the first zero, then the phone number.

Local Calls

Local calls should be made with a *Telefonkarte* (telephone card). This is by *far* the best option available; cards are sold in all post offices. Another option is to feed **coins** to the phone. In the booth, pick up the receiver, deposit coins (even if your call is toll-free) and dial. **Local calls** cost 30Pf. Phones accept 10Pf, DM1, and DM5 coins, but not DM2 or 50Pf. If you only use 10Pf coins, the excess will be returned at the end of the call. At some phones, you can also pay by **credit card.**

Inter-City Calls

Inter-city calls entail dialing the city telephone code (including the first zero that appears in the code) and the number. Do not be confused by the fact that there is no standard length for telephone numbers. The smaller the city, the more digits in the telephone code *(Vorwahl)*, while the telephone number *(Rufnummer)* varies in length. In **Eastern Germany,** the phone system is fluctuating during its integration into the West's. Listings operators dispense information about any German city. The **national information number** is 011 88. For information within the EU, call 00 11 88.

International Calls

You can place **international calls** from most telephones. To call from the U.S., dial the universal international access code (011), followed by the country code (49 for Germany), the city code, and the local number. Country and city codes may sometimes be listed with a zero in front (e.g., 049), but when using 011 (or whatever your international access code happens to be), drop successive zeros (e.g., 011 49). English-speaking operators are often available for local and international assistance. Operators in most countries will place **collect calls** for you. It's cheaper to find a pay phone and deposit enough money to say "Call me" and give your number. In Germany, pay phones marked with a bell allow you to receive calls—the phone number should be printed on the phone.

Some companies, seizing upon this "call-me-back" concept, have created callback phone services. Under these plans, you call a specified number, ring once, and hang up. The company's computer calls back and gives you a dial tone. You can then make as many calls as you want, at rates about 20-60% lower than you'd pay using credit cards or pay phones. This option is most economical for loquacious travelers, as services may include a US$10-25 minimum billing per month. For information, call **America Tele-Fone** (tel. (800) 321-5817), **Globaltel** (tel. (770) 449-1295), **International Telephone** (tel. (800) 638-5558), and **Telegroup** (tel. (800) 338-0225).

A **calling card** is probably your best and cheapest bet; your local long-distance service provider will have a number for you to dial while traveling (either toll-free or charged as a local call) to connect instantly to an operator in your home country. The calls (plus a small surcharge) are then billed either collect or to the calling card. For more info, call **AT&T** about its **USADirect** and **World Connect** services (tel. (888) 288-4685; from abroad call (810) 262-6644 collect), **Sprint** (tel. (800) 877-4646; from abroad, call (913) 624-5335 collect), or **MCI WorldPhone** and **World Reach** (tel. (800) 444-4141; from abroad dial the country's MCI access number). In Canada, contact Bell Canada **Canada Direct** (tel. (800) 565 4708); in the U.K., British Telecom **BT Direct** (tel. (800) 34 51 44); in Ireland, Telecom Éireann **Ireland Direct** (tel. (800) 250 250); in Australia, Telstra **Australia Direct** (tel. 13 22 00); in New Zealand, **Telecom New Zealand** (tel. 123); and in South Africa, **Telkom South Africa** (tel. 09 03).

MCI's WorldPhone also provides access to MCI's **Traveler's Assist**, which gives legal and medical advice, exchange rate information, and translation services. Many other long distance carriers and phone companies provide such travel information; contact your phone service provider.

Remember **time differences** when calling. Germany is on Western European Time (*MEZ* in German), six hours ahead of U.S. Eastern Standard Time. To make a direct international call from Germany, you must use the **international access code: 00**.

OTHER SERVICES

Domestic and international **telegrams** offer an option slower than phone but faster than post. Fill out a form at any post or telephone office; cables arrive in one or two days. Telegrams can be quite expensive; **Western Union** (tel. (800) 325-6000), for example, adds a surcharge to the per-word rate depending on the country. You may wish to consider **faxes** for more immediate and cheaper communication. Major cities have bureaus where you can pay to send and receive faxes.

Between May 2 and *Oktoberfest*, **EurAide,** P.O. Box 2375, Naperville, IL 60567 (tel. (630) 420-2343; fax 420-2369; http://www.cube.net/kmu/euraide.html), offers **Overseas Access,** a service useful to travelers without a set itinerary. To reach you, people call, fax, or use the internet to leave a message; you receive it by calling Munich whenever you wish, which is cheaper than calling overseas. You may also leave messages for callers to pick up by phone. The cost is US$15 per week or US$40 per month plus a US$15 registration fee.

If you're spending time abroad and want to keep in touch with friends or colleagues **email** is attractive. With little computer knowledge and some planning, you can beam messages anywhere. One option is to befriend college students and ask if you can use their email accounts. If you're not the finagling type, **Traveltales.com** (http://traveltales.com) provides free, web-based email for travelers and maintains a list of cybercafes, travel links, and a travelers' chat room. **Katchup** (http://www.katchup.co.nz) offers a similar service for NZ$50 per year. Other free, web-based email providers include **Hotmail** (http://www.hotmail.com), **RocketMail** (http://www.rocketmail.com), and **USANET** (http://www.usa.net). Many free email providers are funded by advertising and some require you to fill out a questionnaire.

If you're already hooked up to the infobahn at home, there should be access numbers for your destination country; check with your internet provider before leaving. If you're not connected, one comparatively cheap, easy-to-use provider is **America Online,** 8615 Westwood Center Dr., Vienna, VA 22070 (tel. (800) 827-6364). The interactive computer service now offers **"GLOBALnet,"** making it possible for net-junkies to access the internet, chat rooms, and email through their home accounts while traveling in 70 countries. The only hurdles for budget travelers are the US$6-12 per hour surcharge and the fact that GLOBALnet only works on computers with AOL software installed; in other words, to use the service you must travel with your own computer or install the software as you go and log on as a guest.

Travelers who have the luxury of a laptop with them can use a **modem** to call an internet service provider. Long-distance phone cards specifically intended for such calls can defray normally high phone charges. Check with your long-distance phone provider to see if they offer this option; otherwise, try a **C.COM Internet PhoneCard** (tel. (888) 464-2266; international access numbers, see attached), which offers internet connection calls for 15¢ per minute, minimum initial purchase of US$5.

History and Culture

It seems appropriate that as the world reinvents itself, Germany is once again at the center of it all. Germany's modern experience encapsulates all the promises and betrayals of life in the 20th century and exposes the fracture line of Western civilization. It has proven a volatile political crucible in recent times, passing through six political systems in 80 years. Events in Germany facilitated the end of the "long 19th century" in 1914 and the end of the "short 20th century" in 1990, when Germany thawed the Cold War through its reunification. All the while, the "German Question" has been formulated and re-formulated. Is there a distinct "German character" that has informed such a peculiar historical path? There are, to be sure, certain German traits—industriousness, efficiency, and a mystifying refusal to cross the street against the light—but the generation of Germans who came of age after the war defy the negative stereotype of the humorless, heel-clicking German authoritarian. Like the broad social and political range of the nation, the German character resists easy categorization. Indeed, the German national character is marked as much by techno as by its gruesome historical past.

Despite its long history of reactionary governments, Germany has always been a wellspring of revolutionaries and innovators—for better and for worse. One of the first heroes of German history, **Charlemagne** (Karl der Große) unified post-Roman Europe under enlightened rule. A small-town German monk, **Martin Luther,** stands as one of the most influential figures in Western history as the author of the pedestal-smashing Protestant Reformation. Socialist pioneers **Karl Marx** and **Friedrich Engels** equipped the revolutionary groundswell of 19th-century Europe with an ideology and a project whose power has been re-channeled but never defused. **Adolf Hitler,** one of the most loathsome figures in history, performed deeds—the seizure of power, the conquest of Europe, the **Holocaust**—which defy explanation. This last image, of course, indelibly colors all subsequent German history. Germans must grapple with the wrenching fact that the cradle of **Johann Wolfgang von Goethe** and **Immanuel Kant** also nurtured **Auschwitz** and **Treblinka.**

These days Germans are busy trying to come to terms with their schizophrenic history and identity. The Wall had barely come down when West Berlin dilettantes started cracking jokes about putting it back up. The "Wall in the Mind" *(die Mauer im Kopf)* may continue to separate Germans for at least a generation. Yet as Germans turn inward, their global position is becoming increasingly significant. In the wake of Europe's most recent revolutions, a newly reunited Germany's pivotal position between East and West is even more important than it was during the

> The "Wall in the Mind" (die Mauer im Kopf) may continue to separate Germans for at least a generation.

Cold War. As a nation forced to face the moral bankruptcy of its nationalism, Germany brings a unique perspective and motivation to recent conflicts and the project of an integrated Europe. It's worth remembering all of this in your travels. The historical and cultural legacies that Germany has offered posterity over centuries of war and division represent a healthy chunk of Western civilization's collective past. There are always bursts of change which seem to have no precedent. There are moments when one seems to be hearing the same story again, to hear the same turns of phrase deployed in different settings, the same insistence and the same denial. It is easy to be caught and lost in what Bertolt Brecht called "this Babylonian confusion of words," the narrative of Germany.

■ History

All history involves conflict, but in Germany it is especially contested ground. Witness the 1996 publication of Daniel Goldhagen's *Hitler's Willing Executioners,* which claimed that Germans were active and knowing participants in the Holocaust. The statement incited an academic brawl which continues to instigate intense debates. Even the starting point of German history is debatable. Ancestors of *homo sapiens* lived in Germany 50,000 years ago; the first remains identified as **Neanderthal Man** were dug up near Düsseldorf in 1856. At the opposite extreme, the first ruler of an entity identified as "Germany" was Heinrich of Sachsen, in the early 10th century. Nominally speaking, "German" history began in 90BC when the Roman author Posidonius first gave that moniker to the peoples that migrated around 1000BC from Southern Scandinavia to territories contained in modern central Europe. That's where we pick up the story.

TIMELINE

800	Charlemagne crowned as emperor of the Holy Roman Empire.
1356	Golden Bull splits authority between archbishops and electors in choosing Emperor
1358	Hanseatic League founded
1517	Luther posts 95 Theses, inaugurating the Protestant Reformation
1618-48	Thirty Years War between Protestants and Catholics, concluding with the Peace of Westphalia
1709	Friedrich the Great establishes Berlin as Prussian capital
1774	Goethe's *Sorrows of a Young Werther* ushers in *Sturm-und-Drang*
1806	Napoleonic Wars begin—decline and fall of the Holy Roman Empire
1815	Congress of Vienna concludes Napoleonic Wars
1824	Beethoven composes his Ninth Symphony
1848	Abortive socialist revolution; Marx publishes the *Communist Manifesto*
1864-71	Bismarck's wars of unification
1871	Wilhelm I crowned *Kaiser* of new, unified Germany—2nd Reich
1914-18	World War I, concluding with the Treaty of Versailles
1918	Socialist revolution in Berlin; Weimar Republic founded
1922-23	Hyperinflation; Hitler's Beer Hall *Putsch*
1933	Hitler appointed Chancellor, declares himself *Führer* of 3rd Reich
1935	Racial Purity Laws, depriving Jews of German citizenship and prohibiting intercourse between "Aryan" and Jew.
1938	Kristallnacht, during which most Jewish property in Germany was destroyed
1939-45	World War II, ending with the Allies' defeat of Germany
1942-45	"Final Solution," the attempted extermination of European Jews
1949	Division of Germany into FRG and GDR
1953	Rebellion in Berlin crushed by Soviets
1961	Berlin Wall constructed
1989	Fall of the Berlin Wall
1990	Germany Reunifies

THE ROMAN ERA: HAIR-BUTTERERS AND THINGS

In early German society, individuals of common ancestry lived communally in clans, the basic social units. All men able to fight were expected to do so to protect the clan's honor. Regular **Things** (general assemblies), usually held outdoors in the absence of convention centers, convened to discuss their leader's proposals. In his chronicle Germania, the Roman author Tacitus memorably vilified the wild, dairy-loving Germans as "barbarians who buttered their hair."

The expanding **Roman Republic** waged war against the German clans for centuries; by 58BC the Rhine was its northeast frontier. A particularly celebrated thumping at the hands of **Hermann** (Arminius) in the Teutoburger Wald in 9AD put an end to Roman expansion. Beginning in 90AD, the Roman Empire built a string of fortifications between the Rhine and the Danube, but these were broken in the 3rd century, and Germanic tribes began to migrate into the Empire, sanctioned as **foederati** (allies): the Romans hired the tribes to protect the outer parts of the empire. Driven by an envy of Roman orgies and luxuries, the non-*foederati* clans accelerated their attacks while *foederati* reneged on their treaties and established their own sovereign

That "ß" Thing,
Plus a Few Necessary German Words

In your travels, it is useful to pick up a number of words for common tourist attractions and services, even if you speak no German. *Let's Go: Germany 1998* uses a fair amount of German words in the text without translation. To read some of them, and many of the titles and phrases in the book, you need to be let in on the mysterious secret of the **"ß,"** a special consonant which Germans call an "ess-tset." **It is pronounced exactly like a double "S"** in English; hence, *Straße,* the German word for street, is pronounced "SHTRAH-ssuh." Meißen, a small town in Sachsen, is pronounced "MIGH-ssen." For details on the future of the "ess-tset," see **Ess-terminate with Ess-treme Prejudice!**, p. 522. With that aside, here is a list of the most essential German tourist terms that you will see used (all over the place) in this text:

das Schloß (SHLOSS) = **castle**
die Altstadt (AHLT-shtaht) = **old city,** the historic section of town
das Rathaus (RAHT-hauss) = **town hall,** often located in the *Altstadt*
der Dom (DOME) = **cathedral** or
das Münster (MYN-stuh) = **cathedral**
die Kirche (KEER-hkuh) = **church**
die Kneipe (k'NIGH-puh) = a **bar** for students or young people
der Hauptbahnhof (HAUWPT-bahn-hohf) = a town/city's **main train station**
die Pension (PAHN-tzee-OHN) = small, cheap, often family-run **hotel**
das Privatzimmer (pree-VAHT-tsim-mer) = a **private room,** in a home
die Jugendherberge (YOO-gent-hair-BARE-guh) = **youth hostel**
die Mensa (MEN-zah) = **cafeteria** (often at a university)
das Imperium schlägt zurück = The Empire Strikes Back

monarchies on Roman territory. Eventually, German tribes laid siege to Rome itself; Visigoths pillaged the city in 410, Vandals seized it in 455, and **Odoacer,** leader of the Ostrogoths, deposed Emperor Romulus Augustus in 476, the date at which the empire is considered to have ended in the west. Despite the decline in Roman authority, Germanic tribes preserved many imperial administrative institutions.

While other German tribes were busy knocking over the ancient equivalents of liquor stores and gas stations, the **Franks** got serious and spent their time expanding their rule in the Rhine Valley. **Clovis** consolidated the power of the Franks over the northwestern territories of modern France. After converting to **Christianity** late in the 5th century, Clovis employed the church to help govern his burgeoning kingdom. Since Clovis issued religious laws and appointed bishops, he essentially controlled the ecclesiastical administration (this entanglement of king and church would be a major sticking point in later centuries). After his death, Clovis's heirs split the kingdom, soon adding Provence, Burgundy, and Bayern to their domains.

THE AGE OF CHARLEMAGNE

In the process of unifying and expanding the territories under their control, the Merovingian royal family turned over administration of the kingdom to **major-domos** (mayors of the palace), who served as heads of the royal household and as the king's chief retainers. The **Carolingian** family dominated the post for generations. The power of the *major-domos* began to visibly eclipse that of the king; in 751, **Pepin the Short** became the titular and effective ruler of the Franks in a bloodless coup. The Carolingian empire reached its zenith under the rule of Pepin's son **Charlemagne** ("Charles the Great"), whom Germans know as **Karl der Große.** By medieval or modern standards, Charlemagne was an extremely busy man; he subdued Sachsen, the Papal States, and Bayern. At the same time, Christian missionaries extended his influence among the Slavs (setting the stage for centuries of conflict). Pope Leo III attempted to reconstitute the lost Roman empire of the west, as well as increase his own influence, by crowning Charlemagne the **Holy Roman Emperor** on Christmas Day 800 (although whether he did so only at Charlemagne's request is a matter of historical debate), and the Byzantine emperor recognized Chuck as his equal in the **Treaty of Aachen.** Charlemagne's rule was relatively enlightened; his administrative wisdom and love of learning were reflected in a variety of legacies. Under his stewardship, monasteries became centers of learning and preservers of classical traditions, and commerce within Europe and with the Arab and Byzantine worlds was revived.

However, this Dark Age "renaissance" did not endure. Several factors caused the empire to crap out: a new wave of **invasions** from Vikings to the north, Magyars to the east, and Arabs to the south; the lack of a sufficient infrastructure to support such a vast empire, encompassing virtually all of Christian Europe; and the end of a long lucky streak in which only one male Carolingian had emerged in every generation to rule. After the death of Charlemagne's son, **Louis the Pious,** the 843 **Treaty of Verdun** split the empire into three kingdoms. Civil wars ensued, further dismembering the Frankish lands. Vassals asserted their independence from their lords, while those remaining loyal demanded greater power. Out of the hundreds of new semi-sovereign principalities emerged a few strong duchies—namely Swabia, Sachsen, Bayern, and Franconia—as a defense against the invasions the center had proven incapable of stopping. **Otto I** defeated the Slavs and pushed the Franks' borders as far east as the Oder River. Otto secured the tacit support of the other lords and made a difficult trek to Rome through hostile territory; he was crowned Holy Roman Emperor in 962, invigorating a title which had been in disrepute for over a century.

THE ROOTS OF DIVISION

The relationship between the church and the empire deteriorated in the following centuries. **Pope Gregory VII** excommunicated **Heinrich IV** twice in fights over the appointment of bishops during the **Investiture Conflict;** ironically both were proponents of church reform. In the 1122 **Concordat of Worms,** Hank's son **Heinrich V** conceded his Italian claims to the Pope and agreed to exert no influence over the elections of bishops other than to attend the ceremonies. Because of the conflict, Heinrich V lost the church's administrative support and its powerful backing. Territorial lords rose up and challenged him, further reducing his imperial authority.

Late in the 12th century, Emperor **Friedrich Barbarossa** united the houses of Guelph and Hohenstaufen and feudalized and federalized the Holy Roman Empire.

> Aspirants to the throne bribed the electors, allowing the electors to make a financial killing every time an emperor died.

He created a new class of **imperial princes** below the emperor and above the other nobles, winning the support of strong territorial lords for his plans by promoting them to these positions. His designs were undermined by his own grandson, **Friedrich II.** In exchange for support from princes and the Pope for his Italian military expeditions, Friedrich ceded significant legal, administrative, and judicial authority to them, further fragmenting German lands. Squabbles between the princes after Friedrich's death in 1250 left the empire without clear leadership. Despite these renewed conflicts and rivalries, the centuries that followed were marked by the construction of cathedrals and the growth of towns.

A compromise between warring factions, the **Golden Bull of 1356,** declared that electors from seven major territories—three archbishops and four secular leaders—would approve the selection of each emperor. Aspirants to the throne bribed the electors, further diluting the power of the emperor and allowing the electors to make a financial killing every time an emperor died. Under these conditions members of the well-heeled **House of Habsburg** maneuvered their way to the top, occupying the throne for the next five centuries (except for one brief interregnum) with the support of their Austrian domains. Meanwhile, settlers moved from western Germany to eastern Germany, Bohemia, and Austria; centuries later, the Nazis resurrected the phrase describing this movement, *Drang nach Osten* (drive to the East). In 1358 several German merchant towns organized the **Hanseatic League,** designed to help its members protect their trading interests. Emperor Maximilian I was the first Holy

Roman Emperor to receive papal permission to be crowned without going to Rome to have the Pope perform the ceremony. As time passed, Italy and other outlying areas of the empire slipped out of its control entirely.

THE REFORMATION AND THE THIRTY YEARS WAR

On Halloween Day 1517, **Martin Luther,** a monk and professor of Biblical studies at Wittenberg University in Sachsen, posted his **Ninety-Five Theses** on the door of the city's castle church. The reverberations created by the unleashing of the **Protestant Reformation** persist today. Luther attacked the Roman Catholic Church for the extravagance of the papal court in Rome and its practice of selling **indulgences**—gift certificates for the soul which promised to shorten the owner's stay in purgatory. Luther insisted that salvation came only through God's grace, not through good works. The stern, indefatigable Luther revolutionized everything he touched; one of the greatest salvos of his war against Catholicism was a **new translation of the Bible,** a document whose publication single-handedly crystallized the patchwork of German dialects into a standard, literary High German language.

Luther's crusade found immediate support with Friedrich the Wise, Elector of Sachsen, who did not permit the sale of papal indulgences. Other princes soon adopted Lutheranism, captivated by hopes of stemming the flow of money to Rome without going to Hell for it. Armed conflicts soon erupted. The disturbances quickly became more than just religious conflicts; the serfs rebelled during the **Peasants' Wars** in 1524-1526. The chaos was too much for Luther, who called upon the princes to crush the bands of peasants. But Lutheranism continued to spread throughout Europe. The Habsburg Emperor **Karl V**—the most powerful monarch since Charlemagne—declared his intention to uproot the subversive doctrine and destroy those who professed it. However, in the 1555 **Peace of Augsburg,** Karl suspended the **Counter-Reformation** and conceded individual princes the right to determine the religion practiced in their territory, a system that led to a number of absurd overnight conversions and further divided and paralyzed the empire.

Karl's successors did not keep the bargain. When Ferdinand of Styria tried to impose Catholicism on Bohemia, Protestants rebelled, leading to the "smashing" **Defenestration of Prague** (the unsuspecting papal legate who was hurled out of a window had his fall broken by a pile of horse dung). The **Thirty Years War** (1618-48) which ensued was a catastrophe for Germany. At least one-third of the Holy Roman Empire population was wiped out, towns were laid to waste, and famine stalked the population in the longest and bloodiest conflict ever to embroil Europe. The **Peace of Westphalia,** which ended the war, granted 300 princes the right to elect the emperor. The Habsburgs retained the right to interfere in intra-state squabbles, but the imperial administration was effectively dismantled. The Holy Roman Empire never had a unified and loyal population; although it lingered for another 150 years, it was a dead institution, and its demise left Germany greatly divided.

THE RISE OF BRANDENBURG-PRUSSIA

The war indirectly benefited the leaders of **Brandenburg-Prussia.** Elector Friedrich Wilhelm of the **House of Hohenzollern** achieved peace with Sweden without estranging the Habsburgs. He gained the support of the landed nobility, the **Junkers,** by making them army officers. His great-grandson, Friedrich II—known as **Friedrich the Great**—consolidated the heartland of the rising Prussian state. Friedrich is revered in German history as an enlightened ruler, notable for administrative and military skill as well as support of the arts. He was also reputedly gay, which did not sit well with his father. When Maria Theresa became empress of the Habsburg domains in 1740, Friedrich seized the opportunity to snatch the prosperous province of **Silesia.** By the end of the Seven Years War in 1763, Prussia was viewed as one of Europe's great powers. Friedrich II and his nephew joined forces with Russia and Austria to **divide Poland** in 1772 and link Brandenburg to Prussia physically for the first time.

These skirmishes paled in comparison to the havoc wreaked by France in the wake of the French Revolution. **Napoleon** conquered and disbanded the Holy Roman Empire, fusing hundreds of territories into the **Confederation of the Rhine** in 1806. Despite incorporating hundreds of thousands of German soldiers, Napoleon's armies bogged down in Russia, and a general rebellion known as the **Wars of Liberation** ejected Napoleon from German territory, culminating in the 1813 Battle of Leipzig. The 1815 **Congress of Vienna** partially restored the pre-war German state system by creating the Austrian-led **German Confederation,** although the princelings didn't return. The congress awarded Prussia portions of Rhineland-Westphalia, Germany's future industrial heartland. In 1834, Prussia sponsored the **Zollverein,** a customs union that linked most German territories—except Austria—in a free trade zone.

In 1848, revolution broke out again in France, and the discontent spread rapidly to other parts of Europe. The German Confederation agreed to let an elected assembly decide the future of the confederation. The Frankfurt **National Assembly** drafted a liberal constitution, and invited Friedrich Wilhelm IV of Prussia to serve as emperor. In a victory of absolutism over democracy, he spurned the offer, saying that he would not accept a cardboard Bürger King crown created by rabble. The assembly disbanded, and the ensuing revolt in Frankfurt was crushed by the Prussian army.

BISMARCK AND THE SECOND REICH

In 1862, Prussian King Wilhelm I appointed a worldly Junker aristocrat named **Otto von Bismarck** as Chancellor. History's most successful practitioner of *Realpolitik,* Bismarck exploited a remarkably complex series of alliances and compromises that were more than once dissolved in favor of more violent tactics—"Blut und Eisen" (Blood and Iron), Bismarck liked to point out, were all that mattered in the long run. Bismarck believed strongly in the cause of German unity, and used war to achieve it.

"Blut und Eisen" (Blood and Iron), Bismarck liked to point out, were all that mattered in the long run.

This he did often and well. In 1864, he fought Denmark and seized control of Schleswig and Holstein. The fallout from this dispute led to conflict with Austria, which Prussia quashed in 1866 at **Sadowa** (Königgrätz). Viewing Austria as a future ally, Bismarck did not impose a humiliating peace. Instead, he made it clear that Prussia would now dominate German affairs; Austria should mind its own affairs in the east. In 1867, he disbanded the German Confederation and replaced it with the Prussiandominated **North German Confederation.** Bismarck realized that France would never willingly acquiesce to a fully united Germany under Prussian domination. Through a series of trivial diplomatic slights he suckered France into a misguided declaration of war in 1870; the technologically superior Prussian army and its allies swept through France and trounced the French army at **Sedan,** capturing Emperor Napoleon III. Parisians declared a republic and vowed to carry on the fight. Bismarck gleefully besieged Paris and had Wilhelm crowned **Kaiser of the German Reich** in the Hall of Mirrors at the Palace of Versailles. Even today, idealized murals depicting this militaristic scene appear in numerous German castles and museums.

With France thus disposed of, Bismarck was free to **unify Germany** on his own terms; the remaining independent German states were unable to resist him. He presented German liberals with an offer they couldn't refuse: unification in exchange for an authoritarian monarchy. Prussia, the dominant state in the empire, retained an anti-democratic **three-class voting system** which preserved the political supremacy of the Junkers despite their clear minority. British Prime Minister William Gladstone suggested that "Bismarck made Germany great, but the Germans small."

The so-called **conservative empire** garnered popular support by fomenting an aggressive nationalism and colonialist sentiment. **Naval leagues** formed to agitate for a German navy that could compete with Britain in the race for overseas colonies. Naval construction, however, represented only a tiny fraction of the breakneck **industrialization** that Germany underwent in the last decades of the 19th century. In the space of less than 40 years, one of the most backward nations in Europe developed the most advanced industrial base on the continent, despite retaining a medieval political system completely incompatible with modern liberal ideals. Many historians have thus dubbed Germany the *"die verspätete Nation"* (belated nation).

By the 1870s, reformist sentiment had gained ground in Germany. Led by a burgeoning trade union movement and the newly founded **Social Democratic Party** (*Sozialdemokratische Partei Deutschlands*—SPD), working-class radicalism began to pose a serious threat to the reactionary order. In one of the world's great instances of political Machiavellianism, Bismarck engaged in a long series of initiatives that alternatively revolved around reforms and repression (known as the **Kulturkampf**). Bismarck pioneered **social welfare programs** for the working class such as unemployment insurance, but harshly repressed trade unions and the Social Democrats with the **Anti-Socialist Laws** of 1878. His 1879 **Alliance of Iron and Rye** brought together the two leading conservative forces in society—the industrialists and the agrarian aristocrats. Traditionally, Junker farmers had been free-traders, while the industrialists were protectionists. But the aristocrats' stance changed when a revolution in shipping technology suddenly made American wheat so competitive on the European market that it threatened to drive them out of business. Bismarck was so successful in his quest that in 1890 the new Kaiser Wilhelm II judged him superfluous—Bismarck had completed the task—and the Iron Chancellor was dismissed.

Such rapid transitions produced tremendous social friction. The numbers of the proletariat exploded, but protectionist tariffs kept food absurdly expensive. Germany accelerated its pattern of foreign adventurism in part to quell unrest at home—a policy derisively known as **"Flucht nach vorn"** (flight to the front). Disputes over colonial issues left Germany diplomatically isolated in Europe, and tension between Germany and its neighbors rose. Meanwhile, democratic opposition began to pose a challenge to the regime. For the *Kaiser* and the elites who supported him, it became clear that dramatic and militaristic action might be required for self-preservation.

WORLD WAR I

On the eve of World War I, Europe was caught in a complex web of alliances in which minor disputes could easily escalate into a full-blown continental war. The German General Staff designed the **Schlieffen Plan** to win a war on two fronts: a lightning thrust through Belgium would deliver a knock-out blow to France, whereupon Germany could turn to the east and defeat the Russian Czar before he could mobilize his backward army. As Russia's rail network modernized, German generals saw their window of opportunity closing; they were strongly inclined to mobilize at the first sign of a crisis. That crisis broke out in 1914, when a Serbian nationalist assassinated the Habsburg heir to the Austrian throne, **Archduke Franz-Ferdinand,** in Sarajevo.

Germany could have persuaded Austria to exercise restraint but did not. Austria marched on Serbia. Russia, playing the champion of its brother Slavs, mobilized. Almost the entire *Reichstag,* including the Social Democratic delegates (who despised the Russian Czar), voted to prepare for war. The decision received popular support from the young generation of German men who were eager to prove themselves on the battlefield. After Russia ignored an ultimatum to rescind the mobilization, Germany entered the war on the side of Austria, prompting France to mobilize. Germany then declared war on France and demanded that Belgium allow its army to cross its frontier. Belgium refused. Britain, which was treaty-bound to defend Belgian neutrality, declared war on Germany. Germany quickly advanced through Belgium and northern France, and suddenly virtually all of Europe was at war.

After advancing within 50km of Paris, the German offensive stalled at the **Battle of the Marne.** Four years of agonizing **trench warfare** ensued. The slaughter was staggering, magnified by new weapons such as machine-guns, tanks, planes, flame-throwers, and poison gas. Germany's policy of **unrestricted submarine warfare** on all ships entering European waters provoked the United States into entering on the side of the Triple Entente. After England checked the imperial navy in the **Battle of Jutland,** a naval blockade rapidly choked Germany. Coupled with the industrial capacity and fresh armies of the U.S., the blockade allowed the Entente to emerge victorious.

THE WEIMAR REPUBLIC

In late 1918, with the German army on the brink of collapse, riots and mutinies broke out on the home front. On November 9, 1918, Social Democratic leader **Philipp Scheidemann** declared a republic in Berlin. **Friedrich Ebert** became its first president. The *Kaiser* and his flunkies fled to the Netherlands. France insisted on a harsh peace in the **Treaty of Versailles** (signed at the spot of Wilhelm's coronation—the Hall of Mirrors at the Palace of Versailles), which imposed staggering reparations payments and a clause ascribing the blame for the war to Germany. The new republican government had little choice but to accept the treaty, as the continuing Allied blockade was starving the country. Even before a constitution was drawn up, the republic was stuck with the stigma of the humiliating treaty; because the war had never reached German soil and the *Kaiser* had promised a smashing victory right up to the end, Germans were psychologically unprepared for defeat. The **legend of the stab-in-the-back** *(Dolchstoßlegende)* found a willing audience.

The newly formed **Communist Party** (*Kommunistische Partei Deutschlands*—KPD) led a revolt in Berlin that found some support. The Republic crushed the revolution by appealing to bands of right-wing army veterans called **Freikorps.** In a fit of reactionary fervor, the Freikorps, led by **Wolfgang Kapp,** turned against the government. Workers demonstrated support for the new republic through a general strike, and a force of 50-80,000 organized against the coup in the Ruhr industrial area. The republic emerged bruised but intact. Its leaders drew up a constitution in **Weimar.** Chosen for its legacy as the birthplace of the German Enlightenment, it now gave its name to a period of intense cultural activity but economic and political uncertainty.

Outstanding war debts and the burden of reparations produced the staggering **hyperinflation** of 1922-23, during which time the *Reichsmark* sunk from four to 4.2 trillion to the U.S. dollar. Eventually, the Republic achieved a degree of stability with help from the American **Dawes Plan,** and an age of relative calm and remarkable artistic activity ensued. But the seeds of authoritarianism never became sterile. The old, reactionary order still clung to power in many segments of society: army, police, big business, civil service, and judiciary. When an Austrian corporal named **Adolf Hitler** was arrested for treason after his abortive 1923 **Beer Hall Putsch,** he was not deported (on the grounds that he "believed he was German") and received the minimum sentence of five years, of which he served only 10 months. During his time in jail, Hitler wrote a book—*Mein Kampf*—and decided that his party, the National Socialist German Workers Party (*Nationalsozialistische Deutsche Arbeiterspartei*—NSDAP), also known as the **Nazis,** would have to seize power by constitutional means. Two aspects of the Weimar constitution, intended to establish a perfectly representative and functional democracy, in fact expedited this process. **Pure proportional representation** encouraged a spectrum of political parties and discouraged stable governments. The infamous **Article 48** (drafted by sociologist Max Weber) gave the chancellor the power to rule by decree during crises.

> After the Great Depression struck in 1929, membership in the NSDAP exploded to more than a million.

The Nazi party expanded its efficient, blindly obedient bureaucracy and nearly quadrupled its membership to 108,000 by 1929. Even so, it was still a fringe party in 1928, receiving only 2.5% of the vote. But when the Great Depression struck in 1929, 25% of the population was unemployed within months. Membership in the NSDAP exploded to more than a million by 1930—the **SA** *(Sturmabteilung),* its paramilitary arm, grew as large as the German army. The Nazis campaigned on an anti-Semitic, xenophobic platform; Hitler failed in a presidential bid against the nearly senile warhero Hindenburg in 1932, but the parliamentary elections that same year made the Nazis the largest party (winning 37% of the vote and seats) in the *Reichstag*. After various political maneuvers, President Hindenburg reluctantly appointed Hitler as chancellor of a coalition government on January 30, 1933.

THE THIRD REICH

The conservatives who backed the Hitler government had always been hostile to the Republic, and naively believed they could control Hitler and establish an authoritarian regime ruled by traditional elites. When Hitler's government formed, the Nazis controlled only two cabinet ministries and one minister-without-portfolio. But during the next two months, Hitler persuaded Hindenburg to dissolve the *Reichstag* and call new elections, allowing him to invoke Article 48 and to **rule by decree** for seven weeks. During this time, he curtailed freedom of the press, authorized the SA and SS Sonderkommando (special commands) as auxiliary police, and brutalized opponents. A week before the elections, the mysterious **Reichstag fire** gave Hitler an occasion to declare a state of emergency and begin rounding up opponents, many of whom were relocated to newly built **concentration camps.** In the election of March 5, 1933, with 44% of the votes, the Nazis fell short of a majority. Nonetheless, they arrested and browbeat enough opposing legislators to pass an **Enabling Act** making Hitler **legal dictator** of Germany, authorized to ban all opposition and rule by decree indefinitely. In a policy known as **Gleichschaltung** (roughly, "coordination"), the Nazis established party control over the country—not just the government, but universities, professional associations, and even chess clubs. Press, radio, books, and every imaginable aspect of public life was "Nazified," that is, strictly regulated by the state.

One of the government's first acts was to institute a **boycott of Jewish businesses** and to expel Jews from professions and the civil service. In 1935, the first of the anti-Semitic **Racial Purity Laws** deprived Jews of German citizenship and prohibited intercourse between "Aryan" and Jew. After a respite during the 1936 Berlin Olympics, the program resumed in earnest in 1938 with **Kristallnacht** (Night of Broken Glass). On November 9, Nazis destroyed thousands of Jewish businesses, burned synagogues, killed scores of Jews, and sent at least 20,000 to concentration camps.

For those fortunate enough not to be Jews, Gypsies, Communists, Social Democrats, artists, free-thinkers, disabled, gay, or concerned about any of them, the early years of the Third Reich were in many ways a marked improvement over the Weimar era. A massive program of industrialization restored full employment. Hitler abrogated the Versailles Treaty, thus freeing Germany from reparations payments and allowing it to re-arm. Although the *Autobahn* highway project was planned during the republic—as were other improvements for which the Nazis claimed credit—Hitler pushed it in earnest, recognizing its military implications. When Hitler boldly **remilitarized the Rhineland,** thousands cheered him in the streets. Next, Hitler stared down Mussolini and the West to annex Austria—the infamous **Anschluß.** Then he demanded territorial concessions from Czechoslovakia, home to thousands of ethnic Germans. British Prime Minister Neville Chamberlain assured Hitler in the notorious 1938 **Munich Agreement** that Britain would not interfere (Czechoslovakia was not consulted). One of the fundamental tenets of Nazi ideology was the necessity of acquiring **Lebensraum** (living space) from the "sub-human" Slavs in the East; many historians suggest that Hitler premeditated war to expand German *Lebensraum.*

WORLD WAR II

On September 1, 1939, German tanks rolled into Poland. Britain and France, bound by treaty to defend Poland, immediately declared war on Germany but did not attack. Germany's new tactic of mechanized **Blitzkrieg** (literally, lightning war) quickly crushed Poland. In a month, Poland was vanquished, and Hitler and Stalin divided it under the terms of a secret agreement. On April 9, 1940, Hitler rolled over Denmark and Norway. A month later, the *Blitzkrieg* roared through the Ardennes Forest of Luxembourg and quickly overwhelmed Belgium, the Netherlands, and France. Only a desperate sea-lift at Dunkirk saved the British army from total destruction. However, the Nazis failed to bomb London into submission in the aerial struggle of the **Battle of Britain.** Preparations for a cross-channel invasion were shelved as Hitler turned his attentions to his most despised enemy, Russia. The German **invasion of the USSR** in June 1941 ended the Hitler-Stalin pact. Despite the Red Army's overwhelming manpower, the invasion came close to success due to the pathetic state of the Soviet officer corps. At the peak of his conquests in late 1941, Hitler held an empire stretching from the Arctic Circle to the Sahara Desert, from the Pyrénées to the Urals.

The Soviets suffered extremely high casualties, but the *Blitzkrieg* faltered in the Russian winter and Hitler sacrificed thousands of German soldiers in his adamant refusal to retreat. The titanic and bloody battle of **Stalingrad** was the critical turning point in the East. Hitler committed a second fatal error when he declared war on the United States after Japan bombed Pearl Harbor. His attempt to save Mussolini in North Africa led to the Nazi's first battlefield defeats, and soon Germany was retreating on all fronts. The Allied landings in Normandy on **D-Day** (June 6, 1944) preceded an arduous, bloody advance across Western Europe. An **assassination attempt** against Hitler led by a group of army officers failed in July 1944, ensuring that the war would continue. The Third Reich's final offensive, the **Battle of the Bulge,** failed in December 1944. In March 1945, the Allies crossed the Rhine. The Red Army overcame bitter resistance to take Berlin in April 1945. With Red Army troops overhead, Hitler married Eva Braun just prior to killing himself in his bunker. The Third Reich, which Hitler had boasted would endure for 1000 years, had lasted only 12.

THE HOLOCAUST

Hitler's twisted ideology regarded history as a series of catastrophic confrontations between racial groups. The German *Volk,* he believed, had to triumph or perish forever. He made no secret of his desire to exterminate all Jews, who, associated with internationalism, communism, pacifism, and democracy, represented the very antithesis of Hitler's fanatic nationalism, militarism, and the myth of the *"Führer."* The Nazis' **"Final Solution to the Jewish problem"** can be seen as an extension of the persecution, deprivation, and deportation to which Jews had been subjected since the first days of the *Reich.* Another precedent was the gassing of the handicapped in the 30s. Nevertheless, the mass gassing of Jews in specially constructed **extermination camps** began only in 1942, although **SS** troops which followed the *Wehrmacht* through Russia had earlier staged mass executions. Seven full-fledged extermination camps, **Auschwitz, Buchenwald, Chelmno, Treblinka, Majdanek, Sobibor,** and **Belzec,** plus dozens of nominal "labor" camps such as **Bergen-Belsen, Dachau,** and **Sachsenhausen** were operating before war's end. Some six million Jews, two-thirds of Europe's Jewish population, mostly from Poland and the Soviet Union, were gassed, shot, starved, worked to death, or killed by exposure. Five million other victims—Soviet prisoners of war, Slavs, Gypsies, homosexuals, the mentally retarded, and political opponents—also died in Nazi camps. The atrocities of the Nazi years reach beyond the scope of tragedy and into the realm of inconceivable horror.

How much did the average German know about the Holocaust? No one can say for sure, but it is certain that the vicious persecution and small-scale murder of Jews in pre-war Germany and the "resettlement" of Jews in the east were clear for all to see. However, the Nazis were careful to keep the grisly details of gas chambers and crematoria out of reach, even among the top party leadership. Many Germans who now express horror at the genocide tolerated—or even approved of—the Nazis' earlier expressions of anti-Semitism. Very few were as daring as industrialist Oskar Schindler or the Scholl siblings, who led the "White Rose" student resistance movement.

As the living memory of the Holocaust slowly fades, the aging remains of concentration camps become the most crucial, tangible testimony available to any audience willing to see and listen. Just as a monument can lose its power to shock by becoming too familiar to passersby, so can the very existence of "museums" and guided tours seem to trivialize what occurred at them. The very fact that concentration camps are noted as points of interest in many travel guides (including this one), must be recognized as somewhat troubling. If you choose to visit one, keep in mind that while some treat these grounds as "just another stop" on a list of things to see, coming in ignorance and leaving unaffected, many visitors come with a knowledge of the camp's past or perhaps a personal memory of a loved one who perished there. Make an effort not to treat them and the grounds with disrespect. In addition, know that the exhibits here do not tell the whole story; no single medium can embrace such a narrative. Read up before you come. Better yet, a discussion with a survivor will shed more light on the dark history of these camps than any exhibit ever can.

OCCUPATION AND DIVISION

Germans call their defeat in the Second World War Null Stunde—"Zero Hour"—the moment at which everything began again. Unlike in World War I, Germany's battle-field defeat was total and indisputable. The Allies occupied and partitioned the country: the east under the Soviets, the west under the British and Americans, and Berlin under joint control. The economy was in shambles. Most cities were bombed into ruin. More than five million German soldiers and civilians died in the war, and millions remained in POW camps. All German territory east of the Oder and Neisse rivers—a quarter of the nation's land—was confiscated and placed under Soviet and Polish administration, while the coal-rich Saarland was put under French control. Ten to twelve million ethnic Germans were expelled from Poland and Sudeten Czechoslovakia; more than two million perished during the exodus. As the details of the Nazi genocidal project became public, "German" became synonymous with "barbaric."

The Allied program for the **Occupation**—demilitarization, democratization, and de-Nazification—proceeded apace, but growing animosity between the Soviets and the Western allies made joint control of Germany increasingly difficult. De-Nazification proceeded in quite disparate ways in East and West, paving the way for total division in 1949. Blaming bourgeois capitalism for the Nazi nightmare, the Soviets purged all former elites, leaving the common people exempt from any responsibility. The Allies, however, prosecuted Nazis individually, yet often so inadequately that many retained their posts. In 1947, the Western Allies merged their occupation zones into a single economic unit known as **Bizonia** (later Trizonia, after a French occupation zone was carved out of the British and American zones). The Western Allies began rebuilding their zone along the lines of a market economy with the aid of huge cash infusions from the **Marshall Plan.** The Soviets, who suffered immeasurably more in the war than the U.S. or Britain, had neither the desire nor the spare cash to help the east rebuild—they plundered it instead, as allowed by the Potsdam agreement. The Soviet Union carted away everything that wasn't fixed in concrete and a lot of things (such as factories and railroads) that were. The Western Allies ceased their contribution to this "giant sucking sound" in 1948 and then effectively severed the East's economy from the West's by introducing a new currency to Bizonia, the **Deutschmark.** Though the imposition of the new *Marks* seemed draconian at the time, most historians agree that it was the single greatest cause of the eventual stabilization of West Germany. The currency reform dispute was the proximate cause of the **Berlin Block-ade** (see **Berlin: History,** p. 89) and the ultimate **division of Germany** in 1949.

THE FEDERAL REPUBLIC OF GERMANY (FRG)

The Federal Republic of Germany (*Bundesrepublik Deutschland*—FRG) was established as a provisional government of Western Germany on May 24, 1949. A **Basic Law,** drawn up by German academics and politicians under the direction of the Western Allies, safeguarded individual rights and established a system of Federal States. Although similar in many ways to the Weimar Constitution, the Basic Law had significant departures: it made the Chancellor responsible to Parliament, banned anti-democratic parties, renounced militarism, emasculated the presidency, and established a more stable parliamentary system. One of the most visionary paragraphs of the Basic Law was the one which established a Right of Asylum, guaranteeing refuge to any person fleeing persecution. Ratification of the Basic Law, however, did not restore German sovereignty; the Allies retained supreme power over the country.

As the only party untainted by the Third Reich, the **Social Democratic Party (SPD)** seemed poised to dominate post-war German politics. Another new party, the **Free Democratic Party** (*Freidemokratische Partei*—FDP), assembled bourgeois liberals and professionals with several former Nazis. Although the FDP remained small and was often disparaged as the *"fast drei Prozent"* (almost 3%) party, it acquired power as a coalition partner. Remarkably, Germany's historically fragmented conservatives and centrists managed to unite in a new party, the **Christian Democratic Union** (*Christliche Demokratische Union*—CDU). With former Köln Mayor **Konrad Adenauer** at the helm, the CDU won a small plurality of *Bundestag* seats.

Adenauer, 73 years old when he assumed office, was perhaps the Federal Republic's greatest Chancellor. He unflaggingly pursued the integration of Germany into a unified Europe and, at the same time, the return of German national self-determination. He achieved both of these aims, first in 1951 with West Germany's entrance into the European Coal and Steel Community—the precursor of the modern European Union (EU)—and then in 1955 when the Western Allies recognized West German sovereignty. The idealistic Adenauer also helped to restore the self-esteem and purpose of his defeated people without rekindling nationalism. By the mid-1950s, Germany's post-war **Economic Miracle** (*Wirtschaftswunder*) was in full swing, and the CDU's dominance of German politics seemed unshakable. Rebuilding progressed rapidly, and Germany's industrial production increased sixfold between 1949 and 1966, with a heavy emphasis on exports. Germany achieved full employment by the late 1950s and soon began recruiting thousands of foreign **Gastarbeiter** (guest workers). Despite SPD opposition, Adenauer aligned Germany with NATO (North Atlantic Treaty Organization) in a common defense bloc.

The SPD, whose fortunes seemed so promising in 1945, wandered in the electoral wilderness without any bread crumbs for over 20 years. The party's Marxist rhetoric prevented it from expanding beyond a working-class base. In 1961, its Bad Godesberg Program jettisoned Marx. The SPD found a dynamic young leader in **Willy Brandt**, the charismatic former Berlin mayor who had worked in the anti-Nazi resistance. Germany's first post-war recession in 1967 badly hurt the CDU and the 1969 *Bundestag* elections launched the SPD into power. With Brandt as chancellor, the **Social-Liberal Coalition** of the SDP and FDP enacted a number of overdue reforms in education, governmental administration, social security, and industrial relations. Its most dramatic policy innovation, however, was in **foreign relations.** Under the old **Hallstein Doctrine,** the Federal Republic refused to recognize the German Democratic Republic, to the point of severing relations with any country that recognized the GDR. This effectively meant that West Germany was entirely cut off from the entire Eastern Bloc. Under Brandt's **Ostpolitik** (Eastern Policy), the Federal Republic actively sought improved relations with East Germany, the Soviet Union, and other Eastern Bloc nations—a policy symbolized by the famous image of a tearful Brandt dropping to his knees in front of a Polish war memorial. Brandt and his foreign minister concluded several important treaties, including an agreement **normalizing relations** with the GDR. For this, Brandt received the Nobel Peace Prize in 1971.

> The idealistic Adenauer also helped to restore the self-esteem and purpose of his defeated people without rekindling nationalism.

After Brandt resigned in the wake of a 1974 spy scandal, **Helmut Schmidt** assumed the chancellorship. West Germany under Schmidt racked up an economic record that was the envy of the industrialized world. Nevertheless, persistent structural problems in heavy industry contributed to **mounting unemployment** and dissatisfaction with the SPD in the late 1970s. In 1982, the FDP and the CDU formed a government under **Helmut Kohl** after FDP leader **Hans-Dietrich Genscher** abruptly abandoned the Social-Liberal coalition.

Kohl's government pursued a policy of welfare state retrenchment, tight monetary policy, and military cooperation with the U.S. Around the same time, a new political force emerged in Germany: the **Green Party** (*die Grünen*), which fought for disarmament and environmentalism, won a surprisingly large following by rejecting the traditional coalition politics of the Left. In 1984, Richard von Weizsäcker of the CDU was elected to the largely symbolic post of Federal President, from which he urged Germans to shoulder fully their moral responsibility for the Third Reich—an implicit rebuke of politicians like Kohl who spoke of "the grace of late birth."

HISTORY AND CULTURE

THE GERMAN DEMOCRATIC REPUBLIC (GDR)

When the Red Army occupied Eastern Germany, a cadre of German Communists who had spent the war in exile came close on their heels. Even before the surrender was signed, these party functionaries began setting up an apparatus to run the Soviet occupation zone. The first party licensed to operate in the Soviet Sector was the communist KPD under Wilhelm Pieck and Walter Ulbricht, but versions of the Western parties were established shortly afterwards. At first, the German Communists pledged to establish a parliamentary democracy and a distinctively "German path to socialism." However, their dependence on Moscow became apparent. The Social Democrats were forced to join them in a common working-class anti-fascist front, the **Socialist Unity Party** (*Sozialistische Einheitspartei Deutschlands*—SED).

In Berlin, the one area where the SPD was permitted to operate freely, the SED was soundly defeated at the ballot box. The Soviets responded by not holding any more freely contested elections, and future elections required voters to approve or reject a "unity list" of candidates that ensured SED dominance. On October 7, 1949, a People's Congress selected by such methods declared the establishment of the **German Democratic Republic** (*Deutsche Demokratische Republik*—GDR), with the national capital in Berlin. Although the first constitution of the GDR guaranteed civil liberties and paid lip service to parliamentary democracy, these were but empty words. Real power lay in the hands of the SED's *Politburo* and the party's general secretary. Although the SPD was nominally an equal partner in the SED, some 200,000 SPD members were purged. Many died in labor camps.

After Stalin's death, political conditions relaxed a bit in the GDR, though the nationalization of industry proceeded without hesitation. Impossibly high work goals, sharpened by the drainage of workers to the West, led to a **workers' revolt** across the GDR on June 17, 1953, which was ruthlessly crushed with the aid of Soviet tanks (see **Berlin: History,** p. 89). The insurrection marked the end of the mildly reformist **New Course.** In response to the FRG's normalization with the West, the GDR was recognized by the USSR in 1954 and became a party to the **Warsaw Pact** in 1955.

In 1961, the GDR decided to remedy the exodus of skilled young workers to the Federal Republic; although borders to the West had been sealed off, escape through Berlin remained a possibility. On the night of August 12-13, the first, rudimentary barriers of the **Berlin Wall** were laid. The regime called it an "anti-fascist protective wall," but Berliners knew which way the guns were pointed. Stanching the flow of refugees gave Ulbricht room to launch his hard-line **New Economic System** and to establish the GDR's **second constitution** in 1968. This document jettisoned most constitutional rights, already ignored in practice, and abandoned all pretense of parliamentary democracy. In 1968, units of the People's Army assisted in the Soviet suppression of the Prague Spring in Czechoslovakia.

Ulbricht's iron grip on power was broken in 1971 when he ran afoul of his Soviet patrons. His replacement, **Erich Honecker,** was a party functionary even more doctrinaire and colorless than his predecessor. He returned East Germany to unquestioning subservience to the Soviet Union and eliminated all reformist experiments. Relations with the West improved remarkably during the era of Willy Brandt's **Ostpolitik,** and many Westerners were permitted to visit relatives in the GDR for the first time. Despite the scars of the war and the shortcomings of central planning, East Germans enjoyed the highest standard of living in the Eastern Bloc by the late 70s. Nevertheless, the hated secret police, the **Stasi,** maintained a network of hundreds of thousands of agents and paid informants that strove to monitor every citizen.

With the ascension of the *glasnost*-minded **Mikhail Gorbachev** to the leadership of the USSR in 1985, reform began to spread throughout the Eastern Bloc—except in the GDR, which adhered to rigid orthodoxy. The foundation for *die Wende* (the turning or the change), as the sudden toppling of the GDR is referred to in Germany, began in May 1989 when Hungary dismantled the barbed-wire border with Austria, giving some 55,000 East Germans a route to the West. By October, Czechoslovakia tolerated a flood of GDR citizens into the West German embassy; thousands emigrated. On October 6, while on a state visit to celebrate the GDR's 40th birthday, Gorbachev publicly reprimanded Honecker and announced that the USSR would not interfere in the GDR's domestic affairs. Dissident groups (supported and protected by the church) such as **New Forum** began to operate more freely, organizing massive **anti-government demonstrations** *(Demos),* which started in Leipzig (see **Leipzig,** p. 170), and spread to Dresden, Berlin, and other cities. The East Germans demanded free elections, freedom of press , and freedom of travel. Faced with rising pressure, Honecker resigned. His successor, **Egon Krenz** (whose name bears an uncanny similarity to the word for "border"), promised reforms. Meanwhile, tens of thousands of GDR citizens—largely young professionals—continued to flee via Czechoslovakia, which completely opened its border with West Germany. The entire GDR Politburo resigned on November 8, and a day later, a Central Committee spokesperson announced the **opening of all borders to the West,** including the Berlin Wall.

REUNIFICATION AND ITS AFTERMATH

The opening of the Wall did not immediately herald the demise of the GDR or the Communist regime. Elected four days after the opening of the wall, Prime Minister **Hans Modrow** pledged to hold free elections. The constitution was re-written to remove references to the SED's leading role, but the party remained in power and the *Stasi* continued to operate despite pressure. Throughout December, *Demos* continued unabated. Honecker was whisked away to the USSR and the SED renamed itself the **Party of Democratic Socialism (SPD).** The year 1990 began with another ecstatic celebration on top of the Berlin Wall, but the apparent community belied a furious political struggle going on in both Germanies. In the East, opposition parties took shape and assumed positions in the existing government, while the West's political parties scrambled to assert their influence; eventually, all of them linked up with like-minded parties in the GDR in preparation for March **elections.** The SPD was crippled by its expressed reluctance about the prospect of reunification, which inhibited it from making allies in the East. Buoyed by Kohl's success at getting Moscow to assent to unification, the CDU-backed **Alliance for Germany** emerged the winner. A broad coalition government of non-Communist parties authorized **economic and social union** with the Federal Republic. On **D-Mark Day** (as July 2 was known in the English press), GDR citizens exchanged their worthless Ostmarks for mighty D-Marks. The signing of the **Four-Plus-Two Treaty** by the two Germanies and the four occupying powers on September 12, 1990 signalled the **end of a divided Germany.**

Despite catch-phrases such as *Wiedervereinigung* (reunification), East and West Germany did not unify on an equal basis to create a new nation-state. Rather, East

Nationalistic euphoria blurred the true state of matters for Germans on both sides of the wall.

Germany was absorbed into the institutions and structures of the Federal Republic, leading some to call the union *der Anschluß* (annexation). Under the Basic Law's paragraph 23, any territory had the power to accede, or simply declare themselves ready to be consumed by, the FRG. This was a faster route to unity, and after a great deal of debate, it was the one Germany took. On **October 3, 1990,** the Allies forfeited their occupation rights, the GDR ceased to exist, and Germany became one united, sovereign nation for the first time in 45 years. Germans now distinguish between East and West with the labels **"new federal states"** and **"old federal states."**

Immediately following the quick pace of events in 1989-90, nationalistic euphoria blurred the true state of matters for Germans on both sides of the wall. The inefficient industries and institutions in the East led to massive unemployment and the Federal Republic's worst-ever recession. Many Westerners have resented the inflation and taxes brought on by the cost of rebuilding the new federal states, while Easterners have had to give up the generous social benefits Communism afforded them. A rightward-moving political climate in the west pulled the east with it, restricting social programs not only in welfare but also in areas such as abortion.

In the years following, the anger spread to an intense distrust of **foreigners,** especially immigrants from Eastern Europe and the *Gastarbeiter,* some of whom have been living in Germany for decades. German law does not automatically grant citizenship to children born in Germany; parentage is considered the paramount factor. This has become more and more of a troubling point as the children of immigrants grow up in Germany, speak only German, know no other home, but are defined as aliens. The violent attacks on foreigners reached horrible proportions in 1992, when wide-scale assaults were launched against immigrants in Mölln and Rostock, resulting in numerous deaths. In June 1993, an arson attack on the home of a Turkish family in the town of Solingen claimed several lives, including those of a number of young children. Soon after Solingen, the liberal Asylum Law was repealed. Fortunately, the violence has decreased significantly in the past few years.

After the dramatic fall of the Berlin Wall in 1989, Kohl and his CDU seemed insurmountable. Carrying their momentum into the first all-German elections, the CDU scored a stunning victory. After that, however, Kohl's popularity plummeted to the point where on one occasion Eastern voters pelted him with rotten fruit during a visit, and his party failed to carry his own state in *Land* elections. But the CDU bounced back, and in 1994 it accomplished a hat trick of victories in the elections for President, the European Parliament, and the German Parliament. Kohl's majority is, however, narrow, and dependent on the increasingly-marginalized liberal FDP.

Europe, or more specifically the new Germany's place in it, is currently the big political question. The burden of the past makes everyone, including the Germans themselves, nervous about German intervention into European foreign policy. The last initiative, an attempt to bring about the diplomatic recognition of the splinter states of the former Yugoslavia, ended in disaster; Germany has been content to stick to the sidelines since. The dominant feeling now, promulgated by Kohl's CDU coalition, is that Germany should stay out of foreign policy, acting instead as a large, benign economic machine at the heart of the European Union. But Germany is not Switzerland; such a neutral stance may not always be possible for the most populous and economically powerful nation in Europe. There are thinkers on the political Left, with some support in the Greens and the SPD, who would like to see the unified Germany take on the mission of embodying a "third way," a corrective to the excesses of both Eastern socialism and Western capitalism.

THIS YEAR IN GERMANY

Kohl, while passing Adenauer for longest tenure of any FRG chancellor, spent 1997 actively promoting the European Union, and remained an ardent supporter of NATO expansion. He and finance minister Theo Waigel have tied the fate of the *Mark* to the coming of the euro, a funky little currency which is supposed to be introduced in Germany sometime in 2002 following a transitional period beginning in 1999. The chancellor's insistence on pursuing monetary union has led to condemnations from Germans (his popularity is distinctly waning) and blessings from foreign tourists, who have been reveling in the slide of the *Mark*. The economy is in the midst of some turmoil, as the government scrambles to balance its budget to meet the requirements of the EU. Some of the victims of this fiscal austerity have been wheezing rheumatics, who suffered from health insurance cuts in their massage subsidies.

In more upbeat news, demonstrating how government is, in fact, the province of fat cats and gourmands, a new law allowed German stores to remain open until 8pm on weekdays and 4pm on Saturdays. Bakeries can even turn out *Brötchen* for three hours on Sundays. Another measure regarding what Germans may ingest is now under consideration, as the SPD is considering a move to de-criminalize heroin consumption. Smacky, smacky. Don't expect to run into main-lining Germans too soon, however, as the likelihood of any such reform is minimal to non-existent.

At the same time that Germany has increased legal restrictions on asylum-seekers, violence has been declining substantially. Since 1992, violent xenophobic crimes have dropped by over 70%, a trend which continued into 1997. Indeed, conflicts between *Länder* (states) are quickly becoming more prominent than those with *Ausländer* (foreigners). Voters in Berlin and Brandenburg voted on a measure to unify their territories, but resoundingly defeated the measure, which would have made

Potsdam the capital of the *Land* (a move comparable to having Albany as the capital of New York). Nevertheless, the two territories are working to increase cooperation, and may again pursue a merger in a few years. More serious and less cordial is the dispute developing in the northern regions of *Freistaat Bayern*, where Frankish secessionists are flashing a big *Stinkefinger* in the face of hegemonic *Lederhosen*. The Franks seek a referendum on the establishment of a *Fränkischer Bund*, with its capital in Nürnberg. While the Federal Constitutional Court considers the validity of a demand for the referendum, independence-minded Franks have come up with witty slogans such as *"Frei statt Bayern"* (Free instead of Bayern).

At the same time that *documenta* X set Kassel and the art world on its head, Germany was wistfully reflecting on the fate of booty—*Kunstbeute* (booty art), that is. Much of the art plundered by the Soviets after World War II remains in Russia, and the Russian parliament passed a measure in the past year making booty removed from other countries in the wake of "the Great Patriotic War" Russian property. While Yeltsin is willing to give up the booty, the Parliament's intransigence means that Germany's not gettin' any for the time being.

FURTHER READING

Gordon Craig's *Germany 1866-1945* provides a definitive history of those years. A more general picture of the modern German character can be found in Craig's excellent *The Germans*, an accessible but never simplistic book. Primo Levi's *Survival in Auschwitz* provides a gripping and poignant account of a Holocaust survivor. For an in-depth look at post-war German history, pick up Henry Ashby Turner's *The Two Germanies Since 1945*, or Peter J. Katzenstein's *Policy and Politics in Western Germany*. Ralf Dahrendorf's *Society and Democracy in Germany* is a great treatment of "the German Question." Also, read anything that novelists Günter Grass or Christa Wolf have written on Reunification. They criticize the rapidity of the process and the forgetfulness and abandonment of the historic lessons Germany might have learned in the years since the war. Both emerged as powerful moral voices in contemporary Germany. Their novels are also excellent (see **Literature,** p. 77).

■ Culture

Germany, the Germans like to say, is the land of *"Dichter und Denker"*—the poet and the philosopher. Poet Bertolt Brecht, with inspired cynicism, claimed that a truer epithet was land of the *"Richter und Henker"*—the judge and the hangman. But Brecht's own literary life helped to belie his statement. German conceptions of culture have always resonated with political ramifications, as both nationalists and humanists invoked the arts to advance their agendas. The significance attached to the humanities allowed Germany to establish fertile ground from which many of the major European artistic movements in the last 500 years have been spawned.

VISUAL ART

Distinctively German painting flourished in the Renaissance. The **School of the Danube** marched into the secular world, giving the landscape or architectural environment primary importance over human subjects. **Lucas Cranach** was particularly taken with the idea of combining the beauty of nature with the sublimity of divine subjects. Cranach was the 15th-century painting equivalent of Stephen King; there's barely a town or city in east-central Germany that doesn't boast a sizable collection of his work. **Hans Holbein the Younger** is renowned for his portraits from both the German and English courts—his *Henry VIII* is an eerie, detached portrait of the noble with the standard *memento mori*. **Matthias Grünewald** clung to medieval forms for his highly symbolic religious works. His medium of choice was the altar dip- or triptych. **Albrecht Dürer,** one of Germany's most renowned Renaissance artists, worked in painting, drafting, and woodcuts; his work in all three is dark in psychological atmosphere and masterful in line. In the fateful year 1500, on a featureless black background, Dürer painted one of the era's great images—Europe's first self-portrait. After the Thirty Years War virtually halted construction and laid Germany to waste, the **Baroque** era invigorated Renaissance architecture with bold, flamboyant decoration.

The cool simplicity of **Neoclassicism** softened into **Romanticism,** harking back to German national idioms and to local Gothic and Romanesque architectural styles. The Wars of Liberation (see p. 63) infused paintings with highly **national themes** of German landscape and legend, some frolicsome and pastoral, others mystical and serious. The intriguing master of the latter type was **Caspar David Friedrich,** whose landscapes obsessed over man's solitude and insignificance. Many of his works capture dramatic, uninhabitable landscapes such as wind-blown cemeteries. The less-bleak **Max Liebermann** began as a master Impressionist and went on to lead the Berlin faction of the **Secession movement** in the 1890s: in two words, decadence and eroticism. This trend became **Jugendstil** (literally, "youth-style"), which rose to popularity in central European metropoli in the early 20th century.

The years of the **Weimar Republic** saw an extraordinary proliferation of artistic genius. The Symbolist tendencies of *Jugendstil* intensified into the larger Expressionist movement, with a deliberately anti-naturalist aesthetic that distorted objects and colors to project deeply personal experiences. **Die Brücke** (The Bridge) was the earliest Expressionist consortium, founded at Dresden in 1905 with the explicit aim of heightening the intensity of expression in art. The Munich-based **Blaue Reiter** (Blue Rider) group emerged in 1909, led by Russian emigré **Wassily Kandinsky** and named after one of his paintings. Kandinsky's epoch-making contribution was a series called *Improvisations* painted in 1910-11, considered the first totally **non-representational paintings** in Western civilization. The Blaue Reiter also included **Franz Marc** and **Paul Klee.** **Max Beckmann** left a large body of Expressionist works (although he shunned the label) focused on the anxieties of a dehumanized culture. The satirical works of **Otto Dix** navigated a tightrope between Expressionism and Dadaism before embracing the **Neue Sachlichkeit** (New Objectivity) movement and its emphasis on the spectator's (and artist's) role as social critic. The smaller German **Realist** movement devoted itself to bleak, critical works such as **Käthe Kollwitz's** posters for social reform. **Ernst Barlach** infused realism with religious themes, inflaming Nazi censors.

> In the fateful year 1500, on a featureless black background, Dürer painted one of the era's great images—Europe's first self-portrait.

The rise of Nazism drove most Weimar artists and their works into exile. They were either the "wrong" race or religion, or their works were branded "decadent and subversive" and banished from view after the Nazis displayed them in an exhibition to showcase its *Entartet* (degenerate) nature. In contrast to the complex and eclectic banned works, wartime art was limited by Nazi ideology. Themes of **Blut und Boden** (Blood and Soil) dominated Nazi visual arts, depicting the mythical union of *völkisch* blood and German soil through idealized images of workers, farmers, and soldiers. A reject from the Vienna School of Art, Hitler favored sterile, bombastic idealism, including nude images of the "master race."

Postwar artistic effort has not spawned any unified movement. Much postwar art from West Germany incorporated intense performative strategies meant to challenge the relation between art and politics. Some of the Weimar masters were still active in the 50s and 60s, but the fragmentation characteristic of "pomo" culture splintered artists into different styles that reshaped—at times shattered—the icons of German culture. The Düsseldorf **Zero Group** produced abstractions after the war. The **Junge Wilde** (Young Savages), a neo-Expressionist group, surfaced in Berlin in the late 70s, using vivid colors and strong movement. **Josef Beuys** was a charismatic, controversial figure who created deliberately low-brow juxtapositions, such as felt and lard.

Art in the GDR had a more nuanced history than the western stereotype of a socialist cultural desert would imply. After an initial flirtation with liberal tolerance, the ruling SED "Stalinized" the arts. The regime-sponsored orthodox style was known as **Socialist Realism,** exemplified by paintings such as **Lea Grundig's** *Coal and Steel for Peace* and **Otto Nagel's** *Jungpioniere.* The painters **Hans Grundig, Rudolf Bergan-**

der, and **Eva Schulze-Knabe** and the sculptor **Fritz Cremer** (who designed the Buchenwald Memorial) were also leading figures in the movement. Ambiguity had no place in Socialist Realism: the GDR and the SED were glorified, and "bourgeois influence" was repressed. East German artists managed a remarkable amount of innovation and experimentation despite the repression.

ARCHITECTURE AND DESIGN

In the medieval period, violent, highly stylized images and masterworks of carving and glasswork ornamented the quiet, somber lines of the cathedrals. The **Romanesque** period followed, spanning the years 1000 to 1300, with a style of architecture that emerged in direct imitation of antique ruins. Outstanding Romanesque cathedrals can be found at Speyer, Trier, and Mainz. The **Gothic** style gradually replaced the Romanesque from 1300 to 1500. The 14th century was a transitional period that spawned the **Köln Cathedral.** Stained glass filled the windows of Gothic cathedrals with ever more elaborate patterns of divine light.

The Lutheran reforms of the 1550s put a damper on the unrestrained extravagance of cathedrals. Although the **Renaissance** saw fits of church-building, efforts were mostly channelled into secular buildings such as the **Augsburg Rathaus** (town hall) and **Heidelberg Schloß.** Early Baroque shows itself in the **Rathäuser** of Leipzig and Bremen, as well as the **Würzburg Residenz.** Baroque developed quickly into the extravagant ornamentation of **Rococo;** Munich's **Amalienburg Palace** and **Residenztheater** are typical of the hyper-ornate flamboyance of that movement. The French Revolution snuffed out the courtliness that fueled Baroque and Rococo, replacing them with ideals of "noble simplicity" (Einfachheit). These ideals spawned a revival of classical forms, visible in the Prussian buildings along **Unter Den Linden** in Berlin.

Wertheim's Department Store in Berlin and the **Exhibition** buildings at Darmstadt are two architectural manifestations of **Jugendstil,** the early 20th-century movement of decorative, stylized design (see **Visual Art,** above). **Erich Mendelsohn** later brought the Expressionist aesthetic to architecture, creating curvaceous structures like the **Einstein Tower** in Potsdam, a structure Einstein himself approved with a single word: "Organic." The ideas behind **Neue Sachlichkeit** revolutionized design. **Peter Behrens** pioneered these ideas, designing objects to suit the efficient new materials of industry through unornamented geometric harmonies. **Walter Gropius** designed several sensational buildings with clean forms, flat roofs, and broad windows, all made possible by new concrete-and-steel construction techniques. In 1919 Gropius founded the **Bauhaus,** a ground-breaking school of design that combined theoretical training in the new principles of efficiency with exposure to the realities of mass production. "Form follows function" was its oft-quoted principle. The school moved to **Dessau** in 1925, where Gropius designed the school's new facility, which became the symbol of the modern style. While *Bauhaus*'s sleek, austere lines informed some of the most brilliant designs of the century, the school must also bear some responsibility for the later abuse of its principles: the soulless, box-like skyscrapers and uniform rows of residences in cities like Frankfurt and New York.

Hitler disapproved of the new buildings; he named a design school reject, **Albert Speer,** as his minister of architecture, and commissioned ponderous, Neoclassical buildings intended to last the "Thousand-Year Reich." Many were intended for public rallies, such as the **Congress Hall** and **Stadium** at Nürnberg. The architecture in the GDR created a Bizarro *Bauhaus* landscape in sterile, Stalinist style. The overblown buildings lining the then-**Karl-Marx-Allee** in Eastern Berlin represent the apogee of **Socialist Realist** architecture. The East's most noted architect, **Hermann Henselmann,** was a former *Bauhaus* member. As Chief of Architecture in Berlin from 1953 to 1959, he designed several of the sterile edifices on **Alexanderplatz** in Berlin and conceived the plan for the TV tower. The "Sharp Tooth" building at the heart of the former **Karl Marx Universität** in Leipzig bears his bite mark as well.

LITERATURE

The history of German literature traces back to pre-Christian times and the earliest records of Germanic gods who were the subjects of heroic tales of warriors told before the advent of writing, like the legendary **Dietrich** and the **Walküre** (battle-maidens). In the 10th and 11th centuries, villagers flocked to hear **Spielmänner,** itinerant poet-entertainers, recite tall tales of the exotic or marvelous. At court, nobles amused themselves with chivalric romances. The 12th-century master, **Gottfried von Strassburg,** concerned himself more with aesthetics than jousting in his version of the *Tristan* legend. **Wolfram von Eschenbach's** *Parzival* is the seminal story of a noble boy who loses his birthright and then regains it before searching for the Holy Grail. Clerics in monasteries transcribed these and earlier tales.

By the 13th century heroic lyrics developed into full-fledged **epics.** The most famous and popular of these is the **Nibelungenlied,** the story of Prince Siegfried, his wooing of the valkyrie Brunhilde, his murder, and the subsequent downfall of the Burgundians. Shorter lyric forms gave rise to the wandering **Minnesänger,** the greatest of whom was **Walther von der Vogelweide.** Lyrics of this era became an art instead of a means of record-keeping, with topics ranging from humorous legend to courtly subjects with an emphasis on originality and form. Although the literature of the following **Reformation** consisted primarily of propagandist prose tracts, Martin Luther's landmark High German **translation of the Bible** brought the German language to great heights of expression and away from Latin influences.

A self-consciously German canon emerged in the 18th century. The dramatist **Gotthold Ephraim Lessing** produced plays which diverged sharply from contemporary French-influenced drama. Lessing broke the ground for the overtly critical and emotional works to come in the series of sub-movements around the turn of the 19th century. The writers of the well-known **Sturm und Drang** (Storm and Stress) movement ventured further into the depths of human emotion. The works of this era emphasize the primacy of individual conscience and emotion over reason. **Johann Wolfgang von Goethe** was the first major success of this movement, and remains a monumental figure in German literature as a whole. His hugely popular *Die Leiden des jungen Werthers* (The Sorrows of Young Werther) spawned a wave of sentimental *Weltschmerz.* This and other early works virtually ignored the principle of dramatic simplicity, instead opting for psychological works with complicated characters and an unrestrained natural form that had been fostered by **Johann Gottfried Herder.** Herder's insistence on originality of image and on a distinctly national style characterized his literary criticism. **Friedrich Schiller** also catapulted to continental fame. By the 1790s the *Sturm und Drang* began to metamorphose into a more refined movement balancing feeling and reason, a tendency that gave the period its **Classical** label. Schiller and Goethe composed masterworks in this mature, innovative period just before the full flowering of **Romanticism.** At Weimar, Goethe completed *Faust* and

Günter Grass: Of Cats, Mice and Tin Drums

Considered Germany's most celebrated contemporary writer, Günter Grass was born in Danzig in 1927. In the immediate post-war period, he quickly came to prominence in the lively and critical literary Gruppe 47. His brilliant works, *Cat and Mouse, Dog Years,* and *The Tin Drum,* were each uncompromising attempts to come to terms with the horrors of the Nazi experience. With dwarves, toads, and flounders serving as his central characters and an incredible eye for detail, Grass's eccentric and humorous literary style launched his career and catapulted him to fame. Grass has never flinched from his opinion that the writer as intellectual must be actively engaged with the political landscape and democratic process. Grass has applied his versatile, often satirically perverse, talents through poetry, essays, plays and drawings. Since 1989, he has consistently professed a strong, and increasingly isolated, criticism of German unification. With Auschwitz, Grass argues, Germany lost for all time the right to reunify. This radical view is contained in his recent *Two States—One Nation?*

Wilhelm Meister, which became a favorite of later Romantics. At the turn of the 19th century, a difficult young poet named **Friedrich Hölderlin** composed sonorous, strangely modern hymns about the disappearance of the Greek gods and the spiritual textures of Germany's hills and rivers. Hölderlin was the college roommate of philosophers Hegel and Schelling; tragedy loomed over his life due to his contemporaries' failure to understand his work and of his gradual descent into madness after 1800. At the same time, the **Brothers Grimm** assembled their famous collection of fairy tales, providing a foundation for German philology. **Heinrich Wilhelm von Kleist** wove pessimistic tales before killing himself; the best known is *Die Marquise von O.*

Many writers, even during the height of Romanticism, were members of the politicized, anti-mystical **Young Germany** school banned as subversive by the *Bundesrat* in 1835. **Heinrich Heine** allied with this movement. His *Deutschland: ein Wintermärchen* considers the stultifying climate engendered by political repression. Heine was also a Jew, and it is hard to say which irritated the patriotic *Bürger*s more—his beautifully ironic criticism of German society or his Judaism. **Georg Büchner** was Heine's counterpart in drama; his *Woyzeck* introduced the first lower-class tragic hero in German literature. Finally, toward the end of the century, the volatile philosopher **Friedrich Nietzsche** took his place among the greatest German writers. In his poetic, apocalyptic discourse *Also Sprach Zarathustra* (Thus Spoke Zarathustra), Nietzsche declared that "God is dead," and introduced his oft-abused notion of an *Übermensch,* trying to create a counter-ideal to what he saw as a mediocre, enervating Christianity. (For more on Nietzsche, see **Philosophy…in 10½ Sentences,** p. 79.)

The turn of the century saw a progression into the **Naturalistic** mode, inspired by the work of the French author Emile Zola. In Germany, the movement was based on finding beauty and value in the objects and patterns of everyday life. **Gerhart Hauptmann** and **Theodor Fontane** were the foremost authors of Naturalism. Conversely, the **Symbolist** movement of the early 20th century, and its leading figure **Stefan George,** rejected Naturalism in favor of fleeting, sonorous image-poems; the **George Kreis** (George circle) was a cadre of passionate, like-minded, well-dressed artists. The truly brilliant works of these years were written by Rilke, Hesse, and Mann. **Rainer Maria Rilke** composed supple rhymes and haunting images that captured fragments of experience. His uncanny poems expressed the difficulty of finding spirituality in the modern era. **Hermann Hesse** had a similar interest; his *Steppenwolf* considers the plight of modernity and the breakdown of bourgeois identity. **Thomas Mann** carried Symbolism to its purest form with *Der Zauberberg* (The Magic Mountain) and *Doktor Faustus,* two allegorical recountings of Germany's fateful history. Thomas' brother **Heinrich,** also a novelist, produced passionate works including *Der Untertan* (The Subject), an attack on the subservience of the Germans.

The **Weimar era** marked an intense and magnificent outpouring of artistic expression, producing more masterpieces in less time than any other period in German history. Germany's version of the Parisian "Lost Generation" articulated its

Nazi propaganda minister Goebbels once sneered, "Whenever I hear the word 'culture,' I reach for my gun."

disillusionment in the *Neue Sachlichkeit* movement. Its most famous novel was **Erich Maria Remarque's** *Im Westen nichts Neues* (All Quiet on the Western Front), a blunt, uncompromising account of war's horrors which became embroiled in the political turmoil of the era. **Bertolt Brecht's** dramas and poems present humankind in all its grotesque absurdity, and sought to awaken the consciousness of his audience. His *Dreigroschenoper* (Three-Penny Opera) was set to music by Kurt Weill. Inspired by the ferment of Viennese Art Nouveau and nonrepresentational art, **Expressionism** picked up the torch of Symbolism after World War I. **Alfred Döblin's** novel *Berlin Alexanderplatz* traces shifts in consciousness in the metropolis. The years of the Third Reich yielded little of artistic note; the official attitude toward literature was summed up by Nazi propaganda minister Goebbels, who once sneered, "Whenever I hear the word 'culture,' I reach for my gun." Some 2500 authors went into exile, and others underwent "internal emigration" and ceased to write.

The experience of war, defeat, and genocide inspired greater social conscience in many Germans. Many authors of the **Social Realist** movement convened formally in 1947 to reform German writing. The resulting coalition, known as **Gruppe 47,** heavily influenced German literature well into the 70s. A major issue for these postwar German authors was how to reclaim their language after its corruption under fascist rule. Gruppe 47's ranks include most of the largest names in contemporary German literature. **Heinrich Böll,** one of the founding members, won the Nobel Prize for Literature in 1972. **Günter Grass** wrote a stunning series of novels relating to recent German history, including *Der Blechtrommel* (The Tin Drum). **Peter Handke** is an on-the-road modern writer; his *Der kurze Brief zum langen Abschied* is set entirely in America. A new school of drama developed through playwrights like **Rolf Hochhuth** *(Die Soldaten)* and **Peter Weiss** *(Marat/Sade).*

The state of letters in the **GDR** followed the same pattern of waxing and waning government control that affected the visual arts (see p. 75). Many expatriate writers, particularly those with Marxist leanings from before the war (such as Brecht), returned to the East with great hopes. But the communist leadership was not interested in eliciting free artistic expression. The combination of personal danger and the burden of censorship led many immensely talented writers to leave, including **Ernst Bloch, Uwe Johnson, Sarah Kirsch,** and **Heiner Kipphardt.** Disillusionment drove many others to emigrate. In the 1970s and 80s, some East German writers were able to publish in the West, though not at home, and took that option as a middle ground. **Christa Wolf,** one of the most prominent German women writers, voluntarily remained in the GDR. Another prominent dissident author was **Stefan Heym.** Radical-left GDR playwright **Heiner Müller** shocked audiences throughout the 70s with the disgusted protagonists and stripped-down scenarios of Beckett-esque plays such as *Hamletmachine.* Since reunification, there has been a period of artistic anxiety and occasional malaise; in the new federal states many authors are caught up in controversies over complicity with the *Stasi.* Others in both East and West have found that just thinking about the future of their country and what it means to be a German today consumes their emotional and creative energies.

PHILOSOPHY...IN 10½ SENTENCES

Germany's philosophical tradition is characterized by revolutionaries. **Martin Luther** defied the whole Christian establishment, the pompous Pope included, spawning the Protestant Revolution. **Gottfried Wilhelm Leibniz** gave the world differential and integral calculus, making high-school a nuisance. **Immanuel Kant,** the foremost thinker of the Enlightenment, inaugurated a new era in the development of thought. His famous categorical imperative today provides the foundation for most non-utilitarian ethics: "Act only according to that maxim by which you can, at the same time, will that it should become universal law." **Karl Marx** set himself against his contemporary capitalist bourgeois society, showing that it is based on brutal exploitation of the masses, and conceived of dialectical materialism, arguing that the natural conclusion of history would be a communist society. **Friedrich Nietzsche,** influenced by the pessimist *par excellence* **Arthur Schopenhauer,** scorned the mediocrity of the masses who were ensnared in the hypocritical creeds of Christianity, setting himself aside from humanity all together: "Not mankind, but superman is the goal." Nietzsche's superman has been used and abused repeatedly by evil men such as Stalin and Hitler. Nietzsche's intensity of thought consumed him prematurely, and he lapsed into *Über*-insanity before kicking the *Über*-bucket in 1900. Max Weber, the father of sociology, frightened the world by announcing that we are trapped in a bureaucratic iron-cage—"please, wait in room 101, fill in the pink and blue forms, and stand next to Mr. DeNiro and his friends from *Brazil*..." **Martin Heidegger,** aligning with the Existentialists, provided the Nazis with the intellectual support they needed to assume power by underscoring the need for national unity and heroes.

German heroes can be found among the German Idealists, a movement spearheaded by **Johann Gottlieb Fichte,** heavily influenced by the Romantic currents flowing through Germany in 18th century, challenged Kant. While Kant believed that it was impossible to find the truth, Fichte saw human self-consciousness as the primary metaphysical fact through the analysis of which the philosopher finds his way to the cosmic totality that is "the Absolute" (Swedish vodka?). **Georg Wilhelm Friedrich Hegel** was inspired by Fichte, adding a dialectical twist to the latter's ideas, but, admittedly had serious writing difficulties—when asked to encapsulate his philosophical theories in a sentence, he responded with 10 volumes of writing, poor even by German standards. Only our contemporary **Jürgen Habermas**—succeeding **Theodor Adorno, Max Horkheimer, and Walter Benjamin** of the Frankfurt School—lives up to Hegel's muddled style with a true German spirit. Habermas spent 3000 pages to say that it is important to talk if there is to be any progress (duh!).

Although philosophy at times seems to diverge from anything logical, Germany has given birth to one of the world's foremost logicians, **Gottlob Frege,** the father of modern mathematical logic. The man behind the man behind phenomenology is **Edmund Husserl,** who strove to make philosophy into a strict science. One of Germany's bad-ass scientists, **Werner Heisenberg,** helped to established quantum mechanics. His grand uncertainty principle tells us that we can't know if a cat in a box is dead or alive…what?! Exasperated, *Let's Go: Germany* seeks solace in…

…FILM

The newborn medium of film was used brilliantly by directors in the **Weimar era.** These early German films persist as central elements of all film study. *Das Kabinett des Dr. Caligari* (The Cabinet of Dr. Caligari), an early horror film directed by Robert Wiene, plays out a melodrama of autonomy and control against brilliantly expressive sets of painted shadows and tilted walls. **Fritz Lang** produced a remarkable succession of classic films, including *M., Dr. Mabuse der Spieler,* and *Metropolis,* a dark and brutal vision of the techno-fascist city of the future (to which *Blade Runner* owes a great debt). **Ernst Lubitsch** and **Josef von Sternberg** also produced silent classics, while **F.W. Murnau's** *Nosferatu* crystallized German pathologies of "the other" in his portrayal of the Dracula legend. Meanwhile, **Carl Zuckmayer** extended the tradition into sound with his satiric and pathetic *Der blaue Engel* (The Blue Angel), based on Heinrich Mann's novel *Professor Unrath*—it starred the immortal Marlene Dietrich as a cabaret singer.

Heeding Hitler's prediction that "without motor-cars, sound films, and wireless, (there can be) no victory for National Socialism," propaganda minister **Joseph Goebbels** became a masterful manipulator. Most **Nazi films** fell into two categories: political propaganda and escapism. *Der ewige Jude* (The Eternal Jew) and *Jud Süss* glorified anti-Semitism. The uncanny, masterful propaganda films of **Leni Riefenstahl,** including *Triumph des Willens* (Triumph of the Will), which depicted a Nürnberg Party Rally, and *Olympiad,* found a wide audience.

Film has been perhaps the most vigorous artistic medium in post-war Germany. The late 60s and the 70s saw the greatest flood of cinematic excellence. The renaissance began in 1962 with the **Oberhausen Manifesto,** a declaration by independent filmmakers demanding artistic freedom and enough new toys to create competitive feature films; within a few years, the government was granting subsidies to a constellation of young talents. **Rainer Werner Fassbinder** made fatalistic films about individuals corrupted or defeated by society, including a mammoth production of Alfred Döblin's mammoth novel *Berlin Alexanderplatz.* Fassbinder's film *Die Ehe der Maria Braun* (The Marriage of Maria Braun) and **Volker Schlöndorf's** *Der Blechtrommel* (The Tin Drum, based on Grass's novel) were the films that brought the new German wave to a wider, international audience. **Margarethe von Trotta** focused mainly on women and politics, notably in her film *Die bleierne Zeit* (The Leaden Time). **Wolfgang Petersen** directed *Das Boot* (The Boat), one of the most successful German feature projects to date. **Werner Herzog's** works, including *Nosferatu,* attempted to revitalize the Expressionist emphasis on oblique cinematic images and very ugly vampires. **Wim Wenders's** restless, romantic quest films, par-

> **Film has been perhaps the most vigorous artistic medium in post-war Germany.**

ticularly his "road films" like *Paris, Texas*, express his fascination with America. In 1983, **Edgar Reitz**, a director of the 60s generation, created the 15-hour epic *Heimat* (Home). The film was a reaction against what Reitz considered the cheap and shallow treatment of German war guilt in the American TV mini-series *Holocaust*.

East German film was subject to more constraints than other artistic media, owing to the difficulty of producing films without the large-scale financial backing which only the state could provide. Just after the war, directors in the Soviet Zone produced several internationally acclaimed films, among them **Wolfgang Staudte's** *Die Mörder sind unter uns* (The Murderers are Among Us), about a Nazi war criminal who evades detection and goes on to lead the good life, **Kurt Maetzig's** *Ehe im Schatten* (Marriage in the Shadows), and **Erich Engel's** *Affaire Blum* (The Blum Affair). The GDR's ministry of culture operated its own studios, the German Film Corporation (DEFA). **Slatan Dudow** produced the first of DEFA's films, *Unser tägliches Brot* (Our Daily Bread), a paean to the nationalization of industry, and went on to make one of the best East German films, *Stärker als die Nacht* (Stronger than the Night), which tells the story of a Communist couple persecuted by the Nazis. After a brief post-Stalinist thaw, few East German films departed from the standard format of socialist heroism or love stories. **Egon Günther's** *Lots Weib* (Lot's Wife), an explicitly feminist exploration of marital breakdown and divorce, was one notable exception. The next year, 1966, saw three major films, Maetzig's *Das Kaninchen bin ich* (The Rabbit is Me), **Frank Vogel's** *Denk bloß nicht, ich heule* (Just Don't Think I'm Crying), and **Frank Beyer's** *Spur der Steine* (Track of Stones). Beyer later made the critically acclaimed *Jakob der Lügner* (Jacob the Liar), which was nominated for an Oscar. Another promising director stifled by the GDR, **Konrad Wolf,** produced such films as *Ich war neunzehn* (I was Nineteen), *Goya*, and *Sonnensucher* (Sun Seekers), the last of which was not permitted to be released until 14 years after its completion. The GDR also devoted a healthy portion of its filmmaking resources to the **documentary** genre. A handful managed to critique the prevailing political situation, although the majority of directors, such as Andrew and Annelie Thorndike, Walter Heynowski, and Gerhard Scheumann, concocted unremarkable films glorifying the Soviet Union and the SED and denouncing the Federal Republic and the United States.

MUSIC

Documented German music goes back to the medieval songs of the **Minnesänger,** the German troubadours, whose tradition of sung poetry passed gradually to the **Meistersänger,** commoners who had passed through five ranks from apprentice to *Meister* (Master). Singers remained in local guilds; their instrumental counterparts were the **town-pipers,** whose own guilds were the forerunners of modern orchestras. Lutheran hymns applied new polyphonic techniques to folk song forms. The 16th century saw both the *cantata* and the passion, a work thematizing a saint's transcendence. **Michael Praetorius** and **Johann Pachelbel** (best known for his *Canon*) worked in these modes. **Georg Friedrich Händel's** passion *Messiah* is now familiar Christmas music throughout the Western world.

Johann Sebastian Bach was the stand-out in a long line of musically successful Bachs. Bach's organ works construct worlds whose meticulous symmetries and regularities reflect a careful spiritual order. In mid-career he produced more secular works; the *Brandenburg Concerti* are famous for their exploration of the happy tensions between solo instruments and the chamber orchestra. After moving to Leipzig in 1723, he returned to the somber Lutheran sound; his *St. Matthew Passion* used Biblical texts with arias and choruses. Explorations of orchestral forms moved farther in the next generation of composers. The Austrians Franz Josef Haydn, Wolfgang Amadeus Mozart, and their contemporaries rejected the institutionalized religious feeling of their musical predecessors and replaced it with personal emotion in keeping with the Romantic ideology of the era.

The 19th century was an era of German musical hegemony. **Ludwig van Beethoven's** symphonies and piano sonatas bridged Classicism and Romanticism. His monumental *Ninth Symphony* and late string quartets were written in the 1820s after he was completely deaf. Influenced by Romantic literature, including lyric poetry and songs, **Robert Schumann** and **Franz Schubert** composed settings for the poetry of Goethe, Byron, Scott, and Heine. The ethereal work of **Felix Mendelssohn-Bartholdy** is well-represented by his overture to *A Midsummer Night's Dream*. Immigrants **Franz Liszt** and **Frederic Chopin** pushed piano music and the symphonic form into still further reaches of unorthodox harmony and arrangement.

The second generation of Romantic composers included **Johannes Brahms,** a Schumann protégé whose talent for variation begat many popular German *Lieder* (songs). **Richard Wagner** embodied both the artistic strengths and ideological weaknesses of late 19th-century Romanticism. He composed many of the world's best-known operas—*Tannhäuser, Die Meistersinger, Der Ring des Nibelungen*—in an attempt to revolutionize the form with topics chosen specially for musical suitability, simple characters, and a mythic plot filled with divinity and the supernatural. He envisioned a stream of "endless melody" distinguishing itself through changes in mood or key, or through the reappearance of a *Leitmotif*. Wagner's plots are highly nationalistic in their simplicity and celebration of Germanic legend, and were easily exploited by German-Aryan supremacists. Eventually, Nietzsche began to write brilliantly satiric tracts about his former mentor's pomposity: he described Wagner's swirling music as a "narcotic" and a "sickness." The center of musical genius shifted to Vienna in the late 19th and early 20th centuries as Romanticism over-ripened into decadence.

The unstable economy of the Weimar Republic and the anti-Romantic backlash encouraged smaller, cheaper musical forms such as jazz. A new movement of *Gebrauchsmusik* (utilitarian music) engendered music for amateur players and film scores. **Arnold Schönberg** disciples **Anton Webern** and **Alban Berg** mastered the possibilities of 12-tone composition. Berg's opera *Wozzeck* described squalor and tragedy through a progression of forms. **Paul Hindemith** headed a group of Neoclassicists influenced by the *Neue Sachlichkeit* and the emphasis on craftsmanship introduced by the *Werkbund* and *Bauhaus*. They embraced the older, variational forms (such as the sonata) most suited to the abstract aesthetic of the time. **Carl Orff,** Hitler's favorite composer, is most noted for his eclectic *Carmina Burana,* a resurrection of bawdy 13th-century lyrics with a bombastic score. The work was later reinterpreted as a well-loved ballet, though Orff's work under the Third Reich tainted his legacy. Music-hall works prior to World War II bred satiric operettas and songs of the political avant-garde. **Kurt Weill's** partnership with Bertolt Brecht produced such masterpieces of the genre as *Die Dreigroßchenoper* (Three-Penny Opera), one of the last good musical pieces that was composed on German soil.

"Germany is not supposed to be rock 'n' roll country," Rudolf Schenker once remarked about his country's modern music, a pop legacy almost as disgraceful as that of France ("ribbet, ribbet..."). Sadly real rock 'n' roll only makes up a small, albeit benign, tumor on the corpus of German music, a body ill with *Schlager* (see **If you play Schlager, I'll go home,** p. 484). Yet dismissing Germany's pop history as one big pile of putrifax would be ignoring their indispensable contribution—techno. The music blasting from black VWs in German cities, the music popularized in the U.S. by the Chemical Brothers and Prodigy, derive from the Ur-techno of **Krautrock,** a genre as quintessentially German as *Schlager*. Krautrock emerged in the 60s with groups like **Neu!** and **Can,** who used primitive keyboards and simple tape loops to create music sounding like stoned people going berserk on dialing pads. **Kraftwerk,** a group of Düsseldorf engineering students designing their own equipment, popularized techno-pop, combining hypnotically catchy melodies with previously unheard of electronic sounds. While they scored an international hit with in 1975 with "Autobahn," their huge influence and importance rest on their earlier albums, such as the seminal *The Man Machine*. Krautrock imploded in the late 1970s with the art noise of **Einstürzende Neubauten** (German for "collapsing new buildings"). After a decade of musical stagnation in Germany, when glam-rock bands churned out stillborn hits akin to **Scorpions'** attempt to political commentary, "The

> Dismissing Germany's pop history as one big pile of putrifax would be ignoring their indispensible contribution—techno.

Winds of Change," **techno** exploded onto the scene in the late 1980s, and it still resounds all over the country.

In terms of popularity with German *Jugend*, **hardcore** comes in a distant second after techno. While American hardcore peaked in the mid-1980s and then fizzled out for a lack of things to be pissed off about, the bleakness of many of the Eastern German cities, the long festering war in former Yugoslavia, and the unpopular neo-Nazi renaissance provide German bands with enough holler fodder to support one of the most effervescent hardcore scenes on the planet. The most raging German hardcore bands are **E.G.A.L.** and **Entrails Massacre**. After hardcore, the German audio-diet consists of a mixture of ska, R&B, rap, and soul, all of which fall under the indelicate heading of "black music."

■ Food and Drink

German cuisine gets bad press. Though it is neither as sophisticated as French cooking nor as sultry as Italian or Hungarian food, *Deutsche Küche* has a robust charm. While vegetarians will have a rough time outside of the major cities, meat-and-potatoes lovers will find the food in Germany hearty and satisfying. And if the local food is not to your taste, Germany's larger cities offer a wide variety of good ethnic restaurants. Be careful when ordering from a German menu if you don't speak the language; ingredients such as *Aal* (eel), *Blutwurst* (blood sausage) and *Gehirn* (brains) are not uncommon, and may represent an acquired taste. Don't let this deter you from taking risks—brains are probably a lot tastier than you think.

The typical German **Frühstück** (breakfast, literally "early piece") is coffee or tea with *Brötchen* (rolls), butter, marmalade, slices of bread, *Wurst* (cold sausage), and *Käse* (cheese). **Mittagsessen** (lunch) is usually the main meal of the day, consisting of soup, broiled sausage or roasted meat, potatoes or dumplings, and a salad or some vegetables. **Abendessen** or **Abendbrot** (supper) is a re-enactment of breakfast, only beer replaces coffee and the selection of meat and cheese is wider. **Dessert** after meals isn't common, but many Germans indulge in a daily ritual of **Kaffee und Kuchen** (coffee and cakes), a snack analogous to English "tea-time," at 3-4pm.

Brot (bread) is the staff of life in Germany; the country's bakeries produce loaves of astonishing quality and variety. *Vollkornbrot* is whole-wheat (which has a completely different meaning in Germany) and *Roggenbrot* is rye bread. *Schwarzbrot* (black bread) is a dense, dark loaf that's slightly acidic and most delicious when it's fresh. Go to a *Bäckerei* (bakery) and point to whatever looks good. Generally they sell you the whole loaf; for half, ask for *ein Halbes*. Those traveling on the cheap can ward off hunger for a few dozen *Pfennigs* by entering a bakery and requesting *zwei Brötchen*, a pair of fresh, warm rolls to take out.

Beer and wine (see below) are the meal-time **beverages.** *Saft* (fruit juice), plain or mixed with *gespritzt* (sparkling water), is an alternative. Germans rarely drink water; if they do, it's carbonated mineral water. If you ask for *Wasser* in a restaurant, you get mineral water (which ain't free). This is one aspect of the national taste that often produces culture shock, especially for Americans who are used to slugging thirst-quenchers in quantity. For tap water, ask for *Leitungswasser* and expect funny looks.

Unpretentious **restaurants** (that's most of them) expect you to seat yourself. If there are no tables free, ask someone for permission to take a free seat (ask *"Darf ich Platz nehmen?"*, pronounced "DAHRF eekh PLAHTS nay-men"). In traditional restaurants, address waiters "Herr Ober," and waitresses (but no one else) as "Fräulein." In a hip *Kneipe* (bar), just say *hallo*. When you're finished, pay at the table. Ask the server *Zahlen, bitte* ("TSAH-len, BIT-tuh": "check, please"). Taxes (*Mehrwertsteuer*) and service are usually included in the price, but it is customary to leave a little something extra, usually by rounding up the bill by a *Mark* or two.

Eating in restaurants at every meal will quickly drain your budget. One strategy is to stick to the daily *prix-fixé* option, called the *Tagesmenu*. A cheaper option is to buy food in **grocery stores,** which *Let's Go* lists in most cities. German university students eat at cafeterias called a **Mensa**. Most *Mensen* require an ISIC (or charge higher prices for non-students), and some are open only to local students, though travelers often evade this requirement by casually strolling in as if they belonged. In smaller towns, the best budget option is to stop by a *Bäckerei* (bakery) for bread and garnish it with sausage purchased from a butcher *(Fleischerei* or *Metzgerei).*

Besides bread, the staples of the German diet are *Wurst* (sausage, in myriad varieties), *Schweinefleisch* (pork), *Rindfleisch* (beef), *Kalbsfleisch* (veal), *Kartoffeln* (potatoes), and *Eier* (eggs). Dairy products, including *Käse* (cheese) and *Butter*—but especially *Schlagsahne* (whipped cream)—are favorites. Some travel guides recommend a portable cholesterol test kit, but the typical budget traveler might survive unaided. Sampling the various **local specialties** around Germany gives a taste of the diverse food tradition. Everyone knows *Wiener Schnitzel* (a breaded veal cutlet) and *Sauerkraut* (pickled cabbage), but there's much more to German cuisine. In **Bayern,** *Knödel* (potato and flour dumplings, sometimes filled with meat) are ubiquitous. *Leberknödel* are filled with liver. *Weißwurst* is also a Bavarian specialty; it is a sausage made with milk. It spoils so quickly that it has to be eaten the day it's made. Thüringen and northern Bayern are famed for their succulent grilled Bratwurst, the classic, garlicky, roasted sausage eaten with potatoes or bought from a street vendor clasped in a roll. The preferred vehicles for starch in **Baden** and **Swabia** are *Spätzle* (noodles) and *Maultaschen* (pasta pockets). German *Pfannkuchen* (pancakes) are much heavier and bigger than the flapjacks back home and come with toppings. *Kaiserschmarren* is a chopped-up pancake with powdered sugar. **Hessians** do amazing things with potatoes, like smothering them in delectable *grüne Soße* (green sauce).

BEER

> *Where does the German begin? Where does it end? May a German smoke? The majority says no ... But a German may drink beer, indeed as a true son of Germania's he should drink beer ...*
>
> —Heinrich Heine

Germans have brewed frothy malt beverages since the 8th century BC, and they've been consuming and exporting them in prodigious quantities ever since. The province of Bayern alone contains about one-fifth of all the breweries in the world. The Germans drink more than 150 liters of beer per person every year, more than any other country. According to legend, the German king Gambrinus invented the modern beer recipe when he threw some hops into the fermenting malt. Brewers still honor him (and Bud Selig). During the Middle Ages, monastic orders refined the art of brewing, imbibing to stave off starvation during long fasts. It wasn't long before the monks' lucrative trade caught the eye of secular lords, who established the first *Hofbraüereien* (court breweries). The variety of beers in Germany boggles the mind. Most beer is **Vollbier,** containing about 4% alcohol. **Export** (5%) is also popular, and stout, tasty **Bockbier** (6.25%) is brewed in the spring. **Doppelbock** is an eye-popping concoction understandably reserved for special occasions (like drinking *in Massen*...see **Ess-terminate with Ess-treme prejudice!,** p. 522). Ordering *"ein Helles"* will get you a standard light-colored beer, while *"Dunkles"* can look like anything from Coca-Cola to molasses.

Though generalizations are difficult, the average German beer is maltier and more "bread-like" than Czech, Dutch, or American beers. (An affectionate German slang term for beer is *flüßiges Brot,* "liquid bread.") Among the exceptions is *Pils,* or Pilsner, which is most popular in the north. Its characteristic clarity and bitter taste come from the addition of extra hops. From the south, especially Bayern, comes *Weißbier,* a smooth, refreshing brew. Despite the name, *Weißbier* is not white, but a rich brown. (The name is a corruption of *Weizenbier,* meaning wheat beer.) The term *Weizenbier* now generally refers to a darker wheat beer, while *Hefe-Weizen* is wheat beer with a layer of yeast in the bottom. *Faßbier* simply means beer from a barrel. Sampling local brews numbers among the finest of Germany's pleasures. In Köln, one drinks smooth *Kölsch,* an extraordinarily refined, light-colored beer; a Düsseldorf specialty is *Altbier,* a darker top-fermented beer. Berliners are partial to *Ber-*

liner Weiße, a mixture of beer and lime-flavored syrup (or *Berliner Rote* with raspberry syrup). On hot summer days, lightweight drinkers prefer *Radler,* a Bavarian mix containing half beer and half lemon-lime soda. *Diesel* is a mixture of *Bier* and cola that will get your engine started.

The variety of places to drink beer is almost as staggering as the variety of brews. The traditional *Biergarten* consists of outdoor tables under chestnut trees. The broad leaves of the trees originally kept beer barrels cool in the days before refrigeration, until one enterprising brewer figured out that they could do the same thing for beer drinkers. The *Bierkeller* is an indoor version of the *Biergarten,* where local breweries dispense their product. During the summer, breweries sponsor carnivals with rides and beer under a tent. To order *"Ein Bier,"* hold up your thumb, not your index finger. Raise your glass to a *"Prost,"* and drink (for more on Beer Halls (in Munich), see **Beer, Beer, and more Beer,** p. 484). Another option for beer drinking is the *Gaststätte,* a simple, local restaurant. It's considered bad form to order only drinks at a *Gaststätte* during mealtimes, but any other time, friends linger for hours over beers. Many *Gaststätten* have a *Stammtisch* (regulars' table), marked by a flag, where interlopers should not sit. The same group of friends may meet at the *Stammtisch* every week for decades, doing nothing but drinking, playing cards, and shooting the breeze; keep in mind that your visa has an expiration date. *Kneipen* are bars where cool young dudes hang out.

WINE AND SPIRITS

Though overshadowed by Germany's more famous export beverage, German wines win over connoisseurs and casual drinkers alike. Virtually all German wines are white, though they vary widely in character. Generally, German wines are sweeter and more fresh tasting than French wines, though not as gusty as Mediterranean wines. Because Germany is the northernmost of the wine-producing countries, the quality of a vineyard's produce can vary considerably with the climate.

The cheapest wines are classified as *Tafelwein* (table wine), while the good stuff (which is still pretty affordable) is *Qualitätswein* (quality wine). *Qualitätswein mit Prädikat* (quality wine with distinction) designates a wine derived from a particular varietal grape. The *Prädikat* wines are further subdivided according to the ripeness of the grapes when harvested; from driest to sweetest, they are *Kabinett, Spätlese, Auslese, Beerenauslese,* or *Trockenbeerenauslese.* The grapes that produce the *Trockenbeerenauslese* are left on the vine until they have shriveled up into raisins and begun to rot—no kidding. The label *Qualitätswein bestimmter Anbaugebiete,* or *Q. b. A.,* designates quality wine from a specific cultivation region.

The major concentrations of viniculture lie along the Rhine and Mosel valleys, along the Main River in Franconia, and in Baden. Rhine wines are bottled in brown glass, all others in green. Of the dozens of varieties, the most famous are *Riesling, Müller-Thurgau,* and *Traminer* (source of *Gewürztraminer*). But don't miss the equally delicious wines made from the *Lemberger, Spätburgunder,* and *Trollinger*

HISTORY AND CULTURE

Das Reinheitsgebot: Germany's Beer Purity Law

One of the most despised characters in medieval Germany was the shoddy brewer who tried to cut costs by substituting lesser grains for the noble cereal at the heart of beer—barley. In 1516, Duke Wilhelm IV of Bayern decreed that beer could contain only pure water, barley, and hops. Wilhelm's Purity Law *(Reinheitsgebot)* has endured to this day, with minor alterations to permit the cultivation of Bayern's trademark wheat-based beers. The law even applies to imports—none of the filler-laden products of the major American breweries (Samuel Adams is an exception) can be imported into Germany. But with the arrival of the European Union, the law was challenged by other European countries, who saw it as an unfair trade barrier. Now the "impure" foreign beers are being admitted to the market, but to the joy of drinkers worldwide, the German breweries have all reaffirmed their full commitment to the *Reinheitsgebot.*

varieties. In wine-producing towns, thirsty travelers can stop by a *Weinstube* to sample the local produce. In Hessen, the beverage of choice is *Äppelwoi* or *Äpfelwein* (apple wine), a hard cider similar in potency to beer. After a meal, many Germans aid their digestion by throwing back a shot of *Schnapps,* distilled from fruits. *Kirschwasser,* a cherry liqueur from the Schwarzwald, is the best known and probably the easiest to stomach, but adventurous sorts can experiment with the sublimely tasty *Black Haus,* delectable, 100 proof, blackberry *Schnapps* also from the Schwarzwald, and which will indeed get you *Haus*ed in most delightful fashion. Each year, unsuspecting tourists are seduced into buying little green bottles of *Jägermeister,* an herb liqueur slightly more palatable than raw eggs flavored with soap.

■ Media

British dailies, such as the *Times* and *Guardian,* are widely available at news stands in major cities. The *International Herald Tribune* and the European edition of the *Wall Street Journal* (DM3) are the most common U.S. papers. American and British armed forces maintain English-language radio stations. German-speakers can keep track of things with the informative, Hamburg-based weekly *Der Spiegel,* one of the world's leading news magazines. *Die Zeit* is a witty, left-leaning weekly journal of opinion. The *Frankfurter Allgemeine Zeitung* is a stodgy newspaper comparable to the *New York Times.* Munich's *Süddeutsche Zeitung* is Germany's best daily paper, though the racy, trashy, semi-rag *Bild Zeitung* is far more popular. For perspective on *Bild,* read Heinrich Böll's *Lost Honor of Katerina Blum,* an open attack on the tabloid and its distinctive style. Coming at you from Berlin are the liberal *Berliner Tagesspiegel* and the iconoclastic, left leaning *Tageszeitung (TAZ).*

■ Social Life

> —*You do not seem to know how rude you are.*
> —*When you're polite in German, you are lying.*
> —Mephisto and Baccalaureus, in Goethe's *Faust, Part II*

An afternoon of relaxation at a park in Berlin or a cafe in any college town will teach you more about Germany than one spent in a museum. Many Germans know Americans and Britons only through contact with NATO soldiers, who haven't always made the best impression. Anti-Americanism is sometimes a powerful sentiment among many young Germans concerned about what they perceive as the American government's failure to exercise moral leadership in the world. If you are sensitive to this concern, you will find that most Germans have a passionate interest in the U.S.

Take the time to actually meet people. A photo of Walter and Gisela Schmidt who put you up for the night in Laßunsgehendorf will contain more memories than a postcard of the Brandenburg Gate. Europeans in general are sincerely interested in other lands and cultures, but have a very strong sense of their own cultural history; if you insult or belittle it, you'll only seem ignorant (and rude). Above all, don't automatically equate "our way" with "better."

The byzantine rules surrounding German etiquette make Ann Landers look like a gas station attendant. Of course, it varies dramatically depending on who you're trying to impress, but it's generally true that the Germans are much more formal than Americans and Australians, and incredibly big on punctuality (especially to meals). Among the older generations, be careful not to use the informal *"du"* (you) or a first name without being invited to do so. *"Du"* is appropriate when addressing fellow students and friends at a youth hostel, or when addressing children. In all other circumstances, use the formal *"Sie"* for "you," as in the question *"Sprechen Sie Englisch?"* Only waitresses in traditional restaurants are addressed as *"Fräulein"*; address all other women as *Frau* (followed by a name). To find out if someone speaks English (many Germans, particularly in the Western *Länder,* do), humbly ask, *"Sprechen Sie Englisch?"* (SPREH-shen zee AYN-glish?) before launching into a question. Better yet, try to learn a little German and don't be afraid to test your talents. The language is intimately related to English, and you can learn the pronunciation system and some useful phrases in about 15 minutes (see **Appendix: Language and Pronunciation,** p. 560). In any case, learn at least two phrases: **please** (*bitte*; BIT-tuh) and **thank you** (*danke;* DAHNK-uh). At the table, Germans eat with the fork in the left hand and the knife in the right. While eating, it is polite to keep the tines of your fork pointing down at all times. An invitation to a German home is a major courtesy; you should bring something for the hostess.

Everything you've heard about the Germans' compulsive abidance of law is true. The first time you see a German standing at an intersection in the pouring rain, with no cars in sight, waiting for the "Walk" signal, you'll know what we mean. Jaywalking is only one of the petty offenses that will mark you as a foreigner (and subject you to fines); littering is another. The younger generation takes matters a bit less seriously. Although **police** are polite and businesslike, they aren't to be messed with. If you fail to treat officers with proper respect (for instance, addressing them with the familiar *"du"* rather than the formal *"Sie"*), they can slap you with on-the-spot fines (see **Insults for Sale,** p. 257). Few officers speak more than a bit of English. The **drinking age** is 16 for beer and 18 for spirits, although both are skimpily enforced; driving under the influence, however, is treated as a severe offense.

Berlin

"Als das Kind Kind war, wüßte es nicht, daß es Kind war."
—*Wings of Desire*

"When the child was a child, it didn't know it was a child." The opening words of Wim Wenders's *Wings of Desire* still piercingly reflect the inchoate tangle of culture and disaster that seeks to define the indefinable entity that is Berlin. The often discordant clash between Berlin's history and present—intellectual personalities and political movements, dignified 18th-century structures, and bold postmodern architecture—echoes in the city's restless, vibrant air.

It has been said that Berliners have experienced more history than any other people in Europe. For 40 years, the divided city personified the undeclared Cold War. Raised in the shadow of global conflict, Berliners responded with a glorious storm of cultural activity and the sort of nightlife you might expect from a population that has its back against the wall. With the collapse of the Berlin Wall in 1989, the city suddenly gained the opportunity to reinvent itself. When Communist governments fell across Eastern Europe, Berlin found itself in a unique position, straddling the border of two distinct but no longer separate worlds. Almost overnight, it became a gateway—*the* gateway—between East and West. Yet at the same time, its two halves were forced to fuse, forming a complex, decentralized metropolis.

Now, as Eastern and Western Europe stitch themselves together, the result will be a new city for a new millennium, redefining Berlin as Germany's cultural capital. Berlin's appeal is thus not only how different it will be in 10 years, but simply that it *will* be different in 10 years. Even so, this self-fashioning must occur without the benefit of an historical umbilical cord, as the pre-division days of the Third Reich cannot absolve Berlin of its role as the symbolic fault line of Western Civilization. Today all efforts to recreate Berlin as it "had been" are illusory amidst the intoxicating whirlwinds of change which characterize the present.

Berlin is both better and worse off as a result of the dizzying transformations. While the post-war West underwent an enormous period of growth fostered by the Marshall Plan and the ensuing *Wirschaftswunder,* the East stood still. The cascade of money flowing eastward since 1991 has turned much of Eastern Berlin into rubble-strewn construction sites; indeed, the giant cranes towering over the horizon at Potsdamer Platz have come to symbolize reunited Berlin as much as the ruined Kaiser-Wilhelm-Gedächtniskirche or the Alexanderpl. television tower. But despite the current plethora of construction jobs, Eastern Berlin suffers from massive unemployment as the transition from communism to capitalism proves more painful than the German government predicted. Tempers flare up frequently as vigorous students protest over contemporary social problems. Unfortunately, economic hopelessness and social alienation have led some young Berliners towards xenophobic neo-Nazi movements.

It will continue to be social chasms and contradictions that represent Berlin in the coming decade, as the radically liberal artist communes continue to coexist with the disaffected, unemployed masses, and the greedy capitalist entrepreneurs. In this sense, Berlin suffers from a disheartening historical continuity, spawning a battleground of social forces that is reminiscent of the later years of the Weimar Republic. Yet it has always been this way in Berlin. After all, this is the home of Christopher Isherwood and the cast of characters he immortalized in *Goodbye to Berlin* (better known as the musical *Cabaret*), of revolutionary playwright Bertolt Brecht, and of Adolf Hitler and his Gestapo. Ironically, the parliament that once tried to seal the destiny of the world let itself be packaged in 1995, when the *Reichstag* was wrapped by the artist-couple Christo and Jean-Claude.

Berlin is not pretty; it has neither the architectural glory of Paris nor the densely packed towers of New York. But, to use a phrase once applied to the Rolling Stones, "it's so ugly, it's beautiful." For now, Berlin is a kaleidoscope of GDR apartment blocks and designer boutiques, decaying buildings pockmarked with bullet holes and

Greater Berlin and Environs

gleaming modern office complexes. The occasional melancholy of the city's tumultuous past is more than made up for by the exhilaration of being on the cutting edge. As Weimar decadent Karl Zuckmayer wrote, "Berlin tasted of the future, and for that one happily accepted the dirt and the coldness as part of the bargain."

■ History

PRUSSIAN KINGDOM TO WORLD WAR I

Berlin took its time to attain international importance. Although populated since the Stone Age, the first mention of a town called "Berlin" appeared in 1237; despite political and economic links, it was not until 1709 that the five towns by the river Spree united into the city of Berlin, capital of the Prussian kingdom. In the 18th century, Berlin flourished under the progressive rule of Friedrich II (the Great), and intellectuals such as Gotthold Ephraim Lessing and Moses Mendelssohn turned the growing city into a center of the Enlightenment. Voltaire, who fled the stifling atmosphere of French absolutism to enjoy Friedrich's patronage, marveled at the transformation of Berlin: "Things have changed visibly: Sparta has become Athens." Berlin suffered a decline in the 19th century as it was conquered by Napoleon and later beset by revolution in 1848. As it grew, it remained a hotbed of political and economic discontent. In 1871, Berlin became the capital of the German Empire established after Bismarck's wars. Its new position as national capital ushered in a period of prosperity, stability, and hypocrisy documented in the novels of Theodor Fontane. The absence of centralized rule in Germany before Bismarck and hundreds of years of political fragmentation left its mark on the country. Imperial Berlin never became the center of the new nation in the same way that Paris was for France or London for Britain. Munich and Frankfurt remained cultural and commercial rivals, and many Germans felt little affection for the Prussian capital. It was not until the end of World War I and the establishment of the first German Republic that Berlin became the undisputed center of national life.

REVOLUTION AND WEIMAR CULTURE

World War I and the Allied blockade brought about near-starvation conditions in Berlin. A popular uprising led to the *Kaiser*'s abdication and Karl Liebknecht's declaration of a socialist republic, with Berlin as capital. Locally, the revolt—led by Liebknecht and Rosa Luxemburg—turned into a full-fledged workers' revolution which wrested control of the city for several days. The Social Democratic government enlisted the aid of radical right-wing mercenaries, the *Freikorps,* who brutally supressed the rebellion and murdered Liebknecht and Luxemburg. But when the *Freikorps* chose the new government as its next target, the workers demonstrated their commitment to democracy and staged a massive strike to defeat the coup. Political and economic instability continued until 1923, when Chancellor Gustav Stresemann's economic plan and generous loans from the United States improved the situation. Meanwhile, Berlin had become one of the major cultural centers of Europe. The Expressionist painters flourished, Bertolt Brecht developed revolutionary new theater techniques, Alexander Döblin applied Joycean method in his novels about Berlin, and artists and writers from all over the world flocked to the city. The city's "Golden Twenties," however, ended abruptly with the 1929 economic collapse. Mass unemployment preceded bloody riots, radicalization, political chaos, and the ascent of the Nazis.

CAPITAL OF THE THIRD REICH

When Hitler took power on January 30, 1933, traditionally left-wing "Red Berlin" was not one of his strongholds. He consolidated his control over the city through economic improvements and totalitarian measures, and found plenty of supporters for the savage anti-Semitic pogrom of November 9, 1938, known as the *Kristallnacht* (Night of Shattered Glass). Berlin was hit extremely hard during World War II; Allied bombing and the Battle of Berlin leveled a fifth of the city. With almost all of the healthy men dead or gone, it was Berlin's women, known as the *Trümmerfrauen* (rubble women) who picked up the broken pieces of the city. The pre-war population of 4.3 million sank to 2.8 million. Only 7000 members of Berlin's once-thriving Jewish community of 160,000 survived the Nazi genocide.

After the war, the Allies took over control of the city, dividing it into French, British, American, and Soviet sectors under a joint Allied Command. On June 16, 1948, the Soviets withdrew from the joint Command and demanded full control of Berlin. On June 26, they began an 11-month blockade of most land and water routes into the western sectors. The population would have starved were it not for a massive Allied airlift of supplies known as the *Luftbrücke* (air bridge). On May 12, 1949, the Soviets ceded control of the western half of Berlin to the Western Allies.

A DIVIDED CITY

On October 5, 1949, the Soviet-controlled German Democratic Republic *(Deutsche Demokratische Republik)* was formally established, with East Berlin as its capital. The city was thus officially divided. Dissatisfaction was great in East Berlin, and it manifested itself in the workers' uprising of June 17, 1953, when widespread popular demonstrations were crushed under Soviet tanks. One result of the repression was an increase in the number of refugees who fled from East to West Berlin—200,000 in 1960 alone. On the morning of August 13, 1961, the government of the East responded to this exodus of many of its most talented citizens with the almost instantaneous construction of the Berlin Wall, which stopped virtually all interaction between the two halves of the city. A commercial center around Breitscheidpl. and the renowned Kurfürstendamm was created and nurtured to become *das Schaufenster des Westens* (the store window of the West).

West Berlin remained under joint French, British, and American control. Although there was an elected mayor, final say rested with the Allied commander-in-chief. The city was not officially a part of the Federal Republic of Germany, but had a "special status." Although Berlin adopted the resolutions of the Federal Parliament, the municipal Senate still had to approve them, and the Allies retained ultimate authority over the city right up until German reunification in 1990. One perk of this special status was the exemption of West Berliners from military conscription. Thousands of German artists, punks, and left-wing activists moved to Berlin to escape the draft and formed an alternative political and artistic scene without parallel anywhere in the world. The West German government, determined to make a showcase of the city, subsidized its economic and cultural life, further enhancing its vitality.

THE WALL OPENS

On November 9, 1989—the 71st anniversary of the proclamation of the Weimar Republic, the 66th anniversary of Hitler's Beer Hall *Putsch,* and the 51st anniversary of *Kristallnacht*—a series of popular demonstrations throughout East Germany, riding on a decade of discontent and a year of rapid change in Eastern Europe, culminated in the opening of the Berlin Wall. The image of jubilant Berliners embracing atop the Brandenburg Gate that night provided one of the most memorable images of the century. Berlin was officially reunited (and Allied authority ended) along with the rest of Germany on October 3, 1990, to widespread celebration. Since then, the euphoria has evaporated. Eastern and Western Berliners have discovered that they don't really like each other as much as they once imagined. Resignation to reconstruction has taken the place of the biting criticism and tasteless jokes that were standard in the early 90s. Eastern Berlin remains politically volatile and economically disadvantaged, and Western Berliners have responded with their own form of xenophobia; in 1995, voters in the western Wedding district voted a handful of far-right nationalists onto the town council. The city is slowly restitching itself, but it may take a long time before its residents truly consider themselves neighbors.

Although the first united, freely elected Bundestag symbolically convened in Berlin in December of 1990, the June 1991 vote to move the parliament back here bodes no immediate action—Bonn remains the seat of government, and the transfer is not expected to be complete until 1999. When this happens, perhaps the "post-war" era in Berlin will have a definitive endpoint, more than 50 years after World War II, and on the doorstep of the 21st century.

■ Orientation

Berlin surveys the Prussian plains from the northeastern corner of a reunited Germany and is again becoming the hub of the national rail network. About four hours southeast of Hamburg by rail and eight hours north of Munich (though ICE trains cut down on travel time), Berlin has a web of rail and air connections to other European capitals. Berlin is well-connected to Eastern European countries—Prague is five hours by rail; Warsaw six hours. Almost all European airlines, Western or Eastern, have frequent service to one of Berlin's three airports. For the time being, West Berlin's **Bahnhof Zoologischer Garten** (almost always called **Bahnhof Zoo**) remains Berlin's major train station and a central focus of Berlin's subway and surface rail systems. The situation is changing, however, as reconstruction is allowing the eastern **Hauptbahnhof** station to supercede the space-constricted Zoo station. Within the next few years, the *Hauptbahnhof*—a 20-minute S-Bahn ride from the Zoo station—should once again become the main station. At the moment, trains from the new federal states and from eastern Europe are evenly split between this station and **Berlin-Lichtenberg,** significantly farther east (about 45min. by S-Bahn from the Zoo). Trains com-

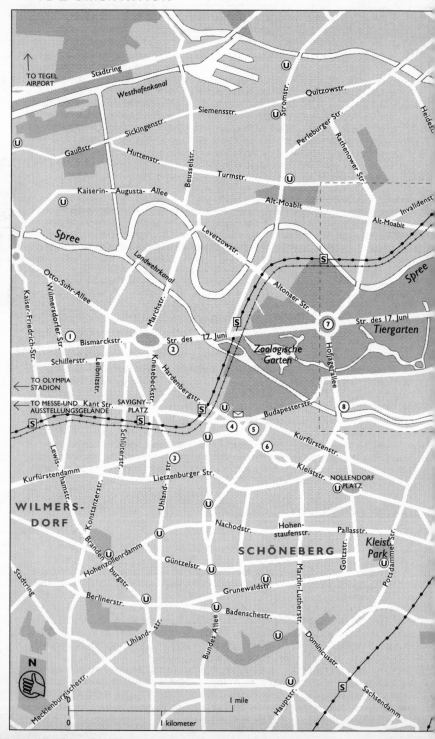

TO TEGEL AIRPORT

Stadtring

Westhafenkanal

Siemensstr.

Sickingenstr.

Gaußstr.

Huttenstr.

Kaiserin- Augusta- Allee

Beusselstr.

Turmstr.

Alt-Moabit

Quitzowstr.

Stromstr.

Perleburger Str.

Rathenower Str.

Heidestr.

Alt-Moabit

Invalidenstr.

Spree

Levetzowstr.

Landwehrkanal

Otto-Suhr-Allee

Wilmersdorfer Str.

Kaiser-Friedrich-Str.

Bismarckstr.

Schillerstr.

Marchstr.

Knesebeckstr.

Str. des 17. Juni

Altonaer Str.

Spree

Str. des 17. Juni

Tiergarten

Zoologische Garten

Hofjägerallee

TO OLYMPIA STADION

Leibnizstr.

Hardenbergstr.

TO MESSE-UND AUSSTELLUNGSGELÄNDE

Kant Str.

SAVIGNY-PLATZ

Budapesterstr.

Kurfürstenstr.

Lewishamstr.

Schlüterstr.

Kurfürstendamm

Lietzenburger Str.

Uhland-str.

Konstanzerstr.

WILMERS-DORF

Nachodstr.

Kleiststr.

NOLLENDORF PLATZ

Hohen-staufenstr.

Pallasstr.

Kleist Park

SCHÖNEBERG

Goltzstr.

Potsdammer Str.

Branden.

Hohenzollerndamm

burgstr.

Güntzelstr.

Grunewaldstr.

Martin-Lutherstr.

Stadtring

Berlinerstr.

Uhland-str.

Bundes Allee

Badenschestr.

Dominicusstr.

Mecklenburgischestr.

Haupstr.

Sachsendamm

N

I mile

0

I kilometer

0

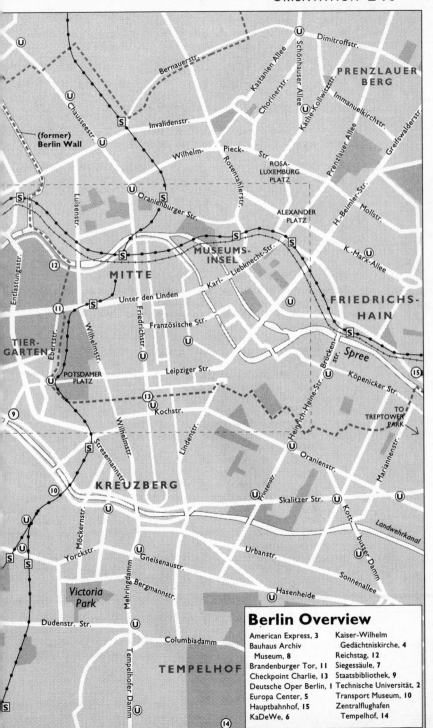

Berlin Overview

American Express, 3
Bauhaus Archiv
  Museum, 8
Brandenburger Tor, 11
Checkpoint Charlie, 13
Deutsche Oper Berlin, 1
Europa Center, 5
Hauptbahnhof, 15
KaDeWe, 6

Kaiser-Wilhelm
  Gedächtniskirche, 4
Reichstag, 12
Siegessäule, 7
Staatsbibliothek, 9
Technische Universität, 2
Transport Museum, 10
Zentralflughafen
  Tempelhof, 14

ing from the west and south arrive either at the Zoo or the *Hauptbahnhof.* **Friedrichstraße** and **Alexanderplatz** are other important eastern stations.

Berlin is an *immense* conglomeration of what were once two separate and unique cities: the former East, which contains the lion's share of Berlin's architectural landmarks and historic sites, and the former West, which functioned for decades as a small, isolated, democratic state and is still the commercial heart of united Berlin. As businesses and embassies are starting to move their headquarters back to the east, however, this situation is changing.

The commercial district of Western Berlin lies at one end of the huge **Tiergarten** park, and is focused around Bahnhof Zoo and **Breitscheidplatz.** It is marked by the bombed-out **Kaiser-Wilhelm-Gedächtniskirche,** adjacent to the boxy tower of the **Europa Center.** A star of streets radiates from Breitscheidpl.: toward the west run **Hardenbergstraße, Kantstraße,** and the great commercial boulevard of modern Berlin, the renowned and reviled **Kurfürstendamm,** or **Ku'damm.** Down Hardenbergstr. 700m is Steinpl. and the enormous Berlin **Technical University (TU).** Down Kantstr. 800m is **Savignyplatz,** home to cafes, restaurants, and *Pensionen.*

The grand, tree-lined **Straße des 17. Juni** runs west-east through the Tiergarten to end at the triumphant **Brandenburg Gate,** which opens out onto **Pariserplatz,** a site of landmark public addresses. Heading south from the Brandenburg Gate and the nearby **Reichstag,** newly asphalted **Ebertstraße** runs uncomfortably along the path of the demolished Berlin Wall to **Potsdamer Platz.** Toward the east, the gate opens onto **Unter den Linden,** Berlin's most famous boulevard and the site of many historic buildings, particularly around the **Lustgarten** plaza. Continuing east, one arrives at teeming **Alexanderplatz,** the center of the East's growing commercial district and the home of Berlin's most visible landmark (an unparalleled example of architectural priapism), the **Fernsehturm.** The alternative **Kreuzberg** and **Mitte,** for 45 years the fringe, back-against-the-wall neighborhoods of the West and East, are once again at the city's heart. Distinctions between east and west are withering away as communication networks—transportation, telecommunication, and utilities—are synthesized and rebuilt to serve the sprawling metropolis reborn with unification.

The ferry-laden **Spree River** snakes its way from west to east through the center of Berlin; it forms the northern border of the Tiergarten and splits just east of Unter den Linden to close off the **Museumsinsel** (Museum Island), East Berlin's cultural epicenter. The windswept waters of the Wannsee, Tegelersee, Niederneuendorfer See, and Heiligensee lap the city from all sides, and are connected by narrow canals.

If you're planning to stay more than a few days in Berlin, the blue-and-yellow **Falk Plan** (available at most kiosks and bookstores) is an indispensable and convenient city map that includes a street index and folds open like a book (DM11). Dozens of streets and transit stations in Eastern Berlin once took their names from Communist heroes and heroines. Many, but not all, have been renamed in a process only recently completed; be sure that your map is up-to-date. In newly united Berlin, many **municipal services** are gradually being joined and coordinated. Novelist Peter Schneider called the East and West Siamese twin cities, with, for instance, two matching television towers as navels. When services are duplicated in both parts of the city, *Let's Go* lists those in Western Berlin first, then their Eastern counterparts.

Safety Warning! Although neo-Nazis represent a tiny minority of Berliners, Africans, Asians, and other conspicuously non-German individuals should be on guard in less-touristed areas of Eastern Berlin. Extreme-right groups have (infrequently) targeted gays and lesbians. Neo-Nazis have been linked to late-night S-Bahn attacks on foreigners. Berlin's neo-Nazis tend to identify themselves according to the traditional skinhead uniform (see **Safety and Security,** p. 14).

BERLIN

Central Berlin

Alte Nationalgalerie, 17
Alte Synagogue, 18
Brandenburger Tor, 8
Bodemuseum, 16
Checkpoint Charlie, 11
Deutsches Historisches
Museum, 14
Fernsehturm, 20
Humboldt Universität, 13
Kongresshalle, 3
Kunstgewerbemuseum, 5
Marienkirche, 19
Martin-Gropius-Bau, 10
Neue Nationalgalerie, 6
Pergamon Museum, 15
Philharmonie, 7
Reichstag, 9
Schloss Bellevue, 2
Siegessäule, 1
Soviet Army Memorial, 4
Staatsoper, 12

■ Practical Information

TOURIST OFFICES AND CITY TOURS

Main Office: Berlin-Touristen-Information, Europa Center, Budapesterstr. 45. From Bahnhof Zoo, walk along Budapesterstr. past the Kaiser-Wilhelm-Gedächtniskirche; the office is on the right (5min.). Helpful staff speaks fluent English. Open Mon.-Sat. 8am-10pm, Sun. 9am-9pm.

Branch offices: In the main hall of **Tegel Airport,** at the Lufthansa Airport Center. Open daily 5:15am-10pm; also inside the **Brandenburg Gate,** south wing. Open daily 9:30am-6pm. Because all three offices are very busy, it is impossible to dial a particular office.

Services: Thanks to recent privatization, the tourist offices no longer provide the plethora of free services and information they used to. However, they all sell a useful city map (DM1) on which sights and transit stations are more clearly marked than on the *Falk Plan.* They book same-day hotel rooms for a DM5 fee—though room prices start at DM50 and rise to stratospheric heights. They also have free copies of the city magazines *030* and (for gays and lesbians) *Serge,* which have reasonably good entertainment listings. *Tip* and *Zitty,* which are *auf Deutsch,* have the most comprehensive listings (DM4 each). The city's main English language magazine, *Berlin* (DM3.50), has good listings for classical music and opera but little else. Dig *Deutsch?* You're better off buying *Tip* or *Zitty.*

Tours: Berlin Walks (tel. 301 91 94) offers a range of English-language walking tours, including their thorough Discover Berlin tour, as well as tours of Infamous Third Reich Sites, Jewish Life in Berlin, and Prenzlauer Berg. Tours last about 2½hr. and meet at 9:15, 10am, and 2:30pm in front of the Zoo station (DM14, under 26 DM10). The **Insider Tour** of Berlin hits all the major sights and enjoys a very good reputation. Tours last 3hr. and leave from the McDonald's by the Zoo station May-Nov. at 10am and 2:30pm (DM10). **Rad Zeit,** a monthly pamphlet (available in bike shops and in some cafes), lists bike tours of Berlin (in German only) and the surrounding countryside—a great way to meet people. **Bus tours** are offered by various companies in English and German (they're rather touristy), leaving somewhat hourly from the Ku'damm near Europa Center and the *Gedächtniskirche.*

BUDGET TRAVEL

Kilroy Travels, Hardenbergstr. 9 (tel. 313 04 66; fax 312 69 75), across from the Technical University. The friendly staff will cheerfully help you navigate through the intricacies of European planes, trains, and buses. **Branch offices** at: Takustr. 47 (tel. 831 50; fax 832 53 76; U-Bahn #1: "Dahlem-Dorf"), Nollendorfpl. 7 (tel. 216 30 91; fax 215 92 21; U-Bahn #1, 2, or 4: "Nollendorfpl."), Mariannenstr. 7 (tel. 614 68 22; fax 614 99 83; in Kreuzberg; U-Bahn #1 or 8: "Kotbusser Tor"), Georgenstr., Stadtbahnbogen 184, in Mitte; S-Bahn or U-Bahn #6: "Freidrichstr." All open Mon.-Fri. 10am-6pm, Sat. 11am-2pm.

STA, Goethestr. 73 (tel. 311 09 50), does the travel agency thing. U-Bahn #2: "Ernst-Reuter-Platz." Open Mon.-Wed. and Fri. 10am-8pm, Thurs. 10am-6pm.

EMBASSIES AND CONSULATES

Australian Consulate: Uhlandstr. 181-183 (tel. 880 08 80). U-Bahn #15: "Uhlandstr." Open Mon.-Fri. 9am-noon.

Canadian Embassy: Friedrichstr. 95 (tel. 261 11 61; fax 262 92 06). S-Bahn or U-Bahn #6: "Friedrichstr." Open Mon.-Fri. 8:30am-12:30pm and 1:30-5pm.

Irish Consulate: Ernst-Reuter-Platz 10 (tel. 34 80 08 22; fax 34 80 08 63). U-Bahn #2: "Ernst-Reuter-Platz." Open Mon.-Fri. 10am-1pm.

New Zealand citizens should contact their embassy in Bonn.

South African Consulate: Douglasstr. 9 (tel. 82 50 11; fax 826 65 43). Open Mon.-Fri. 9am-noon.

U.K. Embassy: Unter den Linden 32 (tel. 20 18 40; fax: 20 18 41 58). S-Bahn #1 or 2: "Unter den Linden." Open Mon.-Fri. 9am-noon and 2-4pm.

BERLIN

U.S. Citizens Service: 170 Clayallee (tel. 832 92 33; fax 831 49 26). U-Bahn #1: "Oskar Helene Heim." Open Mon.-Fri. 9am-noon. Telephone advice available Mon.-Fri. 9am-5pm; after hours, a machine will give you emergency instructions.

TRAINS

Stations: For now, **Bahnhof Zoo** is Berlin's principal station for trains to the west, while the **Hauptbahnhof** is the main source of eastern and southern-bound trains. The stations are connected by S-Bahn. Trains to and from the east also use **Berlin-Lichtenberg.** Exceptions abound, so check before you set off.

Connections: Zoo, Hamburg (IC; 4hr.), Düsseldorf (IC; 5½hr.), Köln (IC; 5½hr.), Munich (ICE; 8hr.), Frankfurt (ICE; 5hr.), Amsterdam (IR; 7hr.), Paris (IC; 12hr.), Zürich (IC; 12hr.). **Hauptbahnhof,** Munich, Hamburg, Leipzig (2½hr.), Warsaw (6½hr.), Krakow (8hr.), and Malmö, Sweden (9hr.). **Lichtenberg,** Hamburg, Dresden, Prague (5hr.), Krakow (9hr.), Rostock (2½hr.), Vienna (10hr.), Budapest (13hr.), Moscow (36hr.), and St. Petersberg (36hr.).

Information: Deutsche Bahn Information (tel. 194 19). Be prepared for a long wait. Also long lines at offices in **Bahnhof Zoo** (open daily 5:30am-10:30pm) and **Hauptbahnhof.** Both stations have recently installed computers to help you figure out your own itinerary but there are lines for these, too—*arrive early.* For **recorded information** about departures and arrivals (in German) there are several lines depending on your destination: Hamburg, Kiel, Rostock, and Scandinavia (tel. 01 15 31); Hanover, Köln, the Netherlands, France (tel. 01 15 32); Halle, Erfurt, Frankfurt, Switzerland (tel. 01 15 33); Leipzig, Munich, Austria, Italy (tel. 01 15 34); Dresden, Czech Republic, Hungary, Romania, Bulgaria (tel. 01 15 35); Poland, Lithuania, Latvia, Russia (tel. 01 15 36). Some timetables confusingly include all stations; make sure you're at the right one.

GETTING AROUND

Buses: ZOB, the central bus station (tel. 301 80 28), is by the *Funkturm* near Kaiserdamm. U-Bahn #2: "Kaiserdamm." Check *Zitty* and *Tip* for deals on long-distance buses—they aren't comfortable but they are often much cheaper than the train. Paris (10hr.; DM109 one-way); Vienna (10½hr.; DM85 one-way).

Public Transportation: The **BVG** (*Berliner Verkehrsbetriebe,* or transit service) is in the midst of a massive spate of construction and renovation which will affect S- and U-Bahn service for the next few years. Under the slogan *"Freie Bahn für Berlin,"* the construction will bring service in Eastern Berlin up to snuff with the West, adding new lines and stops, increasing the frequency of trains to existing stops, and removing unexploded World War II bombs from below the streets. To cushion the blow, the BVG has put up posters everywhere introducing Berliners to **Max,** a bespectacled cartoon mole who will appear on announcements of disruptions to service. In most cases, the worst inconvenience is that you'll wait an extra 30min.

Orientation and Basic Fares: It is impossible to tour Berlin on foot—fortunately, the public transit system is quite efficient (but expensive). The extensive **bus, U-Bahn** (subway), and **S-Bahn** (surface rail) systems of Berlin operate as 1 network, the **BVG.** A single ticket for the combined network (*Einzelfahrschein Normaltarif;* DM3.90) is good for 2hr. after validation. An *Einzelfahrschein Kurzstreckentarif* (short-trip fare; DM2.50) allows travel up to 6 bus stations (with no transfers; not valid on airport bus lines) or 3 U- or S-Bahn stops (with unlimited transfers). A 4-trip *Sammelkarte* (Multiple Ticket) costs DM13; each "click" is good for 2hr. A short-trip 4-ride *Kurzstreckensammelkarte* is available for DM8.50. You can buy tickets from machines, bus drivers, or ticket windows in the U- and S-Bahn stations. Inspections are not as frequent here as in some other German cities, but the cost of cheating is steep (DM60 and tremendous humiliation). Children under 6 accompanied by an adult travel free; children under 14 pay a reduced fare. *All tickets must be canceled in the red validation box marked "hier entwerten" before boarding to be valid.* Tickets bought on the bus are automatically valid.

Special Passes and Maps: Information, maps, and tickets are available at the **BVG Pavillon,** Bahnhof Zoo (24hr. tel. 25 62 25 62). Open daily 8am-8pm. The **Berlin Tagesticket** (DM13, ages 6-14 DM6.50) is a 24hr. pass for the bus, U- and S-Bahn. A

7-Day Ticket (DM40) is a good value for moderate-length stays. An **Umweltkarte** (DM93), valid during the month of purchase (not necessarily 30 days), is good for longer stays. After 8pm on weekdays and all-day Sat. and Sun., this ticket allows you to travel with 1 other adult and 3 children free. The prices listed for the *Umweltkarte* and 7-day ticket are for the basic versions of the passes; more expensive passes allowing you to travel in all 3 tariff zones (not just A and B) and to bring a bike onto the train are also available. The **Kombi-Ticket** is valid for 1 day of unlimited travel on all BVG services as well as the ferry services of **Stern und Kreisschiffahrt** (DM25; also see **Ferries,** below). The extensive **Liniennetz** map can be picked up free at any ticket office and clearly depicts all U- and S-Bahn routes. The *Falk Plan* also demarcates all routes, including buses.

Note: Berlin is divided into 3 transit zones. Zone A encompasses downtown Berlin, including Tempelhof airport. Almost everything else falls into Zone B, with Zone C containing the outer suburbs of Potsdam and Oranienburg. An AB ticket is the best deal, as you can buy regional Bahn tickets for the outlying areas.

Night Transport: U- and S-Bahn lines generally do not run from 1-4am, although some S-Bahn lines run sporadically in central Berlin at night, and the **U9** and **U12** run all night Fri.-Sat. (The U12 line, which only runs Fri.-Sat. night, combines the Rühleben-Gleisdreieck leg of U2 with the Gleisdreieck-Warschauerstr. leg of the U1.) Most regular lines start their final runs by 12:15am. There is an extensive system of **night buses** centered on Bahnhof Zoo that run about every 15min.; you can pick up the free *Nachtliniennetz* map at the BVG pavilion. All night bus numbers are preceded by **N.**

Ferries: Stern und Kreis Schiffahrt, Puschkinallee 16-17 (tel. 536 36 00; fax 53 63 60 99), operates ferry services along the Spree from April-Oct. Ferries leave from locations throughout the city, including Friedrichstr., Museum Island, the *Dom,* and the Nikolaiviertel. Fares depend on distance traveled (DM3.50-22). Pleasure cruises also available. *Berlin Kombi-Tageskarte* is valid on all regularly scheduled services. For further information contact tourist office or BVG Pavilion.

Taxis: tel. 21 02 02, 26 10 26, or 690 22. Call at least 15min. in advance. Women may request a female driver.

Car Rental: Avis, Budapesterstr. 43 (tel. 793 19 80), is closest to Bahnhof Zoo. Open Mon.-Fri. 7:30am-8pm, Sat. 8am-2pm. **Hertz** has an office at the corner of Spandauerstr. and Karl-Liebknecht-Str. (tel. 242 44 40), near Alexanderpl. Open Mon.-Fri. 8:30am-6:30pm, Sat. 8am-noon. Both companies also have offices at Tegel airport.

Automobile Clubs: ADAC (tel. 018 02 22 22 22). 24hr. breakdown service.

Bike Rental: Bahnhof Zoo, next to the lost and found. DM13-23 per day. DM60 for 3 days. DM120 per week. Open daily 6am-11pm. **Herr Beck,** at Goethestr. 7 (tel. 312 19 25), near Ernst-Reuter-Platz. DM12 per day. Mountain bikes DM20 per day. Call for selection and deposit information. Bring passport. No English spoken.

Mitfahrzentrale: City Netz, Joachimstalerstr. 17 (tel. 194 44 or 882 76 04; fax 882 44 20), in the Ku'Dorf Mall, has a computerized **ride-share** database. U-Bahn #1 or 9: "Kurfürstendamm." To Hamburg, DM11 fee for info, DM18 paid to driver; and Vienna, DM18, DM39. Driver fee is less if more than 1 person shares the ride. Open daily 8am-9pm. **Branch offices,** Südstern 2, in Kreuzberg (tel. 693 60 95). U-Bahn #7: "Südstern." Bahnhof Zoo, on the U2 platform (tel. 31 03 31). Both open daily 9am-8pm. **Mitzfahrzentrale Alex,** in the Alexanderpl. U-Bahn station (tel. 241 58 20), specializes in the East. Open Mon.-Fri. 8am-8pm, Sat. 8am-6pm, Sun. 10am-6pm. The **Mitfahrtelephon für Schwule and Lesben,** Yorckstr. 52 (tel. 194 20 or 216 60 21), matches gay and lesbian drivers and passengers. U-Bahn #7: "Yorckstr." Open Mon.-Fri. 9am-8pm, Sat.-Sun. 10am-4pm. Berlin has many small *Mitzfahrzentralen;* check *Zitty, Tip,* or *030* magazines for addresses and phone numbers.

Hitchhiking: *Let's Go* does not recommend hitchhiking as a safe mode of transportation. No, no, no. Those who hitch west and south (Hannover, Munich, Weimar, Leipzig), S-Bahn #1 or 3: "Wannsee," then bus #211: *Autobahn* entrance ramp. Those headed north (Hamburg, Rostock), U-Bahn #6: "Tegel," then bus #224 and ask the driver to be let out at the "Trampenpl." Both have huge crowds, but someone gets picked up every few minutes.

Flights: Flughafen Tegel (tel. 41 01 23 06) is Berlin's main airport. Take express bus X9 (from Bahnhof Zoo) or bus #109 (from Bahnhof Zoo or the Jakob-Kaiser-Platz U-Bahn station: "Tegel"). **Flughafen Tempelhof** (tel. 69 51 22 88), the smallest of Berlin's airports, is mostly used for intra-Germany travel and flights to the former Soviet Union. U-Bahn #6: "Platz der Luftbrücke." **Flughafen Schönefeld** (tel. 60 91 51 66), in Eastern Berlin, is for charters; El Al flies here too. S-Bahn #9 or 45.

GENERAL SERVICES

Currency Exchange: Deutsche Verkehrs-Kredit Bank, on Hardenbergstr. at Bahnhof Zoo (tel. 881 71 17). Long hours, terrible rates—1% commission on traveler's checks (DM7.50 min. fee). Open daily 7:30am-10pm. The **Reisebank** at the *Hauptbahnhof* (tel. 296 43 93) changes traveler's checks for a DM7.50 fee. Open Mon.-Fri. 7am-10pm, Sat.-Sun. 7am-4pm. **Berliner Bank,** in Tegel Airport. Open daily 8am-10pm. You can also change money at most **post offices,** which cash traveler's checks for DM6 per check. **Sparkasse** and **Deutsche Bank** have branches everywhere; their ATMs usually accept Visa and MC, though only a few still take EuroCard. Sparkasse changes cash free, but charges 1% commission on traveler's checks (with a DM7.50 min.). **Citibank** has branches with 24hr. ATMs at Kurfürstendamm 72. S-Bahn or U-Bahn #2 or 9: "Zoo"; Wittenbergpl. 1. U-Bahn 1, 2, or 15: "Wittenbergpl."; Wilmersdorferstr. 133. U-Bahn #2 or 7: "Bismarckstr."; and Karl-Marx-Allee 153. U-Bahn #5: "Strausbergerpl." There's also a Citibank ATM at Tegel Airport. ATMs are the best (and cheapest) way to get money.

American Express: Main Office, Uhlandstr. 173, 10719 (tel. 884 58 80). Mail held, banking services rendered. No commission for cashing AmEx traveler's checks. On Fri. and Sat., expect out-the-door lines of travelers carrying *Let's Go.* Open Mon.-Fri. 9am-5:30pm, Sat. 9am-noon. **Branch offices,** Bayreutherstr. 37 (tel. 21 49 83 63). U-Bahn #1, 2, 12, or 15: "Wittenbergpl." Traveler's checks cashed and sold, but no mail held. Also at Friedrichstr. 172, 10117 (tel. 238 41 02). S-Bahn or U-Bahn #6: "Friedrichstr." Full services. Both branch offices open Mon.-Fri. 9am-6pm.

Luggage Storage: In the **Bahnhof Zoo** train station (lockers DM2 per day, larger lockers DM4, 72hr. max.). If all the lockers at Bahnhof Zoo are full, you can check your luggage at the center near the post office for DM4 per piece per day. Open daily 6am-11pm. At the **Hauptbahnhof** (lockers DM2 per day, larger DM4, 72hr. max.). At Bahnhof **Lichtenberg** and S-Bahnhof **Alexanderplatz** (lockers DM2 per day, 24hr. max.).

Lost Property: Zentrales Fundbüro, Platz der Luftbrücke 8 (tel. 69 95). **BVG Fundbüro,** Lorenzweg 5 (tel. 256 230 40). U-Bahn #6: "Ullsteinstr." For items lost on the bus or U-Bahn. Many, many umbrellas. Open Mon.-Tues. and Thurs. 9am-3pm, Wed. 9am-6pm, Fri. 9am-2pm. **Fundbüro Berlin,** Mittelstr. 20 (tel. 29 72 96 12), at the Schönefeld airport train station.

Bookstores: Marga Schoeler Bücherstube, Knesebeckstr. 34 (tel. 881 11 12), at Mommsenstr., betweeen Savignypl. and the Ku'damm. Large selection of books in English includes politics, history, poetry, lit crit, and fiction. Open Mon.-Wed. 9:30am-7pm, Thurs.-Fri. 9:30am-8pm, Sat. 9am-4pm. The **British Bookshop,** Mauerstr. 83-84 (tel. 238 46 80), by Checkpoint Charlie. An artfully-stocked addition to Berlin's English book club, with well-chosen literature and history sections and English-language newspapers and mags. Open Mon.-Fri. 10am-6pm, Sat. 10am-4pm. **Literaturhaus Berlin,** Fasanenstr. 23 (tel. 882 65 52), is in a wonderful old mansion complete with garden cafe and readings of German and international literature. Their resident bookstore, **Kohlhaas & Co.** (tel. 882 50 44), has many second-hand German books, as well as Berlin's best Judaica *and* Nazi history sections, right next to each other. Open Mon.-Fri. 10am-8pm, Sat. 10am-4pm.

Libraries: Staatsbibliothek Preußischer Kulturbesitz, Potsdamerstr. 33 (tel. 26 61), and Unter den Linden 8 (tel. 210 50). 3.5 million books—one for every Berliner—but not all are stored on site. Some can take 2 days to retrieve. Lots of English-language newspapers. The Potsdamerstr. library was built for West Berlin in the 1960s, after the Iron Curtain went down on the original *"Staabi"* on Unter den Linden, next to the Humboldt University. Now Berliners can choose between them—and so can you. Both open Mon.-Fri. 9am-9pm, Sat. 9am-5pm.

Cultural Centers: Amerika Haus, Hardenbergstr. 22-24 (tel. 31 00 73 or 31 50 55 70). Library includes English-language books and day-old editions of *The New York Times,* and presents readings by visiting American authors. Offices open Mon.-Fri. 8:30am-5:30pm. Library open Tues. and Thurs. 2-8pm, Wed. and Fri. 2-5:30pm.

British Council, Hardenbergstr. 22 (tel. 31 10 99-0), is next door. Enter through the *Informationszentrum* Berlin, 2nd floor. Office open Mon.-Fri. 9am-12:30pm and 2-5pm. Library open Mon., Wed., and Fri. 2-6pm; Tues. and Thurs. 2-7pm.

Language Instruction: Goethe Institut, Friedrichstr. 209, 10969 (tel. 25 90 63; fax 25 90 64 00), is the best known and the most expensive. U-Bahn #6: "Kochstr." All levels of German available. DM1510 for 4 weeks, 25hr. of instruction per week. **Fokus** *(Forum für Kultur und Sprachen),* Haubachstr. 23, 10585 (tel. 341 47 37), also has a good reputation. U-Bahn #7: "Richard-Wagner-Platz." DM360 for 4-weeks, 15hr. per week. *Tip* and *Zitty* are filled with ads for other schools and private tutors—check the classifieds under "Unterricht" and shop around.

Laundromat: Wasch Centers at various locations: **Leibnizstr. 72,** in Charlottenburg. U-Bahn #7: "Wilmersdorferstr"; **Wexstr. 34,** in Schöneberg. U-Bahn #9: "Bundespl."; **Bergmannstr. 61,** in Kreuzberg. U-Bahn #7: "Gniesenaustr."; **Behmstr. 12,** in Mitte. S-Bahn #1 or 2, or U-Bahn #8: "Gesundbrunnen"; and **Jablonskistr. 21,** in Prenzlauer Berg. U-Bahn #2: "Eberswalderstr." Wash DM6 per 6kg, soap included. Dry DM2 for 30min. All open daily 6am-10pm. **Waschcenter Schnell und Sauber,** 61 Uhlandstr. U-Bahn #15: "Uhlandstr." Wash DM6 per 6kg. Open daily 6am-11pm.

Crisis Lines: Sexual Assault Hotline, tel. 251 28 28. Open Tues. and Thurs. 6-9pm, Sun. noon-2pm. **Schwules Überfall** (gay bashing) hotline and legal help, tel. 216 33 36. Open daily 6-9pm. **Drug Crisis,** tel. 192 37. Open Mon.-Fri. 8:30am-10pm, Sat.-Sun. 2-9:30pm. **Frauenkrisentelefon** (women's crisis line), tel. 615 42 43. Open Mon. and Thurs. 10am-noon; Tues.-Wed., and Fri. 7-9pm; Sat.-Sun. 5-7pm. English speakers at all crisis lines.

Pharmacies: Europa-Apotheke, Tauentzienstr. 9-12 (tel. 261 42 44), by Europa Center (close to Bahnhof Zoo). Open daily 9am-9pm. **Münz-Apotheke,** Münzstr. 5 (tel. 241 10 83), just off Alexanderpl. Open Mon.-Fri. 8am-6:30pm, Sat. 9am-1pm. Closed *Apotheken* post signs directing you to the nearest open one. For information about late-night pharmacies call 011 41.

Medical Assistance: The American and British embassies have a list of English-speaking doctors. **Emergency Doctor,** (tel. 31 00 31). **Emergency Dentist,** (tel. 841 91 00). English-speaking dentists available.

Emergency: Police, Platz der Luftbrücke 6 (tel.110 or 69 90). **Ambulance** and **Fire,** tel. 112.

Internet Access: Cyberb@r Zoo, Joachimtalerstr. 5-6 (tel. 88 02 40; email cyberbar-zoo@hotmail.com) in the Karstadt Sport Megastore. 30min. connection DM5. Open Mon.-Fri. 10am-8pm, Sat. 9am-4pm. Also in **Cybermind's Virtuality Cafe** (see **Food,** p. 108).

Post Offices: In the **Bahnhof Zoo** (tel. 313 97 99). Interminable lines, but the best hours. Open Mon.-Fri. 6am-midnight, Sat.-Sun. 8am-midnight. **Poste Restante** (held at window 7) should be addressed: Poste Restante/Hauptpostlagernd, Postamt Bahnhof Zoo, 10612 Berlin. Branch office at **Tegel Airport** (tel. 430 85 23). Open daily 6:30am-9pm. In Eastern Berlin, around the corner from the **Hauptbahnhof,** Postamt Berlin 17, Str. der Pariser Kommune 8-10, 10243 Berlin. Open Mon.-Fri. 7am-9pm, Sat. 8am-8pm. Neighborhood branches are everywhere (usually open 9am-6pm, Sat. 9am-noon); look for the little yellow "POST" signs.

Telephones: When calling Eastern Berlin from overseas, if dialing (30) doesn't work, you'll probably need operator assistance. **Telephone Code:** 030.

■ Accommodations

Even though tourists mob Berlin during the summer, thanks to the ever-growing hosteling and hotel industry, same-day accommodations aren't impossible to find, but, as always, it's best to call ahead. If you plan on visiting during the **Love Parade,** however, you'd better book ahead or plan on dancing all night (see p. 126).

For a DM5 fee, **tourist offices** will find you a room in a hostel, *Pension,* or hotel. Be prepared to pay at least DM70 for a single and DM100 for a double. There are also over 4000 private rooms *(Privatzimmer)* available in the city; the overwhelming majority are controlled by the tourist offices. Expect to pay DM80 for singles, DM100 for doubles, plus a single-night surcharge of DM5. For that price, there's a wide spectrum of locations, comfort levels, and amenities. Press for details, and be sure that they know your language abilities (if any). They often prefer to fill up the *Pensionen* first, so you may have to ask for private rooms.

Although most accommodations are in Western Berlin, the office does have some listings for private rooms in the eastern part of the city. The tourist offices have the pamphlet *Accommodations, Youth Hostel, and Camping Places in Berlin,* which lists hostels and inexpensive guest houses and hotels in English and German (DM2).

For longer visits (over 4 days) the various **Mitwohnzentralen** can arrange for you to housesit or sublet someone's apartment. Prices start at DM40 per night, plus a percentage fee, and go down the longer you stay. The **Mitwohnzentrale,** Joachimtalerstr. 17 (tel. 88 30 51; fax 882 66 94) in the Ku'Dorf mall, is the biggest (open Mon.-Fri. 9am-7pm, Sat. 11am-3pm). **Erste,** Sybelstr. 53 (tel. 324 30 31; fax 324 99 77), tends to be less chaotic (open Mon.-Fri. 9am-8pm, Sat. 10am-6pm). U-Bahn #7: "Adenauerpl." Usually the **Mitwohnzentralen** require you to pay up front unless you have, or can find a friend who has, a German bank account. Keep fees in mind—for short stays (less than a month) the standard commission is 20% of the final sum while for longer stays the rate is usually 25%, although the monthly prices are lower. Leases in Berlin start at any time—you don't need to wait for a new calendar month.

HOSTELS AND DORMITORY ACCOMMODATIONS

Hostels fill quickly with German school groups (especially in summer and on weekends)—always call ahead. All HI-affiliated hostels are for members only. They tend to attract school groups, and are liable to be overbooked. For an extra DM4, some hostels will give nonmembers a stamp and let you spend the night. To buy an **HI card,** head to Tempelhofer Ufer 32, 10963 Berlin (tel. 264 95 20; fax 262 04 37; open Mon., Wed., and Fri. 10am-4pm, Tues. and Thurs. 1-6pm). For non-Germans, membership cards cost DM36. HI-hostels also have curfews which hinder night-ragers and tend to regulate more strictly. Many hostels accept written or faxed reservations.

Kreuzberg

The Backpacker, Köthenerstr. 44, 10963 Berlin (tel. 262 51 40; email ante@aol.com). U-Bahn #2: "Potsdamer Platz"; from the Stresemannstr. exit, turn right on Stresemannstr., then right on Köthenerstr. If you don't mind the worn interior, it's one of the best budget options. Amenities include a kitchen, free map, and a supremely hip staff that updates you on nightlife. Friendly Anglophile atmosphere, close to Mitte's action. Reception open 7am-11pm, but check-in easiest 9-11am. No curfew. First night DM30, subsequent nights DM25. Sheets DM3. Laundry facilities DM5. On January 15, 1998, a **second location** will open in **Mitte,** Chausseestr. 102 (tel. 251 52 02). U-Bahn #6: "Zinnowitzerstr." or S-Bahn #1 or 2: "Nordbahnhof." The new location will offer all the amenities of the old hostel, as well as free pick-up service from the station for groups of 3 or more, discounted public transportation tickets, and **email access.** Doubles DM30 per person; triples and quads DM27. 5- and 6-bed-rooms DM25. Sheets DM4. Breakfast DM5-10.

Die Fabrik, Schlesischestr. 18, 10997 Berlin (tel. 611 71 16; fax 618 29 74). U-Bahn #1: "Schlesisches Tor." *Pension qua* hostel in a beautifully converted factory with lush green interior within walking distance of Kreuzberg's mad nightlife. The hotel rents **bikes** for DM16 per day. Reception open 24hr. Surprisingly comfortable Mehrbettzimmer sleep-in deal puts you up in a 16-bed room for DM30; singles DM66; doubles DM94 (honeymoon suite DM110); triples DM120; quads 144. Breakfast in the cafe downstairs DM10. Reserve or call ahead. Curfew? Rage all night, little pumpkin.

Mitte/Friedrichstr.

Circus, Am Zirkus 2-3 (tel. 28 39 14 33; email circus@mind.de). S-Bahn #3, 5, 7, 9, 75: "Friedrichstr." Brand new and close to Unter den Linden and Oranienburgerstr., Circus makes a heroic effort at hostel hipness, offering email service, **Internet access,** laundry machines, and a disco ball in the lobby. Mostly doubles, with a few 4- and 5-bed rooms. No curfew. Singles DM40; doubles DM62; triples DM86; 4- and 5-bed rooms DM27 per person. Breakfast not included. Sheets DM3.

Schöneberg—Wilmersdorf

Jugendgästehaus (HI), Kluckstr. 3, 10785 Berlin (tel. 261 10 97; fax 265 03 83). From Kurfürstendamm, bus #129 (direction: "Hermannpl."): "Gedenkstätte," or U-Bahn #1: "Kurfürstenstr.," then walk up Potsdamerstr., go left on Pohlstr., and right on Kluckstr. A highly abstract 8m conceptual "DJH" archway stands in front. While the "art" out front recalls the dark ages of 60s modernism, the 4- to 6-bed rooms are clean and modern. Reception open 1-1:45, 2:35-9:45, and 10:15pm-midnight. Curfew midnight; stragglers admitted at 12:30 and 1am. Lockout 9am-1pm; ring the bell later. DM32, over 26 DM41. Sheets and breakfast included. Key deposit DM10. Lockers and laundry facilities available. Call more than 2 weeks in advance.

Studentenhotel Berlin, Meiningerstr. 10, 10823 Berlin (tel. 784 67 20; fax 788 15 23). U-Bahn #4: "Rathaus Schöneberg" or U-Bahn #7: "Eisenacherstr.," or by bus #146 (from Zoo): "Rathaus Schöneberg," walk right on Freiherr von Stein, then cross Martin-Luther-Str. to Meiningerstr. Barren interior feels like a sanitarium, but same day rooms often available if you call from the station. Within walking distance of Schöneberg action. Reception open 24hr. English spoken. Singles DM59; doubles DM86; quads DM156 per person. Breakfast included.

CVJM-Haus, Einemstr. 10, 10787 Berlin (tel. 264 91 00; fax 261 43 08). U-Bahn #1, 2, or 4: "Nollendorfpl." Young men: it's fun to stay at the German YMCA, despite the institutional exterior. Palpably wholesome interior, all in tranquil blue. Act like a macho, macho man in the billiard and casino rooms or recede to the solace of the tea room. Reception open 8-11am and 4-9pm. DM40 per person for singles, doubles and dormitory rooms. Quiet time 10pm-7am and 1-3pm. You can get a key for curfew-free revelry. Breakfast included. Book ahead.

Jugendgästehaus Feurigstraße, Feurigstr. 63, 10827 Berlin (tel. 781 52 11; fax 788 30 51). U-Bahn #7: "Kleistpark," or bus #146 or 148. An unadorned brown stucco building in a busy district. 4- and 6-bed rooms that won't cramp your style. 200 beds. Good location for the bars and clubs of Schöneberg. Reception open 24hr. Dorms DM38 (DM27 after August). Singles DM55; doubles with shower DM90. Breakfast included. Sheets DM5 if staying less than 3 nights, otherwise free. Call from the station.

Steinplatz-Tiergarten

Jugendgästehaus am Zoo, Hardenbergstr. 9a, 10623 Berlin (tel. 312 94 10; fax 401 52 83), opposite the Technical University *Mensa*. Bus #145, or the short walk from the back exit of Bahnhof Zoo straight down Hardenbergstr. Advantage: it's within spitting distance of the Bahnhof Zoo. Disadvantage: the rooms are spartan and poorly lit. It's on the 5th floor; ride up in the elevator with international frat boy graffiti. Reception open 24hr. Check-in 10am. Check-out 9am. No curfew. Small dorms (4-8 beds) DM35; singles DM47; doubles DM85. Over 26 add DM5 to all prices. No reservations, but tends to have room if you call in the morning.

Haus Wichern, Waldenserstr. 31, 10551 Berlin (tel. 396 50 91; fax 396 50 92). The hostel's attractive stone exterior is a mere facade for the unadorned interior filled by school groups. 4-bed rooms with thin mattresses are often available, however. Reception open 24hr., check in by 10pm. No lockout. DM40. Breakfast included.

Tegel

Jugendherberge Ernst Reuter (HI), Hermsdorfer Damm 48, 13467 Berlin (tel. 404 16 10; fax 404 59 72). U-Bahn #6: "Alt-Tegel," then bus #125 (direction: "Frohnau/ Invalidensiedlung"): "Jugendherberge." Distant from the center in a placid suburb, on the edge of the forest. Lots of school groups necessitate reservations. 6-bed rooms. Curfew midnight. Stragglers admitted until 1am. DM26, over 26 DM33. Breakfast and sheets included. DM8 for laundry facilities. Fluent English spoken. Key deposit DM10. Closed Dec. 3-Dec. 28.

Jugendgästehaus Tegel, Ziekowstr. 161, 13509 Berlin (tel. 433 30 46; fax 434 50 63). U-Bahn #6: "Tegel," then bus #222 or night bus N22: "Titusweg." Old brick outside, new and bright inside with linoleum halls. On the north end of town by the Tegel parks. For a more communal experience, check out neighboring Internationales Jugendcamp Tegel (see **Camping,** p. 104). No curfew. Under 27 only. DM38. Breakfast and sheets included. Same-day rooms sometimes available.

Elsewhere in Berlin

Jugendgästehaus Nordufer, Nordufer 28, 13351 Berlin (tel. 451 70 30; fax 452 41 00). U-Bahn #9: "Westhafen," left over the bridge and left onto Nordufer for about 15min. Away from the center, but on the pretty, blue, swimmable Plötzensee Lake. Some singles, but more 4-bed rooms. Reception open 7am-midnight. No curfew. DM38. Breakfast buffet and sheets included. Swim in the adjacent *Freibad* (swimming pool) for DM5, students DM3.

Jugendgästehaus am Wannsee (HI), Badeweg 1, 14129 Berlin (tel. 803 20 35; fax 803 59 08). S-Bahn #1 or 3: "Nikolassee," turn left at the main exit, cross the bridge, and head left for 5min. Far from the center, but Wannsee has its own charm. The tan tile floors, open spaces, white plaster walls, and bright red trim are reminiscent of a municipal swimming pool. 62 4-bed rooms. Toilets shared between 2 rooms, showers between 6. Large groups of jolly kids make it impossible to get a room without booking 2 weeks in advance. DM31, over 26 DM40. Breakfast and sheets included. Key deposit DM20.

HOTELS AND PENSIONEN

Many small *Pensionen* and hotels are within the means of budget travelers, particularly since most establishments listed in *Let's Go* are amenable to *Mehrbettzimmer,* where extra beds are moved into a large double or triple. However, these benefits are really only for groups of three or more; hotels will not usually allow random individuals to crash together (lest an orgy spontaneously erupt). Most affordable hotels are in Western Berlin; the hotels in Mitte are ridiculously expensive, and other areas in the east still lack the facilities to support many visitors. The best places to find cheap rooms are around Savignypl. and down along Wilmersdorfstr. and its sidestreets.

Savignyplatz

Hotelpension Cortina, Kantstr. 140, 10623 Berlin (tel. 313 90 59; fax 31 73 96). S-Bahn #3, 5, 7, or 9 or bus #149: "Savignypl." High-ceilinged, bright, convenient, and hospitable. Reception open 24hr. Extra beds in rooms upon agreement. Small singles DM70; doubles DM120, with shower DM130; *Mehrbettzimmer* DM45-50 per person. Breakfast included.

Pension Knesebeck, Knesebeckstr. 86, 10623 Berlin (tel. 312 72 55; fax 313 34 86). S-Bahn #3, 5, 7, or 9: "Savignypl." Just north of the park. Friendly, large *Alt-Berliner* rooms, with faux Baroque stylings come with offerings for voluptuaries like couches and sinks. Hearty buffet-style breakfast served in a rather flyly decorated dining room. Reception open 24hr. Singles with showers DM85; doubles DM120, with showers DM140; big *Mehrbettzimmer* DM50-60 per person. Laundry machines DM2.50. Phone reservations must be confirmed by fax or letter.

Wilmersdorf-Schöneberg

Hotel-Pension München, Güntzelstr. 62 (tel. 857 91 20; fax 85 79 12 22). U-Bahn #9: "Güntzelstr." *Pension cum* gallery saturated with art by contemporary Berlin artists and sculptures by the owner. Superclean, white-walled rooms with TVs and phones. Singles DM60, with shower DM110; doubles DM80, with bath DM125. Breakfast DM9. Written reservations are best, but try calling before 2pm.

Hotel Sachsenhof, Motzstr. 7, 10777 Berlin (tel. 216 20 74; fax 215 82 20). Small and plainly decorated rooms that are clean and well-furnished in the middle of the Schöneberg cafe scene. Reception open 24hr. Singles DM57, with shower DM65; doubles DM99, with shower DM116, with bath (including an adorable bathtub with feet) DM126-156; DM30 per extra bed. Breakfast DM10.

Frauenhotel Artemesia, Brandenburgischestr. 18, 10707 Berlin (tel. 873 89 05; fax 861 86 53). U-Bahn #7: "Konstanzerstr." Pricey, but a rare bird—an immaculate, elegant hotel for women only. Rooms celebrate famous women in Berlin's history, while an outdoor terrace provides a damn fine view of contemporary Berlin. The **Artemesia Café** serves breakfast (Mon.-Fri. 7:30-10:30am, Sat.-Sun. 8-11:30am) and evening drinks (5-10pm) to an all-female (straight and lesbian) crowd that really digs Tracy Chapman. Reception open 7am-10pm. Singles DM99, with shower DM149; doubles DM169, with bath DM200; extra beds DM45 per person. Breakfast included. Alternatively, try to get the "last-minute, same-day" specials, with singles from DM79 and doubles from DM129 (without breakfast).

Kreuzberg

Pension Kreuzberg, Grossbeerenstr. 64, 10963 Berlin (tel. 251 13 62; fax 251 06 38). U-Bahn #6 or 7: "Mehringdamm" or bus #119. Decently priced rooms, small but well-decorated with things abstract in an old but grand building close to the Kreuzberg scene. Watch your head in the doorway to the bathroom lest you suffer the fate of Dennis Hopper in *Speed*. Reception open 8am-10pm. Singles DM70; doubles DM95; *Mehrbettzimmer* DM42 per person. Breakfast DM5.

Hotel Transit, Hagelbergerstr. 53-54, 10965 Berlin (tel. 785 50 51; fax 785 96 19). U-Bahn #6 or 7: "Mehringdamm," or bus #119 or night bus N19 (every 10-15min.). Party hard and crash gently in this tragically hip *Pension*. Reception area jams to techno. Big-screen MTV lounge open 24hr. Bar open until 2-3am. Rooms adorned with sleek, fake *Bauhaus* furnishings and showers. Reception seems to know its coolness quotient. If you anticipate a hangover, you can request breakfast at noon or later. Curfew? Lockout? Pshaw. Singles DM90; doubles DM152; triples DM140; quads DM180. Their "Sleep-In" deal allows you to share a *Mehrbettzimmer* with any other traveler for DM34. Breakfast included.

Charlottenburg

Charlottenburger Hof, Stuttgarterpl. 14, 10627 Berlin (tel. 32 90 70; fax 323 37 23). S-Bahn #3, 5, 7, or 9: "Charlottenburg" (across the street) or U-Bahn #7: "Wilmersdorferstr." Slick but expensive *Pension* with wall-art: Miró, Klee, and Dalí in the rooms. Spotless modern rooms with phones and TVs, plus a peaceful guest lounge with funky black chairs. Singles DM110 (D'oh!); doubles DM150. Prices for triples (DM180) and quads (DM200) return from orbit. Shower and bathroom in all rooms. Nov.-Dec 20-30% winter discounts. Breakfast in the adjoining Café Voltaire (see **Food**, p. 107) DM6. Laundry DM5. Sometimes has same-day space.

Elsewhere in Berlin

Hotel-Pension Hansablick, Flotowstr. 6 (tel. 390 48 00; fax 392 69 37). S-Bahn #3, 5, 7, 75, or 9: "Tiergarten." Somewhat pricey, but it's an absolute *Jugendstil* pearl, from the decorative ceilings to the marble entrance and lamps gracing the cobblestone streets in front. Breakfast room like a salon. All rooms have bath, hair dryer, phone, and cable TV. Some have patios from which you can watch ferries on the Spree. Few places like this survived WWII bombing, so call, write, or fax ahead for reservations. Reception open 24hr. Singles DM150; doubles DM175-215. In the low season (mid-July to Aug. and mid.-Nov. to Feb.) singles DM125; doubles DM150-170. Extra bed in the big doubles DM55. 5% discount if you mention *Let's Go*. July-Aug. same-day specials are available but without the *Let's Go* discount.

Hamburger Hof, Kinkelstr. 6 (tel. 333 46 02), in the old quarter of Spandau. U-Bahn #7: "Altstadt Spandau" (second-to-last stop). Easily accessible. A tiny, comfortable hotel with only 18 beds, but so far from the action that they usually have room. Small-town charm, but no English spoken. Diminutive singles DM55; more spacious doubles DM100. Breakfast included.

CAMPING

Deutscher Camping-Club runs two of the major campgrounds in Berlin; both are adjacent to the imaginary line tracing the site of the Berlin Wall. Written reservations can be made by writing the Deutscher Camping-Club Berlin, Geisbergstr. 11, 10777 Berlin. Otherwise, call in advance. Both sites charge DM9.50 per person, DM7 for a tent, and DM3.50 for children.

Dreilinden (tel. 805 12 01). U-Bahn #1: "Oskar-Helene-Heim," then bus #118: "Kätchenweg"; follow Kremnitzufer to Albrechts-Teergfen (about 20min.). A city campsite, surrounded on 3 sides by the vestiges of the Berlin Wall. The remains of a stretch of the *Autobahn* which fell into disuse after 1949 can be seen through the trees. The site's bar is an old border checkpoint. Open March-Oct.

Kladow, Krampnitzer Weg 111/117 (tel. 365 27 97). U-Bahn #7: "Rathaus Spandau," then bus #135: "Alt-Kladow" (the last stop). Switch to bus #234: "Krampnitzer Weg/Selbitzerstr.," then follow Krampnitzer Weg 200m. A store and restaurant complement the relaxed atmosphere by a swimmable lake. Open year-round.

Internationales Jugendcamp Fließtal, Ziekowstr. 161 (tel. 433 86 40). U-Bahn #6: "Tegel," then bus #222 or night bus N22: "Titusweg." Next to Jugendgästehaus Tegel (see **Hostels,** p. 102). Far away, but it's the next best thing to rolling a groovy doobie in your VW van, man. Blanket and mattress under a big tent with free showers DM10. Campfire-fire-fire every night, Beavis. Officially under 27 only, but rules are made for conformists, and they aren't into that sort of thing here. Lockout 9am-5pm. No reservations accepted—just show up and dig the far-out experience. Open July-Aug.

■ Food

Berlin's cuisine has joined the melting pot, with many delectable international culinary options saving you from the ubiquitous *Würste* and *Schnitzels* of other German cities. While many offerings from the German cuisine are palatable, Berlin's most notable home-grown option is the tasty, sweet **Berliner Weiße mit Schuß,** a concoction of local wheat beer with a shot of syrup. *Rotes* (red) is the most popular variety, made with fruity *crème de cassis* (blackberry) or *kirsch* (cherry) syrup; be careful when ordering a *Grünes* (green), which sometimes entails lemon-lime syrup, but may also mean a stomach-turning depth charge of *Jägermeister* liqueur.

Unfortunately, Berlin's **beer** offerings are like water compared to other national brews; the ubiquitous locally brewed *Schultheiss* and *Berliner Kindl* are among Germany's more lackluster brands. The breweries east of the former Wall offer little consolation, with the **Berliner Bürgerbrau** providing little for the refined palate. If you must try a Berlin brand, sample **Bären Pils** for a slightly bitter, flavorful experience. Fortunately the city's *Kneipen* offer typical Berlin cosmopolitanism: you'll be too busy sampling *Kölsch,* Guinness, and Munich beers to feel deprived.

Much typical Berlin food is Turkish: almost every street has its own Turkish **Imbiß** or restaurant. The *Imbiß* stands are a lifeline for the late-night partier; most are open ridiculously late, some 24 hours. The *Döner Kebab,* a sandwich of lamb and salad, has cornered the fast-food market, with *Falafel* running a close second. For DM3-5, either makes a small meal. To save money, opt for *Außer Haus* (take-out), as many *Imbiße* tack on an extra DM2 or so for eating on the spot. The second wave of immigration has brought quality Indian and Italian restaurants to Berlin.

There is no clear distinction between *Kneipen,* cafes, and restaurants; indeed , cafes often have better food and a livelier atmosphere than restaurants for much more reasonable prices. A gloriously civilized tradition in Berlin cafes is **Frühstück,** breakfast served well into the afternoon, sometimes 24 hours. Leisurely natives read the paper and linger over their fruit and cheese breakfasts; join them and relax with *Milchkaffee.* New cafes in Mitte and Prenzlauer Berg are rapidly providing stiff competition for their western counterparts; prices tend to be somewhat lower and portions larger, attracting a crowd of starving artists looking for a respite from their ascetic regime. In addition, street vendors with all shapes, sizes, and flavors of cheap eats fill **Alexanderplatz** every day, and the sprawling grocery department on the first floor of the nearby **Kaufhof am Alex** comes with a salad bar.

Aldi, Bolle, and **Penny Markt** are the cheapest **supermarket** chains, along with **Plus** stores, which are omnipresent in Wilmersdorf, Schöneberg, and Kreuzberg. Supermarkets are usually open Monday to Friday 9am-6pm, Saturday 9am-1pm, although the ridiculously strict laws that regulate their opening hours are starting to relax in the face of competition from smaller neighborhood stores, which stay open later. The best **open-air market** fires up Saturday mornings in Winterfeldtpl., though almost every neighborhood has one; there's a kaleidoscopic **Turkish market** in Kreuzberg on the banks of the Landwehrkanal every Friday. U-Bahn #1: "Kottbusser Tor." In Eastern Berlin, markets often set up under S-Bahn platforms.

WESTERN BERLIN

Mensen (University Cafeterias)

Mensa der Freie Universität, in the huge complex at Habelschwerdter Allee 45. U-Bahn #1: "Thielpl." or "Dahlem-Dorf." Conveniently located near the Dahlem museum. Meals from DM2 (ISIC required). Open Mon.-Fri. 11:15am-2:30pm. The **cafeteria** on the first floor has less hot food, more sandwiches, and is somewhat more expensive. Open Mon.-Fri. 8:15am-4pm.

Mensa TU, Hardenbergstr. 34. Bus #145: "Steinpl.," or walk 10min. from Bahnhof Zoo. The mightiest of Berlin's *Mensas*, serving *haute cuisine* (by cafeteria standards), as well as rather good vegetarian *(Bio Essen)* dishes. Meals DM4-5. The cafeteria downstairs has longer hours and slightly higher prices. Meals DM4-6. *Mensa* open Mon.-Fri. 11:15am-2:30pm. Cafeteria open Mon.-Fri. 8am-7:45pm.

Bahnhof Zoo-Ku'damm Area

Café Hardenberg, Hardenbergstr. 10. Big *belle époque* spot, opposite the TU *Mensa,* but with a bit more atmosphere. Funky music, artsy interior, and lots of students. Breakfast served 9am-5pm (DM4-8). Most entrees well under DM13. Also good for a few drinks (grog DM4). Open Sun.-Thurs. 9am-1am, Fri.-Sat. 9am-2am.

Restaurant Marché, Kurfürstendamm 15, just a couple of blocks down from Bahnhof Zoo and the *Gedächtniskirche.* Run by the ubiquitous Mövenpick restaurant company, this place themes itself around a French marketplace. Probably the most affordable lunch on the Ku'damm. The colorful, very *Euro* cafeteria area is full of fresh produce, salads, grilled meats, pour-it-yourself wines, and hot pastries (DM12-25). Free ice water! Open daily 8am-midnight. AmEx, Visa.

KaDeWe, Tauentzienstr. 21 (tel. 212 10). U-Bahn #1, 3, or 4: "Wittenbergpl." Satiate every desire in the 6th-floor food emporium of this tremendous department store. Bright, beautiful stands happily heaped with cabbage and caviar. An entire wing devoted just to tinned fish. The prices? Ah, but such a joy! Open Mon.-Fri. 9am-8pm, Sat.-Sun. 9am-4pm.

Savignyplatz

Schwarzes Café, Kantstr. 148 (tel. 313 80 38), near Savignypl. Knotty interior full of hip young folks. Dark walls, big-band music, and dapper waiters. It's not so cool to pay DM4.20 for 0.2L of apple juice—but hey, they have breakfast at all hours (DM7-13). Open Wed.-Mon. 24hr., Tues. from 6pm on.

Mexico Lindo, Kantstr. 134 (tel. 312 82 18), on the corner of Wielandstr. S-Bahn: "Savignypl." One of the cheaper Mexican restaurants popping up throughout Berlin. Lunch specials (including vegetarian dishes) DM9-13. *Quesadillas* from the *Imbiß* stand (open Mon.-Fri. noon-7pm) DM3.50. Open daily 5pm-midnight.

Schöneberg-Wilmersdorf

Baharat Falafel, Winterfeldtstr. 37. U-Bahn #1 or 2: "Nollendorfpl." Perhaps the best falafel in Berlin. Five plump chick-pea balls in a fluffy pita, covered with veggies and heavenly sesame, mango, or chili sauce, for DM6. Bright shop with Arab pop and watercolors depicting selfless falafel balls leaping into waiting pita. Open Mon.-Sat. 10am-3am, Sun. 11am-3am. Closed last week in July.

Café Belmundo, Winterfeldtstr. 36 (tel. 215 20 70), on a street loaded with bohemians. U-Bahn #1 or 2: "Nollendorfpl." Young crowd, with outdoor tables and breakfast until 3pm. Sun. breakfast buffet (DM14) until 3pm. Salads DM4.50-10. Open Mon.-Sat. 9am-1am, Sun. 10am-whenever.

Rani, Goltzstr. 32 (tel. 215 26 73), behind the church on Winterfeldtpl. U-Bahn #1 or 2: "Nollendorfpl." Very casual and cheap Indian restaurant popular with students. Most dishes DM6-10. Generous portions. Open daily 11am-2am.

Kurdistan, Uhlandstr. 161 (tel. 883 96 92). U-Bahn #15: "Uhlandstr." One of Berlin's most exotic and appetizing offerings. Fabulously spiced *Yekawe* (meat with rice, raisins, and cinnamon) DM15. Most entrees DM15-20. Brush up on your Kurdish with one of the grammar books lying around, or challenge the owner to a game of backgammon. Open Mon.-Sat. after 5pm.

Bella Italia, Maaßenstr. 12, U-Bahn #1 or 2: "Nollendorfpl." Damn cheap Italian food, with some chairs outside on which to sit and watch people go by. The pasta dishes offer the best value for the money; around DM6 gets a plate of spaghetti. Open daily 11am-1am.

Charlottenburg-Tiergarten

Café Voltaire, Stuttgarterpl. 14 (tel. 324 50 28). S-Bahn #3, 5, 7, or 9: "Charlottenburg," or U-Bahn #7: "Wilmersdorferstr." Cafe-bistro-gallery with a talkative crowd. Close to a whole array of cafes and the *Kino Klick,* farther down the street at Winterscheidtstr. An extensive menu with great breakfasts (DM6-8; served 5am-3pm) and warm meals (noon-5am). Open daily 24hr.

Rogacki, Wilmersdorferstr. 145. A gargantuan delicatessen, with everything from stuffed grape leaves to caviar. A nice selection of meats and cheeses for do-it-yourself sandwiches. The fish stands inside are very popular at lunchtime. Soups DM5. Herring with potatoes DM6. Open Mon.-Fri. 9am-6pm, Sat. 9am-1pm.

Ashoka, Alt-Moabit 49 (tel. 313 20 66). U-Bahn #9: "Turmstr." A friendly, entirely vegetarian, neighborhood Indian place. Huge portions DM6-10, including the exotic and delicious banana curry. Open daily 12:30pm-midnight.

Kreuzberg

Morena, Wienerstr. 60 (tel. 611 47 16). U-Bahn #1 or 12: "Görlitzer Bahnhof." A gracious, roomy cafe with some of Kreuzberg's best *Frühstück* (DM5-8.50, served 9am-5pm), as well as a selection of international magazines and newspapers. Spend a leisurely morning or afternoon here, enjoying breakfast and people-watching. Great blue-tiled interior. Open Sun.-Thurs. 9am-4am, Fri.-Sat. 9am-5am.

Die Rote Harfe, Oranienstr. 13 (tel. 618 44 46), in Heinrichpl., the center of Kreuzberg. U-Bahn #8: "Moritzpl." or 1: "Kottbusser Tor." Leftists and grizzled types eating solid German food. The *Schweizer Schnitzel* (DM15.90) and the *Algäuer Käsespätzle* (DM9.90) are bound to spark radicalism, even in stodgy you. Three-course lunch (DM15). Open Sun.-Thurs. 10am-2am, Fri.-Sat. 10am-3am.

Café Abendmahl, Muskauerstr. 9 (tel. 612 51 70). U-Bahn #1: "Görlitzer Bahnhof." While some of the *Ecce Homo* decorative motifs are a touch overbearing, the restaurant is a favorite for gay and lesbian (and even hetero) Berlin with delicious vegetarian and fish dishes. Substantial salads and artichoke dishes run DM9.50-15.50. Open daily 6pm-1am; best to reserve on weekends.

Café V, Lausitzerpl. 12 (tel. 612 45 05). U-Bahn #1: "Görlitzer Bahnhof." Berlin's oldest vegetarian restaurant, not an 80s miniseries. Try the *Tofu-Würstchen* with scrambled eggs and tomato sauce (DM10.50). Open daily 10am-2am.

PowWow, Dieffenbachstr. 11. U-Bahn #8: "Schönleinstr." Large satisfying helpings of "American Indian" food. Yes, many Germans *are* obsessed with the American West. Don't ask why. Dishes have names like "General Custer's Disaster" (steak with herb butter and fries; DM19). Among the Teutonic cowboys are a number of Kreuzberg artists reveling in the campiness of it all. Open summer Mon.-Sat. noon-4am, Sun. 11am-4am; winter Mon.-Sat. 5pm-4am, Sun. 11am-4pm.

Pagode, Bergmannstr. 88 (tel. 691 24 40). U-Bahn #6: "Mehringdamm" or U-Bahn #7: "Gniesenaustr." Thai noodles, salads, and spring rolls made to order in a tiny green

---

What's a Döner?

When this question was posed to Germany's *Döner* dealers, the response was astonishment. After all, everyone knows what a *Döner Kebab* is—chunks of lamb stuffed in a Turkish *Fladenbrot* topped with vegetables and a mysterious sauce. Yet where does the name come from? Vendors in northern Germany unanimously insisted that it comes from Berlin and told us not to get any ideas about this being authentic Turkish food. But we learned that the German "Dön" comes from the Turkish word meaning "to turn," and that the meat is thus named a *Döner* because it revolves as it cooks. The origin of *"Imbiß"* is also intriguing. Today it's used to refer to a snack bar, but the term actually comes from the Middle High German *entbeißen,* which means, literally, "to bite something out of something else"—kind of like picking the lamb out of the *Döner.*

bamboo-decked room. Kreuzberg youth fill the outdoor tables in summer. *Pad thai* DM16. Open daily noon-midnight.

Austria, Bergmannstr. 30 (tel. 694 44 40). U-Bahn #7: "Gniesenaustr." One of the best and most romantic places to get "German" food in Berlin. A classy interior and friendly sidewalk seating make up for slightly higher prices. Gulash DM21.50. Austrian *Kaiserschmarren* (pancake pulled to pieces and sprinkled with powdered sugar and raisins) DM9.50. Open Tues.-Sun. 6pm-1am.

Elsewhere in Western Berlin

Cybermind's Virtuality Cafe, Lewishamstr. 1 (tel. 327 51 43). Taste of the future by checking email, playing virtual reality games, and chomping down vegetarian food. Speakers blasting classics from Snoop Doggy Dog and Tupac let everyone outside know what kind of gat-toting badass puts on yellow goggles and waves his hands to the tune of DM7 per 15min. Open daily from 2pm.

EASTERN BERLIN

University Mensa

Humboldt University Mensa, Unter den Linden 6, in the back of the University's main building. The cheapest *Mensa* in Berlin, and conveniently located for sightseeing in Eastern Berlin. Full meals from DM1.50. Student ID required. Open Mon.-Fri. 11:30am-2:30pm.

Oranienburger Straße-Mitte

Taba, Chausseestr. 106 (tel. 282 67 95). U-Bahn #6: "Zinnowitzerstr." Big portions of delicious, spicy Mexican and Brazilian food are spiced up further by live salsa music Wed. While most of the entrees are DM15-20, you can indulge in great *quesadillas* for DM13.50 or *empanadas* for DM11.50. On Wed., all entrees are DM10. Eat until you yell, with smug satisfaction, "I am the great Cornholio!" Open Sun.-Thurs. from 4pm, Tues.-Sat. from 6pm.

Beth Café, Tucholskystr. 40 (tel. 281 31 35), just off Auguststr. S-Bahn #1 or 2: "Oranienburgerstr." Located in Mitte's small Orthodox Jewish neighborhood, it's a genuine kosher restaurant. Serves inexpensive Israeli specialties and a generous selection of kosher wines. Bagel with lox and cream cheese DM4. Other dishes DM5-15. Open Sun.-Thurs. 11am-10pm, Fri. 10am-6pm (in winter 9am-3pm), Sat. after Shabbat-midnight.

Die Kantine im Abgeordnetenhaus, Niederkirchnerstr. 3-5 (tel. 23 24 19 45). This heavily subsidized cafe in the Preußischen Landtag serves food for German ministers and the public at large. Helmut Kohl-sized portions of good solid food, including vegetarian dishes. Open Mon.-Fri. 1:30-3:30pm, Aug. Mon.-Fri. 8am-3:30pm.

The Oscar Wilde, Friedrichstr. 112a (tel. 282 81 66). U-Bahn #6: "Oranienburger Tor." The home-away-from-home for Berlin's expatriate Irish. Irish Stew, fried eggs, chips (i.e., fries), and Guinness for reasonable prices. Live music, usually of the Irish persuasion (Thurs.-Sat.). Open Sun.-Thurs. 11am-2am, Fri.-Sat. 11am-3am.

Prenzlauer Berg

Die Krähe, Kollwitzstr. 84 (tel. 442 82 91), off Kollwitzpl. U-Bahn #2: "Senefelderpl." Check out the psychedelic "crow" tapestry. Bright crowd orders from changing weekly menu; mighty satisfyin' breakfasts under DM10, whopping salads DM11. The popular Sun. buffet lets you load up until you burst for DM13.50. Open Mon.-Thurs. 5:30pm-1am, Fri.-Sat. 5:30pm-2am, Sun. 10:30am-1am.

Ostwind, Husemannstr. 13 (tel. 441 59 51). U-Bahn #2: "Senefelderpl." Chinese food that seeks to bridge the cultural divide between East and West. Prenzlauer hipsters indulge in the dim sum or *Shao-Lin Min* (noodles with tofu, lotus, broccoli, and carrots) for DM12.50. Open Mon.-Sat. 6pm-1am, Fri.-Sat. 10am-3am.

Daye, Danzigerstr. 24. U-Bahn #2: "Eberswalderstr." Turkish *Imbiß* option with hours to get you through a Prenzlauer Berg night and delectable *Döner*s that are spicy enough to send unprepared Germans reeling. The hearty chicken *Döner* is a good meal (DM4.50). Open Sun.-Thurs. 10am-2am, Fri.-Sat. 10am-3am.

Village Voice, Ackerstr. 1a (tel. 282 45 50). U-Bahn #8: "Rosenthalerpl." Cafe and bar *cum* bookstore trying hard for NYC hipness. Multilingual literature and inexpensive fare; the nachos and tacos beat the campy books. Open Mon.-Sat. 9am-2am, Sun. 11am-2am. Thurs. at 9pm, they show high-brow films, some in English (DM2).

Café Restauration 1900, Husemannstr. 1 (tel. 442 24 94), at Kollwitzpl. U-Bahn #2: "Eberswalderstr." Alternative interior on a street decorated in Potemkin-village-esque 19th-century style. Decent food at reasonable prices. German, French, and Italian wines. Open Mon.-Fri. 11am-2am, Sat.-Sun. 10am-2am.

■ Sights

Berlin can be just as disconcerting in its complexity as it is stunning. For a guide to the city's major neighborhoods, see page 91. Below, the sights are organized into five major sections: **Central** sights, **Western** Berlin, **Eastern** Berlin, **Museums,** and the **Outer Boroughs.** Most of central Berlin's major sights lie along the route of **bus #100,** which travels from Bahnhof Zoo to Prenzlauer Berg, passing the Siegessäule, Brandenburg Gate, Unter den Linden, the Berliner Dom, and Alexanderpl. along the way. A typical way to sight-see is to purchase a four-trip *Sammelkarte* public transport ticket (DM12) and use it to follow the route of the bus, getting off periodically to view sights of interest. Remember that each "click" is good for two hours after validation. This method is cheaper than a package tour, and there's usually an amateur tour guide on the #100 bus trying to impress his friends.

BETWEEN EASTERN AND WESTERN BERLIN

For decades a barricaded gateway to nowhere, today the **Brandenburg Gate** is perhaps the one structure that most symbolizes reunited Berlin. Standing directly in the center of the city, it opens east onto Unter den Linden and west onto the Tiergarten park and Straße des 17. Juni. Built during the reign of Friedrich Wilhelm II as an image of peace, the gate was a symbol of the Cold War east-west division. This locked door embedded in the Berlin Wall did not actually open until December 22, 1989, more than a month after the Wall fell. The images broadcast around the world of East and West Berliners dancing together atop the Wall were all filmed at the Brandenburg Gate, since this section of the wall was the only part with a flat top—everywhere else, the top is curved, preventing would-be escapers from getting a good grip.

The **Berlin Wall** itself is a dinosaur, with only fossil remains still visible. Erected overnight on August 13, 1961 (initially as a fence), the 140km wall separated families and friends, sometimes even running through people's homes. In the early 1970s, a second wall was erected parallel to the first; the space in between them (about the width of a street) became known as the **"death strip."** The 1989 wave of liberalization in other Communist countries and mass demonstrations of East Germans demanding the right to travel freely finally drove the government to open its borders and dismantle the Wall (and itself). Portions of the reinforced concrete structure of the Wall are preserved near the *Hauptbahnhof* and by Potsdamer Platz. The longest remaining bit is the brightly painted **East Side Gallery,** a 1.3km stretch of cement slabs that also passes as one of the world's largest open-air art galleries. S-Bahn: "Hauptbahnhof." The murals are not the remnants of Cold War graffiti, but rather the efforts of an international group of artists who gathered here in 1989 to celebrate the city's openness. The scrawlings of later tourists have been added to their work. Occasionally, late-coming *Mauerspecher* (wall-peckers) nibble at the edges of the Gallery, trying to knock off a chunk for posterity, but most of the pieces you'll see for sale at the tourist stands are fake.

The demolished wall has left an incompletely healed scar across the city center. From the western side, newly planted trees extend the Tiergarten park a few more meters. But the numerous cranes jutting up into the sky on the eastern side have become as much a symbol of Berlin as the TV tower on Alexanderpl. **Potsdamer Platz,** cut off by the wall, was once a major Berlin transportation hub designed under Friedrich Wilhelm I to approximate Parisian boulevards, with the primary purpose of moving troops quickly. The land surrounding the *Platz* is now a chaotic mess of construction machinery and half-dug foundations. The shiny **"InfoBox,"** a temporary, bright-red structure near the Potsdamer Platz U- and S-Bahn station, contains an exhibit describing in exhaustive and enthusiastic detail the future Daimler-Benz-sponsored offices on the site, as well as various railway improvements that will ostensibly make Berlin the transport hub of Europe. The construction was supposed to conclude by 2000, but the date has been pushed back to 2004 (InfoBox open daily 9am-7pm; free). Near Potsdamer Platz, unmarked and inconspicuous, lies the site of the **Führerbunker,** where Hitler married Eva Braun and then ended his life. In macabre irony, the actual bunker site is now a playground (behind the record store at Wilhelmstr. 92); tourists looking for it often mistakenly head for the visible bunker at the southern edge of Potsdamer Platz. Plans to restore the bunker were shelved amid fears that the site would become a shrine for the radical right. As with the re-opening of *Geisterbahnhöfe* ("ghost stations" under East Berlin, once guarded by troops and bypassed by the U-Bahn), reunification has let all sorts of forgotten underground ghosts loose in Berlin.

Just south of Potsdamer Platz, between the center of Schöneberg and the former no-man's-land surrounding the wall, stands the **Martin-Gropius-Bau,** at Stresemanstr. 110. The decorous edifice was designed by Martin Gropius, a pupil of Schinkel and uncle of *Bauhausmeister* Walter Gropius. There's nothing *Bauhaus*-like about the red-and-white Neoclassical building, though it's more graceful than most Prussian turn-of-the-century fare. Today the building holds a museum of applied and fine arts as well as a dynamic **Jewish Museum** (see **Museums,** p. 121). Nearby at Potsdamerstr. 33, funkadelic Modernism rules the exterior of the huge **Staatsbibliothek Preußischer Kulturbesitz** (tel. 26 61), the library that starred in Wim Wenders's *Wings of Desire*—the angels found its main reading room a perfect spot to observe humanity. Good thing they didn't come at exam time, or even they would have had trouble finding a table (open Mon.-Fri. 9am-9pm, Sat. 9am-5pm).

A blood-red Soviet flag hangs over the door of the **Haus am Checkpoint Charlie,** Friedrichstr. 44 (tel. 251 10 31). U-Bahn: "Kochstr." or bus #129. A strange, fascinating museum on the site of the famous border crossing point, with an uneasy mixture of blatant Western tourist kitsch and didactic Eastern earnestness, it is still one of Berlin's most popular tourist attractions. On the ground floor, flashiness is the order of the day; an expensive snack bar is crammed against a ticket desk covered with postcards, mugs, posters, books, and "Communist" baubles. Right by the door stands the car in which Johannes Ehret smuggled his girlfriend across the border in 1988. Upstairs you can find out everything you've ever wanted to know about the Wall or various ways of escaping over it, while studying the history of human rights struggles throughout the world. The exhibits are in German, English, French, and Russian. Documentaries in German are shown daily from 9am to 5:30pm (open daily 9am-10pm; DM7.50, students DM4.50).

WESTERN BERLIN

The Reichstag

Just to the north of the Brandenburg Gate sits the imposing, stone-gray **Reichstag** building, former seat of the parliaments of the German Empire and the Weimar Republic, and future home of Germany's governing body, the *Bundestag*. In 1918 Philipp Scheidemann proclaimed a German republic from one of its balconies with the words *"es lebe die deutsche Republik"* ("the German Republic lives"). His move turned out to be wise, since two hours later Karl Liebknecht, in the Imperial Palace a few kilometers away on Unter den Linden, announced a German Socialist Republic, ironically on the site that later supported the parliament of the GDR. (For more on the Imperial Palace, see **Eastern Berlin,** p. 114.) Civil war followed in Berlin and much of the rest of Germany. The government fled to Weimar to draw up a new constitution, but over the course of the next decade the *Reichstag* became the fractured center of the economically troubled Republic. As the Republic declined, Nazi members showed up to sessions in uniform, and on February 28, 1933, a month after Hitler became Chancellor, fire mysteriously broke out in the building. The fire provided a pretext for Hitler to declare a state of emergency, giving the Nazis broad powers to arrest and intimidate opponents before the upcoming elections. The infamous end result was the Enabling Act, which established Hitler as legal dictator and abolished democracy. A conceptual monument outside recalls the 96 members of the Reichstag executed by the Nazis.

In the summer of 1995, the Reichstag metamorphosed into an artsy parcel, when husband-and-wife team **Christo** and **Jeanne-Claude** wrapped the dignified building in 120,000 yards of shimmery metallic fabric. Tourists and residents alike marvelled at the effect, but after three weeks, the cloth came down and less picturesque scaffolding went up as the effort to restore the building for the government's return by 1999 commenced in earnest. The government held a massive design competition for the building's new dome (the original was destroyed in World War II). The current plans call for a huge glass dome surrounding a large mirror. The design will likely change, however, since a scale model of the design fried the miniature model ministers inside like ants under a magnifying glass.

Tiergarten and Kurfürstendamm

The lush **Tiergarten** in the center of old Berlin is a relief from the neon lights of the Ku'damm to the west and the din and dust of construction work to the east. Spreading over the northeast corner of Western Berlin, the vast landscaped park was formerly used by Prussian monarchs as a hunting ground. As you walk along its canals, notice the old streetlamps; each Prussian city sent one to the capital. In the heart of the Tiergarten, the slender 70m **Siegessäule** (victory column), topped by a gilded statue of winged victory (where Bruno Ganz hung out in *Wings of Desire*), commemorates Prussia's humiliating defeat of France in 1870. In 1938, the Nazis moved the monument from its former spot in front of the *Reichstag* to increase its height and make it more impressive. Despite the bad taste their militarism leaves in the mouth, they did improve the view. Climb 285 steps to the top for a panorama of the city (open April-Nov. Mon. 1-6pm, Tues.-Sun. 9am-6pm; DM2, students DM1). Radiating out from the column, the **Straße des 17. Juni** bisects the park from west to east. At the eastern ends stands the **Soviet Army Memorial** (yes, you're still in Western Berlin) flanked by a pair of giant toy tanks. South of the memorial, Entlastungstr. leads to the highly modern, bright yellow buildings of the **Tiergarten complex,** which includes the Philharmonic, the *"Staabi"* library (above), and a host of museums (see **Museums,** p. 118).

During the city's division, West Berlin centered around **Bahnhof Zoo,** the only train station in the world to inspire a rock album stadium tour (the U2 subway line runs through the station, but this is just a coincidence). At the nearby Breitscheidpl., the shattered **Kaiser-Wilhelm-Gedächtniskirche,** nicknamed "the rotten tooth" by Berliners, stands as a sobering reminder of the destruction caused during World War II. The shattered tower, its jagged edges silhouetted against the sky, serves as one of Berlin's most striking sights. The ruins house an exhibit showing what the church used to look like, as well as shocking photos of the entire city in ruins just after the war (exhibit open Tues.-Sun. 10am-4pm). The ruins have unfortunately been submitted to the eternal torture of juxtaposition with a hideous "modern" church, built in 1960s concrete-and-stained-glass chic (church open daily 9am-7pm). In the summer, Berlin's many leftists, foreigners, young people, and others often gather in front of the church to speak out, converse, sell watches, play bagpipes and sitars (not at the same time), breakdance, perform crude imitations of Chancellor Kohl, and generally act up. Stretching several kilometers to the west from Breitscheidpl., the **Kurfürstendamm** (so damm coo' it's called **Ku'damm**) is Berlin's biggest and fanciest shopping strip, lined with designer boutiques and pricey hotels. The renowned **Zoo** (not the station, but the menagerie) is one of the best in the world, with many animals displayed in open-air habitats instead of cages (main entrance directly across from the train station). The second entrance across from Europa Center is the famous **Elephant Gate,**

Budapesterstr. 34, a delightfully decorated pagoda of pachyderms (open daily 9am-6:30pm; Oct.-Feb. 9am-5pm; March-April 9am-5:30pm; DM11, students DM9, ages 3-15 DM5.50). Next door is the excellent **Aquarium,** Budapesterstr. 32, which houses broad collections of insects and reptiles as well as endless tanks of wide-eyed, rainbow-colored fish. Its pride and joy is its 1000 lb. **Komodo dragon,** the world's largest reptile, a gift to Germany from Indonesia. Also check out the psychedelic jellyfish tanks, filled with dozens of translucent sea nettles. (Open daily 9am-6pm. Aquarium DM8, students and kids DM5. Combination card to aquarium and zoo DM17, students DM14, children ages 3-15 DM8.50.)

Schöneberg

Further south in the district of Schöneberg stands the **Rathaus Schöneberg,** where West Berlin's city government used to convene during the 1960s. U-Bahn #4: "Rathaus Schöneberg." On June 26, 1963, 1.5 million Berliners swarmed the streets beneath the sleek tower to hear John F. Kennedy reassure them of the Allies' commitment to the city. Kennedy's speech ended with the now-famous words, "All free men, wherever they may live, are citizens of Berlin. And therefore, as a free man, I take pride in the words **Ich bin ein Berliner.**" For the record: this is a grammatically correct expression, and it means what Kennedy wanted to say, although a native would say *"Ich bin Berliner."* In 1993, a conceptual art exhibit was set up on the streets near the *Rathaus.* If you look closely, you'll notice some of the street signs have black-and-white placards above them—they state some of the Nazi edicts against Berlin's Jews. A number of these signs can be seen on Grunewaldstr. Not too far away is **Fehrbellinerplatz,** a standard example of Nazi architecture. These gruesomely regular prison-like blocks were meant to be model apartment houses; try to imagine a city full of them. U-Bahn #2 or 7: "Fehrbellinerpl."

Charlottenburg

The borough of Charlottenburg, one of wealthiest areas in Berlin, includes the area between the Ku'damm and the Spree river; like many of Berlin's neighborhoods, it was once a separate town. **Schloß Charlottenburg,** the vast, bright Baroque palace built by Friedrich I for his second wife, Sophie-Charlotte, presides over a carefully landscaped park on the western edge of the region. U-Bahn #2: "Sophie-Charlotte-Platz" or bus #145 from Bahnhof Zoo. The *Schloß's* many buildings include **Neringbau,** the palace proper, which contains many rooms filled with historical furnishings; the **Schinkel-Pavillion,** a museum dedicated to the Prussian architect; **Belvedere,** a small building housing the royal family's porcelain collection; and the **Mausoleum,** the final resting spot for most of the family. The **Galerie der Romantik,** a state museum housing Berlin's first-rate collection of German Romantic paintings, is located in a side wing (see **Museums,** p. 118). (Castle open Tues.-Fri. 9am-5pm, Sat.-Sun. 10am-5pm. Mausoleum open March-Nov. Entire palace complex *Tageskarte* DM15, students DM10, under 14 free.) Seek out the **Palace Gardens** behind the main buildings, with their small lakes, footbridges, fountains, and carefully planted rows of trees (open Tues.-Sun. 6am-9pm; free).

At the western edge of Charlottenburg is the **Olympia Stadion,** one of the more restrained architectural remnants of the Nazi Party. It was erected for the 1936 Olympic Games, in which Jesse Owens, an African-American, triumphed against the Nazis' racial theories by winning four gold medals. Hitler refused to congratulate Owens because of his skin color, but there's now a Jesse-Owens-Allee to the south of the stadium. U-Bahn #2: "Olympia Stadion."

Kreuzberg

Indispensable for a sense of Berlin's famous *alternative Szene,* or counter-culture, is a visit to **Kreuzberg,** an area loaded with cafes and bars. Kreuzberg has long been proud of its diverse population and liberal leanings: this is the place to see anti-Nazi graffiti and left-wing revolutionary slogans (in English, Turkish, Russian, Spanish, and German). During President Reagan's 1985 visit to Berlin, authorities so feared protests from this quarter that they cordoned the whole Kreuzberg district off without warning—an utterly unconstitutional measure. Much of the area was occupied by *Hausbesetzer* (squatters) during the 60s and 70s. A conservative city government decided to forcibly evict the illegal residents in the early 1980s, provoking riots and throwing the city into total consternation.

For a look at the district's more respectable face, U-Bahn #6 or 7: "Mehringdamm" and wander. Particularly interesting is the area around **Chamissoplatz,** bordered by Bergmannstr. and Fidicinstr. Bergmannstr. features an especially large number of old buildings and second-hand shops. At night, many bohemian cafes and punk clubs spill onto **Gneisenaustraße,** which heads west from the intersection with Mehringdamm. The cafes and bars on Oranienstr. boast a more radical element; the May Day parades always start on Oranienpl. U-Bahn #1 or 8: "Kottbusser Tor."

The **Landwehrkanal,** a channel bisecting Kreuzberg, is where Rosa Luxemburg's body was thrown after her murder in 1919. The tree-dotted strip of the canal near Hallesches Tor, **Paul-Linke Ufer,** may be the most beautiful street in Berlin, with its shady terraces and old facades. The east end of Kreuzberg near the old Wall is home to Turkish and Balkan neighborhoods, with a corresponding wealth of ethnic restaurants popular with radicals, students, and shabby genteel gourmets. From the Schlesisches Tor U-Bahn stop, a three-minute walk takes you across the **Oberbaumbrücke,** through a fragment of the wall and into the Friedrichshain district of the former East.

Spandau

Spandau is one of the oldest parts of Berlin. U-Bahn #7: "Altstadt Spandau." Many of the old buildings have been restored, including the massive 16th-century **Zitadelle** (citadel; U-Bahn #7: "Zitadelle"). Surrounded on all sides by water so as to be nearly impregnable, the star-shaped enclosure was the anchor of the medieval town. During the war, the Nazis used the fort as a chemical weapons lab, and in 1945 the Allies employed the *Zitadelle* as a prison to hold war criminals before the Nürnberg trials. Despite its grim name and past, the citadel is now a wistful place filled with old field-cannons, statues, and a **medieval history museum.** The thickly fortified *Juliusturm* tower, dating to circa 1200, is Spandau's unofficial symbol. (Open Tues.-Fri. 9am-5pm, Sat.-Sun. 10am-5pm. DM1.50. Complete tour Sat.-Sun. at 10am. DM3.) You can catch a boat from near the fort, or bus #145: "Johannestift" (the last stop) into the **Spandau Forest.** Also notable is the exceptionally fine **Rathaus,** which Spandauers defiantly constructed from 1911 to 1913 (at a cost of 3.5 million Marks) in a futile effort to stave off absorption into Berlin. U-Bahn #7: "Rathaus Spandau." **Spandau Prison** was demolished after its last inmate, Hitler's deputy Rudolf Hess, hanged himself in 1987 at age 93. Hess, a devoted party member from the beginning (he participated in the Beer Hall Putsch and took dictation for Hitler's *Mein Kampf*) was an unrepentant Nazi until his death. Lately this unsavory character has made a controversial comeback as a latter-day idol for neo-fascist groups; to Berlin's credit, the local anti-Hess response has been even stronger.

To the South: Dahlem, Zehlendorf, and the Grünewald

In the southern suburb of **Dahlem,** Berlin's **Botanischer Garten,** on Königin-Luise-Str., is a delight, especially the tropical greenhouses. Nearby, a sprawling cultural complex holds several important museums (see **Museums,** p. 118). The even more sprawling *Freie Universität* complex is next door. (U-Bahn #1: "Dahlem-Dorf.") Dahlem was the center of the former American Sector, home to many American military personnel stationed in Berlin. Although the Allied forces have almost entirely pulled out of Berlin, a strong American presence in the area persists.

West of Dahlem lies **Zehlendorf,** Berlin's ritziest residential district. At the southwestern corner of the district, the **Glienecker Bridge** crosses the Havel into Potsdam and what was once the GDR. Closed to traffic in Cold War days, it is famed as the spot where East and West once exchanged captured spies. The most famous such incident traded American U-2 pilot Gary Powers for Soviet spy Ivanovich Abel. Bus #116 from the Wannsee bus station to the end of the line.

BERLIN

In summer, clear your head in the nearby **Grünewald,** a 745-acre birch forest. While there, visit the **Jagdschloß,** a restored royal hunting lodge housing a worthwhile collection of European paintings, including works by Rubens, van Dyck, and Cranach. Call the tourist information for further info.

EASTERN BERLIN

Unter den Linden

The Brandenburg Gate opens eastward onto **Unter den Linden,** once one of Europe's best-known boulevards and the spine of old Berlin. All but a few of the venerable buildings near the gate have been destroyed. Farther down stands the statue of Friedrich the Great atop his horse. The designer of the edifice despised Fred; rumor has it that he placed the emperor's visage on the horse's behind. Ah, sweet myth. Many neighboring 18th-century structures have been restored to their original splendor. The pompous architecture can only hint at the Prussian conception of a capital and kingdom, with Unter den Linden as its axis. Past Friedrichstr., the first massive building on your left is the eastern branch of the **Deutsche Staatsbibliothek** (library), with a pleasant cafe inside. Beyond the library is the statue-crested, H-shaped main building of the **Humboldt Universität,** which boasts an imposing history as one of the finest universities in the world. The university's past faculty includes Hegel, Fichte, and Einstein, while the Brothers Grimm and Karl Marx are among its alumni. In the wake of a recent internal ideological *Blitzkrieg,* in which "tainted" departments were radically revamped or simply shut down, international scholars have descended upon the university to take part in its dynamic renewal.

Next door, the **Neue Wache** (new guard house) was designed by Prussian architect Friedrich Schinkel in unrepentant Neoclassical style. During the GDR era, it was known as the **"Monument to the Victims of Fascism and Militarism,"** and, ironically, was guarded by a goose-stepping East German soldier. After reunification, the building closed briefly but was reopened in 1993 as a war memorial. Buried inside are urns filled with earth from the Nazi concentration camps of Buchenwald and Mauthausen as well as from the battlefields of Stalingrad, El Alamein, and Normandy. Inside the dark enclosure, a statue by Käthe Kollwitz ("Mother with Dead Child") broods alone on the stone floor. The statue is not a Kollwitz original but a replica, enlarged by a factor of 30 thanks to a laser-guided lathe and the will of Chancellor Kohl. The replica has caused protests from the Kollwitz estate and other artists, as well as endless academic tussles about the nature of a copy vs. an "authentic original." The inscription reads: "To the victims of war and tyranny."

Across the way is **Bebelplatz,** where on May 10, 1933 the Nazis (aided by local students and faculty) burned nearly 20,000 books by "subversive" authors such as Heinrich Heine and Sigmund Freud—both Jews. The square is now the site of an excellent commemorative piece of art entitled "Bibliothek" (Library), by Israeli artist Micha Ullman; it consists of a hollowed-out chamber lined with illuminated empty white bookshelves. A plaque nearby is engraved with Heine's shockingly prescient 1820 quote: *"Nur dort wo man Bücher verbrennt, verbrennt man am Ende auch Menschen"* ("Wherever books are burned, ultimately people are also burned").

The building with the curved facade is the **Alte Bibliothek.** Once the royal library, it is now used by Humboldt University. On the other side of the square is the handsome **Deutsche Staatsoper,** fully rebuilt from original sketches by Knobelsdorf, the same architect who designed Schloß Sanssouci in Potsdam. The most striking of the monumental buildings is the **Zeughaus,** an old armory across the street near the bridge, which served before the war as the Prussian Army Hall of Fame and military museum; it has calmed down a bit to become the **Museum of German History** (see **Museums,** p. 121). From the museum you can enter the enclosed courtyard and see the tormented faces of Andreas Schlüter's "Dying Warriors."

Gendarmenmarkt

Berlin's most impressive ensemble of 19th-century buildings is a few blocks south of Unter den Linden at **Gendarmenmarkt,** also known as the French Quarter after it became the main settlement for Protestant Huguenots in the 18th century. The twin cathedrals **Deutscher Dom** and **Französischer Dom** grace opposite ends of the square. In the middle, the Neoclassical **Schauspielhaus,** designed by Schinkel, is Berlin's most elegant concert space, hosting international orchestras and classical performers. When first built, the hall was described as "music made solid." Destroyed by an air attack in 1945, it was painstakingly reconstructed and reopened in 1984.

Lustgarten and the Museumsinsel

Unter den Linden, after crossing over a small bridge, passes by the **Museumsinsel** (Museum Island), the home of four major museums and the **Berliner Dom.** Immediately to the left stands the pillared **Altes Museum,** created by Schinkel, who envisioned Berlin as the "Athens on the Spree." The huge granite bowl in front was supposed to adorn the main hall, but it didn't fit through the door. Next door, the beautifully bulky, multiple-domed *Berliner Dom* proves that Protestants can go overboard just as well as Catholics. Severely damaged by an air raid in 1944, the cathedral, built during the reign of Kaiser Wilhelm II, recently emerged from 20 years of restoration. The ornate gold and jewel encrusted interior, with its distinctively Protestant idols (Calvin, Zwingli, and Luther), is stunning if tacky to non-believers. (Open Mon.-Sat. 9am-8pm, Sun. noon-8pm. Admission to *Dom* DM5, students DM3. Comprehensive admission to the *Dom,* tower, and galleries DM8, students DM3. Free organ recitals daily at 3pm. Frequent concerts in summer; buy tickets in the church.) There's also a **Kaiserliches Treppenhaus** upstairs, with exhibits of period art and imperial stuff (open Mon.-Sat. 9am-8pm, Sun. noon-8pm; free).

Behind the Altes Museum lie the complex's three other enormous museums: the **Pergamon,** the **Bodemuseum,** and the **Alte Nationalgalerie** (see **Museums,** p. 118). The current **Altes Museum** was once the **Neues Museum,** but when the Altes Museum was bombed, the Neues Museum became the Altes Museum by default. Now the old museum is being restored and is known as the Alte Nationalgalerie, since the Neue Nationalgalerie is in the Tiergarten complex. Indeed, just like the rest of Berlin, its Museums exhibits an interesting interplay between the new and the old. The cobblestone square in front of the Altes Museum is known as the **Lustgarten.** Once a small park, it became a military parade ground under the Nazis; there are tentative plans to turn it back into a park, but for now it hosts occasional open-air concerts and art exhibits. Across the street, the Lustgarten turns into Marx-Engels-Platz under the glaring, amber-colored **Palast der Republik,** where the GDR parliament once met. In 1990, city authorities discovered that the building was full of asbestos and shut it down, and it remains closed as Berliners argue about whether to demolish it. The problems associated with the building itself are further complicated by the fact that the entire square used to be the site of the **Berliner Schloß,** the Hohenzollern family palace. Remarkably, the palace survived the war, although Soviet authorities demolished it in the 1950s in censure of its royal excess. The **Staatsrat** (Councils of the State) currently resides on the site—look for the modern building with a slice of the palace facade embedded in the middle. This section was preserved because Karl Liebknecht supposedly proclaimed a German socialist republic from the balcony. The newest plans for the site aim to demolish the *Palast der Republik* and rebuild the facade of the palace with a modern entertainment center behind it, but whether this plan will change is anybody's guess.

Crossing the Liebknecht-Brücke leads you to a small park in the right-hand side of the street; in the middle of the park stands a "conceptual memorial" consisting of steel tablets engraved with images of worker struggle and protest surrounding a huge statue of a seated Marx and a standing Engels. In 1990, a graffito appeared on the base of the statue: *"Wir sind unschuldig!"* ("We're innocent!"). The park and the street behind it used to be collectively known as the Marx-Engels-Forum; the park has not been renamed, while the street is now called Rathausstr.

Alexanderplatz and Nikolaiviertel

On the other side of the *Museumsinsel,* Unter den Linden becomes Karl-Liebknecht-Str., and leads into the bustling, concrete **Alexanderplatz.** Formerly the frantic heart of Weimar Berlin, the plaza—known affectionately to Berliners as "Alex" (a very endearing moniker)—was the setting for Alfred Döblin's montage-novel of the modern metropolis, *Berlin-Alexanderplatz.* Friends from all over Berlin often meet at the plaza's **Weltzeituhr,** the international clock—*wie Spät ist es in Schweden?*—but the undisputed landmark of the district is the **Fernsehturm.** The tower, the tallest structure in Berlin, is a truly awkward piece of design: picture the Death Star impaled on a long, thin, candy cane-striped spike. *Fernsehturm* is the German word for television tower, but the literal translation of "see far tower" is just as appropriate in this case—the view from the top (the spherical node 203m up the spike) is magnificent. A crowded elevator whisks tourists to the top. The *Fernsehturm* is the universal point of reference—everywhere in the city, you can pinpoint your location in relation to Alexanderpl. In a city with few tall buildings, it can be seen from almost every part of Berlin, as far west as Charlottenburg and as far east as Pankow and Weissensee (open daily March-Oct. 9am-1am; Nov.-Feb. 10am-midnight; DM8, children DM4).

The buildings surrounding the square include some GDR concrete-block classics, including the **Hotel Forum.** In the 1970s, the East German government made a concession to the people's implacable craving for bright lights by erecting some enormous neon signs, thus giving the area around Alexanderpl. the superficial trappings of a Western metropolis: "Chemical Products from Bitterfeld!" and "Medical Instruments of the GDR—Distributed in All the World!" Now nearly all of the buildings are covered with scaffolding, as the government tries to disguise the blatant GDR-era look of the structures. The constant demolition (or reconstruction) of GDR buildings has annoyed some *Ossies,* who are offended by what they view as an attempt to wipe out their history. In the first post-Communist months, Alexanderpl. was a rough place, the natural meeting ground for antagonistic gangs. But the pedestrians, working Berliners, and tourists prevailed. During the day, the square hums with con artists and vendors selling everything from Turkish *Fladenbrot* to black-market cigarettes smuggled from Russia. Around the U- and S-Bahn stations, the picture becomes seedier. Crowds congregate after dusk; watch your pockets.

The **Marienkirche,** a graceful 15th-century church, stands on the wide open plaza in front of the *Fernsehturm.* Nearby is the ornately gabled **Rotes Rathaus,** Old Berlin's famous 1869 red-brick town hall. Between 1949 and *die Wende,* it was home to East Berlin's city government; since 1990, the *Oberbürgermeister* and senate of the unified city have had their seat here. Behind the *Rathaus,* the twin spires of the **Nikolaikirche** mark Berlin's oldest building. Inside the 13th-century structure, a small museum documents the early history of the city (open Tues.-Sun. 10am-6pm; DM3, students DM1). The church gives the surrounding **Nikolaiviertel,** a carefully reconstructed *Altstadt,* its name. The Nikolaiviertel's narrow winding streets are popular and crowded; among the two dozen historic buildings are the **Knoblauchhaus,** at Poststr. 23, which houses a small museum documenting the life and times of architect Eduard Knoblauch (Tues.-Sun. 10am-6pm; DM2, students DM1) and the **Ephraim-Palais,** at the corner of Poststr. and Muhlendamm. The Nazis used this Rococo building as a sports museum; now it houses a collection of contemporary art from Berlin artists (open Tues.-Sun. 10am-6pm; DM3, students DM1).

Scheunenviertel—Oranienburgerstraße

Northwest of Alexanderpl. lies the **Scheunenviertel,** once the center of Berlin's Orthodox Jewish community. U- or S-Bahn: "Alexanderpl." or S-Bahn #1 or 2: "Oranienbergerstr." Prior to World War II, Berlin never had any ghettos. Jews lived throughout the city, although during the war they were deported to ghettos in Poland. Wealthier and more assimilated Jews tended to live in Western Berlin (Wilmersdorf was once 12% Jewish), while more Orthodox Jews from Eastern Europe settled in the Scheunenviertel (literally, "barn district," because in medieval times barns were placed here, just outside the city walls). Though evidence of Jewish life in Berlin dates back to the 13th century, the community was expelled in 1573 and not invited back for 100 years. Berlin's first synagogue opened in 1714 on the tiny **Heidereute-gasse,** near the corner of Rochstr. and Rosenstr. Remarkably, this synagogue was not destroyed during the *Kristallnacht* because of the presence of a post office which had been renting space in the building—however, it was later bombed during the war, never to be reconstructed. The spot is marked by a huge construction site. The former **Jewish welfare office** was located at Rosenstr. 2-4. In the adjacent park, a terra-cotta memorial was put up in October 1995—on the 54th anniversary of the first deportation of the Berlin Jews.

The shell of the **Neues Synagoge** stands at Oranienburgerstr. 30. This huge, "orien-tal-style" building was designed by the famous Berlin architect Knoblauch; its in-your-face quality reflects the community's heightened status. The synagogue, which seated 3200, was used for worship until 1940, when the Nazis occupied it and used it for storage. This synagogue, amazingly, also survived *Kristallnacht*—the SS torched it, but a local police chief, realizing that the building was an historical monument, ordered the Nazis to extinguish the fire. The synagogue was destroyed by bombing, but its restoration, largely financed by international Jewish organizations, began in 1988. The temple's beautiful gold-laced domes and some of the sumptuous interior have been reconstructed, and were opened to the public in May 7, 1995—the 50th anniversary of Germany's surrender. Two first-class exhibits (tel. 28 40 13 16) are housed here: **The New Synagogue 1866-1995,** chronicling the synagogue's history, and **Jewish History in Berlin,** documenting the history of Jews in Berlin since the 1660s (open Sun.-Thurs. 10am-6pm, Fri. 10am-2pm; DM5, students DM3). It is a som-ber sign of the times that the synagogue has been placed under 24-hour protection by machine gun-equipped Berlin police; to enter, you must pass through a metal detec-tor and, if you have a camera, demonstrate that it is not a weapon. A sign on the side of the building reads "Never forget this."

At the end of Große Hamburgerstr. near the intersection with Monbijoustr. are the remains of the **Alter Jüdische Friedhof** (Old Jewish Cemetery). Destroyed by the Nazis, the site now contains only the restored gravestone of the Enlightenment philos-opher and scholar Moses Mendelssohn; the rest is a quiet park. In front, a plaque marks the site of the **Jüdische Altersheim,** the Jewish old-age home which after 1942 served as a holding place for Jews before their deportation to concentration camps. Next door, yet another plaque marks the location of Berlin's oldest **Jewish school,** where Moses Mendelssohn taught. Mendelssohn, who was known as "the German Socrates," translated the Hebrew Bible into German, and supported interaction between Berlin's Jewish and non-Jewish communities. Corresponding with his humanist outlook, the school's pupils were half-gentile, half Jewish. The building was reopened as a school in 1992; its student body is still half-and-half.

The area around the Berlin Synagogue served as a showpiece for the East German government; many of the old buildings have been restored, and many of the new con-structions have a flair unusual for Berlin. In particular, **Oranienburgerstraße** has become a center of the squatter and artist communities, including many from the West, with a correspondingly rich quality of cultural and cafe life.

North Mitte

If any single man personifies the maelstrom of political and aesthetic contradictions that is Berlin, it is **Bertolt Brecht,** who called the city home. "There is a reason to pre-fer Berlin to other cities," the playwright once declared, "because it is constantly changing. What is bad today can be improved tomorrow." The **Brecht-Haus Berlin,** Chausseestr. 125 (tel. 282 99 16), near the intersection with Schlegelstr., is where Brecht lived and worked from 1953 to 1956. U-Bahn #6: "Zinnowitzerstr." If you understand German, you should take the guided tour, given in flamboyant Brechtian style. The **Brechtforum** on the second floor sponsors exhibits and lectures on artistic and metropolitan subjects; pick up a schedule. (Expected to re-open in late 1997. Open Tues.-Thurs. 9am-noon and 1-4pm, Fri. 9am-noon and 1-3pm. DM4, students DM2. Tours every 30min.) Directly adjacent to Brecht's house, the **Dorotheenstädtis-**

cher **Friedhof** (cemetery) contains the graves of a host of German luminaries, including Brecht and his wife Helene Wegel. Fichte and Hegel are buried side by side a few yards away; both graves are often festooned with flowers by admirers (or pillaged by frustrated students). At the end of the entrance path, next to the chapel on the right, is a map to the locations of the departed (open May-Aug. daily 8am-8pm; Feb.-April and Sept.-Nov. 8am-6pm; Dec.-Jan. 8am-4pm).

Prenzlauer Berg

Northwest of Oranienburgerstr. and Alexanderpl. lies **Prenzlauer Berg,** a former working-class district largely neglected by Eastern Germany's reconstruction efforts. Many of its old buildings are falling apart; others still have shell holes and embedded bullets from World War II. The result is the charm of age and graceful decay, slightly less charming for phoneless local residents with bad plumbing. Don't be surprised, however, at the mind-blowing rate of gentrification underway here; Prenzlauer Berg is one of the most sought-out locales for Berlin's wealthy jetset. Fancy shops and restaurants are popping up left and right, disturbing this neighborhood's reputation as a mellow, low-key retreat for artists and students. Unlike the loud, raucous scene in Kreuzberg and Mitte, Prenzlauer Berg is still more sedate and cerebral—which is not to say that it isn't lively. The streets here are studded with hip but casual cafes, bars, and squats, frequented by an ever-burgeoning crowd.

Especially worthy of a stroll is the restored **Husemannstraße,** home to the **Museum Berliner Arbeiterleben um 1900,** Husemannstr. 12, with a meticulously accurate reproduction of a Berlin working-class family apartment at the turn of the century (open Tues.-Thurs. and Sat. 10am-6pm, Fri. 10am-3pm; DM2, students DM1). The city government's anti-commune policy, heavily supported by the mainstream press, is in danger of destroying this counter-cultural renaissance. Meanwhile, the scene around green **Kollwitzplatz** is especially vibrant—a number of cafes have popped up within the past year. The statue of artist Käthe Kollwitz has been painted over a number of times in the past few years, in acts of affectionate rather than angry vandalism, most notably with big pink polka-dots.

Berlin's Jews found the slightly remote Prenzlauer Berg ideal, slowly gravitating there during the 19th and early 20th centuries. The **Jewish cemetery** on Schonhauser Allee contains the graves of composer Giacomo Meyerbeer and painter Max Liebermann (open Mon.-Thurs. 8am-4pm, Fri. 8am-1pm). U-Bahn #2: "Senefelderpl." Just off Kollwitzpl. stands one of Berlin's loveliest **synagogues,** Rykestr. 53, miraculously unharmed during *Kristallnacht* due to its inconspicuous location in a courtyard. It's generally not open to the public, but you can call 448 52 98 and arrange to be let in.

▨ Museums

Berlin is one of the world's great museum cities, with collections of art and artifacts encompassing all subjects and eras. The **National Prussian Cultural Foundation** (*Staatliche Museen Preußischer Kulturbesitz* or **SMPK**) runs the four major complexes—Charlottenburg, Dahlem, Museumsinsel, and Tiergarten—that form the hub of the city's museum culture. Since these museums are government-run, their prices and opening hours are standardized: Tues.-Fri. 9am-5pm, Sat.-Sun. 10am-5pm; DM4, students DM2. The first Sunday of every month offers free admission. A *Tageskarte* (good for all national museums, including the four above) is DM8, students DM4—a real bargain. Smaller museums deal with every subject imaginable, from sugar to tarts.

MUSEUMSINSEL (MUSEUM ISLAND)

The island holds the astoundingly broad treasure hoard of the former GDR in four separate museums. S-Bahn #3, 5, 7, or 9: "Haeckescher Markt." Unfortunately, a *Tageskarte* doesn't admit you to the Altes Museum.

Pergamonmuseum, Kupfergraben (tel. 20 35 54 44). One of the world's great ancient history museums from the grand old days when archaeology was king and

Heinrich Schliemann traversed the world, uncovering the debris of ancient civilizations. The scale of its exhibits is mind-boggling: huge rooms can barely contain the entire Babylonian Ishtar Gate (575BC), the Roman Market Gate of Miletus, and the majestic Pergamon Altar of Zeus (180BC). The altar's great frieze (125m long and 2.5m high) depicting the victory of the gods over the giants symbolizes the triumphs of Attalus I. The museum also houses extensive collections of Greek, Assyrian, Islamic, and Far Eastern art. Tours of Pergamon Altar at 11am and 3pm. A *Tageskarte* is required for entry. Last entry 30min. before closing. Entrance includes a free and nifty audio tour.

Alte Nationalgalerie, Bodestr. (tel. 220 03 81). 19th-century art in a beautiful historic building. The collection is mostly German but also includes a sizable number of works by French Impressionist painters.

Bodemuseum, Monbijoubrücke (tel. 20 35 55 03; fax 200 46 31). A world-class exhibit of Egyptian art, as well as late-Gothic wood sculptures, early Christian art, 15th- to 18th-century paintings, and an exhibit on ancient history. The *Kindergalerie* holds interactive exhibits designed for kids; it will reopen in 1998.

Altes Museum, Lustgarten. Converted into a special-exhibit museum, it has recently showcased powerhouse exhibitions of 20th-century avant-garde and political art. Regrettably, a *Tageskarte* for the other museums is not valid here. Exhibits run up to DM10, students DM5. Open Tues.-Sun. 10am-5pm, except during major exhibitions when Thurs. hours extend to 8pm.

DAHLEM

The **Staatliche Museen Preußischer Kulturbesitz, Dahlem,** Arnimallee 23-27 and Lansstr. 8 (tel. 830 14 65), looms near the *Freie Universität.* U-Bahn #2: "Dahlem-Dorf." Seven globe-spanning museums cram into one enormous building, plus another across the street. Pick up a map at the entrance; the museums are laid out very strangely. Various connections among the wings make it impossible for them to charge admission to any of the museums except the Gemäldegalerie and the Museum für Volkskunde. All museums operate with standard SMPK times and prices (p. 118).

Gemäldegalerie (Painting Gallery). One of Germany's most famous museums, and rightly so. It houses a stunning collection of Italian, German, Dutch, and Flemish masters. The world-class collection includes 26 Rembrandts (and *The Man with the Golden Helmet,* once incorrectly attributed to him), Bruegel (including *Netherlandish Proverbs*), Vermeer, Raphael, Titian, and Botticelli.

Skulpturen-Galerie (Sculpture Gallery), adjacent to the Painting Gallery. Mostly German statuary, with many gnarled, distraught-looking Gothic pieces, and others intended for churches. Worth a walk through.

Museum für Ostasiatische Kunst (East Asian Art). Mercifully empty of the blue-and-white porcelain you usually see in east Asian museums, this museum possesses a fabulous 17th-century Chinese throne with a representation of the Taoist paradise, as well as some exquisite Japanese screen-printing.

Museum für Islamische Kunst (Islamic Art). The most international of the museums, it follows the culture of Islam around the world. Captivating tapestries hang from ceiling to floor, while the illuminated manuscripts are particularly fascinating.

Museum für Indische Kunst (Indian Art). One of the most extensive collections around, with art and artifacts from all of India and Southeast Asia.

Museum für Völkerkunde (Ethnography). Fascinating collections of tools, artifacts, musical instruments, weapons, and clothing from Africa, Polynesia, Central and South America, and Southeast Asia. The Polynesian exhibit climaxes with a giant display of ornately decorated boats, many of which you can climb into. In the African section, you can play the *baláfon* (xylophone).

Museum für Volkskünde (Folklore), Im Winkel 6/8 (tel. 839 01 01). A hop away from the main Dahlem complex, this museum is dedicated to artifacts of lower- and middle-class life over the past 400 years from all over the world. The exhibit on 50s-80s pop culture is charming—never thought you'd see "Garbage Pail Kids" in a museum, did you? Scheduled to reopen in 1998.

BERLIN

CHARLOTTENBURG

Schloß Charlottenburg, Spandauer Damm (tel. 32 09 11). U-Bahn #2: "Sophie-Charlotte-Platz" or bus #145. The castle's wide-flung wings hold several museums set
against the romantic *Schloßgarten.* The **Kleiner Orangerie** sports special exhibitions.
Admission to the historic rooms of the *Schloß* costs DM8, students DM4, while a *Tageskarte* for the gardens and non-SMPK parts of the *Schloß* costs DM15, students
DM10 (see **Sights,** p. 112, for more on the *Schloß* and its grounds).

Ägyptisches Museum (Egyptian Museum), across Spandauer Damm from the castle.
   This stern Neoclassical building houses a fascinating collection of ancient Egyptian
   art, dramatically lit for the full Indiana Jones effect. The most popular item on display is the stunning 3300-year-old bust of **Queen Nefertiti** (1350BC), thought to be
   the most beautiful representation of a woman in the world.

Sammlung Berggruen, on Schloßstr. (tel. 311 16 14), in an identical building across
   the building across the street from the Egyptian museum. An incredible collection
   of Picasso and other modernists, this newly opened museum replaces the Antiquity
   Collection that was housed here until 1996. Like the Pergamon, an SMPK *Tageskarte* is required for admission.

Bröhan Museum, Schloßstr. 1a (tel. 321 40 29), next door to the Berggruen, features
   two floors of *Jugendstil* and Art Deco furniture, housewares, and paintings in the
   sleekest of surroundings. Bring a martini for full effect. Open Tues.-Sun. 10am-6pm.
   The SMPK *Tageskarte* is laughed at here; admission DM6, students DM3.

Galerie der Romantik, in the palace's Neuer Flügel, holds the Prussian crown's
   dynamic collection of 19th-century art. The unquestioned show-stealers are works
   by early 19th-century Prussian artist Caspar David Friedrich, whose specialty was
   hypnotically beautiful, bleak landscapes with infinite, looming skies and seas with
   tiny human figures precariously placed in their midst.

TIERGARTEN

Tiergarten-Kulturforum, is a complex of museums at the eastern end of the Tiergarten park, near the *Staatsbibliothek* (see **Sights,** p. 114) and Potsdamerpl. Bus #129
from the Ku'damm, S-Bahn #1 or 2, or U-Bahn #2: "Potsdamerpl." All have SMPK
times and prices.

Neue Nationalgalerie, Potsdamerstr. 50 (tel. 266 26 51). This sleek building,
   designed by Mies van der Rohe, now gives quantity its own quality in a collection
   devoted to large art displays. Billboard sized paintings and sculptures heavy enough
   to put Atlas in a truss fill the first two floors. The permanent collection includes
   works by Kokoschka, Barlach, Kirchner, and Beckmann, but these are often put
   away to make room for special exhibits that wouldn't fit through the door in any
   other museum. SMPK times and prices; call ahead to find out what's on display.

Musikinstrumenten Museum (Museum of Musical Instruments), Tiergartenstr. 1
   (tel. 25 48 10). Fittingly next door to the Philharmonic, this museum is a must for
   anyone even remotely interested in classical music. Musical instruments from every
   period, from 16th-century virginals to Pianolas. You can hear recordings of the
   period instruments being played. Tours Sat. at 11am (DM3).

Kunstbibliothek/Kupferstichkabinett (tel. 266 20 02), on Matthaikirchpl. A stellar
   collection of lithographs and drawings by Renaissance masters, including many
   Dürers and Botticelli's fantastic illustrations for the *Divine Comedy.*

Kunstgewerbemuseum (Museum of Applied Arts), Matthäikirchpl. 10 (tel. 26 66 29
   02). Lots of plates, jugs, and china in a museum more or less trace a millenniums
   advances in dining technology. The toasters, folding chairs, and TVs on display
   demonstrate that if you put it behind glass and shine spotlights on it, it's art.

ELSEWHERE IN WESTERN BERLIN

Martin-Gropius Bau, Stresemannstr. 110 (tel. 25 48 60). S-Bahn #1 or 2: "Anhalter
Bahnhof." Walter Gropius's uncle Martin designed this neo-Renaissance wedding

cake as a museum for and tribute to the industrial arts. The building alone is worth the price of admission (DM12, students DM6). Open Tues.-Sun. 10am-8pm.

Berlinische Galerie, on the second floor, is devoted to rotating exhibits of contemporary German art, much of it very famous, much of it very Picasso.

Jüdisches Museum, on the third floor, hosts extremely varied exhibits of painting, sculpture, and design; the only common thread is that the art has something to do with Jews in Germany.

Topographie des Terrors, in back of the Martin-Gropius-Bau, is built on top of the ruins of a Gestapo kitchen; the area used to be the site of the notorious Gestapo headquarters at Prinz-Albrecht-Str. (now Nieder-Kirchnerstr.). Very comprehensive exhibit (in German) details the Nazi party's rise to power and the atrocities that occurred during the war. English guides are available (DM2), but you don't need to understand the captions to be moved by the photographs. Free. Open Tues.-Sun. 10am-6pm. The adjacent **Prinz-Albrecht-Gelände,** a deserted wasteland near the site of the Wall, contains the ruins of most of the Gestapo buildings. Signs describe what once took place. Free. Open during daylight hours. Renovations might be finished by 1998, although there are tentative plans to relocate.

Bauhaus Archiv-Museum für Gestaltung, Klingenhöferstr. 13-14 (tel. 254 00 20). Bus #129 (from Ku'damm): "Lützowpl." or U-Bahn #1, 2, or 4: "Nollendorfpl." A building designed by *Bauhaus* founder Walter Gropius that houses a permanent exhibit devoted to the school's development. The temporary exhibits are based around questions of art theory. *The* place in Berlin to pick up design students. DM5, students DM2. Free on Mon. Open Wed.-Mon. 10am-5pm.

Museum für Verkehr und Technik (Transport and Technology), Trebbinerstr. 9 (tel. 25 48 40). U-Bahn #1: "Gleisdreieck" or "Möckernbrücke." Souvenirs from *Autobahn* speed-devils, medieval printing presses, trains that run on time, World War I fighting planes, and an historic brewery filled with historic empties. Combined admission with a yard of antique locomotives down the street. DM5, students DM2. Open Tues.-Fri. 9am-5:30pm, Sat.-Sun. 10am-6pm.

Käthe-Kollwitz-Museum, Fasanenstr. 24 (tel. 882 52 10). U-Bahn #15: "Uhlandstr." A marvelous collection of works by one of Germany's most prominent modern artists, much of it focusing on the themes of war and poverty. DM6, students DM3. Free on Mon. Open Wed.-Mon. 11am-6pm.

Brücke Museum, Bussardsteig 9 (tel. 831 20 29). From Bahnhof Zoo, bus #249: "Güntzelstr.," then bus #115: "Clayallee/Pücklerstr." (13 stops; 30min.). Along with the *Neue Nationalgalerie,* this is *the* Expressionist museum in Berlin, with wildly colorful works by the Expressionist school *die Brücke.* DM7, students DM3. Open Wed.-Mon.11am-5pm.

Postmuseum Berlin, An der Urania 15 (tel. 21 71 17 17). Bus #109 or 219 from Bahnhof Zoo or a short walk from U-Bahn #1 or 4: "Nollendorfpl." Exposes the Post's growth with lots of historic video and techno-fun—play with the toy mail train, light up an historic mail-route map. Free. Open Tues.-Sun. 9am-5pm.

Zucker-Museum, Amrumerstr. 32 (tel. 31 42 75 74), U-Bahn #9: "Amrumerstr." A cultural history of sugar explores its uses, such as sculpture, records, and alcohol. Yum. DM4.50, students DM2 (or a solemn oath never to buy into the myth of cavities). Open Mon.-Wed. 11am-5pm, Sun. 11am-6pm.

ELSEWHERE IN EASTERN BERLIN

Otto Nagel Haus, Märkisches Ufer 16-18 (tel. 279 14 24). U-Bahn: "Märkisches Museum." A collection of art exploring social themes, taken from the *Preußischer Kulturbesitz* collection. Includes works by Käthe Kollwitz and an exciting collection of photomontage by the famous anti-Nazi satirist John Heartfield. DM4, students and seniors DM2. Open Mon.-Thurs. 9am-3pm, Fri. 9am-noon.

Deutsches Historisches Museum (Museum of German History), Unter den Linden 2, in the former arsenal (tel. 21 50 20; fax 21 50 24 02). Across from the *Museumsinsel.* Permanent exhibits trace German history from the Neanderthal period to the Nazis, while rotating exhibitions examine the last 50 years. Large quantities of GDR art in the "painting-of-a-happy-faced-worker" vein. Tours (in German, *Komrade*) 4-

5 times per day. The *Zeughaus-Kino* on the side shows documentaries and films Thurs.-Sun. at 4, 6:15, and 8:30pm. Open Thurs.-Tues. 10am-6pm. Free.

Friedrichswerdersche Kirche, Werderstr. (tel. 208 13 23), south of Unter den Linden. U-Bahn #2: "Hausvogteipl." 19th-century French and German sculpture in a unique church built by Schinkel. SMPK times and prices.

■ Entertainment

Berlin has one of the most vibrant cultural scenes in the world. Exhibitions, concerts, plays, and dance abound, although cutbacks in government subsidies have recently resulted in slightly fewer offerings and higher prices. Nonetheless, Germany still has a very generously subsidized art scene, and tickets are usually reasonable, especially with student discounts. Varied festivals celebrating everything from Chinese film to West African music spice up the regular offerings.

You can reserve tickets by calling the box office directly. Always ask about student discounts; most theaters and concert halls offer them up to 50%, but only if you buy at the *Abendkasse* (night box office), which generally opens one hour before a performance begins. There are numerous other ticket outlets which will charge you a commission and do not offer student discounts. Remember that while most theaters do accept credit cards, most other ticket outlets don't. The main box offices are **Theaterkasse Centrum,** Meinekestr. 25 (tel. 882 76 11; fax 881 33 32), with branches in all Karstadt department stores and in **KaDeWe,** Tauentzienstr. 21 (tel. 218 10 28; all charge 18% commission; all open Mon.-Fri. 10am-6:30pm, Sat. 10am-2pm). **Theaterkasse Zehlendorf,** Teltower Damm 22 (tel. 801 16 52), also sells Berlin tickets (open Mon.-Fri. 7:30am-6pm, Sat. 8am-1pm). For last-minute 50%-off tickets, contact **Hekticket,** Rathausstr. 1 (tel. 243 12 431), by the Alexanderpl. S-Bahn station. Shows to which tickets are available are posted in the window (open Mon.-Sat. 4-8pm). Unfortunately, major theaters and operas close from mid-July to late August.

CONCERTS, OPERA, AND DANCE

Berlin reaches its musical zenith during the fabulous **Berliner Festwochen,** lasting almost the entire month of September and drawing the world's best orchestras and soloists, and during the **Berliner Jazztage** in November. For more information on these events (and tickets, which sell out months in advance), call or write to Berliner Festspiele, Budapesterstr. 48-50, 10787 Berlin (tel. 25 48 92 50; open daily noon-6pm). In mid-July, **Bachtage** (Bach Days) offer an intense week of classical music; every Saturday night in August, **Sommer Festspiele** turns the Ku'damm into a multi-faceted concert hall with punk, steel-drum, and folk groups competing for attention.

In the monthly pamphlets *Kultur in Berlin* and *Berliner Programm*, as well as in the biweekly *Tip* and *Zitty*, you'll find notices of concerts in the courtyard of the old Arsenal on the **Schloßinsel Köpenick** (castle island) or in the parks. The programs for many theaters and opera houses are additionally listed on huge posters in U-Bahn stations. Tickets for the *Philharmonie* and the *Oper* are often impossible to acquire through conventional channels unless you write months in advance. Try standing out in front before performances with a small sign saying, *"Suche Karte"* (I seek a ticket)—invariably a few people will try to unload tickets at the last moment. Remember that concert halls and operas close for a few weeks during the summer months.

Berliner Philharmonisches Orchester, Matthäikirchstr. 1 (tel. 25 48 81 32; fax 25 48 81 35). Bus #129 from Ku'damm: "Potsdamerstr." and walk 3 blocks north, or S-Bahn #2: "Potsdamerpl." The big yellow building, designed by Scharoun in 1963, is as acoustically perfect within as it is unconventional without. The *Berliner Philharmoniker,* led for decades by the late Herbert von Karajan and currently under the baton of Claudio Abbados, is perhaps the finest orchestra in the world. It is well-nigh impossible to get a seat; check an hour before concert time or write at least 8 weeks in advance. The *Philharmonie* is often closed during the summer months. Tickets around DM30. Box office open Mon.-Fri. 3:30-6pm, Sat.-Sun. and holidays

11am-2pm. Tickets cannot be ordered by phone. Fax or write to: Kartenbüro, Berliner Philharmonisches Orchester, Matthäikirchstr. 1, 10785 Berlin.

Konzerthaus (Schauspielhaus Gendarmenmarkt), Gendarmenmarkt (tel. 203 09 21 01). *Großer Konzertsaal* and *Kammermusiksaal*. U-Bahn #2 or 6: "Stadtmitte." The opulent home of the Berlin Symphony Orchestra, *if* it continues to survive cuts in subsidies. Call for performance info. Last-minute tickets are somewhat easier to come by. Box office open Mon.-Fri. 10am-6pm. Chamber music throughout the summer, but the orchestra goes on vacation late July to mid-Aug.

Deutsche Oper Berlin, Bismarckstr. 34-37 (tel. 341 02 49 for info, 343 84 01 for tickets). U-Bahn #2 or 12: "Deutsche Oper" or 7: "Bismarckstr." Berlin's best opera, featuring newly commissioned works as well as all the German and Italian classics. Student discounts of up to 50% (depending on the price of the ticket) 1 week or less before performance. Tickets DM15-140. Main box office open Mon.-Sat. 11am-1hr. before performance, Sun. 10am-2pm. Evening tickets available starting 1hr. before performance. For tickets, write to Deutsche Oper Berlin, Richard-Wagner-Str. 10, 10585 Berlin or fax 343 84 55. For program info, write to Deutsche Oper Berlin, Bismarckstr. 35, 10627 Berlin. Closed July to mid-Aug.

Deutsche Staatsoper, Unter den Linden 7 (tel. 20 35 45 55; fax 20 35 44 83). U-Bahn #6: "Friedrichstr." or bus #157 or 100. Eastern Berlin's leading opera company, led by Daniel Barenboim (also the conductor of the Chicago Symphony Orchestra). Ballet and classical music, too, although the orchestra fluctuates between good and mediocre. Backstage tours also available daily at 11am. Tickets DM18-35, 50% student discount. Box office open Mon.-Fri. 10am-6pm, Sat.-Sun. 2pm-6pm. *Abendkasse* open 1hr. before showtime.

Komische Oper, Behrenstr. 55-57, 10117 (tel. 20 26 03 60, fax 20 26 02 60). U-Bahn #6: "Französischestr." Its reputation was built by famous post-war director Felsenstein, but in recent years zany artistic director Harry Kupfer has revitalized the opera with clever stagings of the classics. Program ranges from Mozart to Gilbert and Sullivan. Tickets DM10-90. 50% student discounts almost always available 2hr. before the show. Box office open Mon.-Sat. 11am-7pm, Sun. 1-4:30pm.

Tanzfabrik, Möckernstr. 68 (tel. 786 58 61). U-Bahn #7: "Yorckstr." Turn left on Yorckstr., then right onto Möckernstr. Modern dance performances and a center for dance workshops. Box office open Mon.-Thurs. 10am-noon and 5-8pm, Fri. 10am-noon. Tickets DM15. Occasional weekend performances start at 8 or 8:30pm. Often when the main theaters close down for the summer, dance companies take up residence. Check posters at the *Komische Oper* and the *Staatsoper*.

THEATER

Theater listings are available in the monthly pamphlets *Kultur in Berlin* and *Berlin Programm*, as well as *Tip* and *Zitty*. They are also posted in most U-Bahn stations; look for the yellow posters. In addition to the best German-language theater in the country (or in the world), Berlin also has a lively English-language theater scene. Look for theater listings in *Tip* or *Zitty* that say *"in englischer Sprache"* ("in English") next to them. There are a number of privately-run theater companies called "off-theaters," which feature occasional English-language plays. As with concert halls, look out for summer closings *(Theaterferien);* see the introduction to **Entertainment,** p. 122, for box office information. There is an international **Theater Festival** in May.

Deutsches Theater, Schumannstr. 13a (tel. 287 12 25). U-Bahn #6 or S-Bahn #1-3, 5, 6, or 9: "Friedrichstr." or bus #147: "Albrechtpl." The word has spread to Western Berlin: this is the best theater in the country. Max Reinhardt made it great 100 years ago, and it now has innovative productions of the classics and newer works (especially strong on Heiner Müller). Latter-day director Dieter Mann, a virtual deity to GDR theater-lovers, stepped down in 1991. The repertory runs from Büchner to Mamet to Ibsen. The **Kammerspiel des Deutschen Theaters** (tel. 28 44 12 26) has smaller, controversial productions. Tickets DM15-40, but 50% student discounts often available. Box office open Mon.-Sat. noon-6pm, Sun. 3-6pm.

Hebbel Theater, Stresemannstr. 29 (tel. 25 90 04 27). U-Bahn #1 or 6: "Hallesches Tor." The most avant of the avant-garde theaters in Berlin, drawing cutting-edge talent from all over the world. Watch out for tomato-throwers in the audience. Fear the Sandman. Box office open Mon.-Sun. 4-7pm.

Freie Volksbühne/Musical Theater Berlin, Schaperstr. 24 (tel. 88 42 08 84). U-Bahn #2 or 9: "Spichernstr." Avant-garde musical theater, with many English-language productions imported from Britain. You won't find *Katzen* or *Der Phantom der Oper* here. Tickets DM45-135. Box office open Mon. noon-6:30pm, Tues.-Fri. 11am-8pm, Sat. noon-8:30pm.

Friends of Italian Opera, Fidicinstr. 40 (tel. 691 12 11). U-Bahn #6: "Platz der Luft-brücke." The moniker is a joking reference to the flick *Some Like It Hot,* and belies its role as Berlin's leading English-language theater, home to the renowned Berliner Grundtheater company as well as a grab-bag of English-language performances. The locale is neat too—the theater is hidden in a *Hinterhof* (courtyard) in Kreuzberg. Tickets DM15-20.

Berliner Ensemble, Bertolt-Brecht-Platz 1 (tel. 282 31 60). U-Bahn #6 or S-Bahn #2, 3, 5, 6 or 9: "Friedrichstr." The famous theater established by Brecht is undergoing a renaissance. Hip repertoire, including Heiner Müller and some young American playwrights, as well as Brecht's own plays. Also some premieres. Tickets DM12-40, students 50% discounts available 1hr. before the show in the *Abendkasse.* Box office open Mon.-Sat. 11am-6pm, Sun. 3-6pm.

Maxim Gorki Theater, Unter Den Linden 2 (tel. 20 22 11 29). U-Bahn #6 or S-Bahn #2, 3, 5, 6 or 9: "Friedrichstr." Excellent contemporary theater with wonderfully varied repertoire—everything from Molière to Beckett. Tickets DM5-25. Box office open Mon.-Sat. 1-6:30pm, Sun. 3-6:30pm.

Die Distel ("The Thistle"), Friedrichstr. 101 (tel. 204 47 04). U-Bahn #6 or S-Bahn #2, 3, 5, 6 or 9: "Friedrichstr." During GDR days, this was a renowned cabaret for polit-ical satire—but reunification has taken the bite out of some of the jokes. Box office open Mon.-Fri. noon-6pm and 2hr. before performance.

FILM

Berlin is a movie-lovin' town; it hosts an international **Film Festival** (late-Feb. to March), and on any night in Berlin, you can choose from 100 different films, many in the original languages. (*"O.F."* next to a movie listing means original version. *"O.m.U."* means original version with German subtitles. Everything else is dubbed.) Check *Tip, Zitty,* or subway posters. Numerous city cineplexes offer the chance to see dubbed Hollywood blockbusters. **Zoo-Palast,** at Hardenbergstr. 29a (tel. 25 41 47 89), near Bahnhof Zoo, is one of the biggest and most popular, with upwards of a dozen screens. Tuesdays and Wednesdays are *"Kinotage"* at most movie theaters, with prices reduced a few Marks. Bring a student ID for discounts.

Freiluftkino. In summer, Berliners take to open-air film festivals with screenings in parks. Two venues show films in English: **Freiluftkino Hasenheide,** at the Sputnik in Hasenheide Park, screens anything from silent films to *Get Shorty.* U-Bahn #7 or 8: "Hermannpl." **Freiluftkino Kreuzberg,** Mariannenpl. 2 (tel. 238 64 88), screens avant-garde contemporary with films like *Smoke* and *Pulp Fiction.* U-Bahn #1 or 8: "Kottbusser Tor." DM10 for either theater.

Eiszeit, Zeughofstr. 20 (tel. 611 60 16). U-Bahn #1: "Görlitzer Bahnhof." Shows the movie factories' slightly alternative products (e.g., *Crumb*) in English, as well as more independent films and documentaries.

fsk am Oranienplatz, segitzdamm 2 (tel. 614 24 64). u-bahn #1 or 8: "kottbuser tor." this wacky lower-case moviehouse with a flair for self-approbating concretism seeks to void films of meaning by awkwardly juxtaposing incongruous films in dou-ble features. watch primarily original-language screenings of *I Know the Way to the Hofbrauhaus* followed by *From Dusk Till Dawn.* dm10, mon. dm8.

Filmtheater Babylon-Mitte, Rosa-Luxemburgstr. 30 (tel. 242 50 76). U-Bahn #2: "Rosa-Luxemburg-Platz." Shows classics and art films, often in their original lan-guage. DM8, students DM7. The Kreuzberg **Babylon,** Dresdenerstr. 126 (tel. 614 63 16; U-Bahn #1 or 8: "Kottbuser Tor") plays offbeat comedies (such as *Flirting with Disaster*) and, yes, Tarantino.

Blow Up, Immanuelkirchstr. 14 (tel. 442 86 62). S-Bahn #8 or 10: "Greifswalderstr." Always something entertaining going on—see *Unzipped* followed by a fashion show or catch them when they're showing the eternally cool Bogey flicks. They always screen something in English. DM9, Tues.-Wed. DM7.

SHOPPING

When Berlin was a lonely outpost in the Eastern Bloc consumer wilderness, Berliners had no choice but to buy native. Thanks to the captive market, the city accrued a mind-boggling array of things for sale: if a price tag can be put on it, you can buy it in Berlin. The high temple of the consumerist religion is the seven-story **KaDeWe department store** on Wittenbergpl., the largest department store in Europe. The name is a German abbreviation of "Department Store of the West" *(Kaufhaus des Westens);* for the tens of thousands of product-starved Easterners who flooded Berlin in the days following the Wall-opening, KaDeWe *was* the West—prompting warnings such as, "OK now, we're going in. Just act normal," as intrepid children stood on the threshold of consumerism. Even Westerners would do well to follow the advice, with the materialism on display alternatively proving awe-inspiring and sickening. (No photography allowed!) The store's food department, sixth floor, has to be seen to be believed (see **Food,** p. 105).

The entire **Kurfürstendamm** is one big shopping district, but the **Ku'damm Eck,** (the corner of Joachimstalerstr.) and **Ku'damm Block** (around Uhlandstr.) are the most notable areas. Bleibtreustr. has stores closer to the budget traveler's reach, while the hagglers around **Brandenburger Tor** will sell you cheap GDR memorabilia— don't accept their stated prices, and don't fool yourself into thinking the relics are authentic; there just aren't *that* many "real" pieces of the Berlin Wall.

Theodore Sturgeon astutely observed that "90% of everything is crap," and the **flea markets** that regularly fertilize Berlin are no exception. Nevertheless, you can occasionally find the fantastic bargain that makes all the sorting and sifting worthwhile. The market on **Straße des 17. Juni** probably has the best selection of stuff, but the prices are higher than those at a lot of other markets (open Sat.-Sun. 8am-3pm). **Winterfeldmarkt,** by Nollendorfpl., overflows with food, flowers, and people crooning Dylan tunes over their acoustic guitars (open Wed. and Sat. mornings). The market on **Oranienburgerstraße** by Tacheles offers works by starving artists and a variety of other nonsensical Dadaist delights (open Sat.-Sun. 8am-3pm).

Zweite Hand (second-hand; DM3), an aptly named newspaper appearing at news stands for DM3.80 on Tuesdays, Thursdays, and Saturdays, consists of ads for anything anyone wants to resell, from apartment shares and plane tickets to silk dresses and cats; it also has good deals on **bikes. Bergmannstraße,** in Kreuzberg, is a used clothes and cheap antique shop strip. **Made in Berlin,** Potsdamerstr. 106, generally has funky second-hand stuff, all quite cheap. Get your leather jacket here. U-Bahn #1: "Kurfürstenstr." A larger selection of used clothes, albeit with less consistent quality, awaits at **Checkpoint,** Mehringdamm 59. U-Bahn #6 or 7: "Mehringdamm."

■ Nightlife

Berlin's nightlife is absolute madness, a teeming cauldron of debauchery that runs around the clock and threatens to inflict coronaries upon the faint of heart. Bars, clubs, and cafes typically jam until at least 3am and often stay open until daylight; during the weekends, you can literally dance non-stop from Friday night until Monday morning. Take advantage of the night buses from the U-Bahn stations and **U-Bahn #9 and 12,** which run all night on Fridays and Saturdays. The best sources of information about bands and dance venues are the bi-weekly magazines *Tip* (DM4) and the superior *Zitty* (DM3.60), available at all kiosks and newsagents, and the free *030* that's distributed in all *Mensas*, Burger Kings, and many bars. *Arena* is also free and lists the more more minor events which don't make it into *030*, but is hard to find.

In Western Berlin, the best places to look are **Savignyplatz, Schöneberg, Wilmersdorf,** and particularly **Kreuzberg.** The Ku'damm is best avoided at night, unless you enjoy fraternizing with drunken businessmen, middle aged, unenlightened tourists, and dirty old men who drool to the sight of strip shows. The north is a bit more inviting to the youthful: the middle point is Savignypl., which includes Café Hardenberg and the Schwarzes Café (see **Food,** p. 105), both excellent for a drink at night. South of the Ku'damm, the area between Uhlandstr. and Olivaerpl. is littered with crowded late-night cafes. The main focus of Schöneberg nightlife is around **Nollendorfplatz,** encompassing cafe-*Kneipen* on Winterfeldpl. and Goltzstr., and more bars on Kleist-str. Pushing up against the remains of the Wall in the western section of the city is the center of the **Kreuzberg** *Szene.* The scene in East Kreuzberg is wild; in the midst of the heavily Turkish neighborhoods, along Oranienstr. between U-Bahn #1: "Kottbusser Tor" and U-Bahn #1: "Görlitzer Bahnhof," roost a menagerie of radically alternative clubs that range from laid-back to breathtakingly salacious. The area is not well-lit at night and can be somewhat unsafe for those traveling alone.

As funky as Kreuzberg is, its days at the heart of the Berlin *Szene* are over as clubs flee to the east and north. While Mercedes-Benz and Sony build their new European headquarters at Potsdamer Platz, speculators have been dumping capital into the surrounding areas, bringing a wave of massive rent increases that have forced nearby clubs to pick up and head deeper into Mitte and Prenzlauer Berg. The most prominent victims of the rent scourge so far have been the legendary E-Werk, which plans to re-open elsewhere, and Franz-Club, which totters on the verge of shutting down. Rent problems in the west, coupled with a fascinating new "alternative" population, make the East hot. On the other hand, most of the West's clubs are dinosaurs (for example, Metropol and Big Eden), relics of an era when disco was considered a viable weapon against godless communism. Indeed, a military milieu still permeates many Western clubs, which attract divisions of uniformly dressed (tight jeans and no sneakers, private!) high school kids to dance on spotless, spit-and-polish shiny dance floors, watched over by drill sergeant bouncers. Some of the more interesting bars abound in the **Scheunenviertel,** especially along Oranienburgerstr. (not to be confused with Kreuzberg's Oranienstr.) near the old synagogue. The **Prenzlauer Berg** area boasts some fun, interesting places along Schönhauser Allee, Kastanienallee, and especially by the gritty, seedy, bombed-out clubs around the Water Tower. Streetlights are sparse on many of the residential streets of the east, making a midnight club crawl a little creepy. Berlin's very active squatter community lives out in **Lichtenberg** and puts on truly underground punk shows several times a week. Be warned that this area is quite dangerous at night, with muggings and fights occurring regularly. Eastern Berlin is still safer than most American cities, but it's wise to avoid empty alleys and parks and to travel in groups when possible.

If at all possible, try to hit Berlin during the **Love Parade,** usually held in the second weekend of July (see **The Love Parade,** p. 127), when all of Berlin just says "yes" to everything. In that vein, it's also worth mentioning that Berlin has **de-criminalized marijuana possession** of up to eight grams. Smoking in public, however, has not been officially accepted. *Let's Go* does not recommend puffing clouds of hash smoke into the face of police officers.

BARS AND CLUBS

This is the section of *Let's Go: Germany* where we dance.

Savigny- and Steinplatz Area

Quasimodo, Kantstr. 12a (tel. 312 80 86). S-Bahn #3, 5, 7, or 9: "Savignypl." This unassuming basement pub with attached *Biergarten* is one of Berlin's most crucial jazz venues, drawing in big names and lively crowds. Superfly swingers John Abercrombie, Defunkt, and Betty Carter jammed here recently. It's totally dead until 10pm when the shows begin. (An extraordinary fact: the men's bathroom here is lit by fluorescent "black light" bulbs. Why is this extraordinary? Because **human urine glows** under fluorescent light.) Cover depends on performance, ranging from free to DM30. Concert tickets available from 5pm or at Kant Kasse ticket service (tel. 313 45 54; fax 312 64 40). Open daily from 8pm; closed Aug.-Oct.

Big Eden, Kurfürstendamm 202 (tel. 882 61 20). U-Bahn #15: "Uhlandstr." No paradise: 9 planes of disco inferno. Funked out post-Saturday Night Fever crowd shakes to disco, house, and techno. Open Sun.-Thurs. 8pm-4am, Fri. 8pm-5am, Sat. 8am-6am. Cover Sun.-Thurs. DM5 (free drink if you arrive before 9pm), Fri.-Sat. DM12.

Schöneberg

Metropol, Nollendorfpl. 5 (tel. 216 41 22). U-Bahn #1 or 4: "Nollendorfpl.," or night buses N19, N29, or N85. The architecture of Metropol, long one of Berlin's most famous discos, is stunningly reminiscent of The Tower of Babel in Fritz Lang's *Metropolis* (absent are the 50,000 baldies Lang hired for the scene); fractile lights illuminate the dance floor in the loft, where lots of 16- to 25-year-olds groove. Sometimes big-time concerts take place between dances. Cover DM15. Dress nicely, lest the radio-controlled bouncers go berserk at the sight of your sneakers and baggy jeans. Open Fri. 9pm-6am, Sat. 9pm-8am. Concert ticket prices vary; call 216 27 87 for info and prices (Mon.-Fri. 11am-3pm and 3:30-6pm).

M, Goltzstr. 33 (tel. 216 70 92). U-Bahn #7: "Eisenacherstr." One of the more interesting Schöneberg bars, stark and neon-lit, and slightly wild late at night. Black is eternally in. "Karlheinz, you are beautiful and angular." Open daily 8am-whenever.

Kreuzberg

SO 36, Oranienstr. 190 (tel. 61 40 13 06; http://www.SO36.de). U-Bahn #1: "Görlitzer Bahnhof." A mish-mash of wild oeuvres: Sun. is ballroom dancing with tango lessons, Mon. dishes up the techno Electric Ballroom, Wed. means gay and lesbian disco night, Thurs. keeps heads banging with Ska, Metal, Punk, and hardcore. Fri.-Sat., the crowd gets younger for the slightly raucous parties. The name celebrates the pre-war postal code for this part of Kreuzberg, while the venue sends 90210 through the looking glass. Open Sun. after 7pm, Mon. after 11pm, Wed.-Thurs. after 10pm, Fri.-Sat. 11pm 'til mommy takes you home.

KitKat Club, Glogauerstr. 2 (tel. 611 38 33). Lascivious? The word loses its meaning here. Erotic? This implies innuendo, a quality which has no place on this dance floor. Sex. SEXSEXSEX. People with varying degrees of clothing, some copulating, some just digging the cool trance music in the jaw-dropping, fluorescent interior, leave their inhibitions outside. Open Tues.-Sun. after 11pm. Cover DM20. The Sun. after-hours party (8am-7pm) is popular, free, and more fully clothed. On Thurs., the

---

The Love Parade

Every year during the second weekend in July, the Love Parade brings Berlin to its knees, its trains running late, its streets filling with litter, and its otherwise sedate and productive populace dying their hair, dropping ecstasy, and getting down *en masse*. What started off in 1989 with 150 people celebrating a DJ's birthday has mutated into an annual techno Woodstock, the world's only million-man rave, and a massive corporate event. (Get your **free cigarettes** at major sponsor Camel's tent!) A huge "parade" takes place on Saturday afternoon, involving a snail-paced procession of tractor-trailers loaded with blasting speakers and people dancing on top. Speaker- and dancer-laden trucks slowly bust the bass from Ernst Reuter Platz to the Brandenburg Gate. The city-wide party turns Str. des 17 Junis into a raving dance-floor, and the Tiergarten into a garden of original—indeed, sometimes quite creative—sin. Unless you have a fetish for tall people's hairy and sweaty armpits, the best way to see and enjoy the parade is to be up high (literally, of course)—the porta-potties are supreme watch towers. Club prices skyrocket for the event as the best DJs from Europe are imported for a frantic weekend of parties and dancing. It's an experience that you'll never forget, unless you ingest or consume something that leaves you in a hazy cloud of oblivion. While past Love Parades have been held in the Tiergarten, the authorities might move it in 1998 after environmentalists raised concerns about the 750,000 liters of urine which the park absorbed. Regardless of the locale, the techno world trembles in eager anticipation of next year's incarnation.

club cross-dresses as the **Crisco Club** for some serious homoerotics (men only!). Not for the faint of heart.

Yaam, Eichenstr. 4 (tel. 617 59 59). U-Bahn #1: "Schlesisches Tor." Neither a club nor a bar, but rather *the place* to chill on weekends, with an African and Caribbean food market Sun., as well as Berlin's largest pick-up basketball league. Also features a skatepark and headshop right next to the basketball courts where you can fly high and bring the soul to the hole. Open Fri.-Sun. 2pm-10pm. Cover DM5.

Ex, Mehringhof, Gneisenaustr. 2a (tel. 693 58 00). U-Bahn #6 or 7: "Mehringdamm" or night bus N19. A *Kneipe* in an old Berliner courtyard run by a famed collective and hangout for the people from the *Szene*. Anarcho-communists who hate hierarchies proffer cheap drinks and Indian food amid a funk and jazz backdrop well-suited for chillin'. Nascent bands rattle the little stage on weekends. Punk/hip-hop disco on Sat. Open Mon.-Thurs. 5pm-2am, Fri.-Sat. 8pm-2am, Sun. 7pm-2am.

Schnabel Bar, Oranienstr. 31 (tel. 615 85 34). U-Bahn #1 or 8: "Kottbuser Tor." Raucously upbeat swingers shake dat booty non-stop to jungle music. Open 24hr., but the most heated dance scene runs midnight-6am. A *Let's Go* favorite, if only because it features *The Voodoo Lounge* on Thurs.

Flammende Herzen, Oranienstr. 170 (tel. 615 71 02). U-Bahn #1 or 8: "Kottbusser Tor." Angry. Very angry. The regulars sport piercings vicious enough to raise a pierced eyebrow. The decor's a trip: hot orange-and-black walls with huge mirrors and surreal constructions over the bar. Open daily from 11am.

Plantation, Stresemannstr. 69. S-Bahn #1 or 2: "Anhalter Bahnhof" or U-Bahn #2: "Potsdamer Platz." Very, very popular neighborhood bar, with a big *Biergarten* out back where you can barbecue your own steaks. Inside, there's a bar and dance floor packed with locals getting down to salsa and James Brown. (*Ich bin ein* Sex Machine!) Open daily from 6pm. Cover DM5.

Oranienburgerstraße-Mitte

Tresor, Leipzigerstr. 8 (tel. 609 37 02). U-Bahn #2: "Mohrenstr." or "Potsdamer Platz." One of the most rocking techno venues in Berlin, packed from wall to wall with enthusiastic ravers. Its 2 dance floors, both sporting rapidly blinking lights and floor-shaking bass, are enough to bring out the epileptic in all of us. Open Wed. and Fri.-Sun. after 11pm. Cover DM5 on Wed., DM12 on weekends. The garden stays open all day Sat. with free entry after 7am.

E-Werk. The other most rocking techno club in Berlin. This world-renowned club will be relocating from Wilhelmstr. 43 to somewhere in northern Mitte. Techno and British house on weekends. Cover around DM15-20.

Tacheles, Oranienburgerstr. 53-56 (tel. 282 61 85). U-Bahn #6: "Oranienburger Tor." This bombed-out ex-department store that serves as a copacetic congregating point for alternative-type folks is likely the greatest source of artistic pretense in all of Berlin. The art commune that operates Tacheles has decorated the interior from top to bottom with graffiti, collages, and exhibits. Don't even think about taking pictures unless you don't mind being assaulted by some tortured genius yelling about art for art's sake. Bands, films, raves, and 3 bars serve up nightly entertainment. The sculpture garden in the back is like a playground for the *Exorcist*. If you're unimpressed by the art, hang out in the garden's rocketship where you can open your mind and reconsider. Open 24hr.

Café Silberstein, Oranienburgerstr. 27 (tel. 281 28 01). S-Bahn #1 or 2: "Oranienburgerstr." Post-everything art decor offers sushi, ambient music, and a hipper than hip clientele. Dieter, his Sprockets, and even his little pet ("touch my monkey! love him!") come here. Open Mon.-Fri. 4pm-around 2 or 4am, Sat. noon-morn.

Delicious Doughnuts Research, Rosenthalerstr. 9 (tel. 283 30 21). U-Bahn #8: "Weinmeisterstr." A treacherous Homer Simpson bulking up for his latest work-evasion scheme ("I'm an obese man stuck in a fat man's body!") sticks to the cafe up front, while the kids in the back room dig the drum 'n' bass/trip-hop scene. Open daily 10pm-6am. Cover DM5.

Go-Go, on Neue Schönhauser Allee near the intersection with Rosenthalerstr. U-Bahn #8: "Weinmeisterstr." or S-Bahn: "Hackescher Markt." This steel-lined hole in the wall epitomizes the crop of transient clubs creeping up in the east: tiny, hip, and slightly underground. Dub and trance nightly from 11pm. Cover DM5.

Prenzlauer Berg

Subground, Schönhauser Allee 176 (tel. 449 65 34). U-Bahn #2: "Senefelderpl." As the name suggests, this club is at ground level. Less mobbed than E-Werk and Tresor, with DJs spinning a varied mix of drum 'n' bass, jungle, and dub, as well as healthy quantities of techno and British house. After-hours party Sun. starting at 9am. Open Thurs.-Sun. 11pm-8am.

Café-Kunstfabrik Schlot, Kastanienallee 29 (tel. 448 21 60). This respite from the "in-your-face" Berlin night scene serves up jazz Fri.-Mon. and cabaret Tues.-Thurs. Free Mon. jam session; DM5 all other days. Open 7pm-4am; closed July to mid-Aug.

Franz-Klub, Schönhauser Allee 36-39 (tel. 442 82 03). U-Bahn #2: "Eberswalderstr.". The east's most reliable rock venue—a favorite among Prenzlauer Bergers and *Wessies* in the know. Cover varies. Live music every damn night of the year under the gaze of a big sphinx, including world music acts, local ska bands, blues, and rock. Bands usually start around 10pm, followed by dance and a DJ until late.

Knaack-Klub, Greifswalderstr. 224 (tel. 442 70 60). S-Bahn #8 or 10: "Ernst-Thälmann Park." Smaller and more grungy than Franz. In a perpetual state of musical identity crisis, this club waffles between indie rock, disco, techno, and karaoke. Frequent live shows. Its indecisiveness even extends to its shifting opening times. Cover around DM10.

Elsewhere in Eastern Berlin

Insel der Jugend, Alt Treptow 6 (tel. 534 88 51). S-Bahn #8, 9, or 10: "Treptower Park," then bus 265 or N65: "Alt-Treptow." Or bus N65 from the "Schlesiches Tor" U-Bahn stop if the S-Bahn has shut down. The name means "island of youth," and is indicative of the club's location on an island in the middle of the park. Three fiercely decorated floors of dancing have the feel of a fishbowl with fluorescent silver foil and netting all over the place. Very cool. Top 2 floors spin reggae, hip-hop, ska, and house (sometimes all at once), while the frantic techno scene in the basement claims the casualties of the upper floors. Hipsters chill in the cafe during the day and indulge in occasional John Woo and Cheech and Chong classics. An outdoor patio overlooking the trees and river serves as a peaceful venue for the locals to roll mad joints. Cafe open May-Sept. Tues.-Sun. 2-10pm. Club open Thurs.-Sat. after 10pm. Movies shown Thurs. night.

Die Halle, An der Industriebahn 12-16 (tel. 467 42 91). S-Bahn #8 or 10: "Prenzlauer Allee," then bus #156: "Gehringstr./An der Industriebahn." Berlin's rotten, vicious punks cook up brutal hardcore while getting jonesed out in this former tractor factory out in the suburb of Weißensee. OiOiOi.

■ Gay and Lesbian Berlin

Gay and lesbian life in Berlin is out, integrated, and in a word, FABulous. Traditionally, the social nexus of gay and lesbian life has centered around the **Nollendorfplatz,** the so-called "Pink Village." Christopher Isherwood lived at Nollendorfstr. 17 while writing his collection of stories *Goodbye to Berlin,* later adapted as the Broadway musical *Cabaret.* A marble pink triangle plaque outside the Nollendorfpl. U-Bahn station reads: "Beaten to death; abandoned to death," and remembers the thousands of gays and lesbians deported to concentration camps from the station.

The both demure and wild history of homosexuality comes out at the **Schwules Museum,** Mehringdamm 61 (tel. 693 11 72; open Wed.-Sun. 2-6pm; DM7, students DM4). **Spinnobden-Lesbenarchiv,** Anklamerstr. 38 (tel. 448 58 48), tends towards culturally hip lesbian offerings, with exhibits, films, and all kinds of information about current lesbian life (open Wed. and Fri. 2-7pm). U-Bahn #8: "Bernauerstr." **Lesbenberatung,** Kulmerstr. 20a (tel. 215 20 00), offers a library, movie viewings, and counseling on lesbian issues (open Mon.-Wed. 4-8pm). U-Bahn #7: "Kleistpark." The gay info center **Mann-o-Meter,** Motzstr. 5 (tel 216 80 08), off Nollendorfpl., dispenses everything from K-Y jelly to posters for political activities. They have pamphlets and a notice board with listings of apartments and other accommodations and a cafe in back (open Mon.-Fri. 5-10pm, Sat. 5-9pm, Sun. 5-8pm).

The **Prinz Eisenherz bookstore,** Bleibtreustr. 52 (tel. 313 99 36), has lots of information and books, many in English (open Mon.-Wed. and Fri. 10am-6:30pm, Thurs. 10am-8pm, Sat. 10am-4pm). The travel guide *Berlin von Hinten* (Berlin from Behind) costs DM19.80, but details gay life in Berlin extensively in English and German. The free magazine *Siegessäule* details gay events for the month and is available in gay bars and bookstores. **Lilith Frauenbuchladen,** Knesebeckstr. 86 (tel. 312 31 02), is a women's bookstore with a focus on lesbian issues (open Mon.-Fri. 10am-6:30pm, Sat. 10am-4pm). **Marga Schoeller Bücherstube,** Knesebeckstr. 33 (tel. 881 11 22), offers women's issues books in English. *Blatt Gold* (DM5 from women's bookstores and some natural food stores) has information and dates for women on a monthly basis. Many of the *Frauencafés* listed are not exclusively lesbian, but do offer an all-woman setting. Some do have "mixed" nights or days. Berlin's queer population ecstatically celebrates its **Christopher Street Day** Parade in the last weekend of June with parades, floats, and wild parties. Have fun. Berlin is an open city.

Rose's, Oranienstr. 182, U-Bahn #1 or 8: "Kottbusser Tor." One of the most popular and energetic bars in Berlin, gay, lesbian, or otherwise. Amuse yourself while waiting for your drink by playing with the lights on the bar, which turn on and off when you touch them. Or don't. Open daily 10pm-6am.

Café Anal, Muskauerstr. 15 (tel. 618 70 64). U-Bahn #1: "Görlitzer Bahnhof." Spirited alternative gay and lesbian bar in east Kreuzberg. The decor hovers between Salvador Dalí and Pee-Wee's Playhouse: shiny gold ceiling, stuffed-pumpkin light fixtures, plump multi-colored cushions in corner nooks, seashell-shaped canopy. Mon. women only. Open summer daily from 6pm; winter from 8pm.

Drama, Oranienstr. 169 (tel. 614 53 56). U-Bahn #1 or 8: "Kottbusser Tor." Sensual interior of red and black drapes attracts a gay/lesbian/mixed 20-something crowd that delights in dancing to house and funkadelic. Open daily from 8pm on.

90°, Dennewitzstr. 37 (tel. 262 89 94). U-Bahn #1: "Kurfürstenstr." Exceptionally popular gay and lesbian techno dance scene for the sartorially splendiferous (dress sleekly!) on Thurs. and Sun. "Dance! Dance, I say. Now prance! Prance, girl." Open Thurs.-Sun. after 11pm.

Hafen, Motzstr. 19. U-Bahn #1, 2, or 4: "Nollendorfpl." Pay no heed to the sign above the door—this place is really the Blue Oyster bar: rough, raunchy, and raucous. Somewhat seedier than the other clubs listed, with no dress code, so accessorizing with motorcycle helmets and pets is no problem. Open daily from 9pm.

Schocko-Café, Mariannenstr. 6 (tel. 615 15 61). U-Bahn #1 or 8: "Kottbusser Tor." Lesbian women's central; a cafe with a cultural center upstairs, billiards, and dancing every second Sat. of the month. Open Sun.-Thurs. 5pm-1am, Fri.-Sat. from noon in the summer; the rest of the year, Fri.-Sat. from 2pm.

Jane Bond, in SO36, see (p. 127). This lesbian disco of discos knocks the roof off Oranienstr. every 3rd Fri. of the month after 10pm. Octopussy Galore!

Connection, Fuggerstr. 33 (tel. 218 14 32). U-Bahn #1 or 2: "Wittenbergpl." Exceedingly intense gay techno dance scene. The aptly named bar in the basement, The Twilight Zone, serves as a testing ground for the bondage gear showcased in the display window in front. "Bring out the gimp!" Boys and girls the first Fri. of every month, (bad) boys only every other night. Open Mon.-Thurs. 10pm-1am, Fri.-Sat. 10pm-until the gimp gets tired. Cover DM3-5.

Andreas Kneipe, Ansbacherstr. 29 (tel. 218 32 57). U-Bahn #1 or 2: "Wittenbergpl." Popular gay bar, decorated with bizarre murals of men with tank tops, moustaches, and mohawks, all vaguely emblematic of the clientele. Open daily 11am-4am.

■ The Outer Boroughs

The suburbs of Berlin lie within the *Berliner Außenring,* a massive roundabout of highways and train lines which circles the greater metropolitan area. The towns and city districts listed below are generally accessible by public transportation, and make good afternoon or daytrips. (See **Brandenburg,** p. 134, for other excursions.)

WANNSEE

Most Berliners think of the town of Wannsee, on the lake of the same name, as the beach. Wannsee has long stretches of sand along Havelufer Promenade. To reach the lake, take the triangle bus from the Wannsee or Nikolassee S-Bahn stations to "Strandbad Wannsee" (for the beach) or the end of Nikolskoer Weg (for the boats).

Unfortunately, the reputation of the charming village of Wannsee is indelibly tarnished by the memory of the notorious Wannsee Conference of January 20, 1942. Leading officials of the SS completed the details for the implementation of the "Final Solution" in the **Wannsee Villa,** Großer Wannsee 56, formerly a Gestapo Intelligence Center. In January 1992, the 50th anniversary of the Nazi death-pact, the villa reopened as the **Haus der Wannsee-Konferenz** (tel. 805 00 10), an excellent museum with permanent Holocaust exhibits and a documentary film series, as well as a look at the strange history of the villa itself. In fact, until recently, its association with the conference was not generally known. The villa is discomfitingly lovely, and its grounds offer a dazzling view of the Wannsee. (Open Tues.-Fri. 10am-6pm, Sat.-Sun. 2-6pm. Free. Tours and info in English.) Bus #114 from the S-Bahn station: "Haus der Wannsee-Konferenz." Along the shores of the **Kleiner Wannsee,** the brilliant young author **Heinrich von Kleist** and a terminally ill companion committed suicide in 1811. Kleist's works gained acclaim only after his death.

From Wannsee, ferries also run to the **Pfaueninsel** (Peacock Island; DM10.50), where Friedrich the Great's successor Friedrich Wilhelm II built a *trompe l'oeil* "ruined" castle as a private pleasure house in which he and his mistress could play alone. A flock of the island's namesake fowl roams about the gardens surrounding the castle. From Wannsee, ferries also sail to Tegel, Charlottenburg's Schloßbrücke, Spandau, Potsdam, Werder, and Kladow. Contact **Stern und Kreisschiffahrt** (tel. 536 36 00) or visit them at the Wannsee waterfront near the S-Bahn station.

TEGEL AND PLÖTZENSEE

The forest and lake in Tegel are among the most serene in Berlin. You can swim, water-ski, or go boating on the lake (head down Alt Tegelstr.). The forest has been left mostly untouched, and you can follow *Wanderwege* (walking paths) to deserted parts of the woods. U-Bahn #6: "Tegel." From the U-Bahn, walk up Karolinenstr. or take buses #133 or 222 two stops to get into the heart of the forest.

An understated yet haunting monument to the victims of Nazism, the **Gedenkstätte Plötzensee** (Plötzensee Memorial; tel. 344 32 26), housed in the former execution chambers of the Third Reich, exhibits documents recording death sentences of "enemies of the people," including the officers who attempted to assassinate Hitler in 1944. More than 2500 people were murdered within these walls. Still visible are the hooks from which victims were hanged. The stone urn in front of the memorial contains soil from Nazi concentration camps. English literature is available at the office. (Open daily 8am-6pm, Feb. and Oct. 8:30am-5:30pm; Nov. and Jan. 8:30am-4:30pm; Dec. 8:30am-4pm; free.) U-Bahn #9: "Turmstr.," then bus #123 (direction: "Saatwinkler Damm"): "Gedenkstätte Plötzensee."

TREPTOW

The powerful **Sowjetische Ehrenmal** (Soviet War Memorial) is a mammoth promenade built with marble taken from Hitler's Chancellery. S-Bahn 8, 9, or 10: "Treptower Park." The Soviets dedicated the site in 1948, honoring the millions of Red Army soldiers who fell in what Soviets, and Russians today, know as the "Great Patriotic War." Massive granite slabs along the walk are festooned with quotations from Stalin, leading up to colossal bronze figures in the Socialist Realist style, symbolically crushing Nazism underfoot. It's quite moving, despite the pomp. Buried beneath the trees surrounding the monument are the bodies of 5000 unknown Soviet soldiers who were killed during the Battle of Berlin in 1945. The memorial sits in the middle of **Treptower Park,** a spacious wood ideal for morbid picnics. Also in the park is the **Figurentheater,** Puschkinallee 15a, full of figures with wooden expressions on their faces. They usually perform *Märchen* (fairy tales) in German, though in April 1998 they will put on an English-language version of Snow White (tickets DM6-9 depending on the alignment of the planets). The neighborhood adjoining the park is known for its pleasant waterside cafes.

LICHTENBERG

In the suburb of Lichtenberg on Normannenstr. stands perhaps the most hated and feared building of the GDR regime—the headquarters of the East German secret police, the **Staatsicherheit** or **Stasi.** On January 15, 1990, a crowd of 100,000 Berliners stormed and vandalized the building to protest the continued existence of the police state. The building once contained six million individual dossiers on citizens of the GDR, a country of only 16 million. Since a 1991 law returned the records to their subjects, the "Horror-Files" have rocked Germany, exposing informants—and wrecking careers, marriages, and friendships—at all levels of the political and cultural world. The exhibit displays the offices of Erich Mielke (the loathed Minister for State Security from 1957-1989), surveillance equipment employed by the *Stasi*, and loads of *Stasi* kitsch (including innumerable Lenin busts). The **Forschungs- und Gedenkstätte Normannenstr.,** Ruschestr. 59 (tel. 553 68 54), is close to the U-Bahn station. U-Bahn #5: "Magdalenenstr." From the station's Ruschestr. exit, walk up Ruschestr., then take a right on Normannenstr.; it's Haus #1 in the complex of office buildings. Lichtenberg suffers from severe unemployment and has become a somewhat **dangerous** haven for squatters. When visiting the memorial (open Tues.-Sat. 11am-6pm, Sat.-Sun. 2-6pm; DM5, students DM3), be cautious among the remaining emblems of GDR misery. This warning goes for all the eastern outer boroughs, where right-wing and other disaffected youths sometimes roam. Visibly non-German folks should be very careful in these areas or avoid them entirely.

■ Near Berlin

BERNAU AND WANDLITZ

The eastern satellite town of Berlin, **Bernau** is surprisingly provincial considering its proximity to The Big City; it provides a soothing respite from the noise. It offers a well-preserved, 600-year-old city wall, and precious little else. Its saving grace is the nearby forest, accessible by bike or bus. If **biking** is your thing, rent a bike in Berlin and bring it with you on the S-Bahn—bike rental shops do not seem to have made it here yet. Beautiful rides through the woods end at stunning lakes, including **Wandlitz,** the former retreat of East German government bigwigs. To get there from Bernau (6km), follow the bike trail or bus #94 (DM3). When the GDR regime fell, Wandlitz became one of the more notorious symbols of its corruption. Few things angered ordinary East Germans more than the aristocratic **hunting lodges,** complete with stables and stocked with game. Grim, garden-variety totalitarians were bad enough, but hypocritical ones were just a bit too much to bear.

To get to Bernau from Berlin, S-Bahn #8 from Ostkreuz (1hr.; Berlin rapid transit ticket valid; you may have to change in Pankow). From the station, go straight until the first corner, turn left, zigzag right and left until you reach the Marktplatz. The **tourist office** *(Fremdenverkehrsamt),* Burgermeisterstr. 4 (tel. (03338) 36 53 88; fax 87 36), books private rooms for DM3 (from DM25) and provides brochures (open April-Sept. Mon.-Fri. 9am-6pm, Sat. 9am-1pm; Oct.-March Mon., Wed., and Fri. 9am-5pm, Tues. and Thurs. 9am-6pm). The local **Jugendherberge (HI),** Prenzlauer Chaussee 146 (tel.(033397) 221 09), 300m to the left of the bus stop, is in Wandlitz. (Reception open 7am-10pm. DM20, over 26 DM25. Sheets DM6. Breakfast included.)

ORANIENBURG AND SACHSENHAUSEN

The small town of Oranienburg, just north of Berlin, was home to **KZ Sachsenhausen,** a Nazi concentration camp in which more than 100,000 Jews, communists, intellectuals, gypsies, and homosexuals were killed between 1936 and 1945. In 1961, the GDR opened the site as the **Gedenkstätte Sachsenhausen,** Str. der Nationen 222, 16151 Oranienburg (tel. 80 37 15). Parts of the camp have been preserved in their original form, including the cell block where particularly "dangerous" prisoners were kept in solitary confinement and tortured daily, and a pathology department where Nazis performed medical experiments on inmates both dead and alive. Only the foundations of Station Z (where prisoners were methodically exterminated) remain, but the windswept grounds convey the horrors which were committed here. A GDR slant is still apparent; the main museum building features Socialist Realist stained-glass windows memorializing "German Anti-Fascist Martyrs." The museums themselves, however, have been totally overhauled recently. The main one hosts special shows of Holocaust-related art, as well as a fascinating permanent textual exhibit (in English and German) on the history of anti-Semitic practices throughout the world. To get to Sachsenhausen, S-Bahn #1 (direction: "Oranienburg") to the end (40min.). Follow the signs from the station. (Open April-Sept. Tues.-Sun. 8am-6pm; Oct.-March Tues.-Sun. 8:30am-4:30pm. Free.) The **telephone code** is 03301.

BERLIN

Brandenburg

Surrounding Berlin on all sides, the province of Brandenburg is overshadowed by the sprawling metropolis within it. The Hohenzollern family, which eventually ruled the German Empire, emerged from this forest like Natty Bumppo to jump onto the political stage. The stunning palaces in Potsdam stand as reminders of that moment in Brandenburg's past. Many believe that Brandenburg, now an agrarian hinterland, will unite with Berlin in the future, to form a single federal state, Berlin-Brandenburg. Brandenburg's lakes and forests are all easily accessible from Berlin, and provide a soul-saving break from the overloaded circuits of the capital.

■ Potsdam

Visitors disappointed by Berlin's distinctly unroyal demeanor can get their fix by taking the S-Bahn to nearby Potsdam, the glittering city of Friedrich II (the Great). While his dad, Friedrich Wilhelm I (a.k.a. "the Soldier King"), wanted to turn Potsdam into a huge garrison, the more eccentric Friedrich II beautified the city. Although most of downtown Potsdam was destroyed in a 20-minute air raid in April 1945, the castle-studded **Sanssouci Park** still stands as a monument to Fred II's (sometimes dubious) aesthetic taste. Potsdam was Germany's "Little Hollywood" from 1921 until World War II, as the suburb of Babelsberg became one of the capitals of the film industry. As the site of the 1945 conference where the Allies divied up Germany, Potsdam's name became synonymous with Germany's defeat. After serving for 45 years as the home of Communist Party fat cats, the 1000-year-old city finally recovered a sense of dignity in 1991 when Brandenburgers restored its status as the *Land*'s capital.

Orientation and Practical Information The **tourist office,** Friedrich-Ebert-Str. 5 (tel. 27 55 80), is between the streetcar stops "Alter Markt" and "Platz der Einheit"—all trains from the Potsdam Stadt bus/train station go to one of the two stops. To get to the tourist office, go across the *Lange Brücke* (bridge) and head straight on Friedrich-Ebert-Str. The office provides a usable city map (Potsdam is also on the more expensive Berlin "Extra" *Falk Plan*) and info on private accommodations, which they'll book for DM5. (Rooms DM20-40 per person. Private bungalows DM35-50 per person. For accommodations info, call 275 58 16. Open April-Oct. Mon.-Fri. 9am-8pm, Sat. 10am-6pm, Sun. 10am-4pm; Nov.-March Mon.-Fri. 10am-6pm, Sat.-Sun. 10am-2pm). You can buy the **Berlin-Potsdam Welcome Card** (DM29)—it gets you 48 hours on the Berlin-Brandenburg public transport network and reduced or free admission to museums in Berlin and Potsdam.

The tourist office offers three-hour **bus tours** from the **Filmmuseum,** at Schloßstr. 1. (Tours leave Tues.-Sun. 12:45pm, Fri.-Sun. 10:45am; available in English. DM35 with admission to Castle Sanssouci, DM27 without, students DM30.) **City Rad** (tel. 61 90 52), 100m from the Potsdam-Stadt station, offers three- to four-hour **bike tours** every Saturday (11:30am). Tours DM15 (not including bike rental) can be conducted in English if you ask. (**Bike** rental (not permitted in Sanssouci Park) open April-Oct. Mon.-Fri. 9am-7pm, Sat.-Sun. 9am-8pm.) S-Bahn #7 runs from Berlin to Potsdam-Stadt (30min. from Bahnhof Zoo); Potsdam is connected by **rail** to most of Brandenburg. Berlin rapid-transit tickets are valid on the S-Bahn for regular public transportation but are *not* valid for the bus lines to Sanssouci and Neues Palais (another DM3). However, bus #695 stops directly at the *Schloß* and is included in the regular ticket; Sanssouci is within walking distance of the city center. The **post office,** 14476 Potsdam, is at Platz der Einheit (open Mon.-Fri. 9am-6pm, Sat. 9am-noon). The **telephone code** is 0331.

Accommodations and Camping Potsdam has no hostel—the closest is in Wannsee (see **Berlin,** p. 131), 10 minutes away by S-Bahn. Hotels are scarce and dear, but the tourist office finds private rooms. The main campground, **Intercamping-platz**

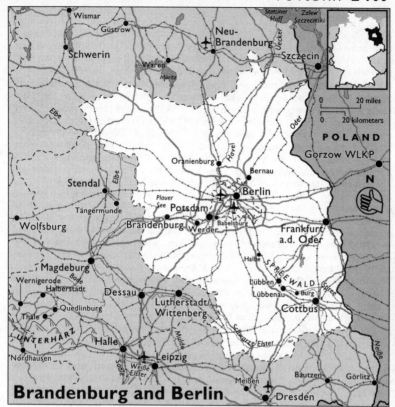

Brandenburg and Berlin

Riegelspitze am Glindower See (tel. (03327) 421 77), lies 13km away, on the other side of Lake Havel. Bus #631 (direction: "Werder") either from the main bus station or from Bassinpl. (Reception open 8am-1pm and 3-10pm. DM5 per person. DM5-8 per tent.) The tourist office also offers a list of campgrounds in the Potsdam area.

Food Bright, renovated Brandenburgerstr., the local pedestrian zone, encompasses most of the city's restaurants, fast-food stands, and grocery shops—including two bakeries that are open on Sunday. One of the street's better cafes, **Märkischer Land-mann,** Brandenburgerstr. 46 (tel. 270 64 36), is a sunny place that whips up big salads for DM11-12 and big German meals for DM14-17 (open Mon.-Sat. 9am-7pm, Sun. noon-7pm). The **Hollandisches Viertel** (see **Sights,** below) is lined with chic little cafes where you can have a civilized afternoon glass of wine or coffee. The merchants at the **flea market,** on Bassinpl., include a number of farmers with fresh produce and fake Levi's (open Mon.-Fri. 9am-6pm).

Sights and Entertainment Friedrich the Great's bizarre and authoritarian personality is on display in every manicured square meter of the 600-acre **Sanssouci Park.** Countless fountains and nudes line the intersecting footpaths that convey tourists between the park's Baroque castles and exotic pavilions. The largest of the four royal castles, the 200-room **Neues Palais** (tel. 969 42 55), was built by Friedrich to demonstrate Prussia's power and, incidentally, to house his guests. Inside is the 19th-century **Grottensaal,** a reception room whose ribbed walls glitter with seashells. The palace also houses a luxurious cafe (open daily 11am-7pm; closed 2nd and 4th Sat. of the month) and a **Sommertheater** (tel. (030) 210 02 10) with occasional classical-music performances (open most of the summer). In a macabre reunification gesture, Fred's remains, spirited away in 1945 to a Hohenzollern estate near Tübingen to save them from the Red Army, were brought back to rest on the grounds of Schloß Sanssouci in 1991. (Open April-Oct. daily 9am-5pm; Feb.-March and Oct. 9am-4pm; Nov.-Jan. Sun.-Mon. and Wed.-Sat. 9am-3pm; closed 1st and 3rd Mon. of each month.)

At the other end of the park's long, long **Hauptallee** (central path) stands the main attraction, the Versailles-esque **Schloß Sanssouci** (tel. 969 41 90), atop an incredible landscaped hill stair-stepped with garden terraces. The orange-tinted palace is small and airy, but richly decorated with figures of Bacchus and other Greek gods; Fred used to go here to escape his wife and drown his sorrows (*sans souci* is French for "without cares"). Unfortunately, visits are not always carefree; reunification has made this truly beautiful site accessible, and thousands of Western tourists and Hohenzollern groupies are making up for lost time. Tours of the castle in German (strictly limited to 40 people) leave every 20 minutes, but the final tour (5pm) usually sells out by 2pm during the high season—come early. If you want an English-language tour, go on the one led by the tourist office, but note that it includes only the main *Schloß* (although you're free to wander around afterwards). Inside, the style is cloudlike French Rococo (Fred was an unrepentant Francophone until his dying day)—all pinks and greens with startlingly gaudy gold trim. A high point is the **Voltairezimmer,** a chartreuse languor of a room decorated with colorful, carved reliefs of parrots and tropical fruit. Voltaire never stayed at the palace, though—the room was only built in his honor. The library reveals another of Fred's eccentricities: whenever he wanted to read a book, he had five copies printed, one for each of his palaces—in French, of course. By the way, the **"ruins"** the castle overlooks are fake: Fred liked the look of ancient ruins, so he had these built in the style of what's left of the Roman Forum. (Open April-Oct. daily 9am-5pm; Feb.-March 9am-4pm; Nov.-Jan. 9am-3pm.)

Next door is the **Bildergalerie** (tel. 969 41 81), whose brilliant collection of Caravaggio, van Dyck, and Rubens recently opened after extensive restoration with gorgeous results (open mid-May to mid-Oct. Tues.-Sun. 10am-noon and 12:30-5pm; closed 4th Wed. of each month). Romantic **Schloß Charlottenhof,** whose park surroundings were a Christmas gift from Friedrich Wilhelm III to Friedrich Wilhelm IV, melts into landscaped gardens and grape arbors at the south of the park. Nearby lie the **Römische Bäder** (Roman baths). Overlooking the park from the north, the pseudo-Italian **Orangerie-Schloß** is famous for its 67 dubious Raphael imitations—they serve to replace originals swiped by Napoleon (open mid-May to mid-Oct. 9am-noon and 1-5pm; closed 4th Thurs. of each month). Next door are the **Neue Kammern** (royal guest chambers), which also served as a recital hall for the dilettante king. The former ball and festival rooms are lavishly decorated; check out the Hohenzollern porcelain collection in a huge gold-trimmed closet room (open mid-May to mid-Oct. Sat.-Thurs. 10am-noon and 12:30-5pm; April to mid-May and mid-Oct. to early-Nov. Sat.-Sun. only 10am-5pm). The most bizarre of the park's pavilions is the **Chinesisches Teehaus,** a gold-plated fantasy, complete with a rooftop Buddha toting a parasol. (Admission to each palace DM8, students DM4. Neue Kammern DM5, students DM3. Pavilions each around DM4, students DM2. Day card to all palaces DM20, students DM15. Compulsory German tours of Sanssouci, Neue Kammern, and Schloß Charlottenhof; in others you can wander on your own.)

Back in town, the **Brandenburger Tor,** a smaller, vanilla cousin of Berlin's Brandenburg Gate, sits amid traffic flowing through Luisenpl. From here, Brandenburgerstr. leads down to the 19th-century **Kirche St. Peter und Paul,** Potsdam's only Catholic church. One block before the church, Friedrich-Ebert-Str. heads left to the **Hollandisches Viertel** (Dutch quarter), streets lined with red-brick Dutch-style houses. Now the most sought-after real estate in the city, Mittelstr. offers many quiet cafes. Towards the waterfront on Friedrich-Ebert-Str., the impressive dome of the **Nikolaikirche** rises above its neighbors. On closer inspection, the dome and the granite cube it sits on don't seem to match. The interior was renovated à la GDR with glass and sound-tiles that somehow lessen the aesthetic impact (open Mon. 2-5pm, Tues.-Sat. 10am-5pm, Sun. 11:30am-5pm). Down Friedrich-Ebert-Str. towards the bridge, the **Filmmuseum** (tel. 29 36 75), housed in the old Orangerie (which also served as Fred I's stables), documents Potsdam/Babelsberg's glory days as a film mecca with artifacts like Marlene Dietrich's costumes and a huge silent film archive (open Tues.-Fri. 10am-5pm, Sat.-Sun. 10am-6pm; DM6, students DM3).

Potsdam's second park, the **Neuer Garten,** nuzzling the Heiligersee, contains several royal residences. The most worthwhile is **Schloß Cecilienhof** (tel. 239 31), built in the image of an English country manor. Exhibits document the **Potsdam Treaty,** signed at the Palace in 1945. Visitors can see the tacky rooms in which the Allied delegates stayed (open Tues.-Sun. 9am-noon and 12:30-5pm; DM3, students and seniors DM2, under 6 free). Bus #695: "Cecilienhof," or tram #96: "Platz der Einheit," then tram #95: "Alleestr."

In the beginning of the 19th century, General Yorck brought 500 Russian soldiers to Prussia, and Friedrich Wilhelm III, a great fan of Russian culture, discovered that many of them had singing talent. Unfortunately, by the 1820s, only 12 of the original group were left—the rest died of homesickness. To make up for the depressing atmosphere, Fred III built each soldier an ornate wooden house. The nearby onion-domed **Kapelle Alexander Newski,** designed by Schinkel, was also intended as compensation. To the northeast, the crumbling villas of the Berliner Vorstadt were luxury homes for politicos during the heyday of the GDR. Berlinerstr. leads through here to the **Glienicker Brücke** (a.k.a. "The James Bond Bridge"), which used to be swallowed up by the "no man's land" between the GDR and West Berlin. Until 1989, it was used for the exchange of spies. Tram #93-95: "Burgstr."

Back in the Golden Age of European cinema, the **UFA Fabrik** in nearby Babelsberg was *the* German studio, giving Marlene Dietrich, Hans Alberg, and Leni Riefenstahl their first big breaks; in addition, Fritz Lang made *Metropolis* there. Tragically, apart from the films, few memorials of this era remain. The Disneylandish **Filmstadt Babelsberg,** August-Bebel-Str. 26-52 (tel. (0331) 721 27 55), built on the UFA lot, makes a feeble attempt to commemorate the greats of early German cinema, dishing out family fun of the worst sort in the form of video arcades and gift shops. The offerings of this theme park are vapid. S-Bahn #3: "Greiebnitzsee," then bus #690: "Bahnhof Drewitz." (Open March-Nov. daily 10am-6pm; DM25, students DM18.)

■ Brandenburg

One-thousand-year-old Brandenburg has long been a reluctant wielder of power; even when it was capital of the province to which it lends its name, it allowed Berlin civic freedom. When Albrecht the Bear ("Grrr...") built the town's cathedral in 1165, the surrounding *Neustadt* and *Altstadt* became the region's political epicenter. The city's industry took off during the 19th century, when the Brennabor bicycle factory and the Lehmann toy factory first began churning out their wares. Today Potsdam has officially usurped Brandenburg's political limelight, leaving the town to fade gently into obscurity. Reconstruction of the decaying buildings is proceeding slowly, and the winding cobblestone streets are wistfully quiet.

Brandenburg is surrounded by lush greenery and water. The river Havel, dotted with rowboats, flows gently by the **Dom St. Peter und Paul,** begun in Romanesque style in 1165, completed in Gothic style, and currently being refashioned late-20th century construction site style, with red bricks swaddled in blue plastic, and hairy construction workers filling in for the temporarily removed gargoyles. Before this major overhaul, architect Friedrich Schinkel couldn't resist adding a few touches: the "Schinkel-Rosette" and the window over the entrance. The cathedral's many wings fold off from the center into darkness, ending in little rooms like the 1235 **Bunte Kapelle** (the name means "colorful chapel"). The **Dommuseum** inside displays an array of relics and local-history treasures (open Tues.-Sat. 10am-4pm, Sun. noon-4pm; DM3, students DM2). The **St. Katharinen Church,** built at the end of the 14th century, is a beautiful example of *Backstein* (glazed brick) Gothic. The carved altar dates back to 1474 (open daily 10:45am-5:15pm). Both churches offer cultural events: St. Katharinen schedules organ concerts and the *Dom* hosts theater in the *Petrikloster* during the summer months. For 500 years a 6m statue of the legendary hero Roland has stood in front of the **Rathaus**—the GDR-era was just a ripple in time to this medieval symbol of free commerce. Several remaining towers from the 12th-century city walls add historic flavor to the *Altstadt* and the streets around **Neustädter Markt.** Incidentally, *Neustadt* (new town) is a relative term—it was founded in 1196.

Two routes run to Brandenburg from Berlin: you can either hop on trains heading towards Magdeburg and Hannover or S-Bahn #3 or 7: "Potsdam-Stadt," then change to the RB #33 (40min.; DM14 round-trip). The **tourist office,** Hauptstr. 51 (tel. 194 33), is just off Neustädter Markt. To get there from the train station, walk along Große Gartenstr., follow it until it turns into Steinstr., and head left on Hauptstr. Or tram #1, 2, or 9 from the station: "Neustädter Markt." The immensely helpful staff will answer questions and book rooms free of charge. Private rooms run DM30 for singles, DM40 for doubles. The tourist office also supplies cultural and historical information and distributes free maps and brochures in English (open Mon.-Wed. and Fri. 9am-7pm, Thurs. 9am-8pm, Sat. 10am-2pm). The **telephone code** is 03381.

The **Jugendherberge "Walter Husemann" (HI)**, Hevellerstr. 7 (tel./fax 52 10 40), sits on a tiny island right across from the *Dom*'s Domlinden entrance. Bus B also stops near here—get off at "Domlinden," and keep walking for a few blocks. The rustic lakeside locale and old volleyball nets in back transcend backwaterhood; this is charm, *Ossie* style. (Reception open 7-9am and 5-7pm. No English spoken. Curfew 10pm, but you can get a key. Members only. DM18, over 26 DM22. Breakfast included.) When the hostel is booked, they've been known to provide overflow housing in tents outside for DM12 per night. **Campingplatz Malge** (tel. 66 31 34) is in the middle of the woods, but only 20 minutes away from the city center. Bus B from Neustädter Markt; ask the driver to let you off at the campground. You can rent boats to fish in the nearby lake. (DM6.50 per person. DM6-8 per tent. Showers included. Fishing permits from campground reception or tourist office. Open April-Oct.) The campground also has a few two-person bungalows for DM30 per night. Inexpensive **restaurants** line the pedestrian area of Hauptstr., which also features a **Spar supermarket,** Hauptstr. 39 (open Mon.-Fri. 8am-6pm, Sat. 7-11am) and an open-air **farmers' market** (open daily 8am-6pm) behind the St. Katharinen Church. **Zum Kaffeekannchen,** Hauptstr. 16, just around the corner from the *Döner Imbiß,* serves coffee and ice cream on a balcony. (Namesake coffee pot DM4. Ice cream DM6-8. Open Mon.-Sat. 10am-7pm, Sat.-Sun. 1:30-6:30pm.)

▓ Frankfurt an der Oder

When writer **Heinrich von Kleist** was born here in 1777, Frankfurt an der Oder was a sleepy locale—even Kleist couldn't wait to skip town for the greater excitement of Dresden, Paris, and ultimately Berlin. Established in 1226 by merchants who found the location on the Oder ideal for trade with Poland and Northern Germany, Frankfurt remained a trading post until the **Universität Viadrina** was established in 1506. The university moved to Wroclaw (Breslau), Poland in 1811, the same year that Kleist committed suicide on the banks of the Kleiner Wannsee in Berlin (for entirely unrelated reasons). Frankfurt became a garrison town in the 19th century, and consequently was flattened in World War II. After the big sleep of the Communist era, the feeling here is not as much of a town *re*-building as of one building for the first time. In 1991, the Viadrina University returned, quickly coming to represent the youthful energy now surrounding "Frankfurt/O." This energy is attributable to the constant traffic of Germans and Poles crossing the border to transact business; though Polish town Slubice is only a 10-minute walk across the Oder bridge, the lines of BMWs and Polski Fiats waiting on either side sometimes extend for kilometers. As Poland becomes an increasingly important trading partner for Germany and the West, Frankfurt an der Oder promises to be a vibrant city in years to come.

Orientation and Practical Information Frankfurt an der Oder is less than an hour from Berlin by frequent **trains.** The **tourist office,** on the main drag at Karl-

Marx-Str. 8a (tel. 32 52 16; fax 225 65), provides maps and information about sights within Frankfurt and the surrounding countryside. From the station, head down the curving Bahnhof Str. and go right at the next major intersection onto Heilbronnerstr. A block later, turn left on Karl-Marx-Str. and the office is on the right (15min.).They find private rooms (DM30-50 with breakfast) for a fee of DM5 per person, or they can give you a free list of Pensions and *Privatzimmer* (open Mon.-Fri. 10am-noon and 12:30-5:30pm, Sat. 10am-12:30pm). There is a 24-hour **ATM** in the train station. The main **post office,** on the far right side of Heilbronnerstr., at the intersection of Linden-str. and Logenstr., is in a beautiful red brick building (open Mon.-Fri. 8am-6pm, Sat. 8am-noon). The **postal code** is 15230. The **telephone code** is 0335.

Accommodations Budget accommodations in Frankfurt an der Oder are sparse and in a state of flux. A *Privatzimmer,* booked through the tourist office, is probably the best option (DM25-45). Otherwise, the **Gästehaus des Bildungszentrums,** Hein-rich-Hildebrand-Str. 20a (tel. 556 32 27), offers an authentic GDR remnant. From the station, walk 15 minutes through the tunnel on the left up Dresdenerstr., then go left at Fürstenbürgerstr. as it becomes Johann-Eichorn-Str. Another 10 minutes of walking awaits; at the streetcar overpass, turn right on Friedensweg, and left on Heinrich-Hildebrand-Str. Or tram #1, 5, 6, or 7: "Johann Eichorn Str." (DM2.20). Tickets are available only at the SVF houses on the corner of Heibronnerstr. and Karl-Marx-Str. or in front of the *Bahnhof.* The rather run-down-looking guest house conceals 20 clean and comfortable rooms. (Open 24hr., but the office closes on weekends and takes no reservations. Singles DM35; doubles DM78. Breakfast included. Call ahead.)

Food Aside from the many outdoor food markets and stands in town, the **Student-enpassage** in the Schmalzgasse, one block down from the tourist office on Karl-Marx-Str., serves good, cheap meals for under DM6 (open Mon.-Fri. 8am-6:30pm, Sat. 8am-1pm). Try **Café Calliope,** Lindenstr. 4 (tel. 32 52 59), for Italian fare (DM6-14) in an outdoor sculpture garden (open Mon.-Fri. 9am-11pm, Sat. 5-11pm). Afterwards stroll in the cool galleries of the **Haus der Künste,** a Neoclassical building erected in 1787. For coffee and ice cream, the delightful **Café im Museum,** Heilbronnerstr. 19 (tel. 227 63), is located inside the Heilbronnerstr. part of the **Museum Junge Kunst** (open Tues.-Sun. 2-4:30pm). Pack for a picnic on the Oder at **Rewe** supermarket (tel. 404 21), at Johann-Eichorn-Str. and Spartakusring (open Mon.-Fri. 8am-6:30pm, Sat. 8am-1pm). Tram #1, 5, 6, or 7: "Johann-Eichorn-Str." A much cooler, and somewhat cheaper dining option is to cross the bridge from Rosa-Luxemburg-Str. and do lunch in Slubice, Poland (passport required). Given that Slubice's economy seems to be based solely on the sale of **cheap cigarettes** (under DM2 per pack), selling food is a low priority, but there are a few cafes on Robotniczejstr. Most restaurants and stores accept both Marks and Zloty, but for better prices, convert Marks into Zloty at the exchange stands *(kontor)* on the Polish side.

Sights Most historical sights in Frankfurt an der Oder are conveniently located within a few blocks of the main Marktplatz. From Karl-Marx-Str. one can easily see the beautiful but scarred **Marienkirche.** Built in the early Gothic style of the 13th century, it was once one of Frankfurt an der Oder's grandest sights. Unfortunately, the deteri-orated cathedral is now closed indefinitely while undergoing renovations.

Brilliant author **Heinrich von Kleist** is the town's claim to fame. Born to a noble but impoverished Prussian military family, young Heinrich enlisted in military school at 14. From 1793 to 1795 he participated in campaigns against the French, but, influenced by Enlightenment ideals, he quit the army in 1799, citing the inequality of conditions between officers and enlisted men. Rejecting his birthright, he lived as a pauper, attempting to start journals in Dresden and Berlin. Meanwhile, he wrote plays—among them his comedy *Der Zerbrochne Krug* (The Shattered Jug) and the intense, imagistic tragedy *Penthesilea*—and short stories (the most famous being his novellas *Michael Kohlhaas* and *Die Marquise von O*). Kleist wrote famously complex prose describing bourgeois society with irony and sympathy. Although his works did not find an audience during his lifetime—his scathing eye may have been too much for contemporaries to take—they are now considered classics of German literature. Penniless and dissatisfied, Kleist and a terminally ill friend committed suicide on the shore of the Kleiner Wannsee in Berlin in 1811.

Kleist's birthplace was destroyed during World War II—all that remains is a plaque on an ugly GDR-era apartment block on Große Oderstr., opposite the *Marienkirche*. The **Kleistmuseum,** on Faberstr. 7 (tel. 53 11 55), at the end of Bischofstr., is housed in a small blue building in which the young Kleist attended school. The musuem is a little disappointing—its three floors feature facts and documents about the Kleist family as well as manuscripts, but very little about Kleist himself. It's understandable that the museum should be so spare in personal information—when Kleist died, his only possession was a black leather *Rucksack* which was sold to pay his debts (open Tues.-Sun. 11am-5pm; DM4, students DM3, kids DM1; audio tours in English DM2).

The **Museum Junge Kunst,** Heilbronner Str. 19 (tel. 53 58 67), is the place to see contemporary paintings and sculpture in Brandenburg. Housed in a beautiful villa, the exhibits are a worthy attempt to bring modern East German art to light (open Tues.-Sun. 11am-5pm; DM2, students DM1.40). The rest of the museum lives in the **Rathaus,** Marktplatz 1 (tel. 552 41 50), and has a similar but larger collection of modern Eastern German art (DM3, students DM2; open Tues.-Sun. 11am-5pm).

■ Spreewald (Spree Forest)

The Spree River splits apart about 100km southeast of Berlin and branches out over the countryside in an intricate maze of streams, canals, meadows, lakes, and primeval forests stretching over 1000kmsq. This is the home of the legendary **Irrlichter,** a sort of Sachsen leprechaun who lights the waterways (for a price) for travelers who lose their way, and leads those who refuse to pay to their deaths. Folklore, tradition, and wildlife have survived here with remarkable harmony in tiny villages and towns first settled in the Middle Ages. Hire a barge, rent a paddle boat, or take to the trails by foot or bicycle to see why locals insist that the Spreewald—not Amsterdam, Stockholm, or St. Petersburg—is the true "Venice of the North."

But this is an agrarian Venice, where farmers row to their fields and noisy children paddle home from school. It's a green Venice as well—the fields and forests teem with owls, storks, kingfishers, otters, and foxes, animals known to most Europeans only through textbooks or television documentaries. In a country infamous for pollution and its *kaputt* environment, the Spreewald is idyllic.

Until the 17th century, these waterways wound through one of Europe's densest forests. The Prussian kings, however, directed a clearing of the trees—they wanted to use the wood for furniture and to sow the newly created fields with pumpkins. Though heavily bombed in World War II, the forest recovered quickly and the rich diversity of flora and fauna flourished once more. But socialist industry was not so kind: until 1990, coal-power stations towering outside of Lübbenau drew their cooling water from these streams as their smoke choked the sky.

Reunification brought the mixed blessing of greater environmental protection and hordes of forest-trampling tourists. The Spreewald is now recognized as a *Biosphär-reservat* (a biosphere nature reserve) by the U.N. Some sections of the forest are closed to the public; other sections are closed during mating and breeding seasons, but not tourist season. **Guided tours** are offered by reservation, camping spots abound, bicycles can be rented everywhere, and excellent hiking trails and footpaths weave their way through the peaceful forest. Each local tourist office has information on these leisure activities. They won't let you forget, however, that the forest is protected by the government; tourists are urged to be environmentally responsible.

Lübben and **Lübbenau,** two tiny towns that open up into the labyrinths of canals that snake through the forest, are the most popular tourist destinations and lie within daytrip range of Berlin. **Cottbus,** close to the Polish border, a bit farther east, offers genuine **Sorb** culture. The Sorbs, Germany's native Slavic minority, originally settled the Spreewald region (see **The Sorbs,** p. 163). Although the traditional Sorbian culture survives in several Lusatian towns, it is (with a few exceptions) otherwise encountered mostly in museums, Sorbian souvenirs, and in the occasional use of Sorbian place names alongside their German counterparts. If your German is shaky, the **Spreewaldbüro,** Zwinglistr. 5a, Berlin 21 (tel. 392 30 22), is your best source of regional information. They speak English and will reserve private rooms in the Spreewald (open Mon.-Fri. 9am-6pm). It's best to make reservations ahead, during the summer, when a mass of tourists invades. U-Bahn #9: "Turmstr."

LÜBBEN

A good base for Spreewald excursions, Lübben is about an hour southeast of Berlin by train or by the Berlin-Cottbus *Autobahn.* The **harbor** is watched over by the ancient **Schloßturm** (castle tower), built in the 15th century by the Brandenburg Prince Friedrich II as an imposing defense against invaders. Even World War II, which destroyed 80% of the **Altstadt,** could not topple the tower.

The *Altstadt's* architectural pride is the newly restored **Paul Gerhardt Kirche,** named for the most famous German hymn writer since Martin Luther. Gerhardt is buried inside (open Wed. and Sun. 10am-noon and 3-5pm). If you wish to wander or picnic in Lübben's lush green park, **Der Hain,** the entrance is at the end of Breite Str. Near Lübben stands **Straupitz,** an otherwise forgotten village where Neoclassical architect Karl Friedrich Schinkel erected a strikingly unusual church. Saved from obscurity by ample transportation, Straupitz is accessible by barge or bus.

Lübben's **tourist office,** Lindenstr. 14 (tel. 41 31; fax 25 43), directly on the harbor, provides trail maps and finds rooms (doubles DM25-35 per person) for a DM5 fee. From the station, head right on Bahnhofstr., left on Logenstr., right on Friedenstr., and left on Spreenferstr., then head to the intersection; it's on the right. They charge DM2.50 for a good map, but it's worth avoiding a mapless meander through town. They also rent **bikes** (1hr. DM1.50, day DM10, ID deposit; open Tues. 9am-noon and 1-6pm, Thurs. 9am-noon and 1-3pm, Fri. 9am-noon). During winter months and after hours, the office posts a list of private rooms just outside the entrance. You can also rent a **bike** at the station for DM10 per day (open daily 7am-9pm). For a **taxi,** call 37 16. The **post office** waits at Poststr. 4, 15907 Lübben. The **telephone code** is 03546.

The **Fährmannsverein Lübben/Spreewald,** Ernst-von-Houwald-Damm 16 (tel. 71 22), offers many different **boat trips** exploring different regions of the Spreewald (open daily 9am-4pm; 1½-8hr., DM4-5 per hour). Trips depart from Strandcafé-Kahnanlegestelle after 9am; the boats leave when full. Go straight from the tourist office down Ernst-von-Houwald-Damm, cross the bridge, and go right. The **Kahnfährhafen "Flottes Rudel,"** Eisenbahnstr. 3 (tel. 82 69), also straight ahead from the tourist office (bear right through the lot before the bridge), offers boat and barge trips with picnics for the same prices as the Fährmannsverein, starting daily at 10am. Alternatively, rent a **boat** at **Bootsverleih Gebauer,** on Lindenstr. (tel. 71 94). From the tourist office, go straight and turn right just before you reach the bridge. (One-seat paddle boat Mon.-Fri. DM24 per day, Sat.-Sun. DM28. Rowboats for up to 4 people Mon.-Fri. DM45, Sat.-Sun. DM49. Canoes for 2 adults and 2 children under 7 Mon.-Fri. DM40, Sat.-Sun. DM45. You can also rent by the hour (DM5-10). Everyone must know how to swim. Lifejackets provided for kids; those under 10 must be accompanied by adult. ID required. Open April-Sept. daily from 9am, Oct.-March daily from 10am.)

The **Jugendherberge Lübben (HI)** is located in the middle of a wheatfield on the outskirts of town, but ostensibly still in this galaxy. Though in the middle of nowhere, the hostel itself is a dream, with cozy 10-bed rooms, nightly entertainment in the form of watching cows stumble into electric fences (Moo!), and a hip regular crowd of sharply dressed *Schülmädchen*. To get there, turn right off Bahnhofstr. until the end of Luckauerstr., then veer right and take a left onto Eisenbahnstr., cross Pushkinstr., and follow Dorfstr. (Reception open after 3pm. No curfew—not that it really matters. DM20, over 26 DM22. Sheets DM6.) It takes a good 30 minutes to reach **camp** at **Am Burglehn** (tel. 70 53). From the station, turn right on Bahnhofstr., left on Luckauer Str., right on Burgtehnstr., and continue along the footpath to the campground. (Reception open 7am-10pm. DM6 per person. Tents DM5-8. 4-person cabins DM30.) While you're in Lübben, sample the Spreewald's particular pickled delicacies, famous throughout Germany. The **Gurken Paule,** Ernst-von-Houwald-Damm-Str. (tel. 89 81), is an outdoor stand offering the freshest of the Spreewald's unique *Gurken* (cucumber) assortment (*Salzdillgurken*—salty, *Senfgurken*—mustard, *Gewürzgurken*—spicy). Pay DM0.50 per pickle, DM5 for a hefty jar (open daily 9am-6pm).

LÜBBENAU

Tiny Lübbenau is actually the largest and most famous of Spreewald towns. For many tourists (and there are tons), the village serves as a springboard for trips into the **Oberspreewald.** Winding streets of the town center open directly onto the wooded paths and villages of the upper forest. The landscape here is much denser than that above Lübben, and intricately interwoven with canals.

The *Altstadt* is a 10-minute trot from the station. Go straight on Poststr. until you come to the marketplace dominated by the Baroque **Church of St. Nikolai.** The carved stone pillar in front served as an 18th-century crossroads post marking the distance in *Stunden,* an antique measurement equalling one hour's walk (circa 4.5km; open Mon.-Fri. 2-4pm). The town's aristocracy met its maker in 1944 when the local Duke was executed after being implicated in an attempt on Hitler's life. After the *Wende,* his three sons returned from the West to restore the familial *Schloß,* now a handsome (but terrifically expensive) hotel and restaurant. The lush castle grounds (*Schloßbezirk*) are open to the public and shelter the **Spreewaldmuseum Lübbenau,** offering a fascinating overview of Spreewald development and its unique customs. Adore traditional Spreewald costumes (open April to mid-Sept. Tues.-Sun. 10am-6pm; mid.-Sept. to Oct. 10am-5pm; DM3, students DM2).

There are two main departure points for **gondola tours** of the forest: the **Großer Hafen** (big harbor) and the **Kleiner Hafen** (little harbor). Follow the signs to either from the town center. The Großer Hafen offers a larger variety of tours, including two- and three-hour trips to Lehde (DM8.50-10, children half-price). Longer trips (4-8hr.) cost around DM5 per hour; for the same price, you can design your own tour. The boats take on customers starting at 9 or 10am and depart when full, continuing throughout the day (2-7hr.; DM8-14; no English tours, but hilarious if you speak German and can decipher Sachsen's dialect). The gondolas are a great way to see the scenery. From the Kleiner Hafen, at the end of Spreewaldstr., tours leave daily from 9am on and last 1½ to 10 hours. Also at the Kleiner Hafen, a beautiful leafy path begins just over the wooden bridge. Stroll or bike down it. If a cruise with drunken elderly Germans doesn't float your boat, rent a **paddle boat** at **Manfred Franke,** Dammstr. 72 (tel. 27 22; DM29 per day for a 2-person boat). To get there from the station, turn right down Bahnhofstr. and left at the next intersection (open 8am-7pm).

Lübbenau lies 13km past Lübben on the Berlin-Cottbus line. The **tourist office,** Ehm-Welk-Str. 15 (tel. 36 68; fax 467 70), left of the church, provides maps, info on bike trails, and finds rooms (DM25-45; open Mon.-Fri. 9am-4pm). **Kowalski,** Poststr. 6 (tel. 28 35), near the station, rents **bikes** (day DM10; open Mon.-Sat. 9am-6pm). For a **taxi,** call 31 43. In an **emergency,** call 81 91 or 22 22. The **telephone code** is 03542.

Even though the closest hostel is in Lübben (10min. by train), finding a room isn't a problem in friendly Lübbenau. Check for *Zimmer frei* signs or knock on the door of **Zimmervermietung-Haus Jerkel,** Max Plessner-Str. 22 (tel. 436 96), just 10 minutes from the station. Take Poststr. straight, then right on Max-Plessner-Str. The Jerkels offer 14 comfortable beds in their white stone house. They often have same-day rooms, but call ahead. (Doubles DM62, with full bath DM72. Breakfast included.) There are two camping options: directly on the road to Lehde, **Campingplatz "Am Schloßpark"** (tel. 35 33; emergency 28 11; in winter (035456) 51 55) offers 300 plots for tents (DM5-8 per night) with cooking and shower installations on site (DM1-3). There are also 55 bungalows (DM25 for up to 6 people) and 21 trailer spots (DM11-13), as well as a store with soap, soup, pickles, and other necessities. (Reception open 7am-10pm. Open May-Oct. and sporadically during the winter—call ahead).

For cheap food and pickles, beets, and beans by the barrel, check out the snack bars and stands along the harbor. On the way to the campgrounds, the **Café-Garten,** on the Lehde stream (tel. 36 22), is a self-service outdoor cafe with Munich potato salad (DM2.50) or pike filet (DM9.80; open daily 9am-10pm). In town, **Spreewald Idyll,** Spreestr. 13 (tel. 22 51), makes specialties like *Wildschweinbraten in Sahnesoße mit Wildpreiselbeeren und Salzkartoffeln* (DM13; open daily 8am-midnight).

LEHDE

It's only a hop and a paddle from Lübbenau to **Lehde,** a UNESCO-protected landmark and the most romantic village of the Spreewald, accessible only by foot, bike, or boat. You can drive to the Lehde outskirts, but cars (except those owned by residents) are banned in the village. By foot, it's a 15-minute trek; follow the signs from the Großerhafen. If you're partial to water, take a boat from the harbor. Most farmers here still depend on the canals for access to the world. Check out the **Freilandmuseum Lehde,** where things remain as they were when an entire Spreewalder family slept in the same room and newlyweds spent their honeymoons heaving in the hay. The museum displays restored farm houses and local art works (open April to mid-Sept. daily 10am-6pm; mid-Sept. to Oct. 10am-5pm; DM6, students, and seniors DM4).

Because Lehde is extremely protective of its landmark status, few guest beds are offered, but a few *Pensionen* cower on the outskirts. Don't expect to stay in Lehde overnight, but if you really want to, talk to the Lübbenau tourist office. Just before you reach the bridge to the museum, you'll see **Zum Fröhlichen Hecht,** Dorfstr. 1 (tel. 27 82), a large cafe, restaurant, and *Biergarten*. Sit upstairs on the wooden benches for a view of the languidly passing boats. Try *Kartoffeln mit Quark* (potatoes with sour curd cheese) in a special Spreewald sauce (DM7) or pickles with a side order of *Schmalz* (lard; DM3), another Spreewald specialty. Say a prayer for your heart, and dig in (open daily 10am-5pm). The **telephone code** is 03542.

BURG

Farther east and accessible only by bike or the Lübben-Cottbus bus, Burg is an amazingly expansive village—over 600 farms and 200 private homes sprawl across 52km-sq. From Lübben, bus #700 (direction: "Cottbus"): "Burg Bleske." From Cottbus, bus #700 (direction: "Lübben") or 46 (direction: "Burg"): "Burg Bleske" (one-way DM4.10). The ride itself is stunning, providing vertiginous views of a tremendous landscape of fields, forests, and farmers oblivious to the industrial towns 30 minutes away. The most impressive view of Burg is from the 27m high 1914 **Bismarckturm** (Bismarck tower) overlooking the surrounding forests and the 300 streams and bridges that thread through them. From the bus, head right on Hauptstr. toward the main harbor. Cross the bridge and follow the trail signs ahead for 1km (open April-Oct. Tues.-Sun. 10am-6pm; DM2, children DM1; closed in bad weather).

The **tourist office,** Am Hafen 1 (tel. 417), is to the left just before the bridge. They find rooms for DM5 (private rooms DM25-35; *Pension* DM50-70) and provide info on Burg and Sorb festivals (open Mon.-Fri. 9am-noon and 1-6pm). To rent **boats**—canoes, paddle boats, or kayaks—try **Bootsverleih Lukas,** Willisaschzaweg 42 (tel. 867). For a **taxi** call 603 65. **Zweiradhaus Schmidt,** Bahnhofstr. 17 (tel. 376), rents **bikes** (open Mon.-Fri. 8am-6pm, Sat. 9am-6pm; day DM10-12 with ID). The Spreewald-Drogerie **pharmacy,** Bahnhofstr. 1 (tel. 232), has a condomat outside (DM5 per pack). In this romantic village, it may be of use. The **telephone code** is 035603.

The local **Jugendherberge (HI),** Dorf 220 (tel. 225), is just a few steps from the bus stop; follow the signs. This pastoral hostel on the river has comfy rooms. (Reception opens at 7pm. Curfew 10pm. DM20, over 26 DM25. Breakfast included. Dinner DM5. Sheets DM6). **Edeka supermarket** on Hauptstr. offers groceries (open Mon.-Fri. 8am-6pm, Sat. 7:30-11am). The tasty bakery **Werner Mieth,** Bahnhofstr. 39 (tel. 348), serves pretzels and pastries (DM2-3; open Tues.-Fri. 6:30am-6pm, Sat. 6:30am-11am).

COTTBUS (CHOSEBUZ)

The second-largest *Burg* in Brandenburg, Cottbus dwells in **Niederlausitz** (Lower Lusatia) on the southernmost edge of the Spreewald. Founded by Sorbs in the 8th century, Cottbus's distinguishing quality is its substantial Sorb population. All street signs are printed in both Sorbian and German, several local Sorbian newspapers and radio stations flourish, and the study of Sorbian is growing popular in local schools. Cottbus's other claim to fame is the tongue-twister every German child knows: *"Der Cottbuser Postkutscher putzt den Cottbuser Postkutschkasten."* (Regardless of your language skills you're probably stumped; it means something like "the stagecoach driver from Cottbus cleans the interior of his Cottbus stagecoach.") The stagecoach is the town symbol, which at least partially explains the aforementioned nonsense.

Orientation and Practical Information Direct trains to Berlin (2hr.) and bus lines to nearby hamlets make Cottbus the nexus for Spreewald tours. The bus station is a 15-minute walk from the train station. Head straight on Bahnhofstr. and right on Marienstr. Or streetcar #1 from the train station: "Marienstr." (two stops, DM2); the bus station is on the right. The **tourist office,** Berlinerstr. 1a (tel. 242 55 or 242 54; fax 79 19 31), at the corner of Bahnhofstr., finds rooms for DM5 (singles DM40-60, doubles DM70-105), and gives out a free but nearly illegible map (open Mon.-Fri. 9am-6pm, Sat. 9am-1pm). **Schenker,** Friedrich-Ebert Str. 15 (tel. 330 95), rents **bikes** from DM5 (open Mon.-Fri. 9am-6pm, Sat. 9am-noon). The **telephone code** is 0355.

Accommodations Cottbus's two **Jugendherbergen** sit kitty-corner to each other on the quiet square behind the Klosterkirche. From the "Stadthalle" tram stop, head up Berlinerstr. toward the *Altstadt,* take a left on Wendestr., and go around the church. The **Bettenhaus (HI),** Klosterpl. 2-3 (tel. 225 58), serves clean and modern three- to 10-bed rooms. (Reception open Mon.-Fri. 8am-1pm and 7-9pm. DM20, over 26 DM25. Non-members DM26.50. Breakfast included.) **Pension Schiemenz,** Karlstr. 22a (tel. 79 12 29), is a sweet deal. It's got six rooms, all luxuriously furnished with TV and telephone. (Reception open until 10pm or by arrangement. Singles DM40-60; doubles DM80-100. Breakfast included.) It's about a 15-minute walk north of the city center. From Berlinerpl., head straight on Friedrich-Ebert-Str. and follow it as it turns into Karlstr. Or tram #1 or 4: "Bonmaskenpl." The **Pension** at Klosterpl. 4 (tel. 225 58) is in a historic building embedded in the town wall. (Singles DM50, with shower DM85; doubles DM85, with shower DM110. Breakfast included.)

Food The restaurant **Buffalo,** Spremburgerstr 27 (tel. 228 38), specializes in German food and potato concoctions such as potatoes with tomatoes and mozzarella for DM9 (open daily 11:30am-when it's really really dark). For a more romantic atmosphere, try **Café Altmarkt,** Altmarkt 10 (tel. 310 36), where you can have a beer and a view of the Altmarkt from beneath the 16th-century arch (cafe open Mon.-Fri. from 9am, Sat.-Sun. from 10am). On the other side of town, **Café Baum,** Marienstr. 6 (tel. 311 20), to the right of the bus station, serves all four food groups: coffee, wine, beer, and ice cream (open Mon.-Fri., Sun. 9am-midnight, Sat. noon-2pm).

Sights and Entertainment Cottbus, like most East German cities, was severely scarred by World War II. But the city's post-war *Neue Sachlichkeit* (New Objectivity) architecture has not penetrated the *Altstadt,* which is liberally sprinkled

COTTBUS (CHOSEBUZ) ■ 145

with historic buildings. Heading down Berlinerstr., the church on the left is the **Klosterkirche** (tel. 248 25), also known as *Wendische Kirche* (*"Wendish"* is German for Sorbian). Built in 1300 by Franciscan monks, it is the oldest church in Cottbus (open Wed. and Fri. 10:30am-4:30pm, Sat. 10:30am-3:30pm). The **Altmarkt** lies a bit farther down Berlinerstr. The **Niederlausitzer Apotheke,** Berlinerstr. 21 (tel. 239 97), first started dealing drugs in 1573. The shop still sells herbal teas and other potions, but the back offers a museum with a poison chamber. (Store open Tues.-Fri. 10am-5pm. Obligatory tours Tues.-Fri. 11am and 2pm, Sat.-Sun. 2 and 3pm or by appointment. DM4, students DM2.) At the eastern end of the Altmarkt, Sandowerstr. leads to the 1400 **Oberkirche St. Nikolai,** the largest church in the Niederlausitz and home to frequent concerts by regional orchestras (open Mon.-Sat. 10am-5pm, Sun. 1-5pm; tickets DM12, students DM6). Sorbian culture buffs can head to the **Wendisches Museum** (Sorbian museum), Mühlenstr. 12 (tel. 79 49 30), down Spremburgerstr., which houses unique Sorbian folk art and costumes, particularly the distinctive headdress. (For more on the Sorbs, see **The Sorbs**, p. 163.) (Museum open Tues.-Fri. 8:30am-6pm, Sat.-Sun. 2-6pm, DM2, students DM1).

Farther down Spremburgerstr. lies the strangely named petite **Schloßkirche**. The Huguenots who rebuilt it had no delusions of grandeur. At the end of the street, the *Altstadt* transmogrifies into the *Neustadt*. The 1908 cherub-sprinkled **Staatstheater Cottbus,** Schillerpl. 1 (tel. 222 73 or 222 75), is Europe's only extant example of late-*Jugendstil* architecture. The program includes works by Verdi, Goethe, and Brecht; call 237 61 for tickets. While the inner city is somewhat congested, Cottbus is surrounded by a beautiful landscape. The riverside panorama leads to **Schloß Branitz** (tel. 751 50), a Baroque castle built in 1772 by Prince Hermann von Pückler-Muskau, a globetrotter with a love of larger-than-life architecture. From the *Altstadt,* follow Spremburgerstr. to Str.-der-Jugend, and bear left at Bautzenerstr., turn left at Stadtring, and right at Gustav-Hermann-Str., which leads you to the park (open Tues.-Sun., 10am-6pm; Nov.-March Tues.-Sun. 10am-5pm; DM5, students DM3). **Branitzer Park,** which surrounds the castle, is peppered with oddities. The landscape in the western park includes several pyramids which will forever bear witness to Pückler-Muskau's Egyptophilia. One appears to float in the center of the lake.

BRANDENBURG

Sachsen (Saxony)

Sachsen is known to foreigners primarily for Leipzig and Dresden, the most fabled cities of Eastern Germany after Berlin, but the entire region provides a fascinating historical stratification that reveals a great deal about life in the former East. The castles around Dresden attest to the bombastic history of Sachsen's prince-electors, while the socialist monuments of Chemnitz and the formless architecture of other major cities depict the colorless world of the GDR. On the eastern edge of Sachsen, Sächsiche Schweiz and the Zittauer Gebirge provide a respite from the aesthetic violence done by East Germany's city planners with hiking trails that march through a land of escapism to the borders of the Czech Republic and Poland.

■ Dresden

Dresden pulses with an historical intensity that is both vicious and sublime, an emblem of everything that was and is Eastern Germany. No matter where you go, you will not be able to forget that Allied bombings shattered the "Baroque Jewel" in February 1945, claiming over 50,000 lives and destroying over 75% of the *Altstadt*. Today, Dresden offers spectacular ruins amidst an array of world-class museums and an unparalleled history as the cultural capital of pre-war Germany. As partially reconstructed palaces and churches burst forth from the surrounding rubble that remained uncleared during the "deep freeze" of the GDR years, Dresden finds itself a focal point for the efforts of reunification; a skyline of over 200 cranes steadily assists the reconstruction, scheduled for completion by 2006, the city's 800-year anniversary. While you'll hear tourists everywhere waxing pretentious about a "phoenix-from-the-ashes" and "the hope of tomorrow," the raw Dresden of today offers a unique vitality that simply goes beyond the process of reincarnation.

ORIENTATION

The capital of the *Bundesland* of Sachsen, Dresden stands magnificently on the Elbe River 80km northwest of the Czech border and 180km south of Berlin. This city of half a million people is a major transportation hub between Eastern and Western Europe—during the mass emigrations from Germany in 1989, Dresden was the most frequented point of departure into Czechoslovakia. From the **Dresden Hauptbahnhof,** travelers shoot off to Warsaw (5 per day, 10hr.), Paris (9 per day, 10-13hr.), Prague (12 per day, 3hr.), Berlin-Lichtenberg (17 per day, 1½-2½hr.), Budapest (4 per day, 11hr.), Munich (14 per day, 7½-9hr.), Frankfurt am Main (8 per day, 5hr.), and Leipzig (37 per day, 1½hr.). Another station, **Bahnhof Dresden Neustadt,** sits on the other bank of the Elbe and bears a striking resemblance to its mate; trains leave from here to Weimar and other eastern cities.

Dresden is bisected by the Elbe. The *Altstadt* lies on the same side as the *Hauptbahnhof;* the *Neustadt,* to the north, escaped most of the bombing, paradoxically making it one of the oldest parts of the city. South of the *Altstadt* are the contrasting suburbs of Plauen and Strehlen. Since Dresden has finished removing socialist-era names from its streets and squares, when you pick up a map at the tourist office or a postcard stand, ask how old it is. Many of Dresden's main tourist attractions are centered between the Altmarkt and the Elbe. From there it's a five-minute scenic stroll to the banks of the *Neustadt.* Five immense bridges (Marienbrücke, Augustbrücke, Carolabrücke, Albertbrücke, and the "Blue Wonder" Loschwitzbrücke) connect the city halves. Watch for pickpockets along Pragerstr. and in department stores.

PRACTICAL INFORMATION

Tourist Offices: Dresden Information, Pragerstr. (tel. 49 19 20; fax 310 52 47; http://www.dresden-online.de). As you exit the *Hauptbahnhof* from the side exit on Wienerpl., cross the *Straßenbahn* tracks and head toward the main square straight ahead. Walk straight on Pragerstr. The office is on the right, behind the McDonald's. Decent

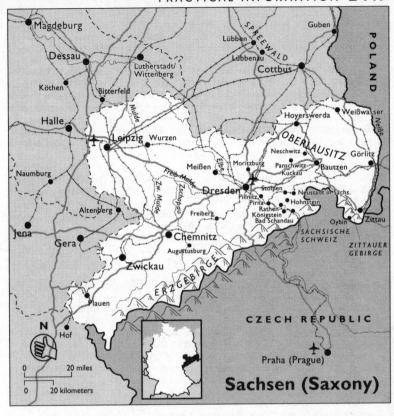

Sachsen (Saxony)

English spoken. They find **private rooms** (DM30-50) or hotel rooms for a DM5 fee, sell theater tickets, and offer guided **tours.** Their free maps cover the sights in a panoply of languages. Open Mon.-Fri. 9am-8pm, Sat. 9am-4pm, Sun. 10am-2pm. If closed, try the ultra-funky automated "Info-Tour" in the window. The **Tourist Information Neustädter Markt** (tel./fax 804 35 39), in the tunnel to the right as you walk off the Augustusbrücke, provides the same services. Open Mon.-Fri.10am-6pm, Sat.10am-4pm.

Discount Card: The **Dresden Card,** available at the tourist office or at DVB public transportation system offices, provides 48hr. of free rides on buses and trains and entry into many major museums (DM22).

Currency Exchange: ReiseBank, in the main hall of the train station. Open Mon.-Fri. 7:30am-7:30pm, Sat. 8am-noon and 12:30-4pm, Sun. 9am-1pm. DM3 charge for cash currency exchange; DM7.50 for traveler's checks. There are also a number of banks on Pragerstr. After hours, the self-service exchange machine in the *Hauptbahnhof* will do, but the rates are poor.

American Express: Hoyerzwalderstr. 20 (tel. 80 70 30), in front of the Frauenkirche in a booth a bit larger than a shoe box. Money sent, mail held, and other standard AmEx offerings. Open Mon.-Fri. 7:30am-6pm.

Flights: Dresden's airport (tel. 88 10) is about 15km from town. The **Airport City Liners** bus (one-way DM8) leave both stations for the airport every hr.; call 251 82 43 for schedules and information.

Trains: For information, call 194 19 or use the computerized schedule center in the main hall of the *Hauptbahnhof.*

Public Transportation: Dresden is sprawling—even if you'll only spend a few days, familiarize yourself with the major bus and streetcar lines. **Punch your ticket as**

you board. Four or less stops DM1.30; 1hr. DM2.50; 24hr. pass DM8; Weekly pass DM22, students DM15. Tickets and maps are available from friendly *Fahrkarten* dispensers at major stops and from the **Verkehrs-Info** stands outside the *Hauptbahnhof*, Postpl, Albertpl. or Pirnaischerpl. (open Mon.-Fri. 6am-7pm, Sat.-Sun. 7am-7pm). Most major lines run every hr. after midnight. Dresden's **S-Bahn** network reaches from Meißen (DM4.80) to Schöna by the Czech border. Buy tickets from automats in the *Hauptbahnhof* and validate them in the red contraptions; insert the ticket and press *hard*. Harder. The Dresden Card (see above) provides comprehensive discounts.

Ferries: The **Sächsische Dampfschiffahrt** (tel. 86 60 90) grooves with a restaurant, band, and dancing. Ships to Pillnitz (11am-5pm, every 2hr.; 1½hr.; DM20), Meißen (1hr.; DM12), and the Sächsische Schweiz (day pass DM27, under 14 DM16).

Taxis: tel. 459 81 12.

Car Rental: Sixt-Budget, in the Hilton by the Frauenkirche (tel. 864 29 72). Open Mon.-Fri. 7am-6pm, Sat. 8am-noon. **Europacar,** in the *Hauptbahnhof* near the Pragerstr. exit. Open Mon.-Fri. 7am-9pm, Sat. 8am-7pm, Sun. 9-11am.

Bike Rental: (tel. 461 32 85) in the *Hauptbahnhof* near the luggage storage. DM10 per day. Open Mon.-Fri. 6am-10pm, Sat. 6am-9pm.

Mitfahrzentrale: Martin-Luther-Str. 23 (tel. 801 05 48). Prices are DM0.03 per km plus a finder's fee. Berlin DM18. Frankfurt am Main DM44. Munich DM46. Hamburg DM46. Call one day in advance. Rides to Prague are easy to come by on weekends. Open Mon.-Fri. 10am-6pm.

Hitchhiking: *Let's Go* does not recommend hitchhiking as a safe mode of transportation. Hitchers stand in front of the *"Autobahn"* signs at on-ramps; otherwise they are heavily fined or smacked by oncoming traffic. To Berlin: streetcar #3 or 6: "Liststr.," then bus #81: "Olter." To Prague, Eisenach, or Frankfurt am Main: bus #72 or 76 to their last stops ("Lockwitz" or "Luga," respectively).

Luggage Storage and Lockers: At both train stations. Lockers DM2-4. 24hr. storage DM4 per piece. Open Mon.-Fri. 6am-10pm, Sat. 6am-9pm.

Bookstore: Das Internationale Buch, Kreuzstr. 4 (tel. 495 41 90), directly behind the Kreuzkirche, puts the State Dept. to shame with its bevy of flags. English books on the 2nd floor. Open Mon.-Fri. 9am-7pm, Sat. 9am-2pm (first Sat. every month 9am-4pm).

Library: Haupt- und Musikbibliothek, Freibergerstr. 35 (tel. 864 82 33), in the World Trade Center. A sparkling new library with tons of info, maps, and books about Dresden and Sachsen. Also offers **internet access** (for those who obtain a library card) and a cool cafe. Open Mon.-Fri. 10am-7pm, Sat. 10am-2pm.

Laundromat: Groove Station, Katharinenstr. 11-13. A laundromat and much, much more. Wash your clothes (DM5-6 per load) while getting tattoos, piercings, drinks, or *"Erektionsbekleidung"* (condoms). Open Sun.-Fri. 11am-2am, Sat. 10am-late. Also at **Jugendherberge Rudi Arndt,** in the cellar. DM3-4 per load.

Women's Center: Frauenzentrum "sowieso," Dornblüthstr. 18 (tel. 33 77 09), focuses on women's issues, with a phone line (tel. 281 77 88) for confidential crisis counseling. Office open Mon. 10am-noon, Tues. 10am-6pm, Fri. 9am-noon. Women's (straight and lesbian) bar night **"Klara Fall"** Thurs.-Fri. 7pm-midnight.

Gay and Lesbian Organizations: Gerede-Dresdner Lesben, Schwule und alle Anderen, Wienerstr. 41 (tel. 464 02 20), in Haus der Jugend, near the station. Also **AIDS-Hilfe,** Floria-Geyer-Str. 13 (tel. 233 73 01), with **"Bunker"** gay night, sponsored by Lederclub Dresden e.V. (Dresden Leather Club) Fri.-Sat. after 10pm.

Pharmacy: Closed pharmacies throughout the *Alt-* and *Neustadt* post signs indicating open ones.

Emergency: Ambulance, tel. 115. **Fire,** tel. 112. **Police,** tel. 110.

Internet Access: Spiel-In, Königsbrücke 56 (tel. 804 47 28), in the kind of arcade that Ms. PacMan could only dream about. Open Mon.-Fri. 6am-11pm, Sat.-Sun. 8am-11pm. 30min. connection and one drink DM5. (Also in **Library,** see above.)

Post Office: The **Hauptpostamt,** Königbrückerstr. 21/29, 01099 Dresden (tel. 444 10), is in Dresden-Neustadt. Open Mon.-Fri. 8am-6pm, Sat. 8am-noon. **Postamt 72,** Pragerstr., 01069 Dresden (tel. 495 41 65), is near the tourist office.

Telephone Code: 0351.

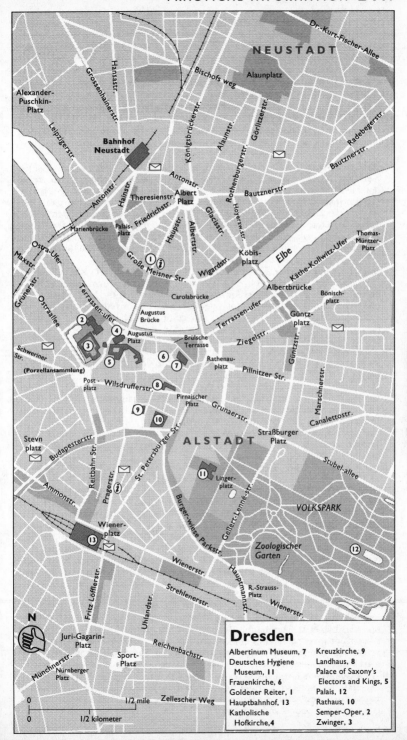

SACHSEN

Dresden

Albertinum Museum, 7
Deutsches Hygiene
   Museum, 11
Frauenkirche, 6
Goldener Reiter, 1
Hauptbahnhof, 13
Katholische
   Hofkirche, 4

Kreuzkirche, 9
Landhaus, 8
Palace of Saxony's
   Electors and Kings, 5
Palais, 12
Rathaus, 10
Semper-Oper, 2
Zwinger, 3

ACCOMMODATIONS AND CAMPING

Dresden is prepared for a convergence of all the citizens of the world, if need be, and the choices are only improving with the coming of two new hostels in 1997/98. For Huck Finn wannabes, a **riverboat hostel (HI)** will open on the Elbe. The plans for this 110-bed Love Boat include all the normal hostel goodies and a bar for DM20-30. Ask the tourist offices or the Hostel Rudi Arndt (below) to find out if its rooms are ship-shape and sea ready. The new **Mondpalast Backpacker** opened its doors in August 1997. The excess of available rooms means that you can often find same-day deals at some of the hotels on Pragerstr. if you don't want to stay in one of the hostels. The tourist offices can also facilitate stays in private rooms (see p. 146).

Jugendgästehaus Dresden (HI), Maternistr. 22 (tel. 49 26 20; fax 492 62 99), formerly the Hotel-kongress-business-center, now an authentic glimpse into pre-fab hotel living. Go out the Pragerstr. exit of the *Hauptbahnhof* and turn left, following the streetcar tracks along Annonstr. to Freibergerstr. Turn right and take another quick right onto Maternistr. Over 400 beds virtually ensure open spaces. The two- to three-bed rooms have a posh feel, and the breakfast buffet will leave you happier than a pig in slop. Singles, family rooms, and apartment-style rooms available. Reception open 4-10pm. No curfew. DM33, over 26 DM38; non-members pay DM5 extra. Breakfast and sheets included.

Mondpalast Backpacker, Katharinenstr. 11-13 (tel./fax 804 60 61), a 5-minute walk from *Bahnhof-Neustadt,* above Groove Station and DownTown (see p. 154). A hostel created by backpackers for backpackers, located at the heart of the *Neustadt* scene but soundproofed for sweet dreams. The artfully decorated theme rooms, the huge kitchen, the absence of a curfew, and the brand-newness of the hostel make it a veritable backpacker's paradise. Reception open 24hr. 4- and 6-bed dorms DM29. Doubles DM 70. Sheets included.

Jugendherberge Dresden Rudi Arndt (HI), Hübnerstr. 11 (tel. 471 06 67; fax 472 89 59). Streetcar #5 (direction: "Südvorstadt") or 3 (direction: "Plauen"): "Nürnbergerpl." Continue down Nürnbergerstr., turn right onto Hübnerstr.; the hostel is at the first corner on right. Or, from the *Hauptbahnhof,* walk down Fritz-Löffler-Str., bear right onto Münchenerstr., turn right onto Nürnbergerstr. Walk 1 block, turn left onto Hübnerstr. Central, comfortable, and pacific with a laid-back staff. Crowded three- to five-bed rooms don't detract from the convenience. Call, fax, or mail reservations for stays between March and August. Check-in 3-10pm. Curfew 1am. Lockout 10am-3pm. DM22, over 26 DM27. HI members only. Mandatory one-time linen fee (DM5).

Jugendherberge Oberloschwitz (HI), Sierksstr. 33 (tel./fax 268 36 72). S-Bahn #3 or 5: "Pirnaischerpl." (7min.) and change to S-Bahn #1: "Schillerpl." After 8pm, streetcar #3: "Albertpl." across the Elbe, then streetcar #6: "Schillerpl." Once at Schillerpl., there are 2 options. **Option 1:** Chill in the *Biergarten,* indulging in libations. Then stumble across the Elbe on the Loschwitzer bridge to Körnerpl. and take the intoxicatingly scenic *Schwebebahn* (hill train, not the *Standseilbahn*): "Siekstr." (DM2.50, covered by bus passes and Dresden Card). **Option 2:** Forget the beer—bus #61 (direction: "Weißeg, Buhlau"): "Steglicherstr." (4 stops), then bus #84: "Malerstr." Either way, this will take you well over an hour. The friendly looking hostel will be up on your right. Big rooms in a lovely setting, but *extremely* remote. It takes less time to get to Prague. Reception open 4-10pm. Get a key to escape curfew. DM24, over 26 DM29. Members only. Breakfast included.

City-Herberge, Lignerallee 3 (tel. 485 99 00; fax 485 99 01). From the Pragerstr. exit of the *Hauptbahnhof,* right on Wienerstr., left on J.-v.-Goethe-Str., which becomes Blüherstr. Turn left on Lignerallee. Great, central location with access to most major streetcar and bus lines. Rooms are well-kept (if somewhat sterile), and keep a high standard, but the bathrooms are shared. The grandiose breakfast buffet makes waking up a lot easier. Singles DM70; doubles DM100. Breakfast included.

Ibis Hotel, Pragerstr. (tel. 48 56 66- 61,62, or 63). Three huge hotel skyscrapers on Pragerstr. just across the street from the *Hauptbahnhof* offer summer same-day specials that are a good bargain for people traveling in pairs. Suites for two (DM99) come with TV, phone, and shower or bath, but no breakfast.

Camping: Campingplatz Altfranken, Altfranken (tel. 410 24 00). Only 7km out-side of Dresden and 1km from the nearest bus stop. Streetcar #7: "Julius-Val-drecht," then bus #70 to the end. Reception open Mon.-Fri. 7am-9pm, Sat.-Sun. 8:30am-4pm. DM10 per tent.

FOOD

Unfortunately, the surge in Dresden tourism yields an increase in prices, particularly in the *Altstadt*. The cheapest eats are at supermarkets or *Imbiß* stands on Pragerstr. The Altmarkt also features good Italian and Turkish restaurants. The *Neustadt* area, between Albertpl. and Alunpl., not only spawns a new bar or second-hand shop every few weeks, but also clearly rules the roost of quirky ethnic and student-friendly restaurants. The monthly **Garçon,** free at the tourist office, details culinary options.

Raskolnikow, Böhmischestr. 34 (tel. 931 72 22). A Dostoevskian haunt in a ram-shackle pre-war brownstone. Hidden beneath a sign for *Galerie Erhard*. Russian and Afghan fare DM8-15. Open daily 7pm-2am.

Café Aha, Kreuzstr. 7, across the street from the Kreuzkirche. Crunchier than Rice Krispies. The upbeat atmosphere celebrates things indigenous and detests things meaty. Spinach and mushroom dishes, as well as *Nudelauflauf* (noodle and cheese casserole; DM6.50-DM14), scream "take on me." Open Tues.-Sat. 11am-midnight, Sun.-Mon. 11am-10pm. Includes "Eine-Welt-Laden" (One World Shop) for consci-entious shopping.

Planwirtschaft, Louisenstr. 20 (tel. 801 31 87). Newly remodeled, refined punk graced with Lenin memorabilia in the *Neustadt*. Steaks, *soljanka* (hearty soup), and mozzarella sandwiches (DM8-14). Open daily 10am until after 3am.

City Center, across from the *Hauptbahnhof* on the Bayerischestr. side. A shopping mall with an **Aldi supermarket** and a cafeteria-style **Fleischerei** (butcher shop) that dishes out huge portions at itsy-bitsy prices. While vegetarians might not appreciate the hanging-slabs-of-beef decor, a heaping plate of mashed potatoes, Hungarian *Paprika,* and tomatoes costs only DM4.50. Most shops open Mon.-Fri. 8am-8pm, Sat. 8am-4pm.

SIGHTS

From the banks of the Elbe, the **Electors of Sachsen** once ruled nearly the whole of central Europe. The extravagant collection of Emperor August the Strong and the magnificent palace he built to house it, the **Zwinger,** once rivalled the Louvre (see **Museums,** p. 153). Today hordes of tourists flock to view its array of decadent Baroque ornaments. The statues that line the museum grounds are still charred, although workers are busily sandblasting everything back to aesthetic perfection. The northern wing of the palace, a later addition, was designed by Gottfried Semper, revolutionary activist and master architect. Semper's famed Opera House, the **Sem-per-Oper,** reverberates with the same robust style as the palace wing. Its painstaking restoration, with original techniques affordable only during the GDR-era, has made it one of Dresden's major attractions. The interior is open for tours between shows every few weeks. (DM8, students DM5. Believe us, it's worth it.) Check the main entrance for tour times (usually mid-day) or call 491 14 96. Many guided **city tours** take off from Theaterpl. for better rates than those offered by the tourist office.

Across from the Zwinger lies the nearly restored **Dresdner Schloß,** the Residential Palace of Sachsen's old time Electors and Emperors. Once the proud home of August the Strong, its restoration has proceeded piecemeal since it was firebombed along with the rest of the *Altstadt* on February 13, 1945. It features a display on the Renais-sance and Baroque eras of the palace and the history of its reconstruction. (Open Tues.-Sun. 10am-6pm. DM5, students and seniors DM3.) Across the street, the Kemp-inski Hotel once served as the **Taschenbergpalais,** the home of August the Strong's mistresses. After poor Countess Cosel was banished to Stolpen (see p. 158) it became a residence for princes. A private walkway once connected the *Schloß* to the **Katholische Hofkirche** (Catholic Royal chapel). The church was built to hide the family's Catholic pageantry from their Protestant subjects, and pageantry it is, with golden chandeliers and a Silbermann organ. (Tours Mon.-Thurs. 11am and 2pm, Fri.-Sat. 1 and 2pm, Sun. 1pm. Open during the day for unguided perusal.) Adorning the **Fürstenzug** (Procession of Electors), the alley leading to the cathedral entrance, is a 105m mosaic in Meißner porcelain tiles tracing Sachsen history since the Middle Ages. If you've been mistaking Friedrich the Earnest for Friedrich the Pugnacious, you may want to double back here for a quick history lesson.

From the Catholic Cathedral, the 16th-century **Brühlische Terrasse** offers a prime photo opportunity of the Elbe. Within its casements, Johann Friedrich Böttger was imprisoned by August the Strong until he finally solved the secret recipe for porcelain (interestingly, Böttger had originally promised he could produce gold). Turn right at the end of the terrace to reach the **Albertinum,** another of Dresden's fabulous museum complexes (see **Museums,** p. 153) that now hosts a courtyard collection of Greek and Roman sculptures. From the Albertinum, a walk to the Neumarkt leads to the ruined shell of the **Frauenkirche,** once a splendid Protestant church, and Dresden's most famous silhouette before construction began to revive the city after the war. The first Protestant celebration of communion in Dresden took place at the **Protestant Kreuzkirche** on the Altmarkt. Now the fourth church to be erected on the site, its interior remains in rough plaster as a reminder of the war's devastation. Some tourists are fortunate enough to catch a performance by the world-famous **Kreuzchor,** a boys choir with a tradition dating back to the 13th century. Climb to the top for a bird's-eye view of the colossal jigsaw puzzle of downtown Dresden. (Church open summer Mon.-Tues. and Thurs.-Fri. 10am-5:30pm, Wed. and Sat. 10am-4:30pm, Sun. noon-4:30pm; winter Mon.-Fri. 10am-4:30pm, Sat. 10am-3:30pm, Sun. noon-4:30pm. Sun. services at 9:30am. Free. Tower closes 30min. before the church. DM2, kids DM1.)

The main promenade of the **Neustadt,** once *Straße der Befreiung* (Street of Liberation), has been renamed **Hauptstraße** (Main Street) in a surge of nomenclatorial genius. The cobblestone pedestrian avenue stretches from the magnificent **Augustus Brücke** over the Elbe past the **Goldener Reiter,** a gold-plated vision of Friedrich August II (a.k.a. August the Strong). The nickname was reputedly an homage to his remarkable (some might say unseemly) virility—legend has it that he fathered over 300 kids, although the official tally sits at 15. Still, the gilded August sports a legendary visage which almost seems to pronounce, *"Ich bin* badder *als der MackDaddy des DaddyMacks!"* (For more on MackDaddies, see **Schloß Linderhof,** p. 499.) At the other end of Hauptstr., **Albertplatz** (formerly Platz der Einheit) is surrounded by handsome 19th-century mansions, and marks the delta of the *Neustadt* bar and restaurant scene towards the north and west. Also see the **Dreikönigskirche** (Church of the Three Kings), one of the oldest original structures in the city, farther down Hauptstr. (open daily 9am-6pm; free organ concerts Mon.-Fri. 5:30-6pm).

In the direction of Blasewitz, Loschwitz, and Striesen, you'll find the old haunts of the author Friedrich Schiller; really, really committed fans (fans who should be committed?) can check out the **Schillerhäuschen,** Schillerstr. 19 (tel. 49 86 60; open May-Sept. Sat.-Sun. 10am-5pm or by appointment; DM1, students and seniors DM0.50). For a taste of Dresden's pre-war atmosphere, venture just a bit farther out to **Blasewitz** and **Loschwitz,** connected by the **Blaues Wunder.** A 19th-century suspension bridge, it is visually resplendent—also the only bridge not destroyed by the SS when the Soviets invaded the city. **Körnerplatz,** on the Loschwitz side, remains one of Dresden's prettiest squares, with its artist-colony ambience still partially intact.

In a particularly dismal section of town, the **Schlachthofringe** (Slaughterhouse Circle) is an original 1910 housing complex. In World War II, the buildings were commandeered as a camp for prisoners of war. Novelist Kurt Vonnegut was imprisoned here during the bombing of Dresden, inspiring his masterpiece *Slaughterhouse Five.* The box-like buildings are chilling, even without any exhibits. Streetcar #9 (direction: "Friedrichstadt") to the last stop and walk up (don't do this at night). On the way, you'll pass one of Dresden's architectural oddities, the former **Zigarrettenfabrik** (cigarette factory). Keep an eye out for its brown, stained glass dome. Built in 1907, it was modeled on a tobacco factory in Turkey.

Theater Junge Generation, Meißner Landstr. 4 (tel. 421 45 67). Shakespeare, opera, fairy tales, and more. Tickets DM6-14, 15-50% student discount. Tickets available Mon.-Sat. 10am-noon, extra hours Wed. 2-6pm, Fri. 2-7:30pm, or 1hr. before show.

Puppentheater der Stadt Dresden, Leipzigerstr. 220 (tel. 84 06 40; fax 840 64 44). Children's performances during the day for young and older folk. DM6, children DM4, family ticket (up to five people) DM18. Occasional evening performance geared more towards older folks DM12, students DM10. Box office open 30min. before shows on weekdays, 45min. before shows on weekends.

Bars and Clubs

Scheune, Alaunstr. 36-40 (tel. 802 66 19). The heart of the *Neustadt* bar scene (Dresden's *Kulturzentrum*), in a former youth center. A Pee Wee's Playhouse complete with beer garden that serves decently priced Indian food (DM10-15) cooked by the German Shiva Team. Open Tues.-Fri. 7pm-2am, Sat. 10am-2pm and 7pm-2am, Sun. 10am-2pm. The culturally eclectic dance floor invites you to disco to West African roots and Baltic and Yiddish piano songs (not at the same time). Club opens at 8pm. Call for schedule of events.

DownTown and Groove Station, Katharinenstr. 11-13 (tel. 801 18 59). *The* place to shake your booty and indulge in Dresden's fluorescent-and-neon techno scene. One of the few night venues capable of convincing skeptics that some Germans *can* dance. Very popular straight, gay, and lesbian scene. In the upstairs Groove Station (see **Laundromat,** p. 148), patrons numb themselves with drink, get tattooed and/or pierced, and return to the fracas below. DownTown open Thurs.-Mon. 9pm-5am with dancin' on all these days except Sun.; Thurs.-Sat. cover DM5, Sun.-Mon. DM3. Thurs. women free, Sat. everyone free before 11pm.

Studentenklub Bärenzwinger, Brühlischer Garten 1 (tel. 495 51 53), not far from the Albertinum. Head towards the Carolabrücke, but make a sharp left down a little hill just before reaching the streetcar stop. Students congregate in this bizarre tunnel under the Brühlische Terrasse to nurse cheap drinks and partake in the disco action. Some hard core interspersed with canonical American "alternative" music. Over 18 only. Bring student ID for discounts. Open Tues.-Thurs. and Sun. 8pm-midnight, Fri.-Sat. 9pm-3am for live shows and dancing.

Fritz-Löffler-Str. 10-12. It's not a name, it's a student apartment complex that has a few clubs geared for its residents (not big spenders) with eminently romantic titles—**M14** (tel. 476 62 44) on the 8th floor of building C/D, and **Club 10** (tel. 476 62 44) in building A, among others. Show up after 9pm and see where the twenty-somethings are heading. Student ID saves money on the cover charges.

Die Tonne, Am Brauhaus 3 (tel. 802 60 17), boasts an offering of "cool drinks and hot jazz" for slightly more refined entertainment. Performances most nights at 9pm. Cover DM8-20. Free on Mon. Open daily 5pm-1am.

■ Near Dresden

MEIßEN

Just 30km from Dresden, Meißen sits on the banks of the Elbe as yet another testament to the frivolity of August the Strong. In 1710, the Sachsen emperor developed a severe case of *Porzellankrankheit* (the porcelain "bug"—an affliction that continues to manifest itself in tourists today) and turned the city's defunct *Schloß* into a porcelain-manufacturing base. Those visitors who would otherwise feel little affinity for the craft now indulge in a couple of glasses of Meißen's fine wines and soon find themselves toasting the beauty of "white gold" (china, not cocaine). Meißen has a distinct aesthetic advantage over its comrade Dresden, as its medieval nooks and crannies were barely scathed by World War II bombs. Meißen is an easy daytrip from Dresden by S-Bahn (45min.; 9hr. card DM9) or scenic cruise (round-trip from Dresden DM23).

Wander the narrow, romantic alleyways of the *Altstadt* and climb up to the **Albrechtsburg** (tel 47 07 10), a castle and cathedral overlooking the city. From *Bahnhof* Meißen, walk straight onto Bahnhofstr. and follow the banks of the Elbe to the aptly-named Elbbrücke (Elbe bridge). Cross the bridge and continue straight to the Markt and turn right onto Burgstr.; at the end of Burgstr., on Schloßstr., you'll find the stairs that lead to the right up to Albrechtsburg. The castle foundations were first built in 929 as fortifications to protect the area's Sorb population (see p. 163). The interior was lavishly redecorated in the 15th century, and once again when porcelain profits started pouring in. Sliding through the gilded vaults to see the porcelain products and royal memorabilia becomes truly sensual in the felt slippers provided to protect the floor. The fantastically decorated rooms also house an extensive medieval sculpture collection. (Open Mar.-Nov. daily 10am-6pm; Dec.-Feb. 10am-5pm; last entry 30min. before closing. DM6, students DM3.) Next door dwells the **Meißener Dom,** an early Gothic cathedral which ensures that its visitors get their money's worth with four priceless 13th-century **statues** by the Naumburg Master, a triptych by Cranach the Elder, and the beautiful metal grave coverings of the Wettins. (Open April-Oct. daily 9am-6pm; Nov.-Mar. 9am-4pm. Last entry 40min. before closing. DM3.50, students DM2.50. Organ music May-Oct. daily noon; DM3, students DM2.)

Meißen's porcelain factory was once more tightly guarded than KGB headquarters for fear that competitors would discover its secret techniques. Porcelain was first discovered here in 1708, and today anyone can tour the **Staatliche Porzellan Manufaktur** at Talstr. 9 (tel 46 87 00). The **Schauhalle** serves as a museum where you can peruse finished products (open daily 9am-5pm; DM7, students DM5), but the real fun lies in the high-tech tour of the Schauwerkstatt (show factory) which shows folks working on different steps of the porcelain-manufacturing process. (English tapes available; open daily 9am-noon and 1-4:45pm; DM7, students DM5.) Meißen's Gothic **Rathaus** stands alongside the **Frauenkirche,** whose porcelain bells chatter every 15 minutes over the main market square (open May-Oct. daily 10am-noon and 1-4pm).

The **tourist office,** Markt 3 (tel. 45 44 70), is across the Markt from the church. Pick up maps or find a room in a private home (DM25-55) for a DM4 fee (open April-Oct. Mon.-Fri. 10am-6pm, Sat.-Sun. 10am-3pm; Nov.-Mar. Mon.-Fri. 9am-5pm). Meißen's **Jugendherberge,** Wilsdrufferstr. 28 (tel. 45 30 65), is a crap shoot—its 45 beds are often booked; should they have space, they'll put you up in a crowded five-bed room. From the station, cross the Elbe footbridge and take Obergasse to the end where it meets Plosenweg. Turn left and continue uphill until you see the small EDEKA Markt; the hostel is across the street. An infrequent bus (line C/C) runs from the train station up the steep hill ("Dr.-Donner-Str."). (Reception open Mon.-Fri. 7am-noon and 4-8pm, Sat.-Sun. 4-8pm. DM18. Breakfast included. Sheets DM5.) In a pinch, Meißen is also close to the hostels of Dresden (see p. 150). The **telephone code** is 03521.

A puffed, almost hollow pastry, the *Meißener Fummel* owes its origin to August the Strong. One of his couriers was a spirited sort whose penchant for Meißen wine became known to the king. To keep tabs on his bacchanalian behavior, August ordereed the Meißen bakers' guild to create an extremely fragile biscuit. The courier was to carry the *Fummel* with him undamaged when delivering messages. Many *Altstadt* bakeries vend this puffery. For less fluff, try **Zum Kellermeister,** Neugasse 10 (tel. 45 40 88). Most *Schnitzels* run DM5-10 (open Mon.-Fri. 11am-9pm). The farmer's **market** is on the main market (open Tues.-Fri. 8am-5pm). In the last weekend of September, Meißen frolics in merriment during its annual **wine festival.**

MORITZBURG

Never one to be bashful about leaving his mark on the Sachsen landscape, August the Strong tore down a little palace in 1723 and replaced it with **Schloß Moritzburg** (tel. 814 39; fax 814 58), his titanic hunting lodge of ribaldry. For his princely comfort, a vast and splendid array of paintings, porcelain, tapestries, and hunting trophies were lugged from Dresden every summer. The immense *Schloß* lounges arrogantly at the end of Schloßallee on an island in an artificial lake. Inside, lavish rooms and leering deer skulls commemorate the courtly hunting penchant, while the ornately embossed and painted leather wallpaper sets the standard for masculine, animal-killing elegance. (Open May-Oct. daily 10am-5:30pm; March and Nov. Tues.-Sun. 10am-4:30pm; April Tues.-Sun. 10am-5:30pm; Dec. Tues.-Sun. 10am-3pm. DM7, students and seniors DM4.) To get to the *Schloß* from the *Schmalspurbahn* train station, join the pilgrimage out to the left then right onto Schloßallee. Near the *Schloß*, the smaller **Fasanenschlößchen** was built by the great-grandson of August the Strong, Friedrich August III, as a more delicate summer residence. Outside, sculptures of moose in tremendous pain remind you that this, too, is a hunting lodge. Unfortunately, the Fasanenschlößchen is closed indefinitely for repairs; ask the tourist office for more information. From Schloß Moritzburg, follow Meißnerstr. to the right until Große Fasanenstr.; the Fasanenschlößchen appears on the left. Farther down Große Fasanenstr., the curious structure peeking out of the forest is the **Leuchtturm** (lighthouse), which once served as a backdrop to the mock sea battles of the decadent princes. Moritzburg is also surrounded by extensive parks in addition to a huge gaming reserve and the **Sächsisches Langestüt** ("Sachsen Stud-Farm"), where animals procreate almost as frequently as did August the Strong—surpassing 300 (see p. 152).

In addition to its monuments of Wettin flight and fancy, Moritzburg also has a rich art tradition as the place where die Brücke artists resided between 1909 and 1911. It continued to serve as a summer residence for many artist who came back to frolic in the waters. One of Germany's most-celebrated 20th-century artists, **Käthe Kollwitz,** resided in the region for a time. After Kollwitz's home in Berlin was bombed near the end of World War II, Prince Ernst Heinrich von Sachsen offered her a place of retreat here. Though Kollwitz passed away in 1945 only one year after her arrival, her house now holds the **Käthe Kollwitz Gedenkstätte,** Meißnerstr. 7. Inside, the museum showcases her powerful sculptures, woodcuts, and drawings, starkly and beautifully depicting the cruelty of war and poverty. Pictures and excerpts from her letters and diaries help fill in the gaps about the remarkable woman. (Open April-Oct. Tues.-Fri. 11am-5pm, Sat.-Sun. 10am-5pm; Nov.-March Tues.-Fri. noon-4pm, Sat.-Sun. 11am-4pm. DM3.50, students and seniors DM2.)

The fastest way to Moritzburg from Dresden is by **bus.** Bus #326 (direction: "Radeburg") from either train station: "Mortizburg, Schloß." The return trip runs from "Maritzburg, Markt" on Marktstr. parallel to the Schloßallee. The most scenic route (but also the slowest, bumpiest, and noisiest) is the 110-year old *Schmalspurbahn* (narrow-gauge railway) which leaves from Radebeul-Ost, accessible by the S-Bahn to Meißen (4 stops, 30min.; S-Bahn and train DM7.40 each way, students DM5). Moritzburg's **tourist office,** Schloßallee 3b (tel. 854 10; fax 854 20), provides information on guided **tours** of the *Schloßpark*, concerts in the *Schloß*, horse-and-carriage rentals, and books rooms for a DM2 fee. (DM25-30 per person. Open May-Oct. Mon.-Fri. 10am-5pm; Sat.-Sun. noon-4pm; Nov.-April Mon.-Fri. 10am-5pm.) For a meaty meal, go to **Zum Dreispitz,** Schloßallee 5 (tel. 822 00), which offers Sächsische meat and mushroom dishes (maybe poached from the stud farm) for DM10-20 (open daily 11am-midnight). Small restaurants and food stands line the parking lot across from the *Schloß*, serving up regional specialties at much lower prices. The hunting-tradition-laden **Hengstparade** (equestrian parade) takes place every year on three consecutive Sundays in September. The **telephone code** is 035207.

PILLNITZ

August the Strong must have led a happy life. Among his many castles (almost as numerous as his mistresses), the magnificent gardens of **Schloß Pillnitz** produce a singularly fantastic effect. The strongman inherited the nearly 300-year-old castle in 1694 and generously passed it on to Countess Cosel a few years later—who says diamonds are a girl's best friend? The Countess lived there from 1713 to 1715 until August decided to imprison her in the more poorly furnished Burg Stolpen (see below) and began the extensive remodeling that gave the complex its characteristic look of today. The turrets of the **Bergpalais** and **Wasserpalais** (modeled on Chinese architectural forms) seem to float above the adjacent Elbe. The residences now house Dresden's **Kunstgewerbmuseum** (arts and crafts museum), some modern art displays, and lots of porcelain amidst the sumptuously sensual and suggestively salacious summer-like colors of the courtly rooms. Outside, brilliantly colored flowers heighten the mystical effect of the architecture. Summer **concerts** take place every Sunday in the garden. (Museum open May-Oct. 9:30am-5:30pm. *Bergpalais* and *Kunstgewerbmu-*

seum closed Mon., *Wasserpalais* closed Tues. DM3, students and seniors DM2. Permission to take photos DM3. Grounds open 5am-8pm.) To reach Pillnitz from Dresden, *Straßenbahn* #14 from Pirnaischerpl. (direction: "Kleinzschachwitz") to the last stop (30min.). Get off the *Straßenbahn* and walk towards the banks of the Elbe, where you'll see a *Fähre* (ferry) shuttling passengers every 15 minutes (DM1.30, children DM1; surcharge DM1 for bicycles, DM5.50 for cars). Bus #85 also runs from Schillerpl. Alternatively, the **Weiße Flotte** fleet can float you there. Head straight through the main garden to the "Alte Woche" **tourist office** for maps of the surrounding gardens, information, and tours (open daily 10am-6pm).

STOLPEN

The Sachsen Emperor August the Strong entertained an extensive array of mistresses, but the most well-known was the Countess Cosel. As a result of a lovers' quarrel about the king's new mistress and his anti-Protestant stance, she was imprisoned without official sentence in the old castle of Stolpen from 1716 to 1765. Her 49 years of confinement were perhaps made bearable, however, by the spectacular views of Bohemia and Sächsische Schweiz from every window of her lonesome look-out. The 13th-century **Burg Stolpen,** Schloßstr. 10 (tel. 23 40), can be reached by bus #261 (direction: "Sebnitz") from Dresden (50min.; DM6.20). Disembark, walk right around the building and up the street into the Markt; go to the uppermost corner of the steeply inclined Marktplatz, then left again onto Schloßstr. where you'll find the fortress entrance. The heavy stone fortifications and utter lack of adornment (the living quarters of the *Burg* were destroyed) among the ruins seem wholly unrelated to other decadent structures in Sachsen. The first of four courtyards houses a **torture chamber** that should delight any S&M reveler (poor, poor Foucault) with its maces and handcuffs. The next three courtyards contain the courtroom, the old castle cannons, the castle tower (which can be climbed), and the castle **chapel and tomb** where Countess Cosel is buried. The **castle well** in the fourth courtyard is the deepest basalt well in the world; it took the castle miners 22 years to find water. (Open daily April-Oct. 9am-5pm; Nov.-March 10am-4pm, weather permitting. Last entrance 30min. before closing. DM5, students and seniors DM3.)

The Stolpen **Tourist Information Center,** Schloßstr. 14a (tel./fax 273 13), offers maps and a list of accommodations (private rooms DM25-35; open April-Sept. daily 9am-5pm; Oct.-March 10am-4pm). **Gar Küche,** on Dresdenerstr., right between the Markt and the Nieder Tor, is Stolpen's oldest *Gaststätte,* founded in 1659. They serve *Schnitzels* with veggies and potatoes for DM9 (open Mon.-Thurs. 10am-2pm and 3:30-10pm, Fri. 10am-2pm and 3-11pm, Sat. 11am-11pm, Sun. 11am-9pm). Alternatively, load up on delicious fruity goodness at the **Gemüse am Tor** grocery store next door (open Mon.-Fri. 8:30am-6pm, Sat. 8-10am). Stoplen's **postal code** is 01833. The **telephone code** is 035973.

▓ Sächsische Schweiz (Saxon Switzerland)

One of Eastern Germany's most beloved holiday destinations, Sächsische Schweiz has become Germany's newest national park since reunification. The region is "Swiss" because of the stunning landscape—sandstone cliffs emerge from dense vegetation, while sumptuous summits and excellent hiking beckon adventurous tourists. The national park is divided into two regions, the *voderer Teil* and the *hintere Teil;* both are easily accessible from the south with Dresden's S-Bahn #1, which runs alongside the Elbe River. The **Wanderwege** coils up the hills, into the heart of the park, connecting all towns in the area in a spidery web. Trail maps of the region are available at any tourist office in the area (DM8-10). The area's vibrant, dense greenery and lovely landscape make this uniquely beautiful yet inexpensive region a must-see for those convinced that Eastern Germany comes only in shades of gray. Visitors can obtain further information from **Tourismusverband, Sächsische Schweiz,** Am Bahnhof 6,

01814 Bad Schandau (tel./fax (035012) 49 50), or **Nationalpark-Verwaltung,** Schandauerstr. 36, 01824 Königstein (tel. (035021) 682 29; fax 684 46).

PIRNA

Pirna gloats in the fame it gleaned from Canaletto's depiction of its Marktplatz. Once a 16th-century trading town that overshadowed its golden neighbor, Dresden, today Pirna is something of a toadstool compared to the more prominent towns higher on the mountains. The city's greatest significance now lies in its role as "the door to Sächsische Schweiz."

Pirna is the last stop on S-Bahn #1 before entering the region, a mere 30 minutes from Dresden. To see the **Markt** that fills the natives with so much pride, walk straight down Gartenstr. from the train station, turn left on Grohmannstr., and right on Jacobäerstr. which turns into Schuhgasse and leads straight to it. The **Rathaus** once served as a mall for merchants purveying the latest in silk tunics. The 16th-century **Marienkirche** on the right of the market place is graced by a huge baptismal font once admired by Goethe. At Obere Burgstr. 1, you can see the 16th-century **Teufelserker** (devil's bay window), named for its three evil overhanging figures. At Barbiergasse 10, its Manichean counterpart, the **Engelserker** (angel's bay window) is adorned with a heavenly gold figure. The **Stadtmuseum Pirna,** Klosterhof 2-3 (tel. 52 79 85), provides a thorough explanation of these architectural oddities, as well as its own collection of tricks and trinkets that vaguely represent the city's history. You can also see the **Schützenröcklein,** one of the oldest military dresses left in the region (open May-Oct. Tues.-Sun. 10am-6pm; Nov.-April Tues.-Sun. 10am-5pm; DM2, students and seniors DM1). **Schloß Sonnenstein** overlooks the city and was its often unsuccessful defender against invading Swedes, militant Prussians, and Napoleonic looters; it now houses bureaucratic offices.

Pirna's **tourist office,** Dohnaischestr. 31 (tel./fax 52 84 97), just off Jacobäerstr., provides free maps and books rooms (DM20-40) for a DM5 fee (open Mon.-Fri. 9am-6pm, Sat. 9:30am-1pm). The **post office** awaits at Gartenstr. 29/30, 01784 Pirna (open Mon.-Fri. 8:30am-noon and 2-6pm, Sat. 9:30am-12:30pm). Bypass the pricey hotel scene at **Jugendherberge-Pirna-Copitz Weltfrieden** (world peace), Birkwitzerstr. 51 (tel.44 56 01). This socialist box holds 160 beds and rents **bikes.** Bus Line F from the *Busbahnhof* across the Elbe: "Sportpl.," then walk in the direction of the yellow phone booth and turn right. (Reception open Mon.-Fri. 8:30am-noon and 2-6pm, Sat. 9:30-11:30am. Lockout 9:30am-noon. DM22, over 26 DM26. Breakfast included.) For a meal, scale the 150 steps up to the **Biergarten,** Schloßhof 4, in Schloß Sonnenstein. Treat yourself to some grill fare (DM4-6:50) and a beer (open May-Oct. Mon.-Thurs. 5pm-midnight, Fri.-Sat. 3pm-2am, Sun. noon-midnight). If you have no interest in hiking up to the castle, grab a quick bite at **Bier-Pub,** Am Markt 16, where burgers and *Würste* run DM3.50-7 (open Mon.-Fri. 8am-7pm). The **telephone code** is 03501.

You can also get to **Liebstadt** by bus to visit the exceptionally curious **Schloß Kuckucksstein,** Am Schloßberg 1 (tel. (035027) 502 83). Once a robber baron's castle, the *Schloß* was taken over by a family devoted to Freemasonry. The museum inside details the history of the lodges, but let it be known: Freemasons rule the world (open July-Aug. Tues.-Sun. 9:30am-4pm; Sept.-June Wed.-Sun. 9:30am-4pm; tours 10, 11am, 2, and 3pm). The **Bonsaigarten,** Liebstädterstr. 53 (tel. 52 77 34), a curious bonzai tree garden, revives old *Karate Kid* dreams (open Tues.-Fri. 2-6pm, Sat.-Sun. 10am-noon and 1:30-5pm).

RATHEN AND WEHLEN

The jagged sandstone cliffs oft-referred to as "those jagged sandstone cliffs," but officially called **Die Bastei,** loom over the dinky town of **Rathen,** connected only by a sturdy sandstone bridge. You can ascend the cliffs either from Rathen or **Wehlen.** The path from Wehlen, starting across the Elbe from the S-Bahn station by the *Ratskeller,* provides a gentle incline that August the Strong used to climb with his carnivorous pals (look for the **Höllengrund am Steinernen Tisch,** his mammoth dining table, at the top). The climb from Rathen is a steep (wheeze) 30 (cough) minutes, but it brings you to the **Basteiaussicht** more quickly. Because of Rathen's prime location at the edge of **Sächsische Schweiz National Park,** hiking trails of varying difficulties abound. One leads to Rathen's **Felsenbühne,** one of the most beautiful open air theaters in Europe, with 2000 seats facing a stage carved into the cliff. Tickets and schedules for performances are available from **Theaterkasse der Felsenbühne** (tel. 704 96; fax 350 24).

The **tourist office** upstairs in the *Gästeamt* (tel./fax 704 22) dishes out maps, stacks of information on hiking trails, and a list of private rooms or area hotels. To get there from the S-Bahn station, take the ferry across the Elbe (DM1, children and bikes DM0.50) and follow the signs to the *Haus des Gastes/Gästeamt;* the office is on the right (open Mon.-Fri. 9am-noon and 2-6pm, Sat. 9am-2pm; winter closed Sat.). Panoramic boat trips on the **Motorschiff "Bastei"** (300 seats) or the more personal **Dampfschiff "Sachsenwald"** (80 seats) leave every two hours from Rathen's shores (one way to Wehlen DM7; round-trip to Bad Schandau DM24). In the absence of a *Jugendherberge* in Rathen, you'll have to stay in the more expensive **Gästehaus** (tel. 76 00; fax 760 02), in the *Burg Altrathen* (Fortress of old Rathen; singles DM35-40; doubles DM65-90; breakfast included). Rathen's **telephone code** is 035024.

HOHNSTEIN

The small village of **Hohnstein** ("high stone" in old Sachsen), with its grand forest vistas on all sides, is a mere hop, skip, and hike from Rathen. The hefty trek (1¼hr.) traverses the inner valleys of the Sächsische Schweiz. To get there from Rathen, follow the **path of the red stripe** (a hiking trail, not a Maoist paramilitary clan) which starts behind the *Gästeamt.* If your stamina fails and grandparents in *Lederhosen* are passing you on the trails, you can settle for public transportation. S-Bahn: "Pirna," then bus #236 or 237 from the *Bahnhof:* "Hohnstein Eiche" (DM4.10).

The town encircles the **Hohnstein Jugendburg** (tel. (035975) 202; fax 203), a fortress which holds a history and nature museum, *Aussichtsturm* (lookout tower), cafe-restaurant, and an outdoor garden. The **Museum der Geschichte des Burg Hohnstein** covers the history of the *Burg* with medieval armor, weapons, and an exhibit on anti-fascist resistance in Dresden and Sächsische Schweiz. The museum commemorates Konrad Hahnewald (the beloved father of Hohnstein's *Jugendherberge* and later the first political refugee of the Hohnstein Concentration Camp). (Open March-Oct. daily 9am-5pm; by appointment at other times. DM2.) The **Naturfreundehaus Burg Hohnstein,** Am Markt 1 (tel. 812 02; fax 812 03), offers singles, quads, and titanic 6- to 18-bed rooms for the same price per person. (DM26-28, non-HI members DM33-37; DM1.30 tax per day; 10% supplement for fewer than 3 nights. Breakfast included.) The **tourist office,** Rathausstr. 10 (tel. 194 33; fax 868 10), in the *Rathaus,* doles out information on trails and the *Burg,* and finds rooms (open Mon.-Fri. 9am-6pm, Sat. 9am-noon). The **telephone code** is 035975.

KÖNIGSTEIN

The next stop on the Dresden S-Bahn journey into the hills and dales of the Sächsische Schweiz is **Königstein.** The *Weiße Flotte* boat also alights on these shores. The **fortress** is incredible—drawbridges, impenetrable stone walls, and a huge complex put this mammoth on the list of legendary medieval royal abodes. An oft-exploited retreat for the kings of Sachsen during times of civil unrest and marital discord (the Sachsen electors tended to flee faster than the French), it was later converted into a feared state prison; Nikolai Bakunin and August Bebel were imprisoned here. During the Third Reich, it was used by the Nazis to stash stolen art, and between 1949 and 1955 it served as a juvenile correctional center. Recently, skeletons were found in the fortress's torture chamber; no one yet knows which of its incarnations produced them. The complex now houses museums on everything from weapons to porcelain. The view from the fortress is worth sweating for—from the city, it's a half-hour struggle straight up from Hainstr. to Kirchgasse then to Goethestr. Around the left side of the rickety movie theater are the stairs, and then the stairs, and then the stairs up to the **fortress.** (Open May-Sept. daily 9am-8pm; Oct. 9am-6pm; Nov.-March 9am-5pm. DM7, students and seniors DM5. 1-1½hr. tours in English available DM2.) The cheeky **Festungs Express** tours Königstein as it drags the lazy bums of sissy tourists who are too tired to make the trek (DM4, kids DM2; round-trip DM6, kids DM3). Rides leave from Reißigerpl. regularly, just to the right down Bahnhofstr. from the S-Bahn station (Festungs Express runs April-Oct. 9am-6pm). Paths also lead from the town up to the challenging 415m **Lilienstein,** hiked by August the Strong in 1708 (the 2km hike takes a steep 30min.).

The **tourist office,** Schreiberberg 2 (tel. 682 61; fax 688 87), on the Marktplatz close to the "Festungs Express" stop, books rooms (DM40-50), but in summer it's wise to call ahead. They have a list of available rooms, vacation houses, and *Pensionen;* prices are in the window when they're closed (open Mon.-Tues. and Thurs.-Fri. 9am-noon and 2-6pm, Wed. 2-6pm, Sat. 9am-noon; Nov.-March may be open shorter hours). Königstein's **Naturfreunde Jugendherberge,** Halbestadt 13 (tel. (035022) 424 32), is a lot nicer than most hostels but also more expensive—the stunning one- to four-bed rooms have showers in them. To get there, cross the river by ferry and turn right. The hostel will emerge on your right in about 10 minutes. (Reception open 7-10am, 3-5:30, and 7-8pm. DM42, over 26 DM50; non-members DM6 extra. Breakfast included.) The **campground** (tel. 682 24) is on the banks of the Elbe about 10 minutes upstream from the station in the shadow of the fortress. It has washing facilities, a small supply shop, and a playground (DM12 per person with tent; open April-Oct.). The **telephone code** is 035021.

BAD SCHANDAU

One stop farther upstream from Königstein lies Bad Schandau, a miniature village sitting daintily between the Elbe and the mountains. **Trains** connect Bad Schandau with the Zittauer Gebirge, with a train to Bautzen every 2 hours. The biggest of the towns in Sächsische Schweiz, Bad Schandau lies wedged between the two parts of the national park. Yet another small-town **Heimat Museum,** Badallee 10 (tel. 21 73), sets you straight on Sachsen geology, geography, shipping, and Bad Schandauer history (open Tues., Thurs., and Fri. 2-5pm, Sat. 9:30am-12:30pm; DM2, children DM0.50). From the train station, take the **ferry** (7:30am-9:30pm, evey hr.; DM1) and cross the street to the **tourist office,** Markt 8 (tel. 424 12), for hiking maps and a list of rooms. City **tours** in German depart from the office. (Tours May-Oct. Mon. 10:30am; DM2. Office open Mon.-Fri. 9am-noon and 1-5pm; Nov.-April Mon.-Fri. 9am-noon and 1-4pm.) Be aware that *the tourist office is scheduled to move in 1998.* **Adler Apotheke,** Dresdnerstr. 2 (tel. 425 08), provides **pharmacy** services (open Mon.-Fri. 8am-12:30pm and 1:30-6pm, Sat. 8:30am-noon). Take the solar-powered, eco-friendly *Kirnitzschtalbahn* train (May-Oct. 31 every 30min.; for info call 423 70 or fax 423 33) to the **Lichtenhainer Waterfall,** a favorite starting point for full-day hikes on the **Schrammsteine.** The office can provide suggestions for shorter or longer hikes. The office also capitalizes on its proximity to the Czech Republic. Bus **tours** to **Prague** are offered weekly (round-trip DM45-49); the Czech towns Decin, Hreusko, and Prebischtor are nearby (office open Mon.-Sat. 8:30am-8:30pm). To rent a **bike,** try **Fahrradverleih,** Poststr. 14 (tel. 428 83; DM14 per day with ID). Overnighters should head up to the **Jugendherberge,** Dorfstr. 14 (tel./fax 424 08), in Ostrau, poised on a plateau above the town. (Reception open 7-10am and 4:30-10pm. DM22, over 26 DM26. Breakfast included.) The **telephone code** is 035022.

■ Oberlausitz (Upper Lusatia)

Between Dresden and the Polish border stretch the rolling hills of Oberlausitz. Dotted with cows, farmers, and cheery-looking villages, this expanse of land borders two former Warsaw Pact neighbors, Poland and the Czech Republic. As a result, throughout the GDR's reign, Oberlausitz remained largely untouched by Western tourism, and the Politburo *apparatchiks* left much of the region's magnificent medieval, Renaissance, and Baroque architecture to decay. As in much of former East Germany, Oberlausitz is currently undergoing extensive restoration in pursuit of its former shine. As the homeland of Germany's only national minority, the **Sorbs** *(die Wenden* in German), the area around Bautzen is rich in customs long abandoned elsewhere.

BAUTZEN (BUDYSIN)

Where in the world can you find a witch's house, a church where Protestants and Catholics can attend church hand-in-hand, and a binational theater that puts on puppet shows in Sorbish and German? Nowhere but Bautzen. A millennium-old cultural capital, with ancient towers on a hill high above the Spree River, Bautzen is the seat of several Sorb institutions and was the home of the first Sorb tribe centuries ago. Bautzen has survived pillage, war, fire, and its use as a GDR repository for political prisoners. Its romantic cobblestone streets now wind peacefully among medieval, Baroque, and Art Nouveau residences. During the unique **Easter Riding Event,** lavishly decorated Sorb horses parade through town. Despite the bilingual street signs, Bautzen's character is very German, evolving into the 21th century with Dresden and the rest of Eastern Germany. In an era of transition and integration into a united Germany, Bautzen today resembles a large archaeological dig slowly modernizing.

Orientation, Practical Information, and Accommodations

Bautzen is a one-hour **train** ride away from Dresden (1 per hr.) The **tourist office,** Hauptmarkt 1 (tel. 420 16; fax 53 43 09), offers listings of accommodations in hotels, *Pensionen,* and private homes, as well as **city tours.** (Tours May to mid-Oct. Wed. 2pm, Sat. 11am. Office open Mon.-Fri. 9am-6pm, Sat.-Sun. 10am-noon; mid-Oct. to April closed on Sun.) At the ancient defense-tower-turned-**Jugendherberge (HI),** Am Zwinger 1 (tel. 440 45), just to the right through the Nikolaiturm, you can get packed into a 20-bed room if the more habitable triples upstairs are not available. Walk around the Kornmarkt, straight ahead as it becomes Wendischer Graben, then follow Vorden Schülertor as it curves left. Follow the left wall until you reach the Schülertor, turn right just before it, and the hostel smiles on your right. (Reception open Mon.-Fri. 7am-8pm, Sat. 8am-8pm. No lockout. Curfew 10pm, but you'll get a key. DM17, over 26 DM22. Breakfast included.) The **post office,** 02607 Bautzen, is located on Postpl. (open Mon.-Fri. 8am-6pm, Sat. 9am-noon). The **telephone code** is 03591.

Food For a lick of local cuisine, **Zum Karasek,** Kornstr. 8 (tel. 430 66), will weigh you down with its *Gegrillter Schweinerücken* (DM13.50), or lift you up with its light salads (DM8-12.50). No tourists—except for you (open Mon.-Sat. 11am-1am, Sun. 11:30am-11pm). For excellent Italian food and an entertaining decor heavy on gangsta motifs, **Al Capone's,** Schülerstr. 4, dishes out pizzas (DM8.50-11) and pastas (DM9-14; open Mon. 5pm-midnight, Tues.-Sun. 11:30am-2pm and 5pm-midnight). **Wjelbik,** Kornstr. 7 (tel. 420 60), serves tasty Sorbian specialities. Try the *Sorbische Stulle* (DM13), or relish a hefty veggie dish (DM16-17; open Mon.-Sat. 11am-11pm, Sun. 11am-8pm). The Hauptmarkt hosts a fresh food **market** (Tues. 8am-1pm, Sat. 7-11am). **Fox Markt** and **Sparmarkt,** both on Rechenstr. 18, double your grocery possibilities (open Mon.-Wed. and Fri. 9am-6:30pm, Thurs. 9am-7pm, Sat. 9am-1pm).

Sights and Entertainment

To reach the *Altstadt* from the station, walk straight through Rathenaupl. and bear left onto Bahnhofstr., then left at the post office onto Karl-Marx-Str. Follow the Marxist path to the intersection up ahead, and on your left will be the **Stadt Museum,** Kornmarktstr. 1 (tel. 498 50), specializing in the regional and cultural history of Bautzen. The museum also displays a collection of wood carvings and copper engravings from the 15th to the 17th century (open Wed.-Sun. 10am-5pm; DM3, children and students DM2). Up Kornmarktstr. from the museum is the leaning tower of Bautzen, the **Reichen Turm,** on Reichenstr. It was built in 1490, with a Baroque top added in 1715. It deviates exactly 1.44m from the perpendicular. Climb up to take in the marvelous view. (Open April-Oct. daily 10am-5pm. Last entrance at 4:30pm. DM1, students and children DM0.50.) A block away, at

The Sorbs

The Sorbs are a Slav minority stemming from Serbian tribes who streamed into the Niederlausitz and Oberlausitz areas between the Spreewald and Lusatian mountains during the 6th and 7th centuries. Sorbish is similar to Czech and Polish but spoken with two basic dialects: *Niedersorbisch* and *Obersorbisch* (Lower and Upper Sorbian). Niedersorbisch is spoken in and around Cottbus and Obersorbisch in the Bautzen region. Since the crystallization of the Sorb nationalist movement in 1848, small Sorbian-speaking communities totalling about 75,000 members have maintained their regional identities. Under Hitler's *Reich*, Sorbian was ruthlessly suppressed as a program of liquidation commenced in 1937; after the war, the *Sorbengesetz* (Sorbs Law) was established to assure the protection and promotion of the culture and language. However, the Sorbs still encountered many barriers as they tried to preserve their unique culture. After reunification, a special bureau was created to guarantee Sorbian civil rights in the German constitution. The Sorbs are particularly renowned for their ornamental Easter eggs, the Easter rides organized throughout various towns, and their traditional love of marriage and weddings. Zapust is a merry Sorbian festival in which dance and music are celebrated from the end of January to the beginning of March.

the intersection of Wendische Gasse and Wendischestr. is the **Alte Caserne** (old barracks), an elegant building designed by Dresden master Gottfried Semper that housed unappreciative 19th-century troops and currently provides business offices.

Left from the Reichen Turm down Reichenstr. is the **Hauptmarkt.** The grand yellow building is the **Rathaus** (built in 1213), with the Fleischmarkt behind it alongside the Gothic **Dom St. Petri.** Also built in 1213, it has been Eastern Germany's only *Simultankirche* (simultaneously Catholic and Protestant) since 1524. The division of the church was a remarkably peaceful compromise (open June-Sept. Mon.-Sat. 10am-4pm; May and Oct. Mon.-Sat. 10am-3pm). Farther along sits the ornate red-and-gold **Domstift**, housing the **Domschatz** (cathedral treasury), a phenomenal collection of jewel-studded gowns, icons, and gold regalia (open Mon.-Fri. 10am-noon and 1-4pm; free). Follow the narrow street An der Petrikirche downhill from the cathedral until you see the **Nikolaiturm** down the hill on your right. Crossing under the gate, note the face carved above the entrance. Locals claim that this is a likeness of a former mayor, who was bricked alive into the tower as retribution for opening the city to Hussite attackers in the 16th century.

If you head back through Nikolaiturm and right onto Schloßstr., you'll find the **Sorbisches Museum,** Ortenburg 3 (tel. 424 03), which details the intriguing history and culture of the Sorbs. Displays include samples of their writing, life-sized costumes, the area's special Sorbian Easter eggs, and those crazy *Dudelsacks* that look like psychedelic water-filtration devices. (For more info on the Sorbs, see **The Sorbs,** p. 163. Museum open daily 10am-12:30 and 1-5pm; Nov.-March 10am-12:30 and 1-4pm. DM3, students DM2, children DM1). From the Nikolaiturm or the Sorbisches Museum, follow the **Osterweg** path around the city walls and along the Spree, taking in the views of the 1480 **Mühlbastei** (mill tower), the 1558 **Alte Wasserkunst** (old water tower), and the spire of the 1429 **Michaeliskirche.** On the way back up the hill, on the other side of the fortress, lies the brown-shingled **Hexenhäusrl** (witches' cottage). This small wooden structure, the oldest house in the area, was the only home in the area to survive two devastating fires; the villagers subsequently shunned the inhabitants as witches (though the fire was actually averted by a well inside the house). If you find the Sorbs particularly absorbing, visit **Sorbische Kultur Information,** Postpl. 2 (tel. 421 05; fax 428 11). Purchase Sorb CDs, Sorb literature, and darling ornamented Easter eggs (open Mon.-Fri. 9am-6pm).

Near Bautzen: Panschwitz-Kuckau, Neuschwitz, and Crostwitz

Today the Sorbian language is seldom heard in the city, but buses leave regularly for villages such as **Panschwitz-Kuckau, Neuschwitz,** and **Crostwitz,** which are roughly

80-90% Sorb, and where both the mother tongue and colorful traditional costumes are alive. If your timing is right, you can witness one of the celebrations held on Catholic holidays. On Easter, the people of Bautzen and neighboring towns gather to ride around on horses, proclaiming the good news. January 25 marks the **Marriage of the Birds** *(Vogelhochzeit)*, during which children act like sycophantic peckers dressed in bird costumes. The children run around to represent local birds' gratefulness for seeds left by their human friends and to celebrate marital merriment. For more information, head to the **Sorbische Kultur-Information** in Bautzen. For regional bus information, go to the terminal at August-Bebel-Platz in Bautzen where the **Überlandlinien** (long-distance) boats depart, and take time to decipher the schedules.

GÖRLITZ

The easternmost town in Germany, Görlitz offers an exquisite, untouristed *Altstadt* that has changed little since Napoleon trudged through it on the way to his unsuccessful invasion of Russia. Many of the elegant pastel Renaissance and Baroque homes of former *Bürgermeister*s still stand. In fact, Görlitz was one of the only German towns to survive completely unharmed after World War II. With straightforward rail connections to Bautzen (1 per hr., 50min.), Dresden (every 2hr., 2hr.), and Zittau (2 per hr., 1hr.), as well as easy access to major bus routes, Görlitz is an excellent starting point for exploring Oberlausitz.

Most of Görlitz's central sites are located around the **Obermarkt.** From the train station, go straight down **Berlinerstraße,** Görlitz's attractive pedestrian and shopping zone. The street intersects **Postplatz,** home to a beautiful central fountain surrounded by a motley collection of flowers, the gloomy and sooted main post office, and the darkly stained **Frauenkirche** (a late Gothic cathedral built in 1431; open Mon.-Tues. and Thurs.-Fri. 2:30-4:30pm, Wed. 12:30-2:30pm). The 5m thick **Dicker Turm,** a squat gray tower, stands tall, fat, and proud at Marienpl. To reach the heart of the city, the **Obermarkt,** walk down Steinstr.

Across the Markt, you'll see the **Dreifaltigkeitskirche.** Originally a 13th-century Franciscan monastery, the church bears marks of frequent expansion. Walking past it down Brüderstr. you will come to the Untermarkt. Practically every side street and alley offers some little landmark—a gargoyle or an historic apothecary. Here you'll find the **Rathaus** (built in 1537, remodeled in 1902-1903). At its top is a clock-face in which a sculptured head's chin yawns with the passing of each minute. House #22 is the **Flüsterbogen** *(Whisper Arch)*—even if you're traveling solo, grab the nearest Görlitzer to stand on the stone steps; put your ear to the stone while your partner whispers his or her darkest secrets. On the corner is the **Ratsapotheke,** a Renaissance building from 1550 that still has an astrology and astronomy chart painted on its crumbling surface—the confluence of tweaked clocks is indicative of Görlitz's position on the 15-degree meridian, the center point of the Central European time zone. Don't miss the **St. Peter and Paul Church** down Peterstr. from the Untermarkt. Its brightly adorned interior, speckled with gilded suns and clocks, is enough to impress even the most jaded of travel guide writers. Enter on the backside (open Mon.-Fri. 10:30am-5pm, Sat. 10am-6pm, Sun. 11:30am-5pm).

The **tourist office,** Obermarkt 29 (tel. 475 70; fax 47 57 27), sells maps and finds rooms (DM30-40) in private homes for free (open Mon.-Fri. 10am-6:30pm, Sat. 10am-4pm, Sun. 10am-1pm). For a **taxi,** call 40 68 93. Görlitz has a sweet, sweet *Jugendstil* **Jugendherberge (HI),** Goethestr. 17 (tel./fax 40 65 10). This villa, poised over beautiful shaded grounds, is one of the coolest hostels for miles around. Take the south exit *(Südausgang)* of the train station, bear left up the hill, turn right onto Zittauerstr., and continue until Goethestr. Turn left, and the hostel is ahead on the right, just before the street curves (15min.). Enter the gate up the stairs to reach the entrance on the right. The huge, stained-glass windows are almost as brilliantly colorful as the comforters (we exaggerate—*nothing* is as colorful as the comforters). Accordions and guitars are supplied for guests' use; you can also rent skis, baby carriages, and grills. Mostly four-bed rooms with balconies. (Reception open Mon.-Fri. 7am-10pm, Sat.-Sun. 7-10am and 4-10pm. No lockout. Curfew 10pm, but keys available. DM20, seniors DM25. Handicap accessible. Breakfast included, but they'll jack you for DM1 if you want coffee, *kakao,* or black tea.) The **telephone code** is 03581.

Many cost-effective *Imbiß* options line Berlinerstr., while the nooks and crannies of the *Altstadt* offer Slavic cuisine. **Destille,** Nikolaistr. 6 (tel. 40 53 02), directly across from the Nikolaiturm, serves *Soljanka* soup with sour sauce, lemons, olives, and toast (DM5) to the many locals who flock to its wooden tables. They also weigh patrons down with a hefty farmer's omelette, served with ham and potatoes (DM10; open Tues.-Sat. 11:30am-midnight, Sun. 11am-10pm). The immaculate chain seafood restaurant **Gastmahl des Meeres,** Struvestr. 2 (tel. 40 62 29), whips up Alaskan fish for DM11.70 (open Mon.-Sat. 11am-10pm, Sun. 11am-3pm). Two **Edeka-Markts** make **supermarket** hunting easy: Steinstr. 1 is in the *Altstadt* (open Mon.-Fri. 8:30am-6pm, Sat. 8-11am), and Goethestr. 17 is but a few doors down from the hostel (open Mon.-Wed. 8am-6:30pm, Thurs. 8am-7pm, Sat. 7:30am-2pm).

■ Zittauer Gebirge

In a sliver of Germany that borders Czech Bohemia and Poland rise the rocky cliffs of the Zittauer Gebirge. Once a favored spot of medieval monks, these beehive-shaped mountains are today conquered by skiers, hikers, and landscape lovers. The sublime yet mystical surroundings acted as a fountain of inspiration for Romantic artists like Ludwig Richter. But matters have not always been so picture-perfect. In 1491, the Gebirge was the scene of the vicious **Bierkrieg** (beer war), when the citizens of Görlitz protested Zittau's success as a beer-brewing town by destroying barrels of the beverage. The Horror! The incensed townspeople stole a menagerie of animals from surrounding Görlitzer farms in retaliation, an example of boar-for-beer justice. More recently, the local forests and workers of this region have experienced a nasty socialist hangover as inefficient factories that belched pollution into the trees are being shut down, leaving many residents unemployed. For more information about touristing possibilities in the region contact **Fremderverhehrsgemeinschaft Zittauer Gebirge,** Hochwaldstr. 29, 02763 Zittau (tel. (03583) 72 25 15).

ZITTAU

Nestled between three lands—Poland, the Czech Republic, and Germany—Zittau served as a trading and cultural center for many years. Under the rule of the Bohemian kings in 1238, Zittau took on an dominant role in Oberlausitz, and later within the textile industry. The more important sites lie along the *Altstadt.* From the train station, follow Bahnhofstr. through Haberkornpl. to Bautznerstr., which will lead you directly to the Johanniskirchepl. There, you can behold the towering **Johanniskirche,** rebuilt in 1837, and climb to the tower (open May-Sept. Mon.-Fri. noon-6pm, Sat. and Sun. 1-6pm; DM2, students and seniors DM1). From the church, walk directly down Bautznerstr. to the grand **Marktplatz.** In the center, the 1585 **Rolandbrunnen** (fountain) gurgles directly across from the Renaissance-style **Rathaus** designed by Prussian architect Friedrich Schinkel in 1843. Heading left down Johannistr., you'll see the late Gothic **Kloster Kirche,** and farther up Klosterstr., the **Stadtmuseum** (tel./fax 51 02 70), housed in a former 13th-century Franciscan monastery. A collection of standard medieval torture devices awaits in the cellar. (Open Tues. and Thurs. 10am-noon and 1-4pm, Wed. 10am-noon and 1-6pm, Fri. 10am-1pm, Sat. 2-4pm, Sun. 10am-noon and 2-5pm. DM3, students DM2.)

Trains roll in from Dresden (every 2hr., 1½hr.) and Görlitz (1 per hr., 1hr.). The **tourist office,** Markt 1 (tel. 75 21 37; fax 75 21 61), rests in the *Rathaus* on the first floor near the left side entrance. It provides hiking maps and a room-finding service (DM20-40) for a DM5 fee (open Mon.-Fri. 8am-6pm, Sat. 9am-1pm, Sun. 1-4pm). A **pharmacy,** Johannis Apotheke, Johannisstr. 2 (tel. 51 21 64), has night services listed on the door (open Mon.-Fri. 8am-6pm, Sat. 8am-noon). The **post office,** 02763 Zittau, is at Haberkornpl. 1 (open Mon.-Fri. 6am-8pm, Sat. 7am-4pm). Head up Johannisstr. from the tourist office for the historic, hearty fare of the **Kloster Stüb'l,** Johannisstr. 4-

6 (tel. 51 25 76). Pictures of merry monks with large glasses of beer greet your entrance into this brewery/restaurant, built in 1810. Try the *Abernmanke mit Brotwurscht* and *Sauerkroattch* (DM8.50), or lighter *Soljanka* soup with toast and lemon (DM4). There's also an all-you-can-eat salad bar for DM9 (open Mon.-Tues. 11am-10pm, Fri. and Sat. 11am-midnight). A myriad of cafes and pastry shops in the Markt provide tasty delicacies, while the **Rewe Markt,** Bautznerstr. 11, satisfies **grocery** needs (open Mon.-Fri. 8am-6pm, Sat. 8am-1pm). The **telephone code** is 03583.

OYBIN

The neighboring *Kurort* of Oybin has been called "the pearl of the Zittauer Gebirge," and is a nice half-day trip to half-timbered houses and bulbous cliffs, entertaining both hikers and skiers. From the Zittau train station, hop on the **Schmalspurbahn** (narrow gauge steam train; 5-6 per day; one-way DM3.50) for a 45-minute ride into scenic Oybin in the 100-year-old coach. This little train has remained in continuous operation as a normal railway line to the present day, making it a premier attraction for locomotive buffs. At the top of the cliffs outside the town are the ruins of a high-Gothic fortress and cloister built in the 14th century. In the summer, concerts are held in the halls of the **cathedral.** From the trails along the top cliffs one can see far into Czech Bohemia. To get there from the station, head right onto Hauptstr. The stairs will be on the right of the church (DM4, students DM2.50). If it's just railroad memorabilia you're after, cross the tracks from the station to visit the **Schmalspurbahn Museum,** where the first tickets ever sold for the adorable train in 1890 are displayed (open Mon.-Fri. 1-4pm, Sat.-Sun. 10am-noon and 1-4pm; DM1, children DM0.50).

The **tourist office,** Freiligrathsstr. 8 (tel. 703 46; fax 702 78), provides hiking maps, town maps, bus schedules, and accommodations (DM20-50) for free (open Mon.-Fri. 9am-5:30pm, Sat. 10am-3pm). If the office is closed, they leave a list of available rooms at **Hotel Oybiner Hof,** Saupstr. 5. The **telephone code** is 035844.

The nearby town of **Jonsdorf** is home to the **Jugendherberge Jonsdorf (HI),** consisting of two houses about 1km apart. The office is at Hainstr. 14 (tel. 702 20); call in advance (DM20, with lunch DM27, over 26 DM24, DM30; reception open 7-9am and 3-8pm). From Zittau, you can take the *Schmalspurbahn:* Jonsdorf (the last station) and then turn down Hainstr. From Oybin, you have to take the *Bahn* to Bertsdorf., then continue on to Jonsdorf, or take the bus (last bus 6:55pm, 6 per day). Jonsdorf's twin hostel in Waltersdorf, **Jugendherberge Waltersdorf** (tel. (035841) 70 26 50), is accessible only by foot from the nearby (*Bahn* accessible) village of Großschonau; if you call ahead, they'll pick you up by car for DM1. (Breakfast DM6; reception open 7am-10pm. DM20, over 26 DM22.)

▓ Chemnitz

If you've ever wanted visible proof of the triumph of capitalism over Communism, visit Chemnitz. Beginning in 1953, the city went by the name "Karl-Marx-Stadt" in a rather unsubtle tribute to the philosopher who never even called it home. In 1990, however, the workers of the city united in a plebiscite to disavow the town of its Marxist associations and return its earlier title. While the city's name no longer serves as a monument to Communism, many of the Communist monuments remain, giving Chemnitz a strange, nostalgic value.

Orientation and Practical Information Tourist Information Chemnitz, Rathausstr. 1 (tel.194 33; fax 450 87 25), lies at the back of the *Stadthalle.* Exit the train station and take the first right on Carolastr. to Straße der Nationen; the *Stadthalle* looms on the right. They find rooms (DM25-40) for a DM2 fee. For a **taxi,** call 44 62 44 or 30 22 51. Chemnitz city magazines *Blitz* and *Stadtstreicher* can point you in the direction of the Chemnitz jet-set. The main **post office,** a Marxist architectural fantasy, is on Straße der Nationen, across from the tourist office (open Mon.-Fri. 9am-6pm, Sat. 9am-noon). The **postal code** is 09009. The **telephone code** is 0371.

Accommodations and Food Accomodations in Chemnitz are relatively expensive. While the **Jugendherberge (HI),** Augustusburgerstr. 369 (tel. 713 31), is stunningly renovated, it is far from town and difficult to reach with public transportation. Bus T-245 from the bus station down the street from the train station: "Walter-Klippel-Str." (Bus runs infrequently 6:25am-6:55pm; on weekends only 5 per day.) Or streetcar #1 or 6 (direction: "Gablenz"): "Gablenzpl." (5 stops). Cross the tracks to the left, follow the road as it curves into a pedestrian walkway, and continue until you reach Augustusburgerstr. It's a 20-minute walk from here. Don't even think of walking from the city. Out here you'll have the opportunity to see the inviting green countryside that surrounds poor old Chemnitz, but precious little hope of exploring any nightlife. (Reception open 2-7pm with reservations, 4-7pm without. DM22, over 26 DM26.50. Breakfast included. Best to call ahead to make sure there's space—in a pinch, you can always head for the hills of Augustusburg (see p. 168).

A good **supermarket** waits in the train station (open Mon.-Fri. 6am-9:45pm, Sat.-Sun. 7am-9:45pm). It's also remarkably easy to find cheap eats of the fast food variety along Straße der Nationen. For simple snacky fare, head to the neighborhood behind the *Stadt Halle.* To find a more satisfying meal, take a stroll down the Brühl, a pedestrian zone lined with moderately priced restaurants. **Bogart's,** Hartmannstr. 7d, serves up a healthy vegetable platter (DM12) as well as tasty blueberry shakes (DM5) amidst Bogey posters (open Mon.-Fri. 4-11pm, Sat.-Sun. 4pm-3am). The intersection of Klosterstr. and Theaterstr. provides some hearty options, with **Central-Eck** offering cafeteria-style German food sprinkled with oom-pah-pah for around DM8 (open Mon.-Fri. 9am-8pm, Sat. 9am-2pm), as well as more refined culinary dishes at **Café Oben,** on the second floor of the *Rathaus.* It's so well established, they even include it on the city map (open Mon.-Sat. 8am-11pm, Sun. 10am-11pm).

Sights There's an interesting Communism-theme-park atmosphere to Chemnitz; its most interesting attractions are the surviving socialist-inspired public artworks, although its museums and conventional tourist attractions are showing renewed signs of life. Every street corner, particularly along **Straße der Nationen,** boasts a statue of frolicking socialist children or happily scrubbed workers. Nothing, however, can outshine the monstrously pompous **bust of Karl Marx** at the corner of Straße der Nationen and Brückenstr. The dour Marx, however, is derided by the McDonald's across the street.

Continuing down Straße der Nationen will take you through the diminished remnants of the city's once-sprawling **Altstadt.** Chemnitz's strategic industrial importance guaranteed heavy Allied bombing in the war. Practically all that remains are the **Roter Turm,** a 12th-century relic of the city walls, and the **old Rathaus.** Closer to the train station is the **König-Albert-Museumsbau,** with the **Städtische Kunstsammlungen Chemnitz** (City Art Exhibit) and the **Museum für Naturkunde Chemnitz** (Natural History Museum). The art exhibit features a nice sampling of 19th- and 20th-century German art, as well as a huge collection of paintings and woodcuts by local Expressionist Karl Schmidt-Rotluff (open Tues. and Thurs.-Sun. 11am-5pm, Wed. 11am-7:30pm; DM4, students and seniors DM2).

To reach the **Schloß Complex,** Schloßberg 12, dash to Straße der Nationen from the train station and turn right, take a left onto Elisenstr., which merges with Mullerstr., which in turn leads to Schloßberg on the right. The castle that stood here was destroyed in the Thirty Years War; the **Schloßbergmuseum** occupies a reconstructed building that approximates the old structure. While the first floor offers medieval artwork and rotating exhibits, the goods reside upstairs in the **Stadtgeschichte** (city history) display. A large room documents the history of Chemnitz from its 12th-century foundation. The posters advertising Hitler's *Entartete Kunst* (Degenerate Art) exhibit, on display in Chemnitz at the outset of World War II, and the collections of Communist kitsch from the Karl-Marx-Stadt days, are particularly intriguing (open Tues.-Sat. 11am-5pm, Sun. 10am-6pm; DM4, students and seniors DM2).

SACHSEN

Entertainment and Nightlife Chemnitz offers a burgeoning theater and film scene. **Chemnitzer Kabarett,** An der Markthalle 1-3 (tel./fax 67 50 90), dishes out the comedy nearly every night. (Performances begin at 8pm. Tickets DM15, DM10 for seniors and students (except Fri. and Sat.). Mon. every seat is DM10.) The **Chemnitz Opern** (opera), Theaterpl. 2 (tel. 488 48 80), does it all, from *West Side Story* to Wagner. (Seats DM10-30; 50% student discount. Open Mon.-Fri. 10am-6pm, Sat. 2-6pm.) For the scoop on Chemnitz's theater scene, check the program at the **Schauspielhaus** (tel. 488 48 15), located at Park der Opfer des Faschismus. **Tanzhaus Heideschänke,** Eubaerstr. 103 (tel. 74 13 27; open Mon.-Fri. 11am-11pm, Sat.-Sun. 10am-11pm), and **Fuchsbau,** Carolastr. 8 (tel. 67 17 17; grooves Wed.-Sun. after 9pm), are where local cats head for disco, techno, and jazz.

■ Near Chemnitz: Augustusburg

A night at the lively and beauteous castle in Augustusburg facilitates recovery from the exhaustion of post-industrialist, post-Marxist, monochromatic Chemnitz. The princely mountaintop hamlet can be reached by bus T-244 or T-245 from the Chemnitz *Busbahnhof,* down Georgstr. from the train station: "Schloßberg." The stop is at the foot of the path leading to the castle (7am-7pm, 45min., DM4.90; check schedules early). The Renaissance **hunting lodge** of the Sachsen Electors is perched 1500m above town with a mesmerizing 360-degree panorama of the surrounding **Erzgebirge** mountains—look for the Czech Republic on the horizon. A guided tour (required) of the royal playhouse will lead you through the **Brünnenhaus** (well house) and the intimate **Schloßkapelle** (church chapel), the only Renaissance chapel left in Sachsen. The altar is graced by a Lucas Cranach painting, portraying the dour Herzog August, his wife Anna, and their 14 pious children; all those damn critters might explain why the Sachsen elector was so stingy—he conscripted poachers into well-digging duties that ran around the clock. (Tours every hr. at 30min. past the hr.; DM5, students and seniors DM3.) Explore the **Motorrad Museum** (Motorcycle Museum), the **Museum für Jagdtier und Vogel kunde des Erzgebirges** (Hunting and Game Museum), or the **Kutschen Museum** (Carriage Museum). A day pass for all museums costs DM9, students and seniors DM5. Tickets for individual museums can also be purchased separately. (*Schloß* open Mon.-Fri. 9am-6pm, Sat.-Sun. 9am-6:30pm; Nov.-March closed Mon.) In the first weekend of August, the *Schloß* offers an American-style **Country Fest** for absolutely no apparent reason—satisfy your lust for bull-riding here. The real treat of a visit to Augustusburg is the **Jugendherberge (HI),** located inside the castle (tel. (037291) 202 56), with high domed ceilings, animal skins on the walls, and a supreme view of the surrounding mountains. Narrow and crooked stone stairways lead from the spacious bunk-bed rooms to the romantic doubles (2 mattresses tucked together in an alcove). The ambience really is medieval—you are the prince or princess of the castle. To reach the reception, turn left as you enter the castle courtyard and knock on the door reading *"Bereiche Herbergsleitung."* (Reception open after 3pm. DM26, students DM21. Breakfast included.)

FREIBERG

For *Dom-* and *Altstadt-*weary travelers, Freiberg offers a subterranean treasure—a 600-year-old silver mine. The **Himmelfahrt Fundgrube** or **Freiberger Silberbergwerk** has been mined since the 14th century, unearthing a major source of wealth for Freiberg and Sachsen. While the first notice of anyone striking silver in the town dates to the Frankish and Thüringer settlers in 1168, the 700m-deep mine has been used for educational purposes since 1765, providing geology and mining students with a "laboratory." Today, the mine attracts down 'n' dirty adventure-seeking tourists who want to toss on an old-school uniform, jump into a pair of Wellington boots, and strap on a headlamp before descending into the dark bowels of the earth.

To get to the entrance of the **silver mine** from the station, walk along Bahnhofstr., take a left on Poststr. and veer right onto Hornstr., which leads to Himmelfahrtsgasse. After passing the cemetery, turn left on Füchsmuhlenweg, which leads to the mine, the **Reiche Zeche Schacht.** The two-hour **tour** begins when everyone sports the

The Greatest Budget Souvenir Ever—Castles for DM1!

Many travelers like to buy postcards of castles, and happily shell out a couple *Mark*s for pretty little pictures of royal abodes. Some travelers, however, prefer to buy their own castle. The state of Sachsen has more royal palaces than it knows what to do with (about 1000), and has begun a novel pilot program to market some of these treasured historical fortifications for a mere DM1. There is, sadly, a slight drawback. Those who purchase the castles must renovate them—40 years of GDR neglect has produced a terrible state of disrepair. The cost of renovation tacks about DM7-20 million onto the purchase costs. Still, the opportunities for those who want to buy something by which to remember their travels in Germany are spectacular. Schloß Gaußig, about 10km from Bautzen, has a newly renovated ballroom with all the posh adornments which one could ever hope for. Its dining room walls provide a *Jägermeister* fantasy, with deer antlers lining the walls. The nearby Schloß Milkel comes with a mausoleum and many remains of ancient royalty. Schloß Lichtenwalde, 10km from Chemnitz, is also up for grabs. Response to the offer has been rather slow, so the opportunity to purchase your very own bit of royalty should endure for a while. Who knows? If the *Mark* continues to slide, those renovation costs might not be so tough to swallow.

GDR-style *Schutzkleidung* (protective clothing). The guide retells the history of the mine as he leads the group through the dark, wet tunnels, illuminated only by headlamps. (Tours May-Sept. Mon.-Fri. 9:30am, Sat. 8, 11am, and 2pm; Sept.-April Mon.-Fri. 9:30am, first Sat. every month 8, 11am, and 2pm. DM15, students DM10.) After a few hours underground, it's a relief to meander the streets of Freiberg. The spectacular **Freiberger Dom** towers at the edge of the Untermarkt, easily reached from the train station: walk straight on Bahnhofstr., turn left on Poststr., which changes names twice (Erbischestr. and Burgstr.) before it reaches Kirchgasse; continue straight to the *Dom*. The *Dom* stores some world-class treasures. The intricately ornate **Goldene Pforte** (Golden Portal), built around 1230, is almost as stunning as the free standing **Tulpen Kanzel** (Tulip Pulpit). A 1510 Hans Witten creation, the pulpit appears to grow from the church-floor—what a tulip! The *Dom* may usually only be visited by complimentary tour. (Tours May-Oct. Mon.-Sat. 10, 11am, 2, 3, and 4pm; Nov.-April daily 11am, 2, and 3pm. Tours with organ demonstration (their organ, not yours) Thurs. 2pm, Sun. 11am. Tour DM3, students DM2; organ tour DM5, students DM3.)

The **tourist office (Freiberg Info),** Burgstr. 1 (tel. 236 02; fax 27 32 60), popping up behind the *Rathaus,* sells tickets and silver trinkets, gives **tours,** and finds **private rooms** (DM30-50) for a small fee (open Mon.-Fri. 9am-6pm, Sat. 9am-noon). On the opposite side of the *Rathaus,* where the bloody chopped head protrudes into the Obermarkt, the **Rats-Apotheke pharmacy** has been pushing pills since 1539 (open Mon.-Tues. and Thurs. 7am-6:30pm, Wed. and Fri. 7am-6pm, Sat. 8am-noon). The post office is at the end of Poststr. on the way to town. The **postal code** is 09599. The **telephone code** is 03731.

For an elegant setting and delicious food, the **Hartmann Café,** at the corner of Obermarkt and Peterstr., cooks up breakfast all day (veggie omelette with *Brötchen* DM7.50) and light meals (tasty quiche DM3.50). They specialize in fantastic baked goods—savor some *Kaffe und Kuchen* (open Tues.-Sat. 8am-6pm, Sun. 11am-6pm). To see geophysics students get their rocks off as you have a drink, dance at **Das Füllort,** the beer garden **Wolfsschlucht,** and the bar **Abgang**—all located on Petersstr. 5 (tel. 26 24 04 for all; disco and bar open Mon. and Sat. 10pm-late; beer garden open daily 2pm-late). For groceries, visit the **E Activ Markt** on the Marktplatz (open Mon.-Wed. 8am-6:30, Thurs.-Fri. 8am-7pm, Sat. 7:30am-1pm).

■ Zwickau

Zwickau is best known as the Motor City of Eastern Germany. For over 35 years, the city's Sachsenring-Auto-Union produced the GDR's ubiquitous consumer car, the tiny *Trabant*. An ill-engineered, two-cylinder plastic jalopy, the *"Trabi"* was Communist industry's inferior answer to the West's *Volkswagen,* and, like cockroaches, the wheezing little cars persist. Officially, the city would prefer to play up its more genteel distinctions, such as its active artistic tradition, which launched composer Robert Schumann and a couple of members of *die Brücke* painting school into the world. But it may be a losing battle; the tinny whine of a *Trabi* laboring uphill is never far from the ears of a visitor.

The dusky-colored, four-story **Schumann Haus** stands at Hauptmarkt 5 (tel./fax 21 52 69). The museum plays up the Romantic composer's childhood in Zwickau before his life as a globetrotting celebrity, performing at the hotspots in Germany, Russia, and Austria. The museum also devotes several parts of the display to Schumann's wife, Clara Wieck, one of the most accomplished pianists of her day—today, Clara is eternalized as "the woman on the DM100 bill." No mention here of Schumann's later insanity, although the less than flattering busts of the composer hint that all was not well. Musicians perform both Robert and Clara's works in the *Klavierhalle* (open Mon.-Sat. 10am-5pm; DM5, students and seniors DM 3).

Amid a smattering of Schumann memorabilia and a dark, imposing, old **cathedral** at the newly-renovated central Platz, Zwickau's unique offering resides in its **Automobilienmuseum.** To find it, make your way north from the Ring on Walther-Rathenau-Str. to an out-of-the-way little building past the auto factory (20min.). Before the days of GDR mediocrity, Zwickau turned out classy cars—its early production days spawned the Audi company, and auto pioneer August Horch designed some roadsters that'll knock your socks off. Over a dozen *Trabant* models are on display, prompting wonder at the design's invulnerability to innovation over the years. The sight of the last *Trabi* ever produced (in 1991) in all of its pink "splendor" and emblazoned with the words, "Trabant: Legend on Wheels," is enough to make even the most ardent Cold Warrior misty-eyed (open Tues. and Thurs. 9am-noon and 2-5pm, Sat.-Sun. 10am-5pm; DM5, students and seniors DM3).

Located in the middle of the busy Sachsen-Thüringen rail network, Zwickau is easily reached by **train** for a daytrip from Leipzig (13 per day, 1½hr.), Dresden (26 per day, 2hr.), or Altenburg (17 per day, 40min.). Its oldest attractions and most beautiful streets are confined to a circular region in the *Altstadt,* bounded by a bustling three-lane roundabout named **Dr.-Friedrichs-Ring.** Zwickau's **tourist office,** Hauptstr. 6 (tel. 29 37 13; fax 29 37 15; email zwickau@lfr-sachsen.imedia.de; http://www.imedia.de), lies in the center of the circle; from the station, head along the left fork which becomes Bahnhofstr. until it ends at Humboldtstr. Turn right, and then quickly left on Schumannstr., which will lead you across the Ring. The street resumes as Innere Plauenschestr., a pedestrian zone, which takes you past the Marien Kirche. Hang a right to the Markt; the first left is Hauptstr. They provide maps and book rooms (DM35; open Mon.-Fri. 9am-6pm, Sat. 9am-noon). The main **post office,** Humboldtstr. 3, 08056 Zwickau, is just outside the Ring. The **telephone code** is 0375.

The monthly *Stadtsreicher,* free at the tourist office, lists the major events in the area, ranging from shows to bars to food. Just outside of the Ring, **Bistro International,** Schumannstr. 10 (tel. 29 88 09), has Turkish pizzas (DM8-10) that please the palate (open daily 10am-midnight). To imbibe some spirits and GDR nostalgia, head to **Roter Oktober,** at the corner of Leipzigerstr. and Kolpingstr. Toast the hammer and sickle if you really feel like getting crazy. The **Markt** serves up food stands (Thurs.-Fri. 8am-6pm). A number of cheap dining options can be found along the Hauptmarkt and Innere Schneebergerstr. during the day, and the **SPAR supermarket,** across from the Schumann Haus, fills your grocery bags (open Mon.-Fri. 8am-6:30pm, Sat. 8am-noon).

■ Leipzig

Leipzig jumps out from the calm Eastern German landscape in a fiery blaze of nowNowNOW. The glitzy nightlife and glassy skyscrapers set amidst concrete blights cast a decidedly Western flavor upon the city. The *Uni*-culture spawned by over 20,000 students keeps the sense of progress alive as it did when Goethe, Nietzsche, and Leibniz stalked these ivory (well…gray) towers.

At the same time, Leipzig's rich cultural legacy adds to its vitality. The echoes of musical genius emanate from the top-notch *Gewandhaus Orchester,* founded by Felix Mendelssohn in 1850 in the spirit of Bach and Wagner, who both preceded him as residents of this city. Goethe revered "L.E.," as Leipzig is known to those who love it, for its cultivated inhabitants who inspired him to set a pivotal scene from *Faust* in Auerbach's Keller—it was here that Mephisto tricked his student.

Simultaneously, the *Uni*-town has not lost touch with reality due to the ephemeral lives of academicians and artists. Leipzig is celebrated as a cradle of German liberty for its role in the "Wars of Liberation," in which the city kicked Napoleon out of Germany in the 1813 Battle of Leipzig. In the abortive revolutions of 1830 and 1848, Leipzig again convulsed in an effort to throw off authoritarian rule. More recently, Leipzig gained fame as Germany's *Heldenstadt* (city of heroes) for its role as the crucible of *die Wende,* the sudden toppling of the GDR in 1989.

Leipzig's half-millennium tradition as a *Messe Stadt* (Fair City) continues to impart international verve (and money) into the city. This Boom town is booming with *style* as it charges through the transformations of the *Neue Bundesländer,* resolutely resisting any threats to the student-hipster vibe by entrepreneurs and speculators.

ORIENTATION AND PRACTICAL INFORMATION

Most of the sights and the entertainment district dwell in the ringed *Innenstadt,* but you'll have to leave the comforting sight of the huge, metal university tower for nightlife and the Leipzig behind the scenes. It's a 10-minute walk from the main train station on the north edge of the *Innenstadt* to the **Augustus Platz,** the center surrounded by the *Gewandhaus,* the university, and the main post office. The cavernous **Leipziger Hauptbahnhof** is a sight in itself—its curved-beam roofs enclose one of Europe's largest train stations and recall the grander days of rail travel. The station has the proud distinction of being the biggest terminus rail station in Europe and is is restructured to include a huge shopping and eating complex (expect some track changes and delays). Fast inter-city trains bring you to Dresden, Halle (20min.), and Berlin (under 2hr.).

Tourist Office: Leipzig Information, Richard-Wagner-Str. 1 (tel. 710 42 60; fax 710 42 65; email lipsia@aol.com). Walk across Willy-Brandt-Platz in front of the station and turn left at Richard-Wagner-Str. Among the gorgeous brochures, there's a useful free map of the *Innenstadt* and suburbs with a street name index. They book rooms in opulent hotels and *Pensionen* for free and sell tickets. Free magazines *Fritz* and *Blitz* fill you in on nightlife, but the superior *Kreuzer* (bought here or at newsstands, DM2.50) puts them to shame. Open Mon.-Fri. 9am-7pm, Sat.-Sun. 9:30am-2pm. Room-finding service (tel. 710 42 75; see **Accommodations and Camping,** p. 172) open Mon.-Fri. 9am-6pm, Sat. 9:30am-2pm.

Tours: The tourist office leads bus tours (2½hr.) daily at 10am and 1:30pm. The Sunday 10:30am tour is in English; the 4:30pm tour is always in both languages. DM28, seniors DM20, students DM16. Walking tours (2hr.), on themes from "the bar mile" to a less alcohol-soaked visit of the fairgrounds, depart daily in the summer at 10am, 4, 5, 7, and 7:30pm. DM10-15. From Oct.-April there are no tours Sat.-Sun. There are also shorter tours available (Tues.-Thurs. 1pm; DM8). Some guides are English-speaking. Ask at the office for details.

Budget Travel: Kilroy Travels Germany, Augustuspl. 9 (tel. 30 30 90), in the university courtyard. Affiliated with STA. Open Mon.-Fri. 9am-7pm, Sat 9am-1pm.

Consulate: U.S. Wilhelm-Seyferth-Str. 4 (tel. 213 84 20). Entrance on Wächstr. behind the Museum der Bildenden Künste. Open Mon.-Fri. 9am-noon or by appointment. Also home to the **Amerika Haus Bibliothek** (tel. 213 84 25). Open Tues.-Fri. 11am-5pm.

Currency Exchange: Dresdner Bank, on Goethestr. between the station and Augustuspl. Open Mon.-Thurs. 8:30am-7:30pm, Fri. 8:30am-4pm. Several **ATMs.**

American Express: Dorotheenpl. 224 (tel. 96 70 00). On the far side of the central city from the station. Head down Schillerstr. from Dittrichring about a block; it's on the left. All AmEx services. Open Mon.-Fri. 9:30am-6pm, Sat. 9am-noon.

Flights: Flughafen Leipzig-Halle (info tel. 492 20 66) in Schkendingasse, about 20km from Leipzig. International service throughout Central Europe. Buses leave Goethestr. near the tourist office, Mon.-Fri. and Sun. 5am-9pm every 30min.; Sat. 5am-8:45pm every 45min., Sun. 3:30am-10:30pm every 30min.; DM4 one-way.

Trains: (tel. 194 19). Leipzig lies on the Berlin-Munich line, with regular InterCity service to Frankfurt am Main. Information counter on the platform near track 15, or ask at one of the many counters in the huge and hugely helpful new *Reisezentrum* at the entrance of the station.

Public Transportation: Streetcars and buses cover the city; the hub is on Platz der Republik, in front of the *Hauptbahnhof*. Tickets come in two varieties: 15min. for DM1.40 and 1hr. (with line changes) for DM2. Streetcars and S-Bahn run from 5:30am-3am, although each line varies in its nightly duration. Free maps at the tourist office. Day passes available for DM7 or four-ride passes for DM5.50.

Taxis: tel. 48 84, 98 22 22, or 42 33.

Car Rental: Avis, Augustuspl. 5/6 (tel. 961 14 00; fax 961 44 01). Open Mon.-Sat. 7am-7pm, Sun. 8am-noon. **Sixt-Budget,** (tel. 26 98 90; fax 269 88 19). Open Mon.-Fri. 8am-6pm, Sat. 8am-noon. **Hertz,** next to the train station in the Hotel Astoria (tel. 128 47 01). Open Mon.-Fri. 7:30am-6pm, Sat. 8am-noon. **Europacar Inter-Rent,** in the west hall of the *Hauptbahnhof* (tel. 211 38 84). Open Mon.-Fri. 7am-9pm, Sat. 8am-noon. More offices at the airport.

Mitfahrzentrale: Rudolf-Breitscheid-Str. 39 (tel. 211 42 22), next door to the *Hauptbahnhof*, organizes ride-shares, a standard deviation from the risks of hitching. Open daily 9am-8pm. Another *Mitfahrzentrale* is located at Universität Leipzig (tel. 973 78 55), near the *Mensa*. Open Mon.-Fri. 9am-6pm.

Hitchhiking: *Let's Go* does not recommend hitchhiking as a safe mode of transportation. Hitchers going to Dresden and Prague, S-Bahn #2, 3, 6, or 8: "Pounsdorfer Allee," turn left down Pounsdorfer Allee to the *Autobahn* interchange. Those hitching to Berlin, streetcar #16 to "Essenerstr.," switch to bus F, get out at Sachsenpark, and walk to the *Autobahn*.

Lost Property: Fundstelle, in the western side of the station (tel. 123 32 70). Open Mon.-Fri. 7am-3:15pm.

Library: British Council, Lumumbastr. 11-13 (tel. 564 67 12), stocks an open reading room with English books a-plenty. Bus stop: "Nordpl." Open Mon. and Thurs.-Fri. 11am-5pm, Tues. 11am-7pm, Wed. 11am-6pm.

Gay and Lesbian Information: AIDS-Hilfe, Ossientzkystr. 18 (tel. 232 31 26), is open daily and features a popular gay cafe on Tues. and Thurs. from 3-10pm. Also offers the updated **Queer Stadtplan,** a map of gay and lesbian nightlife.

Laundromat: Maga Pon, Gottschedstr. 11 (tel. 960 79 22), takes the cake as the jazziest laundromat in Sachsen—it doubles as a hep-cat bar and restaurant, so come in your coolest dirty clothes (unless you want to wash them). Wash DM6, dry DM1. Open daily 9am-3am.

Frauenzentrum: Frauen-Notruf, B.-Göring-Str. 152 (tel. 306 52 46). Open Mon.-Fri. 6am-10pm for advice or help.

Pharmacies: Löwen Apotheke, Grimmaischestr. 19 (tel. 960 50 27). Open Mon.-Fri. 8am-8pm, Sat. 9am-4pm. Whenever the shop is closed, push the button by the door for emergency service.

Emergency: Ambulance, tel. 115. **Police,** tel. 110. **Fire,** tel. 112.

Internet Access: In **Café le bit,** Kohlgartenstr. 2 (tel. 998 20 00; email le-bit@mediagroup.de; see **Food,** p. 174).

Post Office: Hauptpostamt 1, 04109 Leipzig (tel. 212 25 88), across from Augustuspl. on Grimmaischestr. Open Mon.-Fri. 8am-8pm, Sat. 9am-4pm.

Telephone Code: 0341.

ACCOMMODATIONS AND CAMPING

Leipzig's budget accommodations are on the verge of disaster, with both of its hostels giving way to expensive real estate development; one closed in 1997, one is moving. While **private rooms** are tolerable at around DM35 per person, the private *Zimmervermittlung* service, located in the tourist office, rudely sticks you with a DM10 booking fee for the first three nights, followed by a charge of DM5 for each additional

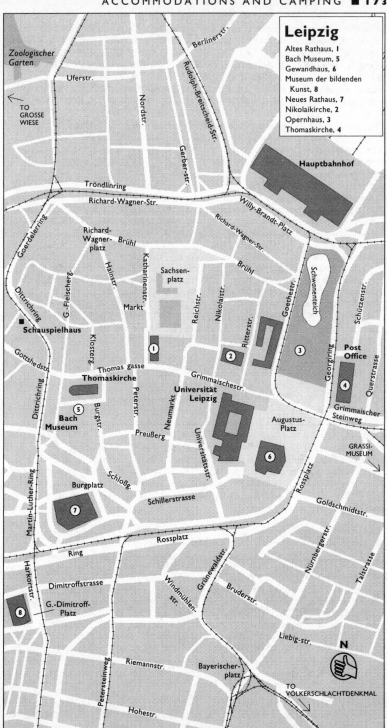

Leipzig

Altes Rathaus, 1
Bach Museum, 5
Gewandhaus, 6
Museum der bildenden
  Kunst, 8
Neues Rathaus, 7
Nikolaikirche, 2
Opernhaus, 3
Thomaskirche, 4

Zoologischer
Garten

Uferstr.

TO
GROSSE
WIESE

Berlinerstr.

Rudolph-Breitscheid-Str.

Nordstr.

Gerberstr.

Hauptbahnhof

Tröndlinring

Richard-Wagner-Str.

Willy-Brandt-Platz

Richard-Wagner-Str.

Goerdelerring

Richard-
Wagner-
platz

Brühl

Dittrichring

Katharinenstr.

Brühl

Schwanenteich

Hainstr.

G.-Fleischerg

Sachsen-
platz

Reichstr.

Nikolaistr.

Goethestr.

Schützenstr.

Schauspielhaus

Markt

Klosterg.

Georgring

Querstrasse

Gottschedstr.

Dittrichring

Thomas gasse

Thomaskirche

Peterstr.

Neumarkt

Grimmaischestr.

Ritterstr.

Universität
Leipzig

Post
Office

Bach
Museum

Burgstr.

Preußerg

Schloßg.

Universitätsstr.

Augustus-
Platz

Grimmaischer
Steinweg

GRASSI-
MUSEUM

Martin-Luther-Ring

Burgplatz

Schillerstrasse

Rossplatz

Goldschmidtstr.

Ring

Rossplatz

Nürnbergerstr.

Talstrasse

Harkortstr.

Dimitroffstrasse

G.-Dimitroff-
Platz

Windmühlen-
str.

Grünewaldstr.

Bruderstr.

Liebig-str.

N

Petersteinweg

Riemannstr.

Bayerischer-
platz

Hohestr.

TO
VÖLKERSCHLACHTDENKMAL

1
2
3
4
5
6
7
8

SACHSEN

night. Ouch! As a result, if you want to stay at a hostel or at a camping sight, be sure to call ahead, especially during tourist high season (June-Aug.). You can save some money by asking at the tourist office desk for a copy of **Übernachten in und um Leipzig,** which can point you to some small and cheap but well-appointed *Pensionen.* The **Jugendherberge Grethen (HI)** in Grethen (tel. (03437) 76 34 49) is a tolerable distance (30min.) by train (direction: "Groß Steinberg"): "Grethen." Call to be picked up at the bus stop or train station at Grethen, or get directions for the 1½km walk to the hostel. (DM20, over 26 DM26.50. Breakfast included. Sheets DM5.) For longer stays, the helpful **Mitwohnzentrale,** Rudolf-Breitscheider-Str. 39 (tel. 90 50 00; fax 980 50 01), has English-speaking staff willing to help you avoid the clutches of the tourist office (open daily 9am-8pm). A church-run **Jugendhospiz** opens its doors at Weißdornstr. 102, just outside the city center, in late 1997. Beds will probably cost somewhere between DM15 and DM20.

Jugendherberge Leipzig Centrum (HI), Käthe-Kollwitz-Str. 64 (tel. 47 05 30; fax 47 58 88). From the station, streetcar #1 (direction: "Lausen") or 2 (direction: "Plagwitz"): "Marchnerstr." (4 stops). Well-worn furniture in a hostel that will keep the name but lose the location around January 1998. This is the third "official deadline," but when the move takes place, it will be onto Volksgarten 24 (cell phone (0172) 910 41 66 or check with the tourist office). Streetcar #17, 27, or 57 (direction: "Schönefeld"): "Löbauerstr." Reception open 24hr. DM24, over 26 DM29. Breakfast included. Sheets DM5. In current location, reception open 6:30-9am, 9:30am-noon, and 12:30pm-1am. Curfew 1am. DM22, over 26 DM25.

Am Auensee, Gustav-Esche-Str. 5 (tel. 461 16 00), in the nearby suburb of Wahren. A budgetary *deus ex machina* in the absense of hostels. From the station, streetcar #10, 28, or 30 (direction: "Wahren"): "Rathaus Wahren." Turn left at the *Rathaus,* and then right at the end of the street onto Gustav-Esche-Str. Reception open 6am-10pm. **Camping** DM6-10 for tents, DM12 for caravans. Small tent-huts function as 2-bed bungalows. DM50 per hut, winter DM55. Two-person huts with bath DM90.

Camping: Campingplatz am Kulkwitzer See, Seestr. in Markrandstadt (tel. 941 13 15). Streetcar #8 (direction: "Lausen") to the last stop, then bear right. Reception open 7am-5pm. Open April 15-Oct. 15.

FOOD

Budget meals are not as hard to find in Leipzig as budget rooms, but it's still no cake-walk (so to speak). The **Innenstadt** is well-supplied with *Imbiß* stands, bistros, and restaurants for consumption on the go. The Brühl, running in front of the Sachsenpl., offers a **Kaiser's supermarket** (open Mon.-Fri. 7am-8pm, Sat. 7am-4pm) and the veritable beacon in the night, **McDonald's,** whose golden arches sing like Heinrich Heine's sirens (open Sun.-Thurs. 6am-3am, Fri-Sat. 24hr.). Sachsenpl. also offers a **market** on Tuesdays and Fridays.

Universität Leipzig Mensa, in the university complex just off Grimmaischestr. Less than astounding university food for DM4-6 for university students…of Leipzig U., that is. A better bet is the **Eck-Café,** also in the university complex across from the *Mensa.* The cafe serves daily specials for about DM3 that are more freshly prepared than the putrifax in the *Mensa. Mensa* open Mon.-Fri 7am-7pm. Eck-Café open Mon.-Thurs. 9am-10pm, Fri. 11am-3pm. Both open Oct.-Feb. and April-Aug.

Maître, Karl-Liebknecht-Str. 62 (tel. 31 17 30), like Maga Pon (below), treads the fine line between bar, cafe, and restaurant. Streetcar #10, 11 or 28 (directions: "Connewitz," "Markleeberg-Ost," or "Markleeberg West," respectively): "Arndtstr." Also serves breakfast buffet Sun. 10am-3pm (DM11.80), but during the week they do it French-style with generous slices of quiche and onion tart (DM4). Revel in the bistro hipness of it all (open Mon.-Fri. 9am-1am, Sat. 2pm-1am, Sun. 10am-midnight).

Alexandrina, Körnerstr. 27 (tel. 213 18 88), a store front on Karl-Liebknecht-Str.; follow directions to Maître and backtrack a bit towards town. An ideal location for satisfying the late-night cravings of patrons at the many nearby bars, but it merits a trip out of the city center even during the day. An obscenely friendly staff slices strips of flavorful lamb-calf-beef kebab into toasted *Fladenbrot* and finishes it off with fresh veggies and tasty sauces (DM4). The exceptional falafel also comes with tasty salad goods, crowned with a large chunk of deep-fried feta cheese and real, live tahini (DM4). You never knew that *Imbiß* stands could live so large.

Maga Pon, Gottschedstr. 11 (tel. 960 79 22), has delicious spaghetti dishes for DM7-9.50 and a fantastic breakfast buffet (Sun. 9am-6pm), but there's an awful lot of liquid refreshment going on 'til the wee hours of the morn (open daily 9am-3am).

Bagel Brothers, Nikolaistr. 42 (tel. 980 33 30), between the *Hauptbahnhof* and the Nikolaikirche, smears all kinds of cream cheese toppings and creates all kinds of sandwiches on 14 different flavors of bagels that are only slightly too light and fluffy for the true connoisseur. Bagel with flavored cream cheese (DM2.90).

Café le bit, Kohlgartenstr. 2 (tel. 998 20 00; email le-bit@mediagroup.de), right off Friedrich-List-Platz; heading towards the train station on Georgiring, turn right on Schützenstr. which becomes Rosa-Luxemburg-Str., leading straight there (10min. from the station). Cyberfreaks check email, or play games, or drink themselves silly just steps from the bar in—what else would you expect from Leipzig?—super-hip surroundings. 10min. connection DM2. A good bar menu with snacks like crepes (DM3-8.50). Open Mon.-Fri. 8:30am-3am, Sat. starting at 10am, Sun. 10am-1am.

Pleißenberg, Schulstr. 2, a couple of blocks from the Thomaskirche. One of the few German meat-and-potatoes restaurants in Leipzig, with good prices and even better hours. Meals DM6-9. Open Mon.-Fri. 7am-5am, Sat.-Sun. 10am-5am.

Kultur Café Alte Nikolaischule (tel. 211 85 01), across the street from the Nikolaikirche. Daily specials DM10-15 come dripping in free pretense. Occasional art exhibits and jazz performances round out the ambience. Open daily 10am-1am.

Messehaus am Markt, just off the Markt, is a food-court with vending windows. **Nudel Macher** offers specials with an all-you-can-eat pizza and pasta buffet (DM9.90) every Mon.-Wed. 3-8pm, all day Sun. Eat until you're comatose.

SIGHTS

Leipzig's historic *Innenstadt* suffered less at the hands of World War II bombers than it did from the poorly planned architectural creations of the socialist era. The heart of the city beats on the **Marktplatz,** a colorful, cobblestone square guarded by the slanted 16th-century **Altes Rathaus,** with its elegant **clock tower** showing four bright-blue faces. Inside, a grand festival hall runs above the **Stadtgeschichtliches Museum Leipzig,** which offers a straightforward look at Leipzig's history and generally entrancing temporary exhibits (open Tues.-Fri. 10am-6pm, Sat.-Sun. 10am-4pm; DM4, students DM2).

Behind the *Altes Rathaus,* on Nikolaistr., the 800-year-old **Nikolaikirche** witnessed the birth of Bach's *Johannes Passion* as well as the GDR's peaceful revolution. The sandstone exterior, an unfortunate product of 19th-century *fin-de-siècle* malaise, hides a truly empyrean interior. The ceilings and columns feature a surprisingly majestic array of pinks and greens—not your usual flavor for a church, but the late-18th-century renovation was, after all, inspired by the not-so-usual *French* Baroque school. The end result is far removed from the days of fire and brimstone; instead, the attempt to make the columns resemble palms proves more evocative of the sunny tropics (open Mon.-Sat. 10am-6pm, Sun. after services; free). What began as regular Monday meetings at the Nikolaikirche in 1989 turned into massive weekly demonstrations *(Montagdemos),* in which ever-growing numbers of Leipzigers called for an end to the Communist government's policies. On October 7, 1989, the nerves of the Communist government erupted in a display of police violence against unarmed citizens. Despite the heightened security measures, over 70,000 people showed up at the church for the demonstration on Monday, October 9. For reasons that remain unclear, the armed forces allowed the protest to pass without a response. The following Monday demonstration drew 120,000 emboldened citizens, and on October 18, SED party chief Erich Honecker resigned.

Continuing away from the Marktplatz, take Universitätsstr. to the former Karl Marx University, now rechristened **Universität Leipzig.** Its "Sharp Tooth" tower, a steel and concrete behemoth, displaced the centuries-old Universitätskirche and other popular buildings following a wave of faculty protests in 1968. Structural renovations are planned, as the cloud-stabbing tower's design has proven increasingly unstable over the years.

Past the university and down Grimmaischer Steinweg is the **Grassimuseum** (tel. 21 42), on Johannispl., an Art Deco home for three small museums. The largest of the three (and we mean *large*), the **Museum fur Völker Kunde** (Museum for Anthropology), seems somehow politically incorrect, but the huge collection of clothing, religious objects, artwork, and just about everything else documenting different "peoples" around the world is strangely fascinating, with collections of clay huts and some disturbingly anatomically correct decorations (open Tues.-Fri. 10am-5:30pm, Sat. 10am-4pm; DM5, students DM2). The university's **Musikinstrumenten-Museum** contains more than 5000 instruments, some dating back to the 16th century (open Tues.-Sat. 10am-5pm, Sun. 10am-2pm; DM5, students DM2). Enter the courtyard to find the **Museum des Kunsthandwerk** (handicrafts), with only 1% of its excellent collection on display. The Art Deco and *Jugendstil* pieces are especially attractive (open Tues. and Thurs.-Sun. 10am-6pm, Wed. noon-8pm; DM4, students DM2). On the far side of the Grassimuseum, the **Ausstellungsraum Grassimuseum** (tel. 214 21 11), on Prager St., is a magnet for international art exhibitions (open Mon. and Sat.-Sun. 10am-8pm, Tues. and Thurs.-Fri. 10am-6pm; DM12, students DM8).

The **Neues Rathaus** on Schillerstr., a former fortress laid to waste in the 17th century and then converted in the late 19th, provides a vexing spectacle—the gray behemoth, which contains over 800 rooms, seems large enough to house its own city. The place is currently closed for repairs while the city tries to figure out what the hell they should do with it. Behind it, cross over Martin-Luther-Ring and walk south on Harkortstr. one block to the **Museum der Bildenden Künste** (Museum of Fine Arts), at Georg-Dimitroff-Platz 1. Built in the former "Reichsgericht" (a sort of Supreme Court for the Wilhelmine Reich), its building alone merits a visit as an excellent example of this self-aggrandizing style of architecture. The museum provides a fairly thorough survey of German art from the late 1700s to the present day, with three rooms completely dedicated to some of the creative art works which developed between 1945 and 1989, in spite of the stifling East German government. Expressionist works are notably absent from the collection as a result of the purging that claimed 394 paintings for Hitler's "degenerate art" exhibit. The recent reacquisition of Otto Mueller's *Liebespaar* and donation of the bold *Teppichhändler* by Max Beckman have commenced the collection's rebuilding. The old *Plenarsaal,* in which the court met, remains covered in intricate wood carvings with the shields of the precursors to the modern *Bundesländer* decorating the room in wood and stained glass. (Open Tues., Thurs.-Sun. 9am-5pm, Wed. 1-9:30pm. DM5, students DM2.50, free on the second Sun. of each month.)

Just north of the *Neues Rathaus* and close to the Marktplatz is the **Thomaskirche,** where Bach served as cantor. When his original burial site was destroyed in World War II, his remains were interred here in front of the altar. The memorial statue, showing Bach with empty pockets, says a lot about the genius's impoverished success. A stained-glass window commemorates Martin Luther's trip here in the early Reformation. Mozart and Mendelssohn also performed in this church, and Wagner was baptized here in 1813 (open daily 8am-6pm; in winter 9am-5pm; services Sun. 9:30am and 6pm). Across the street, the **Johann-Sebastian-Bach-Museum,** Thomaskirchhof 16, chronicles Bach's work and time in Leipzig from 1723-1750. (Open daily 10am-5pm. Last entry 4:30pm. DM4, students and seniors DM2.50. Tours daily 11am and 3pm; with tour, admission DM8 and DM5. The museum's *Sommersaal* hosts concerts 2-3 times per week for DM10-15, students DM6-8.)

In the Mädler Passage, just off the Markt, Leipzig's most famous restaurant, **Auerbach's Keller,** Grimmaischestr. 2-4 (tel. 21 61 00) probably won't make it on the budget travel Top 10 list, with entrees costing DM25-30, but it's worth taking a peak at where Mephisto tricked his student in Goethe's *Faust.* Not far north of the Thomaskirche lies Leipzig's newest, most fascinating museum, the **Museum der "Runden Ecke"** (Museum of the Round Corner), Dittrichring 24, the former headquarters of the East German Ministry for State Security or **Stasi;** its permanent exhibition, *"Stasi-Macht und Banalität"* (Power and Banality, an echo of German philosopher Hannah

Arendt's line on the "banality of evil") provides a glimpse into the eyes of the Panopticon. The sinister tools of the *Stasi* trade included mechanisms for monitoring all mail and phone calls, as well as breath samples which, much like phrenology, were used to determine criminal personalities. While the surveillance equipment is enough to inflict erythmea on any conspiracy theorist, the museum also chronicles the triumph of the resistance that overthrew the *Stasi* terror. The Monday demonstrations in the Nikolaikirche often ended at the *Stasi* headquarters; the wax from candlelight vigils on the front steps can still be seen. On the night of December 4-5, 1989, the people of Leipzig took over the *Stasi* building. Inside they found some 50,000 letters seized over the last 40 years and entire floors devoted to documentation of the actions of suspected resistors (open Wed.-Sun. 2-6pm; free).

Outside of the city, a towering stone monument commemorates Leipzig's first self-liberation. The **Völkerschlachtdenkmal** (tel. 878 04 71) on the *Süd-Friedhof* remembers the 400,000 soldiers engaged in the 1813 Battle of Nations—a struggle that turned the tide against Napoleon and determined many of Europe's present national boundaries. The monument, overlooking a large pool, is an absolutely massive pile of sculpted brown rock that all but conclusively proves that Kaiser Wilhelm had a very small penis. A dizzying 500 steps spiral up in a nearly windowless, one-person-wide passage to the very top of the monument. From the top on clear days, you can see the Harz mountain range. Streetcar #15 or 20 from the *Hauptbahnhof* (direction: "Meusdorf" or "Probstheida"): "Völkerschlachtdenkmal" (20min.; open May-Oct. daily 10am-5pm; Nov.-April 9am-4pm; DM3.50, students DM2).

ENTERTAINMENT

You don't have to be dead to have heard a good concert in Leipzig. Still, most of the theaters, musical and otherwise, have their *Spielpause* (with no performances) during July and August, so many summer visitors come away culturally unfulfilled. The musical offerings are top-notch, particularly at the **Gewandhaus Orchestra,** a major international orchestra since 1843. Kurt Masur will preside through the 1998 season, after which he'll become full-time *Meister* of the New York Philharmonic. Some concerts are free, but usually only when a guest orchestra is playing; otherwise buy tickets (from DM7; 30% student discount) at the *Gewandhaus* **box office,** Augustuspl. 8 (tel. 127 02 80; fax 127 02 22), next to the university (open Mon. 1-6pm, Tues.-Fri. 10am-6pm, Sat. 10am-2pm). Leipzig's **Opera** (tel. 126 10) receives wide acclaim and gives Dresden's *Semper* company a run for its money. Tickets run DM8-50, with a 50% student discount (except for premieres). Head to the ticket counter at Augustuspl. 12 for more information (open Mon.-Fri. 10am-8pm, Sat. 10am-1pm, and 90min. before curtain). **Bach Festivals** every July and August bring the orchestra and opera to the streets with free performances (ask at the tourist office for exact dates).

The opera house is also the entry point to Leipzig's diverse **theater** scene. The opera company hosts the experimental **Kellertheater** (tel. 126 10) in its basement. Known for its theater, Leipzig has unleashed a wave of experimental plays in the wake of the revolution. The **Schauspielhaus,** Bosestr. 1 (tel. 126 80), just off Dittrichring, serves up established plays, including offerings from Euripides, Heiner Müller, and Brecht (open Mon.-Fri. 10am-6pm, Sat. 10am-1pm). The cabaret scene centers around the understated **academixer,** Kupgergasse 6 (tel. 960 48 48), run by the Leipzig student body (open Mon.-Fri. 10am-6:30pm, Sat. 10am-3:30pm), the more brash **Gohglmohsch,** Markt 9 (tel. 961 51 11), and the **Leipzig Pfeffermühle,** Thomas Kirchhof 16 (tel. 960 32 53). While movie theaters are easy to come by, Leipzig also offers serious avant-garbage at its annual **film festival** at the end of October (call 980 39 21 for information, or ask at the tourist office).

NIGHTLIFE

Moritzbastei, Universitätsstr. 9 (tel. 960 51 91; tickets tel. 960 51 92), next to the university tower, is one of the more fascinating sights in Leipzig. In the 16th century it served as a place of execution; now, it houses the largest student club in Europe, with a diverse alternative crowd. Multiple bars and dance floors cater to all tastes in a supercool underground labyrinth with frequent live shows. Above ground, **Café Barbakan** (open Mon.-Fri. after 10am, Sat. after 2pm), an **open-air movie theater** (screenings June-Aug. Mon.-Tues. and Thurs.-Sat. at 10pm, weather permitting), and the outdoor terrace/*Biergarten* (open in nice weather Mon.-Fri. 11:30am-10pm, Sat.-Sun. 2-10pm) provide respite from the wild music scene. Things kick off after 9pm, with a particularly salacious scene for the jam-packed, Wed. night *"Papperlapop"* disco. Cover DM4-10. Bring student ID for discount.

Barfußgäschen, a street just off the Markt, serves as the see-and-be-seen bar venue for everyone from students to *Schicki-Micki*s. **Markt Neun, Steel, gohlgomosch** (whose cobblestones are covered in summer with outdoor seating from all sides), and **Spizz** start to fill up between 8-10pm, and remain packed into the wee hours.

Karl-Liebknecht-Straße is as *Szene*-ic without being quite so claustrophobic as Barfußgäschen. Streetcar #10 or 11: "Arndtstr." During the day, **Boom Town** and **Mrs. Hippie** fill that extra space in your pack with used or otherwise funked-out clothing. At night, bars along the street pour drinks for Irish lovers (**Killiwilly** at #44), Francophiles and Francophones (**Maître** at #62, see **Food,** p. 174), tough art-house film types (**nato** at #46), caffeine addicts (**KAHWE** at the corner of Arndtstr. and Karl-Liebknecht-Str.), and everyone else (**Weisses Rössel,** right next door). Most are open during the day for food and three-martini lunches, but nighttime revelry kicks off around 8pm. nato shows independent films, usually in original language with subtitles.

Blauer Pudel, Katherinenstr. 17, in an alcove just off the street. Bring your pierced and punked-up self here to cast aspersions on the mainstream while flippantly throwing pastries into the abyss; a bar and dance floor for disaffected students screams "alternative" every night after 8pm.

Distillery, on the corner of Kurt-Eisner-Str. and Lößingerstr. Features a dynamite techno and rave scene on Wed. and Fri.-Sat. after 10pm. S-Bahn #5 or 16 (direction: "Lößing") to the "K.-Eisner-Str./A.-Hoffman-Str." stop. Distillery is one block down.

RosaLinde, Lindenauer Markt 21 (tel. 484 15 11). Not exactly in the middle of the Markt, but it features a hellaciously cool gay and lesbian scene on Fri. and Sat. nights in addition to its daily bar. Tues. amply entertains with "Queer Film Night." Reputed to be the epicenter of the gay and lesbian scene. Open daily after 8pm.

Kutsche, on Brandenburgerstr., by the station. Gay bar and disco with a darkroom in the basement that's not as commercial as RosaLinde. Dancing Fri.-Sun., with a mad Wed. pick-up scene dubbed *"Kennen Lernen Party."* Open daily after 7pm.

■ Near Leipzig: Naumburg

The town of Naumburg squats in the "Tuscany of the North," the beautiful scenery between Leipzig and Weimar and beckons visitors with its medieval flavor. Naumburg, one of the 12 "model cities" in the former East Germany, has been saved from destruction and blessed with a phenomenal cathedral. Careful restoration has chipped away the gray legacy of decay and communism, revealing a colorful city center, reminiscent of Naumburg during its medieval days of glory—a trading city, rivaled only by Frankfurt am Main. A relic from those days, the **Naumburger Dom,** undoubtedly merits a pilgrimage if only to gaze upon the lovely Uto, one of 12 striking stone figures put in place in 1250 as the Dom was being completed. Uto is considered to be one of the best examples of realism between Classical times and the Renaissance. Too humble to carve his name in the cathedral's stone, the artist is remembered today simply as the *Naumburger Meister* (the Naumburg Master).

The double-chinned Ekkehard and extremely Snow-White-esque bride Uta, belonging to this collection of extraordinarily detailed sculptures of the cathedral's biggest financiers, were nearly taken from the *Dom* as reparations payments to the French after World War II. The removal proved to be virtually impossible, so Naumburg kept its treasures. The blood-colored paint splashed on the wounds of the master's life-size crucifixion, combined with the freaky winged skulls by the entrance, are spooky but cool. (Open April-Sept. Mon.-Sat. 9am-6pm, Sun. noon-6pm; Nov.-Feb. Mon.-Sat. 9am-4pm, Sun. noon-4pm; March and Oct. Mon.-Sat. 9am-5pm, Sun. noon-5pm. DM4.50, students and seniors DM3. There's a steep fee of DM10 for the right to take photos or use video cameras inside.) The helpful staff at the front desk will provide English-language pamphlets on request. Foreign-language tours are also available. To reach the *Dom*, head down Markgrafenweg from the station, bearing right until you reach the end of the street. To the left is the winding cobblestone path that leads uphill to the town proper. At the top of the path a sign points to the *Dom;* follow it until the cathedral's huge towers poke above the rooftops to guide you.

The rest of Naumburg has recovered amazingly well from its 45 years as a backwater Red Army post to emerge in better shape than most small towns of the former GDR. A jaunt past the *Dom* on Steinweg leads to Naumburg's bright, lively **market.** Just off the market square is the **Wenzelskirche,** the *Dom*'s earnest runner-up. Its peeling walls provide a solemn backdrop for a few paintings by Cranach the Elder and an impressive 18th-century organ that received Bach's approval (open Mon.-Sat. 10am-6pm, Sun. and holidays noon-4pm; last entrance 15min. before closing; free). Lest you think Naumburg functions solely as a bastion of religious relics, Nietzsche, Fichte, and even the world-famous founder of Egyptology, Richard Pelsius, all lived in Naumburg for parts of their illustrious lives. In spite of the pious monuments, Nietzsche spent some of his formative years here from 1850 to 1858 (before he sported the bushy mustache) and returned in 1890 to visit his mother, who wouldn't let little Friedrich leave because he was too darn crazy. The **Nietzsche-Haus,** Weingarten 18 (tel. 20 16 38), a couple blocks from the Markt, offers biographical snippets in addition to displaying exhibits of folks who were inspired by the erstwhile professor (open Tues.-Fri. 2-5pm, Sat.-Sun. 10am-4pm; DM3, students DM1.50).

Naumburg, well-situated along the rail network, is an excellent sidelight during a visit to Leipzig (30min.), Halle (45min.), Weimar (31 per day; 45min.), or Erfurt (31 per day; 30min.). There are two competing **tourist offices** in Naumburg. One is right on the market square at Markt 6 (tel. 20 16 14; open March-Oct. Mon.-Fri. 9am-1pm and 2-7pm, Sat. 10am-4pm; Nov.-Feb. Mon.-Fri. 9am-5pm, Sat. 10am-2pm). The other is right near the entrance to the *Dom* at Steinweg 15 (tel./fax 20 25 14; open daily 10am-5pm). Both are stocked full of brochures and books on Naumburg and the area, and the office on the Markt arranges private rooms for a DM2 fee (most DM26-40).

There are several full-service banks in town, as well as an **ATM** on Markgrafenweg, immediately to the right as you exit the train station. To reach Naumburg's **Jugendgästehaus,** Am Tennispl. 9 (tel./fax 70 34 22), from the Marktplatz, follow Wenzelsstr. out of the old walled city to Bürgergartenstr., which will appear slightly to the right at the end of Wenzelsstr., then go straight and up either through the many paths in the narrow park, or continuing on Niedschützerstr. until reaching signs for the hostel. A monument to good ol' eastern youth-hosteling, this hostel is slowly being remodeled out of its current "GDR-Standard." Double rooms with bath attached (and larger dorms without) all come with breakfast. (Reception open 8-10am and 5-10pm. Dorms DM23 per person, over 26 DM28; doubles DM26, over 26 DM32. Sheets DM6.) Cheap meals await at the Markt and the Holzmarkt areas, within three blocks of each other. For a truly chic cup of coffee or light meal, try **Engelgasse 3—** "What's the address?" you might wonder…(tel./fax 20 07 70). From the *Dom,* go straight on Steinmegstr. towards the Markt, and Engelgasse will be on your right. A cafe, used book store, and art gallery, it has the retro, feel-good, funky style of renowned Leipzig illustrator Thomas Müller, further enhanced by omnipresent posters, menus, paintings, and postcards featuring the artist's work. The equally feel-good and friendly owner, Wieland Hühr, happened to know Müller since his Crayola days and was able to get the full-service treatment for his new venture. Almost all the ingredients on the menu come from small area farms and a *Brötchen* with *Bratwurst* or goat's milk gouda will run DM4.90-DM5.90 (open Mon.-Fri. 10am-7pm, Sat. 10am-4pm). Another interesting culinary surprise is **China-Garten,** Rosbacherstr. 4 (tel. 30 90), near the cobblestone path. An authentic American-Chinese restaurant, it flaunts lacquer trim, mirrors, and pseudo-Asian instrumental pop. The lunch specials (DM9-14) are the best deal—tons of food plus a big veggie-laden, pastry-like spring roll (open daily 11:30am-2:45pm and 5:30-11:30pm). The **telephone code** is 03445.

Thüringen (Thuringia)

Affectionately dubbed the "Green Heart of Germany," Thüringen is the hub of a wheel formed by Bayern, Sachsen, Sachsen-Anhalt, Niedersachsen, and Hessen. Certainly the most beautiful of the new Federal States, Thüringen might also be called Germany's Cultural Belt. Echoes of Thüringen are heard throughout Europe's cultural canon: Bach, Goethe, Schiller, Luther, and Wagner all left their mark on this landscape, which in turn left its mark on their work. The Thüringer Wald is the deep green, hilly nucleus of the *Land*. One route through Thüringen is to follow the necklace of historic cities—among them Jena, Weimar, Erfurt, and Eisenach—joined by a direct east-west rail line. Extending downward from the cities is the forest itself, bisected by the equally historic *Rennsteig* hiking trail. Another way to attack Thüringen is through the state capital, Erfurt, a great "must visit" city. Every summer, Thüringen celebrates its musical giants with a series of concerts; the *Musiksommer* plan of events is available at most regional tourist offices. Relatively unknown to, and unexplored by, foreign tourists, Thüringen is the perfect destination for an authentic and dazzling German experience—are you experienced?

■ Weimar

Weimar thrives on the laurels of daring cultural achievement and spectacular political failure. Intellectual energy resonates throughout the city of Goethe, Schiller, and German philosopher Johann Gottfried von Herder, grandfather of the Romantics. Weimar expanded the boundaries of the avant-garde into the 20th century, spawning both the *Bauhaus* architectural movement and the Weimar Republic's remarkably liberal Constitution of 1919. After the collapse of these latter experiments, however, the city returned to the memory of its majestic past. With its recent selection to be crowned Europe's cultural city in 1999, a gigantic reconstruction process has commenced, and many of the monuments are being packaged in plastic or scaffolding—this time, not by Christo—in preparation for the impending hoopla. The activity bespeaks a new dynamism which has descended upon the city, breathing new life into a city whose intellectual ghosts dominate the setting.

ORIENTATION AND PRACTICAL INFORMATION

Weimar is near the center of Germany, well-situated on the Dresden-Frankfurt (3hr.) and Berlin-Frankfurt (3½-4hr.) rail lines. It also lies on a handy rail route running from Jena in the east to Erfurt (4 per hr.; 15min.) and Eisenach in the west; call 33 30 for more information. Weimar's intelligently designed bus system runs through two nerve centers: the train station and the central **Goetheplatz.** To get to Goethepl. from the station, head straight down Carl-August-Allee (10min.). Walk down the pedestrian **Schillerstraße** to get to the Markt and major sights.

If you are staying 3 or 4 days and plan to use the buses or visit museums, you can save some dough by buying a 72hr. **Weimarcard.** For DM25, you get unlimited free bus travel, free entrance to almost all of Weimar's museums, 50% off city tours, and 10% off theater tickets. The card is available in the tourist office.

Tourist Office: The seriously modern and efficient **Weimar Information,** Marktstr. 10 (tel. 240 00 or 656 90; fax 24 00 40), is within view of the city's *Rathaus.* It provides maps, brochures, souvenirs, and tickets for the *Deutsches Nationaltheater.* The office also books rooms in private homes, hotels, *Pensionen,* or hostels for a DM5 fee. **Walking tours** leave the office daily at 11am and 2pm (DM8, students and seniors DM4). Alternatively, you can guide with a walking-tour brochure (DM1.50), available in numerous languages. Open March-Oct. Mon.-Fri. 9am-6pm, Sat. 9am-4pm, Sun. 9am-4pm; Nov.-Feb. Mon.-Fri. 9am-6pm, Sat. 9am-1pm.

Thüringen (Thuringia)

Currency Exchange: A number of banks line Schillerstr. and Goethepl., but beware—none are open between Sat. afternoon and Mon. morning.

Public Transportation: Weimar's lack of streetcars is more than compensated for by an extensive **bus network.** If you buy tickets from the driver, you'll pay an inflated price (DM2.50). Instead, buy tickets at the *Hauptbahnhof* (open Mon.-Fri. 5:45am-6pm, Sat. 8am-2pm) or at kiosks scattered throughout the city. Buses run until midnight. The Weimarcard (see above) offers free bus travel to its holders.

Taxis: tel. 36 00.

Pharmacy: Bahnhof Apotheke, Carl-August-Allee 14 (tel. 614 24), near the station and the *Jugendherberge.* It has evening hours as well as a *Notdienst* (emergency) buzzer and a list of night pharmacies. Open Mon.-Fri. 7:45am-7pm, Sat. 9am-noon.

Women's Center: Frauenzentrum, Freiherr-von-Stein-Allee 22 (tel. 85 01 86). They host a **Frauen Café** daily 2-6pm, and serve "women's breakfast" Wed. 10am. Office open Mon. 9am-noon, Tues. 2-6pm, Wed. 10am-11pm, and Thurs. 2-5pm.

Help Line: Telefonseelsorge ("Telephone Soul Care") will be of assistance—call toll-free (0800) 111 01 11. Open 24hr.

Emergency: Police, tel. 110. **Fire,** tel. 112. **Ambulance,** tel. 115.

Post Office: Mail postcards of Goethe and Schiller from the *Hauptpostamt,* Goethepl. 7/8, 99423 Weimar (tel. 23 10). Open Mon.-Fri. 8am-6:30pm, Sat. 9am-1pm.

Telephone Code: 03643.

ACCOMMODATIONS

Weimar is home to one of eastern Germany's most extensive tourist industries; unfortunately, that translates into ever-increasing room prices for budget travelers. Thanks to the city's three youth hostels and new "youth hotel," however, finding a cheap place to stay should now be easier than in many Eastern cities. Private accommodations are also available and accessible through the tourist office. Remember that prices vary according to location, not comfort; a room near the city center may cost DM50, while many of the nicer rooms in Weimar's southern suburbs go for DM25-30. Weimar's "finest," **Hotel Elephant,** Am Markt 19 (tel. 80 20; fax 653 10), has catered to such discerning travelers as Napoleon, J.S. Bach, Richard Wagner, Leo Tolstoy, and Thomas Mann (who set his novel *Lotte in Weimar* there). In case you don't have the requisite DM155-285 per person, console yourself: Hitler stayed there, too.

Jugendhotel Hababusch, Geleitstr. 4 (tel. 85 07 37; email yh@larry.scc.uni-weimar.de; http://www.uni-weimar.de/yh). Smack in the middle of the sights, this hostel, run by a bunch of architecture students, is the best-located and coolest place to stay in Weimar. From Goethepl., turn left on Geleitstr. and follow its rightward twist to the clearing with the statue on the left. The hostel *wants* to serve backpackers and travelers, which means no rabid school groups or screaming kids. A common room with couches makes most college students feel at home. Reception open 24hr. DM15. No breakfast, but access to a fully equipped kitchen.

Jugendherberge Germania (HI), Carl-August-Allee 13 (tel. 85 04 90; fax 85 04 91). Arriving exhausted at the train station, head straight down the hill for a mere 2min.; it's on your right. A stately foam-gray vision with newly renovated facilities. Reception open 24hr. DM22, over 26 DM26. Breakfast included. Sheets DM7.

Jugendherberge Am Poseckschen Garten (HI), Humboldtstr. 17 (tel. 85 07 92), is situated near the city center (although fairly distant from the train station). Bus #6 from the station (direction: "Merketal"): "Poseckschen Garten." Make a right onto Am Poseckschen Garten, then a left onto Humboldtstr.; the hostel is immediately on your left. A big turn-of-the-century brownstone with 8- to 10-bed rooms. The hostel tends to fill with school groups because of its proximity to cultural attractions, so come early. Reception open 6am-12:30am. No curfew. DM22, over 26 DM26. Breakfast included. Lunch and hot dinner DM6-10 each.

Jugendgästehaus Maxim Gorki (HI), Zum Wilden Graben 12 (tel./fax 34 71). Bus #8 from the station (direction: "Merketal"): "Wilder Graben." A converted villa in a tranquil Weimar suburb. With only 58 beds, its less than pristine facilities fill quickly. Careful: buses stop running in this direction early—the walk back is poorly lit. Reception open 24hr. DM24, over 26 DM28. Sheets DM7. Breakfast included.

FOOD

Weimar serves up rich cooking for rich tourists, as well as culinary delights for less opulent visitors as well. For cheap delights, try the daily **produce market** at the Marktplatz (open Mon.-Fri. 10am-6pm, Sat. 9am-noon), or the **Rewe grocery store,** in the indoor mall *("Handelhaus zu Weimar")* right of Theaterpl. (open Mon.-Fri. 7am-8pm, Sat. 7am-4pm). Another option is the array of **bakeries** and **bistros** ringing the Markt and along Karl-Liebknecht-Str. towards the train station.

C-Keller-Galerie, Markt 21 (tel. 50 27 55), on the Marktplatz, blends Expressionism and crunchiness in its cafe and art gallery with a small beer garden. The vegetarian dishes are tasty and cheap (DM3-6); the best breakfasts in town can be had here on Sun. noon-6pm. Open Tues.-Sun. noon-11pm.

Da Toni Ristorante Pizzeria, Windsichenstr. 12 (tel. 50 27 19). Delicious, no-foolin' Italian food close to Schiller's house—so Italian they hardly understand German. Pizzas from DM5.50, pastas from DM8.50. Open daily 10am-1am.

Bistro Donecker, Theaterpl. 1. A cafeteria-style restaurant that serves German and international foods (DM5-12). Toast Goethe and Schiller (or at least their statues) while enjoying the comforts of sleek chairs that look like they were ripped off from the Bauhaus Museum. Open Mon.-Sat. 7am-6pm, Sun. 9am-6pm.

Anatolia, Frauenplan 15 (tel. 51 71 93). Ruminate on the immortals while nourishing yourself on a *Döner* kebab (DM5) with a view of a giant park statue and Goethe's house. Open daily 10:30am-10pm.

Bauhaus Universität, on Marienstr., just across the footpath in front of the Bauhaus building. Also accessible from Park an der Ilm. Flee the omnipresent Goethe and

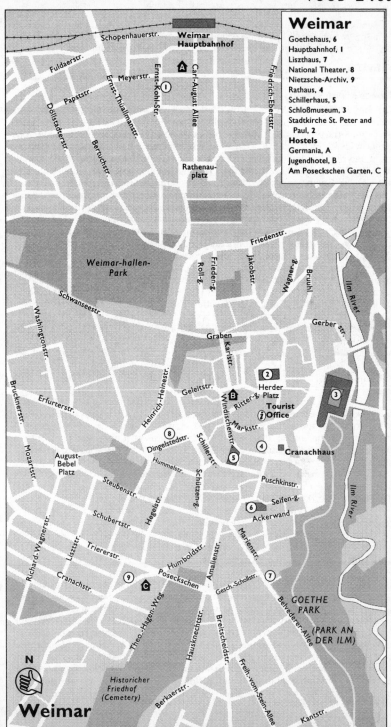

Weimar

Goethehaus, 6
Hauptbahnhof, 1
Liszthaus, 7
National Theater, 8
Nietzsche-Archiv, 9
Rathaus, 4
Schillerhaus, 5
Schloßmuseum, 3
Stadtkirche St. Peter and
Paul, 2
Hostels
Germania, A
Jugendhotel, B
Am Poseckschen Garten, C

THÜRINGEN

Weimar

Schiller in this sanctuary of modernism, and fraternize with the German students in a smoky ambience. The **Mensa** (cafeteria) offers eats that aren't exactly delicious—did we mention it's cheap? Meals DM2-5. Open Mon.-Fri. 6:45am-7pm.

SIGHTS

Goethe and Schiller

One hundred and fifty years after his death, the spirit of the botanist, geologist, doctor, artist, novelist, and poet Johann Wolfgang von Goethe still looms large in Weimar. Such immortality would not surprise the egotistical poet; nor would the numerous sights in his adopted home of Weimar, which dwell upon him and his friend, collaborator, and rival Friedrich Schiller. While countless German towns leap at any excuse to build memorial *Goethehäuser* (proclaiming Goethe slept here, Goethe went to school here, Goethe once asked for directions here), Weimar features the real thing. *The* **Goethehaus,** Frauenplan 1, an elegant butter-colored mansion with a commanding view of the central pedestrian zone, shows off the immaculately preserved private chambers where the poet entertained, wrote, studied, and ultimately died after 50 years in Weimar. It's jammed to the bursting point with busts, busts, and busts, as well as paintings and sculptures from Goethe's 50,000-piece art collection (not all are on display). The master's tastes were pleasantly Bacchanalian: rampant Neoclassical images dominate the collection, including a bottle-stopper in the shape of the bust of Napoleon (apparently, Goethe felt the need to take revenge for the little general's criticisms of his works). To get the most out of the largely unlabeled **Wohnhaus** exhibits, pick up the handy English guide "Goethe's House on the Frauenplan at Weimar" (DM3) at the desk (open Tues.-Sun. 9am-5pm; DM8, senior and students DM5).

The **Schillerhaus,** Schillerstr. 12, sits a neighborly distance from Goethe's pad. This was Schiller's home during the last three years of his life after he resigned from his academic chair at Jena. Showcasing the backgrounds to *The Maid of Orleans* and *William Tell,* both written here, the house offers original drafts and early editions of plays, and a detailed biographical chronicle of its owner's life (open Wed.-Mon. 9am-5pm; Nov.-Feb. 9am-4pm; March-Oct. 9am-5pm; DM5, students DM3). One block away on Hummelstr., Schiller and Goethe are reconciled in bronze before the **Deutsches Nationaltheater** (tel. 75 53 34; fax 75 53 21), which first breathed life into their stage works. The theater is the epicenter of Weimar's cultural and political intensity—in addition to operating as a first-run venue for their plays, it was also the locale from which the Weimar Constitution emerged in 1919. At the **Wittumpalais,** across the square at Palais 3, Goethe, Schiller, and Herder sat at the round table of their patron, Duchess Anna Amalia. Under the same roof, the **Wieland Museum** documents the life and works of the extraordinary duchess (open March-Oct. Tues.-Sun. 9am-noon and 1-5pm, Nov.-Feb. 9am-noon and 1-4pm; DM6, students DM4).

The **Park an der Ilm** ("Goethe Park") flanking the river was landscaped by Goethe. It sports numerous 18th-century pavilions and shelters for grazing sheep and goats (or picknickers). Of particular note are the fake ruins built by the Weimar shooting club and the eerie Soviet war memorial, complete with hammer and sickle. Perched on the park's far slopes is Goethe's **Gartenhaus,** on Corona-Schöfer-Str., the poet's first Weimar home and later his retreat from the city. It was here that Goethe put the moves on a certain *Fräulein* Christiane Vulpius, who later became *Frau* Goethe (open March-Oct. Wed.-Mon. 9am-noon and 1-5pm; Nov.-Feb. 9am-noon and 1-4pm; DM4, students and seniors DM3). South of the town center, Goethe and Schiller lie in rest together at the **Historischer Friedhof** cemetery (open March-Sept. 8am-9pm; Oct.-Feb. 8am-6pm), where twisted black metal crosses protrude from a jungle of unkempt wild-flowers and weeds. Goethe arranged to be sealed in an airtight steel case. Schiller, who died in an epidemic, was originally buried in a mass grave, but Goethe later combed through the remains until he identified Schiller and had him interred in the tomb. Skeptics argued for a long time that Goethe was mistaken, so a couple of "Schillers" were placed side by side for a while. In the 1960s, a team of Russian scientists determined that Goethe was right after all. (Tomb open daily March-Oct. 9am-1pm and 2-5pm; Nov.-Feb. 9am-1pm and 2-4pm. DM4, students DM3.)

Other Attractions in Weimar

The cobblestone **Marktplatz,** straight down Frauentorstr., spreads out beneath the neo-Gothic **Rathaus** and the colorful Renaissance facade of the **Lucas Cranach Haus,** where the prolific 16th-century painter spent his last days. Both are closed to the public, but the *Cranachhaus* shelters an **art gallery** of fairly hip modern paintings, photos, and sculptures by still-to-be-discovered talents (open Tues.-Fri. 10am-6pm, Sat. 11am-3pm). Left of the Marktplatz sits the **Schloßmuseum,** at Burgpl. 4. The first floor is a major-league Lucas Cranach fest; the second floor is a minor-league collection of 19th- and 20th-century German works, along with a Rodin sculpture and one of Monet's Rouen cathedral paintings (open Tues.-Sun. 10am-6pm; DM6, students and seniors DM3). For the morbid: Cranach himself rests in the churchyard of the **Jakobskirche** on Am Graben (open Mon.-Fri. 11am-3pm, Sat. 10am-noon). Down Jakobstr. the **Stadtkirche St. Peter und Paul** features Cranach's last triptych altarpiece (open Mon.-Sat. 10am-noon and 2-4pm, Sun. after services are over until noon and 2-3pm; free). The church is also called the **Herderkirche,** in honor of philosopher and linguist Johann Gottfried von Herder, who preached here regularly in the 1780s. Herder's works spurred two later cultural developments: the Romantics embraced his sermons about freedom, and his groundbreaking discussions of the progression of human history pointed directly to the Hegel's dialectic of the spirit. Herder was buried in the church in 1803. The church's interior is at odds with its solemn exterior: dazzlingly colorful coats of arms painted on all the balconies give the hall a festive air which came in handy in the August 1994 celebration of Herder's 250th birthday.

Directly across from the theater is the slick **Bauhaus-Museum** (tel. 54 60; fax 54 61 01), featuring, in an appropriately well-designed space, historical artifacts about, and works produced by, the *Bauhaus* School of Design and Architecture. Weavings, sculptures, prints, furniture, books, toys, and other nifty objects bear eloquent testimony to the breadth of the school's philosophy and undertakings. A 25-minute documentary (produced by the BBC, then ruthlessly dubbed into German) runs continuously (open April-Aug. Tues.-Sun. 10am-6pm; Oct.-March 10am-4:30pm; DM5, students and seniors DM3). The **Bauhaus Universität,** on Marienstr., ironically offers no exhibits related to the iconoclastic design movement—there is no relation between the two, save the name. Instead, its sleek, prim yellow buildings are the 1911 creation of Henry van de Velde, a pioneer of the *Jugendstil* movement. Steps away is the **Franz Liszt Haus,** where the composer spent his last years. The instruments and furnishings are supposedly original, but given Liszt's torrid love life, the single bed seems improbable (open March-Oct. 9am-1pm and 2-5pm; Nov.-Feb. 9am-1pm and 2-4pm; DM4, students and seniors DM3).

Down Humboldtstr. from the *Jugendherberge* is the **Nietzsche-Archiv,** Humboldtstr. 36. Nietzsche spent the last three wacky years (1897-1900) of his life in this house—he was pretty far gone by the end, as is painfully evident from the cross-eyed glares emanating from the myriad pictures and busts. The archive was founded by Nietzsche's sister Elisabeth, a woman whose misunderstandings set the stage for the Nazis' cynical distortion of her brother's philosophy—she gave Hitler a tour of the house in 1932 (open Tues.-Sun. 1-5pm; DM4, students and seniors DM3).

ENTERTAINMENT AND NIGHTLIFE

Weimar is again emerging as a burgeoning German cultural epicenter, with numerous theatrical offerings livening the setting. The annual art and theater festival in June and July, the Goethe birthday party at the end of August, and the Liszt festival every October maintain a full plate for the high culture connoisseur. The contemporary repertoire in the *Deutsches Nationaltheater* (see **Sights,** above) varies, but still includes works by Weimar's favorite sons, as well as avant-garde favorites like Robert Wilson and Schönberg. Ticket prices vary from DM9 for seating in orbit miles above the the-

THÜRINGEN

ater to DM44 for orchestra seats (with more oxygen). There are 50% discounts for students (box office open Mon. 2-6pm, Tues.-Fri. 10am-6pm, Sat. 10am-1pm and 4-6pm).

While Weimar's nightlife is often dismissed as dead, if you listen closely enough, you'll hear a pulse (or a tell-tale heart). The night scene is more active during the week, since most students flee to Erfurt or the *Uni*-culture of Jena on weekends. The Bauhaus Universität's *Mensa* has posters and bulletin boards directing you to what's going down (see **Food**, p. 182). The **Studentenklub Kasserturm** is in an old medieval tower on Goethepl. opposite the main post office. With a disco up top (Mon.-Sat. nights after 8pm) and a groovy beer cellar below, this is one of the oldest student clubs in town and currently *the* place to go in Weimar (cover varies). The **Studentenklub Schützengasse**, on Schützengassestr., has a disco on Tuesday and Friday nights, and a beer garden outside (open Mon.-Thurs. after 7:30pm, Fri.-Sat. after 9pm). **Gerber III,** Gerberstr. 3, offers straight-up, hardcore punk. Imagine the bus that Dr. Teeth rode around in during "The Great Muppet Caper" being hijacked by the Sex Pistols. Weimar also has a burgeoning gay scene. **Jugendclub Nordlich,** on Staufenbergstr., has a gay disco every other Saturday night (10pm-3am). **AIDS-Hilfe** (tel. 614 51), Erfurterstr. 17, holds a popular gay cafe (office open Mon.-Tues. and Thurs. 11am-3pm, Wed. 11am-8pm; cafe open Tues.-Sat. at 8pm).

■ Near Weimar: Buchenwald

"Why?" Buchenwald lies at the edge of disbelief, its history of atrocity producing only questions. A visit here is difficult not because the locale is horrible, but rather because it is not. It is one of the most bitter ironies of the Third Reich that many *KZ Lager* (concentration camps) were situated within beautiful natural milieux. Buchenwald was built on a hill with a stunning view of Weimar (it was one of Goethe's favorite mountain retreats). It is chilling to realize how easily the woods could reclaim this site and erase all record of the crimes committed here. As Hannah Arendt observed, the most frightening thing about Nazi evil was that it was banal, ordinary, everyday. Buchenwald is just a place—nothing except the relics and monuments maintained here would tell you otherwise. There's no black cloud perpetually hanging over it, it's not surrounded by a ring of thorns, and there are no symbols scorched into the earth. If it weren't for the human labors that preserve the historical value of this place, nature would swallow it up. What makes a visit to Buchenwald so difficult is the effort each visitor must make to remember what could so easily be forgotten.

The best way to reach the camp is bus #6 from the station or from downtown Weimar. Check the bus schedule carefully: half the departures have "EB" after the departure times. They terminate in Etterburg, a full 5km walk from the memorial site. Seek out the buses with a "B" (Buchenwald) after the departure times; they leave every hour (1 per 2hr. on weekends) from the train station and takes you to the camp.

From 1937 to 1945, the concentration camp held over 250,000 Jews, political prisoners, gypsies, and gays (after 1942, there was also a large Communist contingent); most did not survive the Holocaust. What remains is the **Nationale Mahn-und Gedenkstätte Buchenwald** (National Buchenwald Memorial; tel. (03643) 43 00). At the memorial, signs will point to two destinations: the **KZ Lager** and the **Gedenkstätte.** The former refers to the remains of the camp, while the latter is a solemn monument overlooking the valley, a 20-minute walk away.

The film "O Buchenwald" is shown regularly in German, but not even a language barrier can keep you from being moved by the film's images (daily viewings at 11am and 2pm, or by request). Expect apologies from the monument staff for the pre-1989 ideological content of the film, which emphasizes the stories of the Communist detainees over the experience of the many Jews who were murdered here.

Death claimed members of many groups at Buchenwald. A plaque near the former commandant's horse stable matter-of-factly states that an estimated 8000 Soviet prisoners were executed by firing squad in the little space before the war's end. Many Jews were sent here, but after 1942, most were deported to Auschwitz. For the most part, Buchenwald served to detain and murder political enemies of Nazism and prisoners of war. The Soviet Union used the site from 1945 to 1950 as an internment camp in which over 28,000 Germans, mostly Nazi war criminals and opponents of the Communist regime, were held; 10,000 died of hunger and disease. An exhibit detailing the Soviet abuses opened in 1997. In the woods, behind the museum, rests a cementary with the graves of both victims and perpetrators of the Soviet abuses.

The central camp area, downhill from the reception, is now a vast, flat, gravel plain; gone are the ramshackle wooden *Blocks,* which crammed prisoners. The former crematorium building has been preserved with a wrenching suggestion of the terror wrought here; flowers and wreaths are lain at the base of the open-mouthed ovens. Downstairs lurk the dreadful rooms where the corpses were piled before their incineration. In the large storehouse building, a museum documents both the history of Buchenwald (1937-1945) and the general history of Nazism, including German anti-Semitism. The museum sets real documents (most of which are translated into or summarized in English) in wrought-iron boxes visibly riveted together. A moving installation by Polish artist Jòzef Szajna features thousands of photos of inmates pasted onto large silhouettes of human figures. Just outside the museum lies a brutally ironic symbol: the charred stump of the **Goethe-Eiche** (Goethe oak), left standing in the middle of the camp to commemorate Buchenwald's former role as a get-away for Germany's greatest cultural figure. The memorial stones recently embedded in the ground around the former children's barracks read, in English, German, and Hebrew: "So that the generation to come might know, that the children, yet to be born, may rise and declare to their children." Tiny candles and flowers are regularly placed near the stones, just outside the main gate close to the remains of the camp zoo, built for the amusement of the SS officers' children. (Camp open May-Sept. Tues.-Sun. 9:45am-5:15pm; Oct.-April Tues.-Sun. 8:45am-4:15pm). The camp **archives** are open to anyone searching for records of family and friends between 1938 and 1945. Call ahead to schedule an appointment with the curator (tel. (036431) 430 154).

To get to the **memorial bell tower** *(Glockenturm)* from the camp, start by facing the reception at the bus stop and head right. Around the corner of the right-most building is the footpath to the **Mahnmal** (monument). After a short walk through the woods, it emerges at a two-way fork in the street. Head right, and keep walking past a parking lot and a bus stop. Keep going as the street curves left, and soon you'll come to the somber GDR-designed bell tower, with no marking other than an immense "MCMXLV" carved on each side. The plaque inside commemorates the memory of the anti-fascist "resistance fighters of the Republic of Germany." On the great stone plaza behind the tower unfolds a commanding view of the surrounding countryside, overseen by the slightly awkward **Plastikgruppe,** a sculpture of ragged, stern-jawed socialist prisoners claiming their freedom. Like the rest of the grounds outside of the buildings, the memorial can be visited until nightfall.

∎ Jena

Once home to the country's premier university, Jena still triggers intellectual fireworks in the German historical consciousness. Under the stewardship of literary greats Schlegel, Novalis, Tieck, and Hölderlin (Hegel and Schelling's college roommate, who went insane in 1807 and is now considered Germany's greatest post-Goethe poet), Jena first transplanted the Romantic movement to German soil. It was here that philosophers Fichte and Schelling argued for a new conception of intellectual and political freedom, and where, in 1806, a then-unknown junior philosophy professor named Herr Doktor Professor Georg Wilhelm Friedrich Hegel wrote the epoch-making *Phenomenology of Spirit* by candlelight in his ramshackle lodgings by the centuries-old *Collegium Jenense.* Today, the university bears the name of Friedrich Schiller, who in 1789 graced its halls with his lectures on the ideals of the French Revolution. True to its 19th-century tradition, Jena remains a campus town, albeit an increasingly Westernized one, with very little reverence for the past. Students keep this town youthful, left-leaning, and multicultural. Jena's dearth of touristy sightseeing is made up for its dynamism and forward-looking spirit.

THÜRINGEN

Orientation and Practical Information Jena lies in the Saale Valley, 25km east of Weimar (27 trains per day, 1hr.). Trains between Dresden and Erfurt stop at **Bahnhof Jena West** (3-4 per hr., 45min.) while trains on the Berlin-Munich line stop at the more distant **Jena Saalbahnhof** (15min. north of the center). The main transfer point for Jena's bus and streetcar system is the **Zentrum** stop on Löbdergraben near Eichpl. and the Markt. From the Saalbahnhof, turn left down Saalbahnhofstr. and take a right on Saalstr. to arrive at the center of town. Bus #15 also goes here. From Bahnhof Jena West, head toward Westbahnhofstr. until it becomes Schillerstr. Turn left up the street to the towering university building. **Jena-Information,** Holzmarkt 8 (tel. 58 63 20; fax 58 63 22), close to the Zentrum bus stop, slightly past the university tower, hands out maps and schedules of special events. They also book private and hotel rooms (open Mon.-Fri. 9am-6pm, Sat. 9am-2pm). Rent **bikes** for DM15 per day (you must pay in advance and bring a photo ID as collateral) at **Kirscht Fahrrad,** Löbdergraben 8 (tel. 44 15 39), near the Zentrum bus stop and the tourist office (open Mon.-Fri. 9am-7pm, Sat. 9am-4pm). The **Goethe-Apotheke** is conveniently located on Weigelstr., just north of the vast concrete Eichpl.; a sign directs you to other **pharmacies** that are open when it's closed (open Mon.-Fri. 8am-8pm, Sat. 8am-4pm). The **post office** is at Engelpl. 8, 07743 Jena. The **telephone code** is 03641.

Accommodations and Food Jena's two youth hostels are conveniently located right next to each other, albeit about a 10-minute bus ride and 25-minute hike out of town. Bus #10 (direction: "Lobeda Ost") or 11 (direction: "Beutenberg"): "Mühlenstr." Follow Mühlenstr. until it turns into Am Herrenberge. The **Jugendgästehaus,** Am Herrenberge 3 (tel. 68 72 30), has large, sparkling-clean rooms and an in-house cafe, albeit steep prices. (Reception open Mon.-Fri. 24hr., Sat.-Sun. call ahead. First night DM35.50, over 26 DM39.50; additional nights DM10 cheaper. Curfew 12:30am. Breakfast included.) At the **Jugendgästehaus Herrenberge (HI),** Am Herrenberge 9 (tel. 62 50; fax 60 55 54), a little farther down the road, hostel members pay DM36.50 (over 26 DM40.50) for rooms in a hostel that normally cost DM115-135. The *only* difference is that the hostel rooms lack phones, but the bath, TV, and minibar help ease the pain. (Reception open 6am-10pm. Breakfast included. Mandatory sheet fee DM7.) Another competitive option is the many **private rooms** booked by the tourist office for a DM3 fee; many quiet bedrooms with breakfast go for DM25-35.

The **Spar Markt,** across from the *Rathaus* on Eichholzpl., wins the prize for most centrally located **supermarket** (open Mon.-Fri. 8am-6:30pm, Sat. 8am-12:30pm). After five years in India, the owners of **Monsun,** Wagnergasse 7 (tel. 42 03 33), developed a taste for subcontinental food, and today they invite you to an oasis of authenticity in a sea of Asia-*Imbiße.* Daily specials served with Basmati rice, *raita,* and salad DM7-10, including plenty of vegetarian options. Quench your thirst with *Chai* or *Lassi* (open Tues.-Fri. 11:30am-11pm, Sat.-Sun. 5:30-11pm). A crunchier clientele frequents the nuclear-free zone of **Café Immergrün,** Fürstengraben 30 (tel. 44 73 13), tucked inside an old building. An unofficial recycling and environmental center, this intimate cafe is decorated with Green Party pamphlets and worn couches. In bad weather, board games can be borrowed; in good, a few tables are set in the garden outside. Tasty green specialties like veggie pizzas run DM5 (open Mon.-Thurs. 11am-midnight, Fri.-Sat. 11am-1am, Sun. 3pm-whenever). Numerous **bakeries** and **butcher shops** cluster around Eichpl. and the St. Michaelkirche, while *Imbiße* of all sorts park at Hochpl. The **Markt** on Eichpl. provides a panoply of cheap culinary options (open Tues. and Thurs.-Fri. 10am-6:30pm). That huge, round, metal university eyesore actually provides its students with very, very cheap meals in the ground floor **Mensa.** Ask one of them to buy you a ticket and partake in the fun. (Full meals DM2.50-4.50; open Mon.-Thurs. 8am-4pm, Fri. 8am-3pm, Sat. 11am-3pm.)

Sights The **Romantikerhaus,** Unterm Markt 12a, just off the old market square, once bubbled with the raw creative energy of the Romantic period. Once owned by philosopher and fiery democrat Johann Fichte, who lectured here, it later hosted the poetry and philosophy parties of the Romantics. It's a curious and small museum

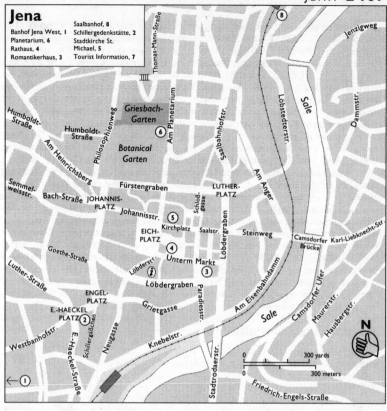

Jena

Banhof Jena West, 1
Planetarium, 6
Rathaus, 4
Romantikerhaus, 3

Saalbanhof, 8
Schillergedenkstätte, 2
Stadtkirche St.
Michael, 5
Tourist Information, 7

where first-edition books and portraits scattered around the interior are interspersed with big stenciled quotes of great thinkers on the walls. Everything is in German. At the center of the museum's strangeness, the **Kritische Guillotine** (critical guillotine) remains frozen in mid-chop of a pile of books. Upstairs hides the unspectacular **Fine Arts Museum of Jena** (open Tues. and Thurs.-Sat. 10am-1pm and 2-5pm, Wed. 10am-1pm and 2-6pm; DM5, students and seniors DM3).

A few blocks to the southwest sits the **Schillergedenkstätte,** Schiller's swank summer home on Schillergäßchen (tel. 63 03 94), just off (you guessed it!) Schillerstr. Another museum where the furniture, including a standing desk, looks like it *could* have been used by Schiller—who knows? A helpful information brochure translated into English brings some history into these recently renovated rooms and delightful sculptured garden (open Tues.-Fri. 10am-noon and 1-4pm, Sat. 11am-4pm; DM2, students and seniors DM1). Jena's most visible structure is neglected as a tourist sight: the cylindrical, 24-story **new university tower.** A product of the late-GDR architectural imagination, it looks like a Buck Rogers-inspired vision of the future. The sky-high lecture halls on the top floor are used for special recitals and events. A competing, more contemporary vision of the future is the **Jenoptik** building, across Leutragraben from the *Uni*-tower. This ultra-slick modern edifice attests to Jena's high-tech corporate aspirations. The **original university building,** just up Oberlauengasse from the *Romantikerhaus,* dates from the 13th century. It housed a Dominican monastery until Wittenberg U. took over, as it temporarily relocated to dodge the plague.

The **Stadtkirche St. Michael,** just off Eichpl., presides proudly over **Luther's tombstone.** He's not resting here, though the stone was intended for him; the folks at the Stadtkirche claim it was shipped here by mistake, while back at the gravesite in Wittenberg, tour guides mutter something under their breath about 17th-century plundering. The 16th-century church is unusually frightening and black outside, but the interior is graceful and light (open Mon.-Fri. 11am-1pm and 3-5pm, Sat. 10am-2pm, Sun. mass 10am). Up Weigelstr., and left onto Fürstengraben, visit the **Botanischer Garten** (open dawn-dusk), or the row of statues of the university's distinguished faculty—notice that teachers and students of **Marx** are given particularly large statues. But there's one glaring exception—Marx's intellectual godfather and Jena's most famous professor, **Hegel**, has no bust at all. In fact, the only mention of him in the entire city is a piddly plaque on the back of the *Romantikerhaus*. Maybe it's a legacy of Communist *Angst* about Hegel, whose writings inspired Marx's work but themselves propounded a spiritual, bourgeois-centered political vision (to make Hegel's theories right, Marx once wrote, you had to "stand him on his head").

The **Wagnergasse**, which extends from Eichpl. is shaping up as Jena's funkiest area, chock full o' bars, shops, and little restaurants. Face the university tower, walk around the right side of the tower, past the small battlement (the *Pulverturm*) on your right, then bear right at the fork. The university energy has clearly been funneled in this direction. Rave culture invades **Backstage** and the adjacent **Stahlwerkt**, clothing stores on Wagnergasse 3 and 4 (both open Mon.-Fri. 11am-6pm, Sat. 10am-1pm). At the end of the street lies the **Studentenhaus Wagner,** Wagnergasse 26 (tel. 63 63 24), the source of the funk, as it were. This university-sponsored bar/hang-out doubles as a performance space for plays, readings, live music, and movie showings (open Mon.-Thurs. 1pm-1am, Fri.-Sat. 7:30pm-1am). The **Zentrum** area is saturated with swinging saloons. Wednesdays at **Kassablanca,** Felsenkellerstr. 13a (tel. 282 60), are all about "Gay-House" disco, beginning at 10pm.

■ Near Jena: Dornburg

Among Jena's attractions is its proximity to the little *Dorf* of **Dornburg** (18km to the north), home to the **Dornburger Schlößer,** a series of three palaces perched high, high, high above the Saale River valley. Parts of the modern village are at *Hauptbahnhof* level, but it takes a hike to see the castle, puny market place, embarrassing church, and supreme view. The castles lie on the very edge of the rose and grapevine covered hillside. First in line is the **Altes Schloß,** the oldest and homeliest castle, built in 937 when the *Kaiser*s still visited Dornburg. The first German *Reichstag* met here,; the building was also used as a prison by both the Nazi and Communist regimes. The interior is closed to the public. The summer residences of the Grand Duke of Sachsen-Weimar-Eisenach, the **Renaissanceschloß** and the **Rokokoschloß,** preside majestically and frivolously (respectively) over the magnificent rose gardens where Goethe practiced his horticultural skills while writing letters to his lover, Charlotte von Stein (see **Großkochberg,** p. 201, for some juicy details). Inside the whitewashed, slate-roofed, 16th-century Renaissance castle, the plain royal belongings are spiced up with stories about Goethe's frequent visits to the *Schlößer* (info tel. 222 91). Goethe never actually napped on the big ottoman in the guest bedroom, since he traveled everywhere at great expense with his portable bed (the bed now sits in the Gärtenhaus in Weimar, p. 180). One look inside the lush chambers of this 1740 Rococo pleasure palace will reveal why Goethe chose its ornate, luxurious, and window-filled rooms for 19 of his 20 visits to Dornburg. Visitors can partake in the voluptuous pleasure of gliding along the slick surface of the main hall in the slippers provided to protect its plumtree wood. The high-Rococo gilded decorations and large porcelain collection border between priceless treasures and gaudy kitsch. The gardens surrounding the castle are kept up according to the 1839 pictures and directions. (Open April-Oct. Tues.-Sun. 9am-noon and 1-5pm; Nov.-March Wed.-Sun. 9am-noon and 1-4pm. Last entry 15min. before closing. Gardens open daily until 8pm. DM6, students DM4.) The castles and the mini-village are a grueling climb up a very steep hill. Fortunately for pedestrians (you can also drive the route), steps also lead partway to the summit. Use them; otherwise you'll face a hike up a mile of winding, steep highway. From the tiny *Bahnhof*, turn left and then take the first right onto Am Born; the stairs will be immediately on your left. When you reach the main road, turn right and continue upwards. When the first houses come into sight, watch on the left for signs to the Markt or *Schlößer*.

Dornburg's also got a bloomin' lot of roses, which are celebrated during the last weekend in June with the **Dornburg Rose Festival,** marking the anniversary of King Karl August's lavish birthday parties held here a century ago. The townspeople elect a sort of homecoming queen who hands out food and candy to spectators. Locals don their party hats again during the last week in August to celebrate **Goethe's birthday.** Dornburg fills up quickly during festivals, but otherwise the helpful staff at the castle has lists of available **private rooms** (DM30-50) and gives good restaurant advice (same hours as castle). To reach Dornburg from Jena, hop a **train** from either the Jena Saalbahnhof or Bahnhof Jena-Paradies, on Kahlaischestr., a 5-minute walk from Bahnhof Jena West. Dornburg is also an easy and attractive **bike ride** from Jena, though you may want to save your strength for the climb to the castles. **Gaststätte am Born,** by the entrance to the stairs, will serve a tasty *Schnitzel* with roasted potatoes and cucumber salad for DM8 (open Mon.-Fri. 8am-9pm, Sat. 9:30am-1pm). The **post office,** right by the castle and on the Markt, doubles as the grocery store (open Mon.-Fri. 8am-1pm and 3-5pm, Sat. 8-10am). The **telephone code** is 036427.

■ Gera

Gera's limited plate of attractions is at odds with its status as the second-largest city in Thüringen. Nevertheless, the city blends the usually less-than-attractive architecture of the GDR with occasional cultural gems to create a happy co-existence between the functionalist aesthetic of the past decades and the rich history of the *Land*. While its most significant contribution to the world was the provision of a birthplace for renowned painter Otto Dix, Gera's handful of art museums make the city a fine daytrip from any number of cities in the region.

Practical Information, and Accommodations Frequent **trains** connect Gera to Erfurt (38 per day, 1¾hr.) running through Jena and Weimar. Lines also steam in from Leipzig (20 per day, 80min.). The **tourist office,** Ernst-Toller-Str. 14 (tel. 61 93 01; fax 61 93 04), finds private rooms (DM25-45) for a DM5 fee, the only real overnight option in the absence of a youth hostel. They also equip patrons with free maps and brochures in English and German. From the *Hauptbahnhof,* head right and then turn left onto Ernst-Toller-Str. (open Mon.-Fri. 9am-7pm, Sat. 9am-2pm). The **post office,** 07545 Gera, lies at Puschkinpl. on Ernst-Toller-Str. (open Mon.-Fri. 8am-6pm, Sat. 8am-noon). The **telephone code** is 0365.

Food Restaurants and food stands abound throughout the center of town, but the real meal deal is at **Gastronom,** close to the Stadtmuseum at the intersection of Reichstr. and Heinrichstr. beneath the Spielpalast in a black building. This self-serve restaurant serves a clientele undaunted by fears of cholesterol, dishing out huge portions of delectable Thüringer home-cooking for DM5.50-6 (open Mon.-Fri. 8am-4pm). A **Kaiser's supermarket,** around Sorge 41 in the basement of the Horton's, fills any remaining gaps (open Mon.-Fri. 9:30am-8pm, Sat. 9:30am-4pm).

Sights Gera's main attractions all lie within 10 to 15 minutes of the *Hauptbahnhof.* Like a vein of pure capitalism running through the heart of the town, **the Sorge** is filled with Western brandnames in a setting not easily mistaken for the more glitzy Köln or Düsseldorf. Heading right from the *Hauptbahnhof* and left onto Ernst-Toller-Str. will bring you to this pedestrian area. Following the Sorge up and then heading right onto Steinweg to Greizerstr. takes you to the **Museum für Angewandte Kunst,** Greizerstr. 37 (tel./fax 287 50). A medium-sized collection of Art Deco and functionalist objects (furniture, posters, tableware, etc.) occupies half the space of this mansion. The other half hosts revolving two-month exhibitions ranging from the serious to the downright silly. Plans for 1998 include "Hats," "Porcelain," "Games," and more. (Standing collection DM4, students and seniors DM1.50; special exhibitions DM9-10,

THÜRINGEN

students and seniors DM3. Open Tues.-Sun. 10am-5pm.) Heading out from the museum onto Böttchergasse and then right through Kornmarkt to the Marktplatz brings you to the center of historic Gera. The Renaissance **Rathaus** has a 300-year-old fountain of Samson wrestling with a lion; despite its age, Samson looks like he's still going strong. The **Stadtmuseum,** Heinrichstr. 2 (tel. 838 14 70), straight down from the Markt on Kloster Kirchstr., houses a small but well-constructed museum documenting Gera's history (open daily 10am-5pm; DM4, students and seniors DM1.50).

Gera recently recognized its import as the birthplace of famed *Neue Sachlichkeit* painter Otto Dix in 1991 with the establishment of the **Otto-Dix-Haus,** Mohrenpl. 4 (tel. 832 49 27). The museum documents Dix's life and career with photos, letters, and a tiny collection of his paintings. (Open Tues.-Fri. 10am-5pm, Sat.-Sun. 10am-6pm. DM4, students and seniors DM1.50; combined admission with Orangerie DM5, DM2.) To get there via a scenic route from the *Hauptbahnhof,* and turn right from the station, take another right under the tracks to Kückengartenallee. Enter the park to the left of the sorbet-colored Neoclassical Theater, head through the Orangerie, cross a bridge, pass grandmother's house, and land directly at the museum. The late-Baroque **Orangerie,** Küchengartenallee 4 (tel. 832 21 47), serves as an exhibition space for a small permanent collection, and displays some fairly avant-garde artists at the head of the beautifully manicured garden park (open Tues. 1-8pm, Wed.-Fri. 10am-5pm, Sat.-Sun. 10am-6pm; DM4, students and seniors DM1.50).

■ Altenburg

Altenburg's fame and hilltop castle are literally built upon a house of cards. Famous for its role as the world's only *Skatstadt,* Altenburg revels in its card-playing glory and savors its status as the birthplace of the card-game *Skat.* Not surprisingly, the city is also the home of a centuries-old playing cards manufacturing industry. The city now serves as the fount of inspiration for travel guide card game puns.

Orientation and Practical Information A web of rail-lines connect Altenburg with Leipzig (45min.) and Zwickau (40min.). To reach the **tourist office,** Moritzstr. 21 (tel. 59 41 74; fax 59 41 79), turn left from the train station and walk to the end of Wettinerstr., then turn right onto Gabelentzstr.; follow it past the *Schloß* until Burgstr. emerges on your right. Turn left from Burgstr. down Weibermarkt, which becomes Moritzstr. The tourist office books rooms for a DM3 fee, provides free maps with information in English, and leads **tours** in both English and German on Mondays at 10am and 3pm (open Mon.-Fri. 9:30am-6pm, Sat. 9:30am-noon). Altenburg's **postal code** is 04600. The **telephone code** is 03447.

Accommodations and Food Altenburg sadly lacks a youth hostel, but booking a private room through the tourist office may cost less than DM30 per person. A novel (and cheap) option is a stay at the **Magdalenenstift,** Stiftsgraben 20 (tel. 31 16 13). The *Stift* is a Lutheran-run home for the elderly partially converted into friendly dormitory-style rooms. It's best to call ahead on weekends to make sure rooms are available. To get there, head left from the *Schloß* on Morstallstr., take a right on Münsterstr.; the *Stift* is to the right as soon as you turn right on Stiftsgraben. The office is on the second floor in entrance G. Heavenly peace reigns under Martin Luther's gaze. (Beds DM23.50 plus a one-time DM7.50 fee for a linen change. Breakfast included.) While the restaurants in the Markt are a touch pricey, the **food markets** throughout the town soften the budget sting (most open Mon.-Fri. 8am-6pm, Sat. 8am-noon). The less expensive restaurant scene resides close to the *Schloß* driveway. **Eiscafé Angela,** Rosa-Luxemburg-Str. 15 (tel. 26 33), has a menu of daily *Thüringer* specials and homemade ice cream (DM6-8.50; open Mon.-Fri. 10am-10pm, Sat. 1-11pm, Sun. 1-10pm). The *Biergarten* and restaurant **Kulisse,** Theaterpl. 18 (tel. 50 09 39), has cheap sandwiches (DM3.50-6.50) to prepare you for the beer they'll foist into your greedy hands (beer garden open Mon.-Sat. after 4pm, Sun. after 2pm; restaurant open Tues.-Thurs. 2pm-1am, Fri.-Sat. 2pm-3am, Sun. 2pm-midnight).

No More Hot Dogs!

In an effort to dip into the high culture of German cuisine, you will undoubtedly be confronted with the dilemma of whether or not to indulge in a *Wurst*. The staple of the German diet, they're tasty, they're cheap, and dammit—they're German! There can be a severe downside, however, to living the life of a German gourmet. Nietzsche, in *Ecce Homo,* described how the German character, particularly its food, necessarily inflicted him with bad digestion. A couple months after writing this testament, he went completely nuts. But *Würste*-lovers got the last laugh—Nietzsche was a vegetarian (as was Hitler). The following brief guide is an attempt to help you navigate through both the perils and the delights that define the *Wurst*. You will be hard-pressed not to make the leap of faith into the unknown world of *Würste*. Just remember to proclaim beforehand, *"Das ist mir Wurst!"* (I don't give a damn!)

Thüringer Bratwurst—The direct ancestor of the American "hot dog" comes cupped in a flaky Brötchen, doused in mustard. Also known as a Roster, Thüringer Bratt, the zesty sausage puts the sickly pink American frank to shame.

Rheinländer Wurst—Some barbaric Rhinelanders have been known to grab a naked, greasy *Wurst* in their bare hands, alternately biting the meaty mass and a roll. It is not known if they bathe or observe any social norms.

Bavarian Weißwurst—The ubiquitous meal is sometimes referred to as *Scheißwurst* (shit *Wurst*), owing to its reputation from the era predating refrigeration, when eating a Weißwurst after noon guaranteed a stomach-buckling experience. Thanks to modern technology, they can now be enjoyed any time of day.

Frankfurter—A legal title referring only to sausages produced following an official recipe within a certain distance of Frankfurt's city center. A gruesome process with tasty results: meat extracted from the tender front legs of a pig are mixed with fatty bacon and bunches of spices before being hand-stuffed in sheep intestines. These hearty concoctions make Oscar Mayer look like a weener.

Sights The wide cobblestone footpath leading up to the looming **Schloß** winds from Theaterpl. in the heart of town. A massive sand-colored enclosure, the castle was begun in the 11th century and expanded over the next 700 years. The architecture ranges from a humbly squatting 11th-century guard tower called the **Flasche** (bottle) to the dazzlingly Gothic 15th-century **Schloßkirche**. The church organ, the **Trostorgel,** was given a thumbs-up by Bach after a trial performance in 1730. Unfortunately, the only way to view the inside of the church, its organ, and some of the castle's gems is through guided **tours** which leave from the second floor of the museum every hour, on the hour. Adjacent to the church is a museum that cunningly combines Altenburg's two claims to fame in one neat package: the **Schloß-und-Spielkartenmuseum** (castle and playing card museum; church and museums open Tues.-Sun. 9am-6pm; DM5, students DM2.50). The *Schloß* amply entertains with its huge, hanging portraits of the Dukes of Sachsen-Gotha-Altenburg. The **Waffenmuseum** (weapons museum) section sports ornately gilded muskets, jagged-edged Bavarian cavalry sabres, and bizarre pointy helmets; the **Stadtgeschichte** (city history) displays, which have yet to recover from their socialist days, place Altenburg in the middle of all rebellious proletarian activities. You'll find a full house in the **Spielkarten** wing, occupying gorgeous, Rococo-ceilinged rooms jammed with excellent giant playing-card displays, representing over 400 years of international gaming history. The most occult elements of the exhibit are the hand-enameled extra-large 15th-century Florentine tarot cards, each the size of a hand. The cards of the former GDR are fascinatingly comical—meant to indoctrinate the incorrigible, frenzied school groups who make life in hostels hell, they come in four suits: the October Revolution, solidarity, anti-Fascism, and the triumph of Communism. Presumably, no kings, queens, or jacks in this set.

Altenburg's ace in the hole is a hidden cultural treasure: the **Lindenau-Museum** at Gabelentzstr. 5. It possesses an unexpectedly sophisticated collection of cutting-edge modern paintings and some representatives of major movements of the past, including many works from the GDR. Sadly, the museum lacks the picture of dogs playing poker (open Tues.-Sun. 10am-6pm; DM3, students DM1.50). Altenburg also has a couple of parties up its sleeve: the highlight of the **Skatbrunnenfest,** during the first weekend in May, is an attempt by four skinny boys to re-enact the statue near the Markt. There are equally lively attractions at the **Schloßfest** in mid-July and the **Altstadtfest** during the first weekend in October.

■ Erfurt

The capital of Thüringen, Erfurt surprises its guests with an exquisitely renovated and quirky *Altstadt,* many cosmopolitan cafes, and an abundance of verdant parks. The city is the point of connection between Thüringen's political and cultural spheres. Hardly an historical cultural powerhouse like Dresden or even Eisenach, it has certainly attracted its fair share of politicos. Napoleon based his field camp here for over a year, Konrad Adenauer lived here before World War II, and more recently, Willy Brandt met here with Erich Honecker, commencing the long and arduous process of German-German reconciliation in 1970. A lot of money has been funneled into Erfurt recently, allowing the cultural offerings to flourish and creating a nearly ideal transportation system. Erfurt also offers a stunning cathedral, a handful of museums, and a civic atmosphere fueled by three educational institutions. While the city at large is strikingly picturesque, giving Erfurt a look all too rare in the cities of the east, it gains additional flavor from those buildings which have not yet been renovated, intermittently appearing eerily similar to sets from *The Cabinet of Dr. Caligari.*

ORIENTATION AND PRACTICAL INFORMATION

Erfurt lies in the heart of Thüringen, only 15 minutes from Weimar (4-5 trains per hr.), 1½ hours from Leipzig (29 per day), and three hours from Frankfurt (20 per day). The city is also properly referred to as the gateway to the Thüringer Wald, with numerous connections throughout the forest. The train station stands south of the city center. Head straight down Bahnhofstr. to reach the **Anger**—the main drag—and then the *Altstadt,* which is cut through by the *Gera River.* Take Schlößerstr. across the river to the **Fischmarkt** square, dominated by the neo-Gothic **Rathaus.** Marktstr. then leads left to the **Domhügel** hill, one of the oldest districts and site of the **cathedral.**

Tourist Office: Erfurt Fremdenverkehrsamt, Schlößerstr. 44 (tel. 562 62 67; fax 562 33 55), next to the *Rathaus.* Pick up the monthly *Erfurt Magazin* with a worthy map in the center, a copy of *In* magazine for nightlife tips, and the *Sales Guide,* which does an excellent job providing the most up-to-date maps, public transportation schedules, and info about sights, museums, movie theaters, and daytrips (in English and German). Maps of the Thüringer Wald are also available. The office reserves tickets and books rooms in costly hotels and affordable private rooms for a DM5 fee (singles DM30-50). Open Mon.-Fri. 10am-6pm, Sat. 10am-1pm. Another **branch** in a narrow half-timbered house on the **Krämerbrücke** (tel. 562 34 36; fax 562 11 16) has weekend hours, though they don't book rooms (open Mon.-Fri. 10am-6pm, Sat. 10am-4pm, Sun. 10am-1pm). **Tours** of the city leave from the Krämerbrücke April-Oct. daily at 1pm; Nov.-March Sat. at 1pm (DM6).

Currency Exchange: Reisebank is located in the train station. It offers money transfer, phonecards, and cash advances on credit cards. Nice hours, but somewhat stiff rates. Open Tues.-Fri. 8:30am-7:45pm, Sat.-Sun. 10am-4pm. Also close to the train station, and with better rates and a 24hr. ATM, is the **Deutsche Bank** on the corner of Bahnhofstr. and Juri-Gagarin-Ring, across from the tourist office. Open Mon., Wed., and Fri. 8am-4pm; Tues. and Thurs. 8am-5:30pm.

Trains: From the *Hauptbahnhof,* trains go to Dresden (every 2hr.), Würzburg (every 3hr., 2½hr.), and Frankfurt am Main (every 3hr., 2½hr.).

Public Transportation: An effective combination of **buses** and silent **streetcars** runs through the pedestrian zones. DM2 per trip. 50% senior discount. Validate your tickets on board. For info call 194 49 or stop by the office at the *Hauptbahnhof.* Most streetcars and buses stop just before 1am.

Taxis: tel. 511 11, or for people with bad memories 555 55, 666 66, or 777 77 77.

Bicycle rental: Velo-Sport, on Juri-Gagarin-Ring. From Bahnhofstr. turn left and walk for about 3min. DM10-15 per day, and you must leave a passport. Open Mon.-Wed. and Fri. 10am-6pm, Thurs. 10am-7pm, Sat. 9am-1pm.

Laundry: Jump for joy at the sight of washing machines across the street and to the left as you exit the *Hauptbahnhof.* Open Mon.-Fri. 6am-10pm, Sat.-Sun. 9am-8pm.

Pharmacy: Bahnhof-Apotheke, on Bahnhofstr. near the Anger, has a wide selection and lists the daily 24hr. pharmacy. Open Mon.-Fri. 8am-6pm, Sat. 9am-noon.

Women's Center: Frauenzentrum, Espechstr. 3 (tel. 562 60 68), in the southwest part of the city, has information, counseling, and a cafe. Open Mon. 2-6pm, Tues.-Thurs. 9:30am-9:30pm, Fri. 9:30am-2pm, Sat. 2-6pm.

Emergency: Police, tel.110. **Fire,** tel 112. **Ambulance,** tel. 115.

Internet Access: Internet-Café, Willi-Brandt-Platz 1, across from the *Bahnhof,* has fast machines (20min. DM5). Open Mon.-Fri. 7am-7pm, Sat.-Sun. 10am-6pm.

Post Office: The main post office, 99084 Erfurt, the focal point of the Anger, occupies an ornate beast of a building probably larger than some of the punier European countries. Open Mon.-Fri. 8am-6pm, Sat. 9am-noon.

Telephone Code: 0361.

ACCOMMODATIONS

Housing options are dicey. The best bet for budget beds is the **Jugendherberge Karl Reiman (HI),** Hochheimerstr. 12 (tel. 562 67 05; fax 562 67 06), an old white-and-maroon mansion in a once-ritzy suburb an easy streetcar ride from the city center. From the station, streetcar #5 (direction: "Steigerstr.") to the last stop. Backtrack a little, turn left onto Hochheimerserstr., and the pillar-fronted hostel is on the left corner at the first intersection. The renovated interior, with sparkling new showers and bathrooms in all new rooms, is more inviting than the "tired" exterior. *Fußball,* billiards, and table tennis in the lounge. Considering Erfurt's size and the hostel's lack of competition, it's a pleasant surprise that it's sometimes possible to book same-day rooms. (Reception open 6-9am and 3-10pm. Curfew midnight. DM24, over 26 DM28. Breakfast included. Sheets DM7. Wheelchair accessible.) If the hostel is booked, the **Zimmervermittlung** at the tourist office (tel. 194 33) can book private rooms costing about double what you'd pay in the hostel. If they're out of rooms, head to the gracious people who run the private agency **Tourismus Agentur Otto,** Schmidstedterstr. 28 (tel./fax 643 09 71), down the road across from the tourist office, which has rooms in private homes for DM36.50 (fee included; open Mon.-Fri. 10am-6pm). In a pinch, Weimar's hostels are a 15-minute train ride away.

FOOD

What it lacks in accommodations, Erfurt makes up for with food. Cheap groceries await at the **Rewe supermarket** on Bahnhofstr., less than 100m from the train station (open Mon.-Fri. 6am-8pm, Sat. 8am-4pm), or fill up at the **market** on Dompl. (open Mon.-Sat. 6am-2pm). But Erfurt does offer some of the better restaurants in the *neue Bundesländer,* with spicy oases at some of the more exotic Chinese, Italian, or Argentine restaurants. The capital of Thüringen is a good place to discuss the region's wondrous specialty: *Thüringer Bratwurst* (DM2-3), served at stands all over the city (see **No More Hot Dogs!,** above). Many budget meals can be had from the fast- and semi-fast-food restaurants on the **Anger,** several of which have appealing late-night hours.

Schmalztopf, Dompl. 12-13 (tel. 646 30 73). Locals in the know come here to dine on native specialties amid the owner's self-congratulatory pictures of hearty customers eating gustily. Dinner specials from DM6.50, with a good view of the *Dom* at no extra charge. Open daily noon-midnight.

Kaffe Mühle, Schlößerstr. 25A (tel. 561 22 79), hanging over the Gera River, clearly commands a supreme location. The apple pie with vanilla ice-cream (DM4.60), and sublime gin and tonics (DM6.50) satisfy any tired traveler. Open Tues.-Sat. 11am-1am, Sun. 11am-10pm. Kitchen closes at 11pm Mon.-Fri. and 10pm Sun.

Kloster Stube, next to the *Kloster,* with outdoors seating, is a supreme place to experience the German tradition of *Kaffee und Kuchen.* The *Stube* serves Goliathan mugs of delicious coffee (DM1.50), and sweet freshly baked cake—apple strudel or the daily special (DM1.50). Open Mon.-Sun. 10:30am-7:30pm.

SIGHTS

The mammoth **Marien-Dom** completely dominates the view from the marketplace at its perch on **Domhügel hill**, impressing even the most ardent heathen. Today a Gothic extravaganza, the church's Romanesque foundation dates back to 1154. Its rusty green spires explode against the sky, conspiring with the adjacent church to create a fantastical, prickly skyline. Inside, the most impressive part of the cathedral is the 15th-century **Hochchor** in the eastern wing; the **altar** is fully 17m high, embellished with miniature oil paintings and intricate carvings. The 15 **stained glass windows** rise higher than the altar and are currently about halfway through a massive cleaning that will make them brighter than they've been in centuries. Already, the density of adornment in the clean parts is enough to make your eyes cross. While the newer, paler windows—designed and made by Quedlinburg native Charles Crodel in the early 1960s—desperately needs some polishing up, Lucas Cranach the Elder's altar painting is in perfect condition. Luther was invested as a priest here, and word has it that his first mass was disrupted by a visit from...*Satan*. In mid-liturgy, the doughty Luther hurled his Bible across the altar, which sent the Dark One fleeing but failed to impress the Bishop. The muted sandstone interior of the neighboring **Church of St. Severi** proves less impressive than its turrets would lead one to believe. The enormous, wooden, Baroque organ appendages scream with flying golden angels, sunbursts, flames, and a pastel palate of fake marble. (Both open May-Oct. Mon.-Fri. 9-11:30am and 12:30-5pm, Sat. 9-11:30am and 12:30-4:30pm, Sun. 2-4pm; Nov.-April Mon.-Sat. 10-11:30am, Sun. 2-4pm. Sun. mass 11am and 6pm. Free.)

From Dompl., Marktstr. leads down to the breezy, open **Fischmarkt,** bordered by restored guild houses with wildly decorated facades. Overlooking the space is the brazenly neo-Gothic **Rathaus,** whose bonanza of **paintings** depicting mythical sequences, including Faust and Tannhäuser portrayals, is open for public gawking. Late-19th-century Thüringians weren't into subtlety (open Mon. and Wed.-Thurs. 9am-4pm, Tues. 9am-6pm, Fri. 9am-2pm; free).

Further down Marktstr. flows the quietly babbling **Gera River,** which provides the *raison d'être* for one of Erfurt's oddest architectural attractions. The little river is spanned by the **Krämerbrücke,** a medieval bridge completely covered by small shops, some of which date back to the 12th century. In the 1400s, this bridge was part of a great trade-route running from Kiev to Paris. When you're walking on the bridge, it is impossible to see the water; it looks for all the world like a "regular," narrow Central European street. Even more fascinating is the view from underneath—take one of the paths leading off the bridge to get a glance up from the water's edge. The **Brückenmuseum,** in a small house on the far end (away from the *Altstadt*), chronicles the bridge's history as well as medieval period costume (open Tues.-Sun. 10am-6pm; DM2, children DM1). On the other side of the river, just beyond the museum, a chalk-written sign announces that the *"Turm"* (tower) of the St. Aegidii church is open for thrill-seeking stair-climbers. For DM2, the tower gives you another perspective of the Krämerbürcke and evidence that Erfurt suffered very little from modern architecture (tower open sporadically, but always Sun. noon-6pm).

From the far side of the bridge, follow Gotthardtstr. and cut left through Kirchengasse to reach the **Augustinerkloster,** where Martin Luther spent 10 years as a Catholic priest and Augustine monk. He got his way, and the cloister now functions as a Protestant college. (Hourly tours April-Oct. Tues.-Sat. 10am-noon and 2-4pm; also on Sun. after morning services, around 10:45am; Nov.-March Tues.-Sat. 10am, noon, and 2pm. The cloister usually won't lead a tour if fewer than five people show up. You may get bumped back an hour or more. DM4.50, students DM3.) The **library** here has one of Germany's most priceless collections, including a number of early Bibles with personal notations by Luther himself. During World War II, the books were moved to make room for a bomb shelter. When U.S. bombers destroyed the library in February 1945, 267 people lost their lives, but the books remained unscathed.

From the Krämerbrücke, head down Futterstr. and turn right on Johannesstr. to reach the **Kaufmannskirche,** where Bach's parents tied the knot (open Mon.-Sat. 10am-6pm, Sun. 11am-5pm; service Sun. 10am). In front of the church, feet planted firmly on a pedestal decorated with scenes from his days here, a squat **Martin Luther** casts an indifferent stare over the **Anger,** Erfurt's wide pedestrian promenade. Beautified with numerous statues and fountains, the Anger is one of the most attractive shopping streets in Eastern Germany. No, it's not Milan (or even Dortmund, for that matter), but the street's collection of shops, mega-cafes, fast food joints, and cinemas bring Erfurt solidly into the realm of conspicuous consumption. The architecture lining the street—most of it 19th-century Neoclassical or *Jugendstil*—is for the most part fascinating, though some GDR-era behemoths mar the effect, refusing to let the recent past go unnoticed. Across from the post office lies **House #6,** where Russian Czar Alexander I stayed when he came to Erfurt to meet with Napoleon in 1808.

The **Angermuseum,** Anger 18, in an immaculate yellow mansion, is dedicated not to chronicling the history of rage, but to displaying a collection of medieval religious art mostly from Erfurt and its vicinity. Don't miss the room designed and painted by Expressionist Erich Heckel in 1922. The bold colors and primitive style tell the tale of the artist's development in a mural. (Open Tues.-Sun. 10am-6pm. DM3, students DM1.50; special exhibits add a few Marks to the price.)

Bear right at the end of the Anger and follow Regierungstr. to the abode formerly known as the **Statthalterei,** the massive Baroque building from which the Communists ruled the city. Here, in a small salon on the second floor, Napoleon had breakfast with Goethe in 1808. Goethe later wrote that Napoleon spent the entire time chastising him for his gloomy tragedies, which the French emperor seemed to know inside and out, while Goethe listened passively; both understood themselves to be immortals—Goethe also realized, however, that Napoleon's immortality was backed by an army. The building is being converted to the Thüringen Minister-President's office and is not open to the public, but the exterior still merits a healthy gawking.

ENTERTAINMENT AND NIGHTLIFE

Erfurt's 220,000 inhabitants manage a fairly indulgent nightlife. The area near the Dompl. and the Krämerbrücke between **Michaelisstraße, Marbachergasse,** and **Allheiligenstraße** glows at night with cafes, candlelit restaurants, and bars. While the Opera House is closed, a victim of stringent German safety regulations, the Theater Erfurt puts on regular shows at the nearby **Schauspielhaus.** The **ticket office** (tel. 223 31 58), Dalbergsweg 2, is in the Opera House (office open Tues.-Fri. 10am-1pm and 2-5:30pm, Sat. 10am-1pm, Sun. 10am-noon, and 1hr. before performances, when prices drop 60% on unsold seats); tickets can also be purchased at the tourist office. Just off the Dompl. the **Theater Waidspeicher** (tel. 598 29 24), charms all with an intricate marionette and puppet theater; cabaret on weekend nights (box office at Dompl. 2 open Tues.-Fri. 10am-2pm and 3-5:30pm; puppet show DM5-7; cabaret DM17-21).

The **Double b,** Marbacher Gasse 10 (tel. 642 16 71), near the Dompl., functions as a hybrid Irish pub, German beer garden, and Amsterdam cafe; all the cool kids in Erfurt show up there to indulge in things fast and decadent—it's dangerously close to *Schicki-Micki* land (open Mon.-Fri. 8am-midnight, Sat.-Sun. 9am-midnight). The **Studentenclub Engelsburg,** Allerheiligenstr. 20/21 (tel. 290 36), just off Marktstr., is down with the disco and moderate punk scene, especially at the frat-like musical grotto within. Live bands from Erfurt and the surrounding area offer their talents as an alternative to the disco in the party room. (Open July-Sept. Wed. and Sat. 9pm-1am, Sun. 10pm-midnight; Oct.-June Wed.-Sat. 9pm-1am; cover DM8, students DM4.)

■ Thüringer Wald (Thuringian Forest)

"The area is magnificent, quite magnificent…I am basking in God's world," wrote Goethe from the Thüringer Wald in a letter more than 200 years ago. Goethe's exuberant exclamation is still accurate; the time-worn mountains make for perfect skiing during the winter and excellent hiking, camping, and walking in the summer. The peaceful pine woods of the Thüringer Wald have attracted Germans for generations, and cradled within these mighty but gentle hills, the small towns and villages have cultivated and inspired many of Germany's composers, philosophers, and poets. Goethe and Schiller composed some of their most brilliant poetry on these slopes (and on the walls of huts). The unspoiled forests stretch south of Eisenach, Weimar, and Erfurt to the border with Bayern. Trains and buses trek regularly from larger cities to the smaller, wood-framed villages.

The **Rennsteig,** a famous scenic hiking trail, snakes through this forest, and before the war, the Rennsteig was one of Germany's favorite wilderness trails. While history books date the trail to 1330, locals claim that it was first trodden by prehistoric hunter-gatherers. During the years of East-West division, much of the route was closed because of its potential as an escape route. Now hikers wander all 168km from Hörschel near Eisenach right into Bayern, and veterans of the five-day hike can't stop talking about the route's delights. **Erfurt,** the new state capital, is without question the door to the Thüringer Wald. The **tourist office** (see **Erfurt: Orientation and Practical Information,** p. 194) equips you with guides and maps for an extended jaunt. Keep in mind that foreign tourists and modern conveniences are rare here. English is only understood in larger tourist offices, although an increasing number of brochures are published in English. Get yourself ready for a true, poetic wilderness experience.

ARNSTADT

The oldest town in Thüringen, the stately **Arnstadt** (founded in 704) lies at the fringe of the forest just beyond Erfurt. After 50 years of GDR-style maintenance, Arnstadt is today going through a face-lift at the behest of John Woo. Cranes and scaffolds are juxtaposed with the city's medieval walkways and buildings. Johann Sebastian Bach began his career here as an organist in **Bachkirche** (open March-Sept. Tues.-Sat. 10am-noon and 2-4pm, Sun. 2-4pm). Before they named holy edifices in honor of him, the local authorities found Bach's license with musical forms as well as local women "shocking to community standards"—just like horse porn. They politely but firmly asked him to leave town for good. Nevertheless, a statue on the Marktplatz—the young Bach slumped on an organ stool, looking mildly displeased—commemorates the life of the trumpeted composer. The Renaissance-era **Haus Zum Palmbaum,** Markt 3 (tel. 60 29 78), serves as a **town museum,** with a strong emphasis on the history of the socialist and communist parties in Germany—a fascinating GDR relic in itself—and **Bach memorial museum** (open Mon.-Fri. 8:30am-12:30pm and 1-5pm, Sat.-Sun. 9:30am-5pm; DM4, students DM2).

The **Neues Palais** (New Palace), Schloßpl. 1 (tel. 60 29 32), houses one of Germany's more fascinating doll museums: **Mon Plaisir.** In the mid-18th century, the local princess whimsically demanded that court employees and craftsmen fashion a miniature panorama of the community. More than 400 wax and wooden dolls are displayed in 24 dollhouses, with a total of 82 furnished rooms decorated with thousands of miniature props from spinning wheels to musical instruments. (Open May-Oct. Tues.-Sun. 8:30am-12pm and 1-4:30pm; Nov.-April Tues.-Sun. 9:30am-4pm; last entry 30min. before close; DM3.50, students and seniors DM2.50.) The old medieval town walls stand in glorious decrepitude throughout the **Schloßgarten.** The magnificent ruins of **Schloß Neideck** are closed for renovations, but you can visit its gardens and theater (call 618 60 for info; ticket sales open Tues. and Thurs. 10am-noon and 4-6pm; tickets DM9-20, students and seniors DM3). The **Liebfrauenkirche** (tel. 74 09 65) makes up for its anonymous history with a brilliant display of stained glass windows. While originally built in the 11th century, the innumerable reparations render the church ageless. (Open March-Sept. Tues.-Sat. 10:30am-12:30pm and 2-4pm, Sun. 2-4pm; otherwise, call the tourist office for opening hours and tours.)

The **tourist office,** Arnstadt Information, Markt 3 (tel. 60 20 49; fax 74 57 48), finds rooms (DM25-40) for a DM3 fee. From the station, turn left and then right on Bahnhofstr., continue down on Erfurterstr., and then walk up Ledermarkt to the Markt. They can tell you about bus and train connections to the **Drei Gleichen** (three matching castles), near Arnstadt. They also provide you with information and maps for hiking,

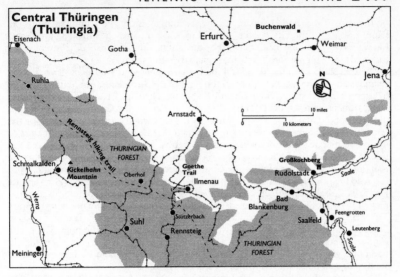

Central Thüringen (Thuringia)

as well as sell a snazzy new bilingual (German and English) city guide and map (DM4.50; open Mon.-Fri. 10am-6pm, Sat. 9am-noon). Arnstadt is best reached by **train** from Erfurt (2-3 per hr.; 20min.) or Ilmenau (1 per hr.; 40min.). The **Apotheke unter der Gallerie,** Marktplatz 15, is located next to the post office (open Mon.-Wed. and Fri. 8am-6pm, Thurs. 8am-7pm, Sat. 8am-noon). **Exchange money** at the **post office,** Ritterstr., 99310 Arnstadt, on the edge of the park off Bahnhofstr. (open Mon.-Fri. 8:30am-6pm, Sat. 8:30am-noon). The **telephone code** is 03628.

The streets of Arnstadt lead to some Thuringian culinary treasure troves. **Feinbäckerei und Cafe am Jakobsturm,** Ried 18, bakes the freshest cakes, breads, and pastries for miles around. Better still, you get a **free cup of coffee** by picking up a postcard of the cafe at the tourist office (open Mon.-Fri. 6:30am-6pm, Sat. 7-11am and 2-5pm, Sun. 2-5pm). At the hearty **Hotel-Restaurant Goldene Sonne,** Ried 3 (tel. 60 27 76), you can dine on *Bratwürstchen* (DM8.80) or *Klopse,* the forest's special meatballs (DM7.80). Most meals run DM7.50-14 (open Mon.-Thurs. 10am-3pm and 6-10pm, Fri. 10am-3pm, Sun. 11am-3pm). For typical Thuringian meals (read: hot sausages) hovering around DM10, try the **Ratsklause,** Ledermarkt 3 (tel. 480 73; open Mon.-Thurs. 7:30am-4pm, Sat. 7:30am-2pm). At night, check out the **Kulisse Cafe,** Kohlenmarkt 8 (tel. 782 88). This joint used to be a brew house; now it swims with locals sitting outside in a cobblestone courtyard surrounded by half-timbered walls (open Mon.-Fri. 10am-midnight, Sat.-Sun. 2pm-midnight).

ILMENAU AND GOETHE TRAIL

The train to Ilmenau blazes through wide verdant valleys, prickled with clusters of red-roofed houses, and occasional patches of wild flowers. Closer to Ilmenau, the pre-fab apartment buildings mar the scenery, providing a bizarre contrast to the mountainous backdrop. The center of this puny university town, however, retains a picturesque, shabby medieval feel. History of a different sort put Ilmenau on the map. Thüringen claims several geniuses, but its favorite offspring by far is Johann Wolfgang von Goethe. Johann's beginnings in the region were tediously bureaucratic. Goethe first worked in Ilmenau reorganizing the regions mining industry while he was a government minister under the Duke of Weimar. Only later did he come back to the area as a poet looking for a place of his own. "Ilmenau cost me much time, effort, and money," he wrote, "but I learned something as well and developed a way of looking at nature which I would not give up at any price." Today, in turn, the main attractions

THÜRINGEN

on the way to the market square are the stunning scenery and a number of his old haunts. South of the city center, parallel to Waldstr., stretches the 18.5km **Goethewanderweg** (Goethe Trail) marked by the author's over-flourished "g" monogram, that leads through the forest to **Stützerbach** (6-8 hr. each way).

The trail starts from the delightful market area, endowed with pedestrian-friendly fountains, and sidewalk cafes, just to the right of the **Amtshaus,** Am Markt 1 (tel. 26 67; open May-Oct daily 9am-noon and 1-4:30 pm; Nov.-April 10am-noon and 1-4pm; DM2, students and seniors DM1). Follow the "g" signs to the **Grab Corona Scröters,** the grave of the first actress to portray Goethe's renowned *Iphigenia*. Next along the trail is the **Schwabenstein,** the rock upon which Goethe wrote Act IV of *Iphigenia*. At this point, practically every rock, stone, and pebble gains fame: Goethe observed this tree in 1779, Goethe reclined on this rocky ledge in 1782, etc. About 4km into the trail (much of which is uphill) is the **Goethehäuschen** on the **Kickelhahn,** where you can read the poetry he scratched on the walls in his youth. Farther along (2hr.) lies the **Jagdhaus Gabelbach** (tel. 20 26 26), often visited by Goethe in summer, with a display of his scientific experiments. (Open May-Oct. Tues.-Sun. 9am-noon and 1-5pm; Nov.-March Wed.-Sun. 9am-noon and 1-4pm. DM4, students DM2.) The hike ends in **Stützerbach,** where the local glass-works magnate often hosted the poet. The house is now a **Goethe memorial,** but as a nod to the patron there are demonstrations of traditional **glass-blowing** (open May-Oct. Tues.-Sun. 9am-noon and 1-5pm, Nov.-April Wed.-Sun. 9am-noon and 1-4pm; DM3, students DM2).

The **tourist office** awaits at Lindenstr. 12 (tel. 20 23 58 or 621 32; fax 20 25 02). From the *Hauptbahnhof,* walk straight ahead on Bahnhofstr. to Wetzlarerpl. and follow the pedestrian zone until it becomes Lindenstr. (15min.). From the Ilmenau-Bad station, turn left on Waldstr., cross the river and continue straight on Lindenstr. (5min.). They provide maps and hiking brochures and book private rooms (DM20-35) for a DM2 fee per person (open Mon.-Fri. 9am-6pm, Sat. 9am-noon). You can obtain a map of the trail from the tourist office, or head for the **Goethe-Gedenkstätte im Amtshaus** (see above). Ilmenau can be reached by **train** from Erfurt (17 per day; 1hr.) and Arnstadt (1 per hr., 40min.). Ilmenau also makes a good starting point for a hike along the 168km long **Rennsteig** (take the train to Schmiedefeld), cutting across a good section of mid- and southern-Thüringen—gorgeous scenery and traditional villages lie scattered along the path. Pick up a map and ask for tips about day-trips at any of the tourist offices along the way. **Rent** a hi-tech sporty **mountain-bike** from **Rad Art,** Lindenstr. 22 (tel. 84 22 25; fax 84 22 35), to the right of the tourist information (day DM25, tandem bike DM40); open Mon.-Fri. 9am-6pm, Sat. 9am-1pm). The **post office,** Poststr., 98693 Ilmenau, is located just uphill from Wetzlarerpl. (open Mon.-Fri. 8am-12:30pm and 2-5:30pm, Sat. 9am-noon). The **telephone code** is 03677.

Ilmenau got a new **Jugendherberge** for its birthday last year. The hostel, Am Stollen 49 (tel. 88 46 81; fax 88 46 82), offers a shower and bathroom for each spacious four-bed room. Leaving the *Hauptbahnhof* to the left, take another left at the dead end, cross the tracks and veer to the right on the path alongside the tracks. After the sharp right curve, cross the bridge on your left, and you are almost on Am Stollen which snakes around the hostel (10min.). (Reception open 10am-10pm. DM20, over 26 DM24. Breakfast included.) **Die Arche,** Str.-des-Friedens 28 (tel. 89 41 11), is half-cafe featuring international cuisine (*paella*—rice with mixed-in vegetables, DM8.20) and half-shop for African and Indian trinkets. Popular with students, the walls on the top floor are covered with teas and herbs. Immerse yourself in the cloud of exotic scents, and enjoy a pot of tea—170 options (cup DM2.50, pot DM3; open Mon.-Fri. 10am-6pm, Sat. 9am-2pm). **Zur Post,** on Wetzlarerpl. at Mühltor 6 (tel. 67 10 27), offers regional specialties at excellent prices (DM9-15). Try *Thüringer Rostbrätel* (roasted sausage) with fresh peasant bread for DM10 (open Mon.-Fri. 8:30am-midnight, Sat.-Sun. 11am-midnight). Behind the Raiffeisenbank on the right side of Bahnhofstr., a **market** offers fresh fruits and vegetables (open Mon.-Fri. 8am-5pm, Sat. 8am-11am).

RUDOLSTADT

Below Jena, the Saale Valley meanders down to Rudolstadt. A litany of famous people have aimlessly strolled on its cobblestone streets. This is the city where Goethe and Schiller first locked pens (Schillerstr. 25), where Schopenhauer furiously scribbled away at his dissertation, and where Richard Wagner's star of musical immortality began its ascent. Apart from its close proximity to the incurably romantic Thüringer Wald (a 40min. bus ride), Rudolstadt offers few mind-blowing attractions.

During the 18th century, social life in Rudolstadt centered on the princes of Schwarzburg-Rudolstadt and the dusty-yellow, Baroque-towered **Heidecksburg palace.** From the tourist office, veer right on Allestr. and turn left twice onto the "Schloßaufgang." Look for the steep *Häbner Treppe* (Chicken steps) on your right, which lead straight to the palace. The **museum** in *Heidecksburg* (tel. 429 00) showcases a frightening weapons collection and an insanely ornate Rococo *Festsaal.* The ceiling drips with chandeliers, while the walls suffocate in gold moulding and four-colored imitation marble. Local craftworkers still deal in hand-painted china dolls (open Tues.-Sun. 10am-6pm; last entrance 30min. before closing; DM6, students and children DM3). The **Volkskundemuseum Thüringer Bauernhäuser** (Thuringian Farmhouse Museum; tel. 42 24 65), is an open-air display of two regional farmhouses, completely restored and furnished. Go right from the station and cross the bridge into the park (open May-Aug. Wed.-Sun. 9am-noon and 1-5pm; Sept.-April Wed.-Sun. 9am-noon and 1-4pm; DM2, children DM1).

Trains and **buses** from Weimar (bus #14) and Erfurt (bus #13) take about an hour to reach Rudolstadt (for bus info call 42 26 12). To reach the **tourist office,** Marktstr. 57 (tel. 41 47 43; fax 42 45 43), from the train station walk straight ahead to the right of the park *(Platz der Opfer des Faschismus),* down Bahnhofsgasse to Marktstr., and turn left. Look through the free brochures on the information rack to find Rudolstadt maps—the ones they try to sell you cost DM1 and up. They find rooms (DM25-40) for a DM3 fee (open Mon.-Fri. 9am-6pm, Sat. 9am-noon). **Exchange money** at **Deutsche Bank,** Marktstr. 45 (tel. 223 51; open Mon. 9am-4:30pm, Tues. 9am-6pm, Wed. and Fri. 9am-4pm, Thurs. 9am-6pm). To explore town, rent a **bike** from **Kern,** Markt 32 (tel. 42 73 71; DM20 with DM20 deposit). The **telephone code** is 03672.

Zum Brummochsen, Altestr. 12 (tel. 243 55), serves heavy food of the Thüringer Wald for DM6-7.50 or small *Wurst* meals for DM4-6; their mascot is a big, smiling cow (open Sun.-Thurs. 11am-10:30pm, Sat. 6-10:30pm). For lighter fare, **Café Brömel,** Bahnhofsgasse 1 (tel. 42 20 76), serves pastries, pies, and meals (salmon filet and salad DM10) in a 300-year-old locale, with "quick lunch" specials between 11am and 2pm DM7.50 (open Mon.-Sat. 8am-6pm, Sun. 1-6pm). Stock up on basics at the **E-Markt** supermarket on Marktstr. 55 (open Mon.-Wed. 8am-6:30pm, Thurs. 8am-7:30pm, Fri. 8am-6:30pm, Sat. 8am-12:30pm). On Wednesdays (6am-6pm) and Saturdays (6am-noon), buy fruits and vegetables at the **farmer's market** on the Marktplatz.

GROßKOCHBERG

From Rudolstadt, big, comfortable buses and bumpy, serpentine foot trails run the 8km north to **Großkochberg** (the bus ride takes 40min.). The moated **Schloß Kochberg,** once the summer home of **Charlotte von Stein,** was the inspiration for many of Goethe's powerful love poems, the proximate source for his sentimental hit novel *The Sorrows of Young Werther,* and in general the *ewig Weibliche* (eternal feminine) of his life—or so he thought. For 10 years Goethe and Frau von Stein frolicked here in the beautiful English gardens while her husband stayed in Weimar with the kids. Goethe fled to Italy to find himself, came back two years later and took up with a simple factory girl twenty years his junior. Understandably a touch bitter, Frau von Stein promptly returned everything Goethe had ever given her. When he did likewise, she publicly burnt her letters to him and composed the nasty tragedy *Dido,* a fictive act of retaliation and character assassination against the poet. The castle lost nothing in the nasty breakup; it did, however, get custody of the children. Just kidding. Today you can wander its 11 furnished rooms to see the first letter Schiller wrote Goethe (June

13, 1794), the first letter Goethe wrote Schiller (June 24, 1794), an odd sketch of Schiller riding a donkey, and sculptures of Goethe's and Charlotte's hands (right or left?). Move on to see the table that supported Goethe's 1700 love letters to her—a man of letters indeed. Behind the castle, the landscaped gardens, soggy with ponds and paths, shelter picnic alcoves. (Castle open May-Aug. Tues.-Sun. 9am-noon and 1-5pm; Sept.-April Wed.-Sun. 9am-noon and 1-5pm; DM6, students DM4.) If you have a moment before the bus comes, visit the church just down the hill with a touching **memorial** to the victims of the Franco-Prussian and World Wars. Eight buses per day bump from Rudolstadt to Großkochberg (6:25am-6:30pm; the last return back to Rudolstadt leaves around 4:30pm; for further info call (03672) 42 26 12). **Rosas Bauernstübel,** a white farm house down the street from the bus stop and the castle on the left, serves delicious and filling *Bauernfrühstück* (farmer's breakfast) at dinnertime (DM7.40; open Tues.-Sun. 11am-9pm). At **Goetheplatz,** on Goethepl. (surprise), meals range from DM4.50-12 for *Schnitzels,* roasted potatoes, and jellied meats—just the way Goethe liked 'em (open Thurs.-Mon. 11:30am-9pm).

LEUTENBERG

Leutenberg remains a scarred city; it was razed and plundered during the Thirty Years War, 200 years before a fire raised hell in the town in the 1850s. While the town itself lacks splendor, its location in the middle of bunches of foothills makes "the city of the seven hills" a magnificent point of departure for hiking excursions. For an in-town excursion, a walk up Schloßstr. and up the path of the Schloßberg will, not surprisingly, bring you to Leutenberg's 9th-century **castle** (15min.). **Schloß Friedensburg** is unspectacular—an old-school type of domain that lacks the jaw-dropping punch of the later German castles. In point of fact, the *Schloß* is now a hospital clinic that proffers little more than a sweet view of the city and a commentary on the sickness of decadence and the decay of lying. The tourist office (see below) provides maps and advice about hiking trails in the area. The free map clearly and colorfully highlights a "Top 10" list of trails around the town. Most trails start at either Leninstr. (not all streetnames where changed after 1989!) or at the **Bayerische Bierstube.**

The **tourist office,** Herrngarten 7 (tel. 222 62), also offers room booking services at no charge (private rooms DM15-20, *Pensionen* DM25-50). To get there from the **train station** after arriving on one of the hourly **trains** from Rudolstadt (40min.-1hr.), take a right at the station down Bahnhofstr., turn left at the post office onto Am Ilmbach, then make a right onto Hauptstr. The office will be on your right directly off the main street (open Mon.-Thurs. 8am-noon and 1-5pm, Fri. 8am-2pm). Leutenberg's **telephone code** is 036734.

For tasty eats of the sit-down variety, **Gute Quelle,** Am Ilmbach 17, will provide you with a *Stammer Max* meal (ham and bread with fried eggs) for DM7.50; for those who love Miss Piggy and Big Bird, they also serve a *Reispfanne* (rice and veggies in a creamy mushroom sauce) for DM9.80 (open Tues.-Fri. 11:30am-2pm and 5-11pm, Sat.-Mon. 11:30am-11pm). Grab grub at **E Aktiv supermarket** at the end of Bahnhofstr. (open Mon.-Wed. 8am-6pm, Thurs.-Fri. 8am-7pm, Sat. 8am-1pm).

"I wish they all could be East German girls ..."

Among the many concerns of lost cultural and social identity that would result from reunification, sex was not the least of them. A professor at University of Leipzig performed a study in the wake of the Wall's shattering which found that "the rate of orgasms in the Eastern part of Germany is "substantially higher" than the rate in the West, with 37% of East German women regularly achieving orgasm against an average of 26% of women in the West. The findings were greeted with such headlines as "Experts Fear Cooling of East German Sex." While this fact is entirely frivolous, it might say something about the very liberated women of the former East: the GDR's many social programs—daycare, guaranteed maternity leave, and virtually certain employment—produced an image of independence that was one of the few things West German women admired about their Eastern counterparts.

THÜRINGEN

■ Eisenach

Birthplace of Johann Sebastian Bach and home-in-exile for Martin Luther, Eisenach boasts impressive humanist credentials. Yet inside the walls of the town's mammoth *Wartburg* Fortress, student fraternities convened in 1817 to promote a bizarre agenda of democracy and xenophobic nationalism; they celebrated their dedication to liberal tolerance by burning conservative books. The writings of Marx and Engels were so well received in Eisenach that the duo called the local communist faction "our party." Adolf Hitler is said to have called the idyllic Wartburg "the most German of German castles," and fought a pitched (and unsuccessful) battle with the local church to replace its tower's cross with a swastika. More recently, the GDR regime tapped into old associations by dubbing its "luxury" automobile the *Wartburg*. It's fitting that Eisenach—this romantic, rationalist, conservative, radical, democratic, despotic bundle of contradictions—should be home to one of the new reunified Germany's most treasured national symbols.

Orientation and Practical Information Eisenach's **tourist office,** Markt 2 (tel. 67 02 60 or 61), smack-dab in the center of the Marktplatz, has plenty of information on the *Wartburg* and books rooms in private homes (DM30-40) for free. From the train station walk on Bahnhofstr. which becomes Alexanderstr. until you reach the Marktplatz (open Mon. 10am-6pm, Tues.-Fri. 9am-6pm, Sat. 10am-2pm). Frequent **train** connections link Eisenach to Erfurt (50 per day; 1hr.) or Weimar (50 per day; 1¼hr.) in the east, and Bebra on the IC or IR in the west. Eisenach's *Bahnhof* provides a world of services for budget travelers; there's **luggage storage,** an **ATM, a grocery store** (open Mon.-Fri. 5:30am-8pm, Sat.-Sun. 8am-8pm), a flower shop, and everything short of a hot tub. For a **taxi,** call 220 220. The **Ost-Apotheke,** Bahnhofstr. 29 (tel. 20 32 42), has a list of night **pharmacies** (open Mon.-Fri. 8am-6pm, Sat. 8am-noon). Send your *Wartburg* postcard from the **post office** on the Markt, 99817 Eisenach (open Mon.-Fri. 8am-6pm, Sat. 8am-noon). The **telephone code** is 03691.

Accommodations and Food Jugendherberge Artur Becker (HI), Mariental 24 (tel. 74 32 59; fax 74 32 60), fills a comfortable old villa located fairly far from the center, a bit beyond the castle. From the station, take Bahnhofstr. to Wartburger Allee, which runs into Mariental. Here you can walk down the street until the hostel comes up on your right, past the pond (35min.). Alternatively, bus #3 (direction: "Mariental"): "Lilienstr." A sign points out the uphill path to the hostel; next comes a stairway on your right. The hostel is a touch worn, and by no means immaculately clean, but there is lots of wood trim, a nice sunny terrace outside, and it's cheap. (Reception open 9am-8pm. Curfew 10pm. DM22, over 26 DM26. Breakfast included. Sheets DM7.) The nearest **camping** is at **Am Altenberger See** (tel./fax 21 56 37), offering showers, a sauna, and a view of the lake in the hamlet of Eckartshausen. From the Eisenach station, take the **bus** toward Bad Liebenstein (4 departures daily 7:35am-5:35pm) and tell the driver your destination. About 10km from town. 13 cabins are available, with four rooms each. (Reception open until 10pm. Person DM6, tent DM5, car DM2, electricity DM3.)

You probably can't afford to stay at the **Hotel Wartburg** (tel. 51 11), just below the castle (DM195-380), although the delicious complimentary breakfast is tempting. If your wallet can accommodate a night here, burn the Bible of the budget traveler; otherwise, marvel at its pseudo-castle styling and its parking lot full of BMWs and Mercedes-Benzes, or indulge in a meal of house-made *Bratwurst, Sauerkraut,* and mashed *Kartoffeln* (DM14.50; restaurant open daily 9am-10pm). For large and delicious ice-cream cones with a mini-Dickman (a chocolate-covered marshmallow, not Howard Stern) on top for a mere DM3, pay a visit to **Dänishe Eiscreme.** They also sell a melange of crepes and danish waffles. From the Marktplatz, walk on Karlstr., and veer right onto Querstr. (open Mon.-Sat. 11am-8pm). Near the train station, **Café Moritz,** Bahnhofstr. 7 (tel. 72 65 75), raises your daily caloric intake with Thüringer specialities (around DM8), served outside if the weather permits. (Open May-Oct.

THÜRINGEN

Mon.-Fri. 8am-10pm, Sat.-Sun. 10am-10pm; Nov.-April Mon.-Fri. 8am-10pm, Sat.-Sun. 10am-8pm.) For a wide array of inexpensive food, head to **Edeka Neukauf supermarket,** on Johannispl. (open Mon.-Fri. 8am-7pm, Sat. 8am-4pm).

Sights High above Eisenach's half-timbered houses, the **Wartburg Fortress** lords over the northwestern slope of the rolling Thüringer Wald. In 1521, this deservedly hyped castle sheltered Martin Luther after his excommunication. To thwart the search, Luther grew a beard and spent his 10-month stay disguised as a noble named Junker Jörg. Burning the midnight oil working on his landmark German translation of the Bible, the reformer was visited by the devil (the perceptive traveler can't help but marvel at how often the Prince of Darkness and Luther's paths crossed during Luther's travels). By Luther's account, it only took a toss of an ink pot to dispel the Beast. Later pilgrims took the fable literally and mistook a smudge of stove grease for the blessed ink spot, gutting the wall (now a big hole) in their search for a souvenir.

Petty vandalism aside, the Romanesque *Wartburg* is notable for the peaceful character of its history—besides sheltering Luther, it was a haven for the 12th-century *Minnesänger,* the originators of German choral music. In one of the castle's restored chambers, a wall-sized copy of lyrics from Wagner's *Tannhäuser* is illustrated with ornate murals of the 12th-century battle of musicians that inspired the opera. Like many of the more dazzling chambers in the *Wartburg,* the mural room is a product of 19th-century imagination, not medieval reality. The Romantics' obsession with Wartburg began in 1777 when Goethe visited, fell in love with the place, and convinced some backers in the nobility to restore the interior and set up a museum. As a general rule, anything you see that's frayed and restrained-looking is old; anything shiny and ornate is the product of the 19th-century fan club. The castle's **Festsaal** preserves the memory of the 1817 meeting of 500 representatives of university fraternities who threw a party, got inspired, and formed Germany's first bourgeois opposition (ruthlessly crushed 2 years later); the flag they toasted still hangs in this room. From the walls of Wartburg's courtyard, trace the line of your path through the countryside below. The view is spectacular—if you turn to the side opposite Eisenach, you can see the Thüringer Wald and all the way across the former East-West border to Hesse. The first floor of the tower is a deep dungeon dating from darker days.

The *Wartburg* sits on the south side of Eisenach; the foot of the hill can be reached by a stroll down **Wartburger Allee** from the train station. A multitude of city-sponsored **tourist buses** run between the train station and the castle (15min.; one-way DM1.50, roundtrip DM2.50). Mini-vans shuttle visitors from parking-lots near the base (one-way DM4). For the more adventurous, there are a number of well-cleared **footpaths** up the incline—hiking downhill is a blast. Arriving at the medieval stronghold after a 30-minute hike through rich-smelling pines and lilacs, you'll wipe your sweat and feel like a pilgrim. If you weigh 60kg (132 lbs.) or less (and have no sympathy for poor Ior), you can opt for a donkey ride for the last stretch (DM5). When eastern Germany was East Germany, West Germans were issued special visas that allowed them to visit the castle and nothing else, and even those visas were hard to come by. Now, legions of sightseers are making up for lost time. On weekday mornings during the summer, expect crowds of schoolchildren; on weekday afternoons, crowds of German pensioners; on weekends, just be prepared for crowds. The interior of the castle can be visited only with a tour, and you may have to wait an hour to enter. (Open March-Oct. daily 8:30am-5pm; Nov.-Feb. 9am-3:30pm. Admission to the whole complex DM11, students and children DM6, seniors and people with disabilities DM8. Admission to museum and Luther study DM6, DM4, and DM5 respectively.) Alternatively, hike around the rich woods and grounds without spending a *Pfennig*.

Back at the base of the mountain, the **Bachhaus,** Frauenplan 21 (tel. 20 37 14), where Johann Sebastian stormed into the world in 1685, recreates the family's living quarters. Downstairs are period instruments such as a harpsichord, a spinet, and a beautifully preserved "house organ" from 1750, about the size of a telephone booth, with a little stool for the player. Around every 40 minutes, one of the museum's guides tunes up for a musical tour, including anecdotes about Bach's life, and spellbinding musical interludes—you can join the tour at any stage. Turn off Wartburger Allee down Grimmelgasse to reach the house (open Oct.-March Mon. 1-4:45pm; Tues.-Sun. 9am-4:45pm; April-Sept. Mon. noon-5:45pm, Tues.-Sun. 9am-5:45pm; DM5, students DM4). The **Reuter-Wagner-Museum,** Reuterweg 2 (tel. 20 39 71), below the Wartburg, is dedicated to the joint memory of writer Fritz and composer Richard (open Tues.-Sun. 10am-5pm; DM4, students and seniors DM2). Town life centers on the pastel **Markt,** bounded by the tilting dollhouse of a **Rathaus** and the latticed **Lutherhaus,** Lutherp. 8 (tel. 298 30), home of young Martin's school days from 1498 to 1501 (open May-Sept. daily 9am-5pm; Oct.-April Mon.-Sat. 9am-5pm, Sun. 2-5pm; DM5, students DM2). If you want to see the showcase of Eisenach's recent past in the form of its *Wartburg* cars, the **Automobilbaumuseum,** Rennbahn 6-8 (tel. 772 12), displays the grandest of GDR performance cars. Leave from the *Hauptbahnhof*'s "Ausgang Nord," and veer left; after a refreshing eight-minute walk, the museum is on the right (open Tues.-Sun. 9am-5pm; DM4, students, seniors, and kids DM2).

■ Gotha

Like many towns in the former GDR, Gotha suffers from troublesome construction and architectural decay. The lively Marktplatz and the extensive castle grounds are both islands of beauty in a sea of industrial filth and dirt. Gotha's past, on the other hand, is more intriguing. Prince Albert, one of the Dukes of Sachsen-Coburg-Gotha, married Queen Victoria of England, and hence Queen Elizabeth and Prince Charles are direct descendants of this house—the royal family's name of "Windsor" is a product of a name change during World War I, when Germany was "out of fashion." The birth of the Social Democratic Party in Gotha made Marx hopping mad, furthering his revolutionary career. When Charlemagne visited the city, he relaxed, spending only a day to scope out the city—more than enough time.

Orientation and Practical Information From the far side of the palace, you'll see the **Hauptmarkt,** a collection of 17th-century homes and businesses set on a 45-degree incline. The wave of renovation scared the **tourist office,** Blumenbachstr. 1-3 (tel. 85 40 36; fax 22 21 34), from the Marktplatz to the low-rent district. Facing the *Rathaus* entrance, go left down the narrow Hützelsgasse past the Socialist-era apartment block until you see the welcoming **"i."** Get information on the *Schloß* and nearby Thüringer Wald (ask about the *Rennsteig* hiking trail), or book a private room (DM35-40 per bed) for free. City **tours** leave on Wednesday at 11am from the steps of Gotha's *Rathaus,* overlooking the market. The tourist office also sells the Gotha *Touristenticket* (DM9.50) which knocks a mark or two off the price of most attractions and is good for one free trip each on Gotha's bus system and the *Thüringer Waldbahn,* which leads from the train station into hiking country. Unless you plan to use the *Waldbahn,* don't bother; Gotha is small enough to see on foot (open Mon.-Fri. 8am-6pm, Sat. 8am-1pm). Gotha is connected by frequent **trains** to Erfurt and Eisenach (20min.). In 1997, five digit phone numbers beginning with "5" had an "8" added in front. The city **postal code** is 99867. The **telephone code** is 03621.

Accommodations and Food Gotha's **Jugendherberge (HI),** Mozartstr. 1 (tel. 85 40 08), rests on the corner of the Schloßpark. From the station, walk an easy two blocks straight ahead; the beige hostel is on the right. Explore your musical side with accordion (DM5) or acoustic guitar (DM3) rentals. In the hallway, school children crowd the 80s arcade games, relics from the pre-Nintendo era. (Reception open 3-8pm. Curfew 10pm, but guests over 18 can ask for a key. DM15, over 26 DM19. HI members only. Breakfast DM5, lunch DM8, dinner DM6. Sheets DM7. Call ahead.)

Load up at the Markt (daily food bonanza open Mon.-Fri. 8am-6pm, Sat. 8am-1pm) and picnic in the palace gardens for an aesthetically pleasing bargain. **Bella Italia Eiscafé/Ristorante,** Erfurterstr. 11/13, provides decent Italian food (pizzas and pastas DM6.50-10) at a sidewalk cafe with a great view of the sparkling ice cream monstrosities that people are crazy enough to consume here (open Mon.-Sat. 9am-11:30pm,

Sun. 11am-11pm). Another solid option is **Kuhn and Kuhn,** Hühnersdorfstr. 14, a few blocks down from the castle and adjacent to the Buttermarkt. They offer cafe fare as well as German standards until the wee hours of the morning (DM7.50-14; open Tues.-Thurs. 9am-2am, Fri. 9am-3am, Sat. 11am-3am, Sun. 11am-1am).

Sights Gotha is saved from being just another castle town by its political history; the Social Democratic Workers' Party (a radical forerunner of Germany's moderate-left SPD party) was founded in a Gotha guest house in 1875. Still, the big draw is definitely the white-and-gray **Schloß Friedenstein,** whose three wings and entrance wall square off an immense gravel courtyard. For sightseers used to the Gothic intricacy or Rococo fantasy of other German castles, the 17th-century *Schloß*'s exterior may be a bit of a let-down. The crisp, unadorned rectangular windows and doors were intended to be built in the early Baroque style, then at the cutting edge of architecture. The lack of glitz, however, is made up for by the castle's sheer size. Duke Ernst I, the ruler who made the decision to build it in contemporary style, was a visionary in other ways as well: his peace initiatives and healthy support for the arts earned him the title *Ernst der Fromme* (the pious). A *Sammelkarte* (DM10, students and seniors DM5) allows entry to the *Schloß* and surrounding museums.

A nice portrait of the duke hangs in the **Schloßmuseum,** which includes the royal family's art collection—a respectable lot of 16th- and 17th-century works highlighted by a series of Cranachs and the serene *Gothaer Liebespaar* (Lovers of Gotha), a late 15th-century work by a German artist known only as "The Master of the Housebook." The collection of ancient and classical artifacts is superb; check out the sepulcher filled with Egyptian sarcophagi and mummies.

Upstairs are the royal apartments, whose splendor contrasts strikingly with the castle's spartan exterior. It's a treat to follow the red carpets that lead through the 16 fully restored, lavishly furnished ducal rooms. The Rococo *Festsaal* (feast hall), decorated with colorful crests from each of the duchy's provinces and cities, houses the original royal silver service. Other highlights include beautifully inlaid walls in the smaller rooms and the royals' bedroom cabinets. It must have been good to be the duke. Also in the palace buildings are the **Museum für Regionalgeschichte,** a small *Waffensammlung* (arms collection) of guns and knives, and the world's first museum of maps, the **Kartographisches Museum.** The Renaissance and early Mercator maps (named for a Flemish cartographer) are especially fascinating: watch the Americas slowly, awkwardly take their correct shape. At the castle corner, clever architectural tricks and optical illusions broaden the tiny stage of the 1683 **Eckhof Theater** (call the tourist office for tickets and information), one of the oldest indoor theaters still in use (open Tues.-Sun. 9am-4:45pm). Gotha's densely grown and resplendent Baroque **palace garden** is the largest in Europe.

The **Haus am Tivoli,** at the intersection of Cosmartstr. and Am Tivoli, was where August Bebel and others got the Social Democratic Party (SPD) together. The modern SPD is the largest political party in Germany and main opposition since the coalition regime, headed by the Chrstian Democrats, took the reigns. A GDR-era **plaque** outside the house commemorates the founding as a "glorious moment in the history of the German working class," even though Marx himself accused the Social Democrats of selling the proletariat short in his scathing *Critique of the Gotha Programme.* Now that Gotha's residents are sorting out their history, they don't know exactly what to do with the Socialist past of the place, and Am Tivoli is closed indefinitely. The SPD does, however, maintain an office in the purple house next door to the Tivoli, but don't go with any big expectations.

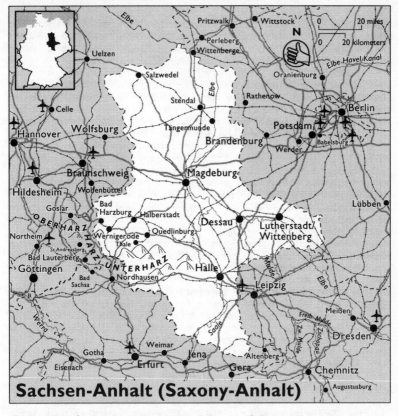

Sachsen-Anhalt (Saxony-Anhalt)

Sachsen-Anhalt (Saxony-Anhalt)

Sachsen-Anhalt's endless, mesmerizing grass plains offer one of the more tranquil landscapes in Eastern Germany. Once serving as the stronghold of the Holy Roman Empire, the region today suffers from the highest unemployment rates in Germany, and is also the most polluted province of the former GDR. Cities here once belched enough toxic filth into the air to make a smoggy day in Los Angeles seem fresh and healthy. But with the help of Western tourist dollars, Sachsen-Anhalt is rapidly cleaning up its act and gradually creating a stable work force. The region contains a number of worthwhile destinations that include Wittenberg, the city of Martin Luther and crucible of the Protestant Reformation, and Magdeburg, home to a splendid gothic *Dom* where the first Holy Roman Emperor is buried. The grand cathedrals filling the skyline attest to the region's former importance, and the many construction sites mushrooming across the *Land* point towards the future.

■ Wittenberg

Wittenberg does everything in its power to milk Martin Luther for what he's worth; in 1938, the town even went so far as to rename itself **"Lutherstadt Wittenberg."**

Luther claimed that Wittenberg was the source and font of his life's work: he preached, taught, married (a scandal to the Catholic clergy), raised children, and led the Protestant Reformation in this picturesque town. The city's fondest memories are of Luther nailing the *95 Theses* to the **Schloßkirche** (castle church) in 1517, and of his scandalous (and exceptionally contrived) wedding, a made-for-TV event that the town re-enacts every June. 1996 witnessed the 450th anniversary of Martin Luther's death—the infamous "Luther Year," an unparalleled tourist extravaganza. If you missed it, don't worry. Martin's remains still remain; although he died in Eisleben in 1546, his body was buried directly beneath the pulpit of the *Schloßkirche.*

Luther managed to hang onto his celebrity status in the officially atheistic GDR; after all, he was a harsh critic of Catholic wealth, inciting early bourgeois revolutions. He also had a presence in the civil sphere—for many East Germans the image of Luther risking his life to nail up his *95 Theses* became an emblem of courageous resistance. A successor of Luther at the *Schloßkirche* pulpit, Pastor Friedrich Schorlemmer, was a key player in the 1989 revolution. Since that time, religious pilgrims have returned in full force to Luther's city. The slow shuffle of Scandinavian church groups has pushed up *Schnitzel* prices while giving a fresh gleam to the architectural remnants. The huge new projects planned for the Expo-2000 spearhead an attempt to widen the spectrum of tourist attractions. But whether a concert park/museum/laser shows-island and a technicolor *Gymnasium* designed by **Hundertwasser** will overshadow the Great Reformer is a question for the next millennium.

Orientation and Practical Information Instead of disembarking at the less-than-central *Hauptbahnhof*, get off at *"Haltepunkt Lutherstadt Wittenberg-Elbtor."* Walk straight down Elbstr., hook a left at the second intersection (Schloßstr.), and walk for 5 minutes to the *Schloß*. Directly across the street, the brand new **Wittenberg Information**, at Schloßpl. 2 (tel. 49 86 10; fax 49 86 11), happily caters to all your map, room, postcard, and info needs (open Mon.-Fri. 9am-6pm, Sat.10am-2pm, Sun. 11am-3pm). The **regional tourist office**, Mittelstr. 33 (tel. 40 26 10; fax 40 58 57), by Lutherhalle, insists that an "ideal" daytrip is different for all individuals—bikers can purchase a great map of the extensive trails in the region (open April-Oct. daily 9:30am-5:30pm; Nov.-March Mon.-Fri. 9:30am-5:30pm). Wittenberg is a mere hour and a half by **train** from Berlin, Halle, or Leipzig, making it an excellent daytrip from any of these cities. The **pharmacy** on the Marktplatz, where painter Lucas Cranach pushed drugs to support his art habit, posts a rotating schedule of all-night pharmacies (open Mon.-Fri. 8am-6:30pm, Sat. 9am-noon). The **post office**, 06886 Wittenberg, is near Lutherhalle on the corner of Friedrichstr. and Fleischerstr. (open Mon.-Fri. 8am-6pm, Sat. 9am-noon). The **telephone code** is 03491.

Accommodations Hotels in the *Altstadt* are overpriced, but **private rooms** provide a reasonable option. The Wittenberg information center finds rooms for a DM3 fee (DM25-75). Alternatively, you can pick up a list of accommodations at the center and dodge the fee. The **Jugendherberge (HI)**, located in the castle (tel./fax 40 32 55), is simultaneously haunted by the ghosts of the Reformation and the rabid kids who tear through the place every summer. All rooms sport snazzy new bunkbeds and closets as part of a renovation campaign, which also left the bathrooms immaculately clean. The staff will wash, dry, and fold your dirty knickers for a mere DM4 per load. Take a left into the castle's enclosure, then trek up the spiraling stairs to the right. There are a few two- to four-bed rooms and a bunch of spacious 10- to18-bed rooms. (Reception open daily 7am-10pm. Lockout 10pm, but keys are available for a DM10 deposit. DM20, over 26 DM25. Breakfast included. Sheets DM6. Reservations recommended, but the hostel offers floor space for a reduced rate if it's full.)

For decently priced private rooms, there's the *Gaststätte-Pension* **"Zum Tender,"** Bahnstr. 5 (tel. 41 39 36). It's far from the center and tricky to find. From the Lutherhalle, head north on Friedrichstr. and stick with it as it kinks right at the intersection with Sternstr. Turn right onto Bahnstr. and follow it all the way to a lot in the railyard overlooking the train station. A building with conspicuous beer signs in the front houses a friendly little *Kneipe.* Call a few days ahead. (Reception open 6-11pm, although it often remains open as long as the bar does. Singles DM35; doubles DM70.) While not centrally located, **Gästehaus Wolter,** Rheinsdorfer Weg 77 (tel. 41 25 78), sings sweet lullabies with its truly homey ambience—complete with playground, family dog, a grill for guests to use, sunny rooms with TV, and spotless bathrooms. Bus #302, 314, or 315: "Elbedruckerei," walk in the direction of the bus, take the first right, and finally veer right on Rheindorfer Weg. If this sounds confusing, call Frau Wolter and she will happily pick you up from town. (Reception open 24hr. Singles DM35; doubles DM70. Breakfast included.)

Food A number of delectable delights at low cost lie along the Colliegenstr.-Schloßstr. strip, and a **City-Kauf supermarket** waits across from Coswigerstr. 15, about 20m from the tourist office (open Mon.-Fri. 8am-6:30pm, Sat. 8am-12:30pm). **Bosphorus,** a Turkish restaurant at Collegienstr. 64, cooks up a filling, spicy *Döner Kebab* platter with a cucumber-tomato salad (DM10); tasty vegetarian entrees, like falafel (DM4) or mixed salad with tzatziki dressing and toasted *Fladenbrot* (DM5), provide a cheap respite from the tyranny of *Schnitzel* (open Mon.-Fri. 9am-10pm, Sat.-Sun. 11am-10pm). Get Guinness on tap and eat pub grub at the **Irish Harp Pub,** Collegienstr. 71, where live English and Irish folk and rock music rumbles on Saturdays (open daily 3pm-3am; cover DM5). Members of Wittenberg's artsy theater crowd occasionally burst into song or soliloquy at **Vis à Vis,** Sternstr. 14 (tel. 40 67 65), a cozy and alternative establishment close to the theater and the cinema. An almost entirely vegetarian menu with main courses around DM10, wine served by the glass, and beer, and tea specialities add flavor to the lively atmosphere. The staff occasionally puts up musical productions, and on the weekends local bands rock da hizzowse (open Mon.-Thurs. 3pm-1am, Fri.-Sat. 3pm-2am).

Sights The town's name does not function as a performative contradiction—the sights provide unending adulation of the eminently historical Luther. Plan your sightseeing around **Collegienstr.;** the street is less than 1.5km long and encompasses all of the major sights. At Collegienstr. 54 lies the (ingeniously named) **Lutherhaus** (tel. 40 26 71; fax 40 29 34), to which Martin moved in 1508. Inside the minister's rather posh digs is a museum that features lots of paintings analogizing Luther to geese; while the metaphor may seem strained (Luther was a dumpy man, not a goose), the representation is supposed to symbolize Luther's triumph in the face of the adversity he encountered in the fallout over his *95 Theses.* Nonetheless, you can see Luther's ground-breaking translation of the Bible, considered a model of the German language, an original **Gutenberg Bible,** and many angry responses to the feisty minister's theses. An obnoxious tourist's graffiti has also been preserved: Russian Czar Peter the Great scribbled his name above the door when he stopped by in 1702 (open April-Oct. Tues.-Sun. 9am-6pm; Oct.-April Tues.-Sun. 10am-5pm; DM6, students DM3). Turn right as you leave the Lutherhaus and stroll down Collegienstr. until you reach Lutherstr. to behold the sickly elm tree under which Luther defiantly burned a papal bull (a decree of excommunication, not a Catholic beast).

    Stadtkirche-St. Marienkirche, known for its dazzling altar painted by pharmacist-*cum*-hometown art genius **Lucas Cranach the Elder,** lies at the end of Mittelstr., near Collegienstr. at the Marktplatz. The interior is a blend of Protestant severity and Catholic adornments—it bears eloquent testimony to the iconoclastic tradition begun here in 1522 (open Mon.-Sat. 9am-noon and 2-5pm, Sun. 11am-noon and 2-5pm). Inside is another branch of the ever helpful Wittenberg **information** (open Tues.-Fri. 10am-4pm). Near the church, Wittenberg's **Rathaus** towers with an imposing facade. Matching statues of Luther and Melanchthon share the square with the **Jungfernröhrwasser** (fountain of virginity), a 16th-century well whose refreshing (and potable) waters still flow through original wooden pipes. The tourist office sells small bottles of this "water of innocence," actually filled with German *Schnapps.*

    Further down Collegienstr., the **Schloßkirche,** crowned by a sumptuous Baroque cupola, holds a copy of the complaints that Luther nailed to its doors. At the front of the church, the man who fought to translate the scriptures into the common man's tongue is interred, ironically, under a Latin plaque. Also featured are the graves of Wittenberg's other important dead folks: Prince Electors Friedrich the Wise and Johann the Steadfast, and Reformation hero Philip Melanchthon the non-adjectivally monikered. In the 1840s, it was arranged that 15 people would check and make sure that old Luther was really buried here. The crypt was opened in secret for fear that failure to find Luther would discredit the church (sort of like Geraldo and Al Capone's vaults). Happily they found the remains—or so they said. (Open May-Oct. Mon. 2-5pm, Tues.-Sat. 10am–5pm, Sun. 11:30am-5pm; Nov.-April Mon. 2-4pm, Tues.-Sat. 10am-4pm, Sun. 11am-4pm. Services Sun. at 9am.) At the top of the castle's enormous tower, you can digest the surrounding lands with pleasure (open Mon.-Fri. noon-3:30pm, Sat.-Sun. 10am-3:30pm; DM1, students DM0.50). Should the view excite your appetite for nature, take a bus from Mauerstr. (11 per day, almost hourly 4:45am-6:15pm) to the **Wörlitzer Park,** built by a local prince who wanted his quaint palace and Gothic house to be surrounded by exotic flora and fauna (open dawn to dusk).

■ Dessau

The postmodern philosopher *par excellence* Homer Simpson dismissed idealism by saying: "In theory Communism works—*in theory*." About 30km west of Wittenberg, Dessau, which houses the sleek Gropius-designed **Bauhaus art school,** suffers from the divide between theory and practice. For a brief period from 1925 to 1932, *Bauhaus* instructors Walter Gropius, Hannes Meyer, Lazlo Moholy-Nagy, and their students struggled with aesthetic representations of modernity and attempted to reconcile human living space with 20th-century industrialization. Ironically, today Dessau is home to some of the least successful building projects of recent memory, with row upon row of soulless GDR-era apartment blocks burdening the city streets.

The history of Dessau stretches back into antiquity. Founded as a medieval fortress in 1341, Dessau became one of the first German Renaissance settlements. With the backing of Princess Henrietta Catharina von Oranien, Dessau flourished as a thriving center of cultural and economic importance. It quickly evolved into a factory town during the late-blooming German Industrial Revolution. When the Nazis seized power in 1933, they transformed Dessau's factory infrastructure into a center for armament production. Dessau subsequently suffered massive damage in World War II—bombing destroyed nearly 80% of the inner town. Nevertheless, Dessau prides itself on a unique civic culture and its two major historical offspring. Moses Mendelssohn, one of the greatest German-Jewish philosophers and a fervent proponent of religious tolerance in the 19th century, lived in Dessau, as did the greatly admired modern composer Kurt Weill (1900-1950), whose critical theater created artistic resistance against Nazism. In effect, Weill's *Verfremdungseffekt* (alienation effect) makes its listeners feel drunk and confused. Every year (Feb. 28-March 3 in 1998), a **Kurt Weill Festival** alienates a new generation of fans with international artists performing his work in media as wide ranging as conventional musicals, big brass bands, chamber concerts, films, and lectures. (Tickets are available by phone ((0810) 321 35 35), fax ((0340) 250 54 10), or in writing to M&P GmbH, Antoinettenstr. 37, 06844 Dessau; DM10-60).

Orientation and Practical Information Hourly trains undertake the journey from Wittenburg (35min.) and Berlin (2hr.), while trains from Leipzig depart about every two hours (1hr.). The local **tourist office,** Zerbsterstr. 2c (tel. 204 14 12; streetcar #1 or 2 from the train station's main exit: "Post") sits across the street from the huge "Rathaus-Center" signs. Walk towards the center, and veer left on Ratsgasse. Take the first right; the office is on your left (open Mon.-Fri. 10am-7pm, Sat. 9:30am-12:30pm). They find rooms for a DM5 fee (DM30-75) and provide free city maps that fulfill all aesthetic expectations in the most organic of forms (some are shaped like *Bauhaus* buildings!). **Bicycle rentals** help navigate the scattered sights of the city and protect you from the perils of pedestrianism. **Fahrradverleih Dieter Becker und Sohn,** Coswigerstr. 7 (tel. 21 61 29), can make you an honorary Sprocket with rentals (4hr DM6, day DM 10-12; open Mon.-Fri. 9am-noon and 2-6pm, Sat. 9am-noon;). In an **emergency,** call 21 44 55. A corner of the restaurant at the Fürst-Leopold-Carée at the *Hauptbahnhof* side of Friedenpl. serves as an **internet cafe,** Friedrich-Schiller-Str. (tel. 251 52 57; fax 251 51 77; 30min. connection DM7, 1hr. DM12, 1½hr. DM16, and 2hr. DM20; prices include a cup of coffee or tea every 30min.). The **post office** is at the corner of Friedrichstr. and Kavalierstr. (open Mon.-Fri. 8am-6pm, Sat. 8am-noon). The **postal code** is 06844. The **telephone code** is 0340.

Accommodations and Food The **Jugendherberge (HI),** Waldkarterweg 11 (tel. 61 94 52), is a bit of a schlepp—a 20-minute winding trek from the train station. Exit from the smaller back entrance of the station (through the underground tunnel), make a left onto Rathenaustr. as you emerge, and follow it to the end; at the intersection zig-zag across and follow the main street (Kühnauerstr.) for about 10 minutes until you cross Kiefern Weg. About 50m further, a small path to your right (Waldkarterweg), marked by a pedestrian sign, will lead you straight to the woodsy entrance. The hostel, brimming with German school kids in the summer, is slightly sterile, but the surrounding residential area, close proximity to the Bauhaus and the Georgium park (10min. walk), well-lit common rooms, and a nourishing breakfast more than make up for it. (Check-in Mon.-Fri. 8-10am and 7-9pm, Sat.-Sun 5-8pm. No lockout. Check-out 9am. DM21, over 26 DM26. Sheets DM6. Breakfast included. Bike rental DM2 for the first hr., DM1 per each additional hr., DM10 per day.)

Affordable restaurants are difficult to come by in Dessau. The stunningly hip **Klub im Bauhaus,** in the *Bauhaus* school basement (tel. 650 84 84), is a delightful place to indulge in angsty pretense over a light meal. To feel like the coolest cat ever to walk the earth, order the **anarchisten Frühstück** (anarchist's breakfast) of a pot of coffee, some bread, and a *Karo* cigarette (DM4). For something less revolutionary, the spaghetti *al pesto spezial* (DM8) with pesto, feta cheese, and fresh tomatoes is enough savory food to make you wish they had doggie bags in Germany. The silver and black *Bauhaus* furniture and students flitting around with huge sketch pads complete the sensory experience (open Mon.-Fri. 8am-midnight, Sat. 10am-1am, Sun. 10am-5pm). The gleaming expanse of the newly built Rathaus-Center satisfies every craving for mall life, and the bakeries, produce stands, and **Tip supermarket** inside provide an easy end to the harrowing search for cheap eats downtown. (All open Mon.-Fri. 8am-8pm, Sat. 8am-4pm, Sun. 11am-6pm; most shops close on Sun.) Just off Kurt-Weill-Str., a 10-minute walk north of the tourist information center (turn right as you are leaving), **Kiez Café,** Bertolt-Brecht-Str. 29a (tel. 21 20 32 or 37; fax 21 20 38; email kiez@misa.uni-magdeburg.de; http://www.misa.uni-magdeburg.de/kiez/), is a good locale for a nightcap in the company of students. For the more ambitious, Kiez is a **one-stop-shop** for all your cultural needs in Dessau, offering a photo lab, theater productions, art studios, a cinema, bike rental, and **internet access.** Call for info and prices.

Sights The *Bauhaus* began in Weimar in 1919, but the conservative local oligarchy pressured it to leave. The school toted its theory of constructive and artistic unity to Dessau in 1925; in 1932 the school fled yet again to the more brash Berlin before being exiled from the country in 1933 by the Nazis. Despite the necessity of remaining itinerant to avoid total dissolution, the *Bauhaus* masters inspired an architectural renaissance that attained its aesthetic zenith with the sleek skyscrapers of America's metropoli. After the war, as Dessau rebuilt, city planners perversely translated the shapely *Bauhaus* legacy into building-block-shaped monotony. Since 1977, the **Bauhaus,** Gropiusallee 38 (tel. 650 82 50; fax 650 82 26), has housed a design school for international architecture. The school currently decorates its sparsely linear walls with the works of legendary *Bauhausmeisters* Gropius, Klee, Kandinsky, Geinger, and Brandt. To get there from the station, turn left and go up the steps, then head left over the railroad tracks. Veer left at the first street onto Kleiststr., then right onto Bauhausstr. (The building is open for a free self-guided tour daily 24hr. and there are rotating exhibits on *Bauhaus* themes; exhibit open Tues.-Sun. 10am-5pm. Last entry 4:30pm. DM4, students and seniors DM2.) Turning left from the Bauhaus entrance, right on Gropiusallee, and left on Ebertallee, brings you to the **Kurt Weill Zentrum,** Ebertallee 63 (tel./fax 61 95 95), located in the former house of designer and painter Lyonel Feininger amidst the famous Bauhaus **Meisterhäuser.** Bau-haus, is a very very very fine Haus. The center has been restored to its original splendor, thus providing lucid insight into the school's musings. Occasional concerts celebrate the wacky Weill (open Tues.-Fri. 10am-5pm, Sat.-Sun. noon-5pm; DM5, students DM3).

On the other side of the intersection of Puschkinallee and Kleiststr., a short walk through the garden, squats the **Schloß Georgium,** home to the **Anhaltische Gemäldegalerie** (tel. 61 38 74). Set in the midst of carefully tended formal gardens, this 17th-century country estate displays a range of lesser-known Old Masters' paintings from the 16th to the 19th century. The tired exterior encases a couple of Lucas Cranach the Elder's star paintings (open Tues.-Sun. 10am-5pm; DM5, students and seniors DM3; gardens open daily 24hr.). The **Rococo-Schloß Mosigkan,** on Knobelsdorfallee (tel. 52 11 81), about 20 minutes by bus from central Dessau, is an historic castle built in 1752 as a summer hangout for the Princess Anna Wilhelmine. Furnished in opulent Baroque style, the castle displays works by such masters as Rubens and van Dyck. For the botanist brewing in us all, there are 100-year-old plants in the surrounding gardens. Bus D or L (direction: "Kochstedt"): "Schloß Mosigkan" (every 30min. from the main train/bus station; avoid the 2-3 D buses that *don't* go all the way to the *Schloß*). (Open May-Sept. Tues.-Sun. 10am-8pm; Nov.-March Tues.-Sun. 10am-4pm; April and Oct. Tues.-Sun. 10am-5pm. Admission DM5, students and seniors DM3.50.)

If Dessau really floats your boat, then visit the **Museum für Stadtgeschichte,** Wolfgangstr. 13 (tel. 21 29 13). Opened after the *Wende*, the museum is located on the third floor of Dessau's *Volkshochschule*. A central room hosts changing exhibitions focusing on Dessau's regional history and contemporary political, historical, and cultural concerns in rather offbeat ways. On the way up to the museum, traverse the 75-year-old *Volkshochschule* building—catch a glimpse of socialist school life. Classes are still held here. (Museum open Mon. 9am-4:30pm, Tues.-Wed. 9am-7pm, Thurs.-Fri. 9am-2pm, Sat. 11am-3pm, Sun. 11am-5pm. DM5, students and seniors DM1.50.)

■ Halle

Halle an der Salle, the town saved by Katrin's drumming in the climactic scene of Brecht's *Mother Courage*, emerged from World War II relatively unscathed, although sometimes it's hard to tell in the dull physical landscape. Three months after the war came to a close, occupying Americans swapped Halle for a bit of Berlin under the terms of the Yalta agreement, and in the post-war decades, it served as Sachsen-Anhalt's political and industrial capital. Although several thousands have lost their jobs since reunification, adding a grim edge to the urban outlook, efforts are being made to salvage Halle's former beauty from the cascade of gray that dominates its streets. While the *Neustadt,* an immense, shoddily constructed district of housing projects built under the Communist regime, stands untouched by capitalist evolution, the *Altstadt* boasts a few sites of historic beauty set amid the crumbling vestiges of socialism. The Moritzburg Fortress, with its meager but well-chosen offerings of 20th-century avant-garde art, the lively university culture, and the contemporary theater scene all help Halle to push toward the future.

Orientation and Practical Information Halle is divided into several town sectors; most significant are the GDR-style Halle **Neustadt** and the historical **Altstadt,** separated by the scenic Saale River. Come nightfall, *Neustadt* is not so secure, as political extremists (both right and left) reportedly roam this area. The train station and major streetcar lines run predominantly through the *Altstadt*. If you haven't come to see the dingy and gray GDR-era housing, stick with the safer, brighter *Altstadt* areas—you'll still get your share.

Though most of Halle is walkable, the streetcar system efficiently covers the town (single ticket DM2.50, day pass DM7). To reach the *Neustadt*, take the bus. The S-Bahn system is easy to use, and all stops are clearly marked. The main street is Große Ulrichstr.; as you move away from the Marktplatz, it becomes Geiststr., then Bernburgerstr. With the cold war a thing of the past, Lenin and Honecker Streets and Squares have been replaced by *Freiheit* (Freedom) and *Geist* (Spirit) Boulevards.

The **tourist office** is in the *Roter Turm* (tel. 202 33 40; room-finding service tel. 202 83 71; fax 50 27 98), on the Marktplatz. From the main station, leave from the E.-Karieth-Str. exit and head right to buses, streetcars, and the pedestrian tunnel to town. Follow the pedestrian tunnel to a left on Leipzigerstr. and past the *Leipziger Turm* to the Marktplatz (15min.). Or streetcar #4 (direction: "Heide/Hubertuspl.") or 7 (direction: "Kröllwitz"): "Markt" (four stops). The office hands out city maps, sells tickets, offers a number of pamphlets on cultural events around Halle, and finds rooms (DM35-50, with shower from DM50) for a DM5 fee. (Open Mon.-Tues. and Thurs.-Fri. 9am-6pm, Wed. 10am-6pm, Sat. 9am-1pm; April-Sept. also Sun. 10am-2pm.) **Tours,** leaving from the Marktplatz, vary in historical theme. (Tours offered May-Oct. and Nov.-April Mon.-Sat. 2pm; DM8.50, students and seniors DM5.) You can **exchange money** at several banks near the Marktplatz, including **Dresdner Bank,** which has a 24hr. ATM (open Mon.-Wed. 8:30am-4:30pm, Thurs. 8:30am-5:30pm, Fri. 8:30am-4pm). A **Mitfahrzentrale** at R.-Paulick-Str. 5 (tel. 202 44 26) arranges ride shares. The **Weiberwirtschaft women's agency,** Robert-Franz-Ring 22 (tel. 202 43 31), complements the usual meetings and lectures with a *Frauencafe* that's co-ed on Wednesdays and Fridays (office open Mon.-Fri. 9am-4pm; cafe open Mon.-Tues. and Thurs.-Fri. 4pm-midnight). For advice on all things queer, **AIDS-Hilfe Halle,** Magdeburgerstr. 34 (tel. 23 09 00 or 19 411) can help. Halle's **post office** is at the corner of Hansering and Große Steinstr., 5min. from the Marktplatz (open Mon.-Fri. 8am-8pm, Sat. 9am-noon). The **postal code** is 06108. The **telephone code is** 0345.

Accommodations Hotels and *Pensionen* are generally far above the budgetary means of simple traveling folk (most singles start at DM100), but the tourist office lists **private rooms.** Halle's **Jugendherberge (HI),** August-Bebel-Str. 48a (tel./fax 202 47 16), rests in a newly restored mansion north of the market. The quiet residential location and hardwood elegance of the common areas enhance the sublime feeling of youth hostel high-life. Streetcar #7 (direction: "Kröllwitz"): "Geiststr.," two stops from the Markt. Follow Geiststr. one block, turn right onto Puschkinstr., and then right onto August-Bebel-Str. at the Hong Kong restaurant. Walk two blocks down; the hostel is on your left. 72 beds. (Reception open 7-10am and 5-11pm, but someone is usually there during the day. Call ahead. Curfew 11pm. DM23, over 26 DM28. Breakfast included, dinner DM7. Sheets DM6.)

Food Affordable sit-down restaurants are a difficult find in this town, but coffeehouses, ice cream parlors, and cafes line Leipzigerstr. and the Marktplatz. Between the Marktplatz and Moritzburg crouch cafes, catering to a young and lively student crowd. And when you get sick of circling the Marktplatz, dive right into its center for one big market and what looks like a little slice of *Imbiß* heaven—heaven? (Markt vendors sell Mon.-Fri. 9am-6pm, Sat. 9am-1pm.) Halle also boasts several outdoor markets and cheap **supermarkets. EDEKA-neukauf** is on Große Ulrichstr., about two blocks from the Marktplatz on the left side of the street, and on Leipzigerstr., approximately one block from the train station (both open Mon.-Fri. 8am-8pm, Sat. 8am-4pm). **Cafe Nöö,** Große Klausstr. 11, at the end of the street facing Domstr., is far töö green-tinted cööl to say nö to. Occupying the ground floor of an entire building filled with social change and environmental groups, the cafe serves cheap breakfast (DM3.90-5.90, with coffee DM8.50) and an updated daily international menu that allows you forget the evils of the world for a while. Vote Green! Salad and spaghetti DM4-8. Ask here for concert info, and read the newspaper *Queer* (open Mon.-Thurs.

8am-1am, Fri. 8am-2am, Sat. 4:30pm-2am, Sun. 4:30pm-1am). At **Café Unikum,** Universitätsring 23 (tel. 202 13 03), there's serious hipster *Uni*-action amidst smoke and modern art. On the menu are cheap salads, sandwiches, and daily specials (DM4.50-10), including baked potato with *tzaziki* sauce and olives (DM5.50; open Mon.-Fri. 8am-midnight, Sat. 4pm-midnight, Sun. 10am-2pm). Local flavor suffers an identity crisis at **Zur Apotheke,** Mühlberg 4a, off Mühlgasse between the *Dom* and Moritzburg Fortress, with Thüringer morsels served in Sachsen-Anhalt (DM5.50-10; open Mon.-Thurs. 8:30am-1am, Fri. 8:30am-2am, Sat. 5pm-2am, Sun. 5pm-1am).

Sights Central Halle revolves around the **Marktplatz,** which bustles with traffic, vegetable stands, and three-card monte con-artists. At its center stands the **Roter Turm,** a 400-year-old bell tower. A number of popular myths surround the origin of the tower's name; some credit the copper roof, while others say the architect was a Herr Rote—what about the *Parrote?* The most gruesome version relates that after it was built (1418-1506), the blood of the people being executed on the adjoining gallows splattered onto the tower, lending it a grisly tinge (tower interior closed to the public, except for the historically insignificant tourist office). Across from the tower lies the **Marktkirche Unsere Lieben Frauen,** whose altar is adorned with a triptych painted by students under the direction of Lucas Cranach. Above the altar swings the organ on which Händel began his musical studies—the organ was silent for over 100 years until recent renovations. (Open Mon.-Fri. 10am-noon and 3-6pm, Wed. 3-4pm, Sat. 9am-noon and 3-5pm. Sun. services 10am. Free 30min. organ concerts Tues. and Thurs. 4:30pm.) The 16th-century **Marktschlößchen,** an unassuming, rather small castle, overlooks the Marktplatz. Inside, you can find the **Galerie Marktschlößchen,** Markt 13 (tel. 202 91 41). Wander these galleries free of charge to see the works of lesser-known contemporary European artists (open Mon.-Fri. 10am-7pm, Sat.-Sun. 10am-6pm). The second floor houses the **Musikinstrumentensammlung des Händel-Hauses** (musical instrument collection of Händel's House), with an impressive collection of keyboard instruments, as well as three majestic music boxes on display (open Wed.-Sun. 1:30-5:30pm; DM2, students DM1, Thurs. free.)

An 1859 centennial memorial to composer Georg Friedrich Händel decorates the Marktplatz, but the most important Händel shrine remains his familial home. The outstanding **Händelhaus,** Große Nikolaistr. 5-6 (tel. 50 09 00; fax 50 09 04 11), is only a short walk from the market down Kleine Klausstr. They offer soundtracks with voice-overs in 20 languages to guide pilgrims through the composer's career in Germany, Italy, and England. (Open Mon.-Wed. and Fri.-Sun. 9:30am-5:30pm, Thurs. 9:30am-7pm; DM4, seniors and students DM2, Thurs. free.) June 4-9, 1998 witnesses the annual **Händel-Festspiele,** a celebration of Baroque music and one of its masters. Tickets are available from the tourist office. From Händel's home, the **Dom** is a five-minute walk down Nikolaistr. This ancient complex, begun in 1250, remains a significant repository of religious relics. Today the church's most treasured offerings, renovations permitting, are 17 life-size figures by Peter Schroh from the 16th century (open irregularly during renovations; check signs outside for hours).

To reach the white-washed **Moritzburg Fortress,** go around the far side of the *Dom* and head downhill, then turn right on Schloßburgstr. and walk up the hill. Most of this 15th-century giant is dedicated to the **Staatliche Galerie Moritzburg Halle** (tel. 281 20 10; fax 202 99 90). The largest art museum in Sachsen-Anhalt, it focuses mostly on 19th- and 20th-century German painters. Halle's once extensive Expressionist collection—including works by Max Beckmann, Paul Klee, Edvard Munch, and Oskar Kokoschka—offended Hitler, who drew heavily from this museum to furnish the infamous exhibit of "degenerate art" that toured Nazi Germany. Although much of the collection was either burnt or sold off by the Nazis, the salvaged works remain an impressive monument to artistic freedom. Lyonel Feininger, *Bauhaus* master and Expressionist painter, lived part-time in the tower at the entrance from 1929-31 while completing his series of paintings of Halle; two still remain in the museum. (Open Tues. 11am-8:30pm, Wed.-Fri. 10am-5:30pm, Sat.-Sun. 10am-6pm; last entry 30min. before closing. DM5, students DM3, Tues. free.)

SACHSEN-ANHALT

Entertainment and Nightlife Halle's swiftly growing theater scene produce the Classics and German contemporary plays. Near the University and around the Moritzburg Turm, you'll find entertainment and gastronomical pleasures. Halle hosts a number of organ concerts in the **Konzerthalle** (affectionately referred to as "Konzert Halle" by the locals), Kleine Brauhausstr. 26 (tel. 202 89 36; tickets on sale Tues.-Thurs. 10am-1pm and 3-6pm, Wed.-Fri. 10am-1pm). To remain on top of Halle's groovin' nightlife, pick up free copies of the **city magazines** *Fritz* and *Blitz* at the tourist office or in cafes and bars.

Completed in 1990, the **neues theater,** Große Ulrichstr. 50 (tel. 205 02 22), features works of a wide palate—everything from Schiller, Shakespeare, Moliere, and Brecht to Halle's own homegrown playwrights. (Orchestra tickets DM15, all others DM10-12.50. Students and seniors 50% off. Box office open on days of performance Mon.-Fri. 8am-8:30pm, Sat. 10am-1pm, Sun. 4-8:30pm; mid-July to Sept. usually no performances.) Halle's satirical theater, **Die Kiebitzensteiner,** in the Moritzburg Turm's South Tower (for tickets tel. 202 39 81), is tucked beneath the fortress and serves as a contemporary forum for criticism, holding spicy and engaging performances, often as benefits for current noble causes. The downstairs restaurant **Kiebitzkeller** offers snacks and spirits for nightly performances. (Theater open Tues.-Sat. from 7pm on. Ticket office open Tues.-Sat. 5-8pm and 1hr. before shows. Restaurant opens at 6pm on evenings of performances.) **Kleines Thalia Theater,** on Thaliapassage (tel. 20 40 50; fax 202 43 57; http://www.halle-online.de/kultur/thalia), off of Geiststr., premiers avant-garde theater productions as well as kiddy performances. (Box office open Tues. and Fri. 10am-noon and 1-4pm, Wed. 10am-noon, Thurs. 10am-noon and 1-6pm. DM12, children and students DM7.) **Turm,** in the northeast tower of the Moritzburg Turm (office tel. 202 51 90, club tel. 202 37 57), hosts the city's *Studentenklub* for the music-loving and grooving literary set in Halle. The music is a mishmash of disco, punk, funk, blues, techno, and rock performed by local bands. A *Biergarten* and grill are outside (open 6-10pm). Foreign students with ID (18 and over) are welcome. (Open Sun., Tues., and sometimes Thurs. from 8:30pm; disco Wed. and Fri.-Sat. from 9pm.) **Pierrot,** Großer Sandberg 10, just off Leipzigerstr., is a popular gay bar and disco (open daily after 5pm; disco open Wed. and Fri.-Sat. after 10pm. Cover Wed. DM3, Fri.-Sat. DM6.) that alternates with **Zoom,** Rudolf-Breitscheid-Str. 92, as the queer hot spot.

■ Harz Mountains

Heinrich Heine wrote that even Mephistopheles stopped and trembled when he approached the Harz, the devil's dearest mountains. It's easy to see why Heine—as well as Goethe, Bismarck, and a host of others—fell in love with these mist-shrouded woodlands. Germany's 45-year political division allowed the Harz Mountains to flourish in an artificial time warp. Since the region straddled the Iron Curtain, both East and West declared much of it off-limits, sparing its natural gifts from development.

Now that the armed border guards have gone, visitors have taken their places and multiplied like mosquitoes; hikers and spa-tourists alike incline to these misty, rugged hills in the heart of the restored nation. The range stretches from the northwestern **Oberharz** to the wind-sheltered, mineral-rich valleys of the south and Wernigerode in the east. All through the Harz, historic villages compete with the lush natural beauty of the mountains and valleys. In summer, the foliage offers great biking and striking hiking. In June, the mountains' famed cherries, *Harzkirschen,* are in season on both sides of the former political division. With the first snow, the terrain becomes a splendid winter playground for skiing, skating, and tobogganing. The **Ostharz,** untouched by the transforming winds of capitalism, is endowed with gorgeous scenery and stubborn, half-abandoned castles. The **Harzquerbahn** and **Brockenbahn,** antique, narrow-gauge railways, steam through gorgeous Harz scenery from Nordhausen to **Wernigerode,** passing through the unfortunately named towns of **Sorge** and **Elend** (Sorrow and Misery) and reaching a 540m peak on **Drei-Annen-Hohne.**

The easiest means of traveling between the Ostharz and Oberharz is by the new **bus** lines between Bad Harzburg and Wernigerode which restore the region's common identity. But who says it's the best? A more strenuous and interesting way involves a little jaunt through the woods. Torfhaus, Braunlage, Schierke, Elend, and Drei-Annen-Hohne all lie within a day's hike of one another. In the Ostharz, **Nordhausen** is technically in Thüringen, but touristically relevant as the *Harzquerbahn* terminus. **Nordhausen Information,** Bahnhofspl. 3a (tel. (03631) 38 25) books rooms. The **regional tourist office** in Goslar (p. 281) and the **regional bus station** in Wernigerode offer a wealth of information for navigating the region. Pick up a copy of the *Fahrplan der Verkehrs und Tarifgemeinsschaft Ostharz* (DM3) to get a comprehensive list of bus and rail lines in the Ostharz. From the main Wernigerode *Bahnhof,* the end of the *Querbahn,* it is a short trek to the regional bus station, whose routes extend like tentacles throughout the Ostharz and provide a convenient means of reaching small mountain towns. The **Harzer Schmalspurbahnen information line** (tel. (039485) 624 23) provides info about Ostharz trains. When in the Harz, always be prepared for bad weather, especially sudden and violent rainstorms. Travelers should call the **Braunlage Wetterstation** at (05520) 13 20 for summertime (April-Oct.) weather conditions (open 5:30am-11pm). During the winter months (Nov.-March), contact the **Schnee Telefon in Goslar** at (05321) 34 04 44 or 200 24.

If possible, dive into the Harz to join in the immense regional celebration of **Walpurgisnacht.** The April 30th hedonistic festivities, immortalized by Goethe, center around legendary **witches** who sweep through the sky on broomsticks to land on **Brocken,** the Harz's highest peak. The legendary witches dance with the devil until midnight, at which point the May King cleans house. For more on regional sorcery, see **Raising Hell! Witchcraft in the Harz,** p. 221.

BAD HARZBURG

The train from Hannover to the mountains ends at the Bad Harzburg *Bahnhof,* 10 minutes past Goslar. The ruins of the imperial castle of Harzburg loom from the hills above, but there isn't much left—just flat piles of stones. Indeed, it may well be the building with some of the worst luck of all time. Built in 1065 by Heinrich IV, a stipulation in the Peace of Gerstugen forced him to destroy it a mere nine years later. In 1215, Kaiser Otto IV hiked up the hill, saw the castle, and died. In 1574, Herzog Julius commenced an ambitious renovation project, but, alas, ran out of *Geld.* Sadly enough, even today Bad Harzburg has little to offer, save good bus connections to greener pastures. The in-town highlight is the **Märchenwald,** a melancholic "fairy-tale forest" with mechanically animated scenes from the Brothers Grimm's fables and shining, smily gnomes (open daily 9am-6pm; DM4, Hänsel and Gretel DM3). In Bad Harzburg's favor, there are plenty of ways to escape the town—get a pair of boots, a backpack, and muster the energy required to scale the gentle, pine-covered hills along the marked hiking routes. The town serves as a gateway to the **Harz National Park;** the rangers at the **Haus der Natur** (tel./fax 17 74), a few steps towards town from the *Bergbahn,* will tell you all about the wonders of the wild (open daily 10am-5pm). Trains connect Bad Harzburg to Wernigerode and Halberstadt in the Ostharz.

The **tourist office** (tel./fax 29 27) to the left of the station will find rooms (DM30-50) for a DM5 fee (open Mon.-Fri. 9am-1pm and 3-6pm, Sat. 10am-1pm). **Deutsche Bank,** at the start of pedestrian zone, provides **currency exchange.** (Open Mon. 8am-1pm and 2-4:30pm, Tues. and Thurs. 8:30am-1pm and 2-6pm, Wed. 8:30am-1pm, Fri. 8:30am-1pm and 2-3:30pm.) The **post office,** 38667 Bad Harzburg, is next door in the **pedestrian zone** where Bummel Allee meets Herzog-Wilhelm-Str. (open Mon.-Fri. 8am-12:30pm and 2:30-5:30pm, Sat. 8:30am-noon). Take in some spectacular treetop scenery with the **Bergbahn,** located at the end of the pedestrian zone. Hauling skiers in the winter and snap-shooting tourists in the summer, this cable car runs up the Burgberg every 15 minutes to a whopping 482m above sea level (DM4 to go up, DM3 to come down, DM6 round-trip; open mid-Dec. to mid-Nov.). Once on top, you can scope out the defunct castle and the stern black 1877 obelisk (dedicated to Bismarck) at the main viewpoint. The **telephone code** is 05322.

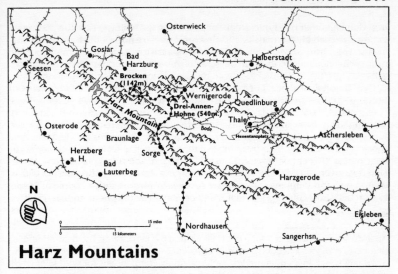

Harz Mountains

A retreat owned by the "Naturfreunde" society, **Braunschweiger Haus,** Waldstr. 5 (tel. 45 82; fax 18 76), doubles as Bad Harzburg's **Jugendherberge.** From the station, bus #73: "Lärchenweg" (the bus drives in two rings around the town and may not hit Lärchenweg until the second go-round), then take Im Bleichental to Waldstr. and go up the stone steps at the "Naturfreunde" sign. On foot, head right from the station to Silberbornstr. and follow its curves uphill to Im Bleichental (about 35min.); follow the above directions to the mountainside complex. A quintessential "cabin camp" feel. (Reception open 9am-7pm. DM25, ages 12-18 DM20.50. Nonmembers DM29, ages 12-18 DM26. Breakfast included. Sheets DM7. Call ahead.) The bus to Goslar only stops at **Campingplatz Göttingerode** (tel. 812 15) if you ask the driver ahead of time. At the stop, head left. All the modern amenities: pool, sauna, hot showers, solarium, restaurant. (DM9 per tent, DM7 per person. Call ahead. Closed Dec. 16-26.)

There is a cheap, well-stocked **Mini Mall supermarket** to the right of the train station (open Mon.-Fri. 9am-6:30pm, Sat. 8am-1pm); people heading to Torfhaus and trails beyond should pick up food and camping supplies here or in the pedestrian zone, because none can be found in Torfhaus. A mountain-produce **market** appears in the park at Herzog-Julius-Str. and Schmiedstr. (open Thurs. 8am-1pm). Vegephobic Germans arrive later at the cleverly named **Biergarten,** also in the market (tel. 62 30), to watch the vendors over a *Reichelbräu* (DM2.80) and a pair of Bavarian *Weißwürstchen* with sweet mustard and potato salad (DM5). (Open April-Nov. daily 10:30am-10pm; Nov.-April Tues.-Sun. 10:30am-6pm.) To quench the travel-induced thirst, head right from Biergarten to the 19th-century **Trinkhalle** to guzzle any of a surprising variety of waters from a selection of Bad Harzburg's finest springs (DM0.50 a glass; open Mon.-Fri. 8am-3pm, Sat.-Sun. 8am-noon).

TORFHAUS

When Goethe began his first hike to the peak of the **Brocken mountain** in 1777, **Torfhaus** was nothing more than his launching point; nothing much has changed since then. The town, a humble crossroads 3km from the former inter-German border, offers worldly sophisticates little more than an airy mountain hostel, near-perfect hiking trails, and, at 1142m, the Harz's highest mountain. Buses arrive in Torfhaus from Bad Harzburg (20min.; DM4.70) and Braunlage (20min.; DM4.50) every 90 minutes (Mon.-Fri. 7:45am-9pm). A left turn at the "Altenau-8km" sign will take you to the **Goetheweg;** the 16km path to Brocken's peak (6hr. there and back) hops the stream that used to divide Germany and occasionally follows the old patrol road along the

Iron Curtain. About two hours from Torfhaus along the trail, you can stop and check out the **Brocken Museum** inside the **electronic warfare post** of the former East German state security service. The **Brockenbahn,** a narrow-gauge train, runs from the peak of the mountain to the Ostharz; scramble up and slide down the other side into Schierke, or chug to Wernigerode with the connecting **Harz Schmalspurbahn.**

The **Nationalparkhaus Torfhaus,** Torfhaus 21 (tel./fax 263), provides maps of Brocken's trails (open daily 9am-5pm). **Ski-Verlieh,** near the bus stop, rents cross-country skis for DM20 per day (open daily 8am-5pm when snow adorns the ground). Walking away from Bad Harzburg, turn right at the "Altenau-8km" sign for the **Jugendherberge (HI),** Torfhaus 3 (tel. 242; fax 254). The rooms are designated by species of avian rather than by number. Proprietors will guide non-ornithologists to their rooms. (Reception open 8:15-9am, 12:15-1pm, and 6:15-7pm. Curfew 10pm. DM22.30, over 26 DM27.30. HI members only. Various levels of breakfast available; the top one, the strapping *"Öberharzer Brockenfrühstuck"* adds a couple of *Mark*s to your bill. Cross-country ski rental DM10 per day.) The **telephone code** is 05320.

BRAUNLAGE

An ideal stop for hikers working the trails around the fantabulous Brocken mountain, Braunlage provides a needed rest from other excessively cute Harz villages. What the town might lack in architectural panache, it amply compensates for with kilometers and kilometers of excellent trails and the luxury of an ice-skating rink, as well as spas at backpacker prices. Braunlage is also a likely bus stop for those traveling from the Oberharz in the West to the Ostharz.

The **Wurnbergseilbahn** open-air chairlift provides an exhilarating means of approaching the hiking paths around Braunlage. In the summer, the open-air lift flies above the trees to two different stations on the Wurnberg as the wind energizes passengers for a quick jaunt to the **Brocken** (2½hr. from the Bergstation) or **Schierke** (1½hr. from Mittelstation). The lift departs from the mountain base at the huge parking lot behind the ice rink; from the tourist office, turn left, then take the first right to its end. (Open May-Oct. 9am-5pm. One-way to Bergstation DM8, round-trip DM13; to Mittelstation DM5, DM8; DM0.50-2 extra for more sedate closed cabins.) When winter hits, the appeal of the open-air cabins diminishes, as everyone cowers inside the closed lifts on their way back up the slopes. (Open Dec.-Jan. 8:45am-4:15pm; Feb.-April 9am-4:45pm. 5 one-way stops in open cabin DM18, closed cabin DM20, day pass for open cabins and other ski lifts DM32, closed cabins and lifts DM35.) **Skis** and **boots** are rented at the cafe **Zur Seilbahn** (tel. 600; open daily 9am-5pm; DM20 per day). An **Eisstadion** (ice rink; tel. 21 91) on Harzburgerstr. fulfills the need for winter sports year-round. (2hr. DM5, skate rental DM4.50. Open Mon. 10am-noon and 2-4pm, Tues. and Thurs.-Fri. 10am-noon, 2-4pm, and 5-7pm, Wed. and Sat. 10am-noon, 2-4pm, and 8-10pm, Sun. 10am-noon, 1:30-3:30pm, and 4-6pm.) The **Kurmittelhaus,** Ramsenweg 2 (tel. 22 41), and the adjacent **Hallen- und Freizeitbad** (tel. 27 88) soak, steam, massage, and mud-pack the weary into a clean and relaxed state of mind and body. (Sauna open Mon.-Fri. 9am-12:30pm and 2-6:30pm, Sat. 9am-6:30pm, Sun. 9am-5pm. DM15 with 3hr. of swimming. Pool open Mon., Wed., and Fri. 7-8am, 9am-12:30pm, and 2-6:30pm, Tues. 9am-12:30pm and 2-6:30pm, Thurs. 9am-12:30pm and 2-8:30pm, Sat. 9am-6:30pm, Sun. 9am-5pm. 3hr. swimming DM9.)

Buses cruise from Bad Harzburg (40min.; DM8.30) and Torfhaus (20min.; DM3.60) to Braunlage. Disembark at the "Von-Langen-Str." stop to land in the center of town. The **Altenhöner-Reisedienst travel office,** Bismarckstr. 37 (tel. 10 74; fax 10 48), finds private rooms (from DM20) and happily details transportation connections (open Mon.-Tues. and Thurs.-Fri. 9am-12:30pm and 3-6pm, Sat. 10am-noon).

The view through the wall of windows in the dining room of Braunlage's **Jugendherberge (HI),** Von-Langen-Str. 28 (tel. 22 38; fax 15 69), provides reason enough to crash in its ideal location. It's real popular with the kids—the hostel often fills with school groups and single travelers, so call ahead. From the bus stop, follow Von-Langen-Str. uphill for about 15 minutes (reception open noon-10pm; DM23, over 26 DM28. Breakfast and *Kurtaxe* included. Sheets DM6.) A **Penny Markt,** Marktstr. 22, fulfills your grocery needs for long hikes (open Mon.-Fri. 8am-7pm, Sat. 8am-2pm). **Rhodos,** Elbingeröderstr. 3 (tel. 22 23), heaps yer plates with Greek specialties (DM10-15) and pizzas (DM8.50-13.50; open 11:30am-3pm, 5pm-midnight).

WERNIGERODE

Wernigerode was one of Goethe's secret spots in the hills, and in some ways, it's still the same small town he visited on trips through the Harz, packed with half-timbered houses and crowned with the cool stone of a magnificent hilltop castle. This *Bergstadt* (mountain city) is a well-preserved, well-worth-it destination for riders of the **Querbahn.** Wernigerode is the natural crossing-over point from Western to Eastern Harz, establishing it as the region's most-touristed town. Recently, the town has employed a cosmopolitan artifice in an effort to increase tourism, and the subsequent flood of visitors constantly pushes prices up in the picturesque *Stadt.*

Wernigerode's **Schloß** (tel. 50 03 96; fax 50 03 99), on its looming perch in the wooded mountains above town, is a plush and pompous monument to the Second Reich. Though the place was maintained by the GDR as a museum of feudalism, its guiding spirit was much more recent. Graf Otto, one of Bismarck's main flunkies, hosted Kaiser Wilhelm I here for wildly extravagant hunting expeditions. The perfectly preserved **Königszimmer** guest suite, where the Kaiser stayed, oozes inbred, masculine luxury down to the deep green and gold brocaded wallpaper in the bedroom. The other regal rooms include a chapel, two drawing rooms, and the jaw-dropping *Festsaal* (dining hall) featuring a sky-high inlaid wooden ceiling, panoramic murals of glorious Teutonic dukes, and the heaped wealth of the ducal table service. Outside on the flower-trimmed terrace, cannons are still poised in defense, and a fountain is angled to catch the sun; from here, you can see straight to the peak of the **Brocken,** the Harz's highest and supposedly most haunted mountain. (Castle open May-Oct. daily 10am-6pm; Nov. Sat. and Sun. 10am-6pm; Dec.-April Tues.-Sun. 10am-6pm. Last entry 5pm. DM7, students DM6, under 14 DM3; add DM1 for a tour.) Ride up to the *Schloß* on the bumpy **Bimmelbahn,** a train-truck that leaves from the clock at the intersection of Teichdamm and Klintgasse behind the *Rathaus.* (May-Oct. 9:30am-5:30pm Mon.-Sat. every 20min., Sun. every 40min.; Nov.-April 10:30am-4:30pm every 45min. daily 10:30am-4:30pm. One-way DM3, under 10 DM2.) To walk it, take the gravel *Christiantalweg* path or follow the white brick road marked "Burgberg," and ascend the wooded park to the castle (20min. from town center).

Back in town, the newly renovated **Rathaus** looms over the *Fachwerk* (half-timber) madness. The colorful town hall dominates the Marktplatz with its steep spire and sharply pitched roof. Small figurines of saints, virgins, miners, and other Wernigerode notables decorate the facade of the 500-year-old building. The **Krummelsche Haus,** Breitestr. 72, is so completely covered with ornate wood carvings that the original *Fachwerk* is hardly visible. The **Älteste Haus,** Hinterstr. 48, is the oldest house in the city, having survived fires, bombs, and various acts of God since its construction in the early 15th century. The **Normalste Haus,** Witzestr. 13, has no distinguishing traits. The **Kleinste Haus,** Kochstr. 43, is 2.95m wide, 4.2m to the eaves—and for the diminutive, the door is only 1.7m high (DM1; open daily 10am-4pm).

Wernigerode's busy **tourist office,** Nikolaipl. 1 (tel. 194 33; fax 63 20 40), around the corner from the *Rathaus,* books rooms in private homes or hotels (DM30-40) for a 10% commission (open May-Oct. Mon.-Fri. 9am-7pm, Sat.-Sun. 9am-3pm; Oct.-April Mon.-Fri. 9am-6pm, Sat.-Sun. 9am-3pm). It also sells a small town guide with an excellent pull-out map (DM3)—if your wallet is on a diet, ask for the free map. **Tours** leave the tourist office Tues. and Sat. at 10:30am, Wed., Thurs., and Sun. at 2pm. To reach Wernigerode from Magdeburg, change trains at Halberstadt (18 per day, 30min.); trains also run directly from Halle (10 per day, 2hr.); and a bus travels from Bad Harzburg. The town has two **train stations** that serve its 37,000 citizens. **Wernigerode-Westentor** is the next-to-last stop on the *Harzquerbahn* and close to the city center—just head up Mittelstr., and then right on Bahnhofstr. to arrive at the Markt. The antique steamer also stops at the main **Bahnhof Wernigerode,** next to the regional **bus terminal** (see p. 215). To get to the Marktplatz and the tourist office

SACHSEN-ANHALT

from the *Bahnhof,* take a right on Schreiberstr., another right on Bahnhofstr., follow it as it becomes G.-Petri-Str. which leads directly to the *Altstadt* (15min.). **H. J. Haller-man,** located in the alcove above Breitestr. 27 (tel. 63 25 08), offers street and mountain **bike rentals** (day DM10-15) for roughshod running over Goethe's walking paths (open Mon.-Fri. 9:30am-12:30pm and 1:30-6pm, Sat. 9:30am-noon). **Exchange currency** and mail cards at the **post office,** Marktstr. 14, 38855 Wernigerode (open Mon.-Fri. 8:30am-1pm and 2-5:30pm, Sat. 8:30am-12:30pm). The **telephone code** is 03943.

To reach Wernigerode's **Jugendgästehaus,** Friedrichstr. 53 (tel. 63 20 61), bus #1, 5, or 7: "Kirchstr.," or walk from the Westerntor station right on Unter den Zindeln and turn right on Friedrichstr. (25min.). The rooms have recently been refurbished and sport modern facilities and warm mountain *Gemütlichkeit* (coziness). All you can say is "quaint," even if you hate yourself for doing so. (Reception open 8am-10pm. DM15. Breakfast DM6. Dinner DM7. You *must* buy one meal. Sheets DM5. Reservations strongly recommended.) **Frucht-haus Lucke,** Westernstr. 36, a 5-minute walk from the Marktplatz, stocks fresh fruits and other groceries (open Mon.-Fri. 9am-6pm, Sat. 8am-noon). There is a **farmers' market** in the pedestrian zone (Tues. and Thurs. 10am-5pm). An upscale *Imbiß* (dig the oxymoron!), the **Schlemmerbox,** around the corner on G.-Petri-Str., keeps the Marktplatz from draining your pocket too quickly. The **Kochöffel,** just a few minutes away at the intersection of Breitestr. and Große Bergstr., fulfills cheap food fantasies: after 7pm hamburgers cost a mere DM1.50 (open Mon.-Fri. 8am-10pm, Sat. 9am-10pm, Sun. 11am-10pm).

HALBERSTADT

If you plan to travel any farther east than Wernigerode, chances are good you'll have to make a connection here. Halberstadt, known before the devastation of World War II as a producer of cigars, gloves, and sausages (everything a gentleman needed), emerges as a grimy town from the moment you enter the train station. En route to Halberstadt's only attraction—a large Romanesque cathedral—your apprehensions are confirmed. Block after block of textbook GDR-depression assault you while meandering on the streets of the stagnant *Stadt.* Follow Bahnhofstr. and turn left on Magdeburgerstr. to reach the multi-colored bricks of **Breiter Weg;** this pedestrian lane rests at the **Fischmarkt,** where citizens gather to sell their wares (open Tues. and Fri. 8am-5pm, Sat. 8am-noon). To get directly to the **tourist office,** streetcar #1 or 2: "Am Johannisbrunnen." Behind the Fischmarkt, a **Roland statue,** dating from 1433, scarred with time- and war-wounds, guards the front of the **Martinikirche** which, despite the name, is not a shrine to olive-garnishing intoxicants.

The unquestioned focus of the city center is the **Domplatz,** framed by the superflying buttresses of the 13th-century **Dom St. Stephanus** and the not-so-flyly-buttressed Romanesque **Liebfraukirche.** The effect of the former's midnight-sooted spires is heightened by the sheer bulk of the edifice: it's a couple sizes too large for a city center like Halberstadt's. The only way to see the **Dommuseum** and its **treasury,** complete with gilded everything and the oldest known tapestries in the world (dating from 1150) is to take a combined tour of it and the *Dom.* (Open May-Oct. Mon.-Fri. 10-11:30am and noon-5pm, Sat. 10-11:30am and noon-4:30pm, Sun. noon-4:30pm. Tours Mon.-Fri. at 10am, 11:30am, 2pm, and 3:30pm, Sat. 10am and 2pm, Sun. 11:30am and 2:30pm; Nov.-April Mon.-Sat. 10am and 2pm, Sun. 11:30am.) The *Dom*'s enormous **organ** belches out concerts every weekend from June until September (prices and times vary, but there are discounts for students and seniors). In the 1930s, the *Dom* was the sight of several *Hitler-Jugend* rallies. In an act of *Vergangenheitsbewältigung* (coming to terms with the past), a group of quartz-like stones placed in front of the cathedral pay tribute to Halberstadt's once-thriving Jewish community, completely wiped out in the Holocaust. On the night of the dedication in 1992, the memorial was plastered with fascist and neo-Nazi symbols; the *Denkmal* (monument) was fully cleaned the following morning. Follow the *Dom*'s **rose garden** out and around to the **Städtisches Museum** (tel. 55 14 71; fax 55 10 48), a scrapbook of Halberstadt history, and the **Museum Heineanum** (tel. 55 14 61; fax 55 14 69), a gallery of our feathered friends. (Both open Tues.-Fri. 9am-5pm, Sat.-Sun. 10am-5pm. Admission to both museums DM5, students DM2.50.)

The newly renovated **tourist office,** Düsterngraben 3 (tel. 55 18 15; fax 55 10 89), down an alley just in front of the *Dom,* has information on these sights and more, and will find you a room (from DM30) in one of the three hotels or myriad of guest houses for free (open Mon.-Fri. 9am-1pm and 2-6pm, Sat. 10am-2pm). There's no *Jugendherberge* here, but the juicy exoticism of the words **Campingplatz SH 200** (tel. 60 93 08) will surely lure you to the *Halberstädter See* (Lake) in the northeast part of town. From the station follow Bahnhofstr., go right on Magdeburgerstr., and left on Warmholzberg (30min; reception open daily 10am-8pm; DM7.50 per person, DM8 per tent). Cheap food is a bit hard to come by, although there are food stores on Düsterngraben: **Votwitzkei,** a bakery (open Mon.-Fri. 6:30am-6pm, Sat. 6:30am-noon); and **Ahrens** (open Mon.-Fri. 7am-6pm, Sat. 7am-noon). The **Museumscafé** in the Dompl. offers light meals for DM5-10. On the street behind the tourist information, the **internet cafe Deja Vu,** Lichtengraben 7 (tel. 57 04 25), surfs (1hr. DM10, 2hr. DM16, 3hr. DM20; open daily 2pm-2am). The **telephone code** is 03941.

QUEDLINBURG

For sheer authenticity, no other destination in the Harz can match Quedlinburg. This town gets medieval on your ass, coming complete with spires, castles, torture chambers, and half-timbered houses that look as though they've been around since 919, when Heinrich I waited in the market square for the news that he'd been chosen as emperor. In 1994, the city was crowned by UNESCO as one of the world's most important cultural treasures. Quedlinburg has been a bit run-down for the past forty years, but locals are busy painting and patching. Unfortunately, navigational difficulties will no doubt survive the renovations: the tiny alleys, bends, kinks, and crazily oblique intersections are the price of Quedlinburg's historic charm. Get a free map from the tourist office as soon as you arrive, and use it. If you have to ask for directions, try to get the person to show you the route to your goal on the map; this is not the place to test your grasp of German prepositions.

Recently, Quedlinburg gained a modicum of notoriety as party to an international art-theft scandal. In 1945, ecclesiastical gems from the church were hidden in a basement to protect them from the bombing. An American G.I. came across them, threw the lot in his pack, and took it all home to Texas. The story came out only after his recent death, when his heirs tried to dispose of the goods. German government officials mounted a knock-out legal battle, and this small town got the prize, now on display in the church in the *Burgberg* castle above town.

Raising Hell! Witchcraft in the Harz

German ritualism is not limited to beer drinking. In prehistoric times, nomadic German tribes who weren't concerned about public infamy would gather atop the highest neighborhood mountain on the eve of April 30 to celebrate the wedding anniversary of Wodan and Freja (Nordic gods who controlled the seasons). In celebrations that would make most decadents blush, shepherds and farmers danced naked around live human and animal sacrifices in hopes of receiving a good harvest. (Ozzy Osborne's bark at the moon doesn't compare.) The pagan rituals persisted into the modern era; Charlemagne and other zealous missionaries weren't enamored of the blasphemous celebrations, so they attempted to usurp the occasion by proclaiming the events of April 30-May 1 **Walpurgisnacht,** in memory of St. Walpurga whose May 1 birthdate offered a convenient excuse for the *legerdemain.* Even Charlemagne's efforts to quiet the madness failed; the festivities later came to celebrate witchcraft and the devil. In 1484, Pope Innocent VIII decided to put a vicious end to the infernal games. A crusade against witchcraft over the next century tortured and slaughtered over 7000 *"Hexen"* (witches). The campaign brought activity to a halt until Goethe's interest in witchcraft and things Faustian inspired historical societies to spring up in this century and spread the myths of devilish delight anew. Today, the *Hexen* are still raising hell.

Heinrich I died within the original walls of the **Burgberg** (tel. 27 30), an old Saxon stronghold, in 936. The current 13th-century structure has been a favorite residence-in-exile for the ruling family's widows and inconvenient relatives. The castle complex consists of three parts: the **Schloßmuseum,** the **Schloßgarten,** and the **Stiftskirche.** The museum depicts city history from the Paleolithic era until the present, all according to good old Marxist historiography. Several rooms, decorated according to 17th- and 18th-century fashion, allow you to cruise back in time, while a wooden box with two tiny peepholes cut in the sides—built as a show prison—gives you the creeps. (Open May-Sept. Tues.-Sun. 10am-6pm; Oct.-April Tues.-Sun. 9am-5pm and Sat.-Sun. 10am-5pm; DM5, students DM3.) The **Stiftskirche** is the castle church, where the purloined art treasures are on permanent display. (The church is only accessible by guided tour. There are tours every 30min. May-Sept. Tues.-Sat. 10am-3:30pm, Sun. noon-3:30pm; Nov.-April Tues.-Sat. 11am-3:30pm, Sun. noon-3:30pm.) Loiter in the gardens around the *Schloß,* or walk down the castle path past an impressive row of old houses, cramped together on the hillside.

Underneath the castle, the **Lyonel Feininger Museum** is tucked away in a smart, more modern-looking white house at Finkenherd 5a (tel. 22 38). Inside is an *Angst*-heavy selection of works by the artists in the *Die Brücke* artistic circle, including Feininger's own bleak landscapes and portraits vivisected by characteristic fracture-like lines (closed until late 1997; ask the tourist office for information). The unavoidable stone statue of **Roland** guards the ivy-covered **Rathaus,** after nearly four centuries underground: the statue was smashed and buried as punishment for the people after a failed insurrection in the mid-14th century. The neighboring **Benediktikirche** graces the Markt with its 13th-century base; the twisting Solomonic columns of the altar are truly exceptional. The **Schreckens-Turm,** at the end of Neuendorf, served as Quedlinburg's 14th-century S&M torture palace; now, it disintegrates amidst ghost-like, virtually abandoned blocks. The **Wipertikirche** (tel. 77 30 12), a squat, mostly rebuilt Romanesque church, a short walk from the *Schloß,* stands guard over the 1000-year-old crypt, resting on the site of Heinrich I's court (open 11am-5pm).

Quedlinburg's **tourist office,** Markt 22 (tel. 77 30 13; fax 77 30 16), finds private rooms for no fee (from DM20), sells museum tickets, leads tours, and provides everything short of a massage. (Open May-Sept. Mon.-Fri. 9am-8pm, Sat.-Sun. 9am-6pm; Oct. Mon.-Fri. 9am-6pm, Sat.-Sun. 10am-3pm; Nov.-Feb. Mon.-Fri. 9am-5pm; March-April Mon.-Fri. 9am-6pm, Sat.-Sun. 10am-3pm.) **Exchange money** at decent rates or use the ATM in the **Deutsche Bank,** Am Markt 3 (open Mon. and Wed. 8:30am-4pm, Tues. and Thurs. 8:30am-6pm, Fri. 8:30am-1:30pm). **Trains** shuttle between Halberstadt and Quedlinburg (every 2hr.), Thale (every hr., 9min.), Magdeburg (every hr., 2hr.), and Halberstadt (every hr., 20min.). The main **post office** stamps 'n' sends at the intersection of Bahnhofstr. and Turnstr. (open Mon.-Fri. 8am-noon and 2-6pm, Sat. 8:30am-noon). The **postal code** is 06484. The **telephone code** is 03946.

On the way to the castle, grab some local brew at the **Brauerei Lüdde,** Blassistr. 14 (tel. 70 52 06). The interior is a high-ceilinged, circular wooden brewing hall with a bar, filled with shiny copper brewing kettles. You can also elect to sip your tasty, light Pilsner (DM3.30) or the excellent, nutty **Lüdde-Alt** (ale; DM3.30). They also offer a cheap, low-alcohol *Pils* beer called *Pubarschknall* (a name which hardly merits translation; maybe something about bad digestion) for DM1.90 per tiny glass. Tasty snacks and meals at around DM12 may improve that rumbling down under (open Mon.-Thurs. 11am-midnight, Fri.-Sat. 11am-1am, Sun. 11am-10pm). **Pasta Mia,** Steinbrücke 23 (tel. 21 22), faces the Marktplatz and serves up inexpensive Italian meals. Pizzas DM5.50-12. Pastas DM8.50-13.50. Mondays are pasta days (any pasta DM6), and Tuesdays are pizza days (any pizza DM6; open Mon.-Sat. 11am-10pm). Local **farmers** sell their most treasured foods at the Marktplatz (Wed. 7am-5pm, Sat.7am-noon).

THALE

Above the dramatic front of Thale's flowing rivers, jagged cliffs, and lush mountainside scenery lurks a region of myths, legends, witches, and demons. Like most towns in the Harz, Thale boasts that Goethe fancied its **Bodetal** valley—hence, the *Goet-*

beweg. However, Goethe's literary genius and love of hiking is overshadowed by the rich folklore of the region and its overwhelming natural beauty. Thale is a mystic land whose reality blurs into legend and myth.

Legend dates Thale's cultic history back to prehistoric times, when a sorceress named **Watelinde** led pagan rituals that forced incorrigible youths down a path of destruction in the fast-lane lifestyle of witchery. A few thousand years later a Harz resident named **Hilda** got lost in the woods for a couple of years—her re-appearance was, by all accounts, a touch sketchy. Watelinde freaked out at the sight of Hilda and begged God to save her from the frightening countenance before her. Amidst explosive thunder and lightning, a whirlwind threw poor Watelinde into some rocks, which now comprise the nifty attraction **Hexentanzplatz** (witches' dance place). Amidst the celebrated spot of splattering are statues of demonic and ghoulish creatures adorned with parasitic animals. Adjacent to Hexentanzpl. is the wildly entertaining **Walpurgishalle,** a museum commemorating the Harz history of witchcraft through displays of Thale's cultic ceremonies, as well as animal heads with pentagrams attached (open May-Sept. daily 9am-5pm, Oct.-Apr. 9am-1pm; DM3, students DM1). Also located on the Hexentanzpl. is the rather impressive **Harzer Bergtheater Thale** (tel. 23 24), a huge outdoor amphitheater vacillating between the sublime and the infernal, the sacred and the profane, with performances ranging from broadway musicals and operas to Goethe's *Faust* and the *Hexenkonzerts* (witches' concerts). (Shows run sporadically May-Sept. Starting times also vary. 30% discount for students.) One can ascend to the Hexentanzpl. either by following the adventure-filled **winding trail** that begins by the hostel (30min.)—on foggy days its teeming life and poor visibility are reminiscent of Yoda's cave in the Degoba system—or by means of the **Kabinenbahn,** a cable car which crosses the Bodetals to Hexentanzpl. A **Sessellift** (chair lift) heads up to the **Roßtrappe,** a mythical place in its own right. (Open May-Sept. daily 9:30am-6pm, Oct.-April 10am-4:30pm; DM8, students and youths DM5.)

Across the street from the train station, the **tourist office,** Rathausstr. 1 (tel. 25 97 or 22 77; fax 22 77), can hook you up with a private room (DM25-40 per person) for no charge. You can also purchase spirits in the form of the *Hexen Gesoff* alcohol sold in cute little bottles (DM2.50). (Open Oct. and Dec.-April Mon.-Fri. 9am-6pm; May-Aug. Mon.-Fri. 9am-6pm, Sat.-Sun. 9am-4pm; Nov. Mon.-Fri. 9am-4pm.) **Trains** leave for Thale from Halberstadt (30min.) and Quedlinburg (7min.) hourly. A **Sparkasse,** on Bahnhofstr. close to the train station, takes care of your money-exchanging needs. The **Hubertus-Apotheke,** Poststr. 15, is easily reached by walking left as you exit the train station (open Mon.-Fri. 8am-6pm, Sat. 8am-noon). The **post office,** Poststr. 1, 06502 Thale, lies across from the *Apotheke* (open Mon.-Fri. 9-11:30am and 2:30-5:30pm, Sat. 9-11:30am). The **telephone code** is 03947.

Writing for *Let's Go: Germany 1884,* Theodor Fontane described Thale as a place where "one is up-lifted, well-served, and well-nursed." He was immediately fired for his bland depiction. Nevertheless, the **Jugendherberge,** Bodetal Waldkater 1 (tel. 28 81), deserves the lofty laud; its cavernous eight-bed rooms look out into the mountains and the running river below. The *Jugendherberge* may or may not be haunted; check with the tourist office for more details. (Reception open 7am-10pm. DM22, over 26 DM27. Great breakfast buffet included. Sheets DM6.) From the train station, cut diagonally through the park, past the *Opfer des Fascismus* statue on the right and the cute cathedral on the left; then go right and continue walking along the river and until you reach it (15min.). The hostel's cafeteria has lunch and dinner specials (DM7.50-9). Otherwise, the many food stands by Hexentanzpl. can fill your need for cheap eats. Straight ahead of the Sparkasse, Karl-Marx-Str. provides each according to his needs with shops, restaurants, and amusements. The **Wolf and Sohn supermarket** (open Mon.-Fri. 7:30am-1pm and 2:30-6pm, Sat. 7:30-11am), and the **J. Goethe bakery,** fill the gaps for the needier ones. Left on Bahnhofstr. from the train station, continue until it becomes Eisenbahnstr. Thale goes crazy every year on April 30 for the **Walpurgisnacht,** but only go if you dare commit yourself to an orgy of sin.

■ Magdeburg

Magdeburg has three claims to fame: it has a spectacular cathedral, it's the birthplace of 18th-century composer Georg Phillipp Telemann, and it was devastated in both the Thirty Years War and World War II. On May 10, 1631, one of the most gruesome battles of the Thirty Years War decimated the city after Protestant town leaders refused to cut a deal with Catholic troops. As a major German industrial center, it was a prime target for the Allied forces in World War II. After the war, Magdeburg was rebuilt GDR-style—blessed with enviably broad boulevards and parks but cursed by concrete cookie-cutter apartment blocks. In the months before reunification, Magdeburg had the good luck to triumph over Halle, becoming the new capital of Sachsen-Anhalt. Now brightness and shine have invaded. Magdeburg offers its visitors a *Dom* and historical sites, all set in a cosmopolitan shopping district. Yet Magdeburg's increased popularity has brought increased trouble—skinheads congregate here, instigating various problems. Despite some of the bumps of reunification, Magdeburg increasingly resembles its sister-in-Domness, Köln, with a vibrant university life and cultural *Szene* surrounding the humongous heart of the city. Construction throughout the city bodes well for this German rookie.

Orientation and Practical Information In the cold days of the Iron Curtain, Magdeburg was one of the few rail links between West Germany and West Berlin's centrally located Bahnhof Zoo. As a result, travelers en route to Berlin from eastern cities can often save time by traveling through Magdeburg to avoid the Berlin Hauptbahnhof (a 20min. S-Bahn ride to the city center) or Bahnhof Lichtenberg (a good 45min. away). ICE bullet trains also connect Magdeburg with Hanover and Munich. The city is conveniently configured for pedestrians: most of the sights and museums are located on Otto-von-Guericke-Str. and Breiter Weg, parallel streets that lie less than 15 minutes away from the train station via Ernst-Reuter-Allee. A **Touristenkarte,** available in the tourist office and at many museums, provides cover charge for most of the sights (DM8).

The **tourist office,** Alter Markt 9 (tel. 540 49 03; fax 540 49 10; email mi@magdeburg.de; http://www.magdeburg.de), is on the main market square. From the train station, head straight on Ernst-Reuter-Allee (a bit to the left from the front doors) then left at the second intersection onto Breiter Weg; turn right onto the market. Inquire about tours and maps in English. Pick up a copy of *Dates* magazine, which has hotel and *Pension* listings, as well as an up-to-date schedule of cultural and nightlife activities (free). The **Zimmervermittlung** (tel. 540 49 04), in the same building, finds rooms (DM25-75) for a DM3 fee. (Office open Mon.-Fri. 10am-1pm and 1:45-6pm, Sat. 10am-1pm. Tours Mon.-Fri. 11am; DM5.) If it's late and the many banks in town are closed, you can use **Reise Bank** in the train station for **currency exchange,** but you'll pay a commission of DM20 minimum on traveler's checks, DM3 for cash exchanges. Cash advances on AmEx, EC, Diners, MC, and Visa (open Mon.-Fri. 7am-7:30pm, Sat. 8am-noon). For towns near Magdeburg, the **bus** station is to the right of the train station. For **bicycle rental, Zweirad-Schulz,** Frankefeldel (tel. 631 21 82), charges DM18 per day. Bus #53 or 54: "Am Teich" (open Mon.-Sat. 9am-12:30pm and 1:30-6:30pm, Sun. 9am-1pm). The **Women's Communication Center, Courage** is at Porsestr. 14 (tel./fax 404 80 89). **Internet access** is available in *Cyb@r* (see **Food,** below) and *Orbit cyber cafe* (see **Nightlife,** p. 226). The **post office** is a dark hulk on Breiter Weg, 39104 Magdeburg, towards the *Dom* (open Mon.-Fri. 8am-6pm, Sat. 9am-noon). The **telephone code** is 0391.

Accommodations and Camping A frightful gap in the Magdeburg budget housing scene was filled in 1997 when the **Jugendherberge Magdeburger Hof,** Leterstr. 10 (tel. 53 21 01; fax 53 21 02), opened a centrally located, rainbow colored hostel. Construction on the hostel should be completed in 1998, culminating in TV-rooms and workout equipment. Follow the S-Bahn tracks to the right from the main train station, and when they end, walk up the stairs under the cement covering and the hostel is on the right 150m ahead. (Reception open daily 2-10pm; DM27, over 26 DM32. Breakfast included. Sheets DM6.) Camp at **Campingplatz Am Barleber See** (tel. 50 32 44); streetcar #10 (direction: "Barleber See") to the last stop, continue down the main street, then cross underneath the highway bridge. **Bike rental** available for DM5 per day. (Reception open daily 7am-9pm. DM4 per person; DM2 per tent; DM2.50 for showers, bathroom, and water.)

Food Many of the cheaper restaurants crowd the streets around the intersection of Breiter Weg and Einsteinstr. in Hasselbachpl. This was the only section of the downtown area to survive wartime bombing. The **Alter Markt** proffers up a bounty of flea market doo-dads and cheap food—half roasted chickens (DM3.50), cheese, *Bratwurst,* and more (open Mon.-Fri. 8am-5pm, Sat. 7am-noon). The **Karstadt Restaurant-Cafe,** Breiterweg 128, across from the market, offers groceries as well as an international selection of food sold by weight (100g Asian DM2.40, Italian DM2.75, Salad DM2; open Mon.-Fri. 9am-8pm, Sat. 9am-4pm). Next door, the **Cyberb@r** allows you to surf the **Internet** (30min. DM3; same hours as the restaurant). **Ratskeller,** Alter Markt (tel. 568 23 23; fax. 568 23 99), is a historical set-up in the basement of the Baroque *Rathaus.* If you play your cards right, this can be the best food deal in Magdeburg: while *à la carte* dinners are prohibitively expensive, the restaurant offers two special deals. Each weekday features a different *Stammessen* (lunch special) from noon-2pm including an entree, starch, and dessert for a delightful DM8-10. Get there by 1pm if you can. The other sweet deal occurs every day: 3-5pm is *Ratsherrenzeit,* when all entrees are reduced to half-price plus DM1. Late eaters can get flavorful steaks and copious traditional meat-heavy dishes for DM6-15 (open Mon.-Sat. 11am-11pm, Sun. 11am-9pm). **Mausefalle,** Breiter Weg 224 (tel. 543 01 35), at the north end of the lively Hasselbachpl., attracts a young crowd, particularly students. The big wall over the bathroom doors is decorated with old newspaper clippings and vintage car memorabilia. Solid spaghetti dishes for DM10; extensive liquor and mixed-drink selection (open Mon.-Sun. 8:30am-3am; kitchen open until 2am). A **SPAR supermarket** waits at the corner of Breiter Weg and Julius-Brenner-Str. (open Mon.-Fri. 8am-7pm, Sat. 8am-2pm).

Sights Dominated by modern grays and beiges, Magdeburg's urban neutrality offers no challenge to the city's few dazzling sights. The main landmark and city symbol is the sprawling **Magdeburger Dom,** adjacent to the old square on Breitestr. In fact, the *Dom* was famed as the largest cathedral in the nation until reunification forced it to yield that honor to Köln. But there's nothing second-rate about the spectacle of the wide **courtyard** quadrangle with the cathedral's twin dark towers spearing the skies above. At the front of the cathedral lies an inconspicuous tomb, the 973 grave site of Otto I, the second Holy Roman Emperor (after Charlemagne). Local ghost stories credit the *Kaiser*'s spectral guardianship with preservation of the *Dom* during the destruction of 1631 (Catholic raiders) and 1945 (B-17 bombers), though the bombs did in fact give the cathedral quite a buzz. Ernst Barlach's famous wooden memorial to the victims of WWI, originally designed for the spot it now occupies, was removed by the Nazis, fortuitously spending the war years stored safely in Berlin's National Gallery. (Open Mon.-Sat. 10am-6pm, Sun. 11:30am-6pm. Tours Mon.-Sat. 10am and 2pm, Sun. 11:30am and 2pm. Free; tours DM4, students DM2.)

Near the *Dom,* between the many faceless apartments, lies the ancient **Kloster Unser Lieben Frauen,** Regierungstr. 4/6 (tel. 56 50 20). An 11th-century nunnery, it now serves as a museum for visiting exhibitions and a concert hall. The grounds about the cloister still shimmer in sheltered peacefulness; sit and cogitate on the benches or on the remains of stone walls (open Tues. and Thurs.-Sun. 10am-5pm, Wed. 10am-8pm; DM4, students and seniors DM2). Heading away from the *Dom* and crossing Breiter Weg on Danzstr., the **Kulturhistorisches Museum,** Otto-von-Guerike-Str. 68-73 (tel. 53 65 00; fax 543 26 46), will pop up on your left. You can view everything from a potato bug model 15 times the bug's actual size to the city's history through the late 17th century (open Tues.-Sun. 10am-6pm; admission DM1, students

DM0.50). The ruins of the **Johanniskirche**, almost on the Elbe behind the Alter Markt, best seen from the walkway along the river, stand as a memorial to the 1945 bombing. The skeletal remains of the church's main part, including the empty patterned stain-glass window frames, are slowly being rebuilt, transforming the church into a cultural center. The statues and the frightening bronze doors juxtapose the terror of the bombings with the image of a **Trümmerfrau** (rubble woman), providing an emblem of the city's efforts to recover from its difficult past. Climb the **tower** for a magnificent view of the city (open daily 10am-5pm). Across from the Johanniskirche rises the clock tower of the elegantly proportioned 17th-century **Rathaus.** Directly on the Marktplatz in front of the *Rathaus* is a replica of the **Magdeburger Reiter** (built in 1240), the oldest free-standing equestrian figure in northern Europe. The original rides off into the sunset at the Kulturhistorisches Museum. Giddy-up. Behind the cathedral lies the Elbe River; follow the Remtergang just off the Dompl. and look out over the river from **Auf dem Wall,** the ramparts of the old city fortifications.

Entertainment   For bars, restaurants, and the inexpensive sport of people-watching, there are three superior areas in Magdeburg: **Hasselbachplatz** (see **Food,** p. 225), **Sudenburg,** along Halberstädtlerstr. and its cross streets (S-Bahn #1 or 10, or Bus #53 or 54: "Eiskellerpl." or "Ambrosiuspl."), and **Diesdorfstr.** (S-Bahn #1 or 6: "Westring" or "Arndstr."). As well-prepared for emergencies as its namesake predecessor, the **Feuerwache** (Fire Station), Halberstädtlerstr. 140 (tel./fax 60 28 09), answers calls for theater, art exhibits, and concerts while serving as a winter cafe and a casual summer beer garden (beer garden open Mon.-Sun. 7pm-midnight). Heading left from Feuerwache on Halberstädtlerstr., you will pass a **movie theater.** Take a right on Heidestr., where **Orbit cyber café,** Heidestr. 9 (tel. 609 17 11) offers to beam you up to a land with funky decorations, drinks of all sorts, occasional live DJs, and **Internet access** (open Mon.-Fri. 6pm-1am, Sat.-Sun. 6pm-2am; 30min. connection DM5). The clientele at **Layla,** Lessingstr. 66 (tel. 731 70 28), gulp down pints of Guinness in an indistinct but relaxing setting, where *Uni*-students and expatriates gather to indulge in German bar food (daily specials DM7.90, salads DM 5.50) and the weekly English fest Thursdays at 8:30pm (open Mon.-Thurs. 11am-1am, Fri. 11am-2am, Sat. 10am-2am, Sun. 10am-1am). The Magdeburger *Kabarett* (cabaret) **Die Kügelblitze,** Breiter Weg 200, around the corner from the youth hostel, was well known during the GDR era, and the last eight years have fed its sardonic sensibility. (Nightly performances start around 8pm. Tickets DM20, students and seniors DM10. Call 543 47 66 for ticket information.) There's also straight-out drama at the **Freie Kammerspiele Theater,** Otto-von-Guericke-Str. 64 (tel. 598 82 26).

Mecklenburg-Vorpommern

Over 1700 lakes, the marshy coast of the Baltic Sea, and labyrinthine medieval towns characterize the lonely landscape of Mecklenburg-Vorpommern. Once a favored vacation spot for East Germans, this sparsely populated northernmost province of the former GDR retains the sturdy, raw-boned natural beauty of the *Bundesboonies*. Cyclists and hikers flock to the Mecklenburg Lake Plain and Rügen Island, which offer some of Germany's most spectacular scenery. As restoration work in the region's main cities continues, dramatic Hanseatic architecture begins to emerge from the rubble. Though many visitors pass through this region en route to the Baltic Sea beaches or Scandinavia, Mecklenburg-Vorpommern's cities remain economically and politically troubled, and the presence of neo-Nazis is, unfortunately, palpable.

■ Schwerin

A keepsake of Heinrich the Lion's 12th-century march through the East, Schwerin is a rejuvenating stop on the way to the swarming Baltic seacoast. With reunification, the city regained its status as capital of Mecklenburg-Vorpommern. Schwerin again administers this *Land* of fallen *Junkers*, rye bread, and brick churches. As a precursor

227

to the Thirty Years War, the Swedes burned much of it to the ground in 1616, but the Allies spared it in World War II. Today's *Altstadt* is therefore well preserved, with an elegant look of shabby gentility. Surrounded almost completely by lakes and largely free of Communist "architectural innovations," Schwerin's *Altstadt* and *Schloß* are also unmarred by tourist-trap capitalism.

Orientation and Practical Information Schwerin lies on the Magdeburg-Rostock rail line and is easily accessible from all major cities on the Baltic coast. Hourly **trains** connect Schwerin to Rostock (1¼hr.) and other major cities in the East. **Schwerin Information,** Am Markt 11 (tel. 592 52 12; fax 55 50 94), sells maps for DM1 and books private rooms (DM25-50) for free; cheap rooms go quickly, so call ahead. From the station, go right on Gründthalpl., continue as it turns into Wismarchestr., left on Arsenal, right on Bischofstr., and left on Schmiedestr. (open Mon.-Fri. 10am-noon and 1-6pm, Sat. 10am-2pm). The **Apotheke am Markt,** Puschkinstr. 61 (tel. 592 350), just off the Marktplatz, posts addresses of pharmacies and has an emergency bell (open Mon.-Fri. 8am-6pm, Sat. 8:30am-1pm). At the **SB Münz Wasch Center,** Werderstr. 6, wash 6kg for DM6, soap included; dry for DM1 per 15min. Bus #10 (direction "Knaudtstr."): corner of Werderstr. and Knaudtstr. (open daily 6am-11pm). **Goethe Fahrradverleih** (tel. 834 78) rents bikes at the Platz der Jugend, near the train station (walk right on Wismarchstr.). The main **post office** resides at Mecklenburgstr. 6, 19053 Schwerin. From the Markt, go down Schmiedestr. and turn right (open Mon.-Fri. 8am-6pm, Sat. 9am-noon). The **telephone code** is 0385.

Accommodations and Food The **Jugendherberge (HI),** Waldschulenweg 3 (tel. 21 30 05), lies south of town in the woods by the lake. Bus #15; get off at the end and walk towards the zoo (see p. 229). It's on the left. With Schwerin's increasing popularity, the friendly hostel frequently fills, so phone first. (Reception open 4-10pm. Curfew 10pm. DM20, over 26 DM25. Tasty breakfast included. Sheets DM6.) **Kaiser's,** on Schmiedestr., is the most convenient supermarket (open Mon.-Fri. 8am-6pm, Thurs. 8am-8pm, Sat. 8am-4pm). The fancy **Friesenhof Restaurant,** on Mecklenburgerstr., next door to the post office, parts the seas of foody goodness with 40% discounts from 3-5pm daily; steaks and seafood dishes miraculously become a reasonable DM9-12 (open daily 11:30am-10:30pm). **Boomerang** on Mecklenburgstr., across from McDonald's, offers breakfast seven days a week for DM5-8, with more expensive Australian fare later in the day (opens Mon.-Fri. at 8am, Sat.-Sun. at 9am).

Sights Schwerin's strangely Byzantine **Schloß** (tel. 56 57 38) is situated just south of the city center, over the bridge at the end of Schloßstr. This castle served as the seat of the Dukes of Mecklenburg, who ruled the area until the 1918 upheaval chased the *Kaiser* from power The castle's intricately gilded Baroque cupolas runneth over with luxury—the red silk wallpaper and mahogany floors pale in comparison to the sumptuous throne room, with its gilt and marble columns (open Tues.-Sun. 10am-6pm; DM6, students DM3). Across from the *Schloß*, the **Alter Garten** square was the site of mass demonstrations preceding the downfall of the GDR in 1989. Atop a cascade of stairs on the right sits the **Staatliches Museum,** which houses a good collection of 15th- to 19th-century Dutch and German art, including a few works by Rembrandt, Cranach, and Rubens (open Tues.-Sun. 10am-5pm; DM7, students DM5.50). The striking cream pillared building next door is the **Mecklenburgisches Staatstheater Schwerin** (tel. 530 00), currently in the midst of a dramatic revival (box office open Tues.-Fri. 10am-1pm and 2-6pm, Sun. 10am-1pm; tickets DM15-25, students DM10). Looking uphill, the nearest spire belongs to the 13th century **Gothic cathedral,** am Dompl. For DM2 you can sweat your way up the 110m tower. (Open Mon.-Fri. 11am-noon and 2-3pm, Sat. 11am-1pm and 2-4pm, Sun. noon-3pm. Services Sun. 10am.) Schwerin's former **synagogue** reposes silently at Schlachterstr. 3, off the Marktplatz; the temple was destroyed in a pogrom in 1938. The building used to house the region's memorial to its Jewish community, but closed several years ago after an interior looting by local skinheads. The town keeps its own historical house with permanent exhibits on Schwerin's checkered past in the **Heimatmuseum** (tel. 56 09 71) on the Markt (open Tues.-Sun. 10am-6pm).

If you're looking for something on the wilder side, the **Schweriner Zoo** (tel. 20 80 30) borders the *Jugendherberge,* adjoining the **Fauler See.** The zoo specializes in waterfowl, but it has its share of large ferocious mammals, plus some giraffes who stare wistfully at the adorable, dinky heads of ostriches. (Open April-Sept. Mon.-Fri. 9am-5pm, Sat.-Sun. 9am-6pm; Oct.-March Mon.-Fri. 10am-4pm; DM8, students DM5.) Another option for nature lovers is the reserve on **Kaninchenwerder Island,** set in the midst of the Schweriner See. In summer, ferries leave at least once an hour from the docks left of the *Schloß* to visit the island's rabbits (one-way DM2.80, children DM1).

■ Mecklenburgische Seenplatte (Mecklenburg Lake Plain)

When things got hectic in Berlin, Otto von Bismarck often found refuge among the reserved but sincere folk of the Mecklenburgische Seenplatte. Around the necklace of lakes in this sparsely populated region of the country, nature has conquered civilization—a light in the gloom of modernity. With the exception of Neubrandenberg, the reminders of the GDR are not as painfully obvious here as in other regions of Eastern Germany, perhaps because the socialist-era architects were wise enough to leave the forests and hills alone. A popular vacation area for more than a century, the Seenplatte attracts plenty of summer crowds; consider advance reservations.

WAREN

Conveniently located within an hour of Rostock and two hours of Berlin, Waren draws many German tourists to the northern edge of the **Müritz,** Germany's second-largest freshwater lake. Smaller streams weave from the lake into **Müritz National Park,** a unique preserve of rare birds and marshland. The Waren tourist office has tons of info about guided tours of this paradise for hikers or bikers, ranging from early-morning bird-watching jaunts to all-day canoeing, biking, and hiking triathlons.

Since Waren's primary attractions are nature-related, it's not suprising that restoration of the former *Altstadt* is not a top priority. The weather-beaten 14th-century **Altes Rathaus,** the crumbling **Speicher** (granary) that presides over the harbor, and the 290-year-old **Altes Schulhaus** (old schoolhouse), have all seen better days. Next door, the **Georgenkirche** lost its roof to fire in 1699 and received only a modest, flat replacement. The **Müritzmuseum Waren,** Friedenstr. 5 (tel. 66 76 00), houses a natural history museum. Under the Herrenseebrücke lives Müritz's modest aquarium and garden (open Tues.-Fri. 9am-6pm, Sat.-Sun. 9am-noon and 2-5pm; Oct.-April Tues.-Fri. 10am-4pm, Sat.-Sun. 10am-noon and 2-5pm; DM4, students DM2).

Waren Information, Neuer Markt 21 (tel. 66 61 83; fax 66 43 30), in the town square, has maps of the park, brochures, and a free room-finding service (rooms DM25-30). They offer tours in the park and guided tours in German through the town (Mon.-Wed., and Fri. 10am; DM3, students DM2). From the train station, take the Schweriner Damm exit and walk left, then turn right on Friedenstr. and left on Langestr. (open Mon.-Fri. 10am-noon and 2-6pm, Sat. 10am-noon and 1-4pm; winter Mon.-Fri. 10am-4pm). **Warener Schiffahrtsgesellschaft GmbH,** Kietzstr. 14a (tel. 12 56 24; fax 12 56 93), and **Müritzwind Personenschiffahrt,** Strandstr. (tel. 66 66 64; fax 66 58 79), both offer boat **tours** of the Müritz lake that vary in length from one to four hours (DM7-22, children half-price). **Bikes** can be rented at the train station (tel. 590; open Mon.-Fri. 6am-10pm, Sat.-Sun. 8am-8pm; DM10-12). A **pharmacy** (*Löwenapotheke;* tel. 66 61 53) cohabits with the tourist office (open Mon.-Fri. 8am-6:30pm, Sat. 9am-noon). The **post office,** Güstrowerstr. 24, 17192 Waren, can be reached by turning right as you exit the train station and following the road along the tracks (open Mon.-Fri. 10am-noon and 2-6pm, Sat. 10am-noon and 1-4pm). Waren's dinky **supermarket** lies on Friedenstr. near the natural history museum (open Mon.-Fri. 9am-6pm, Sat. 9am-1pm). The **telephone code** is 03991.

The **Jugendherberge (HI),** Auf dem Nesselberg 2 (tel. 66 76 06), dwells in the woods south of town. From the station's Schweriner Damm exit, go left on Schweriner Damm, bear right at the fork in the road, and then walk along the harbor down the successive streets Zur Steinmole, Strandstr., Müritzstr., and Am Seeufer. When you reach the wooded hill on the left, head straight up the path (25min.). Or simply go 100m to the left as you leave the train station and bus #3 from the Schweriner Damm (direction: "Ecktannen"): "Wasserwerk." The 60 beds in barracks book quickly, but the hostel boasts a lovely location, and the friendly management will try to set up tents outside if they're full. (Reception open briefly at 9am, 3, 6, and 8pm. DM20, over 26 DM26. Breakfast free, lunch or dinner DM7. Sheets DM7. Open March-Nov.) There is regular camping at **Azur,** on Fontanestr. (tel. 26 07). Follow the directions to the youth hostel (above), but keep going on Am Seeufer until you reach Fontanestr. The **City Ristorante,** Friedenstr. 8 (tel. 66 87 03), offers big and small pizzas (DM5-12) and other dishes (open Mon.-Thurs. 10am-10pm, Fri.-Sun. 10am-11pm).

NEUBRANDENBURG

Poet Fritz Reufer referred to the city as "the pearl of the Mecklenburg realm," and perhaps it once was. But after Allied bombers blew up the entire *Altstadt* in 1945, only the medieval wall around the city remained intact; now the fortified wall protects a city center crammed with "workers' paradise" architecture ripe for the wrecking ball. Ranked on UNESCO's list of international cultural treasures, the 2.3km long medieval fortifications *(Wehranlage)* with four arched gates *(Tore)* are the landmarks of the town. Countless biking and hiking trails connect Neubrandenburg with the nearby lake **Tollensee,** making it a good base for exploration of the lake area.

The city center is bounded by Friedrich-Engels-Ring (old habits die hard), a huge traffic circle (on the outside), and the cobblestone Ringstr. following the wall on the inside. The best way to get a sense of the structure and its four main gates is to walk around—literally. Crossing Friedrich-Engels-Ring from the train station puts you at the foot of **Stargarderstraße,** the main north-south street; from here head in either direction around the ring. Turning right leads you to the 19m-high **Fangelturm,** a prison tower remining one of of Bentham's tales. *Fear the Panopticon!* Turning left takes you to the **Friedländer Tor,** the city's oldest gate, now home to an art gallery. Look for the 26 meticulously maintained *Fachwerk* houses built directly into the wall.

Head around the wall to pass the **Neues Tor** (521-years-old) and the **Stargarder Tor,** whose facade is ornamented with nine female figures—what do they represent. The **Treptower Tor,** the tallest of the gates, is now home to the **Regionalmuseum Neubrandenburg** (tel. 582 29 06) which hosts exhibits on the town's archaeology (open Tues.-Fri. 9am-5pm, Sat.-Sun. 1-5pm; DM2, students DM1). The Gothic **Marien-kirche,** in the southern part of town, has recuperated nicely from World War II damage and is now open to the public (Tues.-Sun. 11am-5pm). Mecklenburg's oldest theater, the **Schauspielhaus,** Pfaffenstr. 22, is housed in two huge *Fachwerk* houses joined by an Art-Deco glass pavillion (call 544 26 17 for a schedule). Though the **Neubrandenburger Philharmonie** occasionally performs at the *Schauspielhaus,* its permanent home is the hideous **Haus der Kultur und Bildung,** on the Marktplatz (call 559 50 for listings). The **"Latücht" Kommunales Kino,** Gr. Krauthöferstr. 16 (tel. 544 25 70), in the former Catholic church, mixes art movies and Hollywood blockbusters.

Neubrandenburg is connected by **train** to Rostock (3hr.), Dresden (4½hr.), and Berlin (1½hr.). The **tourist office,** Turmstr. 11, 17033 Neubrandenburg (tel. 19 43 31; fax 582 22 67), offers maps and a find rooms for no fee (rooms DM25-40). From Stargarderstr., turn left on Turmstr. before the *Kaufhof* department store (open April-Sept. Mon.-Fri. 9am-6pm, Sat. 9am-noon; Oct.-March Mon.-Fri. 10am-5pm, Sat. 9am-noon). **Fahrradhaus Jürgen Leffin,** Friedrich-Engels-Ring 22 (tel. 36 75 30), rents bikes, 7-speed cruisers, or 21-speed mountain bikes for DM15 per day (open Mon.-Fri. 9am-6pm, Sat. 9:30am-noon). Neubrandenburg's nifty **Spar supermarket** hides inside the *Kaufhof* department store on Stargarderstr. (open Mon.-Fri. 9am-8pm, Sat. 9am-4pm, Sun. 11am-6pm). The **post office** is at Stargarderstr. 6, 17033 Neubrandenburg (open Mon.-Fri. 8am-6pm, Sat. 8am-noon). The **telephone code** is 0395.

The **Jugendherberge** is at Ihlenfelderstr. 73, 17034 Neubrandenburg (tel./fax 422 58 01). From the bus station adjacent to the train station, bus #7 (direction: "Trollenhagen" or "Monckeshof"): "Wolgasterstr." On weekends, bus #5 (direction: "Monckeshof"): "Ihlenfelderstr." By foot, go left on Friedrich-Engels-Ring and cross the bridge onto Demminerstr.; at the first intersection head right on Torgelowerstr. Ihlenfelderstr. is the first left (25min.). It could use a fresh coat of paint, but it has clean beds and big breakfasts. (Reception open Mon.-Fri. 5-10pm, Sat.-Sun. 6-10pm. Curfew 10pm. DM19, over 26 DM23. Sheets DM6.50. Breakfast included.) The adorable **Tor Café,** in front of the mighty Friedländer Tor, takes *Gemütlichkeit* to as yet unheard of levels (meals DM8-15; open Mon.-Sat. 11am-midnight, Sun. 3pm-midnight). **Lake Tollensee,** a wonderful afternoon swimming and tanning respite, is only 20 minutes by foot outside the city wall. To get there, walk through the Treptower Tor onto Rostockerstr. for 1.25km, make a left onto the trail along the little canal.

GÜSTROW

Were it not home to a huge collection of works by the prolific 20th-century artist **Ernst Barlach,** Güstrow would be like most of Mecklenburg-Vorpommern's towns— a bleak mass of crumbling buildings with satellite dishes and *Imbiße* poking out of the brick work. In addition to filling Güstrow with pacifist sculptures, Barlach fiercely opposed German nationalism and fascism, causing the Nazis to condemn his work as *Entartete Kunst* (Degenerate Art). Güstrow is also the hometown of **Uwe Johnson,** the GDR author subjected to constant surveillance and eventually forced into exile in 1959 for "subversive" writings which criticized the divisions between East and West.

Orientation and Practical Information Central Güstrow lies south of the train station. To get there, follow Eisenbahnstr. until it becomes Lindenstr., then go about 45 meters farther on Lindenstr. before turning left onto Pferdemarkt. *Geradeaus* (straight ahead). **Güstrow Information,** Domstr. 9 (tel. 68 10 23), finds rooms (DM20-30) for a DM3 fee (open Mon.-Fri. 9am-6pm, Sat. 9:30am-1pm; May-Sept. also Sun. 9:30am-1pm). The office offers guided city **tours** (DM4, students DM2) that leave from the *Rathaus* at 11am (June-Sept.). **Fahrrad Dräger,** Langestr. 49 (tel. 68 40 10), rents **bikes** for DM8-10 per day. Do laundry across the street at **SB Waschsalon,** Pferdemarkt 34 (wash DM6 per 7kg; dry DM2; open 7am-10pm). The **post office,** Pferdemarkt 52-56, 18271 Güstrow, close to the Markt, is extraordinary (open Mon.-Fri. 8am-6pm, Sat. 9am-noon). The **telephone code** is 03843.

Accommodations and Food Güstrow's **Jugendherberge (HI),** Heidberg 33, is rather inconvenient, a one-hour walk, and serviced only by a bus that comes every three hours. Take the same route as to the Barlach Atelierhaus, but stay on the path until it hits Heiberg, instead of cutting onto Bukower Chausee (curfew 10pm). Also consider using the **Zimmervermittlung** at the tourist office (tel. 84 00 44). **Cafe Küpper,** on Domstr., boasts a 143-year history of serving up sweets, sandwiches, and (more recently) pizza (DM7; open Mon.-Fri. 8am-7pm, Sat. 11am-7pm, Sun. 1-7pm).

Sights The Barlach tour of Güstrow begins on the southwest side of town with the **Dom,** which houses Barlach's most famous work, *Der Schwebende Engel* (The Hovering Angel). Created as a testament to the horrors of war, it was originally designed to hang above the pews of the *Dom* but is now tucked away in a corner. The statue was originally cast in 1926, but was then publicly melted down and cast into bullets by the Nazis in 1941; the Nazis intended to show the futility of pacifism while defaming the dangerously popular artist. After World War II, a plaster cast of the statue was found buried in Western Germany, and in 1952, the angel was restored and rededicated to the war's victims (open Tues.-Sat. 10am-noon and 2-4pm, Sun. 2-4pm).

Walking back to Domstr., the recently renovated towers **Schloß** ahead. A grand example of Renaissance architecture, it is complete with a cute **Schloßgarten** surrounded by an ingenious shrub wall (gates and windows included). The **Schloßmuseum** (tel. 75 20) brims with Italian and Dutch paintings from the 15th to the 17th century, as well as works by Barlach (open April-Oct. Tues.-Sun. 10am-6pm; Nov.-March Tues.-Sun. 10am-5pm; DM5, students DM3). On the west side of town, the **Gertrudenkapelle,** Gertrudenpl. 1 (tel. 68 30 01), houses an excellent collection of Barlachs in its octagonal white chapel and peaceful garden. From the station, walk down Eisenbahnstr.; take a right on Gertrudenstr. (open March-Oct. Tues.-Sun. 10am-5pm; Nov.-Feb. Tues.-Sun. 11am-4pm; DM3, students DM2). The only church in town neglecting Barlach is the **Pfarrkirche St. Marien.** Sitting in the shadow of the *Dom*, the church is still artistically rich, displaying an impressive, recently restored altarpiece from 1522, and over 180 sculpted figures by Brussels artist Jan Borman, narrating the Passion of Christ on the stage. Organ music echoes in the church on Wednesdays at 12:15pm (open Tues.-Sat. 10am-noon and 2-4pm, Sun. 2-4pm).

Barlach's **Atelierhaus** (studio), Heidberg 15 (tel. 822 99), hosts the largest collection of his works in the very house in which they were created (open Tues.-Sun. 10am-5pm). It's a one-hour walk from the *Altstadt*, and bus #4a comes here every three to four hours, so renting a bike is the best way to visit. Head down Glevinerstr. from the Marktplatz and follow it as it turns into Planerstr. until you see the bike path signs for "Barlachweg." Follow this path all the way around the lake until you reach the "Boots-Verleih," then head down to the parking lot on the left and cut up to Bükoner Chausee; the museum is 200m to the right.

WISMAR

Wismar still reels from a vicious one-two combination of war damage and 50 years of neglect. Leprous buildings blackened from the fires of war, and scabs of exposed masonry still lightly pepper the *Altstadt*. Only the shells of two grand cathedrals stand with the rest of the buildings amputated by Allied bombers. Though restoration of old buildings was a low priority during the GDR days, the Marktplatz area has been fully cleaned up, and the rebuilding of the two cathedrals progresses, albeit at a sluggish pace. Off the Marktplatz on Sargmacherstr., the 80m **Turm** (tower) of the **St. Marien-kirche** is the only remaining shred of a beautiful 14th-century *Basilika* that was destroyed in World War II. The four clocks of the lovely tower still chime daily at noon, 3, and 7pm. The **St. Georgenkirche,** west of the St. Marienturm, was once the local church for craftsmen and traders and is now the local construction site during its renovation. The **Nikolaikirche,** nearer the port on Hinter der Chor, with its disproportionately small tower (the original was destroyed in a 1703 hurricane), provides a hint as to how Wismar's churches once appeared. Its interior contains one of the oldest organs in Mecklenburg (open Mon.-Sat. 1-6pm; information available in English). Closer to the Marktplatz, the **Heilige Geist Kirche,** Wismar's other intact church, also contains medieval art (open Mon.-Sat. 10am-noon and 1-5:30pm, Sun. 1-6pm).

The Marktplatz itself boasts a slightly dizzying juxtaposition of architectural styles. The citadel-like **Rathaus,** dating from the 14th century, was rebuilt in 19th-century Neoclassical style after its roof collapsed in 1807 and destroyed most of the original building. The medieval brick house with all the windows and the overgrown Punch and Judy head above the door is the **Alter Schwede,** the town's oldest *Bürgerhaus* (pub). The **Wasserkunst,** a metal mushroom built in Dutch Renaissance style in front of the Alter Schwede, was the village spigot for 300 years. Running downhill from the Marktplatz on ABC-Str., the **Schabbelhaus museum** features the works of local artists and an extensive medical history museum. Its gory centerpiece is a display case full of the most deformed teeth pulled by a local dentist. *Let's Go* recommends brushing your fangs at least twice a day (open Tues.-Sun. 10am-8pm; DM3, students DM1.50).

Frequent **trains** connect Wismar to Schwerin and Rostock. From the train station, follow Bahnhofstr. right, make a left on Am Poeler Tor, and follow it past the Nikolaikirche to reach the Marktplatz. Wismar has no youth hostel, so finding a place to sleep requires a visit to the **tourist office,** Stadthaus am Markt 11 (tel. 25 18 15; fax 28 29 58). It will find rooms (DM25-40) for a DM5 fee, and provide helpful brochures and maps (some in English). Call ahead (open daily 9am-6pm). For a bite to eat, head to **Das Kittchen** (slang for prison), Vor dem Fürstenhof 3 (tel. 259 43 20). It's decorated with cheerfully black humor in a jailhouse motif. Enjoy the *Sauerfleisch Knas-*

tfrüder (prisoners' pickled meat; DM11) or *goulash à la gulag* while waiting for your parole (open Mon.-Sat. from 5pm, Sun. from 10am. Meals DM6-12). The **Spar supermarket,** Lübschestr 21, off the Heiligenkirche corner of the Marktplatz, sells groceries (open Mon.-Fri. 8am-6pm, Sat. 8am-12pm). The **post office,** Mecklenburgerstr.18, 23966, is around the corner from the Marktplatz. The **telephone code** is 03841.

Cheap (DM2), uncrowded beaches stretch around the nearby island of **Poel.** Bus #460 goes from Große Schmiedstr. just off the Alter Schwede corner of the Marktplatz: "Timmendorf Strand" (DM4.60). Aside from its beaches, Poel has little to offer aside from views of horses galloping in rolling fields and grassy marshes by the sea.

■ Rostock

East German schoolchildren were always taught to think of Rostock, the largest and most active port of Eastern Germany, as socialist GDR's "gateway to the world." This red-bricked Hanseatic trading town has had a rocky history, but after reunification, Rostock's booming business declined as industrial ships began to shift their home harbors to Hamburg. Then, six years ago, an event occurred that would change the way the world viewed the city. On August 24, 1992, a hostel for foreigners seeking political asylum in Germany was attacked and set ablaze by neo-Nazis and other right-wing youths. The tension caused by an immigratory flood finally caused the dam to break here in Rostock. "The chanting was filmed and syndicated abroad... There were no distractions this time, not Kabul, not Sarajevo. ROSTOCK it said in big letters wherever you looked," wrote Günter Grass.

As far as the events of 1992 are concerned, today most Rostock natives would like to place them in the past; many walls spray-painted with swastikas also carry the more comforting message, *"Nazis raus!"* ("Nazis out!"), added by a later hand. Both psychologically and physically, the people here have made an effort to move on. Reconstruction and restoration work can be seen in most quarters of the *Altstadt* and the number of tourists flocking to the beaches is once again high. Indeed, what happened in 1992 should not discourage you from a visit to Rostock, but rather leave you aware of continuing problems in the new Germany. You might come to see the old church towers, or pass through on your way to Scandinavia; whatever the case may be, recall Grass's words, "since Rostock, Germany has changed."

ORIENTATION AND PRACTICAL INFORMATION

The majority of Rostock's sights lie in the downtown area, with the exception of **Warnemünde,** a peaceful fishing village and resort town to the northwest. If you spend a night in Rostock, it will be impossible to avoid the newer city suburbs, which consist of huge brick-and-concrete apartment blocks linked by long, wide roads. These areas are not well-lit, and their residents have been known to be hostile and aggressive toward foreigners. **Single travelers, particularly women, should avoid these areas at night.** Rostock is well-served by an extensive network of S-Bahn trains, buses, and trams; they run less frequently during the late hours and at night, so check schedules before you set out. Rostock is also a regional transportation hub.

Tourist Office: Schnickmannstr. 13/14, 18055 Rostock (tel. 194 33; fax 497 99 23). Streetcar #11 or 12: "Langestr.", then follow the signs to the right. **Room service** finds rooms for a DM5 fee (free if you call in advance). They also lead 1½hr. **tours** through the town (May-June and Sept. Wed. and Fri.-Sun. at 2pm). Open Mon.-Fri. 10am-6pm, Sat.-Sun. 10am-2:30pm. There is also an office in **Warnemünde,** Heinrich-Heine-Str. 17 (tel. 511 42). Walk across the bridge from the train station, cross Kirchenpl., and turn right on Heinrich-Heine-Str. Open Mon.-Fri. 10am-5pm, Sat. 10am-noon.; Sept.-June Mon.-Fri. 10am-4pm.

Currency Exchange: Citibank, on Kröpelinerstr. near Universitätspl., charges a 1% fee for exchanging cash. ATM open 24hr. Bank open Mon. and Wed. 9am-1pm and 2-4:45pm, Tues. and Thurs. 9am-1pm and 2-6pm, Fri. 9am-1pm.

Trains: Hourly connections to Schwerin (1hr.), Stralsund (1½hr.), and Wismar (1¼hr.). Daily connections to Berlin (2½hr.), Hamburg (3hr.), and Dresden (7½hr.). Call 493 44 54 for information.

Public Transportation: Streetcars #11 and 12 shuttle from the main station to the *Altstadt.* Single ticket DM2. *Tageskarte* (combined 1-day ticket) for streetcar, bus, and S-Bahn DM7.50. The S-Bahn leaves from the main station for Warnemünde and the newer suburbs every 15min. To get to the bus station for lines to smaller towns, exit the station through the Südstadt exit. Bus service peters out at night, leaving only the *Fledermaus* buses connecting a few central strops. Schedules of late night buses have blue circles with pictures of bats on them.

Ferries: Boats for **Scandinavia** leave from the **Überseehafen** docks. **TT-Linie,** Hansakai (tel. 67 07 90; fax 670 79 80) runs to Trelleborg, Sweden (3 per day, 5hr.; peak season July-Oct. one-way DM60, students and children DM36). **Scandlines Europa GT Links** (tel. 670 06 67; fax 670 66 71) sails to Gedser, Denmark (5 per day, 2hr., one way DM8, children DM4). Ferries also leave from the **Warnemünde** docks; the **DFO** (tel. 514 06; fax 514 09) sails to Gedser, Denmark, with special trips to other Scandinavian ports (8 per day; one-way DM10-16, children DM5-8; round-trip DM20-32, children DM10-16).

Mitfahrzentrale: Am Kabutzenhof 21 (tel. 493 44 38). Matches riders and drivers. Generally open 10am-4pm, but call ahead. Prices start at DM0.06 per km.

Bike Rental: Fahrradverleih Strandläufer, (tel. 45 28 27) in the Inter-City Hotel next to the train station. DM12 per day, DM8 per day for five or more days. ID required. Open Mon.-Fri. 9am-6pm, Sat. 10am-1pm.

AIDS-Hilfe Rostock: tel. 45 31 56.

Women's Hotline: Frauen in Not, Kinderkrippe Lichtenhagen, E. Warnkestr. 10 (tel. 711 167).

Pharmacy: Rats-Apotheke, Neuer Markt 13 (tel. 493 47 47), posts a list of 24hr. pharmacies. Open Mon.-Fri. 9am-6pm, Sat. 9am-1pm.

Emergency: Ambulance, tel. 115. **Police,** tel. 110. **Fire,** tel. 112.

Post Office: *Hauptpostamt,* Neuer Markt, 18055 Rostock. *Postlagernde Briefe* at counter 8. Open Mon.-Fri. 8am-6pm, Sat. 8am-noon.

Telephone Code: 0381.

ACCOMMODATIONS

Rostock has two hostels, both of them situated inconveniently far from the sights in the *Altstadt.* Past travelers have complained of harassment by local thugs while walking to the Jugendgästeschiff. Since booking guests into rooms in the rough end of the boonies is bad for business, the **Zimmervermittlung** (tel. 194 14) at the tourist office finds rooms with better safety and proximity.

The **Jugendherberge Rostock-Warnemünde (HI),** Parkstr. 46 (tel. 54 81 70), is fairly new and provides spacious rooms. S-Bahn (direction: "Warnemünde") to the end, cross the bridge, and head straight on Kirchenstr. which becomes Mühlenstr. and then Parkstr. (20-25min.). To avoid the walk, S-Bahn: "Lichtenhagen" and bus #36 (direction: "Warnemünde-Strand") to the end of Parkstr. Most rooms are doubles. Reception open 24hr. DM19.50, over 26 DM23. Sheets DM5. Breakfast and resort tax included. The **Jugendgästeschiff Rostock-Schmarl,** (tel. 71 62 24; fax 71 40 14), is a massive breakthrough in leisure technology, containing a hostel, a museum, and a bar. Leaving the boat is never necessary, and at night, not advisable, as the harbor neighborhood is dangerous. S-Bahn (direction: "Warnemünde"): "Lütten Klein," then bus #35: "Schmarl-Fähre," then take the buoy-lined road across from the bus stop to the end of the street. The bus stops running at 8pm. Alternatively walk out of the train stop, follow the foot path alongside the off ramp, then left on Warnower Allee for 30min., left again on the road full of buoys by the Schmarl-Fähre bus stop. DM20, over 26 DM25. Sheets included. Breakfast DM6.

FOOD AND NIGHTLIFE

While no one will ever accuse Rostock of being a gastronome's heaven, eating here doesn't necessarily mean choking on *ein Whopper* and *Pommes Frites* and chasing it down with a paper cup of Happy Daddy beer at the Universitätspl. Burger King. **Supermarket Spar,** Kröpelinerstr. 37 near the Kröpeliner Tor, offers a sizeable selection (open Mon.-Wed. and Fri. 8am-6pm, Thurs. 8am-8pm, Sat. 8am-1pm). In Warnemünde, several restaurants along the beach fish up the bounties of the ocean. If you're trying to stay financially afloat, try the fast food joints on Kirchpl.

Mensa, on the corner of Südring and Albert-Einstein-Str. From the train station or the *Altstadt*, tram #11 (direction: "Neuer Friedhof") to the end and bus #27 (direction: "Biestow") or 39 (direction: "Stadthalle/ZOB"): "Mensa" (one stop). Generous helpings of good food. With college ID DM2-4, others DM4-6. Open Mon.-Fri. 11:15am-2pm. Downstairs a bulletin board advertises all major parties and club shows, while on weekends the *Mensa* holds what students claim is the best **disco** in Rostock. Open Thurs.-Sun. after 10pm. Cover DM5 and up. The **Filmclub** shows movies every Tues. and Wed. at 9pm. DM2. Call 459 12 48 for the program.

Studentenkeller, Universitätspl. (tel. 45 59 28). Rostock's students go to unlearn in this Clark Kent *Keller*. A mild mannered cafe by day jumps into its phone booth, emerging as a rock club and disco by night. Cafe open daily 8:45am-5:30pm (closed in March and Aug.). Club open Mon.-Thurs. after 9pm, Fri.-Sat. after 10pm.

Mo Mo, Barnstorfer Weg 36. Tram 11: "Doberanerpl." Serves Middle Eastern noodle dishes along with tasty hip hop. Word. All you can eat brunch every Sunday (DM14.50; 9am-noon). Open daily 9am-2am.

Wespennest, Karlstr. 19 (tel. 492 21 93). A women-only cafe and women's center. Open Tues.-Sat. 7pm-midnight.

In Warnemünde:

Café 28, Mühlenstr. 28 (tel. 524 67), on the way to the hostel, is a shiny, happy hangout. Soups, salads, and small but tasty dishes run DM4-20. Vodka and coffee served (separately). Open May-Oct. Mon.-Sat. 10am-late.

Seehund Warnemünde, Am Strom 110 (tel. 511 93), is a cheerful and relatively cheap oasis of drinks built organically into the promenade of the *Alter Strom* (you can tread its roof on the upper road). Open daily 10am-2am or later.

SIGHTS AND ENTERTAINMENT

In the 12th century, Rostock's Baltic harbor made it a proud Hanseatic League member, and relics of this mercantile past still stand. Although half of the city was destroyed in World War II, many of the half-timbered and glazed-brick houses and Gothic churches have been restored. **Kröpelinerstraße,** the main pedestrian mall, lined with 16th-century *Bürger* houses, runs east to the **Kröpeliner Tor,** the former town gate. The main buildings of the **Universität Rostock,** one of the oldest universities in North Central Europe, are just a bit farther down Kröpelinerstr. Next to the university, along the remains of the city wall, sits the **Kloster zum Heiligen Kreuz,** a restored cloister originally built by the Danish Queen Margaret in 1270. The museum contains medieval art, sculptures by the omnipresent Ernst Barlach, and special exhibits (open Tues.-Sun. 10am-5pm; DM4, students DM2).

The principal landmark in Rostock is the 13th-century **Marienkirche,** a beast of a brick basilica near the main square at the Steintor end of Kröpelinerstr. (open Mon.-Sat. 10am-5pm, Sun. 11am-noon; DM2, students DM1). In the final days of the 1989 turmoil, the services here overflowed with political protesters who came to hear the inspiring sermons of Pastor Joachim Gauck. In one of his more heroic gestures, Pastor Gauck began to publicly chastise the secret police by calling out the names of those *Stasi* members whom he could identify from the pulpit; after reunification, Gauck was entrusted with the difficult job of overseeing the fate of the *Stasi* archives. The 12m **astronomical clock** behind the altar dates from 1472. At noon and midnight, mechanical apostles strut in a circular procession.

Rostock's Renaissance **Rathaus,** a strawberry-pink eyesore on Neuer Markt, was originally composed of three separate *Bürger* houses visually united by a Gothic wall with seven towers; elaborate detailing can still be seen above some of the portals. The **Steintor, Kuhtor,** and **Lagesbuschturm** sit in close proximity to Steinstr., connected

MECK.-VORPOMMERN

by remnants of the recently renovated town wall. The **Alter Markt,** Rostock's commercial center before the war, now buzzes with the hammering sounds of extensive restoration. Strike a Quasimodo pose as you ascend the tower of the **Petrikirche,** atop which you can see all of Rostock including its Springfield-esque nuclear power plant. D'oh! (Open Mon.-Fri. 9am-noon and 2-5pm, Sat.-Sun. 11am-5pm; tower DM2.) Rostock's **Zoo** (tram #11: "Zoo") deserves the adoration of the 800,000 visitors who flock here annually; the animals in residence include polar bears, elephants, and other biggies (open May-Aug. daily 9am-6pm, April-Sept. 9am-5pm, Oct.-March 9am-4pm; DM9, students DM7, children DM5). The **Schiffahrtmuseum der Hansestadt,** August-Bebel-Str. 1 (tel. 492 26 97), tram #11: "Steintor," tells tales of wild seafaring along the rocky Baltic coast (open Tues.-Sun. 9am-5pm; DM4, students DM2).

Rostock was once home to a very large Jewish population; many American and European Jews still carry the last name "Rostock." Little remains, however, of Rostock's Jewish community. The S.A. razed the synagogue on Augustenstr., and the S.S. annihilated the community soon after. Only partially destroyed in the war, the **Jewish cemetery** still stands. In the 1970s, the government decided to embed the gravestones face-down into the earth in order to create the city's **Lindenpark.** Pressure from the international Jewish community forced the city to right most of the stones and to include a memorial in 1988. Tram #1, 3, or 11: "Saarpl.," then south through the park. The sign outside claims that Rostock began renovating the cemetery in 1945 and completed the work in 1988—no mention of the detour along the way.

To the north of Rostock and accessible by S-Bahn lies the schizophrenic beach town **Warnemünde.** The **Alter Strom** (old harbor), across the bridge from the train station, rings with the sounds of fishing boats, fish hawkers, and the shattering of teeth on rock candy, creating the Nantucket side of the town's personality. Warnemünde's sunny side lies along the **Parkstraße,** with tan concrete houses on one side facing sandy beaches of the crystal-clear blue Baltic behind the woods. Along the *Alter Strom* toward the sea stands a **watch tower** whose middle platform is accessible during the day (DM3). For a comprehensive survey of those tiny, colorful *Pfister* houses, visit Warnemünde's **Heimatmuseum,** at Alexandrinerstr. 31, just off the Kirchenpl. (open Wed.-Sun. 9am-12:30pm and 1-5pm; DM3, students DM1.50).

■ Stralsund

Albrecht von Wallenstein, commander of the Catholic army during the Thirty Years War, lusted after Stralsund. "Even if it were chained to heaven, I'd want to have it," he panted, but Stralsund resisted his advances. The beauty that seduced Wallenstein is now unfortunately obscured by dust and rubble; as in so many eastern German medieval towns, restoration work is far from complete. Even though it may be crumbling around the edges, the once-spectacular architecture is still a poignant testimony to Stralsund's former wealth. As a free city, Stralsund helped to found the Hanseatic League in 1293, and quickly asserted itself as a trading hub and ship building center. Today the key to Stralsund's charm is its unique geography; the hill of the *Altstadt* is bordered to the south and west by two natural ponds and slopes gently north toward the *Strelasund,* the strait that separates the mainland from Rügen Island.

ORIENTATION AND PRACTICAL INFORMATION

Stralsund is directly connected by trains to Rostock (1 per hr.), and to Binz and Bergen on Rügen; trains also leave several times daily for Hamburg and Berlin. The major sights and attractions are concentrated in the *Altstadt,* where the distinctive spires of the city's three churches make excellent navigational beacons. **Ossenreyerstraße** is the main pedestrian zone; it runs north-south and encompasses a department store, **supermarkets,** and bakeries. Two of the city's former gates, the **Kutertor** and the **Kniepertor,** sit to the west and north, respectively. If you are planning on going to Rügen Island, **Der Touristen Paß** (The Tourist Pass; DM19, students DM9) gives you six coupons, each one good for either a museum entry, tour, ride on the Arkonabahn, or a boat rental, and is a wise investment.

Tourist Office: Ossenreyerstr. 1/2 (tel. 246 90; fax 24 69 49). From the station, head straight on Jungfernstieg, turn right onto the dirt path at the X intersection about 1km from the *Bahnhof* to transverse Knieper Teich, continue straight through the Kütertor, and turn left on Ossenreyerstr. Or bus #4 or 5: "Kütertor." The office distributes free maps, finds private rooms (DM25-100) for a DM5 fee, and sells tickets for **tours** through the *Altstadt* (DM7). Open Mon-Fri. 9am-7pm, Sat.-Sun. 9am-2pm; Oct.-May Mon.-Fri. 10am-6pm, Sat. 10am-2pm. The office in the **train station** (tel. 29 38 94) books rooms (DM5 fee). Open daily 10am-8pm.

Public Transportation: Bus lines #1-6 circle the *Altstadt*, serving the outskirts of town. Single fare DM2. The central **bus station** at Frankenwall is the departure point for **intercity buses** to Rügen and other surrounding areas (although trains are usually cheaper); check the **information desk** at the train station.

Ferries: Water tours of the harbor and the Strelasund depart daily from the dock behind the conspicuously floating hotel (1hr.; DM6, children DM5). **Reederei Hiddensee** (tel. 28 81 16) runs 3 times per day to the ports of Kloster, Vitte, and Neuendorf on Hiddensee (round-trip DM22-26, children DM12, bikes DM10) and to Schaprode on Rügen's west coast (DM3, children DM1.50).

Bike Rental: (tel. 28 01 55), in the train station. DM11-13 per day. Technically open Mon.-Fri. 6am-9pm, Sat. 7am-2:30pm, Sun. 9am-4:30pm, but you may need to ask at the tourist office in order to track somebody down.

Pharmacy: Bahnhofsapotheke, Tribseer Damm 6 (tel. 29 23 28), by the station.

Emergency: Ambulance, tel. 115. **Police,** tel. 110. **Fire,** tel. 112.

Post Office: Main Office, Neuer Markt, 18439 Stralsund, in the red-brick building opposite the Marienkirche. Also exchanges **currency.** Open Mon.-Fri. 9am-6pm, Sat. 9am-noon.

Telephone Code: 03831.

ACCOMMODATIONS

Jugendherberge Stralsund (HI), Am Kütertor 1 (tel. 29 21 60; fax 29 76 76). From the station, turn right onto Tribseer Damm and go straight to the "Hauptbahnhof" bus stop. Bus #4 or 5: "Küter Tor" (the 2nd stop), then turn right and take the first left onto Heilgeiststr.; the hostel is just before the big gate on the left. By foot, it's a gorgeous 10min. walk from the *Bahnhof*. Follow the directions to the tourist office (above), but stop at Küter Tor. Located in an old town hall with a courtyard, the hostel is convenient, but watch those strange angles and low ceilings. Many school groups in summer. Reception open 7-9am and 3-10pm. Lockout 9am-3pm. Curfew 10pm, but you can ring the bell until 1am. DM20, over 26 DM24. Buffet breakfast included. Sheets DM6.50. Closed Dec.15-Jan.15.

Jugendherberge Stralsund-Devin (HI), Strandstr. 21 (tel. 49 82 89). From the station, bus #3 or 60: "Devin" (25min.; DM2.50), then walk straight into the woods; take the trail on the left side of the dreary-looking Kurhaus-Devin, and left when you hit Strandstr. (5min.). Located in the nearby village of Devin, this place is bigger and more modern than the Stralsund hostel, but much harder to reach. The 20 buildings are close to the beach, and they're sometimes generous even when "full." Bikes rentals to guests DM10 per day. Reception open 3-8pm. Curfew 10pm. DM22, over 26 DM26. Breakfast included. Sheets DM7. Open March-Oct.

FOOD

Large portions and decent prices rarely keep company in Stralsund these days; even the supermarkets are pretty steep. While Stralsund waits for a McDonald's to drive down prices, **Teddybär** on Ossenreyerstr. handles the town's need for cheap, fast, and greasy food (open daily 8am-6pm). Get **groceries** at **Lebensmittel-Feinkost,** Ossenreyer 49, in the Ost West Passage (open Mon.-Fri. 8am-7pm, Sat. 8am-1pm).

Stadtbäckerei und Café, Ossenreyerstr. 43 (tel. 29 40 82). A cheap place to indulge in *Kaffee und Kuchen.* Open Mon.-Fri. 7am-6pm, Sat. 8am-5pm, Sun. 1-5pm.

Café Lütt, Alter Markt 12 (tel. 29 23 48), serves brightly-iced little cakes (DM3-5), including some Northern German rarities. Open daily 9am-6pm.

MECK.-VORPOMMERN

Zur Kogge, Tribseerstr. 26 (tel. 29 38 46). Fish and matching maritime interior. Open Mon.-Fri. 10:30am-3:30pm and 6-11pm, Sat.-Sun. 11:30am-11:30pm.

Al Porto, Seestr. 4 (tel. 28 06 20). Stralsund's beautiful people get their noodles at this mildly pretentious restaurant/cafe by the harbor. While much of the food is on the pricey side, the decent pizza is affordable (DM8-14). Open daily 11am-11pm.

SIGHTS

Stralsund's compact *Altstadt* island is unpolluted by GDR-era architecture. The **Alter Markt,** to the north, is surrounded by several of the town's oldest buildings. The remarkably well-preserved 14th-century red-brick facade of the Gothic **Rathaus** displays the coats-of-arms of the other major players in the Hanseatic League, such as Rostock and Hamburg, as well as Stralsund's trademark green and gold 12-point stars. The courtyard was designed in 1680 after a devastating fire precipitated the decision to transform this former warehouse into the town hall. The interior is closed to visitors, but you can catch a glimpse of it from the outside.

Behind the *Rathaus* loom the unmatched towers of the **St. Nikolaikirche,** built in the same French gothic style as Lübeck's Marienkirche. After a fire in 1662, one of the towers received a sophisticated Baroque dome while the other kept its flat roof. Restoration proceeds at a flying pace, with the astronomical clock and mast of the inside already refurbished and the tower scheduled to re-open in 1998. (Church open Tues.-Fri. 10am-5pm, Sat. 10am-4pm, Sun. 2-4pm; services Sun. 10am).

From the Alter Markt, Ossenreyerstr. (right at the end) leads to the **Neuer Markt** and the Gothic **Marienkirche.** Besides the usual large church attractions like a huge organ (concerts every other Wed. 8pm; DM7, DM5), graves (open Mon.-Sat. 10am-5pm, Sun. 11am-5pm, services Sun. 10am), and a painfully phallic Soviet Memorial out front, the church also offers the best view of Stralsund from its tower. Getting to the top is an adventure; after climbing the narrow, winding staircase, ladders ascend the last 150 feet to the top. The third of Stralsund's monumental churches, the **St. Jakobi,** on Böttcherstr., was heavily damaged in 1944 and is currently being restored.

Between the Alter and Neuer Markt, Stralsund's two major museums have replaced the monks in the adjoining buildings of the **St. Katharinen Monastery.** A good use for a **Touristen Paß** coupon is a visit to Stralsund's big aquarium, the **Deutsches Museum für Meereskunde und Fischerei,** Katharinenberg 14 (tel. 29 51 35), which contains many tanks of tropical fish, a shark tank, and the mandatory collection of Baltic Sea fish. Bring a camera, as the gift shop doesn't sell any postcards of the **five-foot-long whale penis** on display (open May-Oct. daily 10am-5pm; Nov.-April, Tues.-Sun. 10am-5pm; DM7, students DM3.50). Next door at the **Kulturhistorisches Museum** (tel. 29 21 80), you can see some beautiful old photographs and paintings of Stralsund when it was in better shape (open Tues.-Sun. 10am-5pm; DM4, students DM1.50).

A stroll along the **Sundpromenade** at sunset reveals a glowing red Rügen across the bay. Another beautiful walk runs along **Knieperwall,** alongside the **Knieperteich** (pond) and the remains of the **town wall.** The gates **Kniepertor** and **Kütertor** date back to the 13th century. An alternate route from the Alter Markt follows Külpstr. to Schillstr., ending at the **Johanniskloster,** a Franciscan monastery built in 1254—45 years after Francis of Assisi founded the order. Nestled down by the harbor, the monastery is a glory of Gothic hallways, 14th-century mosaics, murals (rescued from 30 layers of peeling paint), roses, and red-brick walls. The former **Johanniskirche,** ruined in 1944, now hosts occasional open-air concerts. The quiet courtyard (usually locked, but they'll open it if you ask) contains a dramatic Ernst Barlach *pietà*, as well as a **memorial** to Stralsund's lost Jewish community. The sculpture used to sit on the Apollonienmarket, near the former site of the synagogue, but was placed in the cloister for safe-keeping after it was vandalized by neo-Nazis in 1992; graffiti marks still remain. (Open Tues.-Sun. 10am-6pm. DM3, students DM2, including a tour that tells you neat stuff. Free last Wed. of every month.)

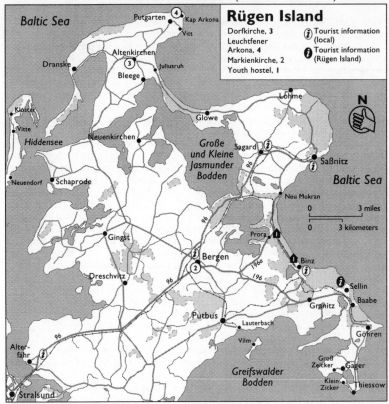

Rügen Island

Dorfkirche, 3
Leuchtfener
Arkona, 4
Markienkirche, 2
Youth hostel, 1

i Tourist information (local)
i Tourist information (Rügen Island)

■ Rügen Island (Insel Rügen)

Bathing in the Baltic Sea northeast of Stralsund, Germany's largest island wears an intricate mantle of beautiful coastline. The island's wildly varied landscape offers white beaches, rugged chalk cliffs, farmland, beech forests, heaths, and swamps. But Rügen is not all unsettled wilds; the island's history is long and occasionally tumultuous. Stone Age ruins and megalithic graves (easily identified piles of big stones) are scattered about like enormous paperweights. Teutonic tribes were pushed out by Slavs during 5th-century migrations; 500 years later, the rule of the pagan Slavs was broken by invading Danes, who bestowed the joys of Christianity upon the not-so-eager Slavs. In the 19th century, the island was discovered by the nobility and transformed into a resort stacked with expensive Neoclassical buildings that are now showing their age after decades of neglect.

The most striking architectural achievement of the island is understandably understated in the official tourist literature. An important part of Hitler's racial purification plan was the **Kraft durch Freude** (*KdF;* strength through joy) initiative, intended to cultivate Aryans for the new Germany. As part of this plan, the Nazi authorities designed a 3.5km complex of interconnected five-story buildings at **Prora** (5km north of Binz) that were intended to provide seaside lodging for 20,000 German workers at the negligible cost of three *Reichsmarks* per day. After the war, the nearly finished complex fell into the hands of the GDR, which intended to dynamite the whole thing. But after two unsuccessful attempts at demolition, the durability of the armored-concrete walls proved stronger than the will of East German authorities to purge the past. The buildings lodged the military until 1989. Except for a hotel, a youth hostel (see p. 242), a *Kindergärten,* and a few cafes, the mile-long hallways are now empty.

Today the tourist industry in Rügen is treading water. Once the prime vacation spot for East Germans, tourism has decreased somewhat as the Easterners explore Western Germany for vacations. Still, summer months are busy. *Let's Go* strongly recommends that you book a room in advance by phone or by writing ahead; be sure to specify how many people you need lodging for, how long you want to stay, and what you're willing to pay. If you don't speak German, write in English. For groups of three or more (sometimes even couples), a *Ferienwohnung* (vacation apartment) can be a surprisingly practical option (DM20-30 per person). There are only two hostels, one in **Prora** and the other in **Binz,** and the latter is almost constantly booked. The campgrounds peppering Rügen, however, provide a viable option. A handy helper is the *Wander und Freizeitkarte von Rügen und Hiddensee* map (DM9.90) which includes hiking trails, campgrounds, and sights—you can pick it up at any bookstore. Many tourist offices provide a free brochure of the island's campgrounds as well.

Rügen is so close to Stralsund's coast that you could almost swim there; since **trains** leave hourly for Bergen, Binz, and Saßnitz, however, you can probably leave your water wings at home. It's only an hour from Stralsund to Saßnitz, which makes daytrips feasible, especially if the hostels on Rügen are booked. **Buses** connect Stralsund with Rügen's largest towns, and a **ferry** runs to Schaprode, near Hiddensee, on Rügen's west coast. Major towns on the island include **Bergen** in the center, **Putbus, Binz,** and **Göhren** in the south, and **Saßnitz** in the north.

Once on the island, public transportation gets to be little tricky—most visitors come with cars. The *Deutsche Bahn* connects Bergen with Binz, Prora, Saßnitz, Putbus, and Lauterbach. To get to Kap Arkona in the north or Göhren in the south, however, you'll have to take the bus (which runs somewhat infrequently); check schedules carefully, and make sure you know when the last bus leaves, lest you get stuck. The **Rasender Roland,** a narrow-gauge rail line, runs from Putbus to Göhren with stops in many spa towns—unfortunately, the railway is more of a tourist attraction than a means of practical transportation. Although the island is large, the major points of interest generally lie no more than 20km from one another. The best way to get around is by combining the train and buses with walking, hiking, and biking. **Trails** are well-marked and cover the entire island.

BERGEN

With the majority of Rügen's seldom running buses and trains passing through it, Bergen serves as the island's waiting room. As transportation hub, this landlocked town, short on natural beauty and charm, cannot be avoided. Because it lacks a beach—the main reason to visit Rügen—Bergen is not heavily touristed and therefore usually has private rooms when the rest of the island has filled up. As Bergen is smack dab in the middle of the island, most points of interest on Rügen are within 30 minutes by train or bus. For those brave souls daring enough to leave the *Bahnhof,* turn left on Bahnhofstr. and follow it uphill, then take a left on Marktstr., the following insanity awaits: The **Marienkirche,** a Romanesque basilica built around 1200, is Rügen's oldest building. Apart from the usual faded frescoes, large organ, and big collection box, the most remarkable feature of the church are the outwardly splayed pillars. The architectural equivalent of platform shoes, the angled supports were intended to make the diminutive church look taller. (Open May-Sept. daily 9am-6pm; April and Oct. 10-11am and 2-3pm; to arrange a tour, call 231 00.) Behind the church lies the colossal (by Rügen standards) **Städtmuseum Bergen,** with three rooms full of habits, pictures of nuns, and other religious sundries (open May-Sept. Mon.-Sat. 10am-12:30pm and 1-4:30pm; Oct.-April Mon.-Fri. same hours; DM1.50, students DM1). On the hillside stands the pawn-shaped **Ernst-Moritz-Arndt-Turm,** containing a memorial to the 19th-century writer and revolutionary (open May-Oct. daily 10am-6pm; in winter 10am-5pm; DM2, children DM1). To get there from the Marktplatz, take Vieschstr. straight into the woods, and then follow the signs (20min.).

Trains and buses run every hour from Bergen to Binz and Saßnitz, and about every two hours to Putbus. The friendly **tourist office,** Markt 11 (tel. 25 60 95), in the *Rathaus,* finds private rooms (DM25-35) for a DM10 fee. To get there, take a left from the station to Bahnhofstr., then take a left onto the Markt (open June-Oct. Mon.-Fri. 10am-8pm, Sat. 10am-2pm; winter Mon.-Fri. 10am-6pm). **Fahrradverleih Richter,** Königstr. 18 (tel. 25 44 83), rents **bikes** (open Mon.-Fri. 10am-noon and 2-6pm, Sat. 9-11am). The **Rügard Apotheke,** Markt 26 (tel. 220 12), is a **pharmacy** with a 24-hour emergency bell outside (open Mon.-Fri. 8am-6:30pm, Sat. 8am-noon). **Rügenscher Hof,** Bahnhofstr. 5 (tel. 228 34), serves reasonably priced meals starting at DM7.80 (open Mon.-Sat. 7am-11pm). Deaden the pain of being in Bergen at **Bibo Ergo Sum,** Markt 12, which serves drinks at reasonable prices (DM5 for 0.5L beer), Italian food, and a decent selection of vegetarian food (open Mon.-Fri. 11am-2:30pm and daily after 6pm). Slightly north of Bergen in the small town of **Ralswiek,** a huge open-air theater hosts the yearly **Störtebeker Festspiele** (end of July to late-Aug.), a big theatrical production loaded with special effects that tells the tale of the *Seeräuber* Klaus Störtebeker, a local legend who was a Robin Hood-style rowdy (call 311 00 or fax 31 31 92 for exact dates and prices). The **post office,** 18528 Bergen, is at Markt 25 (open Mon.-Fri. 9am-6pm, Sat. 9-noon). The **telephone code** is 03838.

PUTBUS

Colloquially known as *"Weiße Stadt"* (White Town), **Putbus** was founded by Prince Walter von Putbus as a private residence and resort in 1810. Its most striking architectural landmark is the **Circus,** a now-empty plaza encircled by crumbling Neoclassical villas. Between the Circus and the shabby Marktplatz lies Rügen's only **theater,** a white building tastelessly adorned with paintings of Greek gods and goddesses. Alleestr. leads past the Marktplatz to the English-style **Schloßpark,** a more pastoral manifestation of the Prince's personal aesthetic. The statue of the prince still stands, though the palace, condemned as "decadent" by the Communists, was torn down in 1962. Walking south through the park, the glass-cupolaed **Affenhaus,** on Kastanienallee, served as a huge monkey cage for the amusement of the primates outside until the turn of the century. The **Rügener Puppen-und-Spielzeug-museum,** on Kastanienallee (tel. 609 59), lives there today with a kitschy collection of antique bisque dolls, doll houses, and teddy bears (open daily 10am-8pm; Oct.-March noon-5pm; DM5, students DM3). The area's best attraction may be Kastanienallee itself, which branches into dozens of hiking trails that lead to fields, ponds, and wildflowers.

The **Putbus tourist office,** August-Bebel-Str.1 (tel. 431), off the Marktplatz, gives out free maps and has a bulletin board where people post room listings. **Room booking** is monopolized by **Rolf Kempe,** Bahnhofstr. 2 (tel. 605 13; fax 613 95), who charges a DM10 fee (rooms DM30-65) and has lots of info on recreation activities in the area (open Mon.-Fri. 9am-6pm, Sat.-Sun. 10am-4pm). Rent **bikes** from **Albert's Fahrrad-Service,** Bahnhofstr. 5 (tel. 429), for DM8-10 per day (open Mon.-Fri. 9am-noon and 1:30-6pm, Sat. 9am-noon). Putbus is also the start of the line for the **Rasender Roland,** the narrow-gauge steam train that wheezes and its way through south Rügen at "whirlwind" speed (one way DM3-12, children 50% off; railpasses valid). Putbus's **Spar Supermarket** is on E. Güstelitzerstr.; from the Marktplatz with your back to Alleestr., head left (open Mon.-Fri. 8am-6:30pm, Sat. 8am-noon). The **post office,** on Marienstr., 18581 Putbus, is right off the Circus (open Mon.-Fri. 9am-noon and 1-5pm, Sat. 9-11am). The **telephone code** is 038301.

Three kilometers east of Putbus lies the minute and unremarkable town of **Lauter-bach.** Ferries to **Vilm,** a tiny island once owned by Prince Putbus that now houses a nature reserve, leave from Lauterbach's harbor at 10am, 1 and 3pm (tel. 618 96; 1½hr.; DM14, children DM6). To get to Lauterbach harbor from Putbus, take Lauterbachstr., which intersects Bahnhofstr. near the Circus.

BINZ AND PRORA

"They paved paradise and put up a parking lot." Joni Mitchell's words ring painfully true in describing Binz, the main beach town on Rügen Island. The beat on the street here is the sound of jackhammers working furiously to resurrect Binz as Germany's "other Sylt." Decrepit seaside mansions offer the ghost-like remains of Binz's former incarnation as a fashionable, aristocratic resort along the **Strandpromenade,** and are rapidly opening as spiffed-up luxury hotels. While there isn't much to see in Binz, there is plenty to do, with miles of sandy beach suitable for swimming, sunbathing, windsurfing, or playing badminton with accountants from Düsseldorf. There are also two **nude beaches** tastefully situated at the far ends of the town beach, suitable for just hanging out. Equally gritty fun can be found at the **Kurhaus;** once Binz's biggest hotel and hottest hotspot, it now smolders with family entertainment, as crooners and oompah bands dish out tunes that may leave you in tears. Luckily, Binz leaves a better taste in the mouth than in the ears, as it teems with restaurants, bars, and ice cream stands. The **Strandcafé Binz/Pizza Ristorante da Barbara,** Strandpromenade 29, serves pasta and herring specialties (DM8-15; open daily 11am-midnight). More restaurants and a **crazy billiards** game (miniature golf with pool cues, DM2.50 for 18 holes) are in the **Vitarium,** a greenhouse-type building at the north end of the beach.

Accommodations in Binz fill up quickly and are DM10-15 more expensive than other parts of the island. To deal with this, the town abounds with **Zimmervermittlung** offices, many of them charging immodest fees, although the office at Jasmunderstr. 2 (tel. 27 82) finds rooms free of charge (open Mon.-Fri. 9am-5pm, Sat. 9am-noon). Equally plentiful in Binz are **tourist offices;** the most convenient is in the *Bahnhof* (tel. 22 15), offering free maps and advice (open Mon.-Fri. 9am-5pm, Sat.-Sun. 9am-1pm). Getting around Binz is best done by on a **bike,** which may be rented at **Zweirad-Haus Deutschmann** (tel. 22 90) near the train station (DM10 per day; open Mon.-Fri. 9am-noon and 2-6pm, Sat. 9am-1pm). The **Rasender Roland** stops in Binz, but not at the *Hauptbahnhof* (where the trains from Bergen and Stralsund stop); there's a separate train station, **Binz-Ost,** responsible for the *Roland.* From the main station, head east on Dollahnerstr., continue on Jasmunderstr., and then turn onto Bahnhofstr. (20min.).The **post office,** Zeppeliastr. 3, 18609 Binz, is good (open Mon.-Fri. 9am-noon and 2-6pm, Sat. 9am-noon). The **telephone code** is 038393.

The scarcity of rooms worsens at the better-located of Rügen's two youth hostels, the **Jugendherberge Binz (HI),** Strandpromenade 35, 18609 Binz (tel. 325 97; fax 325 96), located directly on the beach. (Reception open 8am-noon and 7:45-9:30pm. Curfew 10:30pm, but you can get an access code. DM24, over 26 DM29.50. Sheets DM6. Breakfast included.) More dependable but exponentially less attractive accommodations await in the **Jugendherberge Prora (HI)** (tel. 328 44), a 400-bed beast of a hostel. Its bleak, Orwellian hallways have the acoustics of a stethoscope, enabling guests to hear the beating of the tell-tale hearts of school groups that stay here. To its credit, it does have a **bar** on the first floor. To get there, take either the Bergen-Binz train or the Binz-Saßnitz bus: "Prora-Ost," (not "Prora") cross the tracks and follow the signs. (Reception open 7am-9am and 4-10pm. Curfew 11pm. DM22, over 26 DM26. Call ahead or show up by 4pm.) This hostel has an even stranger definition of the word "full" than most German hostels; even if they swear they are, keep begging. They hold mail for guests. The **Edeka supermarket,** on Schillerstr. and Zeppeliastr., boasts long hours (open Mon.-Fri. 8am-7pm, Sat. 8am-6pm, Sun. 10am-6pm).

SAßNITZ

Saßnitz was a 19th-century seaside resort so popular it prompted Theodor Fontane to pen in *Effi Briest:* "To travel to Rügen means to travel to Saßnitz." Today, *visiting* Saßnitz means *leaving* Saßnitz to explore the nearby **Jasmund National Park,** a nature reserve containing the *Große Stubbenkammer,* as well as other spectacular chalk cliffs. The Jasmund peninsula, which sits to the northeast of the main port of Rügen, is surrounded by the *Große und Kleine Jasmunder Bodden* and the Baltic Sea; *Bodden* are shallow salt-water lakes that are scattered over Rügen and divide it into several peninsulas. The National Park covers one-third of Jasmund peninsula and incorporates two *Bodden* and the accompanying wildlife. Several marked hiking trails run through the **Stubnitz beech forest,** also part of the park.

Saßnitz's **tourist office,** Seestr. 1 (tel. 51 60; fax 516 16), is in the Rügen Hotel. From the train station, walk down Bahnhofstr. and left on Hauptstr. The staff books rooms (DM30-40) for free (open Mon.-Fri. 8am-7pm; April-Oct. also Sat. and Sun. 3-7pm). **Ferries** leave Saßnitz for Trelleborg, Sweden, the Danish island of **Bornholm,** and Poland. The **Arkona-Reederei,** Am Hafen (tel. 578 50; fax 578 52), has ships that leave Saßnitz at 9am, reach Bornholm 3½ hours later, and leave Bornholm at 4:30pm (May-Sept. round-trip DM32, children DM16). **DFO-Linie,** Trelleborgerstr. (tel. 641 80; fax 642 00), offers trips to Trelleborg (5 per day, 4hr.; DM30, under 11 DM20). Other companies send boats on **water tours** around the *Stubbenkammer* and to Kap Arkona (daily 9am-5pm; DM10-15). Rent a **bike** at Birkenweg 12 (tel. 350 75), about 500m right of the train station (DM10-15 per day; open Mon.-Fri. 9:30am-1pm and 2-5:30pm, Sat. 10am-noon). The **post office,** 18546 Saßnitz, is at Hauptstr. 34 (open Mon.-Fri. 8am-5pm, Sat. 9am-noon). The **telephone code** is 038392.

The closest campground is **Campground Nipmerow,** under ancient beech trees next to the National Park (tel. (038302) 92 44), near the *Königstuhl.* Catch the *Stubbenkammer* bus from Saßnitz and ask the driver to let you out at the camp. (Reception open 6am-10pm. DM7.50 per person. DM3-5 per tent. Wash DM5; no dryers.) **Am Kai** fries fish (DM8-12) directly on the harbor (open daily 10am-midnight).

GROßE STUBBENKAMMER

The spectacular chalk cliffs rising just north of Saßnitz and culminating in the famous **Große Stubbenkammer** (Great Chests of Drawers) were forged by massive glaciers 12,000 years ago; despite some erosion, they'll still give you the chills. There are a couple options for approaching the cliffs. The most direct (but also the least fun) is to take the **bus** from the stop outside the Saßnitz train station (DM2.50); it runs hourly during the summer and lets you off about 500m away from the **Königstuhl** (king's chair), the most famous of the cliffs. You can also follow one of the **bike trails** through the forest from Saßnitz to the *Königstuhl* (8km), but these bypass the most dramatic scenery. For the best views, take the **Hochuferweg** (high coastal trail) all the way from Saßnitz to the *Stubbenkammer.* Despite the intimidating name, the 8.5km trail (a 2½hr. hike) is fairly easy and runs from one incredible scenic lookout to the next. To pick up the trail, follow the "Stubbenkammer" signs through Saßnitz up the hill until you reach the parking lot, where there's a detailed map of the park showing all of the trails and their corresponding blazes—follow the ones for "Hochuferweg."

The trail takes you first to the **Wissower Klinken** (3km), which you might recognize from Caspar David Friedrich's paintings—these were his favorite chalk cliffs. Even though they've lost about 3m to erosion since he painted them, their beauty still seems almost supernatural. Continuing for another 5km, you'll reach the **Victoria-sicht** lookout, named after a German empress, and then the famous *Königstuhl,* which is anticlimactic after all the beautiful views. If you follow the mob to the lookout area, you'll have to pay for the view, which isn't much better than what you've already seen for free (DM2, students DM0.50).

Legend has it that the kings of Röf had to climb up to the top of the 110m *Königstuhl* to be crowned upon the stone chair. If you look up to the left, you'll notice a small guard post once used by GDR authorities to make sure no one escaped by boat to Sweden. For a bit of solitude, walk down the steep and windy paths to the flint-covered beach. Another trail leads from the *Königstuhl* to the lovely **Herthasee,** a lake named after the German harvest goddess Hertha. According to myth, Hertha drowned her mortal servants in this lake, and their spirits supposedly still gather on the banks each night, although we didn't stick around to find out. Nearby, the **Herthaburg,** a U-shaped earth wall built by the Slavs in the 7th century, recalls the less peaceful periods of this violently beautiful landscape.

GRANITZ AND GÖHREN

The **Jagdschloß Granitz** is a cheesy castle-like hunting lodge designed and built in 1836 by Prussian architect Schinkel, whose unmistakable creations can be discerned all over the island. Built atop the *Tempelberg* hill, its 38m tower offers a breath-taking panorama of the island. Bambi's family tree is mounted on the walls of the **Jagdmuseum** (hunting museum) inside the "castle" (open Tues.-Sun. 9am-5pm; DM4.50, students DM3.50). The *Roland* stops at the Jagdschloß, as does the **Jagdschloßexpress,** which makes round-trips from the *Kurhaus* in Binz (DM10, children DM6). From the "Jagdschloß" *Roland* stop, head uphill on the trail off to the right to reach the castle. To walk or bike the 5km from Binz, pick up the trail near the "Binz Roland" station. If you head south from the *Roland* "Jagdschloß" stop to the village of Lancken-Granitz, you'll pass by a bunch of huge prehistoric graves; one dates back to 2300BC.

The *Roland's* final stop is **Göhren,** on the easternmost tip of the forested **Münchgat peninsula,** which looks like a four-fingered glove. The peninsula was settled in the 13th century by monks, who believed in total self-sufficiency; the area thus developed unique customs and costumes. Things move at a noticeably slower pace than the rest of Rügen. Göhren, like every other town worth its salt on Rügen, has a nice beach; it's also the base of numerous **hiking and biking trails** leading through beautifully empty beaches, forests, and the rolling hills of the **Zickersche Alpen.** Göhren's main attraction is the **Münchguter Museum,** composed of four tiny museums scattered about the town. The **Heimatsmuseum,** on Theissowerstr., muses over local customs with exhibits of clothing, artifacts, and furniture (don't miss the antique loom). A few blocks down, the **Museumshof** is an old thatched-roof barn filled with strange farming implements. The **Rookhus** is a 17th-century thatched-roof fishing cottage. The **Museumsschiff,** a testament to traditional freight shipping, is a 1906 Dutch ship stashed behind the dunes on the southern shore outside of town. The **Schulmuseum,** in a one-room schoolhouse, recalls the days of simple education. (Each museum DM4, students DM3. Day card for all 4 museums DM14, students DM10. All open May-June and Sept.-Oct. Tues.-Sun. 10am-5pm; July-Aug. daily 10am-6pm.)

Navigating in Göhren requires little effort, as almost everything lies either on **Strandstraße** or right off it, and signs abound pointing to all areas of interest. To get to the center of town from the train station, follow Strandstr. up the hill. **Buses** connect Göhren to Binz and Bergen, and to Saßnitz and Klein Zicker in the south. The **tourist office** *(Kurverwaltung),* Schulstr. 8 (tel./fax 21 50), provides information and helps find rooms for a 10% fee. From the train station, follow Strandstr. up and to the left, then go right on Waldstr., and right again onto Schulstr. (open Mon.-Thurs. 8am-6pm, Fri. 8am–12pm and 4-6pm, Sat.-Sun. 4-6pm). **Sparkasse Rügen,** on Strandstr., cashes traveler's checks for free and has an ATM (open Mon.-Tues. and Fri. 8:30am-12:30pm and 2-4pm, Wed. 8:30am-12:30pm, Thurs. 8:30am-12:30pm and 2-6pm). Get groceries at **Aktiv Markt,** on the corner of Strandstr. and Waldstr. (open Mon.-Fri. 8am-6pm, Sat. 8am-1pm). **Tilly Fahrräder,** Schulstr. 7 (tel. 22 40), rents sturdy one-speed **bikes** for DM7 and touring bikes for DM9 (open Mon.-Fri. 9am-6pm, Sat.-Sun. 9am-noon and 5-6pm). The **post office,** 18586 Göhren, is at Poststr. 9 (open Mon.-Fri. 11am-noon and 3-5pm, Sat. 11am-noon). The **telephone code** is 038308.

The **campground** (tel. 21 22) is near the train station and the beach. From the station, turn right and follow the signs. They have **bike rental,** a cinema, restaurants, and a **laundromat.** (Reception open 7am-10pm. DM6 per person. DM3.50-6 per tent.) **Haus Norstrand,** Strandstr. 14, a big white restaurant with Christmas lights, serves hearty half-chickens and other standard German fare (open daily 11:30am-7pm).

KAP ARKONA AND VITT

At the northern tip of Rügen, Kap Arkona—Germany's only cape, flanked on either side by the villages of Putgarten and Vitt—stretches into the Baltic. **Buses** run (sort of) hourly from Saßnitz to Altenkirchen (45min., DM4.60) where you can transfer to the Putgarten bus, which also runs (sort of) hourly (15min., DM2). Infested with tour buses and gift shops, **Putgarten** serves as the transportation hub and tourist center of Kap Arkona. The two main attractions on the cape are accessible from Putgarten: the **lighthouses** and the town of **Vitt.** The **Arkonabahn,** a cheesy motorized train, connects to Putbus, Vitt, and the lighthouses for a modest DM8 (students DM5). **Horse drawn carts** offer even less efficient transportation between Putgarten and the lighthouses for the same prices as the slightly faster *Arkonabahn*. Before reunification, the two lighthouses on Kap Arkona resided in a restricted area belonging to the GDR's National People's Army. The **Leuchtfener Arkona,** designed by Schinkel, has been open to the public since 1993. Built in 1826, it guarded the GDR's sea borders. Nearby, the **Marinepeilturm** was built in 1927 and rigged up with a fancy electronic system that could eavesdrop on British radio communications. Now it houses archaeological finds from the former **Tempelburg Arkana,** a Slavic fortification built in the 8th century and destroyed by the Danes in 1168 (lighthouses open daily 10am-4pm; DM5). Buses back to Saßnitz leave every 2 hours or so.

The new **tourist office,** in the parking lot by Kap Arkona (tel. 419; fax 419 17), 300m down the road from Putgarten's bus stop, finds rooms for a DM15 fee (open Jan.-March daily 11am-5pm; March-May 10am-5pm; June-Oct. 10am-7pm). Pick up a free guide to Kap Arkona or rent a **bike** to wheel around (1hr DM2.50; day DM10). The **Drewoldke campground** (tel. 124 84) is east of Altenkirchen (reception open 8am-9pm; person DM6; tent DM4-6; open April-Oct.). The **telephone code** is 038391.

■ Near Rügen: Hiddensee

West of Rügen lies the slender island of Hiddensee, known in the *Plattdeutsch* dialect as *dat söte Länneken* (the sweet island). Free of youth hostels, campgrounds, motor vehicles, and other sources of pollution, Hiddensee remains the same sliver of untrammeled, unadulterated natural beauty that drew Sigmund Freud, Albert Einstein, and Käthe Kollwitz here. Ferries serve Hiddensee's three towns, Neuedorf, Vitte, and Klöster. Of the three, **Neuendorf** is the lest spectacular; like the heath surrounding it, Neuendorf rests silently except during the winter, when a local plant is picked for *Sanddorn,* a rust-colored, honey-like drink (DM5 per bottle, DM15-25 for the alcoholic variant). North of Neuendorf lies **Vitte,** the island's main town with the island's sandiest beach and tourist office, Nordereude 1662 (tel. 42 26; fax 642 25; open Mon.-Fri. 7am-5pm, Sat. 10am-noon). As Hiddensee has neither a hostel nor a campground, a visit to the **Zimmervermittlung** at the tourist office, which finds rooms for a 10% fee, or to **Stralsund** tourist information, which has a free list of houses with rooms for rent, is essential. The island's beauty and action climax in **Klöster,** the northernmost town. The great naturalist author and social dramatist Gerhardt Hauptmann summered in Klöster from 1930 to 1943 and is buried here, where there is a memorial to him and his work (open daily 10am-5pm; DM3, students DM1.50; closed Dec.-Feb.). The huge wine cellar reveals that Hauptmann loved the bottle nearly as much as letters. The nearby **Heimatmuseum,** Kirchweg 1, contains an eclectic, if small, collection of local art, amber, stuffed birds, and fishing nets (open April-Oct. daily 10am-4pm; Nov.-March Mon.-Fri. 10am-4pm, Sat.-Sun. 11am-2pm; DM4, students DM1).

Klöster's museums and sandy beaches are mere appetizers for the hills above the town which make up the **Dornbusch,** an area so pristine not even bikes are allowed. Follow the trails (hay-covered to avoid erosion) which run along the grassy hillsides carpeted with wildflowers to reach the **Leuchtturm,** atop which you can see the entire island (open May-Oct. daily 10:30am-6pm; April Mon.-Thurs. 10:30am-6pm; Fri.-Sun. 10:30am-3pm; DM4). Fully enjoying Hiddensee requires renting a **bike,** preferably a burly one with plenty of gears and nice fat tires (à la *Fear and Loathing in Las Vegas*), as the majority of the island's roads are either muddy country trails or sandy beach paths. Bike rentals *(Fahrradverleih)* are everywhere on the island, with DM10 per day the standard rate for a three-speed. Provided you get up very early, you can go bombing down the path from the *Dornbusch* to Klöster, a winding 1.6km descent over gnarly, pot-holed cement. At the bottom, buy a thirst-quencher at the **Spar supermarket,** Hatenweg 6 (open Mon.-Fri. 8am-7pm, Sat. 8am-6pm).

Ferry connections are available to Hiddensee from Stralsund on the mainland (see Stralsund, p. 236) and Schaprode on Rügen's west coast. Ferries leave Schaprode approximately four times per day (45min.; DM8, children DM6; round-trip DM12, children DM8; bikes DM10). The **telephone code** is 038300.

MECK.-VORPOMMERN

Schleswig-Holstein

Between Schleswig-Holstein's twin coastlines lies a flat, green, and lush countryside of tiny towns populated primarily by cows. Scenic cycling paths wind from the North Sea beaches, across the cobblestone hills of Lübeck, and on to the vivaciously gritty port of Kiel. Schleswig-Holstein became a Prussian province in 1867 following Bismarck's defeat of Denmark and chose to remain part of Germany at the end of World War I. However, the state retains close cultural and commercial ties with Scandinavia. Numerous Danish libraries and schools (and plenty of tourists) are scattered within its borders. The state's major ports are connected by ferries to Danish, Swedish, and Norwegian docks. Hamburg, the sultry, progressive metropolis on the region's southern border, is a politically autonomous *Land*, but looms influentially over the region.

■ Hamburg

The largest port city in Germany, Hamburg radiates an inimitable recklessness. Calling its atmosphere "liberal" or "alternative" does not do the city justice. With a licentious sex industry comparable only to Amsterdam's and a fiercely activist population of squatters, Hamburg is a crazy coupling of the perverse and the progressive. As a busy port Hamburg gracefully grew over the centuries into an industrial center of nearly two million inhabitants. Gaining the right to navigate the Elbe in 1189, Hamburg held off pirates and trading rivals, emerging by the 13th century as a leading power of the Hanseatic League. Straddling several rivers, it was an early hub for overland trade from the Baltic Sea, and the growing profits of the lucrative shipping trade led to dabbling in other financial concerns. The first German stock exchange convened here in 1558, and the Bank of Hamburg dates back to the early 1600s. In 1618 Hamburg gained the status of Free Imperial City, and a proud tradition of autonomy endures to this day. The commercial city's insistent neutrality protected it through the Thirty Years War, when the rest of northern Germany was ravaged.

Poised on the crest of Germany's breakneck industrialization and naval construction drive, Hamburg became one of Europe's wealthiest metropoli by World War I. The *Hamburg-Amerika Linie* ruled the oceans of industry as the largest shipping firm in the world. The city suffered a severe pummeling at the outset of World War II, when it became the first stop for the Royal Air Force's wrath. Because the port was the primary Allied target, a single air raid killed more than 50,000 civilians, many of whom lived in crowded tenements along the waterfront. The conflagration in the streets reached temperatures of 1800°F (1000°C), leaving nearly half the city's buildings in ruins. Fortunately, Germany's richest city could afford the reconstruction of much of its copper-roofed brick architecture. Since the late 1960s, an active conservation movement has steadily lobbied for the restoration of historic buildings, including museums, hotels, and houses. In the early 80s, violent riots erupted when police attempted to evacuate warehouses occupied by anarchists and left-wing intellectuals protesting property speculators' acquisition of the real estate. Today, Hamburg expresses its restlessness less violently; instead, it exudes the excitement of a city which has become a mecca of contemporary artists and reveling party-goers who absorb Germany's self-declared "capital of lust."

ORIENTATION AND PRACTICAL INFORMATION

Hamburg's fame as a North Sea port relies upon its huge harbor 100km inland, on the north bank of the **Elbe River.** The city is squeezed between the river and the two city lakes (**Außenalster** and **Binnenalster**) formed by the confluence of the Alster and Bille Rivers with the Elbe. Most major sights lie between the **St. Pauli Landungsbrücken** ferry terminal in the west and the *Hauptbahnhof* in the east. Much of the city around the docks is part of the *Freihafen* (duty-free zone), so be prepared for

Schleswig-Holstein and Hamburg

customs stops when leaving this area. Both the **Nordbahnhof** and **Südbahnhof** S-Bahn stations exit onto the *Hauptbahnhof.*

The **Hanse Viertel** is a mall thick with shops, art galleries, and auction houses. The mall's glamour turns otherwise humdrum window-shopping into an aesthetic adventure. Students aimlessly meander in the area around **Sternschanze,** where quirky shops selling everything from junk jewelry to exotic spices crowd the sidewalks. A flea market sells its junk here every Saturday. The **Altona** district, with its own major train station, was once an independent city ruled by Denmark; as Hamburg grew, the Danes were ousted. At the south end of town, an entirely different atmosphere reigns in the **Fischmarkt** along the Elbe at **St. Pauli.** Near the mural covered houses veritable anarchy reigns as vendors haul in and hawk endless varieties of fish, produce, CDs, and other goods. The Fischmarkt fascinates in the morning, as early risers mix with revelers from St. Pauli who rally to keep the night going. Listen for cries of *"Ohne Geld!"* ("No Money!") and look sharp—to grab attention, the fruit vendors toss free pineapples into the crowd (market open Sun. 5-10am, off season 7-10am; U- or S-Bahn: "Landungsbrücken" or S-Bahn: "Königstr.").

The **Hamburg Card,** available at the tourist offices, offers a great means of exploring the city. It provides unlimited access to public transportation and discounts of up to 50% on city tours and museum admission (day DM12.50, 3 days DM24.50).

Tourist Offices: Hamburg's two main tourist offices supply free maps and various pamphlets. The **Hauptbahnhof office,** Kirchenallee exit (tel. 30 05 12 01; fax 30 05 13 33; http://www.hamburg-tourism.de) books rooms for a DM7-8 fee. Open daily 7am-11pm. The less crowded **St. Pauli Landungsbrücken office** is located between piers 4 and 5 (tel. 30 05 12 00). Open daily 10am-7pm; Nov.-Mar. 9:30am-5:30pm. A third office is in the **Hanse Viertel** mall. Open daily 9am-6pm.

Tours: Sight-seeing tours *(Stadtrundfahrt)* leave several times daily from Pier 4-5. Tours last 2hr., include all major sights, and are conducted in English (DM24, children under 14 DM10; discount for *Hamburg Card* holders). For an additional DM5-10, they'll throw in a tour of the port. Call 10 24 43 39 or ask at the tourist office for times. **Alster-Touristik** (tel. 34 11 41), across from the Hotel Atlantic on the Außenalster (S-Bahn: "Dammtor"), will lead you on a one hour jaunt around the lakes (daily 10am-5pm, every 2hr.; DM12, children DM6).

Consulates: Ireland Feldbrunnenstr. 43 (tel. 44 18 62 13). U-Bahn: "Hallerstr." Open 9am-noon. **New Zealand** Heimhuderstr. 56 (tel. 442 55 50). **U.K.** Harvestehuder 8a (tel./fax 448 03 20) U-Bahn: "Hallerstr." Open 9am-noon and 2-4pm. **U.S.** Alsterufer 27-28 (tel. 41 17 13 51), on Außenalster's west side. Open Mon.-Fri. 9am-noon.

Currency Exchange: The **bank** at the Kirchenallee exit of the train station boasts long hours but bad exchange rates and high commissions (DM5 on transactions of DM100 and less, DM10 on transactions above DM100, DM7.50 for American Express). Open daily 7:30am-10pm. Better rates are available at downtown banks (usually open 9am-1pm and 2:30-4pm, Thurs. 9am-1pm and 2:30-6pm).

American Express: Ballindamm 39, 20095 Hamburg (tel. 30 90 80, refund service tel. (0130) 85 31 00; fax 30 90 81 30). Mail held for cardmembers up to four weeks (no charge). All banking services. Open Mon.-Fri. 9am-5:30pm, Sat. 10am-1pm.

Flights: For information call 507 50 or contact individual carriers. **Lufthansa** (tel. (01803) 80 38 03) and **Air France** (tel. 50 75 24 59) are the two heavy hitters that fly to Hamburg. Buses zoom off to **Fuhlsbüttel Airport** (serving most major European and German cities) from the Kirchenallee exit of the *Hauptbahnhof* (5am-9:20pm, every 20min., 30min.; DM8, ages 12 and under DM4, family DM18). The bus leaves for the *Hauptbahnhof* from terminal 4 in the airport (every 20min. 6:30am-11pm). Alternatively, the U-Bahn heads to "Ohlsdorf," from which a bus departs for the airport (daily 5:30am-11pm, every 10min., DM3.90).

Trains: The **Hauptbahnhof** handles most traffic with connections to Berlin (3½hr.; IC), Bremen (1hr.), Munich (5½hr.; ICE), Copenhagen (6hr.) and Zurich (9½hr.; ICE). For **train information** call 194 19. **Dammtor** station is across the Kennedy/ Lombards bridge, and **Altona** station is in the west of the city. Most trains to and from Kiel, Schleswig, Flensburg, and Westerland stop only at **Altona.** Frequent trains and the S-Bahn connect the 3 stations.

Buses: The long-distance bus station is located on Adenauerallee, around the corner from the *Hauptbahnhof.* Buses go to Berlin several times daily (3½hr.; one way DM39, round-trip DM62). Prices vary slightly by carrier. **Eurolines** (tel. 24 71 06; fax 280 21 27) travels to Amsterdam (6½hr.; DM63 one way, DM95 round-trip), Paris (28hr.; DM 90 one way, DM155 round-trip), and London (15hr.; DM90 one way, DM155 round-trip). **Becker Reisen** (tel. 31 43 41; fax 317 45 07) sends buses as far away as Krakow, Poland (3 per week, 16hr.; DM100 one way, DM170 round-trip; students under 26 DM90 one-way, DM155 round-trip).

Public Transportation: The efficient public transportation system (buses, U-Bahn, and S-Bahn) charges DM2.50-15, depending on distance. All public transit effectively shuts down from midnight to 4:30am. While regular **day tickets,** *Ganztageskarte,* (DM9.20-13.90) for the U-Bahn and the S-Bahn are readily available the **Hamburg Card** is a better deal (see above). The new **9-Uhr-Tageskarte,** a 9hr. ticket, costs DM7.70-12.40. A **family day ticket** (DM13.20-17.70) is good for up to 4 adults and 3 children under 12. A **3-day ticket** sells for DM22.30. All cards can be purchased at tourist offices; day tickets can also be bought at orange *Automaten.*

Ferries: Scandinavian Seaways, Van-der-Smissenstr. 4 (tel. 38 90 30; fax 38 90 31 41), about 1km west of the Fischmarkt (U-Bahn: "Königstr."), sets sails to England and Ireland. Overnight ferries run to Harwich, England (20hr.) every other day. The cheapest tickets cost DM183, students DM147; Fri.-Sat. DM183, students DM163. Other destinations include Copenhagen, Oslo, and Amsterdam—call for details.

Boat Rental: You can rent sailboats, paddleboats and rowboats on the Außenalster from **Kpt. Pieper,** An der Alster (tel. 24 75 78), directly across from the Hotel Atlantic at the foot of the Kennedy bridge. S-Bahn to "Dammtor," then east along Alsterglacis. Sailboats DM26 per hour for 1-2 people (additional DM3-4 apiece), paddleboats and rowboats DM18 per hour. Sailing license required to rent sailboats.

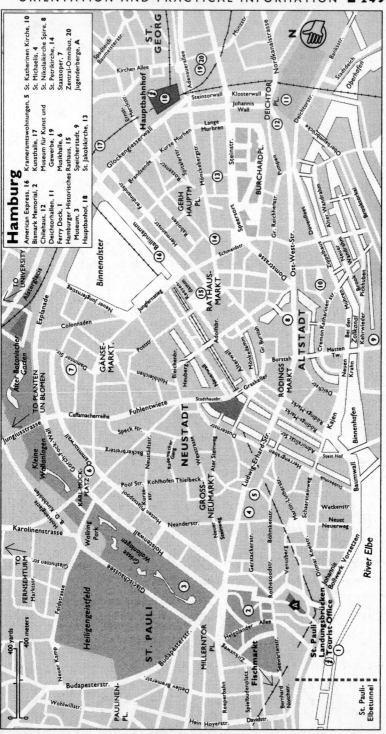

Hamburg

American Express, 16
Bismark Memorial, 2
Chilehaus, 12
Deichtorhallen, 11
Ferry Dock, 1
Hamburger Historisches Rathaus, 15
Hauptbahnhof, 18
Krameramtswohnungen, 5
Kunsthalle, 17
Museum für Kunst und Gewerbe, 19
Musikhalle, 6
Museum, 3
St. Katherinen Kirche, 10
St. Michaelis, 4
St. Nikolaikirche Spire, 8
St. Petrikirche, 14
Staatsoper, 7
Speicherstadt, 9
St. Jakobikirche, 13
Zentral-Omnibus, 20
Jugenderberge, A

Car Rental: Hertz, Kirchenallee 34-36 (tel. 280 12 03), is opposite the *Hauptbahnhof.* Open Mon.-Fri. 7am-6pm, Sat. 8am-4pm, Sun. 10am-4pm.

Bike Rental: O'Niel Bikes, Beethovenstr. 37 (tel. 531 177 44), offers German-language bike tours of the city and environs. Prices range from DM49 for 3hr. to DM129 for an all-day extravaganza. They also rent bikes (DM19 per day).

Hitchhiking: *Let's Go* does not recommend hitchhiking as a safe mode of transportation. Those headed to Berlin, Copenhagen, or Lübeck take U-Bahn #3 to "Rauhes Haus," then walk up Hammerstr. to Hamburg Horn (a treacherous traffic rotary at the base of the *Autobahn*). Hitchers aiming for points south take S-Bahn to "Wilhelmsburg" and wait at Raststatte Stillhorn.

Mitfahrzentrale: City Netz Mitfahrzentrale, Gotenstr. 19 (tel. 194 44). U-Bahn #3: "Berliner Tor," offers high-tech matching. Open daily 9am-7pm. DM0.10 per km.

Bookstores: English Books Second Hand, Stresemannstr. 169 (tel. 851 44 78), a few blocks to the left of the Holstenstr. S-Bahn stop. Somewhat disorganized but inexpensive. Open Mon.-Fri. 9:30am-6:30pm, Sat. 10am-4pm. **Heinrich-Heine-Buchhandlung,** Grindelallee 24-28 (tel. 441 13 30; fax 44 11 33 22; http://www.buchkatalog.de), in the university district, has a superb selection of German literature. Open Mon.-Fri. 9:30am-7:30pm, Sat. 10am-1pm.

Library: Staats- und Universitätsbibliothek, Von Melle Park 3 (tel. 41 23 22 33), in the vicinity of the university. Fine English-language section. Borrowing cards can be acquired between 10am and 4pm. Photo ID required. Open Mon.-Fri. 9am-9pm.

Lesbian and Gay Center: Magnus Hirschfeld Centrum, Borgweg 8 (tel. 279 00 69). U-Bahn #3 or bus #108: "Borgweg." Daily films and counseling sessions. A good source of info on the gay and lesbian community. Evening cafe, open daily 5pm-midnight. No men allowed Wed.-Thurs. 3-7pm. Center open Mon.-Fri. 9:30am-1pm. **Hein und Fiete Gay & Lesbian Information Center** (tel. 24 03 33), Kleiner Pulverteich 17-21, open Mon-Fri. 4-9pm, Sat. 4-7pm.

Laundromat: Schnell und Sauber, Grindelallee 158, in the university district. S-Bahn #21 or 31: "Dammtor." Wash 6kg DM6, soap included. Dry DM1 for 15min. Open daily 6am-11pm. There are also several laundromats on Simon-von-Utrecht-Str., heading towards the Altona station from St. Pauli.

Rape Crisis Line: tel. 25 55 66, Mon. and Thurs. 9:30am-1pm and 3-7pm, Tues.-Wed. 9:30am-1pm and 3-4pm, Fri. 9:30am-1pm. **Opferhilfe Beratungstelle,** Paul-Nevermann-Platz 2-4 (tel. 38 19 93), offers advice to victims of sexual crimes. Phone line open Mon.-Thurs. 9am-5pm, Fri. 9am-2pm. Personal appointments can be arranged.

Pharmacy: Central Apotheke, Rödingsmarkt 1 (tel. 378 67 30), is open Mon.-Wed. and Fri. 7:30am-6:30pm, Thurs. 7:30am-7pm, Sat. 8am-2pm.

Emergency: Police, Kirchenallee 46, opposite the train station (tel. 110). **Ambulance,** tel. 112. Headquarters at the Berliner Tor U-Bahn station.

Internet Access: In the **Regionales Rechenzentrum der Universität Hamburg,** Schlüterstr. 70 (tel. 412 31).

Post Office: Branch at the Kirchenallee exit of the *Hauptbahnhof,* 20099 Hamburg (open Mon.-Fri. 8am-8pm, Sat. 8am-6pm, Sun. 10am-4pm). **Poste Restante** *(Postlagernde Briefe),* 20097 Hamburg, in the main branch on Gr. Burstah 3. Open Mon.-Fri. 8am-6pm, Sat. 8am-12pm.

Telephone Code: 040.

ACCOMMODATIONS AND CAMPING

Hamburg's single rooms, from DM60, reflect the cost of the city's accommodations. Many establishments are tawdry with few comforts. A slew of small, relatively cheap *Pensionen* line **Steindamm, Bremer Weg,** and **Bremer Reihe,** the north of the *Hauptbahnhof.* Be aware: Herbertstr. isn't the only place in Hamburg where you can pay and get screwed. The tourist office's *Hotelführer* (DM1) offers a good means of navigating past the filth. For longer stays, try the **Mitwohnzentrale** at Lobuschstr. 22 (tel. 194 45; open Mon.-Fri. 9am-5:30pm, Sat. 9am-1:30pm). Passport required, as well as a deposit of either DM100 cash or DM50 and a bank account number.

Hostels and Camping

Jugendherberge auf dem Stintfang (HI), Alfred-Wegener-Weg 5 (tel. 31 34 88; fax 31 54 07). S-Bahn #1, 2, or 3, or U-Bahn #3: "Landungsbrücke." Follow the signs in the U-Bahn and hike up the steps to the hill above. A great location near the Reeperbahn and the subway, a beautiful view of the harbor, free storage lockers, and kitchen facilities. However, what really draws travelers to this hostel is the **Fantasy Island chessboard,** with 1m high pieces!—"Checkmate, Mr. Rourke." Call ahead, since not even clout with Tattoo can score a bed during busy weekends. Reception open noon-1am. Curfew 1am, stragglers admitted at 2am. Check-out 9am. DM24, over 26 DM29. Sheets and breakfast included.

Jugendgästehaus-und-Gästehaus Horner-Rennbahn (HI), Rennbahnstr. 100 (tel. 651 16 71; fax 655 65 16), U-Bahn #3: "Horner-Rennbahn." From the main exit of the station, turn right—the hostel is about 10min. by foot, at the corner of Tribünenweg. Located a bit farther from the sights than auf dem Stintfang but about the same distance from the *Hauptbahnhof.* Extremely clean and secure. Soundproof walls ensure that you won't hear a peep from the disco downstairs. Reception open 7:30-9am and 1pm-1am. Curfew 1am, stragglers admitted at 2am. DM26 for HI-members, DM36 for non-members, members over 27 DM34.50. Sheets and excellent breakfast buffet included.

Camping: Campingplatz Buchholz, Kielerstr. 374 (tel. 540 45 32). S-Bahn #3 (direction: Pinneberg) or S-Bahn #21 (direction: Elbgaustr.): "Stellingren." Walk straight on Volksparkstr. and turn right on Kielerstr. Reception open 7am-10pm. DM7 per person. Showers DM1.50. Call ahead.

Hotels

Schanzenstern Übernachtungs-und-Gasthaus, Bartelsstr. 12 (tel. 439 84 41; fax 439 34 13). U- and S-Bahn: "Sternschanze," left onto Schanzenstr., right on Susannenstr., and left to Bartelsstr. Located in the student district. Friendly staff. Dorms DM35; singles DM60; doubles DM90; triples DM 110. Breakfast buffet DM10.

Pension Sarah Peterson, Lange Reihe 50 and 98 (tel./fax 24 98 26). The eminently charming Frau Peterson decorates every room of her small, artsy *Pension* with original works of a bohemian flair, a TV, and a phone. Musically inclined guests occasionally perform in the dorm at Lange Reihe 98. Singles DM60; doubles DM85; three people in a double DM85; triples DM180; quads DM240. Breakfast included.

Hotel Terminus Garni, Steindamm 5 (tel. 280 31 44; fax 24 15 18). From the *Hauptbahnhof*'s Kirchenallee exit, turn right. Almost always has vacancies. Reception open 24hr. Doubles DM45, with shower DM60; triples with bath DM165. Breakfast included. Major credit cards accepted.

Hotel Alt Nürnberg, Steintorweg 15 (tel. 24 60 23; fax 280 46 34). From the station, go straight ahead from Kirchenallee, veering off toward Steintorpl. on the right, then look for Steintorweg on the left. TV and phone in each of the small, clean rooms provide an island of sanity amidst the drug-ridden chaos of the *Hauptbahnhof* and the nearby Bremer Allee. Reception open 8-11pm. Singles DM60, with shower DM90; triples DM135.

Hotel Annerhof, Lange Reihe 23 (tel. 24 34 26). From the station's Kirchenallee exit, take the second left. Singles DM48; doubles DM82. Breakfast DM8. Call ahead.

FOOD

Small seafood restaurants and fry stands squat along St. Pauli's Quai, **Landungsbrücke.** For less fishy fare, the **Rathausmarkt** serves up food at easy-to-swallow prices. A generous portion of *Swäbische Spätzle* (noodles with onions, ham, and cheese) costs about DM8. Better deals reside in the inexpensive cafes and restaurants of the university area. **Renteelstr., Grindelhof, Grindelallee,** and **Schanzenstraße** The *Fußgängerzone* (pedestrian mall) in **Altona** leading up to the train station is packed with ethnic food stands and produce shops. The **Safeway grocery store** in the Mercado Mall, Altona offers basic foodstuffs (open Mon-Fri. 10am-8pm, Sat. 9am-4pm). No stomach has visited Hamburg until it absorbs a plate of the city's specialty stew, *Labskaus.* An affront to the eyes and arteries, it consists of a mash of fried potatoes, pickled beets, cucumbers, and herring, topped with a fresh egg. It's delicious—proof of the culinary truth Germans have known for ages: grease is the soul of flavor.

Geo Pizza aus dem Holzbackofen, Beim Schlump 27 (tel. 45 79 29). Delectable pizzas (DM8-15), baked in an oven hot enough to make steel glow, highlight the large vegetarian selections. The Inferno Pizza (DM11.80-13.80), topped with an incendiary blend of jalapenos, red peppers, beef, onions, salsa, and corn, transforms humans into fire-belching beasts. Open Sun.-Thurs. 11am-1am, Fri.-Sat. 11am-2am.

Mensa, Schlüterstr. 7. S-Bahn: "Dammtor," then head north on Rothenbaumchaussee, left on Moorweidenstr., then right onto Schlüterstr. A place to catch up with students and check bulletin boards for special events. Student ID required. Meals DM1.70-6. Serves lunch Mon.-Fri. 11am-2pm and dinner 4-7pm.

Machwitz, Schanzenstr. 121 (tel. 43 81 77). Despite the name, their foot-long croque sandwiches are savory and filling. Join the hip (but not tragically so) student crowd in the mayhem of table *Fußball*. Occasional concerts from local bands. Open daily from 10am until everyone leaves.

Libresso Antiquariat, Binderstr. 24 (tel. 45 16 63). U-Bahn: "Hallerstr.," south on Rothenbaumchaussee, then right onto Binderstr. Bookstore and cafe mixes its dark espresso with a high grade of used printed matter, served up for students at the nearby university. Open Mon.-Fri. 9am-6pm.

Frauenbuchladen und Café, Bismarckstr. 98 (tel. 420 47 48). U-Bahn: "Hoheluftbr." A women-only establishment. Pick up the *Hamburger Frauenzeitung* (DM6) if you can read German. Open Mon.-Fri. 10am-7:30pm, Sat. 10am-2pm.

Gorki Park, Two locations: Grindelallee 1 (tel. 45 70 17), near the university at Bundesstr. across from the Staatsbibliotek; and on Hans Henry Jahn Weg (tel. 220 07 15). Bus #106: "Muhlenweg." At both locations, Gorki Park provides enough booze to send capitalists into delirium. Decorated in kitschy red velvet and adorned with socialist propaganda, the restaurants feed the revolution every Sunday with their big brunch buffets (DM16; 11am-3pm). All you can eat, comrade! Open Mon.-Thurs. 5pm-2am, Fri. 5pm-3am; Sat. 6pm-3am, Sun. 11am-3pm.

Asia Imbiß Bok, Bartelstr. 29. U-Bahn #3: "Sternschanze." *Imbiß* is a misnomer here—this joint serves real restaurant food. Try the spicy Thai noodles, or some of the other savory Korean and Chinese options (circa DM7). Open daily 10am-noon.

Noodles, Schanzenstr. 2-4 (tel. 439 28 40). U-Bahn #3: "Sternschanze." Noodles serves nothing but noodles amidst concrete furnishings and trippy ambient music. Regular crowd of local artists and dapper *poseurs*. Wear black—lest you clash with the decor. Open Sun.-Thurs. 10am-1am, Fri.-Sat. 10am-3am.

Arkadasch, Grindelhof 17 (tel. 44 84 71). U-Bahn #3 or S-Bahn #3: "Dammtor." Fiery Indian food—viciously spicy curries. Ample vegetarian offerings. Swinging student crowd indulge during Arkadasch's "happy hours" when most dishes go for DM12 (Mon.-Fri. 3-6pm and midnight-2am); at other times the prices are somewhat steep (DM15-20). Open daily 11am-2am.

Café Planet, Große Brünnerstr. 55a (tel. 39 77 14). S-Bahn: "Altona." Art collective cafe that frequently puts on plays and concerts; also serves a delectable breakfast. Open daily 10am-damn late.

SIGHTS

The **Hamburg Hafen,** the largest port in Germany, lights up at night with ships from all over the world. More than 100,000 dockers and sailors work the ports, and their presence permeates the entirety of Hamburg. After sailing the East Indies, the 19th-century **Windjammer Rickmer Rickmers** (tel. 319 59 59) was docked at Pier 1 and restored as a museum ship. Old navigation equipment, all brass and polish, is juxtaposed with modern nautical technology (open daily 10am-5:30pm; admission DM5, students DM3, children ages 4-12 DM2). Inside the building behind Pier 6 resides the elevator to the Old Elbe Tunnel. With all of its machinery exposed, the building looks like a nautilus machine built for the gods. East of the docks near the copper dome of the **St. Katherinenkirche,** across the river from Zippelhaus, lies the historic warehouse district known as the **Speicherstadt.** These elegant late 19th-century brick storehouses are filled with cargo, spices, and swarms of stevedores.

The copper spire of the **Rathaus,** a richly ornamented, neo-Renaissance monstrosity, rises above the city center. The *Rathaus,* located at the *Rathausmarkt* at the end of Mönckebergstr., has a fountain in the small stone courtyard. Shields representative of each continent embellish the facade of the building, showcasing Hamburg's international flavor. (Tours in German every 30min. Mon.-Thurs. 10am-3pm, Fri.-Sun. 10am-1pm. Tours in English and French leave every hr. Mon.-Thurs. 10:15am-3:15pm, Fri.-Sun. 10:15am-1:15pm. Call 36 81 24 70 for details.) Built in 1932, the **column** to the left of the *Rathaus* stands in memorial to the 40,000 Hamburg men who died in World War I. The extraordinarily sad statue of poet Heinrich Heine overlooks the square. Hamburgers have tried to bring a smile to his somber face for ages. Recently, citizens pursued this goal by covering Heine in aerosol string and replacing the inscription at the base of the statue with a sign reading "Heine dances."

To the north of the *Rathaus,* the two **Alster lakes** are bordered by tree-lined paths. Elegant promenades and commercial facades surround **Binnenalster,** while windsurfers, sailboats, and paddleboats dominate the larger **Außenalster.** Ferries, more personal than the bigger Hamburg boats, sail from here. To the west of the lakes, the **Planten un Blomen park** extends close to the harbor and provides a home for flowers, ponds, ducks, fountains, and water games. Near the Karolinenstr. entrance a medicinal herb garden provides elaborate explanations of the particular therapeutic value of each plant. *Let's Go* does not recommend stealing herbs to ease your aches and pains. Free concerts shake the nearby outdoor **Musikpavillon** nearly every day throughout the summer. Check the *Oxmox* (DM4.30) for listings.

After a fire destroyed much of old Hamburg in 1842, the city government launched an ambitious reconstruction project that created the current urban landscape, including its familiar six green copper spires. Just south of the *Rathaus,* off Ost-West-Str., rest the somber ruins of the old **St. Nikolaikirche.** The Allied bombing of 1943 flattened this early example of neo-Gothic architecture. City officials have left the ruins unrestored as a memorial to the horrors of war. The 12th-century **St. Petrikirche** (tel. 32 44 38; open Mon.-Fri. 9am-6pm, Sat. 9am-5pm, Sun. 9am-noon and 1-5pm; English services first Sun. of every month at 5pm) and **St. Jacobikirche** (tel. 536 60 79), known for its 14th-century **Arp-Schnittger organ** (open daily 10am-5pm) stand next to the *Rathaus.* On the other side of the bustling Ost-West-Str., on a breezy side street, looms a fourth copper tower; it rises up from the medieval **St. Katharinenkirche,** built by three generations of townspeople from 1350 to 1420 (U-Bahn: "Meßberg"; open daily 9am-6pm; Oct.-April 9am-4pm). Way up north by the Hallserstr. U-Bahn towers the new **St. Nikolaikirche,** whose marvelous mosaic altar is based on one of Expressionist Oskar Kokoschka's designs (open daily 9am-5pm).

The gargantuan 18th-century **Große Michaelskirche** (tel. 31 10 26 24) is the granddaddy of all Hamburg churches. It is affectionately and somewhat fearfully referred to as *"der Michael."* While the exterior is a bit imposing—the statue of St. Michael above the doorway mischievously grins at the passing tourists—the inside looks like a wedding cake with its scalloped walls. *Der Michael*'s bulbous Baroque tower is the official emblem of Hamburg; it's also the only one of the city's spires that can be ascended—by foot or by elevator. (Tower and church open April-Sept. Mon.-Sat. 9am-6pm, Sun. 11:30am-5:30pm; Oct.-March Mon.-Sat. 10am-4:30pm, Sun. 11:30am-4:30pm. Church entrance DM1; elevator DM4, students and children DM2; crypt DM2.50 (for the living). Organ music April-Aug. daily at noon and 5pm.)

Farther east along Ost-West-Str., the **Chilehaus** showcases architecture of a different generation. This striking *trompe l'oeil* office building is the work of Expressionist architect Fritz Höger, who also designed the **Sprinkenhof** building across the street. The Great Fire of 1842 consumed many splendid 17th- to 19th-century office buildings, which are carefully restored today. On hot summer afternoons, locals gather in the quiet sidewalk cafes. The last block of **Peterstraße,** up Neanderstr. from the Michaelskirche and then left, is a pedestrian zone for the ages. It is a quiet cobblestone street lined with 17th- and 18th-century High Baroque houses.

Beyond the city center, various and sundry monuments bear eloquent testimony to harsh reality of the Holocaust. In 1923, Communist labor leader Ernst Thälmann led a march on the police headquarters, setting off a riot that resulted in the death of 61 protestors and 17 police officers in addition to nearly 1000 arrests. Thälmann was later murdered by the Nazis at Buchenwald. His life and times are chronicled at the

Ernst-Thälmann Gedenkstätte, on Ernst-Thälmann-Platz (tel. 47 41 84; open Tues.-Fri. 10am-5pm, Sat.-Sun. 10am-1pm; free). In the midst of warehouses stands the **Gedenkstätte Janusz-Korczak-Schule,** Bullenhuser Damm 92 (tel. 78 32 95), S-Bahn: "Rothenburgsort." Walk north from the station and make a right onto Bullenhuser Damm; the school is 200m down on the right. It serves as a memorial to 20 Jewish children brought here from Auschwitz for "testing" and murdered by the SS only hours before Allied troops arrived. Visitors are invited to plant a rose for the children in the flower garden behind the school (open Mon.-Thurs. 9am-5pm, Fri. 9am-3pm, Sun. 10am-5pm; free). An idyllic agricultural village east of Hamburg provides the backdrop for the heinous **KZ** (concentration camp) **Neuengamme,** Jean-Doldier-Weg (tel. 723 10 31). Take S-Bahn #21: "Bergdorff," then bus #227 (about 50min. from Hamburg). The bus stops at the base of the road on its way there, so watch for the sign; it makes several stops along Jean-Doldier-Weg on its return trip. Here the Nazis murdered approximately 50,000 prisoners through slave labor. In 1948 Hamburg prison authorities took over the camp and demolished all of the buildings to construct a German prison on the site; the mayor at the time believed that the facility would cleanse Neuengamme's sullied reputation. In 1989 the Hamburg Senate moved the prison in order to build a more appropriate memorial on the site. Banners inscribed with the names and death-dates of the victims hang in the **Haus des Gedenkens,** located on the road to the camp. Maps of the camp can be picked up here.

MUSEUMS

Hamburg's many museums exhibit everything from erotica and high *Kunst* to history and folk art. The one- or three-day **Hamburg Card** (see p. 246) allows access to most of these museums, with the exception of the Deichtorhallen and the Erotic Art Museum. Hamburg also has a thriving and exciting contemporary art scene; pick up a list of the city's galleries and their current exhibits at either tourist office.

Hamburger Kunsthalle, Glockengiesserwall 1 (tel. 24 86 26 12), 1 block north of the *Hauptbahnhof.* This first-rate art museum is three-pronged: the first part of the collection contains a superb exhibition of German and Dutch art, from the medieval era through the 19th century. The next assortment contains works by 19th century French painters such as Millet, Courbet, Manet, and Monet. The newly built **Galerie der Gegenwart** displays Warhols, Picassos, and a pair of Levi's nailed to the wall. Open Tues.-Wed. 10am-6pm, Thurs. 10am-9pm. DM10, students DM5.

Deichtorhallen Hamburg, Deichtorstr. 1-2 (tel. 32 10 30). U-Bahn: "Steinstr." Follow signs from the subway station; look for two entwined iron circles. Hamburg's contemporary art scene resides here in the former *Hauptbahnhof.* New exhibits each season showcase artists such as Warhol amidst mind-boggling architecture. Open Tues.-Sun. 11am-6pm. DM10, students DM8.

Museum für Kunst und Gewerbe, Steintorpl. 1 (tel. 24 86 26 30), is a large and yellow building one block south of the *Hauptbahnhof.* A fantastic, rich collection of handicrafts, china, and furnishings ranging from ancient Egyptian and Roman to Asian and *Jugendstil.* The collection is sure to inspire you to new heights of interior decoration. The aristocratic bric-a-brac gains vitality with clever exhibits such as *"Geheimnisse des Pharaohs,"* a depiction of the life and times of ancient Egyptians constructed out of Legos. Open Tues.-Wed. and Fri.-Sun. 10am-6pm, Thurs. 10am-9pm. DM10, students and seniors DM5.

Erotic Art Museum, Nobistor 12 (tel. 31 34 29). S-Bahn: "Reeperbahn," U-Bahn #3: "St. Pauli." Follow the silver sperm painted on the floor as they lead you through four floors of tactful iniquity. The first two floors examine post-card sized sketches of assorted aristocrats and their voluptuous maids, while the top two focus on the art of bondage. The exhibit is in surprisingly good taste, as evidenced by the Haring originals on the 4th floor and the sonorous classical music. The Reeperbahn peepshow crowd tends to head elsewhere. Needless to say, a stimulating collection. Open daily 10am-midnight; admission DM15, students DM10.

Hamburgisches Museum für Völkerkunde, Rothenbaumchaussee 64 (tel. 44 19 55 24). U-Bahn #34: "Hallerstr." With two floors of glass cases brimmed with weapons, clothing, and cooking utensils, the exhibit is a treasure trove of imperial plunder. Open Tues.-Wed. and Fri.-Sun. 10am-6pm, Thurs. 10am-9pm. DM8, students DM4.

ENTERTAINMENT

As the cultural capital of the North, Hamburg magnanimously patronizes the arts with money and attention. The lavish subsidies of high culture in Germany lower the ticket prices significantly. In addition most box offices and concert halls offer generous student discounts. The **Staatsoper,** Dammtorstr. 28, houses one of the best opera companies in Germany (vying with Munich and Dresden). For **tickets,** call 35 17 21. S-Bahn #28: "Dammtor." For the past decade John Neumeier directed the associated **ballet company,** transforming it into the acknowledged dance powerhouse of the nation. Pompous **orchestras** abound—the **Philharmonie,** the **Nord-Deutscher-Rundfunk Symphony Orchestra,** and **Hamburg Symphonia,** the big three, all perform at the **Musikhalle** on Karl-Muck-Platz (tel. 34 69 20), U-Bahn: "Gänsemarkt" or "Messehallen." The Musikhalle also hosts **chamber music** concerts on a regular basis. Hamburg's many churches offer a wide variety of classical concerts (usually free)—pick up a schedule at any of the major churches. The German **cabaret** tradition is still alive and kicking at a number of venues, including **Das Schiff,** on Holzbrückestr. (tel. 36 47 65), U-Bahn: "Rödeingsmarkt," and at the drag theater **Pulverfass,** Pulverkich 12 (tel. 24 97 91), U-Bahn: "Hauptbahnhof." Call the tourist office for information.

The **Deutsches Schauspielhaus,** Kirchenallee 39 (tel. 24 87 13), U-Bahn: "Hauptbahnhof," competes with the many musicians of the city. Peter Zadek, a virtuoso director who emerged as a major German dramatic figure in the 1980s, produces eclectic plays. His productions bear an intimately personal and shocking stamp. The **Thalia,** Alstertor 1 (tel. 32 26 66), S-Bahn: "Jungfernstieg," sets up adventurous avant-garde musicals, plays, and staged readings. Most theaters sell half-price tickets to students at the regular box office as well as at the evening box office, which generally opens one hour before performance times. In July and August, many theaters close down, but only to make way for the **Hamburger Sommer** festival of the arts. The **Theaterkarten Last-Minute** kiosk in the Hanse-Viertel tourist office (see p. 246) sells tickets for regular and special events. The **English Theater,** Lerchenfeld 14 (tel. 227 70 89), U-Bahn: "Mundsburg," entertains both natives and tourists with its English-language productions. Performance schedules can be found at the tourist office.

The movie scene in Hamburg is dauntingly diverse, expanding beyond the realm of American blockbusters dubbed into German. The **Kommunades Kino Metropolis,** Dammtorstr. 30a (tel. 34 23 53), a non-profit cinema, features new independent films and revivals from all corners of the globe, focusing on pieces from the U.S., France, Germany, and Italy. **Kino 3001,** Schanzenstr. 75 (tel. 43 76 79), U-Bahn: "Sternschanze," also shows artsy alternative flicks.

Live music prospers in Hamburg, satisfying all tastes. Superb traditional jazz for both the amateur and the connoisseur swing at the **Cotton Club** (see **Nightlife,** below) and on Sunday mornings at the Fish Auction Hall of the **Fischmarkt.** Rock groups jam at **Große Freiheit,** Große Freiheit 36 (tel. 31 42 63), and at **Docks,** Spielbudenpl. 19 (tel. 319 43 78). The renowned **Fabrik,** Barnerstr. 36 in Altona (tel. 39 10. 70), features everything from funk to punk. For more info, check the 'zines *Szene, Oxmox,* or *Prinz* (available at newsstands for DM5; hostels keep free copies).

The **Hafengeburtstag,** or "Harbor Birthday," is the city's biggest bash. Hamburg owes its prosperity to May 7, 1189, when Friedrich Barbarossa granted the town the right to open a port. The city still celebrates the anniversary for a weekend in early May featuring music and other events. In 1998, the party will run May 8-10.

For a month, three times every year, the **Heiligengeistfeld Square** just north of the Reeperbahn metamorphoses into the **Dom,** a titanic amusement park with funbooths, kiosks, and merry-go-rounds. In 1998, the *Frühlingsdom* (Spring Fair) will be held from the end of April until the end of May; the *Sommerdom* (Summer Fair) throughout August; and the *Winterdom* throughout December. The festival's offerings of beer and wild parties have submerged its historical connection to the church.

NIGHTLIFE

St. Pauli, the Sternschanze, and Altona areas virtually monopolize Hamburg's crazy nightlife scene. The infamous **Reeperbahn,** a long boulevard, is the spinal cord of St. Pauli; sex shops, strip joints, peep shows, and other establishments seeking to satisfy any libidinal desires compete for space along the sidewalks. Crowds meander up and down the Reeperbahn like ants, occasionally crossing the street to curiously peek into a shop window or dodge one of the many gruesome greaseballs who beckon passersby to enter the erotic interiors of their stripclubs. Though the Reeperbahn is reasonably safe for both men and women, it is not recommended to walk alone or, if a woman, venture to the adjacent streets. Herbertstr., Hamburg's only remaining legalized prostitution strip, runs parallel to the Reeperbahn, and is open only to men over 18. The prostitutes flaunting their flesh behind large windows on Herbertstr. are licensed professionals required to undergo health inspections, while the streetwalkers are venereal roulette wheels. Needless to say, men and women flock to this district to revel all night long in an atmosphere simmering with sultry energy. Although the sleaze peddlers commodify women, they have failed to stifle the vital spark of the many clubs that cater even to those not seeking sex for sale. Indeed, St. Pauli houses many of Hamburg's best bars and clubs.

Students trying to avoid the debauchery of the Reeperbahn head north to the spliffy streets of **Sternschanze** and **Altona.** Unlike St. Pauli, these areas are centered around cafes and weekend extravaganzas of an alternative flavor. The sheer artistic quality of the posters and the graffiti adorning the exterior and interior of the cafes bespeak an intensity and coherence that far surpasses the Reeperbahn's superficiality. Much of the Hamburg gay scene is located in the **St. Georg** area of the city, near the *Hauptbahnhof.* For gay or straight persons, some of the bars in this area are more welcoming and classier than those in the Reeperbahn. In general, clubs open late and close late, with some techno and trance clubs remaining open until noon the following day. *Szene, Oxmox,* and *Prinz* list events and parties. Lesbians and gays alike are clued in on special events by the *Dorn Rosa* journal.

> **Rote Flora,** Schulterblatt 71 (tel. 439 54 13). Held together both figuratively and literally by the graffiti and posters which cover all of its vertical surfaces, this venue serves as the nucleus of the Sternschanze scene. A cafe during the week, the Flora lights up on weekends, with huge dub and drum 'n' bass parties inside the spooky and decrepit shell of an old mansion; political plays with a leftist spin also take place in this squatter's community center. Cafe open Mon.-Fri. 5-10pm; weekend cover DM 6-8, opening times vary (call ahead for a schedule).
>
> **Große Freiheit 36/Kaiser Keller,** Große Freiheit 36 (tel. 31 42 63). U-Bahn: "St. Pauli"; S-Bahn: "Reeperbahn." The Beatles played on the small stage downstairs during their early years. Today the Wu-Tang Clan stomp about on the big stage upstairs. Go figure. Open daily. Call for show times and ticket prices.
>
> **Molotow,** Spielbudenpl. 5 (tel. 31 08 45), parallel to the Reeperbahn. This basement lives on the fringes of Hamburg's club scene. While mildly committed to funk with "Der Motor Booty Club" playing every Sunday, the club's DJ spins an eclectic mix of rock, hip-hop, garage, and industrial Thurs.-Sat. There is a small bar, and as the complimentary case of joints by the door clearly indicates, the crowd sometimes forgets to "just say no." Cover varies. Open Thurs.-Sat. at 11pm, Sun. at 9pm.
>
> **Mojo Club,** Reeperbahn 1 (tel. 319 19 99), has more attitude than it knows what to do with. Called the best club in Germany by MTV. Go Mojo. The attached **Jazz Café** attracts the trendy. Features jazz, dance-floor jazz, and acid-jazz. Open Fri.-Sat. from 11pm; cover usually DM10. Cafe open Wed.-Sat. from 10pm; no cover.
>
> **Cave,** Reeperbahn 6. Hamburg's house for "house" (meta-house!), Cave spins nothing but wild, raving techno at a hundred beats per minute with enough bass to turn your eardrums inside out. More than a great club, Cave is also one of Hamburg's best accommodation deals (see **Accommodations,** p. 250). In exchange for a DM15 cover charge, you can stay from opening time at 1am until the close at noon without having to worry about any curfew. Breakfast not included.
>
> **Cotton Club,** Alter Steinweg 10 (tel. 34 38 78; fax 348 01 23); U-bahn: "Rödingsmarkt." Gives a different jazz, swing, or skittle band a chance every night. Smoky

atmosphere, mostly older crowd. Great jazz. Open Mon.-Sat. 8pm-midnight. Shows start at 8:30. Cover varies, usually DM5-10.

Logo, Grindelallee 5 (tel. 410 56 58). If you can play it live, you can play it at Logo. Nightly live music at this smoky club near the university gives locals a chance to be rock stars. Occasional Britpop superstars such as Oasis prevent the place from degenerating into karaoke *Quatsch*. Open nightly from 9:30pm. Cover varies.

EDK, Gerhardtstr. 3. U-Bahn #3: "St. Pauli." Small but furiously intense techno club. Open Fri.-Sat. 11pm-sunrise.

Basement in the **Powerhouse** club, Simon von Utrechtstr. 42 (tel. 317 18 48). U-Bahn: "St.Pauli." A powerful club that boasts the fastest techno and trance (160 bpm!) in town, and strobe lights designed to leave clubgoers catatonic. Open Fri.-Sat. 11pm-until you leave.

Front, Heidencampsweg 32 (tel. 23 25 23), U-Bahn #3: "Berliner Tor." House and jungle for Hamburg's gay and lesbian scene interspersed with straight people just trying to stay hip. Opens Wed. and Fri.-Sat. 11pm. Cover DM10-12.

Frauenkneipe, Stresemannstr. 60 (tel. 43 63 77). A bar and meeting place for women. Visitors who are disconcerted by the Reeperbahn and drunken-sailor scene will discover here that red-lighters do not represent the whole of Hamburg. Men are distinctly unwelcome, but women, gay or straight, will feel comfortable. Open Mon.-Fri. and Sun. 8pm-1am, Sat. 9pm-3am.

Insults for Sale

The concept of free speech in Germany does not imply *kostenlos* (cost-free) speech. While doling out compliments requires no budget, dropping insults will unload your wallet in no time. Public humiliation in Germany carries such destructive and belittling force that officials have created an insult price list. Angry, offended, or drunk budget travelers should beware. The heaviest fines will be incurred by mouth-flappers who put down a female police officer's respectability: belting out *Trottel in Uniform* (slut in uniform) costs DM3000, while the lesser insult *Dumme Kuh* (dumb cow) requires a mere DM1200 payoff. Call any uniformed official *Idioten* (idiot), and you'll be out a whopping DM3000. The budget traveler's insult, *Holzkopf* (wood-headed), goes for DM1500. If you give another driver the *Stinkefinger* (middle finger)—deservedly, of course—and he or she can round up witnesses, you'll be DM2200 poorer. Equivalent insults in English are not exempt; stories abound of policemen who've doled out thousands of *Marks* in fines to tourists who think that Germans don't understand what "asshole" means. We tell you this merely as a warning—and prices are, of course, subject to change, you idiot.

■ Lübeck

With a prickly skyline of green medieval spires, each of them giving a defiant *Stinkefinger* (see **Insults for Sale,** above) to the ugly cement and ribbonglass face of modernity, Lübeck is easily Schleswig-Holstein's most beautiful city. Local heroes and literary giants Heinrich and Thomas Mann grew up here and ran through its labyrinth of cobblestone streets lined with old brick buildings. While the city gates ward off soulless modern architecture, Lübeck retains the pulse and energy of a city with bustling businesses beyond the bubble-gum and ice-cream tourist industry.

ORIENTATION AND PRACTICAL INFORMATION

Because water surrounds Lübeck, getting into serious navigational trouble requires getting wet first. However, getting around Lübeck can be a very Kafkaesque experience, particularly at night when everything looks the same and you're never sure where you are or whether you've been there before. When lost, a good rule of thumb is to head uphill, returning to Königstr. and Breitestr., the two main streets.

Tourist Office: In the train station (tel. 86 46 75; fax 86 30 24). Open Mon.-Sat. 9am-6pm. Grab a free map here, then make for the larger **main office,** Breitestr. 62 (tel.

122 81 06), which books rooms for a DM3 fee and is located in back of the *Marien-kirche*. Open Mon.-Fri. 9:30am-6pm, Sat.-Sun. 10am-2pm.

Trains: Lübeck is a main transfer point for crossing the former East/West border. Frequent departures for Schwerin (1½hr.), Rostock (2hr.), Hamburg (40min.), Berlin (4hr.), Munich (9hr.), Copenhagen (5½hr.), and Amsterdam (6½hr.).

Public Transportation: Although the *Altstadt* is easily seen by foot, Lübeck has an excellent bus network. The **ZOB** (central bus station) is across from the train station. A single ride costs DM2-2.80, children DM1.50. **Mehrfahrkarten,** books of 6 tickets, cost DM10-14. The best value is the **Lübeck-Karte**—it's valid for 24hr. on all local buses, including those going to Travemünde (DM9).

Ferries: Cruises around the *Altstadt* and harbor depart several times every day from the bridge in front of the *Holstentor* (DM10, students DM8). The best deal on ships to Scandinavia are found in Travemünde (see p. 261).

Taxi: Tel. 811 22. Available 24hr., but best to call at least 30min. ahead.

Car Rental: Hertz, Willy-Brandt-Allee 1 (tel. 717 47), by the train station, next to Mövenpick hotel. Open Mon.-Fri. 7am-6pm, Sat. 7am-1pm, Sun. 9-10am.

Bike Rental: Buycycle, Muhlenbrucke 1 (tel. 75 757), *rents* bikes, despite the name. DM12 per day. ID required. Open Mon.-Sat. 10am-6:30pm.

Bookstore: Buchhandlung Weiland, Königstr. 67a (tel. 16 00 60), has a great stock of English-language paperbacks in the basement. Open Mon.-Wed. 9am-7pm, Thurs. 9am-8pm, Sat. 9am-4pm.

Laundromat: McWash, on corner of An der Mauer and Hüxterdamm. Wash 7kg DM7. Dry 10kg DM1 per 15min. Open Mon.-Sat. 6am-11pm. No burgers.

Rape Crisis Line: tel. 70 46 40. Pick up a copy of **Zimtzicke,** a women's events calendar containing other important numbers and addresses, at the tourist office.

Pharmacies: Adler Apotheke, Breitestr. 71 (tel. 798 85 15), is located across from the *Marienkirche*. Open Mon.-Fri. 9am-6pm, Sat. 9am-1pm. Late-night pharmacies are listed in the windows of all *Apotheken*.

Emergency: Fire/Ambulance, tel. 112. **Police,** tel. 110.

Post Office: Königstr. 44-46, 23552 Lübeck, near the Marktplatz. Currency exchange and 24hr. ATM. Open Mon.-Wed. 8am-6pm, Thurs.-Fri. 8am-7pm, Sat. 8am-2pm.

Telephone Code: 0451.

ACCOMMODATIONS AND CAMPING

Jugendgästehaus Lübeck (HI), Mengstr. 33 (tel. 702 03 99; fax 770 12). From the train station head for the *Holstentor*, cross the river and make a left on An der Untertrave, and then right on Mengstr. Though slightly more expensive, this superb hostel is ideally located. The historic building *qua* hostel has doubles, triples and quads. Reception open 7:30am-midnight. Lockout midnight, but guests over 18 can get a key. 3- or 4-bed dorms DM29 first night, DM26.50 each additional night, guests over 26 DM37.50, DM35; 2-bed dorms DM31, DM28.50, over 26 DM40, DM37.50. Breakfast included. Call ahead.

Sleep-In (CVJM), Große Petersgrube 11 (tel. 719 20), near the *Petrikirche*. Walk past the *Holstentor*, turn right on An der Obertrave, left on Große Petersgrube, look to the right for the sign. Germany's answer to the YMCA comes complete with pub and *Fußball*. In the old town, 10min. from the station. Whip up some slop in the guest kitchen. Reception open July-Aug. daily 8am-noon and 5-10pm; Sept.-June Mon.-Fri. 9am-noon and 5-10pm, Sat.-Sun. 9-10am and 5-10pm. 10-bed dorms DM15; doubles DM40. Sheets DM5. Breakfast DM5.

Rucksack Hotel, Kanalstr. 70 (tel. 70 68 92), on the north side of the *Altstadt* by the canal. From the station walk past the *Holstentor*, left on An der Untertrave, right on Beckergrube which becomes Pfaffstr. and then Glockengießerstr. On the corner of Glockengießerstr. and Kanalstr. (20min.). The Wulfs welcome you to their friendly ski-chaletish abode. Reception open 9am-10pm. 8-bed dorms DM22, 6-bed dorms DM25; doubles with bath DM80; quads with bath DM122. Self-serve kitchen. Breakfast DM10, served in Café Affenbrot (see **Food,** below). Wheelchair access.

Jugendherberge Lübeck (HI), Am Gertrudenkirchhof 4 (tel. 334 33; fax 345 40), northeast of the historic center. From the *ZOB*, bus #34 or 39 (direction: "Roter Hahn"), 31 (direction: "Travemünde"), or 3 (direction: "Brandenbaum"): "Gustav-Radbruch-Platz." Walk approximately 100m along Travemünder-Allee and turn left, then right. In a calm neighborhood just outside the *Altstadt*. Its dirty co-ed bath-

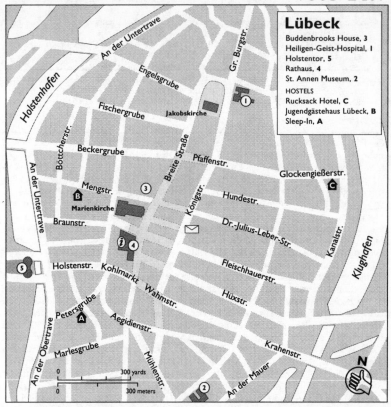

Lübeck

Buddenbrooks House, **3**
Heiligen-Geist-Hospital, **1**
Holstentor, **5**
Rathaus, **4**
St. Annen Museum, **2**

HOSTELS

Rucksack Hotel, **C**
Jugendgästehaus Lübeck, **B**
Sleep-In, **A**

rooms in no way diminish the charm of its battered, cramped 8-person rooms. Happily, a new modern wing will open in 1998. Reception open 7:35-9am and 12:05-11:30pm. Lockout 9-11:30am. Curfew midnight. DM22, over 26 DM27. Sheets DM7. Breakfast included. Closed Dec.10 to Jan. 10.

Camping: Campingplatz Lübeck-Schönböcken, Steinraderdamm 12 (tel. 89 30 90 or 89 22 87), on a grassy site northwest of the city, is somewhat distant. Showers, washing machines, and cooking facilities available. From the *ZOB*, bus #8 (direction: "Bauernweg") to the end; then walk 300m along Steinraderdamm toward the city. DM6 per tent, DM7 per person.

FOOD

While the rest of Germany swims in beer, Lübeck drowns in coffee, with no point more than a saucer's throw away from a caffeine fix. Of course this is still Germany, so Lübeck's cafes function as the nightlife venue of choice by staying open until the wee hours serving beer. Hipper, more popular cafes lie along **Muhlenstr.** in the eastern part of the city. A local specialty is *Lübecker Marzipan,* a gratifying candy made with sugar and almonds. The confectionery **I.G. Niederegger,** Breitestr. 89 (tel. 530 11 26), across from the *Rathaus,* is renowned for its beautifully-shaped marzipan. The **Mädchen und Frauencafé,** on the second floor at An der Untertrave 97 (tel. 122 57 46), is a friendly women-only cafe that serves coffee, tea, and cake, and hosts a "Women's breakfast" (Wed.-Thurs. 10am-1pm; also open Sun. 3-8pm). A **supermarket** at Sandstr. and Schmiedstr. is open Mon.-Wed. 9am-7pm, Thurs.-Fri. 9am-8pm.

Café Affenbrot, Kandstr. 70 (tel. 721 93), on the corner of Glockengießerstr., is a popular vegetarian cafe. Dine on *Salattasche* (salad in pita bread; DM6) at tables made from old-fashioned sewing machines. Vegetarian meals DM8-11. Open daily 9am-midnight, but the kitchen closes at 11:30pm.

Café Amadeus, Königstr. 26 (tel. 70 53 57). If the name conjures up images of a sophisticated cafe in Vienna, think again—the decor is as cheesy as the pizza. Good Italian meals for DM6-14. Open Sun.-Thurs. 8am-12:30am, Fri.-Sat. 8am-2am.

Bei Ulla, Mühlenstr. 19 (tel. 764 41). Ulla serves hearty German fillers such as *Bratkartoffeln mit Spiegeleier* (fried potatoes and eggs; DM9). Are there German fillers which aren't hearty? Open daily 11am-12:30am.

SIGHTS

On the eve of Palm Sunday, 1942, Allied bombers flattened most of Lübeck. Since then, the city has been renovating its beautiful historic *Altstadt.* The core of the *Altstadt* is the **Rathaus,** a striking 13th-century structure of glazed black and red bricks (DM4, students DM2; *Rathaus* tours leave Mon.-Fri. at 11am, noon, and 3pm). Behind the Marktplatz towers the schizophrenic **Marienkirche,** begun in the Romanesque style around 1200 but finished as a Gothic cathedral in 1350. Inside, the bent and broken pieces of the church bells rest where they fell during the 1942 raid. The church's music comes from the **largest mechanical organ** in the world. Free 10-minute soundbites of world-famous organ concerts occur daily at noon; prices vary for Saturday evening organ concerts (6:30pm). The saints literally come marching in, also at noon, on the church's newly restored **astronomical clock.** The famous medieval **Totentanzbild** (death-dance mural) used to encircle the chapel opposite the astronomical clock, but it was destroyed in 1942; all that remains is a reproduction, including one of the *Kaiser* holding hands with skeletons, representing the plague. (Church open daily 10am-6pm; winter 10am-4pm. Services Sun. at 10am and 6pm.)

Opposite the *Marienkirche* is the **Buddenbrooks Haus,** Mengstr. 4 (tel. 777 88), where literary giants Thomas and Heinrich Mann lived as children, and from which Thomas Mann's 1911 novel took its name. The house is now a museum dedicated to the life and works of both brothers and their dear friend Michael Knittel. While Thomas received the Nobel Prize for Literature in 1929, his brother also wrote a number of important works including *Professor Unrat,* on which the famous Marlene Dietrich film *Der Blaue Engel* (The Blue Angel) is based. The brothers had a falling-out during World War I, when Thomas attacked his sibling in a difficult tract called *Betrachtungen eines Unpolitischen* (Reflections of an Unpolitical Man), which espoused the superiority of German *Kultur* to French *Zivilisation.* Thomas's later works, however—most notably *Der Zauberberg* (The Magic Mountain), a tale of life in a Swiss sanitorium—were built on his deep ambivalence about German culture and his fierce opposition to Nazism; he wrote: "Such musicality of the soul must be paid for dearly in other spheres—in the political, the sphere of the common life of human beings." Much of the exhibit is textual and includes original manuscripts and letters (open daily 10am-4pm; DM5, students DM3). The house holds special summer events, including a "literary walk" through Lübeck every Sunday from June to September (DM10, students DM8); pick up a schedule of events at the museum.

The medieval **Jacobikirche,** farther north on Breitestr., traditionally a church for seafarers, contains an old, beautifully ornamented organ. (Open Tues.-Sun. 10am-6pm; services Sun. at 9:40am. Organ recitals Sat. at 5pm. DM3, students DM2.) Behind the Jacobikirche stands the **Heiligen-Geist-Hospital,** Am Koberg 9. The long corridor of tiny cabins was built as a hospital in 1280 and served as an old-age home from 1518 to 1970. The neighboring **cloister** contains a small medieval mural (open Tues.-Sun. 10am-5pm; Oct.-April Tues.-Sun. 10am-4pm; free). Heading south on Königstr., the **Katharinenkirche** (tel. 122 41 80), which served as a Franciscan monastery from 1225 to 1531, now houses modern art exhibitions (open April-Sept. Tues.-Sun. 10am-1pm and 2-5pm). A block away at Königstr. 11, the **Museum Behnhaus/Drägerhaus** (tel. 122 41 42) consists of two townhouses presenting the Expressionist works of Max Liebermann, Edvard Munch, and Ernst Barlach (open Tues.-Sun. 10am-5pm; DM5, students DM3; free first Fri. of every month).

Between the inner city and the station is the massive **Holstentor,** one of the four gates built in the 15th century to guard the entrance to Lübeck. Inside, the **Museum**

Holstentor (tel. 122 41 29) displays exhibits on ship construction, trade, and quaint local implements of torture (open Tues.-Sun. 10am-5pm; Oct.-March 10am-4pm; DM5, students DM3, under 18 DM1). The **Petrikirche,** east on Schmiederstr., is about 750 years old. An elevator climbs to the top of the steeple for a sweeping view. (Church open Tues.-Sun. 11am-4pm. Tower open April-Oct. 9am-6pm. Admission DM3, students DM1.50.) At the southern end of the inner island lies the **Dom,** on Domkirchhof (tel. 747 04), founded by Heinrich the Lion in 1173 as evidenced by his trademark lion statue. (Open April-Sept. 10am-6pm; March and Oct. 10am-5pm; Nov. 10am-4pm; Dec.-Feb. 10am-3pm; services Sat. at 6pm and Sun. at 10:40am; free.)

The **Lübeck Marionette Theater und Puppet Museum,** Kleine Petersgrube 4-6 (tel. 700 60, museum tel. 786 26), just below the Petrikirche, has 13 rooms filled with more than 700 puppets (open daily 10am-6pm; DM6, students DM5, children DM3). The **St. Annen-Museum,** St.-Annen-Str. 15 (tel. 122 41 37), off Mühlenstr., displays crosses, tablets, and other paraphernalia of the opiate of the masses, as well as an exhibit recounting Lübeck's cultural history (open Tues.-Sun. 10am-5pm; DM5, students and children DM3; free first Fri. of every month).

ENTERTAINMENT AND NIGHTLIFE

Lübeck is world famous for its **organ concerts.** At least two per week are held in various churches throughout the summer; schedules are available in churches or at the tourist office. For entertainment listings, pick up *Piste, Zentrum,* or (for women) *Zimtzicke* from the tourist office. Lübeck's two major theaters offer generous student discounts: the huge **Theater Lübeck** puts on operas, symphonies, and mainstream German and American plays, while the smaller **Theater Combinale,** Hüxstr. 115 (tel. 788 17) gets down with avant-garde works.

Finnegan, Mengstr. 42 (tel. 711 10), an Irish pub, serves Guinness and other dark, yeasty beers guaranteed to make you go Bragh the next morning. Very popular with the locals (open weekdays 4pm-1am, weekends 4pm-whenever). While most Lübeckers shun clubs like the plague, **In Bad Taste,** an der Untertrave 3A, draws healthy crowds to watch local bands rock out under camouflage netting and disco balls. Something obnoxious every night, with weekends reserved for particularly vicious events like tattooing and piercing nights. Times and cover vary.

■ Near Lübeck

TRAVEMÜNDE

The attractive town of Travemünde (15km north of Lübeck) is a land of beaches, sun, casinos, and spas. Boutiques line the town streets and *Strandkorben* (wicker chairs) clutter the stretch of beach near the north pier. The **Aqua-Top,** Strandpromenade 1b (tel. 804 42), a fun-filled glass complex of spas and swimming pools, will pamper you with saunas, massages, and waterslides (open daily 10am-9pm; day pass DM16, children DM8; with sauna DM22, children DM16; massage extra). Cross the harbor to the nearby island of **Priwall** (ferries depart every 15min. near the Aqua-Top, DM0.60). Also across the inlet, the four-mast trade ship **Passat** is moored (open May-Sept. 18 daily 10am-4:30pm; admission DM4, students and children DM2). From the deck, look back on the 16th-century **lighthouse** situated on Trelleborg Allee (tours March-Sept. Wed. at 5pm; admission DM2). **Travemündewoche** takes place every year in the last week of July and includes outdoor concerts and sailing activities.

Travemünde is easily accessible from Lübeck by **train** (hourly; 20min.) or by **bus** #30 or 31 from the *ZOB* (45min.; day pass valid); trains also run from Hamburg (hourly; 1¼hr.). There are three main train/bus stops: **Skandinavienkai** accesses the Scandinavia-bound ferries, **Travemünde-Hafen** is close to the town center, and **Travemünde-Strand** leads directly to the beach. The overworked but friendly **tourist office,** Strandpromenade 1b (tel. 804 30; fax 804 60), is located in the Aqua-Top building that faces the beach. Walk from the Travemünde-Strand station down Bertlingstr. and turn right on Strandpromenade. They'll find rooms free of charge or give you an accommodations list (open Mon.-Sat. 10am-6pm, Sun. 10am-1pm). **Boat tours** of Travemünde run every hour from various spots along the pier (DM7, children DM4). **TT-Line** runs daily to Trelleburg, Sweden (DM60, students DM45; round-trip DM120, students DM90). For more information, contact **TT-Line** in Hamburg (tel. (040) 360 14 42), or **Nordische Touristik Information** in Travemünde (tel. 66 88; open Mon.-Fri. 9am-5pm). Travemünde's **telephone code** is 04502.

The **Jugend-Freizeitstätte Priwall**, Mecklenberger Landstr. 69 (tel. 25 76; fax 46 20), is right across the inlet. Take the ferry to Priwall, walk along the beach path for 300m; it's on your right. Surrounded by a standing army of green tents, the hostel makes you feel like a member of the *Bundeswehr*. They also rent bikes to guests for DM8 per day. (Reception open 2-10pm. Curfew Sun.-Thurs. 10pm, Fri.-Sat. midnight. DM14, over 26 DM19. June-Sept. *Kurtax* DM5, other times DM2. Sheets DM5. Breakfast DM6. Open April to mid-Oct. Call ahead.) Pitch your tent next door at **Strand-camping-Priwall**, Dünenweg 3 (tel. 28 35; reception open 9am-noon and 3-7pm; DM9 per tent, DM7 per person; open April-Sept.). Decent fast food and bakeries decorate the downtown beach path; similar options lie along Düneweg on the Priwall.

RATZEBURG

The island town of Ratzeburg, founded in the early Middle Ages by Heinrich the Lion, lies about 15km from Lübeck near the top of the former Lübeck-Lüneburg salt trail. The natural beauty of the town and the surrounding area hypnotically draws bicyclists and hikers. The German Olympic crew team trains daily on the huge lake surrounding the island. Other than the scenery, Ratzeburg's main attraction is its art culture—two small but significant museums offer unique collections by 20th-century artists A. Paul Weber and Ernst Barlach, who lived in the town, as well as Günter Grass, who resided in the nearby town of Behlendorf.

Weber's astounding, satirical lithographs and watercolors are on permanent display at the **A.-Paul-Weber-Haus**, Domhof 5 (tel. 88 83 26). Weber is perhaps best remembered for his depictions of Hitler, as in the pamphlet *Hitler—ein deutsches Verhägnis* (a German disaster; open Tues.-Sun. 10am-1pm and 2-5pm; admission DM2, students DM1). Ratzeburg's **Dom**, built by Heinrich the Lion soon after he colonized Schleswig-Holstein, houses galleries containing religious works. (Open April-Sept. daily 10am-noon and 2-6pm; Oct.-Mar. Tue.-Sun. 10am-noon and 2-4pm; services Sun. at 10:15am.) Between the Weber-Haus and the Dom lies the **Kreismuseum** (regional museum; tel. 123 25), filled with a random mishmash of Biedermeier furniture, art by Weber, Grass, and Barlach, and the obligatory pointy Prussian helmet display (open Tues.-Sun. 10am-1pm and 2-5pm; DM2, students DM1). A larger collection of Barlach's work sits across the Marktplatz in the **Ernst-Barlach-Museum**, Barlachpl. 3 (tel. 37 89); haunting, meditative bronzes and manuscripts are on display (open Tue.-Sun. 10am-noon and 3-6pm; DM3, students DM1.50; closed Dec.-Feb.).

To reach Ratzeburg's **Jugendherberge (HI)**, Fischerstr. 20 (tel. 37 07; fax 847 80), take any bus from the train station to the Marktplatz, or embark on a 45-minute journey along Bahnhofsallee as it becomes Lüneburger Damm, Unter den Linden, Herrenstr. and finally empties out into the main square. Continuing straight, turn right onto Große Wallstr. and follow it until it becomes Fischerstr.; it's at the end of the street. (Reception open 7am-10pm. Curfew 10pm, but you can ring the bell until 11:30pm. DM20, over 26 DM25. Sheets DM6. Laundry DM6, soap included.)

The **tourist office**, Schloßwiese 7 (tel. 80 00 80; fax 53 27), is between the train station and the Marktplatz. From the station, head down Bahnhofsallee until it becomes Lüneburger Damm (15min.); it's in a huge parking lot on the left. They book **private rooms** (DM30-40) for free (open Mon.-Wed. and Fri. 9am-5pm, Thurs. 9am-6pm, Sat.-Sun. 10am-4pm). Hourly **trains** connect Ratzeburg with Lübeck (15min.) and, via Lüneburg, with Hamburg (1hr.). Join the hordes of nature-lovers by renting a **bike** from the **Fahrrad Verleih Schloßweise** (tel. 44 66) on the lake, just past the tourist office (DM8 per 3hr., DM15 per day). A combined bike rental and ferry ticket (DM12) will take you to the other side of the lake, where there are additional bike paths. Get groceries at the **Aktiv Markt** on the corner of Herrenstr. and Barlachstr. (open Mon.-

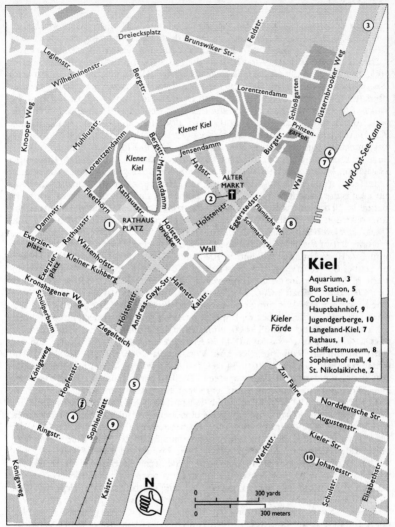

Kiel

Aquarium, 3
Bus Station, 5
Color Line, 6
Hauptbahnhof, 9
Jugendgerberge, 10
Langeland-Kiel, 7
Rathaus, 1
Schiffartsmuseum, 8
Sophienhof mall, 4
St. Nikolaikirche, 2

Fri. 8am-6:30pm, Sat. 8am-2pm). The **post office,** Herrenstr. 12 (tel. 239 09), is around the corner from the Marktplatz (open Mon.-Fri. 8am-noon and 2-6pm, Sat. 10am-noon). The **telephone code** is 04541.

■ Kiel

Site of the 1936 and 1972 **Olympic sailing events,** the waters around Kiel swim ceaselessly with brightly colored sails. The last full week of June sees the annual **Kieler Woche,** an internationally renowned regatta that enlivens the harbor and floods the town with music, food, and beer, particularly around the Olympia Zentrum (bus #44 north). Kiel's mainstay shipping industry thrives on the traffic through the world's busiest artificial waterway, the **Nord-Ostsee-Kanal** (North-Baltic Sea Canal). A 700-year-old port, Kiel's history is bonded to the sea. Kiel's most heroic moment came in 1918, when a mutiny of sailors touched off the revolution that sent the *Kaiser* packing at the conclusion of WWI. The city was also home to Germany's first submarine, built in 1850, as well as the base of Germany's deadly **U-Boot** (submarine) warfare in World War II. Thus, Allied bombings here were ruthless, destroying 80% of the city.

The sights and sounds of the harbor, the city's focal point, are omnipresent in stolid, modern Kiel, the capital of Schleswig-Holstein. The highlight is the largest team of **canal locks** in the world. The view of the canal and the harbor is amazing. The tour offers the island's full effect—nothing but trees and machinery are visible from the banks. (Bus #4 north: "Kanal," then the ferry that runs every 15 minutes; free. Walk right 10min. along Kanalstr. from the ferry dock to the *Schleuseninsel*, or Lock Island). Alternatively, land-lubbers can take bus #1 or #41: "Schleuse" (30min.; obligatory tours daily 9am-3pm, every 2hr., DM3, 50% off with *Kieler Karte*, students DM1.) Hugging the west coast of the **Kieler Förde** (Kiel Harbor), the **Schiffahrtsmuseum** (Navigation Museum; tel. 98 10) displays authentic-looking model ships (open daily 10am-6pm, mid-Oct. to mid-April Tues.-Sun. 10am-5pm; free). North of the ship museum is the **aquarium** (tel. 597 38 57), home to a smallish collection of Nordsee's marine life. The persistent residents of the herring tank have been swimming in the same direction for a year now with no signs of dizziness or fatigue. (Open daily 9am-7pm, Oct.-March 9am-5pm; DM2.50, students DM1, children DM0.50.)

To the left of the **St. Nikolaikirche** (tel. 950 88; open Mon.-Fri. 10am-1pm and 2-6pm, Sat. 10am-1pm; services Sun. at 10am and 7:30pm; free) stands Barlach's haunting statue, *Der Geistkämpfer* (ghost-fighter; see Güstrow, in Mecklenburg-Vorpommern, p. 231, for more on the controversial artist). Every February, Kielers celebrate the *"Umschlag,"* when a flag, *"Der Bürgermeister sin Büx"* (that's *Plattdeutsch* for "the mayor's pants"), is hung outside of the Nikolaikirche. The nearby **Rathaus,** whose steeple can be climbed for DM2, also sports a strangely clad statue of a soldier.

Kiel's **tourist booth** (tel. 67 91 00) is located in the *Sophienhof* mall across from the train station. It finds rooms for a DM3.50 fee; maps are a stingy DM1 (open Mon.-Sat. 9am-6:30pm, Sun. 9am-1pm; Oct.-April Mon.-Fri. 9am-6:30pm, Sat. 9am-1pm). The **Mitfahrzentrale,** Sophienblattstr. 54 (tel. 194 40), two blocks south of the train station, matches riders and drivers for a fee of DM0.10 per km, paid to the driver (open Mon.-Wed. and Fri. 9am-7pm, Thurs. 9am-8pm, Sat. 10am-3pm, Sun. 11am-3pm). At DM3.10 per ride, Kiel's extensive public transportation system will quickly result in a massive cash hemorrhage. Avoid the fiscal bloodletting by investing in a **Kieler Karte,** which comes with coupons for sights and restaurants (one-day DM12, three-day DM17); available in hostels, the tourist booth, and the KVAG (Kiel Transit Authority) office at the *Bahnhof*. Most of Kiel's buses pass through the rows of stops outside of the train station; the ones on the train station side of the street *generally* head north, while the ones on the *Sophienhof* side go south. A **bus** leaves from the *ZOB*, around the corner from the train station, every two hours for the Hamburg **airport** (1½hr.; DM20); buses also go to the Hamburg train station. **Ferries** leave from the piers on the west side of the harbor. **Baltic Line** (tel. 98 20 00) will take you to Sweden (weekly; 60hr.; DM430), **Color Line** (tel. 97 40 90) sails to Oslo (daily, 18hr.; DM150, students 50% off on selected sailings), and **Langeland-Kiel** (tel. 97 41 50; fax 945 15) will ship you to Bagenkop, Denmark (2½hr.; DM7, in July DM9). The **post office,** Stresemannpl. 1-3, 24103 Kiel, is a block to the right of the train station (open Mon.-Fri. 8am-6pm, Sat. 8:30am-1pm). The **telephone code** is 0431.

Kiel's boss hostel, **Jugendherberge Kiel (HI),** Johannesstr. 1 (tel. 73 14 88; fax 73 57 23), has uncrowded four-person bedrooms, each with its own shower and bathroom. A bus stop nearby motors passengers to the *Hauptbahnhof* every 15 minutes. Bus #4 from the train station on the *Sophienhof* side: "Kielerstr.," and backtrack one block, then turn right on Johannesstr. (Reception open 7am-11:30pm. Curfew 1am. DM24, over 26 DM 29. Sheets and breakfast included.) Camping is distant at **Campingplatz Falckenstein,** Palisadenweg 171 (tel. 39 20 78), about 10km north of the city center. Bus #44 (direction: "Strand"): "Seekamp." Backtrack to Scheidekoppel and hike for 20 minutes through wheat fields until Palisadenweg, then turn left down toward the beach (DM6 per tent, DM7 per person).

Get groceries at **Kaiser's,** a supermarket on the ground floor of the *Sophienhof* (open Mon.-Fri. 9am-8pm, Sat. 8am-4pm). Holstenstr. and the Marktplatz are the best places in town for a meal. **Sandwich,** Holstenstr. 92, counts on tourists' thirst for expensive Coca-Cola, but if you fight the power by bringing your own drink, you can go berserk on the yummy little sandwiches noted in the appellation (DM2.50-3.50 each; open Mon.-Fri. 6:30am-6pm, Sat. 7am-2pm).

■ Near Kiel

LABOE AND MOLFSEE

While it is possible to mix it up with the crowds and swim in the **Kieler Förde,** warmer water and beach basketball await in nearby **Laboe.** Use of the beaches requires a **Strandkarte** (DM4), which must be purchased at the *Automaten* to avoid a DM10 fine. Bus #54 from the *Sophienhof* side of the bus stop (direction: Laboe) will take you on a tour through the 'burbs to the beach (1hr.; DM3.10, *Kieler Karte* valid). Although inconveniently located about a mile down the beach from the bus stop, U-Boot 995, with eight-person rooms the size of phone booths, is a tourist attraction, not a hostel. Used in the Nazi campaign of submarine warfare during World War II, U-Boot 995 is now open to a democratized assembly of tourists. (Open daily May-Oct. 9:30am-6pm, Nov.-April 9:30am-4pm. DM3, DM2.50 with *Kieler Karte,* free for German soldiers in uniform. *Let's Go* does not recommend enlisting in the German army as a means of obtaining discounts.) Across the street, winning no awards for architectural subtlety, stands the **Marine-Ehrenmal** (tel. (04343) 87 55), a 72m concrete erection commemorating "the sailors of all nations who died on the seas." While the exhibits are little more than dioramas and flags, the building is an amazing study in fascist aesthetics, particularly the "Hall of Commemoration," a veritable symphony in cement. (Same hours as the U-Boot. DM4.50, with *Kieler Karte* DM2.50, kids DM2.50.) Laboe's **tourist office,** Strandstr. 25 (tel. (04343) 16 63) on the boardwalk, will hook you up with a tanning bed or a room (DM30-40, breakfast included) for a 10% fee. (Open May-Aug. Mon.-Sat. 11am-4pm.)

Molfsee's main attraction is the **Schleswig-Holsteinisches Freilichtmuseum** (tel. 655 55), a miniature ghost town of transplanted cottages from all over northern Germany, some more than 200 years old, filled with original furniture, farming tools, and other artifacts. To give the museum an authentic, old-fashioned feel, chickens run around the footpaths, while behind ye olde electrick fence, cattle and some nappy goats graze. Bus #1680 from the *Sophienhof* stop (direction: "Flintbek"): "Rammsee-Freilichtmuseum" or 1 (direction: Schulensee) to the end and walk the last 1.5km along the road. (Open daily 9am-6pm; Nov.-March Sundays and holidays 11am-4pm; DM7, DM3 with *Kieler Karte,* students DM5.)

▓ Flensburg

Flensburg is Germany's northernmost city, with the Danish border lying only a hop, skip, and a stumble away. The presence of a large and international student population from the university and lots of locally brewed alcohol injects some pulse into the staid northern German atmosphere. You can't go anywhere in northern Germany without having a face-to-face encounter with **Flensburger Pilsner** on tap; the town itself is swimming in it. Flensburg is located around the perfect harbor that forms the tip of the **Flensburger Förde;** the streets run along the water to wind into the hills. If you can't understand what the people around you are saying, don't blame it on that extra glass of *Pils*—they're either locals speaking *Plattdeutsch*, a North German dialect, or Danes on a serious beer run. The local greeting, "*Moin, Moin,*" is a *Plattdeutsch* variation of "*Guten morgen,*" but you'll hear it throughout the day.

Heading straight down Bahnhofstr. from the station and zigzagging across Friedrich-Ebert-Str. will lead you to the lively *Altstadt* and Flensburg's huge pedestrian zone along **Holmstr.** and **Großestr.** Along the way you'll pass the **Deutsches Haus,** a *Bau-*

haus-style concert hall donated to Flensburg in recognition of the city's loyalty in the 1920 referendum, quite contrary to the Kieler rebellion (see p. 263). In the **Süder-markt,** the beautiful 14th-century **Nikolaikirche** boasts a gargantuan organ, the *Organ Maximus*—Sexus, Plexus, and Nexus don't stand a chance (open Tues.-Fri. 9am-5pm, Sat. 10am-1pm; free). Just beyond the **Nordermarkt** stands the **Marien-kirche,** with its superb stained-glass windows (open Tues. and Thurs.-Fri. 10am-4pm, Wed. and Sat. 10am-1pm; free). Pining for Carlsberg? At Norderstr. 50, next to the Danish library is the **Marientreppe,** which offers a glimpse of Denmark from atop its 146 stairs. Along the pier, at **Museumshafen,** several retired ships have been turned into museums. At Schiffbrücke 39, a 150-year-old customs house has become the **Schiffahrtsmuseum** (Navigation Museum; tel. 85 29 70), documenting Flensburg's nautical history and role in Denmark's once-thriving Caribbean trade. The **rum** exhibit is impressive. *Ahhrr!* Whar's the booty? (Open Tues.-Sat. 10am-5pm, Sun. 10am-1pm; DM2, students DM1.) The last weekend of May sees the **Rum Regatta,** an event for traditional boats and sober sailors only.

The **tourist office,** Speicherlinie 40 (tel. 230 90; fax 173 52), lies off Großestr.; follow the signs through the courtyard (open Mon.-Fri. 9am-6pm, Sat. 10am-1pm). They'll find a room (DM20-35) without a fee and can arrange summer tours of the brewery for DM5. Flensburg's high-tech bus system saves a lot of uphill walking; practically all buses circulate through the *ZOB* (central bus station) close to the city center (one-way fare DM2.30, 24hr. *Tageskarte* DM6). **Trains** link the city to Hamburg (2hr.) and Kiel (1½hr.) at least every other hour, while others head north to Copenhagen (5hr.) and many other Danish cities. **Buses** from the *ZOB* bus station also cross the border to the Danish towns of Sønderborg (1¼hr.) and Aabenraa (50min.). From the west bank of the harbor, ferries country-hop between Flensburg and Glücksburg in Germany and Gravenstein and Kollund in Denmark (DM3). **Ferries** also leave for Sønderberg from the nearby town of **Kappeln** (reachable by bus). The main **post office,** near the train station at Bahnhofstr. 40, 24939, **exchanges currency** (open Mon.-Fri. 8am-6pm, Sat. 8am-1pm). The **telephone code** is 0461.

Flensburg's **Jugendherberge (HI),** Fichtestr. 16 (tel. 377 42; fax 31 29 52), offers no escape from exercise, whether it be running laps on the nearby track, making the long walk into town, or shivering off calories in the chilly showers. From the train station, bus #1 (direction: "Lachsbach") or 4 (direction: "Klueshof"): *"ZOB"* and change to #3 or 7 (direction: "Twedter Plack"): "Stadion," then follow the signs. (Reception open 8-8:45am, 5-6pm, and 9:30-10pm. DM22, over 26 DM26. Sheets DM7.)

The **Nordermarkt** simmers with a slew of cafes and bars. For those itching to see what a metric hangover feels like, **Hansen's Brauerei,** Großestr. 83 (tel. 222 10), serves home-brewed beer by the meter (DM26) and German food in equally absurd quantities. Their whopping Sunday special bloats you with 1kg of ribs for DM13.90.

Just 10km away from Flensburg, **Glücksburg** boasts beautiful beaches (DM4) and a fairytale **Schloß** (tel. (04631) 22 13) surrounded by a looking-glass lake. Unlike Wonderland, Glücksburg can be reached by bus from Rathausstr. at the end of Flensburg's sprawling *ZOB* (35min.; DM3.50) or by ferry via Kollund, Denmark (6 per day, 50min.; DM3; passport necessary). From the Glücksburg *ZOB,* walk down towards the post office and follow the signs left to the *Schloß,* or get off at the beach (one stop earlier) and follow the signs around the lake (2.5km). Skate around the waxed floor in the slippers provided while discovering just how inbred—and from looking at the beds, short—19th-century royals were. On the third floor, Gobelin tapestries depict scenes from Ovid's *Metamorphoses.* Don't miss the "corpses" in the dungeon (open April-Oct. 10am-5pm, Nov.-March 10am-4:30pm; DM7, students DM5).

■ Husum

A town of modest historical import, Husum's big claim to fame is the 19th-century novelist and hometown hero Theodor Storm. Prior to Storm (who dismissed the city as "the grey town by the sea"), the only thing Husumers could brag about was their ability to transform their city name into a misspelled anagram of "hummus." The hamlet on the Wattenmeer now successfully resists both modernization and the construction of a tourist trap, offering a genteel flavor livened by its crabbing industry.

The **Marktplatz** is the epicenter of Husum. From the train station, head up Herzog-Adolf-Str. and turn left on Ludwig-Nissen-Str.; head right through the shopping center (5min.). At one end of the square stands the solemn and plain **Marienkirche**, built between 1827 and 1832 from the designs of Danish master Christian Frederik Hansen. Across the square is the 17th-century **Rathaus**. Everywhere in Husum statues, paintings, and restaurants are dedicated to Theodor Storm. He cried and wet his diaper for the first time on September 14, 1817 at Marktplatz 9, next to the *Rathaus*. The building is now a bank. The **Theodor-Storm-Haus**, Wasserreihe 31 (tel. 66 62 70), was the writer's residence from 1866 to 1880 and is now a museum with original furnishings and manuscripts. (Open April-Oct. Tues.-Fri. 10am-noon and 2-5pm; Mon., Sat., and Sun. 2-5pm; Nov.-March Tues., Thurs., and Sat. 2-5pm; DM3, students DM2.) Completing our tour of the three ages of Man, Storm is buried in the *Klosterkirchhof* in Osterendestr., east of the Marktplatz.

The **Schloß vor Husum** (tel. 897 30), two blocks in the opposite direction from the Marktplatz, was built by the Gottdorfer dukes at the end of the 16th century but was set upon by Bob Villa's 18th-century ancestors, who gratuitously converted it into a Baroque castle. Instead of the usual diet of swords, crests, and other medieval party favors, the *Schloß* offers kinder and gentler exhibits in its special art exhibitions from German and international talents. The castle also hosts summer evening concerts (open April-Oct. Tues.-Sun. 11am-7pm; admission DM5, students DM2.50, special exhibitions DM1 extra). The **Nissenhaus**, Herzog-Adolf-Str. 25 by the *ZOB*, was donated by a wealthy German-American and houses the **North Frisian Museum** (tel. 25 45). Its collection focuses on dike building, dike breaking, and offers part of a real dike as a *coup de grace*. The rest of the museum depicts artworks from North Frisians who make Klaus Theweleit's head spin with their fetish of floods and naked people (open daily 10am-5pm, Nov.-March Mon.-Fri. 10am-4pm; DM5, students DM2, under 14 DM1). Husum's answer to Sotheby's, the **Tabak-und-Kinderspielzeug-Museum** (Tobacco and Children's Toy Museum), Wasserreihe 52 (tel. 612 76), contains a full rack of Bavarian mountain pipes and rare matchbooks. Rising high above the clutter and putting the local head shop to shame stands a **5-foot hookah** (open daily 10am-6pm; DM3, students DM2.50, children DM1.50).

Husum has hourly rail connections to Hamburg (1¾hr.) and Kiel (1½hr.). The **tourist office** (tel. 89 87 30; fax 47 28) in the *Rathaus* books rooms in private homes; call ahead (open Mon.-Thurs. 9am-noon and 2-4:30pm, Fri. 9am-noon and 2-3pm). Rent **bikes** from **Koch Fahrräder**, Schulstr. 4 (tel. 44 65; DM10 and a photo ID). A bike is particularly useful if you want to visit Husum's gorgeous **swimming pool**, Flensburger Chaussee 28 (tel. 899 71 55), the center of the town's weekday nightlife, has two heated pools, a waterslide, and a sauna (open Tues.-Fri. 2-10pm, Sat. 8am-5pm, Sun. 8am-6pm; DM6). The **post office** is at Marktplatz 5 (open 9am-6pm); Husum's **postal code** is 25813. The **telephone code** is 04841.

To reach the **Jugendherberge Theodor Storm (HI)**, Schobüllerstr. 34 (tel. 27 14; fax 815 68), head left from the tourist office and make a right onto Neustadtstr., which turns into Marktstr. Make a left at Adolf-Brütte-Str. and continue as it turns into Schobüllerstr. Or bus #51 from the *ZOB* just down the street from the train station: "Westercampweg" (DM2). Though the farmhouse exterior suggests rural charm, German *Schulkinder* frequently terrorize the fortress. Still, the ample **kitchen facilities** provide some sanity. (Reception open intermittently from 4:30-10pm. Curfew 10pm. DM22, over 26 DM26. Breakfast included. Closed Jan.15-Feb.15. Call ahead.) The area around the harbor is filled with restaurants and *Imbiß* stands, while a **grocery store** sits by the post office (open Mon.-Wed. 8:30am-6pm, Thurs.-Fri. 8:30am-7pm, Sat. 8am-2pm). Sustain yourself with a crab sandwich, the local specialty (DM15). Feast on cheap eats at **Porto Bello**, Hafenstr. 3, which serves 30cm pizzas for DM8.50-15 (open daily 11am-11pm). Thursday is **farmer's market** day—from 8am-1pm stands sell the weekly harvest of fruits, vegetables, fish, and leather wear in the Marktplatz.

■ Schleswig

At the southernmost point of the **Schlei inlet,** Schleswig is a quiet town bordered by fields and the bluest of waters. Once a major Viking settlement, Schleswig became an important fishing and trade center in the Middle Ages. The city subsequently became the seat of the Gottorfer dukes, lesser German nobles who, despite their social status, built a grandiose castle on the Schlei banks. When Bismarck annexed Schleswig-Holstein from Denmark in 1867, he made Schleswig the region's capital, a post it retained until 1945. After a millennium of history, Schleswig has retired to live like an old man—quiet, mellow, and primarily concerned with fishing.

The large, Baroque **Schloß Gottorf** is on a tiny island off the Schlei, a pleasant 20-minute walk along the harbor from the *Altstadt;* it now houses a complex of museums. The *Schloß* itself contains a collection of 19th-century Realist and Impressionist German art, and artifacts dating back to the mad, mad world of medieval Schleswig-Holstein. To the left of the *Schloß,* the **Nydamhalle** museum (partially open as some exhibits are renovated) boasts a hoard of unusual archaeological finds dating back to the last Ice Age, including a complete Viking ship and, for those drawn to the macabre, the remains of four big Vikings who were preserved in the sea for more than 1200 years. The **Kreuzstall Museum** (tel. 81 30), on the right, houses an extensive collection of works by artists from the *Brücke* School, including Ernst Ludwig Kirchner, Emil Nolde, and Max Pechstein. The other building samples every major 20th-century German artist, including Oskar Kokoschka, Käthe Kollwitz, and the haunting sculptures of Ernst Barlach and Hans Wimmer. (All museums open daily March-Oct. 9am-5pm, Nov.-Feb. Tues.-Sun. 9:30am-4pm. DM7, students DM3.)

If you find yourself longing for more breast plates and horned helmets, ferries travel from the Stadthafen port near the *Dom* to the **Wikinger Museum Haithabu** (tel. 81 33 00). The museum, next to an archaeological dig of a former **Viking settlement,** covers all aspects of Viking life. (Open daily 9am-6pm, Nov.-March Tues.-Fri. 9am-5pm, Sat.-Sun. 10am-6pm. Admission DM2, students DM1. Ferries DM3.50, round-trip DM6.) About five minutes south of the *Schloß,* the **Städtisches Museum,** Friedrichstr. 9-11 (tel. 81 42 80), houses documents and *objets trouvés* from Schleswig's history, including an unbearably cute collection of teddy bears. On a darker note, it also documents the 1920 *Schleswiger Putsch,* during which soldiers occupied the *Schloß* and government buildings. In response, all of Schleswig's workers went on strike. The tension peaked when the workers encircled the *Schloß* until the soldiers yielded, turning the castle over to the people. Back toward the harbor, the copper steeple of the 12th-century **St. Petri Dom** towers above Schleswig's *Altstadt.* (Open Mon.-Thurs. 9am-5pm, Fri. 9am-3pm, Sat. and Sun. 1-5pm; Oct.-April Mon.-Thurs., Sat. 10am-4pm, Fri. 10am-3pm, Sun. 1-4pm; organ concerts DM5-8.) East of the *Altstadt* lounges the **Holm** district, a postcard-perfect fishing village.

The **tourist office,** Plessenstr. 7 (tel. 248 78 or 207 03), is up the street from the harbor; from the *ZOB,* walk down Plessenstr. towards the water. They book private rooms and hotels (DM30-60) for a DM10 fee and a 10% charge. (Open May-Sept. Mon.-Fri. 9:30am-12:30pm and 1:30-5pm, Sat. 9am-12:30pm; Oct.-April closed Fri. afternoon and Sat.) Schleswig's **train station** is located quite a distance from the city center; take any bus from the stop outside to the *ZOB,* which is close to the *Altstadt* (single ride DM1.70, 6-ride card DM8.50). The **post office,** Poststr. 1, 24837, **exchanges money** at counter 5 (open Mon.-Fri. 9am-12:30pm and 2:30-6pm, Sat. 9am-noon). The **telephone code** is 04621.

The **Jugendherberge (HI),** Spielkoppel 1 (tel. 238 93), lies close to the center of town. Bus #2 (direction: "Hühnhauser-Schwimmhalle") from either the train station or the *ZOB:* "Schwimmhalle;" the hostel is across the street. It's on the right across from the school. Great location and a view of the Schlei inlet, but the eight-bed rooms are *extremely* cramped. "I sleep in a drawer!" (Reception open 7:30-8:30am, 12:30-1pm, 4:30-5pm, and 6-10pm. Curfew 10pm. DM22, over 26 DM24. Sheets DM6. Breakfast included.) For a night in a former *Fischerhaus* overlooking the water (or the TV in each room), try **Pension Schleiblick,** Hafengang 4 (tel. 234 68). To get there from the *ZOB,* head west on Königstr., right onto Domweg, zigzag left around the church, and keep going straight until turning left on Hafengang. (Singles DM65; doubles DM90-115. All have showers. Breakfast included.) **Da Paolo,** Stadtweg 65 (tel. 298 97), serves up traditional pizza and pasta on red-checkered tablecloths (DM8-15; open Mon.-Sat. noon-7pm, Sun. 1-7pm). For German food, **Panorama,** up the street from the *ZOB,* at Plessenstr. 15 (tel. 239 46), has lunch specials for DM8.50.

■ North Frisian Islands

SYLT

The sandy, windswept island of **Sylt** stretches far into the North Sea, culminating in Germany's northernmost point. A 10km railtrack built in the 1920s connects Sylt—traditionally a favorite spot for government luminaries and other wealthy vacationers, but now a more democratic affair for all kinds of riffraff—to the mainland. The beauty of Sylt's dune-ridden shores attracts large crowds, and nowhere is this phenomenon more apparent than in **Westerland.** The mother of all Kurtowns and the largest town on the island, Westerland is Germany's answer to Martha's Vineyard, abuzz with bourgeois types on vacation. In the midst of the hubbub sits the town's signature statue which looks like a female Buddha bathing placidly in the main square.

From Westerland, the best way to explore the island is by bicycle. The main **bike path** follows the highway, making it good for intertown travel, while the smaller dirt and gravel paths meander through the dunes, affording stunning views of the ocean. The streets of **Westerland,** the main tourist town, are stuffed with designer shops and spa-hotels. Outside the recreational chaos of the main town, however, Sylt offers sparsely populated beaches, including the (in)famous **Bühne 16,** whose nude bathers reveal that water wings do not a swimsuit make. Sylt's beaches also provide the only locale in Germany where **surfing** is possible. While they're no Waikiki, the beaches of **Wellingstedt, Hörnum,** and **Standhalle** all produce rideable surf.

The **tourist office** (tel. 99 88; fax 99 81 00) in the train station reserves rooms for a 10% fee and DM5 deposit (DM30 and up) and gives you a super-beachin' island map for DM4.90 (open daily in the summer 9am–8pm). The beaches euphemistically designated *"FKK"* (*Freie Körper Kultur,* or "free body culture") are strictly nude; the others are bathing suit-optional. Trains from Hamburg **Altona** travel to Westerland via Niebüll (about 18 per day; 3hr.). **Public transportation** on the island is quite expensive (DM6 to reach either hostel from Westerland, day card DM20). Buses leave from the *ZOB* terminal to the left of the Westerland station. **Rent a bike** at the Westerland train station, across from gate 1 (DM9 per day, DM49 per week; open daily 8:30am-6:30pm). Sylt imposes a levy called a *Kurtaxe* on any easy riders hoping to hit the beaches (May-Oct. DM5.50; Nov.-April DM3; under 18 free). The **post office** is at Kjeirstr. 5, around the corner from the train station (open Mon.-Sat. 9am-6pm, Sun. 9am-1pm). The **postal code** is 25992. The **telephone code** is 04651.

Ferries run hourly from the List harbor to **Havneby** on the Danish island of **Rømø** (less frequently in winter; round-trip DM8, seniors and children DM6). Call **Rømø-Sylt Linie** (tel. 87 04 75) in List for reservations and information. **Adler-Schiffe,** Boysenstr. 13 (tel. 987 00), runs daytrips to the Halligen Islands (see below) from Hörnum, as well as excursions to Denmark's lovely **Legoland** theme park (every Thursday at 7:15am; DM70, children DM60). Passport required, or you'll have to deal with the Legoland border guards, who tote menacing Lego Uzis.

Sylt offers two youth hostels. Those neither wayward nor lucky enough to earn a spot in Hörnum's reform school will have to settle for the adjacent **Jugendherberge Hörnum (HI),** Friesenpl. 2 (tel. 88 02 94; fax 88 13 92). The hostel offers convenient location next to a bus stop and a **SPAR grocery store** (open Mon.-Fri. 8am-noon, 2:30-6pm, Sat. 8am-1pm). From the *ZOB* take the bus (direction: "Hörnum") to "Hörnum-Nord" and continue along Rantumerstr., turning left at the *Jugendherberge* sign. Behind the hostel, a sheltered, secluded beach stretches for miles. (Reception open noon-1pm and 5-10pm. Curfew 11pm. DM22, over 26 DM26. Reservations strongly recommended.) List's **Jugendherberge Mövenberg** (tel. 87 03 97; fax 87 10 39) lies over the hills and out in the boonies, although it is close to a beach. Like the Hörnum hostel, it's close to a **grocery store.** Catch the bus (direction: "List") from the Westerland *ZOB:* "List-Schule." If you're lucky you can change for the infrequent List-Strand bus: "Mövenberg;" otherwise, return to the intersection, turn right and follow the *Jugendherberge* sign about a mile, past the sheep and dunes. (Reception open 7-9am, noon-2:30pm, and 4-10pm. Curfew 11pm. DM19.60, over 26 DM24.10. Breakfast included. Written reservations strongly advised: write to Jugendherberge Mövenberg, 25992 List/Sylt. Definitely call ahead. Closed Nov. to mid-March.)

HALLIGEN ISLANDS

South of Sylt stretch the clean beaches and marshy green plains of the **Halligen Islands.** A mini-archipelago surrounded by the *Wattenmeer* (cotton-sea) the Halligens are part of the **Schleswig-Holstein Wattenmeer National Park,** a sanctuary for rare breeds of wildlife—sea lions, wild birds, and naked vacationers. The islands are equally well-known for their popularity as a spa-cure destination for wealthy Germans who flock to the revitalizing sea air.

Föhr, the largest island and the closest to the mainland, features numerous spas and miles of sandy beach dotted with naked folk; look for the Speedo-sized *"FKK"* signs designating the *al fresco* portions of the beach. In **Wyk,** the island's biggest town, those looking to remain clothed can go **windsurfing** or peruse the expensive boutiques. The closest island to Sylt, **Amrum** is also somewhat commercialized, but it manages to preserve a bit more of the natural atmosphere. Getting there provides its own excitement, as folks can run to Amrum at low tide. The path connecting the two islands contains a few **quicksand** pits, making it advisable to take a guided tour (tel. 14 85; DM6). The other Halligens—**Hooge, Pellworm, Langeneß,** and **Gröde**—are nearly uninhabited, and rarely see action outside of the sea lions' mating season. **Adler-Schiffe** (tel. 987 00; fax 263 00) runs daytrips to the Halligens (Hooge, Amrum, and Föhr) from **Hörnum** and **List,** on Sylt (DM32-34, under 14 DM16-17). The ferries usually leave about 10am, returning by 6pm and allowing five hours on the islands; call for schedules and reservations. To reach Föhr from **Husum,** ask the *Hauptbahnhof* to set it up—for DM40, they'll take care of the whole thing, including connections to private railways and the ferry from Dägebull to Wyk (railpasses valid).

Föhr's **tourist information** (*Kurverwaltung;* tel. 30 40) is in the *Rathaus* across from the port (open daily 9am-12:30pm and 1:30-5pm). They book rooms in private homes for a 10% fee (DM30-80 per person); you can also surf for the info yourself on their nifty little computer. Since Föhr is as flat as last week's soda, and the size of a frisbee, a **bike** is a great way to see the island. **Fahrrad Verleih Fehr,** Badestr. 6 (tel. 38 64), rents 'em for DM6 per day. Föhr's **telephone code** is 04681; Amrum's is 04682.

Föhr's Jugendherberge, **Haus-Atlantis (HI),** has risen from the sea at Fehrstieg 41 (tel. 23 55; fax 55 27). Bus #1 from pier 3: "Schullandheim" (every 30min.; DM1.50). The hostel is about a block straight ahead, then right around the first corner. The hostel requires reservations one year in advance. (Reception open 7am-10pm. Curfew 10pm. DM35. Breakfast, sheets, and *Kurtaxe* included. Laundry DM5, including soap.) Amrum's **Jugendherberge Wittdün,** Wandelbahn 9 (tel. 20 10), is filled to the gills with stuffed island wildlife and clean rooms. Follow the signs from the ferry dock. (Reception open 11:30am-1pm and 4:30-9:30pm. DM22, over 26 DM24.10, *Kurtaxe* DM0.80. Sheets DM7.) Even the fast food on Föhr is overpriced—the **co-op** is your best bet. Follow Rundföhrstr. from the harbor to the big green monstrosity (open Mon.-Fri. 8am-6:30pm, Sat. 8am-6pm).

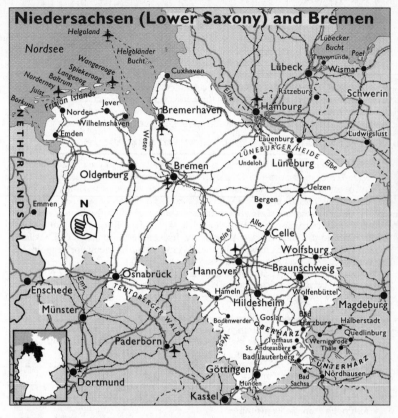

Niedersachsen (Lower Saxony)

Extending from the Ems River to the Harz Mountains and from the North Sea to the hills of central Germany, Niedersachsen has two distinct flavors. Along the northern coast, descendants of the Frisians run their fishing boats from ports built on foggy marshland. The vast remainder of the *Land* is a broad plain which supports agricultural communities. Since the Middle Ages, the region has been the seat of intense individualism and unbridled innovation. Christianity found a foothold here in the wake of Charlemagne's march through the fringe of the deep-purple Lüneburger Heide. Niedersachsen still treasures its autonomy, harkening back to the Hanseatic traders who made the region's fortune. A pocket of its area belongs to Bremen and Bremerhaven, two seafaring cities united in a unique case of state federalism to form Germany's smallest *Land*.

■ Hannover (Hanover)

Despite its relatively small size, Hannover puts on a magical display of culture and cosmopolitan charm, rivaling that of cities twice as large. As the most important railway center in Northwest Germany, the city's myriad attractions easily lure in travelers moving through the Berlin-Hamburg-Köln triangle. But Hannover has seen darker times. Because of an unusual marriage that bound the Hannoverian royalty to the United Kingdom, the city found itself repeatedly attacked by foreign powers striking at the British throne. Later, under Prussian domination, Hannover thrived under the prosperity of a unified empire. World War II saw the end of that, as 60% of the city was flattened. Yet resilient Hannover, accustomed to severe poundings, emerged like a jack-in-the-box, leaping joyfully from the ashes. Today, with great economic vigor, a wealth of museums, a supreme opera hall, and a tradition of outdoor festivals, Hannover reigns proudly as the political and cultural capital of Niedersachsen.

ORIENTATION AND PRACTICAL INFORMATION

The old Sachsen "Hon overe" means "High Bank," referring to the city's position on the river Leine. In the heart of Hannover lies the *Hauptbahnhof,* where a statue of Ernst August, first king of Hannover, beams from the saddle of his horse, surveying the city he founded. **Bahnhofstraße** extends from the hooves of his horse, leading to the landmark **Kröpcke Café.** Below the statue's feet sprawls the underground **Passerelle,** a bizarre conglomeration of cheap diners doing the tango with souvenir shops. Behind the station is the **Raschplatz,** home to a disco and a club scene. A pedestrian zone connects most of the middle city, including the major shopping districts along **Georgstraße,** and the *Altstadt.*

The **Hannover Card** (DM14), available at youth hostels and **ÜSTRA** offices, provides public transportation within the city and to the airport, as well as free admission or discounts for several museums.

Tourist Office: Hannover Information, Ernst-August-Platz 2 (tel. 30 14 22; fax 30 14 14). Outside the main entrance of the train station, facing the large rear of the king's splendid steed, turn right. In the same building as the post office. The superb staff finds rooms for any budget for a steep DM10 fee, provides maps and information on cultural events, sells tickets to concerts and exhibits, and runs a full travel agency. Open Mon.-Fri. 9am-7pm, Sat. 9:30am-3pm.

Student Travel Office: RDS, Limmerstr. (tel. 44 60 37), and Asternstr. 34 (tel. 70 24 54). Basic bargains for the budget traveler, including flights and train packages. Both open Mon.-Fri. 9am-6pm.

Consulate: U.K. Berliner Allee 5 (tel. 388 38 08). Behind the train station, across Raschpl., inside the DG-Bank building.

Currency Exchange: DVB, in the train station, is the most convenient with the longest hours and decent commissions. Open Mon.-Fri. 7:30am-7pm, Sat. 7:30am-5pm, Sun. 9am-12:45pm and 1:30-4:30pm.

American Express: Georgstr. 54, 30159 Hannover (tel. 36 34 28), across from the Opera House. Travel agency and full cardmember services. Mail held for a maximum of 4 weeks for cardmembers, traveler's check clients, and travel agency customers. Open Mon.-Fri. 9am-6pm, Sat. 10am-1pm.

Flights: The Hannover airport is 15-20min. from the *Altstadt.* By car, highway B522 from the *Innerstadt. Schnellbusline* (express bus line) #60 runs from the *Hauptbahnhof* to the airport (Mon.-Fri. 5am-10pm, every 20min.; Sat.-Sun. every 30min.; DM9). Flights depart to Berlin, Dresden, Frankfurt, Leipzig, Munich, Nürnberg, and Stuttgart, as well as other European cities. For flight information call 977 12 23.

Public Transportation: ÜSTRA, Hannover's mass-transit system, is extremely thorough and fast. As soon as you arrive, walk to the lime green stand in front of the King or at the "Raschpl." bus stop behind the station, and pick up the free map of the U-Bahn and bus lines. Single-ride tickets DM3, children 4-11 DM1.50. Blocks of 6 tickets can be purchased at discount rates, but the best deal for travelers is either a **24hr. Pass** (DM7.50) or a **Schuler-Wochen** card, which opens up the magical world of public transportation to students for one week (DM17). All tickets can be purchased from drivers or in vending machines at stations. For more info and maps, call the **ÜSTRA Customer Service Office** in the Kröpcke station (tel. 166 82 38). Open Mon.-Wed. and Fri. 8am-6pm, Thurs. 8am-7pm, Sat. 9am-2pm. The **Hannover Card** provides more comprehensive savings (see above).

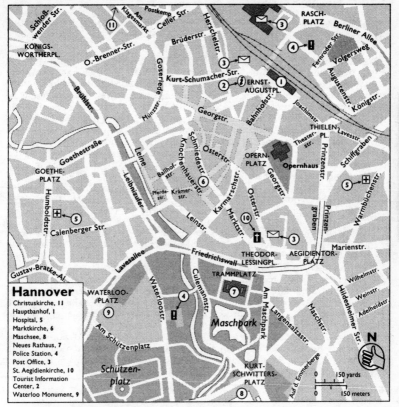

Hannover

Christuskirche, 11
Hauptbahnof, 1
Hospital, 5
Marktkirche, 6
Maschsee, 8
Neues Rathaus, 7
Police Station, 4
Post Office, 3
St. Aegidienkirche, 10
Tourist Information
Center, 2
Waterloo Monument, 9

Bike Rental: Prorad, Friesenstr. 48 (tel. 31 39 67), a 10min. walk behind the train station, sends you zipping past the ÜSTRA for DM9-18 per day. Open Mon.-Wed. 2-6pm, Thurs.-Fri. 10am-1pm and 2-6pm, Sat. 10am-1pm.

Mitfahrzentrale: Citynetz, Weißekreuzerstr. 18 (tel. 194 44), matches drivers with riders. Open Mon.-Fri. 9am-6pm, Sat. 9am-1pm, Sun. 11am-2pm.

Bookstores: Georgsbuchhandlung, Georgstr. 52 (tel. 32 16 12), has English-language novels downstairs. Open Mon.-Fri. 9:30am-8pm, Sat. 9:30am-4pm.

Rape Crisis Line: tel. 33 21 12.

Women's Shelter: tel. 66 44 77.

AIDS-Hilfe: tel. 62 45 68, counseling 66 46 30.

Pharmacy: Europa Apotheke, Georgstr. 16 (tel. 32 66 18; fax 363 24 63), near the train station. 14 languages spoken, including English. Open Mon.-Fri. 8am-8pm, Sat. 8am-4pm. Info about emergency service *(Notdienst)* posted when closed.

Emergency: Police, tel. 110. **Medical Information,** tel. 31 40 44.

Internet Access: In Daily Planet (see **Nightlife,** p. 277).

Post Office: In same building as the tourist office, 30159 Hannover. Open Mon.-Fri. 9am-8pm, Sat. 9am-4pm, Sun. noon-3pm. Mail held, currency exchanged.

Telephone Code: 0511.

ACCOMMODATIONS

Finding budget accommodations in Hannover is difficult but not impossible. The youth hostel and two *Naturfreundehäuser* (similar to hostels, but not part of HI) provide affordable respites, as do private accommodations through the tourist office. Should all else fail, traveling to the hostels in nearby Braunschweig or Celle may be cheaper than bedding down in one of Hannover's royally-priced hotels. As always, calling ahead to ensure a bed is recommended.

Jugendherberge Hannover (HI), Ferdinand-Wilhelm-Fricke-Weg 1 (tel. 131 76 74; fax 185 55). U-Bahn #3 or 7 (direction: "Mühlenberg"): "Fischerhof/Fachhochschule." Cross the tracks and walk to the left of the school; follow the bike path as it veers left and over a bridge. Turn right; the hostel is 50m down on the right (15min.). Within walking distance of the Maschsee and the Schützenfestpl. The walk at night is poorly lit—take care. Rooms of 6 or 12 with bathrooms down the hall, but a scenic location and bunnies outside (Wile E. Coyote would have a field day) make for a pleasant stay. Reception open 7:30-9am and 2-11:30pm. Checkout 9am. Curfew 11:30pm. When there's night service, door is opened every hour from midnight to 7am. DM22, over 26 DM27. Sheets DM5.70. Small lockers. **Camping sites** available for DM13.25, over 26 DM15.50. Breakfast included.

Naturfreundehaus Misburg, Am Fahrhorstfelde 50 (tel. 58 05 37; fax 958 58 36). U-Bahn #4 (direction: "Roderbruch"): "Misburgerstr.," then bus #631: "Misburg Waltfriedhof." Stroll up am Fahrhorstfelde to the very end. Go 10m straight ahead on the trail and follow the sign. On a beautiful lake brimming with ducks. 4- to 6-bed rooms decked out in homey brown. Reception open Tues.-Fri. 3-10pm, Sat.-Sun. 10am-10pm. No curfew. DM14, nonmembers DM24. Breakfast DM8. Sheets DM7.50 The *Häus*'s 30 beds fill quickly—reservations are necessary.

Naturfreundehaus Stadtheim, Hermann-Bahlsen-Allee 8 (tel. 69 14 93; fax 69 06). U-Bahn #3, 7, or 9 (direction: "Lahe" or "Fasanenkrug"): "Spannhagengarten." Walk 15m back to the intersection and follow Hermann-Bahlsen-Allee to the left for about 5min.; follow the sign to your right down the paved road 200m to the hostel. Tiny rooms, with a superior breakfast. Reception open 8am-noon and 3-10pm. No curfew. DM33.80, nonmembers DM28.80. Full *Pension* DM19.50.

Hotel am Thielenplatz, Thielenpl. 2, 30159 Hannover (tel. 32 76 91; fax 32 51 88). Luxurious furnishings in the lobby and 160 beds in well-maintained rooms, all with TV. Check-out 11:30am. Singles with shower DM78-140; doubles with shower DM160-215. Breakfast included.

FOOD

Kröpcke, the world-renowned foodcourt/cafe at the center of the pedestrian zone, can hook you up with small snacks (from DM2.50) or nice sit-down meals (from DM13.50). The *Imbiß* stands around the adjacent subway stop are surprisingly good. The Lister Meile area behind the train station also offers an interesting selection of cafes with pleasant seating options. A **Spar supermarket** sits by the Lister Meile U-Bahn stop (open Mon.-Fri. 8am-7pm, Sat. 8am-2pm). For a more international flavor, ride on down to the **Markthalle,** where a wild variety of snacks, meals, and booze awaits (open Mon.-Fri. 7am-6pm, Sat. 7am-1pm).

Nudel Holz, Köther Holzweg 25 (tel. 21 21 22). U-Bahn #10: "Leinaustr." Award-winning Italian restaurant offers huge pasta dishes (DM9) and 11 potato dishes (DM11). 28 wines available, from French to Californian. Open daily 11am-1am.

Mensa (tel. 768 80 35) on Schneiderbergstr. U-Bahn #4 or 5: "Schneiderberg." Take a right up Schneiderbergstr., just past the small bridge in the green-trimmed building. DM3 gets you the non-refundable card on which you can deposit however much you wanna spend. Meals DM2.20-3.70. Open Mon.-Sat. noon-2:10pm.

Uwe's Hannen Faß Hannover, 36 Knochenhauerstr. (tel. 326 16). Located in the center of the *Altstadt*, in the timber-framed house where the master brewer of Hannover once lived. The steaming *Niedersachsenschmaus* (DM7.50), a potato casserole, steadies the stomach while a *Bowle* of the house-brewed *Hannen Alt* lightens the head. Also a popular nightspot overseen by attention-starved DJs. Foot-long sandwiches DM9.50. Salad bar DM5.50. Daily specials served noon-3:30pm. Open Mon.-Sat. noon-2am, Sun. 3pm-2am.

Bö 29, Bödekerstr. 29 (tel. 31 90 05). A big bistro full of vegetarian specialties puts the crunch in you. Almost 200 dishes (DM5-23). Open Mon.-Thurs. 11:30am-midnight, Fri.-Sat. 11:30am-2am, Sun. noon-midnight.

Peach Pit, Lister Meile 5 (tel. 34 34 32). A late night/early morning haven for the drunk, tired, and hungry. Although you won't run into Brenda or Brandon, you will likely see happy inebriates (Hi Eric!) looking for a sandwich (DM5), milkshake (DM3.50), or more beer. Open Sun.-Thurs. 6am-2pm, Fri.-Sat. 24hr.

SIGHTS

In 1714, the son of Electoral Princess Sophie ascended the throne of the United Kingdom as George I, and his descendents continued as the rulers of Hannover and the United Kingdom until 1837 when the Hannoverians refused to accept a queen—Sophie's great-great-great-great-granddaughter Victoria. The city owes much to Sophie, who furnished the three paradisiacal **Herrenhausen Gardens.** The Baroque landscaping is wild and ambitious. U-Bahn #4 or 5 (direction: "Stöcken"): "Herrenhausengarten." The centerpiece is the **Großegarten** (Great Garden). Its **Herrenhausen Palace,** built in the 18th century, hosts frequent concerts and ballets (snap up advance tickets from DM16 at the tourist office, or buy tickets at the door on the evening of the performance). During the "illuminations," geyser-like fountains shoot from the ground to glow in the warm backlighting—gushing in their midst is Europe's highest garden fountain, the **Große Fontäne.** Originally 32m high, it has been gradually built up to 80m. Adjacent to the Großegarten, the smaller **Georgengarten** and **Berggarten** offer equally bewitching vegetation. Various *Feuerwerkswettbewerbe* (fireworks contests), held during the summer, provide dazzling displays with musical accompaniment. (Georgengarten always open; free. Großegarten and Berggarten open April-Oct. Mon.-Tues. 8am-8pm, Wed.-Sun. 8am-11pm; Nov.-Mar. daily 8am-dusk; DM3. Explosives Wed.-Sun. 10-11pm. Fountains Mon.-Fri. 11am-noon and 2-4pm, Sat.-Sun. 11am-noon and 2-5pm; admission DM3, 2½hr. before fireworks DM4, students DM2.) The 14th-century **Marktkirche,** Hans-Lilje-Platz, presides over the almost totally reconstructed *Altstadt.* From the station, follow Bahnhofstr. to the Markt (open daily 10am-4pm; check for concerts). City government outgrew the **Altes Rathaus** (Old Town Hall), just off the Markt in 1913, but its trellised facade and mosaic work are kept bright. Walking back towards Knochenhauerstr. and a making a quick left down Krämerstr. brings you to Holzmarkt and the **Leibnizhaus,** a beautifully restored Baroque mansion, home to brilliant mathematician, philosopher, man of letters, and royal advisor Gottfried Wilhelm Leibniz until his death in 1716. Tread carefully—this site cost DM22 million to restore (open Sun. 10am-1pm and 1:30-6pm). A jog down Leinstr. brings you past the magnificent **Leineschloß,** seat of the Diet of Niedersachsen, to the ivy-covered shell of the crumbling **St. Aegidienkirche.** The massive damage suffered during World War II was intentionally left untouched as a grim reminder of the folly of war.

Against the ruined remains of Hannover's medieval fortifications, the **Friedrichswall,** down Marktstr. from the *Altstadt,* rises the more modern, spectacular **Neues Rathaus.** Hannoverians painstakingly recreated this palatial turn-of-the-century complex after World War II. Step inside to see models of the city in 1689, 1939, 1945, and today. Take the slanted elevator up the tower to gawk at the real thing. (Open 10am-5pm. Elevator open April-Oct. daily 10am-12:15pm and 1:30-4:15pm. DM3, students DM2.) From up high, you can scout out Hannover's many parks, including the woods around the **Maschsee.** This artificial 2km long lake just south of the *Rathaus* is covered with sailboats and rowboats during the summer and ice skaters in winter. Hannover's links with Britain are espoused in the **Waterloo Monument** (from the *Neues Rathaus,* cross the Leine River bridge or walk through the tunnel near the subway), a high column commemorating the Niedersachsen citizens who fought with the Brits, Russians, Austrians and Prussians against Napoleon. To fully experience Hannover, follow the **Red Thread,** a 4km. walking tour guided by a painted red line connecting all the major sites. The accompanying *Red Thread Guide* (DM3) details the tour in English—available from the tourist office. Your very own Freedom Trail in Germany!

MUSEUMS

Sprengel Museum, Kurt-Schwitters-Platz (tel. 168 38 75), next door to the Landes-museum. A modern art lover's dream: James Turrell, Henry Moore, Dalí, Picasso, Magritte, and Horst Antes. Check out the light experiments by Turrell. Be patient—the results will amaze you. Permanent collection and the special exhibit DM8.50 and DM4.50, respectively. Open Tues. 10am-8pm, Wed.-Sun. 10am-6pm.

Wilhelm-Busch Museum, Georgengarten 1 (tel. 71 40 76). U-Bahn #4 or 5 (direction: "Stöcken"): "Schneiderberg." See wit and sarcasm channeled onto paper in vivid colors. Just as fun are the art books and postcards from past exhibitions—don't miss the Sebastian Krüger pieces or the history of Max and Moritz. DM4, students and kiddies DM2. Open Tues.-Sat. 10am-5pm, Mon. 10am-6pm.

Historisches Museum am Hohen Ufer, Pferdestr. 6 (tel. 168 30 52), next to the Leibnizhaus, sits in a 1960s replica of a 10th-century fortress. A very thorough exposition of Hannover's history and its cultural links with Britain. Also houses a huge collection of dioramas depicting scenes from battlefields, as well as one from "Dances With Wolves"—Lieutenant Dunbar is omnipresent. DM5, students and children DM3. Open Tues. 10am-8pm, Wed.-Fri. 10am-4pm, Sat.-Sun. 10am-6pm.

Kestner-Museum, Trammpl. 3 (tel. 168 21 20), through the park behind the *Rathaus*. Numismatics will go dizzy over the ancient coin collection. The center-piece is the Greco-Roman and Egyptian art. DM5, students DM3. Free on Wed. Open Tues. and Thurs.-Fri. 10am-4pm, Wed. 10am-8pm, Sat.-Sun. 10am-6pm.

Landesmuseum, Willy Brandt Allee 5 (tel. 980 75), near the *Neues Rathaus*. This place is the jack-of-all-trades, and the variety amuses. Stare down ugly fish in the aquarium, dig into excavations of the Leine Valley, or check out the art of Max Beckmann. DM3, students and children DM1.50. Open Tues.-Wed. and Fri.-Sat. 10am-5pm, Thurs. 10am-7pm. Special exhibits in the **Forum des Landesmuse-ums,** Am Markt 8 (open Tues.-Wed. and Fri.-Sun. 10am-5pm, Thurs. 10am-7pm). Closed until fall 1998.

Kubus Museum, Theodor-Lessing-Platz 2 (tel. 168 57 90), an der Aegidienkirche. A museum organized around the alphabet. TE*x*T aS IMAgE. Syntagm? We don't need no stinking syntagm. Free. Open Tues.-Fri. 10am-6pm, Sat.-Sun. 10am-4pm.

ENTERTAINMENT

If you're within a 100km radius of Hannover between July 3 and July 12, detour to its **Schützenfest** (marksmanship festival), the largest such *fête* in the world. Every summer since 1539, Hannoverians have congregated—weapons in hand—to test their marksmanship and retreat to the beer gardens to get *Schützen*-faced. In that order. The 10-day festival comes complete with parade, fireworks, chintzy stuffed animals, and rickety amusement park rides, but its main attraction is the *Lüttje Lage*, a feisty traditional drink. Without spilling, you must down the contents of two shot glasses simultaneously, holding them side by side in one hand; one glass contains *Weißbier*, the other *Schnapps*. And if this isn't enough fun for you, Hannover delivers a nifty one-two punch. After giving the liver a brief respite, the **Maschseefest** (July 29-Aug. 16, 1998) hits you with another wild combination of concerts, masked balls, and street performances. For anyone left standing and capable of walking a straight line, the knockout blow falls with the **Altstadtfest** in the first or second weekend in August. All the big *Kneipen* and cafes convene for one last hurrah until next year.

Over 20 theaters make their homes in Hannover, supplying ballet, opera, dramas, and Broadway musicals. The **Opera House,** Opernpl. 1, the **Ballhof,** Ballhofstr. 5, the **Schauspielhaus,** and the **Theater am Aegi,** on Aegienterpl., are the four largest. Tick-ets for most of the theaters (from DM12) are sold at the tourist office. (Advance tick-ets for the Opera house and the *Schauspielhaus* are also sold at the Opera House Mon.-Fri. 11am-7:30pm, Sat. 11am-1pm, or by calling 368 17 11 for the opera or 32 11 33 for the *Schauspielhaus* 1 hour after the box office opens.) Most theaters offer stu-dent tickets 30 minutes before each show. For the official line on theater listings, fes-tival dates, and other items of interest, pick up the monthly *Hannover Vorschau* from the tourist office (DM3). The **Kino am Thielenplatz,** Lauesstr. 2 (tel. 32 18 79) shows movies in English. The **Flohmarkt** (flea market) on the **Leibnizufer** hits town every Saturday from 7am to 4pm.

NIGHTLIFE

When the sun goes down, Hannover lets 'em rip with an impressive array of packed cafes and pumping discos. Kröpcke buzzes with an alternative scene in the small plazas. The happening university crowds swarm the area of Linden North, between Goethepl. and Leinsustr., filling the cafes and *Kneipen*. For parties, snoop around the **Mensa** for signs or check either *Prinz* (DM4.50) or *Schädelspalter* (DM5), outstanding guides to nightlife in the city, listing more concerts, performances, and get-togethers than you'll know what to do with. The free *MagaScene* lists dance clubs and concerts. Each university *Fach* (department) throws monthly parties, and the best ones, believe it or not, are held by the *chemistry* students.

The Capitol, Schwarzer Bär 2 (tel. 92 98 80), sets the floor thumping with dance hits. Loosen up in a sea of bumping bodies. Next to the bar, a smaller floor for hard rock gets heads banging. Opens Fri.-Sat. 10pm. DM8. Other times, find live music, movies, or a locked door. Call for a schedule.

Daily Planet, Aegidientorpl. 1 (tel. 32 30 04). Jump out of your phone booth and stop the friggin' presses. A cool news bar with **Internet access,** burgers, and beers (DM3.30). Open Mon.-Sat. 10am-midnight.

Waterloo Biergarten, Waterloopl. 1 (tel. 156 43). Walk under the highway toward the Waterloo monument. Fun, beer-drinking-song atmosphere. Stands around the *Garten* sell pretzels and hot dogs. Open daily 11am-whenever.

Finnegan's Wake, Theaterstr. 6 (tel. 32 97 11). A place to chill with real Dubliners, where everybody knows Ulysses's name. Daily happy-hour (4-6pm) and live Irish music (Fri.-Sun. 9pm) liven the scene. Open Mon.-Fri. 4pm-late, Sat.-Sun. noon-late.

Osho Disco, Raschpl. 7L (tel. 34 22 17), caters to a similar crowd as The Capitol. A lounge area surrounding the dance floor is a great place to meet (read: pick-up) folks. Every Wed. is "over 30-night"—no cover for survivors of the "Stayin' Alive" years. Cover Wed.-Thurs. and Sun. DM5, Fri.-Sat. DM8. Open Wed.-Sun. at 10pm.

Schwul Sau, Schaufeldstr. 29 (tel. 700 05 25). U-Bahn #6 or 11: "Kopernikusstr." Don't even try to translate the name; we'll do it for you (it means "gay pig"). One of the most popular gay and lesbian bars in Hannover, located in the university district. On good nights, the 3-person sofa in the corner seats 15. Tues. ladies only. Wed. men only. Open Fri.-Sat. 8pm-late; other days, call ahead for times.

▓ Göttingen

Contemporary Göttingen remains a college town to the bone, serving as home to Europe's first free university. The Georg-August-Universität boasts Otto von Bismarck as an alumnus and the Brothers Grimm as faculty members, but its real fame comes from its spectacular track record in hard Science. Forty-one Nobel laureates have been students or faculty members, including Max Planck (the father of quantum mechanics) and Werner Heisenberg (the brilliant but eccentric head of the German A-bomb project). Heisenberg may have been one of World War II's unsung heroes, reputedly disclosing information to Allied scientists while leading his research teams down fruitless paths to keep the Bomb out of the Hitler's hands. Such anti-authoritarianism is a Göttingen tradition—in the years after its founding in 1737, the university was one of the most liberal in the German lands. By the 1920s, however, it degenerated into a hotbed of reactionary nationalism. After World War II, the pendulum briefly swung the other way as Göttingen earned a reputation as a *"rote Uni"* (red university). The ideological sparks have now subsided as the town exudes a serene yet cosmopolitan air for its students and visitors.

ORIENTATION AND PRACTICAL INFORMATION

Tourist Office: Fremdenverkehrsverein Göttingen, Markt 9 (tel. 540 00; fax 400 29 98), is located in the *Rathaus*. From the station, cross busy Berlinerstr. to pick up the perpendicular Goetheallee. Follow it for several blocks as it becomes Prinzenstr., turn right onto Weenderstr. which runs into the market square. From there, the *Rathaus* will be visible. The office has maps and hotel and restaurant lists. They will also book a private room (DM35) for free. Open April-Oct. Mon.-Fri. 9:30am-6pm, Sat.-Sun. 10am-4pm; Nov.-March Mon.-Fri. 9am-6pm, Sat. 10am-1pm. A smaller **branch office,** Berlinerstr. 11 (tel. 560 00), is located across from the train station. Open Mon.-Fri. 10am-1pm and 2-6pm, Sat. 10am-1pm.

Tours: Leave from the main hall of the *Rathaus* daily at 2:30pm if 5 or more folks attend. DM5, students DM3. Tours in English available for large groups only.

Currency Exchange: Commerzbank, Prinzenstr. 2 (tel. 40 80), has the best rates in town. Open Mon.-Wed. 8:30am-4pm, Thurs. 8:30am-4pm, Fri. 8:30am-3:30pm. The **Postamt** in the *Bahnhof* exchanges currency on weekends.

American Express: Goethealle 4a (tel. 52 20 70). Open Mon.-Fri. 9am-6pm, Sat. 9:30am-12:30pm.

Car Rental: Sixt-Budget, Groner Landstr. 336 (tel. 54 75 70). Open Mon.-Fri. 7:30am-6pm, Sat. 8am-1pm.

Bike Rental: The youth hostel (see below) rents bikes to guests for DM9 per day. DM50 deposit or ID required.

Mitfahrzentrale: Mitfahrbüro Cheltenham House, Friedrichstr. 1 (tel. 48 59 88), hooks up riders and drivers, and includes a **budget travel office** (tel. 575 08). English spoken. Open Mon.-Fri. 10am-6pm, Sat.-Sun. 10am-2pm.

Bookstore: Deuerlich, Weenderstr. 33 (tel. 49 50 00), is the main store. Smaller, specialized branches at Weender Landstr. 6 and Theaterstr. 25. If you're feeling down, let the amazing wit and verve of *Let's Go* soothe your jangled nerves. Open Mon.-Wed. and Fri. 9am-7pm, Thurs. 9am-8pm, Sat. 9am-4pm.

Laundromat: Wasch-O-Center, Ritterplan 4, opposite the Städtisches Museum. Wash DM5, soap included. Dry DM1 per 12min. Open Mon.-Sat. 7am-10pm. There are also washers, but no driers, at the hostel (see below).

Women's Concerns: Frauenhaus (tel. 483 20). Open daily 24hr.

AIDS-Hilfe/Gay Information: tel. 833 55.

Post Office: Heinrich-von-Stephan-Str. 7, 37073 Göttingen (tel. 498 61 50), to the left of the train station. Open Mon.-Fri. 8am-6:30pm, Sat. 8am-1pm.

Telephone Code: 0551.

ACCOMMODATIONS

The abundance of students and visitors in Göttingen makes the long-term housing market tight but not unreasonable. Fortunately, the hostel is excellent and generally has available rooms, while those wishing to stay a few days or even a few months can check the **Mitwohnzentrale,** Judenstr. 10 (tel. 194 45), which matches up potential roomies (open Mon., Wed., and Fri. 10am-4pm; Tues. and Thurs. 10am-1pm).

Jugendherberge (HI), Habichtsweg 2 (tel. 576 22; fax 438 87). From the station, turn left onto Berlinerstr., which becomes Nikolausberger Weg, and follow the signs (30min.). Or, bus #8, 10, 11, 15, or 18: "Kornmarkt;" and then either bus #6: "Jugendherberge" or #9: "Hermann-Föge-Weg." This place puts most *hotels* to shame with immaculate rooms, many singles, with new sinks and furnishings. Reception open 6:30am-11:30pm. Curfew at midnight, but get a key with a DM50 deposit. DM22, over 26 DM27. Room keys require DM20 deposit. Breakfast included. Sheets DM5.70. Washers DM4.50 (no driers). Bikes for rent.

Hotel "Zum Schwan," Weender Landstr. 23 (tel. 448 63). Walk left from the station and left onto Weender Landstr. (10min.). Cool tie-like patterns cover the walls of some pretty darned big rooms. Hallways clean and furnished. Reception open Mon.-Fri. 7am-10pm, Sat. 7am-2pm, Sun. 7am-2pm and 7-10pm. Singles DM46, with shower DM56; doubles DM73, DM87. Breakfast included.

Hotel-Gastätte Berliner Hof, Weender Landstr. 43 (tel. 38 33 20; fax 383 32 32). Down the street from the above and neatly tucked up next to the university. Floral comforters make your dreams cozy. Reception open 7am-1pm and 3-11pm. Singles DM55, with bath DM70; doubles with the works DM98.

FOOD

Göttingen is blessed with museum-quality specimens of the **Mensa** and the vegetable **Markt,** Germany's two great budget-food institutions. An impressive array of farm-fresh peddlers haggle in the area between Lange and Kurze Geismarstr., including a fruit market adjacent to the Deutsches Junges Theater (Tues., Thurs., and Sat. 7am-1pm) and in the square in front of the *Rathaus* Thurs. 2-8pm). The most central **supermarket** is **Plus,** Prinzenstr. 13, across from the library (open Mon.-Fri. 8am-6:30pm, Sat. 8am-2pm). **Goetheallee,** running from the station to the city center, has late-night Greek, Italian, and Turkish restaurants.

Zentral Mensa, follow Weender Landstr. onto Platz der Göttinger Sieben, turn right into the university complex, and walk to the dusty central plain to the cavernous *Studentenwerk* building off to the left. Swarming with people and plastered with events listings, the plain, dependable cafeteria serves meals for DM2-5, guests (non-students) DM6.80. Meal tickets are sold downstairs—buy one or you can't eat. Select one of the four menus from the wall opposite the ticket booth; e.g., Stammessen 1 or Wahlessen 2. Food served Mon.-Fri. 11:30am-2:15pm, Sat. 11:30am-2pm; baguettes and snacks available Mon.-Fri. 9am-2:15pm, Sat. 10am-2pm.

Nudelhaus, Rotestr. 13 (tel. 442 63). Oodles of noodles, with a fully stocked international menu (most DM7-13). A beer garden in back facilitates the eupeptic merriment. Open daily noon-midnight. Beer garden open Sat.-Sun until 2am.

Cron & Lanz, Weenderstr. 25 (tel. 560 22), under a conspicuous sign, is one of Germany's sweetest pastry shops and a real diet buster since 1876. The window displays of gorgeous dark *Torten* and *petit-fours* will make you drool. The white-glazed, cherry-laced *Baumkuchentorte* ("tree-cake"; DM3) is their speciality. Open Mon.-Fri. 8:45am-6:30pm, Sat. 8:30am-6:30pm, Sun. 1-6:30pm.

Shucan, Weenderstr. 11 (tel. 48 62 44). Just follow your nose to the giant toucan out front. A hip cafe and bar with hundreds of outdoor seats overlooking the Marktplatz behind the *Rathaus*. Baguettes (DM5-7) are an afterthought; their overornate, neo-Gothic/Baroque ice cream concoctions tower over the central city (from DM3.70). No Fruit Loops. Open Sun.-Thurs. 10am-2am, Fri.-Sat. 10am-3am.

Asia-Imbiss, at the corner of Johanisstr. and Pandektengasse. Nothing fancy—just *really* cheap Chinese food (DM3-7). Open Mon.-Fri. 11am-8pm, Sat. 11am-4pm.

SIGHTS

The courtyard of the **Altes Rathaus** serves as the meeting place for the whole town: punker, professor, and panhandler alike. The little 1m high **Gänseliesel** (goose-girl) on the fountain in front of the *Rathaus* is Göttingen's symbol, renowned as "the most-kissed girl in the world"; graduating students, particularly budding doctors, line up to kiss the promiscuous bronze beauty after receiving their diplomas. The repressed city council imposed a "kissing ban" in 1926, prompting one incensed (or perhaps just frustrated) student to sue. He lost, but town officials now turn a blind eye to extracurricular fountain activities. The bronze lion-head doorknob on the south portal of the **Rathaus** was crafted in 1300, making it the oldest town hall door knob in Germany. (So it's not the Pyramids. Oh well.) Inside elaborate murals depict 19th-century working-day life in Göttingen. Tours of the city depart from the *Gänseliesel* (see **Practical Information**, p. 277). The renowned **university** is outside the Ernst-Hönig-Wall (indeed a modest attempt at a wall). The campus fills an area bounded by Weender Landstr. and Nikolausberger Weg. Göttingen's student body is diverse, representing many styles, outlooks, and nationalities; still, you won't meet the cast from *Animal Haus* here. This is Deutschland.

The **Bismarckhäuschen** (tel. 48 58 44) is a tiny stone cottage built in 1459 outside the city wall where 17-year-old law student Otto von Bismarck took up residence after authorities expelled him from the inner city for boozing it up (open Tues. 10am-1pm, Thurs. and Sat. 3-5pm; free). A **Bismarckturm,** in Kleperberg (tel. 742 13), along the Stadtforest, commemorates the larger-scale trouble making of his later career (see **Bismarck and the Second Reich,** p. 64). From the top of the old stone tower, there's a Göttingen-wide view. Bus A: "Bismarckstr./Reitsall" (open Sat.-Sun. 11am-6pm; free). Göttingen also flaunts a few notable medieval churches. At the corner of Prinzenstr. and Weenderstr., next to the stone lambada sculpture called "Der Tanz," thrusts **St. Jacobi's** 72m tower. Inside, a miniature model of the impressive 1402 altar triptych is fun to play with (open daily 10am-noon; free organ concerts Fri.

at 6pm). Down Weenderstr. behind the *Altes Rathaus* stands the fortress-like **St. Johanniskirche.** The unexceptional interior is open daily 10:30am-12:30pm (the more interesting tower, where students have lived since 1921, is open Sat. 2-4pm). On Untere Maschstr. stands a spiraling pyramid erected as a **memorial** to the Göttingen synagogue that was razed in 1938. Viewed from above, the structure spirals into a monumental Star of David. Elsewhere, venerable *Fachwerk* mark the town's zenith, constructed when Göttingen was a member of the **Hanseatic League** (1351-1572).

The **Städtisches Museum,** Ritterplan 7 (tel. 400 28 45), one block north on Jüdenstr. from the Jacobikirche, gives a detailed examination of the city over the last several millennia or so (with stuff on Captain Caveman and friends). It starts off a bit weak, with an exhibit of bizarre **Göttinger religious art** from the 16th to the 18th century. Much more interesting is the third floor **Göttingen History** wing; the limited scope here tells the story well. After a sharp display of medieval town artifacts, the museum features the Nazi years of Göttingen. Hostel-sleepers will get a strange chill from a display of *Hitlerjugend* memorabilia which includes a number of *Deutsche Jugendherbergswerk* pins complete with swastikas on them. There's also a display of dozens of cover pages from Göttingen's Nazi-run local newspaper that offer a rather distorted view of history. The propagandists' allusions to the Pearl Harbor attack as "American war-mongering" must be read to be believed. A Nazi shadow also falls over the **university history** room. Much is made of Göttingen's intellectual distinction and liberal sentiments: in 1837, on the 100th anniversary of the university's founding, a group of professors known as the **Göttingen Seven** made German history by sending a public letter of protest to King Ernst August, who had revoked the liberal constitution established four years previously by his predecessor. Courageous signers included the Brothers Grimm, then well-known professors of literature; as expected, the Seven were all removed from office. Several were exiled. The museum does not miss the irony of comparing Göttingen's heroic first centennial with the ignominy of its bicentennial: 1937 saw the streets covered with swastikas while Goebbels and other intellectual "luminaries" renamed Theaterpl. "Adolf-Hitler-Platz." The extravaganza was held at a university devoid of Jewish faculty or students; most had emigrated or been imprisoned. A special side room exhibit commemorates the loss (open Tues.-Fri. 10am-5pm, Sat.-Sun. 10am-1pm; DM3, students DM2).

ENTERTAINMENT AND NIGHTLIFE

Göttingen's entertainment industry covers the entirety of the theatrical spectrum. For world-class performances, the renowned **Deutsches Theater** (tel. 49 69 11; fax 530 97) puts on the classics with tickets as low as DM11. Check out the slick **DT** catalog for the schedule, available at the box office (open Mon.-Fri. 10am-1:30pm and 5-7pm, Sat. 10am-noon, and 1hr. before shows). To sample the youthful perspective, head down to the **Junges Theater** (tel. 551 23; fax 530 64), which presents both the classic and the innovative (DM19, students DM13; on Wed. DM14, DM10). *All theaters close for the summer from July to mid-September.* Otherwise shows run daily Wednesday to Sunday (box office open Mon.-Sat. 11am-1pm and 2hr. before showtime). Film buffs can indulge in the perverse pleasure of ruthlessly dubbed blockbusters and German-language flicks at **Capitol 3 Cinema,** Prinzenstr. 13, or at the gigantic **Cinemaxx** complex behind the *Bahnhof* with nine movie screens. The artsy **Lumière,** Geimarlandstr. 19 (tel. 48 45 23), is more cosmopolitan and foreign-language friendly.

Although, Göttingen's disco and pub scene primarily occupies the *Altstadt,* a few popular clubs perch on the outskirts of the university, notably **Luloid,** Kreuzbergring 13. The aptly named **Outpost,** Königsallee 243, reputedly the best dance club in the city, keeps jumping until 1am, making it accessible only by cab (open Fri.-Sat.). Within the *Altstadt,* the best place to hear music and hang with students is the **Blue Note** (tel. 469 07), under the *Alte Mensa* in Wilhelmspl. There's a new musical theme every day, and live bands at least once a week. Jazz, reggae, and African pop are all well represented (open Mon.-Sat. 8pm-3am; when big-name DJs hop into the fray, cover DM12, students DM8). **Irish Pub,** Mühlenstr. 4, serves as one of the most popular student watering holes with a seemingly infinite supply of Guinness and a ton of Gaelic *Gemütlichkeit* (open daily 6pm-2am). **Graffiti,** Weenderstr. 58 (tel. 597 75) by the Jacobikirche, keeps rocking on Wednesday and Thursday nights while most other discos snooze. (God-sent happy hour Fri.-Sat. 11pm-midnight. Open Oct.-June Wed.-Sun. 10pm-5am; July-Sept. Fri.-Sat. only. Cover DM3.)

■ Goslar

Goslar flaunts a winning hand. The *Altstadt* is congested with immaculate half-timbered houses and winding narrow streets, encircled by the divinely lush, green Harz Mountains. Exciting museums and provoking sculptures, designed and crafted by artists such as Henry Moore and Botero, are scattered throughout the village, enchanting the most jaded art lover. In addition, as the hub of an extensive bus network, Goslar spins you to any part of the region.

During the 11th century, Heinrich II governed Goslar from the solemn **Kaiserpfalz** (Imperial Palace). However, when the Swabians deposed Kaiser Heinrich IV in 1077, Goslar's good fortune went with him. In the 13th century, the town hit the jackpot again: the **Rammelsberg,** a tall hill at the southern edge of town, turned out to be loaded with high-quality silver ore. Soon, prosperity hit Goslar broadside, and a powerful guild class took control of the city council. The mines sustained the boom until the 16th century, when Free Goslar began to spend all of its time and money fighting off the covetous dukes of Braunschweig. Finally, in 1552, Goslar crapped out again: it was occupied and forced to cede its mine-mountain to Braunschweig.

This loss 450 years ago now creates an extraordinary windfall for tourists: all building halted after the occupation, and Goslar's immense 16th-century *Altstadt* section was effectively frozen in time. During World War II, Goslar's citizens proclaimed it neutral and free of soldiers, painting red crosses atop the pointy *Fachwerke.* Under the Geneva convention, this rendered the town a non-target for bombing, saving it from destruction. UNESCO recognized Goslar's unique character by declaring virtually the entire town a historic site, beckoning tourists and Diva Fortuna back.

Orientation and Practical Information Trains from Hannover (16 per day) and Göttingen (14 per day) stop at Goslar. Perched near the defunct border with the East, Goslar is a good base for a bus or hiking tour of the Harz Mountains. The **tourist office,** Markt 7 (tel. 780 60; fax 230 05), across from the *Rathaus,* finds rooms (from DM30) for no fee. From the station, turn left and walk to the end of Rosentorstr.; it becomes Hokenstr. (Open March-Oct. Mon.-Fri. 9am-6pm, Sat. 9am-2:30pm; Nov.-April Mon.-Fri. 9am-5pm, Sat. 9am-1pm.) There is also a **Harz regional tourist office** in Goslar: the **Harzer Verkehrsverband,** Markstr. 45 (tel. (05321) 340 40), inside the *Industrie und Handels Kammer* building (open Mon.-Fri. 8am-4pm). Their indispensable *Grüner Faden für den Harz-Gast* pamphlet (DM5) lists attractions and everything from ski schools, rentals, and lifts to tours on horseback. *Jugend und Freizeitheime im Harz und im Harzvorland* is a complete guide to hostels and student centers in the area. The *Museumsführer: Harz und Umgebung* booklet describes every museum in every town. Also pick up the *Auto und Wanderkarte der ganzen Harz,* the map to hiking, biking, or driving through the region (DM12.80). (The tourist office is open Mon.-Fri. 8am-5pm.) **Harzbike Goslar-Baßgeige,** Bornhardtstr. 3-5 (tel. 820 11), rents **bikes** for DM35 per day (open Mon.-Fri. 9:30am-6pm, Sat. 9am-4pm). The **Frauenzentrum Goslar,** Breitestr. 15a (tel. 422 55), provides counseling for women. The entrance is on Bolzenstr. (open Mon. 9am-noon and 3-5pm, Wed. 9am-noon, Fri. 9am-noon). The **post office** is at Klubgartenstr. 10, 38640 Goslar (open Mon.-Fri. 8am-5:30pm, Sat. 9am-noon). The **telephone code** is 05321.

> **Note:** While the Oberharz Mountains loom over Niedersachsen and Thüringen, information about the entire Harz region can be found in Sachsen-Anhalt (see **Harz Mountains,** p. 215).

Accommodations and Camping The half-timbered Goslar **Jugendherberge (HI),** Rammelsbergerstr. 25 (tel. 222 40; fax 413 76), wins the prize for being the most confusingly located hostel in the book. Non-locals and patsies try to reach the hostel via the streets; they suffer for it. There's a **shortcut:** from the Marktplatz, take twisty Bergstr. southwest until it ends at the large east-west Clausthalerstr. Directly across the street, between the trees, a stairway marked with a "Wanderweg" sign awaits. Take this pleasant path through the pines, head right at the fork at the path's midpoint, and you'll find yourself in the hostel's backyard (5min.). Keep in mind that the path is poorly lit at night. The hostel features smallish two- and six-bed rooms with new furniture and newly equipped bathrooms. (Reception open 8:30am-10pm. Check-in after 3pm. Curfew 11:30pm. HI members only. DM20, over 26 DM25. Breakfast included. Vegetarian meals available.) **Campingplatz Sennhütte,** Clausthalerstr. 28 (tel. 224 98), 3km from town along the B241, has a restaurant (tel. 225 02) and sauna (person DM5.50, tent DM4, showers DM1).

If you've a bit more money to spare, Goslar proffers several excellent *Pensionen.* Next to the Markt is the impressive **Gästehaus Schmitz,** Kornstr. 1 (tel. 234 45). While Schmitz has all of the quirky architectural details of an authentic half-timbered house, the rooms are nicely decorated and comfortably modern. All rooms have access to a fully equipped kitchen, sauna, solarium, whirlpool, and a sunny breakfast area. From the Markt, turn left on Kornstr. (Reception open 9am-7pm. Singles DM55; doubles DM68. Spartan two-person apartments DM55; luxurious apartments DM60 per person.) **Gästehaus Elisabeth Möller,** Schieferweg 6 (tel. 230 98), has been a family affair for 24 years. An immense, shady garden (3000msq.), with a complete patio, invites afternoon lounging. Take Klubgartenstr. and Am Heiligen Grabe west from the train station, cross Von-Garssen-Str., and turn right on Schieferweg (singles DM35, with bath DM45; doubles with bath DM85-100).

Food and Entertainment The town's mountain **Markt** yodels every Tuesday and Friday (open 8am-1pm). The beautiful market square is ringed with cafes and restaurants; unfortunately, most are of the DM5-per-beer variety. Cheaper bistros and cafes can be found along Hokenstr., where *Imbiß* stands provide meals for DM4-8. **Don Camillo Pizza-Bistro,** Bergstr. 60 (tel. 462 62), will meet the needs of the cheaper than cheap: pizzas run DM3-10, while pasta dishes consume DM10 (open Mon.-Fri. 11am-midnight, Sat.-Sun. 4pm-midnight). To explore Goslar's sordid underbelly, across the street from Don Camillo's, but also on Bergstr., is **Himmel Blaue Trichter Winde,** identifiable by the "Café Theater Livemusik Café" painted in hideous neon graffiti on the window. This place has all the feel of an S&M dungeon, complete with hanging skulls and hard-core Goth music (open Tues.-Sat. after 8pm).

Sights Guarded by a pair of bronze Braunschweig lions, the austere **Kaiserpfalz,** Kaiserbleek 6, is a massive Romanesque palace that served as the ruling seat for 11th- and 12th-century emperors. The palace fell into sad decay by the 19th century but was extensively restored by nationalistic 1870s Prussian aristocrats. The interior of the **great hall** is plastered with 19th-century murals; the huge paintings display carefully selected historical incidents in the mythic pompous manner that only 19th-century Germans could properly pull off. Their unsubtle purpose was to link the ancient Kaisers, through Friedrich Barbarossa and Wilhelm the Great, to Kaiser Wilhelm I, who appears flanked by Bismarck on the left and his son behind, with "Father Rhine" poised like Poseidon below. In the palace's **Ulrichskapelle,** Heinrich III's heart lies tucked away inside a massive sarcophagus. (Museum and tomb open April-Oct. daily 10am-5pm; Nov.-March 10am-4pm; last entry 30min. before closing; tours in German every 15min. past the hour 10:15am-3:15pm; DM3.50, students DM2.) Below the palace at Kaiserbleek 10 is the **Domvorhalle** (Cathedral Foyer), the sad remains of a 12th-century imperial cathedral destroyed 170 years ago. The plaque on the wall is the engraved equivalent of a scrawled "Heinrich Heine wuz here."

The central **Marktplatz** is delightful: as far as the eye can peer, it finds a rush of ornate woodwork and trellises. The **Hotel Kaiserworth,** a former guild house, was for many years an eccentric but striking addition to the square, with its superb tapering gable spires and the copious wooden statues of emperors gracing the facade. Recently, however, its elegant white front has been repainted a vulgar red. The hotel's statues have been painted up, too; in full comic-book color, it's now easier to see the coarsely humorous smaller figures on the corners. Each day in the market square, small **Glocken- und Figurenspiel** figures of court nobles and the miners whose work made the region prosperous dance to the chime on the treasury roof (9am, noon, 3, and 6pm). The **Rathaus** has a few really great things inside that will remain secret until it reopens in 1999.

The twin towers of the reconstructed 12th-century **Marktkirche** poke up from right behind the *Rathaus*. Inside, see the stained-glass saga of St. Cosmas and St. Damian, 3rd-century twin doctors and martyrs. In a classic instance of the Roman empire's overkill, the saints were disciplined and punished by drowning, burning at the stake, stoning, crucifixion, and transfixion (open Tues.-Thurs. and Sat. 10:30am-3:30pm, Fri. 10:30am-2pm, Sun. noon-3:30pm). The **Mönchehaus**, Mönchestr. 3 (tel./fax 421 99), exhibits a grand modern art collection, including Anselm Kiefer, Calder, Miró, and Joseph Beuys. And long before he wrapped the *Reichstag*, Christo came to Goslar to wrap the last wagon of coal from the now-closed mine (open Tues.-Sat. 10am-1pm and 3-5pm, Sun. 10am-1pm; free, but donation requested). On the way back from the *Kaiserpfalz*, don't miss the fantastic **Puppen-und-Musikinstrumente Museum** (Puppet and Musical Instrument Museum), Hoherweg 5. The owner has spent more than 40 years assembling the largest private instrument collection in Germany, including one of the **world's first accordions,** and a 50s Wurlitzer jukebox. Also visit the **meta-museum** tucked inside, billed as the "smallest musical instrument museum in the world," with a small box featuring models of miniature models of instruments. Your ticket will also get you into the antique doll and toy exhibit, and the racier "Beauty" porcelain exhibit of naked women hidden in the basement (open daily from 11am-5pm; DM4, children DM2). Goslar gets funky every year from August 30 to September 1 with its **Altstadtfest**—a kind of watered-down *Oktoberfest*.

▨ Hameln (Hamelin)

In the 700 years since the Pied Piper first strolled out of town, Hameln has transformed from a rat trap to a tourist trap. The original story was sordid enough: after Hameln failed to pay the piper his rat-removal fee, he walked off with 130 children in thrall. But today the legend of the *Rattenfänger*, as he is known in Germany, draws tourists as mysteriously as his flute drew rodents in 1284. What do people find so attractive about this legend? Its allegorical link to the settlement of the eastern regions (the so-called *"Drang nach Osten"*), to which many of medieval Hameln's citizens were lured? The cynical delight of comparing children to rabid rodents? Whatever the case may be, the appeal of the dancing rats is a certainty upon which Hameln has built a good deal of prosperity. Along the souvenir-choked streets today, you can almost hear the town mayor consoling grieving parents, "You haven't lost a child, you've gained a tourist industry."

Orientation and Practical Information The **tourist office,** on the Bürgergarten at Deisterallee 3 (tel. 20 26 17 or 20 26 18; fax 20 25 00), tracks down rooms (from DM25) for a DM2 fee. From the station, cross Bahnhofpl., go up Bahnhofstr., and turn left onto Deisterstr., which becomes Deisterallee (open Mon.-Fri. 9am-1pm and 2-6pm, Sat. 9:30am-12:30pm and 3-5pm, Sun. 9:30am-12:30pm; Oct.-April Mon.-Fri. 9am-1pm and 2-5pm). A smaller booth in the **Hochzeithaus** has summertime **information** (open mid-April to mid-Oct. Tues.-Fri. 11am-2pm and 2:30-4:30pm, Sat.-Sun. 10am-2pm). City **tours** take off from the Bürgergarten (Mon.-Sat. 3pm, Sun. 10am and 3pm; DM5, kids DM3). Hameln bridges the Weser River, 45 minutes from Hannover by frequent **trains** (daily 4:23am-10:23pm, 26 per day). When riding **buses** in Hameln, check the schedule carefully. If there is a "T" next to the time, a bus does not come. Instead, you must call 194 19 and tell the operator at least 45 minutes prior to departure that you would like a **taxi;** a Mercedes will then roll up and take you along the bus route (DM2-4). **Oberweser-Dampfschiffahrt,** Inselstr. 3 (tel. 220 16; fax 230 40), runs **ferries** up and down the Weser River (April.-Sept.), offering a complete package of tours (1hr. expeditions DM7.50, students DM5; call for a schedule and prices). **Rent a bike** (DM15 per 24hr.) from the **Troche Fahrräder repair shop,** Kreuzstr. 7 (tel. 136 70; open Mon.-Fri. 9:30am-1pm and 2:30-6pm, Sat. 9:30am-12:30pm). The hostel (see below) also rents bikes to guests (DM8 per day). **Matthias Buchhandlung,** Bäckerstr. 56 (tel. 947 00), has a decent selection of English paperbacks. The **post office** is at Am Posthof 1, 31785 Hameln (open Mon.-Fri. 8am-1pm and 2-5:30pm, Sat. 8am-1pm). The **telephone code** is 05151.

Accommodations and Camping The beautifully located but regrettably Piper-festooned **Jugendherberge (HI),** Fischbeckerstr. 33 (tel. 34 25; fax 423 16), sits on a dreamy bend in the Weser. From the station, bus #2: "Wehler Weg," and turn right onto Fischbeckerstr. By foot (35min.), cross Bahnhofpl. to Bahnhofstr., turn left on Deisterallee, right around 164-er Ring (along the Hamel rivulet) to Erichstr., as it bends into Fischbeckerstr. German school children *love* dreamy bends in rivers, so call a couple of months in advance if possible. Crowded rooms, but a sweet view from the outdoor patio makes a stay enjoyable. (Reception open 5-10pm. Curfew 10pm, but key available with DM30 deposit. DM20, over 26 DM25. Breakfast included; magic flute to lure away schoolkids is not. Sheets DM5.50. Laundry DM6.)

Hameln's tourist boom has resulted in a large number of *Pensionen.* The **Pension Grölling,** Fuchsbau 11 (tel. 671 53), is a 40-minute walk from the train station, but bus #31: "Fuchsbau," stops right at the door (DM25-40). Closer to the center is **Pension Wiese,** Alte Marktstr. 44 (tel. 39 72), directly across the street from the *Redenhof.* If you tire of watching that piper prance around, ask Wiese to tell you how he escaped from the Russians in 1942 by faking nature's call—the visual accompaniment is very entertaining. (Reception open until 10pm. DM35-40. Reservations highly recommended.) Southeast of the city center, on the Tönebön Lake, lies **Campground Jugendzeltplatz,** Tönebönweg 8 (tel. 262 23), equipped with a sauna. From the *Bahnhof* or the *Altstadt,* bus #51: "Sädbad." (Reception open Mon.-Fri. until 10pm, Sat.-Sun. until 11pm. DM5. Open May-Sept.)

Food The streets of the *Altstadt* around Ostenstr. and Pferdemarkt are lined by restaurants and cafes, but chances of finding a bargain are slim. A few good deals loom along Bäckerstr. near the *Münster.* Duck into **Julia's Restaurant,** Bäckerstr. 57 (tel. 444 32), which serves spaghetti (DM8.50) and eight scrumptious potato dishes (DM9.50-11; open daily 11am-2:30pm and 5:30-8pm). *Hamelners* flock for fruit, vegetables, and other treats to the open-air **market** on the Bürgergarten (open Wed. and Sat. 8am-1pm). Hameln boasts an impressive array of edible rodents (if you swallow them whole, the fur will tickle your throat...lovely!). To catch these rats, pay to the tune of DM0.35 for tiny marzipan critters and up to DM6 for a jumbo pastry rat. Little crusty bread-rats cost DM3 at **Schnelz Reformhaus,** Osterstr. 18 in the *Altstadt.* The *Haus* also sells all-natural foodstuffs of every sort, a delight for the vegetarian with some cooking equipment (open Mon.-Wed. 8:30am-6pm, Thurs.-Fri. 8:30am-6:30pm, Sat. 8am-1pm). **Plus supermarket,** Bahnhofstr. 34-36, sells the basics.

Sights If you cringe at the thought of small rodents or little flute players in motley capes, Hameln is probably not the best vacation spot; the Piper motif is inescapable. One of the few buildings unadorned by Pied Piper paraphernalia is the modern **Rathaus** (did we say RAT Haus?). In the courtyard out front, however, several elfin children hang suspended in mid-air, following a piper statue to the **Rattenfänger-Brunnen.** The **Bürgergarten,** right down the street, is a small but soothing relief from the tourist rat race. Chess players will enjoy the massive game board and 3-foot-high pieces. (Garden open daily 7am-midnight; fountains run mid-May to mid-Sept. daily 11am-noon, 3-4, and 7:30-8pm.) Walk back down Kastanienwall and turn right into the massive auto-free zone that is the *Altstadt.* Off to the left, the **Rattenfängerhaus**

(built in 1602) is decked out with dozens of startled-looking figureheads recalling the sudden surge in the average age of townsfolk. Trek down another 100m to the 1589 **Leiesthaus**, Osterstr. 9 (tel. 20 22 15), where the **Museum Hameln** exhibits the Piper in 20 poses and 20,000 books (open Tues.-Sun. 10am-4:30pm; DM2, students and children DM1). The grim *Rättenfänger* tale is re-enacted each Sunday at noon (May-Sept., weather permitting) in a **Freilichtspiel** (open-air show) at the 1610 **Hochzeith-aus** (wedding house). Small children dressed as rats chase a man with a large wooden instrument in his mouth wearing a multicolored suit and tight pants. At 10:05am the **Glockenspiel** on the *Hochzeithaus* plays the *Rattenfängerlied* (Pied Piper Song); at 11:05am you're serenaded by the *Weserlied*; and at 1:05, 3:35, and 5:35pm, a tiny stage emerges from the *Hochzeithaus* and "rats" circle around a peculiar wooden flautist.

■ Hannoversch Münden

Hannoversch Münden, known to groupies as "Hann. Münden", lies between forested hills where "the Fulda and the Werra kiss one another"—the newborn Weser River popping out as a result of the consummation. Alexander von Humboldt called it "one of the seven most beautifully located cities in the world." With over 700 preserved *Fachwerkhäuser*, this is one of the most attractive among Germany's six zillion half-timbered towns. The impeccable *Altstadt* remains refreshingly free of tourists despite its picture-book setting at the foot of the *Deutsche Märchenstraße* (German fairy tale route). To taste the flavor of the town, strolling aimlessly through the *Altstadt* might offer a richer palate than dragging yourself between sights. Either way, Hann. Münden offers a tiny world of architectural beauty and authenticity.

Orientation and Practical Information Get hiking maps and the *Weg & Fähre*, a free and complete guide with information for the town and its environs, from the **tourist office** (tel. 753 13; fax 754 04) in the *Rathaus*. The staff will book you a room (from DM40) for free. (Open Mon.-Fri. 8:30am-1pm and 2-5pm, Sat. 8:30am-12:30pm; Oct.-April Mon.-Thurs. 8:30am-1pm and 2-4pm, Fri. 8:30am-1pm.) Help is also on hand from the *Auskunftschalter* (information counter; tel. 750), in the same building, after the office closes (open May-Sept. daily until 9pm; Oct.-April daily until 8pm). Hann. Münden is easily accessible by **train** from Göttingen (35min.) or Kassel (20min.). **Ferries** navigate the Fulda and Weser rivers with water tours of Hann. Münden (DM10). A confusing web of boat companies run the ferries, but the tourist office has a special department (tel. 753 13 or 753 14) to do all the work for you at no cost. Walking **tours** of the *Altstadt* are given mid-May to October (Wed. and Sat. 10am, Sun. 9:30am; DM4). Rent **bikes** at **Campingplatz Münden** (see below; open 8am-10pm; DM15 per day). Paths along the Weser River lead to the *Tilly-schanze* and continue on toward the **Reinhardswald forest** area. **Hiking maps** are available at the hostel and the tourist office (DM10). The **telephone code** is 05541.

Accommodations, Camping, and Food The lace-curtained **Jugendher-berge (HI)**, Prof.-Oelkers-Str. 8 (tel. 88 53; fax 734 39), sits just outside the town lim-its on the banks of the Weser. From the station, walk down Beethovenstr., turn left at Wallstr., cross the Pionierbrücke, turn right along Veckerhägerstr. (B3; 25min.); or from the *Bahnhof* bus stop, bus #135 or (on Sun.) 134 (direction: "Veckerhäger/Kas-selerstr."): "Jugendherberge." (Bus #135 Mon.-Fri. hourly until 7pm, Sat. hourly until 2pm. Bus #134 June-Sept. Sun. 10:15am, 1:15, and 5:15pm only.) A BahnCard gets you a 40% discount on all travel in the *Altstadt*. (Reception open 5-7 and 9:45-10pm. Curfew 10pm. DM20, over 26 DM25. Breakfast included. Sheets DM6. Call ahead. Closed two random weekends per month June-Sept.) Pitch your tent in view of the city walls at **Campingplatz Münden**, Oberer Tanzwerder (tel. 122 57), 10 minutes from the train station on an island in the Fulda River off Pionierbrücke. There is a small **restaurant** on the premises, **canoe and bike rentals** are available, and hot showers are on tap. (Reception open 7am-10pm. DM8.50 per person. DM7.50 per tent. DM3.50 per auto. Open March 15-Oct.) The cheapest eats can be found at bakeries along Langestr. or at the **Markt** behind the *Rathaus* (Wed. and Sat. 7am-1pm). For some historic action, dine at the **Tillyhaus,** Marktstr. 15 (tel. 42 48), where the infamous French general lived for five years during the town's occupation. Beer from DM1.90 (open Mon.-Sat. 10am-2am, Sun. 2pm-2am). For cheap eats to top off the beers, **Pizza Eck,** Rosenstr. 14 (tel. 209), serves hefty pizza and pasta plates (DM6-9; open Mon.-Sat. 11am-11pm, Sun. 5-11pm). **Plus,** Marktplatz 5, satisfies grocery needs (open Mon.-Fri. 8am-6:30pm, Sat. 8am-2pm).

Sights Weave through the angled sidestreets to admire the 14th-century *Fachwerkhäuser;* some of the oldest and most impressive are tucked away on **Ziegelstraße.** The 16th-century **Hinter der Stadtmauer 23,** a Jewish School since 1796, was gutted in 1938. A plaque stands outside in memoriam. Recent owners restored it and uncovered a *Mikwe* (ritual bath) in the basement. The ornate **Rathaus** is a prime example of the Weser-Renaissance style that originated in the area around 1550. To reach the **Rathaus** from the train station, walk straight down Bahnhofstr., take a right at Burgstr., and continue on until you reach Markstr.; take a left here, and the *Rathaus* is on your left. Centuries-old markings of Weser flood heights mark the *Rathaus* corner walls, but more artistic coloring book scenes out of the city's past line the **Rathaushalle** walls inside. Outside, figurines appear from the upper windows of the *Rathaus* to dance to the merry melodies played on the bells hanging from the facade daily at noon, 3, and 5pm. Also outside is the wagon of Hann. Münden's former resident and favorite tourist gimmick, **Doctor Eisenbart,** an 18th-century traveling physician whose ability to treat many illnesses was overshadowed by his reputation as a quack and a swindler. The comic story of his life is played out every Sunday from June to August on the stage in front of the *Rathaus* (at 11:15am; DM4). The striking **St. Blasiuskirche,** opposite the *Rathaus,* is decked out in periwinkle and emerald, with ornate Solomonic columns surrounding the altar, a somber *Rittergrabmal,* and a 15th-century crucifix (open Mon.-Fri. 11am-12:30pm and 2-5pm, Sat. 11am-12:30pm, Sun. 2-6pm).

Hann. Münden's three islands—**Doktorwerder, Unterer Tanzwerder,** and **Oberer Tanzwerder**—are all easily accessible by small, historic bridges on the outskirts of the *Altstadt.* The U.K.'s hired guns, the famed Hessian mercenaries, took off from the islet's former pier to face off against the upstart American colonists. The best view of the valley is from across the Fulda atop the 1882 **Tillyschanze** tower, built to commemorate May 30, 1626. On this day during the Thirty Years War, General Tilly stormed through Hann. Münden, slaughtering over 2000 citizens. The path is unmarked; follow the occasional concrete-slab steps and wire fences. Ask at the adjacent *Gasthaus* kiosk to magically open the door (tower open 7am-dusk; DM1). On the banks of the Werra, the austere **Welfenschloß** proves that not all Weser Renaissance buildings look like over-iced birthday cakes. The gray parts of the building are remnants of the original Gothic structure that burned down in 1560. The sumptuous interior can only be admired on a guided tour (Sat. 2:30pm; meet in front of the *Rathaus;* DM4). It also houses the **Städtisches Museum** that boasts a sizable antique fayence collection (18-19th centuries) and several of Gustav Eberlein's neo-Baroque sculptures. (Open Wed.-Fri. 10am-noon and 2:30-5pm, Sat. 10am-noon and 2:30-4pm, Sun. 10am-12:30pm. DM2, students DM1.) Wander along the city walls that still show seven of the original defense towers, as well as the 1329 **Alte Werrabrücke** and the **St. Aegiden Kirche,** built in the 12th century but another victim of Tilly—a nearby *Pulverturm* (gun powder tower) exploded and ignited the church.

■ Hildesheim

The **Tausend Jähriger Rosenstock** (The Thousand-Year-Old Bush), symbolizes the prosperity of the town of Hildesheim. According to legend, Emperor Ludwig der Fromme (the Pious) lost his way after a hunt and fastened his Marian relic to the branch of a conspicuous rose bush. He managed to find his way home, and the next day, remembering his relic, returned to find it still clinging to the branch. He interpreted this as a divine sign and erected a chapel on the site, around which grew the majestic **Dom** and the town of Hildesheim. As long as the bush flourishes, so will Hildesheim. On March 22, 1945, Allied bombers flattened the town, yet the remarkable bush survived. The collapsed ruins of the *Dom* sheltered the roots from the flames. Eight weeks later, 25 buds were growing strong.

Orientation and Practical Information Hildesheim is 45km southeast of Hannover, with good *Autobahn* connections and almost hourly **trains.** The **tourist office,** Am Ratsbauhof 1c (tel. 179 80; fax 17 98 88), two blocks from the *Rathaus,* offers brochures and also books rooms for a DM5 fee. From the *Hauptbahnhof,* walk straight up Bernwardstr. which becomes Almsstr., turn left onto Rathausstr., and turn right down Ratsbauhof (open Mon.-Fri. 9am-6pm, Sat. 9am-1pm). There is also a **branch office** in the **Kirchturm** of St. Andreas Church that passes out maps and city guides (open Sat. 10am-5pm, Sun. noon-6pm). Enjoy the two-hour city **tours** (April-Nov. Sun.-Fri. 2pm, Sat. 10am; DM5). **Bus** tickets cost DM2.20 and are good for one hour of unlimited rides. **Internet access** awaits in the **Internet-Café,** Judenstr. 3 (open daily 10am-11pm; 30min. connection DM5). The **post office,** 31134 Hildesheim, sits next to the *Hauptbahnhof* (open Mon.-Fri. 8am-6pm, Sat. 8am-1pm). The **telephone code** is 05121.

Accommodations Hildesheim's pastoral **Jugendherberge (HI),** Schirrmanweg 4 (tel. 427 17; fax 478 47), perches on the edge of a bucolic farm, with a beautiful view ●f the city, although its four- to six-bed rooms are cramped. Breakfasts are ample and there's a backyard disco. Bus #1, 2, 6, or 11 (direction: "Himmelstür"): "Schuhstr." and switch to bus #4 (direction: "Bockfeld"): "Triftstr." Cross the street and climb uphill (10min.) to the hostel. (Reception open Mon.-Sat. 8-9:30am, 5-7, and 9:45-10pm, Sun. 6-7 and 9:45-10pm. Curfew 10pm, but key available for DM50 deposit. DM20, over 26 DM24.50. Breakfast included. Sheets DM5.70.) A little further out, but well worth the extra trouble, rests **Maria Schröder's Pension,** Bleckenstedterstr. 2 (tel. 434 21). From the train station, bus #1 (direction: "Hammelstür"): "Am Dammtor." Backtrack and turn left down Schützenweisestr. and turn right down Bleckenstedterstr. Frau Schröeder has got to be one of the nicest ladies in Germany, and amazingly enough, her rooms are almost as big as her heart. Plush sofas will have you feeling like a million *Marks*—enough to buy a slimy mint in 1923 (DM35). Another good pick is **Hotel Marheineke,** Peiner Landstr. 189 (tel, 526 67). Line #10 (direction: "Bauenstedt"): "Alt Drispenstedt," backtrack 10m, make a right onto Peiner Landstr., and then a quick left through the pedestrian tunnel. Or bus #1 (direction: "Bavenstedt"): "Ehrlicherstr.," walk back 50m, right on Peiner Landstr., and follow the above. (Reception open until 10pm. Singles DM45-50; doubles DM80, with shower DM90.)

Food and Entertainment Hildesheim has a diverse culinary scene, with plenty of variety and reasonable prices. The **Knochenhauer-Amtshaus** (tel. 323 23), on the Marktplatz, serves German dishes from DM10 (open daily 11am-11pm). **Dolphin,** Weinhagonstr. 4 (tel. 51 78 72) serves Turkish staples (falafel, *Döner,* etc.) from DM5 (open daily noon-2am). **Paulaner im Kneip,** Marktstr. 4 (tel. 360 13), offers a piece of Munich in Hildesheim. Lunch dishes *(Bratwurst, Schnitzel)* from DM6.80, but the real draw is the beer—sweet *Münchener* Paulaner (0.5L DM5.80; *Maß* DM10.50). The students in the area get down at **Vier Linden,** Alfolderstr. 55b (tel. 252 55), a hip, *jung* dance-mecca with a popular bar (club open Mon. and Thurs. 10pm-3am; bar open daily 6pm-1am). More relaxing but as fun is the Irish *Kneipe* **Limerick,** Klaperhagen 6 (tel. 13 38 76). Open Mon.-Thurs. 11am-1am, Fri.-Sat. 11am-2am, Sun. 11am-midnight).

Sights Ludwig's favorite chapel, the **Annenkapelle,** and the famous *Tausend-Jährige Rosenstock* bush, are featured in the *Dom*'s courtyard (open Mon.-Sat. 9:30am-5pm, Sun. noon-5pm; DM0.50, children DM0.30). The **Diözesan Museum** (tel. 16 89

50), around to your left as you exit the *Dom,* showcases the Marian relic of old Ludwig—it's #8 on the "Schlacht bei Dinklar" exhibit—and other ecclesiastical goodies. (*Dom* open Mon.-Sat. 10am-5pm, Sun. noon-5pm. Museum open Tues.-Sat. 10am-5pm, Sun. noon-5pm. DM4, students DM1.50.) The **Marktplatz** is a plaza of reconstructed half-timber buildings and archways featuring the majestic **Knochenhauer-Amtshaus** (Butcher's Guild House), reputed to be the "most beautiful wooden structure in the world." The facade is lavishly decorated with colorful paintings and German proverbs (e.g., *arm oder reich, der Tod macht alles gleich—*poor or rich, death treats all the same). South of the city center at the intersection of Gelber Stern (Yellow Star) and Lappenberg, lie the remains of Hildesheim's **synagogue.** The temple itself was torched on *Kristallnacht* in 1938, and a memorial has been erected on the site. The warped facade of the 1606 **Wernerhaus** (down from Gelber Stern to Brühl) rests untouched by bombs or modernization. The 14th-century **Tempelhaus,** in the Marktplatz, is a visually arresting bookstore (unfortunately, a small English-language section).

Looping back around the western tip of the city, drop in at the **Römer- und Pelizaeus-Museum,** Am Steine 1 (tel. 936 90), featuring a colorful collection of Egyptian art and artifacts (including mummies), as well as frequent and extensive special exhibits, ranging from "The World of the Whale" (presented by Greenpeace) to the history of ancient Persia (open Tues.-Sun. 9am-4:30pm; DM12, students DM5).

■ Bodenwerder

In the land of **Baron von Münchhausen,** the King of Liars, you might not be sure what to believe. Here on the banks of the Weser, the Baron first told his hunting buddies his fabulous adventure stories of flying to the Moon and sailing through a sea of milk to an island of cheese. But is this Baroque Jon Lovitz himself a fabrication of Bodenwerder's tourist industry, an attempt to out-fable Hameln? Verily not: the little town's church ledgers have birth and death listings for Baron Hieronymus Carolus Friedericus von Münchhausen. More useful truths can be found on the carved wooden signs which point out the various sights of Bodenwerder.

On Münchhauspl., the mansion-turned-**Rathaus,** the Baron's birthplace, holds the **Münchhausenzimmer Museum** (tel. 405 47). Inside, you'll find color illustrations of his exploits along with the legendary pistol with which he shot his horse off a steeple (DM2, students and *Kindern* DM1.50). The same ticket gets you into the **Heimat Museum,** on the other side of the *Rathaus,* where you can see pictures of Bodenwerder as an island in the Weser before it was dammed up (both open April-Oct. daily 10am-noon and 2-5pm). The landmark **fountain** outside shows the Baron watering his horse, whose hindquarters were sliced off in battle, and later retrieved. As the story goes, the Baron's farrier sewed the poor animal's booty together with twigs and laurels, which sprouted into a tree, providing the rider shade for the rest of his expeditions (and a nasty splinter affliction). The streets lining the **Fußgängerzone** (pedestrian zone) are riddled with 114 half-timbered houses; the oldest dot Königstr., Homburgstr., and Grossestr. Further up the pedestrian zone is a beautiful fountain depicting three of the Baron's most outrageous adventures.

For a list of events in Bodenwerder, pick up a copy of *Weg und Fähre* at the **tourist office,** Weserstr. 3 (tel. 405 41; fax 405 40; open Mon.-Fri. 9am-12:30pm and 2:30-6pm, Sat. 9am-noon). City **tours** start at 3pm every Wednesday out front (DM3). Bodenwerder is 24km northeast of Hameln. Take **bus** #48/520 or #48/523 (Bahn Card valid) to visit. Rent **bikes** from **Karl-Heinz-Greif,** Danzigerstr. 20 (tel. 33 34; fax 931 45), for DM10 per day (open Mon.-Fri. 8:30am-12:30pm and 2:30-6pm, Sat. 8:30am-1pm, Sun. 9-10:30am).The **post office,** 37619 Bodenwerder, is located across the street from the *Rathaus* (open Mon.-Fri. 8:30am-noon and 2:30-5pm, Sat. 8:30-11:30am). The **telephone code** is 05533.

The **Zimmernachweis,** on the corner of Weserstr. and Münchhausenpl., lists updated information on room addresses and vacancies. As always, check the room before agreeing; after all, the town hero is a con artist. Bodenwerder's **Jugendher-**

berge (HI), Richard-Schirmann-Weg (tel. 26 85; fax 62 03), is a 10-minute walk from the *Fußgängerzone,* but the last 100m is steep, steep, steep. See if you can get a local to shoot you up there via cannonball, or walk across the Weser River (via bridge, that is) and turn left, then right on Siemenstr., and follow the signs up Unter dem Berge. The institutional exterior conceals a fun-filled interior brimming with *Fußball* and ping-pong. (Reception open 3-10pm. Curfew 10pm. 6-bed dorms DM20, over 26 DM25. Breakfast included. Lunch DM6.70. Sheets DM5.70.) *Pension* rooms and private rooms are generally inexpensive and easy to come by. Most *Pensionen* run DM25-35; several hotels cost less than DM45. Ask the tourist office for details.

Cheap meals in Bodenwerder are not too hard to find, yet even the locals take advantage of the food service in the youth hostel's dining hall (DM6.50-8.50; lunch at noon, dinner at 6pm). The **Goldenhähnchen Grill,** Königstr. 19, has plenty of greasy, authentic German food. *Bratwurst* and fries DM4.70, *Wienerschnitzel* and fries DM8.70 (open daily noon-11pm). **Pennymarkt,** Grossestr. 37, has groceries at prices even the Baron can't believe! (Open Mon.-Fri. 8:30am-7pm, Sat. 8am-2pm). On the first Sunday of each month at 3pm, from May to October, a **free play** in the Spa Gardens reenacts Münchhausen's exploits. On the second Saturday of August, Bodenwerder sets the Weser ablaze with its pyrotechnic **Festival of Lights.**

■ Braunschweig

Now that Braunschweig's Cold War border town duties are over, this middleweight city is pumping up its cultural attractions. The history of Braunschweig (sometimes called "Brunswick" in English) began in 1166, when Heinrich the Lion settled here. After hanging up his hat, Heinrich set about building a kingdom: he erected the famous Braunschweig lion statue (now the city's most visible symbol) and inaugurated Braunschweig's metamorphoses into a thriving religious and commercial center. The town is saturated with gargantuan cathedrals and other religious monuments that once marked the free city's economic importance to the Holy Roman Empire. An alumnus of the Hanseatic League, Braunschweig's robust economy and brash bids for tourism make it one of Lower Saxony's most vital cities.

ORIENTATION AND PRACTICAL INFORMATION

Braunschweig crouches between the Lüneburger Heide and the Harz Mountains. It serves as the crossing point for high-speed trains connecting Frankfurt and Hannover to Berlin and other lines. The *Hauptbahnhof* lies southeast of the city center, essentially an island ringed by the Oker River. Walking straight from the *Bahnhof* brings you across Berlinerpl. to the wide **Kurt-Schumacher-Str.** This curves to the left to meet **John-F.-Kennedy Platz** (also JFK Platz or Kennedypl.), a major crossroad at the southeast corner of the central city. Following Auguststr. northwest from JFK Platz leads to the center city. Braunschweig's downtown attractions are mostly within the great circle formed by the branching Oker River. Streetcars and buses criss-cross the city; most lines pass through either the "Rathaus"/"Bohlweg" stops (downtown) or "JFK Platz"/"K. Schumacher-Str." stops (a 10min. walk from the *Bahnhof*).

Tourist Offices: There are two tourist offices in town; one is inside the train station (open Mon.-Fri. 8am-6pm, Sat. 9:30am-noon) and the other a block from the *Rathaus,* Bohlweg (tel. 27 35 50 or 273 55 30; fax 273 55 19 or 273 55 39; open Mon.-Fri. 9am-6pm, Sat. 9:30am-12:30pm). An excellent free map of the bus and streetcar system is available from the ticket booth outside the station. A wide range of tours (DM4-DM27) depart from the Bohlweg branch; both offices help to find rooms in hotels and *Pensionen* for a DM3 fee (DM39 and up).

Mitwohnzentrale: Heinrichstr. 37 (tel. 194 45), in the suburbs of town. From the *Hauptbahnhof,* bus #19 (direction: "Europl."): "Jasperallee." Walk up Hagenring two blocks and turn right on Heinrichstr.—the office is on the right. Friendly and effective for long-term arrangements as well as overnight stays. They ask a commission of 15% of the first-night price for stays of less than a week, and the percentages go down from there. Open Mon.-Tues. and Thurs. 11am-6pm, Wed. 10am-4pm, Fri. 10am-1pm.

Currency Exchange: The **post office** offers decent rates and cashes traveler's checks for DM3 per check.

American Express: Casparistr. 1 (tel. 242 83 10; fax 428 39), in the center of town near the "Rathaus" and "Bohlweg" stops. Cashes and sells traveler's checks and exchanges money. Open Mon.-Fri. 9am-7pm, Sat. 10am-2pm.

Public Transportation: A thorough system of **streetcars** and **buses** laces Braunschweig and its environs. 90min. tickets, valid for any number of line changes, are sold as single cards (DM2.80), double cards (DM4.80), or in packs of 10 (DM22); 24hr. cards (DM7); weekly, monthly, and yearly passes are also available. Pick up a network **map** *(Liniennetzplan)* at the booth in front of the main train station.

Taxis: call 555 55 or 621 21. Call 444 44 for **Frauennacht-Taxi** (women's taxi).

Car Rental: Hertz, Berlinerpl. 1D (tel. 710 55), near the station. Turn left from the *Bahnhof* and you'll see the office. Open Mon.-Fri. 7am-6pm, Sat. 8am-noon.

Bike Rental: Glockman und Sohn, Ölschulägernstr. 29/30 (tel. 469 23), in the Magni quarter (DM10 per day). Open Mon.-Fri. 9am-6:30pm, Sat. 10am-2pm.

Mitfahrzentrale: ADM, Wollmarkt 3 (tel. 194 40), is the local ride-share place. Open Mon.-Fri. 10am-6pm, Sat. 10am-1pm.

Bookstores: Pressezentrum Salzman, in the Burgpassage Galerie mall, sells paperback pulp novels as well as a limited selection of English and American magazines and newspapers. Open Mon.-Fri. 9:30am-8pm, Sat. 9am-4pm.

Library: Öffentliche Bücherei, Hintern Brüdern 23 (tel. 470 68 38), right off Langestr. Main building open Mon.-Fri. 11am-7pm, but the **foreign language library** is only open Tues. noon-6pm and Fri. 11am-4pm.

Student Agency: ASTA (tel. 391 45 55), to the right of the cafeteria on Katharinenstr. This university-sponsored office finds summer housing and has information on women's and gay and lesbian activities. Open Mon.-Fri. 10am-2pm.

Pharmacy: Apotheke am Kennedy Platz, corner of Auguststr. and Kurt-Schumacher-Str., right on the JFK Platz. Open Mon.-Fri. 8:30am-6:30pm, Sat. 9am-1pm. **Emergency service** *(Notdienst)* information posted on the door.

Emergency: Police, tel. 110. **Ambulance and Fire,** tel. 112.

Post Office: The main office, 38106 Braunschweig (tel. 709 27 96), is in the 16-story building to the right of the train station. Open Mon.-Fri. 8am-6pm, Sat. 8am-1pm.

Telephone Code: 0531.

ACCOMMODATIONS

Considering its size, Braunschweig's budget accommodation cupboard is pretty bare. Little that is inexpensive can be found within walking distance; most affordable *Pensionen* and private rooms require a 10- to 15-minute bus or streetcar ride. Pick up a free copy of *Hotels und Gaststätten* at the tourist office. It includes a listing of accommodations and some cafes with prices, phone numbers, and city maps.

Jugendgästehaus (HI), Salzdahlumerstr. 170 (tel. 622 68 or 622 69; fax 636 54). Bus #11 (from the station, direction: "Mascherode"): "Klinikum," or bus #19 (direction "Lieferdestr."): "Klinikum Salzdahlumerstr." By foot, walk left from the station on Berlinerpl. to H.-Büssing-Ring, turn left on Salzdahlumerstr., under the overpass, and continue for 20min. Far from town, these antiseptic buildings contain bright, spacious rooms, a huge backyard, and kitchen facilities. Members only. Reception open 7am-10pm. DM18-36, depending on number of roomies and bathroom facilities, over 26 DM22-36. Breakfast DM7. Sheets included. Key deposit DM30.

Hotel-Pension Wienecke, Kuhstr. 14 (tel. 464 76; fax 464 64). From the station, walk up Kurt-Schumacher-Str. to JFK Platz, bear right onto Auguststr. and then Kuhstr. (15min.). Quiet, comfortable rooms with big windows, private bathrooms, and TVs. Singles DM58-95; doubles DM99-145. Breakfast included. AmEx, MC, Visa.

FOOD

A plethora of *Kneipen* (bars) and *Imbiß* kiosks along **Bohlweg,** the eastern boundary of the *Innenstadt,* proffers pizzas, salads, soups, and small sandwiches at reasonable prices. There's a produce market in the *Altstadt* every Wednesday and Saturday 8am-1:30pm. The **Kohlmarkt** area, southeast of the *Altstadt Markt* in the city center, is a bustling, open space with many pleasant (though not terribly cheap) cafes and restaurants. The **Magni Quarter's** winding streets, boutiques, and half-timbers provide a great setting for a meal or drink.

Student-Mensa, Katharinenstr. Hardly gourmet, but five selections are offered (DM1.60-3.90). Ask a student to buy you a meal ticket, technically only available to university affiliates. Open for lunch Mon.-Fri. 11:15am-2:25pm, Sat. 11:15am-1:55pm; dinner Mon.-Thurs. 4:30-8pm.

Delicato, Münzstr. 9 (tel. 40 07 16), straight down 3 blocks from Burgpl., protruding from the corner of Münzstr. and Kattreppeln. A top-notch Turkish specialty deli with colorful salads and fresh-baked lasagna. Specials like fat, warm eggplant half with spiced lamb and tomatoes, plus potato salad sells for DM7.90. Have them cater your next party in Niedersachsen. Open Mon.-Fri. 9am-8pm, Sat. 9am-4pm.

Café L'Emigré, Hinter Liebfrauen, near St. Ägidienkirche. A *papier-mâché* centaur is the centerpiece of this Turkish bistro, which features a fully stocked vegetarian menu that includes falafel and Greek salads, in addition to a large selection of kebabs. Meals DM5-15. Open Mon.-Thurs. 3-8pm, Fri.-Sun. 3pm-3am.

Vegetarisches Vollwert-Restaurant Brodocz, Stephanstr. 1 (tel. 422 36), across from the Karstadt perfume department, will help clear clogged arteries with vegetarian meals. Serves a delectable daily menu with salad, main course, and dessert (DM15), and daily specials (DM8.50). Open Mon.-Sat. 11am-11pm, Sun 3-10pm.

Cafe MM, Kuhstr. 6 (tel. 422 44), near Hotel-Pension Wienecke, offers omelettes, salads, and pastas (DM5.50-13.80). The ritzy sidewalk cafe has antipasto specials and many other tasty morsels (DM6-10.50) from noon-2pm and after 5pm. Open Mon.-Thurs. 8am-midnight, Fri.-Sat. 8am-2am, Sun. 10am-midnight.

Atlantik's Früchtchen, in the Burgpassage Galerie mall, is a fruit stand with frequent sales and unbelievably low prices. An impressive assortment of fresh fruits and veggies with a sprinkler-mist system simulating sparkling morning dew. Open Mon.-Fri. 10am-8pm, Sat. 10am-4pm.

SIGHTS

All of Braunschweig was once crowded on a small island surrounded by offshoots of the Oker River; the streams now form a moat-like line around the *Altstadt*. Braunschweig's medieval sights encircle the cobbled **Burgplatz,** over which the city's (and Heinrich's) emblem, a **bronze lion,** stands guard. First cast in 1166 as a symbol of Heinrich's regional dominance, the lion is challenged by the **St. Blaze Cathedral,** which towers over the city center. The 12th-century **Dom,** erected on the spot of another church, shows only one telltale sign of its inheritance: a wooden crucifix pendant above the Nave. The faded but motley paintings adorning the rear end of the church are remains from 13th-century murals, illustrating the lives of John the Baptist, Thomas of Cantebury, Christ, Mary, and St. Blaze. The first level looks like an elegant, eerie meeting ground for vampires. A couple of steps below in the gloomy granite **crypt** rest the sarcophagi of Heinrich the Lion and his consort Mathilde (*Dom* open daily 10am-5pm; crypt DM2). The original Braunschweiger lion has retreated to the confines of the **Dankwarderode Castle,** also on the Burgpl. Originally Heinrich's 12th-century den, it now keeps a modest trove of saints' relics. The newly renovated **Rittersaal** dazzles with its golden technicolor paintings, covering virtually every inch of the room. (Rittersaal open Tues.-Sun. 10am-11pm; museum open Tues.-Wed. and Fri.-Sun. 11am-5pm, Thurs. 10am-8pm; DM5, students DM2.50.) To reach the historic center, take streetcar #1 from the train station; or walk (15min.) along Kurt-Schumacher-Str., then bear right at JFK Platz through Ägidienmarkt onto Bohlweg. **St. Martini's Cathedral,** in the Altmarkt, was built concurrently with the St. Blaze Cathedral. Its magnificently ornamented interior includes sculptures of the Wise and Foolish Virgins, who look like they carry larger than life Martini glasses. The biblical story says that they were waiting for their grooms; the smarter bunch had enough lamp oil and the less cerebrally gifted...well, didn't, and will thus continue to practice the safest form of safe sex (open Tues.-Fri. 10am-1pm and 3-5pm, Sat. 10am-1pm, Sun. 10am-noon; free).

The **Braunschweig Landesmuseum** (tel. 484 26 02), across from the castle, also has a copy of the bronze lion; more copies can be found at the *Rathaus* in the *Altstadt*, in squares of neighboring villages, and, *ad nauseum*, at the tourist office. If the sight of the cat grows tiresome, direct your cat-eyes elsewhere—behold an entire room full of *Bieder Maier* furniture, love letters from the 1880s, little Nazi toy soldiers (including an angry man with a puny dark mustache), or a 1960s living room rimmed with avocados (open Tues.-Wed. and Fri.-Sun. 10am-5pm, Thurs. 10am-8pm; DM5, students DM2.50). The Landesmuseum also has a branch at Hinter Ägidien devoted to **Jewish culture** (tel. 484 26 25). A reconstruction of the main room of the old synagogue hauntingly complements memorials to victims of the Holocaust. The furniture is all authentic, rescued from the deteriorating synagogue (open Tues.-Wed. and Fri.-Sun. 10am-5pm, Thurs. 10am-8pm; DM5, students DM3.50). The **Herzog Anton Ulrich Museum**, Museumstr. (tel. 484 24 00; fax 484 28 08; http://www.dhm.de/museum/havm), in the eastern part of town, was the first European museum to open its doors to the general public. Its galleries are papered with Dutch masterpieces, including works by van Dyck, Vermeer, and Rubens. A special room sets aside a group of five Rembrandts, charting the artist's stylistic development over the decades (open Tues. and Fri.-Sun. 10am-5pm, Wed. 10am-8pm; DM5, students DM2.50). Down the street, the world's first motorcycle is poised at the entry to the **Städtisches Museum,** Am Löwenwall (tel. 470 45 05). It's a specialized "domestic museum;" holdings include historical originals of furniture, appliances, and things in your living room (open Tues.-Wed. and Fri.-Sun. 10am-5pm; free).

The **Neues Rathaus,** at the "Rathaus" bus stop on Bohlweg near the Burgplatz, is a textbook example of the neo-Gothic style. The 1900 edifice boasts jutting spires, golden sandstone walls, russet roof tiles—the works. Possibly the most relaxing place in Braunschweig, the **Löwenwall** is an oval-shaped park in the eastern part of the Innenstadt Island, near the Städtisches Museum. The obelisk flanked by lions between two splashing fountains is a monument to the city nobles who died in the Napoleonic Wars. The **Staatstheater,** built in 1861 to replace the Court Theater on Haymarkt where Lessing's *Emilia Galotti* and Goethe's *Faust* premiered, offers an extensive, inexpensive repertoire. Decent seats for good shows run DM15-46, but students get all tickets at half-price. Write or call (tel. 484 28 00) one month prior to the show, or get leftover seats one hour before the performance (box office open Mon.-Fri. 10am-6:30pm, Sat. 10am-1pm).

NIGHTLIFE

Braunschweig has several free monthly magazines that provide the skinny on local events: *Subway, Da Capo,* and *Extra Dry.* It's telling that these magazines sometimes direct readers to cities as far away as Hamburg. Still, the Braunschweig scene heats up to a steady simmer on the weekend. The most lively area is the square formed by the intersection of Sack, Vor der Burg, and Schuhstr., as well as the nearby Neuestr. **Movie,** Neuestr. 2 (tel. 437 26), will not serve you buttered popcorn. Lots of beer on tap, cheap bar food (2 *Wieners* DM4.50), and rock and blues constitute the "feature presentation" (open Sun.-Thurs. 10am-2am, Fri.-Sat. 10am-3am). The titanic premises of **The Jolly Joker,** Broitzemerstr. 220 (tel. 28 14 60), hold a large dance floor, six bars, a beer garden, a cheap restaurant (fast-food meals DM5), and a Brechtian movie theater that offers a bar and pop-culture flicks. Buses #5, 6, and 19: "Broitzemerstr." (Open Mon. 9:30pm-2am, Tues. and Thurs. 9:30pm-2:30am, Fri. 9:30pm-4am, Sat. 9pm-4:30am; cover DM3; movies free.) The **Pink Cadillac,** Breitestr. 23 (tel. 416 61), just off the *Altstadt Markt,* has pool tables and **Internet access** that should be working in 1998 (open Mon.-Thurs. 1pm-midnight, Fri.-Sat. 1pm-2am, Sun. 3pm-midnight). The **Magni Quarter,** around the St. Magni church, south of the Ulrich Museum, abounds with restaurants, bars, and genuine Braunschweig charm.

▓ Wolfenbüttel

Just a few kilometers from Braunschweig lies Wolfenbüttel, its pretty little sister city (bus #21 from the *Hauptbahnhof*). Most of Wolfenbüttel's meticulous Baroque-era urban planning remains intact. Though a few of the city's old half-timbers show their age, the dominant aura is one of well-kept prosperity; the good vibes swell from the **Schloßplatz,** the riverside enclave within the city that features shady lawns and a bevy of brightly colored historical attractions. If you want to feel like you really have experienced Germany, Wolfenbüttel's medieval streets, jutting red-tiled houses, and the occasional canal sure beat Epcot. Although the town attracts plenty of visitors, it retains a feeling of authenticity.

The sights of Wolfenbüttel capture the atmosphere of Candyland—the pink **Trinitatiskirche** (in the Holzmarkt), the wildly tilting half-timber houses of the inner city, and the **Kanzlei** (Royal Chancellery), on Kanzlerstr., look like the results of architects fighting over the gingerbread man. The *Kanzlei* can only be described as an absurdist mini-castle, with red walls and a bizarre metal statue perched outside defying architectural jargon (it looks like a wascally wabbit). Walking from the Schloßpl. down Löwerstr., keeping left, you will see a sign for "Kleiner Venedig." Two more absurdities lurk through the entryway: at #15 a house a mere 1.7m wide humbly rests, and a little further up on the right on Schiffwall porches hover over canal remnants.

Once a stately, pure-white vision, the ducal **Schloß** (tel. 57 13) has been repainted in crimson with white trim. Go Crimson. The cheery castle has its roots in a 13th-century fortress of the Guelphs, but its current appearance is pure Baroque with a beautifully proportioned 17th-century clock tower. A small **Schloßmuseum** displays restored rooms from the ducal living quarters (be sure to indulge in a view of the ceilings!). In good weather, the **Braunschweig Staatstheater** puts on open-air performances in the castle enclosure. There's only room for a few hundred seats, so call the Wolfenbüttel tourist office for dates and ticket reservations (museum and castle interior open Tues.-Sat. 10am-5pm, Sun. 10am-1pm; museum DM3).

Across the street from the *Schloß* is the C-shaped **Lessinghaus** (tel. 80 80), a compact mansion that was the local duke's gift to big-time *littérateur* Gotthold Ephraim Lessing, the court librarian of the nearby August-Bibliothek. The museum inside recalls Lessing's life and work through manuscripts, letters, and paintings (open Tues.-Sun. 10am-5pm). Across a tree-dotted lawn from the Lessinghaus, the stern **Herzog-August-Bibliothek** guards a priceless collection of medieval and Renaissance books. Under the loving care of bookworm Duke August (who reigned 1634-1666), the library became the largest in Europe. A series of medieval manuscripts culminates with a facsimile of the famous **Braunschweiger Evangelier,** a kaleidoscopically illuminated gospel drawn up in the late 12th century at the request of Heinrich the Lion; Lower Saxony shelled out millions of *Marks* for the manuscript in 1983. The original is locked safely away. Across from the castle is the 17th-century **Zeughaus;** the high-gabled facade belies its former role as an armory. It now serves as a library annex holding the other half of the Herzog-August collection. (Open Tues.-Sun. 10am-5pm. The two libraries and the Lessinghaus each sell admission tickets for DM6, students DM3, family DM12; a ticket from one attraction is good for the other two.)

The city's other major sight, the **Hauptkirche Beate Mariae Virgins,** throws up its spires across town in the Heinrichstadt section. An aggressive stone-gray edifice, a jutting four-faced clock tower, and full-sized statues of saints grace the church's exterior (open Tues.-Sun. 10am-noon and 2-4pm, Sat. 10am-12:30pm and 2-4pm; free, but they encourage a donation of DM1 for the pamphlet). The Wolfenbüttel **tourist office** (tel. 864 87; fax 864 42), hides around the corner from Kornmarktpl., just off Komißstr. From the station, head left on Bahnhofstr. across the Oker River, continuing to the intersection where Komißstr. bears slightly left. They lack a room-finding service, but they book rooms in hotels for no fee and lead **tours** from the Schloßpl. for DM5. (Office open Mon.-Fri. 9am-12:30pm and 2-4pm, Sat. 9am-1pm. Tours April-Sept. Sat. 2:30pm and Sun. 11am; Oct.-March Sun 11am.) Wolfenbüttel's **postal code** is 38300. The **telephone code** is 05331.

Wolfenbüttel has a first-class **Jugendgästehaus,** Jägerstr. 17 (tel. 271 89; fax 90 24 45; http://www.tigersof.de/wf-net/wolfenb/jbg/jbg.html). Take Bahnhofstr. to Schulwall and turn left; keep going until the Schloßpl. From there, walk east across the river on the long Dr.-Heinrich-Jasper-Str., and take little Glockengasse left until it stops at Jägerstr. Turn right, and look for the *Fachwerk* on the far side of the street. Everything is new; you get free access to **laundry machines** and you can rent a **bike** for DM2 per day or DM10 per week. Four-person canoes can also be rented for DM15 per day. (DM22, over 25 DM28. Breakfast included. Sheets DM2.50. Call ahead.) The **market** displays its bounty every Wednesday and Saturday with fresh fruit stands (open 8am-1pm). Krambudenstr., just off the center of the *Stadtmarkt*, has many a bistro and bakery. **Casablanca Billard Bistro,** Okerstr. 17, serves sandwiches (DM5) and soups (DM4.50) under the shade of artificial palms and a Bogey poster (open Mon.-Thurs. 10am-2am, Fri.-Sat. 10am-3am, Sun. 4pm-2am). Close by, **Kaiser's supermarket** (tel. 18 28) sells inexpensive foodstuffs. While in Wolfenbütte, don't miss the delicious coconut macaroons (DM1.20) served in the **Altstadt-Bakeries** around town.

■ Lüneburger Heide (Lüneburg Heath)

Between the Elbe and Aller rivers stretches the shrub-covered Lüneburger Heide. The symbolic power of the *Heide* is evidenced by many German literary greats: the delicate *Heideröslein* (wild rose) found a role in one of Goethe's *Lieder* while Heine charmingly compared one lady's bosom to the "flat and bleakly desolate" landscape of the *Heide*. Journeying by bicycle or horseback from one mist-shrouded town to the next in the morning is a tranquil escape from the worries of backpacking. The undulating countryside moves quickly back and forth from farm to forest; green gives way to purple from July to September, when the bushes flower. The area around the town of **Wilsede** is perhaps the most charming stretch in the entire *Heide*.

If you want to see the grassy *Heide* during the flowering season, but would prefer not to sleep on it, put down the book and make reservations now. All of Germany comes here to bike, hike, motor, and otherwise frolic in the late summer. *Tourist offices typically recommend making reservations up to six months in advance.* The most important regional towns are Lüneburg and Celle. In Lüneburg, the **Fremdenverkehrsverband Lüneburger Heide,** Barckhausenstr. 35 (tel. (04131) 737 30; fax 426 06), finds rooms in remote hamlets barely on the map, including overnight stays at barnyard bed-and-breakfasts and horse farms. Their list even tells you which animals you can expect to encounter. Biking and hiking maps as well as calendars of *Heide* events are also available (office open Mon.-Thurs. 7:30am-5pm, Fri. 7:30am-1pm). For those without a bike, rentals abound. Trains along the Hannover-Hamburg line run frequently but provide access to only a handful of towns. Most other towns are serviced by occasional buses. Check the threadbare schedules carefully.

LÜNEBURG

Perhaps because there is no salt-god, or perhaps because the name Salzburg was already taken, Lüneburg derives its name from the moon-goddess Luna. Regardless, this is a city built, literally and figuratively, on salt. The city made a 13th-century fortune with its stores of "white gold." The *Bürgers'* salt monopoly held Northern Europe in an iron grip until granny blew it all in a high stakes poker game, and the plague and the war that struck the town in the 1620s. Although "salt shocks" no longer pose a threat to the world economy, and Lüneburg's wealth and power have faded, neither the salt nor the town are obsolete. The former is channeled into the city's famed rejuvenating baths, and the latter, with its Gothic brick *Altstadt* and elegant half-timbered houses, retains its ancient grace. It was in Lüneburg that native poet Heinrich Heine penned Germany's greatest and most melancholic Romantic *Lied* (epic song), the *Lorelei*.

Orientation and Practical Information Lüneburg serves as the main transportation axis for the *Heide.* The 60,000-strong city lies between Hamburg (30min.) and Hannover (1hr.). The **tourist office** (tel. 30 95 93 or 322 00; fax 30 95 98), Am Markt in the *Rathaus,* books rooms for a DM5 fee. From the station, head downhill away from the post office, take a left onto Lünertorstr., and then turn left onto Bardowickerstr. at the end (open Mon.-Fri. 9am-6pm, Sat.-Sun. 9am-1pm; Oct.-April Mon.-Fri. 9am-1pm and 2-6pm, Sat. 9am-1pm). Daily **tours** of the *Altstadt* start at 11am from the tourist office (DM5, children DM2.50). A separate **regional tourist office** serves the entire *Heide* area (see above). Rent **cars** at **Sixt Budget,** Bardowicker Tore 21 (tel. 350 75; fax 367 95; open Mon.-Fri. 7:30am-6pm, Sat. 8am-noon). For a **bike,** try **Laden 25,** Am Weder 25 (tel. 379 60; day DM12, week DM60; DM50 deposit and ID required; open Mon.-Fri. 9am-noon and 1-5:30pm, Sat. 9am-12:30pm). The main **post office,** 21332 Lüneburg, is on the corner of Soltauerstr. and Saltztorstr. (open Mon.-Fri. 8am-6pm, Sat. 8am-noon). The **telephone code** is 04131.

Accommodations Hotels fill up rather quickly when the *Heide* blooms in July, August, and September. At **Jugendherberge Lüneburg (HI),** Soltauerstr. 133 (tel. 418 64; fax 457 47), cheap and charming go hand in hand. During the week and Saturday morning until 1pm, bus #11 (direction: "Rettmer/Hecklingen") runs from the train station to the hostel stop: "Scharnhorststr./DJH." During off hours, bus #7 from "Auf dem Klosterhof" behind the *Rathaus:* "Ginsterweg," and walk 200m further along Soltauerstr. Or, brace yourself for a long haul from the station (30min.)—turn left on Bahnhofstr., right at the bottom onto Altenbrückerstr, then left onto the very long Berlinerstr. Follow the street as it turns into Uelzenarstr., make a right at Scharnhorst-str., and continue until you meet Soltauerstr. (Reception open until 10pm. Curfew 10pm, but pocket a housekey with DM10 deposit. DM20, over 26 DM25. Breakfast included. Sheets DM5.70. Laundry available, DM5. Call ahead.) For accommodations in the *Altstadt,* **Hotel "Stadt Hamburg,"** Am Sande 25 (tel. 444 38), will put a grin on your face. Portraits of famous Lüneburgers line the stairway. (Singles DM40, with shower DM45; doubles DM80, with shower DM90. Call ahead.)

Food and Nightlife Although salt is plentiful in restaurants here, the real staple in town is another of mankind's ancient preservatives: beer. At **Kronen-Brauerei,** Heiligengeiststr. 39-41 (tel. 71 32 00), you can imbibe freshly brewed beer (from DM3.50) in a late 15th-century beer hall (open daily noon-10pm). For cheap food visit the local college **cafeteria** and the **Café Vamos.** The cafeteria, *Building 9,* serves the Pizza Diablo (*Dio Mia!* DM8.50; open Mon.-Thurs. 10am-6pm, Fri. 10am-3pm). The cafe, *Building 26,* features live music. From #9, walk away from the street and turn left.The cafe is in the building with the funky windows (open Mon.-Thurs. 10am-7pm, Fri. 10am-7pm and from 8pm, Sat. only if there's a party, Sun. 11am-3pm). **Sam-urai,** Backerstr. 8 (tel. 39 07 48) serves tasty *Gyoza,* sweet and sour pork, and vegetar-ian dishes, all for under DM7. During the week, nightlife piles up around the Lüner Bridge, while locals pack the cafes along am Stintmarkt. The patios offer cheap food and beer, and if you feel more like dancing, check out **Garage,** auf der Hude 76-80 (tel. 358 79). Frequent live acts, raves, and theme parties complement the regular dance scene. (Open Wed. and Fri.-Sat. after 10pm. Cover Wed. DM2; Fri. DM2 before 11pm, DM6 after; Sat. DM2 and DM8.)

Sights Legend has it that Lüneburg's salt stores were discovered when a wild boar fell into a pit and, clawing his way out, shook salt loose from his bristles. At the **Deut-sches Salz Museum,** Sülfmeisterstr. 1 (tel. 450 65), you can see, touch, taste, smell, mine, melt, and generally be one with salt. From the *Rathaus,* take Neue Sülze to Salzstr.; at Lambertipl., take the path behind the supermarket. The piquant museum features exhibits on salt production, ancient salt ships, salt use, and a medieval salt mill. (Open May-Sept. Mon.-Fri. 9am-5pm, Sat.-Sun. 10am-5pm; Oct.-April daily 10am-5pm. 1hr. tours Mon.-Fri. at 11am, 12:30pm, 3pm, Sat.-Sun. at 11:30am and 3pm. DM6, students DM4, children DM3.50. With the tour, tack on DM1.50 for adults, DM1 for students and children.)

The **Kloster Lüne** (cloister; tel. 523 18), on Domänehof, just over the Lünetor bridge, proudly displays its 15th-century face (open April-Oct. Mon.-Sat. 10am-12:30pm and 2:30-5pm, Sun. 11:30am-12:30pm and 2-5pm; DM5). Side streets with old, ivy-covered houses and boutiques lead to the Gothic **Michaeliskirche** (tel. 314 00), on Johann-Sebastian-Bach-Platz in the *Altstadt*. This imposing brick, wood, and ceramic church was built in 1418 on a foundation of salt; the massive pillars have warped somewhat since then (open Mon.-Sat. 10am-noon and 2-5pm). Over the gables of the streets soars the **Johanniskirche** spire, Am Sande (tel. 445 42). Late 13th-century walls protect a Gothic altar and Baroque organ (open daily 10am-5pm).

The **Brauereimuseum** (Brewery Museum), Heiligengeistr. 39-41 (tel. 410 21), was a working brewery for 500 years until its copper vats became museum pieces in 1985. The museum shows you exactly how hops, malt barley, and a few extras make the magic potion that keeps Germany going, going, and going (going daily 10am-noon and 3-5pm; free). The **Ostpreußiches Landesmuseum,** Ritterstr. 10 (tel. 418 55), celebrates the sometimes troubling history and culture of East Prussia, with everything from bear hunting equipment to the Königsberg philosopher Kant (a mausoleum?!). Lüneberg's two other offbeat museums should be taken with a grain of…never mind (open Tues.-Sun. 10am-5pm; DM3, students and children DM2).

CELLE

The powerful prince electors of Lüneberg moved to Celle in 1398 after the Lüneberger War of Succession and remained here until 1705 when the last duke croaked. During those 307 years, the royalty spent lavishly on their residence, building a massive castle and promoting the city's growth. Celle celebrates this rich cultural past with its cobblestone streets lined with half-timbered houses. In the heyday of *Fachwerk*, residents were taxed by the number of crossed diagonal beams on their houses; they quickly became coveted status symbols—until the advent of the BMW.

Some of the finest *Fachwerk* houses are tucked away on side streets; to find them wander down any of the smaller streets radiating from Schloßpl. or Großerpl. in the *Altstadt*. The **oldest house** in the area is at Am Heiligen Kreuz 26. The **Stadtkirche** stands just outside the massive pedestrian zone that dominates the *Altstadt*. The climb up the church tower rewards with a view of red- and brown-shingled roofs fading into the countryside (tower open April-Oct. Tues.-Sat. 10am-noon and 3-4pm; DM2, students and children DM1). In the *Altstadt*, the **Rathaus** is richly wrought in the *Weserrenaissance* style. Directly across the road, fine figures out of Celle's colorful history mark the hour on the **Glockenspiel** (at 10, 11am, noon, 3, 4, and 5pm).

The **Herzogschloß**, Schloßpl. 13 (tel. 123 73), just west of the *Altstadt*, flaunts foundations that date back to 1292. One of the most renowned residents of the castle was Caroline-Mathilde; she was granted asylum here in 1772 after her politically expedient marriage to the King of Denmark collapsed and her affair with the King's minister was exposed. (Caroline-Mathilde's personal rooms open Tues.-Sun. 10am-4pm. Tours of the ducal staterooms Tues.-Sun. hourly from 10am; last tour starts at 4pm; Oct.-April tours at 11am and 3pm. DM5, students and children DM2.50. Castle open Mon.-Fri. 10am-1pm, Sat.-Sun. 10am-noon; phone service Mon.-Fri. 9am-2pm and Sat.-Sun. 9am-noon). Caroline-Mathilde's weeping likeness is found in the **Französischer Garten,** south of the *Altstadt*, but it's hard to figure out why she's crying. The 1740 Baroque **synagogue,** Kriese 27, survived even the Nazi cruelties, and persists as a memorial to Celle's once thriving Jewish community (open Tues.-Thurs. 3-5pm, Fri. 9-11am, Sun. 11am-1pm; free).

The **tourist office,** Markt 6 (tel. 12 12; fax 124 59), reserves rooms for a DM2 fee, and distributes the *Jahresveranstaltungen,* a list of concerts and musical productions, as well as "The Wonderful Nine," a huge, full-color English brochure, describing Niedersachsen's historical highlights. From the train station, walk up Bahnhofstr. as it becomes Westcellertorstr., turn left onto Schloßpl., then take the second right onto Stechbahn, and finally take the second left onto Markt. Or bus #2 or 3: "Schloßpl." and follow the signs (open May to mid-Oct. Mon.-Fri. 9am-6pm, Sat. 9am-1pm and 2-5pm; mid.-Oct. to April Mon.-Fri. 9am-5pm, Sat. 10am-noon). City **tours** start from the bridge in front of the *Schloß* (April-Oct. Mon., Wed., and Sat. 2:30pm, Sun. 11am; DM3). Celle, a self-proclaimed "Romantic Half-Timbered City," is 40km northeast of Hannover, 35 minutes by frequent **trains** (DM11.20). **Rent cars** from **Auto-Hansa,** Braunschweiger-Heerstr. 43 (tel. 290 44). Or rent a **bike** from **2-Rad-Meier GmbH,** Neustadt 42a (tel. 413 69; fax 48 10 18). Follow Neustadt behind the train station for 10 minutes (DM15 per day, ID required; open Mon.-Fri. 8am-1pm and 2:30-6pm, Sat. 8am-1pm). The **post office,** 03100 Celle, is on Schloßpl. (open Mon.-Fri. 8am-6pm, Sat. 8am-1pm). The **telephone code** is 05141.

The *Herbergeltern* at the **Jugendherberge (HI),** Weghausstr. (tel. 532 08; fax 530 05), may have an obsession with plants, but you can use this to your advantage. To hide from the roving mob of ferocious schoolchildren, wear jungle camouflage clothing and stand amidst the greenery. From the train station, bus #3 (direction: "Boye"): "Jugendherberge." Turn left out of the station, walk up the pedestrian/bike path as it becomes Biermannstr., turn left on Bremer Weg, and turn up the first right onto Petersburgstr. (Reception open until 10pm, but best time for check-in is 5-7pm. Curfew 10pm; housekeys available with a DM50 deposit. DM20, over 26 DM24.50. Breakfast included. Sheets DM5.70.) At **Pension Luhmanns Hof,** Dorfstr. 8 (tel. 530 94), a little chocolate on each bed adds the touch of elegance. From Petersburgstr., it's the first building on the right after you pass Weghausstr. (Reception open until 9pm, reservations recommended. Singles DM70; doubles DM110. Breakfast included.) **Hotel Blühende Schiffahrt,** Fritzenwiese 39 (tel. 227 61), is considerably closer to the *Altstadt* (DM65 per person. Breakfast included. Call ahead). **Campingplatz Silbersee** (tel. 312 23) lies 7km northeast of the town proper; bus #6 (direction: "Vorwerk"): "Silbersee" (DM5.50 per person. Showers included).

Café Fricke, Neuestr. 14 (tel. 21 49 18), at the intersection with Brandpl., sets a merry table with artsy decorations, where you can enjoy crepes from DM5 (open daily 10:30am-6pm). The Disenfranchised Youth, Celle Chapter, breaks bread at the chic **Alex's Antik Cafe,** Schuhstr. 6 (tel. 21 75 40), and it's easy to see why—cheap, simple food (soup and sandwich combo DM10), a spectrum of alcohol (this time it will go down…) and coffee drinks, and smoky surroundings. Even Bohemians need food (open Mon.-Sat. 9am-2am, Sun. 9am-9:30pm). During Celle's **market** (Wed. and Sat. 7am-1pm) the *Altstadt* fills with people carrying cloth-lined baskets in search of bargains on meats, fruits, vegetables, socks, and flowers.

BERGEN-BELSEN

Near the town of Bergen, 20km north of Celle, lies the site of the **Bergen-Belsen concentration camp.** Fear of a typhus epidemic led British military authorities to raze the camp buildings in May 1945, but memories of what they had witnessed inspired the construction of a monument in November the same year. The German government agreed to care for and expand it in 1952. A somber stone obelisk commemorates the 30,000 Jewish victims. Mass graves flank the memorial erected in memory of the 50,000 Soviet prisoners of war who perished here. Bergen-Belsen claimed more than 100,000 lives. Most inmates of the concentration camp were Western political insurgents and Western European Jews. The document room details the camp's history; the photographs taken by liberating British troops are powerful, moving reminders of what must not be forgotten. One of the camp's victims was young **Anne Frank,** immortalized by her diary, describing her terrifying experiences as a Jew in hiding. She wrote, "in spite of everything I still believe that people are really good at heart." The camp is difficult to reach, and the regional authorities do not publicize it well. The **Bergen-Belsen Memorial** (tel. (05051) 60 11) is open daily 9am to 6pm, but you must take two buses to get there from the station. Bus #2: "Bergen Cellerstr." (daily 11:55am and 2:55pm), then #9: "Belsen-Gedenkstätte." Schedules change regularly and buses run infrequently; for schedule information contact **Kraftverkehr Celle** at (05141) 88 11 80. By car take the B3 toward Hamburg to Hinweisschild (about 20km from Celle), then turn left and continue straight to Bergen-Belsen by following the *Gedenkstätte* (memorial) signs.

■ Bremen

Happy is the man who has reached the harbor and left the sea and storm
behind and now sits warm and peaceful in the good Ratskeller of Bremen.
—Heinrich Heine, "Im Hafen"

Much like Hamburg, its Hanseatic sister city to the North, Bremen has given over its once famed medieval ambience to a thriving cosmopolitan society in which internationalism and mass consumerism displace *"echtes"* German culture. The donkey, dog, cat, and rooster of the Brothers Grimm's fairy tale *Die Bremer Stadtmusikanten* (The Musicians of Bremen) were en route to Bremen when they terrified a band of robbers with their singing. The transients singing for attention at the city's train station still put a charge in the atmosphere. Closer to the *Altstadt,* more talented artists ply their crafts, creating beautiful murals with charcoal and spray paint as musicians provide accompaniment on a mind-boggling array of instruments.

The most enduring *bremisch* trait is a strong desire for independence: despite continuing struggles, Bremen and its daughter city Bremerhaven remain their own tiny, autonomous *Land* in the middle of Lower Saxony. This activism creates a strongly liberal political climate which erupted into violent battles between police and demonstrators in 1980. People here flaunt high-flying, don't-tread-on-me attitudes—Bremen is one of the few places in Germany where jaywalkers will feel more at home.

ORIENTATION AND PRACTICAL INFORMATION

Bremen lies south of the portal of the Weser River at the North Sea, a little over an hour from both Hamburg and Hannover by frequent trains. The city is perfect for meandering, but beware of the blocks surrounding Ostertorsteinweg and Am Dobben; as you move out of the *Altstadt,* bong shops replace bakeries for several blocks, and sirens drown out singers on the streets.

A **Tourist Card Bremen,** available at the tourist office, provides free travel on city transportation, 20% discounts to theater shows and city tours, and 50% off the cost of admission at many of Bremen's museums. (2-day card for 1 adult and 1 child DM19.50, 3-day card DM26; 2-day group card for up to 5 folks DM35, 3-day DM46.)

Tourist Office: The souvenir-jammed central office (tel. 308 00 51; fax 308 00 30), across from the *Hauptbahnhof,* books rooms for DM3 plus a DM10-20 deposit. It also offers guides to museum exhibits and theater schedules, and sells tickets for concerts and festivals. Open Mon.-Wed. 9:30am-6:30pm, Thurs.-Fri. 9:30am-8pm, Sat.-Sun. 9:30am-4pm.

Consulate: U.K. Herrlichkeit 6 (tel. 590 90). Open Mon.-Thurs. 8:30am-12:30pm and 2:30-3:30pm, Fri. 8:30am-12:30pm.

Currency Exchange: DVB, in the train station, exchanges currency and cashes traveler's checks for a 1% commission, minimum DM10. Open Mon.-Fri. 7:30am-7pm, Sat. 8am-4pm.

American Express: Am Wall 138, 28195 Bremen (tel. 17 46 00). Get off at Schüssel Korb and walk away from the Deutsche Bank. Follow the curve to the right and then go left onto Am Wall; it's 30m to the left. Open Mon.-Fri. 9am-5:30pm, Sat. 9am-noon.

Flights: Bremen's international airport (tel. 559 51) is only 3.5km from the city center; take S-Bahn #5 (20min.) or drive south on Oldenburger Str. and follow the signs (15min.). Frequent flights to major German cities, the East Frisian Islands, and other countries.

Public Transportation: An integrated system of streetcars and buses covers city and suburbs. Information and the hub of the main connections in front of the train station. The best deal by far is the **Bremer Kärtchen** (Little Bremen Card), with unlimited rides for 2 adults for 1 calendar day (*not* 24hr. from time of purchase), DM8. Single rides DM3.20, children under 16 DM1.60. Four-ride ticket DM9.60.

Ferries: Ferries from **Schreiber Reederei** (tel. 32 12 29; fax 32 61 36) shuttle to the suburbs and towns along the Weser, ending up at Bremerhaven. (May 16-Sept. 14

Bremen

Hauptbahnhof, 1
Kunsthalle, 6
Post Office, 3
Rathaus, 4
St. Petri Dom, 5
Tourist
Information, 2

NIEDERSACHSEN

Wed.-Thurs. and Sat. at 8:30am. One way to Bremerhaven DM21, round-trip DM34.) More info is available at the tourist office. From Bremerhaven, ferries are available to scenic Helgoland.

Car Rental: Avis, Kirchbachstr. 200 (tel. 21 10 77). Open Mon.-Fri. 7am-6pm, Sat. 8am-1pm.

Bike Rental: Leave a DM50 security deposit and a photo ID, and pedal away from the **Fahrrad Station** (tel. 30 21 14), a bright red stand with bright bikes, on your left as you exit the station. DM15 per day, children DM9; DM60 per week, children DM45. Biker's city map DM9.80. Open June-Sept. Mon. and Wed.-Fri. 10am-5pm, Sat.-Sun. 10am-noon and 5-5:30pm; March-May and Oct.-Dec. Mon.-Fri. 10am-5pm.

Bookstores: Storm, Langestr. 10 (tel. 32 15 23). Impressive selection of English books, dictionaries, and travel guides. Open Mon.-Fri. 9am-7pm, Sat. 10am-3pm. **Frauenbuchladen Hagazussa,** Friesenstr. 12 (tel. 741 40), stocks over 3000 titles of particular interest to women. Only women admitted. Open Mon. 10am-2pm, Tues.-Fri. 10am-6pm, Sat. 10am-2pm.

Gay Information Line: (tel. 70 41 70), provides information about gay events and services. Open Mon.-Wed. and Fri. 10am-1pm, Thurs. 4-5pm.

Women's Center: The offices at Am Hulsberg 11 (Streetcar: "Am Hulsberg"). Info pertinent to travelers is available in the lobby. **Frauen Taxi** runs a women's taxi service daily 7pm-6am. Call 144 33.

Laundromat: Wasch Center, Vor dem Steintor, 30m in the direction opposite the *Hauptbahnhof.* Streetcar #2, 3, or 10: "Brunnenstr." DM6 for wash, soap, and spin dry; another DM1 to dry in a standard machine. Open daily 6am-11pm.

Pharmacy: Päs Apotheke, Bahnhofpl. 5-7 (tel. 144 15). Pick up a map of the city's pharmacies with their rotating schedule of late and emergency openings. Open Mon.-Fri. 8am-6:30pm, Sat. 8am-2pm.

Emergency: Police: tel. 110. **Fire:** tel. 112.

Post Office: Main office at Domsheide 15, 28195 Bremen (tel. 367 33 66), near the Markt. Open Mon.-Fri. 8am-6pm, Sat. 9am-1pm. Another office is on Bahnhofpl. 21, by the train station. Open Mon.-Fri. 8am-8pm, Sat. 8am-2pm, Sun. 9am-2pm.

Telephone Code: 0421.

ACCOMMODATIONS AND CAMPING

The key phrase is "call ahead." Inexpensive hotels exist, but they fill fast. The tourist office's *Hotel-Liste* (free) lists a few rooms in the DM20-40 range, but prices quickly rocket into the DM100 range. New bus connections have made direct links with the somewhat distant campsite possible.

Jugendgästehaus Bremen (HI), Kalkstr. 6 (tel. 17 13 69; fax 17 11 02). Bus #26 or streetcar #6: "Am Brill," then walk along Bürgermeister-Smidt-Str. to the river, turn right, and walk 2 blocks. To walk from the train station, take Bahnhofstr. to Herdentorsteinweg, go right at Am Wall, then turn left on to Bürgermeister-Smidt-Str. and right along the water to the 162-bed hostel. The linen is clean, the ping-pong is fun, and the glowing Beck's brewery sign across the Weser lulls you to sleep with visions of malt dancing in your head. Reception open 24hr. Check-out 10am. No curfew. DM27, over 26 DM32. Breakfast and sheets included.

Jugendherberge Bremen-Blumenthal (HI), Bürgermeister-Dehnkamp-Str. 22 (tel. 60 10 05), in Blumenthal. Bus #10 from the *Hauptbahnhof* (direction "Gropelingen") to the end of the line, then change for the #70 or 71 (direction "Farge/Neuenkirchen" or "Blumenthal"): "Kreinsloger" (45-50min.). Bürgermeister-Dehnkamp-Str. is down the stone steps through the trees. An oasis on the busy wharf, the hostel's small park overlooks the river. Call ahead to make sure it isn't filled with schoolchildren. Reception open 7am-10pm. Check-out 9am. Curfew 10pm. DM20, over 26 DM22.50. Sheets DM5. Breakfast included.

Hotel Enzensperger, Brautstr. 9 (tel. 50 32 24). Bus #24: "Am Neuenmark," then right on Brautstr. Or, from the *Markt*, cross the Wilhelm-Keisen Bridge over the Weser, turn right on Osterstr., and right on Brautstr. Lots of space and lots of plaid. Singles DM48, with shower DM49; doubles DM70, with shower DM92. Breakfast included. Call a few days ahead.

Hotel-Pension Garni Weidmann, Am Schwarzen Meer 35 (tel. 498 44 55). If Elizabeth Taylor were as young as she tries to look, she would have no qualms about living in this *Pension*. The plush comforters and feet-tickling bathroom rugs are just her style. Such pampering at bargain prices (singles from DM40; doubles from DM80) is in demand. Two-week advance reservations are recommended.

Hotel Weltevreden, Am Dobben 62 (tel. 78 015; fax 70 40 91), just off Ostertorsteinweg. Comfortable rooms, good prices, close to Bremen nightlife. Reception open Mon.-Sat. 7am-10pm, Sun. 7:30am-1pm and 5-10pm. Singles DM60; doubles DM100, with shower DM120. Breakfast included. Call a few days ahead.

Camping: Am Stadtwaldsee I (tel. 21 20 02). Bus #26: "Hemmstr.," then #28 to the door. DM7.50 per person, DM4.50 per child; two-person tent DM5, bigger tent DM9.50. Washers and dryers DM4 each. Free showers and electrical hookup. Open from one week before Easter until Nov. 1.

FOOD

In the *Rathaus*, visit Bremen's renowned **Ratskeller** (tel. 32 16 76). Dating back to 1405, it's one of the oldest wine bars in Germany. Settle in a cozy leather-and-wood booth or among huge barrels to enjoy one of 600 German wines; most are reasonably priced (from DM4.60 per 0.2L glass), but the elegant beef and fish meals run around DM40 (open daily 11am-midnight, kitchen open noon-2:30pm and 6-11pm). A cheaper way to eat well is in the open-air **market** daily from 8am to 2pm. The restaurants that pack the **Schnoorviertel** are silly, charming, and exceedingly pricey, so shop around. Bronze pigs herd pedestrians into shops and take-out cafes on **Sögerstraße,** where they sell everything from chocolate truffles to *FischBrötchen*. Student pubs proliferate farther east, on and around **Ostertorsteinweg** (see Nightlife, p. 302).

Henry J. Beans, Pieperstr. 16 (tel. 169 26 74). An American bar and grill with that delightful if unrefined taste of the States. Entrees are reasonable (DM12 and up), but the main draw is the all-you-can-eat Sunday brunch (11am-3pm, DM15.80), something generally unheard of in a land of artery-damning, hearty eaters. Open daily 11am-1am.

Ada, Ostertorsteinweg 99 (tel. 783 57). "Ardor" is this joint's subtitle. Try a *tzatziki* pizza (DM4) and chase it down with a Turkish mocha (DM3). Always open.

Café Torno, Am Dobben 71 (tel. 70 06 11). Relax nerves to Western showdown music. Their hefty gyros (DM6-10) will scare hunger from your stomach. Pasta dinners DM9-12. Open Mon.-Thurs. noon-2am, Fri.-Sat. noon-4am, Sun. noon-1am.

Café Harlekin Bookshop, Lahnstr. 65b (tel. 50 19 11). Bus #5: "Theater am Leibnizpl." Walk in the direction away from the *Hauptbahnhof,* past the centaur; take the second right and cross the street. Bremen's best breakfast selection (served all day) is flanked by an alternative bookstore. The generous *Türkisches Frühstück* ("Turkish Breakfast"; *Fladenbrot,* feta, olives, and cucumbers for DM7.50) makes an invigorating lunch. Cafe open daily 10am-6:30pm.

Engel, Ostertorsteinweg 31/33 (tel. 766 15). Simple, elegant dining, and prime people-watching facilities provided by the terrace's *Ostertor* location. Lunch specials (DM10.50) even include dessert. Other artful entrees cost DM10-15. Concerts on the terrace on summer weekends. Open Sun.-Thurs. 7am-2am, Fri.-Sat. 7am-3am.

Schnaare Schnoor Bäckerei, Landherrnamt 7 (tel. 337 93 02). Was JFK a Berliner? No. Taste the real *Berliner* (a yummy donut, DM1.60), or indulge yourself with a drop-dead gorgeous *Sahne Desserttörtchen* (creamy dessert tarts, DM2.50). A good deal since 1890. Open Mon.-Fri. 7am-6:30pm, Sat. 7am-2pm.

SIGHTS

The best way to see Bremen is to casually meander on the many historic streets. The *Altstadt* revolves around the **Rathaus,** its 15th-century base decorated by a startlingly ornate Renaissance facade. It survived World War II only because the English pilot who bombed the area deliberately missed this target. (Tours occasionally available Mon.-Fri. at 10, 11am, and noon; Sat.-Sun. at 11am and noon. Ask at the tourist office for more details.) Just left of the town hall is the 1951 sculpture by Gerhard Marcks, *Die Musikanten,* which shows the Grimms' donkey, dog, cat, and rooster in their model-mugging, robber-foiling stance. Also a war survivor, the **St. Petri Dom,** Sandstr. 10-12 (tel. 36 50 40), next to the *Rathaus,* has a mosaic interior of orange, gold, and gray stone arches. The foundation dates to 798, when Charlemagne had the first stone placed there. If gilded chandeliers and artwork are too overwhelming, descend into the subterranean crypts at the front and rear of the church. (Cathedral open Mon.-Fri. 10am-5pm, Sat. 10am-1:45pm, Sun. 2-5pm. Free. Tower, all 265 steps, open May-Oct. Mon.-Fri. 10-11:20am and 12:20-4:20pm, Sat. 10am-noon, Sun. 2-5pm. DM1.) In a corner of the cathedral is the **Dom Museum** (tel. 365 04 75), housed in part of the original foundation with frescoes dating back 500 years (open May-Oct. Mon.-Fri. 10am-5pm, Sat. 10am-noon, Sun. 2-5pm; Nov.-April Mon.-Fri. 1-4:30pm, Sat. 10am-noon, Sun. 2-5pm; DM3, students and children DM2). Your ticket from the museum is good for DM1 discount on the ticket for the **Bleikeller,** in the basement of the **Dom.** The mummified corpses of workers who fell from the roof of the cathedral were discovered here in 1695 and have been on exhibit for three centuries. (Open May-Oct. Mon.-Fri. 10am-5pm, Sat. 10am-2pm, Sun. 2-5pm; Nov.-April daily 1-5pm; DM2, children DM1; admission ticket likewise good for DM1 discount at museum above.) A symbol of Hanseatic freedom and an emblem of Bremen's liberal tradition, the Bremer Roland gazes across the Marktplatz.

Just past the *Domshof,* turn left on Domsheide for the medieval **Schnoorviertel,** a district of red-roofed gingerbread houses, dainty shops, and dog salons. Between the Marktplatz and the Weser lies the narrow red brick and cobblestone **Böttcherstr.** Once a crowded artisanal quarter, the street offers a winding labyrinth of gilded archways, stained-glass windows, boutiques, and craft shops. It's worth standing with all the tourists at noon, 3, or 6pm for the magic of the Böttcherstr. **Glockenspiel.** Bells ring and part of the building swings open to deliver a performance by mechanical figures, re-enacting wild sea and air exploits from the building's early memory. Come early—the prime gawking spots fill up fast. Modern offices are now housed in some of the city's beautiful Renaissance structures; look for the **Gerichtsgebäude** (municipal court), Domsheide 16. The smell of brewing beer lures the helpless lush across the Weser to the **Beck's Brewery** (tel. 50 94 55 55). The mysterious has lifted its veil of mystery, offering tours to a thirsty public (DM5, children under 12 free). Unlike its exported counterparts, *bremisch* Beck's offers the famous full bouquet expected in a German beer.

MUSEUMS

Neues Museum Weserburg Bremen, Teerhof 20 (tel. 59 83 90), across the Wilhelm Kaiser Bridge, then right on Herrlichkeit on the small island that splits the Weser River. The initiated savor the irony of works by Assig, Darboven, and Warhol as they expose the hollowness of modernity. The novices wonder why the heck the paintings aren't finished. Bring a black turtleneck. Open Tues.-Fri. 10am-6pm, Sat.-Sun. 11am-6pm. DM6, students and children DM3.

Übersee Museum, Bahnhofplatz 13 (tel. 361 91 76), next to the train station. With the motto "the world under one roof," this collection brings a fifth-grade social studies textbook to life. Exhibits ranging from a Shinto garden to a South Seas fishing village attempt to show the wonders of the world outside Germany's borders. Open Tues.-Sun. 10am-6pm. DM4, students and children DM2.

Gerhard Marcks Haus, Am Wall 208 (tel. 32 72 00), next to the Kunsthalle. An indoor and outdoor sculpture garden of works by the sculptor of *Die Musikanten*. Seven display rooms and an outdoor area house changing exhibitions of modern sculpture and graphic art. Open Tues.-Wed. and Fri.-Sun. 10am-6pm, Thurs. 10am-5pm. DM4, students and children DM2.

Rundfunkmuseum, Findorffstr. 85 (tel. 35 74 06 or 35 37 97). A large-scale center depicts the progress of telecommunications with exhibits that light up and whirl when touched. Open Mon.-Tues. and Thurs.-Fri. 9:30am-5pm. DM2, children DM1.

Böttscherstrasse Art Collections, Paula-Becker-Modersohn Haus and Roselius Haus (tel. 336 50 77). Located at the corner of Böttscherstr. and Martinistr., these two collections represent the work of local sculptor Bernhard Hoetger and seven centuries of arts and crafts linked to Bremen. No mats or juice. Open Tues. 11am-9pm, Wed.-Sun. 11am-6pm. DM10, students and children DM7.

ENTERTAINMENT AND NIGHTLIFE

You want singing barnyard animals? Bremen delivers. Plus there's opera in the **Theater am Goetheplatz,** Am Goethepl. 1-3 (tel. 365 33 33), new drama in the **Schauspielhaus,** Ostertorsteinweg 57a (tel. 365 33 33), and the **Bremer Shakespeare Company,** Theater am Leipnizplatz (tel. 50 03 33). The **Theater im Schoor,** Wüste Stätte 11 (tel. 32 60 54), does cabarets and revues, from postmodern Shakespeare (is nothing sacred?) to parodies of the *Wehrmacht*. Summertime brings performances to parks around the city. Discount tickets are usually held for students. Check the tourist office, the theaters, or *Bremer Umschau* (DM3) for schedules and prices, as well as information on free performances. *Belladonna* lists cultural events of special interest to women. Two free publications available at the tourist office, *Mix* and *Bremer Lokal,* provide great leads on what's shakin' in Bremen.

During the last two weeks of October, Bremen drinks beer and eats lard cakes in honor of its trading heritage and freedom as a *Land* with the colorful **Freimarkt** fair, an annual event since 1095. And Bremen rocks—big concerts are often held in the **Weserstadion** (tel. 43 45 00) behind the train station. Tickets and information for small- and large-scale events are available at the tourist office. Many clubs host live music nights that feature American bands making their European debut. **Modernes Complex,** Neustadtswall 28 (tel 50 55 53), hosts cinema, theater, concerts, and dancing (times and cover charges vary).

Bremen offers a well developed and raucous pub culture. The long and densely populated **Ostertorsteinweg** is the place to find the true pulse of the nightlife. Bremen also possesses a lively gay and lesbian nightlife scattered throughout the city.

Litfass, Ostertorsteinweg 22 (tel. 70 32 92). An all-day, all-night bastion of alternative chic which poses as a bar. As the eyes of the supermodel on the wall cast flirting glances, coolly take down one of their piping hot coffees. The extensive outdoor terrace and open facade make it the place to see and be seen. Open Sun.-Thurs. 10am-2am, Fri.-Sat. 10am-4am.

Moments Bar, vor dem Steintor 65 (tel. 780 07). An intimate jazz bar which, like the Energizer Bunny, just keeps going and going.... The music invariably improves during happy hours (10-11pm) with half-price drinks. Open daily 10pm-whenever.

Café Engel, Ostertorsteinweg 31/33 (tel. 766 15). A hip indoor/outdoor bar and restaurant whose patrons lack nothing in style, sophistication, or libations. Open Sun.-Thurs. 11am-1am, Fri.-Sat. 11am-4am.

Aladin, Hannoverschestr. 11 (tel. 41 23 04). Bar that hosts live music and popular disco events. Open Wed. 9pm-2am, Fri.-Sat. 9pm-7am, sporadically for other performances. Cover DM7.

Confession, Humboldtstr. 156 (tel. 738 22). A swinging, swank gay and lesbian club featuring live blues, jazz, and alternative bands. Open Sun.-Thurs. 7pm-2am, Fri-Sat. 9pm-late. Sat. women-only.

TheaLit, Im Krummen Arm 1 (tel. 70 16 32). Evening club and center for women's and lesbian events. Also contains a bar. Women only. Information office open Tues. 10am-noon, Wed.-Fri. 4-6pm. Bar opens Mon.-Fri. and Sun. at 5pm, and closes when everybody goes home.

■ Bremerhaven

ARRR, matey! Founded in 1827 as a port for land-locked Bremen, Bremerhaven is a younger and saltier version of its bigger sister city. The harbor, once the city's commercial *raison d'être,* serves as a tourist hub. The city itself has added a modern architectural veneer to its maritime foundations. Ferries sail daily for Helgoland, Germany's own Fantasy Island, at 9:45am (see **Helgoland,** p. 305). The harbor also houses the **Deutsches Schiffahrts-Museum** (German Maritime Museum; tel. 48 20 78), which pays tribute to boats, boats, and more boats, with models and relics inside the building and real full-scale *Museumschiffe* (museum ships) outside. (Open Tues.-Sun. 10am-6pm. Ships open April-Sept. Tues.-Sun. 10am-6pm. Admission DM5, students, seniors, children, and soldiers DM2.50.) Docked nearby, but with separate admission, is the **U-Boot Wilhelm Bauer,** the only German submarine (U-Boat) from World War II that was neither sunk nor scrapped (open April-Oct. daily 10am-6pm; admission DM3, under 18 DM2). At the **Zoo am Meer,** further up the harbor, German schoolchildren hoot and dash about frantically, while animals on the other side of the bars (polar bears, sea lions, monkeys) sit calmly and watch (open May-Aug. daily 8am-7pm; April and Sept. 8am-6:30pm; Oct.-March 8am-5pm; DM4, students and children DM2; free tours available with prior reservation). Should you lose your way, info centers abound which can help you to navigate the city's maritime and technical museums. Each year the city celebrates numerous festivals. In 1997, the Bremerhaven **Fest Woche** (Festival Week) will be held July 19-August 2.

The **tourist office,** in the Columbus Center, finds rooms gratis (tel. 430 00; open Mon.-Wed. 9:30am-6pm, Thurs.-Fri. 9:30am-8pm, Sat. 9:30am-4pm). Bus # 2, 5, 9, or 12: "Große Kirche," then take the escalators to the second floor. The office is in the back on the left side. The **Verkehrsamt,** Van-Ronzelenstr. 2 (tel. 94 64 60; fax 460 65), does the same with different hours (open Mon.-Fri. 8am-4pm). Bremerhaven is 30 minutes from Bremen by **train; a ferry** leaves Bremen each morning at 8:30am (see Bremen, p. 298). To **rent a bike,** visit the **BBU** (tel. 860 23), in a train car at the entrance to the harbor, near the zoo (DM10 per day, DM42 per week; children DM6 per day, DM30 per week; open April-Sept. Tues.-Sun. 10am-6pm). The **post office,** 27570 Bremerhaven, directly to the left as you leave the *Hauptbahnhof,* offers a currency exchange and cashes traveler's checks for a DM6 fee and provides the regular services (open Mon.-Fri. 8am-6pm, Sat. 8am-1pm). The **telephone code** is 0471.

Bremerhaven's combination **Jugendgästehaus/Jugendherberge (HI),** at Gaußstr. 54-56 (tel. 856 52; fax 874 26), bus #2 or 9: "Gesundheitsamt," offers a dazzling array of conveniences. As your clothes whirl in the washer and dryer (DM2.50 each), you can borrow one of the management's TVs or clock-radios for free. For a few *Marks* extra, work out in the mini-gym followed by a trip to the sun lamp and a Volkswagen-sized spa (for *Jungendgästehaus* guests only). Incidentally, the hostel also offers beds to sleep in. (Reception open 7am-6am. *Jugendherberge* DM28, over 26 DM31.50. *Jugendgästehaus* DM29.90. Breakfast and sheets included.)

■ Cuxhaven

Just like the old rock song by Boston, the brochures for nearby Cuxhaven boast that the town is "more than a feeling." Actually, it's a play on words: in German, that would be *"mehr als ein Gefühl,"* but salty Cuxhaven emphasizes *"Meer* (the German word for 'sea') *als ein Gefühl."* Clever. Unfortunately, both the band and the island have wealthy groupies who make the procurement of a cheap seat or accommodation deal rather difficult. Still, Cuxhaven offers the sinking ground of the **Watt**, Northern Germany's unusual sand-marsh landscape. When the tide is out, *Wattwanderers* have the unique opportunity to walk across the semi-permanent landbridge to **Neuwerk Island**. Guides start at DM3, and can be contacted through the tourist office or found on the beach—they are highly recommended (crossing alone is *dangerous*). For those too unmotivated to make the 11km trek by foot, the horse-drawn **Wattwagen** cart accesses all that wet sand (DM25, ages 10 and under DM12.50). If you find yourself hindered by several tons of water during high tide, the **MS Flipper** makes several daily trips to the island (DM20, round-trip DM28; ages 4-17 DM21, round-trip DM15). Once on the island, it's possible to tour with a guide (DM3, children DM2). For more info on transportation and schedules, contact the tourist office.

Pick up your schedule of high and low tide times at the **tourist office** (tel. 360 46; fax 525 64), at Lichtenbergplatz (bus #1, 4, or 21, direction "Duhnen"; open July-Aug. Mon.-Fri. 9am-5pm, Sat. 9am-1pm and 2-4pm; Sept.-June Mon.-Fri. 10am-5pm). Trains run frequently from Cuxhaven to Bremerhaven (50min.). Ferries run to Helgoland daily at 10:30am (see p. 305). For intra-Cuxhaven cruising, try renting a **bike** from **Zweirad-Paulsen**, Schillerstr. 47 (tel. 362 66), for DM9 per day with ID (open Mon.-Fri. 10am-5pm). Bus #1, 5, or 21: "Kasernenstr." Walk away from Kasernenstr. on Marienstr., then veer right onto Schillerplatz, left on Schillerstr. The **post office** lies at Rohdestr., 27472 Cuxhaven; traveler's checks cashed. The **telephone code** is 04721.

Cuxhaven's **Jugendherberge (HI)** (tel. 485 52; fax 457 94) is 1½ blocks from the deep, blue sea. From the station take bus #1, 2, or 4 (direction "Döse-Duhnen"): "Seelust," and backtrack to the *Jugendherberge* sign (reception open 12:30-1pm and after 7pm). The rooms are clean and cheery. Save your room receipt to get onto the beach for free; otherwise you'll pay DM5. Wash your laundry (DM5 with soap) and hang it to dry. (Curfew 11:30pm. DM16, over 26 DM23.70. Sheets DM6. Breakfast DM6. Partial wheelchair access. Call one week ahead.) **Camping** is available just down the street at **Nordsee Campingplatz**, Cuxhavenstr. 17 (tel. 489 51; DM7.50 per tent, DM6 per person). While Cuxhaven offers little for the frugal palate, **Hansagrill**, 14a Nordersteinstr. (tel. 252 70) offers grilled and fishy food (not to be confused with fish food) for DM9-13 (open daily 10am-10pm).

■ Lauenburg

Eight-hundred-year-old Lauenburg an der Elbe was one of the minor lights of the Hanseatic League. It still shines quietly, with picturebook ferry docks, half-timbered houses painted with posies, and winding cobblestone streets. Easy transport to Lauenburg is one of many remnants of the town's past; the town earned its bread as a stop on the great medieval canals connecting the mines of Lüneburger Heide to the perversely salt-starved towns of the Baltic coast. Lauenburg is still on the train route from Lüneburg to Lübeck, with connections to Hamburg and Berlin at either end (2 per hr.). The duck-decked **Elbe** River, gently flowing through Lauenburg, once formed the border between East and West Germany.

The Lauenburg *Altstadt* consists of two halves—the **Unterstadt** (lower city) down by the river, and the **Oberstadt** up above, joined by pathways of narrow steps. The apartment complexes of modern Lauenberg loom above. Most of the sites are located in the *Unterstadt*, an uninterrupted half-timbered strip built over a stone embankment (the *Sperrmauer*). The **Uferpromenade** runs along the river's edge, ideal for walking or biking. Lauenberg's houses, many of which date back to the 16th century, are distinctive for their elaborately painted wood-and-brick framework. The **Mensingschehaus,** Elbstr. 49, off the Kirchpl., is one of very few survivors of a catastrophic 1616 fire that charred the Duke, his young wife, and most of the posher houses in town. The former **Rathaus,** Elbstr. 59, stands tall, and now houses the **Elbschiffahrts museum,** which documents the town's shipping industry (open March-Oct. daily 10am-1pm and 2-5pm; Nov.-Feb. Wed.-Sun. 10am-1pm and 2-5pm). The house at Elbstr. 97, only about 6 ft. wide, is one of the smallest in Germany; if you've ever wondered about what a house would look like in a fun-house mirror, look no further. Up the cobblestone hills of the *Altstadt*, the **Maria-Magdalena Kirche,** Kirchpl. 1, stands tall and solid over the city; the church tower was a signal to returning sailors that they were home at long last. The 13th-century building was commandeered by the French for a celebration in May 1804 on the day Napoleon crowned himself Emperor (open Thurs.-Tues. 9am-5pm; services Sat. 5pm, Sun. 10am). Just beyond the church at the Amtspl. is the **Schloßturm,** built between 1457 and 1477. After the town burned down in 1616, the tower served as a state-of-the-art vantage point from which vigilant watchdogs observed the town burning down six more times. Recognizing the observation post's uselessness, the town has closed the tower. Nothing remains from the **Schloß** except one wing, now used to house government offices.

The **tourist office** (tel. 59 09 81) sits across from the *Schloßturm* on Amtspl. The fastest way there from the train station is across the bridge, then left down Hafenstr., which turns into Bahnhofstr. and then Elbstr. Then turn right up the *Fahrtreppe* (stair-street), and finally left onto the Amtspl. (open Mon.-Fri. 8:30am-12:30pm and 1:30-6pm). The **Jugendherberge Lauenburg (HI),** Am Sportpl. 7 (tel. 25 98), is a pleasant hike—if a long one (40min.)—from the *Hauptbahnhof.* Cross the bridge and take Hafenstr. left; keep following it as it turns into Bahnhofstr. and Elbstr. At the fork in the road at Elbstr. 20, follow the "Radweg zur Jugendherberge" sign left to the *Uferpromenade* (river path). After about 10 minutes the paved promenade will end; make a right here onto Kuhgrund (unmarked). Turn left at the *Jugendherberge* sign and take the dirt path through the woods (5min.). The hostel is the big brick building at the top of the hill. The brightly colored hostel, packed with school groups, offers game rooms with ping pong and a TV. (DM19, over 26 DM23.50. Breakfast included. Sheets DM6. Closed Dec. 15-Jan. 15. Call ahead. The hostel also plays host to a summer cooking school; DM7 to test the budding talents of young chefs.) *Pensionen* abound in the *Altstadt*, mostly closer to the train station; look for "Fremdenzimmer" or "Zimmer frei" signs. A persistent reminder of Lauenburg's shipping life is the local consumption of *Eierspunch*, an old sailor's drink made according to an ancient alchemical recipe to keep sniffling sailors warm (and wasted) in the winter. Faintly reminiscent of Rocky's raw egg cocktail, it packs a punch meaner than Apollo Creed. For food, try one of the outdoor cafes on the waterfront, such as the **Schifferbörte Café and Restaurant,** Elbstr. 82 (tel. 27 73). Enjoy Elvis-esque German music while sitting by the large windows in your blue suede shoes, surveying the open seas. Fish dishes DM15-25. The **telephone code** is 04153.

■ Helgoland

Helgoland is both a resort island and a game show—"The Duty-Free Dash." The contestants (hordes of greedy German tourists) pile onto ferries, ride small skiffs to the island, and dash frantically from store to store snatching up all of the cigarettes, cheeses, and meter-tall bottles of liquor that they can legally carry before the skiffs head back to the ferry at 4pm. A different kind of mayhem reigned at the conclusion of World War II, when the British navy evacuated the strategically valuable island and attempted to disintegrate it with thousands of tons of dynamite. Despite the real-life game of Risk, the resilient sandstone base withstood the assault and a teeming cauldron of humanity descended upon the island in the 1950s.

NIEDERSACHSEN

Helgoland now attracts nature-loving bargain-hunters. If you have only a day to see it, don't go. "Getting there is half the fun" is a cliche, not an axiom, and three hours on this admittedly lovely island can't justify the 4-6 hour round-trip ferry ride. An open-ended ticket (DM13 more than a daytrip) will give you time to push through the throngs and enjoy the view. The extra time will also allow you to find tiny trails and quiet corners to admire the red cliffs that give Helgoland poetic cachet equal to that of its pale English cousin Dover. *Rot ist die Wand, weiß ist der Sand, Grün ist das Land; Das sind die Farben von Helgoland* (Red are the cliffs, white is the sand, green is the land; these are the colors of...). Today's tourists are the latest incarnation of an imperialist assault on the island, previously controlled by pirates, Frisians, the Hanseatic League, Danes, and Britons. The small **Museumswerkstatt Nordseehalle,** located between the Nordost-Bohlwerk and the Northeast harbor, documents the legacy of plunder. (Opening times vary.)

The cheapest and most reliable way to get to Helgoland is through Cuxhaven, Norddeich, or Bremerhaven; ferries also leave from some of the Frisian Islands (including Norderney and Langeoog), but their schedules are erratic. The **MS Wappen von Hamburg,** which sails from Cuxhaven's *Fährhafen* harbor, is probably your best bet. The ride is relatively short (2 hr.) and the price is competitive. (Departs daily May-Sept. at 10:30am. Open-ended round-trip DM 68, ages 12-18 DM40. Day excursions DM 55, ages 12-18 DM36.) The **MS Frisia III,** operating from Norddeich, offers a lower fare but a longer ride (4hr.) and a skimpier schedule. (Departs May-June Tues. at 8am, July-Aug. Tues. and Fri. at 8am. Daytrips only DM43, 12 and under DM27.) Finally, ships depart and return earlier to **Vogosack,** albeit at a slightly higher price. (Departs April-Sept. daily at 7:30am. Open-ended round-trip DM70, ages 12-18 DM36. Day excursions DM62, ages 12-18 DM42.) The **telephone code** is 04725.

With thousands of visitors coming each year, Helgoland's **tourist office** (tel. 81 37 11) greets travelers as they step off the skiff. Their free prospectus offers a wealth of info, including a list of hotels and other accommodations (open Mon.-Fri. 9am-4pm, Sat. 11am-3pm). Helgoland's **Jugendherberge "Haus der Jugend" (HI),** Postfach 580 (tel./fax 341), sits right on the beach, a short 15-minute walk from the ferry dock following the signs. (Reception open April-Oct. 10am-2pm and 5-7pm. Curfew 10pm. DM42, over 26 DM37. Three meals included. Sheets DM10. Call 4-6 weeks ahead.)

Matjes

Matjes (MAH-ches), the Scandinavian word for herring, is all the rage in northern Germany during the first few weeks of June, which are officially dubbed the *"Matjes-Wochen"* (Herring Weeks). Several varieties exist: *nederlandisch* (Dutch), with cream sauce and vegetables; *hausfrau* (housewife), in sour cream with onion and apple; and sweet and sour, doused in sugared vinegar—but any restaurant worth its salt has its own secret recipe. Look for *Matjes* advertised everywhere, from the dives in the train station to the hip Schanzenstr. cafes in Hamburg. The fish has a very strong, sweet taste that is not acquired—you'll either love it or hate it. Wash it down with a glass of *Alsterwasser*—literally "water from the Alster" (one of Hamburg's lakes), but actually a gentle mix of beer and lemonade which tastes a lot better than it sounds.

■ Oldenburg

The city of Oldenburg, founded in 1108, was spared the destruction of the Thirty Years War largely because its head honcho at the time, Count Anton Günther, raised the most beautiful horses in all of Germany. Today's Oldenburg is much more than a one-trick pony; the Frisian *Stadt* has become an international cultural and political hub of Northwest Germany, maintaining close ties to sister cities in Denmark, France, Russia, the Netherlands, and Israel.

Orientation and Practical Information Oldenburg is easily accessible from Bremen (35min.). The old, moated city lies along an offshoot of the Weser

River, opening the way to East Frisia and serves as the take-off point for most excursions. The **tourist office,** Wallstr. 14 (tel. 157 44), finds rooms (from DM35) for a DM4 fee (call ahead) and plies visitors with numerous North Sea brochures (open Mon.-Fri. 9am-6pm, Sat. 9am-noon). You can also visit the **Fremdenverkehrsverband Nordsee-Niedersachsen-Bremen,** Bahnhofstr. 19-20 (tel. 92 17 10), for invaluable information on the East Frisian islands as well as regional information for the area between Holland and Hamburg (open Mon.-Thurs. 8am-5pm, Fri. 8am-4pm). **Rent bikes** at the **Fahrradstation,** on Neuesstr. (tel. 163 45), right across the street from the tourist office on Wallstr. (Open Mon.-Thurs. 7am-11pm, Fri. 7am-3pm, Sat. 8am-3pm; DM12 per day, DM42 per week; passport or other personal ID required.) **AIDS-Hilfe** (tel. 194 11) offers information on AIDS and gay concerns, with a separate line (tel. 122 39) for lesbian concerns. Oldenburg's **postal code** is 26123. The **telephone code** is 0441.

Accommodations and food The city's modern **Jugendherberge (HI),** Alexanderstr. 65 (tel. 871 35), is 1.5km from the station. Go down Moslestr. and turn right on Am Stadtmuseum; as Am Stadtmuseum disintegrates into an impossible jumble of intersecting streets, head in the general direction in which you were previously moving until you reach the greens of the Gertruden-Friedhof cemetery, with Alexanderstr. veering to your left. Or bus #7, 9, or 12: "Lappen," and then #2 or 3: "Von Finckstr." (Reception open 5-10pm. Curfew 10pm. DM22, over 26 DM26. Breakfast included. The hostel fills quickly, so call several weeks ahead.) The **Hotel Hegeler,** Donnerschweerstr. 27 (tel./fax 875 61), has clean rooms and a bowling alley. From the station, cross the pedestrian bridge over the tracks (near the post office) and follow the road to Donnerschweerstr.; then turn left and walk 150m. (Singles DM45, with shower and toilet DM75; doubles DM90, with shower DM130. Call a few days ahead.)

If you want to go where everybody knows your name, take a hike up around Wallstr., where almost every restaurant boasts "American-style" cuisine with Harley Davidson decor to match. **Taking it Easy,** Wallstr. 12 (tel. 158 27), down the street from the tourist office, can remind you of what happy hour is like. Experience American Budweiser as an exotic phenomenon (open daily after 6pm). Alternatively, chill in the sun while drinking German beer (despite its lack of a born-on date) at **Marvin's Biergarten,** Rosenstr. 8. Head up Bahnhofstr. and go left on Rosenstr. (open Mon.-Thurs. and Sun. 7pm-2am, Fri.-Sat. 8pm-3am). Those experiencing the *ennui* induced by modernity head to **Zauberkessel,** Kurwickstr. 6 (parallel to Wallstr.) to get medieval with live bards, and not-so-medieval with an ample vegetarian menu (open Sun.-Thurs. noon-1am; Fri.-Sat. noon-3am).

Sights and Entertainment Every morning, the city's residents jockey for position with hundreds of tourists as daily markets bustle in two different squares: one on the **Pferdmarkt,** an erstwhile horse-showing arena near the yellow brick state library, the other on the main square surrounding the 1888 **Rathaus.** The adjacent 13th-century **Lambertikirche** has gracefully endured baroque and neoclassical additions to its Gothic structure (open Tues.-Fri. 11am-12:30pm and 2:30-5pm, Sat. 11am-12:30pm; free). The **Landesmuseum,** Schloßpl. 26, housed in the yellow-and-white *Schloß* with gingerbread trim, exhibits an extensive painting collection with special emphasis on Goethe's friend and fan, Johann Tischbein (open Tues.-Fri. 9am-5pm, Sat.-Sun. 10am-5pm; DM4, students, children and seniors DM2). The **Augusteum,** Elisabethstr. 1 (tel. 220 26 00), is an extension of the *Landesmuseum* with two floors of groggy surrealist dreamscapes and Kirchner's Expressionist street scenes (open Tues.-Fri. 9am-5pm, Sat.- Sun. 10am-5pm; DM4, students, children, and seniors DM2). For a little less esoteric action, walk another 300m to the **Naturkunde and Vorgeschichte Musuem** (Natural and Prehistory Museum), Damm 40-44 (tel. 924 43 00), and meet some real-life bogey (not Bogey) men, whose macabre appearances persist through the millennia (open Tues.-Thurs. 9am-5pm, Sat.-Sun. 10am-5pm; DM3, students and children DM1.50). Where Wallstr. turns into Lappan, **Alte Schmiede am Lappan,** an old-style blacksmith shop offers a glimpse of craftspeople at work (open Mon.-Fri. 9:30am-6pm, Sat. 10am-1:30pm). Further down Lappan and crossing at Am Stadtmuseum 4-8, the **Stadtmuseum** holds everything from period-based studies of Oldenburg's long history to the naturalist and expressionist collections of local notable Theodor Francksen (open Tues.-Fri. 9am-5pm, Sat. 9am-noon, Sun. 10am-5pm; free).

Oldenburg's nightlife centers around a curious man named "Popeye" who runs the club **JFK's** on Wallstr. Despite the campy and strangely morbid motif, Popeye injects some pulse into Oldenburg after hours. He organizes numerous raves, dance parties, and beach parties (no pajama-jammy-jams); just ask him what's goin' on. Oldenburg also offers **Pulverfass,** Kaiserstr. 24 (tel. 126 01), a popular men-only gay disco (open Tues.-Thurs. 10pm-2am, Fri.-Sat. 11pm-5am; Fri.-Sat. DM5 cover).

■ Wilhelmshaven

Crazy Kaiser Wilhelm II, spurred by megalomaniacal dreams of creating a "place in the sun" for Germany, built the modestly named Wilhelmshaven in an attempt to lay the groundwork for German military and naval expansionism. Today, the somber statue of the Kaiser on **Friedrich Wilhelm Platz** oversees a jovial and bustling seaport whose docks are purely pacific. The city's location on the **Jadebusen** and its excellent harbor enable the town to pursue its three passions—eating, drinking, and boating—in close proximity. The **Südstrand** beach is accessible by taking Ebertstr. east from the *Hauptbahnhof* and crossing the **Kaiser-Wilhelm-Brücke** (open May-Sept. daily 8am-6pm; admission DM4, children DM1). Right by the Kaiser-Wilhelm Brücke floats the bright red **Feuerschiff,** used until 1981 to fight boat fires (open Tues.-Sun. 11am-10pm, free).The boat houses a bar and grill (open daily 11:30am-3pm and 6-10pm). For more active *Schiffvergnügen* (ship pleasure), rent a sail, paddle, or rowboat at the **Boatverleih** (tel. 20 26 22; open April-Sept. daily 11:30am-9pm, boats DM18 per hour). The adjacent *Gaststätte* serves delicious *Bockwurst* and beer. From the Pumpwerk stop, go south on Jadestr. then right onto Ems for 10 minutes, follow the signs left onto Henschelstr., then walk 200m.

For something completely different, and *extremely* disturbing to the *Kaiser,* visit the **Pumpwerk Kulturzentrum,** An der Deichbrücke (tel. 438 77). Witness the decline of Western civilization daily with some of Germany's most egregious pop bands, or revel in the death of theater with productions like "Stories from the Belly of the Moon," in which the comical Frau Mond (Mrs. Moon) tells tales of her observations of the Earth. Times, prices, and quality of entertainment vary. A *Pumpwerk* program is available at the ticket office. A few rungs higher on the hipness ladder stands the **Hotel Kling Klang,** Böxsenstr. 73 (tel. 133 22), just up the street from the tourist center. By day, it's a pleasant, unassuming cafe with spray-painted stools. By night, the small stage showcases acts ranging from a KISS revival to original hip-hop and DJs, with live music on Fridays (open daily 10am-late). Not even Gene Simmons can rock all night on an empty stomach; that's why there's *Auflauf* at **Pumpwerk I** (not to be confused with the Kulturzentrum), Ahrstr. 24 (tel. 445 90). Line 3 (or line A after hours): "Kaiser-Wilhelm-Brücke." Choose ingredients from broccoli to salami to add to the starchy mash that is *Auflauf* (DM11.80). Open daily from 6pm.

Walk straight out of the station along Virchowstr. (which is to the left of the *Reisezentrum*) and make a left on Börsenstr. to the **tourist office,** Börsenstr. 55b (tel. 92 79 30), which can find you a private room (open Mon.-Fri. 9am-6pm, Sat. 9am-1pm). Conveniently located down Gökerstr. from the hostel is **Oeltermann's,** Holtermanstr. 2 (tel. 321 54), where you can rent a **bicycle** for DM9 per day (open Mon.-Fri. 8am-1pm and 3-6pm, Sat. 8am-1pm). Wilhelmshaven's **postal code** is 26382. The **telephone code** is 04421.

The **Wilhelmshaven Jugendherberge (HI),** Freiligrathstr. 131 (tel. 600 48; fax 647 16), sits on the city outskirts by the botanical gardens. Take bus #1 (or bus A after hours) to Friedenstr. and follow the sign 200m. (Reception open 24hr. Curfew 11:30pm, but you get a house key. DM20, over 26 DM24. Breakfast included. Sheets DM5. Closed in Nov.). While there are a number of inexpensive *Pensionen,* **Privat-**

Pension Heine Lübben, Rheinstr. 25 (tel. 434 19), is close to the beach and the city. From the station, walk along Virchowstr. toward the water and turn left on Rheinstr. Go down three blocks and look to your left. If you find yourself standing in the Jadebusen, you've gone too far. (Reception open daily 10am-10pm. Singles DM40; doubles DM80.) From Wilhelmshaven you can sail away to the sun and surf of the German vacation paradise **Helgoland** (see p. 305).

■ Jever

Jever is the small town equivalent of a happy drunk—often charming, occasionally vulgar, and wholly kept afloat by beer. The astute observer can't help but notice, next to the town water pump in the city center, a sculpture of a dog answering nature's call on the pump. To uncover the town's frothy foundations, follow your nose to the **Jever Brewery** (tel. 137 11) for a **tour** of the complex that puts Jever on the map, and on tap, in *Kneipen* all over northern Germany. A trifling DM10 gets you the tour, a souvenir mug, a tasty *Langenbrezel* (big soft pretzel), and 0.6L of sharp *Jever* lager. (Tours every 30min. April-Oct. Mon.-Fri. 9:30am-12:30pm; Nov.-March Tues.-Thurs. 10:30am only; DM10. Call several weeks ahead to reserve a place.)

Like most lushes in denial, Jeverians dismiss their barley fetish, claiming that their finest offering is the castle located across from the tourist office at Alter Markt 18. The rose-colored, 15th-century **Schloß** houses an engaging museum filled with art and trinkets dating back five hundred years. (Open March 1-Jan. 15 Tues.-Sun. 10am-6pm; admission DM4, students DM2, children DM1.) The beautiful Renaissance **Rathaus** towers in the main square. After being burned down and reconstructed nine times, the **Stadtkirche,** on Kirchplatz, is now fully modernized.

The **tourist office,** Alter Markt 18 (tel. 710 10; fax 93 92 99), across from the *Schloß,* books rooms for free and directs the smell-impaired to the brewery. (Open May-Sept. Mon.-Fri. 10am-6pm, Sat. 10am-2pm, Sun. 10am-noon; Oct.-April Mon.-Thurs. 10am-5pm, Fri. 9am-1pm.) The **Jugendherberge Jever (HI),** Mooshütterweg 12 (tel. 35 90), idles on a small street behind the *Schloß.* The rooms, holding up to 10 beds, are a bit cramped, but plaid quilts and colored curtains brighten the atmosphere. Unlike most other hostels in the region, rooms are generally available. (Reception open 5–9:45pm. Curfew 10pm. DM18, over 26 DM24. Breakfast included. Sheets DM5. Open April-Oct.) The **telephone code** is 04461.

NEAR JEVER: HOOKSIEL

A small coastal port to the Northwest of Jever, Hooksiel is one of the preeminent bathing spots on the East Frisian mainland. Famed for its beaches, one-third of which are **nude,** and its cozy camping grounds, Hooksiel magnanimously offers 4km of sweet sandy coast.

The best way to get to Hooksiel is by bus from Jever. Weekend trips require reservations. Ask the tourist office in Jever for times, or call the bus line (tel. (04461) 949 00). Hooksiel's **tourist office,** Hohe Weg 1 (tel. (04425) 958 00), finds rooms and offers information on bike, ski, and tent rentals (open Mon.-Fri. 8:30am-6:30pm, Sat. 9am-noon, Sun. 10am-noon).

■ East Frisian Islands

Seven sandy islands bracelet the East Frisian *(Ostfriesische)* North Sea coast. Control of the dunes has shuffled between Russia, Prussia, Holland, and various Scandinavian countries for several centuries, but today their value is more therapeutic than strategic—flash floods of Germans come here to be healed by the purifying air. Bikers abound, furiously pedaling in observance of the car ban (enforced on all islands except Norderney and Baltrum). For those seeking a less strenuous route, pungent aromas provide the direction to one of the many old-fashioned horse carriages. Although often called the *"Land mit still Plätzen"* (land of silent places), the Frisian islands are livened by the *Seehünde* (seals) flapping their tails at passing ferries. Natives become disgruntled if the seals' greetings go unanswered; diplomatic visitors holler, *"Moin! Moin!"* (the North German phrase for hello), to impress them (the natives, that is).

When the tide is out, the marshy landscape of the *Watt* appears, connecting the mainland to Baltrum, Norderney, Spiekeroog and Langeoog. *Never* venture out onto these *Watts* without a guide—the tide's quick return can be *extremely* dangerous. Under the careful watch of a guide, the trek (8-10km) allows folks to witness the vast and splendid desolation of the ocean floor. The tourist offices in cities with *Watt* terrain have information about guides *(Wattführer)* in their area. (Tours cost about DM5 for 2hr.) The region's specialty is *Matja* (baby herring); it's cheap and everyone eats it (see **Matjes,** p. 306).

Six of the islands—Borkum, Juist, Norderney (two hostels), Langeoog, Spiekeroog, and Wangerooge—have **HI youth hostels,** and there are several more on the mainland coast. Swarms of German schoolchildren crowd the hostels. Call or write weeks, even months, in advance. Most of the hostels require you to purchase *Vollpension* (full board; 3 meals per day); in addition a resort tax slithers its way onto the accommodation bills. The most vexing problem of East Frisian tourism is getting there: a variety of small companies run **ferries** to individual islands from separate mainland ports (railpasses not valid). However, there is no inter-island transport, and the budget traveler might smart from the expensive sting of the region's costly ferries (DM35 and up for round-trips).

NORDERNEY

As Germany's oldest North Sea spa, the island **Norderney** has served as a retreat for illustrious illuminaries like the Hannoverian monarchs, Otto von Bismarck, and Heinrich Heine. An endless stream of ferries from Norddeich dumps loads of luggage-toting tourists at the port (July-Aug. 14 daily departures, Sept.-June at least 9 daily; open-ended round-trip DM25, ages 11 and under DM14.25; call (04931) 987 24 for information). The beautiful beaches now bear a certain resemblance to Coney Island. While there's no roller coaster or Nathan's Famous, dozens of skateboarders tackling a half-pipe and cheesy beachside diners create an impression of a seaside Brooklyn. The desolate dunes and endless beaches in eastern Nordeney are free from the hustling hordes of tourists. The **Fahrradverleih am Hafen** (tel. 13 26), 300m down Hafenstr. as you step off the ferry, rents **bikes** at an unbeatable location (open daily 9am-6pm; DM9 for 4hr., DM12 for the day, children DM6 and DM9 respectively).

If you want to spend the night, the friendly folks at the **tourist office,** Bülowallee 5 (tel. 918 50; fax 824 94), sniff out rooms in *Pensionen* (DM40) or private homes (longer stays only, DM30) for a DM7.50 fee. (Open March-Oct. Mon.-Fri. 9am-12:30pm and 2-6pm, Sat. 10am-12:30pm and 2-4pm, Sun. 10am-12:30pm; Nov.-Feb. Mon.-Fri. 9am-12:30pm and 2:30-6pm.) The **telephone code** is 04932.

Norderney's two **Jugendherbergen (HI)** are both excruciatingly crowded and expensive; they require you to pay for full pension (3 meals) for the duration of your stay. The owner of the hostel at **Südstraße** (tel. 24 51; fax 836 00) takes pains to provide a haven for stranded travelers. Follow Zum Fähranleger to Deichstr., then onto Südstr. (Reception open 8:30-9am, 5:15-6pm, and 9:45pm. DM37.50, including both the local tourist tax and full board. Members only. Sheets DM5. Open March-Oct.) Somewhat less inviting, due to its inconvenient location, is the hostel **Am Dünensender 3** (tel. 25 74; fax 832 66); if you miss the bus (destination: "Leuchtturm"; 1 per hr.), you'll have to rent a **bike** in town or suffer the1½-2-hour walk. Follow Deichstr. to its end, and head left on Karl Reger Weg, where signs point you to the hostel. (Reception open 8:30am-10am. DM35.50, over 26 DM43.50. Full board included. Open March-Oct.) **Camping** is available in summer for HI members only (DM11 per person with breakfast). **Camping Booken,** Waldweg 2 (tel. 448), is expensive, but the next best thing to the hostels. Call ahead. (Reception open 10am-noon. DM12 per person, DM12 per tent. DM10 per mobile home. Warm showers included. Washer DM6, dryer DM5.)

BORKUM, JUIST, AND BALTRUM

Borkum is proud of its long history as the Baden-Baden of the North Sea, the *Hauptinsel* of the asthmatic and consumptive. Bring us your tired, your sick, your huddled masses...as long as you're not poor, of course. The clean and invigorating climate delights the happy folk who take to the **nude beach** ("FKK Strand"), accessible by bus. Make reservations for **private rooms** and pick up a bus map at the **tourist office,** Goethestr. 1 (*Kurverwaltung;* tel. 30 30; for rooms call 841). Hours fluctuate wildly. The **ferry** ride leaves from the dock in Emden, the first port on the train from Oldenburg. (Ride lasts 2hr. Departures March-Oct. and last week in Dec. daily at 8, 11am and 2, 5pm; Jan.-March and Oct.-Dec. Mon.-Thurs. and Sat. 8am and 3:30pm, Fri. and Sun. 8am and 4:30pm. Day excursion DM25, children 4-11 DM12.50; round-trip DM47, children DM23.50. Weekend ticket (depart Fri., return Sun.) DM35, children DM17.50.) Double-hulled **catamarans** also skim across to the island. (Trip lasts 1hr. Departures irregular. DM15 surcharge on regular prices.) A second ferry runs from Borkum to **Eemshaven** in the Netherlands (day excursion DM21, children DM10.50; round-trip DM38, children DM19). Schedule varies from year to year. For more information and specific dates, call **Reederei Aktien-Gesellschaft** (tel. (04921) 89 07 22). The **telephone code** is 04922.

Borkum's **Jugendherberge (HI),** Jann-Berghaus-Str. 63 (tel. 579; fax 71 24), a five-minute walk from the dock, fills up quickly. To get a room, a written request one month in advance is necessary. (Curfew 10:30pm, but house keys are available. With *Vollpension* DM34.70, over 26 DM38.55.) **Insel-Camping,** at Hindenburgstr. 114 (tel. 10 88), is 15 minutes from the train station by foot. (DM20 per person, tent included. Open mid-March to Oct.)

Juist is merely 17km long, 500m wide, and famous for its birds. First settled in 1398, it's a bit tough to settle there now unless you camp in a nest. Ferries leave from the port at Norddeich at odd times, depending on tides and season; call (04931) 98 70 for details. (Ferries June-Oct. roughly 2 per day. Day excursion DM28.50, round-trip DM40, children ages 4-11 half-price.) The **tourist office,** Friesenstr. 18 (*Kurverwaltung;* tel. 80 92 22; fax 80 92 23; email juist@t-online.de), has maps and a free room-finding service (rooms DM30-60 per person; open May-Sept. Mon.-Fri. 8:30am-noon and 3-5pm, Sat. 10am-noon; Oct.-April Mon.-Fri. 3-6pm). The rental shop **Germania,** Wilhelmstr. 17 (tel. 297), has over 600 **bikes** to lease (from DM12 per day, ID required; open daily 9am-6pm). The tiny island also has its own **Jugendherberge,** Loogster Pad 20. (Tel. 929 10; fax 82 94. Reception open 8-10pm or whenever a boat arrives. DM29.20 with breakfast and dinner, over 26 DM34.20. Open March-Dec.) The **telephone code** is 04935.

The smallest of the Frisian Islands, with a population of 500, **Baltrum** is the ideal escape from civilization. First mentioned in the 14th century, Baltrum still maintains a Luddite ambience, supported by a total ban on cars and the absence of bike rentals. To reach **Baltrum** take the bus from the Norden train station (one short stop from Norddeich) to **Neßmersiel** to meet the ferry (open-ended round-trip DM36, children DM17; day excursion DM22, DM11). Train, bus, and boat are all timed for a convenient rendezvous (June-Nov. 2-3 per day; last ferry to the island does not have a corresponding ferry back). For more information, check the schedule, call the ferry company at 235, or visit the **tourist office,** Rathausstr. 130 (tel. 800; for rooms call 80 48; fax 80 27) in the *Rathaus*. The office also offers hotel information and books private accommodations for a 5% commission (open March-Oct. Mon.-Fri. 8:30am-noon and 2-5pm; Nov.-Feb. Mon.-Fri. 9am-noon). The **telephone code** is 04939.

LANGEOOG, SPIEKEROOG, AND WANGEROOGE

The bus from Norden (DM7.50) or from **Esens** (DM3.50) travels to Bensersiel, the departure point for ferries to "Long Island"—not the one in New York, but **Langeoog,** which served as a base for 18th-century pirates. (May-Sept. 7 daily departures; Oct.-April 4; open-ended round-trip DM34, children DM17; daytrip DM28.) For more info or to book a room (DM30), visit the **tourist office** in front of the *Bahnhof*, at

Hauptstr. 28 (tel. 69 32 01; fax 65 28; open Mon.-Sat. 9am-7pm, Sun. 10am-2pm; winter Mon.-Fri. 9am-5pm). Rent a bike next door at **Fahrrad Verlein** (tel. 64 74; open daily 9am-12:30pm and 1:30-6pm).

Langeoog's **Jugendherberge Domäne Melkhörn (HI)** is smack-dab in the middle of the island (tel. 276; fax 66 94). One can only reach the hostel by foot, bike, or horse and buggy—motor vehicles are prohibited on the island. (DM33.55, over 26 DM35.55. Members only. Full board included.) The hostel also runs a **campground.** (Curfew at 10pm, but if you're 18 or older, you can get a key. DM28.35, over 26 DM29.75. Members only. Full board included. Reservation required. Open April-Sept.) The **telephone code** is 04972.

The **Bäderbus** goes to Neuharlingersiel, the departure point for **Spiekeroog**, the island that takes pride in its historic shipwrecks and its natural silence—"No festivals celebrated here," brags the official brochure. Its **tourist office,** Noorderpad 25 (tel. 919 30; for rooms call 919 25), has information on ferries, rooms for as little as DM16, and dune paths (open April-Sept. Mon.-Fri. 9am-noon and 2-5pm, Sat. 9am-noon; Jan.-March Mon.-Fri. 9am-noon). Spiekeroog's **Jugendherberge,** Bid Utkiek 1 (tel. 329), is a trifling 10-minute walk from either the port or the beach. (DM35.50 per person. Full board included. Written reservations are required 1 year in advance! Open April-Oct.). The **telephone code** is 04976.

The journey to **Wangerooge** is a Herculean labor, but worth it if you're desperate to avoid the crowds which plague the other islands in the enjoyment of the beach and the sea of solitude. From Norden take a 90-minute ride on the *Bäderbus* to the town of **Harlesiel.** Boats leave the dock two to five times daily from April to October and once or twice daily the rest of the year; exact times vary widely with the season. (Open-ended round-trip DM44, children 4-11 DM22; day excursion DM29.) Wangerooge's **tourist office** on the Strandpromenade (tel. 990; for rooms call 948 80; fax 991 14) has ferry information (open Mon.-Fri. 9am-noon and 2-5pm, Sat.-Sun. whenever a ferry arrives.) They can also direct you to the haunting **Westturm,** a landmark that's been converted into a striking **Jugendherberge (HI)** (tel. 439), a 20-minute walk from the station (tel. 439). Look for the stone tower. (Reception open 7-9am, 1-3pm, and 5-7pm. Curfew 10pm for those under 18. DM34.10 with full board, over 26 DM38.10. Open May-Sept. Call weeks in advance.) The **telephone code** is 04469.

EMDEN

A large seaport, **Emden** has a history as a thriving trading centre. Today the town is pleasant but unremarkable, and is important chiefly because of its Volkswagen plant. From the *Hauptbahnhof,* head to the *Innenstadt* (bus #3001: "Rathaus" or a 15min. walk along Grossestr.). The **tourist office,** Am Stadtgarten across from the *Rathaus* (tel. 974 00; fax 974 09), gives out free brochures and sells a bargain ticket that lets you into four of city museums (DM9, under 18 DM4.50; open May-Sept. Mon.-Fri. 9am-6pm, Sat. 10am-1pm, Sun. 11am-1pm; Jan.-April Mon.-Fri. 9am-1pm and 3-5:30pm, Sat. 10am-1pm). The **Landesmuseum** in the *Rathaus* offers a menacing display of 16th- and 17th-century weapons (open Mon.-Sat. 1-5pm, Sun. 11am-5pm). The **Kunsthalle,** Hinter dem Rahmen 13 (tel. 209 95), is a perfect afternoon outing; the permanent collection includes Picasso, Franz Marc, and an impressive gathering of *Neue Sachlichkeit* works. It also hosts great special exhibits. Rooms atop the museum's spiral staircases offer crash courses in 20th-century art. (Open Tues. 10am-8pm, Wed.-Fri. 10am-5pm, Sat.-Sun. 11am-5pm; DM7, students and seniors DM4.)

The newest museum in town is the highly-acclaimed **Bunker Museum** (tel. 271 06; open May-Oct. Tues.-Fri. 11am-1pm and 3-5pm, Sat.-Sun. 1-2pm). For only DM3 (students DM1) you can explore six floors of an old air-raid shelter stocked with memorabilia, tracing the sad fate of Emden's population from 1941 to 1944, when the city was firebombed, and 85% of its buildings destroyed. For a more light-hearted experience, a visit to **Das Otto Haus** is in order. The three-story edifice is a shrine to comedian, children's entertainer, and **living legend Otto Waalkes,** a native Emdener. The first floor is free; see kissing elephants (Otto's symbol) and buy images of Otto on everything from rubber to silicon. To see the second and third floors, featuring photos of Otto clowning with Boris Becker and Steffi Graf, and other madcap antics, pilgrims must pay (DM4, children DM1.50). (Open April-Oct. Mon.-Fri. 9:30am-6pm, Sat. 9:30am-1pm and 3-6pm, Sun. 10am-4pm; Nov.-March Mon.-Fri. 9:30am-1pm and 3-6pm.) Call 862 390 to get on a tour of the town's mammoth **Volkswagen plant** (open Mon.-Thurs. 9:30am-1:30pm). The **telephone code** is 04921.

Jugendherberge Emden (HI), An der Kesselschleuse 5 (tel. 237 97; fax 321 61), overlooks a small stream and offers bikes and canoes for rent. If you miss Bus Linie 3003 to Herrentor (Mon.-Sat. 1 every hr.), it's a 20-minute walk from the *Rathaus* along am Herrentor. The hostel caters to the kiddies with comical paintings of cartoon animals in some of the bed rooms. (Reception open 5-10pm. Curfew 10pm. DM20, over 26 DM24. Breakfast included. Sheets DM6.)

NORDEN AND NORDDEICH

Norden is the transportation polestar for any excursion around Frisia. By train, it connects to Emden and Norddeich (every hr., DM3-5), and as the anchor of the **Bäderbus** and the only public link to Neßmersiel, it provides easy access to every other port town. Call or visit the **tourist office** (*Kurverwaltung;* tel. 986 02; fax 98 62 90), next to the *Rathaus* (open Mon.-Fri. 8am-3pm, Sat. 9am-1pm) for specific transportation info, or to book rooms (from DM25) for no fee.

From the *Rathaus,* not even a Gomer Pyle could miss the gigantic steeple across the market. The spire belongs to the 15th-century **Ludgerkirche,** famed for its exquisite organ. (Open April-Sept. Mon. 10am-12:30pm, Tues.-Sat. 10am-12:30pm and 3-5pm. Organ concerts mid-June to mid-Sept. Wed. 8pm.) One of the peculiarities of the North Sea coast is its natives' great love of **tea;** perhaps this is because of the region's proximity to Britain, or the sobriety required for sound nautical exploits. You can revel in the gift of the leaves at the one and only **East Frisian Tea Museum,** am Markt (tel. 121 00), in the town square. For DM1 on Wednesdays (May-Aug. only), you can participate in an East Frisian **tea ceremony,** which resembles its Japanese counterpart only in its placid atmosphere. The ceremony takes place at tea time (2 and 3pm), of course (open March-Oct. Tues.-Sat. 10am-4pm; DM4, children DM1.50). In the same building is the **Heimat Museum,** which shows the early culture of *Ostfriesland,* including dike construction and shoemaking.

Ten minutes away by bus or rail, the suburban port of **Norddeich** provides an adequate **Jugendherberge (HI),** Strandstr. 1 (tel. 80 64; fax 818 28). It teems with the terror that is German *Schulkinder.* From the station, facing the sea, follow the road behind the dike, walk 30m past the Hotel Regina Maris, and left on Strandstr. (Reception open 5-8pm; DM23, over 26 DM28. Breakfast included.) The hostel's backyard tent sleeps eight (DM17.50 per person); they'll also let you pitch your own (DM14.75 per person). **Nordsee-Camp,** Deichstr. 21 (tel. 80 73; fax 80 74), is 20 minutes farther down Badestr., which turns into Deichstr. Impressive views, but dike-side camping gets chilly (Day DM5; Person DM8.25, *Kurtaxe* DM3; open mid-March to Oct.).

The Norddeich **tourist office,** Dörperweg 22 (tel. 98 62 00), finds rooms in *Pensionen* (DM23-35). From the train station, head down Badestr. and turn left on Dörperweg (open Mon.-Thurs. 8:30am-1pm and 2-4:30pm, Fri. 8:30am-4pm, Sat. 10am-4pm). The **postal code** is 26506; the **telephone code** for both cities is 04931.

■ Osnabrück

October 24, 1998 marks the 350th anniversary of the signing of the Peace of Westphalia in Osnabrück. The city still emanates pacific vibes, complete with tourist brochures that beam, "Have a Nice Day." Inside Osnabrück's stunning **Rathaus** is the perfectly preserved **Friedenssaal,** the site of the historic negotiating table from which the Thirty Years War was ended. (For more on the Thirty Years War, see p. 63. *Rathaus* open Mon.-Fri. 8:30am-6pm, Sat.-Sun. 10am-1pm. Tours Sun. 10:30am. Free.) Next to the *Rathaus* stands the **Marienkirche,** completely destroyed during the war, but now fully rebuilt (open Mon.-Sat. 10am-noon and 3-5pm; Oct.-March

Mon.-Sat. 10:30am-noon and 2:30-4pm). The **tower** can be toured Sundays from 11:30am to 1pm (admission DM2, children DM1). The immense **Dom,** Kleine Doms-freiheit 24, has been collecting priceless religious relics for nine centuries (open Tues.-Fri. 10am-1pm and 3-5pm, Sat.-Sun. 11am-2pm; DM2, children DM1).

The warm afterglow of Westphalia quickly fades amidst the permanent **Felix Nuss-baum** (1904-1944) exhibit at the **Museum of Cultural History;** Nussbaum's paintings depict the tragedy of the Holocaust with heart-wrenching symbolism (open Mon.-Fri. 8:30am-6pm, Sat.-Sun. 10am-1pm; DM3, students and children DM1.50). Osnabrück's most famous son is Erich Maria Remarque, the acclaimed author of *Im Westen nichts Neues* (All Quiet on the Western Front). Though Allied bombing completely destroyed his house on Hafenstr., literary diehards are welcome to see the new **Erich Maria Remarque-Archiv,** Alte Münze 16 (tel. 969 45 11), which documents his life and times (open Mon.-Thurs. 9am-noon, also open Tues. 2-4pm).

The **tourist office,** Krahnstr. 58 (tel. 323 22 02; fax 323 42 13), stands between the *Dom* and the *Marienkirche* (open Mon.-Fri. 10am-6pm, Sat. 10am-2pm, Sun. 11am-1pm). From the station, walk up Möserstr. as it turns into Herrenteichsstr., follow the curve around, and turn onto Krahnstr. The office will book you a room (from DM30 per person) for free. The **Fahrradverleih,** in the train station (tel. 25 91 31), leases the *Rikscha-Fahrrad* (rickshaw cycle), the Euro-Asiatic equivalent of a go-cart (day DM70, week DM299); it also rents more modest **bikes.** (Day DM8, week DM35. Open Mon.-Fri. 6am-8pm, Sat. 7am-2pm. ID and DM20 deposit required.) The **bus** travels around the city center (DM2) and to the outer zones (DM2.50). Launder your dirty duds at **Wasch Center,** on the corner of Kommenderiestr. and Petersburger-Wall (open 6am-11pm). The **telephone code** is 0541.

South of the city center is the newly outfitted **Jugendgästehaus Osnabrück,** Iurger-str. 183a (tel. 542 84; fax 542 94). From the station, bus #13, 15, 62, or 83: "Neu-markt," then change to #23, 25 or 27: "Kinderhospital;" turn left and follow the signs up a tree-lined path. (Reception open 5-10pm. DM26, over 26 DM30.50. Breakfast and sheets included. Wheelchair accessible. Call ahead.) Clean rooms fill the **Hotel Jägerheim,** Johannistor-Wall 19a (tel. 216 35). From the station, turn left on Konrad-Adenauer-Ring, which becomes Petersberger-Wall and then Johannistor-Wall. (Reception closes at 9pm; call ahead. DM39 per person, with shower DM44, with shower and toilet DM61.) For **camping,** try **Freizeitpark Attersee,** Zum Attersee 50 (tel. 12 41 47). From the station, bus #22: "Attersee." (DM5.50 per person. No tent rentals. Showers included.) In a pinch, rooms are almost always available at the **Bad Essen Jugendherberge,** easily accessible by bus #302 (tel. (05472) 21 23; reception open 5-10pm; DM22, over 26 DM25; breakfast included; *Kürtaxe* DM2.50).

Students attending the local university stimulate the nightlife in Osnabrück. **Uni-cum,** Neue Graben 40 (tel. 224 92), proffers a student disco, music bar, and home-made treats, including *Auflauf* (open Mon.-Sat. 7pm-3am). Liberace has nuthin' on the **Pink Piano,** Lotterstr. 99 (tel. 428 23), which offers live blues (open daily after 10am; in winter Mon.-Fri. after 2pm, Sat.-Sun. after 10am).

In 1998, Osnabrück will host a number of special events to commemorate the 350th anniversary of the Peace of Westphalia. Always looking for an excuse to party, the city will also commemorate Remarque's 100th birthday in 1998 with special exhibits in the *Stadtbibliothek,* Am Markt 6-7 (tel. 323 21 09). Contact the tourist office for details.

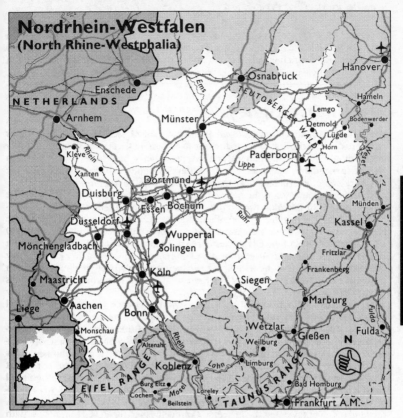

Nordrhein-Westfalen (North Rhine- Westphalia)

In 1946, the victorious Allies attempted to speed Germany's recovery by merging the traditionally distinct regions of Westphalia, Lippe, and the Rhineland to unify the economic nucleus of post-war Germany. The resulting *Land,* Nordrhein-Westfalen, meets no typical German stereotype, a fact which has unfairly tarnished its image. True, the avant-garde multiculturalism of Berlin, the *Lederhosen* and beer halls of Bavaria, and the unspoiled natural beauty of the Black Forest are all far from here, but the region's dense concentration of highways, raillines, and people connect and unite the diverse traditions. With its 17 million inhabitants and the mighty Ruhr Valley, North Rhine-Westphalia is the most heavily populated and economically powerful area in Germany. But industry has brought strife to the region in the past: the industrial boom of the late 19th century sparked social democracy, trade unionism, and revolutionary communism—the popular moniker "Red Ruhr" didn't refer to the color of the water. Despite downturns in heavy industry and persistently high unemployment, the great industrial wealth of the region continues to support a multitude of cultural offerings for the citizens and visitors of its lively towns and beautiful river valleys. And while the region's industrial squalor may have inspired the philosophy of Karl Marx and Friedrich Engels, the natural beauty of the Teutoburg and Eifel and the cultural and intellectual energy of Köln and Düsseldorf have spurred the muses of writers from Goethe to Heine to Böll.

■ Köln (Cologne)

Founded as a Roman colony (*colonia*, hence Köln) 48AD, Köln was Petrarch's "city of dreams" when the rest of Germany was just wilderness. The city's location at the intersection of several international trade routes ushered in a Golden Age during the Middle Ages and the Renaissance; this position contributes to Köln's present status as Germany's commercial, technical, and communications center *par excellence*.

Köln's major attraction is the majestic and legendary *Dom*. Designed to exceed all other churches in splendor, the Gothic structure took an amazing 632 years to build. During World War II, at least 14 bombs struck the *Dom*. Surprisingly, it survived and has since become a powerful symbol of Köln's miraculous recovery from the allied raids which left 90% of the city center in ruins. Today, Köln is the largest city in Nordrhein-Westfalen and the most important culturally, with a full plate of world-class museums and theatrical offerings. It is a prosperous, modern city with a grip on the past and a penchant for bibulous celebrations, such as the annual *Karneval* (like *Mardi Gras*, but with more drinking).

Modern Köln is also the city of Nobel Prize-winning novelist Heinrich Böll, who set *The Lost Honor of Katharina Blum* and the scandalous *Clown* here. The novels concern the venom of press slander and the violation of civil liberties—topics appropriate to a city steeped in literary and journalistic tradition. Köln is the base of many national media networks, just as it was during the days of Karl Marx, who began his revolutionary career here as a local newspaper editor, although Karl did not get to host a TV program when orchestrating the Gotha program. Though Köln's citizens conduct their own communications in the impenetrable "Kölsch" dialect, a locally brewed *Kölsch* beer offers a savory experience that can bring to all visitors' taste buds the kind of experience that the heavenly *Dom* delivers to their eyes.

ORIENTATION AND PRACTICAL INFORMATION

Eight bridges carry Köln, Germany's fourth-largest city and located north of Bonn, across the Rhine. Direct train lines connect Köln with Düsseldorf (30min.), Frankfurt (2½hr.), Munich (6-8hr.), Hamburg (4hr.), and Berlin (5½-7½hr.).

The **Dom Hotel**, across from the *Dom*, sells the **Köln Bonbon**, a packet of vouchers entitling the holder to a print of the 1531 town panorama woodcut, discounts on Rhine cruises, reduced admission to area attractions, and a three-day pass for free entry into all of the city's museums (DM15; with voucher for 2hr. **city bus tour** DM26). You can also pick up several brochures that aren't free at the tourist office.

Tourist Office: Verkehrsamt, Unter Fettenhennen 19 (tel. 221 33 45; fax 221 33 20; http://www.koeln.org.verkehrsamt), across from the main entrance to the *Dom*, provides a free city map (you must pay for most other brochures), books rooms for a DM5 fee, and tries to sell posters. Ask about English **tours** of the city and *Dom*. Pick up the *Monatsvorschau* (DM2), a booklet with essential info and a complete monthly schedule of events. Open May-Oct. Mon.-Sat. 8am-10:30pm, Sun. 9am-10:30pm; Nov.-April Mon.-Sat. 8am-9pm, Sun. 9:30am-7pm.
Budget Travel: STA Travel, Zülpicherstr. 178 (tel. 44 20 11).
Currency Exchange: There's an office at the **train station** (open daily 7am-9pm), but the service charges are lower at the post office.
American Express: Burgmauerstr. 14 (tel. 925 90 10), near the *Dom*. **ATM.** Cardmembers' mail held free for 4 weeks. Open Mon.-Fri. 9am-5:30pm, Sat. 9am-noon.
Flights: Flights depart from **Köln-Bonn Flughafen** for 50 destinations non-stop; a shuttle to Berlin leaves 24 times per day. Call (02203) 40 25 38 for more information. Bus #170 leaves stop #4 of the *Hauptbahnhof* at 5:40, 6, and 6:30am, and

NORDRHEIN-WESTFALEN

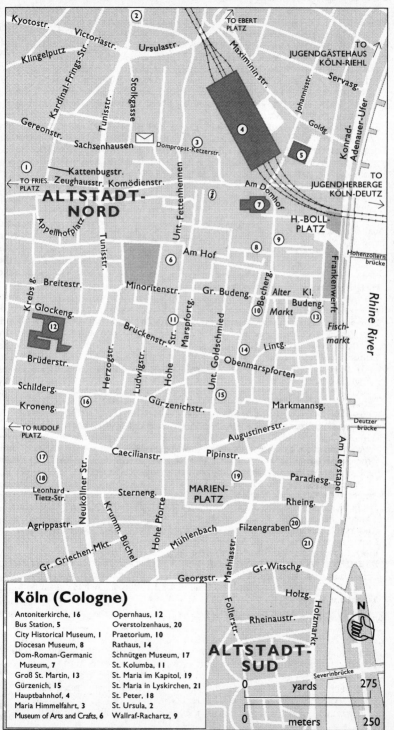

Köln (Cologne)

0   yards   275

0   meters   250

then every 15min. 7am-8pm, and every 30min. 8-11pm; it stops at Köln-Deutz 5min. later, then proceeds to the airport (15min.; DM8.20, children DM4.50).

Public Transportation: Any **VRS** *(Verkehrsverbund Rhein-Seig)* office has maps of the S- and U-Bahn lines throughout the Köln-Bonn area, as well as maps of city bus and streetcar lines. One is downstairs in the train station near the U-Bahn. Major convergence points include the *Hauptbahnhof,* Köln-Deutz, Appellhofpl., and Barbarossapl. Tickets priced by distance: 1-ride tickets DM1.55-13.50; day cards DM11-33; the DM11 card gets you anywhere in Köln. Determine the zone you want (A-D), as prices vary widely.

Ferries: Köln-Düsseldorfer (tel. 258 30 11; fax 208 82 38) sails to 40 Rhine landings between Köln and Mainz, including the cliffs and waterfalls at Königswinter (round-trip DM39.80). Connections to Mosel River ferries. Seniors half-price on Mon. and Fri. Students and children ages 4-12 half-price. Most trips (excluding the super-cool hydrofoils) are covered by Eurail and German rail passes.

Gondola: Rheinseilbahn (tel. 76 20 06), Europe's only river-crossing **gondola lift,** spans the Rhine north of the city, between the zoo on the west bank and the Rheinpark. DM6.50, kids DM3.50; round-trip DM9.50, DM5. Times change daily.

Taxi: Funkzentrale (tel. 28 82). Funk is as deep as an elephant's trunk.

Car Rental: Avis, Clemensstr. 29 (tel. 23 43 33); **Hertz,** Bismarckstr. 19-21 (tel. 51 50 84).

Bike Rental: Kölner Fahrradverliehservice, Sedanstr. 27 (tel. 72 36 27). From the station, walk along the shore towards Deutzer Bridge. Go right at the spiral staircase. DM4.50 per hr. DM21 per day. Open Mon.-Sat. 8am-8pm, Sun. 11am-8pm.

Mitfahrzentrale: Citynetz Mitfahrzentrale, Maximinstr. 2 (tel. 194 40), to the left of the train station, lists rides. Open Mon.-Fri. 9am-6pm, Sat. 9am-2pm.

Hitchhiking: For all destinations, hitchers say to take bus #132 to the last stop.

Bookstore: Mayerische Buchhandlungs, Hohestr. 68-82 (tel. 257 57 85), has a fine paperback selection, including English language books. Open Mon.-Wed. and Fri. 9:30am-6:30pm, Thurs. 9:30am-8:30pm, Sat. 9:30am-4pm.

Cultural Centers: Amerika Haus, Apostelnkloster 13-15 (tel. 20 90 10; fax 24 45 43), offers English cultural activities. English-language **library** open Tues.-Fri. 2-5pm. The **British Council,** Hahnenstr. 6 (tel. 20 64 40), on Neumarkt, offers the same services with a British accent and a better Monty Python collection. Open Mon.-Wed. and Fri. 1-5pm, Thurs. 1-7pm (closed for 6 weeks in July and Aug.).

AIDS-Hilfe: Beethovenstr. 1 (tel. 194 11). **Hotline,** tel: 20 20 30.

Laundry: Öko-Express, Neue Weyerstr. 1, is ökey-dökey. Wash DM6. Dry DM1 per 10min. Soap included. Open Mon.-Sat. 6am-11pm. Also available at Zülpicher Wall 2 and at the Köln-Deutz hostel (same times and prices).

Women's Resources: The municipal **Frauenamt,** Markmansgasse 7 (tel. 221 64 82), fields questions on cultural opportunities and services. Open Mon.-Thurs. 8:30am-1pm and 2-4pm, Fri. 8:30am-12:30pm, but it's best to call for an appointment. **Women's crisis hotline,** tel. 420 16 20.

Pharmacy: Dom Apotheke, Komodienstr. 5 (tel. 257 67 54), near the station. Their *Pharmacie-Internationale* advises in English, and has a list of other after-hours pharmacies posted outside. Open Mon.-Fri. 8am-6:30pm, Sat. 8:30am-4pm.

Emergency: Police, tel. 110. **Ambulance,** tel. 112.

Internet Access: In **Jam-Store** (see **Nightlife,** p. 324).

Post Office: Main office, WDR Arkaden, 50667 Köln. From the *Dom* exits of the train station, head down Breitestr. and then An den Ruhr. Open Mon.-Fri. 8am-6pm, Sat. 8am-6pm, Sun. 8am-1pm. Limited service Mon.-Fri. 6-8pm, Sun. 1-6pm.

Telephone Code: 0221.

ACCOMMODATIONS AND CAMPING

The brisk convention and tour business in Köln produces a wealth of rooms; the trick is pinning one down. Hotels fill up (and prices set sail) in the spring and fall when trade winds blow conventioneers into town. Summer is high season for Köln's two hostels, both of which brim to the beams from June to September. The main hotel haven, on the less interesting side of the *Bahnhof,* centers around Brandenburgerstr. The **Mitwohnzentrale,** An der Bottmühle 16 (tel. 32 70 84), is an alternative matching service for longer stays (open Mon.-Thurs. 8:30am-1pm and 2-4pm,

Fri. 8:30am-12:30pm). Scrounging for a last minute room during *Karneval* is futile—most people book a year or more in advance for the festivities. If all else fails, schlepp to Bonn. In general, call a few weeks to a few months ahead of time, if possible, because that's exactly what conventioneers will be doing. Also calculate the time and transportation cost if you stay in Bonn. A roundtrip generally consumes 1½-3 hours and DM8-15.

Jugendherberge Köln-Deutz (HI), Siegesstr. 5a (tel. 81 47 11; fax 88 44 25), just over the Hohenzollern Bridge. From the main exit of the train station, walk down Neuhöfferstr., the first street to the left of the mirrored building, and take the first right; the hostel is tucked behind the courtyard with big trees (2min.). Or S-Bahn #6, 11, or 12: "Köln-Deutz" (1 stop). Cramped rooms and wimpy showers, but a good location, with two pinball machines and free access to washing machines (soap DM1). The 374 beds fill quickly and the staff is overworked. Best check-in is 6-9am. Later is riskier, but reception open again 12:30pm-12:30am. Curfew 12:30am. DM27, over 26 DM32. Breakfast buffet DM8. Sheets included.

Jugendgästehaus Köln-Riehl (HI), An der Schanz 14 (tel. 76 70 81; fax 76 15 55), on the Rhine north of the zoo. U-Bahn #16 or 18 (direction: "Ebertpl./Mülheim"): "Boltensternstr.," or walk along the Rhine on Konrad-Adenauer-Uferstr. until it becomes Niederländer-Ufer and finally An der Schanz (40min.). Huge common areas, with plush sofas, 4-6 bed rooms, and lockers big enough to hide in. Reception open 24hr. No curfew. DM37. Breakfast and sheets included. The **Köln-Treff Café** sells beer, baguettes, and fries (open 8pm-12:30am).

Hotel Im Kupferkessel, Probsteigasse 6 (tel. 13 53 38; fax 12 51 21). From the station bear right; follow the street as it changes from Dompropost-Ketzer-Str. to An den Dominikern to Unter Sachsenhausen to Gereonstr. and on to become Christophstr., then turn right on Probsteigasse. Newly renovated building with sharp-looking rooms. Reception open 7am-9pm, or call. Singles from DM44, with bath phone, and TV DM78; doubles with all the goodies DM125. Breakfast included.

Jansen Pension, Richard-Wagner-Str. 18 (tel. 25 18 75). U-Bahn #1, 2, 6, 15, or 19: "Rudolfpl." and head west out of the underground (2-3 blocks). Only 18 rooms with few amenities (no breakfast), but a few as low as DM40 in a good location. Reception open for reservations 9am-noon.

Hotel Heinzelmännchen, Köln-Riehl, Hohe Pforte 5-7 (tel. 21 12 17; fax 21 57 12). Bus #132 (direction: "der Frankenstr."): "Waidmarkt," or walk down the Hohestr. shopping zone until it becomes Hohe Pforte. Bright hallways and firm mattresses. Reception open 10:30pm. Singles DM62, with bath DM70; doubles DM95, with bath DM110; triples DM135. Less for stays over 2 days. Breakfast included.

Hotel Hubertus Hof, Mühlenbach 30 (tel. 21 73 86; fax 21 55 89). Follow directions to Hohe Pforte, then left onto Mühlenbach. Monster-size rooms and fuzzy carpets. Showers and toilets are off the hall. Reception open 7am-9pm. Singles DM60; doubles DM80-85. Breakfast included.

Hotel Berg, Brandenburgerstr. 6 (tel. 12 11 24; fax 139 00 11). Bear left onto Johannisstr. from the back exit of the train station and take the third left onto Brandenburgerstr. A standout for its well-kept rooms and down-home breakfast room. Reception open 24hr. Singles start at DM52, with shower DM90; doubles DM90, with shower DM160. Breakfast included. AmEx, Diners, MC, Visa.

Am Rathaus, Burgstr. 6 (tel. 257 76 24; 258 28 29). Right outside the *Dom,* this small hotel has 9 rooms in the DM50-65 range, but virtually nothing else. Still, price and location are hard to beat. Reception open 24hr.

Das kleine Stapelhäuschen, Fischmarkt 1-3 (tel. 257 78 62; fax 257 42 32). Three nifty houses with a great view of the Rhine. Classic oak furniture and color-coordinated sheets. For huge medieval oaken mill wheels suspended above your bed, ask for the *historisches Turmzimmer* (DM220). Singles DM70-80, with shower DM102, with bath DM110; doubles DM105, with shower DM165, with bath DM185. Breakfast buffet included. AmEx, Eurocard, Visa.

Camping: Campingplatz Poll, Weidenweg (tel. 83 19 66), on the Rhine, southeast of the *Altstadt.* U-Bahn #16: "Marienburg" and cross the Roddenkirchener Bridge. Reception open 8am-noon and 3-10pm (later in the summer). Person DM6, tent DM5, car DM5.

FOOD

Small cafes packed by students and cheap restaurants offering quick meals line **Zülpicherstraße** all the way to the university complex. U-Bahn #12, 14, 16, or 18: "Neumarkt," then U-Bahn #7 or 9: "Zülpicherpl." Mid-priced restaurants with a fine selection of ethnic cuisine are concentrated around the perimeter of the *Altstadt,* particularly from Hohenzollernring to Hohenstaufenring. For glitzy cafes, the city's wealthy patrons head to **Neumarkt.** Don't pass through Köln without sampling the city's eponymous and extraordinarily smooth **Kölsch beer,** served in little glasses (0.2L—Munich this is not). Local brews of the delightful stuff include *Sion, Küppers, Früh,* and the devout *Dom.* Köln offers hungry visitors the *Rievekoochen* ("potato pancakes"), a slab of fried potato dunked in *Apfelmuß* (apple sauce). A number of authentic German-style places, generally well-priced, surround the Dompl. The most interesting area for inexpensive eats is the Turkish district on Weidengasse. An open-air **Markt** on Wilhelmspl. takes over the northern Nippes neighborhood to offer farm-fresh joys (open Mon.-Sat. 7-11:30am). **Deutsche Supermarkt,** Hohenzollernring 20 (tel. 25 47 74), a good grocery store, is open Mon.-Fri. 8am-8pm, Sat.-Sun. 9am-4pm.

Café Rendezvous, Heinsberg 11a (tel. 23 34 98), at the corner of Heinsberg and Zülpicherstr. As Marilyn Monroe and Clark Gable look blissfully on, let pizzas and pastas be intimate with your stomach (all under DM10). Breakfast spreads served all day. Open Sun.-Thurs. 8am-1am, Fri.-Sat. 8am-3am.

Schlotzky's Deli (tel. 920 13 20), at the corner of Hohenzollern Ring and Edro Palmstr. It's rather difficult to get a decent pastrami sandwich in Germany, but this burgeoning chain has all the classics, including a large vegetarian selection (DM6.50-9.50). Open Mon.-Thurs. and Sun. 11am-1am, Fri.-Sat. 11am-3am.

Café Waschsalon, Friesenstr. 80 (tel. 13 33 78), is filled with washers; turn on the spin cycle in your head with their fine assortment of drinks. Breakfast (DM6.50 and up) served until 4pm. No dryers—let the balmy breezes dry you instead. Open Mon.-Thurs. 8am-1am, Fri. 8am-3am, Sat. 10am-3am, Sun. 10am-1am.

Momotaro, Benëssisstr. 56 (tel. 257 14 32), at Ehrenstr. and Rudolfpl. An excellent Japanese restaurant without the financial bite. Sushi specials start at DM24 (lower during lunch) and more terrestrial fare runs DM12-15. Cozy surroundings and a friendly sushi chef. Open Mon.-Sat. noon-3pm and 6-10pm.

Prager Frühling, Bonnerstr. 335 (tel. 340 53 95). Despite the name (Prague Spring), this place has little to do with the Cold War and a lot to do with quality Bohemian fare, from gulash to baked *Nudeln,* for reasonable prices (DM15 and up). Open Sun.-Wed. and Fri. noon-3pm and 6-11pm, Sat. 6-11pm.

Brauhaus Früh am Dom, Am Hof 12-14 (tel. 258 03 97). This *echtes* establishment arguably offers the best *Kölsch* in town and an excellent place to eat. Enjoy a number of Kölner and German specialties (*Schnitzel, Brats, Kartoffeln,* it's all here) while basking in the warm glow of a lit *Dom* and "lit" Germans in the outdoor beer garden. Most dishes DM9-22. Open daily 8am-midnight (later for drinks).

SIGHTS

The Dom

When sightseeing in Köln, it's impossible to save the best for last. Most train stations offer only drunks, beggars, and transients, but visitors exiting Köln's *Bahnhof* are immediately treated to the beauty, power, and sorrow that emanate from the colossal **Dom,** Germany's greatest cathedral. Dedicated to St. Peter and St. Mary, visually overwhelming in intricacy and scale, the edifice took six centuries to build before reaching completion in 1880. Moreover, Köln's *Dom* is a pure example of High Gothic style, the largest of its kind in the world. For 500 years, the giant wooden crane, now kept inside, was as much Köln's trademark as the two massive towers. The stunning stained glass windows—enough to cover the floor twice—cast a harlequin display of colored light over the interior. Moving toward the front, the section to the right of the center altar bears the **Dombild triptych,** a masterful painting and gilded altarpiece from the 15th-century Kölner School; the enormous sculpture shining brilliantly in the dim light is the **Shrine of the Magi,** a reliquary of the Three Kings in blinding gold, brought to the city in 1164. The Three Kings are the town's holy patrons; they stand behind the altar in a magnificent 1531 woodcut of the town by Anton Woensam, and their three crowns grace Köln's official heraldic shield. Tapestries of Rubens' *Triumph of the Eucharist* line the central nave. While in the *Dom,* look for the 976 **Gero Crucifix,** the oldest intact sculpture of **Christus patiens** (depicting Christ during crucifixion with closed eyes) in the world. (Cathedral open daily 6am-7pm. Tours in German Mon.-Sat. 10 and 11am, 2 and 3pm, Sun. 2 and 3pm. Free. English tours Sun.-Fri. 2pm, Sat. 10:30am; for info call 52 19 77; DM6, children DM4. Free organ concerts mid-June to Sept. Tues. 8pm.)

Five hundred and nine steps and 15 minutes are all it takes to top the **Südturm** (south tower), and peer down at the river below. Catch your breath at the *Glockenstube* (400 steps up), a chamber for the tower's nine bells. Four of the *Glocken* date from the Middle Ages, but the 19th-century upstart known affectionately as **Der große Peter** (at 24 tons, the world's heaviest swinging bell) rings loudest. Hailed as "Germany's bell on the Rhine," it bears an engraved call for national unity. (Tower open May-Sept. 9am-6pm; March-April and Oct. 9am-5pm; Nov.-Feb. 9am-4pm; DM3, students DM1.50.) The **Domschatzkammer** in a corner of the cathedral holds the requisite clerical artwork and reliquaries: thorn, cross, and nail bits as well as pieces of 18 saints. (Open April-Oct. Mon.-Sat. 9am-5pm, Sun 12:30-5pm; Nov.-March Mon.-Sat. 9am-4pm, Sun. 1-4pm; DM3, under 18 and students DM1.50.) Find more ecclesiastical favors in the **Diözesan Museum,** Roncallipl. 2, just outside the south portal in the red building (open Fri.-Wed. 10am-5pm; free).

The allure of the cathedral illuminated from dusk 'til midnight is irresistible, drawing natives and tourists alike to the expansive **Domvorplatz** for a daily carnival of relaxation, art, and activism. Since time and acid rain have corroded much of the *Dom's* original detail, every piece is gradually being reproduced and replaced with new, treated stone. To expedite this task, you can play the *"Dom* lottery" at posts around the plaza and save a statue's fingernail (DM1-2).

Central City

In the shadow of the cathedral, the **Hohenzollern Brücke** crosses the Rhine. The majestic bridge empties out onto a promenade guarded by equestrian statues of the imperial family. A monumental flight of stairs leads to the **Heinrich Böll Cultural Center** (see p. 323), a piece of modern architecture that actually complements the *Dom.* Farther on, the squares and crooked streets of the old **Fischmarkt** district open onto paths along the Rhine; the cafe patios give way to a wide expanse of grass along the river, perfect for a picnic serenaded by musicians.

The **Rathaus** (Town Hall), partially bombed in World War II, has been reconstructed in its original mongrel style. The Gothic **tower** stands guard over Baroque cherubs flying around an ornate 1570 Renaissance arcade called the *loggia,* the only section to survive the war. The tower is adorned with a diverse array of historical and cultural figures; Marx and Rubens loom above rows of popes and emperors. On the *Rathaus* facade, a **Glockenspiel** offers a titillatingly tintinnabulary experience daily at noon and 5pm (open Mon.-Thurs. 7:30am-4:45pm, Fri. 7:30am-2pm; tours Wed. at 3pm). Classical historians and *Ben Hur* fans will be more impressed by the **Römisches Praetorium und Kanal,** the excavated ruins of the former Roman military headquarters from the province of Niedergermania (Lower Germany). To get there from the *Rathaus* porch, take a right towards the swarm of hotels and then a left onto Kleinen Budengasse. Looking like an abandoned set from a gladiator movie, the museum displays the remains of various Roman gods and a befuddling array of rocks left by the city's early inhabitants (open Tues.-Fri. 10am-4pm, Sat.-Sun. 11am-4pm; DM3, students DM1.50). The glass pyramid visible to your left as you exit the *Rathaus* shelters the **Mikwe Judenbad,** a 12th-century Jewish ritual bath that burrows 15m down to groundwater. Medieval bathers generally went in naked, but you'll need at least a passport (carry it everywhere!) to obtain a key from the *Rathaus* (open Mon.-Thurs. 8am-4pm, Fri.-Sat. 8am-2pm; free).

Goethe, the original 18th-century *grenouille*, noted "how grateful the women are for the fragrance of Eau de Köln." This magic water, once prescribed as a drinkable curative, made the town (or the oft-mimicked export) a household name. Be sure your tourist bottle says *"Echt kölnisch Wasser"* (real Köln water) if you're after the authentic article; or look for the world-renowned "4711" label. Its name comes from the Mühlens family house, labeled **House #4711** by the Napoleonic system that abolished street names. It has now been converted into a perfect boutique, with a small fountain continually dispensing the famous scented water. Visit regularly and you'll be torn apart by worshipful throngs. The house is on Glockengasse, at the intersection with Tunisstr.; from Hohestr., turn right on Brückenstr., which becomes Glockengasse. The house **Glockenspiel** chimes hourly from 9am to 10pm to the tunes of old German songs (open Mon.-Fri. 9am-6:30pm, Sat. 9am-2pm).

The **Rheinseilbahn** (gondola; see p. 318) touts a terminus near Köln-Riehl's **zoo** (open daily 9am-6pm; in winter 9am-5pm), **aquarium** (open daily 9:30am-6pm), and **botanical garden** (open daily 8am-dusk). U-Bahn #16 or 18: "Zoo/Flora." (Combined admission DM15, students DM8.50, children DM7.50. Sorry Lassie, you can't come.) Köln-Bayenthal, south of the city center, hosts the **Historische Braustätte der Küppers-Kölsch-Brauerei,** Alteburgerstr. 157, the brewery where the refined *Küppers* beer is made as it has been for 100 years; bus #132: "Bonntor" (open Sat. 11am-4pm).

Churches

Köln's success in building awe-inspiring churches began hundreds of years before the idea for the *Dom* was even conceived. The Romanesque period from the 10th to mid-13th century saw the construction of 12 churches roughly in the shape of a semi-circle around the *Altstadt*, using the holy bones of the saints to protect the city. The churches attest to the sacred glory and tremendous wealth of what was, at the time, the most important city north of the Alps. The city's piety even received poetic embodiment in a Samuel Taylor Coleridge poem: "In Köln, a town of monks and bones/ And pavements fanged with murderous stones/ And rags, and hags, and hideous wenches/ I counted two-and-seventy stenches…" Probably the perfume.

One of the first medieval structures to use the unique decagon layout, **St. Gereon** (tel. 13 49 22) houses a floor mosaic of David hacking off Goliath's head (open Mon.-Sat. 9am-noon and 1:30-6pm, Sun. 1:30-6pm). Along with the majestic *Dom,* **Groß St. Martin** (tel. 257 79 24) defines the legendary Rhine panorama of Köln. The church was completely rebuilt in 1963 after its total destruction in World War II. Crypts downstairs house an esoteric collection of stones and diagrams (open Mon.-Sat. 11am-6pm, Sun. 2-4pm; church free; crypt DM1, students and children DM0.50). Visitors to the **St. Maria im Kapitol** (tel. 21 46 15) are treated to amazingly ornate carved wooden panels detailing the life of Christ (open daily 9:30am-6pm). On the portal behind **St. Cäecilian** (tel. 221 23 10) stands "Death"—the masterpiece of a professional sprayer, not drunken vandals (open Tues.-Fri. 10am-4pm, Sat.-Sun. 11am-4pm).

The **St. Ursula** church (tel. 13 34 00), north of the *Dom*, commemorates Ursula's attempts to maintain celibacy despite her betrothal. She and 11 virgins under her tutelage were mistaken for Roman legionnaires and burnt at sea. The Latin record of the tale indicated "11M," meaning 11 martyrs, but was later misread as 11 *thousand* virgins. Over 700 human skulls and innumerable reliquaries line the walls of the **Goldene Kammer.** (Church and *Goldene Kammer* open Mon. 9am-noon and 1-5pm, Wed.-Sat. 9:30am-noon and 1-5pm. Chamber DM2, children DM1.)

Albeit of modest fame, churches of various styles and times are scattered throughout Köln. **St. Peter's** church, a tiny construction by St. Cäecilien (entrance on Leonard-Tietz-Str.), provides a rare opportunity to see a masterwork in its original position. Rubens's **The Crucifixion of St. Peter,** above the main altar, beautifully illuminates the tiny church (open Tues.-Sun. 11am-6pm). Behind the *Rathaus,* inside the overgrown ruins of the bombed **Alt St. Alban** church, parents mourn the lost children of war in a statue created by Käthe Kollwitz.

MUSEUMS

Köln's cultural, religious and economic significance in Europe stocks this rich city's museums with a vast and impressive array of holdings. The main museums are free with the **Köln Bonbon** (see p. 316). Many smaller, more specialized "museums" stretch the definition of the word to its limit. Look around before you plunk down DM2; some museums might be gems, while other offer nothing more than a peek in someone's junk drawer. 1998 is also the **Gothic Year in Köln** celebrating the cathedral's foundation 750 years ago. Look for special exhibits detailing sights and collections from the middle ages.

Near the Cathedral

Römische-Germanisches Museum, Roncallipl. 4 (tel. 221 44 38), built over the ruins of a Roman villa. The displays include the world-famous Dionysus Mosaic, the tomb of Publicus, an intimidating six-breasted sphinx, and some naughty candleholders. DM7, students and kids DM4. Call about tours (usually Sun. 11:30am). Open Tues.-Wed. and Fri. 10am-5pm, Thurs. 10am-8pm, Sat.-Sun. 11am-5pm.

Heinrich-Böll-Platz, Bischofsgartenstr. 1, behind the Römische-Germanisches Museum (tel. 221 48 02). This unusual building, designed to maximize the natural lighting, houses three complementary collections. The **Wallraf-Richartz Museum** (tel. 221 23 72) features crackly masterpieces from the 13th to the 19th century, from the Italian Renaissance to the Flemish and Dutch masters and up to Renoir and Manet. The **Museum Ludwig** (tel. 221 23 70) travels from Impressionism through Picasso, Dalí, and Roy Lichtenstein, to art where the glue and paint have yet to dry. The **Agfa Foto-Historama** (tel. 221 24 11) chronicles chemical art of the last 150 years, including a rotating display of Man Ray's works. Comprehensive admission DM10, students DM5. A dazzling array of tours. Free with the *Bonbon.* All open Tues. 10am-8pm, Wed.-Fri. 10am-6pm, Sat.-Sun.11am-6pm. Tours for Wallraf and Ludwig Wed. 4:30pm, Sat.-Sun. 11:30am.

Museum für Andgewandte Kunst (Museum of Applied Art), An der Rechtschule (tel. 221 67 14), west of the *Dom* across Wallrafpl. A giant arts and crafts fair spanning seven centuries with a fabulous 20th-century design display but no tie-dye stand. Lots of English captions. Tours Tues. 6:30pm, Sun. 11:30am. DM5, students and children DM2.50. Free with *Bonbon.* Open Tues. and Thurs.-Fri. 11am-5pm, Wed. 11am-8pm, Sat.-Sun. noon-5pm.

Elsewhere in Köln

Das Museum (Imhoff-Stollwerk Museum), Rheinauhafen 1a (tel. 931 88 80), near the Severins bridge. Better than Willy Wonka's Chocolate Factory. Salivate at every step of chocolate production from the rainforests to the gold fountain that spurts streams of silky, heavenly, creamy… As you view the provocative photos, resist the urge to slobber uncontrollably on yourself. Free petite samples. Exhibits in German. Tours (DM3) Sat. at 2 and 4pm, Sun. at 11:30am, 2, and 4pm; DM10, students, seniors, and children DM5. Open Mon.-Fri. 10am-6pm (last entry 5pm), Sat.-Sun. 11am-7pm (last entry 6pm).

NS-Dokumentations-Zentrum, Am Appellhofpl. 23/25 (tel. 43 40). From the side of the Stadtmuseum, follow the angel's wing, which points down Appellhofpl. Once a citadel for perpetrators of Nazi terror, the museum now houses a shrine to its victims and 1200 wall inscriptions by political prisoners. Tours first Sat. of each month at 2pm. Open Tues.-Fri. 10am-4pm, Sat.-Sun. 11am-4pm. Free.

Beatles Museum, Heinsbergstr. 13 (tel. 21 25 98), off Zülpicherstr. U-Bahn #12, 16, or 18: "Barbarossapl." Crammed with Fab Four nostalgia. With new 60s-style cafe, it's bigger—bigger than Jesus? Not in Köln (see **Sights:** the *Dom*, p. 320). Free coffee and souvenir sack with admission (DM5). Open Sept.-July Wed.-Sat. 10am-7pm.

Käthe Kollwitz Museum, Neumarkt 18-24 (tel. 227 23 63), in the Neumarkt-Passage. U-Bahn #9, 12, 14, 16, or 18: "Neumarkt." The world's largest collection of sketches, sculptures, and prints by the brilliant artist and activist. Her images chronicle the sadness of early 20th-century Berlin in stark black-and-white. Tours Sun. at 11am. DM5, students and children DM2. Open Tues.-Wed. and Fri.-Sun. 10am-5pm, Thurs. 10am-8pm.

Schnütgen Museum, Cäecilienstr. 29 (tel. 221 36 20), in St. Cecilia Church. U-Bahn: "Neumarkt." Ecclesiastical art from the Middle Ages to the Baroque, notably tapestry and priestly fashion displays. Tours Sun. at 11am, Wed. at 2:30pm. DM5, students DM2.50. Free with *Bonbon.* Open Tues.-Fri. 10am-4pm, Sat.-Sun. 11am-4pm.

ENTERTAINMENT

Köln explodes in celebration during **Karneval,** a week-long pre-Lenten festival. Celebrated in the hedonistic spirit of the city's Roman past, *Karneval* is made up of fifty major and minor neighborhood processions in the weeks before Ash Wednesday. **Weiberfastnacht,** on the Thursday before Ash Wednesday (Feb. 19 in 1998), is the first major to-do; the mayor mounts the platform at Alter Markt and abdicates leadership of the city to a trio of fools. For the rest of the day, the city's *Weiber* (an archaic and not too politically correct term for women) are given rule of the roost. In the afternoon, the first of the big parades begins at Severinstor. The weekend builds up to the out-of-control, dancing-in-the-streets parade on **Rosenmontag,** the last Monday before Lent (Feb. 23, 1998). Everyone's in costume and gets and gives a couple dozen *Bützchen* (Kölsch dialect for a kiss on a stranger's cheek). Arrive early, get a map of the route, and don't stand anywhere near the station or cathedral—you'll be pulverized by the lollapaloozian crowds. While most revelers nurse their hangovers on Shrove Tuesday, pubs and restaurants set fire to the straw scarecrows hanging out of their windows. For more information on the festival and tickets to events, inquire at the **Festkomitee des Kölner Karnevals,** Antwerpenerstr. 55 (tel. 57 40 00). Also pick up the *Köln, Karneval* booklet at the tourist office (available in December).

Köln's traditional entertainment offers fierce competition, with over 30 theaters including the **Oper der Stadt Köln** (*Abendkasse* (evening box office) tel. 221 82 48) and the **Kölner Schauspielhaus** (*Abendkasse* tel. 221 82 52), near Schildergasse on Offenbachpl. For more on Köln's theaters, check the *Monatsvorschau.* The **Cinemanthek** (tel. 257 59 21) entrance is on the ground floor of the three-museum building in Heinrich-Böll-Platz; current movies show almost daily, with most films in the original English. The **Metropolitan,** Ebertpl., shows movies exclusively in English and offers a selection of gay and lesbian pieces. The 200-seat **Philharmonic Hall** (tel. 28 01) is located in the basement of the same building; check the tourist office for info. The brand new 3000-seat **Cinedom** (tel. 95 19 51 95 98), with 13 screens, is part of the **Media Park.** A converted train station, it opened its doors in 1992. From April to October, catch the **craft market** the last weekend of every month in the *Altstadt,* around Groß St. Martin church.

NIGHTLIFE

Celebrating life with lavish festivities has long been a tradition in Köln. Roman mosaics dating back to 3AD record the wild excesses of the city's early residents. But instead of grape-feeding and fig-wearing, modern life in Köln now focuses on house music and a more sophisticated bump-and-grind. Remember that even though Köln does everything, including nightlife, on a large scale, the closer you venture to the Rhine and the *Dom,* the more that scale applies directly to your wallet. The nightly jazz at **Papa Joe's Jazzlokal,** Buttermarkt 37 (tel. 21 79 50), near Fischmarkt and the Rhine, is as good as jazz gets in these parts, although Coltrane fans should beware: German "jazz" is ultra-traditional, bordering on ragtime (open Mon.-Sat. 7pm-2am, Sun. 3:30pm-1am; jazz from 8:30pm). For diehards, "Four o'clock Jazz" starts every Sunday at 4pm and goes for eight hours.

Students congregate in the **Quartier Lateng**, a.k.a. the *Bermuda Dreieck* (triangle). The area is bounded by Zülpicherstr., Zülpicherpl., Roonstr. and Luxemburgstr. The center of gay nightlife runs up **Matthiasstraße** to Mühlenbach, Hohe Pforte, Marienpl., and up to Heumarkt in the area by the Deutzer Brücke. Radiating westward from Friesenpl., the **Belgisches Viertel** is spiced with slightly more sophisticated and expensive bars and cafes.

The worshippers of Dionysus boozed themselves into stupors here, and the tradition of getting plastered is still highly respected in Köln. At the various *Brauhäuser,* where the original *Kölsch* is brewed and served in-house, the *Köbes* will bring one glass after another until you fall under the table unless you place your coaster over your glass. Saying *"Ich bin nicht zum Spaß hier"* ("I'm not here to fool around") informs the *Köbes* of your serious intentions; just watch that the lines on your coaster correspond to the number of beers you actually drank—it's said they might count on the fact that you won't be able to count.

Museum, Zülpicherpl. 9 (tel. 23 20 98). No temple of science is complete without a two-story **dinosaur** looking out over blood alcohol experiments. Order your own 10 liter mini keg of *Kölsch*. RRRRAWR! Popular Köln University field trip. Open Sun.-Thurs. 6pm-1am, Fri.-Sat. 6pm-3am.

MTC, Zülpicherstr. 10 (tel. 240 41 88). A veritable smörgasbord of olfactory and ol' factory fun. The musical offerings are schizophrenic, alternating between techno/house, punk/grunge, live concerts, and recorded bar music. Cover, including one drink, DM6. Open Mon.-Thurs. and Sun. 9pm-2am, Fri.-Sat. 9pm-3am.

Café Magnus, Zülpicherstr. 48 (tel. 24 16 69). Brimming with students drinking and gettin' down to booty jams. Open daily 9am-3am.

The Corkonian, Alter Markt 51 (tel. 257 69 31), is an authentic Irish corner in Köln—as Irish as it gets beyond County Cork. Trade your lager for some dark beer, topped with a clover. Open Sun.-Thurs. noon-1am, Fri.-Sat. noon-3am.

Päffgen Brauhaus, Friesenstr. 64-66 (tel. 13 54 61). A local favorite since 1883. Legendary *Kölsch* is brewed on the premises and consumed in cavernous halls or in the *Biergarten* (0.2L shot DM2.20). Follow *Brauhaus* rules as enumerated above. Open 10am-midnight. Kitchen open 11am-11pm.

Jam-Store, Breitestr. 116 (tel. 257 30 79; email info@jamstore.de; http://jamstore.de). By day a pacific cafe with **Internet access,** the place turns it up a notch at night as DJs spin house in a multi-media circus. Cafe open Mon.-Thurs. 10am-midnight, Fri.-Sat. 10am-1am. 30min. connection DM5.

42 D.P. ("Don't Panik"), Hohenstaufenring 25-27 (tel. 24 79 71). Popular, smoky, and very *noir.* All flavors of techno. For novices who can't distinguish between goth and ambient, "The Basics of Techno" is offered Wed. (cover DM10). Cover on other nights varies, often DM15 Fri.-Sat. Open Wed.-Sun. 11pm-4:30am.

Star-Treff, Alte Wallgasse (tel. 25 50 63), at the corner of Ehrenstr. Not quite the hangout for the crew of the *Enterprise,* the pink building contains a transvestite cabaret. Excellent performances by Tina Turner and Diana Ross. DM35 buys you a ticket (call ahead) to a night you'll never forget. Showtimes Wed., Thurs., and Sun. 8pm, Fri.-Sat. 7pm and 10:10pm. Call to drag out more information.

Café Stövchen, Ursula Kloster 4-6 (tel. 13 17 12), in the shadow of the St. Ursula church. Sink into a swank couch, beer in hand, and dish out a schoolin' to some suckas at Monopoly. Local flavor. Open Mon.-Fri. 11am-1am, Sun. 10am-1am.

Joe Champs, Hohenzollernring 1-3 (tel 257 61 65; fax 258 12 00). A two story sports bar, serving huge burgers and motley cocktails. Shows major US sporting events—the Superbowl, World Series, NBA finals, and more. Open Sun.-Thurs. noon-1am, Fri.-Sat. noon-3pm.

Broadway, Ehrenstr. 11 (tel. 25 52 14). The hip joint for local artists and painters. To fit in, wear a black coat and a red scarf. Open daily 10am-1am.

Gloria, Apostelnstr. 11 (tel. 25 44 33). Crowded and popular gay and lesbian cafe offering theater, film, and dancing in a converted porn theater. Call for a schedule. Cover averages DM10. Cafe open Sun.-Thurs. 9am-1am, Fri.-Sat. 9am-3am.

■ Bonn

Derisively called the *"Hauptdorf"* (capital village) by Germans, Bonn has been the whipping boy of Germany for 50 years simply because it's not Berlin. Founded by the Romans, Bonn remained a non-entity for most of its 2000-year history before arriving in the limelight by chance. Konrad Adenauer, the Federal Republic's first chancellor, resided in the stumbling suburbs, and the ever-considerate occupying powers made Bonn the "provisional capital" of the Western Occupation Zone before they baptized it as the *Hauptstadt* (capital) of the fledgling Republic. The summer of 1991 brought headlines of "Chaos in Bonn" as Berlin fought for the right to reclaim the seat of government in a political catfight that cleaved every party from the CDU to the Greens. By the narrowest of margins, Berlin won; the *Bundestag* will pack up and move within the next few years, although the exact date changes frequently. Bonners have taken the loss well. Although Berliners joke that Bonn is "half the size of a Chicago cemetery and twice as dead," the sparkling streets of the *Altstadt* bustle with notable energy and eclecticism. The well respected university and excellent museums bolster a thriving cultural scene matched by few cities of similar size.

PRACTICAL INFORMATION

The **Bonncard,** available in the tourist office for DM12 per day, covers transportation costs after 9am (all day Sat.-Sun.) and admission to the city's museums.

Tourist Office: Münsterstr. 20 (tel. 77 34 66 or 19 44 33; fax 77 31 00), in a passageway near the train station in the pedestrian zone. Take the "Stadtmitte" exit from the station, walk 60m up Poststr. to Münsterstr., and turn left; the office is to the right. The staff will make same-day hotel reservations for a DM3-5 fee. They give out more info than you could shake a stick at. Inquire about the many tours, from the *"Heißluftballon"* (hot air balloon) to the "Political Bonn" tour (same thing, minus balloon). Open Mon.-Fri. 9am-6:30pm, Sat. 9am-5pm, Sun. 10am-2pm.

Budget Travel: STA Travel, Nassestr. 11, inside the Mensa building. Open Mon.-Fri. 10:30am-4pm.

Embassies and Consulates: The tourist office has a 140-page list. **Australia** Godesberger Allee 105-107 (tel. 810 30; fax 37 62 68). U-Bahn #16 or 63: "Max-Löbne." Open Mon.-Thurs. 8:30am-1pm and 2-5pm, Fri. 8:30am-1pm and 2-4:15 pm. **Canada** Godesberger Allee 119 (tel. 81 00 60; fax 37 65 25). Open Mon.-Fri. 8am-noon and 1-4pm. **Ireland** Godesberger Allee 119 (tel. 95 92 90; fax 37 35 00). Open Mon.-Fri. 9am-1pm and 2:30-5:30pm. **New Zealand** Bundeskanzlerpl. 2-10 (tel. 22 80 70; fax 22 16 87). U-Bahn #16 or 63: "Heussallee." Open Mon.-Thurs. 9am-1pm and 2-5:30pm, Fri. 9am-1pm and 2-4:30pm. **South Africa** Auf der Hostert 3 (tel. 820 10; fax 820 11 48). Open Mon.-Fri. 8am-4:30pm. **U.K.** Friedrich-Ebert-Allee 77 (tel. 916 70; fax 916 72 00). Open Mon.-Fri. 9am-5:30pm. **U.S.** Deichmanns Aue. 29 (tel. 33 91; fax 339 26 63). U-Bahn #16 or 63: "Rhineallee," then bus #613: "Deichmanns Aue." Open Mon.-Fri. 8:30am-5:30pm.

Flights: International departures from the **Köln-Bonn Flughafen.** Bus #670 runs there from the train station (5am-10pm, every 20min.; DM7.70, children DM3.90).

Public Transportation: Bonn is linked to Cologne and other riverside cities by the massive **VRS** (Verkehrsverbund Rhein-Sieg) S-Bahn, U-Bahn, and Bundesbahn network. Areas are divided into **Tarifzonen;** the farther you go, the more you pay. Single tickets (DM2-13.50), 4-ride tickets (DM7.60-49.60), and day tickets (DM11-33) are available at *Automaten* and designated vending stations. Open Mon.-Fri. 7am-8pm. With the *Minigruppenkarte* (DM9 per day), 5 people can ride Mon.-Fri. after 9am, and all day on weekends. Stop by the **Kundenzentrum** under the *Hauptbahnhof* for network maps and more information.

Taxi: Funkzentrale (tel. 55 55 55). The funk never grows old. Or?

Car Rental: Hertz, Avis, InterRent Europcar, and **Budget** have airport offices.

Bike Rental: Kurscheid, Römerstr. 4 (tel. 63 14 33), charges DM16 per day and offers a DM20 weekend special (Sat. morning-Sun. night). Cars rented here as well. ID required for both. Open Mon.-Sat. 7am-7pm, Sun. 9am-1pm and 5-7pm.

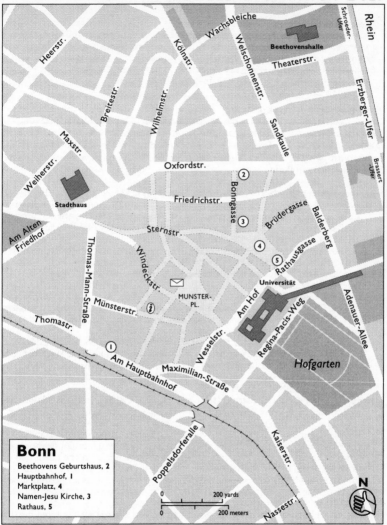

Bonn

Beethovens Geburtshaus, 2
Hauptbahnhof, 1
Marktplatz, 4
Namen-Jesu Kirche, 3
Rathaus, 5

Mitfahrzentrale: Herwarthstr. 11 (tel. 69 30 30), behind the *Bahnhof.* Open Mon.-Fri. 10am-6:30pm, Sat. 10am-2pm, Sun. for phone calls only 11am-2pm.

Bookstore: The mammoth **Bouvier,** Am Hof 28 (tel. 729 01 64), across from the University *Schloß,* has a wide range of foreign books on the top floor. **Concert tickets** sold. Open Mon.-Fri. 9:30am-8pm, Sat. 9:30am-4pm.

Gay and Lesbian Center: Schwul & Lesben Zentrum (tel. 63 00 39) is located in a Mobil Autoöle parking lot. For counseling call 194 46; gay assault hotline 192 28. From bus stop "Kunsthalle," cross the street and go towards the Kunst Forum. In its *Cafe "Z,"* Mon. is gay night, Tues. is lesbian night, and Wed. and Thurs. are mixed. Open Mon.-Tues. and Thurs. 8pm-midnight, Wed. 9pm-midnight.

Laundromat: Wasch Center, on the corner of Breitestr. and Kölnstr. Wash DM7, soap included. Dry DM1 per 10min. Open Mon.-Sat. 7am-11pm.

Women's Resources: The **Frauenberatungstelle,** Doretheenstr. 1 (tel. 65 95 00), near Wilhelmpl., will answer questions, provide help, and direct women to other agencies Mon. and Thurs. 9am-1pm, Wed. and Fri. 10am-noon.

Rape Crisis Line: tel. 63 55 24.

Pharmacy: Bahnhofs Apotheke dispenses the goods right next to the tourist office. Open Mon.-Wed. and Fri. 8am-7pm, Thurs. 8am-8pm, Sat. 9am-4pm.

Emergency: Police: tel. 110. **Fire:** tel. 112.

Post Office: Münsterpl. 17, 53111 Bonn. Big. Yellow. Different. Walk down Poststr. from the station. Open Mon.-Fri. 8am-8pm, Sat. 8am-4pm.

Telephone Code: 0228.

ACCOMMODATIONS AND CAMPING

National capitals attract transients, and Bonn has responded with a fine stock of hotels to take them in. Most hotel prices are suited to wealthy tax-subsidized politicians. With two *Jugendgästehäuser* but no *Jugendherberge,* even hosteling gets financially taxing in Bonn.

Jugendgästehaus Bonn-Venusberg (HI), Haager Weg 42 (tel. 28 99 70; fax 289 97 14), is far from the center of town. Bus #621 (direction: "Ippendorf Altenheim"): "Jugendherberge" (18min.). A sparkling, super-modern place in the suburbs; it even has glass doors that slide open automatically (*a la* your local supermarket). The hostel's "Bistro Come Together" serves up a smooth *Kölsch* beer (0.2L for DM1.60) nightly 8pm-12:30am. Reception open 9am-1am. Curfew 1am. DM37. Breakfast and sheets included. Laundry DM7.50. Wheelchair access.

Jugendgästehaus Bonn-Bad Godesburg (HI), Horionstr. 60 (tel. 31 75 16; fax 31 45 37), even farther from downtown. U-Bahn #16 or 63: "Rhein Allee" or the DB train: "Bonn-Bad Godesberg Bahnhof," then bus #615 (direction: "Stadtwald/Evange-lische Krankenhaus"): "Vennerstr."; look for the sign on the opposite side of the street. Neat, modern rooms and a suave staff. Reception open 8am-5pm and 8pm-1am. Curfew 1am. DM34.50. Breakfast and sheets included.

Hotel Mozart, Mozartstr. 1 (tel. 65 90 71; fax 65 90 75). From the south exit of the station, turn right onto Herwarthstr., left on Bachstr., then right on Mozartstr. It's around the corner from Beethovenpl. Matches unbeatable convenience with first class rooms in a pleasant, quiet area. Singles DM65-75, with bath DM110-135; doubles DM110, with bath DM195.

Hotel Bergmann, Kasernenstr. 13 (tel. 63 38 91; fax 63 50 57). From the station, follow Poststr., turn left at Münsterpl. onto Vivatgasse, then right on Kasernenstr.; after 10min. the hotel is on the left. Cozy, elegant rooms. *Very* pink bathrooms in the hall. Reception hours sporadic—call ahead. Singles DM60; doubles DM95.

Hotel Virneburg, Sandkaule 3a (tel. 63 63 66). U-Bahn #62, 64, or 66: "Bertha-von-Suttner-Platz" or walk up Poststr. and bear right on Acherstr. at the north end of Münsterpl. Turn left on Rathausgasse and left again onto Belderberg, which runs into Sandkaule. Statuettes pepper the hallways, while the rooms are spartan albeit convenient and comfortable. Singles DM35-45, with shower DM55-65; doubles DM65-70, with shower DM90. Breakfast included.

Hotel Haus Hofgarten, Fritz-Tillman-Str. 7 (tel. 22 34 82; fax 21 39 02). From the station, turn right onto Maximilianstr., continue on Kaiserstr., and then turn left on Fritz-Tillman-Str. Just like granny's house, but everyone gets 96 channels of cable TV. Singles DM75-135; doubles DM110-175. Breakfast included. Call ahead.

Camping: Campingplatz Genienaue, Im Frankenkeller 49 (tel. 34 49 49). U-Bahn #16 or 63: "Rhein Allee," then bus #613 (direction: Giselherstr.): "Gunterstr." Turn left on Guntherstr. for 120m and right on Frankenkeller for 300m until you reach the site. Rhine-side camping in the Mehlem suburb. Tents DM5-8; each sleeper DM8. Reception open 9am-noon and 3-10pm.

FOOD

The market on **Münsterplatz** teems with haggling vendors and determined customers trying to get the best meat, fruit, and vegetables at the lowest prices. At the end of the day voices rise and prices plummet (Mon.-Sat. 9am-6pm). Further from the *Altstadt,* along Max and Dorothenstr., ethnic restaurants sustain high quality at low cost.

University Mensa, Nassestr. 11, a 15min. walk from the train station along Kaiserstr. In Bonn's glory days it swung with cosmopolitan flair. Reagan would sip *Dom Perignon* out of Maggie Thatcher's stilleto heels, and Helmut Kohl would lead the crowd in a round of bawdy German drinking songs. Now, it's just another *Mensa*. Cheap, edible meals DM2-4. DM1 extra for non-students. Lunch served Mon.-Thurs. 11:30am-2:15pm, Fri. 11:30am-2pm, Sat. noon-1:45pm. Dinner served Mon.-Fri. 5:30-8pm. Open Sept. to mid-July.

Pizzeria la Piccola, Bonngasse 4 (tel. 63 78 16), only a few steps from the Beethovenhaus and Marktplatz. The insidious scent curls out and drags in the unsuspecting. Pizzas aplenty and large salads (DM10). Ubiquitous dark wood decor enlivened by hilarious waiters. Open daily 11am-1am. Visa, MC, Diners.

Cassius Garten, Maximilianstr. 28d, at the edge of the *Altstadt* facing the station, with a back entrance in the court of the tourist office. A futuristic veggie bar where zealous disciples of health consume salads, noodles, and bread in a stark, white-glossed atrium. My God, Jim, that was our own planet! 50 kinds of salad, 30 teas and juices, and a whole-grain bake shop. Pay DM2.58 per 100g and seat yourself at a booth. Open Mon.-Wed. and Fri. 9am-8pm, Thurs. 8am-9pm, Sat. 9am-4pm.

Café Blan, an Franziskanerstr. across from the *Uni*. Ultra-*ultra*-hip clientele and a trendy, colorful design scheme combine with a wide variety of coffees and light fare to form a surprisingly laid-back and amiable intellectual atmosphere. *Haus Musik* played in the evenings. Beer DM3.50-6, desserts DM5-8, light foods (snacks and breakfast cereals) under DM10. Open daily 9am-1am.

Brauhaus Bönnsch, Sterntorbrücke 4 (tel. 65 06 10), pours its own highly civilized *Bönnsch*, the smooth-as-butter illegitimate son of Köln's *Kölsch* (DM2.30 for 0.2L). For DM6 you can buy their beer glasses—contoured to your hand for easy imbibing. They serve *Bönnsche Flammkuchen* made from a 250-year-old Alsatian recipe (DM10-17). Open Mon.-Thurs. and Sun. 11am-1am, Fri.-Sat. 11am-3am.

SIGHTS

Bonn's old town center winds into a lively pedestrian zone puddled with historic niches. Piano students and teachers can indulge their fantasies at the **Beethoven Geburtshaus** (Bonn's biggest draw after the *Bundestag*), Bonngasse 20 (tel. 63 51 88), where busts and portraits, manuscripts, mementos, and musical instruments add spice to the collection; they even have the trumpets Beethoven stuck in his ears to improve his hearing. U-Bahn #62, 64, or 66: "Bertha-von-Suttner-Platz" or follow the signs through the pedestrian zone. (Open Mon.-Sat. 10am-5pm, Sun. 11am-4pm. Admission DM8, students DM4. Call ahead for English tours.) The symphonic ghost haunts Bonn annually during the **Beethoven Festival.** The first fête, organized by Franz Liszt in 1845, was a riot, with Liszt brawling with French nationalist Berlioz while King Ludwig's mistress Lola Montez spontaneously table-danced. Call the tourist office for information.

Farther down Bonngasse is the **Namen-Jesu Kirche.** The church suffers from an identity crisis, combining Romantic, Gothic, and Baroque elements. The primarily Gothic facade plays second fiddle to the pink marble Baroque altar complete with gilded starbursts. The market takes place in the shadow of the voluptuous pink **Rathaus**—reminiscent of an overdone birthday cake—presiding over the Marktplatz; in the similarly colorful 60s, de Gaulle, Kennedy, and Elizabeth II visited together for a photo-op. Though it is indeed a sight to behold, one might be better off beholding the **Münster basilika.** The cathedral holds three stories of arches within arches that finally yield a gorgeous gold-leaf mosaic; a 12th-century cloister laced with crossways and latticed passages branches off. Keep an eye out for the incongruous blue-red Expressionist windows. The church stands tall right on (surprise) Münsterpl. (cloister open daily 9:30am-5:30pm; *Münster* sleeps 7pm-7am).

The castles, palaces, and museums that lend the area its cultural wealth lie just outside the city center. Forty thousand students study within the **Kurfürstliches Schloß,** the huge 18th-century palace now serving as the center of Bonn's Friedrich-Wilhelms Universität. The *Schloß* is the gateway to the refreshing **Hofgarten** and **Stadtgarten,** forever filled with students and punks. To uncover Bonn's "other" palace, stroll down the Poppelsdorfer Allee to the 18th-century **Poppelsdorfer Schloß.** This castle touts a French facade and an Italian courtyard, plus beautifully manicured **Botanical Gardens.** (Gardens open Mon.-Fri. 9am-6pm, Sun. 9am-1pm; Oct.-April Mon.-Fri. 9am-4pm. Greenhouses open Mon.-Fri. 10:30am-noon and 2-4pm; Oct.-March Mon.-Fri. 10:30am-noon and 2-4pm. Free.)

No visit to Bonn is complete without the obligatory governmental romp. The vaguely *Bauhaus* **Bundestag,** Bundeshaus, Eingang V (tel. 16 21 52), has earned the coveted title of "Least Prepossessing Parliament Building" in the world. U-Bahn #16, 63, or 66: "Heussallee/Bundeshaus" or bus #610 from the main station: "Bundeshaus." Alas, you can't just stroll in and table a motion or exercise the ol' pocket veto; you must take a less than thrilling tour which begins on the hour at Hermann-Ehlers-Str. 29, opposite the Hochhaus. (Tours Mon.-Fri. 9am-4pm, Sat.-Sun. 10am-4pm; Jan.-mid-March Mon.-Fri. 9am-4pm. Bring your passport.) For those hungry for more functional buildings, the **Bundeshaus** (Germany's Parliament) is visible on Görresstr. from the bank of the Rhine. Notice how the postwar architectural mandate to turn this small city into a world-class capital has produced goofy results. A wacky example is the old **Post Ministry,** at Zweite Fahrgasse on the river. The Rhine-side face sports the interpretive relief *Tier-Symbole der Fünf Kontinente* (Animal Symbols of the 5 Continents), with a megalithic eagle (America), bull (Europe), elephant (Africa), kangaroo (Australia), and a big friendly wildcat for Asia. An elaborate joke, you think? No, this happens when you give people money and tell them to build a national capital.

On Adenauerallee, south of the city center, rest the **Villa Hammerschmidt,** home of the German chancellor, and **Palais Schaumburg,** home of the German president. The less majestic **Denkmal** (monument) was erected in honor of Konrad Adenauer, one of Germany's and Bonn's most prominent personas. Nicknamed *"der Alte"* (the old guy), the postwar chancellor was Bonn's guiding light, but the 3m hollow-cheeked bust at Adenauerallee 135-141 looks like a skull lifted from a pirate flag. Engraved into his cranium are allegorical figures—various animals, a pair of bound hands, and two French cathedrals. This is how Bonners commemorate their *heroes,* mind you. Don't get on their bad side.

MUSEUMS

While the parliamentary side of Bonn sight-seeing leaves something to be desired, the museums are superb. Bonn has enjoyed nearly 50 years of generous federal funding and much of the public wealth was channeled into the expansion of the town's museums. The **"Museum Mile"** begins at the **Museum Alexander Koenig.** To get there, take U-Bahn #16, 63, or 66. A **Bonncard** provides free admission to seven museums (see p. 326).

Museum Mile

Kunstmuseum Bonn, Friedrich-Ebert Allee 2 (tel. 77 62 60). U-Bahn #16, 63, or 66: "Heussallee." A superb selection of Expressionist and modern German art transplanted from the old city museum. So much Max Ernst that by the end of the day you will be Ernst. DM5, students DM3. Open Tues.-Sun. 10am-6pm.

Kunst-und Ausstellungshalle der BRD, Friedrich-Ebert Allee 4 (tel. 917 12 00), takes you to utopia. U-Bahn #16, 63, or 66: "Heussallee." The art here is so new you can smell the glue; they even have a media-art room. The 16 columns flanking the *Ausstellungshalle* represent the 16 *Bundesländer* of united Germany. DM8, students DM4. Open Tues.-Wed. 10am-9pm, Thurs.-Sun. 10am-7pm.

Museum Alexander Koenig, south of the city (tel. 912 22 11). U-Bahn #16, 63, or 66: "Museum Koenig." If taxidermy has a Louvre, this is it. People who dislike animals will take pleasure in the stuffed, sterilized, glass-encased exhibits. Snakes and lizards crawl in the basement. DM4, students DM2. Open Tues.-Fri. 9am-5pm, Sat. 9am-12:30pm, Sun. 9:30am-5pm.

Haus der Geschichte, 1 block from the Kunstmuseum Bonn (tel. 916 50). A brand new, futuristic museum dedicated to critical and "interactive" German history. Beautiful exhibits are highlighted by some antique VWs and a black enclosure with the scrolling names of Holocaust victims. Free. Open Tues.-Sun. 9am-7pm.

Elsewhere in Bonn

Frauenmuseum (tel. 69 13 44). The vast galleries glitter with interactive, modern art pieces by women. U-Bahn #61: "Rosental/Herrstr." (Herrstr.?) The 2nd floor covers medieval art. Peculiar pieces on the grassy roof and a Yoko Ono room provide the more thought-provoking works. Open Tues.-Wed and Fri.-Sat. 2-5pm, Thurs. 2-8pm, Sun. 11am-5pm.

Akademisches Kunstmuseum (tel. 72 77 38) on the far side of the *Hofgarten.* Lazy sculpture fans can forget about going abroad to see the masterpieces because they're all here, in the largest collection of plaster casts in Germany. Exhibits include Venus de Milo, the Colossus of Samos, and Laocöon. Better than the real thing. DM1, students free. Open Sun.-Wed. and Fri. 10am-1pm, Thurs. 10am-1pm and 4-6pm.

NIGHTLIFE

Bonn's bombastic and versatile nightlife forcefully debunks myths suggesting that Bonn is boring. Savvy students, joyful journalists, and vibrant visitors more than compensate for the city's conservative civil servants (70% of Bonn's population). Of Bonn's monthly glossies, **Schnüss** is unbeatable when it comes to "who, what, when, and where;" it is more complete than the free *Bonner Gästeführer* and *Szene Bonn.*

Bubbles, Bornheimerstr. 20-22. The most quirky club in Bonn, its themed evenings (different every night) range from bubble-gummy Britpop parties to gothic-industrial "funerals." Opens Tues. and Thurs. 11pm, Wed. 9pm, Fri.-Sat. 10:30pm, Sun. 7am and 9pm. Stays open late.

The Jazz Galerie, Oxfordstr. 24 (tel. 63 93 24), becomes a concert hub nearly every night. Cover for concerts DM10-20, for discos DM5. On concert nights opens at 8pm, but the show begins around 9:15pm. Open daily 9pm-3am.

Sharon, Oxfordstr. 20-21, is a soul discotheque for those who haven't quite had enough. "What's missin' we got it" is their slogan. If the only things missin' are strobe lights and a disco ball, then that's good advertising. 21 and over. Clean clothes required. Cover DM10. Soul and funk Fri.-Sat. 10pm-5am.

The Pantheon, Bundeskanzlerpl. (tel. 21 25 21). Even though it's dangerously close to the *Bundeshaus,* the clientele of this popular disco, which also hosts concerts, stand-up comedy, and art exhibits, tends to be younger, hipper, and more attractive than your average politician. Open Mon.-Sat. 8pm-3am. Cover DM10.

Maxim and Kleopatra Discotheque, Maxstr. 18-20 (tel. 65 77 98), is the budget traveler's option. Get a load of DJ Ben. Cover DM5. House, soul, funk, and dance groove on Fri. Soul, reggae, hip hop, and house on Sat. Open Fri.-Sat. 10pm-5am.

Rochehouen, Sterntorbrücke, next door to *Brauhaus Bönnsch,* is billed as *"Bonns Nacht Rock Cafe."* Escape from the staid atmosphere next door. Open Tues.-Sun. 9pm-5am.

■ Aachen

Aachen jives day and night in four different languages, exuding a youthful internationalism that belies its old age. Charlemagne sang the mantra of multiculturalism when he made the city the capital of his Frankish empire in the 8th century, and the tunes are still heard today—a flux of students and international travelers continually renew the vibrant atmosphere of Aachen. Despite this dynamism, the city maintains strong ties to its Roman, medieval, and Renaissance past. The 14th-century *Rathaus* and the medieval Marktplatz still have their own stories to tell.

ORIENTATION AND PRACTICAL INFORMATION

At the crossroads between Germany, Belgium, and the Netherlands, Aachen is close to Köln (1 hr. by train), Brussels, and Amsterdam. In addition, many cross the Dutch border (a 15min. bike ride) to stock up on cheese.

Tourist Office: Aachen's central tourist office, **Atrium Elisenbrunnen** (tel. 180 29 60; fax 180 29 31) on Friedrich-Wilhelm-Platz, dispenses literature and finds rooms (from DM35) for DM3. From the train station, cross the street and head up Bahnhofstr., turn left into Theaterstr., which becomes Theaterpl., and then right onto Kapuzinergraben, which becomes Friedrich-Wilhelm-Platz; the atrium is on your left. Check here for city **tours,** like the DM2 guided stroll through the *Dom.* Open Mon.-Fri. 9am-6:30pm, Sat. 9am-2pm.

Currency Exchange: At the post office in the train station. Open Mon.-Fri. 9am-6pm, Sat. 9am-1pm, Sun. 10am-noon.

Public Transportation: Tickets are priced by distance with one-way trips running DM2.30-9.30. *24-Stunden* tickets provide a full day of unlimited travel for DM8-20, but the DM8 kind gets you anywhere in Aachen. For those under 21, a weekend pass for all buses can be purchased on Saturdays for DM5. Some hotels also offer a DM7 *Hotelgastkarte* good for 2 days of unlimited travel. Call for details.

Bike Rental: Park & Bike, Parkhaus Wirichsbongardstr. 47 (tel. 312 43). Go up the street directly across from the tourist office; it's in the blue parking garage. Prices start at DM8 per 3 hours, DM20 per day. Open 24hr.

Mitfahrzentrale: Roesmonderstr. 4 (tel. 194 40). Matches riders and drivers. After hours, call 15 20 17. Open Mon.-Thurs. 10am-6pm, Fri. 9am-7pm, Sat. 10am-4pm.

Bookstore: Mayersche Buchhandlung, at Ursulinerstr. 17-19 (tel. 477 70), at the corner of Buchkremerstr. A decent English section. Open Mon.-Wed. and Fri. 9:30am-6:30pm, Thurs. 9:30am-8:30pm, Sat. 9:30am-2pm.

Laundromat: Waschcenter, Heinrichsallee 30. Wash DM6, soap included. Dry DM1 per 15min. Open Mon.-Sat. 6:30am-11pm; last call at 10pm.

Emergency: Police, tel. 110.

Post Office: The *Hauptpostamt,* Kapuzinergraben, is to the left of the station. Walk down Lagerhausstr., right down Franzstr., and then right on Kapuzinergraben. Open Mon.-Fri. 9am-6pm, Sat. 9am-1pm. The **postal code** is 52064.

Telephone Code: 0241.

ACCOMMODATIONS AND CAMPING

Aachen has too much history for a town of its size, and the oodles of visitors push the lodging prices up. Call ahead. The **Mitwohnzentrale,** Süsterfeldstr. 24 (tel. 87 53 46), sets up lodging for longer stays. Bus #7 (direction: "Siedlung Schönau") or 33 (direction: "Vaals"): "Westbahnhof" (open Mon.-Fri. 9am-1pm and 3-6pm).

Jugendherberge (HI), Maria-Theresia-Allee 260 (tel. 711 01; fax 70 82 19). Two buses go to the hostel leaving from the "Finanzamt" bus stop. To get to this departure point from the station, walk left on Lagerhausstr. until it intersects Kareliterstr. and Mozartstr.; the bus stop will be on the other side of the street. Bus #2 (direction: "Preusswald"): "Ronheide" or 12 (direction: "Diepenbendem"): "Colynshof." Cooped up like chickens in old rooms, you'll enjoy the company of interesting travelers (8 per room) and the good cheer of the staff. E-I-E-I-O. Reception open until 10pm. Curfew 11:30pm. DM25, over 26 DM30.

ETAP-Hotel, Strangenhäuschen 15 (tel. 91 19 29; fax 15 53 04). From the *Bushof,* bus #5: "Strangenhäuschen." Though remote, this discount hotel chain is an unbeatable bargain. Fri.-Sun. all rooms (singles and doubles with showers) only DM60. Mon.-Thurs. singles with shower DM60; doubles with shower DM70. Reception open 6:30-10am and 5-11pm.

Hotel Marx, Hubertusstr. 33-35 (tel. 375 41; fax 267 05). Just a hop, skip, and jump from the station. Hop left on Lagerhausstr. which becomes Boxgraben, skip right on Stephanstr., and jump left on Hubertusstr. Nice-looking furniture and rather bourgeois comforter designs. Singles DM60, with bath DM85; doubles DM100, with bath DM130. Breakfast included.

Hotel Cortis, Krefelderstr. 52 (tel. 15 60 11; fax 15 60 12). From the central bus station *(Bushof),* bus #51: "Rolandstr." Continue down Paßstr., then turn left on Krefeldstr. Farther out, but bright and comfortable with access to a multitude of umbrellas. Reception open 24hr. Singles from DM50, with shower DM67; doubles DM75-89, with shower DM110-114. Breakfast included.

Hotel Rütten, Krefolderstr. 86 (tel. 15 73 45). A cool, small place. From the tourist office, bus #51: (direction: "Sportpl.") "Tivoli"; the hotel is on the right. All rooms come with bath. Singles DM55; doubles DM100. Breakfast included.

FOOD

The hungry mouths of the book- and beer-laden are fed by a dense concentration of student restaurants and pubs that line **Pontstr.** from the edge of the pedestrian zone to the medieval Pont Tor. But beware—this region is also the prowling ground of the *Bahkauv,* a fearsome mythical blend of dog, puma, and dragon, which inexplicably derives its name from *"Bachkalb"* (stream calf) and pounces on the throats of drunken revelers, inducing head-splitting hangovers. The remarkable Aachen *Printen,* a spicy gingerbread biscuit (a refinement of an old Belgian recipe) is frightfully appetizing. It's now a world-famous snack with an annual production of 4500 tons—try it at any bakery. For the parsimonious traveler, **Kaiser's,** Markt 24-31 (tel. 332 21), provides a well stocked **supermarket.**

Katakomben Studentenzentrum, Pontstr. 74-76 (tel. 470 01 41), encloses **Café Chico Mendes,** a vegetarian co-op cafe of the Catholic College. DM7 or DM10 for the larger portion. Half-off a very long list of drinks during Happy Hour (Sun. 8:30-9:30pm). Open Mon.-Fri. 4:30pm-1am, Sat. 6pm-1am.

Tam-phat, Pontstr. 100 (tel. 250 80), offers primarily Thai and Chinese dishes. Even slim budgets can afford their phat meals, including numerous vegetarian options (DM7-14). Open Mon.-Fri. 11am-3pm and 5pm-11pm, Sat.-Sun. noon-11pm.

Egmont, Pontstr. 1 (tel. 40 60 44). Just off the *Rathaus.* Droves of Aacheners come here to eat and drink under the watchful eye of Charlemagne. The bar is popular come nightfall. Bring student ID for discounts. Open daily 9am-1am.

Mensa, in the green-trimmed building on Pontwall (tel. 80 37 92), near the Pont Tor. Meals DM3-3.80. Guest meals DM6.20-7.50. Open Mon.-Thurs. 11:30am-2:15pm, Fri. 11:30am-2:15pm.

Van Den Daele, Büchel 18 (tel. 357 24), just off the Markt. The finest selection of baked goods in Aachen's oldest house. Built in 1655, this *Printen* factory was made famous by artist/baker Leo van den Daele. The house specialty is *Reisfladden* (rice pudding)—DM3.80 gets you one momma of a slice. Open Mon.-Fri. 9am-6:30pm, Sat. 9am-6pm, Sun. noon-6pm.

SIGHTS

In 765, the Frankish King Pepin the Short took a dip in the hot springs north of Aachen's present city center. When his son, **Charlemagne** (Karl der Große), assumed power, he made the family's former vacation spot the capital of the rapidly expanding kingdom, and later of the Holy Roman Empire. The emperor's presence still dominates the city and local legends claim that in World War II, a bomb aimed at the **cathedral** was deflected by a statue of Charlemagne. The 8th-century dome at its center tops three tiers of marble arches that separate the gilded roof from the mosaic floor. The neo-Byzantine structure demonstrates Charlemagne's attempt to transplant the grandeur of Constantinople into his own capital. Charlemagne's throne is a simple chair of marble slabs. Stained glass rings the 15th-century Gothic choir, and beneath the chancel lie the bones of the big guy himself. Their place is marked by the gold-and-gem *Karlschreine* with a blinking doll-sized effigy. (Cathedral open daily 7am-7pm. Individual tours Mon. at 11am and noon; Tues.-Fri. 11am, noon, 2:30, and 3:30pm; Sat.-Sun. 12:30, 2:30, and 3:30pm. DM3. For group tours or English-speaking guides, call 47 70 91 27. The gateway to the throne and shrine open for tours only.)

Old Karl cuts more of a figure in the **Schatzkammer,** around the corner to the right from the *Dom* exit, tucked into the Klostergasse. The most famous likeness of the emperor, a solid gold bust *(die Karlsbüste)* shines in this exceptionally rich treasury. Not bad-looking. Among the other golden tidbits of Chuck, you'll find Christ's alleged belt and scourge rope as well as the Imperial Crown Jewels. Groupies shouldn't miss Charlemagne's wall-size "Missionary Man" tour map. (Open Mon.

NORDRHEIN-WESTFALEN

10am-1pm, Tues.-Wed. and Fri.-Sun. 10am-6:30pm, Thurs. 10am-9pm. Last entrance 30min. before closing. DM5, students, seniors, and children DM3.)

The 14th-century stone **Rathaus** (tel. 432 73 10), built on the ruins of Charlemagne's palace, looms over the wide Marktplatz beside the cathedral. Seventeeth-century citizens with a decorative obsession added Baroque flourishes to the facade. On the northern face stand 50 statues of former German sovereigns, 31 of whom were crowned in Aachen (open daily 10am-1pm and 2-5pm; DM3, students and children DM1.50). A copy of the famed **Charlemagne statue** draws a picnicking, multi-colored-hair crowd to the fountain on the square; the real thing is inside the *Rathaus* along with copies of the Imperial Crown Jewels. The **Puppenbrunnen,** a fountain whose lovable characters represent Aachen's clever townspeople (see "No Sympathy for the Devil," above) is at the intersection of Krämerstr. and Hofstr.

MUSEUMS

Although the range of museums in Aachen is limited, the streets, especially in the *Altstadt,* shelter numerous little galleries worth browsing.

Ludwig Forum für Internationale Kunst, Jülicherstr. 97-109 (tel. 180 70). Look for the large clown in drag. The *Forum* scorns the title "museum"; it's more of a works-in-progress arena. The converted *Bauhaus* umbrella factory provides the setting for all modern musts, from Andy Warhol to Barbara Kruger. The *Forum* thrusts itself at the avant-garde with a recent Eastern European collection. DM6, students DM3. Free tour Wed. at 8pm. Open Tues. and Thurs. 10am-5pm, Wed. and Fri. 10am-8pm, Sat.-Sun. 11am-5pm. Last entrance 30min. before closing.

Internationales Zeitungsmuseum, Pontstr. 13 (tel. 432 45 08), just up from the Markt. "What's black and white and re(a)d all over?" This museum houses over 120,000 different international newspapers, including press from the revolutions of 1848, World War I, World War II, and the day Hitler died. Free. Open Tues.-Fri. 9:30am-1pm and 2:30-5pm, Sat. 9:30am-1pm. Last entry 30min. before closing.

Suermondt-Ludwig-Museum, Wilhelmstr. 18 (tel. 47 98 00), a recently expanded museum, holds 44 galleries of sculptures, paintings, engravings, and crafts, commencing with the modern and ending with the medieval. DM6, students and children DM3. Open Tues. and Thurs.-Fri. 11am-7pm, Wed. 11am-9pm, Sat.-Sun. 11am-5pm. Last entry 30min. before closing.

ENTERTAINMENT AND NIGHTLIFE

Aachen has a lively theater scene, beginning with the **Stadttheater,** on Theaterpl. (tel. 478 42 44), in the central city (box office open Mon.-Sat. 9am-1pm, 5-7pm, and 30min. before performances). A small strip of newer, unconventional theaters line Gasbornstr., spearheaded by the **Aachener Kultur und Theater Initiative,** at Gasborn 9-11 (tel. 274 58). At night, the streets come alive as swarms of students hit the cafes and pubs for a study break with the *Bahkauv* (see Food, p. 333). **Klenkes Magazine** (DM3.50) offers readers a few hundred ways to have fun with movies and music listings galore. **Stonewall TAC** has a thorough listing of gay and lesbian events.

Tangente, Pontstr. 141 (tel. 224 67). Catch the hip crowd and snag a delicious shake (DM3.90) while you're at it. But beware: **B**ahkauv **A**lert **R**ating very high, prime stalking ground. Open Sun.-Thurs. 9:30am-1:30am, Fri.-Sat. 9:30am-2:30am.

Domkeller, Hof 1 (tel. 342 65). Standing at the Puppenbrunnen and facing away from the *Dom,* bear right and cross the small square. A silly array of fish and groovy jazz music magically attracts all types: *Bahn* workers, businesspeople, and, of course, you. Open Sun.-Thurs. 9:30am-1am, Fri.-Sat. 9:30am-3am.

Till Eulenspiegel, Pontstr. 114 (tel. 373 97). Named after the mischievous German elf, this club is proud of its laminated Ted Nugent album adorning the wall. On Thursday nights locals and tourists alike revel in *Kölsch* (DM2), Hofewerzen (DM3), and Guinness (DM3). What a bargain! Open daily 6pm-3am (or later).

Café Kittel, 39 Pontstr. (tel. 365 60). Posters smother the walls with announcements for live music, parties, and special events. Enjoy bowls of coffee in the outdoor

Biergarten, in the greenhouse, or amid tightly packed flat rock stars. Che Guevara is watching you. Vegetable quiches DM4.50. Daily menu DM5-10. Take it down with the house specialty, milk coffee (DM4.80). Open Mon.-Thurs. 10am-2am, Fri.-Sat. 10am-3am, Sun. 11am-2am.

▓ Eifel Massif

These wooded hills rise just north of the Mosel Valley and stretch to Aachen in the north and Belgium and Luxembourg in the west. On the Belgian side of the border, the Eifel becomes the Ardennes, remembered as the site of the Battle of the Bulge, the last German offensive of World War II. While tourism is still the main industry, visitors to the Eifel Massif tend to be less obtrusive, blending quietly into the countryside in their hiking knickers and thick socks. It's undeniably more peaceful and relaxed than the *Schwarzwald.* Transportation, however, is difficult; nearly all the rail lines are closed, and the bus lines are tryingly slow. The most heavily traveled part of the Eifel is the **Ahrtal,** south of Bonn, most scenic around the tiny town of **Altenahr.** The **Hohe Eifel** in the center of the Massif is notable for its crater lakes and odd rock formations that dormant volcanoes produced as recently as 10,000 years ago. The **Nordeifel** is home to the Seven Lakes—popular, albeit artificial, venues for fishing and water sports. The Eifel is famous for its *Schinken* (ham), a Roman specialty. The only rival to the popular swine is *Ahrtalwein,* the titillating fruit of the valley's vineyards. Do it the Roman way—devour the swine and drink the wine.

MONSCHAU

The tiny town of Monschau subtly blends the French with the Rhenish, assuming a hybrid character. In the 17th century a deluge of Huguenots fleeing Catholic persecution settled in this region, plying their traditional skills to stimulate a thriving cloth industry. In 1794, Napoleon captured the town, kicking off 12 years of occupation. After some international horse-trading, Monschau again became part of Germany; yet many residents still have French names, and the local cuisine offers many delicious treats from Germany's friendly neighbor to the west. However, Monschau still *looks* distinctly North Rhine-Westphalian. In a narrow, secluded valley cut by the swift-flowing Ruhr about 30km south of Aachen, the town is a visual compendium of gray slate roofs, cobblestones, and brickwork. The surrounding hills are filled with hiking trails. In the city proper, the Ahr winds around tall, stone houses with small, flowered balconies, and the streets are lined with lovely cafes and terraces.

The serene beauty of the landscape is juxtaposed with the gloomy **Burg,** the ruins of a massive castle perched above Monschau. A steep set of stairs leads to the castle from the town center. Midway up, the beauteous gray 1649 **Alte Katherine Pfarrkirche** stands with its shingled onion-turret. The fragile **Glashütte** (glassworks museum), Burgaustr. 15 (tel. 32 16), has demonstrations every hour on the half-hour between 10:30am and 5:30pm (open daily 10am-6pm; DM3, students and children DM2). On the path leading down from the *Burg,* the **Rotes Haus,** Laufenstr. 10 (tel. 50 71), a pinkish building, provides a Hendrixian break in the color scheme. Built by a local cloth merchant in 1760, the building now contains a museum of period pieces (Jimi is nowhere to be seen). (Tours Easter-Nov. Tues.-Sun. at 10, 11am, and 2, 3, and 4pm; DM5, students and children DM3.) Across the bridge, the **Evangelische Pfarrkirche** chapel urges visitors to seek divine salvation.

On the other end of town, the authentic 19th-century **Senfmühle** (mustard mill), Laufenstr. 18 (tel. 22 45), can leave you delirious. Monschau is famous for its mustard (open for demonstrations March-Oct. Wed. at 11am and 2pm; DM4, students and children DM2). As you greedily sample the shop's twelve varieties, the townspeople escape on the hourly bus #163 to Aachen (DM5.80 one way), arriving safely at the Aachen *Bushof.* The **tourist office,** Stadtstr. 1 (tel. 33 00; fax 45 34), reposes across from the steps leading to the *Burg* (open Mon.-Fri. 9am-noon and 1-4pm, Sat. 11am-3pm, Sun. 11am-2pm; Oct.-Easter Mon.-Fri. 9am-noon and 1-4pm). To help you recover from the mustard shock, the amicable staff book rooms (from DM25) for a

DM5 fee and give out maps. The **Jugendherberge Monschen (HI)**, Auf dem Schloß 4 (tel. 23 14; fax 43 91), in the *Burg*, teems with rebellious school children who shriek in German, French, and Flemish. (Reception open 8:30-9am, 12:30-1pm, 6:30-7pm. Curfew 10pm, but keys are available. DM24, over 26 DM29. Breakfast is included. Sheets DM6.) A calmer haven, the larger, more modern **Jugendherberge "Monschau-Hargard" (HI)**, Hargarasgasse 5 (tel. 21 80; fax 45 27), lies outside of town. Bus #163 or 166 (direction: "Hargard") from in front of the post office: "Hargard," backtrack 100m, and follow the sign. (Reception open until 9pm. Curfew 10pm. DM25, over 26 DM30. Breakfast included. Sheets DM6.) **Hotel-Café Flosdorff**, am Markt 7 (tel. 23 03), is also on the main square next to the river. The rooms are brighter-colored versions of the picturesque town (singles DM30; doubles DM65). To satisfy the royal appetite without emptying the royal treasury, feast on pizzas (DM4.50-9) at **Tavola**, Stadtstr. 42 (tel. 72 17 63; open daily 10am-9pm). The **telephone code** is 02472.

THE AHRTAL

The string of tiny hamlets that dots the serene Ahr River refers to itself as *"Rotwein Paradies Deutschlands"* (Germany's red wine paradise). Unlike most cheesy bureau slogans, the Ahrtal lives up to its claims; in many picturesque places the vineyards climb up and *over* the area's craggy hills, continuing straight down the other side. Wine cellars and itty-bitty family-owned wineries abound, and the bulk of information in the valley's tourist offices helps guide those in search of vinic pleasures (the *"Erlebnis Ahrwein"* pamphlet is the boozehound's bible).

Trains travel into the region from **Remagen** (see p. 408), halfway between Bonn and Koblenz. Trains depart approximately once every hour; the *"Linie 42"* pamphlet in Remagen's *Reisezentrum* explains it all. As the train chugs west, the hills become more rocky and steep, culminating in the violent, craggy peaks that surround the town of **Altenahr**. Developed to supply peasants for the royalty of the local castle, **Burg Ahr** (reached by a trail beginning at the *Rathaus*), the town today caters to a different force—the ubiquitous tourist industry. To satisfy thrill-seeking, fun-loving folks, the town boasts a couple of riotous amusements. The **Sommer-Rodelbahn** (tel. 23 21) resembles a luge, without the cold, snow, or embarrassingly tight suits. Cables pull your sled to the summit and then let you rip down a 500m slippery steel track. A brake is provided for the meek. At DM3.50 per ride, DM5 for two (cheaper for more rides or more people), it's a cheap kick. The 4km hike from Altenahr (follow *Autobahn* 357 towards Bonn) doesn't seem to dissuade crowds, especially on Sundays. (Open April-Oct. Sun.-Fri.10am-6pm, Sat. 10am-sundown; Nov.-March Sat. afternoons and Sun.) Lazy and well-heeled blue-bloods take the taxi from the station (DM2.50 per person, 4 person minimum). Another example of the strange interaction between cheesy technology and mountainsides is the **Seilbahn** (tel. 83 83), an 8-minute walk to the left from the train station (follow the signs). They'll haul you up to mountaintop trails (DM3.50, children DM2; round-trip DM6, DM3). For less mechanical pleasures, sample the sweet juices of the Ahr through a *Weinprobe* (local wine tasting) at **Mayschloß-Altenahr**, on Tunnelstr. (tel. 936 00). Probe each delicate *Ahrtal* vintage, inhale the aromatic flavor, or just chug 'em (open Mon.-Sat. 8am-noon and 1-6pm, Sun. 10am-6pm).

Information on hikes, lodgings, and train tickets is available at the **tourist office**, Altenburger 1a (tel. 84 48; fax 35 16), located in the station. (Open Mon.-Fri. 9am-noon and 2-5pm, Sat. 9am-noon; Nov.-April Mon.-Fri. 10am-noon and 3-5pm.) The 24km *Rottweinwanderweg* begins here; follow the red grapes for a comprehensive tour of the valley. The **Jugendherberge Altenahr**, Langfigtal 8 (tel. 18 80), is in a nature reserve 20 minutes from town by foot. From the station, cross the bridge and turn right on Brückenstr., which becomes Tunnelstr. Don't go through the tunnel; walk along the river, cross the green pedestrian bridge, and follow the promenade through the woods. (Reception open daily 8am-10pm. Curfew 10pm. DM19.50. Breakfast included. Sheets DM5. Call ahead.) The town is a good base for area hiking. On the Ahr, the **Camping Schulz campground** (tel. 85 03) offers its bosom to your tired sole. Head right as you face the tracks, follow them on the footpath, and take a left when you reach Altenburgerstr. The campground is on your right across the river. (Reception open 8am-10pm. Adults DM6, children DM4. Tents DM5.) Altenahr is a virtual paradise for the winebiber and traditional food *bon vivant*. To stay below the DM10 barrier without using a plastic *Imbiß* fork, visit **Im Weinhäuschen,** Brückenstr. 27 (tel. 31 15). This homely restaurant serves savory specials for less than DM10, and potato pancakes with ambrosial apple sauce for a mere DM6.50. At night, loud locals populate the bar (open daily 11am-bedtime). The **telephone code** is 02643.

■ Düsseldorf

As Germany's mod-ish fashion hub, advertising center, and multinational corporation base, as well as capital of the densely populated province of Nordrhein-Westfalen, Düsseldorf runneth over with German patricians and wanna-be aristocrats. Founded in the 13th century, the city has endured a series of terrific pummelings. After suffering calamitous destruction during the Thirty Years War, the War of Spanish Succession, and World War II, Düsseldorf rebounded each time with an indefatigable resilience and renewed independence that translates into fierce pride among the city's residents. Set on the majestic Rhine, Germany's "Hautstadt" (a pun on *Hauptstadt*, the French *haute* meaning superior, and the German *Haut* meaning skin) is a stately, modern metropolis. Residents claim that Düsseldorf is not on the Rhine, but on the Königsallee (the central promenade, a.k.a. "the Kö"), a kilometer-long fashion runway that sweeps down either side of the old town moat. At night, propriety (and sobriety) are cast aside as thousands of Düsseldorfers flock to the 500 pubs in the *Altstadt*, trading their monacles and Rolexes for beer goggles and a damn good time.

ORIENTATION AND PRACTICAL INFORMATION

Tourist Office: Main office, Konrad-Adenauer-Platz (tel. 17 20 20; fax 35 04 04). Walk up and to the right from the station and look for the towering Immermanhof building. Their free monthly *Düsseldorf Monatsprogram* is packed with information. Open for ticket sales (12% fee) and general services Mon.-Fri. 8:30am-6pm, Sat. 9am-12pm; hotel reservations (DM55 and up) for a DM5 fee Mon.-Sat. 8am-8pm, Sun. 4-10pm. The **branch office,** Heinrich-Heine-Allee 24 (tel. 899 23 46), specializes in cultural listings. Open Mon.-Fri. 9am-5pm.

Budget Travel: Council Travel, Graf-Adolf-Str. 64 (tel. 36 30 30). Open Mon.-Fri. 9am-1pm, Sat. 10am-1pm.

Consulates: Canada and **U.K.** Yorckstr. 19 (tel. 944 80). Open Mon-Fri. 8am-noon.

Currency Exchange: Deutsche Verkehrs Credit Bank, in the *Hauptbahnhof* or at the airport. Open Mon.-Sat. 7am-9pm, Sun. 8am-9pm.

American Express: Neusserstr. 111 (tel. 90 13 50). Mail held up to 4 weeks for card members. All financial services. Open Mon.-Fri. 9am-5:30pm, Sat. 8:30am-noon.

Flights: Frequent S-Bahns and a Lufthansa shuttle travel from the station to the international **Flughafen Düsseldorf.** Call 421 22 23 for flight information. Open 5am-12:30am. 24hr. emergency service tel. 421 66 37.

Trains: All trains arrive at **Düsseldorf Hauptbahnhof** (tel. 194 19).

Public Transportation: The *Rheinbahn* includes subways, streetcars, buses, and the S-Bahn. **Single tickets,** DM1.90-11.70, depending on distance traveled. The *Tagesticket* (DM10; higher prices for longer distances) is the best value—groups of up to 5 people and one dog can travel 24hr. on any line. Tickets are sold mostly by vending machine; pick up the *Fahrausweis* brochure in the tourist office for instructions. Düsseldorf's S-Bahn is integrated into the mammoth regional **VRR** *(Verkehrsverbund Rhein-Ruhr)* system, which connects Bochum, Dortmund, Duisburg, Essen, Hagen, Krefeld, Mönchengladbach, Mühlheim, Oberhausen, Solingen, and Wuppertal. **Schedule Information,** tel. 582 28.

Taxi: tel. 21 21 21.

Car Rental: Hertz, Immermannstr. 65 (tel. 35 70 25). Open Mon.-Fri. 7am-6pm, Sat. 8am-noon.

Bike Rental: Zweirad Egert, Ackerstr. 143 (tel. 66 21 34). S-Bahn #6 (direction: "Essen"): "Wehrbahn" and walk 10min. Call ahead to check availability. Bikes

NORDRHEIN-WESTFALEN

DM18.50 per day, DM42 per week. DM50 deposit and ID required. Open Mon.-Fri. 9:30am-6:30pm, Sat. 9am-2pm.

Mitfahrzentrale: Konrad-Adenauer-Platz 13 (tel. 37 60 81), to the left as you exit the station, and upstairs over a tiny travel office. Open Mon.-Fri. 9am-6:30pm, Sat.-Sun. 11am-3pm. **City-Netz Mitfahrzentrale,** Kruppstr. 102 (tel. 194 44), is a more professional chain with slightly higher prices. Open Mon.-Fri. 9am-7pm, Sat. 10am-2pm, Sun. noon-3pm.

Bookstore: Stern-Verlag, Friedrichstr. 24-26 (tel. 388 10). A good selection of English paperbacks. Open Mon.-Fri. 9am-6:30pm, Sat. 9am-2pm.

Women's Agency: Any questions or concerns regarding women's issues can be directed to the **Frauenbüro,** Mühlenstr. 29, 2nd floor (tel. 899 36 03), at the municipal office. Walk-ins Mon.-Thurs. 8am-4pm, Fri. 8am-1pm.

AIDS-Hilfe: Oberblicker Allee 310 (tel. 726 05 26). Open Mon.-Thurs. 10am-1pm and 2-6pm, Fri. 10am-1pm and 2-4pm. Advice and assistance hotline tel. 194 11.

Laundromat: Wasch Center, Friedrichstr. 92, down the street from the Kirchpl. S-Bahn. Wash DM6. Dry DM1 per 15min. Soap included. Open daily 6am-11pm. Also available at **Jugendherberge Düsseldorf** (wash DM9; free soap and drying) and **Jugendherberge Duisburg-Wedau** (wash and dry DM2.50 each).

Pharmacy: In the *Hauptbahnhof.* Closed pharmacies post lists of nearby open ones. **Emergency pharmacy,** tel. 115 00. **Emergency Doctor,** tel. 192 92.

Emergency: Police, tel. 110. **Ambulance** and **Fire,** tel. 112.

Internet Access: g@rden, Rathausufer 8 (tel. 86 61 60; email gsg@garden.de; http://www.garden.de). Open daily 11am-1am. DM5 per 30min. Also at **Café InterNezzo,** Fichtenstr. 40 (tel. 973 00 25; http://www.zakk.de/internez.htm). In the "zakk" (Zentrum für Aktion, Kultur, und Kommunikation), which hosts many cultural activities and fun fests. Open Mon.-Thurs. 6-11pm. DM5 per hr.

Post Office: Hauptpostamt, Konrad-Adenauer-Platz, 40210 Düsseldorf, a stone's throw to the right of the tourist office. Open Mon.-Fri. 8am-6pm, Sat. 9am-2pm, Sun. noon-1pm. Limited service Mon.-Fri. 6pm-8pm, Sun. 10am-2pm. **Branch office** in *Hauptbahnhof* open Mon.-Fri. 8am-6pm, Sat.-Sun. 2pm-midnight.

Telephone Code: 0211.

ACCOMMODATIONS AND CAMPING

The old saying goes, "piss-poor planning leads to piss-poor performance," but in Düsseldorf, it can be slightly modified to "piss-poor planning leaves one piss poor." **Call ahead,** at least a month ahead if possible. Düsseldorf is a convention city where corporate crowds make rooms scarce and costly; it's not unusual for hotels to double their prices during a convention. If you're considering a budget hotel stay, call the tourist office for trade fair *(Messe)* dates and show up during a lull. Most spots go for at least DM50 per person even in the off-season. Check around the train station or consider the hostels in Duisberg, Mönchengladbach, Neuss, or Ratingen (all within 30min. by S-Bahn). Most hotels accept major credit cards.

Jugendgästehaus Düsseldorf (HI), Düsseldorferstr. 1 (tel. 55 73 10; fax 57 25 13), is conveniently located in the Oberkassel part of town, just over the Rheinkniebrücke from the *Altstadt.* U-Bahn #70, 74, 75, 76, or 77: "Luegpl.," then walk 500m down Kaiser-Wilhelm-Ring. Unbeatable location with private lockers and cool key cards. Reception open 7am-1am. Curfew 1am, but doors opened every hour on the hour 2-6am. DM33.50, over 26 DM37. Laundry available.

Jugendherberge Duisburg-Wedau, Kalkweg 148E (tel. (0203) 72 41 64; fax 72 08 34). S-Bahn #1 or 21: "Duisburg Hauptbahnhof," then bus #934: "Jugendherberge." Düsseldorf is accessible by frequent trains and buses, but all public transportation closes by 1am, and it's too far for a taxi. Old but clean rooms and those mysterious self-flushing toilets. Reception open 8:30-9am, 12:30-1pm, and 6:30-7pm. DM22.50, over 26 DM27.50. Laundry available. Open mid-Jan. to mid-Dec. Closed one weekend of every month.

CVJM-Hotel, Graf-Adolf-Str. 102 (tel. 17 28 50; fax 361 31 60), down the street to the left of the train station. A lot of money for the "why?" but at least it has clean, spacious rooms with hot water and inspirational messages on the walls. Reception

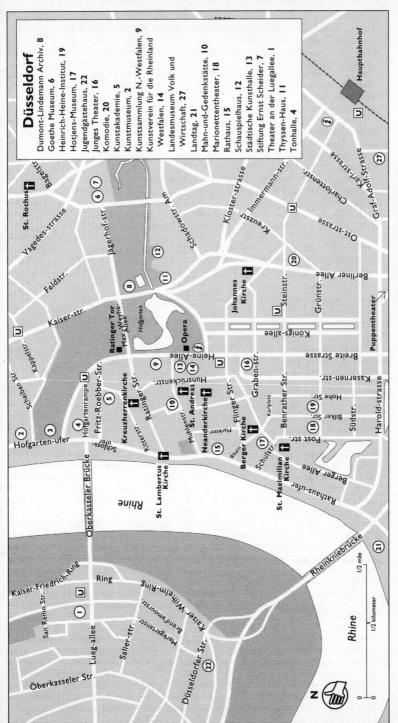

NORDRHEIN-WESTFALEN

Düsseldorf

Dumont-Lindemann Archiv, 8
Goethe Museum, 6
Heinrich-Heine-Institut, 19
Hetjens-Museum, 17
Jugendgästehaus, 22
Junges Theater, 16
Komödie, 20
Kunstakademie, 5
Kunstmuseum, 2
Kunstsammlung N.-Westfalen, 9
Kunstverein für die Rheinland Westfalen, 14
Landesmuseum Volk und Wirtschaft, 27
Landtag, 21
Mahn-und-Gedenkstätte, 10
Marionettentheater, 18
Rathaus, 15
Schauspielhaus, 12
Städtische Kunsthalle, 13
Stiftung Ernst Scheider, 7
Theater an der Luegallee, 1
Thyssen-Haus, 11
Tonhalle, 4

open 24hr. Singles DM62; doubles DM101. Noisier streetside rooms DM65, DM111. Breakfast DM8. No credit cards.

Hotel Diana, Jahnstr. 31 (tel. 37 50 71; fax 36 49 43), five blocks from the station. Head left down Graf-Adolf-Str., left on Hüttenstr., and then a quick jog to the right on Jahnstr. Small but comfortable rooms with phone and TV. Reception open 8am-7pm. Singles DM55; doubles DM85, with bath DM125. Breakfast included.

Hotel Manhattan, Graf-Adolf-Str. 39 (tel. 37 71 38; fax 37 02 47), two blocks from the station. The mirror-plated lobby (with a touch of neon) shines of 1970s dance fever, but the clean, desk-equipped rooms are surprisingly un-metropolitan in their charm. Reception open 24hr. Singles DM68-120; doubles DM100-180, depending on ritziness and whether it's convention time. Breakfast buffet included.

Hotel Amsterdam, Stresemannstr. 20 (tel. 84 05 89; fax 840 50), between Oststr. and Berliner Allee. From the station, start up Graf-Adolf-Str. and turn right at Stresemannpl. Blue baroque rooms and princess-style furniture. Reception open 7am-midnight. Four walls and a bed DM70, with shower, TV, and breakfast DM90; doubles from DM120.

Hotel Bristol, Aderstr. 8 (tel. 37 07 50; fax 37 37 54), one block south of Graf-Adolf-Str. at the bottom tip of the Königsallee. A well-appointed, friendly place to retire and watch TV after a stroll on the Kö. Singles DM60-70, with shower DM120, with bath DM130. Breakfast included.

Camping: Kleiner Torfbruch (tel. 899 20 38). S-Bahn: "Düsseldorf Geresheim," then bus #735 (direction: "Stamesberg"): "Seeweg." Person DM6; tent DM9.

FOOD

For a cheap meal, the conglomeration of dives in the **Altstadt** can't be beat. Endless rows of pizzerias, *Döner Kebabs,* and Chinese diners reach from Heinrich-Heine-Allee to the banks of the Rhine. The **Markt** on Karlspl. offers shoppers lots of foreign fruits and a local favorite, *Sauerbraten* (pickled beef). For *trés chic* cafes that provide the beautiful people with abundant atmosphere and high prices, hit the **Kö. Olto Mess** (tel. 200 10), a popular food chain, should satisfy all grocery needs. The most convenient location is probably the eastern corner of Karlspl. in the *Altstadt* (open Mon.-Fri. 8am-8pm; Sat. 8am-4pm).

Linanon Express, Bergerstr. 21 (tel. 32 95 93), in the *Altstadt.* Where else can you find Lebanese food but in Düsseldorf? Well, probably in Lebanon. Enjoy a falafel (DM4.50) in a hip setting. Open daily noon-midnight.

Heine Geburtshaus, Bolkerstr. 53 (tel. 13 32 00). Pop off a lid and drain a beer where the great poet burst into the world. Read a selection from Heine's brilliantly satirical *Wintermärchen* (A Winter's Tale) while waiting to be served. Enough pictures on the walls to make a comic flip book. The *Speisekarte* does not offer much of a selection (a few salads and meat dishes), so sit back, sip wine, and enjoy the atmosphere. Open daily noon-midnight.

Zum Uerige, Bergerstr. 1 (tel. 86 69 90). Some pheromone in the air attracts the cool Germans here. Try house specialties of *Blutwurst* (blood sausage) for DM3.50 and *Mainzer* (Mainz cheese) for DM4. When you're finished eating, settle down with a *Schlossor Alt* beer and soak up the crisp Rhenish zephyrs. Open daily 10am-midnight. Kitchen open Mon.-Fri. 6-9pm, Sat. 11am-4pm.

La Copa, Bergerstr. 4 (tel. 323 84 58). Sammy, Deano, and Barry Manilow have left the building, but not without bequeathing their beloved Copa with 50 tasty dishes (DM8-15). Hep cats wash it down with a glass of Sangria. Open daily noon-1am.

Marché, Königsallee 60 (tel. 32 06 81), in the Kö-Galerie mall. The only way to dine on the Kö and keep your savings intact. Red stripes and funny hats. Entrees start at DM6.80, including fried chicken, swine, fish, and noodles with zany sauces, all in generous portions. Cafe-bar open daily 7:30am-11pm, restaurant 8am-11pm.

Galerie Burghof, Burgallee 1-3 (tel. 40 14 23), in Kaiserwerth next to Friedrich's Rhine ruins. U-Bahn #79: "Klemenspl." Like IHOP putting on the ritz. Specializes in matrimony between beer and pancakes (DM9.50). A packed *Biergarten,* often jammed in every nook and cranny. Open daily 11am-1am, but pancakes only come out Mon.-Fri. 6-10:45pm, Sat. 2-10:45pm, Sun 2-11pm.

Gatzweiler's Brauhaus, Belsenpl. 2 (tel. 55 93 39) in the Oberkasseler *Bahnhof.* A huge local brewery serving a wide variety of homegrown hops, beverages, and Düsseldorf variations of German culinary specialties, such as *Wurst,* chicken, and sauerkraut (DM15-25). Open daily 11am-1am.

SIGHTS

The glitzy **Kö** located just outside the *Altstadt* embodies the vitality and glamour of Düsseldorf. No bargains here, but the Kö sports the best of everything; you, too, can window-shop at Armani or ogle the Lotus parked outside. To get there, head down Graf-Adolf-Str. from the station (10min.). Properly called the Königsallee, the *belle époque* expanse was laid out over a century ago. Stone bridges span the little river that runs down the middle to trickle at the toes of a decadent statue of the sea god Triton. Three shopping guides for the Kö are printed by the tourist office. Midway up is the awesome **Kö-Galerie**—in Nietzschean terms, an *Übermall* (with *über*-prices). Items *start* at US$100 here, and even the mannequins have attitude. At the upper end of the Kö, the **Hofgarten** park is an oasis of green and culture inside urban Düsseldorf. **Schloß Jägerhof,** at the western end, houses the **Goethe Museum** behind its pink facade and white iron gates. The Hofgarten meets the Rhine at the **Ehrenhof,** a plaza of museums (see below). The **Deutsches Oper am Rhein** (opera house) is here, as is the Neoclassical Napoleonic **Ratinger Tor** gate house. Twilight walks along the east bank of the Rhine are breathtaking. Head north along the Hofgarten-Ufer to the left of the Hofgarten and then veer off onto the adjacent Ufer.

Düsseldorf has had mixed luck with its cultural heroes. Famed composer **Robert Schumann** was so miserable here that he tried to drown his sorrows by jumping off a town bridge. Beloved poet **Heinrich Heine** is a more popular, if equally melancholic, son. His birthplace and homestead are marked by plaques, and every third restaurant and fast-food stand on his Bolkerstr. block bears his name. **The Heinrich Heine Institut,** Bilkerstr. 12-14 (tel. 899 55 71), is the official shrine with a collection of manuscripts and a discomfiting death mask (open Tues.-Fri. and Sun. 11am-5pm, Sat. 1-5pm; DM4, students DM2). In addition to many works of contemporary artists honoring Heine, the institute holds a vast array of the author's correspondence, which show the intellectual and artistic development of the literary master. Further up the *Altstadt,* the **Burgpl.** used to be the site of a glorious castle, but tired citizens have saved only a single tower. The castle was built in 1324, burnt in 1490, rebuilt in 1559, razed in 1794, rebuilt in 1851, and flattened in 1872, at which point the townsfolk gave up—only the tower was reconstructed in 1900, and *that* was bombed to rubble in World War II. The pessimistic citizens waited until 1984 to rebuild the tower. Tread carefully. The **Radschlager,** the legendary Düsseldorf "somersaulting boys," top a fountain on Burgpl. and grace every city manhole cover. For bargain shopping, visit the **Radschlagermarkt am Grossmarkt.**

North on the Rhine but still in Düsseldorf dwell the **ruins** of Emperor Friedrich's palace in the tiny town of **Kaiserwerth.** Built in 1184, the palace was destroyed in 1702 in the War of Spanish Succession, but the gloomy *Kaiserpfalz* frame remains. U-Bahn #79: "Klemenspl.," then follow Kaiserwerther Markt to the Rhine, and walk left another 150m (open daily 8am-12:30pm; free). Just in case you're curious, the seemingly out-of-place **tower** with the blinking lights visible from the Rhine at night is actually a clock called the **Rheinturm.** From bottom to top, the dots represent 1 second, 10 seconds, 1 minute, 10 minutes, 1 hour, and 10 hours.

MUSEUMS

This is a city of museums. Most cluster around the Hofgarten. Internationally important holdings abound in the string of museums along Grabbepl. and Ehrenhof. These museums are expensive, however, so choose carefully.

Grabbeplatz

Kunstsammlung Nordrhein-Westfalen, Grabbepl. 5 (tel. 838 10), is the black, reflecting, glass thing west of the Hofgarten. U-Bahn #70, 75, 76, 78, or 79 "Heinrich-Heine-Allee" and walk north 2 blocks, or bus #725: "Grabbepl." Skylights lavish sunshine on the exhibits—Matisse, Picasso, Surrealists, and Expressionists. The collection of works by hometown boy Paul Klee is one of the most extensive in the world. Tours Sun. 11am and Wed. 3:30pm. DM5, students DM3. Special exhibits DM10, students DM8. Open Tues.-Thurs. and Sat.-Sun. 10am-6pm, Fri. 10am-8pm.

Kunsthalle, Grabbepl. 4 (tel. 889 62 40), across the square from the Kunstsammlung Nordrhein-Westfalen. Quality visiting exhibits of every shape and size, specializing in the bizarre. Admission depends on the exhibit; usually DM10, students and buckaroos DM7. Open Tues.-Sun. 11am-6pm.

Ehrenhof—Hofgarten

Kunstmuseum Düsseldorf, Ehrenhof 5 (tel. 889 24 60 or 892 90 46), surrounding the fountain. A spectacular collection of sculpture, painting, prints, weaving, and crafts spanning 2 stories and 11 centuries. Don't miss the stunning glassware or the Baroque and Renaissance drawings. DM5, students and children DM2.50. Open Tues.-Sun. 11am-6pm. The **Kunstpalast** is an extension of the Kunstmuseum across the fountain at Ehrenhof 5, devoted to rotating contemporary exhibits.

Landesmuseum Volk und Wirtschaft, Ehrenhof 2 (tel. 492 11 08), dissects every nugget of the area's development, including a mini-mineshaft, with a side order of economic and social history. DM2, students DM1. Open Mon.-Tues. and Thurs.-Fri. 9am-5pm, Wed. 9am-8pm, Sun. 10am-6pm.

Goethe Museum, Jakobistr. 2 (tel. 899 62 62), in Schloß Jägerhof, at the east end of the garden. Streetcar #707 or bus #752: "Schloß Jägerhof." The museum makes up for its lack of hometown advantage with the extent of its collection—30,000 souvenirs of the poet and his friends. Goethe was Heine's idol, and in Germany, that is ground enough to claim a connection—he is the German Shakespeare, after all. Everything in the mini-palace is furnished as Goethe would have wished it: to evoke his character. DM4, students and children DM2. Open Tues.-Fri. and Sun. 11am-5pm, Sat. 1-5pm. Library open Tues.-Fri. 10am-noon and 2-4pm.

Elsewhere in Düsseldorf

Film Museum/Hetjens Museum, Schulstr. 4 (tel. 899 42 00), south of the *Schloß-turm* on Rheinuferstr. Hetjens provides a comprehensive history of ceramics, while the film museum showcases 4 floors of costumes, photos, and even clips of classics (alas, all dubbed in German). Admission to each DM6, students and children DM3. Both open Tues. and Thurs.-Sun. 11am-5pm, Wed. 11am-9pm.

Stadtmuseum, at Berger Allee 2 (tel. 899 61 70), by the Rheinkniebrücke. The new building clashes with its turn-of-the-century surroundings, but the exhibits summarize Düsseldorf's culturally rich consumer history perfectly. DM5, students DM2.50. Open Tues. and Thurs.-Sun. 11am-5pm, Wed. 11am-9pm.

Mahn- und Gedenkstätte, Mühlenstr. 29 (tel. 899 62 06). Stark museum and document collection commemorating victims of the Third Reich. Free. Open Tues.-Fri. and Sun. 11am-6pm, Sat. 1-5pm.

Neanderthal Museum, Thekhauser Quall (tel. (02104) 311 49), in the suburb of Erkrath. S-Bahn #8: "Hochdahl," then bus #741: "Neanderthal." A museum where low-brows, thick-skulls, and knuckle-draggers can feel comfortable. The first remains of an entity identified as "Neanderthal Man" were found here; the museum allows you to meet his 60,000-year-old relatives. DM2, students DM1. Open Tues.-Sat. 10am-5pm, Sun. 11am-6pm.

ENTERTAINMENT AND NIGHTLIFE

Folklore holds that Düsseldorf's 500 pubs make up *"die längste Theke der Welt"* (the longest bar in the world). **Bolkerstr.** is jam-packed nightly with street performers of the musical and beer-olympic varieties. *Prinz* magazine (DM4.50) is Düsseldorf's fashion cop and scene detective; it's often given out free at the youth hostel; *Facolte* is the gay and lesbian nightlife magazine and is available at most newsstands. The free cultural guides *Coolibri* and *Biograph* are less complete but more than sufficient to keep it (your thang, that is) shakin' all night long. **Das Kommödchen** ("The Little Commode"; tel. 32 94 43) is a tiny, extraordinarily popular theater behind the Kunsthalle at Grabbepl. (Box office open Mon.-Sat. 1-8pm, Sun. 3-8pm; tickets DM33, students and children DM23; call at least 2 days ahead.) Ballet and opera tickets are best bought (without service charge) at the **Opernhaus** (tel. 890 82 11), on Heinrich-Heine-Allee (box office open Mon.-Fri. 11am-6:30pm, Sat. 11am-1pm, and 1hr. before performances). Tickets can be purchased by phone (Mon.-Fri. 9am-5pm). **Black Box,** Schulstr. 4 (tel. 899 24 90), off Rathaus-Ufer along the Rhine, serves the art-film aficionado with unadulterated foreign flicks (DM8, students DM6).

Stahlwerk, Ronsdorfer 134 (tel. 73 03 50). U-Bahn #75: "Ronsdorferstr." Facing away from downtown turn right onto Ronsdorferstr. A bizarre combination of a trippy multi-floor dance hall and an old-fashioned beer patio filled with fresh-faced Düsseldorfers. An average night draws 1500 of the city's coolest and most bizarre. Cover DM10. Opens Fri.-Sat. and last Sun. of every month at 10pm.

Poco Loco, Mortengasse 2 (tel. 13 33 30), in the *Altstadt.* Take a typical twentysomething watering hole with a dance floor, add a tequila bar and a Latin feel, then throw in a few hundred horny Germans and you have a Poco Loco, renowned for its pick-up scene and party atmosphere. Whether you're in the market for Euro-*fleisch* or just want to dance, this *Kneipe* is a lot of fun. Thursday is singles night; only the tequila bar is open. Open Tues.-Thurs. 7pm-3am, Fri.-Sun. 7pm-5am.

Tor 3, Ronsdorferstr. 143 (tel. 733 64 97). More techno and younger than Stahlwerk, which is just across the street, Tor 3 still rocks around the clock. Prepare alternate transport home from this factory-turned-disco—the S-Bahn stops running far too early. Cover DM15. Open Fri.-Sat. 10pm-5am.

Brauerei Schumacher, Bolkerstr. 44 (tel. 32 60 07), is Düsseldorf's oldest house brewery. It gets packed with a fresh Boomer crowd every night. A truly cross-generational *Treffpunkt.* Open Mon.-Thurs., Sun. 10am-midnight, Fri.-Sat. 10am-1am.

McLaughlin's Irish Pub, Kurzestr. 11, loads up on live bands and Anglophiles loading up. Don't even try to speak German here—practice your brogue instead. Open Sun.-Thurs. 11am-1am, Fri.-Sat. 11am-3am.

Zum Uel, Rattinger 16 (tel. 32 53 69), in the *Altstadt.* Papered with listings for musical happenings. Drink that *Schlösser Alt* (DM2.30 for 0.2L). On good nights the crowd of students blocks traffic, but there's also a pastoral beer garden and good food. Open Sun.-Tues. and Thurs. 10am-1am, Wed. and Fri. 10am-3am.

Engelchen, Kurzestr. 11 (tel. 32 73 56). Raphael's cute cherubs get red in the face with alterna-trendies. Weekdays tend towards Britpop, while weekends offer more grunge. Open Mon.-Fri. 9am-1am, Sat. 10am-3am, Sun. 10am-3am.

Café Rosa, Oberbilker-Allee 310. The socio-cultural mecca of Düsseldorf's queer community. A bar, disco, *Kulturzentrum,* and cafe rolled into one, Rosa, much like Dolemite, hosts parties, self-defense classes, and activities. Tues., Thurs., and most Sat. mixed; Fri. lesbians only; last Sat. of each month gays only. Call 77 52 42 for gay programs and 54 42 for lesbian events. Daytime hours vary (call hotlines); evenings Tues.-Sat. 8pm-1am, sometimes later on weekends.

Fire Club, Grupollostr. 8 (tel. 369 48 16), in the city center. *Kneipe* and disco for the gay-trendy set. Open daily at 5pm until they feel like closing.

■ Near Düsseldorf

MÖNCHENGLADBACH

Eighteen kilometers west of Düsseldorf lies Mönchengladbach, a refreshing respite from the industrial scenery of the *Ruhrgebiet*. Standing out prominently against the skyline is the **Abteiberg,** the hill Archbishop Gero chose as the site of a Benedictine monastery in 974. About 800 years later, the French kicked the monks out, and since then the deserted building has served as the **Rathaus.** Next door towers the 11th-century **Münster** whose ecclesiastical treasures include a portable altar and a bust of the Saxon St. Vitus, the city's guardian (church open Mon.-Sat. 8am-6pm, Sun. noon-6pm; museum open Tues.-Sat. 2-6pm, Sun. noon-6pm). Around the corner, the mirrored **Städtisches Museum Abteiberg,** Abteistr. 27 (tel. 25 26 37), just beyond the *Rathaus*, houses a hip collection of 20th-century art including pieces by Andy Warhol, Roy Lichtenstein, and George Segal (open Tues.-Sun. 10am-6pm; DM5, students and children DM2.50). Also at the top of the Abteiberg is the **Alter Markt,** an old cobblestone square now studded by small diners and craft shops. Gaze down at the residential district, a dense blanket of pastel decorated houses with flowers spilling out of windows. To reach the Alter Markt, turn left out of the train station and head up Hindenburgstr. past the snazzy new stores or take bus #13 or 23 up the hill. MG (em-gay), as even the natives call it, is more garden than city. Five **parks**—Geropark, Brundespark, Kaiserpark, Hardtor Wald, and Volksgarten—lie within MG proper, but most affecting is the **Bunter Garten** (Garden of Colors), in the center of town, three blocks northwest of the Alter Markt on Kaldenkirchenorstr.

Just outside of town stands the majestic **Schloß Rheydt** (tel. 66 92 89 00). From the station, bus #6: "Bonnenbroich" and then bus #16: "Sparkasse" (30min. ride, but worth it). This beautifully preserved Renaissance castle swims in a lily-padded pond surrounded by winding hiking paths and the castle's famous peacocks. Inside, a museum displays 15th- to 17th-century artifacts, including a special exhibit on card games and changing displays of lesser-known but accomplished pre-war artists (open Tues.-Sat. 2-8pm, Sun. 11am-8pm; DM5, tykes DM2.50).

MG is best seen as a day trip from Düsseldorf. Nevertheless, the **tourist office,** Bismarckstr. 23-27 (tel. 66 92 89 00; fax 27 42 22), left of the station, finds rooms (from DM45) for free (open Mon.-Fri. 9:30am-6pm, Sat. 9:30am-12:30pm). The **Jugendherberge Hardter Wald,** Brahmstr. 156 (tel. (02461) 55 95 12; fax 55 64 64), lies at the boundary of a wheat field and a forest. From the station, bus #13 or 23: "Hardtmarkt" (20min.), walk straight and make a left at the *Jugendherberge* sign onto Brahmstr. (1.2km). Newly renovated, the hostel boasts well-kempt rooms and amenities; unfortunately, it's in the middle of nowhere. Aside from frolicking with the resident chickens, there are few nightlife options (reception open noon-10pm;. DM22.50, over 26 DM27.50; breakfast included; sheets DM6). The **telephone code** is 02161.

FAIRY-TALE CASTLES

The Rhineland is the *Schloß*-capital of the world. Castles prickle the urban and rural landscape like fireworks scattered throughout the night sky. From Schloß Bennrath in Düsseldorf to Burg Stahlock in Bacharach, there are literally dozens of castles and *schloßlich* structures worth peeking at, accessible by train, car, or footpath.

Schloß Benrath, in the suburbs of Düsseldorf (S-Bahn #6 (direction: "Köln"): "Benrath"), is a large 18th-century castle which recovers from its excess of pink paint by staring into the looking glass pool of its flowering gardens (castle open Tues.-Sun. 10am-5pm; tours every half hour; DM7, students and children DM3.50). In nearby **Zons, Schloß Friedestrom** is accessible by ferry (tel. (012133) 421 49) or fairy. The real attraction is the summer production of plays based on Grimm's Fairy Tales. For more information, call the **Freilichtbühne Zons** (tel. 422 74). Most of the Rhineland castles are accessible by boat from the larger cities along the Rhine and Mosel rivers. From Köln, one can reach Schloß Friedestrom and **Drachenfels** (see p. 408) in Königswinter (call (02212) 58 30 11 for details). Continue down the Rhine by ship through the **Köln-Düsseldorfer Deutscher Rheinschiffahrt A6** (tel. (02212) 208 83 18; tours available March-Oct; times and prices vary from month to month).

▓ Ruhrgebiet (Ruhr Region)

It was from the coal and steel of the Ruhr Valley that Germany's modern wealth and working class were forged. After 1850, the Ruhr provided the source of railroad expansion and the immense manufacturing demands of a newly unified (and bellicose) Germany, quickly becoming the foremost industrial region in Europe. Not everything was ticky-boo in this era, however; the growing proletarianization and exploitation of the workers led to numerous strikes and strong socialist leanings. Nevertheless, the workers remained loyal to the government, and the Ruhr was torn apart not by Marxist revolution but by Allied bombers in World War II. The reconstruction program in the following years yielded numerous parks and gardens to brighten the region's smoggy visage. At the same time, the Ruhr's sprawling conglomeration of the streetcar, S-Bahn, bus, and U-Bahn systems, linking many of the region's cities, offers the densest concentration of rail lines in the world, providing a snapshot of the industrial past.

ESSEN

For a millennium, Essen was just another German cathedral town. By the eve of World War I, however, Essen had advanced to become the industrial capital of Germany, relying on its seemingly limitless deposits of coal and iron. After its destruction in World War II, the city reformed its image as a soot-belching monstrosity by returning to an emphasis on its religious and cultural offerings. At the same time, Essen's high-tech factories remain the industrial cornerstone of the Ruhr.

Infamous 19th-century arms and railroad mogul **Alfred Krupp** perfected steel-casting in industrial Essen. **Villa Hügel,** the Krupp family home for decades (tel. 48 37), was given to the city in the 1950s in order to brighten the company's image, which was tarnished by affiliation with the Nazis. While exhibits and concerts showcase the villa's magnificent mahogany halls, the house itself reflects Krupp's gaudy arrogance. S-Bahn #6: "Essen-Hügel." (Grounds open daily 8am-8pm. Villa open Tues.-Sun. 10am-6pm. Special exhibits open Mon. and Wed.-Sun. 10am-7pm, Tues. 10am-9pm. DM1.50, students and seniors DM0.50.) Essen's **Münster Kirche,** close to the city center on Burgpl., is an ancient, cloistered string of flowering courtyards and hexagonal crypts. The 1000-year-old doll-like *Goldene Madonna* stands beside the nave (open daily 7:30am-6:30pm; DM2, students DM1). Although Nazis eviscerated Essen's **Alte Synagoge** (tel. 452 80) in 1938, it stands today as the largest synagogue north of the Alps. Inside, slides, pictures, and objects from the Third Reich era make up the *Dokumentationsforum,* a monument to the Jews of Essen. U-Bahn: "Porschepl." and follow the signs to the Schützenbahn; as you head south on the Schützenbahn, the synagogue is on your left (open Tues.-Sun. 10am-6pm; free. Tours DM1, free for students with a call one day in advance.)

The **Deutsches Plakat Museum** (German Poster Museum), on the third floor of the shopping mall at the intersection of Rathenaustr. and Am Glockenspiel, features everything from the unusual (a one-eyed nude) to the downright bizarre (two pig heads eating a human heart). Exhibits rotate every two months (open Tues.-Sun. noon-8pm; DM2, students, handicapped, and children free). The **Design Zentrum Nordrhein Westfalen,** Hindenburgstr. 25-27 (tel. 82 02 10), will fascinate design freaks for hours. Check out futuristic TVs and stereos from the 80s. U-Bahn #17 or 18: "Bismarckpl." (open Tues.-Fri. 10am-6pm, Sat. 10am-2pm; free). **Museum Folkwang,** in the *Museumszentrum* at Goethestr. 41 (tel. 884 53 00), drops all the big names in modern art, although the pre-1945 collections are off-limits until 1998 due to construction. The Folkwang's **Fotographische Sammlung,** in the same complex, takes on camerawork from the early days. Streetcar #101, 107, or 127, or U-Bahn #11: "Rüttenscheider Stern." Follow signs to the Museumzentrum and continue (north) on Rüttenscheiderstr., then turn left on Kuhrstr., and right onto Goethestr. (Both open Tues.-Wed. and Fri.-Sun. 10am-6pm, Thurs. 10am-9pm. *Fotographische Sammlung* closed during summer holidays. Combined admission DM5, students and children DM3.) The **Ruhrland Museum,** Goethestr. 41 (tel. 884 51 28), exhibits the Ruhr in its industrial heyday. Experience the life of a coal miner in the Weimar Republic without getting your hands dirty (open Tues.-Wed. and Fri.-Sun. 10am-6pm, Thurs. 10am-9pm; DM5, students DM3).

The **tourist office,** located in the *Rathaus* (tel. 881 31 06), has lots of maps and other goodies but doesn't make hotel reservations. U-Bahn: "Porschepl." (open Mon.-Tues. 7:30am-4pm, Wed. 7:30am-3:30pm, Thurs. 7:30am-6pm, Fri. 7:30am-3pm). Essen's **U-Bahn** and **streetcar** lines cost DM3.10 per ride. Essen's **Mitfahrzentrale,** Freiheit 4 (tel. 194 40), pairs riders with drivers (open daily 9am-7pm). The **Jugendherberge (HI),** Pastoratsberg 2 (tel. 49 11 63; fax 49 25 05), home to the 8th-century **Abteikirche** and the **Luciuskirche,** the oldest parish churches north of the Alps, sits in a park in the Werden district. S-Bahn #6: "Bahnhof Werden," then bus #190: "Jugendherberge." If you feel like playing Alpine mountain climber, cross the bridge, take the second right onto Bungerstr., and follow Kemensborn uphill as it winds all over the map to a sharp right at Pastoratsberg. The *Jugendherberge*'s grounds contain a grass basketball court. (Reception open 7am-11:30pm. Curfew 11:30pm. DM24, over 26 DM29. Breakfast included, sheets DM6.) The basic, comfortable **Hotel Kessing,** Hachestr. 30 (tel. 23 99 88; fax 23 02 89), is close to the train station; turn left on Hachestr. (Singles DM59, with shower and toilet DM85; doubles DM118, with bath DM138. Breakfast included.) Camp at **"Stadt-Camping" Essen-Werden,** Im Löwental 67 (tel. 49 29 78), on the west bank of the Ruhr. S-Bahn: "Essen-Werden" and continue south along the river. (Reception open 9am-1pm and 3-9:45pm. DM15 per tent, adult DM7.50, child DM5.) The **telephone code** is 0201.

There's a **grocery store** to meet basic food needs in the trains station (open Mon.-Sat. 6:30am-9:30pm; Sun. 9am-9:30pm). The maze of stairs and escalators at **Porscheplatz,** near the *Rathaus,* is Cheap Food Central. U-Bahn: "Porschepl." The **Mensa** (tel. 18 31) is in the green-rimmed building at the university. U-Bahn: "Universität" and follow the signs to the building (open Mon.-Fri. 7:30am-4pm, Sat. 7:30am-3:30pm). Just across the street from the *Mensa,* **Beaulongerie,** on Segerothstr. (tel. 32 62 12), offers huge (30cm), freshly baked baguettes (DM4.50) with a variety of fillings and sauces (open Mon.-Thurs. 11am-11pm, Fri.-Sat. 11am-1pm). Soak up the city ambience and marvel at sculptures crawling out of the walls at **Platz,** Salzmarkt 1 (tel. 22 67 76), near Kennedypl., where they offer daily specials (from DM7) and jazz on Tuesday nights (open Sun.-Thurs. 11am-1am, Fri.-Sat. 11am-3am).

DORTMUND

Take Milwaukee out of Wisconsin, put it in Germany, and you've got Dortmund (except that Dortmund has a better baseball team). With the exception of its American soul-twin, Dortmund annually produces more beer than any other city in the world: 1000L for each of its 600,000 citizens (you do the math). The best known of Dortmund's sudsy brood is the ubiquitous *Dortmunder Union* beer. As part of Germany's industrial backbone, Dortmund was a tempting target for Allied bombers, and 93% of the city center was leveled in World War II. Today, the city is still largely industrial. But there is more to this town than brewing and drunken bowling—Dortmund's cultural assets are significant, and the post-war greening outside the city center has added a new face to this classic *Hendelstadt.* The city gleefully follows its soccer team, **BVB09** (among the best in Europe) with a passion: walk down any street, and when you hear gnashing of teeth, the BVB has just given up a rare goal.

Museum am Ostwall, Ostwall 7 (tel. 502 32 47), was built in 1947 over the ruins of the *Altstadt* in order to make room for modern art, especially the kind suppressed by the Third Reich. The plastic-fruit-and-wooden-grass exhibit make the museum's Picasso look downright conventional. The German Expressionist canvases assemble a definitive collection of the *Blaue Reiter* and *die Brücke* schools (open Tues.-Sun. 10am-5pm; DM4, seniors, students, and children DM1). The Lennies and Squiggies of the world, who may be intimidated by high culture, will be more comfortable in the **Brauerei-Museum,** Märkischestr. 81 (tel. 541 32 89), located in the Kronen Beer Works, southeast of the city center. It's four floors of German art in the form of kegs, steins, and 5000 years of brewing history. U-Bahn #41, 45, or 47: "Markgrafenstr." and walk along Landgrafenstr. in the direction of the tower (open Tues.-Sun. 10am-5pm; free, but no samples). The **Adlerturm,** at Kleppingstr. and Südwall, near the *Rathaus,* is the last remaining section of the old city walls (open Tues.-Sun. 10am-5pm; DM2, seniors, students, and children DM1). The tower has been bisected to show the layers of foundation. Dortmund's 12th-century **Marienkirche,** also in the city center, is known for the artistic brilliance of its altar and the enthroned figure of Christ (open Tues.-Fri. 10am-noon and 2-4pm, Sat. 10am-5pm). The **Dortmunder Tierpark** houses over 2500 animals, including a special South American exhibit in the three-tiered Amazon House. U-Bahn #49: "Hacheney" (open daily 9am-6:30pm; DM8, the small creatures called "children" DM4).

Dortmund is on the eastern edge of the tangle of cities in the Ruhr River area. The S-Bahn (#1 and 21) connects it to Essen and Düsseldorf. The **tourist office,** Königswall 20 (tel. 502 56 66, room booking 14 03 41; fax 16 35 93), across from the station, will book rooms (DM55 and up) for a DM3 fee (open Mon.-Fri. 9am-6pm, Sat. 9am-1pm, Sun. 10am-noon). **ADFC,** Hausmannstr. 22 (tel. 13 66 85), **rents bikes** for DM9 per day (open Wed.-Mon. 10am-6pm). The **post office,** 44137 Dortmund (tel. 98 40), is located outside the north entrance of the *Hauptbahnhof* (open Mon.-Fri. 8am-6pm, Sat. 8am-1pm, Sun. 10am-11am). Send letters and then feast your eyes on the statue outside, depicting two hands fighting with legs. The **telephone code** is 0231.

Hotel prices in Dortmund are high (singles from DM50), and there is no hostel or campground, but hostelers can easily jump the train to nearby Essen (see p. 345). Close to the station, **Hotel-Garni Carlton,** Lütge Brückstr. 5-7 (tel. 52 80 30; fax 52 50 20), has big, comfy rooms. Head left on Königswall as you exit the station, take a right on Gnadenort and then another right on Lütge Brückstr. (Reception open Mon.-Fri. 7am-4am, Sat. 7am-2pm and 6:30pm-4am, Sun. 6:30pm-4am. Singles DM50, with bath DM65; doubles DM90, with bath DM110. Breakfast included.) After satisfying your curiosity about beer mechanics at the Brauerei Museum, go for some interactive experience at **Hövels Hausbrauerei** (tel. 14 10 44), whose light brew is a town favorite (open daily 11am-1am; kitchen open 11am-12:30am). The **Daily am Hambrucher Markt** on Harkortstr. (tel. 71 64 50), has an outdoor cafe with meals under DM10. U-Bahn: "Hambrucher" (open Mon.-Fri. 7am-7:30pm, Sat. 7am-3pm).

WUPPERTAL

The **Schwebebahn,** a renowned suspension rail which was likened to a "flying milli-pede" when its tracks were laid down, was the glue that, in 1929, cemented together the mill towns that now form Wuppertal, and it remains the number one tourist attraction today. As you ride this orange-and-green roller-coaster railway, you'll float over the crowded pedestrian zone and see the many church steeples scattered throughout the modern buildings; then you'll skim along the Wupper River, lined with green trees and bushes on one side and pastel-colored warehouses on the other. Any local will gleefully tell you about Tuffi, the circus elephant who, on a promotional ride on the *Schwebebahn,* shocked everyone by jumping out of his train into the river below. There are actual pictures of the baby elephant landing in the water, but the reporters were too stunned to capture the train's journey on film.

A statue of stone proletarians sits in front of the slate **Engels-Haus,** Engelsstr. 10, where Marx's co-author and pamphleteer Friedrich Engels grew up. Works of this most famous Commie sidekick saturate the house, while multilingual devotions fill the guest book. The **Museum für Frühindustrialisierung** (early industrialization), in an old textile mill to the rear of the house, explains some of Fred's political ire, documenting inhumane working conditions. Guides operate the old machinery, explaining every whirr. (Open Tues.-Sun. 10am-1pm and 3-5pm. Admission DM3. Ring the doorbell to enter.) This **Historisches Zentrum** (tel. 563 64 98), a house and a mill, is easily accessible from the Schwebebahn "Adlerbrücke" stop, the Wuppertal-Barmen train station (go down Flügelstr. and right past the Opera), and bus #610. **Friedrich-straße,** lined with bars, pubs, and cafes, ends at the copper tower of the Elberfeld *Rathaus* and a huge, flamboyant fountain of Neptune. Follow the sea-king's imperious gaze through Kirstenpl. as it curves to Poststr. 11, where a *Glockenspiel* chimes (Mon.-Sat. at 10am, noon, 4, and 6pm; Sun. at noon, 4, and 6pm). The **Von der Heydt-Museum,** Turmhof 8 (tel. 563 22 23), houses an impressive array of works by artists from the Dutch masters to the French Impressionists (including Degas) and moderns (Dalí, Kokoschka, and Picasso, among others; open Tues.-Wed., Fri.-Sun. 10am-7pm, Thurs. 10am-9pm; DM6, students and buckaroos DM4.)

You can get a hotel reservation (from DM35) at the **tourist office,** in the Döppersberg Pavillon (tel. 563 21 80; fax 563 80 52), at the foot of the *"Hauptbahnhof Schwebebahn"* stop. Take the tunnel from the station to the pedestrian zone, and turn right upon exiting (open Mon.-Fri. 9am-6pm, Sat. 9am-1pm). Wuppertal's **Jugendherberge (HI),** Obere Lichtenplatzerstr. 70 (tel. 55 23 72; fax 55 73 54), is in a park in Barmen, south of the city center. From the Barmen station, bus #640: "Jugendherberge" or walk right on Winklerstr., turn right on Fischertal, walk up the hill, and make a right on Amalienstr. Turn left on the path opposite Fischerstr.—the hostel is up the dirt path on the right. The six-bed rooms have sinks and new wood furnishings. (Reception open until 10pm. Curfew 11:30pm. DM22.50, over 26 DM27.50. Members only. Sheets DM6. Breakfast included.) From the *Hauptbahnhof*, go past the end of Poststr. and continue on Friedrichstr. past countless cafes to get to **Café-Téatro**, Albrechtstr. 5 (tel. 44 61 45). This crepe club is a popular hangout with event schedules lining the walls (entrees DM8-17.50; open Sun.-Thurs. 5pm-1am, Fri.-Sat. 5pm-3am). Those seeking mass quantities without the atmosphere should veer off Friedrichstr. at the sign for **Akzenta,** the province's largest grocery store (open Mon.-Wed. 9am-6:30pm, Thurs. 9am-8:30pm, Fri. 8am-8:30pm, Sat. 8am-2pm). The **telephone code** is 0202.

SOLINGEN

Prized throughout the world for quality of the highest caliber, cutlery from Solingen has been a tradition for six centuries. Surviving even the harsh Treaty of Versailles, which barred the production of bladed weapons, the Solingen tradition persists to this day—look for the city's name or the ubiquitous "Zwilling" emblem (two stock figures walking like Egyptians) on a pair of scissors near you. In recent times, the people of Solingen have emphasized the good deeds of businessman **Hermann Friedrich Grähe,** the Solinger "Schindler," whose actions saved a lot of Jews from Auschwitz.

The **Kotten at Balkhausen** (tel. 452 36), just outside of Solingen, has been preserved as a monument to early knife-grinders. From the Solingen station, bus #681: "Hästen," then left on Balkhauser Weg (400m). Learn how to grind (but not bump) for free. (Open Tues.-Sun. 10am-5pm, or by appointment. Workshop and Grinder's Museum open Sat.-Sun. 10am-5pm.) The **Klingenmuseum,** Klosterhof 4 (tel. 598 22), is also a monument to cutlery. Exhibits include baguette-sized pocketknives and exotic African swords—very big and bad. Bus #683: "Täppken," then follow the signs. Look for the 20ft. pair of silver scissors rooted in the courtyard (open Tues.-Thurs., Sat.-Sun. 10am-5pm, Fri. 2-5pm; DM5, students and children DM2.50).

The **tourist office,** in the *Rathaus* on Cronenbergerstr., Room 24 (tel. 290 23 33; fax 290 24 79), happily offers information on the town and the surrounding area—useful, since **Burg an der Wupper** (below) has no tourist office (open Mon.-Tues. and Thurs. 7:30am-5pm, Wed. 7:30am-4pm, Fri. 7:30am-1pm). The **Jugendherberge Solingen-Gräfrath,** Flockertsholzerweg 10 (tel. 59 11 98; fax 59 41 79), labels its rooms with cute pictures of animals. Bus #695 (direction: "Abteiweg"): "Eugen-Maurer-Heim," then walk uphill, and turn right onto the street labeled with the f-word. Inside, the 2-, 4-, 6-, and 8-bed rooms are extremely clean (reception open until 10pm; curfew midnight; DM21.60, over 26 DM26.60; sheets DM6). For accommodations closer to the scenic Burg an der Wupper, consider the **Hotel-Landhaus Arnz,** Burger Landstr. (mmm...burgerland) 249 (tel. 440 00; fax 479 14). Bus #683 (direction: "Burg"): "Jagenberg" and get off right at the door. (Reception open Sun.-Thurs. 5-10pm. Singles DM45, with bath DM65; doubles DM80, with bath DM110.) An impressive array of cheap cafes and grocery stores line **Konrad-Adenauer-Straße** between Kronprinzstr. and Kölnerstr. The **telephone code** is 0212.

BURG AN DER WUPPER

In a setting straight out of a Grimms' fairy tale, the Burg an der Wupper perches majestically 110m above the softly flowing waters of the Wupper. The castle, erected in the 12th century by **Count Englebert II of Berg,** Archbishop of Köln, is surrounded by a lush forest in a valley untouched by time. The little town below touts *Fachwerk* houses with blossoming *Blümchen* billowing out of the windows. Wander the cobblestone streets along the river and pick a little bakery to sample the local *Bretzeln*. To reach the **castle,** walk up the gently sloping paths through the forest or ride the **Seilbahn Burg** to experience the bizarre feeling of riding a chair lift without skis (open daily 10am-6pm; one way DM3, children DM1.50; round-trip DM4.50, children DM2.50). From Solingen, bus #683: "Burg Brücke" and then cross the street and follow Schloßbergstr. up the mountain. As you approach the peak, the ivy-covered *Schloß* turrets will appear. Look back for a full view of the lush Wupper Valley. The castle is now a museum detailing many aspects of castle life from the cool defensive arrow slits in the battlements to the medieval privies (open Tues.-Sun. 10am-6pm, Mon. 1-6pm; Nov.-Feb. Tues.-Sun. 11am-5pm; DM6, students DM4.50).

Scents of a more pleasant nature waft from **Café-Restaurant Burghof,** Wermelskirchenerstr. 2 (tel. 410 24), behind the castle. As you sit in the 17th-century half-timbered house on a tapestry chair, gaze over the rolling hills and devour a waffle (DM4) made from a secret *Burg* recipe (open Tues.-Sun. 8:30am-7pm). To reach the **Jugendherberge Burg an der Wupper,** An der Jugenherberge 11 (tel. 410 25; fax 494 49), walk to the bus stop behind the castle. Bus #266: "Jugendherberge." Or for a little Alpine breathing exercise, trudge up the hill, turn left on Jorgensfeld, make another left on Graf-Adolf-Str., and follow the curve around (10min. from the castle). Adequate rooms with two beds and a sink (reception open 2-6pm; curfew 10pm; DM21.60, over 26 DM26.60; sheets DM6). The **telephone code** is 0212.

▓ Teutoburger Wald (Teutoburg Forest)

The frolicking hills and the towering trees of the Teutoburger Wald expand between the Ems and Lippe rivers. It was in this virescent forest in 9AD that Teutonic chief Hermann (or Arminius, in Latin) lured Roman general Quintilius Varus into a trap, killing him and his three legions—20,000 men—in a victory so devastating that no one came to bury the dead for six years. The event left an indelible stamp on Emperor Augustus, who never again tried to conquer the land east of the Rhine, halting the spread of Roman influence. Later, the image of the heroic Hermann was used to rally a German national consciousness. The military braggadocio has since dissipated, and the Teutoburger Wald now offers biking and hiking through the towns scattered about the woods. Only a few existing establishments offer bicycles, although public transportation in the region is excellent. Numerous buses run frequently, and trains connect Bielefeld, Detmold, and Attenbeken.

DETMOLD

Towering over the dense forest, the striking **Hermannsdenkmal** commemorates the Teutonic chief Hermann, proclaiming him liberator of the German people. Overeager nationalists erected Hermann's monolithic likeness on an old encampment in 1875, and Kaiser Wilhelm I came to cut the ribbon. Complete with winged helmet, the statue wields a 7m sword with the disconcerting inscription, "German unity is my power, my power is Germany's might." The memorial also serves as a source of Germanic historical confusion: research continually re-locates the battle to other hills. The only consensus reached is that the colossus does *not* mark the spot of the battle. Climb up the pedestal or mingle just below Big H's humongous toes (open March-Oct. daily 9am-6:30pm; Nov.-Feb. 9:30am-4pm; DM2, children DM0.70). If the timing's right, you can catch a film at the small theater next door (1 per hr. 9am-5pm; Nov.-Feb. 1 per hr. 10am-3pm). The hike is beautiful, but rather steep for the inexperienced (or lazy) hiker. For those afraid to break a sweat, bus #792 makes the ascent from the train station. (May-Sept. Mon.-Fri. 8:10, 9:10am, 3:10pm, Sat. 9:10am and 3:10pm; Sun. and holidays 10:30am and 2:30pm.)

No less impressive and far more exhilarating is the **Adlerwarte** (Eagle's Watch; tel. 471 71), featuring over 80 birds of prey. Time your arrival with bus #701 from Detmold (direction: "Weidmüller"): "Adlerwarte" to catch a free flight exhibition. The falcons strafe the crowd, passing inches above startled faces and causing children and adults alike to shriek. (Park open March-Oct. 9:30am-5:30pm; displays at 11am, 3, and 4:30pm; Nov.-Feb. park open 10am-4pm; flights at 11am, 2:30pm, and 3:30pm. DM6, students DM4.50, children DM2.50—it's worth every *Pfennig*.)

In the *Altstadt*, cannons still arm the courtyard of the **Fürstliches Residenzschloß** (tel. 700 20), a Renaissance castle in the town's central park. Its **Rotersaal** remains red and decadent. Just down the hall are the **Jagdwaffen** (Hunting Weapons), an array of 400-year-old hunting equipment. (Hourly tours April-Oct. daily on the hr. 10am-5pm; Nov.-March at 10, 11am, 2, 3, and 4pm. Written English translations available. DM6, children DM3, group members DM4.50.)

Detmold's unbeatable location makes it an ideal base for exploring the Teutoburger Wald. The staff at the **tourist office,** Rathaus am Markt (tel. 97 73 28; fax 97 74 47) supplies you with everything you need. From the station, head left on Bahnhofstr., turn right on Paulinenstr., then left on Bruchstr. into the pedestrian zone, and walk another five minutes to the *Rathaus.* The tourist office is on the right side of the building (the front entrance is usually locked). The city brochure is excellent, with a map thorough enough for hikes to the *Denkmal* and the surrounding area. For in-depth info for exploration by bike, pick up the "Lipperland" map (DM14.80). Rooms in town start at DM35, but the tourist office doesn't make reservations. (Open Mon.-Thurs. 9am-noon and 1-5pm, Fri. 9am-4pm, Sat. 10am-noon; Nov.-March Mon.-Thurs. 9am-noon and 1-5pm, Fri. 9am-noon.) **City tours** of the *Altstadt* take off from the main entrance of the *Residenzschloß* (April-Oct. Sat. at 10am, Sun. at 11am; DM4, students DM2). To make the best use of the outstanding **bus** connections, swing by the **SVD** office, Langestr. 70 (tel. 97 77 44), at the "Rosental" bus stop and pick up little cards for each bus line (open Mon.-Fri. 9am-6pm, Sat. 9am-1pm). From the tourist office walk north on Langestr. and then onto Richthofenstr. 14, where **Fahrradbüro Detmold** (tel. 97 74 01; fax 30 02 01) rents out old **bikes.** (DM6 per day, DM30 per week. Passport or ID and DM50 deposit required. Open Tues. and Thurs. 5-7pm, Sat. 10am–1pm). It might be a good idea to pick up a bike in neighboring Lemgo or Horn and bring it here on the bus. The **telephone code** is 05231.

In addition to the regular pack of wild school children, the **Jugendherberge "Schanze" (HI),** Schirrmannstr. 49 (tel. 247 39, fax 289 27), features its own mule in a bucolic setting with standard four-bed rooms and cable TV. From Bussteig 3 at the train station, bus #704 (direction: "Hiddesen"): "Auf den Klippen," and walk 10 minutes down the trail. By foot from the station, walk up Hermannstr., continue onto Fürstengartenstr., turn right on Freiligrathstr. (which becomes Bandelstr.), and then left on Bülowstr. Take a shortcut by turning right up Schützentwete and then right onto Schützenberg (35min.). (Reception open until 10pm. Curfew 10pm, but guests are provided with keys. DM19.30, over 26 DM23.30. Breakfast included. Lunch DM7.40. Dinner DM6.40.) A **Kaiser's supermarket,** Bruchstr. 18-20, serves as the friendly neighborhood grocery store. It's located on the way to the city center from the station (open Mon.-Fri. 8am-7pm, Sat. 8am-2pm).

LEMGO

From the Detmold *Hauptbahnhof,* hike, bike, or take bus #790 or 791 along the 12km trail to Lemgo, where the Weser Renaissance lives again. Those wondering what a Weser Renaissance is and why it should choose to happen here could do no better than to visit the aptly-named **Weserrenaissance Museum** (tel. 945 00) right inside **Schloß Brake** (central castle; open Tues.-Sun. 10am-6pm; DM4, students DM2, under 6 free). Follow the signs as you enter the city, or bus #790: "Schloß Brake." The current castle was built under Graf Simon VI zur Lippe from 1584 to 1592; his chambers and other period rooms are on display in the seven-story castle tower. If you find a revival of the classical fine arts less interesting than, say, burning people alive, head down to the **Hexenbürgermeisterhaus Lemgo,** Breitestr. 19 (tel. 21 32 76), a collection of historical odds and ends focusing on the **witch-trial** era. Get off at the "Waisenhauspl." bus stop and walk (5min.) up Breitestr. (open Tues.-Sun. 10am-12:30pm and 1:30-5pm; DM1.50, students DM1). Nearby, the 800-year-old **St. Nicolai Kirche** dominates the Marktplatz with twin towers. Check out the cross above the bronze door knob—it's made from wood fished out of the wreckage of England's Coventry Cathedral. For room-finding assistance (from DM35 per person), contact the **tourist office,** at Papenstr. 7 (tel. 21 33 47; fax 21 34 92; open March-Oct. Mon.-Fri. 10am-5pm, Sat. 10am-1pm; Nov.-Feb. Mon-Thurs. 10am-5pm, Fri. 10am-2pm). City tours leave every Saturday at 11am (April-Oct.) from the main portal of the *Nicolaikirche* (DM4, students DM2). Papenstr. branches off to the right of Breitestr. as you head away from the train station. Accommodations can also be found at the **Campgrounds,** Regenstorstr. 106 (tel. 148 58). From Breitestr., turn right onto Orpingstr.; when Orpingstr.

becomes Regenturstr., the camp is to the left 100m ahead (adults DM7, children DM3, tents DM3-9). The **telephone code** is 05261.

HORN AND LÜGDE

Horn is the point of departure for an excursion to the **Externsteine** ("Outer Stones"), the mysterious craggy monoliths which jut from the forest floor, scarred by the ravages of millennia. Covered in the half-forgotten pagan imagery of *Ur-Germanic* tribes, these stones trace Druidic symbols of the ancient Celtic tribes who were forced across the English channel well before the first century. The big rocks are also fun to climb (open April-Oct. daily 9am-6pm; DM2, students DM1; tours by appointment). To get there from the *Rathaus,* walk left on Mittelstr., then bear right on Externsteinestr. and follow the signs (25min.).

Horn lies a hilly 12km from Detmold (1 stop before Detmold on the train from Alterbeker), in the southern Teutoburger Wald. To learn more about the *Externsteine,* visit the **Horn Burgmuseum** in the imposing **Burg Horn,** Burgstr. 13 (tel. 20 12 00), following the signs from the *Rathaus* (open Tues.-Wed. 2-4pm, Thurs. 2-5:30pm, Fri.-Sun. 10am-noon; DM1.50, students DM1). Info on rooms (from DM23) and sites is available at the **tourist office,** Rathauspl. 2 (tel. 20 12 62), in the startlingly ugly building next to the big yellow town hall (open Mon.-Wed. and Fri. 9am-noon, Thurs. 9am-noon and 3-5:30pm). From the Horn-Bad Meinberg train station, bus #782 (direction: "Detmold"): "Mittelstr." and backtrack five minutes. Or walk out the station door 20m and turn left. This short road becomes Kampstr.; follow it until it deadends into Mittelstr. and take a right (20min.). Horn's **telephone code** is 05234.

To reach the **Jugendherberge (HI),** Jahnstr. 36 (tel. 25 34; fax 691 99), follow the above instructions to the *Rathaus* and trek up Mittelstr., bearing left onto Paderbornerstr., then turn right onto the second "Jahnstr." sign. From the train station, bus #782: "Mittelstr." and continue in the same direction on foot, following the above directions. From Detmold, bus #356 (direction: "Paderborn/Bus/Hauptbahnhof"): "Jahnstr." *Herbergsvater* Herr Lenzing wakes you with a song on the intercom. (Reception open 5-10pm. Curfew 10pm. DM21, over 26 DM26. Breakfast included. Full *Pension* DM35, over 26 DM39. Sheets DM6.)

Easter Sunday is the best time to visit the hamlet of **Lügde.** After a bacchanalian feast, townspeople hurl giant wheels stuffed with flaming straw (**Osterräder** or Catherine wheels) downhill. The rest of the time, Lügde reverts to being a placid little Christian town with a 13th-century church. The Lügde **tourist office,** Forderestr. 81 (tel. 780 29), offers brochures (open Mon.-Sat. 9am-12:30pm and 2:30-6pm). Lügde is on the **train** line from Hannover to Alterbeker. Lügde's **telephone code** is 05281.

▧ Münster

After its christianization by an envoy of Charlemagne in 805, Münster endured a checkered history of fiery schism, fanatical heresy, and swift and terrible retribution rife with the passion, if not the virtue, of religious fervor. As the capital of the old Kingdom of Westphalia, Münster presided over the 1648 Peace which brought the Thirty Years War to an end, defining the borders of scores of German mini-states for centuries. But the Münster of today offers much more than towering cathedrals and historic checkpoints: the 55,000 students of the **Wilhelmsuniversität** know how to put those 9th-century reveling monks to shame. Still, the monks do their damnedest to keep the students in line, with the sporadically enforced 1am curfew providing a powerful reminder of the ecclesiastic legacy.

ORIENTATION AND PRACTICAL INFORMATION

Münster is located at the confluence of the lower channels of the Ems River, in the midst of the Münsterland plain. Frequent trains, running from Düsseldorf and Köln to the southwest, and from Bremen to the northeast, stop in Münster.

Tourist Office: Klemensstr. 10 (tel. 492 27 10; fax 492 77 43). Cross Bahnhofstr. and head left, taking a sharp right onto Windthorstr., and veer right onto Stubengasse;

the office is on your left as Stubengasse crosses Klemenstr. and becomes H.-Bruning-Str. The office books rooms for free (from DM50 per person), and offers tours and theater tickets. Open Mon.-Fri. 9am-6pm, Sat. 9am-1pm.

Flights: Flughafen Münster-Osnabrück, located to the northeast of the city, has flights daily to Berlin, Frankfurt, Munich, and Zürich, Sun.-Fri. to London, and Mon.-Fri. to Paris and to Amsterdam. Bus #S50 shuttles between the train station and the airport (board to the right of the station); the schedule is posted in the station. For **flight information,** call (02571) 940.

Car Rental: Hertz, Hammerstr. 186 (tel. 773 78). ID required. Open Mon.-Fri. 7:30am-7pm, Sat. 7:30am-2pm, Sun. 9:30-11:30am.

Bike Rental: Münster's train station has an impressive bike rental service (tel. 69 13 20), with 300 bikes up for grabs. DM7, non-DB customers DM11. You can reserve your wheels by phone. Open daily 7:30am-9:30pm.

Boat Rental: Soverschmidt Yachtschule Aasee (tel. 803 03) rents sailboats (DM15), rowboats and paddleboats (DM13) and offers lessons. Bus #4: "Golden Brücke." Open daily 9am-6pm.

Mitfahrzentrale: des AStA runs a ride-share office, Schloßpl. 1 (tel. 405 05). Open Mon.-Fri. 8:30am-4pm.

Laundromat: Wasch Center, Moltekestr. 5-7. Wash DM6. Open Mon.-Fri. 6am-11pm. Another branch at Wolbeckerstr. 81 has the same prices and hours. Bus #11, 320, 330, 311, or 313: "Sophienstr."

Emergency: Police, tel. 110.

Post Office: Berlinerstr. 37, 48001 Münster. Located directly to the left of the train station. Open Mon.-Fri. 8am-6pm, Sat. 8am-5pm.

Telephone Code: 0251.

ACCOMMODATIONS AND CAMPING

Some travelers hit up **students** for a place to sleep, because this little town isn't cheap. The shiny *Jugendgästehaus* is no steal, and hotels fill up quickly; be sure to call days ahead. In a pinch, there's a hostel in **Nottuln,** a 50-minute bus ride away (tel. (02502) 78 78; fax 96 19). Bus #560 or 561: "Rodepl.," then follow the signs. (Reception open until 10pm. DM21, over 26 DM26. Breakfast included. Sheets DM6.)

Jugendgästehaus Aasee, Bismarckallee 31 (tel. 53 24 70; fax 52 12 71). Bus #10 or 34: "Hoppendamm." An Orwellian vision of our hosteling future: huge brick and mirror-glass compound with **security cameras** and strict key policy. Still, it keeps you comfortable, with a toilet and bath in each room. 4-bed room DM37.50 per person, 2-bed room DM46 per person; less if you stay 5 days or more. Reception open 7am-1am. Lockout 1am. Breakfast buffet and sheets included.

Haus vom Guten Hirten, Mauritz-Lindenweg 61 (tel. 378 70; fax 37 45 44), to the right of the train station. Go right onto Wolbeckerstr., left onto Hohenzollern-Ring, right onto Manfred-von-Richthofen-Str., and then left on Maurits-Lindenweg. Or bus #14: "Stadion," then turn left onto Maurits-Lindenweg. It's a considerable distance from both the station and the *Altstadt,* but spacious, immaculate rooms and a relaxing TV make it worth the extra effort. Reception open 6am-9pm. Singles DM55; doubles DM94; triples DM129. Breakfast included.

Hotel Bockhorn, Bremerstr. 24 (tel. 655 10), a 5min. walk from the train. Go left out of the train station, turn left on Hamburgerstr. (made of asphalt, not beef), and then right on Bremerstr. Tidy rooms and powerful showers compensate for the dim hallways. Singles DM55; doubles DM110. Full-service breakfast included.

Hotel An'n Schlagbaum, Woselerstr. 269 (tel. 79 21 80). Bus #7, 15, or 16: "Kappenburger Damn. Despite the silly name, this intimate hotel of eleven rooms remains affordable. Singles DM50-60. Breakfast included.

Camping: Campingplatz Münster, auf der Laer 7 (tel. 31 19 82). Bus #320: "Wersewinkel." Reception open daily 8am-1pm and 3-6pm. DM4 per person. Tents DM4. Showers DM0.50.

FOOD

On Wednesdays and Saturdays, a farmer's **market** takes over the plaza in front of the *Dom,* vending fresh fruit, fresh meat, and fresh clothes (open 7am-2pm). The **Kuhvi-**

ertel (old student quarter) is lined with *Kneipen* and fairly inexpensive eateries. A grocery store sits on Bahnhofstr. 15 (open Mon.-Sat. 8am-8pm, Sun. 8am-4pm).

Diesel, Harsewinkelgasse 1-4 (tel. 57 96), by the intersection of Windhorststr., Stubengasse, and Loerstr.; look for the 2.5m pedestal surmounted by 0.5m cherries. Gobble down daily specials (DM6-12) next to fuel pumps amid fumes of cheap booze. Pool, darts, and an extensive magazine collection. Breakfast served daily 10am-4pm, dinner 7-11pm. Bar open Sun.-Thurs. 11am-1am, Fri.-Sat. 11am-3am.

Cavete Akademische Bieranstalt, Kreuzstr. 38 (tel. 457 00). Founded *by* students *for* students in 1959, this first student pub in Westphalia serves dark carnivalesque decor and delicious homemade spinach noodles in a variety of sauces (DM8-10). Open daily 7pm-1am, kitchen closes Sun.-Thurs. 11pm, Fri-Sat. midnight.

The Pilgrims Irish Pub, Nienberger Kirchpl. 2-4 (tel. 41 24). A real-deal Irish pub with live blues and jazz, darts, and billiards. Open daily 6pm-1am.

John Doe's Diner, Spiekerhoff 44 (tel. 51 84 06). An apple pie slice of 50s Americana, reminiscent of Jackrabbit Slim's. Nostalgic kitsch complements a full selection of burgers, buffalo wings, and American "beer." Open daily 9:30am-1am.

SIGHTS

When Goethe's carriage turned onto the tree-lined **Promenade** encircling the Münster *Altstadt,* he would slow it and smell the seasonal flowers and fruits. It's an inexpensive literary habit worth imitating. To get there, continue through the Baroque facade of the **Schloß,** now the administrative center of **Wilhelmsuniversität,** into the Botanical Gardens (open March-Oct. daily 8am-7pm, Nov.-Feb. 8am-4pm).

In the center of the *Altstadt,* on Dompl., towers the **St.-Paulus-Dom,** a grandiose cathedral. The *Dom* was dilapidated in World War II but has since been beautifully restored; the Bishop's inner courtyard is open to the public (open Tues.-Sat. 10am-noon and 2-6pm, Sun. 2-6pm). A stone from the similarly bombed Cathedral of Coventry stands in the entranceway, carrying a wish for mutual forgiveness between Britain and Germany. From his pulpit in the cathedral, Bishop Clemens von Galen delivered a courageous sermon against the Nazi program of **euthanasia** for so-called "incurables." After wide distribution of the sermon, pressure from the church prompted a rare partial retreat by Hitler. The speech can be read in the **Domkammer** (open Tues.-Sat. 10am-noon and 2-6pm, Sun. 2-6pm; DM1). Inside, a statue of St. Christopher points its massive toes to the 16th-century **astronomical clock,** which recreates the movements of the planets and plays a merry *Glockenspiel* tune (Mon.-Sat. noon, Sun. 12:30pm; *Dom* open Mon.-Sat. 6am-6pm, Sun. 6:30am-7:30pm).

The seamy underbelly of the city's religious fervor is evidenced by the three cages hanging above the clock face of **Marktkirche St. Lamberti,** just off the Prinzipalmarkt. In the 16th century, rebel Anabaptists took over the town, led by the self-styled Prophet Jan van Leiden. He had 16 wives, and killed all who refused to surrender their property to his "New Zion" in Münster. After a bloodbath of episcopal reconquest, van Leiden and his two cohorts were executed, their bodies then hung in cages on the steeple. The authorities finally cleaned the cages out but left them hanging as a "reminder." Also suspended here is Germany's only free-hanging organ. Free concerts are given the first Saturday of every month at noon. Next door to the church is the **Friedenssaal** (Hall of Peace), which kept one unknown woodcarver very busy for a very long time. The treaty that ended the Thirty Years War was sworn here. Among the many elaborate carvings are a mysterious withered human hand and the Golden Cock, a ceremonial carafe used to honor distinguished visitors. (Open Mon.-Fri. 9am-5pm, Sat. 9am-4pm, Sun. 10am-1pm. DM1.50, children DM0.80.) Pick up a guide in English from the front desk; call 83 25 80 for group rates.

MUSEUMS

Like Osnabrück (see p. 313), Münster gears up for the commemoration of the 350th anniversary of the Peace of Westphalia—they'll party like it's 1998. Contact the tourist office for celebratory and pyrotechnical details. Other items of historical interest can be found in Münster's many museums. Ask the tourist office for information about all of the city's offerings, including a **Railway Museum,** a **Carnival Museum,** and a **Museum of Organs** (unrelated to the Leprosy Museum) located in the suburbs.

Landesmuseum für Kunst und Kultur, Dompl. 10 (tel. 59 07 01). Contains modern sculptures and ancient paintings, arranged on 3 floors around a central atrium. Call ahead to find out about special exhibits. DM5, students and children DM2. Free on Fri. Open Tues.-Sun. 10am-6pm.

Mühlenhof-Freilichtmuseum, Sentruperstr. 223 (tel. 820 74), is a completely restored industrial village with a bonus *Don Quixote*-style windmill, which sells pointy wooden shoes for DM20. DM5, students and seniors DM3, children DM2. Open April-Oct. daily 10am-5pm; Nov.-March 11am-4pm.

Museum of Leprosy, Kinderhaus 15 (tel. 285 10), to the northwest of the *Altstadt,* is a little far away, but you should definitely drop by. The exhibits, including playful little leper-puppets, are strictly hands-off. Open Sun. 3-5pm. Free. Call for an appointment on other days.

Museum für Lackkunst, Windthorstr. 26 (tel. 41 85 10), just off the Promenade. The banana painted on the door leads to the world's only exhibition of all things **lacquered,** with videos and explanations of how to try this safely at home. Revolving modern exhibits in the basement. DM3, students and children DM1.50. Free on Tues. Open Tues. noon-8pm, Wed.-Sun. noon-6pm.

NIGHTLIFE

Kneipen line the streets across from the *Schloß* in the student quarter and discos abound farther southwest between the train station and the harbor. **Ultimo** provides semi-weekly print coverage of night-life and art openings in Münster and the surrounding area (free at the AStA and Diesel; DM3 at newsstands).

Blechtrommel, Hansaring 26 (tel. 651 19), features live music and a menu that changes weekly. The name refers to the famous post-war Günter Grass novel, "The Tin Drum." *Fußball* tournaments on Mon. and darts on Sat. Pizzas DM11-17.50. Open daily 6pm-1am. Kitchen open 7-11:30pm.

Cuba-Kneipe, Achtermannstr. 10-12 (tel. 582 17). Sip rum drinks to reggae and gear up for the Cuba-*fête* every 1st, 3rd, and 4th Sat. of the month. Young, hip crowd comes 11pm-3am. Otherwise open daily 6pm-1am.

Gaststätte Pinkus Müller, Kreuzstr. 7 (tel. 451 51). About as hip as an elbow, but one of Germany's acutest joys is drinking beer in the house where it's brewed; the *Pinkus Alt* (DM5) here is a fine beer, with a fine name. Peruse the genealogy of the Müllers, including Carl "Pinkus" Müller himself, as you steel yourself for the *Szene.* Open Mon.-Fri. 11:30am-2pm and 5pm-midnight, Sat. 11:30am-midnight.

■ Lower Rhine

XANTEN

If all the cities of the lower Rhine Valley were to become people, Xanten would be the granddaddy of them all. Founded by Roman Emperor Augustus in 15 BC, Xanten's ancient settlement served as the mythical birthplace of Siegfried after the Romans skipped town in the fourth century. The city weathered the centuries until Canadians decided that "X" marked the spot and flattened the city in World War II. Despite the raid, the Roman ground plan remains intact at the creatively named **Archäologischer Park** (tel. 29 99), offering visitors a rare glimpse of the living past; the enormous structures demonstrate the skill of the Roman architects and the park's big budget (open March-Nov. daily 9am-6pm; Dec.-Feb. daily 10am-4pm; DM7, students DM4, children DM2.50). Every summer, the park hosts live concerts and musicals (but no gladiator fights) in grand Roman style. Ask the tourist office for details.

During the Middle Ages, Xanten flourished as a satellite to Köln. To build the fortifications, the townspeople cleverly carted the walls of the Roman ruins down the street. The **Klever Tor,** in the southwest corner of the town, represents this era in the city's history, as do the buildings surrounding the cobblestone square in the **Markt.** Towering above is the 12th-century **Dom St. Viktor** (tel. 71 31 34), whose two Romanesque towers and vast Gothic cathedral were built on the grave site of an early Christian martyr (open Mon.-Sat. 10am-6pm, Sun. 12:30-6pm; closed Jan.-Feb. noon-2pm). Next door, the **Regionalmuseum,** Kurfürstenstr. 7-9 (tel. 77 22 98), exhibits artifacts recovered from the archaeology dig, including funny Roman helmets (open May-Sept. Tues.-Fri. 9am-5pm, Sat.-Sun. 11am-6pm; Oct.-April Tues.-Fri. 10am-5pm, Sat.-Sun. 11am-6pm; DM3, students and children DM1.50).

Xanten is a 5-minute bus ride from Kleve (every hr.; DM5.50), making it an easy daytrip. To reach the town from the train station, walk up Bahnhofstr. to the Markt. The **tourist office,** at the far end of the square (tel. 372 38; http://www.nissy.com/xanten), is in the *Rathaus.* There is no hostel, but the friendly staff at the tourist office books hotel rooms (from DM60) with a 12% deposit (open Mon.-Sat. 10am-4:30pm, Sat.-Sun. 10am-4pm). If the office is closed, have fun with the computer outside. **Rent bikes** from **Reineke,** Marsstr. 19 (tel. 14 74), just off the Markt, for DM12 per day or DM8 after 3pm. **Dom Stübchen,** Kleverstr. 14 (tel. 907 88), serves cheap gyros and pizzas (DM6-8.50; open daily noon-10pm). The **telephone code** is 02801.

KLEVE (CLEVES)

The town of **Cleves** is famed for its daughter, **Anne of Cleves,** the local princess whom Henry VIII *didn't* make the happiest woman in the world. Henry's third wife had just died, so he sent Hans Holbein out to bring back paintings of eligible princesses. Henry chose Anne, but when she arrived in England, he decided he'd been misled. Henry insulted her looks until she left and banished Holbein from court. Even so, Kleve retains a link to England, with red British mailboxes and telephones throughout the city complemented by miles of well-kempt gardens.

The 11th-century **Schwanenburg** (Swan's Castle) perches upon a steep-hill overlooking the city. Legend tells of Princess Elsa: the Knight of the Swan won her love, but the condition of marriage was that she could never inquire as to his identity. When curiosity got the better of Elsa, a large swan came to lead her true love away; the legend is cast in bronze in the city center. The entire valley can be seen from the top of the castle's long-necked tower (open daily 11am-5pm; Nov.-March Sat.-Sun. 11am-5pm; DM2, students DM1, children DM0.50). Kleve's recently opened **Museum Kurhaus,** Tiergartenstr. 41 (tel. 750 10), offers a fascinating collection of modern art, including a special exhibit of the Rhineland's modernist *Ewald Mataré* movement. To get there from the castle, turn right on Großestr. then left on Minoritenstr. which turns into Tiergartenstr. (open April-Sept. Tues.-Fri. 10am-6pm; Oct.-March 10am-5pm; DM6, students and seniors DM3, under 14 free). Close to the hostel, the **Reichswald nature preserve** is ideal for hiking or chilling.

Kleve is accessible by **rail** from Krefeld or by hourly **bus** from Xanten (50min.). The town is also right on the Dutch border, and buses run regularly to museum-rich **Arnheim.** The **tourist office,** on Kavarinerstr. in room 217 of the *Rathaus* (tel. 842 67; fax 237 59), gives out city maps, gossip about Anne and Henry, and a list of rooms (DM30 and up) in the city (open Mon. and Wed. 8:30am-12:45pm and 2-5pm, Tues. and Thurs. 8:30am-12:45pm and 2-3:30pm, Fri. 8:30am-12:45pm). The **Sport & Reise Animation** (tel. 201 10) rents **bikes** with reservations only (DM10 per day, DM12.50 on weekends). The **Jugendherberge Kleve (HI),** St. Annaberg 2 (tel. 236 71; fax 247 78), sits in the west end of town, next to the Netherlands. From the station, bus #57 (direction: Richtung Haus Ida): "Annabergstr." and walk uphill. After 6:30pm, you've gotta hike it (30min.): follow Großestr. as it becomes Hagschestr. and veer right onto Steichban. When this ends, pick up the trail on Römerstr. which becomes Merowinger, then turn right onto Königsallee and trudge uphill to the hostel. (Reception open 4-4:45pm, 7:15-7:30pm, and 9:45-10pm. Curfew 10pm. DM22.50, over 26 DM26.50. Sheets DM6. Call ahead). **The Mandarin,** Hoffmannallee 1, offers Chinese food in the heart of Kleve, with sweet lunch specials (open Mon.-Sat. 11:30am-2:30pm and 5:30-11pm, Sun. 11:30am-11pm). The **telephone code** is 02821.

NORDRHEIN-WESTFALEN

Hessen (Hesse)

Prior to the 20th century, Hesse was known for exporting mercenary soldiers to rulers such as King George III, who sent them off to put down an unruly gang of colonial hicks in 1776. Absorbed by Bismarck's Prussia in 1866, Hesse ceased to exist as a political entity until the Allies resurrected it in 1945. Somewhere along the line, the Hessians made an ostensible collective decision to exchange their guns for briefcases. Today, Hesse is the busiest commercial center in the country, led by the banking metropolis of Frankfurt. Overshadowed by Frankfurt, the rest of Hesse attracts little attention from tourists, leaving the medieval delights of Marburg's *Uni*-culture and the fascination of Kassel blessedly off the beaten path.

■ Frankfurt am Main

Skyscrapers loom over crowded streets, investment bankers scurry to and fro—it's not hard to see how Frankfurt acquired the derisive nicknames "Bankfurt" and "Mainhattan," although the city's reputation as a financial center reaches back for centuries. Many visitors view Frankfurt as the most Americanized city in Europe, apparent from the flashy McDonald's on every street corner. Despite its notoriety as the crime capital of Germany, however, Frankfurt is still *Kindergarten* compared to New York City.

The city just celebrated its 1200th birthday, and with it the remarkable achievements and contributions of its people. Anne Frank and Goethe lived here, families such as the Oppenheims and Rothschilds influenced Frankfurt's economic development, and Erich Fromm and Frankfurt School members Theodor Adorno, Max Horkheimer, and Walter Benjamin enriched the city's intellectual landscape.

Martin Luther once remarked that Frankfurt resembles a pot of silver and gold, and today the city government spends more on cultural attractions and tourism than any other German city. The *Kulturszene* is also naturally rich—nearly a full third of the Frankfurters you pass on the street are likely to speak Turkish or English as they munch on cuisine of an international flavor. Frankfurt mysteriously manages to retain an aura of hipness, gravity, and agelessness all at once. If that isn't enough to make you visit, the likelihood of arriving in Germany at Rhein-Main Airport probably is.

ORIENTATION AND PRACTICAL INFORMATION

A sprawling conglomeration of steel, concrete, glass, and scaffolding, Germany's fifth-largest city bridges the **Main River** 35km east of its confluence with the Rhine. Frankfurt's airport and *Hauptbahnhof* are among the busiest in Europe. The train station lies at the end of Frankfurt's red-light district, which in typical Frankfurt fashion brings together sex bars, international airline offices, and banks. From the station, the town center is a 20-minute walk down Kaiserstr. or Münchenerstr., crossing from the newer part of the city to the *Altstadt*. The *Altstadt* is compactly fenced off on three sides by a u-shaped strip of park and on the fourth by the Main, and it is easily approached on foot. The commercial heart of the city centers around **Hauptwache** (S-Bahn #1-6 or 8, 2 stops from the main station). The historical center revolves around the **Römerberg.** U-Bahn #4 (direction: Seckbacher Landstr.): "Römer". Students, student cafes, stores, and services cluster in **Bockenheim,** as does the angry, very angry graffiti demanding *Aktion, Solidarität,* and *Freiheit.* U-Bahn #6 or 7: "Bockenheimer Warte". Across the Main, **Sachsenhausen** draws the *Ebbelwei*-lovers, the pub-crawlers, and the museum-goers (U-Bahn #1, 2, or 3: "Schweizerpl."). On a nice day, Sachsenhausen is a delightful walk directly across the bridge.

A **Frankfurt Card** (available at tourist offices and in most travel agencies; DM15) allows two days of travel on all trains and buses, including the airport line; it also gets you 50% off admission to 15 museums, the *Palmengarten,* the zoo, and that veritable carnival funhouse, the airport visitors' terrace. Eurailpasses valid on all S-Bahn trains.

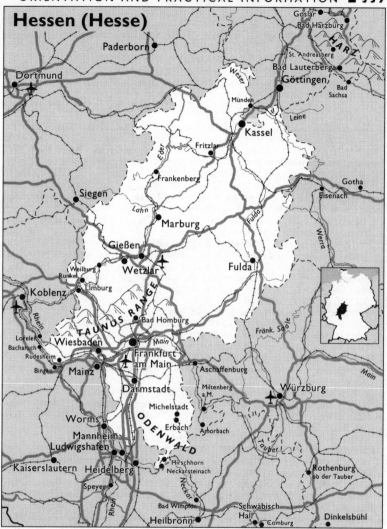

Hessen (Hesse)

HESSEN

Tourist Office: In the *Hauptbahnhof,* across from track 23 (tel. 21 23 88 49). Maps, brochures, souvenirs, tours, and lots more. Books rooms for a DM5 fee (tel. 21 23 08 08). Open Mon.-Fri. 8am-9pm, Sat.-Sun. and holidays 9am-6pm. The other branch borders Römerpl. at Römerberg 27 (tel. 21 23 87 08); no room reservations. Open Mon.-Fri. 9:30am-5:30pm, Sat.-Sun. 10am-4pm.

   Consulates: Australia Gutleutstr. 85 (tel. 273 90 90; fax 23 26 31). Public hours Mon.-Thurs. 9am-1pm and 2-4:30pm, Fri. 9am-1pm and 2-4pm. **U.K.** Bockenheimer Landstr. 42 (tel. 170 00 20; fax 72 95 53). Open Mon.-Fri. 9am-noon and 2-4pm; phone hours Mon.-Thurs. 8:30am-1pm and 2-5pm, Fri. 8:30am-1pm and 2-4:30pm. **U.S.** Siesmayerstr. 21 (tel. 753 50). Open to the public Mon.-Fri. 8-11am; phone hours Mon.-Fri. 8am-4:30pm.

   Currency Exchange: In Airport Hall B (open daily 7:30am-9pm) or the *Hauptbahnhof* (open daily 6:30am-10pm). Better rates at the post office or any of the banks.

American Express: Kaiserstr. 8 (tel. 210 50, 24hr. hotline (0130) 85 31 00; fax 28 33 98). Holds mail for 4 weeks. Services are free. Also exchanges foreign money, handles travelers' checks, and arranges hotel reservations and car rentals. Open Mon.-Fri. 9:30am-5:30pm, Sat. 9am-noon.

Flights: Flughafen Rhein-Main (tel. 69 01) is a major hub. From the airport, S-Bahn #8 and 5 travel to the *Hauptbahnhof* every 15min. Buy tickets (DM5.80) from a green automat marked *"Fahrkarten"* before boarding or face a stiff fee (DM20-80); Eurailpass valid. Most public transport vehicles depart from Terminal 1; a free tram runs from Terminal 2 to Terminal 1.

Trains: Trains from most of Europe frequently roll in and out of Frankfurt's *Hauptbahnhof.* Munich (every 30min., 3½-4½hr.), Berlin (every 30min., 5-6 hr.), Paris (every 2hr., 6-7 hr.). Call 194 19 for schedules, reservations, and information.

Public Transportation: For unlimited access to S-Bahn, U-Bahn, and buses, 24hr. passes (DM9) are available from machines in every station. S-Bahn #1-6 and 8 and U-Bahn vehicles depart from the level below the *Fernzüge* long distance train). Buses depart from the main bus station outside: #10, 11, 16, 19, and 21 pass by the island platform directly outside the main (west) entrance; #35, 37, and 46 leave from just outside and to the right of the main entrance. The Frankfurt Card offers wicked awesome discounts (see above).

Bike Rental: Holger's Rad-Laden, Eschersheimer Landstr. 470 (tel. 52 20 04). U-Bahn #1, 2, or 3: "Lindenbaum." DM20 per day. Bikes are allowed on the subway. Open Mon.-Tues. and Thurs.-Fri. 9am-1pm and 3-6:30pm, Wed. and Sat. 9am-1pm.

Hitchhiking: *Let's Go* does not recommend hitchhiking as a safe mode of transportation. Hitching on the highway itself is strictly forbidden. Masochists heading to Munich from Konstablerwache south, buses #36 or 960: *Autobahn* interchange; to Cologne or Düsseldorf, S-Bahn #1 or 8: Wiesbaden *Hauptbahnhof,* then a local train to Auringen-Medenbach, turn right, walk 800m, proceed under the *Autobahn,* and take the access road to the *Autobahn* rest stop; all other directions, S-Bahn #19 or bus #61 and continue along Mörfelder-Landstr.

Mitfahrzentrale: Baselerstr. 7 (tel. 23 64 44 or 23 61 27). Take a right on Baselerstr. at the side exit of the *Hauptbahnhof* (track 1), and walk two blocks. Connects riders with drivers for a fee. Call ahead. Open Mon.-Fri. 8am-6:30pm, Sat. 8am-2pm.

Bookstores: Süssman's Presse und Buch, Zeil 127 (tel. 131 07 51; fax 131 01 49). Mostly English titles of all kinds for those who can't live without Shakespeare or Clancy. Open Mon. and Wed.-Fri. 9am-7pm, Thurs. 9am-8pm, Sat. 9am-4pm. **British Book Shop,** Börsenstr. 17 (tel. 28 04 92). All-English offerings of classics and popular novels. Open Mon.-Fri. 9:30am-7pm, Sat. 9:30am-4pm.

Laundromat: Wasch Center, Wallstr. 8, in Sachsenhausen near the hostel. Wash DM6, dry DM1 per 15min., soap included. Change machine. Open daily 6am-10pm. **SB Wasch Center,** Große Seestr. 46 (tel. 77 35 80). U-Bahn #6 or 7: "Bockenheimer Warte." From the station, head down Adalbertstr. and right on Große Seestr. Wash DM8, dry DM1 per 10min., soap included. Open daily 6:30am-10pm.

Rape/Battered Women's Hotline: tel. 70 94 94.

Pharmacy: In the basement of the train station by the subway entrances (tel. 23 30 47). Open Mon.-Fri. 6:30am-9pm, Sat. 8am-9pm, Sun. and holidays 9am-8pm. If pharmacies are closed, call 192 92 for emergency prescriptions.

Emergency: Police: tel. 110. **Fire** and **ambulance:** tel. 112.

Internet Access: CybeRyder Internet Cafe, Töngesgasse 31 (tel. 92 08 40 10; fax 28 79 29; email info@cyberyder.de). 6DM per 30min. Mon-Fri. 10am-9pm, Sat. 10am-10pm. More access in **Cyber's** (see **Entertainment and Nightlife,** p. 363).

Post Office: Main branch, Zeil 110, 60313 Frankfurt (tel. 21 11; fax 29 68 84). U- or S-Bahn: "Hauptwache." Send and be sent. Fax and be faxed. Open Mon.-Fri. 9am-6pm, Sat. 9am-1pm. **Branch office** also on the upper level of the *Hauptbahnhof.* Open Mon.-Fri. 6:30am-9pm, Sat. 8am-6pm, Sun. 11am-6pm.

Telephone code: 069.

ACCOMMODATIONS

The cheapest options are the hostels and *Pensionen* in the Westend/University area. If all else fails, there are four other hostels less than 45 minutes away: Bad Homburg (S-

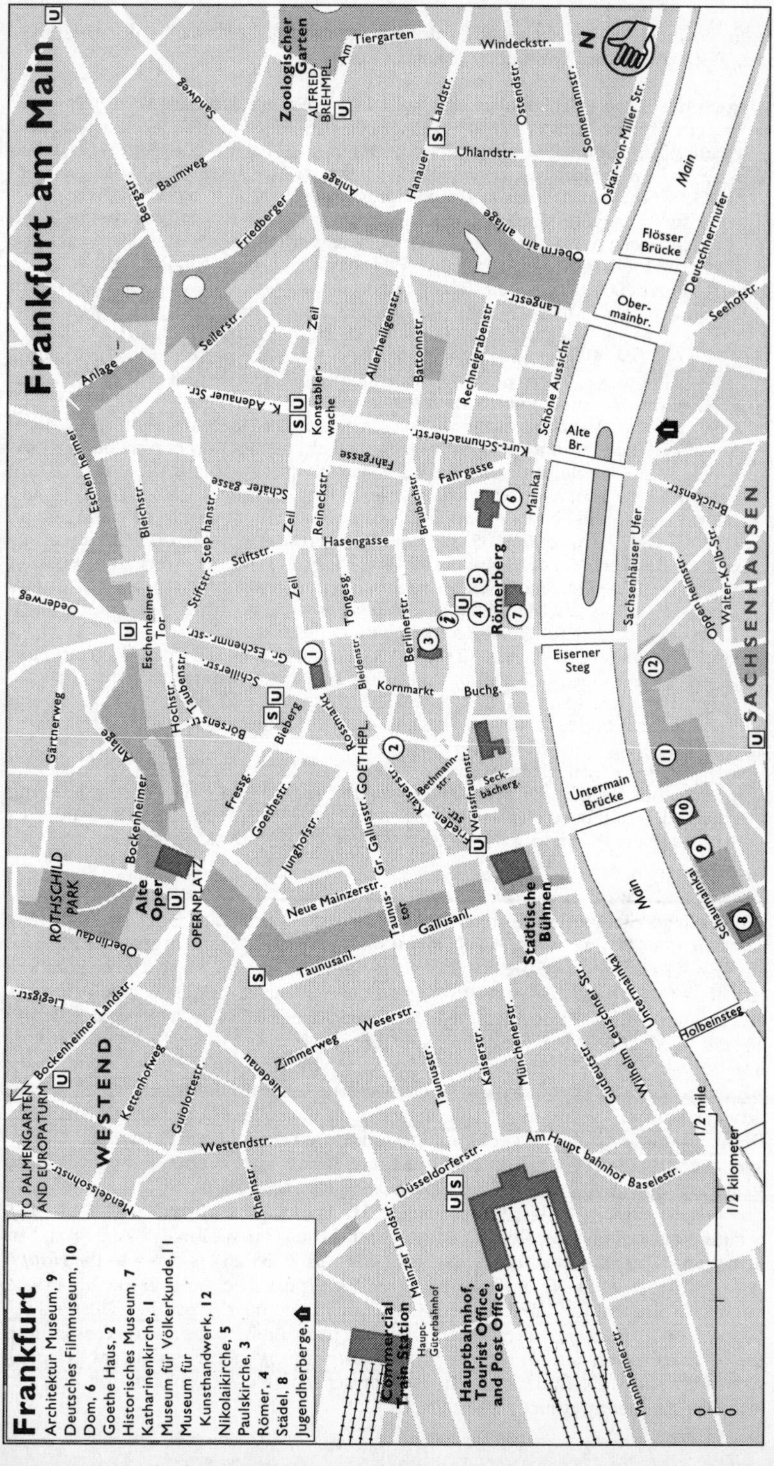

Frankfurt am Main
Frankfurt
Architektur Museum, 9
Deutsches Filmmuseum, 10
Dom, 6
Goethe Haus, 2
Historisches Museum, 7
Katharinenkirche, 1
Museum für Völkerkunde, 11
Museum für Kunsthandwerk, 12
Nikolaikirche, 5
Paulskirche, 3
Römer, 4
Städel, 8
Jugendherberge, 1
TO PALMENGARTEN AND EUROPATURM
WESTEND
ROTHSCHILD PARK
Alte Oper
OPERNPLATZ
GOETHEPL.
Römerberg
Städtische Bühnen
Hauptbahnhof, Tourist Office, and Post Office
Commercial Train Station
Zoologischer Garten
ALFRED-BREHMPL.
Konstablerwache
SACHSENHAUSEN
Main
Alte Br.
Eiserner Steg
Untermain Brücke
Obermainbr.
Flösser Brücke
Holbeinsteg
1/2 mile
1/2 kilometer

Bahn #5, direction: Friedrichsdorf), Darmstadt (S-Bahn #12), Mainz (S-Bahn #14, direction: Wiesbaden), and Wiesbaden (S-Bahn #1 or 14).

Jugendherberge (HI), Deutschherrnufer 12, 60594 Frankfurt am Main (tel. 61 90 58; fax 61 82 57). Bus #46 from the main bus station (DM2.90, morning and evening rush hours DM3.30): "Frankensteinerpl." The hostel is 50m west in the large yellow building. After 7:30pm, S-Bahn #2-6 or tram #16: "Lokalbahnhof" (DM1.90) then turn right on Darmstädter Landstr., which becomes Dreieichstr. (bear right), then turn left on Deutschherrnufer. Newly renovated hostel near the Sachsenhausen pub and museum district. Neighborhood and hostel alike tend to be lively and loud. Breakfast on the glassed-in veranda is free if unfilling, while lunch and dinner (DM 8.70) come in big portions for *große Schulkinder*. Vegetarian meals available. 3 to 5-day max. stay during the summer. Reception open 24hr. Check out 9am. Lockout 9am-1pm. Official curfew is midnight—try begging to extend it. DM24, over 26 DM29.50; doubles DM42 per person (additional nights DM40), but they are *very rarely* available. Required sheet deposit of DM10. Written reservations accepted, but phone reservations are not.

Pension Brüns, Mendelssohnstr. 42 (tel. 74 88 96; fax 74 88 46). From the *Hauptbahnhof*, take a left onto Düsseldorferstr., and after 2 blocks veer right on Beethovenstr. At the circle, go right on Mendelssohnstr. (10-15min.). Located in the Westend near *Palmengarten* and the university. Ring the bell—it's on the 2nd floor. Homey, with sunny rooms and high ceilings. All rooms have TV and phone. Doubles DM79; triples DM105. Showers DM2. Free breakfast in bed! Call ahead.

Pension Backer, Mendelssohnstr. 92 (tel. 74 79 92), up the street from Pension Brüns. U-Bahn: "Westend." Smaller rooms, but they're bright, clean, and cheap. Singles DM50; doubles DM60; triples DM68. Showers available 7am-10pm (DM3). Breakfast included. Reservations taken with deposit.

Hotel Wiesbaden, Baselerstr. 52 (tel. 23 23 47 or 23 23 48; fax 25 28 45). Turn right as you leave the *Hauptbahnhof* and follow Baselerstr. towards the river. Upscale place that offers spacious, neat rooms. All rooms have TV and phone. Reception open 24hr. Singles DM65, with shower DM95; doubles DM90, with shower DM125; triples with shower DM150.

Hotel-Pension Gölz, Beethovenstr. 44 (tel. 74 67 35; fax 74 61 42). One street east of Pensions Backer and Brüns. Big breakfast served in a quiet, beautiful dining room. All rooms have TV and phone. Singles DM65, with shower DM79-94; doubles with shower DM135-148; triples with shower DM175. Breakfast included.

FOOD

While cheap eats in Frankfurt are not nearly as rare as cheap beds, light eats may prove harder to come by, especially if you stick to the local culinary gems. Traditional German *Würste* and beers are popular in Frankfurt, but the region also treasures some fare of its own: *Handkäse mit Musik* (curd cheese with raw onions), *grüne Sosse* (a green sauce with various herbs, usually served over boiled eggs or potatoes), and *Ebbelwei*. Ah, *Ebbelwei*. Large mugs of this apple wine (also called *Ebbelwoi*, or *Äpfelwein* up north) should never top DM3. Don't expect anything akin to the sharp sweetness of cider or the dryness of chardonnay; this ain't no sippin' wine. In your drunken stupor, don't forget to take advantage of the cuisine of Frankfurt's large non-German population. If you get around to looking up the fat content of those *Würste* and swear them off for life or if you just miss home, tasty crepes and even T-bone steaks are right at your fingertips, as are *Döners* (less than DM6).

For those seriously looking to economize, **HL Markt,** Dreieichstr. 56 (tel. 59 56 44), is a fully-stocked grocery store near the youth hostel (open Mon.-Fri. 8am-8pm, Sat. 8am-9pm). **Tengelmann,** Münchenerstr. 37 (tel. 24 27 85 26), is closer to the *Hauptbahnhof* (open Mon.-Fri. 8:30am-7pm, Sun. 8am-2pm). The most reasonably priced kitchens surround the university in Bockenheim and nearby parts of Westend (U-Bahn #6 or 7: "Bockenheimer Warte"), though many of the pubs and taverns in both the Sachsenhausen and Alt Sachsenhausen districts serve food at a decent price (U-Bahn #1, 2, or 3: "Schweizerpl."). In the warmer months, Bockenheim, the Zeil, and Römerpl. frequently attract carts and stands.

The Kleinmarkthalle, on Hasengasse between Berlinerstr. and Töngesgasse, is a 3-story warehouse with several countershops: bakeries, butchers, fruit and vegetable stands, and more. Cutthroat competition between the many vendors pushes prices way down. Buy some fresh *Spargel*, a steaming *Wurst*, or a skinned rabbit ("Kill da wabbit!"). Open Mon.-Fri. 7:30am-6pm, Sat. 7:30am-3pm.

Zum Gemalten Haus, Schweizerstr. 67 (tel. 61 45 59; fax 603 14 57). One of the most famous joints in Sachsenhausen, it drips with *gemütlich* greasiness. Serves up copious amounts of home-brewed *Ebbelwei* (DM2.50 for 0.3L) and the full canon of regional specialties (DM5-18). A glance at the, uh, well-padded clientele lets you know that the food is good. Open Wed.-Sun. 10am-midnight.

Adolf Wagner, Schweizerstr. 71 (tel. 61 25 65; fax 61 14 45). Another famous Sachsenhausen haunt, 4 doors down from Zum Gemalten Haus. Owned and operated by the same family since 1931. Proffers *Ebbelwei* (DM2.50 for 0.3L), hot meals, *Würste,* and all the Frankfurt specialties in heart-warming and heart-burning portions (DM7.50-21). Open daily 11am-midnight.

Römer-Bembel, Römerpl. 20/22 (tel. 28 83 83; fax 55 76 44). At the center of Frankfurt's *Altstadt,* across from the Römer. Pretend to be a local and raise your *Pilsner* (DM4.50) each time a tour group passes by. The popular restaurant also serves Frankfurt specialties at decent prices: *Rippchen* (ribs, DM12.50) and *Oschenbrust* (boiled beef brisket) with green sauce (DM17.50). Open daily 11:30am-11pm.

Lorsbacher Taf, Große Rittergasse 49-51 (tel. 61 64 59), in the cobblestone area of Sachsenhausen. Quiet and relaxing inside, loud and jolly outside. Distinctive ivy overhang creates a cozy feel. Entrees DM8-25, *Ebbelwei* (DM2.40) in abundance.

SIGHTS

"Everywhere one looks," wrote 18th-century author Johann Kaspar Riesbeck, "one sees the signs of a high standard of living. The furnishings of the houses, the yards, the carriages, the clothes, the jewelry of the women—in short, everything exceeds the bourgeois and borders on the most unimaginable splendor." Frankfurt's glamorous glitziness crumbled during World War II, when the Allied forces leveled the city. Industrious Frankfurters rebuilt and restored many of the city's original structures within a few years and have successfully returned the city's gilded brilliance.

The logical starting point for a tour of this city of conspicuous consumption is the **Römerberg,** the cluster of partially surviving historical buildings in the city center. The eastern end of the *Römerberg* is dominated by the **Dom,** a huge red sandstone Gothic cathedral with several splendidly elaborate altarpieces. It served as the site of coronation ceremonies for German emperors between 1562 and 1792 (open June-Aug. daily 9am-noon and 2:30-5pm; Sept.-May 9am-noon and 2:30-5:30pm). The view of the Main valley and the city's bustling vitality is well worth the punishing climb (round and round and round you go) to the top (tower open daily 9am-1pm and 2:30-6pm; admission DM3, children DM1; closed in winter). The **Dom Museum** inside the main entrance contains some venerated robes of the imperial electors (open Tues.-Fri. 10am-5pm, Sat.-Sun. 11am-5pm; DM2, students DM1). Directly in front of the *Dom* is the **Historischer Garten,** with ruins from Roman to medieval times, discovered when workers were digging a sewer line. Ahhhh, the miasma of history.

The **Römer,** a distinctively gabled red sandstone structure at the west end of the Römerberg, has been Frankfurt's city hall since 1405. Only the upper floors (not the council chambers) are open to the public. Visit the **Kaisersaal,** a former imperial banquet hall adorned with portraits of the 52 German emperors from Charlemagne to Franz II, 13 of whom were coronated here (open daily 10am-1pm and 2-5pm; obligatory hourly tour DM3). Next to the Römer on Paulspl. stands the **Paulskirche** (St. Paul's Church; open daily 10am-5pm). In the wake of the waves of revolution that swept through Europe in 1848-49, Germany's first democratic National Assembly convened in the church to draw up a constitution for a German republic. Cognizant that Germany could not unify without the assent of powerful Prussia, the liberal assembly attempted to cajole Prussia's Friedrich Wilhelm IV into accepting the crown of a constitutional monarchy. The king replied that he ruled by the grace of God, and the whole episode ended with the bloody repression of the democratic movement.

HESSEN

Of the half-dozen or so German cities that claim Goethe as their native son, Frankfurt legitimately possesses his early years. The master was born in Frankfurt in 1749, found his first love (a girl named Gretchen, said to be the inspiration for Marguerite in *Faust*), and penned some of his best-known works here, including *The Sorrows of Young Werther*. A few blocks northwest of the Römer stands his birthplace and family home, the aptly named **Goethe Haus,** Großer Hirschgraben 23-25 (tel.13 88 00; fax 13 88 02 22). After renovations last year, the house is again open to the public. Enter through the *Volkstheater*. The sumptuous interior shows that you don't have to suffer from poverty to be angst-ridden. Everybody hurts. (Open April-Sept. Mon.-Sat. 9am-6pm, Sun. 10am-1pm; Oct.-March Mon.-Sat. 9am-4pm, Sun. 10am-1pm. Tours Mon.-Sat. 10:30am and 2pm, Sun. 10:30am. DM4, students DM3.)

The **Museumsufer** is home to a number of high-powered museums (see Museums, below), Frankfurt's weekly **flea market** (open Sat. 9am-2pm during the warm months), and the **Museumsuferfest,** a huge cultural jamboree which draws more than a million visitors over three days in late August. In the northwest part of town, tourists, children, businesspeople, and an extensive variety of German birds take refuge in the sprawling, lush **Palmengarten,** Siesmayerstr. 61 (tel. 21 23 39 39; fax 21 23 78 56; http://www.stadt-frankfurt.de/Palmengarten). U-Bahn #6 or 7: "Bockenheimer Warte." Rent a wooden boat and pretend you're rowing on the Main (DM4 per 30min.). The garden's greenhouses contain seven different "worlds," from the tropics to the plains. In summer, the grounds host a number of performances and exhibitions. (Open daily March-Oct. 9am-6pm; Nov.-Jan. 9am-4pm; Feb. 9am-5pm. Admission DM7, students DM3; with U-Bahn ticket DM5 and DM2.50, respectively.) Check out the exhibit of a human housewife in the *Exotarium,* then *machen Sie* some *Spaß* at the playground. For animal lovers, over 650 species ranging from the commonplace to the exotic are represented at the **Zoo** (tel. 21 23 37 35), on the eastern side of town. U-Bahn #6 or 7. The feeding of the apes (daily at 4:30pm; winter 4pm) and the piranhas (Sun. and Wed. at 11am) excites a certain blood-thirsty pleasure. (Open mid-March to Sept. Mon.-Fri. 9am-7pm, Sat.-Sun. 8am-7pm; Oct. to mid-March daily 9am-5pm. DM11, under 18 and students DM5; with U-Bahn ticket DM9 and DM4, respectively).

MUSEUMS

On the south bank of the Main, between the *Eiserner Stag* and the Friedensbrücke, sits an eclectic collections of museums: the **Museumsufer** on the Schaumainkai. Unified by geography, if not by content, these seven culturally stocked museums offer an extensive range of media—sculpture, film, plants, and old German postal trucks. Frankfurt also has a spectacular scattering of commercial art galleries—nearly 50, many of which are concentrated along the Braubachstr./Saalgasse area. Pick up a Frankfurt Card for big savings.

Museumsufer

Museum für Kunsthandwerk, Schaumainkai 17 (tel. 21 23 40 37 or 21 23 85 30; fax 21 23 07 03). Arts and crafts from Europe (the Middle Ages to the present), the Near East (9th to 19th centuries), and the Far East (Neolithic to the present). One division is devoted entirely to icons. DM8, students DM4. Free on Wed. Open Tues. and Thurs.-Sun. 10am-5pm, Wed. 10am-8pm.

Galerie 37, Schaumainkai 37. The only portion of the **Museum für Völkerkunde** left open while they renovate the large site at Schaumainkai 29, scheduled for completion sometime over the next 3 years. Brazilian, Aboriginal, and Kenyan art from the 1980s and 90s. Interesting, but very small. DM6, students DM3.

Deutsches Filmmuseum, Schaumainkai 41 (tel. 21 23 88 30). Exhibits on the development of filmmaking. Old movies shown on the 3rd floor. Film friends in Sam Spade's office or see yourself flying on a carpet high above the Frankfurt skyline. Swanky and correspondingly pricey **Cafe Kino** adjoins the museum. DM5, students DM2.50; free on Wed. Films DM8, students DM6. Open Tues., Thurs.-Fri., and Sun. 10am-5pm, Wed. 10am-8pm, Sat. 2-8pm. Tours Sun. 3pm.

Architektur Museum, Schaumainkai 43 (tel. 21 23 88 44). A 3-floor survey of the last 10 years in European architecture in a beautifully designed space of white surfaces and right angles. DM8, students free with ID. Open Tues. and Thurs.-Sun. 10am-5pm, Wed. noon-8pm.

Deutschespostmuseum, Schaumainkai 53 (tel. 606 01). A history of German travel and communication in a bright and spacious but somewhat haphazardly designed building. Interactive and video displays in German only. Open Tues. and Thurs.-Sun. 10am-5pm, Wed. 10am-8pm. An amateur radio booth (ask for *Funkstation*) on the top floor is open Wed. 10am-5pm, Thurs. 10am-1pm, and the first Sun. of each month 2-5pm. Museum and radio free.

Städel, Schaumainkai 63 (tel. 605 09 80; fax 61 01 63), between Dürerstr. and Holbeinstr. One of Germany's leading art museums with an excellent collection of Old Masters, housed in a stately mansion. Almost all exhibits are currently inaccessible due to renovations (scheduled for completion in 1999), but the public may still view the 19th- and 20th-century exhibits and rotating special exhibits. Use the side entrances. Admission to permanent exhibits DM8, students DM4. Admission to special exhibits varies. Open Tues. and Thurs.-Sun. 10am-5pm, Wed. 10am-8pm.

Liebieghaus, Schaumainkai 71 (tel. 21 23 86 17). Asian and Egyptian art, and sculptures from the Medieval, Renaissance, Baroque, Rococo, and Classical periods. Admission DM5, students DM2.50, free on Wed. Open Tues. and Thurs.-Sun. 10am-5pm, Wed. 10am-8pm. Tours Wed. 6:30pm and Sun. 11am.

Elsewhere in Frankfurt

Museum für Moderne Kunst, Domstr. 10 (tel. 21 23 04 47; fax 21 23 78 82). Not to be missed. The triangular building's interior (the "slice of cake") is an architectural wonder, an ideal setting for the stunning modern art housed within, including impressive works by Claes Oldenburg, Roy Liechtenstein, and Jasper Johns. Art in every medium imaginable. The basement shows films and slides. DM7, students DM3.50, free on Wed. Open Tues. and Thurs.-Sun. 10am-5pm, Wed. 10am-8pm.

Schirn Kunsthalle, next to the *Dom*, its entrance in a narrow alley (tel. 299 88 20). A postmodern art gallery hosting visiting exhibits with self-satisfied titles like "The Occult and the Avant-garde." DM9, students DM7. DM6 and DM4 on Sundays. Open Tues. and Fri.-Sun. 10am-7pm, Wed.-Thurs. 10am-10pm.

Historisches Museum, Saalgasse 19 (tel. 21 23 55 99), back toward the river from the *Römer*. Presents a first-rate series of exhibitions on the history of Frankfurt, including a permanent "Äpfelwein Museum," an exhibit of Frankfurt porcelain, and a comparative display of the city before and after the bombing of WWII. DM5, students DM2.50. Open Tues. and Thurs.-Sun. 10am-5pm, Wed. 10am-8pm.

Naturmuseum, Senckenberganlage 25 (tel. 754 20). U-Bahn #6 or 7: "Bockenheimer Warte." Features a fully-mounted dinosaur skeleton, dinosaur bones, and some big whales thrown in. The largest natural museum in Germany attracts the largest school groups in Frankfurt. DM7, students DM3, free on Wed. Open Mon.-Tues. and Thurs.-Fri. 9am-5pm, Wed. 9am-8pm, Sat.-Sun. 9am-6pm.

ENTERTAINMENT AND NIGHTLIFE

Frankfurt wields a nightlife commensurate with its size. There are two major theaters, the **Alte Oper** (by no means limited to opera) and the **Städtisches Theater,** in addition to many smaller venues. Shows and schedules of the city's stages are detailed in several publications, including *Fritz* and *Strandgut* (free at the tourist office), and the *Journal Frankfurt* (DM2.80, available at any newsstand). Students can often buy leftover tickets at reduced prices one hour before a performance. Frankfurt has a renowned **jazz** scene (it was once the jazz capital of Europe and jazz musicians like Albert Mangelsdorff and Volka Knegel began their jazz careers here) that centers around Kleine Bockenheimerstr., also known as **Jazzgasse** (Jazz Alley).

If you're looking for a drinking night, the **Alt Sachsenhausen** district, between Brückenstr. and Dreieichstr., is home to a huge number of rowdy pubs and taverns specializing in *Äpfelwein,* the local drink of choice. The complex of narrow cobblestone streets centering on **Kleine Rittergasse** teems with canopied cafes, bars, and restaurants, buzzing with natives and tourists alike, especially during the summer. Irish pubs with gregarious Irish lads also abound.

Frankfurt has a number of thriving discos and a hyped-up techno scene. Wear something dressier than jeans—unless they're *really* hip jeans—if you plan to try your luck with the neurotic bouncers. Don't think you'll escape cover charges, either—most clubs make you pay upon exiting. A recent, revolutionary offering of nightclub organizers Schüler and Pestinger increases partying options while lowering costs dramatically. Pay the cover at one of their five popular discos—including **Europaturm**, located on the 200th floor of Frankfurt's TV tower, and its through-the-looking-glass *Doppelgänger* **Dorian Gray**, an expansive club whose three dance floors encompass the basement of a wing at the airport—and gain free entrance to all of their other clubs and free transportation between them (Fri. DM10, Sat. DM15). Gay nightlife in Frankfurt centers around the area between Zeil and Bleichstr.

Der Jazzkeller, Kleine Bockenheimerstr. 18a (tel. 28 85 37). Hidden at the end of the blues alley in the Rodeo Dr. area lies Frankfurt's most renowned jazz club. Cover usually DM10-25. Call for a schedule. Wed. and Fri. nights boast a "cool music mix"; cover DM8-10. Open Tues.-Sun. 9pm-3am.

Die Jazzkneipe, Berlinerstr. 70 (tel. 28 71 73). U-Bahn #1, 2, 3, or 4: "Willy-Brandt-Platz." Offers a more intimate, funkier bar with live blues and jazz every night from 10pm-3am. Cover DM4-15. Drinks DM4-14. Open daily 8pm-4am.

Shamrock Pub, Kleine Rittergasse 4-8 (tel. 62 39 12). A mixture of merry Irish folk music and disco accompany traditional Irish cuisine (DM5-15) and Guinness (DM6). Open Sun.-Thurs. 5pm-2am, Fri.-Sat. 5pm-3am; winter daily 6pm-1am.

Omen, Junghofstr. 14 (tel. 28 22 33). With a boomin' techno line-up, Omen is *the* place to disco. Cover varies. Open Fri.-Sat. 10pm-6am.

Cyber's: the Inter-n-Active Cafe, Zeil 112-114 (tel. 29 49 64; email cybers@internet.de), on the 6th floor of the Zeil Galerie. For those of you who get that sudden (and perhaps addictive) urge to check your email while dancing the night away. Virtual reality booths will excite and disorient you without the flashback. DM8 per 30min. on-line. Open Mon.-Wed. 11am-midnight, Thurs.-Sun. 11am-whenever.

Cooky's, Am Salzhaus 4 (tel. 28 76 62), off Goethepl. For the alternative crowd, there is no alternative. Live music Mon. Soul, acid jazz, and reggae tracks on other days. Cover varies. Open Sun.-Thurs. 10pm-4am, Fri.-Sat. 10pm-6am.

Gaslicht, 15 Paradiesgasse (tel. 472 11 44), is located in the cobblestone area. Smaller, but great atmosphere. Patrons, packed in like sardines on the weekends, wildly dance on the tables. Drinks DM4-6.

Zum Schwejk, Schäfergasse 20 (tel. 29 31 66). A relaxed, popular, gay men's bar named after the good Czech soldier. Open daily 11am-1am.

L.O.F.T. House, Hanauer Landstr. 181-185 (tel. 943 44 80), S-Bahn #11. Located in the eastern outskirts of the city, this club is for women only.

■ Wiesbaden

Wiesbaden is a city Edith Wharton would have understood. From its tiny designer boutiques to the ritzy casino which consititutes its center of gravity, the city speaks of the heady years of the 19th century when the aristocracy of Europe came to frolic away its time and money in brainless consumption and amusement. When the royalty fell from grace, so did Wiesbaden; today it is remarkable mostly for its U.S. military base, from which the Berlin airlift was launched. Though it is still possible to find less costly amusements, a bit of the old Wiesbaden is here for the taking. You can still test the curative waters of the thermal baths and, provided that you're formally attired, gamble away your life's savings at the casino.

The original **Kurhaus,** now used for events ranging from business conventions to old-timer parades to exhibitions of art by local schoolchildren, is situated off of Wilhelmstr. and bordered on two sides by the expansive and serene **Kurpark,** where locals sprawl under century-old willow trees during the summer. Bus #1 or 8: "Kurhaus/Theater." The **casino** *(Spielbank)* is inside the *Kurhaus* (tel. 53 61 00). Compulsive gambler Fyodor Dostoevsky squandered the last 30 rubles that stood between him and destitution while visiting Wiesbaden, and so can you (coat and tie rental DM10; open daily 3pm-3am; 21 or over). Or, if your dingy hiking shorts just won't come off, try next door at **Kleines Spiel**, which houses all sorts of electronic money-eating machines and has no dress code. Opposite Kleines Spiel, on the other side of the *Kurhaus* is the stately **Staatstheater** (tel. 13 23 25), inscribed with the ominous instruction *"Der Menscheit Würde ist in Eure Hand gegeben, bewahret Sie"* (the dignity of mankind is in your hands, preserve it). The Staatstheater and neighboring **Kleines Haus** present traditional and modern ballets, operas, and plays; tickets occasionally sell for as little as DM9-15 (Staatstheater box office open Tues.-Fri. 11am-2pm and 4-6pm, Sat.-Sun. 11am-12:30pm; Kleines Haus box office open Tues.-Fri. 11am-2pm and 5:30-7pm, Sat. 11am-12:30pm; tickets can be purchased 1hr. before show). On Burgstr. west of the Staatstheater warbles the **world's biggest cuckoo clock,** which, strange as it seems, is topped by a giant moosehead. The birdies strut their stuff every half hour from 8am to 8pm. Towards the *Bahnhof* on Friedrich-Ebert-Allee, the **Museum Wiesbaden,** reminiscent of a train station, houses temporary exhibits of modern German art (open Tues. noon-8pm, Wed.-Fri. 10am-4pm, Sat.-Sun. 11am-5pm; admission DM5, students, seniors, and children DM2.50).

The **Neroberg,** a low hill at the north end of town, provides an alternative to Wiesbaden's hustle and bustle. Bus #1: "Nerotal," and from there take the **hydraulic funicular** (DM2; round-trip DM3) or walk to the summit of the 254m hill. Take a dip in the *Bauhaus*-style swimming pool (open 9am-8pm; DM8). 100m beyond the pool stands the **Russische-Griechische Kapelle,** easily the most impressive monument in the city. This painstakingly decorated Greek Orthodox chapel was built in 1855 as a mausoleum for Princess Elizabeth of Nassau, the niece of a Russian Czar who was married off to a local duke and died in childbirth at age 19. Her tear-jerking tomb dominates the chapel's inspiring interior (open daily April-Oct. 11am-4pm; admission DM1).

Wiesbaden's **tourist office** offers its services on Marktstr. 6 (tel. 172 97 90; fax 172 97 98). It books rooms (singles DM70 and up) for a DM6 fee (open Mon.-Fri. 9am-6pm, Sat.-Sun. 10am-4pm). At the train station, the **DB Service Desk** dispenses terrific city and hotel maps and glossy propaganda about Wiesbaden. They also offer a telephone line to the tourist office. Wiesbaden makes a natural destination for a day-trip from Mainz (see p. 391), as the two cities share a **public transportation** system. The **Mitfahrzentrale,** located in a camper on Bahnhofstr. 9 (tel. 33 35 55 or 194 40), halfway between the pedestrian zone and the train station, connects riders with drivers (open Mon.-Fri. 7:30am-6pm, Sat. 7:30am-noon). If a stranger tries to tempt you with *Strüdel* and *Süße,* call the **International Help Line** (tel. 194 33). The **post office,** Kaiser-Friedrich-Ring 81, to the left as you come out of the *Bahnhof,* changes money and sells traveler's checks (Mon.-Fri. 8am-6pm, Sat. 8am-noon). Victuals can be obtained at the **supermarket** on the second floor of the *Kaufhalle* on the corner of Langgasse and Mittestr. The **telephone code** is 0611.

Wiesbaden's plate of inexpensive accommodations offers slim pickings. The **Jugendherberge (HI),** Bluchterstr. 66 (tel. 486 57; fax 44 11 19), provides the city's cheapest beds with high-quality facilities, including a bar. From the station, bus #14: "Gneisenaustr." or "Elsasserpl." (Reception open until midnight. Lockout midnight-6:30am. Lockers DM10 deposit. DM24, over 26 DM29. Sheets DM6. Breakfast included.) The *Fußgängerzone* (pedestrian zone) west of the *Kurhaus* is brimming with pubs and restaurants, and spice abounds in the ethnic joints around Schwalbacherstr. from the Platz der Deutschen Einheit to Einserstr. The **Kebab House,** Schwalbacherstr. 61 (tel. 30 63 45), dishes out gigantic servings of ready-made Turkish food for unbeatable prices (DM5-8; open daily 10am-1am). **The Irish Pub,** Michelsbergstr. 17, rocks with live music every night and serves beer, wine, and coffee (DM3.50-7), and an enormous Irish breakfast (DM14) on Sundays (11am-3pm).

■ Darmstadt

From the bevy of trendy alterna-cafes and budding academics who study at the local university to the well preserved examples of *Jugendstil* architecture that serve as the city's main tourist attractions, Darmstadt radiates youthful charm and energy. Yet the city is not only for the young; it is also the seat of the venerable German Academy of Language and Literature which awards the annual Georg-Büchner Prize, the most prestigious honor in German letters.

The mecca of Darmstadt's *Jugendstil* architecture is **Mathildenhöhe**, an artists' colony on a hill 800m west of the city center founded by Grand Duke Ernst Ludwig in 1899. The Duke fell in love with *Jugendstil* during his travels and paid for a lavish complex to demonstrate how the style could transform the urban landscape. The seven original artists of the colony were members of the movement, which is reflected in everything from the grumpy-looking statues in the garden to the five-fingered **Hochzeitsturm** (wedding tower). The 48m tower was the city's wedding present to Grand Duke Ernst Ludwig in 1908. From the top, gaze down on the civic spread. To reach the tower and all of Mathildenhöhe, walk east from the Luisenpl. along Erich-Ollenhauer-Promenade, or take bus F: "Lucas," and walk south on Lucasweg (open March-Oct. Tues.-Sun. 10am-6pm; DM3, students DM1). The Mathildenhöhe also hosts two art museums, the **Austellungsgebäude,** Sabaispl. 1 (tel. 13 27 78; open Tues.-Sun. 11am-6pm; admission DM6, students DM3) and the **Museum der Künstlerkolonie** (tel. 13 27 78; open Tues.-Sun. 10am-5pm, tours 11am on the first Sunday of each month; admission DM5, students DM2), both of which house rotating exhibits of modern art and sculpture. A gilded, three-domed Russian Orthodox Church, the **Russische Kapelle** (Russian Chapel), Nikolai Weg 18 (tel. 42 42 35), rests on the Matildenhöhe. The chapel was imported stone by stone from Russia at the behest of Czar Nicholas II upon his marriage to Darmstadt's Princess Alexandra (open summer daily 9am-6pm; admission DM1, students DM0.80). Just south of the Mathildenhöhe, the **Institut für Neue Technische Form,** Eugen-Bracht-Weg 6 (tel. 480 08), contains the Braun Design collection, which documents the evolution of the company's many products since 1955, including razors, toasters, and stereos (open Tues.-Sat. 10am-6pm, Sun. 10am-1pm; free). Spread throughout this area of the city is the **Rosenhöhe,** a verdant park whose nebulous borders circumscribe a rose garden and a mausoleum of the city's deceased dukes. The garden was planted in 1810 at the request of Grand Duchess Wilhelmine, who wanted a garden that breathed "the free, noble Spirit of Nature." It is questionable whether the garden lives up to Wilhelmine's dreams.

The gigantic yellow **Schloß** is smack-dab in the middle of the city. Modeled after the voluptuous Versailles and built between 1716 and 1727, it is the creation of a French architect. Since World War II, the *Schloß* has served as a public university library. A small **Schloßmuseum** tucked in the eastern wing holds 17th- to 19th-century ducal clothing and furniture. (Open Mon.-Thurs. 10am-1pm and 2-5pm, Sat.-Sun. 10am-1pm; obligatory 1hr. guided tour; last tour begins 1hr. before closing; admission DM3.50, students DM3.) And what's a *Schloß* without a *Garten?* **Herrngarten,** a lush expanse of well-maintained greenery north of the *Schloß* provides space for procrastinating students, gamboling dogs, and ducks (which you can't feed). Even more exquisite is the **Prinz Georg Garten,** arranged in Rococo style and maintained by a brigade of six gardeners (open daily 7am-9pm). Next to it, the **Porzellanschlößchen** (little porcelain castle) flaunts an extensive collection of porcelain; the exhibit is closed until the fall of 1998. Those with a geological, paleontological, or zoological bent will appreciate the **Landesmuseum,** at the northern end of the Herrngarten (open Tues.-Sat. 10am-5pm, Sun. 11am-5pm; DM5, students DM2.50).

Darmstadt is accessible from Frankfurt by frequent **trains** (25min.) or by S-Bahn #12 (DM6). **S-Bahn** and **bus** tickets cost DM2, DM7 for 24 hours, or DM17 for a 7-day ticket (students DM13). The **tourist office,** in front of the main train station (tel. 13 27 82), provides good city maps and hotel guides, and finds rooms (open Mon.-Fri. 9am-6pm, Sat. 9am-noon); a **branch office,** at Luisenpl. 5 (tel. 13 27 80 or 13 27 81), is located in the Luisencenter (open Mon.-Fri. 9am-6pm, Sat. 9am-noon). For **taxi,** call **Funk** (tel. 194 10) any time of the day or night; the funk never stops. **Bike rental** *(Fahrradverleih)* is available at **Prinz-Emil-Garten,** Heidelbergerstr. 56 (tel. 632 78). S-Bahn #1: "Prinz-Emil-Garten." Rent before noon at the *Nachtbarschaftsheim,* up the hill, and after noon at the *Minigolfplatz,* up the hill and to the left (DM7 per day; ID required; open 8am-8pm). **AIDS-Hilfe Darmstadt,** Saalbraustr. 27 (tel. 280 73), in addition to providing an array of AIDS-related services, also deals with gay and lesbian concerns. The **post office,** 64293 Darmstadt, **exchanges currency** and sells traveler's checks. There are two branches: Postamt 1, to your left as you exit the main train station; and Postamt 11, at Louisenpl. 3 (both open Mon.-Fri. 8am-6pm, Sat. 8am-noon). The **telephone code** is 06151.

The **Jugendherberge (HI),** Landgraf-Georg-Str. 119 (tel. 452 93; fax 42 25 35), maintains spotless, recently repainted facilities and bright but cramped rooms. Bus D: "Großer Woog." (Reception open until 10pm. Lockout 1-7am. Members only. DM23.50, over 26 DM28.50. Breakfast included.) **Zentral Hotel,** Schuchardstr. 6 (tel. 264 11; fax 268 58), behind the *Neues Rathaus* at Luisenpl., offers small but cozy rooms. (Singles DM60, with shower DM90; doubles DM120, with shower DM150.) The *Jugendherberge* overlooks **Großer Woog** (tel. 13 23 93), an artificial lake doubling as a *Freibad* (outdoor pool). (Open mid-May to mid-Sept. Mon. and Sat.-Sun. 9am-7pm, Tues.-Fri. 8am-7pm; admission DM3.50, students DM2; boats DM6 per hr.)

Eating in Darmstadt can be pricey. Try **Plus,** the grocery store across from the *Schloß* (open Mon.-Thurs. 8:30am-6:30pm, Fri. 8:30am-8pm, Sat. 8:30am-2pm). Most of the city's inexpensive dining can be found in the two student areas: the *Cohannesviertel,* northwest of the city center, and the *Martinsviertel,* northeast of the city center. The university Bistro dishes out cheap meals. With your back to the northern side of the *Schloß,* cross the street, walk right past the five-story building, take a left, then go down the stairs straight ahead, and turn right. Once inside, go upstairs. A decent selection of sandwiches and light fare cost DM3-6. (Open Mon.-Thurs. 9am-5pm, Fri. 9am-3:45pm; kitchen open 11:45am-2pm.) **Efendi's,** 13 Landgrof-Georg-Str. (tel. 29 38 09), has generous, spicy portions, occasional vegetarian options, and large salads (DM6-8; open 10am-1am daily). The **Student Innenkeller** (tel. 16 31 17), a hopping and off-beat locale tucked inside the *Schloß,* is a favorite meeting place for students. It hosts piano and jazz concerts, and it has a disco with sporadic gay and lesbian nights. (Cover for concerts DM5-10, for discos DM3; open daily after 9pm.)

ERBACH AND MICHELSTADT (ODENWALD)

In the heart of the densely forested Odenwald, along a secondary rail line connecting Darmstadt and Heilbronn, rest the tiny, super-cute, hyper-quaint *Dörfer* of Erbach and Michelstadt. Everything about these villages is tiny and cute, from the postage stamp Marktplatz to the itty-bitty buses that putter about the cities to the simply precious German word for the region's star tourist attraction: *Elfenben* (ivory; literally, "elf bone"). And, unlike many similar villages, the seclusion of the two towns ensures that tourist populations remain quite small.

Erbach is the more appealing of the two towns, mainly because it is home to the spectacular **Elfenbeinmuseum,** Otto-Glen-Str. 1 (tel. 64 64; fax 64 63), which boasts over 1000 ivory works. Walk uphill on Hauptstr. and continue straight on Obere Markstr. (15min.); the museum appears on your left (open daily 10am-5pm; DM8, students DM5). The ivory exhibits range from a 30,000-year-old carving of a girl's head made from mammoth ivory to complex Asian masterpieces. Demonstrations feature masters breathing life into new works. The ethical and ecological problems of ivory carving were legally recognized in 1989 with a ban on hunted ivory. However, the workshops at the museum received special permission to use hunted ivory already in storage at the time of the ban, and they can provide permits for those wishing to bring such goods through customs. Next to the town's *Rathaus* lies the **Erbacher Schloß** (tel. 37 00), which holds the antique art and medieval weapons and armor collection of Franz I, Count of Erbach-Erbach (1754-1823), and the **African Hunting Museum** (open daily 8:30-11am and 1:30-4pm; Nov.-Feb. by appointment only).

Erbach is linked by train to Darmstadt and Heilbronn (over Eberbach). From the train station, turn right on Bahnhofstr., then left on (careful!) Bahnstr. to reach the Marktplatz. The **tourist office,** Marktplatz 1 (tel. 943 30; fax 94 33 17), doles out free city maps. Bring your German phrasebook—not much English spoken (open Mon.-

Fri. 9am-6pm, Sat.-Sun. 10am-5pm). The **post office,** 64711 Erbach, across from the Sportpl. on Michelstädterstr., has **currency exchange** and sells traveler's checks (open Mon.-Fri. 8am-noon, 2:30-6pm, Sat. 9am-noon). The **telephone code** is 06062.

If you intend to spend several days in the region, the tourist office can help find very cheap lodging on local **Bauernhöfe** (farms). Browse through a menu of fabulous farmwork and friendly families while you milk cows, brush horses, or bake bread. No experience required; language skills are preferred, though hand-waving sometimes works. If waving isn't your thing, try the local **Jugendherberge (HI),** Eulbacherstr. 3 (tel. 35 15; fax 628 48), next to the sports park. From the Marktplatz, take a left after the bridge and follow Hauptstr. uphill to the right; take a left onto Michelstädterstr., and about 300m later turn right on Eulbachestr. (DM15.50, over 27 DM20.50; Breakfast DM6. Call ahead; lots of young ones.) Another alternative is the central **Hotel Gebhardt,** at Jahnstr. 32 (tel. 32 86), over the bridge and one or two blocks to the right. (Singles DM39, with shower DM43; doubles with shower DM78. Breakfast included.) For a cheap meal, try **Schmucker Stube** just off the Marktplatz on Bahnstr. 7-9 (tel 74 23). For historic dining, cross the bridge from the Marktplatz to **Restaurant Erbacher Brauhaus,** Jahnstr. 1 (tel 57 32), with its own *Biergarten.* Regional specials for DM9.50-16 (open daily 10am-midnight; closed Tues. Oct.-March).

Within walking distance of Erbach (45min.), the town of Michelstadt joins the cutefest. Though its *Altstadt* is more picturesque than Erbach's, it houses no particularly striking attraction akin to Erbach's ivory museum. Visitors come just to absorb the quaintness. Buses from Erbach roll into town every hour Mon.-Fri. 7am-6pm, Sat. 10am-1pm. The same Darmstadt-Heilbronn trains that stop in Erbach also stop here.

▓ The Lahn Valley

The Lahn Valley is reminiscent of France's Rhone Valley, replete with verdant hills, bounteous vineyards, and dinky *Dörfer.* It is a "secluded" valley, breathing with a refreshing absence of tourists; locals frequently greet one another on the street or on the bus with hugs and kisses. Rail service runs regularly between Koblenz and Wetzlar at the eastern extremity of the valley, as well as between Frankfurt and Limburg.

LIMBURG

Limburg an der Lahn flourished during the Middle Ages as a bridge for merchants and journeymen traveling from Köln to Frankfurt. Today, it serves much the same function, but for a different region—as the most important train station between Koblenz and Gießen, Limburg is an excellent base from which to explore the Upper Lahn Valley. Often confused with a notoriously cheesy Dutch city of the same name, Limburg an der Lahn, or "L.L." (no Cool J here—he's goin' back to Cali), is known for the **St. Georg-Dom,** a majestic cathedral sporting a conspicuous dark-orange paint job. In addition to serving as the seat for the bishop of the Limburg diocese, this architectural hybrid of Romanesque and Gothic styles shelters a series of galleries and carefully restored frescoes. Next to the *Dom,* in a beautifully renovated building from 1544, the **Diözesanmuseum,** Domstr. 12 (tel. 29 53 27), displays a small but significant collection of medieval religious artifacts dating back to the 12th century. The *Staurothek* is a Byzantine reliquary cross that a local knight spirited away from Constantinople during the Crusades (open mid-March to mid-Nov. Tues.-Sat. 10am-1pm and 2-5pm, Sun. 11am-5pm; DM2, students DM1). Limburg, left largely unscathed by World War II, prides itself on many well preserved *Burgmannenhöfer* (medieval town houses), scattered throughout the *Altstadt.*

The **tourist office** *(Verkehrsverein),* Hospitalstr. 2 (tel. 61 66; fax 32 93), finds rooms (from DM30) for a DM10 fee. Turn left on the street in front of the station, then make a quick right between the red and green trimmed buildings. Ask for details about the local **Octoberfest,** beginning the third week in October, and the **Wine Festival** in late July; more than 30 vineyards will participate in 1998 (July 24-27). (Open April-Oct. Mon.-Fri. 8am-12:30pm and 2-6pm, Sat. 10am-noon; Nov.-March Mon.-Thurs. 8am-12:30pm and 2-5pm, Fri. 8am-1pm.) The newly renovated **Jugendher-**

berge (HI), auf dem Guckucksberg (tel. 414 93; fax 438 73), in Eduard-Horn-Park, has fuzzy green beds. By foot, walk through the tunnel just to the right of the station exit. When you emerge from the tunnel, walk 10m and turn right down Gartenstr., then right on Wiesbadenerstr. and left down the first paved walkway into the park 10m past Goethestr. Trek down the trail to Frankfurterstr. and follow the signs to the hostel (30min.). Or bus #3 from the "Hospitalstr." (direction: "Am Hammerberg"): "Jugendherberge." (Reception open 5-10pm. Curfew 11:30pm. DM23.50, over 26 DM28.50. Sheets DM6.) There's a **Campingplatz** (tel. 226 10) in a riverside location on the far side of the Lahn. From the station, take Bahnhofstr. into the city. When it ends in the *Altstadt,* turn left on Salzgasse, and take the first right over the Alte Lahnbrücke; turn right and follow the Lahn up to the *Campingplatz.* Or bus #4 from the train station: "Alte Lahnbrücke." (Reception open 8am-7pm. DM5 per person. DM4-5.50 per tent. Open May to mid-Oct.) The **telephone code** is 06431.

WEILBURG

As the Lahn crosses through the Taunus hills and the Wester Forest, the river bends itself into a shape not unlike that of Gumby's head. Sprawled across a high ridge, Weilburg's 14th-century **Schloß** and its terraced surroundings dominate the valley below. The residence of the Counts and Dukes of Nassau from 1355 to 1816, the castle now houses the **Schloßmuseum** (tel. 22 36), which flaunts a 10th-century Frankish foundation, a Romanesque interior, and a princely Baroque garden. (Open Tues.-Sun. 10am-4pm; Nov.-Feb. Tues.-Sun. 10am-3pm. DM6, children DM4, includes a 1-hr. guided tour. Free access to courtyard 10am-5pm.) In case you're feeling old and lethargic, your heart will skip a beat when you see the thousands of glittering crystals at the **Kubacher Kristallhöhle,** Germany's highest and only crystal cave, with limestone chunks more than 350 million years old (open April-Oct. Mon.-Fri. 2-4pm, Sat.-Sun. 10am-5pm; DM4.50, students and children DM3). The **Bergbau-und-Stadtmuseum** allows you to gawk at the Weilburg mineshafts (active until the 1950s) and speed through the city's economic and social history. (Open April-Oct. Tues.-Sun. 10am-noon and 2-5pm; Nov.-March Mon.-Fri. 10am-noon and 2-5pm; DM4, students DM2.) The **Weilburger Schloßkonzert** brings a dizzying array of international musicians to Weilburg every June and July. The yearly festival features performers such as returning favorites *Württemburg Chamber Orchestra* and a fresh ensemble of talented up-and-comers.

The **tourist office,** Mauerstr. 10 (tel. 76 71; fax 76 75), rents **bikes** (DM12 per day) and reserves rooms (from DM30) for free. From the *Busbahnhof* in front of the train station, City Bus Weilburg: "Landtor," and then walk uphill along Vorstadtstr., which becomes Mauerstr. By foot from the train station, walk left along the tracks and over the bridge and veer right at the yellow restaurant. When you reach the 18th-century Landtor gate, turn right and walk up Vorstadtstr. (open Mon.-Fri. 9am-noon and 2-4:30pm, Sat. 10am-noon). The newly-renovated **Jugendherberge Weilburg-Odersbach (HI),** Am Steinbühl (tel. 71 16; fax 15 42), is comfortable, spacious, and clean. From the *Busbahnhof,* City Bus Weilburg: "Steinbuhl," and then walk up the path. (Reception open 5-10pm. DM23.50, over 26 DM29. Sheets DM6.) Inexpensive gyro- and pizza joints rest across the street from the *Bahnhof* (DM6-8), but for an *echtes Hessische* meal, the **Weilburgerhof,** Schwanengasse 14 (tel. 71 53; fax 383 50), right of the Markt behind the *Schloß,* serves regional delicacies (DM12-25; open daily 11am-2:30pm and 5pm-1am). The **telephone code** is 06471.

WETZLAR

Wetzlar peaked in political stature at the end of the 17th century when the imperial legal court of the Holy Roman Empire established itself here. This, in turn, led to the city's even bigger cultural claim to fame when, in 1772, Goethe came to study at the court. The young and naive author found the courtly pretensions dull and decided to pursue a more exciting interest—a young woman named Charlotte Buff. Though she was already engaged to Kestner, a local diplomat and Goethe's friend, the poet endeared himself to the happy couple for many years. Finally, unable to continue the fruitless *Spiel*, he left for Frankfurt where he learned that his good friend Jerusalem had just committed suicide. Goethe intertwined this and his own tale of woe into the enormously popular novel *The Sorrows of Young Werther*, dissolving the real Lotte Buff into literary legend and setting off a wave of suicides referred to as "Young Werther syndrome." The **Lottehaus,** Lottestr. 8-10 (tel. 992 21), enshrines numerous *Werther* first editions in the brown-trimmed home where Lotte lived with her parents, just up Pfaffengasse from the top of the Dompl. (open Tues.-Sun. 10am-1pm and 2-5pm; free). Literary die-hards might also dig the **Jerusalemhaus,** Schillerpl. 5 (tel. 992 69), where Goethe's poor friend shot himself (open Tues.-Sun. 2-5pm; free; access to library Fri. 3-4:30pm). The Wetzlar **Dom** serves as town mascot. Begun in 897 and repeatedly altered and enlarged over the centuries (by Friedrich Barbarossa, among others), the *Dom* was never actually finished; it remains a perpetual architectural history lesson (open until dusk). The **Reichkammergerischtsmuseum,** Hofstatt 19 (tel. 996 12), showcases original documents, explaining the clockwork of the most complex, inefficient, and Byzantine legal system of all time; most documents are accompanied by English translations (open Tues.-Sun. 10am-1pm and 2-5pm).

Wetzlar's **tourist office** *(Verkehrsamt),* Dompl. 8 (tel. 993 38; fax 993 39), in the pre-1350 *Rathaus,* is itself an aesthetic and historical attraction. Bus #18 from the station: "Dompl.," or schlepp uphill for half of the steep 25-minute walk: exit the station, walk through the passageway, and continue on Bahnhofstr. to Buderuspl. Turn left on Brückenstr., cross the bridge, and take the first right, the first left, and then the first right again. The Dompl. is just over the crest of the hill. Signs lead you all the way from the bridge. The tourist office is behind the left face of the *Dom.* (Open Mon.-Wed. and Fri. 8am-noon and 2-4:30pm, Thurs. 8am-noon and 2-5pm, Sat. 9:30-11:30am.) The **Jugendgästehaus (HI),** Richard-Schirmann-Str. 3 (tel. 710 68; fax 758 26), offers an incredible view of the valley from its spacious confines. From the station, bus #12 (direction: "Krankenhaus"): the *second* "Sturzkopf"—there are two and the correct one is a 25-minute ride. Walk in the same direction as the curve. (Reception open 8am-1pm and 2pm-12:30am. Curfew 12:30am. DM26.50, over 26 DM31.50. Breakfast included. Sheets DM6.) The **telephone code** is 06441.

▓ Marburg

Almost two centuries ago, the Brothers Grimm spun their tales around these rolling hills, and from a distance, Marburg an der Lahn seems more of their world than ours. The city's isolation in the Lahn Valley allowed Landgrave Philipp to found the first Protestant university here in 1527. Its alumni list now reads like a syllabus for an intellectual history course: Martin Heidegger, Boris Pasternak, T.S. Eliot, Richard Bunsen (of burner fame), and the Spanish philosopher José Ortega y Gasset, to name a few. Those less familiar with Nobel Prize winners will recognize alumni **Jakob and Wilhelm Grimm,** who briefly attended the university from 1802 to 1805; their philological studies led them to collect the fairy tales that brought them fame. Today, 15,000 students pore over books, conversation, and each other on the banks of the Lahn. The rest of the Marburgers enjoy a slightly less academic but no less invigorating activity—beer. Things get hopping on the first Sunday in July, when costumed citizens parade onto the Markt for the rowdy **Frühschoppenfest** (Early Beer Festival). Drinking officially kicks off at 11am when the brass rooster on top of the 1851 **Rathaus** flaps its wings. Unofficially, however, the kegs of *Alt Marburger Pils* are tapped at 10am when the ribald old Marburger *Trinklieder* (drinking ballads) ensue.

ORIENTATION AND PRACTICAL INFORMATION

Built around a bend in the river, Marburg is served by frequent **trains** from Frankfurt (1hr.) and Kassel (1hr.); it also serves as the starting point for trips to Frankenberg, and from there to the Waldecker *Land.* The heart of the city is the *Oberstadt.* All buses run through Rudolphspl., the base of the wishbone formed by Pilgrimsteinstr. and Biegenstr. To reach Rudolphspl. from the train station, take buses #1-6.

HESSEN

Tourist Office: Pilgrimsteinstr. 26 (tel. 991 20; fax 99 12 12), is located a mere 150m. from Rudolphspl. Bus #1-6: "Rudolphspl.," and exit to the north along Pilgrimsteinstr.; the office is at your left. They sell maps and hotel lists for DM0.50-1.50, and book rooms (from DM35) for free. If they are closed you can call **hotel information** at 194 14. Open Mon.-Fri. 9am-6pm, Sat. 9am-1pm.

Trains: Information office across from the ticket counters. Open Mon. and Wed.-Fri. 10:25am-6:40pm.

Public Transportation: Single tickets (DM2) get you anywhere in the *Oberstadt*.

Taxi: Funkzentrale (tel. 477 77). Funk is long, life is short.

Bike Rental: Velicoped, Auf dem Wehr 3 (tel. 245 11), just over the bridge from Rudolphspl., off the riverside path. DM15 per day. Open Mon.-Fri. 10am-4:30pm.

Bookstore: N.G. Elwert, Pilgrimstein (tel. 17 09 34), one block from Rudolphspl. An annex of the store above it at Reitgasse 7 has a good selection of classics and English books. Open Mon.-Fri. 9:30am-7pm, Sat. 9:30am-4pm.

Laundromat: Wasch Center, at the corner of Gutenbergerstr. and Jägerstr. Sip a beer (DM2.50-5) in its adjacent **Bistro Waschbrett** during the rinse cycle. Wash DM6. Dry DM1 per 15min. Open Mon.-Sat. 8am-10pm, Sun. 1-8pm.

Women's Concerns: Frauenhaus, Schloßsteig 1 (tel 214 38). Open Mon. 5-8pm. At other times, leave a message.

AIDS-Hilfe: Bahnhofstr. 38 (tel. 645 23). Visits Mon. 2-4pm and Thurs. 8-9pm; otherwise, call.

Emergency: Police, tel. 110. **Fire,** tel. 112. **Ambulance,** tel. 192 22.

Post Office: *Hauptpostamt,* Bahnhofstr. 6, 35037 Marburg, a 5min. walk from the train station and on the right. Open 9am-6pm, Sat. 9am-noon.

Telephone Code: 06421.

ACCOMMODATIONS AND CAMPING

Although tiny, Marburg boasts more than 30 hotels and *Pensionen;* competition hasn't done too much to keep prices down. Most reasonably priced accommodations range DM70-85; plan ahead if you intend to spend under DM60.

Jugendherberge (HI), Jahnstr. 1 (tel. 234 61; fax 121 91). From Rudolphspl., cross the bridge and immediately turn right onto the riverside path. Continue until reaching the small wooden bridge (5min.). Newly remodeled rooms, some with bath. The *Jugendherberge* catches the nighttime music of the *Altstadt* from across the Lahn. Reception open 9am-noon and 1:30-11:30pm, but house keys available with ID or DM50 deposit. DM24, over 26 DM29. Breakfast buffet included. Sheets DM6.

Tusculum-Gästehaus, Gutenbergerstr. 25 (tel. 227 78; fax 153 04). Blazing colors and cool stripes decorate this artsy, well-kept hotel, renovated to embody the fanciful aesthetic of Joan Miró. Follow Universitätstr. from Rudolphspl. and take the first left onto Gutenbergstr. Singles DM55-65, with shower DM100; doubles DM75-80, with shower DM125. Kitchen available 24hr.

Hotel Garni im Quelle-Haus, Bahnhofstr. 14 (tel. 656 44), a 3min. walk from the station. Tastefully furnished and fastidiously kept rooms in a homey atmosphere, though the rooms overlooking Bahnhofstr. can be noisy. Reception open 7am-9pm. Singles DM65, with bath DM85; doubles DM125, with bath DM150. Breakfast included. Closed for Christmas. AmEx, MC, Visa.

Camping: Camping Lahnaue, on the Lahn River (tel. 213 31). Follow directions to the *Jugendherberge* and continue down river for another 2min. Person DM6, tent DM6. Closed periodically in winter, when the Lahn overflows its banks. Call ahead.

FOOD

Marburg's cuisine caters to its large student population. Most establishments offer *Würste* or hefty pots of pasta. See **Nightlife** (p. 373) for cafes with food as sidelights to drinks. The **Markt** gets crowded with vendors every Saturday (8am-1pm). **AIDI supermarket,** Gutenbergstr. 15 (tel. 027 52), caters to all your grocery needs when your wallet is on a diet and you're not (open Mon.-Fri. 9am-6:30pm, Sat. 8am-2pm).

HESSEN

Mensa, Erleuring 5, directly across the pedestrian bridge from Wolffstr., will satisfy your hearty appetite. Tripartite meals DM2.90-4.60. Open Mon.-Thurs. 11:30am-8pm, Fri. 11:30am-2:15pm and 5:45-8pm, Sat. 11:30am-2:15pm. Most lunches require a *Schlußel* (key). Get one with a DM10 deposit.

Rathausgockel, Wettergasse 14 (tel. 122 82), serves quality grub in an upscale setting. Walk along Reitgasse as it crosses Barfüßerstr. Breakfast baguettes, lamb leg, sirloin steak, and other delicacies (DM7.50-16.80). Open daily 10am-1am.

Cafe Barfuß, Barfüßerstr. 33 (tel. 253 49), gets packed every day with locals. Big breakfast menu (under DM12) served until 3pm. Amusing menu with very funny cartoons helps digest any of the 5 beers on tap (DM2-5.50). Open daily 10am-1am.

Café Vetter, Reitgasse 4 (tel. 258 88), is a traditional cafe, quite proud of its terrace overlooking Pilgrimstein. *Kaffee und Kuchen* (coffee and cake)—Germany's 4pm sugar rush—around DM7. A town favorite for 80 years. Open Mon. and Wed.-Sat. 8:30park-6:30pm, Tues. 11am-6:30pm, Sun. 9:30am-6:30pm.

SIGHTS

Climbing the hillside **Oberstadt's** dizzying maze of narrow staircases and alleys would melt Cindy Crawford's buns of steel. You can save yourself part of the climb by taking the **Oberstadt-Aufzug** (elevator to the upper city) from Pilgrimstein (less than a block from Rudolphspl.) to Reitgasse (open daily 7am-11:30pm, free). **Enge Gasse,** an old sewer, is now as scenic and half-timbered as the rest of town. Climb more than 250 steps or bus #16 from Rudolfspl. (every 45min.) to the exalted **Landgrafenschloß,** former haunt of the infamous Teutonic knights. Count Philip brought rival Protestant reformers Martin Luther and Ulrich Zwingli to his court in 1529 to convince them to kiss and make up; he verged on success when an epidemic made everyone grumpy and uncooperative. Towering over Marburg, the castle is illuminated until 11pm. It houses the university's **Museum für Kulturgeschichte** (Cultural Museum), which exhibits Hessian history and religious art, as well as the recently unearthed wall remnants in the *Westflügel* (West Wing) that move the castle's construction date back to the 9th century (open Tues.-Sun. 10am-6pm; Nov.-March Tues.-Sun. 11am-5pm; DM3, students DM2). Occasional performances are given in the open-air theater of the **Schloßpark,** the gardens stretching to the west of the fortress (tickets DM20); check for schedules at the tourist office.

Past a strikingly ugly boar's head, down the 140 steps of the "Ludwig-Bickell-Treppe" stairway, rests the 13th-century **Marienkirche** (tel. 252 43), with amber-colored stained glass and an elaborate organ (open daily 9am-5pm; free organ concerts Oct.-July Sat. at 6:30pm). Down Kugelgasse the 15th-century **Kugelkirche** (sphere church) owes its peculiar name not to its shape but to the hats *(cuculla)* worn by the religious order that founded it. Save some ecclesiastical awe for the oldest Gothic church in Germany, modeled on France's cathedrals in Rheims and Amiens (c. 1235-83), the **Elisabethkirche** (tel. 655 73), named for the town patroness, a widowed child-bride (engaged at 4, married at 14) who took refuge in Marburg, founded a hospital, and snagged sainthood four years after she died. The **reliquary** for her bones is so overdone, it's glorious (in the *Kunstschätze*). To get there, cross the bridge opposite the train station and take a left at Elisabethstr. (Church open April-Sept. daily 9am-6pm; Oct. 9am-5pm; Nov.-March 10am-4pm, Sun. after 11am. Church free; reliquary admission DM3, students DM2.) The church is the starting point for the free guided tour of the town (April-Oct. Sat. at 3pm). Walk up the stairs across from the Elisabethkirche to get to the 13th-century **St. Michaelskapelle** surrounded by a medieval pilgrim cemetery that looks like a time-forsaken oasis.

Today's university building was erected in 1871, but the original **Alte Universität** on Rudolphspl. was built on the rubble of a monastery conveniently vacated when Reformation-minded Marburgers ejected the resident monks. The nearby houses with technicolor flags are **fraternities,** now home to a few fine collections of old fencing equipment that belie their former historical importance (see **Animal Haus: deutsche F-F-Frats,** below). Across the Lahn is the **Universitätsmuseum für Bildende Kunst** (Museum for Fine Art), Biegenstr. 11 (tel. 28 23 55), with a variety of paintings including masterpieces by Cranach, Picasso, and Kandinsky. The section on Expressive Realism depicts the lost generation of talented artists who matured during the Nazi period (open Tues.-Sun. 11am-1pm and 2-5pm; free). In the Markt, the **Rathaus** boasts some curiosities that are worth the short hike. Greeting you is a horseman slaying a figure that tragically resembles Puff the Magic Dragon.

ENTERTAINMENT AND NIGHTLIFE

Because of the student population, bars and pubs in Marburg breed faster than bunny rabbits. In the **Oberstadt** there are over 60 such establishments, giving Marburg the proud distinction of having the densest concentration of *Kneipen* in Germany. Live music, concert, theater, and movie options are listed in the weekly *Marburger Express* (free at hotels and the hostel); also ask at the tourist office about the bi-monthly program of live music and theater in the *Schloßpark.*

Kult Lager, Temmlerstr. 7 (tel. 941 85). Bus A1 (direction: "Pommernweg") or A2 (direction: "Cappeler Gleiche"): "Frauenbergstr." The only disco in town, this place gets 'em all, bringing in DJs from England and the U.S. with mad skillz. Cover DM3 weekdays, DM5 on weekends. Open Tues.-Wed. 9pm-3am, Fri.-Sat. 9pm-4am.

Café News/Hemingways/Down Under Dance Club, Reitgasse 5 (tel. 212 05 or 25). **Café News** is a trendy *Treffpunkt* with a mesmerizing view of the Lahn Valley. **Hemingway's,** down the spiral staircase, serves special drinks and American fare (Happy hour daily 6-7:30pm; both open daily 6pm-1am). **Down Under** raves on the weekends—a dance haven. Hurrah! (Open Fri.-Sat. 9pm-1am.)

Bolschoi Café, Ketzerbachstr. 25 (tel. 644 42). From Rudolfspl., walk up Pilgrimstein and turn left onto Ketzerbachstr. You'll find it on the left side of the street. Then prepare for the *real* Left—the Communist kitsch here will warm the cockles of any Cold Warrior's heart with its red candles, red walls, a red foil ceiling, and 19 brands of domestic and imported vodka (DM3.50-5.80). Lenin's bust is stenciled on the wall. The *Rollmops* (raw pickled herring; DM1) may boost your tolerance. Open Sun.-Thurs. 8pm-1am, Fri.-Sat. 8pm-2am.

Hinkelstein, Markt 18 (tel. 064 21 or 242 10), a classic hangout for locals and students, was built when Columbus discovered America. While listening to Hendrix and Jackson Brown, the patrons enjoy a game of darts. This traditional club provides a respite from Germany's omnipresent techno scene. Open daily 6pm-1am.

KFZ *(Kommunikation Freizeit Zentrum),* Schulstr. 6 (tel. 138 98), hosts an impressive schedule of multicultural events, including concerts, theater, cabaret, parties, and gay/lesbian events. Cover varies from free to DM15. Call for a schedule.

SLOT, Steinweg 9 (tel. 655 26), reopened in 1997 after a brief hiatus. Dancing and drinking. Say no more. Dancing Wed. and Fri.-Sat. Open daily 8pm-1am.

Animal Haus: deutsche F-F-Frats

While American fraternities have lost their ideals and stumbled into a puddle of bad beer, "Cocks" baseball caps, and a general abuse of the Greek alphabet, their German *Brüdern* still retain some integrity (and their liquor)—admirable or not. The origin of fraternities traces back to medieval knightly orders, such as the Teutonic Knights, and master guilds, prominent in the Hanseatic cities of northern Germany. These societies, often secret, required members to go through formidable initiation rituals, far superseding the modern "keg-stand" or the Stonecutters' "Leap of Faith." Among the well-heeled, belonging to a fraternity was the norm rather than the exception in the glory days, and many of these clubs wreaked more of aristocratic pretension than stale beer. Riled by nascent nationalism in the early 19th century, German frat boys fought regular "duels" to defend their sections of the sidewalk. The pinnacle of pride resided in a facial scar "acquired" during a violent duel. At the same time, they also became substantial players on the political scene, as their commitment to German unity played a critical role in forming national consciousness. Today, German frats are elitist and conservative, but students still strut around town in overdone suits and colorful ribbons to match their house colors before returning to their *Haus* to pound another *Maß.*

■ Near Marburg

FRITZLAR

The birth of the town of Fritzlar as *Frideslar* (Place of Peace) dates to a not-so-peaceful act of St. Boniface, who in 723 chopped down the huge **Donar's Oak,** the pagan religious symbol of the tribal Chats. The "Apostle of the Germans" used the timber to build his own wooden church, which today is the beautiful St. Peter *Dom.* It was also here that Heinrich I was proclaimed king in 915, inaugurating the medieval incarnation of the Holy Roman Empire. Since then this diminutive medieval town has become isolated from the main routes of buzzing commerce and affluence. Nevertheless, Fritzlar is content with its role as a postcard friendly *Fachwerkstadt* (a town of half-timbered houses) sitting on the *Märchenstraße,* the German fairy tale road.

The gem of Fritzlar is the 12th-century **St. Peter Dom,** with its two massive red sandstone towers and the sizeable *Domschatz* (cathedral treasury) that includes the diamond- and pearl-covered **Heinrich Cross** (created around 1020), as well as numerous precious robes and relics (open May-Oct. Mon.-Sat. 10am-noon and 2-5pm, Sun. 2-4pm; Nov.-April Mon.-Sat. 10am-noon and 2-4pm, Sun. 2-4pm; DM4, students DM2). Just around the corner lies the Marktplatz, with a **Rolandbrunnen** (Roland fountain) symbolically standing watch. This graceful fountain represents such noble concepts as justice, religious freedom, and the laws governing fruit-selling. The angel on the pedestal faces the *Kaufhäuschen,* the guild and merchants' house occupied by the brotherhood of St. Michael. On the western extremity of the still-standing medieval city wall, the 35m **Grauer Turm** (grey tower) seems fully aware of its majestic distinction as the tallest defense tower in Germany. If your lungs and legs cooperate, you can climb it and enjoy the unique view (get the keys from the tourist office; ID required). The **Hochzeitshaus** (tel. 98 86 28), on Burggrabenstr., has hosted weddings and festivals since the 16th century. It also houses the **Regional Museum,** which does its best to reflect all aspects and stages of Fritzlar's bumpy history (open Sun.-Fri. 10am-noon and 3-5pm, Sat. 10am-noon; DM3, children DM1).

Fritzlar is an ideal daytrip. The town is best reached by train from Wabern on the Frankfurt-Kassel line (10 per day; 10min.). The **tourist office** (tel. 98 86 43; fax 98 86 38), sits in the *Rathaus*—the oldest official building in Germany, built in 1109. From the station, walk to the main road (creatively named B450) and turn right up a hill. Take the second left onto Gießenerstr, through the Marktplatz, and left onto Zwischen den Kuamenstr. The office has lists of rooms (from DM25), but makes no reservations (open Mon.-Thurs. 10am-1pm and 2-4:30pm, Fri. 10-11:30am). City **tours** are also available (May-Sept. Tues.-Sat. at 11am and 3pm, Sun. at 3pm; DM5). **Dom-Grill,** Gießenerstr. 2 (tel. 26 55), just off the Marktplatz on the way to town, is the place to catch up on local gossip (if you can decipher Hessian accents) and fill up on greasy kebabs, burgers, *Würste,* and fries (DM3.50-8; open Mon.-Fri. 10am-8pm, Sat. 10am-1:30pm). Little towns seem to like big festivals, and Fritzlar is no exception. The **Pferdemarkt** (2nd weekend in July) and the **Altstadtfest** (Aug. 15-17, 1998) draw out *Lederhosen,* traditional music, and beer goggles. The **telephone code** is 05622.

FRANKENBERG

Frankenberg an der Eden (pop. 16,200) offers travelers a surprisingly big bag of goodies for a town of its tiny size. Dominating the skyline is the 13th-century **Liebfrauenkirche** ("Church of Our Lady"). From the station, follow Bahnhofstr. as it leads into the pedestrian zone to Neustadterstr.; continue trudging uphill as Neustadter becomes Ritterstr. Take the first right onto Neue Gasse, then right again, and then a left onto Kirchberg. The church is graced by 14th-century glass panels depicting the life of Christ and a 6.5m high statue of the Virgin Mary. Upon exiting, head directly onto Obermarkt to the 1509 **Rathaus.** With its whopping 10 towers, it ranks as one of the most attractive townhouses in Germany. Despite the entrancing exterior, the inside is disappointingly empty except for a sobering plaque dedicated to the Jews of Frankenberg. **Free city tours** depart here (Wed. 2:30pm, Sat. 10:30am). The bright red **Steinhaus** ("Stone House"), Pferdemarkt 20 (tel. 99 69), dates 1270; as the oldest house in Frankenberg, it now shelters an Italian restaurant with surprisingly reasonable prices (DM12-24; open Wed.-Mon. noon-2:30pm and 6pm-midnight). The ominous 13th-century **Hexenturm** (Witches' Tower), the sole survivor of an original 20 towers and five gates, stands out sharply against the residential houses and blossoming flowers. Peek inside at the walls to see where *very* unlucky crooks did their time. To get there, disconnect yourself from *Oberstadt* and take a left on Auf der Heide; then take a right and then another right onto Gadengasse. To enter the tower, one has to organize a tour with the tourist office (more than 15 people required).

The **tourist office,** Obermarkt 13 (tel. 50 51 13; fax 50 52 03), passes out nifty maps and brochures (open Mon.-Thurs. 8:30am-noon and 2-4pm; Fri. 8:30am-12:30pm). There is no hostel in Frankenberg, but Marburg is only 40 minutes away (the last train leaves at 6:30pm during the week, at 5:30pm on weekends). Admire your bulging quadriceps as you gobble down ice cream (DM0.70) at **Eis Café San Marco,** Neustadterstr. 32 (tel. 16 55), with its outstanding view down the entire pedestrian zone (open daily 9am-midnight). The **telephone code** is 06451.

■ Fulda

In the grim old days of the East-West division, Fulda earned a dubious distinction as the most likely target for a Warsaw Pact invasion, gaining the undesirable nickname of the "Fulda Gap." While its infrastructure and central location between Hamburg, Berlin, Munich, and Köln once fixed an albatross above the city, reunification sent the nasty bird flying away and turned Fulda into a transportation hub. Today Fulda is rich in culture and serves as the economic and political center of eastern Hesse. The result of this unsteady evolution is a strange contrast: in startling proximity to the marvelous historical treasures which maintain a steady flow of tourists are mini-malls, McDonald's joints, and a Super-Sized extra-value plate of commerce.

The local Prince-Abbots who dominated Fulda's spiritual and secular life for almost 700 years commissioned the construction of the compact Baroque quarter. Inside the **Stadtschloß,** built as the centerpiece of the quarter and the residence of the Prince-Abbots, the white **Kaisersaal** displays the portraits of 16 Habsburg emperors, while its **Historischen Raümen** include the **Fürstensaal** (festivity hall) and the famous collection of Fulda porcelain. To reach this sprawling yellow behemoth from the main train station, head down Bahnhofstr. and turn right in front of the church onto Friedrichstr. (Open Sat.-Thurs. 10am-6pm, Fri. 2-6pm. DM5, students DM4; DM0.50 extra for a guided tour. Tours Sat.-Thurs. at 10:30am and 2:30pm, Fri. at 2:30pm; Nov.-March Mon.-Fri. at 2:30pm, Sat.-Sun. at 10:30am and 2:30pm.) Climb the **Schloßturm** (tower) to admire the lush greenery carpeting Fulda (DM2, students DM1). Behind the palace lies a luxurious **park** lined with terraces and home to the 18th-century **Orangerie** (built 1722 to 1725). The Floravase, one of the most treasured baroque sculptures in Germany, sits atop the wide staircase in front.

Across the street from the **Schloß** stands the magnificent 18th-century **Dom** housing the tomb of St. Boniface, an 8th-century English monk and missionary known as "the apostle of Germany" who founded the Fulda abbey. An alabaster Baroque memorial edged with black marble supposedly depicts St. Boniface surrounded by angels lifting his coffin lid on Judgment Day, though it looks more like the cherubs are trying to stuff him back in. The cathedral, built in the late 18th century as the largest in central Europe, was recently renovated at great expense. (Open Mon.-Fri. 10am-6pm, Sat. 10am-3pm, Sun. 3-6pm; Nov.-March Mon.-Fri. 10am-5pm, Sat. 10am-3pm, Sun. 3-5pm. Free.) The **Dommuseum,** accessible through the courtyard, displays the dagger by which the head of St. Boniface (shake it, shake it Salomé) and the dagger by which he died in 754, as well as Lucas Cranach's *Christ and the Adulteress.* (Open Tues.-Sat. 10am-5:30pm, Sun. 12:30-5:30pm, Nov.-March Tues.-Sat. 10am-12:30pm and 1:30-4pm, Sun. 12:30-4pm; closed in January. Admission DM2, students DM2.) Visitors can purchase a **Museum Passport** from tourist information good for admission to the Historical Rooms, Cathedral Museum, German Fire-Brigade Museum, and the Vonderav

Museum (which puts Fulda's cultural history on exhibit) for DM12, students and children DM8 (DM10 and DM7, respectively, if you take public transportation).

Due to its strategic position, Fulda offers good rail connections. Many of the departing trains are ICE—super-fast but expensive. **Trains** go from Fulda to Hamburg (every hr., 3hr.), Nuremburg (every hr., 1hr.), and Frankfurt (2-3 every hr., 1hr.). The main **tourist office** (*Verkehrsbüro;* tel. 10 23 45; fax 10 27 75) 36037 Fulda, lies through the courtyard of the *Schloß*. They have free maps and book rooms (free in person, DM5 by mail; open Mon.-Wed. and Fri. 8:30am-4:30pm, Sat. 9:30am-2pm), even if they don't speak a word of English. If you need a map and they aren't open (or if your German is rusty), stop by the **Deutsche Bahn Service Point** at the train station, which has tons of maps, though they don't book rooms. The **telephone code** is 0661.

Fulda's **Jugendherberge (HI),** Schirmannstr. 31 (tel. 733 89; fax 748 11) offers quietude, a friendly staff, and standard rooms. Bus #1B (direction: Niederrode) from the bus station at the side of the *Schloß:* "Stadion" (DM2.10) and walk two minutes up the hill—it will be on your left. (Curfew 11:30pm. DM24.50, over 26 DM27. Breakfast and sheets included.) Frau Kremer runs a spartan but delightfully inexpensive ship at the **Gasthaus Zum Kronhof,** Am Kronhof 2 (tel. 741 47), behind the *Dom* just outside the old city walls. From the *Schloß,* cross the street and walk downhill on Kastanian-Allee, which becomes Wilhelmstr. to the left of the *Dom.* Take a right along the city wall on Kronhofstr. and look for a raspberry-pink building three blocks down on the left. (Singles DM35; doubles DM69, with shower DM94. Breakfast included.)

▓ Kassel

After Napolean III and his soldiers were trounced by Prussian troops at the Battle of Sedan in 1870, the unlucky French emperor was captured. While crossing the Franco-German border on his way to the Schloß Wilhelmshöhe prison, Aacheners jeered *"Ab nach Kassel"* ("off to Kassel") at the crestfallen Frog. The slogan echoed throughout Germany. Today, hordes of travelers still answer the call, coming to see the many treasures the ultra-sophisticated metropolis of Kassel has to offer. Kassel's eclecticism produces both contemporaneous and historical delights which gain vibrancy through their intermingling. The steeped traditons of Wilhelmshöhe, the grand hillside parks, and the fairy-tale atmosphere which inspired the Grimm Brothers to create their famous **Kinder- und Hausmärchen** are enriched by the cutting-edge intrigues of the **documenta** modern art exhibitions and a pulsating *Uni*-setting.

ORIENTATION AND PRACTICAL INFORMATION

Kassel is a diffuse city, the product of a nightmarish building boom which followed the postwar housing shortage. Somehow the boom never stopped. The *Deutsche Bahn* powers-that-be have chosen Kassel to be an InterCity Express connection, and have rebuilt the **Bahnhof Wilhelmshöhe-Kassel** with streamlined contemporary specs. The Wilhelmshöhe station is the point of entry to Kassel's ancient castles and immense parklands on the west side; the older **Hauptbahnhof** is the gateway to the tightly packed and entirely modernized *Altstadt.* The *Hauptbahnhof* is now a model of extravagant hipness; its remodeling in the past year saturated it with (post)modern adornments and one of the *documenta* exhibitions, the **caricatura.** IC, ICE, and most IR trains only stop at Wilhelmshöhe. Frequent trains and the RKH buses shuttle between the stations; you can catch most other bus and streetcar lines at either the "Rathaus" or "Am Stern" stops. Kassel is in northern Hessen on the banks of the Fulda River, accessible by trains from Hannover (1hr.) and Frankfurt (1½-2hrs.). The underground walkway in front of the *Hauptbahnhof* is often full of shady-looking folks; don't walk there alone after dark. Instead, explore around **Treppenstraße,** Kassel's original pedestrian zone and the first in all of Germany, or around **Königsstraße,** the current pedestrian zone—both attract brighter crowds.

Tourist Office: Kassel-Service, Königspl. 53, 2nd floor (tel. 707 71 62; fax 707 71 69), gives out free maps, a hotel list (DM0.50; rooms from DM45), and brochures in

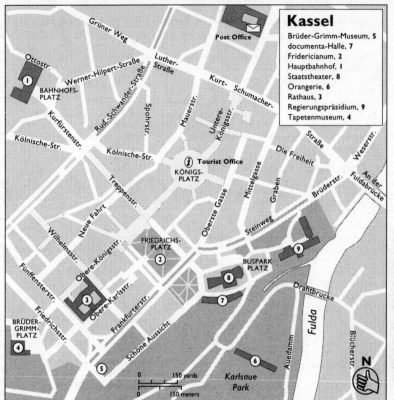

Kassel

Brüder-Grimm-Museum, 5
documenta-Halle, 7
Fridericianum, 2
Hauptbahnhof, 1
Staatstheater, 8
Orangerie, 6
Rathaus, 3
Regierungspräsidium, 9
Tapetenmuseum, 4

HESSEN

English. Open Mon.-Thurs. 9:15am-6pm, Fri. 9:15am-4:30pm. **Branch office** in the Wilhelmshöhe *Bahnhof* (tel. 340 54; fax 31 52 16). As super-modern as the rest of the station. Doles out slick catalogs and maps and finds rooms for a DM5 fee. Open Mon.-Fri. 9am-1pm and 2-6pm, Sat. 9am-1pm.

Public Transportation: Kassel's ultra-sophisticated system is integrated into the NVV (Nordhessischer Verkehrsverbund). Tickets are priced by distance with **one-ride cards** ranging DM2.40 (short trips) to DM4.30 (anywhere in the area). The **Multiticket** (DM8) is valid for 2 adults and 3 kids for a weekday or a weekend. Questions can be directed to the NVV counter in the train station or to their service number (tel. (0180) 234 01 80).

Ferries: Personenschiffahrt Söllner, Die Schlagd/Rondell (tel. 77 46 70; fax 77 77 76), just across Leipzigerstr. from the *Altstadt,* offers Fulda Valley tours (3hr.) mid-June to Aug. daily 2pm, May to mid-June and Sept. Wed. and Sat.-Sun. 2pm. One-way DM10, round-trip DM16, children half-price. You can also sail to the junction of the Fulda and Werra rivers (May to mid-Sept. Sun. and Wed. at 9:30am). One-way DM20, round-trip DM30, children half-price.

Mitfahrzentrale: City Netz Kassel, Friedrichstr. 18 (tel. 194 40). Open Mon.-Fri. 9am-6pm, Sat.-Sun. noon-3pm.

Car Rental: Avis, 77 Leipzigerstr. (tel. 57 10 06), on the other side of the Fulda from the *Altstadt.* Must be 21 to rent. Open Mon.-Fri. 7am-6pm, Sat. 8am-noon.

Bike Rental: In the Kassel-Wilhelmshöhe station (tel. 31 30 83). Bikes from DM20 for 24hr., DM80 for 5 days. Open Mon.-Fri. 9am-1pm and 2-6pm, Sat. 9am-1pm.

Bookstore: Buchladung Vaternahm, Königsstr. 7 (tel. 78 98 40). Broad selection of paperbacks in English from Hobbes to *Calvin and Hobbes.* Open Mon.-Wed. and Fri. 9:30am-6:30pm, Thurs. 9:30am-8pm, Sat. 9am-2pm.

Laundromat: Schnell & Sauber, Friedrich-Ebert-Str. 83, near the hostel, is ecologically friendly and computerized. The future is *now.* Wash DM6. Dry DM1 per 15min. Open Mon.-Sat. 5am-midnight.

Women's Concerns: FIF-Women's Information, Westring 67 (tel. 89 31 36). Open Mon. and Fri. 2-4pm, Tues. and Thurs. 10am-noon, Wed. 5-8pm.

Rape Crisis Hotline: tel. 77 22 44.

AIDS-Hilfe: Frankfurterstr. 65 (tel. 28 39 08).

Emergency: Police, tel. 110. **Fire** and **Ambulance,** tel. 112.

Internet Access: In New York (see **Entertainment and Nightlife,** p. 381).

Post Office: Hauptpostamt, Untere Königsstr. 95, 34117 Kassel, between Königspl. and the university. Open Mon.-Fri. 8am-6pm, Sat. 8am-noon.

Telephone Code: 0561.

ACCOMMODATIONS AND CAMPING

Hotels in Kassel actively seek conventioneers and business crowds, but the large accommodation industry generally has a surplus of moderately priced rooms. The **Mitzwohnzentrale,** LaSallestr. 10 (tel. 194 45), sublets apartments.

Jugendherberge am Tannenwäldchen, Schenkendorfstr. 18 (tel. 77 64 55; fax 77 68 32). Streetcar #4 (direction: "Ottostr." or "Lindenberg"): "Annastr.," walk back one block, and turn right on the tree-lined Querallee; the hostel is at the top of the hill. Or walk from the *Hauptbahnhof;* leave from the *Südausgans,* turn right on Kölnischerstr., and turn right again onto Schenkendorfstr. Huge common areas, 8-bed rooms, and a tasty breakfast buffet. Reception open until 11pm. Sunday and winter curfew 12:30am. DM24, over 26 DM29. No phone reservations.

Hotel-Restaurant Palmenbad, Kurhausstr. 27 (tel./fax 326 91). Streetcar #3 or 4: "Wiganstr." and walk 5min. uphill. Or walk from *Bahnhof* Wilhelmshöhe up Wilhelmshöher Allee (towards Herkules), left on Baunsbergstr., right on Kurhausstr. Comfortable and clean. Reception open Mon. 5:30-11pm, Tues.-Sat. 9am-11pm, Sun. 9am-2pm. Singles DM49, with bath DM58; doubles DM86, DM99.

Hotel-Restaurant Lenz, Frankfurterstr. 176 (tel. 433 73; fax 411 88), is too far to walk from either main station, but the *Bahnhof* Niederzwehren station and bus stop right around the corner is serviced by DB trains or bus #24 (from Wilhelmshöhe) and streetcar #7 (from the *Hauptbahnhof*). Sharp-looking rooms and bathrooms big enough for Herkules. Reception open daily 4-10pm. Singles DM49.50, with bath DM85; doubles DM85, DM150.

Hotel Am Rathaus, Wilhelmsstr. 29 (tel. 97 88 50; fax 978 85 30). Bus #1 or 3: "Rathaus" on Fünfenstr., turn left down Obere Karlstr., and hang a left where the statue of Landgraf Karl is striking a pose. Alternatively, bus #2 or 4: "Rathaus," walk uphill to Fünfenstr., take a left, and follow the above directions. Stained-glass windows and snug rooms. Reception open until 9pm. Singles DM61, with shower DM75; doubles with shower DM110.

Camping: Kurhessen-Kassel, Giesenallee 7 (tel. 224 33), has a stunning spot right on the Fulda and is pleasantly close to the "Island of Flowers" in the Karlsaue park. Reception open daily 7am-noon and 3-10pm. DM5 per person, under 15 DM3. DM5 per car. DM6.50 and up per tent. Open March-Oct.

FOOD

Many of Kassel's culinary offerings take a bite out of ye olde budget. Friedrich-Ebert-Str. and the upper part of Wilhelmshöher Allee have supermarkets and cafes sprinkled among department stores and fashion boutiques. To go easy on your wallet, shop in the **Markthalle,** on Wildemangasse off of Steinweg (open Thurs.-Fri. 7am-6pm, Sat. 7am-1pm). Or pick through goodies at the humongous **Markt,** on Königspl. (Tues.-Wed. 10am-5pm; more sparse pickings on other days). Inexpensive meals await in the university complex. From Wilhelmshöhe train station, streetcar #1: "Holländischerpl.," cross through the underground passage, and continue in the same direction; walk along the left side of the university to the back and hang a right onto Arnold-Bode-Str. As in most large German cities, Kassel's *Altstadt* possesses numerous food stands, bakeries, and fast food restaurants.

documenta X

Hordes of art-lovers, didactic dilettantes, and camera-toting curiosity seekers descended upon Kassel in the summer of 1997 to take part in the world's preeminent exhibition of contemporary art, *documenta* X. As the world careens towards a new millennium, artists of the exhibition struggled to critique art's modern political function. Viewing contemporary art as a means of "social regulation or indeed control through the aestheticization of information and forms of debate that paralyze any act of judgment in the immediacy of raw seduction or emotion (what might be called 'the Benetton effect')," the contributors to *documenta* X emphasized the soul-searching and democratic potential of new media which subvert traditional notions of artistic form. Amidst collections of giant Chia Pets and ironic images of "ideal" cityscapes, the show included a bevy of internet pieces which were broadcast worldwide in real-time (http://www.documenta.de). While the political posturing could be both enrapturing and excruciating, the exhibit represented the ultimate postmodern dream (evidenced by the insistence of the organizers that no label could describe the event) whose influence will resonate in the art world for decades, or millennia, to come.

Student Mensa (tel. 804 25 87), on Arnold-Bode-Str. in the back left corner of the University, 100m across a gorge from the big red brick tower. Look for the "Mensa" sign—it's the only way to tell this brick building from the 50-odd others. Students with ID DM2.60-3.30, others tack on DM2.20. Lunch Mon.-Fri. noon-2pm. The **Moritz-Restaurant** in the same building serves a slightly more elaborate lunch with much shorter lines. Students DM4.70, others DM6.90. Open Mon.-Fri. 11am-2:30pm. Just around the corner the **Studentwerke-Pavillion,** Diagonale 13, slaps together meals later in the day for the same prices (open 5-9pm). The cafe downstairs sells the cheapest ice cream around (DM0.70 per *Kugel*, or scoop).

Lohmann Biergarten, Königstor 8 (tel. 122 90) on the Fulda, two minutes from the *Rathaus.* One of Kassel's oldest beer gardens is also one of its largest. Wide variety of entrees ranges from spaghetti bolognese to *Bratwurst* (DM7.50-11), washed down with *Apfelwein* (DM3). Open Sun.-Thurs. noon-11pm, Fri.-Sat. noon-1am.

Ristorante-Pizzeria Pinocchio, Friedrich-Ebert-Str. 96 (tel. 165 65), about 3min. downhill from the youth hostel. Pizza! Pasta! *Mamma mia!* Under the eye of our long-nosed guardian, feast on fish, wine, salads, and desserts on the outdoor terrace. Entrees DM6-16. Open Wed.-Mon. 11:30am-2:45pm and 5pm-midnight.

Wok, Kölnischerstr. 124 (tel. 71 11 44), on the way to the youth hostel. Surprisingly good and spicy Thai food in an appropriate atmosphere awaits those who have had their fill of *Schnitzel* and *Wurst.* Lunch entrees DM9.50-13.50. Beer DM3.80-4.90. Open Tues.-Sun. noon-2:30pm and 5:30-11:30pm. Make reservations if possible.

SIGHTS

Kassel's sights fall into three categories: those associated with *documenta,* those at Wilhelmshöhe, and those near the *Rathaus.* The museums and galleries of *documenta* are scattered downhill of Königsstr. between the *Rathaus* and Königspl. towards the Fulda River. The sights at Wilhelmshöhe Park lie at one end of the long Wilhelmshöher Allee. At the other end stands the *Rathaus,* just after Wilhelmshöher Allee becomes Obere Königsstr. This latter road runs through Königspl. to the *Uni.* Most of the museums—Schloß Wilhelmshöhe, Ballhaus, Hessisches Landesmuseum, Neue Galerie, and Orangerie—belong to **Staatliche Museen Kassel** and are covered by a good package deal: the *Tageskarte* (day pass) is good for all of these attractions and available at any one of the museums (DM5, students DM3, families DM15); the *Verbundkarte* (combination ticket) lets you visit the museums on different days (DM10, students DM7). Admission to all *Staatliche Museen Kassel* is **free on Fridays.**

documenta

The concept behind the **documenta** is to confront and address the controversies behind expression. In 1997, the city hosted the exhibition for the 10th straight time since 1955. The leftovers from past *documentas*—Claes Oldenburg's "Pickaxe" near the Orangerie or Borofski's "Man Walking to the Sky" in front of the Fridericianum, mere skeletons of the original exhibits—still draw the attention of critics and continue to captivate the art world. The works of sculptor Josef Beuys, including his "7000 Oaks" are particularly intriguing. *documenta* 11 awaits those patient enough for its June 2002 showing. Contact the tourist office for details. The remainders of previous exhibitions sprawl across the city center; even the *Hauptbahnhof* spites its ICE brethren by getting a piece of the action. The **Fridericianum,** Friedrichspl. 18 (tel. 561 70 72 70) contains the lion's share of *documenta* related exhibitions.

Wilhelmshöhe

Wilhelmshöhe is a hillside park with one giant Greek hero, two castles, three museums, and five waterfalls, punctuated with rock gardens, mountain streams, and innumerable hiking trails. The whole park experience—a cross between the halls of Montezuma and a Baroque theme park—takes up half a day in itself; approach it with humor, cynicism, or a bike (see **Bike Rentals,** p. 377). Streetcar #1 stops at the foot of the park near **Schloß Wilhelmshöhe,** the mammoth former home of the rulers of Kassel. Napoleon III was imprisoned here after being captured in the Battle of Sedan. The **Schloß Museum** (tel. 330 86), in the right wing, records the extravagant royal lifestyle. (Open March-Oct. Tues.-Sun. 10am-5pm; Nov.-Feb. Tues.-Sun. 10am-4pm. Tours of private suites leave when there are "enough" people. DM6, students DM4.) The **Ballhaus,** nextdoor, offers changing exhibits (open May-Oct. Tues.-Sun. 10am-5pm; DM3). One of the main attractions at the *Schloß,* **The Gallery of Old Masters** (tel. 937 77), displays the works of Dürer, Rubens, Jerdaeus, Rembrandt, and other artistic bigwigs. Alas, the gallery will be closed for roof repairs until 1999, but some of the famous works can be seen at the Fredericianum museum (see above).

All paths lead up to the monumental **Riesenschloß** (giant's castle), a massive octagonal amphitheater topped by the figure of **Herkules**—Kassel's emblem. The mighty Herkules jeers at his conquered foe, the giant Encelades, whose head pokes out of the rocks at the top of the cascades. An English author traveling in the 18th century described it as "one of the most splendid structures in all of Europe, not excluding those in Versailles, Frascati, or Tivoli." Climb the scores of steps to the feet of the statue past the spectacular steps of the water **Cascades.** Or streetcar #3: "Druseltal" and bus #43 to the rear of the monument. Unfortunately, public transportation within the park is rather unreliable. Once there, climb up onto Herkules's pedestal, and if you're brave enough, into his club (access to the base of the statue free; extra altitude available March-Nov. Tues.-Sun. 10am-5pm; DM2, students DM1). If you arrive at the top of Herkules on a Sunday or Wednesday, you'll see the **fountain displays** *(Wasserspiele)* that start at 2:30pm; they're timed so that a walk down the clearly designated path lands you at the next waterfall as the show begins. The grand finale comes at 3:45pm in the backyard of the *Schloß* when the *Wasserspiele* end in a 52m-high geyser (not quite like Reykjavik…). Stake out a vantage point early (Easter-Sept. only).

The more subtle **Schloß Löwenburg** is an amazing piece of architectural fantasy. It was built by Wilhelm in the 18th century with stones deliberately missing to achieve the effect of a crumbling medieval castle; to add to the ancient look, the material used was a rapidly deteriorating basalt. For some reason this Teutonic Don Quixote was obsessed with the year 1495 and fancied himself as a time-displaced knight. In order to supplement the credibility of this pretense, he even built a Catholic chapel on the *Schloß* to date it before the Reformation, even though he himself was Protestant. Despite his pretense of chivalry, the castle was built as a love cottage for his favorite concubine who bore him 15 children—13 more than his wife.

Near the Rathaus

The English Garden of **Karlsaue Park** sprawls along the Fulda. At its north end, the bright yellow **Orangerie** manor house, built in 1701, is home to the **Museum of Astronomy and Technological History** (tel. 715 43), crammed full of mechanical and optical marvels along with a planetarium. (Open Tues.-Sun. 10am-5pm. Museum

DM5, students DM3. Free on Fri. Shows Tues., Thurs., and Sat. 2pm; Wed., Fri., and Sun. 3pm. Planetarium shows DM5, students DM3.) Lavishly illustrated, the **Brüder Grimm Museum** in Palais Bellevue, Schöne Aussicht 2 (tel. 787 20 33) near the Orangerie, exhibits the Brothers' handwritten copy of *Kinder- und Hausmärchen*, their fabled collection of fairy tales, and translations into dozens of languages (open daily 10am-5pm; DM5, students DM3). Nothing quite matches the **Deutsches Tapeten Museum** (German Wallpaper Museum), Brüder-Grimm-Platz 5 (tel. 784 60), in the yellow **Hessiches Landesmuseum** close to the *Rathaus*. The only museum of its kind in the world this place is *great!* Surprises include 16th-century embossed leather-and-gold Spanish hangings, a rare depiction of the battle of Austerlitz, a six-color wallpaper printer, and a letter from Goethe to Schiller mentioning an order of wallpaper. Shadow box scenes display the fascinating development of styles from the Middle Ages to the 1930s. (open Tues.-Fri. 10am-5pm, Sat.-Sun. 10am-1pm; DM5, kids DM3).

ENTERTAINMENT AND NIGHTLIFE

Dozens of music bars, pubs, cafes, and discos litter the *Altstadt*. The stretch along Ebertstr. and Goethestr., between Bebelpl. and Königspl., extending south along Rathenau-Allee towards the *Rathaus* packs in the party *Geist*. The free magazine INFOTIP, available at the hostel or tourist office, details the *Szene*.

The city fosters a lively film culture. Theaters cluster the *Altstadt; **Capitol** (tel. 729 09 66) on Wilhelmstr. screens films in English (Fri.-Sat.). Kassel hosts an **open-air film fest** every summer in the **Hof von Dock 4** (tel. 787 20 67). Streetcar #1 or 3: "Friedrichpl." Shows range from the artsy pretense of Godard to pure blockbuster mayhem (e.g. *Star Wars* and *das Imperium schlägt zurück;* tickets DM10). The **Staatstheater, Schauspielhaus, and Opernhaus** (tel. 109 42 22) hosts plays, operas, ballets, and concerts.

Salzmanns Factory, Sandershäuserstr. 36 (tel. 57 17 73), pumps it up with the phattest house and techno tracks. Fri. nights in **Aufschwung Ost** are famous in Germany for their thumping techno beat. Open Fri.-Sat. 10pm-4am. Cover DM5.

New York, Obere Königsstr. 4. Sleek, hip young crowd jams to hip-hop, rock, and house, with DJs who represent from Berlin and Hamburg. Also home to an **Internet Cafe** on the bottom floor. Club open Mon.-Thurs. 10pm-2am, Fri.-Sat. 10pm-5am. Cafe open Mon.-Sat. 1pm-midnight. Cover DM8.

Mr. Jones, Goethestr. 31 (tel. 71 08 18). An ultra-hip, ultra-modern bar and restaurant flaunting giant fluorescent insects. Excellent food of the Tex-Mex and grilled varieties (sandwiches DM8-12). Open Sun.-Thurs. 10am-1am, Fri.-Sat. 10am-2am.

Musik Theater, Angersbachstr. 10 (tel. 840 44). A disco-party mecca located on the other side of the tracks (from the hostel, bus #27: "Angersbachstr."). Three humongous dance floors—one for techno, one for hip-hop/Haus, one for rock/pop—occupy two city blocks. Open Wed. and Fri.-Sat. after 10:30pm. Cover DM5.

Knosel, Goethestr. 25 (tel. 77 06 08). Genuine Kassel townies hang out in this classic beer-drinking environment. They love their beer and their *Fußball*. Open Mon.-Fri. 4pm-1am, Sat. 5pm-1am.

Cafe Suspekt, Fünffensterstr. 14 (tel. 10 45 22). Popular gay and lesbian pub enjoys a laid-back and friendly ambience. Open Sun.-Thurs. 8pm-1am, Fri.-Sat. 8pm-2am.

Rheinland-Pfalz (Rhineland-Palatinate)

A trip to the Rheinland-Pfalz to see the castles and wine towns along the Rhine is an obligatory tourist tromp. The region is a visual feast—the Mosel River curls downstream to the Rhine Gorge, a soft shore of castle-backed hills. Trier is a millennia-old collage of sights, while the medieval towns of Worms and Speyer bow down around glorious cathedrals. Politically potent since the days when its electors were the king-makers of the Holy Roman Empire, the Rheinland-Pfalz is now the home of the Federal Republic's large leader, Chancellor Helmut Kohl.

THE RHINE GORGE

> At present, the sun and moon alone cast their light upon these old buildings famed in story and gnawed by time, whose walls are falling stone by stone into the Rhine, and whose history is fast fading into oblivion. O noble tower! O poor, paralyzed giants! A steamboat packed with travelers now spews its smoke in your faces!
>
> —Victor Hugo

Though the Rhine River runs all the way from Switzerland to the North Sea, the Rhine of the imagination exists only in the 80km of the gorge stretching from Bonn to north of Mainz. As the river rolls out to the sea, treacherous whirlpools and craggy shores surround the castles of aristocrats. This is the Rhine of sailors' nightmares, poets' dreams, and the rhetorical storms of nationalism. From the famed Lorelei Cliffs, legendary sirens lured passing sailors to their deaths on the sharp rocks below. Heinrich Heine immortalized the spot with his 1823 poem *"Die Lorelei,"* but he can hardly take sole credit for the literary resonance felt all along this river. The renown of Rhine wines from the hillside vineyards have inspired many a lesser illusion. Two different train lines (one on each bank) traverse this fabled stretch; the line on the west bank that runs between Koblenz and Mainz sticks closer to the water and provides superior views. If you're willing to put up with lots of tourists, the best way to see the sights is probably by **boat**. The **Köln-Düsseldorfer (KD) Line** makes the complete Mainz-Koblenz cruise three times per day during the summer, while more frequent excursions travel along shorter stretches of the river (see **Köln: Orientation and Practical Information**, p. 316).

■ Koblenz

The etymology of "Koblenz," a corruption of the Latin word for "confluence," illuminates the city's volatile history. Over the past 2000 years, Rome, France, Prussia, and Germany all fought to control this beautiful city where the Rhine and Mosel rivers converge. Though wars of conquest have died down in recent years, the frenetic activity has not. Trains rattle along both sides of the Rhine, and barges ringed by flirtatious speedboats plough through the water. For tourists, the rivers may be shining paths of history and legend, but they also serve as the conduits of modern German industry. Before reunification, the city served as the Bundesrepublik's largest munitions dump; today, the pyrotechnics that light up the city are decorative, not destructive. During the annual **Rhein in Flammen** (Rhine in Flames), held in August, the city is transformed into one grand pyrotechnic spectacle.

Rheinland-Pfalz
(Rhineland-Palatinate) FRANCE
and Saarland

ORIENTATION AND PRACTICAL INFORMATION

Koblenz's *Altstadt* merges with the Rhine and the Mosel, connected to the more southern *Hauptbahnhof* by Löhrstr. To the east, the Pfaffendorfer Brücke spans the Rhine, while the Europabrücke and the Balduinbrücke cross the Mosel in the north.

Tourist Offices: The **main office,** across the street from the train station (tel. 313 04 or 331 34; fax 129 38 00), hands out boat schedules and city maps with hotel, restaurant, and pub listings, as well as a simpler walking map. They find rooms for a DM2 fee (using the same list they give you for free if you ask politely). Open May 1-Sept. 30 Mon.-Fri. 9am-8pm, Sat.-Sun. 10am-8pm. The **Konrad-Adenauer-Ufer** branch (tel. 129 16 30), overlooking the river next to the docks, has the same service but with shorter hours. Open June-Sept. Tues.-Sun. noon-6pm. A **walking tour** leaves from this office June-Oct. Sat. at 2:30pm. Call ahead to arrange for groups or foreign language tours. **Rheinland-Pfalz information office,** Lohrstr. 103-105 (tel. 915 20 40), on the 3rd floor of an office building (or 4th floor, for Americans) has enough glossy brochures to outrage a *Grüne*. Open Mon.-Tues. and Thurs. 8am-5pm, Wed. and Fri. 8am-3:30pm.

Public Transportation: The only option for public transit in Koblenz: ride the magic bus. Ten main lines bust you around the city and into the 'burbs for DM1.80-5 per ride. Children's discount 50%. Day pass DM8. Tickets available from the driver. The **Hauptbahnhof, Zentralplatz,** and **Böhr Center** are the bus hubs.

Taxi: Funk Taxi (tel. 330 55). Be aware, funk is its own reward.

Bike Rental: Biking the Rhine and Mosel is more satisfying (and wetter) than travel by boat or train. See the tourist office pamphlet *Rund ums Rad*. **Radschlag Fahrrad,** the cheapest option, has a selection that ranges from one-gear cycles (DM7 per day) to mountain bikes (DM18 per day), tandems, and the *Rikscha*, a 3-wheeled Laff Mobile (DM35 per day). Passport and DM30, DM50, or DM100 deposit, respectively, required. Open April-Jan. 10 Mon.-Fri. 8:30am-noon and 2-6pm, Sat. 9am-1pm; otherwise by appointment. **Fahrrad Franz,** Hohenfelderstr. 7 (tel. 91 50 50), has full service (open Mon.-Wed. and Fri. 9:30am-6:30pm, Thurs. 9:30am-8pm, Sat. 9am-2pm). **Vélo,** on Konrad-Adenauer-Ufer 1 (tel. 151 02), and **Campingplatz Rhein Mosel** will also outfit you (DM10-13 per day).

Bookstore: Reuffel, Löhrstr. 92 (tel. 30 30 70), has bunches of English paperbacks. Open Mon.-Wed. and Fri. 9am-7pm, Thurs. 9am-8pm, Sat. 9am-4pm.

Laundromat: Wash that stink right out of your clothes at **Wasch Center,** on the corner of Rizzastr. and Löhrstr. Wash DM6, soap included. Dry DM2 per 15min. Open Mon.-Sat. 6am-midnight, last call 11pm.

Pharmacy: Posen Apotheke, up Löhrstr. to the left when leaving the train station, posts a list in its front window of other pharmacies providing emergency services. Open Mon.-Fri. 8am-6:30pm, Sat. 8:30am-1pm.

Emergency: Police, tel. 110.

Post Office: Hauptpostamt, to the right of the train station exit, **exchanges currency** and cashes traveler's checks. Open Mon.-Fri. 8am-6pm, Sat. 8am-noon. Limited services rendered Mon.-Wed. and Fri. 7-8am and 6-8pm, Thurs. 7-8am, Sat. 7-8am and noon-4pm, Sun. 10am-1pm. **Postal Code:** 56068.

Telephone Code: 0261.

ACCOMMODATIONS AND CAMPING

Koblenz's *Judendherberge* is blessed by a sumptuously scenic location—even folks who can afford to stay elsewhere want to sleep here. The hostel sits at the zenith of Koblenz, but the difficult trek deters few, so call a day or two ahead. If the hostel is full, they'll send you straight back down the hill with your heavy pack. Some of the hotels nearer to the station offer inexpensive rooms, but they also go quickly—always call ahead.

Jugendherberge Koblenz (HI), in the castle (tel. 97 28 70; fax 972 87 30). Mailing address: Festung Ehrenbreitstein, 56077 Koblenz. Housing both a youth hostel and a museum, the *Festung* is a worthy destination for any visitor. Unfortunately, until very recently, it was also a crucial **military installation;** "easy access" was the furthest thing from its designers' minds. Fortunately, *Let's Go*'s crack intelligence squad has found breaches in the fortress's defenses for soldiers of every rank and budget. To storm the fortress, five options are available: **Generals:** bus #8, 9, or 10 (marked by "Jugendherberge" signs at the *Hauptbahnhof*): "Ehrenbreitstein" (DM3), or take the ferry from the *Altstadt* (Mon.-Fri. 7am-6:55pm, Sat.-Sun. 8:30am-6:55pm). From here the *Sesselbahn* (chairlift) will carry your shiny stars and fat purse to the fortress. This is the least grueling option, if you can spare the cash (March-Sept. daily 9am-5:50pm; DM4, roundtrip DM6). **Privates** (troopers with a big pack and DM3): Ride the bus or ferry with the generals, then continue north and take the main footpath on your right, a somewhat steep 15min. walk. **Ninjas:** Sneak aboard bus #9: "Neudorf/Bergstr." (DM3). Creep up Bergstr. to infiltrate the fortress from the rear. The steep hike levels out, no problem for a lightly-encumbered shadow warrior like you. Follow the signs. The 4- to 10-bed rooms are standard issue. Reception open 7am-11pm, so call ahead. Curfew 11:30pm. DM23.50. Breakfast included, dinner DM9. No lockers.

Hotel Jan-van-Werth, Van-Werth-Str. 9 (tel. 365 00; fax 365 06). This classy family-run establishment is among the best values in Koblenz. From the station, walk through Bahnhofpl. to Emil-Schuller-Str. up on your left. At the end take a left onto Hohenzollernstr. and then left (5min.) onto Van-Werth-Str. Reception open daily 6:30am-10pm. Singles DM35, with shower and toilet DM65; doubles DM85, with shower and toilet DM100-120. Gummi bears and breakfast included.

Zur Kaul, Heffensteinstr. 64, at the corner of Charlottenstr and Heffensteinstr. (tel. 752 56; fax 768 72). A bit unkempt, but in a relaxed sort of way. It's quite a bargain, and it's the closest fallback if the hostel is full and you have (inexcusably) forgotten to call ahead. Singles DM30; doubles DM60.

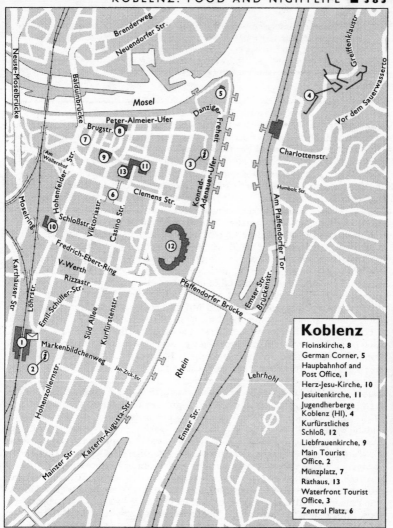

Koblenz

Floinskirche, 8
German Corner, 5
Haupbahnhof and Post Office, 1
Herz-Jesu-Kirche, 10
Jesuitenkirche, 11
Jugendherberge Koblenz (HI), 4
Kurfürstliches Schloß, 12
Liebfrauenkirche, 9
Main Tourist Office, 2
Münzplatz, 7
Rathaus, 13
Waterfront Tourist Office, 3
Zentral Platz, 6

Camping: Campingplatz Rhein-Mosel, Am Neuendorfer Eck (tel. 827 19), across the Mosel from the Deutsches Eck. A ferry journeys across the river during the day (DM0.60). Reception open daily 8am-12pm and 2-8pm. DM5.50 per person, DM4.50-6 per tent. Open April-Oct. 15.

FOOD AND NIGHTLIFE

Restaurant-Café Dubrovnik, Obere Löhrstr. 91 (tel. 129 50), is a 10min. walk to the left of the train station on Löhrstr. Turn right immediately after *Herz-Jesn-Kirche.* Elegant decor with a taste of *Miami Vice.* Daily specials (noon-3pm) are a steal (DM10-18 for soup and entree); evening dining is pricier, but quality is consistently high. Open daily 9am-midnight.

Salat Garten, where Casinostr. becomes Gymnasiumstr. in the *Altstadt.* The arteries (and taste buds) cry out for the vegetarian wonders that crop up here. Good salad bar. Self-service keeps prices low (daily specials DM8). Open Mon.-Wed. and Fri. 11am-7pm, Thurs. 11am-9pm, Sat. 11am-3pm.

Altes Brauhaus, Braugasse 4 (tel. 15 10 01). Wide selection of hearty, traditional German dishes for circa DM15. Home brew between meals. Open Mon.-Sat. 10:30am-10pm. Kitchen open 11:30am-2:30pm and 5:30-10pm.

Tatort, Münzpl. 15 (tel. 42 19), occasionally turns Münzpl. into a ground for local bands—otherwise it's a popular rock 'n' roll bar. Open daily 4pm-late.

SIGHTS

The focal point of Koblenz is the **Deutsches Eck** (German Corner). A peninsula at the confluence of the Rhine and Mosel, it purportedly witnessed the birth of the German nation when the Teutonic Order of Knights settled here in 1216. The tremendous, somewhat creepy **Mahnmal der Deutschen Einheit** (Monument to German Unity) stands on the right, commemorating a rather different sort of union. Erected in 1897, it stands in tribute to Kaiser Wilhelm I for forcibly reconciling the internal conflicts of the German Empire (though the *Kaiser* played second fiddle to Bismarck). The 14m high equestrian statue of the *Kaiser* which once topped the monument was toppled in 1945. In a move that raised questions about German aesthetic sensibilities, not to mention resurgent nationalism, the statue was replaced by a duplicate in 1993.

Attractions of a less fervent sort can be found in Koblenz's many churches, many of which were restored after WWII. The **Florinskirche** towers shine with bursts of vibrant color (open daily 11am-5pm; free). The curvaceous **Herz-Jesu-Kirche,** on the corner of Moselring and Löhrstr., has free organ music the first Wednesday of every month at 5:45pm. In the north end of the city's pedestrian zone is the **Liebfrauen-kirche,** built on the ruins of a hall from the 4th century. Its oval Baroque towers, emerald and sapphire stained glass, and intricate ceiling latticework are stunning; the choir windows document the role of women in the *Heilsgeschichte* (Passion and Salvation of Christ). The **Florinskirche** inside traces back to the 12th century. Napoleon used it as a military depot, but beautifully preserved windows and frescoes endure from the 13th century. Another part of the Liebfrauenkirche, the **St.-Kastor-Kirche,** was rebuilt after World War II and stylistically refined to eliminate eleven centuries of ornamental accumulations. The **Jesuitenkirche,** on the Marktplatz, is a strange symbiosis of a modern interior and a masterful *Rheinisch* facade from the early 17th century. Light streaming through the blazing rosette window interrupts the still darkness of the interior (open daily 7am-6pm). Behind the *Mahnmal,* in the beautiful, unassuming **Blumenhof** (flower garden), lurks more blatant national braggadocio, though this time not on the Germans' part. Napoleon erected the **fountain** to commemorate his "certain impending victory" in the Russian campaign. The Russians, after routing the French army, added the mocking inscription "seen and approved."

All of this ground-level viewing got you down? The best way to see Koblenz is from atop the battlements of **Festung Ehrenbreitstein,** an old Brobdingnagian fortress. The Prussians used it to accommodate the French troops stationed in Koblenz. (For more on reaching the fortress, see **Jugendherberge Koblenz,** p. 384.) In the valley below the fortress, at Wambachstr. 204, just off Hofstr., sits a typically German example of cultural obsession: a **museum** (tel. 129 25 02) in the birthhouse of **Beethoven's mother.** (Open April 15-Oct. 14. Thurs.-Sat. 11am-4pm, Sun. noon-4pm; call for appointments in the winter; free.) All but the most ardent Ludwig van groupies will be disappointed by the few letters on display.

Both the **Kurfürstliches Schloß,** next to the Rhein Bridge, and the **Alte Burg,** next to the Baldwin Bridge, are castles now used for administrative purposes; they are best seen as you walk along the docks outside. The **Schängelbrunnen** is best seen from afar—a statue of a boy, standing defiantly near the *Rathaus,* spews water on passers-by and drives kids into frenzied glee (like Mr. Jolly who lives next door). **Theater** information and tickets are available at the *Rathaus* box office (tel. 129 28 40). Ask about student discounts (open Tues.-Fri. 11am-1pm and 2-4pm, Sat. 11am-1pm).

MUSEUMS

Museum Ludwig im Deutschherrenhaus, Danziger Freiheit 1 (tel. 30 40 40), is right behind the *Mahnmal.* The bias is toward contemporary French artists, but expect anything and everything from the revolving collection, including Picasso and Christo, the infamous *Reichstag* Wrapper. DM5, students DM3. Open Tues.-Wed. and Fri.-Sat. 11am-5pm, Thurs. 11am-7pm, Sun. 11am-6pm.

Mittelrheinisches Museum, next to the *Florinskirche,* contains four diverse floors of art, from 16th-century sculpture to 19th-century painting. They've got Klimt! Good special exhibits. DM5, students DM3. Open Tues. and Thurs.-Sat. 11am-5pm, Wed. 11am-7pm, Sun. 11am-6am.

Landesmuseum Koblenz, Hohe Ostfront, in Festung Ehrenbreitstein (tel. 970 30). A dangerous combination of cannons, wine, tobacco, and autos documents either a 13-year-old's fantasy or the region's industrial past. Alas, no live ammo or tasty samples. DM3, students DM2. Open mid-March to mid-Nov. daily 9am-12:30pm and 1-5pm, last entrance 15min. before closing.

Mittelrheinisches Postmuseum, Friedrich-Ebert-Ring 14-20 (tel. 128 20 60), in the Oberpostdirektion building. Enter on Friedrichstr. The evolution of stamps, mailboxes, and telephones from the days when mailmen carried sabers and bugles. Also documents the unholy alliance between the German post and telephone systems. Free. Open through rain, hail, sleet, and snow Mon.-Thurs. 10am-4pm.

Rhein Museum Koblenz, Charlottenstr. 53a (tel. 70 34 50). Bus #9 or 10: "Charlottenstr." A private museum devoted to all things *Rheinisch,* including old boats, engines, fish (dead!), and even an old captain's seat. Four floors of marine history. A good double-header with Beethoven's mother's house. DM4, children DM3. Open daily 10am-5pm.

■ Lorelei Cliffs and Castles

"Art is a temptation, a seduction, a *Lorelei,*" wrote H.L. Mencken. The mythic distortion of the Rhine explodes into rocky frenzy along the **Cliffs of the Lorelei.** This section of the river, with its switchbacks and boulders, was so difficult to navigate that a sailors' song, immortalized by Heinrich Heine, developed about a siren *(Lorelei)* who seduced sailors with her intoxicating song, disastrously distracting them. Protected by the plush interiors and tinted windows of the gigantic and ubiquitous "Loreley Express" tourbuses, most of today's Rhine travelers avoid such grim fates. However, it is still possible to be seduced if you climb the marked path that begins ten minutes south of **St. Goarshausen.** Though these cliffs are remarkably similar to those just upstream, the view almost lives up to the romance.

Directly above St. Goarshausen the fierce **Burg Katz** (Castle Cat) eternally stalks its prey, the smaller **Burg Maus** (Castle Mouse). Fortunately, the mouse escapes the Kafka-esque little fable by hiding away upstream in the Wellmich district of Goarshausen. About an hour by foot from the station, the smaller castle keeps eternally vigilant, sometimes with hour-long displays of **Raubvogeldressur,** featuring eagles, falcons and other scary carnivorous birds, circling and sometimes landing on tourists' shoulders.

Two minutes away from the Lorelei Cliffs the hostel **Tuner-und-Jugendheim Loreley** (tel. 26 19; fax 81 89) lures travelers in with friendly ditties of hip hostelers, only to drown them in crashing waves of school children. It boasts a picnic area, sports facilities, and an open-air stage nearby. (Curfew 10pm. DM18.50, over 26 DM20. Breakfast included.) Turn left and hug the Rhine to reach the **Campingplatz Loreley-stadt** (tel. 25 92; fax (02137) 49 98), an eight-minute walk from the *Bahnhof.* (DM7, children DM4, dogs DM3). The **telephone code** is 06771.

Across the river, the town of **St. Goar** provides a pleasant home base for Lorelei explorations. The view from the cliffs on the eastern side is spectacular, and the castle **Burg Rheinfels** is dazzling. A sprawling, half-ruined castle with endless layers of fortification, the Burg welcomes all visitors who dares to wander through the monstrosity without joining a tour. (Open daily 9am-6pm, last entrance 5pm. Admission DM5, children DM3.) The laid-back **Fußgängerzane** downtown supplies the non-climber with a sweet option.

St. Goar's **tourist office** (tel. 383; fax 72 09) is located at Heerstr. 86. The town has a convenient **Jugendherberge (HI),** Bismarckberg 17 (tel. 388; fax 28 69), with somewhat strict management 10 minutes from the train station. (Reception open 5-6, 7-8pm. Curfew 10pm. DM19.50. Breakfast included. Sheets DM5.) On the **Marktplatz, Hotel Hausen** (tel. 333; fax 14 64) offers spotless, relaxing rooms at cheap prices. (Singles DM44, with bath DM55-75; doubles DM100-110. Breakfast included.) St. Goar's **postal code** is 56329. The **telephone code** is 06741.

■ Bacharach

With modest German skills and a basic knowledge of Roman mythology, it is a piece of cake to decipher the name of the city: Altar to Bacchus. Natives and barbarians alike prostrate themselves to the god of wine and revelry in the town's numerous **Weinkeller** and **Weinstuben** (wine cellars and pubs), scattered throughout the impeccably preserved village on the Rhine; see the tourist office (below) for a detailed list (DM1.50). View the source of the precious liquid from the **Wernerkapelle,** a red sandstone chapel that took 140 years to build (1294-1434) but only a few hours to destroy in the War of Palatine Succession in 1689. It's a short climb up the steps of the Gothic **Peterskirche.**

The **tourist office,** Overstr. 1 (tel. 12 97; fax 31 55), in the *Rathaus,* a three minute walk up to the right from the station, provides maps of hiking trails (open Mon.-Fri. 10am-noon and 3-5:15pm, Sat. 10am-1pm). Hostels get no better than the unbelievable **Jugendherberge Stahleck (HI)** (tel. 12 66; fax 26 84), a gorgeous 12th-century castle that provides an unbeatable panoramic view of the Rhine Gorge for its 40,000 yearly visitors. With a recently remodeled interior and a bar serving local brews and wines until midnight, the hostel feels like a Hilton taken over by rabble-rousers of all ages. The steep, exhausting 20 minute hike to the hostel is worth every painful footstep. Call ahead; they're usually full by 6pm. To reach the hostel from the station, turn left at *Peterskirche* and take any of the marked paths leading up the hill. (Curfew 10pm. DM23.50. Breakfast included, all-you-can-eat dinner with vegetarian option DM9.) For those growing weary of too many uphill treks, **Haus Dettmar,** on Overstr. 8. (tel. 26 61 or 29 79), is clean and right in town. (Singles DM30; doubles DM50.) Turn right immediately after leaving the station (heading downhill towards the river), then walk south for 10 minutes to reach **Campingplatz Bacharach** (tel. 17 52), where you can camp directly on the Rhine for DM5 per tent and DM7.50 per person inside it. The price is right at the uniquely named **Cafe Restaurant,** on Overstr. 40, where three-course meals go for DM11-17.50. The **telephone city code** is 06743.

■ Rüdesheim

Seen from the other side of the Rhine, Rüdesheim is a romantic's dream come true. The terraced vineyards stretch steeply up from the river, while a checkerboard of green lifts the heart. Across the river, however, the cruel ogre of commercialism has found a home. Rüdesheim's location in the heart of the Rheingau wine-producing region has made the town a formidable tourist magnet, and you can now almost set your watches by the fleets of tour buses that pour into the valley when they roll out the first barrels at 9am. The picturesque 12th-century **Brömserburg Fortress,** Rheinstr. 2, like the rest of Rüdesheim, now succumbs to Bacchanalian indulgence—it's a **wine museum** (tel. 23 48) just five minutes from the train station along Rheinstr. The fortress boasts all important styles of architecture, from the Middle Ages through the Renaissance, Baroque, Rococo, Empire, Biedermeyer, *Jugendstil,* and Art Deco periods. (Open mid-March to mid-Nov. daily 9am-6pm. Last admission 5:15pm. Admission DM5, students and children DM3.) Servings are available along the nearby **Drosselgasse,** a tiny alley occupied solely with souvenir shops and "authentic" German restaurants. Up Drosselgasse to the left are signs for **Siegfrieds Mechanisches Musikkabinett,** Oberstr. 29 (tel. 492 17; fax 45 87), a museum of automatic musical instruments with one of the largest collections of music boxes and player pianos in the world. (Open mid-March to mid-Nov. 10am-10pm. Obligatory tours leave every 15min.; English tours available. Admission DM9, students DM5.) The **Mittelalterliches Foltermuseum** (medieval torture museum), Grabenstr. 13 (tel. 475 10), displays

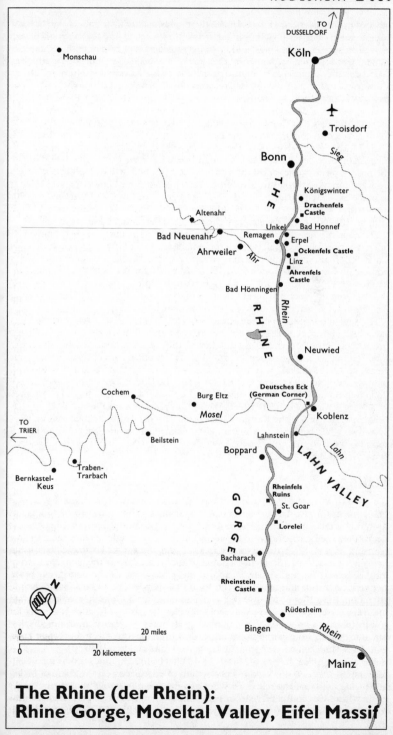

The Rhine (der Rhein):
Rhine Gorge, Moseltal Valley, Eifel Massif

devices prisoners endured to "salvage" their souls. Eighty instruments (including a *Säge*, a saw used to slice victims in half while they dangled upside down, still alive), as well as paintings, drawings, and etchings provide a delightfully grisly exhibition. (Open May-Sept. daily 10am-6pm; Oct.-April Sat.-Sun. 10am-6pm; DM6, children DM3.) Another esoteric exhibit insidiously lurks in the **Motorroller Museum,** Rheinstr. 5 (next to the post office), where over 120 displays illustrate the history of the most dorky of all modes of transport—the moped! (Open daily 10am-8pm; DM8.)

The **Niederwalddenkmal,** a 38m tall monument crowned by the unnervingly nationalistic figure of *Germania* wielding a 1400kg sword, looms high above the town. Erected to commemorate the establishment of the Second Reich in 1871, the central frieze features legions of 19th-century aristocrats pledging loyalty to the *Kaiser* flanked by winged emblems of war and peace. For the heavy of foot and purse, the bronze piece of allegorical extremism is best reached by the **chairlift** *(Seilbahn)* from the top of Christofelstr. that carries 1200 people every hour. (Open mid-March to mid-Nov. daily 9:30am-5pm; DM5.50, children, large dogs, and luggage DM3.50, round-trip DM10.) To reach the chairlift, take a left directly before the tourist office (10min.). By foot, take Oberstr. from the station to the footpath leading uphill.

The **tourist office,** Rheinstr. 16 (tel. 29 62; fax 34 85), couches along the river. It offers walking-tour pamphlets and a room-finding service (10% fee; cheapest rooms DM40-50). It also exchanges money, cashes traveler's checks (no commission), and houses the **AmEx office** (open Mon.-Fri. 8:30am-6:30pm, Sat. 10:30am-5:30pm, Sun. 11:30am-3:30pm; Nov.-April Mon.-Fri. 8:30am-6:30pm). The **post office,** towards Brömserburg on Rheinstr., also exchanges money (open Mon.-Fri. 8:30am-noon and 2:30-5pm, Sat. 8:30-11:30am). The **telephone code** is 06722.

The **Jugendherberge (HI),** am Kreuzberg (tel. 27 11; fax 48 284), is in the vineyards high above the town, but the 25min. walk through flowers, vines, and silence proves aesthetically rewarding. Call ahead—they're often booked solid. From the train station, walk down Rheinstr. and make a left on any street that catches your fancy, up to and including Löhrstr. At Oberstr., turn right and bear left at the fork onto Germaniastr. and follow it to Kuhweg and the "Jugendherberge" signs. (Reception open 8-9am, 1-2, and 5-11pm. Curfew 11:30pm. Members only. DM21.50, over 26 DM26. Breakfast included. Sheets DM6.) **Campingplatz am Rhein** (tel. 25 28) has prime riverside real estate for those with portable roofs. From the train station, walk past town while hugging the Rhine, past the **Asbachbad** (swimming pool), and you'll run into the campsite. (Reception open 8am-10pm; DM6.40 per person, children DM4.20, tents DM6.10-8.20. Open May-Sept.)

■ Bingen

On an island near the village of Bingen, downstream from Rüdesheim, the **Mäuseturm** (Mouse Tower) leans over the winding Rhine. According to legend, Archbishop (and arch-villain) **Hatto II** of Mainz was challenged by starving peasants demanding the food he hoarded during a famine. He proceeded to lock them up in a barn and set it on fire. Hearing their shrieks of pain, the sadistic Hatto cackled, "listen to my mice squeaking." Suddenly, a horde of mice rushed out of the barn, chased him into the tower, and ate him alive. Unfortunately, the tower can be visited only twice per year on a tour announced in the local newspaper. The town's main daytime attraction, **Burg Klopp** (tel. 149 86), is five minutes from the **tourist office** through maze-like streets (follow red mice signs). Besides the castle cafe, affordable only for royalty (entrees start at DM22.50), Burg Klopp features the **Heimatmuseum,** displaying third-century Roman milestones and a view from the top of its tower (open April-Oct. Tues.-Sun. 9am-noon, 2-5pm; DM1, students and children DM0.50).

The **tourist office,** Rheinkai 21 (tel. 18 42 05; fax 162 75), finds rooms for a DM3 fee (singles start at DM31) and offers a wealth of information on the 20km of hiking and biking trails that encircle the town. From the *Hauptbahnhof,* stick by the tracks as they head east to Rheinkaistr. or get off at the Bingen station and head towards town for five minutes (open Mon.-Fri. 9am-6pm, Sat. 9am-12:30pm; Dec.-March

Mon.-Fri. 9am-4pm). Bingen offers the best access to the Rhein Gorge, with two **train** stations, good connections to Frankfurt and Koblenz, and docks from which several brands of **ferries** depart; ferries go to Rüdesheim (every 40min.; one way DM1.60, round-trip DM2.80, bikes, dogs, and strollers DM0.80). The ubiquitous **Kölner-Düs-seldorfer** ferry sails to Koblenz (DM66.20) and Bacharach (DM22). For a **taxi,** call 356 49 or 145 00. The **Rettungsdienst** (ambulance) can be reached by dialing 437 37. The **telephone code** is 06721.

To get to the **Jugendherberge Bingen-Bingerbrück,** Herterstr. 51 (tel. 321 63; fax 340 12), follow the signs from the *Hauptbahnhof* across the bridge and bear left (15min.). The hostel boasts a great view of the shore. (Check-in 5-10pm, curfew 10pm. DM19.50, with 2 meals DM28.20, with 3 meals DM32.50. Breakfast included. Sheets DM5.) **Prina's Pizzeria,** Fruchtmarktstr. 8, cooks authentic Italian fare, and most of the menu is under DM10; the notable exception is the "Pizza Bombe," chock full of toppings, for DM15. Even a pizza bomb pales in comparison to **Pallazzo,** Bingen's renowned **mega-disco.** The club's pulsating lasers and music attract hostelers all along the Gorge. The hours often change, though the club always hops on Saturday nights. The disco is right on the river—you can't miss it.

▓ Mainz

As the capital of the Rheinland-Pfalz, Mainz has metamorphosed into a modern metropolis, but the monumental dome and the maze of minuscule streets in the *Altstadt* are still the center of the city. Mainz successfully combines modernity and antiquity as concrete and cobblestone seamlessly mesh to carry people of every stamp through the vibrant city. Mainzers are known to be more friendly than their bureaucratic neighbors (we won't mention any names).

Orientation and Practical Information To maneuver in the Mainz maze, streets running parallel to the Rhine sport blue nameplates, while streets running perpendicular to the river bear red ones. Mainz's well-developed transportation system makes it user-friendly and offers easy daytrips to Wiesbaden (S-Bahn #6). Recently moved into a swanky new office on the ultramodern *Rathaus's Brückenturm*, the **tourist office** (tel. 28 62 10; fax 286 21 55) doles out free maps and reserves rooms for DM5, but singles start at DM50 and quickly rocket into the stratosphere (open Mon.-Fri. 9am-6pm, Sat. 9am-1pm). The **Köln-Düsseldorf Ferries** (tel. 22 45 11; fax 23 69 36) dock in Mainz and depart from the nearby docks on the other side of the *Rathaus*. Purchase tickets to dance, theater, and concerts (DM12-25) at the **Mainzer Kammerspiele,** Emmerich-Joseph-Str. 13 (tel. 22 50 02; fax 22 50 04), off Schillerpl. (open Tues.-Fri. noon-6pm). Mainz's **AIDS-Hilfe** hotline (tel. 22 22 75) has the scoop on gay and lesbian life in the city. Bike rentals are available at **CityPort,** a stone's throw away from the *Hauptbahnhof* toward the university at the "Hallenbad/City-Port" bus stop. The **post office,** 55116 Mainz, is down Bahnhofstr. from the station (open Mon.-Tues. 8am-6pm, Sat. 8am-noon). The **telephone code** is 06131.

Accommodations, Food, and Entertainment Mainz's **Jugendgäste-haus (HI),** Otto-Brunfels-Schneise 4 (tel. 853 32; fax 824 22), is in Weisenau at the far right corner of the *Volkspark*. Bus #1: "Jugendherberge" or 22: "Viktorstift." The hostel is large and well-maintained but can be noisy. (Reception open 5-10pm. Lockout midnight-6:30am. DM21, over 26 DM26.20; doubles DM48.40, over 26 DM53.20. *Gästehaus* rooms with showers and toilets DM25.20, doubles DM34.50. Breakfast included. Sheets DM5.) **Hotel Stadt Coblenz,** Rheinstr. 49 (tel. 22 76 02), has inexpensive, finely furnished rooms near the city center. Take your choice of several buses to "Rheingoldhalle."(Singles DM75; doubles DM95, with bath DM140; triples DM125, with bath DM170. Breakfast included.)

Near the *Dom,* the **Central Restaurant,** on the corner of Rheinstr. and Hengasse (tel. 22 56 66), cooks up a wide variety of *Essen*, from burgers to traditional German fare to vegetarian dishes, and almost everything on the menu is under DM10 (open

Sun.-Thurs. 10am-midnight, Fri.-Sat. 10am-1am). At the *Uni*, **Taverne Academica** caters to the student crowd, serving cheap food and drinks. Bus: "Universität" and make a left (open Mon.-Fri. 11am-midnight, Sat. 11:30am-3pm and 6-11pm).

KUZ (*Kulturzentrum*), Dagobertstr. 20b (tel. 28 68 60), mixes cultural events and hip crowds, hosting such dance gigs as "Perfect Beat Party" (open Wed. 9pm-3am and Fri. 9pm-4am; Sept.-June also Sat. 9pm-4am). After the city holiday of *Johannistag* in late June, Mainz celebrates **Johannisnacht**—three days of old-fashioned revelry dedicated to Gutenberg. Movable type and Bacchanalian revelry do not easily combine, but Mainz manages it in high style.

Sights At the heart of Mainz lies the colossal sandstone **Martinsdom,** the resting place of the archbishops of Mainz, whose extravagant tombs line the walls. (Open April-Sept. Mon.-Fri. 9am-6:30pm, Sat. 9am-4pm, Sun. 12:45-3pm and 4-6:30pm; Oct.-March Mon.-Fri. 9am-5pm, Sat. 9am-4pm, Sun. 12:45-3pm; free.) The adjacent **Dom Museum** houses artifacts dating from the beginning of the Holy Roman Empire. (Open Mon.-Wed. and Fri. 10am-4pm, Thurs. 10am-5pm, Sat. 10am-2pm; free. Special exhibits DM4, students and tots DM1.)

Behind the *Dom,* the *Altstadt* stretches for a few blocks in and around Augustinerstr. On a hill several blocks south, moving away from the river, stands the Gothic **Stephanskirche,** notable for its stunning stained-glass windows created by Russian artist-in-exile **Marc Chagall** in the eight years prior to his 1984 death. On sunny days (sweepin' the clouds away), the windows bathe the church in an eerie blue light (open daily 10am-noon and 2-5pm). Favorite son Johannes Gutenberg, the father of movable type, is immortalized at the **Gutenberg Museum,** Liebfrauenpl. 5 (tel. 12 26 44), along with his most important creations. The museum contains woodcuts, lithographs, early printing presses, and some of the first books ever printed, including several **Gutenberg Bibles.** (Open Tues.-Sat. 10am-6pm, Sun. 10am-1pm; admission DM5, students and children DM2.50, free on Sun.) Near the museum, the **Experimental Print Shop,** at Fischtorstr. 2 (tel. 12 26 86), lets visitors try their luck at Gutenberg's craft by setting and printing their own designs (open Mon.-Fri. 10am-5pm; free, but call ahead to make sure that *Schulmädchen* haven't taken over). North of the Gutenberg Museum, on Rheinstr., is the **Brückenturm-Galerie der Stadt Mainz**—a city-funded modern art museum that displays the works of regional artists (open Tues.-Fri. 11am-6pm, Sat.-Sun. 11am-2pm).

North of the Marktplatz, along Schurterstr. from the *Dom* and right on Christophstr., is the **Pfarrkirche St. Cristoph,** a thought-provoking illustration of several centuries of history. The site of Gutenberg's baptism, the church was seriously damaged in World War II; the former tower is still used for services, but the main body is a ruin supported by concrete pillars that seem to sprout from the bed of greenery within. Along the river near the Theodor-Heuss-Brücke rests the **Kurfürstliches Schloß,** former palace of the archbishopric and home to the **Römisch-Germanisches Museum's** smallish collection of Roman-era miscellany (open Tues.-Sun. 10am-6pm; free). A more comprehensive collection of art and archaeology, including a Judaica division and enormous Roman arches, awaits in the **Landesmuseum,** up the street at Große Bleiche 49-51 (open Tues. 10am-8pm, Wed.-Sun. 10am-5pm; DM5, free on Sat.). To the northwest of the *Schloß* stands the commanding **Christuskirche.** Flanked by fountains and a flower-filled promenade, the gray-brick church (rebuilt in 1951 after its partial destruction during World War II) looks more like the United States Capitol building than a place of worship. If you have some time to spare when you've exhausted Mainz, Wiesbaden (see p. 364) conveniently commends itself.

■ Worms

Of course you've heard of Worms. It was in European history class, when an unfortunate student (maybe it was you) raised his hand and asked what the whole class was thinking: "What's a diet of worms?" The teacher chuckled for a little longer than necessary and replied with characteristic wit, "I don't know what a diet of worms is, but

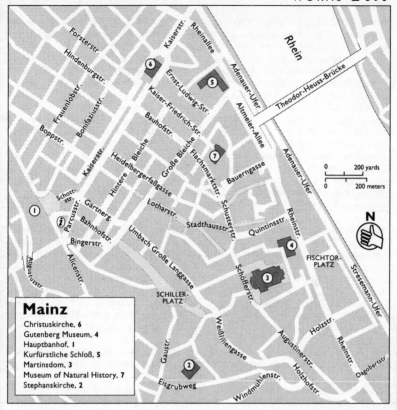

Mainz

Christuskirche, 6
Gutenberg Museum, 4
Hauptbahnhof, I
Kurfürstliche Schloß, 5
Martinsdom, 3
Museum of Natural History, 7
Stephanskirche, 2

the DEET of VOHRMS *(the Diet of Worms)* was the imperial council that sent Martin Luther into exile for refusing to renounce his heretical doctrines." Remember how funny that was? No? No matter—a visit to Worms will certainly refresh your memory, especially since little else of importance has happened here in the centuries since the famous gathering. Today's Worms is a fairly modern conglomerate of businesses with several fantastic historical and architectural sites scattered throughout. Though the city lacks any sort of core (no jam-packed *Altstadt* here), the many churches, monuments, and puny museums warrant a daytrip for anyone in the area.

Practical Information and Accommodations The **tourist office**, Neumarkt 14 (tel. 250 45), is in a small shopping complex across the street from the *Dom St. Peter* (open Mon.-Fri. 9am-6pm, Sat. 9am-noon; Nov.-March closed Sat.). Guided German walking **tours** meet at the south portal of the *Dom* Saturdays at 10am (2hr.; DM5, students DM2.50). To walk to the **Jugendgästehaus (HI),** Dechaneigasse 1 (tel. 257 80; fax 273 94), follow Bahnhofstr. right from the main train station to Andreasstr., turn left and walk until the *Dom* is on your left. This well-equipped very comfy hostel has bright two-, four-, and six-bed rooms, each with private bath (DM26.30, over 26 DM31.50; strict curfew 11:30pm). A relaxed staff runs **Weinhaus Weis** (a *Pension,* not a drinking establishment), Färbergasse 19 (tel. 235 00), supplying soft beds in spacious rooms. (Reception generally opens whenever you call them. Singles DM38; doubles DM68. Breakfast included.) The **telephone code** is 06421.

Food and Entertainment The Worms University **Mensa** is your ticket to cheap food—tastier than the notorious diet of worms (open March-July and Oct.-Jan.

Mon.-Fri. 11:45am-1:45pm). Travelers technically need an ID, but they often get by with language ability or high caliber bluffing. To reach the campus, turn right as you exit the station, go right across the bridge, walk down Friedrich-Ebert-Str., and turn left on Erenburgerstr. It's a block and a half up on your right, past the U.S. Army ("We want YOU!") barracks. Lots of posters about impending events cover the walls. In the basement of the building opposite the *Mensa* is the **Taberna,** a groovy *Studenten Kneipe* with a weekly **disco.** (Taberna open Mon.-Thurs. 3pm-1am. Disco open Thurs. 9pm-1am or later. Any student ID will suffice.) A swank young crowd swims in colorful tropical drinks at **Ohne Gleich,** Kriemhildenstr. 11 (tel. 231 01), down Bahnhofstr. to the right of the station. The place will make you feel like you've stepped into a Magritte painting (banana juice DM3.80; open Mon.-Thurs. 9am-1am, Fri.-Sat. 9am-2am, Sun. 10am-1am). Screams and laughter from intense haggling at the **farmer's produce Markt** echo across the Marktplatz on Monday, Thursday, and Saturday mornings. The Worms open-air **jazz festival** takes place every year in the beginning of July. The **Backfischfest** brings a party of 70,000 people to Worms for nine days beginning the last weekend in August.

Sights The site of Luther's confrontation with the *Diet,* during which he shocked the membership by declaring, *"Ich stehe hier. Ich kann kein anders"* (Here I stand, I can do no other), is memorialized at the **Lutherdenkmal,** a larger-than-life statue erected in 1868 three blocks southeast of the station along Wilhelm-Leuschner-Str. Across the southeast intersection stands the **Kunsthaus Heylshof** art museum, distant from package tours, which houses a small collection of late Gothic and Renaissance art including Rubens's *Madonna with Child* (open Tues.-Sun. 10am-5pm; Oct.-April Tues.-Sun. 2-4pm; DM3, students DM2). The lush, inviting greenery and deserted paths of the **Heylshofgarten** surround the museum, providing a welcome bit of solitude amid Worms's day to day clamor.

Chief amongst Worms's architectural treasures is the **Dom St. Peter,** a magnificent Romanesque cathedral with a spooky crypt. Let your vampire fantasies run wild or stand and face the hounds of hell. According to the *Nibelungenlied,* Siegfried's wife Kriemhilde had a spat with her sister-in-law Brunhilde in the square in front of the *Dom.* (Open daily 8am-5:45pm; free, but a usurious DM0.50 donation, students DM0.20, is requested.) Not as heavenly, but of great historical importance, is the tiny, 1200-year-old **Magnuskirche,** the oldest Protestant church in Germany and the starting point for the Reformation in Worms (open daily March-Nov. 10am-6pm). The late-Gothic **Liebfrauenkirche,** Liebfrauenring 21 (tel. 442 67), several blocks to the north of the *Altstadt* off Mainzerstr., is also gorgeous (open 9am-6pm; Nov.-March 9am-5pm). The vineyards surrounding the church produce the soft, sweetly lingering *Liebfraumilch* (known in its export variety as "Blue Nun").

The 900-year-old **Heiliger Sand** (Holy Sand), the oldest Jewish cemetery in Europe, is the resting ground for sundry rabbis, martyrs, and celebrities. Enter the cemetery through the gate on Willy-Brandt-Ring, just south of Andreasstr. and the main train station. On the opposite end of the *Altstadt,* the area around the **Judengasse** stands witness to the thousand-year legacy of Worms's Jewish community, which prospered during the Middle Ages but was wiped out in the Holocaust. The **synagogue,** just off Judengasse, houses the *yeshiva* of the famous Talmudic commentator Rabbi Shlomo Ben-Yitzhak, better known as Rashi (open Tues.-Sun. 10am-noon and 2-4pm). Behind the synagogue is the **Judisches Museum** (tel. 85 33 45 and 85 33 70) in the *Raschi-Haus.* A modest collection traces the history of Worms's Jews (open Tues.-Sun. 10am-noon and 2-5pm; DM3, students DM1.50, free first Sun. of the month).

▓ Mannheim

For nearly a thousand years, Mannheim contentedly served as a simple fishing village. In 1770, however, history took a step forward when Elector Karl Phillipp made the city the capital of the Rheinland-Pfalz. Mannheim's heady days as capital came to an end a mere 57 years later when the court packed up and marched off to Munich, as

Elector Karl Theodor bid farewell—*Auf Wiedersehen*, baby. The desertion appears to have had little effect on the city; today's Mannheim is one of the most urbanized locales in Southeast Germany. Besides the many grand buildings which the nobility left behind, Mannheim flaunts a substantial cultural scene and a virtual shoppers' paradise. The easily navigated streets and almost nonexistent tourist population make Mannheim a worthy destination for city-loving independent travelers.

Orientation Mannheim perches on a peninsula partitioned by the **Kaiser-ringstraße** (directly in front of the *Hauptbahnhof*); the **Innenstadt** lies to the west and the rest of the city lies to the east. The *Innenstadt* is divided into a grid of 144 blocks along a central axis, the **Kurpfalzerstraße,** which runs from the center of the *Residenzschloß* northward to the *Kurpfalzerbrücke* (bridge) on the Neckar River. Each block is designated by a letter and a number. Streets to the west of Kurpfalzer-str. are designated by the letters **A** through **K** (running from south to north) while streets to the east are similarly lettered **L** through **U.** The blocks on the central axis are numbered 1; the number of the block increases as you move away from Kurpfalz-erstr. The giant grid is bounded by Bismarckstr. to the south, Parkring to the west, Luisenring to the north, and Friedrichsring and Kaiserring to the east. East of Kaiser-ringstr., streets assume regular names; perhaps the Pfalz electors discovered a more poetic side, or saw that they were running out of letters. Mannheim's train station is large and busy with ICE and international trains making frequent stops. It's only a 15-minute ride from Heidelberg by train, 1 hour from Frankfurt, and 1½ hours from Stuttgart. The **A** and **M** streets will keep you well oriented.

Practical Information The **tourist office,** Willy-Brandt-Platz 3 (tel. 10 10 11), a block from the *Hauptbahnhof*, distributes maps (necessary despite the well-planned streets), information on accommodations, and tickets to upcoming events; it also offers a **Mitfahrzentrale** ride-share service (open Mon.-Fri. 9am-5pm, Sat. 9am-noon; DM5 fee for reservations) and **bike rentals** (DM8 per day). A **laundromat** waits for you on block G7 on the Luisenring side. (Wash DM6, soap included. Dry DM1 per 15min. Open daily 6am-11pm, last entry 10pm.) The **post office** is one block east of the main station, easily within sight. *Postlagernde Briefe* is at counters 10 and 11 (open Mon.-Fri. 8am-6pm, Sat. 8am-noon). A **pharmacy,** Bahnhof Apotheke, dispenses therapeutic goods at block L15, across from the station and to the left (open Mon.-Fri. 7am-8pm, Sat. 7:30am-4pm). The **telephone code** is 0621.

Accommodations Mannheim's **Jugendherberge (HI),** Rheinpromenade 21 (tel. 82 27 18), provides somewhat cramped rooms. But its delectable breakfast (they even have cheesecake!) and super-convenient location, 10 minutes from the train station, more than make up for the aging facilities. Walk through the underground passage (towards Gleis 10) and exit at the back of the train station, then take a right, follow Joseph-Kellner-Str., cross the tracks, continue down the street with the park on your right for about a block, and enter at the first official entrance, by the mailbox. (Reception open 8:30-9:30am, 1-2, 4-6, and 7:30-10pm. Curfew 11:30pm. Members only. DM20, over 26 DM25. Breakfast included. Sheets DM5.50.) The next best value is the spotless and conveniently located **Pension Arabella,** block M2, #12 (tel. 230 50), two blocks north of the *Schloß* (singles DM35-40; doubles DM70-80; triples DM100; breakfast DM7.50). **Goldene Gans,** Tattersallstr. 19 (tel. 10 52 77; fax 422 02 60), two blocks northwest of the train station, has its entrance around the corner. Friendly and efficient service in pleasant rooms with phones and sinks is marred only by traffic noise, audible in street-side suites. (Reception open Mon.-Sat. 5am-midnight, Sun. 7am-8pm. Singles from DM55; doubles from DM100. Breakfast included.)

Food and Nightlife The cheapest meals in town are at the government-subsidized **Studentenwerk Mannheim Mensa** (open Mon.-Fri. 11:30am-2pm and 5-7pm) and the adjacent, slightly more expensive **cafeteria** (open Mon.-Thurs. 8:30am-4pm, Fri. 8:30am-3:45pm). The *Mensa* is located behind the *Residenzschloß* in the southwest corner. An old piano, theater posters, and antique bicycles and clocks fill **Harlekin,** Kaiserring 40 (tel. 10 33 54), on the corner of Moltkestr. It boasts an extensive menu with most meals under DM13 (open Mon.-Fri. 9am-1am, Sun. 5pm-1am; closed Sat.). **Rick's Café,** N5, #2 (tel. 10 69 58), serves simple meals on an ivy-enclosed terrace, but its specialty is nightlife, with a cover-free **disco;** Wednesday is soul/rap/funk night. What kind of man is this Rick? Just like any other man, only more so. (Cafe open Mon.-Thurs. 9am-1am, Fri.-Sat. 9am-2am, Sun. 10am-1am. Disco open Wed.-Thurs. 11pm-3am, Fri.-Sat. 11pm-5am.) For a respite from Rick, eat at **Max und Moritz,** S4, #17-22 (tel. 273 48). Salads, soups, and generous entrees are served with a smile for DM10-18. Frequent foreign theme weeks and cocktail parties every Friday and Saturday (cocktails DM7.50). The decor is a jolly yellow, but Mr. Jolly is nowhere to be found (open daily 9am-midnight; kitchen open 10:30am-11pm). Satisfy both your email and caffeine (or, well, alcohol) cravings at the **Neworld Internetcafé,** S3, #11 (tel. 12 95 00), a 32-computer techno-playing cyber-everything two-floored place that claims to be Europe's largest internet cafe (15-minute connection DM3; open Mon.-Wed. 5pm-1am, Thurs.-Sat. 5pm-3am, Sun. 5pm-midnight). Butchers, bakers, and grocers gather at the **market** in the square at the intersection of Kurpfalzstr. and Kirchstr. at the center of the city grid (open Tues., Thurs., and Sat. 7am-2:30pm).

Sights Mannheim's real attraction is its bustling commercial area, which centers around the **Paradeplatz** at block O1 and extends for several bristling blocks in all directions, though most densely north and east. Restaurants, department stores, cafes, movie theaters, and lots and lots of people combine with the decidedly American city layout to form an urban space of an intensity rarely found in antiquated European cities. If the milieu of metropolitan Mannheim leaves you feeling guilty for not taking in enough Old Europe, the city has several substantial offerings, beginning with its emblematic masterpiece, the **Wasserturm** (water tower) and surrounding gardens of **Friedrichsplatz.** Restored to its original glory in 1956, the elegant sandstone tower topped by a statue of Amphitrite almost lives up to its billing as "the most beautiful water tower in the world." On the south side of the manicured foliage and crystalline fountains of Friedrichspl. crouches the **Kunsthalle,** a museum surveying art from the mid-19th century to modern times (open Tues.-Wed. and Fri.-Sun. 10am-5pm, Thurs. noon-5pm; DM4, students DM2). To reach Friedrichspl., walk straight out of the station for ten minutes north on Kaiserring.

Along with a bizarre street-naming scheme, the Palatinate left the giant **Residenzschloß.** The largest palace of the Baroque period, it now houses the **Universität Mannheim.** In the oddly gaudy **Schloßkirche** (tel. 292 28 90), the sleek coffer of the crypt holds Karl Phillip's third wife, Violante von Thurn und Taxis. Even odder, a Masonic symbol (and a post horn) decorates the altar, suggesting a bizarre link between efficient mail and eventual Masonic world domination—Mucho, Mucho Maas cometh... (Tours Tues.-Sun. 10am-1pm and 2-5pm; Nov.-March Sat.-Sun. 10am-1pm and 2-5pm. DM4, students DM2.50). The **Reiß Museum** consists of three buildings located around C5, northwest of the *Schloß*, which contain exhibits on archaeology, ethnology, and natural science (open Tues.-Wed. and Fri.-Sun. 10am-5pm, Thurs. noon-5pm; DM4, students DM2, free on Thurs. afternoons; special exhibitions have separate entrance fee). Between the museum and the *Schloß* at block A4 stands the **Jesuit Church,** built as a symbol of the Pfalz court's reconversion to Catholicism. The poet Friedrich Hölderlin called it "the most splendid building I have encountered during my travels." This is perhaps poetically licentious, but the church is fantastic (open daily 8am-noon and 2-6:30pm).

On the other side of the *Innenstadt,* several blocks northeast of the *Wasserturm,* sprouts the 100-acre **Luisenpark** (tel. 41 00 50; fax 410 05 55). The greenhouses, flower gardens, aviary, zoo, water sports, mini-golf, and frequent afternoon concerts offer something for everyone (open daily 9am-dusk; May-Aug. closes at 9pm; DM5, students DM4). South of Luisenpark, due east of Friedrichspl. on the *Augustanlage,* lies the terrific **Landesmuseum der Technik und Arbeit** (State Museum of Technology and Labor), Museumstr. 1 (tel. 429 89; fax 429 87 54). Bus: "Friedenspl.," and when Augustanlage branches, take the left branch. In its six stories, connected by tunnels and ramps, the museum covers "250 years of technical and social change and industrialization in Southwest Germany" through hands-on exhibits of large, creaky, rusty things. Get a tetanus shot. A working waterwheel, printing presses, and BMWs galore (open Tues. and Thurs.-Fri. 9:15am-5pm, Wed. 9:15am-8pm, Sat.-Sun. 10am-5pm; DM4, students DM2, families DM6). The Landesmuseum's largest exhibit floats in the Neckar—the paddle steamer **Mainz** which sank in 1956. It has since been retrieved from the Rhine's murky depths and now offers a history of navigation.

▓ Speyer

Speyer's political star rose and fell early. During the reign of the mighty Salian emperors in the 11th century, the town served as a principal meeting place for the Imperial Diets. As the emperors' power waned, Speyer slipped in significance until ultimately the entire city was burned to the ground during the Palatinate War of Succession. By the time the two World Wars rolled around, Speyer didn't merit destruction; its gracefully ramshackle **Altstadt** and several glorious churches, until recently well off the beaten path of mass tourism, were spared from the bombings.

Since its construction in the 12th century, the **Kaiserdom** (Imperial Cathedral) has been the symbol of Speyer. The immense Romanesque cathedral is noted for its main portals flanked by seven statues on each side, recounting the tale of Christ's crucifixion. The crypt under the east end coddles the remains of eight Holy Roman Emperors and their wives (open daily 9am-7pm; Nov.-March daily 9am-5pm; services at 7, 9, 10:30am, and 6pm on Sun. and holidays). Just south of the *Dom,* the newly renovated **Historisches Museum der Pfalz,** Dompl. D (tel. 132 50), offers a comprehensive presentation on Palatinate history and has a penchant for pop art; it has hosted comprehensive collections of works by both Andy Warhol and Keith Haring in the past few years. The collection includes beautiful and well-preserved artifacts from the first to the 16th century, one of the ostensible highlights being the **oldest bottle of wine in the world**—a slimy leftover from some wild Roman blowout in the 3rd century. Speyer just couldn't down it all (as opposed to Speier). (Open Tues.-Sun. 10am-6pm, Wed. 10am-8pm. DM8, students and children DM5, more for visiting exhibitions.) A left down Große Pfaffengasse and a right down the Judengasse alley lead to the **Judenbad,** a Jewish ritual bathhouse *(mikwe)* dating from the 12th century (open April-Oct. Mon.-Fri. 10am-noon and 2-5pm; Sat.-Sun. 10am-5pm; DM1.50).

Speyer's main thoroughfare of Maximilianstr. spreads eastward from the *Dom,* culminating in the medieval **Altpörtel,** an exquisitely preserved four-story village gate. From the *Altpörtel,* a southward jaunt on Gilgenstr. leads to the **Church of St. Joseph** and its sister across the street, the **Gedächtniskirche.** The latter sends even jaded hearts soaring (open Mon.-Sat. 10am-noon and 2-6pm, Sun. 2-6pm). For those seeking something slightly more up-to-the-minute, the **Technik-Museum-Speyer,** Geibstr. 2 (tel. 670 80; fax 67 08 20), fills a gigantic warehouse with 30,000 cubic meters of trains, planes, and automobiles, as well as an IMAX theater (program hotline tel. 67 08 50) and the "Adventure-simulator." City shuttle: "Technik Museum." (Museum open daily 9am-6pm; admission DM12, children DM8; IMAX DM12, children DM10; combination ticket DM22, children DM15.)

Speyer is easily reached by rail from Mannheim (15-30min.) and Heidelberg (1-1½hr.). Also, bus #7007 from Heidelberg (1½hr.) deposits passengers at the steps of the cathedral. The helpful **tourist office,** Maximilianstr. 11 (tel. 143 92), two blocks ahead of the cathedral's main entrance, distributes maps and lists of *Pensionen.* From the train station, city shuttle: "Maximilianstr." (open Mon.-Fri. 9am-5pm, Sat. 10am-4pm). **Tours** of the city depart from in front of the tourist office (April-Oct. Sat.-Sun. 11am; DM5). The **shuttle bus** runs the length of the city every 10min. (1-day ticket DM1). The **post office** is on Postpl., next to the Altpörtal. It **exchanges money** and cashes traveler's checks (open Mon.-Fri. 7:30am-6pm, Sat. 7:30-noon). The **postal code** is 67346 The **telephone code** is 06232.

In January 1997, Speyer was blessed with the construction of an incredible new **Jugendherberge,** Geibstr. 5 (tel. 753 80), which fills its super-clean and spacious rooms with schoolchildren and travelers. Fun is guaranteed by the nearby *Schwimm-bad* and the hostel's very own indoor ball pit. (Reception open 5-7 and 9:30-10pm. Lockout 9-11am. Curfew 10pm. Members only. DM26.30.) Affordable housing is not common in Speyer. **Pension Grüne Au,** Grüner Winkel 28 (tel. 721 96, fax 721 96), has comfortable rooms with gleaming sinks. From Maximilianstr., go left in Salzgasse, continue to St. Georggasse, left through Fisch Markt, and right onto Grüner Winkel (singles DM50; doubles DM70). The side streets of Korngasse and Große Himmels-gasse, just north of Maximilianstr., shelter excellent small restaurants. The **Gaststätte "Zum Goldenen Hirsch,"** Maximilianstr. 90a (tel. 726 94), offers German and regional specialities (DM9.50-16.50; open Thurs.-Tues. 11am-midnight).

On the second weekend in July (Friday to Tuesday) Speyer celebrates its **Bret-zelfest** (pretzel festival). The festivities involve all sorts of music, parades, and special events. During the second weekend of August, the **Kaisertafel Speyer** takes place—tables are set up along the streets and visitors are herded along and stuffed full of regional specialties. (To *Let's Go*'s knowledge, they are not then roasted and eaten.) Start your engines for the **car race** which takes over the Airbus airport in mid-April.

■ Trier

Older than any other German town and vastly older than Germany itself, Trier has weathered two millennia in the western end of the Mosel Valley, stubbornly refusing to act its age. Founded by the Romans during the reign of Augustus, Trier reached the height of its prominence in the early 4th century as the capital of the western Roman Empire. Having lived through many epochs, Trier is a patchwork quilt of uncommon design and grace. The vitality of its visitors and students blends harmoniously with the dignity and beauty of its Roman ruins and well-preserved *Altstadt.* The birthplace and boyhood home of Karl Marx, Trier is one of the few places in united Germany stubbornly refusing to give up its "Karl-Marx-Straße."

ORIENTATION AND PRACTICAL INFORMATION

Trier lies less than 50km from the Luxembourg border on the Mosel River. Most of the sights sit in the vicinity of the compact *Altstadt.* The gate to the *Altstadt,* **Porta Nigra,** is a 10-minute walk from the train station down Theodor-Heuss-Allee or Chris-tophstr. Although most sights are within walking distance, the bus system can carry you anywhere for DM2.40. A **Trier Card,** available at the tourist office, offers admission to 7 museums and reduced rates on theater performances and tours (among other things) over a 3-day period (single DM17, family (2 adults, 3 children) DM32). A **Trier Card Plus** also includes free public transportation (single DM25, family DM44).

Tourist Office: Tourist-Information (tel. 97 80 80; fax 447 59) in the shadow of the *Porta Nigra,* offers daily **tours** in English at 1:30pm (DM9). Open Jan.-Feb. Mon.-Fri. 9am-5pm, Sat. 9am-1pm; March Mon.-Sat. 9am-6pm, Sun. 9am-3:30pm; April-Nov. 15 Mon.-Sat. 9am-6:30pm, Sun. 9am-3:30pm; Nov. 16-Dec. Mon.-Sat. 9am-6pm, Sun. 9am-1pm. Whew! During these constantly fluctuating hours, the staff hands out free maps and books rooms for free (5% deposit required).

Wine Information: Konstantinpl. 11 (tel. 736 90), near the Basilika. Staff and com-puters help you make decisions about **wine tasting** in the Mosel region (and in the amply stocked office). Woody? Has legs? Open Mon.-Fri. 10:15am-6:30pm, Sat. 10am-4pm, Sun. 1-5pm.

Trains: Frequent trains to Koblenz (1½hr.), rosy Luxembourg (approximately 1 per hr., 45min.; day excursion DM12.80), and Saarbrücken (1½hr.).

Ferries: Personen-Schiffahrt (tel. 15 15) sails to Bernkastel-Kues from the Kaiser-Wilhelm Brücke. May-Oct. daily at 9:15am. Round-trip DM44, under 13 DM22.

Taxi: Taxi-Funk (tel. 330 30). Whoever smelt the funk dealt the funk.

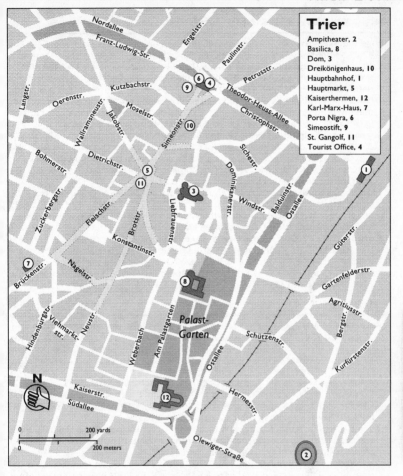

Trier
Ampitheater, 2
Basilica, 8
Dom, 3
Dreikönigenhaus, 10
Hauptbahnhof, 1
Hauptmarkt, 5
Kaiserthermen, 12
Karl-Marx-Haus, 7
Porta Nigra, 6
Simeostift, 9
St. Gangolf, 11
Tourist Office, 4

RHEINLAND-PFALZ

Bikes: Lasso yourself a two-wheeled filly at the station (tel. 200 25 18). DM10 per day with railpass or ticket. Bike rental open Mon.-Fri. 7am-7pm. Or forget the filly and strap on some **in-line skates** at **Skate Away** (tel. 30 90 82), on the riverside bike path at Schotterpl./Messpark. 1hr. DM8, 2hr. DM15, 3hr. DM21, each additional hour DM4. DM20 deposit and ID required. Open Tues.-Fri. 3pm-dusk, Sat.-Sun. 10am-dusk.

Mitfahrzentrale: Mitwohn- und Mitfahrzentrale, Kaiserstr. 13 (tel. 474 47; fax 492 32). The double whammy: rides and room rental hooked up in one office. Open Mon.-Tues. 10am-1pm, Wed.-Fri. 10am-1pm and 4:30-7pm, Sat. 10am-1pm.

Bookstore: Akademische Buchhandlung, Fleischstr. 62 (tel. 97 99 01). Open Mon.-Fri. 9am-7pm, Sat. 9am-4pm.

Gay and Lesbian Concerns: Lesbentelefon (tel. 491 33) for the ladies, **Schwule Männerinitiative** (tel. 425 14) for the gents.

Laundry: Wasch Center, Brückenstr. 19-21, down the street from Karl Marx's old house. Contemplate your relationship to the means of production as you wash (DM8) according to your abilities, dry (DM3 per 25min.) according to your needs. Although there will be a need for proletarian leaders, there's no need to bring your own soap—it's included! Open Mon.-Sat. 8am-10pm.

Post Office: Most convenient is the branch office on Bahnhofpl., 45292 Trier, to the right of the train station. Open Mon.-Fri. 8am-6pm, Sat. 8am-noon. Limited services open Mon.-Fri. 7-8am and 6-8pm, Sat. 7am-2pm, Sun. 11am-noon.

ACCOMMODATIONS AND CAMPING

Jugendgästehaus (HI), An der Jugendherberge 4 (tel. 14 66 20; fax 14 66 230). Bus #2 or 8 (direction: "Trierweilerweg" or "Pfalzel/Quint"): "Moselbrücke," and walk 10min. downstream on the path along the river embankment. Or take the 30min. walk from the station. Follow Theodor-Heuss-Allee as it becomes Nordallee, forks right onto Lindenstr., and ends at the bank of Mosel. Extensive array of ping-pong tables and vending machines, and loud early morning punk music to get your butt outta bed. Reception open sporadically 7pm-midnight. Loose midnight curfew. Quads with toilet and shower DM26.50. Breakfast and sheets included.

Jugendhotel Kolpinhaus/Hotel Kolpinhaus, Dietrichstr. 42 (tel. 97 52 50; fax 975 25 40), is conveniently located one block off the Hauptmarkt. Lovely location and inexpensive prices. Reception open 8am-11pm. Beds in the dorm housing DM27; singles DM37; doubles DM74; four-bed dorms DM25 per person. Key available for late returns. Breakfast included. Call as far ahead as possible.

Hotel Haus Runne, Engelstr. 35 (tel. 289 22). Follow Theodor-Heuss-Allee from the train station and turn right on Engelstr. after the *Porta Nigra.* Did Mike Brady design the interior? Large rooms with shower, toilet, and TV. Singles DM45; doubles DM90; quads DM160. Breakfast included.

Camping: Trier City Campingplatz, Luxemburgerstr. 81 (tel. 869 21). From Hauptmarkt, follow Fleischstr. to Bruckenstr. to Karl-Marx-Str. to the Römerbrücke. Cross the bridge, head left on Luxemburgerstr., and then left at camping sign. Reception open daily 8-11am and 6-10pm in Gortätle Kranich, up from the river. DM7, ages 4-12 DM3, under 4 free, dogs DM2.

FOOD

Astarix, Karl-Marx-Str. 11 (tel. 722 39), is squeezed in a passageway next to Miss Marple's. If you get to the dreadfully tasteful sex shops, you've gone too far. Many students happily munch on cheap food here. Tortellini DM6.90. Gorgonzolatomato garlic toast DM5.90. Open Mon.-Thurs. 11am-1am, Fri.-Sat. 11am-2am, Sun. 6pm-1am. Kitchen closes daily at 11:30pm.

Warsberger Hof, in the Kolpinhaus Hotel, Dietrichstr. 42 (tel. 97 52 50). Walk from *Porta Nigra* to the Hauptmarkt and turn right. Lunch specials and vegetarian fare for DM12.50. Evening menus available in English. Open daily 11am-midnight; kitchen closes at 11:30pm. Visa, MC, EuroCard, Diners.

Zum Domstein, Am Hauptmarkt 5 (tel. 744 90), across from the cathedral's main entrance. An excellent wine tasting opportunity (DM8-10.50). When you see two *Doms,* you've had enough. Open daily 9am-11pm.

Bierakademie, Bahnhofstr. 28 (tel. 729 22), half a block down from the train station. Around the world in 100 beers. For those who foolishly insist that man cannot live on beer alone, simple combinations of meat, cheese, and bread are available for under DM10. An array of specialty coffees served in the mornings. Open Mon.-Fri. 10am-1am, Sat. 11am-1am.

SIGHTS AND ENTERTAINMENT

Trier is fraught with reminders of its Roman past, the most impressive of which is the **Porta Nigra** (Black Gate). Built in the 2nd century, the massive stone gate gained its name from the centuries of grime that metamorphosed its originally light yellow sandstone face into uneven sallow shades of gray. In the past, the gate served as the strongest line of defense against attacks on the city. (Open Jan.-Palm Sunday and Oct.-Nov. daily 9am-5pm; Palm Sunday-Sept. 9am-6pm; Dec. 10am-4pm. Admission DM4, students DM2, children DM1.50. **One-day ticket** for admission to all Roman monuments DM9, DM4.50, and DM4 each season, respectively.) The **Simeonstift,** an 11th-century monastery, enveloped by the courtyard, now holds the **Städtisches Museum** (tel. 718 24 40; open April-Oct. daily 9am-5pm; Nov.-March Mon.-Fri. 9am-5pm, Sat.-Sun. 9am-3pm; admission DM6, students DM5).

Fruit stalls, florists, and ice-cream vendors crowd the **Hauptmarkt** in central Trier. A variety of architecturally diverse buildings adorn the remarkably large pedestrian shopping district. The colorful Gothic **Dreikönigshaus** (House of the Three Magi), once a medieval merchant's home, bears eloquent testimony to the class antagonisms in old Europe. The front door is located on the second story above street level, accessible only by a ladder, and was pulled inside when angry *Lumpenproletariat* besieged the lavishly adorned home. Growing up in such a neighborhood, it's no surprise that young Karl Marx was inspired to write his theory of class conflict. The **Karl-Marx-Haus**, where young Karl first walked, talked, and dreamed of labor alienation, still stands at Brückenstr. 10 (tel. 430 11), and is a must-see for indefatigable Marxists. Busts and copies of the *Manifesto* abound. (Open April-Oct. Mon. 1-6pm, Tues.-Sun. 10am-6pm; Nov.-March Mon. 3-6pm, Tues.-Sun. 10am-1pm and 3-6pm. Admission DM3, students DM2.) For the next leg of *Let's Go*'s "Fathers of Communism" Tour, see **Wuppertal** (birthplace of Friedrich Engels), p. 347. On Nagelstr., around the corner from the Karl-Marx-Haus, placate your inner child at the **Spielzeug Museum** (toy museum) with two centuries of dolls, teddy bears, and automata. (Open April-Oct. daily 11am-5pm; Nov.-March Tues.-Sun. noon-4pm. Admission DM7.50, ages 10-18 DM4, under 10 DM3.)

Close to the Marktplatz through the passage between two houses lurks **Markt und Bürgerkirche St. Gangolf.** Begun in 964, it was rebuilt and restyled over the centuries. A left turn onto Sternstr. from the produce stands of the Hauptmarkt brings you to the 11th-century **Dom,** whose interior design is delightfully impressive. Its many nooks and crannies contain the tombs of archbishops. Reputedly the **Tunica Christi** (Holy Robe of Christ) is enshrined at the eastern end of the cathedral. Tradition tells that this relic was brought from Jerusalem to Trier around 300 by St. Helena, mother of Emperor Constantine. It was last shown to the public in 1996 (open daily 6:30am-6pm; Nov.-March 6:30am-5:30pm; daily tours at 2pm; free). Also in the *Dom,* the **Schatzkammer** touts a treasury of religious artifacts (open April-Oct. Mon.-Sat. 10am-5pm, Sun. 2-5pm; Nov.-March Mon.-Sat. 10am-noon and 2-4pm; admission DM2, students and children DM1). Adjacent to the *Dom* is the magnificent Gothic **Liebfrauen-kirche.** Its stained glass windows turn the interior of the cathedral a dark red and splash the floor with color. Also next to the *Dom* is the **Bischöfliches Dom-und Diözesanmuseum,** Windstr. 6-8 (tel. 710 52 55), a surprisingly modern building which showcases holy art of all types, from ancient sculpture to contemporary abstract painting. The museum also boasts one of the largest archaeological collections of any diocesan museum (open Mon.-Sat. 9am-1pm and 2-5pm, Sun. 1-5pm; DM2, students DM1).

Liebfrauenstr. leads to the **Konstantin Basilika,** originally the location of Emperor Constantine's throne room. Lavishly decorated in its 4th-century prime, this one-room monstrosity is now about as exciting to look at as an airplane hangar (open Mon.-Sat. 9am-6pm, Sun. 11am-6pm; free). Next door lies the bubble-gum pink **Kurfürstliches Palais,** a former residence of the archbishop-electors of Trier that today houses municipal government offices. It overlooks the well-kept **Palastgarten** where the statues have abnormally elongated toes. Along the eastern edge of the garden lies the **Landesmuseum,** Ostallee 44, an impressive collection of Roman stonework, sculpture, and mosaics, as well as a few other random relics, including a 2700 year-old Egyptian casket complete with mummy (open Tues.-Fri. 9:30am-5pm, Sat.-Sun. 10:30am-5pm; admission DM5, children DM3). At the southeast end of the park are the **Kaiserthermen,** the ruins of the Roman baths where Constantine once scrubbed, with long dark underground passages that are easy to get lost in (same hours and admission as *Porta Nigra*). It's a 5-minute walk uphill from here along Olewigerstr. to the remains of the 2nd-century **Amphitheater.** Had the Rolling Stones toured in 169, this 20,000-seat venue (one of the largest in the Roman Empire) certainly would have been on the itinerary. Instead, it hosted a spectacle far more appalling than even aged rock stars belting out the oldies: the agents booked the acts that demonstrated the most spectacular and gruesome ways of inflicting pain (and death) on humans and animals. (Open April.-Sept. daily 9am-5:30pm; Oct.-March 9am-4:30pm. Admission DM4, students DM2, children DM1.50.) If you're simply not impressed, ride the **Kabinen Schwebelbahn** (gondola; tel. 14 72 30) across the Mosel to the Stadtwald and

RHEINLAND-PFALZ

admire the forest primeval, the murmuring pines, and the hemlocks. (Open Mon.-Fri. 9am-6pm, Sat.-Sun. 9am-7pm. Round-trip DM8, kids DM4; one way DM4.50, DM3.)

Several annual festivals spice up Trier's atmosphere. Every fourth weekend of June **Altstadtfest** brings live music, wine, and beer to the streets. The second weekend in July welcomes the **Moselfest,** with Saturday night fireworks over the water. The first August weekend witnesses the arrival of the **Weinfest,** kicked by Friday fireworks.

NIGHTLIFE

Pubs, clubs, and *Kneipen* of all flavors fan out from the Hauptmarkt, with a dense collection at the northwesternly Pferdemarkt. Trier is exceptionally well-postered for a city of its size; keep watch for the many announcements of special concerts and themed nights at clubs.

Blaues Blut, Pferdemarkt (tel. 412 53). Mellow blue lighting and tiles on the tables make you feel like you're drinking on the floor of a swimming pool. Instead of getting an eyeful of chlorine, you can gawk at the sleek crowd and enjoy the house and techno music. Open Mon.-Thurs. 9am-1am, Fri.-Sat. 9am-2am, Sun. 10am-1am.

Exil, Zurmainer Str. 114 (tel. 251 91). Huge, graffiti-adorned complex with a *Biergarten.* A bewildering array of dance parties, as well as Trier's best concert venue. Hours and cover vary. Check posters or call for info.

Palais Walderdorff, across from the *Dom* (tel. 410 62). By day, a mellow cafe, by night a disco with creative and beautifully advertised themes. Open Mon.-Fri. 10am-6:30pm, Sat. 11am-3pm. Party times vary, but posters are everywhere.

Lucky's Luke Filmkneipe, Luzemburgerstr. 6, at the Römerbrücke. Sip fine drinks while watching foreign films, or just get real drunk and scream for more nudity. Open daily 8pm-4am. Movies at 8:15 and 10:30pm.

MOSELTAL (MOSEL VALLEY)

Trying to avoid its inevitable surrender to the Rhine at Koblenz, the Mosel River slowly meanders past the sun-drenched hills, pretty towns, and ancient castles of the softly cut Moseltal. The headwaters of the Mosel flow from the Vosges Mountains of France, following a northeasterly course that winds over 200km of German territory from Trier to Koblenz. The slopes aren't quite as steep as the Rhine's narrow gorge, but the countless, less-touristed vineyards of the gentle hillsides have been pressing quality vintages since the Romans first cultivated the vines 2000 years ago. The only local complaints heard about the region is that the summers are too dry (the least of worries for a visitor) and the winters too wet. Periodically, the mellow Mosel goes berserk, flooding and making the valley Venetian for a few days. In December 1993, many of the towns were buried under 2m of water.

The best way to view the valley's scenery is by boat, bus, or bicycle; the train line between Koblenz and Trier strays frequently from the course of the river, cutting through the unremarkable countryside. Although passenger **boats** no longer make the complete Koblenz-Trier run, several companies run daily trips along shorter stretches through the summer; local tourist offices can provide details. Some train stations will rent you a rugged three-speed **bike** for DM11 per day (bring or buy a ticket or railpass, otherwise rental prices double).

COCHEM

Like so many precious German wine-making villages, the hamlet of Cochem has become a repository of German nostalgia, its quintessential quaintness eaten up voraciously by busloads of elderly German city-dwellers. Despite an overwhelming tourist presence, Cochem's impressive vineyard-covered hills and immaculate **Reichsburg castle** (tel. 255) simply can't be cheapened into run-of-the-mill tourist fodder. Perched high atop a hill adjacent to the village, the castle is visible from afar, with its majestic and elaborately painted turrets lending the town a pleasantly pervasive fairytale quality enhanced by oodles of clapboard architecture that lines the curvy streets.

Originally built in the 11th century, the castle was destroyed in 1689 (like much of the Palatinate) by French troops under Louis XIV. In 1868, a wealthy Berlin merchant rebuilt it in neo-Gothic style. The view from the castle grounds alone warrants the 15-minute climb along Schloßstr. from the Marktplatz. Unfortunately, a peek into the castle's opulent interior can only be taken today as part of a guided tour. (Open March 15-Oct. daily 9am-5pm. Frequent 40min. tours; written English translations available. Admission DM6, students DM5, children DM3.) The tiny lane to the **Peterskapelle** (left as you walk down from the castle), built in 1422, is enclosed by high walls and the ubiquitous vine-covered trellises. The other popular hillside attraction in town is the **Sesselbahn** (chairlift; tel. 226) on Edenstr., which runs to the **Pinnerkreuz**, a lone cross standing on a high peak (lift runs June-Oct. daily 9:30am-7pm; Nov.-May 10am-6pm; one-way DM6.90, round-trip DM8.90; DM3.20 and DM4.50 for tykes, respectively). For even more theme-park style thrills 'n' spills, head across the river and follow the signs for the *Freizeitzentrum* to reach the gigantic **Moselbad** (tel. 979 90), a sprawling complex of pools, saunas, jacuzzis, and waterslides located five minutes north of the Nordbrücke (the bridge near the train station). They've even got a wavepool that let's 'em loose for five minutes every hour. Hang ten, Big Kahuna. (Open Mon. 2-10pm, Tues. and Thurs. 9am-10pm, Wed. and Fri. 10am-10pm, Sat.-Sun. 10am-7pm. All-inclusive day ticket DM16, ages 12-17 DM9, ages 6-11 DM6, younger kids free. Outdoor heated pool only DM5, DM3, DM3, free respectively.) Cochem overlooks a bend in the river one-third of the way between Koblenz and Trier. Unlike much of the Mosel Valley, Cochem is easily accessible by train from these two major cities. Though Cochem is equidistant to the two cities, the route to Koblenz hugs the Mosel, making for some spectacular views; the trip to Trier traverses serene but non-fantastic countryside. About two trains per hour in each direction roll into the station; pick up the handy *Moselbahn* schedule at Koblenz, Cochem, or Trier.

The **tourist office,** on Endertpl. 1 (tel. 39 71 or 39 72; fax 84 10) next to the bridge, makes same-day room reservations for free and doles out brochures. From the train station, go to the river and turn right (open May-Nov.15 Mon.-Fri. 10am-1pm and 2-5pm, Sat. 10am-3pm). Along the way, you'll pass **Fahrrad-Shop Kreutz** (tel. 911 31), tucked in behind the Shell gas station along the river, which leases an array of two-wheeled chrome beauties (DM14 per day, DM70 per week; open Mon.-Fri. 9am-6pm, Sat. 9am-1pm, Sun. 10-11am and 5-6pm). The **post office** is at the corner of Ravenestr. and Josefstr., one block from Endenpl. They cash travelers checks and exchange money (open Mon.-Fri. 8am-noon and 2-5pm, Sat. 8am-noon). The **telephone code** is 02671.

Cochem's friendly but unadorned **Jugendherberge (HI),** Klottenerstr. 9 (tel. 86 33; fax 85 68), is 10 to 15 minutes from the station on the opposite shore. Cross the Nordbrücke (to the left as you exit the station); the youth hostel is next to the bridge on the right. Beware of the wicked echoes that make the schoolchildren seem much louder than usual. (Reception open noon-1pm and 5-10pm, but someone's always around. Curfew 10pm. DM21, with dinner DM29.20. Breakfast included. Sheets DM5.) There are also plenty of rooms available in town; look for the *"Zimmer Frei"* signs, or use the tourist office's Lite-Brite-esque hotel finder. If you've got your own portable palace (i.e., a tent), walk down the path below the hostel to the **Camping-platz am Freizeitzentrum,** on Stadionstr. (tel. 44 09). (Reception open 8am-9pm. DM6.50 per person, DM6-12 per tent. Easter-Oct. 4min. warm shower DM1.50. Washing machine and dryer DM2.) Indulge in food at the cheesy, good-hearted **Weinhexenkeller** (wine witches' cellar), on Hafenstr., across the Moselbrücke. Local legend says that guests who imbibe too much wine in the cellar fall under a witch's spell. Modern science says they only become drunk. Either way, you'll have a perfect excuse to go nuts when the live music kicks in at 7pm (open daily noon-1am).

The **Mosel-Wein-Woche** begins a week and a half after Pentecostal Monday and features some of the Mosel's finest vintages (DM1-2 per 100ml taste). During the last weekend in August, the **Heimat-und-Weinfest** takes place, culminating in a dramatic Saturday night fireworks display. During the wine harvest in September and October visitors can often find work (ranging from days to weeks) if they can do the back-breaking labor of wine harvesting. Ask the tourist office which vineyards are hiring.

BEILSTEIN

Beilstein reposes 10km upstream from Cochem. A tiny hamlet with half-timbered houses, crooked cobblestone streets, and circa 170 residents, Beilstein takes pride in being the smallest official town in Germany (it received town rights in 1319). Spared in World War II, Beilstein's untarnished beauty has made it the idyllic backdrop of several movies and political summits. Adenauer and DeGaspari met here during the negotiations that created the European Economic Community (now the European Union). Beilstein's natural charm draws a tourist crowd that exponentially increases its population, and there has been the expected exponential rise in the number of hotels and restaurants. Fortunately, the delicious Mosel wine flows freely, mellowing the crowds and dampening the touristy vibes.

Burg Metternich is the resident castle; the French sacked it in 1689, but the view is still spectacular (open April-Oct. daily 9am-5pm; DM2, students DM1.50, children DM0.50). Also worth a look is the Baroque **Karmelitenkirche,** with its intricately carved wooden altar and the famous **Schwarze Madonna von Beilstein** (black Madonna), a 16th-century Montserrat sculpture left behind by Spanish troops reintro-ducing Catholicism to the region. The town can be reached by public buses that depart approximately once an hour from both Endertpl. and the station in Cochem (DM3.50 each way) or by a private bus line that makes five trips per day. The boats of **Personnenschiffahrt Kolb** (tel. 15 15) also float there, though the one- hour trip often takes longer than expected due to traffic jams at the locks on the way (4 per day May-Oct., 1hr.; one way DM12, round-trip DM19). Cafe Klapperburg, uphill a block on the left from the bus stop, is the home of Beilsteins's **tourist office** (basically a friendly manager with a couple of brochures). Lay down your sleepy head at the comfortable **Pension Erna Burg,** Moselstr. 2 (tel. 14 24), next to the highway along the river. (DM32 per person per night. Breakfast included.) The **telephone code** is 02673.

■ The Middle Mosel Valley

Less accessible than much of the rest of the Mosel valley, the towns of the *"Mittel-mosel"* retain something that the other villages in the region lack—a sense of seclu-sion. Although the ubiquitous German megabuses do make stops in the area, the *Dörfer* here have a much more local feel than their more touristy brethren; supermar-kets stand next to cafes as residential areas blend seamlessly into historical districts.

TRABEN-TRARBACH

The twin towns of Traben-Trarbach anchor the eastern part of the region. Despite occasional architectural gems and the eroded ruins of a hilltop castle, the towns are of modest attraction. The low tourist population allows independent travelers a break from the herds of Euro-trekkers. The towns are also well-connected to other regions by rail, bus, and ship, making them an ideal base for exploring the valley. The Traben-Trarbach **Jugendgästehaus** (tel. 92 78) is a table *Fußball*-filled facility with standard four-bed rooms, located on the Traben side of the river. Check out the mondo fireplace in the lobby. From the station, head uphill on Poststr. until Kirchstr. Turn right and keep walking through the tract housing while the road turns into Spanheimerstr. Turn left uphill on Laugasse, right on Am Laubloch, and then left uphill on Hirtenpfad. (15min. Reception open 8am-midnight. Curfew midnight. DM25.10, singles DM43.60. Sheets included. Laundry facilities in basement.) The standard range of pamphlets and brochures, as well as the towns' disproportionately mammoth 60-page prospectus are available at Traben-Trarbach's **tourist office,** Bahnstr. 22 (tel. 90 11; fax 29 18), about a block from the train station (open May-Oct. Mon.-Fri. 8am-5pm, Sat. 1-4pm). The **telephone code** is 06541.

Bikers (the ones in spandex, not black leather) flock to the area, and **Zweirad Wagner,** Alte Marktstr. 4 (tel. 16 49), gives them what they want: **bike rentals** for DM10 per day (open Mon.-Fri. 8am-12:30pm and 2-6pm, Sat. 8:30am-1pm, Sun. 9:30-10am). The tiny trains of the Moselbahn roll into Traben once an hour from Bullay, a stop on almost all Koblenz to Trier routes.

BERNKASTEL-KUES

Yet another finalist in *Let's Go*'s Beautiful Double-*Dörfer* of the Mosel River Valley Pageant is Bernkastel-Kues. Our esteemed panel of judges is not alone in recognizing the beauty here—the towns are another favorite stop of the huge German motorcruisers. The **Bernkastel Marktplatz,** located one block from the bridge, is a 400-year-old half-timbered *tour de force*. Around the corner, the narrow, steep-roofed edifice of the **Spitzhäuschen** leans to one side; it looks like it came straight out of a children's cartoon. A scenic but grueling 20-minute climb along a vine-laden path leads to the ruins of **Burg Landshut** above the town and valley. A summer home for the archbishops of Trier until it was gutted by fire in 1693, the ruins have since been rudely usurped by an outdoor cafe-restaurant. The gorgeous view remains the same (and DM0.50 augments it by allowing you to climb the tower). Back in town, walk north from the Marktplatz onto Graacherstr. to reach the **Graacher Tor,** the only preserved gate from the city wall of 1300. During the upheavals of 1848, revolutionaries from Trier met here. Today their meeting hall houses the **Heimat Museum** (tel. 72 60), which covers local history and culture (significantly more interesting for German speakers; open Easter-Oct. Thurs.-Sun. 3-5pm; DM2, students DM1).

Across the river lounges the poor relative of **Kues.** A few stately 19th-century mansions tower along the river and the **Cusanusstift** reposes next to the bridge. Also known as the **St.-Nikolaus-Hospital,** this home for the aged and destitute was founded in the 15th century by a local philanthropist and includes an elaborately decorated chapel. The number of boarders is kept at a constant 33 in honor of the life expectancy of itinerant messianic Nazarene carpenters. Next door, the **Moselweinmuseum,** at Cusanusstr. 1, pays tribute to the tools of the wine-making trade (open April 16-Oct. daily 10am-5pm; Nov.-April 14 2-5pm; DM2.50, students DM1.50).

By some freak of nature (or provincial engineering) the road connecting Traben-Trarbach and Bernkastel-Kues curls around the Mosel for some 24km, but a footpath makes a bee-line between the two towns in 7km. The path is too steep to trek with a heavy backpack, but it's otherwise an easy and gorgeous hike. Rail service no longer connects Bernkastel-Kues to the world; instead, a private **bus** runs to Trier (DM13.20) and Traben-Trarbach (every 2hr.; DM7.30). Passenger boats also make the trip (May-Oct. daily; round-trip from Trier DM45, from Traben-Trarbach DM21). The **tourist office,** Am Gestade 5 (tel. 40 23; fax 79 53), across the street from the main bus stop in Bernkastel, finds rooms for a DM3 fee. (Open May-Oct. Mon.-Fri. 8:30am-12:30pm and 1-5pm, Sat. 10am-4pm; closed Sat. Nov.-April.) The **telephone code** is 06531.

Bernkastel's **Jugendherberge,** Jugendherbergstr. 1 (tel. 23 95; fax 15 29), shares the advantages and disadvantages of its neighbor **Burg Landshut** (this is not to imply that the hostel is in ruins): a scenic location but a traumatic 30-minute uphill trek to get there. Just follow the signs. (Reception open 7:30-9am, noon-1pm, and 5-7pm. Curfew 10pm. DM20.50, over 26 DM24.50. Breakfast included. Sheets DM5.) Otherwise, snuggle in at **Campingplatz Kueser Werth,** Am Hafen 2 (tel. 82 00), on the Kues side of the river. From the bridge, turn left and follow the road along the river for 1.5km. (Reception open 8am-noon and 3-7pm. DM6 per person, DM5 per tent. Open April-Oct.) **Kapuzinerstübchen,** Römerstr. 35 (tel. 23 53), serves traditional German meals without traditional tourist trap prices. Soups DM2.50, entrees DM8-17 (open Tues.-Sat. 11:30am-2pm and 5:45-8:45pm). Thousands arrive into town for Bernkastel-Kues's **Weinfest** the first week of September (Sept. 2-5 in 1998).

■ Saarbrücken

Once again, Saarbrücken is in shambles. For centuries, the city's proximity to the French border has made it a center of one violent conflict after another, leaving virtually none of the *Altstadt* intact and clearing the way for rampant industrial development. Fortunately, the news in Saarbrücken today is of a much less malignant variety—legions of bulldozers and jackhammer-wielding construction workers are tearing the city's streets apart to build a slick new DM500-million rail transit system, scheduled for completion by 2000. Focus on the future exists everywhere in Saarbrücken. Without the ancient architecture that keeps many German cities obsessed with the past, Saarbrücken has had no choice but modernization. Postmodern architecture abounds, factories and power plants spread endlessly throughout the city's outskirts, and the core of the downtown area beats with a cosmopolitan pulse. If you're looking for history, Saarbrücken isn't the place, but with an intense urban atmosphere and a plethora of punks and other young progressives, Saarbrücken may be one of the last undiscovered centers of the modern European cultural scene.

Orientation and Practical Information The **tourist office,** Am Hauptbahnhof 4 (tel. 365 15; fax 905 33 00), lies to the left of the station. They find rooms for DM3 and provide free brochures and maps (open Mon.-Fri. 9am-6pm, Sat. 9am-3pm). The handy **Saarbrücken Card** (DM12.90) provides transportation, free entrance to several sights, and theater discounts. **Der Fahrradladen,** Nauuriserstr. 19 (tel. 370 98), rents bikes. **Mitfahrzentral,** Rosenstr. 32, near the Alte Sammlung, will hook you up with a chauffeur (open Mon-Fri. 10am-6pm, Sat. 10am-2pm, Sun. noon-3pm). Do your **laundry** at Eisenbahnstr. 8. (Wash DM6, soap included. Dry DM1 per 10min. Open Mon.-Sat. 7am-10pm.) The **post office,** 66111 Saarbrücken, is to the right of the station. (Open Mon.-Fri. 8am-6pm, Sat. 8am-1pm; limited services Mon.-Fri. 6am-7:30pm, Sat. 6am-3pm, Sun. 10am-2pm.) The **telephone code** is 0681.

Accommodations and Camping Though Saarbrücken is on few foreign tourists' itineraries, its hostels and hotels do brisk business; it's always good to call ahead. The **Jugendherberge,** Meerwiesertalweg 31 (tel. 330 40), is a 25-minute walk from the station; head downhill and left, at the intersection veer left onto Ursulinenstr., take a left at the huge **supermarket,** and cross the parking lot. The eastern exit flows to Meerwiesertalweg. Or bus #19: "Prinzenweiher" and backtrack to the hostel. The light flickers on magically as you walk down the hall. Wicked modern. Also, private toilets and showers! (Reception open 4–11pm. Curfew 11:30pm. Doubles DM33.50 per person; quads DM26.30 per person. Breakfast and sheets included.) **Gästehaus Weller,** Neugrabenweg 8 (tel. 37 19 03; fax 37 55 65), offers huge rooms with bath, phone, TV, and amazing color coordination. Go down Ursulinenstr, right on Mozartstr., carry on to Schumannstr., left on Fichtestr., and cross the bridge to Neugrabenweg. (Reception open Mon.-Sat. 8am-11pm, Sun. 6-11pm. Singles DM59-69; doubles DM79-98. Call ahead.) **Hotel Atlantic,** Ursulinenstr. 59 (tel. 310 18; fax 37 45 03), is a 5-minute walk along Ursulinenstr. One of those lovely "chocolate-on-the-big-white-fluffy-comforter" places. (Reception open 24hr. Singles DM86 and up; doubles DM108 and up. Breakfast included. AmEx, MC, Diners.) **Hotel Schlosskrug,**

Schmollerstr. 14 (tel. 354 48; fax 37 50 22), at the corner with Bruchwiesenstr., is 10-15 minutes from the station in a quiet location near the hippest part of town. Go left onto Ursulinenstr., right on Richard-Wagner-Str., and right on Schmollerstr. (Singles with shower DM55, with bath DM65; doubles with shower DM100, with bath DM120; triples with bath DM170.) **Campingplatz Saarbrücken,** Am Spicherer Berg (tel. 517 80), is far from the station. How far? Far. Bus #42: "Spicherer Weg," cross Untertürkheimstr., and head right uphill on Spicherer Weg. (Reception open daily 7am-1pm and 3-10pm. DM6 per person. DM8 per tent. Open April-Sept.)

Food The streets around **St. Johannis Markt** brim with bistros, beer gardens, and ethnic restaurants. Walk down Reichstr. and turn left on Bahnhofstr. **Schmokeloch,** on Kappenstr. (tel. 333 97), serves pizza and pasta for DM8.50-10.80 (open Mon.-Fri. noon-3:30pm and 6pm-1am, Sat. noon-1am, Sun. 6pm-1am). Come nightfall, students fill *Kneipen* in the **Chinesenviertel** between Rotenbergstr., Richard-Wagnerstr., Dudweilerstr., and Großherzog Friedrichstr. Traditional German food (DM8-15) is served at **Spaten am Alten Brunnen,** on Türkenstr., right before the church (open Mon.-Fri. noon-1am, Sun. 5pm-1am). **Blue Moon** (tel. 317 80), on the corner of Schmollerstr. and Martin-Luther-Str., serves up entrees for DM9-14 and such kitsch as *Crêpes Elvis* (open Mon.-Fri. 10am-midnight; dinner starts at 6pm). **Hela,** at the end of Ursulinenstr., is a supercalifragalistic supermarket-drugstore-hair salon rolled into one (open Mon.-Fri. 8:30am-6:30pm, Sat. 8:30am-2pm).

Sights and Entertainment The dozens of post-war matchbox buildings around the train station swirl together into a blurring mundanity, but several structures around the St. Johanner's Markt are aesthetically pleasing. Since the details on the bronze doors of the **Basilika St. Johann** have faded since its 1754 construction, it's difficult to tell whether the engraved figures are writhing in hell-fire or heavenly ecstatic bliss (open Mon., Wed., and Fri. at 8:30am; Tues., Thurs., and Sun. 9:30am-evening mass; Sat. 9am-evening mass). To get there, take Kappenstr. from the market and then turn right at the intersection with Katherinen-Kirche-Str.; the *Basilika* will be on your left. The massive mustard **Staatstheater,** south of the market next to the Alte Brücke, rears its ugly head even today; it was presented to Hitler after the Saarland was re-integrated into Germany in 1935. A walk along Am Stadtgarten with the river on the right leads you to the **Saarland Museum,** Bismarckstr. 11-19 (tel. 996 40), which showcases works by Picasso, Matisse, and Beckmann. Medieval Madonnas from Lorraine are in the **Alte Sammlung,** Karlstr. 1, across the street. (Both museums open Tues. and Thurs.-Sun. 10am-6pm, Wed. noon-8pm. Joint admission DM3, students and children DM1.50; for special exhibits DM8, DM4.)

The **Saarbrücker Schloß** (tel. 50 62 47), on the other side of the Saar river, has morphed many times since the 9th century and now has tall sparkling glass columns on either side of its entrance. (Tours in German given Wed.-Sun. at 4pm; free.) Its plaza (the Schloßplatz) is officially the **Platz des unsichtbaren Mahnmals** (Place of the Invisible Reminder) and home to one of the most interesting monuments you'll never see. In 1990, students at a nearby art school, under cover of darkness, dug up 2196 stones in the plaza and carved the names of former Jewish cemeteries on their undersides. Three museums surround Schloßpl. To the south, adjacent to the *Schloß*, the **Historisches Museum** (tel. 50 65 49) includes cars, chairs from the 70s, and a disturbing collection of war propaganda (open Tues.-Sun. 10am-6pm; free; special exhibits DM4, students DM2). To the north, the **Museum für Vor-und Frühgeschichte** (pre- and early history), at Schloßpl. 16 (tel. 584 96 34), has finds that includes a Celtic countess's grave and jewelry from the 4th century BC. (Open Tues. and Thurs.-Sat. 9am-5pm, Wed. noon-8pm. Sun, 10am-6pm. Free. Special exhibits DM5.) The 1498 **Rathaus** west of the *Schloß* hosts the wacky **Abenteuer-Museum** (tel. 517 47), which displays loot from the travels of the original globetrotter (take that, Sweet Lou Dunbar) Heinz Rox Schulz (open Tues.-Wed. 9am-1pm, Thurs.-Fri. 3-7pm; DM3, children DM2). The **Ludwigskirche** is only a five-minute walk down Schloßstr. and to the right. Although the church is still a gem, after World War II only two of its four galleries were rebuilt, giving it an unusual rectangular hall. The decor, with its bright white interior, is a radical departure from the usual gothic gloom. Watch for its high-powered concert series. Saarbrücken is the proud birthplace of renowned filmmaker Max Ophüls, and the town honors him annually with the **Max Ophüls Preis** film festival in late January. The *Kakadu* is Saarbrücken's free culture calendar. Ask for it by name (heh-heh!) at the tourist office.

■ Remagen

After Koblenz, the castles stop appearing around every corner, and the landscape mellows into a less tourist-frenzied atmosphere. Just upstream from the confluence of the Rhine and Ahr Rivers is **Remagen.** In March 1945, as Nazi engineers busily demolished historic bridges across the Rhine to slow the Allied advance, the G.I. Joes preparing to ford the river found the bridge at Remagen intact. Under heavy fire, U.S. troops crossed the explosives-laden bridge and held off a German counterattack until the crossing was secured. The German and American governments acknowledged the site's significance with monuments. Remagen Mayor Hans Kuerten sold souvenir-sized chunks of the now-demolished bridge to fund the **Friedensmuseum** (Museum of Peace) that inhabits the restored bridge tower (tel. 218 63). Poems, letters, pictures, and artifacts inhabit the many rooms and tell the bridge's history (open daily May-Oct.; DM2.50, students DM1). Despite Kuerten's efforts, the grimly blackened bridge ruins remain the most potent warning against war.

To reach the museum, take any street down to the Rhine, turn right on the promenade, and keep going. To get to the Marktplatz from the train station, follow Drususstr. and right onto Bachstr. A few houses down from the tourist office lies the small **Römisches Museum** (Roman Museum, tel. 2010), Kirchstr. 9. The tickets are copies of worthless currency printed during the hyperinflation of 1921. Excavations underneath the 16th-century chapel revealed Roman columns (open March-Oct. Wed.-Sun. 3-5pm; DM2, students DM1, under 14 free). The jewel of Remagen remains the gorgeous mountainside **Apollinariskirche,** whose distinctive Gothic spires can be seen both from the Rhine and the town center. Shining Nazarean frescos cover nearly every surface; hike uphill on Bergstr. to visit the serene crypt. On the way, admire the quiet **St. Peter and Paul** church and nearby 12th-century Romanesque gate.

The **tourist office,** right on the Marktplatz at Kirchstr. 6 (tel. 20 10), hands out maps and books rooms (starting at DM30) for a 10% fee (open Mon.-Thurs. 8:30am-noon and 2-4pm, Fri. 8:30am-noon). To reach the **Campingplatz Goldene Meile** (tel. 222 22) head east (right as you face the Rhine) on Marktstr. As it becomes Altestr. and Goethestr., turn left at the sign (15min.; reception open daily 7:30am-noon and 2-6pm; DM7.50, ages 6-16 DM6.50; per tent DM6-13.) If you're feeling too sweaty, head to the swimming pool and aspiring water park, **Allwetterbad Remagen,** up the road toward Goethestr. The **telephone code** is 02642.

■ Nonnenwerth andDrachenfels

At the northernmost end of the Rhine Gorge, between Bad Honnef and Königswinter, the Rhine Gorge is richly seasoned with legend and beauty of multifarious tastes. The ivy-covered archway, high above the Rhine directly west of Bad Honnef, is all that remains of the **Rolandsbogen** castle, perhaps Europe's greatest monument to sexual frustration. Legendary hero Roland returned from the battle at Roncevalles to find that his wife, upon the (greatly exaggerated) news of his death, had taken a vow of chastity and retreated to the convent on **Nonnenwerth Island.** He channeled his sexual energy into building the **Rolandsbogen** in hopes of catching occasional glimpses of her. Today, too late for Roland but convenient for modern convent peepers, ferries depart from Königswinter, running from the east to west banks, and from the west bank to the island (1½hr.). Call (0228) 63 63 68 for more info.

The cultured tourist making his way past all the gummi dragons here might be inclined to sniff haughtily. The origins (and the view) of the **Castle Drachenfels,** however, are nothing to snuffle at. "The castled crag of Drachenfels frowns o'er the wide and winding Rhine," penned Lord Byron in "Childe Harold's Pilgrimage." In the *Nibelungenlied,* Siegfried slew a dragon here and bathed in its blood, which would have made him invincible if a leaf on his back hadn't left a vulnerable spot. Imbibing enough of the local *Drachenblut* (dragon blood) wine, cultivated on the mountain where the dragon lived, produces a similar feeling of strength. The ruins and the incredible view can be reached by U-Bahn #66 from Bonn and from **Königswinter.** Simply follow Drachensfelsstr. It's officially a 45-minute walk, but Siegfried wannabes hustle up in under 25 minutes. The less heroic take the **Drachenfelsbahn,** Drachen-felsstr. 53 (tel. (02223) 920 90), a railway leading to the top (DM10 up, DM9 down, DM13 round-trip; ages 4-13 DM6 up and DM5 down; dogs DM1). There are also donkey and carriage rides to the top. The **Nibelungshalle,** where the dragon once munched on tasty young virgins, is now a **reptile zoo** and **museum** (tel. (02223) 24150) relating the saga, complete with a 13m mock dragon (DM5, children DM4; open May 15-Nov. 15 daily 10am-7pm). Between the ruin and the museum, **Schloß Drachenburg** (tel. 261 55) reveals its ornate, exquisitely maintained 19th-century interior by way of hourly tours (April-Oct. Tues.-Sun. 11am-6pm; DM3, rug-rats DM2).

The Königswinter **tourist office** is at Drachenfelsstr. 11 (open Mon.-Fri. 9am-5pm, Sat. 10am-2pm). Bad Honnef's **Jugendherberge,** Selhoferstr. 106 (tel. (02224) 713 00; fax 792 26), provides a base to explore the mythical surroundings. From the train station, head up and left, following the "Stadtmitte" signs onto Menzenbergerstr.; when this ends, go left on Linzerstr., and Selhoferstr. will be the first (unmarked) right. From the U-Bahn, walk under the pedestrian overpass and over the next bridge to the left to Menzenbergerstr. Either way, it's almost a half-hour walk; keep on truckin'. (Reception open 9am-10pm. Curfew 11:30pm. DM25, over 26 DM30. Breakfast included. Sheets DM7.) Also in Bad Honnef is the **Bundeskanzler-Adenauer-Haus,** Konrad-Adenauer-Str. 8c, where Herr Adenauer, then mayor of Köln, retired in 1937 after being driven from office by local Nazis. The exhibits tell the story of his personal and political survival. (Open Tues.-Sun. 10am-4:30pm. Last entry 4pm.)

RHEINLAND-PFALZ

Baden-Württemberg

Two powerful German stereotypes—the brooding romantic of the Brothers Grimm and the modern *homo economicus* exemplified by Daimler-Benz—battle it out in Baden-Württemberg. Pretzels, cuckoo clocks, and cars were all invented here, and the region is as diverse as its homegrown products. Baden, Württemberg-Hohenzollern, and Württemberg-Baden—three distinct states—were integrated at the founding of the Federal Republic in 1951 in a shotgun wedding masterminded by the Allies. Baden-Württemberg was meant to act as a conservative counterweight to socialist-leaning Nordrhein-Westfalen. Although the merger was legitimated by a referendum, the Badeners and the Swabians (*never* "Württembergers") proudly proclaim their distinct identities. Rural custom and tradition live on in the lush hinterlands of the Schwarzwald and the Schwäbische Alb, while the modern capital city of Stuttgart celebrates the latter-day ascendancy of the German industrial machine. The province also hosts the ritzy millionaires' resort of Baden-Baden, the lovely vacation getaways of the exquisite Bodensee, as well as the exuberant, historic university towns of Freiburg, Tübingen, and Heidelberg.

■ Heidelberg

One among the countless German cities that flaunt their ancient architecture in glossy tourist propaganda, Heidelberg is surrounded by magnificence that truly shines. From the crumbling walls of the once-majestic *Schloß* to the historic, gabled buildings and romantic, hodge-podge cobblestone streets of the *Altstadt,* Heidelberg has retained the spirit that once lured numerous writers, poets and artists—including Mark Twain, Goethe, Friedrich Hölderlin, Victor Hugo, and Robert Schumann—to the woodsy idyll. Today, during the high season (June-Aug.), roughly 32,000 tourists *per day* (many of them English-speaking) also answer the call. Even in the most "off" of seasons, legions of camera-toting fannypackers (and *Let's Go* readers) fill the length of Hauptstr., where postcards and T-shirts sell like hotcakes and every sign is in at least four languages. However, the incessant buzz of mass tourism is truly worth enduring, as Heidelberg's beautiful hillside setting, endless list of attractions, and lively nightlife actually live up to its well-known reputation.

ORIENTATION AND PRACTICAL INFORMATION

About 20km east of the Neckar's confluence with the Rhine, Heidelberg stretches along the river's shores for several kilometers, with almost all of the city's attractions clustered in the eastern quadrant on the southern shore. To get to the *Altstadt* from the train station, take almost any bus or street car to "Bismarckpl.," where **Hauptstraße** leads into the city's heart. Known as the longest shopping street in Germany, Hauptstr. is undoubtedly the city's backbone; an unending stream of tourists, locals, and the businesses that keep them happy.

Tourist Office: Tourist information (tel. 277 35; fax 167 318), directly in front of the station. Pick up a copy of the mags *Meier* (DM2) or *Fritz* (free) to figure out what's up. Rooms reserved (7% deposit) and maps sold (DM1). You may want to call lodgings yourself as the tourist office steers guests toward more expensive places. Open Mon.-Sat. 9am-7pm, Sun. 10am-6pm; Jan.-Feb. Mon.-Sat. 9am-7pm.

Currency Exchange: If banks and the post office are closed, try the *Hauptbahnhof,* where the exchange office stays open later. On holidays, one can change cash at the *Sparkassen* on Universitätspl. and Bismarckpl.

American Express: Brückenkopfstr. 1 (tel. 450 50; fax 41 03 33), at the north end of the Theodor-Heuss-Brücke (bridge). They hold mail for card members and owners of AmEx traveler's checks. Open Mon.-Fri. 10am-6pm, Sat. 10am-1pm.

Baden-Württemberg

N

FRANCE

SWITZERLAND

AUSTRIA

Trains: Frequent trains run from Stuttgart (45min.) and Frankfurt (1hr.); Mannheim is less than 10min. away. Other trains run regularly to towns in the Neckar Valley.

Public Transportation: To get into, out of, and around Heidelberg, buy a **24hr. pass** that's good on all streetcars and buses (DM10). Passes are available at the tourist office or at the HSB Kiosk, located halfway across the street on Gneisenaustr., the street that runs by the side entrance to the train station. Or, more simply, buy a pass on any bus or streetcar. Single-ride tickets DM3.20.

Ferries: Rhein-Neckar-Fahrgastschiffahrt, down at the southern bank in front of the *Kongresshaus,* runs Neckar cruises. A popular destination is **Neckarsteinach** (May-Sept. 7 per day 9:30am-5:30pm; 1¼hr.; round-trip DM16.50). **Rent** paddle-boats and **rowboats** on the north shore of the Neckar by the Theodor-Heuss-Brücke at **Bootverleih Simon.** Three-person boat 30min. DM9, 1hr. DM15. Four-person boat DM11, DM18. Open daily 10am-sundown.

Taxi: tel. 30 20 30.

Bike Rental: Per Bike, Bergheimerstr. 125 (tel. 16 11 48; fax 16 11 09), has city, mountain, and children's bikes. Half-day DM15, full day DM25, additional days DM20. DM55 Fri.-Mon. weekend special. DM120 per week. DM50 deposit or ID required. Open Mon.-Fri. 9am-6pm; April-Oct. also open Sat. 9am-1pm.

Hitchhiking: *Let's Go* does not recommend hitchhiking as a safe mode of transportation. Hitchers walk to the western end of Bergheimerstr. for all directions.

Mitfahrzentrale: Bergheimerstr. 125 (tel. 246 46 or 194 44; fax 14 59 59), matches riders and drivers in an orderly fashion. Paris DM51, Köln DM28, Hamburg DM54, Freiburg DM24. Open Mon.-Fri. 9am-5pm, and April-Oct. Sat. 9am-noon.

Bookstores: Potter Books, Plöck 93 (tel. 18 30 01), is a hardwood-floored English-only bookstore that stocks a wide variety of new and used titles, from classics to trashy romances, all at reasonable prices. Open Mon.-Fri. 10am-8pm, Sat. 10am-4pm. **Old Bridge Books,** Kettengasse 1 (tel. 121 26; fax 106 68), has recently moved to a convenient location near the university and expanded its operations. New and used books, all in English. Open Tues.-Fri. 10am-6:30pm, Sat. 10am-2pm.

Laundromat: Wasch Salon SB, Poststr. 49, next to Kurfürst Hotel. Wash DM7. Dry DM1 per 20min. Beware: the machines do not give change—you could be forced to dry your clothes for hours. Open Mon.-Sat. 7am-11pm, Sun. 9am-8pm.

Women's Resources: Information, tel. 33 30 88. **Frauennotruf** (women's emergency hotline), tel. 18 36 43. **Buchhandlung Himmelheber,** Theaterstr. 16 (tel. 222 01; fax 230 52), stocks books by, for, and about women, and also hosts readings. Open Mon.-Wed. and Fri. 9am-6:30pm, Thurs. 9am-8pm, Sat 9am-2pm.

AIDS-Hilfe: tel. 194 11.

Emergency: tel. 110. **Police,** Römerstr. 2-4 (tel. 990).

Post Office: *Hauptpostamt,* Belfortstr., 69115 Heidelberg, diagonally to the right across from the front of the station. Held mail can be picked up at counters 15-17. Open Mon.-Fri. 8am-6pm, Sat. 8am-1pm. Limited services Mon.-Fri. 6-8pm.

Telephone Code: 06221.

ACCOMMODATIONS AND CAMPING

Finding a place to sleep in Heidelberg is a task not unlike spinning straw into gold, and the bill could demand your first-born. During the summer, save yourself a major headache by arriving early in the day or, better yet, calling ahead. Possible options for those with some ingenuity and a railpass are the countless little towns and villages scattered around Heidelberg. There are **Jugendherbergen** in: Neckargmünd (10 min. away); Reilscheim (18min.); Mauer (20min.); Hirschhorn (20min.); Eberbach (25min.); and Zwingberg (35 min.). All these Neckar Valley towns lie along the Heidelberg-Heilbronn railroad; train service is reliable and regular between them. Better yet, the **Mannheim Jugendherberge** is only five minutes from Mannheim's *Hauptbahnhof,* 15-20 minutes from Heidelberg, and is close to an array of goings-on right in Mannheim (p. 394). Best of all, a single room in a **private home** in these outlying areas can cost only a fraction of an impersonal place in one of Heidelberg's hotels.

Jugendherberge (HI), Tiergartenstr. 5 (tel. 41 20 66; fax 40 25 59). From Bismarckpl. or the train station, bus #33 (direction: "Zoo-Sportzentrum"): "Jugendherberge" (first stop after Zoo; 10min.). "The Jugendherberge is full today" sign on the tourist office door is practically permanent. Calling less than a week ahead rarely works. Become one of the lucky to stay in this teeming hostel by faxing your reservation. Crowded and noisy, but its small **disco** can be fun (open nightly). Reception open until 11:30pm. Lockout 9am-1pm. Curfew 11:30pm (negotiable). Members only. DM22, over 26 DM27. Sheets DM5.50. Partial wheelchair access.

Jeske Hotel, Mittelbadgasse 2 (tel. 237 33). From the train station, bus #33 (direction: "Köpfel") or 11 (direction: "Karlstor"): "Bergbahn," then follow Zwingerstr. west back towards the *Hauptbahnhof* (don't go back up the hill). Mittelbachgasse is the first right after Oberbadgasse. English-speaking Euro-roamers galore fill this delightfully antiquated *Altstadt* facility, and for good reason—it's the best value in Heidelberg. Truly unbeatable location for just a few more marks than the hostel. Reservations not accepted, but you can call to save a space the day of arrival. Arrive

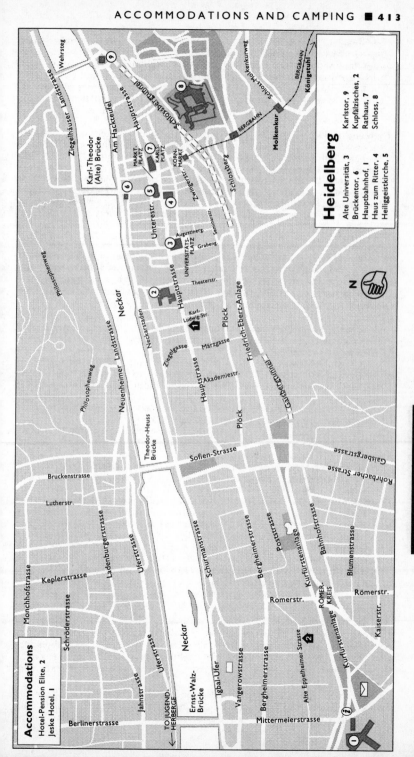

Heidelberg

Alte Universität, 3
Brückentor, 6
Hauptbahnhof, 1
Haus zum Ritter, 4
Heiliggeistkirche, 5

Karlstor, 9
Kupfälzisches, 2
Rathaus, 7
Schloss, 8

Accommodations

Hotel-Pension Elite, 2
Jeske Hotel, 1

BADEN-WÜRTTEMBERG

early! Two- to five-bed rooms DM24 per person. Showers DM2. No breakfast. Open Feb. to mid-Nov. Other times call ahead.

Hotel-Pension Elite, Bunsenstr. 15 (tel. 257 33). From Bismarckpl., follow Rohr-bacherstr. away from the river and turn right onto Bunsenstr.; the *Pension* is on the left. Truly nice rooms with high ceilings, elegant Victorian decor, billowy curtains, and pastoral views. Narrow single DM75; doubles for one DM85; doubles for two DM100; DM15 per extra person. Bath and TV in each room. Breakfast included. DM5 credit card surcharge.

Camping: Haide (tel. (06223) 21 11; email camping.haide@t-online.de), between Ziegelhausen and Kleingmünd. Bus #35: "Orthopedisches Klinik," then cross the river and turn right; the campground is on the right 10min. away. "No-flood" guarantee. Reception open 8am-noon and 4:30-7:30pm. Person DM8; tent DM6; car DM2. Cabins DM14-16 (depending on number of people). Open April-Oct. 31. If this side of the river doesn't float your boat, head to **Camping Heidelberg-Schlierbach,** located on the other bank (tel. 80 25 06), near the Clinic. Bus #35 (direction: "Neckargmünd"): "Im Grund." Person DM10; tent DM4-12; car DM2.

FOOD

Eating out tends to be depressingly expensive in Heidelberg; most of the restaurants on and around Hauptstr. are exorbitantly priced. However, just outside this central area are historic student pubs that offer better values. Fill up a picnic basket at **Handelshof supermarket,** Kurfürsten-Anlage 60, 200m in front of the train station on the right (open Mon.-Fri. 7:30am-8pm, Sat. 7:30am-4pm).

Mensa, in the *Marstall,* on Marstallstr. Bus #35: "Marstallstr." or from the Alte Brücke take a left along the river; it's the huge stone installation on the left. State-subsidized cafeteria turns into a cafe in the afternoon. Cheap food, beer, and cheesecake. If you've forgotten your student ID, ask one of the students hanging out on the green in front to buy you *Mensa Marks* (DM3 each; sold in fives). Open Mon.-Fri. 11:30am-2pm, Sat. 11:30am-1:30pm. During vacations, it alternates with the *Mensa* on Universitätspl. There's also a popular cafe next door serving coffee, snacks, and beer (DM2.70-3) amidst board games. A student crossroads for after-dusk doings. Open Mon.-Fri. 9am-midnight, Sat. 11am-1am.

Gaststätte Essighaus, Plöck 97 (tel. 224 96), has tasty food and service that's quite quick by German standards. Specials include soup, salad, and entrees (DM10-20). Open daily 11:30am-12:30am, food available until 11:30pm.

Café Trotzkopf, Bergheimerstr. 71 (tel. 252 34), is a classy little cafe with *Biergarten* that offers warm, inexpensive food, stained glass windows, and mellow candlelit evenings. *Chili con carne* DM9.80. Open daily 9am-1am.

Zum Schwarzen Wal, Bahnhofstr. 27 (tel. 201 85). *The* place in Heidelberg for big, delicious breakfasts. Each meal is given a nationality (the *Amerikanisches Frühstück* inexplicably includes a crepe). Also serves lunch and dinner (DM10-20). Full breakfast DM6-15. Open Mon.-Fri. 7:30am-1am, Sat. 8:30am-1am, Sun. 9am-1am.

Falafel Store, Kornmarkt 9 (tel. 270 91). A well-stocked vegetarian fast food-*cum*-convenience store. Falafel DM6, exotic coffees DM3. Mention *Let's Go.*

Vater Rhein, Untere Neckarstr. 20-22 (tel. 213 71), near the Stadthalle. Cheap food and drinks in a dark wood-paneled restaurant with a very local feel. *Goulash* DM6. Pizza DM11.50, *Pilsner* DM4. Open daily 8pm-3am.

SIGHTS

American author Mark Twain's description of Heidelberg is the highlight of his 19th-century travelogue *A Tramp Abroad.* Twain recorded, with rare respect, his impressions of this university town's beauty. In the ensuing years, Heidelberg has lost none of the stateliness captured so well in Twain's description; its streets still bustle with an energy that would do a much younger city proud. Presiding over all the majestic elegance are the ramparts of the **Heidelberger Schloß** (tel. 53 84 14 or 538 40), the jewel in the crown of an already striking city. Its construction began early in the 13th century and lasted over 400 years. The conglomeration of styles ranges from Gothic to High Renaissance. Thrice destroyed, first by war (1622 and 1693) and later by nature (lightning in 1764), the castle's regal state of disrepair is best viewed from the **Philosophenweg** (Philsopher's Way) high above the northern bank of the Neckar. From the castle's broad terraces, the red roofs of the town act as the anchor to the far-reaching hills rolling in the distance; the castle's spacious gardens are striking in their measured symmetry. On the first Saturday in June and August and the second Saturday in July, fireworks illuminate the surrounding sky in the **Schloßbeleuchtung.** The *Schloß* is easily accessible by foot or by **Bergbahn** (cable car), which runs from the "Bergbahn/Rathaus" bus stop to the castle (round-trip DM4.50) and continues on to the Königstuhl TV tower (round trip DM7). Trams take off from the Kornmarkt parking lot next to the bus stop every 10 minutes from 9am to 7:45pm. Bus #11: "Köpfel" or 33: "Karlstor." Once atop the hill, shell out the marks for admission to the grounds (open daily 8am-dusk; DM3, students DM1.50, charged 8am-5pm only). Actually, getting inside the *Schloß* is possible only with an obligatory tour, which includes a visit to the *Faß*, a brutally large wine barrel. Local lore tells of a court jester and *Faß* guardian who drank nearly 18 bottles per day and finally perished after accidentally drinking a glass of water (tours in English, German, and French 11am-3pm; DM4, students DM2). The **Apothekenmuseum** (tel. 258 80), also in the castle, stopped dishing out the goods in 1693 but still has all sorts of drug-related displays, including a reconstructed 17th-century pharmacy and alchemists' laboratory (open daily 8:45am-5:45pm; free with entrance to castle grounds).

The *Altstadt* centers on the **Marktplatz,** a cobbled square where **Hercules' Fountain** stands, and where, in the 15th century, accused witches and heretics were burned at the stake; now a legion of plastic chairs spreads across the cobbles while a **market** (Wed. and Sat.) purveys fruit. The two oldest structures in Heidelberg border the Marktplatz. The 14th-century **Heiliggeistkirche** (open to visitors Mon.-Thurs. and Sat. 11am-5pm, Fri. 1-5pm, Sun. 1:30-5pm; free) is the largest Gothic church in the Palatinate and contains the tomb of Ruprecht I as well as an ancient library. Across from the church's southern face, the ornate facade of the swanky **Hotel zum Ritter,** built by a wealthy Huguenot refugee, dates from the 16th century. The stately **Rathaus** overlooks the entire spectacle from the far end of the square.

Walking west from the Marktplatz down Hauptstr. yields views of trendy shops and cafes, while history hides behind them; five blocks down, the **Universitätsplatz,** centered about a stone-lion fountain, is the former headquarters of the **Alte Universität** (Old University). In the aristocratic tradition, students were exempt from prosecution by civil authorities; instead, the crimes of their misspent youth were tried and punished by the university faculty. Between 1778 and 1914, naughty students were jailed in the **Studentenkarzer** (tel. 54 23 34; enter via Augustinergasse behind the old university). Covered with graffiti, the wall tells of a group of honest students who were unjustly imprisoned for returning a loose cobblestone to its rightful owner—through a window. (Open Tues.-Sat. 10am-noon and 2-5pm; Nov.-March Tues.-Fri. 10am-noon and 2-5pm, Sat. 10am-1pm, Sun. 10am-1pm; DM1.50, students and children DM1.) The **Kurpfälzisches Museum,** Hauptstr. 97 (tel. 58 34 02 or 58 34 00), is crammed with artifacts such as the jawbone of an unfortunate *homo Heidelbergensis,* a.k.a. "Heidelberg man," one of the oldest humans yet discovered. Elsewhere stand well-preserved works of art by Dürer, and a spectacular Gothic altarpiece by 15th-century sculptor Tilman Riemenschneider (open Tues. and Thurs.-Sun. 10am-5pm, Wed. 10am-9pm; DM5, students DM3, children free; Sun. DM3, students DM2). No trip to Heidelberg would be complete without a visit to the northern bank of the Neckar, opposite the *Altstadt.* Walk across the modern **Karl-Theodor-Brücke;** on the south side of the bridge stands a plump statue of the Prince-Elector himself, which he commissioned as a symbol of his modesty. On the left side of the bridge stretches a perfect picnic park. On the other side, in the direction of the Marktplatz, lies the shining path to enlightenment: the **Philosophenweg.** Contemplate the Nietzschean *Übermensch* as you gaze upon the masses of pions in the city, or bring yer sweetheart and smooch 'til sunrise. Either way, the view is one of the best in the city.

BADEN-WÜRTTEMBERG

Atop the **Heiligenberg,** the mountain traversed by the *Philosophenweg,* lie ruins of the 9th-century **St. Michael Basilika,** the 13th-century **St. Stephen Kloster,** and an **amphitheater** built under Hitler in 1934 on the site of an ancient Celtic gathering place. The ascent of this mountain is best tackled near the **Tiefburg,** a moated castle in neighboring Handschuhsheim, reached by Straßenbahn #1 or 3.

Heidelberg is home to a number of merry festivals. The **Faschings Parade (Carnival)** struts through the city on Shrove Tuesday (Feb. 24, 1998). The **Spring Festival** provides another excuse for having fun, this time amid the blooming greenery of awakening spring (May 15-24 in 1998). In the third weekend in June after-hours revelers in Heidelberg head to the town of Handschuhsheim across the Neckar, for the Saturday, Sunday and Monday of the **Handschuhsheim Fest.** For five weeks from late-July to late-August, **Schloßfestspiele Heidelberg** features a series of concerts and plays (call 58 35 21 for info and tickets). On the third Saturday of September (Sept. 26, 1998), the **Heidelberger Herbst** takes over town with a fair and fleamarket.

NIGHTLIFE

Even at night, Heidelberg's Marktplatz is the heart of the city's action; most popular nightspots fan out from here. **Unterestraße,** on the Neckar side of the Heiliggeist-kirche, boasts the most prolific—and often congested—conglomeration of bars in the city. During fair weather, drunken revelers fill the narrow way until 1 or 2am. **Hauptstraße** also harbors a fair number of venues, though it is not as densely filled as Unterestr.; the majority are within two or three blocks of the Marktplatz.

Roter Ochsen, Hauptstr. 217 (tel. 209 77). A popular student hangout since 1703. Bismarck and Mark Twain used to get plastered here; so can you for DM4.50-25. But don't let the beer foam stick to your walrus mustache. The pervasive antiquity is even visible in the clientele. Meals DM12-31. Open Mon.-Sat. 11:30-2pm and 5pm-midnight, Nov.-March Mon.-Sat. 5pm-midnight.

Zum Sepp'l, Hauptstr. 213 (tel. 230 85). Next door to Roter Ochsen with a similarly loud crowd that's been partying since 1634. Look for the (yes, it's true!) "Adolf-Hitler-Platz" sign on the wall. Meals DM8-25. Beer DM4.80, "the Boot" (2L of beer) DM6.20. The Boot can kick yer butt. Open daily 10am-midnight.

Reichsapfel, Unterestr. 35 (tel. 279 50), is a popular bar, filled with a fairly diverse crowd of locals. *Pils* DM4.60. Open daily 6pm-1am.

Cave 54, Krämergasse 2 (tel. 278 40), occasionally jumps with 70s retro disco. Check the posters around town. Beer DM5-5.50. Live jazz on Sundays at 9:30pm. Cover DM5. Open daily 9:30pm-3am.

Little Heaven, Fahrtgasse 18 (tel. 226 61). Heidelberg's local outpost of Euro-dance music culture. Jungle, techno, house, and the occasional "Sex Music Special." Open daily 10pm-3am.

Blue Note, Neckarstaden 24 (tel. 14 31 10). In the basement of the *Kongresshaus,* this intimate club hosts nights that range from Havana-themed fiestas to Thursday's All-you-can-drink DM20. Fickle schedule; call ahead. Open Wed.-Sat. 10pm-3am.

Schwimmbad Musik Club, Tiergartenstr. 13 (tel. 47 02 01), across the river. Conveniently located up the street from the hostel, it's the city's main catwalk for underground bands. The Pharcyde and, umm, Humungus Fungus both played here recently. Mainstream music on Fri. and Sat. nights. Open Wed.-Thurs. 8pm-2am, Fri.-Sat. 8pm-4am.

Mata Hari, (tel. 18 18 08), on Zwingerstr. near the corner of Oberbadgasse. Small, subdued gay and lesbian bar; red lighting. Tues. men only. Open daily 10pm-3am.

■ Neckartal (Neckar Valley)

A scenic stretch of narrow, thickly-wooded ridges embraces the Neckar River as it meanders from Heilbronn to Heidelberg—the Neckartal. The **Burgenstraße** (the German Castle Road), traveling all the way to Nürnberg in the heart of Bayern, circumscribes the Neckartal. The hills hugging the river are sprinkled with medieval castles built to protect merchant vessels from pirates. Largely unspoiled by tourism, the valley is an excellent daytrip from Heidelberg, and its charms can be absorbed by both land and water. Two train lines connect Heidelberg and Heilbronn hourly, with stops in the many smaller towns along both sides of the valley. Heilbronn itself is touristically relevant only as the delta of the rail lines through the valley. One of the best ways to explore the valley is by biking along the well maintained 85km route.

Bike rentals are available at the **train station** in Neckargmünd, 12 minutes by train from Heidelberg (DM13 per day, DM9 with a train ticket). In Hirschhorn (see p. 417), **Josef Riedel,** Hainbrunnerstr. 6 (tel. (06272) 20 17), has 'em for DM5 per half-day, DM10 per day. Finally, there's the **train station** in Eberbach (tel. (06271) 22 20), 30 minutes from Heidelberg. Also check **Per Bike** in Heidelberg (see p. 410). The **Rhein-Neckar Fahrgastschiffahrt** runs **boat tours** from Easter through late-October between Heidelberg (departing from the *Stadthalle*) and Neckarsteinach (daily; round-trip DM16.50) as well as between Heidelberg and Hirschhorn (Tues., Thurs., and Sun.; round-trip DM22.50). For information and departure times, call (06221) 201 81 or (06229) 526.

NECKARSTEINACH

At the north end of the valley, 14km upstream from Heidelberg, lies Neckarsteinach, notable for its four medieval **castles** all within three kilometers of one another along the north bank of the Neckar River. They were built by the same ruling clan, the Steinachs, during the 12th and 13th centuries. The two westernmost castles stand in ruins, while the two to the east tower and shine in their splendor; they are privately occupied, however, and visitors are not allowed inside. All can be reached by foot via the **Burgenweg** (castle path)—a journey of 30 minutes to several hours, depending on the strength of your legs and the weight of your backpack. Tourists may visit all but the first castle on the path. From the train station, turn right on Bahnhofstr. until you reach Hauptstr., turn left and follow the bend in the road to the Pizzeria Castello; the *Schloßsteige* begins at the brick path leading upward to the right and connects to the Burgenweg, whose trees are studded with identifying plaques (open March-Oct. Mon.-Sat. 9am-8pm). Neckarsteinach's **tourist office**, Hauptstr. 7 (tel. 920 00), inside the *Rathaus,* is one block down from Bahnhofstr. in the same direction as the *Schloßsteige.* The office lists hotels, *Pensionen,* and private homes offering inexpensive rooms (open Mon.-Wed. 8am-noon and 1:30-3:30pm, Thurs. 8am-noon and 1:30-5pm, Fri. 8am-noon). The **postal code** is 69239. The **telephone code** is 06229. Fireworks emblazon the sky above the town on the last Saturday in July during the **Vierburgenbeleuchtung** (four-castle lighting). *Rhein-Neckar-Fahrgastschiffahrt* organizes trips for the fiery festivities, and also makes daily trips from Heidelberg (see p. 410) all summer long.

HIRSCHHORN AND BURG GUTTENBERG

Just south of Neckarsteinach lounges Hirschhorn am Neckar, ruled for centuries by the Knights of Hirschhorn. In 1200, the knights built their castle on Stockelberg Mountain, cruelly displacing a happy herd of reindeer from their favorite grazing spot. History repeated itself many hundreds of years later, when an enterprising young capitalist bought the knights out; the mountain is now a posh hotel/restaurant complex. Nevertheless, the surrounding countryside is excellent for hiking, and the former **castle of the knights of Hirschhorn** is still worth a peek. By foot, follow the gray brick of Schloßstr. upward from the *Bürgerhaus* intersection (15min.). Unless you are in a car, do not follow the road signs. The castle's terraces offer a fine panorama, and an even better one can be had at the top of the tower for a mere DM0.30. Stone stairs curl from the castle down into the *Altstadt;* along the way, they pass the 15th-century **Karmeliter Klosterkirche,** with a Gothic interior and graceful altar. Some days, monks' chants echo softly through the church, mesmerizing passersby.

Detailed maps of the local trails are available at the **tourist office,** Alleeweg 2 (tel. 17 42 or 92 31 40), which books rooms for free. From the station, turn left on Neckarsteinacherstr. and follow it to the intersection as it curves to the right. Turn right

BADEN-WÜRTTEMBERG

and walk downhill towards the river, just past the hotel. The office is in the rear of the next building on the right (open Mon.-Fri. 8am-noon and 2-5pm; April-Oct. Sat. 9am-noon). The office's home, the **Haus des Gastes,** also houses an **art and natural history museum** with a collection of 17th- and 18th-century wooden statues, weaponry and a truly terrifying diorama that crams over 100 native fauna into a space the size of a king-size bed (open Tues. and Thurs.-Sat. 2-4pm, Sun. 10am-noon and 2-4pm; DM1, kids DM0.50). The **post office,** down Alleeweg, is to the left of the tourist office (open Mon.-Fri. 8:30am-noon and 2-5pm, Sat. 8:30-noon). The **telephone code** is 06272. For overnight accommodations, check the hotels and *Pensionen* along Hauptstr. and the board outside the tourist office. **Haus La Belle,** Hauptstr. 36, has cushy rooms (with bath and TV) from DM30 per person. Camp between April and mid-October at **Odenwald Camping** (tel. 809 or 36 58), one kilometer outside of town in the direction of the castle; follow signs from the tourist office (person DM7).

Thirty kilometers south of Hirschhorn along the *Burgenstraße* towers **Burg Guttenberg.** The castle has gracefully and miraculously survived the sackings, sieges, bombings, and general plunder that laid waste to its less sturdy comrades along the *Burgenstraße.* More distinctive is the aviary for **birds of prey,** maintained by prominent ornithologist Claus Fentzloff. Twice per day (at 11am and 3pm; March and Nov. at 3pm only), Fentzloff sends eagles and vultures flying inches above the heads of the crowds, plucking poor little chickens out of the sky, while he launches into lengthy scientific diatribes. (Museum open March-Oct. daily 9:30am-5pm. Aviary open 9am-6pm. Admission for aviary and bird show DM12, for castle and aviary DM15.) To reach Burg Guttenberg by rail, get off at Gundelsheim (along the Heidelberg-Heilbronn run), cross the big bridge past the camping site, and walk 2km following the signs along the road (15min.).

BAD WIMPFEN

Just downstream from Heilbronn along an alternative rail route on the road to Heidelberg reposes the village of Bad Wimpfen, long one of the best-kept secrets in Southwest Germany. In the past few years, however, the infamous megabuses have infiltrated the area. Though this seems to be just one more innocuous village set against the sweeping backdrop of fields, the town opens unexpectedly into four gnarled bumpy streets and rough-worked, half-timbered houses built atop the ruins of a Roman imperial castle on a ridge high above the Neckar.

From the recently renovated train station, the immaculately preserved *Altstadt* is a 10-minute walk. Go straight ahead and follow Karl-Ulrich-Str. as it bends right. Or, if your calves need toning, take the steep hiking trail to the right of the station. Up we go. Laid out along the southern side of the old castle walls, easily accessible points on the ancient battlements offer incredible views of the valley and surrounding countryside. Along the castle ruins between the Marktplatz and the train station are the **Blauer Turm** and the **Steinhaus.** The former offers another view of the town and its environs to those willing to climb the 169 steps. The tower's dramatic 1984 decapitation by lightning is documented on the way up the stairs. Next door, the sandstone *Steinhaus* contains a museum of artifacts left behind by the Romans (both open Tues.-Sun. 10am-noon and 2-4:30pm; Nov.-April Mon.-Fri. 10am-noon; DM2, students DM1). The **Kulturamt,** Hauptstr. 45 (tel. 531 51), distributes information on cultural events in town. An itty-bitty **Spielzeug Museum** (toy museum) is located on Salzgasse 6. Bears and toys for the *Kind* in all of us. From the *Kulturamt,* take 50 steps, say "Mother, may I?" and turn immediately right around the corner; it's on the right (open Tues.-Thurs. and Sat.-Sun. 2:30-4:30pm; DM4, students DM2). Bad Wimpfen also has claim to the world's only **Pig Museum,** Kronengäßchen 2 (tel. 66 89), off Hauptstr. near the *Kulturamt,* detailing the history of swine (considered a good luck symbol in Germany) with collector's items and lucky charms—meet the real Miss Piggy. (Open daily 10am-5pm. DM4.99, students DM2.49, children under 1m DM0.99—a lucky *Pfennig* on each ticket.)

The **tourist office** is in the train station (tel. 972 00; fax 97 20 20). They do not find rooms, but they allow you to leave your luggage while you explore the town (open

Mon.-Fri. 10am-1pm and 2-5pm, Sat.-Sun. 10am-noon and 2-4pm). Bad Wimpfen's splendid *Jugendherberge* has recently closed its doors; the cheapest option is to pick up the **Gastgeberverzeichnis** (guest room catalog) at the tourist office, which lists private homes that offer inexpensive rooms (DM25-30 per person), as well as *Pensionen* and hotels. **Hotel Garni Neckarblick,** Erich-Salier-Str. 48 (tel. 70 02; fax 85 48), offers affordable luxury with a capital "L," very hospitable management, and a stunning view of the valley. From the Marktplatz, follow Mathildenbadstr. from the pedestrian zone out to the street, then hang a right. Proceed for 15 minutes along Erich-Salier-Str. as it curves around the hillside (past the park); the hotel is on the right. All rooms include TV, telephone, and bath. (Singles DM80; doubles DM115-130; triples DM175. Call ahead or fax reservations.) Along the same street, closer to town, stands **Pension Panorama,** Erich-Sailer-Str. 23 (tel./fax 222), a less cushy and less expensive but still good alternative (singles with bath DM55; doubles DM90, with bath DM100). The **telephone code** is 07063.

For traditional German fare, try **d'Wimpfener Dobel,** Hauptstr. 61 (tel. 82 12), where *Maultaschen* (Swabian pasta pockets) are the house specialty (DM9-13). Their salad bar (DM5) is a rare source of green fiber in the Neckar Valley (open Mon.-Sat. 10am-midnight, Sun. 10am-10pm). **Grocery stores** are located on the other side of the *Altstadt* along Rappenamerstr.

▓ Schwäbisch Hall

Riding into the Schwäbisch Hall station on one of the hourly trains from Heilbronn is like opening a pop-up fairy tale book. After nearly an hour of monotonous German countryside, the windows suddenly fill with hundreds of red-tiled roofs, soaring cathedral towers, and crumbling stone walls. Virtually ignored during the world wars, Schwäbisch Hall's steeply sloping *Altstadt* is one of the most expansive and well-preserved in Germany. In fact, the only bomb to hit the city struck the decrepit *Rathaus,* which was promptly rebuilt to greater grandeur than ever. Though tourism is present, it has yet to reach large proportions, leaving the city almost entirely to its residents and the few independent travelers who wander the ancient streets.

Orientation and Practical Information Schwäbisch Hall has two **train** stations. The *Hauptbahnhof* is close to town, but the larger and more important station is in **Schwäbisch Hall-Hessental,** which lies on the main rail line to Stuttgart. If you're coming from the south, you'll probably end up arriving here. Although you will be 3km away from the salty pleasures of the *Altstadt,* do not panic—bus #1 frequently connects the Hessental station to Schwäbisch Hall proper (DM2; every 20-30min.). Schwäbisch Hall's **tourist office,** Am Markt 9 (tel. 75 12 46; fax 75 13 75), next to St. Michael's, has maps and finds rooms for free (open April-Oct. Mon.-Fri. 9am-6pm, Sat. 10am-3p). To **rent a bike,** useful in navigating this very steep city, try **Radstation,** Langestr. 40 (tel. 87 72), where you can get a two-wheeler for DM15 per day (open Mon.-Fri. 10am-6pm). The **post office,** Hafenmarkt 2, 74523 Schwäbisch Hall, hides behind the *Rathaus* (open Mon.-Fri. 8:30am-noon and 2:30-5:30pm, Sat. 8:30am-noon). The **telephone code** is 0791.

Accommodations and Food Schwäbisch Hall's **Jugendherberge (HI),** Langenfelder Weg 5 (tel. 410 50), is past the Marktplatz on the *Galgenberg* ("Gallows Mountain"). Follow Crailsheimerstr. up to take a left onto Langenfelderstr. A legion of couches decks the halls of an unbeatably clean hostel. (Reception at desk open 4:30-7pm, in the kitchen until curfew at 10pm. DM22, over 26 DM27. Members only. Breakfast included. Sheets DM5.50.) **Gasthof Dreikönig,** Neuestr. 25 (tel. 74 73; fax 87 12), offers large, sparse rooms with creaky floors, but is centrally located and a good bargain. Yes, it does look like a restaurant—just barge right in (singles DM45; doubles DM88, with shower DM98). There is a **Campingplatz** (tel. 29 84) at Steinbacher See. Bus #4: "Steinbach/Mitte," then backtrack slightly and follow the signs (person DM7, under 18 DM5; tent DM9; shower DM1; open April to mid-Oct.). **Tav-**

erne bei Vangele, Bahnhofstr. 15, serves a bewildering array of Grecian specialities with a sizable vegetarian section (entrees DM8.50-15; open Thurs.-Tues. 5pm-midnight, Wed. 11:30am-2pm). **Ilge,** Im Weiler 2 (tel. 716 84) is a picturesque setting in which to drink a delectable yogurt shake (DM4-5.20; open daily 11am-1am).

Sights To reach the marvelously preserved *Altstadt* from the Schwäbisch Hall train station, cross Bahnhofstr. and head down the stone steps and footpath toward the river. Turn left on Mauerstr. and cross the wooden footbridges that connect the islands in the Kocher. Finally, follow the winding cobblestone streets to the **Marktplatz.** Use the church tower as a beacon. From the Schwäbisch Hall-Hessental train station, bus #1: "Spitalbach Ost," the last stop (DM2; 20min.). The restrained Baroque *Rathaus* confronts the **Kirche St. Michael,** which perches precariously atop a treacherously steep set of stone stairs. The church's high altar is a Dutch-influenced series of painted panels; one of the paving stones behind the altar has been removed to reveal a medieval **ossuary.** The **Turmzimmer** (tower room) atop the church's high tower provides an incredible view of the perfect rug of red-tiled roofs sloping down into the valley. (Open Mon. 2-5pm, Tues.-Sat. 9am-noon and 2-5pm, Sun. 11am-noon and 2-5pm; mid-Nov. to April Tues.-Sun. 11am-noon. No visits during church services. Entrance to church free, tower DM1.)

A Gothic spire tops the 16th-century **fountain** that stands to one side of the market square. A number of 15th- and 16th-century *Fachwerk* edifices occupy narrow Obere Herrngasse, which leads off the Marktplatz. The old **Keckenburg** harbors the eight-story Romanesque **Keckenturm** and **Hällisch-Fränkisches Museum,** on Keckenhof, one street lower. The museum houses a distinguished set of wood carvings and a smashing Baroque room. (Open Tues. and Thurs.-Sun. 10am-5pm, Wed. 10am-8pm. Tours Sun. at 11am and Wed. at 6:30pm. Free, with varying fees for special exhibits.) The covered **Henkersbrücke** (Hangman's Bridge), down Neuestr. from the Marktplatz, delivers a view of Schwäbisch Hall's bubbling brook of a river with crooning ducks; look for the two old ladies who've set up a fortune telling booth right on the bridge. A few blocks farther into the lower city is the **Henkersturm** (Hangman's Tower—sense a trend here?), with a disappointingly less than grisly appearance. In the northern part of the *Altstadt,* the old street **Gelbinger Gasse** is the town's most beautiful section. For a relaxing walk along the river, the gardens of the **Ackeranlage** back the tremendous architectural vista with tall, shady trees.

Above town on an adjacent hill, the **Comburg** (tel. 25 48)—monastery, castle, and now an institute for teacher training—dates to the 11th century. The fully preserved wall provides peep holes for views of the valley, and the 18th-century Baroque truffle of a church, marble-gold flavor, satiates any craving for Bavaria. Bus #4: "Steinbach/Mitte," cross the street, and head left around and right up Bildersteige. (Open April.-Oct. Tues.-Sat. 10am-noon and 1:30-5pm, Sun. 1:30-5pm; Nov.-March call for appointment. DM2, students DM1.) The **Hohenloher Freilandmuseum** (open-air museum) in Museumsdorf Wackershofen (tel. 97 10 10) packages a tiny 50-building village into a delectable morsel of *Vergangenheit,* with all sorts of animals and vegetables (including humans and pigs) taking part in a cheerful reenactment of an old German agricultural village. Watch Schnapps being made. *Prost!* Touch a cow. (Open May-Sept. daily 10am-6pm; April-Oct. Tues.-Sun. 10am-5:30pm.)

Entertainment On summer evenings between mid-June and mid-August the **Freilichtspiele,** a series of old and modern plays running from Shakespeare to Brecht, are performed on the steps of the Kirche St. Michael. For schedules and tickets (DM20-45, student discounts DM6-10; some concerts run only DM7-10), contact **Freilichtspiele Schwäbisch Hall,** Am Markt 8 (tel. 75 13 11; open Mon.-Fri. 9am-noon, 2-5pm; during Freilichtspiele open Mon.-Fri. 9am-noon and 3-8:30pm, Sun. 3-8:30pm). When rehearsals occur on the steps (quite frequently), you can watch the directors do their thing for free. On the Saturday, Sunday, and Monday of Pentecost and again on the following Monday, Schwäbisch Hall celebrates the **Brunnenfest** (fountain festival), during which locals don 16th-century salt-boilers' costumes to dance a traditional jig. During **Sommernachtsfest** in the last weekend of August, 30,000 little candles light patterns along the Akeranlage. Live music and fireworks brighten these summer nights.

■ Schwäbische Alb (Swabian Jura)

The limestone plateaus, sharp ridges, and pine-forested valleys stretching from Tübingen in the north to the tropical Bodensee in the south are collectively known as the Schwäbische Alb, a region often considered an ugly cousin of the adjacent Schwarzwald. But the periphery is colored by the brush of the exotic and a bit of the uncanny. Its rough-hewn landscape is scenic yet stubborn, with a harsh climate that often vents its wrath on travelers. The powerful medieval dynasties that held the area in their sway found the Swabian peaks perfect sites for fortification, as they command panoramic views of the surrounding valleys. Big-time families like the Hohenstaufens filled the region with castles and abbeys. The **Schwäbische Albstraße** (Swabian Jura Road) bisects the plateau, intersecting the Romantische Straße at Nördlingen. A web of trails serves hikers; maps are available at regional tourist offices in major towns. These towns have a tranquil aura that is ideal for rest and rejuvenation; nightlife doesn't have much of a place in the *Alb*. Train service to many points is roundabout and often incomplete, but bus routes pick up the slack.Schwäbische Alb

SCHWÄBISCH GMÜND

Schwäbisch Gmünd, located on the northern cusp of the range, provides a base for excursions into the region. The town itself has been a center for metalworking—particularly silversmithing—since the 18th century. Beautifully wrought jewelry and ornaments can be found in many shops in the town center. The blossoming of this industry in the 18th century resulted in a building boom that left the town with a market square surrounded by Baroque plaster facades and *Fachwerk* buildings dating from the 15th and 16th centuries. An American military base once inhabited Schwäbisch Gmünd's Mutlangen suburb. Here protests erupted in the early 80s over the stationing of U.S. Pershing missiles in Germany, drawing the likes of brilliant writer and political activist Günter Grass to the town. However, the GIs left after the fall of East Germany, and the former barracks have now transformed into a campus for the University of Maryland. Go Terps.

The 14th-century **Heiligkreuzmünster** (Holy Cross Cathedral), on Münsterpl., is one of the most compellingly freakish churches every built. The roof was too weak to support any towers, and the boxy compromise renders the building decidedly nonecclesiastic in appearance. Perhaps to compensate for this shortcoming, the powers-that-be have covered the exterior in frightening and amusing statues that protrude horizontally in every direction. The bizarre collection ranges from screaming, tortured human figures to large-fanged beasts of all varieties to one bright green frog. The **Silberwaren- und Bijouteriemuseum** (Silver and Jewelry Museum), across from the tourist office (tel. 389 10), features real, live silversmiths tooling silver in the traditional style. Exhibits cover the history of the silver trade, Silver Age, and silver arts (open Wed. and Sat. 2-5pm, Sun. 10am-noon and 2-5pm; DM5, students DM2).

The 16th-century **Kornhaus,** an old grain storage building right off the Marktplatz, two blocks behind the *Rathaus,* now houses a **tourist office** (tel. 60 34 55; fax 60 34 59). They book rooms for a 5% fee and sell a large selection of maps (open Mon.-Fri. 9am-5:30pm, Sat. 9am-noon). The **post office** is across from the train station (open Mon.-Fri. 8am-noon and 2:30-5:30pm). The **telephone code** is 07171.

Schwäbisch Gmünd's **Jugendherberge (HI),** Taubentalstr. 46/1 (tel. 22 60), is located on the edge of an idyllically forested region criss-crossed by footpaths, only 10 minutes from the train station, and has 4-6 beds in each standard issue, reasonably clean room. Turn left and pass underneath the railroad tracks; follow the road, then veer left onto Taubentalstr. and keep on truckin' uphill. At the end of the street, immediately before the recreational park parking lot, turn right up the path towards the large cream-colored building obscured by trees. (Reception open 5-8pm. Curfew 10pm. DM20, over 26 DM25. Sheets DM5.50. Breakfast included. Call ahead.) **Gasthof Weißer Ochsen,** Parlerstr. 47 (tel. 28 12), has discreet singles (DM35) and one double (DM62). Another accommodation option is the hostel in Hohenstaufen (see below). **Gasthaus "Zum Lamm,"** Rinderbachgasse 19 (tel 26 61), has a nonde-script daily menu (DM8.50-14.50) of Swabian specialties. (Open Mon. 4:30pm-mid-night, Tues. 10:30am-2pm and 6pm-midnight, Wed.-Fri. 10:30am-2pm and 4:30pm-midnight, Sat.-Sun. 11am-2pm.) An open-air **market** fills the Münsterpl. every Wednesday and Saturday (7am-noon).

THE KAISERBERGE

Just south of Schwäbisch Gmünd lie the three conical peaks, **Hohenstaufen, Hohen-rechberg,** and **Stuifen,** which make up the **Kaiserberge.** This curtain of mountains marks the beginning of the Schwäbische Alb. Hohenstaufen was named after the cas-tle that once graced its summit, built by the Hohenstaufens, one of Germany's great medieval dynastic families. The castle is gone, but the view of the other two Kaiser-berge peaks and of the Schwäbische Alb in the distance is spectacular. To reach Hohenstaufen, take bus #12 from Schwäbisch Gmünd to either Straßdorf or the vil-lage of Hohenstaufen (bus #13 on Sun. and holidays only). The trail to the top takes about 30 minutes. Or, take the bus to the Hohenstaufen: "Juhe," and put yourself right in the middle of hill action around **Jugendherberge Hohenstaufen,** Schotten-gasse 45 (tel. (07165) 438; fax 14 18), which has six- and eight-bed rooms on a gently sloping plain. (DM22, over 26 DM27. Sheets DM5.50. Breakfast included. Call ahead.)

Hohenrechberg, to the east, has a mysterious **castle ruin** and a Baroque **Wallfahr-tskirche** (pilgrimage church). The old castle wall now functions as the foundation for a footpath. To reach Hohenrechberg, take the bus from Schwäbisch Gmünd to the village of **Rechberg.** It's about a one-hour climb from there. **Stuifen,** also close to Rechberg, can also be hiked, but there are no flashy ruins, and the view is nowhere near as compelling as it is from the other peaks. The **tourist office** in Schwäbisch Gmünd has a number of hiking maps with routes. All buses to the Kaiserberge from Schwäbisch Gmünd run from the train station.

HAIGERLOCH AND HECHINGEN

Haigerloch exemplifies both the rural charm and the isolation that mark much of the Schwäbische Alb. The layout of the tiny but colorful hamlet defies all logic. Built along a single road, coiling its way from the *Oberstadt* (upper city) to the *Unterstadt* (lower city), an enormous jagged cliff inexplicably cuts Haigerloch in half. This bizarre environment acts as a magnet for creative individuals—a group of young art-ists occupies the local **Schloß,** jutting upward on a ridge opposite the *Oberstadt.* The beautiful interior of the *Schloß* displays works by these and other contemporary Ger-man artists. The castle also sponsors a series of jazz and classical performances (for schedules of the events, contact the local tourist office). While the *Schloß*-terrace offers an awesome view of the sharp cliffs and the weeping valley, an easy three-minute hike along the path marked "Kapf" offers an even more striking panorama.

Between the *Schloß* and the *Unterstadt,* along the stone stairway that leads up from the Marktplatz, lurks the deceptive **Schloßkirche** (open daily 9am-6pm). While the exterior of the church is anonymous with its classical red roof and white facades, the interior is a flashy cacophony of flamboyant biblical and historical paintings, bright pink walls, and endless shiny gold ornaments. Mmm…tastes like birthday cake. The back wall of the **Evangelische Kirche** sports an imitation of da Vinci's *The Last Supper,* which, as the church's sole decoration, deserves a glimpse. From the Marktplatz, walk over the Noyaler Bridge to Hechingerstr. and climb the pedestrian path marked "Steigle" to Oberstadtstr. The church is 200m uphill. The building far-ther uphill from the Evangelische Kirche (visible from the *Schloß*) is the **Römerturm.** If your thirst for views remains unsatiated, you can ascend it and glance around (open April-Oct. Sat.-Sun. 10am-6pm). Around the corner from the bottom of the *Schloß* stairway, in an old beer cellar tucked into the cliff, hides the **Atomkeller Museum** (atom-cellar; tel. 18 00). Near the end of World War II, the German physicists Heisenberg and von Weizsäcker struggled, albeit unsuccessfully, to generate a self-sustaining nuclear chain reaction. Their reactor can be seen much as it was when American troops stormed it in April 1945. The museum itself is a single cold room with bare rock walls and cold water dripping from the ceiling (open May-Sept. daily 10am-noon and 2-5pm; March-April and Oct.-Nov. Sat.-Sun. 10am-noon and 2-5pm; DM2). More along the lines of the Schloßkirche is the **St. Annakirche,** farther up Oberstadtstr. Not quite as gaudy as its sister across the valley, St. Anna has her own charm, flaunting ceilings entirely covered in garish paintings of Heaven's glowing gates.

Omnibus #10 connects Haigerloch to the rest of the world, via Horb to the northwest (30min.; DM5.50), and Hechingen to the east (35min.; DM6.40) only a few times per day. The easiest place to catch the bus from either town is at the train station (next to the phone booth in Hechingen and at Steig 6 in Horb; make sure it's obvious that you're waiting or the bus will speed by). Buses drop passengers at several points in Haigerloch; the most common are the Marktplatz in the *Unterstadt* and the *Obere Apotheke* on the outskirts of the *Oberstadt.* All stops are close to the town center. The **tourist office,** Oberstadtstr. 11 (tel. 697 26 or 697 27), inside the *Rathaus,* has maps, information, and an exhibit on the guy who plagiarized *The Last Supper* (open Mon.-Fri. 9am-noon, Mon.-Wed. 2-5pm, Thurs. 2-6:30pm). To reach the tourist office from the Marktplatz, cross the bridge, turn right onto Oberstadtstr. From the *Obere Apotheke,* follow Oberstadtstr.'s curvy descent for 10-15 minutes. Watch out for the "S" on bus schedules; it indicates buses that run only on school days. Overnight visitors might head to **Krone,** Oberstadtstr. 47 (tel. 954 40; fax 95 44 44), between the Römerturm and St. Anna, which has handsome rooms with white fluffy pillows, all with TV and phone (singles with shower DM55-65; doubles DM100-120; breakfast included; AmEx, MC, Visa). The **telephone code** is 07474.

In trying to get to or from Haigerloch, you will probably end up in **Hechingen,** a town that's nearly free of tourists. In the distance, often ringed by mist, **Burg Hohenzollern** rises majestically above a carpet of trees. The castle is the ancestral home of the Hohenzollern family, which "ruled" a unified Germany from 1871 to 1918 under Kaisers Wilhelm I and II. The current edifice (most of it built during the first half of the 19th century) is a tremendous conglomeration of spiraling towers and imposing battlements that makes Snow White's castle pout with envy. It seems impossible to associate it with the modern world, even though it was inhabited through the first half of the 20th century. An incredible panoramic view extends to the Swiss Alps on clear days. Admission to the castle includes a 45-minute tour in which participants are required to wear enormous slippers to protect the floors (open daily 9am-5:30pm; mid-Oct. to mid-March 9am-4:30pm; DM7, students DM3). Unfortunately, no public transportation connects Hechingen to the castle. Taking a taxi will cost DM15 (some penny-pinching travelers split the cost or hitch the distance). The one-and-a-half-hour walk from the train station through beautiful country is also an option. From the *Rathaus* (see below) walk down Heiligkreuzstr., take a left at the Heilig-Kreuz-Frischof (cemetery), go under the railroad bridge, and take the first right towards the woods. There are a myriad of trails through the woods to the castle. If you keep heading up, you'll probably get there. This is facilitated by the map distributed at the **tourist office,** Marktplatz 1 (tel. (07471) 94 01 14; fax 94 01 08), in the *Rathaus.* From the train station, go straight into the city and keep walking up. A golden ball adorns the *Rathaus* (open Mon.-Thurs. 8am-12:30pm and 2-4pm, 8am-12:30pm).

The best value for overnight accommodations in Hechingen is at the comforting **Hotel Mohren,** Schloßstr. 18 (tel. (07471) 23 93), which has a well-worn wooden staircase, pleasant bathrooms, and spacious rooms with soft beds. (Singles DM35, with shower DM45; doubles DM70, with shower DM90. Breakfast included.)

BADEN-WÜRTTEMBERG

■ Stuttgart

Visiting Stuttgart is like stepping into a little piece of the archetypal utopian ideal. Blown to bits in World War II, the city had nowhere to move but the future, to which it heads with unmitigated optimism. Despite the rampant modernization, Stuttgart gloats in one of the most verdant settings of any major German city. Surrounded by green hills, criss-crossed by leafy parks, and laced by a vineyard that stretches to the *Hauptbahnhof,* the city swathes all traces of urban blight in a cloak of lush green. The fertile ground also sowed the seeds for a number of highly successful businesses. Sleek glass and steel buildings extend to the farthest suburbs, connected by the remarkably comprehensive regional rail system. Porsche, Daimler-Benz, and a host of other corporate thoroughbreds graze here. Still, as the capital of Baden-Württemberg, Stuttgart maintains a thriving cultural scene, maintaining an aura of tranquility and repose that create a blissfully livable metropolis.

ORIENTATION AND PRACTICAL INFORMATION

At the heart of Stuttgart lies an enormous pedestrian zone where shops and restaurants stretch as far as the eye can see. **Königstraße** and **Lautenschlagerstraße** are the main pedestrian thoroughfares; from the train station, both are accessible through the underground **Arnulf-Klett-Passage.** To the left lies the tranquil swath of green called the *Schloßgarten,* to the right the thriving business sector. Stuttgart sells itself as a compact city, and in comparison to many American sprawlers, it is. But sooner or later you will have to ride a train or U-Bahn.

Tourist Offices: I-Punkt, Königstr. 1 (tel. 222 80; fax 222 82 53), directly in front of the escalator down into the Klett-Passage. Books rooms for free, sells excellent maps (DM1), distributes bus and train schedules, and speaks English. Their *Monatsspiegel* (in German; DM3.50) lists museum hours, cultural events, and musical performances, and includes a guide to food and nightlife. Open May-Oct. Mon.-Fri. 9:30am-8:30pm, Sat. 9:30am-6pm, Sun. and public holidays 11am-6pm; Nov.-April same hours but Sun. and holidays only 1-6pm. **Tips 'n' Trips,** Rotebühlpl. 26/7 (tel. 222 27 30; fax 222 27 33; email jugendinformation@tips-n-trips.s.shuttle.de; http://www.s.shuttle.de/tips-n-trips), in the underground U-Bahn passage at Theodor-Heuss-Str. and Fritz-Elsas-Str. Hip and ultra-helpful staff hands out reams of youth-oriented pamphlets (in German and English) about travel and the Stuttgart scene. A great resource. Open Mon.-Fri. noon-7pm, Sat. 10am-4pm.

Consulates: South Africa, Erich-Herren-Str. 27 (tel. 58 64 41) **U.K.,** Breitestr. 2 (tel. 16 26 90).

American Express: Lautenschlagerstr. 3 (tel. 187 50; fax 187 51 32), one block south of the station. Holds mail and cashes traveler's checks. Open Mon.-Fri. 9:30-6pm, Sat. 9:30am-12:30pm. Another second branch, Schillerpl. 4 (tel. 162 49 20; fax 162 49 22), by the Schloßpl. offers the same services and hours.

Flights: Flughafen Stuttgart flies to every Germany city and to other countries (tel. 948 33 88 for schedule info). S-Bahn #2 or 3 to the city (30min.; DM4.60 one way).

Trains: tel. 194 19 for 24hr. schedule information. A public transportation office (tel. 79 30 24) can be found at the station and at the airport, 1 floor downstairs from arrivals. Open Mon.-Fri. 7am-1pm and 1:30-6:40pm, Sat. 8:30am-2pm. The transportation hub of southwestern Germany, Stuttgart has direct rail links to most major German cities. Trains roll to Munich (30 per day, 2½hr.), Berlin (12 per day, 6hr.), Frankfurt (every hr., 1½hr.), and Paris (10 per day, 6hr.).

Public Transportation: Information office, Arnulf-Klett-Passage (tel. 250 53 03), next to the escalator up to Königstr. Look for the *"Kundenberatung"* sign. Bus, streetcar, U-Bahn, and S-Bahn maps and schedules, along with needed map-and-schedule deciphering. Open Mon.-Fri. 9am-6pm, Sat. 9am-noon. A **single-ride ticket** runs DM3.20-9.60. 4-ride *Mehrfahrkarten* range DM10.20-33.20; they save 10% off single ride rates. *Tageskarten*—day passes for trains and buses (except night buses)—are DM18.50; these handy passes also entitle you to free transport of 2 kids and a dog. A *Kurzstrecke* pass (DM1.70) covers short distances. Railpasses

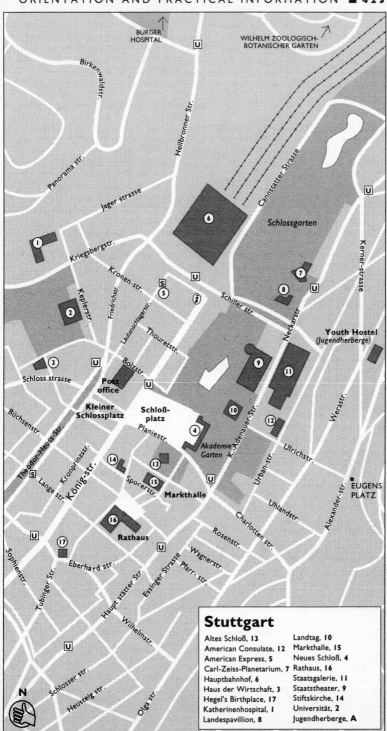

Stuttgart

Altes Schloß, 13
American Consulate, 12
American Express, 5
Carl-Zeiss-Planetarium, 7
Hauptbahnhof, 6
Haus der Wirtschaft, 3
Hegel's Birthplace, 17
Katherinenhospital, 1
Landespavillion, 8

Landtag, 10
Markthalle, 15
Neues Schloß, 4
Rathaus, 16
Staatsgalerie, 11
Staatstheater, 9
Stiftskirche, 14
Universität, 2
Jugendherberge, **A**

are valid *only* on the S-Bahn. **Nachtbus** (night bus) stops are marked with purple-and-yellow signs. The tourist office has a free schedule. Those staying in city accommodations are eligible for a **great deal**—DM12 for 3 days of U-Bahn travel, DM19 for 3 days of travel on the entire transportation system. More info at the tourist office.

Ferries: Neckar-Personen-Schiffahrt (tel. 54 10 73; fax 54 50 80). Boats cruise from Bad Cannstatt (across the river) to little towns along the Neckar (1-2 per day). Round-trip DM9.60-49.60. They're good for alternative transportation. Many older folks take the boats to dance polka and recall the good old days; bring your accordion or a good set of earplugs. Harbor **tours** Sun.-Fri. 9am and 11am (2hr.; DM14).

Car Rental: Europacar (tel. 223 71 36; fax 223 88 05), **Hertz** (tel. 226 29 21; fax 226 27 10), **Avis** (tel. 223 72 58), and **Sixt/Budget** (tel. 223 78 22) share an office at the *Hauptbahnhof* next to track 16. Open Mon.-Fri. 8am-6pm, Sat. 8am-noon.

Bike Rental: Rent a Bike (tel. 209 90). 1hr. DM8, 6hr. DM18, 24hr. DM25, weekend (Fri.-Sun.) DM65, week DM100.

Mitfahrzentrale: Two of 'em: **Stuttgart West,** Lerchenstr. 65 (tel. 636 80 36). Bus #42 (direction: "Schreiberstr.): "Rosenberg/Johannesstr." **Hauptstätterstr. 154** (tel. 60 36 06). U-Bahn #14 (direction: "Heslach/Vogelrain"): "Marienpl." Both open Mon.-Fri. 9am-6pm, Sat. 9am-2pm, Sun. 11am-2pm.

Lost and Found: Fundbüro der Stadtverwaltung, Eberhardstr. 61f (tel. 216 20 16). Open Mon.-Wed. 8am-1pm, Thurs. 8:30am-3:30pm, Fri. 8:30am-12:30pm. **Fundbüro der Deutschen Bundesbahn,** (tel. 20 92 or 24 68) in the *Hauptbahnhof.* Open Mon.-Thurs. 8am-noon and 1-3:30pm, Fri. 8am-noon and 1-2:30pm.

Bookstore: Buchhaus Wittwer, Königstr. 30 (tel. 250 70), right off the Schloßpl., has a truly gigantic selection of English language books and a bevy of bargain bins outside. Open Mon.-Fri. 9:30am-8pm, Sat. 9am-4pm.

Cultural Center: James-F.-Byrnes-Institut, Charlottenpl. 17, Innenhof, Eingang 3 (tel. 22 81 80; fax 228 18 40). Offers a full range of lectures, movies, and discussion groups about American culture and U.S.-German relations.

Gay Information Line: Rosa Telefon (tel. 194 46). Fri. 7-9pm or leave a message.

Laundromat: SB Wasch Salon, Kienbachstr. 16 (tel. 52 30 08). S-Bahn #13 (direction: "Giebel-Hedelfingen"): "Kienbachstr." Wash DM8, dry DM2 per 10min. Open daily 8am-10pm.

Pharmacies: For a schedule of 24hr. pharmacies, buy *Amtsblatt* for DM1.20 from the tourist office, or have a look at the copy posted at the *Rathaus.* **Internationale,** Königstr. 70 (tel. 22 47 80), is a centrally-located pharmacy. Open Mon.-Wed. and Fri. 8:30am-6:30pm, Thurs. 8:30am-8:30pm, Sat. 8:30am-2pm.

Hospital: Bürgerhospital, Tunzhoferstr. 14-16 (tel. 253 00).

Emergency: tel. 110. **Police,** Hahnemannstr. 1 (tel. 899 01).

Internet Access: On the 3rd floor of the **Karstadt department store,** 1 block from the Königstr. tourist office. 30min. DM5. Open Mon.-Fri. 9am-8pm, Sat. 9am-4pm.

Post Office: At the *Hauptbahnhof,* 70001 Stuttgart (tel. 226 03 30). Open Mon.-Fri. 8am-8pm, Sat. 8am-2pm, Sun. 10am-2pm. To mail packages, use the post office at Bolzstr. 3, 18750 Stuttgart (tel. 225 43 31); does not hold mail. Open Mon.-Fri. 9am-8pm, Sat. 9am-2pm.

Telephone Code: 0711.

ACCOMMODATIONS AND CAMPING

Most of Stuttgart's budget beds are located on the two ridges surrounding the downtown area and are easily accessible by streetcar. Accommodations around the pedestrian zone and train station cater to customers used to paying top *Mark* for creature comforts. Make "call ahead" your mantra. Contact Tips 'n' Trips (see **Tourist Offices,** above) for information on cheap overnighting in Stuttgart. WHile further away, the *Jugendherbergen* in Esslingen and Ludwigsburg are good alternatives.

Jugendherberge Stuttgart (HI), Haußmannstr. 27 (tel. 24 15 83; fax 236 10 41). Take the "ZOB" exit of the Klett-Passage, continue through the *Schloßgarten,* and follow the signs leading uphill via the paved path. Or U-Bahn #15 (direction: "Heumaden"): "Eugenspl." and go down the hill, bearing left down Kernerstr. Entrance on Kernerstr. A lively mix of nationalities shacks up in slightly crowded 6-bed rooms, most offering spectacular city views. The 220 beds are often completely full; *always* call ahead. Reception open 7-8:45am and noon-11pm. Lockout 9am-noon. Curfew 11:30pm, but doors re-open for 5min. at 1am. DM22, over 26 DM27. Sheets DM5.50. Breakfast included.

Jugendgästehaus Stuttgart, Richard-Wagner-Str. 2 (tel. 24 11 32). Straßenbahn #15 (direction: "Heumaden"): "Bubenbad." Continue in direction of the U-Bahn on the right side of street and veer right immediately; the place is on the right. *Right.* Excellent dorm-hostel situated in a quiet residential neighborhood offers spotless rooms with a great view. The location far from the city center and the endless climb that makes walking impossible are drawbacks. Reception open Mon.-Fri. 9am-8pm, Sat.-Sun. 11am-8pm. No curfew. Singles DM35, with bath DM50; doubles DM70, DM90; triples DM90, DM105. DM5 extra per person for single-night stays. Breakfast and lockers included. Dinner 6pm (DM7). Key deposit DM20.

Haus Berg, Karl-Schurz-Str. 16A (tel. 26 18 75; fax 286 46 39). U-Bahn #14: "Mineralbäder," then cut diagonally left through the Mineral Bad-Berg parking lot on the right side of the tracks and climb the hill. Neat rooms managed by a youthful, friendly staff. Reception open 24hr. Singles DM55, with bath DM70; doubles DM85, with shower DM100. DM5 cheaper on weekends. Discounts for longer stays and breakfast skippers. Call ahead if arriving after 10pm.

Pension Märklin, Friedrichstr. 39 (tel. 29 13 15). Convenient, period. Take a right from the station and turn left on Friedrichstr. Singles DM45-50; doubles DM80-90. No breakfast, but you can avail yourself of the showers and the bathtub. No lockouts, few rules—get your keys and kick back.

Tramper Point Stuttgart, Wienerstr. 317 (tel. 817 74 76; fax 237 28 10). U-Bahn #6 (direction: "Giebel"): "Sportpark Feuerbach," then go left. It's the mural-covered wood structure on the right. Funkiest alternative accommodations in town: shack up here on one of 25 cots in a crescent-shaped room, or an *Iso-matte* in case of overflow. Reception open 5-11:30pm. 3-night max. stay. Ages 16-27 only. DM13. Wool blanket DM1.50, or bring your own sleeping bag. Breakfast and shower included. Open late-June to early-Sept.

Camping: Campingplatz Cannstatter Wasen, Mercedesstr. 40 (tel. 55 66 96; fax 48 69 47), on the river in Bad Cannstatt. S-Bahn #1, 2, or 3: "Bad Cannstatt." Exit through the back of the station and follow the signs for "Wasen." After the tunnel, head diagonally left across the huge parking lot. Reception open 7am-noon and 2-10pm. Adults DM8, kids DM4. Tent DM6-8. Car DM4. Pets DM4.

FOOD

Due to a sizable contingent of *Gastarbeiter* (guest workers), Stuttgart's restaurant scene is heartily spiced with Greek, Turkish, African, and Asian eateries as well as an astounding variety of snack bars. But the cuisine of the *Schwaben* region is itself one of the most successful forms of German food. *Spätzle* (thick noodles) and *Maultaschen* (pasta pockets filled with meat and spinach) are especially prevalent. Ask at Tips 'n' Trips for a list (in German or English) of inexpensive eateries and pubs (see **Tourist Offices,** p. 424). The Wochenmarkt is on Marktplatz and Schillerpl. (Thurs. and Sat. 8am-3pm). For groceries, try the basement of **Kaufhof,** two blocks from the train station (open Mon.-Fri. 9am-8pm, Sat. 9am-4pm).

University Mensa, Holzgartenstr. 11. From the *Bahnhof,* take Kriegsbergstr. to Holzgartenstr., turn left, and go down the right side of the street over the underpass; it's on the right. A plain but functional place where quantity compensates for quality (meals DM4-5). Open during school (mid-April to late-July and mid-Oct. to mid.-Feb.) Mon.-Fri. 11am-3pm.; the rest of the year Mon.-Fri. 11:15am-1:30pm.

Iden, Eberhardstr. 1 (tel. 23 59 89). U-Bahn: "Rathaus." Cheap, good vegetarian fare served cafeteria-style. Fifty kinds of salads (DM2.65 per 100g), noodles, and potatoes, served in a bright atmosphere with lots of Nordic furniture. Open Mon.-Fri. 11am-9pm, Sat. 10am-5pm.

Academie der Schönsten Künste, Charlottenstr. 5 (tel. 24 24 36). U-Bahn: "Charlottenpl." High ceilings, art-covered walls, a garden, and fewer seats than necessary at

BADEN-WÜRTTEMBERG

such a cool place. Light fare, mellow atmosphere, and breakfast served in the afternoon (DM3-15). Open Mon.-Fri. 7am-midnight, Sat.-Sun. 9am-4pm.

Weinhaus Stetter, Rosenstr. 32 (tel. 24 01 63). U-Bahn: "Charlottenpl.," walk down
Esslingerstr. and take a left onto Rosenstr. Offers intriguing Swabian specialties
(DM7-9), all to be washed down with an incredible wine selection (DM5-7). Open
Mon.-Fri. 3-11pm, Sat.-Sun. 10am-2pm.

Waschsalon, Charlottenstr. 27, at the corner of Charlottenstr. and Alexanderstr. U-
Bahn: "Olgaeck." A *Kneipe* that suffers from a severe identity crisis—it thinks it's a
laundromat! Schwäbisch dishes, crepes, and other light fare adorn the tables, while
articles of clothing grace the walls. Wild potatoes (like home fries with veggies and
special sauce) DM7. Open Sun.-Fri. 10am-1am, Sat. 4pm-1am.

Restaurant Marché, Königstr. 16, is a self-service chain restaurant with salad, pasta,
seafood, and meat selections in a Disney-esque space with themed dining areas and
an enormous synthetic tree (open daily 8am-11pm).

SIGHTS

Stuttgart's sparkling modern architecture hides a paucity of historical attractions. Still,
the city possesses several sights and museums that fascinate. The **Schloßgarten,** Stuttgart's main municipal park, runs from the station southward to the *Neues Schloß* and
northeast to the Neckar; it's crammed with fountains and beautifully tended flower
gardens. The north end of the *Schloßgarten* contains the expansive **Rosensteinpark,**
which also holds the **Wilhelma** (tel. 540 20), a large zoological/botanical garden with
over 1000 species of animals and plants (open daily 8:15am-5:30pm; Nov.-Feb.
8:15am-4pm; DM11, students DM5). The *Schloßgarten* runs to the **Schloßplatz,** off
Königstr., upon which reposes the elegant, Baroque **Neues Schloß,** now home to
stodgy bureaucrats.

The 16th-century **Altes Schloß** (across the street on Schillerpl.) is Stuttgart's only
other architecturally notable sight. To interface with the *Weltgeist* (world-spirit),
head to **Hegel's birthplace,** Eberhardstr. 53 (tel. 216 67 33), a couple blocks from
Königstr.—just a few doors down from **a busy porn shop** (there was always something obscene about the philosopher...). The house provides a thorough, if somewhat inscrutable, exegesis of the philosopher's life through letters, manuscripts, and
notes (open Mon.-Fri. 10am-6:30pm, Sat. 10am-5pm).

Stargazers feast their eyes at the **Karl-Zeiss-Planetarium,** Willi-Brandt-Str. 25. (tel.
162 92 15; fax 216 39 12). U-Bahn #1, 4, 9, or 14 or streetcar #2: "Staatsgalerie" or
simply walk from the south exit of the main train station down into the *Schloßgarten*
for about 200m. For DM9 (students DM5) you can attend one of the shows inside the
big cupola with plenty of cool visual effects—stars falling, comets shooting, black
holes sucking. (Shows Tues. and Thurs. 10am and 3pm, Wed. and Fri. 10am, 3, and
8pm, Sat.-Sun. 2, 4, and 6pm.) During nice weather, would-be astronomers can peer
through the telescope at the canopy of heavens (Mon. and Wed.-Sat. 9-10pm).

MUSEUMS

An outstanding and diverse collection of museums compensate for a scarcity of old,
beautiful, and impressive buildings. In addition to the magnificent art galleries, the
city offers notable displays of beer and cars in a rare instance in which drinking and
driving mix quite well. The monthly *Monatsspiegel* (see **Tourist Offices,** p. 424)
details visiting exhibitions and permanent collections.

Staatsgalerie Stuttgart, Konrad-Adenauer-Str. 30-32 (tel. 212 40 50; fax 212 40 68),
across from the *Schloßgarten*. An absolutely superb collection housed in two separate parts: the stately paintings in the **old wing** span from the Middle Ages to the
19th century; the **new wing,** a controversial stroke of colorful postmodern architecture, contains an essential collection of moderns including Picasso, Kandinsky,
Beckmann, and Dalí. Open Wed. and Fri.-Sun. 10am-5pm, Tues. and Thurs. 10am-
8pm. DM5, students DM3.

Württembergisches Landesmuseum (tel. 279 34 00) in the Altes Schloß, details the Schwäbische region and people, with an emphasis on archaeological exhibits. From skulls and crown jewels to displays of chains from the 17th to 20th centuries, the museum quenches historical cravings. Special exhibits occasionally housed in the Hauptbahnhof. Open Tues. 10am-1pm, Wed.-Sun. 10am-5pm. DM5, students DM3. Wheelchair accessible.

Mercedes-Benz Museum, Mercedesstr. 137, Stuttgart-Bad Cannstatt (tel. 172 25 78). S-Bahn #1: "Neckarstadion," and walk left under the bridge and left at the next intersection. Residing in the actual workshop where Herr Daimler built the first generation of Mercedes-Benzes (named after his daughter Benz), the exhibit covers the history of the automobile, from its invention to the super-sleek James-Bond-mobiles now on the drawing board. Tight security weeds out BMW spies; you even need to take a special bus from the parking lot to the entrance. Open Tues.-Sun. 9am-5pm. Free.

Porsche Museum, Porschestr. 42, Stuttgart-Zuffauhausen (tel. 827 56 85). S-Bahn #6 (direction: "Weil-der-Stadt"): "Neuwirtshaus;" exit the station to the right (don't go under the tracks). Tells much the same story as the Mercedes museum with curvier and racier cars. Housed in a bright pink factory looking like it should be making cosmetics instead of world-class sports cars for Schicki-Mickis. Open Mon.-Fri. 9am-4pm, Sat.-Sun. 9am-5pm. Free.

Württembergischer Kunstverein, Schloßpl. 2 (tel. 22 33 70; fax 29 36 17), directly across from the *Altes Schloß.* Ultra-modern paintings and sculptures in a somewhat small but very intriguing museum. Every year, eight to 10 exhibits document the art of our time. Open Tues. and Thurs.-Sun. 11am-6pm, Wed. 11am-8pm. Free, but DM8 for special exhibits, students DM5.

Schwäbisches Brauereimuseum Stuttgart, Robert-Koch-Str. 12, Stuttgart-Vaihingen (tel. 737 02 01). U-Bahn #1, 3, or 6, or S-Bahn #1-3: "Vaihinger Bahnhof." Only in Germany could an entire museum be devoted to beer. Five millennia of the frothy beverage's history culminate in an exhibit on current brewing techniques. Sorry, no free samples. Open Wed.-Sun. 10:30am-5:30pm.

Deutsches Spielkarten-Museum, Schönbuschstr. 32 (tel 160 03 35). U-Bahn #5: "Leinfelden." The most thorough of its kind in Europe, this playing-card museum carries a fully international deck. Open Tues.-Fri. 2-5pm, Sun. 10am-1pm.

Keplermuseum, Keplergasse 2, Weil-der-Stadt. S-Bahn #6: "Weil-der-Stadt" (30min.; DM7.60), right down Bahnhofstr., left on Poststr. as it becomes Scheergasse, leading to the Markt. The birthplace of astronomical genius Johannes Kepler, who first imagined the planets' orbits as ellipses, is the only thing keeping this Stuttgart satellite from drifting off into uncharted regions of outer space. Mechanical models explain the difference between circles and ellipses—oh, so difficult. Open Tues.-Fri. 10am-noon and 2-4pm, Sat. 11am-noon and 2-4pm, Sun. 11am-noon and 2-5pm. Oct.-May closed Sun. DM1, students DM0.50.

ENTERTAINMENT

The **Staatstheater,** just across the plaza from the *Neues Schloß,* is Stuttgart's most famous theater, with opera, ballet, plays, and concerts by the dozen (24hr. ticket information tel. 197 03; box office tel. 22 17 95; telephone lines open Mon.-Fri. 10am-1pm and 2-5pm; box office open Mon.-Fri. 10am-6pm, Sat. 9am-1pm; DM16-90; student discounts available.) There are 25 other local theaters, and tickets for them are usually much cheaper (DM10-25, students DM5-15). The tourist office provides schedules and sells tickets, which can also be purchased at the **Kartenhäusle,** Kleiner Schloßpl. (tel. 29 55 83; open Mon.-Fri. 9am-6pm, Sat. 9am-1pm; telephone lines open 9am-noon and 2-5pm). Also check out a *Lift* brochure from the tourist office.

Corso Kino, Hauptstr. 6 (tel. 73 49 16), shows primarily original versions of movies—not dubbed into German—with frequent special festivals and revivals. Make sure you're not paying to see a Japanese movie with German subtitles. *"O.m.U."* means the movie is original with subtitles; *"O.V."* means it's the original version. U-Bahn #1: "Schillerpl." or S-Bahn: "Vaihingen Bahnhof." Schedules in English are available at the tourist office.

BADEN-WÜRTTEMBERG

Stuttgart harbors a number of amazing **mineral baths.** Mineralbad Leuze, Am Leuzebad 2-6 (tel. 216 42 10), is the closest to the city. U-Bahn #1, 2, or 14: "Mineralbäder," and continue in the same direction along the paths on the right side of the tracks (open daily 6am-9pm; a 2hr. healthy bath DM15.50, students DM10.50; massage DM36). Another equally posh facility is **MineralBad Cannstatt,** Sulzerrainstr. 2 (tel. 216 92 40). U-Bahn #2: "Kursaal." Both places offer spectacular arrays of pools, saunas, and showers—the perfect remedy for budget traveler exhaustion. Look for the occasional comical statuette spurting water and puffing steam on the rolling hills (Cannstatt open Mon.-Fri. 9am-9:30pm, Sat. 9am-9pm, Sun. 9am-5pm).

NIGHTLIFE

From pleasant chats over fine Italian coffee to hypnotic, hyperspeed, techno-fueled hysteria, Stuttgart fulfills a full spectrum of nightlife whims. Serious night-prowlers should pick up either *Prinz* (DM5) or *Stuttgart Lift* (DM4.50) at any city newsstand; both contain detailed indices to happenings (but only in German). Tips 'n' Trips (see **Tourist Offices,** p. 424) publishes *Discos* and *Kneipen,* dual language guides to the evening scene. Be assured, Dionysus never sleeps in this city. The area along Königstr. and Calverstr. is stayin' alive in the early evenings with lazy chatter (and beers) spilling from numerous cafes onto sidewalk tables.

Palast der Republik, Friedrichstr. 27 (tel. 226 48 87). An island in the middle of a toiling sea of stylish after-hours aficionados waxing ultra-hip and downing reasonably priced drinks. Beer DM4-6. Come back the next morning for crepes (DM5). Open daily 10am-3am; winter 11am-3am.

The Buddha, *Schwabenzentrum* (tel. 23 52 27). Large, locally famous club with lots of twentysomethings grooving to mainstream dance music and Techno Lite. Big, sweaty, noisy, fun. Open Tues.-Wed. 9pm-2:30am, Thurs. 9pm-3am, Fri. 9pm-5am, Sat. 8pm-6am, Sun. 8pm-3am.

Café Stella, Hauptstätterstr. 57 (tel. 640 25 83). Laid-back cafe with good, cheap food and savvy crowds. Occasional jazz performances add to the hipster atmosphere. Open Mon.-Thurs. 9am-1am, Fri. 9am-2am, Sat. 10am-2am, Sun. 10am-1am.

Zenit, Königstr. 49 (tel. 223 81 64). One of Stuttgart's more bombastic dance locales, Zenit pumps cutting-edge techno and trance to big funky crowds. It's like the Love Parade (see **Love Parade,** p. 127), except that it's smaller, indoors, and not in Berlin. Open Tues.-Fri. after 9pm, Sat. after 8pm, Sun. after 6pm.

Kings Club, Calwerstr. 21 (tel. 226 45 58). Stuttgart's premiere gay disco. Energetic boys jam to happy music of the Erasure genre. Open Wed.-Sun. 10pm-5am.

Laura's Club, Lautenschlagerstr. 20 (tel. 29 01 60). Kings Club's lesbian sister. New diverse, intriguing, and obscure themes every night; call for information. Women only. Open daily 10pm-5am.

■ Near Stuttgart

ESSLINGEN AM NECKAR

Though Esslingen's primary role is as a night-home for thousands of Stuttgart's commuters, it does not scream suburbia. Bounded by steep, terraced vineyards on one side and the Neckar River on the other, Esslingen nurtures an *Altstadt* surrounded by the remnants of the original town fortifications. Though it has a population of over 100,000 and lies within Stuttgart's hegemonic industrial sprawl, Esslingen is a cozy town that defiantly celebrates its independence with many festivals, including the fearsome **Zwiebelfest** (Onion Festival) with its own eye-wateringly delicious mascot—the **Esslingen Zwiebel.**

Esslingen is on the **train** line between Stuttgart and Ulm, and can also be reached by S-Bahn #1 from Stuttgart (every 15-20min.; 20min.; DM4.30, railpasses valid). The **tourist office,** in the *Neues Rathaus* (tel. 35 12 24 41), provides maps and books rooms for free (open Mon.-Fri. 8am-12:30pm and 1:30-5pm, Thurs. until 6pm, Sat. 10am-3pm). The **postal code** is 73728. The **telephone code** is 0711.

To reach the *Altstadt* from the train station, walk down Berlinerstr. over the bridge and to the right. The blazing mauve Renaissance facade of the **Altes Rathaus** looks out over one corner of the square. The **Glockenspiel** sitting atop it has a repertoire of more than 200 songs, including "Yankee Doodle." The asymmetrical towers of the **Stadtkirche St. Dionys,** connected by a small footbridge, guard the other corner of the Marktplatz. The church holds a gorgeous 15th-century rood screen and *pietà* (open daily 8am-6pm; enter through door 4). Up on the hill rises the Gothic stone spire of the **Liebfrauenkirche,** which contains luminous 14th-century stained glass (open daily 8am-7pm; enter through front door). Farther up the ridge among the vineyards stands the **Burg.** The squat, round, half-timbered tower at the right of the *Burg,* appropriately named **Dicker Turm** (fat tower), has a restaurant that can make you round and squat (adjectives, not verbs), too. A romantic view of the town super-imposed on the Swabian Jura backdrop is often accompanied here in the evening by chirping crickets and sounds of giggling couples. Put on your love-goggles and "cou-pleate." Footpaths criss-cross the *Weinberge,* and maps identifying the grape-type for each section of the vineyard are available free at the tourist office. Every first Saturday of the month (April-Dec.), there is a **Flöhmarkt** in Blauerpl. where practically every-thing from vacuum hoses to *Lederhosen* is sold (call 37 15 47 for info). A **market** fills the square with fruit and vegetable stalls (Wed. and Sat. 7-11am).

Esslingen's clean **Jugendherberge (HI),** Neuffenstr. 65 (tel. 38 18 48), is in the Zoll-berg section of town, a grueling 30-minute uphill trek; sane people take bus #118, 119, or 120 to "Zollbergstr." (2-3 per hr.), then cross the street and follow the signs (10min.); overflow from Stuttgart's hostel is usually sent here. (Reception open 3:30-5pm, 6:45-7:30pm, and 8:30-9:45pm. Curfew 10pm, but keys available with DM20 deposit. DM20, over 26 DM25. Members only. Breakfast included. Sheets DM5.50.) **Gasthof Falken,** Bahnhofstr. 4 (tel. 35 72 88), has good clean rooms. Go right from the station until Bahnhofstr. (singles DM30; doubles DM50; no breakfast). Esslingen's cup runneth over with *Weinstuben.* A mosey down Herrgasse takes you past numer-ous notable eating and potable drinking establishments. **Weinkeller Einhorn,** Heu-gasse 17 (tel 35 35 90), serves Swabian specialties (DM8.50-16.50) and cool wine (DM5.80-6.80) from a 700-year-old cellar. Open Mon.-Sat. 6pm-midnight. Esslingen is a young town, and youth must have its fun. **Cafe Mayer,** Unterer Metzgerbach 18/1 (tel. 35 69 60), sports stylish people in stylish chairs. (Beer DM2.50-4.50. Open Mon. 10am-6pm, Tues.-Fri. and Sun. 10am-midnight, Sat. 10am-1am.) **Krokodil,** Rossmarkt 9 (tel. 35 66 23), universally known as "Krok," is a popular bar. Martini, Mr. Sinatra? (Open Mon.-Sat. 11am-1am, Sun. 2pm-1am.)

LUDWIGSBURG

Ludwigsburg popped out of the blue in the early 18th century at the behest of Duke Eberhard of Ludwig. His modest idea: to erect a residential castle in the Duchy's new capital bearing his own name. Unfortunately, Ludwig died before his playground was born, and although his successors finished decorating the castle, they preferred to live in Stuttgart. Even without the aristocratic element, Ludwigsburg lived on to become a lively Baroque city with a lovely little trio of palaces.

The opulent Baroque **Residenzschloß** is worth seeing, even if you find yourself lost among German office fieldtrips. (Open mid-March to mid-Oct. daily 9am-noon and 1-5pm; Nov.-Feb. Mon.-Fri. 10:30am-3pm. Tours in English daily at 1:30pm. The 75min. guided journey is the only way to see Ludwig's three meter long bed (he was almost larger than life: 2m 10cm tall) and the rest of the lavish gold, marble, and velvet inte-rior. The palace is situated in an expansive 30-hectare garden that earned Ludwig's complex the tourist brochure epithet **Blühendes Barock** (Blooming Baroque; open mid-March to mid-Dec. daily 7:30am-8:30pm; DM11, students DM5.50). In addition to various summer festivals held here, a perennial **Märchen Garten** recreates scenes of major fairy tales in a large park of wild vegetation. Join 100 kids yelling, *"Rapunzel, Rapunzel, laß deinen Zopf herunter."* The **Favoritschloß** is an excellent destination for a stroll or picnic (open mid-March to Oct. daily 9am-noon and 1:30-5pm; Nov. to mid-March 10am-noon and 1:30-4pm). This smaller Baroque gem was built as a hunting lodge and big-time party venue for Duke Carl Engler. (Combination tickets are also available; tours of both the *Residenzschloß* and the *Favoritschloß* DM11, students DM5.50.) If you are a genuinely dedicated castle fiend, continue for 30 minutes up the alley through the **Favoriten Park** and marvel at the third of the Ludwig palaces—the Rococo **Montrepos** (tel. 225 50). Unfortunately, the castle is now a luxury hotel and closed to visitors, but you can calm your frustrations by renting a **boat** and rowing on the peaceful lake (open April-Sept.).

To reach Ludwigsburg from Stuttgart, S-Bahn #4 or 5 towards Marbach or Bietigheim (20min.; DM4.30). Another option is to take a **boat** run by Neckar-Personen-Schiffahrt (see **Stuttgart: Practical Information,** p. 424). The **tourist office,** across from the *Rathaus* at Wilhelmstr. 10 (tel. 91 02 52), provides plenty of information and books rooms for free (open Mon.-Fri. 9am-5pm, Sat. 9am-4pm). The only cheap place in town is the **Jugendherberge Ludwigsburg (HI),** Gemsenbergstr. 21 (tel. 515 64; fax 594 40). Bus #422: "Schlößlesfeld." It's the story, of a lovely hostel, with six beds per room, and lots of horizontal lines included for free. (Reception open 9am-1pm and 5-7pm. Curfew 10pm. DM22, over 26 DM27. Breakfast included. Cold meal DM7.50, warm meal DM9.) The **telephone code** is 07141.

There are several restaurants on or near the Holzmarkt. **Corfu,** Holymarktstr 2, serves daily specials in the Greek idiom, including the *Gigante*—a giant bean salad (DM5) and vegetarian entrees (DM8.50-11.50; open daily 11:30am-2:30pm and 5pm-midnight). Grocery stores and bakeries run rampant along Myluisstr. and Arsenalstr.

MARBACH

Friedrich Schiller was born in Marbach, a fact that is difficult to ignore; from drugstores to hair salons, the name of the Jena professor and prolific poet is ubiquitous. The **Schiller Geburtshaus,** Niklastorstr. 31 (tel. 175 67), is where Schiller was born in 1759 (open daily 9am-5pm, except Dec. 25-Dec. 26; DM3, students DM1.50). To get there, follow the signs from the right corner of the railroad station. A live cat resting on a chair on the first floor and a golden pair of Schiller's clubbing pants are somewhat more absorbing than the displays of his birth certificates and cutlery. Unless you are a die-hard Schiller devotee, the **Schiller-National Museum,** Schillerhöhe 8-10 (tel. 60 61), will prove more exciting. Follow the signs from the train station (open daily 9am-5pm, except Christmas and New Year's Day; DM4, students DM2). The museum offers not only a detailed account of Schiller's life and work, but also teaches something about his Swabian contemporaries. The audio-visual room at the end of the first-floor plays the authentic voice of Bertolt Brecht singing *"Mackie Messer,"* his wicked German song known to English-speakers as "Mack the Knife"— swing it Louie, swing it! The **Rathaus** has big racks of material, including walking tours and hotel and restaurant maps. The **telephone city code** is 07144. For **food,** head to Marktstr., where most of the restaurants in Marbach are located. To reach Marbach from Stuttgart, take S-Bahn #4 until they kick you off at the very end. Byebye!

■ Tübingen

Tübingen gracefully rises like a nymph out of the conjunction of the willow-lined Neckar River and the edge of the Schwarzwald, retaining the aloofness of its intellectual past. With nearly half the city's residents affiliated with the 500-year-old university, there is no doubt that Tübingen is venerably academic, a place for relaxed contemplation from which literary giant Hermann Hesse launched his book-dealing career. Things have not always been so peaceful in the forests of academe. The university has been a source of unpredictability, from the Middle Ages to the student uprisings of the late 60s and beyond; students have boycotted classes to protest everything from the educational system and the Nazi past of many politicians to American involvement in the Vietnam War. The *Altstadt,* a snail shell sheltering a lively student life both by day and night, has successfully avoided the fate of over-touristed Heidelberg.

ORIENTATION AND PRACTICAL INFORMATION

30km south of Stuttgart, Tübingen stands guard over the Neckar River, on the edge of the Schwarzwald. Easily reachable by rail, it is one of the larger cities in the Schwarzwald area; it is connected by bus and train to many small towns in the Schwäbische Alb and the Schwarzwald.

Tourist office: Verkehrsverein, on Neckarbrücke (tel. 913 60; fax 350 70). From the front of the train station, turn right and walk to Karlstr., turn left and walk to the river. The office books rooms in hotels or **private rooms** (DM30-100) for a DM5 fee, sells maps (DM1-10), and acts as a box office. Open Mon.-Fri. 9am-7pm, Sat. 9am-5pm, Sun. 2-5pm.

Tours: Ask at the tourist office for the comprehensive pamphlet listing all tour offerings. **City tours** (DM5, in English DM10) leave from the tourist office April-Oct. Wed. 10am, Sat.-Sun. 2:30pm. Just show up.

Trains: Service to and from Stuttgart every 30-45min.

Boat Rental: Bootsverleih Märkle, on the river under the tourist office (tel. 31 52 29). Boats for 1-6 people 1hr. DM3.50-4 per person. Open mid-April to mid.-Oct. daily 11am-8pm.

Taxis: Taxi Centrale, tel. 243 01.

Bike Rental: RADlager, Lazarettgasse 19-21 (tel. 55 16 51), in the *Altstadt*. DM18 per day; less for each additional day. Open Mon.-Tues. and Thurs.-Fri. 9:30am-1pm and 2-6pm, Wed. 2-6pm, Sat. 9:30am-1pm.

Mitfahrzentrale: Münzgasse 6 (tel. 267 89 or 50 81). Rides to Munich DM24 (including gas). Open daily 9am-2pm and 4-7pm. Call 1-2 days in advance.

Mitwohnzentrale: Wilhelmstr. 2/3 (tel. 55 10 20; fax 55 10 70). For stays of 1 month or longer. Open Mon.-Tues. and Fri. 10am-noon, Wed. 10am-noon and 3-5pm, Thurs. 10am-noon and 4-6pm. Also check the bulletin boards in the *Mensa*.

Bookstores: The venerable, 400-year-old **Osiandersche Buchhandlung,** Wilhelmstr. 12 (tel. 920 16; fax 92 01 92), carries an enormous selection of English and American literature. Open Mon.-Fri. 9am-8pm, Sat. 9am-4pm. **Bücherkabine Antiquariat,** Bachgasse 13 (tel. 237 35), houses used books in precious stacks that threaten to overwhelm the friendly proprietor. Open Mon.-Fri. 10am-7pm.

Laundromat: City Wascheservice (tel. 843 66), at the corner of Rupperstr. and Herrenbergerstr. Student clientele. 7kg DM7. Open Mon.-Sat. 8am-9pm.

Cultural Center: German-American Institute, Karlstr. 3 (tel. 340 71).

Women's Resources: Women's cafe *(Frauencafé)*, Poststr. 3, is also a hopping, women-only night spot. Open Mon.-Fri. 8pm-midnight. **Women's bookstore** *(Frauenbuchladen)*, Bursagasse 2 (tel. 265 90 or 511 29—also the number for **women's information**). Open Mon.-Fri. 10am-7pm, Sat. 10am-2pm.

Rape Hotline: Frauenhaus tel. 666 04.

Emergency: Police, tel. 110. **Fire,** tel. 112.

Internet Access: H@cker's Internet Café, Neustadtgasse 11 (tel. 219 19).

Post Office: Europapl. 2, 72072 Tübingen, 100m right of the train station. Open Mon.-Fri. 10am-7pm, Sat. 10am-2pm.

Telephone Code: 07071.

ACCOMMODATIONS AND CAMPING

Most of the lodgings in the city are not priced to please, yet rooms rented out by **private families,** listed at the tourist office, are usually economical. Call ahead.

Jugendherberge (HI), Gartenstr. 22/2 (tel. 230 02; fax 250 61), is just a 12-minute walk from the station. Cross the bridge past the tourist office and make a right. Or bus #11: "Jugendherberge" (DM2.50). Cramped rooms and showers with strange water pressure are compensated for by a great breakfast with huge cereal bowls. Reception open 5-8pm, and 10-10:15pm. Sporadically enforced lockout 9am-5pm. Curfew midnight. Members only but you can join the club when you check in. DM22, over 26 DM27. Lockers in the basement (DM5 deposit). Breakfast included. Wheelchair access.

Hotel am Schloß, Burgsteige 18 (tel. 929 40; fax 92 94 10), on the hill leading to the *Schloß*. Great location and newly renovated rooms. The sign above the bench outside is exaggerated Schwäbisch dialect for "here sit those who always sit here" *(dohoggeddiadiaemmerdohogged)*. Singles DM50, with shower DM65, with bath DM99-130; doubles with bath DM124-148. All rooms with cable TV and telephone. Heck, you can even send a fax. Breakfast included.

Hotel Kürner, Weizsäckerstr. 1 (tel. 227 35; fax 279 20), offers friendly management, fun 70s decor, and a restaurant downstairs, near the *Uni* but 20min. from the *Altstadt*. Follow Wilhelmstr. past the university and go right on Weizsäckerstr. Or bus #2, 3, 5, or 7: "Brechtbau." Singles DM45; doubles DM95. Breakfast included.

Camping: Rappenberghalde, on the river (tel. 431 45; fax 350 70). Go upstream from the old town or left from the station, cross the river at the Alleenbrücke, and turn left (20-25min.). Follow the blue camping signs. Reception open daily 8am-12:30pm and 2:30-10pm. Person DM9.50. Tent DM5.50-7. Open April to mid-Oct. Bike rentals DM15 per day.

FOOD

With the smell of pungent herbs and fresh bread in the air, Tübingen's students keep a number of superb restaurants busy. Most of the inexpensive eating establishments cluster around the Metzgergasse/Am Lutznauer Tor area. To buy your own bread and Nutella, go to **Pfannkuch,** Karlstr. 3, which lies next to the tourist office on the Neckarbrücke (open Mon.-Fri. 8:30am-7pm, Sat. 8am-4pm). The *Altstadt* bristles with grocery stores and bakeries.

Marquardtei, Herrenbergerstr. 34 (tel. 433 86). Bus #8 or 9: "Rappstr." Run by a gang of enterprising students; serves pizzas, Schwäbisch specialties, and various vegetarian dishes to an equally varied student clientele. Entrees DM9.50-14.30. Open Mon.-Sat. 11:30am-1am, Sun. 10am-1am.

Mensa, on Wilhelmstr. between Gmelinstr. and Keplerstr. (on the left with teal trimming). Offers generic fare at low prices for the severely budget-conscious. Meals under DM5 for Tübingen students, DM8.80 for guests. Pick up a menu in the lobby. Open late Aug. through July Mon.-Thurs. 11:30am-2pm and 6-8:15pm, Fri. noon-2pm, Sat. 11:45am-1:15pm. Equally cheap is the ID-less **cafeteria** downstairs with cold food, sandwiches, and big chunks o' cheesecake all under DM5. Open Mon.-Thurs. 8am-8pm, Fri. 8am-6:30pm.

Da Pino, Mühlstr 20 (tel. 551 086), is a small but eminently delicious eatery. Crust 'n' cheese in all shapes and sizes. Pizzas DM7-10. Take out or stand at the counter. Open daily 11:30am-2:30pm and 4:30pm-12:30am.

Die Wurstküche, Am Lustnauer Tor 8 (tel. 927 50). Dishes up regional specialties in a gorgeous dining room, with plenty of high *Schwäbisch* camp and friendly service. Entrees DM9-25. Vegetarian dishes DM13-15. Open daily 11am-midnight.

SIGHTS

Winding alleys and gabled houses surround the 15th-century **Stiftskirche,** the focal point of the old city. In the chancel lie the tombs of 14 members of the House of Württemberg. Life-size stone sculptures of the deceased top the tombs—men in their finest suits of armor. From an entryway to the left of the chancel, the rickety stairs of the church tower lead to a view of red-tiled roofs and the surrounding green countryside. (Church open daily 9am-5pm. Chancel and tower open April-July and Oct. Fri.-Sun. 10:30am-5pm; Aug.-Sept. daily 10:30am-5pm. Admission to the chancel and tower DM2, students DM1.) On the square is **Buchhandlung Heckenhauer Antiquariat,** at Holzmarkt 5, where Hermann Hesse worked from 1895 until 1899. It's still selling rare books. Down street from Kirchgasse, any day of the week, a mind-boggling array of vendors sets up shop beneath the *Rathaus*'s incredibly ornate facade.

Speaking of world culture, dwelling just down the road from the Stiftskirche on Kronenstr. is the **Tübingen Evangelischer Stift.** Built as an Augustinian monastery in 1260, it has served as a seminary since 1547, and achieved great intellectual prominence for a brief period in the early 19th century. It boasts among its alumni such academic luminaries as Kepler, Hölderlin, Hegel, Schelling, and Mörike. Down

Bursagasse from the Evangelischer Stift is the **Bursa,** a gargantuan pink building which once served as a dorm and philosophy lecture hall. Here, *Stift* roommates Hegel and Schelling would sit through boring theology lectures, then retreat to their room for conversation and a bottle of Rhine wine. Unfortunately, the historic interest of these buildings rather outweighs their visual splendor.

On top of the hill that rudely isolates the university from most of the city stands the **Schloß Hohentübingen,** a castle with a rough stone balcony overlooking the old town and valley beyond. The upper floors of the castle are occupied by various institutes, while the spooky basements are closed to protect the huge bat family currently inhabiting it. From the *Rathaus,* follow the signs marked "Schloß" leading up to the right in order to reach the castle. Along the river, the tree-lined path of the **Platane-nallee**—which runs the length of a man-made island on the Neckar—makes for a pleasant walk with a view of the *Altstadt.* On the northern river bank is the **Hölder-linturm,** a tower where the great 18th- and 19th-century poet Friedrich Hölderlin, Hegel and Schelling's other roommate at the *Stift,* lived out the final 36 years of his life in a state of clinical insanity. The tower now contains a museum dedicated to his life. (Open Tues.-Fri. 10am-noon and 3-5pm, Sat.-Sun. 2-5pm. Tours Sat.-Sun. 5pm. DM3, students DM2.) Hardcore Hölderlinists may want to contact the **Hölderlin-Gesellschaft,** Bursagasse 6 (tel. 220 40), a society/support group dedicated to helping those addicted to the poet's life and work.

ENTERTAINMENT AND NIGHTLIFE

Tübingen's nightlife is laid-back and easy-going. It mostly revolves around cafes in the *Altstadt* that begin brewing quiet cups of coffee at 10am and remain open well into the night, serving beer to groups of students. The *Altstadt* also houses some sublime bars. **Sudhaus,** Hechingerstr. 203 (tel. 746 96), is a "Socio-cultural Center" which screens wacky art films and hosts dance parties and live acts. Schedules are available at the tourist office and are also plastered all over town. **Jazzkeller,** Haaggasse 15/2 (tel. 55 09 06; fax 221 63), goes from jazz to funk to salsa (often live) and back again. Tübingen also has two major theaters: the small progressive **Zimmertheater,** Bursagasse 16 (tel. 927 30), and the larger, more conservative **Landestheater,** Eberhardstr. 8 (tel. 931 31 49). Tickets and schedules are available at the tourist office and at the box office at Eberhardstr. 6 (open Tues.-Fri. 3:30-7pm, Sat. 10am-1pm).

Tangente-Night, Pfleghofstr. 10 (tel. 230 07), by the Stiftskirche steps. A premier Tübingen student hangout for beer and company at night or a book and cappuccino in the morning (0.3L *Pils* DM3.50; coffee DM3). Most fun Sept.-April Thurs.-Sun., when a DJ spins house, acid jazz, and techno. Sun. is cocktail night and once a week there's live music, a cabaret, or a theme party. Open daily 10am-3am.

Marktschenke, Am Markt 11 (tel. 220 35). Happy students spill out onto Tübingen's largest square. Cartoons on the wall will keep you amused. *Hefe-Weizen* (wheat beer) DM4.90 for 0.5L. Coffee DM3.30. Open daily 9am-1am.

Neckarmüller, Gartenstr. 4, (tel. 278 48), is close to the youth hostel. Young and old alike drink and schmooze at picnic tables under big shady trees by the banks of the river. The only way to get closer to the Neckar is to rent your own boat. They serve their own brew: light or dark, DM3.30 for 0.25L. In case you want to send some to Uncle Jack, a 5L oaken cask is DM45. Open daily 10am-1am.

Ammerschlag, Ammergasse 13 (tel. 515 91). Narrow, noisy bar on a beautiful little street, brimming with hipsters. Blues and jazz on Sun. night; Caribbean or American theme party Thurs. night. Open Mon.-Sat. 10:30am-1am, Sun. 3pm-1am.

■ Karlsruhe

By European standards, Karlsruhe was born only yesterday. In 1715, nobleman Margrave Karl Wilhelm built a castle retreat for himself and his mistresses (hence the name, meaning "Karl's Rest"). He then designed a planned city radiating out from the castle in the shape of a fan. It has been an architectural sensation ever since, perhaps owing to the refreshingly spacious and navigable streets. Karlsruhe is the home of

Germany's two highest courts, the Federal Supreme Court and the Federal Constitutional Court. Relatively overlooked by tourists, modern Karlsruhe is an honest portrayal of modern German society without a quaint little *Altstadt* to conceal the day-to-day doings of its citizens. For travelers, the city offers an impressive selection of museums and a break from the burden of antiquity. For residents, Karlsruhe offers something even better—over 1700 hours of sun per year, earning the title of "Sun City."

Orientation and Practical Information From the station, the town center is a 25-minute walk away from the train tracks on Ettlingerstr. and Karl-Friedrich-Str., or you may take any of the streetcar lines to "Marktplatz" or "Europapl." The **tourist office,** Bahnhofpl. 6 (tel. 355 30), located across the street from the train station, finds rooms for free. They have lots of events information and give out the amazing **Karlsruhe Extra,** an annually updated city bulletin and site guide (in English) with great maps (open Mon.-Fri. 9am-6pm, Sat. 9am-1pm). The **S-Bahn** costs DM3 per ride within the city, DM8 for a 24hr. ticket. If staying in the city for at least one night, you are entitled to a 35% discount on your train ticket (but *not* on the S-Bahn); call the tourist office to make arrangements. **Braunsche Universitäts Buchhandlung,** Kaiserstr. 120 (tel. 232 96), has a small but top-notch selection of English-language books. For a **taxi,** call 94 41 44. For an **ambulance,** call 192 22. The main **post office,** 76133 Karlsruhe, sprawls at Europapl. *Postlagernde Briefe* (Poste Restante) is at booths 21-24 (open Mon.-Fri. 8:30am-6:30pm, Sat. 8:30am-1pm). The **telephone code** is 0721.

Accommodations If looking for a bed in Karlsruhe, ask the tourist office for their thorough guide to accommodations. Karlsruhe's **Jugendherberge (HI),** Moltkestr. 24 (tel. 282 48), is conveniently near the *Schloß* and university, although it's far from the train station. S-Bahn #1, 3, or 11: "Europapl.," then follow Karlstr. until it ends. Turn left onto Seminarstr. and turn left again on Moltkestr.; it's behind #20. (Reception open briefly at 5, 7, and 9:30pm. Quiet 4- and 6-bed rooms. Curfew 11:30pm. Lockout 9am-5pm. Members only. DM22, over 26 DM27. Breakfast included.) The tiny **Pension am Zoo,** Ettlingerstr. 33 (tel. 336 78), is a couple blocks from the station and a camel chip's throw from the zoo. Spacious, well-furnished rooms with TV and decorated hallways feel like home (singles DM55; doubles DM100, with bath DM120; doubles for one person DM65). **Camping** is available at **Türmbergblick,** Tiengererstr. 40 (tel. 440 60), in the nearby village of Durlach. S-Bahn #3: "Durlacher Tor," then S-Bahn #1 or 2: "Durlach." (Reception open 8am-1pm and 3-9pm. Person DM8.80. Children DM6.40. Tent DM11.60.)

Food and Nightlife Karlsruhe is home to a very large *Fachhochschule* (trade school) that brims with students. To get to the school's **Mensa,** go up Karlstr. from Europapl., continue up Seminarstr., and turn left into the bleak blue-gray school complex (open Mon.-Thurs. 8:30am-4pm, Fri. 8:30am-2pm). For reasonably priced German fare, try **Goldenes Kreuz,** Karlstr. 21a (tel. 220 54), where entrees go for DM10-20 (open daily 11am-midnight). Around the corner on Ludwigpl. is the hangout **Krokodil,** Waldstr. 63 (tel. 273 31), a restaurant and cafe offering salad buffets for DM7 (open daily 8am-1am). On a lazy afternoon, **Eiscafé Period,** Kasierstr 33, offers up ice cream confections (DM1.50-12) and rad interior design (open Mon.-Fri. 9am-6:30pm, Thurs. 9am-8:30pm, Sat. 9am-2pm). The **main market** caters to Durlach campers (open Mon.-Sat. 7:30am-12:30pm). Many cafes on Ludwigspl. stay open until 1am, and the tourist office has a list of all local pubs, discos, and live music venues. **Harmonie,** Kaiserstr. 57 (tel. 37 42 09), is a hip pub that serves cheap eats (sausages or pasta DM9; beer DM3.50-5) and features live music (open Mon.-Fri. 8am-1am, Sat. 10am-1am, Sun. 9:30am-1am).

Sights The the most spectacular sight in Karlsruh is the loci of the city—all roads (literally) lead to the classical yellow **Schloß.** The *Schloßgarten,* with its impeccably maintained swathes of green and inviting benches, stretches out behind the castle for nearly 0.5km. The *Schloß* houses the **Landesmuseum** (tel. 926 65 14 or 926 65 42;

Die Kur

In Germany, "The Cure" is not a British rock band, but a venerated excuse for going to the beach. The well-funded German health care system subsidizes trips to spa towns for those over 50, which might explain why more than six million Germans take spa vacations each year. Yet German doctors are divided about the value of the *Kur.* Some believe it to be mostly psychological therapy, while others lend it more credence. The *Kurschatten* (spa romance) has become such a tradition that it's not always admissible as grounds for divorce in Germany, and probably invigorates vacationers more than anything else. This might explain why so many spa towns have at least one *"FKK" ("Freie Körper Kultur"),* better known to English speakers as a nude beach.

---

fax 926 65 37 or 926 65 49), a collection of antiques dominated by the third floor's *Türkenbeute* (Turkish Booty). Examine the booty, behold the booty, desire the booty, but don't touch the booty. Other exhibits recount the history and fashion of head scarves. A tower affords an aerial view of Karlsruhe (open Tues. and Thurs.-Sun. 10am-5pm, Wed. 10am-8pm; DM5, students DM3). The same entry fee allows you admission to the **Museum beim Markt,** Karl-Freidrich-Str. 6 (tel. 926 64 94), dedicated to design and illustration since the turn of the century (open Tues. and Thurs.-Sun. 10am-5pm, Wed. 1:30-8pm). Around the corner are the **Kunsthalle,** Hans-Thomas-Str. 2, and **Kunsthalle Orangerie,** Hans-Thomas-Str. 6, two top-notch art museums (tel. 926 33 55; fax 26 67 88). European masterpieces from the 15th to the 19th centuries adorn the Kunsthalle—don't miss Grünewald's *Crucifixion*—while the Orangerie contains a smaller collection of modern art (both open Tues.-Fri. 10am-5pm, Sat.-Sun. 10am-6pm; DM5, students DM3). The **Kunstverein,** Waldstr. 3, exhibits a smaller, more modern collection (open Tues.-Sun. 10am-1pm and 2-6pm, Thurs. also open 7-9pm; DM4, students DM2).

The Marktplatz, designed by architect and city planner Friedrich Weinbrenner, is bordered on the west by the rose-colored **Rathaus** and on the east by the imposing columns of the **Stadtkirche.** The red sandstone pyramid towering in the center of the Marktplatz is the symbol of the city and Karl's final resting place.

Occupying the upper floors of a former mansion, the **Prinz Max Palais** museum, Karlstr. 10 (tel. 133 44 01 or 133 42 30), has loaned exhibitions and a local history display that includes the purported **first bicycle in the world** and bathrooms coolly lit by black lights. Check with the tourist office for current exhibits (open Tues. and Thurs.-Sun. 10am-5pm, Wed. 11am-8pm; DM5, students DM3.50). The quirkiest of Karlsruhe's museums is indisputably the **Oberrheinisches Dichtermuseum** (Upper Rhine Poets' Museum), Röntgenstr. 6 (tel. 84 38 18), dedicated to lyrical legends such as von Scheffel, Hebel, and Flake. Flake? (Open Tues.-Fri. 11am-5pm. Free.) More accessible is Karlsruhe's **Zoo,** in the *Stadtgarten* across the street from the train station. The overpasses afford free glimpses of llamas, goats, and elephants during feeding times (10:30am and 3pm; zoo open daily 8am-6:30pm; DM5, students DM4).

The visually unremarkable **Bundesverfassungsgericht** (Federal Constitutional Court) stands next to the *Schloß.* Take a moment to consider this edifice—it embodies Germany's strongest legal safeguard against the return of totalitarian rule. Near Friedrichspl., the **Bundesgerichtshof** (Federal Supreme Court) has a security apparatus that makes its counterpart five blocks to the north look open-armed by comparison. Germany's most sensational postwar criminal trials were held here, including those of the infamous Baader-Meinhof terrorist gang. With good imagination, these ugly buildings possess a mystique born of betrayal and humanity gone bad.

Every year in mid- to late-February, Karlsruhe hosts the **Händel-Festspiele,** a 10-day series of concerts of Händel's works. The appetizing **Brigande-Feschd** takes place in late May and brings with it a huge display of dishes from local specialty restaurants. As with all German festivals, the local breweries play an essential role in the reveling— *Prost!* **Unifest** (known as *Das Fest*) is a 10-day orgy in late July of live music, food stands, and roaming students clutching tumblers of beer that takes place at the end of Günther-Klatz-Anlage, and is the **biggest free open-air concert in Germany.**

■ Baden-Baden

You don't have to be fabulously wealthy to have a good time in Baden-Baden, but it sure helps. In its 19th-century heyday, Baden-Baden's guest list read like a *Who's Who* of European aristocracy. Although its status has declined, this spa town on the northern fringes of the Schwarzwald remains primarily a playground for the well-to-do; minor royalty, *Wirtschaftswunderkinder,* and the like gather here year-round to bathe in the mineral spas and drop fat sums of money in the elegant casino. In fact, slightly scruffy backpackers often draw stares from the blazer-wearing wannabe aristocrats who hobble from one exclusive shop to another. The *hochnäsig* (conceited) atmosphere is worth tolerating, if only for the chance to experience the incredible (and affordable) Caracalla baths and the immaculate downtown area.

Orientation and Practical Information Baden-Baden's **train station** is inconveniently located 7km from town. If you're not up for the 1½-hour walk along the park path, take bus #201 (direction: "Lichtental/Oberbeuren"): "Augustapl." (one-way DM3; 24hr. pass DM8). The **tourist office,** Augustapl. 8 (tel. 275 20; fax 27 52 02), in the building next to the Kongresshaus, offers maps, city guides, and a hotel list (open daily 9:30am-6pm). **TaxiFunk** (tel. 621 12 or 538 88) provides taxi service. Even rich folks need the funk. The **post office** on Leopoldpl., 76486 Baden-Baden (open Mon.-Fri. 8am-6pm, Sat. 8am-noon, Sun. 10:30am-11:30am) **exchanges money,** as do the casino and the spas. The **telephone code** is 07221.

Accommodations and Food The cheapest bed in town is at the modern, five-floor **Jugendherberge (HI),** Hardbergstr. 34 (tel. 522 23; fax 600 12), halfway between the station and the town center. Bus #201: "Grosse-Dollen-Str." and follow the signs uphill. The hostel has family apartments. The strange paucity of showers is perhaps explained by the overabundance of bathing facilities in town and the large public swimming pool next door (see **Sights and Spas,** below). (Reception open 5-6pm and briefly at 8 and 10pm. Curfew 11:30pm. Members only. DM22, over 26 DM27. Wheelchair-accessible. Call ahead.) Rooms in the center of the town are appropriately ritzy and expensive, with a couple of exceptions. **Hotel am Markt,** Marktplatz 18 (tel. 270 40; fax 27 04 44), is next to the Friedrichsbad and the Stiftskirche. Family managed for decades and smack in the middle of the pedestrian zone, it has lovely views of the city and a restaurant downstairs for guests. (Reception open 7am-10pm. Singles DM54-60, with shower DM80; doubles DM100-105, DM135. Breakfast included. Dinners DM8-15. Restaurant open for guests only 6-9pm.) The unassuming **Hotel Löhr,** Adlerstr. 2 (tel. 26 20 43; fax 383 08), has its reception 1½ blocks away at **Café Löhr,** Lichtentalerstr. 19, across the street and back towards the *Bahnhof* from the "Augustapl." bus stop. The rooms are spotless but small. (Singles DM45-65; doubles DM100-120.)

Most restaurant prices in Baden-Baden aren't compatible with budget travel, but **daily specials** often run under DM12. Another option is to fill up a picnic basket at **grocery stores: Plus,** on Albrecht-Dürer-Str. next to the *Altes Bahnhof;* **Pfannkuch,** at Augustapl.; or **Pennymarkt,** at the Grosse-Dollen-Str. bus stop. **Deniz Restaurant,** Gernsbacherstr. 18 (tel. 223 64), is one of the few affordable eateries in town, offering an eclectic menu with a Turkish accent and some vegetarian dishes (DM7.80-10.50; open daily 9:30am-1am.) While **nightlife** in Baden-Baden is designed for the rich, reasonably priced cafes along the pedestrian zone stay open at least until midnight. If you're in search of young, rich, available Europeans, look no further than **Griffin's,** in the basement of the *Kurhaus* under the casino. Beer is DM6 for 0.3L, if you know what we mean; *water* is DM7.50. *Um gottes Willen!* (Admission a similarly steep DM10. Open 9pm-3am.)

Sights and Spas Baden-Baden's history as a resort goes back nearly two millennia, to the time when the Romans built the first **thermal baths** here, the remains of which are located in the parking garage underneath the Friedrichsbad, visible behind a glass wall. The **Friedrichsbad,** Römerpl. 1 (tel. 27 59 20), is a beautiful 19th-century bathing palace where visitors are parched, steamed, soaked, scrubbed, doused, and pummelled by trained professionals for three hours. It's a marvelous experience, especially since not a stitch of clothing is permitted. (Open Mon.-Sat. 9am-10pm, Sun. noon-8pm. Last entry 3hr. before closing. Baths are co-ed Tues. and Fri. 4-10pm, all day Wed., Sat., and Sun. Standard Roman-Irish Bath DM36, with soap and brush massage DM48, with cream massage DM46, with both DM56. DM6 discount with hotel coupon. Credit cards accepted, of course.) The Friedrichsbad is the more traditional; its atmosphere of soothing silence re-creates the Baden-Baden of old. More modest or budget-minded cure-seekers should try next door at the also astounding **Caracalla-Thermen,** Römerpl. 11 (tel. 27 59 40), which is cheaper and more public, and allows bathing suits (except in the superb collection of saunas, whirlpools, and sun beds upstairs). Indoor and outdoor pools of all shapes, sizes, and temperatures provide ideal therapy for weary travelers at a very reasonable price. (Open daily 8am-10pm. 2hr. DM19, 3hr. DM25, with a youth hostel coupon DM15.50, DM21.) Whichever bath you choose, the experience will be unforgettable. The large public **swimming pool** next to the hostel has a curvy slide and is the cheapest way to take to the waters in Baden-Baden (open 10am-8pm; DM4.50, students DM3; after 5pm DM3, students DM2; hot shower DM1, deck chair DM4.50).

When they're not busy pruning themselves at the baths, Baden-Baden's affluent guests head to the **oldest casino in Germany;** the opulent decor, modeled after the palace at Versailles, can be viewed via daily guided tours. (Open April-Sept. daily 9:30am-noon; Oct.-March 10am-noon. Last tour leaves at 11:30am. English-language tours by special arrangement. Admission DM3.) Just walk across the river from Leopoldpl. Attendance during gaming hours (Sun.-Thurs. 2pm-2am, Fri.-Sat. 2pm-3am) costs DM5 with a laundry list of restrictions: you must be 21 (or the spouse of someone who is) and wear appropriate dress (coat and tie for men; dress or suit for women). Technically, students are not allowed. Minimum bet is DM5, maximum bet DM20,000 (yeah, we were disappointed, too). If you live in Baden-Baden and want to bet, you need a note from the mayor. There are slot machines in a separate wing (open Sun.-Thurs. 2-11pm, Fri.-Sat. 2pm-midnight; admission DM2). Next to the casino is the massive Neoclassical **Trinkhalle** (Pump Room), which contains a gallery of paintings immortalizing area folk tales and flaunts a gold-plated fountain. The *Heilwasser* (healing water) is warm and slightly saline; it tastes like it's good for you (open daily 10am-6pm; free). A few blocks in the opposite direction down the paths of the **Lichtentaler Allee** is the **Kunsthalle,** which houses visiting exhibits of modern art (open Tues. and Thurs.-Sun. 11am-6pm, Wed. 11am-8pm; admission varies with exhibit but usually DM5, students DM2).

The **Schwarzwaldhochstraße** (see p. 453) begins in Baden-Baden. For a view of rolling green hills, mount the 68m **Merkur** peak east of town. Bus #4 or 5 from Leopoldpl.: "Merkurwald," then tackle the steep railway to the top (combined round-trip DM10). On the hill above the baths and the pedestrian zone, accessible by a steep set of stairs, sits the ivy-covered **Neues Schloß,** occupied by a museum of the town's history. (Open Tues.-Sun. 10am-12:30pm and 2-5pm. Tours Mon.-Fri. 3pm. Admission DM2, students DM1.) Baden-Baden lies at your feet from the neighboring garden. The view from the 12th-century **Altes Schloß** (tel. 269 48), however, extends all the way to France. The castle is a good walk behind the *Neues Schloß,* but bus #15 makes two loops on Sundays and holidays at 1:15pm and 4:15pm between Augustapl. and the *Schloß* (open Tues.-Sun. 10am-10pm; free).

■ Freiburg Im Breisgau

Freiburg may be the "metropolis" of the Schwarzwald, but it has not succumbed to the hectic rhythms of city life. Part of this serene flavor may derive from the persistent Austro-French influence in Freiburg—it was not until the 19th century that it was integrated into Prussia. Some say the influence of the two peoples helps to make Freiburgers more genial and humor-loving than "typical" dour Germans. This international quality, however, helped to cause disaster in May 1940, when a squadron of

Luftwaffe pilots accidentally bombed Freiburg, mistaking it for a French border town. Nevertheless, the resilient town rebuilt itself with a palpably relaxed air resulting from its proximity to the surrounding hills, which brim with greenery and fantastic hiking trails. Trails link the Schwabentor directly to the entire German trail network, and all traces of urbanity dissolve into countryside a few kilometers from the city center. The atmosphere is correspondingly liberal and crunchy, with a bevy of student-populated cafes and used CD stores scattered throughout cobblestone streets filled with Birkenstocked bicyclists.

ORIENTATION AND PRACTICAL INFORMATION

Freiburg lies between Karlsruhe (2hr.) and Basel, Switzerland (1hr.), and is connected to both by frequent trains. Local trains and buses leave regularly for scattered Schwarzwald towns. Most of the city's sights and restaurants lie within walking distance from one another in the *Altstadt*, a 15-minute walk from the main train station.

Tourist Office: Rotteckring 14 (tel. 388 18 80; fax 370 03), two blocks down Eisenbahnstr. from the station. Helpful staff finds rooms for DM5, sells tickets to area events, and has free maps, but prefers to sell the comprehensive *Freiburg Official Guide* (in German or English) for DM6 or a small guide for DM1. The entire desk on the left side is devoted to the Schwarzwald: hiking maps, flashy color brochures, and an amazing trilingual expert on the region. Open June-Sept. Mon.-Fri. 9:30am-5pm, Sat. 9:30am-6pm, Sun. 10am-noon; Oct.-May Mon.-Fri. 9:30am-6pm, Sat. 9:30am-2pm, Sun. 10am-noon.

Currency Exchange: At the main train station. Open Mon.-Sat. 9:15am-12:30pm and 1:15-6:15pm, Sun. 9am-1pm. Slightly better rates available at the post office.

Public Transportation: Single fares on Freiburg's many bus and streetcar lines are DM3.20, 24hr. adult ticket DM7.50, 2 adults DM10. Get the scoop on regional travel at **PlusPunkt,** Salzstr. 3, in the *Altstadt,* which serves your every transportation need. Open Mon.-Fri. 8am-7pm, Sat. 8am-4pm. Another branch is below the *Straßenbahn* platform at the station.

Taxis: tel. 444 44. Four you.

Mitfahrzentrale: Belfortstr. 55 (tel. 194 44), south of the station, just off Schnewlingstr. You're going to vacation in Germany without riding on the *Autobahn?* No, no. Get a chauffeur. Paris DM45, Zurich DM17, Munich DM37. Open Mon.-Fri. 9am-7pm, Sat. 9am-1pm, Sun. 10am-1pm.

Hitchhiking: *Let's Go* does not recommend hitchhiking as a safe means of transportation. Hitchers take public transportation to points of departure. **North:** S-Bahn #5 (direction: "Zähringen"): "Reutebachgasse" and walk back 50m. **West:** S-Bahn #1: "Padua-Allee," then bus #31 or 32: "Hauptstr." **East:** S-Bahn #1 (direction: "Littenweiler"): "Lassbergstr.," then bus #18 (direction: "Langwatten"): "Strombad."

Bookstore: Walthari, Bertoldstr. 28 (tel. 387 70). A fairly large collection of English-language paperbacks. Carries guides to the Schwarzwald region and a few editions of *Let's Go.* Yay! Open Mon.-Sat. 9am-4pm.

Laundromat: Café Fleck, Predigerstr. 3 (tel. 268 29). Laundro-cafe—get a sandwich at the adjacent bar. Wash DM7, soap included. Dry DM1 per 10min. Laundromat open Mon.-Fri. 7am-1am. Cafe open Mon.-Fri. 7am-6:30pm, Sat. 8am-2pm.

Rape Crisis Hotline: tel. 333 39.

Gay Hotline: Rosa Hilfe, tel. 251 61.

Emergency: Police and **Ambulance,** tel. 110. **Fire,** tel. 112.

Post Office: Eisenbahnstr. 60, 79098 Freiburg, one block straight ahead from the train station. Open Mon.-Fri. 8:30am-6:30pm, Sat. 8:30am-2pm.

Telephone Code: 0761

ACCOMMODATIONS AND CAMPING

Most of Freiburg's hotels and *Pensionen* are expensive and are often located outside of the city center. The tourist office books cheaper rooms (DM25-45 for singles; DM45-80 for doubles) in private homes, but a stay of at least three nights is usually required. Unfortunately, Freiburg's youth hostel is large, nondescript, and far from

Freiburg

Alte Universität, 7
Augustiner Museum, 4
Library, 2
Münster, 3
Museum of Modern Art, 5
Neue Universität, 8
Paulus Kirche, 6
Rathaus, 1

the *Altstadt*. If your accommodation is far away, purchasing the 24hr. ticket for buses and streetcars will ultimately save money (see **Public Transportation,** above).

Jugendherberge (HI), Kartäuserstr. 151 (tel. 676 56; fax 603 67). S-Bahn #1 (direction: "Littenweiler"): "Römerhof," cross the tracks and backtrack 20m, then walk down Fritz-Geiges-Str., cross the stream, and follow the footpath to the right. Rampant schoolchildren sleep in packed, cramped rooms amidst bright colors and an arboreal setting. Feels more like a dorm than most hostels. Reception open 7am-11:30pm. Curfew 11:30pm. Members only. DM22, over 26 DM27. Sheets DM5.50. *Gästehaus* DM35, sheets included.

Hotel Zum Löwen, Breisgauerstr. 62 (tel. 846 61; fax 840 23), up the street from Gästehaus Hirschen (see below). An *awesome* deal. Friendly management and large sunny rooms, some with TV. Pretend you're in California with the marble floors and white stucco walls—it sure don't feel like budget travel. Entrance in the court; the front door of the building is also labeled "Löwen" but leads into a more expensive place. Singles DM45, with shower DM50; doubles DM80, DM100-130.

Haus Lydia Kalchtaler, Peterhof 11 (tel. 671 19). S-Bahn #1 (direction: "Littenweiler"): "Lassbergstr.," then bus #17: "Kleintalstr." Turn around and follow Peterhof up and to the left to the large wooden farmhouse with the water trough in front. Operated by the tireless and loquacious Lydia Kalchtaler, this is a rest from institutional living at an unbeatable price. A long trip from the center of town, but neighborly atmosphere and usable kitchen make it worthwhile. DM20-25, some rooms with showers. Call ahead.

Gästehaus Hirschen, Breisgauerstr. 47 (tel. 821 18). S-Bahn #1: "Padua-Allee," backtrack 30m along the tracks, and walk down Breisgauerstr. for 5min. Be careful: this *Gasthaus* is on the other side of town from the hotel of the same name; also, it isn't the same as Hirschengarten-Hotel, which is right next door. Old house in a quiet farm neighborhood with rooms as cozy as the exterior would lead you to believe. Spotless pink tile bathroom. Reception open Fri.-Wed. Singles DM40, with shower DM56; doubles DM70, DM90; triples DM110.

Hotel Schemmer, Eschholzstr. 63 (tel. 27 24 24; fax 220 10). From the train station, take the overpass that crosses the tracks, then go past the church and turn left. Friendly management and superb location. Looks like grandpa's den circa 1965 in bright blue and orange. Some rooms look out on the garden, some on the street. Singles DM55, with bath DM65; doubles DM85, DM95. Breakfast included.

Pension Gisela, Am Vogelbach 27 (tel. 811 52; fax 811 52). Bus #10: (direction "Padua-Allee"): "Hofackerstr.," then double back two blocks and turn left, walk 250m, and turn right on the unmarked street before the train tracks. The tacky Schwarzwald-themed mural on the outside wall conceals large, hotel-quality rooms in a quiet residential neighborhood. Singles DM45; doubles DM85-90. Breakfast included. Apartments available for longer-term guests.

Camping: Hirzberg, Kartauserstr. 99 (tel. 350 54; fax 28 92 12), has sparkling new camping facilities and is only 20min. from the *Altstadt* by foot. Endlessly helpful English-speaking staff. S-Bahn #1: "Stadthalle," then cross the street to the left via the underpass and walk straight (north) on Hirzbergstr. Cross the river at Max-Miller-Steg, walk across stream, then go 30m to the left. Near a quiet residential area. DM8 per person. DM5 per child. DM5-7 per tent. Summer tent rentals DM10-15 per day. Trailer rentals DM20-30. Bikes DM12 per day. **Mosle Park,** Waldeseestr. 77 (tel. 729 38; fax 775 78). S-Bahn #1: "Hasemannstr.," then a 15min. walk, as follows: backtrack to Jahnstr. and then turn left. Follow Jahnstr. until it ends, then go left on Hammerschmiedstr. Follow that, cross the train tracks, then turn right on Littenweilerstr. Beautiful forested location, ideally situated for hiking. Reception open 8am-noon and 3-10pm. DM8 per person. DM5 per child. DM4 per tent. Laundry facilities available: wash and dry DM13.

FOOD

In the early 15th century, the humanist Dietrich von Nieheim noted admiringly that in Freiburg "the supply of victuals is good and readily available." With more than 23,000 university students to feed, Freiburg's budget eateries carry on the fine tradition. During the daytime, the **Freiburger Markthalle** next to the Martinstor is home to food stands serving ethnic specialties for under DM12 (open Mon.-Fri. 9am-6:30pm, Sat. 9am-2pm). At the open-air **market** on Münsterpl., you can find everything from fresh radishes to folks who'll scratch your name onto a grain of rice (open Mon.-Sat. 7:30am-1pm). You can get your groceries at the **Edeka City Market,** Eisenbahnstr. 39, across from the post office (open Mon.-Fri. 8am-8pm, Sat. 8am-4pm).

Mensa: Two university *Mensen*—the blue-trimmed building on **Rempartstraße** in the *Altstadt* (serves only lunch) and **Hebelstraße** on the main campus north of the city center (lunch and dinner). It's true you need a Freiburg student ID to buy *Menukarten* (5 for DM16.50 gets you a hot meal) and *Eintopfkarten* (5 for DM10.50 gets you a bowl of stew or fries), but local students are willing to help out. One flavor fits all. Rempartstr. location open Mon.-Fri. 11:30am-2pm, Sat. 11:30am-1:30pm. Hebelstr. location open Mon.-Fri. 11am-2pm and 5:30-7:30pm.

Freiburger Salatstuben, Löwenstr. 1 (tel. 351 55), near Martinstor. A health-food haven with an array of imaginatively smart salads belies the absence of vegetarian pretension (100g DM2.20). Even the desserts (DM4-5) are smart (but no Smarties). Open Mon.-Fri. 11am-8pm, Sat. 11am-4pm, first Sat. of the month 11am-6pm.

Milano, Schusterstr. 7 (tel. 337 35), with its salmon-leather interior and prime location, feels more high-brow than the prices might indicate. Pizza (DM7-18), and pasta (DM7.50-15.50). Service with Italian flair. Open daily 11am-midnight.

Hausbrauerei Feierling, Gerberau 46 (tel. 266 78). Two enormous copper vats form the centerpiece of this Freiburg institution. Across the way, the *Biergarten* sports thick-shade chestnut trees. Excellent beer (*Inselhof* DM5.50 for 0.5L) and good food (DM12.50-20). Open Sun.-Fri. 11am-midnight, Sat. 1pm-midnight. Kitchen open noon-2pm and 6-10pm.

Papalapub, Moltkestr. 30. Near the *Stadttheater*. Certainly a place to be for the ever-alternative students of Freiburg. Beer (of course), rock 'n' roll on the radio, and the rise and fall of conversation accompanies the excellent pastas and pizzas (DM6-10). Open Mon.-Sat. noon-1am and Sun 10am-1am.

Brennessel, Eschholzstr. 17 (tel. 28 11 87). A plucky student tavern that fills the student gullet without emptying the student wallet. Spaghetti (DM3.50), *Pfannkuchen* (DM5). Open daily 6pm-1am; kitchen open until midnight.

SIGHTS

The majestic Freiburg **Münster** and its 116m spire tower above tourist hordes fighting to get a good view of the impressive erection. With sections constructed between the 13th and 16th centuries, the chapel's interior is a gorgeous melange of architectural and artistic achievement. While many of the stained-glass windows represent different medieval guilds which financed the cathedral's construction, the sculptures on the interior west porch depict Biblical characters. You can stumble up more than 300 steps to ascend the tower, from which you can see all 27 tons of bells swing into motion and catch a 360-degree view of the city. From atop, it's impossible not to marvel at the delicate, lattice-like stonework framing the view that made philosopher Wilhelm von Humboldt say that "one cannot conceive of a more beautiful view than the blue heavens peeking through the thousand openings of this cupola." But be warned that the passage is extremely tight, so claustrophobia and big backpacks are best left behind. Near the south entrance jutting from the wall, gargoyles moon the city. (Cathedral open Mon.-Sat. 10am-6pm, Sun. 1-6pm. Tower open Mon. and Wed.-Sat. 9:30am-5pm, Sun. 1-5pm; Nov.-April Wed.-Sat. 9:30am-5pm. DM2, students DM1.)

What buildings the errant *Luftwaffe* bombers didn't hit, the Allies decisively finished off one night in 1944, obliterating most of the old city. Since then, the citizens of Freiburg have painstakingly recreated the city's architecture and public spaces. On the south side of Münsterpl. haggles the pink-tinted **Kaufhaus,** a merchants' hall dating from the 1500s. Two medieval gates—the **Schwabentor** and the **Martinstor**—stand within blocks of each other in the southeast corner of the *Altstadt*. Sadly, the latter gate has been indelibly profaned by a golden McDonald's sign (boo Ronald!).

From the Schwabentor, you can take the pedestrian overpass across the heavily trafficked Schloßbergring and climb up the glorified **Schloßberg** (castle mountain) for a superb view of the city. Tucked away in the blocks between the *Münster* and the tourist office is the **Rathaus,** an amalgam of older buildings whose bells chime daily at noon, and the oddly named **Haus zum Walfisch** (House of the Whale), where Erasmus of Rotterdam lived in exile from Basel for two years following the Reformation. This gold-trimmed wonder is actually a careful recreation of the original which was destroyed during World War II.

Freiburg's museum circuit is diminutive but diverse, home to occasionally fascinating special exhibits. The **Augustiner Museum,** Salzstr. 32 (tel. 201 25 31), Am Augustinerpl., housed in a former monastery two blocks south of the *Münster*, has a large collection of medieval artifacts. Many original works of stained glass and statuary from the *Münster* are housed here along with other religious art, and there is a section devoted to folk art from the Schwarzwald (open Tues.-Sun. 10am-5pm; DM4, students DM2; free 1st Sunday of each month). Farther south is the **Museum für Neuekunst** (Museum of Modern Art), Marienstr. 10a (tel. 201 25 83), which displays the works of 20th-century German artists such as Otto Dix inside a clean-lined modern building (open Tues.-Sun. 10am-5pm; tours Sat. 3pm and Sun. 11am; free). Eat cake and discuss art in the cafe—or just eat cake (DM3-6). Along Eisenbahnstr. between the station and the tourist office stands an immaculate, early Victorian *Schloß* atop a hill of vineyards and wildflowers, housing the **Museum für Ur- und Frühgeschichte** (tel. 201 25 71). Lots of ancient, crumbling odds and ends focus on the prehistory of the South Baden region. (Open Tues.-Sun. 10am-5pm. Technically free, but DM3.50 donation requested, students DM2.) **Museum für Völkerkunde,** Gerberau 32 (tel. 201 25 66), presents many interesting artifacts, with an excellent depiction of the past and present of non-European cultures—look for an exhibit on

BADEN-WÜRTTEMBERG

Chinese healing practices in early 1998 (open Tues.-Sun. 10am-5pm; free). Conveniently located at the same-name stop of streetcar #1, **Brauerei Ganter,** Schwarzwaldstr. 43 (tel. 218 51 81), conducts tours tracking the production process of the malt beverage. The grand finale of the one-hour tour consists of a portion of *Fleisch-Käse,* bread, potato salad, and **lots of beer** atop one of the factory buildings. The view of the factory, the food finale, and the beer bash are all free (hint, hint). Call the above phone number ahead of time to get in on the group tours (Tues. and Thurs. 1:30pm). Unique to Freiburg is a system of narrow streams—known as **Bächle**—that run through the city. During medieval times, these swift-flowing gutters served as open-air sewers. Today they are the bane of any tourist studying his map *too* hard. But there are compensations for sodden footwear; legend has it that any visitor whose feet are wetted by them will one day marry a resident of Freiburg.

ENTERTAINMENT AND NIGHTLIFE

Freiburg proclaims itself to be a city of wine and music. True to its word, it is awash with *Weinstuben* and *Kneipen,* though club offerings are less abundant. For the current events in town, pick up a free copy of *Freiburg Aktuell* (DM5.50) or *F&K (Freizeit und Kultur)* at the tourist office. **Freiburger Weinfest** is a two-day festival held during the last weekend of June. The annual three-week **Zeltmusikfestival** (Tent Music Festival), held in late June to early July, brings big-name classical, rock, and jazz performers to two circus tents pitched at the city's edge. Tickets (DM15-40) sell surprisingly fast. S-Bahn #5: "Bisserstr." and catch the free shuttle bus to the site. **Freiburger Weintage** (Wine Days) is a 10-day festival held on Münsterpl. in late June and early July where you can stagger around from sample to sample of some 300 different vintages (DM3-6 per glass). In addition, the **Narrenfest** (Fools' Festival) is held the weekend before Ash Wednesday, and the **Weihnachtsmarkt** (Christmas Market) runs from late November until just a few days before Christmas.

Freiburg's nightlife keeps pace with the city's students—afternoon cafes stretch into pubs and discos at night. The streets around the university (Niemenstr., Löwenstr., Humboldtstr., and the accompanying alleyways) form the hub of the city's scene. To find out about popular hangouts, get a free copy of Freiburg's *Nachtleben* at the tourist office. Nightlife also revolves around the Martinstor, where pubs and clubs keep things hopping until the morning hours.

zum Schlappen, Löwenstr. 2, near Martinstor (tel. 334 94). Serious beer drinkers head here. For DM15 you can flex your mettle by polishing off the 2L **Stiefel,** a fearsome vessel known to English-speakers as "The Boot." Lots of posters, rather on the alternative side. Pizza DM6-8.50. Pasta DM6-11. Open Mon.-Thurs. noon-1am, Fri.-Sat. noon-2pm, Sun. 3pm-1am.

Jazzhaus, Schnewlingstr. 1 (tel. 349 73; fax 38 11 59), across from the *Bahnhof* and to the right, features live performances almost every night. Open Sun.-Thurs. 8pm-2am, Fri.-Sat.8pm-3am. Cover under DM10 for small acts, DM10-25 for more well-known performers.

Dampfross, Löwenstr. 7 (tel. 259 39). Tiny student bar, with dark wood and American movie posters. *Pils* DM3.60 for 0.3L. Steak DM10.50-15.50. The most popular dish is *Pommes mit Kräutercreme* (fries with herb cream; DM5.50). Divine. Connected through the back door to the cafe **Savo,** Löwenstr. 3-5 (same tel.), which plays stylish and mod to *Dampfross*'s earthy and traditional. Drinks and food a bit more upscale. More room, too. Both open daily 10:30am-1am.

Uni-Cafe, Niemenstr. 7 (tel. 259 39). A strange mixture of hipsters discussing Kierkegaard over cappuccino and families with frantic kids spilling into the shady square. Open Mon.-Thurs. 8am-midnight, Fri.-Sat. 8am-1am, Sun. 10am-midnight.

Cafe Atlantik, Schwabentorring 7 (tel. 330 33). Spacious pub that grooves to American alternative tunes. Angsty writers in booths who have no dressed-in-black pretensions. *Echt grell.* Packed in the winter, when the beer gardens close. Cheap spaghetti DM6.50-8.50. Guinness on tap. Open daily until 1am.

Agar, Löwenstr. 8 (tel. 38 06 50), next to Martinstor. Get down with Flower Power and the 80s. Tuesday and Wednesday are student nights—free with student ID.

Lots of Attitude. See or be seen, pick up or be picked up. Open Sun. and Tues.-Thurs. 10pm-2:30am, Fri.-Sat. 10pm-4am. Last entry 2hr. before closing.

Greiffenegg-Schlößle, Schloßbergring 3 (tel. 327 28). Drink, eat, and look down over Freiburg from a terrace above the city. Faaabulous view. Far more relaxed than a disco. Beer (DM5-7). Seats 800 and fills up when the weather cooperates. Great view. Half-price salad buffet, happy hour on weekdays 11am-1pm. Entrance in from of the Schwabentor. Open April-Oct. Tues.-Sun.11am-midnight. And how 'bout that view!

■ Near Freiburg: Breisach and the Kaiserstuhl

Thirty-kilometers west of Freiburg, along the portion of the Rhine that divides the German Schwarzwald and the French province of Alsace, lies the sleepy—nay, exhausted—hamlet of Breisach. Life moves at a rather slow pace here, but manages to do so with of style, perhaps because of its border-hugging location and its beautiful pieces of old Europe. The exquisite *Altstadt,* filled with curvy cobblestone streets, a flamboyantly colored *Rathaus,* and crowded clapboard houses, covers a small hill, atop which perches the **Cathedral of St. Stephan,** Breisach's most prominent sight. The unassuming 12th-century facade of this beast hides 15th-century frescoes and a writhing, twisting altar, the work of the mysterious 16th-century artist known only as Master H.L. From the church's promenade, the view stretches east and south to the rolling hills of the Schwarzwald and westward into France. Across the *Altstadt* stand the remains of the town's fortifications, the well-preserved 13th-century **Kapftor,** and the 17th-century **Rheintor,** currently home to the **Museum für Stadtgeschichte,** Rheintorpl. 1 (tel. 8 32 65). Inside, a fairly large collection of city artifacts includes 3000-year-old ceramics and some chain-link undergarments from the 15th century—kinky stuff (open Tues.-Fri. 2-5pm, Sat. 11:30am-5pm, Sun. 11:30am-6pm; free).

Connoisseurs should register for a tour of the largest wine cellar in Germany, **Badischer Winzerkeller** (tel. 90 00; fax 90 02 32; English speakers should call the tourist office in advance (3-7 samples DM5-9.50). It's a 1km walk east of town. Go right from the train station on Bahnhofstr. and keep truckin' on Im Gelbstein. Closer by is the **Graflich von Kageneck'sche Wein & Sektkellerei,** Kupfertorstr. 35 (tel. 90 11 37; fax 90 11 99), specializing in sparkling wine *(Sekt).* Buy yourself a crate (closed Sun.; call tourist office for tour times). Jaunts along the Rhine in big white ships are available through **Breisacher Fahrgastschiffahrt,** Werd 16 (tel. 79 47). Two-hour joy rides are DM14, and the company also runs ships to Strasbourg and Basel that can be used for one-way travel when not fully booked.

Near Breisach is the **Kaiserstuhl,** a clump of lush green hills that were volcanoes in their heyday. Now they attract hikers and bikers who come to see the flora and fauna, many of which are normally found only much farther south. The Freiburg-Breisach **train** stops at the towns of Ihringen and Wasenweiler, both located on the range's southern fringes. **Buses** handles the route straight into the hills; check the schedule at the Breisach *Hauptbahnhof.* The Breisach **tourist office** (tel. 94 01 55; fax 94 01 58),on the Marktplatz, finds rooms for a DM1 fee, and offers maps and hiking and biking information, as well as guides to the nearby French towns of Colmar and Neuf-Breisach (English and French spoken). From the train station, turn left onto Bahnhofstr. and continue going; with the fountain with the huge spinning globe on your right, go down Rheinstr. into the Marktplatz (office open Mon.-Fri. 9:30am-1pm and 1:30-5pm). There is a **market** next door (open Sat. 8am-noon). **Rent bikes** at **Firma Schweizer,** Neutorstr. 31 (tel. 76 01), on the main pedestrian thoroughfare (open Mon.-Fri. 8am-12:30pm and 2:30-6:30pm). The **post office** is one block from the train station (open Mon.-Fri. 8am-noon and 2:30-5:30pm, Sat. 8:30am-noon). The **telephone code** is 07667.

Breisach's superbly modern **Jugendherberge,** Rheinuferstr. 12 (tel. 76 65; fax 18 47), boasts an equally stunning Rhine-front location. From the train station, take a left and then left again at the intersection. After 20m, take the path leading under the main road. Cross the bridge to turn right, then walk along the river. A hostel sign is on the left, facing away from you; turn left when you see it. (20min. Reception open 5-

10pm. Curfew 11:30pm. Members only. DM22, over 26 DM27. Meals DM8.70. Sheets DM5.50.) For a bite of German-meets-French cuisine, try **Daisy's,** Rheinstr. 18 (tel. 86 82; open Mon.-Sat. 11am-10pm, Sun. 4-10pm).

■ Schwarzwald (Black Forest)

Throughout its rocky development, the German cultural consciousness has shown a love of the sinister, a craving for the ominous, a collective dream of the dark. From the earliest fairy tales to Franz Kafka's disturbing fiction, there is an obsession with the more *unheimlich* aspects of life. Nowhere are such nightmarish desires more at home than in the Schwarzwald, a tangled expanse of evergreen covering the southwest corner of Baden-Württemberg. While the Schwarzwald owes its foreboding name to the eerie darkness that prevails under its canopy of vegetation, it is the source of inspiration for the most quintessential German fairy tales, including the adventures of Hänsel and Gretel, as well as a slew of poetry and folk traditions. Many of these regional quirks are now exploited at the pervasive "cuckoo-clock, *Lederhosen,* bratwurst, key-chain, and ice-cream" kiosks, which conspire with the devastation of acid rain to erode the region's authenticity. The hordes of tourists are easily avoided, however, as trails wind through the region leading willing hikers into the dense forest in mere minutes. Skiing is also available in the area; the longest slope is at Feldberg (near Titisee), and smaller hills smatter the Schwarzwald Hochstraße.

The main entry points to the Schwarzwald are Freiburg, in the center; Baden-Baden to the northwest; Stuttgart to the east; and Basel, Switzerland to the southwest. Most visitors cruise around in (or on) their own set of wheels, as public transportation is sparse. Rail lines encircle the perimeter, with only one main **train** actually penetrating the region (from Donaueschingen in the southeast to Offenburg in the northwest). The **bus** service is more thorough, albeit slow and less frequent. The best source of public transportation information is the **Südbaden public transport office** at the Freiburg *Hauptbahnhof* (a copy of the indispensable *Fahrplan* costs DM1). The **Freiburg tourist office** (see p. 440) is the best place to gather information about the Schwarzwald before your trip. The most scenic route through the Schwarzwald is the stretch from northern Waldkirch to southeastern Hinterzarten, where the vistas extend to the Alps in the south and the Rhine Valley in the west.

■ Hochschwarzwald (High Black Forest)

High, rounded mountain tops and a thick carpet of trees maintain the centuries-old isolation of the remote villages of the Hochschwarzwald. Hospitable and traditional residents will confound you with their dialect and impress you with their generosity. The best source of general information about the area is probably the **Freiburg tourist office,** Rotteckring 14 (tel. (0761) 368 90 90; fax 37 00 37). The tourist offices of all the local towns will provide maps and information.

Schwarzwald has given birth to some of Germany's best skiers. When successful, these skiers pay homage to **Feldberg,** at 1493m the Schwarzwald's highest mountain —there is Olympus and there is Feldberg. The ski lift runs in summer and winter (round-trip DM5). At 1234m above sea level, Feldberg's **Jugendherberge Hebelhof (HI),** Passhöhe 14 (tel. (07676) 221; fax 12 32), may be the highest in Germany. Take the Titisee-Schluchsee train to Feldberg-Bärental, then the bus to the Hebelhof stop. (Reception open 8am-10pm. Curfew 10:45pm. Members only. DM18.50, over 26 DM23.50. *Kurtaxe* DM2.10. Reserve in advance for winter.) For tourist information about Feldberg and 16 other ski lifts in the area, call or fax the **tourist office** (tel. (07655) 80 19; fax 801 43); for a **ski report,** call (07676) 12 14.

TITISEE AND SCHLUCHSEE

On hot summer days in Baden-Württemberg, Titisee is mobbed by Germans—the very young, the very old, the leather-clad, and everyone else, all seeking to soak up a little sun. Even cold and cloudy days bring in the mobs, filling the pedestrian zone

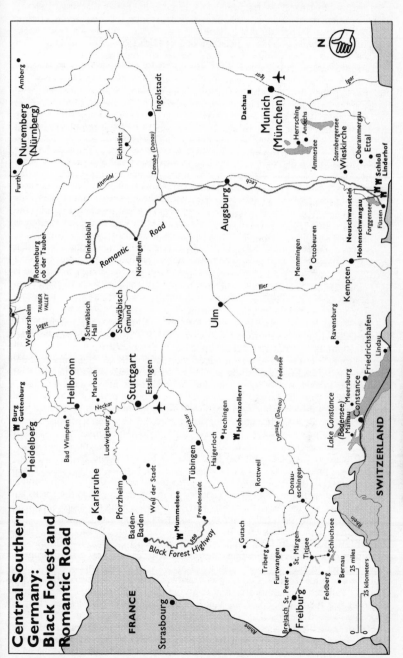

with souvenir-buying, camcorder-wielding German vacationers. Hourly trains connect Freiburg to Titisee; the train ride along through the **Höllental** (Hell's Valley) is scenic now and then, but most of the time is spent in tunnels. Titisee itself is an attractive lake set against a backdrop of dark pine-forested ridges. The most accessible portions of the lake, however, have been invaded by hordes of visitors, making it near impossible to experience any sort of "pure" natural surroundings here.

The **tourist office,** Strandbadstr. 4 (tel. 980 40; fax 98 04 40), is in the *Kurhaus;* to reach the building, turn right in front of the train station, walk to the first intersection and turn left, then turn right before the entrances to the pedestrian zone. Look for a brown modern building and flags dotting the lawn in front. The office books rooms for a suggested DM3 fee, rents bikes (DM15 per day), and arranges horse and carriage rides (1½hr. trip DM80). Also available are maps of the 130km of hiking trails surrounding the lake. (Maps DM1-15. Open May-Oct. Mon.-Fri. 8am-6pm, Sat. 10am-noon and 3-5pm, Sun. 10am-noon; Nov.-April Mon.-Fri. 8am-noon and 1:30-5:30pm.) Rent **paddleboats** from vendors along Seestr. (1hr. DM11-15). Guided boat tours of the lake depart from the same area, run by **Bootsverleih Winterhalder** (tel. 82 14; 25min.; DM6). Titisee's **telephone code** is 07651.

Titisee's **Jugendherberge Veltishof (HI),** Bruderhalde 27 (tel. (07652) 238; fax 756), is inconveniently located at the far end of the lake. From the train station, Südbaden bus #7300 (every 1-3hr.; DM3): "Feuerwehrheim." By foot, it's a 30-minute walk along the main road from the *Kurhaus.* At DM8.50, the hostel serves the cheapest meal in town. (Reception open 5-8pm. Curfew 10pm. Members only. DM22, over 26 DM27. Sheets DM5.50. *Kurtaxe* DM2.10.) **Naturcamping Weierhof,** Bruderhalde 26 (tel. (07652) 14 68; fax 14 78), has great, tree-shaded places to pitch a tent, as well as laundry facilities (person DM8, tent DM6.50; free showers; *Kurtaxe* DM2.10; open mid-May to Sept.). The grocery store **Edeka,** Jägerstr. 5, is down from the tourist office (open Mon.-Tues. and Thurs.-Fri. 8am-12:30pm and 2:30-6pm, Wed. and Sat. 8am-12:30pm). You can practice your synchronized swimming routine at the heated **Freibad,** down Strandbadstr. from the *Kurhaus* (tel. 82 72; open daily 9am-7pm, last entry 6:30pm; DM5, students DM2.50; open late May to mid-Sept.).

If the tourist density in Titisee is too great, go south to the much more serene and picturesque **Schluchsee.** An hourly double-decker train makes the 30-minute jaunt from Titisee to the towns of Schluchsee and Seebrugg, both on the lake. Schluchsee's **tourist office** (tel. 77 32; fax 77 59) is a block into the pedestrian zone in the *Kurhaus.* From the *Bahnhof,* turn right, walk under the underpass, and turn left up the brick sidewalk of Kirchsteige. Sitting on the corner of Fischbacherstr. and Lindenstr., the office provides sight-seeing guides (DM0.50) and hiking maps, and finds accommodations. (Open July-Aug. Mon.-Fri. 8am-6pm, Sat. 10am-noon and 4-6pm, Sun. 10am-noon; Sept.-Oct. and May-June Mon.-Fri. 8am-noon and 2-6pm, Sat. 10am-noon; Nov.-April same hours, except closed Sat.) The **Jugendherberge Schluchsee-Wolfsgrund (HI)** (tel. 329; fax 92 37) is ideally situated on the shore with a stunning lake-view and sparkling, not-too-old facilities; from the station, cross the tracks and hop the fence (easier the farther away you get from the station toward Seebrugg), and then follow the path right, over the bridge parallel to the tracks, directly to the hostel's front door. (Reception closed 2-5pm. Curfew 11pm. DM22, over 26 DM27. Dinner DM8.50. Laundry DM7.) Pick up a list of inexpensive *Pensionen* (DM24-30) at the tourist office. **Haus Bergfrieden,** Dresselbacherstr. 23 (tel. 309), is uphill from the village center. Its tidy rooms are a steal at DM25-28 per person, breakfast included. Doubles and a few singles. **Camping** is available at **Campingplatz Wolfsgrund** (tel. 77 39). Walk left up Bahnhofstr. and continue onto Freiburgerstr., take a left on Sägackerweg, follow it out past Am Waldrain, and then take another left. Stock up on groceries close to the hostel at **Schmidt's Markt,** Im Rappennest 2 (tel. 15 54). **Boat rental** near the hostel is considerably cheaper than in Titisee (30min. DM6, 1hr. DM10). Rent **bikes** at the train station or at **Pension Süßen Winkel Faulen,** Fürsterstr. 4 (tel. 206), just across the bridge (DM10 per day; open daily 8am-7pm). Rent **wind-surfboards** from **Surfschule Ernst Pohl** in Aha-Schluchsee (tel. (07656) 366) for DM15 per hour, DM60 per day (open 10am-5pm).

Three kilometers down the lake at the end of the train line, **Seebrugg** consists of nothing but a train station, a beach, and the **Jugendherberge Schluchsee-Seebrugg (HI),** Seebrugg 9 (tel. 494). Then again, what more could you want? This splendid, recently retouched building (with an intensely green fireplace) is a five-minute walk along the paved path from the train station. (Reception open 12:30-1, 5-6, and 6:30-10pm. Curfew 10pm. Members only. DM22, over 26 DM27. Sheets DM5.50. *Kurtaxe* DM1.65.) Wear your speedos at the **Spaßbad Aqua Schluchsee** (tel. 77 38). Go right from the train station up to the big sign (open daily 9am-7pm; last entry 6:30pm; DM5.50, students DM3.50). Schluchsee's **telephone code** is 07656.

ST. PETER AND ST. MÄRGEN

St. Peter and St. Märgen, only 15km from Freiburg, exude an air of tranquility, and seem to be worlds away from the hectic, student-packed cobblestone city. Sunk deep into the valley between great green hills, the villages are a haven from the sweaty Eurailpass-clutching hordes. **Bus** #7216 runs occasionally from Freiburg to St. Märgen via St. Peter, but the more common route requires a **train** ride along the Freiburg-Neustadt line to "Kirchzarten" (the 3rd stop), where bus #7216 whisks you up to St. Peter. Only half of the buses continue on to St. Märgen; always double check by asking the driver. The *"Südbadenbus Fahrplan"* provides all the schedules; pick one up at the Freiburg bus office (DM1).

St. Peter, designed by architect Peter Thumb, juts high in the curative air, where a halo of green farmland breaks through the dark crust of pine. Its **Klosterkirche** (tel. (07660) 910 10) is yet another contender in the contest for gaudiest church in Southern Germany: a whirlwind of gold, mauve, and almost offensive turquoise mixed with some beautiful Baroque statues of ethereal beings. **Tours** are offered sporadically; call the tourist office for schedules. To get to the **tourist office,** Klosterhof (tel. (07660) 91 02 24; fax 91 02 44), get off the bus at Zähringer Eck and walk up the street for 100m, and the office is on your right, under the arch leading to the Klosterkirche. The office has a list of affordable accommodations starting at DM20 (but it does not book rooms), and maps. Unfortunately, the St. Peter tourist office has only one hiking map for sale. You're better off buying a map in Freiburg or at the gift shop next door (tourist office open Mon.-Fri. 8am-noon and 2-5pm; June-Oct. Sat. 11am-1pm). The **post office,** 79271 St. Peter, is across the street. Many paths begin at the tourist office and abbey; they are well-marked with colored triangles, circles, and diamonds. A relatively easy, but very scenic 8km path (follow the blue diamonds of the *Panoramaweg*) takes you over to St. Märgen.

The wall of white signs speckled with colored shapes of all sorts indicating various *Wanderwegmöglichkeiten* (hiking possibilities) that stands next to the bus stop in the hill-top hamlet of **St. Märgen** is the focus of nearly every visitor's attention. Sporting a large number of easy but gorgeous one- to four-hour trails, as well as links to all the major Schwarzwald trails, the town rightfully calls itself a *Wanderparadies* (hiking paradise). The **tourist office** (tel. (07669) 91 18 17; fax 91 18 40) sits 100m from the St. Märgen "Post" bus stop in the *Rathaus* (open Mon.-Fri. 8am-noon and 2-5pm; June-Aug. also Sat. 10am-noon; Nov.-Dec. closed afternoons). Good hiking and biking maps are available (DM4-5) and they find rooms for free. Upstairs is the inevitable **clock museum,** tracing St. Märgen's role in the Schwarzwald clock-industry with more than 100 endearing locally produced clocks from the 17th to the 19th century crammed into two rooms. The **Heimat Museum** holds equally charming bits of local history and a couple of patiently assembled crucifixion scenes-in bottles. All of these sights dwell in the former Augustinian monastery (watch the doorways—they're short, to encourage the resident monks to stay hunched in humility), whose focal point is the two-tower Baroque church on the right. Unless you have extremely good timing, however, you'll probably miss these wonders. (Clock museum open Wed. 4:30pm. Museum open Fri. 4:30pm. Admission DM2 with a group. Call for arrangements.) The annual **Schwarzwälder Fohlenbrennen,** the annual branding of the young foals, takes place in mid-August—don't say we didn't inform you.

BADEN-WÜRTTEMBERG

■ Mittelerer Schwarzwald (Central Black Forest)

DONAUESCHINGEN AND VILLINGEN-SCHWENNIGEN

At the tender but prodigious age of 10, while traveling from his native Vienna to Paris, Wolfgang Amadeus Mozart stopped in Donaueschingen and played three concerts in the castle. Since that time a variety of other famous personalities have passed through Donaueschingen; most, like Mozart, were on their way somewhere else. Located on the Baar Plateau between the Schwarzwald and the Schwäbische Alb, Donaueschingen acknowledges and even flaunts its status as a rest-stop, its official city brochure emblazoned with the motto, "Donaueschingen: The Princely Destination between the Schwarzwald and Lake Constance." Though the city itself boasts only a few noteworthy sights, its geographical distinction makes Donaueschingen an ideal starting place for forays into the Schwarzwald, the Lake Constance region, and the Wutach Schlucht (Watach Gorge) 15km to the south.

The town's renown comes from its status as the "source" of the 2840km Danube River, the second-longest in Europe and the only major European river to flow west to east. Donaueschingen's claim has little geological validity (the nearby convergence of the Brigach and Brey Rivers is the actual beginning of the Danube), but the town built a monument to the Danube anyway. The **Donauquelle** (Source of the Danube) is a shallow, rock-bottomed basin encased by mossy 19th-century stonework in the garden of the **Fürstenberg Schloß,** conveniently located next to the obligatory 20th-century Fürstenberg Souvenir Booth. The tapestries in the *Schloß* are spectacular, as is the bathroom—a shining marble cave with a massage-shower (no, you don't get to try it). The obligatory tour departs hourly (open Easter-Sept. Wed.-Mon. 9am-noon and 2-5pm; DM5, students DM4; garden always open). Just behind the *Schloß* muses the **Fürstenberg Sammlungen,** Karlspl. 7, a museum displaying collections of former princes of Fürstenberg. The collection's strong late-Gothic holdings kick it old school with works by masters such as Hans Holbein the Elder and Cranach the Elder. (Open Dec.-Oct. Tues.-Sun. 9am-noon and 1:30-5pm, last entrance 30min. before closing. DM5, students DM4.) The museum, the *Schloß,* and the adjacent puddle are all within a 10-minute walk of the train station; take a right in front of the station and walk one block before turning left at Josefstr., then cross the bridge and walk a few hundred meters more. On the way, you'll pass the **Johanniskirche** just above and behind the *Donauquelle;* the church's tame exterior conceals Baroque innards with an intricate gold-and-marble altar. And what would a princely residence be without an opportunity to get royally smashed? **Free beer samples** are available a little farther down the street at the **Fürstliche Fürstenberger Brauerei,** between Haldenstr. and Poststr. (tel. 862 49), which supplies its brews to folks throughout the Schwarzwald (open Mon.-Fri.; call for daily tour schedules). For bike fiends: one end of the **Danube bicycle trail,** trailing along the river, connects Donaueschingen to Vienna. The tourist office (see below) sells a full-length map-*cum*-guide for DM18.80. Take Josefstr. from the station, turn right onto Parkanlage, cross a bridge to the left and follow the path to where the official trail begins.

To reach the **tourist office,** Karlstr. 58 (tel. 85 72 21; fax 85 72 28), veer right up the hill past the *Schloß* and turn left at Karlstr. They book rooms for free. (Open June-Aug. Mon.-Fri. 8am-noon and 1:15-5pm, Sat. 9am-noon; Sept.-May Mon.-Fri. 8am-noon and 2-5pm.) Information about Donaueschingen's annual **Internationales Dressur-, Spring-, und Fahrturnier,** a four-day tournament of show, jumping, and racing horses (Sept. 17-21 in 1998), and the **Musiktage,** (Oct. 16-18 in 1998), a modern music festival, is available at the tourist office. The **post office,** on Bahnhofstr., 78166 Donaueschingen, is across the street and to left of the train station (open Mon.-Fri. 8am-noon and 2:15pm-5:15pm, Sat. 8:30am-noon). The **telephone code** is 0771.

Hotel Bären, Josefstr. 7-9 (tel. 25 18), offers snug rooms to "Baggage-Wanderers" (i.e. those slouching around with big backpacks) for a mere DM25 (DM45 per person without the deal; optional breakfast DM10). More personal service is offered at the itty-bitty **Haus Dilser,** Käferstr. 22 (tel. 46 21), where singles with shower go for DM40; doubles DM80. Pitch a tent (hee hee, you known what we mean) at **Reidsee Camping,** Reidsee 11 (tel. 55 11; fax 151 38), about 8km east of town (DM8 per person and tent). Donaueschingen is well-supplied with restaurants (especially along Josefstr.), and although the price of *Wienerschnitzel* can jump into the DM25 range, most have specials running DM10-14. **Pizzeria da Alfredo,** Villingenstr. 6 near the *Rathaus,* has a gigantic menu which satisfies every craving for Italian (including vegetarian ones) for DM6-20. (Open Mon.-Fri. 11am-3pm and 5:30pm-midnight, Sat. until 1am.) You can get your *Lebensmittel* at **Tengelmann,** a **grocery store** 40m down Karlstr. beyond the tourist office (open Mon.-Fri. 8am-6:30pm, Sat. 7am-1pm).

A 15-minute train ride connects Donaueschingen with **Villingen,** the more curious half of **Villingen-Schwennigen.** Although most of the city is architecturally limp, a handful of well-preserved city gates stand erect. The gorgeous **Münster Unserer lieben Frau** (Cathedral of our dear Lady), features a resplendent golden altar, gigantic wooden organ pipes, and a slew of religious oil paintings beneath the ornate, Victorian ceiling panels. Religious artifacts and pieces (literally) of Villingen-Schwennigen's history can be perused at the **Franziskanermuseum,** Reitgasse 2 (tel. (07721) 82 23 51), which houses various trinkets, ranging from wooden jewelry boxes to shards of prehistoric eating utensils. (Open Tues. and Thurs.-Fri. 10am-noon, Wed. 10am-noon and 2-8pm, Sat. 2-5pm, Sun. 1-5pm. DM3, students DM1.50.) Tucked in a corner of Schwennigen is the well-assembled and surprisingly interesting **Uhrenindustriemuseum** (clock industry museum), Bürkstr. 39 (tel. (07720) 380 44). Watch raw materials miraculously transform into ticking, turning time-keeping devices at the museum's in-house production line, or discuss the intricacies of clock industry labor relations at the cafe (museum open Tues.-Sun. 10am-noon and 2-6pm; DM5, students DM3). Back in Villingen, the local **Jugendherberge (HI),** St. Georgenerstr. 36 (tel. (07721) 526 16), makes a good starting point for Schwarzwald shenanigans. Although it's a 30-minute walk outside of town and serviced only by infrequent buses, it's a good resting place if the kids haven't grabbed all the spaces. Four to six beds per clean, well-worn room (DM20, over 26 DM25; sheets DM5.50; members only).

TRIBERG AND FURTWANGEN

Nestled in a lofty valley 800m above sea level, the touristy whistle stop of **Triberg** has attitude about its altitude. The inhabitants brag in superlatives about the highest **waterfalls** in Germany, a series of bright white cascades tumbling over moss-covered rocks for 162 vertical meters. Tame by Niagara standards and swarming with over 500,000 visitors every year, these swirling falls might fail to impress. The somewhat steep climb dissuades the less-than-fit from ascending, thus leaving the fanny packs behind at lower altitudes (park admission DM2.50, students DM2). The signs within the park for the Wallfahrtskirche point to a trail leading to the small **Pilgrim Church,** a rather plain chapel with white walls and eroded wooden benches, a baffling juxtaposition to the enormous, brashly golden altar. Back in town directly across the street from the waterfalls is the well-stuffed **Schwarzwald Museum,** Wallfahrtsstr. 4 (tel. 44 34). Every room of the rather small building is jam-packed with Schwarzwald paraphernalia of every imaginable variety, from re-enactments of the daily life of the *Schwarzwald Volk* (complete with slimy wax people) to a Schwarzwald model railroad that chugs away among a highly detailed cardboard landscape (DM1 to watch it go), and of course, plenty of clocks (open daily 9am-6pm; Nov.-April 10am-5pm; DM5, children DM2). Beyond these attractions, the region's splendid natural surroundings of mountains, streams, and human-friendly squirrels prove inviting. **Hiking trails** abound throughout the outskirts of town, including a portion of the Pforzheim-Basel *Westweg.* The tourist office (see below) sells hiking maps for DM5.50, and more detailed guides are available at the town's bookstores, souvenir shops, and *Schnitzel* stands. Avoid using the normal town maps for hiking, since the sketched trails are vague and sometimes inaccurate.

Triberg's **tourist office** (tel. 95 32 30; fax 95 32 36) hides on the ground floor of the local *Kurhaus.* They dish out brochures, sell town maps (DM1), and dispense a mammoth catalog of all hotels, *Pensionen*, and private rooms in the region (open Mon.-Fri. 9am-5pm; May-Sept. also Sat. 10am-noon). The town's sparkling, modern **Jugendherberge (HI)**, Rohrbacherstr. 35 (tel. 41 10; fax 66 62), requires a grueling 30-minute climb up Friedrichstr. (which turns into Rohrbacherstr.) from the tourist office. Everything is sleek, and each four- to six-bed room has running water. (Reception open 5-7pm and at 9:45pm. DM22, over 26 DM27. Sheets DM5.50. Call ahead.) For those apprehensive about the climb, the **Hotel Zum Bären**, Hauptstr. 10 (tel. 44 93), offers worn-in rooms, most with showers, closer to the town center. The jolly staff has been dealing with American students for 25 years (singles DM46; doubles DM86). The **telephone code** is 07722.

Bus #7270 makes an hourly run between Triberg and the less idyllic city of **Furtwangen**. Here ticks the **Deutsches Uhrenmuseum**, Gerwigstr. 11 (tel. 92 01 17), the granddaddy of all Schwarzwald shrines to time-keeping. Over 4000 clocks are on display, from decrepit 18th-century cuckoos to gaudy Victorian contraptions to hypermodern timepieces that double as postmodern art (open daily 9am-5pm, Nov.-March 10am-5pm; DM4). After watching the universe wind down meticulously with German-style precision, thank the powers-that-be for the man, the myth, the legend that is Don Bosco. Who is Don Bosco, you ask? Why, the man who made possible the ultra-comfortable and unbeatably cheap **Don Bosco Jugendgästehaus**, Am Engelgrund 2 (tel. 65 08 46). Though the hostel is officially only for groups and families, the gracious owner often lets weary stragglers stick around if there are empty beds. Dig the mod sheet-metal decor and awesome bedrooms with running water (curfew midnight; DM12; breakfast DM5). Furtwangen's **telephone code** is 07723.

■ Nördlicher Schwarzwald (Northern Black Forest)

The dark, meandering valleys of the Nördlicher Schwarzwald, replete with an extensive network of trails, make for wonderful hiking. The area is easily accessible from the north; direct trains make the two-hour trip from Karlsruhe to Freudenstadt hourly, and the final 45-minute stretch is a gorgeous trip through deep valleys and the surrounding heavily forested hills. The tourist office in Baden-Baden (tel. (07221) 27 52 00) is only marginally helpful. Far better is the **tourist office** in **Freudenstadt**, Promenadepl. 1 (tel. 86 40; fax 851 76), which bulges with hiking maps (DM5) and provides information on excursions of every sort (open Mon.-Fri. 10am-6pm, Sat. 10am-1pm). From the *Hauptbahnhof* follow Bahnhofstr. to Turnhallestr. and make a left. The tourist office is at the end of the street, on the left near the *Kurhaus*. From the Stadt *Bahnhof*, follow Martin-Luther-Str. as it turns into to Loßburgerstr. to the Kurhaus plaza; it's on the corner to the left. The **Kurhaus**, Promenadepl. 2 (tel. 86 40), across from the tourist office in the main square, rents **bikes** and books rooms when the tourist office is closed. (Bikes ½day DM10, full day DM7, week DM65. For mountain bikes day DM28, week DM125.) **Katz Reisebüro**, Marktplatz 44 (tel. 89 50), leads daily excursions to far off places like Strasbourg, France (DM25) and Switzerland (DM49), as well as the Europapark amusement park (DM50 includes admission). Pick up a brochure at the tourist office for details. The tourist office is probably the highlight of Freudenstadt ("Town of Joy")—the town is impeccably maintained and little else. It does, however, have **Panorama Bad**, Ludwig-Jahn-Str. (tel. 89 06 20), a swimming complex with several pools and waterslides. From the youth hostel follow Ludwig-Jahn-Str. up and to the right (2½hr.; DM2.50, students DM2; open Mon.-Fri. 9am-10pm, Sat.-Sun. 9am-8pm). The cheapest beds in town are at the standard but well-maintained Freudenstadt **Jugendherberge (HI)**, Eugen-Nägele-Str. 69 (tel. 77 20; fax 857 88). From the *Stadtbahnhof*, hang a left and follow the train tracks to a set of steps (10min.), then pass under the bridge and turn right at Gottlieb-Daimler-Str. (Reception open 5-6:30pm and 9-9:30pm. Curfew 10pm. Members only. DM22, over 26 DM27. Sheets DM5.50. Sleep-sack DM3. Laundry DM5.) Another overnight option in Freudenstadt is **Hotel Adler**, Forststr. 17 (tel. 915 20; fax 91 52 52), which has handsome rooms and accepts credit cards. (Singles DM56, with bath DM65; doubles DM92, with bath DM110.) Buy groceries at **Pfannkuch**, across from the *Stadtbahnhof*. The **telephone code** in Freudenstadt is 07441.

■ Schwarzwaldhochstraße (Black Forest Highway)

The **Schwarzwaldhochstraße** stretches 65km from Freudenstadt in the south to Baden-Baden in the north. It contains some of Germany's most stunning scenery, as well as parts of the two *Bundesstraßen* (federal highways) B28 and B500. Even more arresting, however, is the accompanying footpath **(Westweg)** that spans the spine of the mountains overlooking the Rhine Valley and the Vosges Mountains of France. Along the Westweg, 17km northwest of Freudenstadt and 2km from the crossroads at Alexanderschanze, stands one of Germany's most comfortable youth hostels, the **Jugendherberge Zuflucht (HI)** (tel. (07804) 611; fax 13 23). A large, converted hotel built in the style of a Schwarzwald farmhouse, the hostel lets lodgers bask in spotless, carpeted six-bed dorm rooms; it also rents ski equipment and bikes. Bus #12 leaves from the *Hauptbahnhof Freizeitverkehr* and connects the hostel to Freudenstadt twice daily May-Oct. 11:07am and 5:07pm, returning 9:35am and 1:35pm. (No lockout. Curfew 10pm or by prior arrangement. Members only. DM22, over 26 DM27. Sheets DM5.50.) From the nearby settlement of **Ruhestein,** the Westweg leads over **Seiblesecke** and the **Mummelsee** to **Unterstatt,** traversing the **Hornisgrinde** (1164m), the highest peak in the region. Unbeknownst to the busloads of tourists who are unwittingly dumped here, the Mummelsee is tiny and has little to recommend it save the possibilities inherent in a lovely little lake. Buy your *Walliser Brot* here (kg DM7.20). Bus #7106 departs daily from Augustpl. in Baden-Baden at 9:03am and 1:43pm (50min.; DM6.60) and returns to Baden-Baden at 10:25am and 4:40pm. There are better ways to spend your time, however. Down the hill after a rigorous hike rests the **Wildsee,** a more attractive lake devoid of cars and Europabuses.

▓ Rottweil

Known in Roman times by the name *Alae Flaviae* (Flavius' Altar), Rottweil bears the distinction of being the oldest city in Baden-Württemberg. A free and independent city under the Holy Roman Empire, Rottweil's contributions to the world's wellbeing have included both flameless gunpowder (the unfortunate brainchild of one Herr Duttenhofer) and certain disagreeable and pernicious canines. It comes as no surprise to discover that the city itself is still a bustling, ferocious little village that knows how to party. Chief among its swingin' shindigs is Rottweil's famous, traditional **Fasnet** celebration, which draws gawkers from all over Germany to watch 4000 *Rottweil Narren* (fools) storm through town in wooden masks and expensive costumes in a festive attempt to expel winter (the next outbreak is February 23-24, 1998). The **Fronleichnam** ceremony (June 1 in 1998) reignites old Protestant-Catholic feuds in an innocent re-enactment, in which Protestants do some hard-core housecleaning to whip up dust, sullying the roving bands of Catholics.

Rottweil's fanatic adherence to old traditions is not limited to celebrations. The town is a living architecture museum—contrasting colors, meticulously crafted oriel windows, and historic murals gracing the facades transform nearly every building into a work of art. At the summit of the hill on which the town perches looms the 13th-century **Schwarzes Tor** (Black Gate). In this town of venerable buildings, the ancient *Tor* was built in 1289, and enlarged in 1571 and 1650. Halfway up Hauptstr., across from the **Altes Rathaus,** is the **Stadtmuseum,** Hauptstr. 20 (tel. 49 42 56). Its possessions include a 15th-century treaty between Rottweil and nine Swiss cantons—still valid to this day—and a collection of wooden masks from the *Fasnet* celebrations (open Tues.-Sat. 10am-noon and 2-5pm, Sun. 10am-noon; DM1).

To scale the ancient **Hochturm** and gaze out upon the rippling hills of the Schwäbische Alb, pick up the key from the tourist office in exchange for an ID deposit (on weekends, key available next door at **Café Schädle**). Behind the *Altes Rathaus,* the Gothic **Heilig-Kreuz-Münster** (Cathedral of the Holy Cross) houses an enormous interior and a sparsely dignified altar. One block from the *Münster,* the innocuous pink exterior of the **Evangelische Predigerkirche** conceals a huge Baroque interior. Next to the Predigerkirche, the newly constructed **Dominikaner-**

museum collection, on Kriegsdamm (tel. 78 62), includes a wide variety of religiously inspired sculptures and a large exhibit documenting Rottweil's Roman past, highlighted by a 2nd-century mosaic comprised of 570,000 tiles (open Tues.-Sun. 10am-1pm and 2-5pm; DM3).

Lying on the Stuttgart-Zurich rail line, Rottweil is easily accessible by hourly regional trains connecting the city with Stuttgart in the north and Singen in the south. The train station lies in the valley below the town center, which translates into an unfortunate 20-minute uphill climb. Turn right upon leaving the station and head upward. When you reach the bridge, take another right to cross it. Hauptstr., the cross-street at the second block on your left is the center of the town's action. Halfway up the street on the right-hand side, is the **tourist office,** Hauptstr. 23 (tel. 49 42 80 or 49 42 81; fax 49 43 55); they book rooms for free and offer maps, an English guide to the city, and *Freizeit Spiegel*—a free publication detailing the artistic, theatrical, and musical offerings (open Mon.-Fri. 9am-12:30pm and 2-5pm; May-Oct. also open Sat. 10am-noon). Free 90-minute **city tours** are also available every Saturday at 2:30pm from the tourist office and culminate, if the group is in a sudsy mood, in a round of pub-crawling (May-Oct. only). **Alfred Kaiser,** Balingerstr. 9 (tel. 89 19), will cater to all your **bike rental** desires. The **post office** is on Königstr. 12 (open Mon.-Fri. 8am-noon, 2:30pm-6pm, Sat. 8am-noon). The **telephone code** is 0741.

Inexpensive accommodations are difficult to find in the summer months. Call early and often. To find the small and homey **Jugendherberge (HI),** Lorenzgasse 8 (tel. 76 64), walk left on Lorenzgasse (while walking downhill on Hauptstr.), go right at the ivy-covered building, and left at the *"Jugendherberge"* sign. Many of the cramped six- to eight-bed rooms in this half-timbered house face out onto the terrifically steep plunge into the Neckar. (Reception open 5-10:30pm; DM21, over 26 DM25). The *Pension* **Goldenes Rad,** Hauptstr. 38 (tel. 74 12), is often booked solid several weeks in advance. (Reception open Thurs.-Tues. 11:30am-3pm and 5pm-on. Singles DM40; doubles DM72.) Across the street, **Gasthof Lamm** (tel. 450 15) provides a good deal, offering sparkling clean rooms and a groovy modern art stained glass window in the first floor lobby (singles from DM50; doubles DM78). For traditional regional cooking, head to **Zum Goldenen Becher,** Hochbrücktorstr. 17, a hearty family restaurant where meals run DM12-30 (open Tues.-Sun.11am-midnight). At **Rotuvilla,** Hauptstr. 63 (tel. 416 95), feast on many incarnations of wood-oven pizza (DM9-16) in a half-timbered dining room (open Wed.-Mon. 11:30am-2pm and 5pm-midnight).

■ Bodensee (Lake Constance)

Land-locked Germany has suffered from a Mediterranean-complex for centuries. The white sand beaches of the Riviera, the sparkling waters of the Greek Islands, the white stucco architecture of Italy, all stand in sharp contrast to the colder, grayer German landscape. However, the stretch of Southern Baden-Württemberg that borders the exquisite Bodensee provide an outlet for pent-up *Mittelmeerlust,* an opportunity for Italian fantasies to be enacted and Grecian longings to be satisfied. Potted palms line the streets, public beaches are filled with sunbathers tanning to a melanomic crisp, and daily business is conducted with a thoroughly un-German casualness. Looking out across the lake, one easily sees how the deception works so smoothly, as the surprisingly warm waters glow an intense turquoise blue more typically found in the Caribbean than European lakes. Whatever the case, the beautiful towns surrounding the lake seem more tropical than Teutonic. With the snow-capped Swiss and Austrian Alps soaring beyond the sparkling *See,* Bodensee is one of Germany's most stunning destinations.

Getting to the region by **train** is easy; the cities of Konstanz and Friedrichshafen have direct connections to many major German cities. Transport within the region can require long rides and tricky connections due to the absence of a single route which fully encircles the lake. In many instances, the bright white boats of the **BSB** (Bodensee-Schiffsbetriebe) and several other smaller lines, known collectively as the *Weiße Flotte* (White Fleet) are a quicker and more beautiful alternative. Ships leave

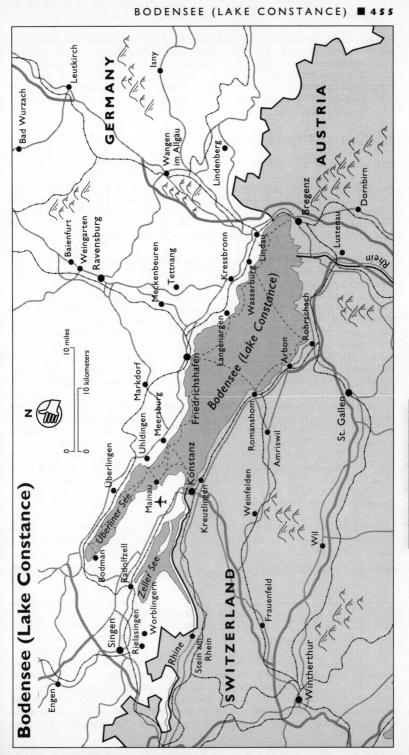

Bodensee (Lake Constance)

BADEN-WÜRTTEMBERG

hourly from Konstanz and Friedrichshafen for all ports around the lake, departing every 1-3 hours. A detailed schedule *(Schiffsfahrplan)* is available free at every ticket counter. Those who plan to spend at least a week here should seriously consider the 7-day **Bodensee-Pass,** which includes two days of free ship travel and a 50% discount on all rail, bus, and gondola-lift tickets (DM57, available at all ship ticket counters). A **15-day card** for 50% off ship, rail, bus, and gondola travel runs DM48. For all ship related information, call the BSB office in Konstanz (tel. 28 13 98).

■ Konstanz (Constance)

Spanning the Rhine's exit from the Bodensee, the elegant university city of Konstanz has never been bombed. Part of the city extends into neighboring Switzerland, and the Allies were leery of accidentally striking neutral territory. The proximity of Switzerland and its possession by Austria until 1805 give the place an open, international character. The narrow streets wind around beautifully painted Baroque and Renaissance facades in the central part of town, while along the river promenades, gabled and turreted 19th-century houses gleam with a confident gentility.

Orientation and Practical Information The **tourist office,** Bahnhofspl. 13 (tel. 13 30 30; fax 13 30 60), in the arcade to the right of the train station, provides an excellent walking map (DM0.50) and lots of information about the area. They find rooms for a DM5 fee in private homes for a three-night minimum stay. (Open May-Sept. Mon.-Fri. 9am-6:30pm, Sat. 9am-1pm; Oct.-April Mon.-Fri. 9am-noon and 2-6pm; April and Oct. also Sat. 9am-1pm.) **Buses** in Konstanz cost DM2.40 per ride, DM10 for a five-ride ticket, and DM7 for a one-day ticket for two adults and three children. The **Gästekarte,** available at any accommodation in the city, including the youth hostel, costs DM1.50 per night and gives you bus fare within Konstanz and free or discounted admission to some sights. The tiny but spunky **Mitfahrzentrale,** Münzgasse 22 (tel. 214 44; fax 166 60), can help find you a ride. (To Munich DM23, Freiburg DM16, Stuttgart DM20. Open Mon. 2-6pm, Tues.-Fri. 9:30am-12:30pm and 2-6pm, Sat. 10am-2pm.) The posh **English Bookshop,** Münzgasse 10 (tel. 150 63; fax 150 66), has superb selection of books (open Mon.-Fri. 9am-6:30pm, Sat. 9am-2pm).

Tickets for the **Weiße Flotte** are on sale in the building behind the train station (open Sun.-Fri. 7:40am-6:15pm, Sat. 7:40am-8:30pm). Otherwise, buy your tickets on the ship. The tourist office offers a two-day pass (DM32) including transportation on buses, the ferry, the *Weiße Flotte* ship line to Meersburg and Mainau and back, as well as a bag o' brochures and admission to Mainau (see p. 458). **Giess Personenschiffahrt** runs private boats hourly from behind the train station to **Freizeitbad Jakob** and **Freibad Horn** (45min.; June-Aug. daily 10:50am-5:50pm; May and Sept. Sun. only; DM8, children half-price). **Paddleboats and rowboats** can be rented at Am Gondelhafen (tel. 218 81) for DM14-16 per hour (April-Oct. daily 10am-dusk). **Rent bikes** from **Velotours,** Mainaustr. 34 (tel. 982 80; day DM20, week DM100; open March-Oct. daily 9am-5:30pm). Remove your disgusting body odor from your clothing at **Waschsalon and Mehr,** Hofhalde 3 (wash DM7, dry DM2 per 10min; open Mon.-Fri. 10am-7pm, Sat. 10am-4pm). The **telephone code** is 07531.

Accommodations Commanding the tip of a small lakefront hill like a manor in the old American South is the marvelous **Jugendherberge Kreuzlingen (HI),** Promenadenstr. 7 (tel. from Germany (0041) 71 688 26 63, from Switzerland (071) 688 26 63; fax 688 47 61). Located south of the border in Kreuzlingen, **Switzerland,** the hostel is actually closer to downtown Konstanz than the official Konstanz hostel. It's also more luxurious, with cushy leather furniture in a wood-paneled library, a scrumptious breakfast spread, and a multilingual staff practically breaking their necks to serve you. The best way there is by foot (20min.); leaving the *Bahnhof,* turn left, cross the metal bridge over the tracks, turn right, and go through the parking lot to the checkpoint "Klein Venedig." Keep walking along Seestr. until the sharp right curve. Instead of following the street, continue straight ahead on the gravel path through the gate, past the billy goats, right through the Seeburg castle parking lot, and right up the hill to the building with a flag on top. (Reception open 8-9am and 5-9pm. First night SFr21.20 (about DM26.50—they also accept *Deutschemarks*), subsequent nights SFr18.70 (DM23.40). SFr2.50 cheaper in March-April and Nov.-Oct. Curfew 11pm. Breakfast and sheets included. Rents mountain bikes for SFr12.50 per day, kayaks for SFr10 per 2hr. Open March-Nov.)

Jugendherberge "Otto-Moericke-Turm" (HI), zur Allmannshöhe 18 (tel. 322 60), has cramped rooms in a former water tower next to a graveyard. There's a terrific view of the lake from the bathrooms. Bus #4 from the "Markstätte" stop (just around the corner from the post office in front of the station): "Jugendherberge." (Reception open 3-10pm. Curfew 10pm. Lock-out 9am-4pm. DM21.50, over 26 DM26.50. Members only. Breakfast included. Sheets DM5.50. Call ahead.) **Jugendwohnheim Don Bosco,** Salesianerweg 5 (tel. 662 52; fax 606 88), is an excellent, quieter alternative to the hostels. From the station, bus #1: "Salzberg." Go back 25m and take the path on the left that becomes Brandesstr.; at the intersection, take Händelstr. until it reaches the alley, turn left, walk 150m, and look for the big yellow building on your left. Choose from 39 channels (MTV Europe, of course) in the comfortable dayroom. (Doubles DM30 per person. Bigger rooms DM25 per person. For young'uns (under 18), curfew 10pm.) **Campingplatz Konstanz-Bruderhofer,** Fohrenbühlweg 50 (tel. 313 88 or 313 92), is even cheaper. Bus #1: "Staad." The campground is along the water front. Call ahead, as it also fills up fast (person DM6.50; tent DM5.50-8.50).

Food The **University Mensa** dishes out Konstanz's cheapest food. Lunches, including dessert and a view of the lake, cost DM8-9 (open Mon.-Fri. 11:15am-1:30pm). The **cafeteria** on floor K6 has lighter fare, like sandwiches and desserts, with no ID required (DM1-4; open Mon.-Thurs. 8am-5pm, Fri. 8am-3pm). Bus #9 from the station: "Universität" (open Mon.-Fri. 8am-6pm; Aug. Mon.-Fri. 11am-2pm). Also with a view is the **Volkshochschule Mensa.** You need an international student ID to get yourself a changecard; ask the attendant. The hassle is worth it—meals cost DM4.40 (open Mon.-Fri. 8:30am-4pm). Stroll through the small streets surrounding the *Münster's* northern side: it is the oldest part of Konstanz, and now the center of its vibrant alternative scene, with health-food stores, left-wing graffiti, and student cafes. There is a **Tengelmann grocery store** at the corner of Münzgasse and Brotlaube (open Mon.-Fri. 8:30am-6:30pm, Sat. 8am-2pm). **Sedir,** Hofhaldestr. 11 (tel. 293 52), serves bowls of delectable vegetarian noodles for DM9.50, and lots of other meat and non-meat dishes for under DM12. The photographs on the wall take you to Turkey, the music to vintage 1970 America (open Mon.-Fri. 11:30am-2pm and 6pm-1am, Sat.-Sun. noon-2:30pm and 6pm-1am).

Sights Konstanz's **Münster,** built over the course of 600 years, has a soaring Gothic spire and 17th-century vaulting as well as a set of organ pipes that look like they were ripped off from Barnum and Bailey's. (Church open daily 8am-5:30pm. Free. Tower open Mon.-Sat. 10am-6pm, Sun. 1-6pm. DM2, students DM1.) The elaborate frescoes on the **Rathaus** depict Konstanz history. Wander down **Seestraße,** near the yacht harbor on the lake, or down **Rheinsteig** along the Rhine, to two picturesque waterside promenades. The tree-filled **Stadtgarten,** next to Konstanz's main harbor, provides peace and an unbroken view of the Bodensee. Across the Rhine from the *Altstadt,* near the "Sternenpl." bus stop, is the great **Archäologisches Landesmuseum,** Benediktinerpl. 5 (tel. 51 038), a three-floor assemblage of all things ancient from Baden-Württemberg—if it was found underground, it qualifies for display: jewels, spearheads, and re-assembled skeletons (open Tues.-Sun. 10am-6pm; DM4, students DM3). The building that houses the **Rosgarten Museum Konstanz,** Rosgartenstr. 3-5 (tel. 90 02 46; fax 90 06 08), is the most exciting thing about this museum of knick-knacks related to the vague "local history and culture" theme. Built in 1324, its low ceilings, creaky floors, and carved wood paneling whisk you back through the centuries (open Tues.-Thurs. 10am-5pm, Fri.-Sun. 10am-4pm; DM3, students DM1.50). To get there, go up Marktstr. from the station and then left on Rosgartenstr.

Konstanz boasts a number of **public beaches:** all are free and open from May to September. **Strandbad Horn** (tel. 635 50; bus #5), the largest and most crowded, sports a section for nude sunbathing modestly enclosed by peek-proof hedges. In inclement weather, head next door to **Freizeitbad Jakob,** Wilhelm-von-Scholz-Weg 2 (tel. 611 63), an ultra-modern indoor-outdoor pool complex with thermal baths and sun lamps. Walk 30 minutes along the waterfront from the train station, or bus #5: "Freizeitbad Jakob" (open daily 9am-9pm; DM8, students DM5). **Strandbad Konstanz-Litzelstetten** and **Strandbad Konstanz-Wallhausen** can both be reached via bus #4. The twenty something set frolics on the beach at the university. Bus #4: "Egg" and walk past the *Sporthalle* and playing fields, or take a 10-minute walk down through the fields from the youth hostel.

NEAR KONSTANZ: MAINAU

The rich and magnificently manicured garden covering the island of Mainau is the result of the horticultural prowess of generations of Baden princes and the Swedish royal family. An arboretum, greenhouses, and **huge animals made of flowers** surround the Baroque palace built by the Knights of the Teutonic Order, who lived here from the 13th to the 18th century. Now thousands of happy little tourists scamper across the foot bridge from Konstanz to pose with the blooming elephants and ooh at the 30 different varieties of butterflies fluttering about the tropical-climate greenhouse. Truly amazing are the dozens of fully grown palm trees planted around the palace, able to survive year-round due to the lake's moderating effect on the climate and the magic green fingers of the island's massive gardening army. From the Konstanz *Hauptbahnhof,* bus #1: "Staad." Or take a romantic boat trip from behind the train station (one-way DM5.40, round-trip DM9). The busiest time on the island is during its official opening hours. (Open 7am-8pm; DM16.50, students DM9, seniors DM13, children DM5.50; Nov. to mid-March 9am-5pm; DM5, children free.) For more information call (07531) 30 30 or fax 30 32 48.

FRIEDRICHSHAFEN

A former construction base for Zeppelins, Friedrichshafen was almost entirely leveled by Allied bombing in 1944. The current town was rebuilt with sweeping, wide promenades and tree-lined boulevards which open up onto breathtaking panoramas of the Alps across the water. The city's flagship attraction is the superb **Graf-Zeppelin-Museum,** Hafenbahnhof, Seestr. 2 (tel. 380 10), which details the history of the flying dirigibles and their inventor. The fleet of nine scale models is overshadowed by an original-size (38m) reconstruction of a section of the unfortunate Hindenburg, which went up in flames in New Jersey in 1936. Climb aboard and check out the authentically recreated passenger cabins—so *that's* how they went to the bathroom. Oh, the humanity! (Open Tues.-Wed. and Fri.-Sun. 10am-5pm, Thurs. 10am-8pm. DM10, students DM4). **Schulmuseum Friedrichshafen,** Friedrichstr. 14 (tel. 326 22), documents school life in Germany over the last five centuries and includes hordes of schoolchildren from this century. Don't miss the "punishment" exhibit, or the report cards of Bertolt Brecht and Karl Marx, whose teacher once commented, "In history and geography, Karl is a bit lost" (open daily 10am-5pm; mid-Nov. to mid-March Tues.-Sun. 2-5pm; DM2, students DM1). The 17th-century **Schloßkirche,** on Friedrichstr., to the right of the station, was practically burned to the ground in 1944; it was restored to its former glory, complete with stucco ceiling and Baroque altar, in 1950. The high altar and the pulpit, however, are made of imitation marble (open Sun.-Thurs. 9am-6pm, Fri. 10am-6pm). The beach is at the **Strandbad,** Königsweg 11 (tel. 280 78); take the path to the right of the Schloßkirche entrance (15min.; open mid-May to mid-Sept. daily 9am-8pm; DM2).

Ask which hotels rent bikes at the **tourist office,** Bahnhofpl. 2 (tel. 300 10; fax 725 88), across the square to the left of the train station. From the harbor, follow Seestr. to the left and cross the park at the Zeppelin monument. The office provides excellent free town maps, an extensive library of biking routes, and reserves rooms for a

DM5 fee, though they encourage you to do it yourself and provide all necessary information to do so (open Mon.-Fri. 8am-noon and 2-5pm; brochures available at the *Schulmuseum* if office is closed). The town has unusually good tourist orientation signs pointing to almost everything noteworthy from the *Bahnhof*. Friedrichshafen is connected by frequent **buses and boats** to Lindau and Meersburg; the boat from Konstanz takes 1½ hours and costs DM12. The city has amazing rail connections, with hourly trains east to Munich and west to Radolfzell (which connects to Konstanz). There is a **boat** from Konstanz. **Rent bikes** at the train station (*Fahrkartenausgabe* counter; DM13 per day). The **telephone code** is 07541.

Friedrichshafen's **Jugendherberge "Graf Zeppelin" (HI),** Lindauerstr. 3 (tel. 724 04; fax 749 86), is clean, renovated, and 50m from the water's edge. Call ahead; this place fills up just like the rest, especially in summer. Walk down Seestr.from the harbor (15min.). (Reception open 1-7:30, 8:30-9:30, and 9:45-10pm. Curfew 10pm. DM22.50, over 26 DM27.50. Breakfast included. Sheets DM5.50.) Well-touristed Friedrichshafen has virtually no affordable restaurants, so *Imbiß* stands, located along Friedrichstr., are your best bet. The **Naturkost am Buchhornplatz,** Buchhornpl. 1 (tel. 243 35), serves up home-cooked vegetarian food in warm brown light and also offers a brisk take-out business (spinach pizza DM4.50). A **supermarket, Norma,** has a branch on Friedrichstr. (open Mon.-Fri. 8:30am-6:30pm, Sat. 8am-2pm).

MEERSBURG

Directly across the lake from Konstanz, the gorgeous medieval town of Meersburg hugs the steep hillside, every crooked little house and curvy little street overshadowed by the massive stone exterior of Germany's oldest inhabited castle—the **Meersburg.** Begun in the 7th century, the huge, medieval edifice now houses a pile of armor and an extensive collection of deer antlers. (Open March-Oct. daily 9am-6:30pm; Nov.-Feb. 10am-6pm; last entrance 30min. before closing. DM9, students DM8, children DM5.50.) In the 18th century, a prince bishop declared the *Altes Schloß* unfit to house his regal self—so he commissioned the sherbet pink **Neues Schloß** to be built by architect Balthasar Neumann. The town's art collection and the **Dornier museum,** with models of Dornier airplanes, are housed there (open April-Oct. daily 10am-6pm; DM5, students and children DM3). Meersburg's quirky and packed **Zeppelin Museum,** Schloßpl. 8 (tel. 79 09), 20m below the old castle, presents two full-sized mannequins decked out in Zeppelin flight attendant uniforms, as well as anything else remotely connected with Zeppelins, including commemorative porcelain and a 30-minute video on the history and development of the flying cigars (open April-Oct. daily 10am-6pm; DM4.50, children DM3.50). Beyond the new castle along the **Uferpromenade,** catch a mind-boggling view of the Bodensee against a backdrop of the Alps. Climb the steep Steigstr. left from the harbor past the crowded half-timbered houses.

The **tourist office,** Kirschstr. 4 (tel. 43 11 10; fax 43 11 20), at the top of the climb, provides free city maps, useful for the tangled *Altstadt,* and a list of accommodations, though it doesn't make reservations (open Mon.-Fri. 9am-noon and 2-5:30pm, Sat. 10am-2pm; Nov.-April Mon.-Fri. 8am-noon and 2-4pm). Meersburg is half an hour from Konstanz by **boat** (DM5.40). It has no train station but uses the one in Uhldingen-Mühlhofen; Friedrichshafen is 25 minutes away. **Haus Mayer Bartsch,** Stettene 53 (tel. 60 50), has balcony rooms with TVs. From the Marktplatz, go up Obertorstr. through the gate, then head straight and bear right onto Stetterstr. Keep on truckin'; it's on the left past the gas station. (Singles DM38, with bath DM50; doubles DM85, with bath DM130-135.) For tasty and honestly priced pizza and spaghetti (DM9-16.50, slices DM3) in this city of sky-high prices, **Da Nico,** Unterstadtstr. 41 (tel. 64 48), across the street from the harbor, offers organic Italian food (open daily 11:30am-11pm). The **telephone code** is 07532.

BADEN-WÜRTTEMBERG

LINDAU IM BODENSEE

Connected to the lake shore by a narrow causeway, the romantic medieval city of **Lindau im Bodensee** looks out across the Bodensee, where the aquamarine waters and the small but oh-so-significant detachment from the mainland contribute to the city's resort-like ambience. Though most of the Bodensee borders Baden-Württemberg, Lindau is technically part of Bayern. The central part of town around **Maximilianstraße** features captivating half-timbered houses, and the view of the Alps is almost the same as the one you see on good chocolates. The **Städtische Kunstsammlung** (town art museum) is located in **Cavazzen-Haus,** an ornate Baroque mansion (open April-Oct. Tues.-Sun. 10am-noon and 2-5pm; DM4, students DM1). The harbor is framed by a rather imposing 19th-century **Bavarian Lion** and the **New Lighthouse,** the latter offering an illuminating overview of the neighborhood (open daily 10am-7pm; DM2, students DM1). The **Rathaus,** halfway along Maximilianstr., is a fruity blend of frescoes. A walk down the less touristed equivalent of Maximilianstr.—In der Grube (In the Pit)—will lead you to the **Diebstahl Turm** (robbery tower). Covered with ivy and newly renovated, the color-speckled tin-roofed turret looks more like Rapunzel's tower than a former prison. For those over 21 and possessing a coat and tie or a formal dress, the **casino** on the island (one of four in Bayern) is an entertaining option. The bet ceiling is DM12,000, so don't worry about losing too much money (open 3pm-2am; admission DM5 and a passport—please daaarling, no jeans).

The **tourist office,** Am Hauptbahnhof (tel. 26 00 30; fax 26 00 26), across from the station, finds rooms for a DM5 fee (open Mon.-Sat. 9am-1pm and 2-7pm). **Tours** leave from the office at 10am (Tues. and Fri. in German, Mon. in English; DM5, students and overnight guests DM3). **Ferries** link Lindau with Konstanz, stopping at Meersburg, Mainau, and Friedrichshafen (5-7 per day, 3hr., one-way DM18). The **train** takes two hours (one-way DM13). Crazy kids can rent **boats** 50m to the left of the casino, right next to the bridge (tel. 55 14; open mid.-March to mid.-Sept. daily 9am-9pm; paddleboats DM12-15 per hr. for up to 5 people; power boat DM45). One-hour excursions (tel. 781 94) on a small boat leave from the dock behind the casino at 11:30am, 1, 2:30, and 6pm (DM12, children DM6). **Rent bikes** at the train station (tel. 212 61) for DM15 (open Mon.-Fri. 9am-noon and 2:30-6pm, Sat. 9:30am-noon).The **post office,** 88101 Lindau im Bodensee (tel. 277 70), is 50m right from the train station (open Mon.-Fri. 8am-6pm, Sat. 8:30am-noon). The **telephone code** is 08382.

The spectacular **Jugendherberge,** Herbergsweg 11 (tel. 967 10), lies across the Seebrücke off of Bregenzerstr. Sleekly modern interior sports a staff that is just as hip. The *only* downside of this place is their policy for single travelers—they don't hold beds for same day arrivals beyond those already reserved. Call as soon as you know that you will arrive. (Reception open 9am-midnight. Curfew midnight. Under 27 and families with small children only. DM27.50. Breakfast, sheets, and *Kurtaxe* included.) You could eat off the floor in the fine rooms at **Gästehaus Holdereggen,** Näherweg 4 (tel. 65 74). Follow the railroad tracks across the causeway to the mainland (after the bridge, the path continues to the left of the tracks); turn right onto Holdereggengasse and left onto Jungfernburgstr. Näherweg is on the left (20min.). (Singles DM38; doubles DM70. DM3 extra per person for one-night stands. Showers DM2.) **Campingplatz Lindau-Zech,** Frauenhoferstr. 20 (tel. 722 36), 3km south of the island on the mainland. It's within spitting range of the Austrian border and a beach. Bus #1 or 2 from the station: "Anheggerstr.," then bus #3 (direction: "Zech"). (Person DM9.50. Tent DM4. *Kurtaxe* DM1.50. Showers included. Open April-Oct.)

Lindau has three beaches (all open June to mid-Aug. and weekends year round daily 10am-8pm; other times 10:30am-7:30pm; last entrance 1hr. before closing). **Römerbad** is the smallest and most familial, located left of the harbor on the island (admission DM5, students DM3). To reach the quieter **Lindenhofbad,** bus #1 or 2: "Anheggerstr." and then bus #4: "Alwind" (admission DM4, students DM3). Lindau's biggest beach is **Eichwald,** about a 30-minute walk away to the right facing the harbor along Uferweg. Alternatively, bus #1 or 2: "Anheggerstr.," then bus #3: "Karmelbuckel" (admission DM5, students DM3). Sit down for Greek at **Taverna Pita Gyros,**

Paradiespl. 16 (tel. 237 02), which offers big platters (DM6-15) on the sidewalk or inside (open daily 10am-9pm). There is a **Plus grocery store** in the basement of the department store at the conjunction of In der Grub and Cramergasse (open Mon.-Fri. 8:30am-6:30pm and Sat. 8am-1pm).

RAVENSBURG

Ravensburg is a fairly unexceptional hamlet nicknamed the "town of towers." The **Mehlsack** (flour sack), soaring above all other towers, was built by the citizens of Ravensburg to keep tabs on the constable of the **Veitsburg,** the castle that once stood farther up the bluff. Ravensburg itself has been a free city since the Middle Ages, but the higher castle remained in the hands of the former lords of the town as the truce between them grew uneasy (the castle is long gone; a restaurant stands in its place). Reach the Mehlsack up the hill via the steps from Marktstr. close to the fountain (open every 3rd Sunday March-Oct. (except July) 10am-noon; free). During the last week of school, Ravensburg's pupils and teachers act out their enmity with the hill lords in the humorous **Rutenfest.** Look at the **Humpis-Haus** (if you need to be urged) at the corner of Rossbachstr. and Burgstr. A half-timbered residence dating from the 15th century, it was the home of Ravensburg's richest medieval family, the Humpis.

The vibrant 15th-century windows come as a surprise in the simple, clean lines of the Gothic **Evangelische Stadtkirche** (Protestant town church), on Seestr., just below the Veitsburg. One block farther is the long **Marienplatz,** the central market square lined with historic buildings and sidewalk restaurants. Here you'll find the late-Gothic **Rathaus** and the charming, colorful Renaissance **Lederhaus,** the former quarters of the leather workers' guild.

Ravensburg is easily reached by **train** from Ulm (1hr.; DM20) and from Friedrichshafen (30min.; DM5). The **tourist office,** Kirchstr. 16 (tel. 823 24 or 823 26; fax 824 66), is in the Weingartner Hof building. From the train station, walk straight down Bahnhofstr., which becomes Eisenbahnstr., and take a left on Marienpl. Then walk toward Herrenstr. to the side of the church; the office is on your right. The staff finds rooms for free (open Mon. 8am-12:30pm, Tues.-Fri. 8am-12:30pm and 2-5:30pm, Sat. 9am-noon). **Rent bikes** (DM13) at the train station. The main **post office** is at Eisenbahnstr. 44, 88212 Ravensburg (open Mon.-Fri. 8am-noon and 2-6pm, Sat. 8am-noon, Sun. 10-11am). The **telephone code** is 0751.

A friendly **Jugendherberge (HI),** Veitsburgstr. 1 (tel. 253 63; fax 137 69), in the Veitsburg, offers a breathtaking view of the valley with clean quarters which have the feel of a barracks. The quickest way up from the city center is to take the steep stairway to the Mehlsack and follow it to the Veitsburg area. (Reception open 5-7pm. Curfew 10pm. Lockout 9:30am-11:30am. DM22, over 26 DM27. Breakfast included. Sheets DM5.50. Open April-Oct. Call ahead.)

WANGEN IN ALLGÄU

Brightly painted buildings along the town square preserve this sleepy resort town's medieval flavor. The astonishingly pretty Herrenstr., lined with muraled houses dating from the late-16th century, leads from the *Frauentor* to the **Rathaus,** whose architecture runs the gamut from Romanesque to Baroque. Since the 15th century, Wangen has sported delightfully refreshing **public fountains**—there are a total of 11. The **Donkey Fountain** on Spitalstr., whose four groups of figures display Aesopic anecdotes, is a recent addition. **Der Wahrheitssucher** (The Truth Seeker) depicts a man desperately trying to decipher a Magic Square atop a pile of books that include such heavy authors as Humboldt, Plato, Socrates, Sappho, and Goethe. The **Amtsschimmelbrunnen** features a bucking horse vomiting water at a circle of humans, supposedly representing "bureaucracy's contribution to self-irony." Very witty.

Well-to-do tuberculosis victims once visited Wangen to take a *Luftkur* (fresh air cure) in the pristine countryside; take a deep breath and you'll understand why. Excellent **hiking** and **cycling** possibilities are a major attraction of Wangen—more than 350km of marked trails meander through the lush forest and fields. The **tourist**

office (tel. 742 11; fax 741 11), in the *Rathaus,* offers hiking and cycling maps, simple city maps, and brochures on the area. They also find rooms for free and **rent bikes** to visitors staying in town up to three days (DM6 per day; open Mon.-Fri. 9am-noon and 2-5pm, Sat. 10am-noon). If closed, purchase an information packet for DM1 from the machine 30m to the right of the office. From the station's right side, go straight on Bahnhofstr. to the end, then go left through the orange *Martinstor,* and the office will be on the opposite side of the building. **Freibad Stephanshöfe** (tel. 12 25) has half a dozen pools, a twisting slide, and a 5m diving board; it's a short bus ride north of town. A free **tour** of the town departs every Tuesday and Thursday (in winter Thurs. only) at 3:30pm from the tourist office. Wangen im Allgäu is an 80-minute **bus** ride from Ravensburg (RAB #7545; possible transfer in Tettnang; DM8) and has **trains** to most towns on thr Bodensee (Lindau; 30min.; DM7). The **telephone code** is 07522.

▓ Ulm

Perhaps best known as the birthplace of Albert Einstein (though he lived here only a year), Ulm was also home to another, less rigorously scientific dreamer, the ill-fated **"Tailor of Ulm."** Albrecht Ludwig Berblinger, tailor by day, inventor by night, nearly drowned in 1811 while trying to fly across the Danube with his "kite-wings*"* in one of the earliest serious attempts at human flight. Citizens of Ulm apparently didn't appreciate his ingenuity, and poor miserable Berblinger was banished irrevocably from intelligent society for the remaining 16 years of his life. The tailor's destination, Neu Ulm, was originally part of Ulm until Napoleon designated the Danube the border between Bayern and Württemberg, splitting the 800-year-old city. Despite the cartographical nitpicking, the two halves of the city remains a united metropolitan area, the flagship city of the gently rolling surroundings of the Schwäbische Alb, and home to the **world's tallest church steeple.**

Orientation and Practical Information The **tourist office,** Münsterpl. 50 (tel. 161 28 30; fax 161 16 41), can be found by walking toward the *Münster;* it's the voluptuous white building next to the tall spire. They sell maps (DM0.50), the comprehensive and helpful *Gästemagazin* (DM2), and a do-it-yourself cardboard *Münster* sculpture kit (DM54.80). They also find rooms for free (open Mon.-Fri. 9am-6pm, Sat. 9am-12:30pm). The automat outside vends a list of accommodations (DM1). Ulm is connected to all of southern Germany; hourly trains head to Munich and Stuttgart; several trains travel daily to Berlin, Hamburg, and most other big German cities. **Rent bikes** for DM15 per day from **Ralf Reich,** Frauenstr. 34 (tel. 211 79). Satisfy pharmaceutical fancies at the **Bahnhof Apotheke,** Bahnhofstr. 16 (tel. 600 74), or check the posted list there to find out which pharmacies in town are open after hours (open Mon.-Fri. 8am-7pm, Sat. 8am-2pm). The **post office,** Bahnhofpl. 2, 89073 Ulm, is left of the station (open Mon.-Fri. 8am-6pm, Sat 8am-1pm). The **telephone code** is 0731.

Accommodations and Food Ulm's **Jugendherberge "Geschwister Scholl" (HI),** Grimmelfinger Weg 45 (tel. 38 44 55; fax 38 45 11), has a pleasant dark wood exterior, while the four- to eight-bed rooms inside look like a high school. Any bus from the train station: "Ehinger Tor," and change to bus #4 or 8 (direction: "Kuhlberg"). Walk through the underpass just up the road, and follow the signs for the "Sport Gaststätte" to a set of stairs on the right side of the building. Descend. Cut through the grass to the right of the tennis courts, and turn left on the paved path. Follow the lone *Jugendherberge* sign. The hostel is named in memory of a brother and sister, students at the University of Munich who were executed in 1943 for conspiring against Hitler. (Reception open 5-6:30pm and 8-8:15pm. Lockout 9-10am. Curfew 10pm. DM22, over 26 DM27. Breakfast included. Sheets DM5.50.) **Münster-Hotel,** Münsterpl. 14 (tel. 641 62), is located (surprise!) to the left of the *Münster.* Spotless, somewhat small rooms with maps of Europe on every desk. (Singles DM45, with shower DM65; doubles with shower DM90, with bath DM110.) Across the river in Neu Ulm, **Gasthof Rose,** Kasernstr. 42a (tel. 778 03), has lovely rooms in a quiet district. (Singles DM40; doubles DM70, with shower DM80. Breakfast included.)

Ulm's restaurants reflect the culinary influences of both Swabia and Bayern. For cheap and greasy *Imbiß* fare, wander around Bahnhofstr. and Hirschstr. on the way to the *Münster.* For the largest variety and the densest collection of restaurants, the territory between Neuestr. and the river is prime strolling ground. Across from the *Rathaus,* the **Erstes Ulmer Weizenbierhaus,** Kronengasse 12 (tel. 624 96), pours more than 20 varieties of *Weizenbier* and serves up a number of decent dishes for DM5.50-12.80 (open daily 4pm-3am). Next to the Ulm Museum, **Dinea Restaurant,** on Neuestr., offers a dazzling and very tasty buffet of fresh salads, pasta, and fish. Daily specials DM6-12. Local brews from the tap DM2.90 (open Mon.-Sat 8am-10pm, Sun. 10am-9pm). Both Schwäbisch and Bavarian dishes are served up in an inviting local-joint atmosphere at **Restaurant "Zur Zill,"** Schwörhausgasse 19. Meals DM9-14, *Gold Ochsen Bier* (the local brew) DM4.40 per 0.5L. (Open Mon.-Fri. 11am-2pm and 5pm-midnight, Sat. 11am-2pm and 5pm-1am.) A **farmer's market** springs up on Münsterpl. on Wednesday and Saturday mornings.

Sights At 161m, the steeple topping the **Ulm Münster** is the tallest in the world, and the soaring ceilings of the chapel are almost as astonishing. Next to the front portal of the cathedral is *The Man of Sorrows,* a famous representation of Christ by 15th-century sculptor Hans Multscher. Inside the Gothic walls, extravagantly carved choir stalls (by Jörg Syrlin the Elder) contain a community of busts: the lowliest tier depicts Greek and Roman philosophers. Climb the 768 dizzying corkscrew steps of the spire on a clear day to see the Alps. (Open daily 8am-7:45pm. Church free. Free organ concerts Mon.-Fri. 11am-noon. Spire DM3.50, children DM2.50.) Toward the river along Neuestr., the **Rathaus,** built in 1370, is decorated with brilliantly colored murals and an elaborate astronomical clock, both from 1540. The old **Fischerviertel** (Fishermen's Quarter) down Kronengasse from the *Rathaus,* has classical half-timbered houses, narrow cobblestone streets, and canal-spanning footbridges.

On the other side of the *Rathaus* in a former *Patrizierhaus* is the **Ulmer Museum,** Marktplatz 9 (tel. 161 43 00), with a historical exegesis of the region from prehistory to the present. (Open Tues.-Sun. 10am-6pm, Thurs. 10am-8pm. DM5, students DM3. Free on Fri. Special exhibits DM7, students, children, and seniors DM5.) The **Deutsches Brotmuseum** (German Bread Museum), Salzstadelgasse 10, documents 6000 years of bread-making and waxes philosophical about "the *Leitmotiv* of Man and Bread." Very well put together, it's a cultural history fan's dream-come-true. Don't miss "Cake—the pride of the housewife," or "Corn and bread in arts and crafts." (Open Tues. and Thurs.-Sun. 10am-5pm, Wed. 10am-8:30pm. DM5, students DM3.50.) A simple monument marking **Albert Einstein's birthplace**, donated to Ulm by India, stands in front of the station. The house has long since given way to a glass-and-chrome savings-and-loan establishment. Every year on the penultimate Monday of July, the mayor of Ulm takes the stand at the **Schwörhaus** (Oath House) to carry on a centuries-old tradition by swearing allegiance to the town's 1397 constitution. The whole affair is accompanied by excessive drinking—that is, merrymaking.

BADEN-WÜRTTEMBERG

Bayern (Bavaria)

Bayern is the Germany of Teutonic myth, Wagnerian opera, and fairy tales. From the villages of the Bayerische Wald and the Baroque cities along the Danube to the turreted castles perched high in the Alps, the region beckons more tourists than any other part of the country. Indeed, when most foreigners conjure up images of Germany, they are imagining Bayern, land of beer halls, oom-pah-pah bands, and trendy *Lederhosen*. This is in part a relic of Germany's 45-year division, which shifted Western perceptions southward and prevented avant-garde Berlin from acting as a counterweight to strait-laced Munich. Though mostly rural, Catholic, and conservative (save Munich), this largest of Germany's federal states nurtures flourishing commerce and industry, including such renowned companies as the Bayerische Motor Werke (BMW). The region's independent residents have always been Bavarians first and Germans second. It took wars with France and Austria to pull the Kingdom of Bayern into Bismarck's orbit, and it remained a kingdom until 1918; local authorities still insist upon using the *Land*'s proper name: *Freistaat Bayern* (Free State of Bayern). In a plebiscite, Bayern was the only state to refuse to ratify the Federal Republic's Basic Law, and the ruling CDU still abides by a long-standing agreement not to compete in Bavarian elections (instead, a related party, the Christian Social Union, represents the Right). The insistent preservation of its independent tradition and history, amply demonstrated by the impenetrable dialect used sporadically throughout the region, animates the wildest stereotypes about *echtes* German culture.

> **Reminder:** HI-affiliated hostels in Bayern generally do not admit guests over age 26, although families with young children are usually allowed even if parents are over 26.

▧ Munich (München)

Munich is Germany's Second City. The capital and cultural center of Bayern, it is a sprawling, relatively liberal metropolis in the midst of solidly conservative southern Germany. The two cities of Munich and Berlin are emblematic of the two poles of the German character. Munich, exuding a sensual yet traditional air of merriment, stands in sharp contrast to Berlin, thriving on its sense of the fragmented avant-garde, and characterized by its dizzying reconstruction.

Munich shines unabashedly with Western German postwar economic glory. World-class museums, handsome parks and architecture, a rambunctious arts scene, and an urbane population collude to create a city of astonishing vitality. An ebullient mixture of sophistication and earthy Bavarian *Gemütlichkeit* keeps the city awake at (almost) all hours. The *Münchener* party zealously during *Fasching*, Germany's equivalent of Mardi Gras, and during the legendary *Oktoberfest* (Sept. 19-Oct. 4 in 1998). Before reunification, Munich was the shadow capital of West Germany; since the Wall fell, its popularity has been eclipsed by the cutting-edge energy of Berlin and eastern cities like Prague and Budapest. Though it may no longer be the beginning and end of the line, Munich continues to reel in visitors; the fascinating character of the city, with its gaze fixed firmly on the future and its consciousness focused on the past, is more intoxicating than its beer.

■ History

The stately monuments and public buildings that survived World War II testify to the imperial aspirations of the **House of Wittelsbach,** the dynasty that ruled Bayern from the 12th to the early 20th century through dukes, prince-electors, and kings. Though the *Münchener* are loath to admit it, their city was actually founded by a northerner, Heinrich the Lion. He built a bridge across the Isar in 1158 to consolidate his hold on

Bayern (Bavaria)

the Austrian salt trade by rerouting major trading routes, which previously passed through Freising to the north. The building of the bridge marked the official founding date of the city, and its name—literally "to the monks"—refers to the city's pre-1158 inhabitants, who lived in a monastery on the site of today's St. Peter's Church. In 1180, control passed to the Wittelsbachs. Although they moved their court to Munich in the late 13th century, sundry other cities like Landshut and Straubing remained rivals for Bavarian supremacy. The dynasty's ruthless acquisition of territory and privileges, however, translated into wealth and grandeur for Munich at the same time that the Wittelsbachs mercilessly suppressed the Reformation. When Protestant King Gustavus Adolphus II of Sweden occupied Munich in the Thirty Years War, the city barely managed to save itself by paying ransom in blood, seeing several prominent heads roll. Periodic wars, revolts, and intrigues, however, failed to shake Wittelsbach rule through the 18th century as Prussian Emperor Friedrich the Great kept Munich from falling under Austrian control. Napoleon's romp across Europe included a brief occupation of Munich, which then sided with the French against the Holy Roman Empire. When Napoleon dissolved the anachronistic empire, Bayern was awarded Kingdom status, with Munich as its capital.

The Kingdom period is vividly remembered as the **Bavarian Golden Age,** when "enlightened" absolutists rationalized state administration, promoted commerce, and patronized the arts. Ludwig I and Maximilian I contributed immensely to the expansion and evolution of the city, while its most famous king, Ludwig II, spent very little time in Munich, preferring his extravagant castles. In 1871, after Bismarck's successful wars solidified Prussian dominance of Germany, Ludwig presided over the absorption of Bayern into the greater *Reich* (a process lubricated by Prussia's generous subsidization of Ludwig's wild building schemes). Bayern became a kingdom in name only. Munich, however, remained a cultural powerhouse rivalling hated Berlin (a city that the *Münchener* (the citizens are not called Munchkins) regarded as a glorified garrison town). Franz Wedekind, Paul Klee, Franz Marc, and others stimulated the artistic and intellectual scene of Munich at the turn of the century.

The Golden Age came to an abrupt end with Germany's defeat in World War I. Amidst the **post-Versailles chaos,** Munich briefly reigned as the capital of an independent Bavarian Soviet Republic until the revolutionaries were brutally suppressed by right-wing *Freikorps.* Weimar Munich was something of an incubator for reactionary and anti-Semitic movements: **Adolf Hitler** found the city such a fertile recruiting ground for the new National Socialist German Workers Party (Nazis) that he later called Munich "the capital of our movement." In 1923, Hitler attempted to overthrow the municipal government and lead a march on Berlin to topple the Weimar Republic. His **Beer Hall Putsch** was quickly quashed and its leaders arrested, but Germany had not seen the end of the Austrian corporal. Munich is haunted by a number of other associations with the Third Reich: Neville Chamberlain's attempted appeasement of Hitler over the Sudetenland is remembered as the **"Munich Agreement,"** and one of the Nazis' first concentration camps was constructed just outside the city at Dachau.

Despite Munich's fortuitous location deep inside the German air defenses, Allied bombings destroyed the city. By 1944, less than 3% of the city center remained intact; since then, much of it has been rebuilt in the original style. When Munich hosted the **1972 Olympics,** it was hoped that the city's tattered image would at last be restored. The city went to great lengths to revolutionize itself: it pedestrianized big chunks of the city center, extended the underground subway system, and brought the city's resources to their current status. But a tragic attack by the Palestinian terrorist group *Black September* during the Games led to the death of 11 Israeli athletes in a police shoot-out and dashed Munich's hopes.

More recently, a potentially momentous upheaval was defused, at least for the time being, when 20,000 enraged citizens took to the streets in protest of a recent court ruling concerning—what else?—beer. The issue at hand in this first-time "Bavarian Beer Garden Revolution" was the **Waldwirtschaft beer garden,** which can accommodate 2000 customers but only has 100 parking places. Numerous neighborhood complaints had finally led to a draconian court decision mandating a 9:30pm closing time for the beer garden. After *Müncheners* marched on Marienpl. in good revolutionary spirit a few years back, the court reversed its decision and they won back a half hour—enough time to chug at least one more *Maß.*

■ Orientation

Munich rests on the banks of the Isar River in the middle of South-central Bayern. Mad King Ludwig's castles, the Bayerische Alpen, and the weekend paradises of the Lake Region are in the vicinity—a short trip through the purgatorial squalor of Munich's industrial outskirts and you're there.

A map of Munich's center looks like a skewed circle quartered by one horizontal and one vertical line. The circle is the main traffic **Ring,** which changes its name again and again as it bounds the city center. Within it lies the lion's share of Munich's sights. The east-west and north-south thoroughfares, in turn, cross at Munich's epicenter, the **Marienplatz** (home to the **Neues Rathaus**), and meet the traffic ring at **Karlsplatz** (called **Stachus** by locals) in the west, **Isartorplatz** in the east, **Odeonsplatz** in the north, and **Sendlinger Tor** in the south. The **Hauptbahnhof** is just beyond Karlspl. outside the Ring in the west. In the east beyond the Isartor, the **Isar River** flows by the city center, south to north. To get to Marienpl. from the station, go straight on Schützenstr. to the yellow buildings of Karlspl. Continue straight through Karlstor to Neuhauserstr., which becomes Kaufingerstr. before it reaches Marienpl. (15-20min.). Or S-Bahn #1-8 (two stops from the *Hauptbahnhof*): "Marienpl."

At Odeonspl., the giant **Residenz** palace sprawls over a hefty piece of downtown land; **Ludwigstraße** stretches north from there toward the university district. **Leopoldstraße,** the continuation of Ludwigstr., reaches farther toward **Schwabing.** This district, also known as "Schwabylon," is student country; it lies to the left of the maddeningly mobbed Leopoldstr. Here Türkenstr., Amalienstr., Schellingstr., and Barerstr. meander through the funk. To the east of Schwabing sprawls the **Englischer Garten;** to the west is the **Olympiazentrum,** the hyper-modern complex constructed for the 1972 games, surrounded by the verdant **Olympiapark.** Further west sits the posh **Nymphenburg,** built around the eponymous **Nymphenburg Palace.** Southwest of Marienpl., **Sendlingerstraße** leads past shops to the Sendlinger Tor. From there, Lindwurmstr. proceeds to Goethepl., from which Mozartstr. leads to **Theresienwiese,** the site of the *Oktoberfest*—the annual beer extravaganza.

There are several publications to help you find your way around Munich. The most comprehensive one (in English) is the monthly *Munich Found* (DM4), available at the "Internationale Presse" booth in the center of the station across from track 24, at the Anglia English Bookshop (see p. 472), and elsewhere; it provides a list of services, events, and museums. The tourist office distributes the encyclopedic *Monatsprogramm* (DM2.50), with a list of city events in chronological order. The bi-weekly *in München* (free) gives a more intensive insider's look at the Munich *Szene* in German, providing detailed movie, theater, and concert schedules. *Prinz* (DM5) is the hip and hefty monthly with endless tips on shopping, art, music, film, concerts, and food. EurAide's free publication *Inside Track* provides updated information in English on train connections as well as basic tips on getting started in Munich; it's available at EurAide (see below) or at the train-ticket *Reisezentrum* in the main hall of the station.

■ Practical Information

TOURIST OFFICES

Main office: The Munich **Fremdenverkehrsamt** (tel. 23 33 02 56 or 23 33 02 57; fax 23 33 02 33; email Munich_Tourist_Office@compuserve.com; http://www.munich-tourist.de) is located on the front (east) side of the station, next to ABR Travel on Bahnhofpl. Usually inundated with tourists, so expect curt service and a weary smile at best—have your questions ready, and don't expect to chat it up. The staff speaks English, but for more in-depth questions, EurAide (see below) will probably better suit your needs. The tourist office books rooms for a DM5 per room fee (plus DM3-9 deposit), sells accommodations lists (DM0.50), and gives out excellent free city maps. You can also buy bilingual maps (DM8). The English/German young people's guide *München Infopool* (DM1) lists beer gardens, *Mensas*, cinemas, and more. Their web site provides the low-down on *Oktoberfest*, accommodations, city tours, and more. Call for recorded information in English on museums and galleries (tel. 23 91 62) or sights and castles (tel. 23 91 72). Open Mon.-Fri. 10am-1pm. A **branch office** lies at the new ultra-modern airport, **Flughafen Munich** (tel. 97 59 28 15), in the *Zentralgebäude*. Provides general information, but no room bookings. Open Mon.-Sat. 8:30am-10pm, Sun. 1-9pm.

EurAide in English: (tel. 59 38 89; fax 550 39 65; http://www.cube.net/kmu/euraide.html), along track 11 (room 3) of the *Hauptbahnhof*, near the Bayerstr. exit. This is the magic mushroom of *Wunderland*—delve into the intricacies of Munich with one (sound) byte from EurAide's Mad Hatter, Alan R. Wissenberg; a solace for frazzled English-speaking tourists, he's a nearly omniscient American who points you (free of charge) in the right direction, and make room reservations for a DM6 fee. *Inside Track* available (free), Thomas Cook Timetables sold (DM38), and Eurail passes validated. EurAide also offers an outing to the *Königsschlösser* called the "Two Castle Tour" (see **Tours,** below). Open from June-*Oktoberfest* daily 7:45am-noon and 1-6pm; Oct.-April. Mon.-Fri. 7:45am-noon and 1-4pm, Sat. 7:45am-noon; May daily 7:45am-noon and 1-4:30pm.

TOURS

Mike's Bike Tours: tel. 651 42 75. Ponder the "Eunuch of Munich," "hunt" lions, have lunch at a *Biergarten* in the *Englischer Garten*—and see the sights of the city. The eponymous Mike, an American emigré, and his loyal disciples herd small groups of English-speaking bikers through Munich's cycling paths. Tours leave (rain or shine) from the *Altes Rathaus* by the Spielzeugmuseum; the 4hr. 6.5km Standard

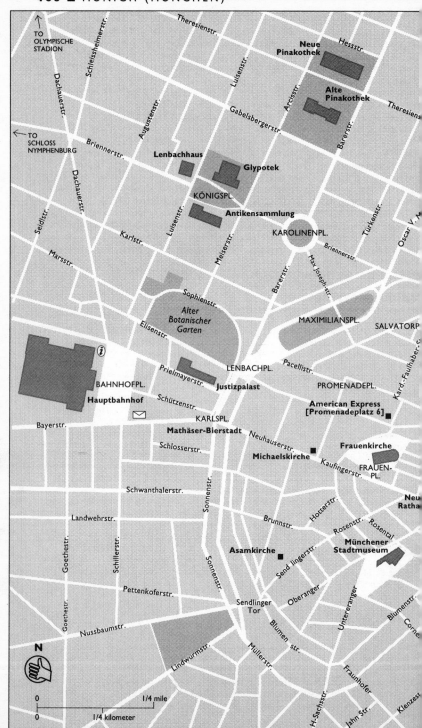

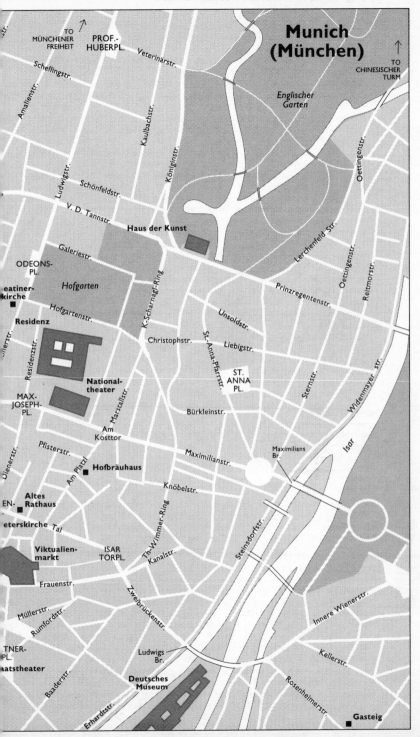

Munich (München)

TO MÜNCHENER FREIHEIT

PROF.-HUBERPL.

TO CHINESISCHER TURM

Schellingstr.

Amalienstr.

Veterinärstr.

Englischer Garten

Kaulbachstr.

Königinstr.

Ludwigstr.

Schönfeldstr.

V. D. Tannstr.

Oettingenstr.

Galeriestr.

Haus der Kunst

Lerchenfeld Str.

ODEONS-PL.

eatiner-kirche

Hofgarten

K.-Scharnagl-Ring

Prinzregentenstr.

Oettingenstr.

Reitmorstr.

Hofgartenstr.

Residenz

Christophstr.

Unsoldstr.

St.-Anna-Pfarrstr.

Liebigstr.

ST. ANNA PL.

Sternstr.

Residenzstr.

National-theater

Marstallstr.

Bürkleinstr.

Widenmayer str.

MAX-JOSEPH-PL.

Am Kosttor

Maximilianstr.

Maximilians Br.

Isar

Pfisterstr.

Am Platzl

Hofbräuhaus

Knöbelstr.

Dienerstr.

Altes Rathaus

EN-

eterskirche

Tal

Th.-Wimmer-Ring

Steinsdorfstr.

Viktualien-markt

ISAR TORPL.

Kanalstr.

Frauenstr.

Zweibrückenstr.

Innere Wienerstr.

Müllerstr.

Rumfordstr.

TNER-PL.

aatstheater

Baaderstr.

Ludwigs Br.

Deutsches Museum

Kellerstr.

Erhardtstr.

Rosenhelmerstr.

Gasteig

City Tour includes a lunch break and runs June-Aug. daily 11:30am and 4pm; April-May and Sept. to early Oct. daily 11:30am and 4pm; March and late Oct. daily 12:30pm. DM31. The 6hr. 16km. all-day "greener" cycling tour includes 2 beer garden breaks, a frisbee hacky-sack break, and runs June-Aug. daily 12:30pm. DM45. All prices include bike rental and rain gear.

Munich Walks: tel. (0177) 227 59 01. Native English speakers give guided historical walking tours of the city with 2 different slants: the comprehensive introductory tour of the *Altstadt* hits all the major sights (May-Oct. daily 10am and 3pm; Nov. to late-Dec. daily 10am), while a more specialized tour visits infamous Nazi sites (Jun-Oct. Mon.-Tues., Thurs. and Sat. 10am; mid- to late May and Nov. to late Dec. Mon. and Sat. 10am). The 2½hr. tours costs DM15, under 26 DM10, under 14 free.

Panorama Tours: Arnulfstr. 8. Offers staid bilingual **bus** tours that leave from across the street from the station's main entrance, in front of the Kaufhaus Hertie store on Bahnhofpl. One-hour tour in an open-topped double-decker bus May-Oct. daily 10, 11:30am, 2:30, and 4pm (DM15, children DM8). A 2½hr. tour leaves daily at 10am and 2:30pm; on Tues.-Sun., the 10am tour goes to the *Residenz* or the Olympic Park, while the 2:30pm tour visits the Peterskirche, the Olympic Park, or the Nymphenburg Palace (DM30, children DM15). They offer six other trips leaving from the Neptune Fountain on Elisenstr. Tickets sold on the bus, in some hotels, or in advance. Hotel pick-up available. 10% off day excursions with Eurailpass. Open Mon.-Fri. 7:30am-6pm, Sat. 7:30am-noon, Sun. 7:30-10am. For day excursions call 59 15 04 or fax 59 81 60. For city excursions call 20 44 18.

Two Castle Tour: For those who want to enter the magical realm of Mad King Ludwig II, two options await: **Panorama Tours** offers a 10½hr. bus excursion (in English) to Schloß Linderhof leaving April-Oct. daily 8:30am; Nov.-March Tues., Thurs., and Sat.-Sun. 8:30am. DM75; with Eurailpass, Europass, InterRail, or German Railpass DM68, with ISIC DM59; *Schloß* admission not included. Book in advance. **EurAide** leads an English-speaking half-bus, half-train *Schloß*-schlepp that also includes an extra stop at the Rococo *Wieskirche*. Meet June-July Wed. at 7:30am by track 11 in front of EurAide. DM70; with Eurailpass, InterRail, or flexipass DM55; admission not included, but EurAide will get you a DM1 discount. Or drop by EurAide for train and public bus schedules and see the castles on your own (see **Hypertravel to the Castles**, p. 500).

CONSULATES

Australians should go to the consulate in Bonn (tel. (0228) 81 30; see **Bonn,** p. 326).
Canada: Tal 29 (tel. 219 95 70). S-Bahn: "Isartor." Open Mon.-Thurs. 9am-noon and 2-5pm, Fri. 9am-noon and 2-3:30pm.
Ireland: Mauerkircherstr. 1a (tel. 98 57 23). Streetcar #20 or bus #54 or 87. Open Mon.-Thurs. 9am-noon and 2-4pm, Fri. 9am-noon.
New Zealanders see the consulate in Bonn (tel. (0228) 22 80 70; see **Bonn,** p. 326).
South Africa: Sendlinger-Tor-Platz 5 (tel. 231 16 30). U-Bahn #1-3 or 6: "Sendlinger Tor." Open Mon.-Fri. 9am-noon.
U.K.: Bürkleinstr. 10 (tel. 21 10 90), fourth floor. U-Bahn #4 or 5: "Lehel." Consular section open Mon.-Fri. 8:45-11:30am and 1-3:15pm.
U.S.: Königinstr. 5 (tel. 288 80). Bus #53. Open Mon.-Fri. 8-11am.

TRANSPORTATION

Trains: *Hauptbahnhof* (tel. 22 33 12 56). The transportation hub of Southern Germany, Munich has connections to all major cities in Germany and throughout Europe several times per day. To: Frankfurt (every hr., 3½hr., ICE only); Berlin (1-2 per hr., 7½hr.); Köln (every hr., 6hr.); Hamburg (18 per day, 6hr.); Prague (6 per day, 3 direct: 6:57am, 2:08, and 11:06pm, 6-7½hr.); Zürich (6 per day, 4-5hr.); Vienna (1 per hr., 4-5hr.); Paris (14 per day, 3 direct: 7:46am, 1:46, and 9pm, 9½-10hr.); Amsterdam (17 per day, 9hr.); Füssen (7 direct per day, 14 via Buchloe or Kaufbeuren, 2hr.). Call for **schedules and fare information** (tel. 194 19; open 6am-11pm) and **reservations** (in German only; tel. 13 08 23 33) Mon.-Fri. 8am-6pm, Sat.-Sun. 8am-3pm. **EurAide** (see **Tourist Offices**, p. 467), in the station, provides free train information in English. Otherwise, the best source is a **destination booklet** (*Städteverbindungen*) available at the counters in the *Reisezentrum*. These list all the possible connections between Munich and scores of other cities. Station open daily 4am-12:30am. Use entrance on Arnulfstr. to reach trains. **Reisezentrum** information counters open daily 6am-10:30pm. Reservation desk open 7am-9pm.

Public Transportation: Munich's public transport system **(MVV)** runs Mon.-Fri. 5am-12:30am, Sat.-Sun. 5am-1:30am. A few lines run hourly through the night; double check the posted schedules. Eurail, InterRail, and German railpasses are valid on any S-Bahn (commuter rail) but *not* on the U-Bahn (subway), *Straßenbahn* (streetcars), or buses. **Einzelfahrkarten** (single ride tickets) are valid for 3hr. as long as you don't backtrack, DM3.40 if you stay within the *Innenraum* (city center). **Kurzstrecke** (short trip) tickets cost DM1.70 and can be used for 2 stops on the U-Bahn or S-Bahn, or for 4 stops on a streetcar or bus. Buying rides in bulk will save you money; a *Streifenkarte* (11-strip ticket) costs DM15 and can be used by more than 1 person. Cancel 2 strips per person for a normal ride, or 1 strip per person for a *Kurzstrecke*. Beyond the city center, cancel 2 strips per additional "zone"—these 5 *Außenraum* zones appear as concentric rings around the *Innenraum,* and the entire area together constitutes the *Gesamtnetz.* Most places you will probably want to go (and all of the places listed in the Munich section of *Let's Go* unless otherwise noted) will be covered by an *Innenraum* ticket. **Single-Tages-Karte** (single-day tickets) give 1 person unlimited travel until 6am the next day (*Innenraum* DM8, *Gesamtnetz* DM16). A **Partner-Tages-Karte** (DM12 and DM24 respectively) can be used by 2 adults, 3 children under 18, and a dog. Buy an *Innenraum* **3-day pass** (DM20) from the MVV office in the *Hauptbahnhof.* Children under 15 pay reduced fares, and children under 4 ride free. Buy tickets at the blue *"MVV-Fahrausweise"* vending machines and be sure to stamp your ticket in the boxes marked with an "E" **before you go to the platform** (except on the bus; cancel after you board). If you plan to jump the fare or don't validate correctly, bring along an extra DM60 for the fine. **Transit maps** can be picked up in the tourist office or EurAide, and at MVV counters near the subway entrance in the train station. The U-Bahn is safe, clean, and punctual; most trains run every 10min. during the day. *"Bitte Zurückbleiben"* means "please stand back."

Taxi: Taxi-Zentrale (tel. 216 11 or 194 10) has large **stands** in front of the train station and every 5-10 blocks in the central city. Women can request a female driver. Each piece of luggage DM1. Train station to airport costs about DM100.

Car Rental: Flach's Leihwagen, Landsbergerstr. 289 (tel. 56 60 56), rents cars for DM60-112 per day with no mileage charges. Open Mon.-Fri. 8am-8pm, Sat. 9am-noon. **Swing,** Schellingstr. 139 (tel. 523 20 05), rents from DM45 per day. **Europcar/National** (tel. (0180) 52 21 22), **Sixt Budget** (tel. (0180) 525 25 25), **Hertz** (tel. 550 22 56), and **Avis** (tel. 550 12 12) have offices upstairs in the *Hauptbahnhof.*

Bike Rental: Radius Touristik, squats in the rear of the *Hauptbahnhof* (tel. 59 61 13; fax 59 47 14), behind the lockers opposite tracks 30-31. Chat it up with Patrick Holder, the gregarious English owner. 2hr. DM10. 10am-6pm DM25. 24hr. DM30. 48hr. DM45. Week DM95. Mountain bikes 50% more. Deposit for 3-6 speed bikes DM100, for mountain bike DM200; passport or a credit card also acceptable. Students and Eurailpass holders receive a 10% discount; discounts also for all-day rentals Tues.-Thurs., or any day for 4hr. rentals, 2-6pm only. Self-guided tour packet DM3. Open daily April to early-Oct. 10am-6pm. **Aktiv-Rad,** Hans-Sachs-Str. 7 (tel. 26 65 06), rents 'em out at DM18 per day. U-Bahn #1 or 2: "Frauenhoferstr." (open Mon.-Fri. 9am-1pm and 2-6:30pm, Sat. 9am-1pm).

Hitchhiking: *Let's Go* does not recommend hitchhiking as a safe mode of transportation. But, those looking to share rides scan the bulletin boards in the **Mensa,** on Leopoldstr. 13. Otherwise, hitchers try *Autobahn* on-ramps; *those who stand behind the blue sign with the white auto may be fined.* Hitchers who've gotta get to *Autobahn Salzburg* (E11; direction: "Salzburg-Vienna-Italy"), U-Bahn #1 or 2: "Karl-Preis-Platz." For *Autobahn Stuttgart* (E11; direction: "Stuttgart/France"), U-Bahn #1: "Rotkreuzpl.," then streetcar #12: "Amalienburgstr.;" *or* S-Bahn #2: "Obermenzing," then bus #73 or 75: "Blutenburg." Thumbers who want to get to the *Autobahn Nürnberg* (E6) interchange north to Berlin, U-Bahn #6: "Studentenstadt" and walk 500m to the Frankfurter Ring. For *Autobahn* A96/E54 to Bodensee and Switzerland, U-Bahn #4 or 5: "Heimeranpl.," then bus #33: "Siegenburgerstr." For Garmisch-Partenkirchen (E6), hitchers head for the *Autobahn* A95/E533 south, U-Bahn #6: "Westpark," then bus #33: "Luise-Kiesselbach-Platz."

BAYERN (BAVARIA)

Mitfahrzentrale: McShare Treffpunkt Zentrale, Klenzestr. 57b and Lämmerstr. 4 (tel. 59 45 61), near the train station matches McDrivers and McRiders (Frankfurt DM41, Berlin DM54, Heidelberg DM34, additional insurance DM2). Open daily 8am-8pm. **Känguruh,** Amalienstr. 87 (tel. 194 44), is in the Amalienpassage near the university (Frankfurt DM40). Open Mon.-Fri. 8:30am-7pm, Sat. 9am-3pm, Sun. 10am-7pm. **Frauenmitfahrzentrale,** Klenzestr. 57b, is for women only. U-Bahn #1 or 2: "Fraunhoferstr.," then walk up Fraunhoferstr. away from the river, and turn right. Open Mon.-Fri. 8am-8pm.

Flights: Flughafen München is accessible from the train station by S-Bahn #8, running daily every 20min. (3:22am-12:42am; DM13.60 or 8 stripes on the *Streifenkarte;* Eurail, InterRail and German railpasses valid). Alternatively, a Lufthansa shuttle bus runs between the *Hauptbahnhof* and the airport (40min.), with a pickup at the "Nordfriedhof" U-Bahn stop in Schwabing. Buses leave from Arnulfstr., on the northern side of the train station 6:50am-7:50pm, every 20min. Buses return from Terminal A *(Zentralbereich)* and Terminal D 7:55am-8:55pm, every 20min. One-way DM15, round-trip DM25. For flight info, call 97 52 13 13.

GENERAL SERVICES

Budget Travel: Council Travel, Adalbertstr. 32, 80799 München (tel. 39 50 22; fax 39 70 04), near the university, sells ISICs. Open Mon.-Fri. 10am-1pm and 2-6:30pm. **abr Reisebüro,** (tel. 12 04 46) is located in the train station and at 16 other locations city-wide. Open Mon.-Fri. 9am-6pm and Sat. 9am-noon.

Currency Exchange: The cheapest way to change money is to head to American Express; otherwise pick up a copy of EurAide's free publication *Inside Track* and take it to the Reise Bank. Two locations: in front of the main entrance to the main station on Bahnhofpl. (open daily 6am-11pm); and around the corner from EurAide at track 11 (open Mon.-Sat. 7:30am-7pm). Those with *Inside Track* get a 50% discount on commission if cashing US$50 or more in U.S. traveler's checks. Otherwise, pay regular DVB traveler's check commissions: DM5 for transactions of DM100 or less; 10% or DM7.50—whichever fee is higher—for transactions above DM100 with AmEx checks, DM10 for other brands. All cash transactions DM3. Western Union services available. Credit card operated phone and fax.

American Express: Promenadepl. 6 (tel. 29 09 00; 24hr. hotline (0130) 85 31 00; fax 29 09 01 18), in the Hotel Bayerischer Hof. Holds mail, cashes traveler's checks, no *kiquebaque.* Open Mon.-Fri. 9am-5:30pm, Sat. 9:30am-12:30pm. **Branch** office also at Kanfingerstr. 24 (tel. 22 80 13 87; fax 22 80 13 83), by the Frauenkirche. Open Mon.-Fri. 9am-5:30pm, Sat. 10am-1pm.

Luggage Storage: At the **train station** (tel. 13 08 50 47) and **airport** (tel. 97 52 13 75). There's a staffed storage room *(Gepäckaufbewahrung)* in the main hall of the train station. Open daily 6am-11pm. DM4 per piece per calendar day. Lockers opposite tracks 16, 24, and 28-36 DM2-4 per 24hr.

Lost and Found: Fundamt, Otztalerstr. 17 (tel. 23 34 59 00). U-Bahn #6: "Partnachpl." Open Mon.-Wed. and Fri. 8:30am-noon, Tues. 8:30am-noon and 2-5:30pm. For items lost on trains, **Fundstelle der DB,** Bahnhofpl. 2 (tel. 13 08 66 64), across from track 24 in the *Haupbahnhof,* can help. Open daily 6:30am-11:30pm. For items lost on S-Bahn/local trains, see **Fundstelle im Ostbahnhof** (tel. 12 88 44 09). Open Mon.-Fri. 8am-5:30pm, Sat. 8am-11:45pm. For the airport, call 97 52 13 70.

Mitwohnzentrale: An der Uni (tel. 286 60 66; fax 28 45 16), in tunnel passage of U-Bahn #3 or 6: "Universität," has apartments available for 1 month or more. Open Mon.-Fri. 10am-1pm and 2:30-6pm, Sat. 11am-1pm. **City Mitwohnzentrale,** Klenzestr. 57b (tel. 194 40; fax 201 63 11), or Lämmerstr. 4 (tel. 194 22; fax 59 45 64), has apartments and houses from 4 days to eternity throughout Germany.

Bookstores: Anglia English Bookshop, Schellingstr. 3 (tel. 28 36 42), offers reams of English-language books in a gloriously chaotic atmosphere. U-Bahn #3 or 6: "Universität." Open Mon.-Fri. 9am-6:30pm, Sat. 10am-2pm. **Words' Worth,** Schellingstr. 21a (tel. 280 91 41), a bit farther down, carries obscure English novels as well as a full range of literature from the greats. Open Mon.-Tues. and Fri. 9am-6:30pm, Wed.-Thurs. 9am-8pm, Sat. 10am-2pm. **Lillemor's Frauenbuchladen,** Arcisstr. 57 (tel. 272 12 05; fax 272 09 98), is a women's bookstore/center for women's events. U-Bahn #2: "Max-Joseph-Platz." Open Mon.-Fri. 10am-6:30pm, Sat. 10am-2pm.

Libraries: Many of Munich's city libraries have a hefty English section. Anyone with ID can get a library card. **Bayerische Staatsbibliothek,** Ludwigstr. 16 (tel. 28 63 80; fax 28 63 82 93), one of the largest libraries in Germany with 6.5 million books, has endless magazines and newspapers. Open Mon.-Fri. 9am-7:30pm, Sat. 9am-4:30pm. **Universitätsbibliothek der Universität,** Geschwister-Scholl-Platz 1 (tel. 21 80 24 28). Open Dec.-July Mon.-Thurs. 9am-8pm, Fri. 9am-4pm; Aug.-Nov. Mon.-Thurs. 9am-7pm, Fri. 9am-noon. **Munich City Library,** Rosenheimerstr. 5 (tel. 48 09 83 13). S-Bahn #1-8: "Rosenheimerpl." Open Mon.-Fri. 10:30am-7pm.

Cultural Centers: Amerika Haus, Karolinenpl. 3 (tel. 552 53 70; fax 55 35 78), is the cultural extension of the consulate. U-Bahn #2: "Königspl." They have cultural resources and advice for Americans wishing to teach, a library for reading and research, and language courses. Open Mon.-Fri. 10am-1pm and 2-4:30pm. **British Council,** Rosenheimerstr. 116b, Haus 93 (tel. 290 08 60). For Canadians, **Deutsch-Kanadische-Gesellschaft,** Hildeboldstr. 5 (tel. 307 33 45). **Munich Scottish Association,** Keferstr. 246 (tel. 39 12 53).

Women's Centers: Kofra *(Kommunikationszentrum für Frauen),* Baaderstr. 30 (tel. 201 04 50). Job advice, a research job library, *Kaffeetrinken,* tons of magazines, lesbian politics, and books. Open Mon.-Fri. 4-10pm. **Frauentreffpunkt Neuperlach,** Oskar-Maria-Graf-Ring 20-22 (tel. 670 64 63), is an environmentally conscious women's cafe/shop. Open Tues. and Thurs.-Fri. 10am-1pm, Wed. 10am-1pm and 3-6pm. **Fraueninfothek,** Johannispl. 12 (tel. 48 48 90). Open Mon. 10am-1pm, Tues. 10am-1pm and 2-5pm, Thurs. 2-5pm.

Gay and Lesbian Organizations: Gay services info tel. 26 92 08. Lesbian info tel. 725 42 72. Also for lesbians, **Lesbentraum LeTra,** Dreimühlenstr. 23 (tel. 725 42 72). Open Thurs. 1:30-4pm; telephones open Thurs. 7-10pm.

Ticket Agencies: Advance tickets for concerts in the Olympiapark and soccer games are available at the **Kaufhof** department store either on Marienpl., 3rd floor (tel. 260 32 49) or at Karlspl., ground floor (tel. 512 52 48). Both open Mon.-Wed. and Fri. 11am-6:30pm, Thurs. 11am-8:30pm, Sat. 9am-2pm. To order tickets by phone call **München Ticket** (tel. 54 81 81 81; fax 54 81 81 54). **Hertie Schwabing,** Leopoldstr. 82, 4th floor (tel. 33 66 59), sells tickets for smaller rock, pop, and theater events. Open Mon.-Fri. 9am-6:30pm, Sat. 9am-2pm.

Laundromat: The **Waschsalon Prinz,** Paul-Heyse-Str. 21, is close to the station; right on Bayerstr., then left on Paul-Heyse-Str. for 1½ blocks. Wash DM7, soap included. Dry DM2. Open daily 6am-10pm. **Münz Waschsalon,** Amalienstr. 61, near the university. Wash DM5.20, soap DM1. Dry DM1. Open Mon.-Fri. 8am-6:30pm, Sat. 8am-1pm. **Waschcenter** is at Landshüter Allee 77. U-Bahn #1: "Rotkreuzpl." Wash DM6. Dry DM1 per 15min. Open 24hr. *Bring your own change for laundromats.*

Swimming Pools: Pool season is May to mid-Sept. Choose among 16 local dives. **Michaelibad,** Heinrich-Wieland-Str. 24 (tel. 40 76 91), is a huge pool complex with slides and 5 swimming areas. U-Bahn #2 or 5: "Michaelibad." Open Mon. 10am-6pm, Tues.-Sun. 7am-9pm. **Müllerisches Volksbad,** Rosenheimerstr. 1 (tel. 23 61 34 29), has Art Nouveau indoor pools and Irish-Roman steam baths (sweat away with Caligula, his horse, and a pint o' Guinness). S-Bahn #1-8: "Isartor." Open Mon. 10am-5pm, Tues. and Thurs. 8am-7:30pm, Wed. 6:45am-7:30pm, Fri. 8am-8:45pm, Sat. 8am-5:30pm, Sun. 9am-6pm. The outdoor, heated **Dantebad,** Dantestr. 6 (tel. 15 28 74), in Neuhausen, is excellent and less crowded—hardly hellish. Streetcar #20 or 21: "Baldurstr." Open daily 8am-7:30pm.

Weather Conditions: *(Wettervorhersage)* tel. 11 64.

Rape Crisis: Frauennotruf München, Güllstr. 3 (tel. 76 37 37).

AIDS Hotline: tel. 520 73 87 or 520 74 12 (Mon.-Thurs. 8am-3pm, Fri. 8am-noon). Or 194 11 (Mon.-Sat. 7-10pm).

Pharmacy: Bahnhof Apotheke, Bahnhofpl. 2 (tel. 59 41 19 or 59 81 19), on the corner outside the station. Open Mon.-Fri. 8am-6:30pm, Sat. 8am-2pm. The hours of all other pharmacies posted in the window. 24hr. service rotates among the city's pharmacies—call 59 44 75 for recorded information (German only). The tourist office and EurAide also have free monthly schedules.

Medical Assistance: Klinikum Rechts d. Isar, clinic across the river on Ismaningerstr. U-Bahn #4 or 5: "Max-Weber-Platz." STD/AIDS tests are free and anonymous at the **Gesundheitshaus,** Dachauerstr. 90 (tel. 520 71). Open Mon.-Thurs. 8-11am and 1-2pm, Fri. 8-11am. U.K. and U.S. consulates carry lists of English-speaking doctors.

Emergency: Police, tel. 110. **Ambulance,** tel. 192 22. **Emergency medical service** tel. 55 77 55. **Fire,** tel. 112. **Poison Control,** tel. 192 40.

Internet Access: In **Hotel Kurpfalz** (see **Accommodations,** p. 476) and the two **Internet Cafes** (see **Food,** p. 479).

Post Office: Post/Telegrafenamt, Arnulfstr. 32, 80074 München (tel. 54 54 23 36). *Poste Restante* and money exchange (DM6 per $20 traveler's check—it's cheaper at AmEx). Go out of the train station and turn left onto Arnulfstr.; the post office will be on your right. Open Mon.-Fri. 8am-8pm, Sat. 8am-noon. **Postamt 31,** up the escalator in the train station (tel. 552 26 20), sells stamps and phone cards, but doesn't exchange money. Open Mon.-Fri. 7am-8pm, Sat. 8am-4pm, Sun. 9am-3pm. EurAide offers a "message-forwarding service" (see p. 58).

Telephone Code: 089.

■ Accommodations and Camping

Munich's accommodations usually fall into one of three categories: seedy, expensive, or booked solid. During times like *Oktoberfest,* there is only the last category. During summer, the best strategy is to start calling before noon or to book a few weeks in advance. Most singles (without private bath) range DM55-85, doubles DM80-120. If you're planning an extended stay in Munich, call the *Mitwohnzentrale* (see p. 472) or try bargaining with a *Pension* owner. Remember: **Bavarian HI hostels do not accept guests over age 26.** The enforcement of this rule varies. At several of Munich's hostels you can check in all day, but try to start your search well before 5pm.

Sleeping in the *Englischer Garten* is unsafe and illegal. Be aware, the police often patrol. Subway stops are similarly patrolled. Many wandering backpackers arrive too late to find lodging and end up cluttered in the main train station; this is extremely unsafe. If you sleep in the *Hauptbahnhof*'s *Warteraum* (waiting room), you'll awake to the racket of railway police scurrying you away. A few options for the roomless do exist: the Augsburg youth hostel is 30 to 45 minutes away by train (until 11pm, 4- to 0-per hr.; DM10), but be mindful of the 1am curfew. Or, you can throw your luggage into a locker and party until 5am, and come back to re-evaluate the hotel lists afterwards. For railpass holders, a final option is to catch the 11:17pm train to Heidelberg and, upon arriving at 3:12am, catch the 3:19am train back to Munich. Arrive in Munich at 7:16am, and start looking for a real room immediately. Be sure to *double check* an up-to-date train schedule before attempting this stunt.

HOSTELS

Jugendherberge München (HI), Wendl-Dietrich-Str. 20. (tel. 13 11 56). U-Bahn #1: "Rotkreuzpl." Cross Rotkreuzpl. heading towards the Kaufhof department store, then go down Wendl-Dietrich-Str. The entrance is ahead on the right. This is the most "central" of the HI hostels. Safes in the reception area—*use them,* and keep keys on your person at *all* times. Check-in starts at 10:30am, but the lines form before 9am. Reception open 24hr. Big dorm (37 beds) for men only DM23; 4- to 6-bed coed rooms DM25.50. Breakfast and sheets included. Mandatory DM20 key deposit. DM50 deposit for the use of safes. Reservations only accepted a week in advance; if you get one, arrive by 6pm or call first.

Jugendlager Kapuzinerhölzl ("The Tent"), In den Kirschen 30 (tel. 141 43 00; fax 5 41 06 18). Streetcar #17 from the *Hauptbahnhof* (direction: "Amalienburgstr.") "Botanischer Garten" (15min.), straight on Franz-Schrank-Str., left at In den Kirschen. The Tent is on the right. Night streetcars run at least once an hour all night. Sleep with 400 fellow "campers" under a big circus tent on a wooden floor. Reception open 5pm-9am—come and go as you please, just don't sleep without registering first (no hostel ID required, but you'll need your passport as deposit). DM10 gets a foam pad, blankets, bathrooms, a shower (not necessarily warm), a rudimentary breakfast (plenty of granola here, but none to eat), and enthusiastic management. The best part about staying here is the super deal on public transportation—rent a *Grüne Karte* that covers everything in the *Innenraum* (DM4 per day), or the *Gestantnetz* (DM6). Spontaneous merrymaking around a bonfire at night. Bike rental DM10 per day (Mon.-Sat. 8-10am), free city tours (Wed. 9am), volleyball ping-pong, and yes—a beer garden. Under 24 only (under 27 if there's room). Actual "beds" DM17. Lockers provided, but bring a lock. Reservations only for groups over 10, but rarely full. Open mid-June to early Sept.

Jugendherberge Pullach Burg Schwaneck (HI), Burgweg 4-6 (tel. 793 06 43; fax 793 79 22), in a castle 12km outside the city center. S-Bahn #7 (direction: "Wolfrat-shausen"): "Pullach" (20min.), and follow the signs (8min.). Unmajestic but entirely adequate. Romantic surroundings swarm with schoolchildren. Reception open 4-11pm. Curfew 11:30pm. 6- to 8-bed rooms DM19.50; 4-bed rooms DM22.50; coed dorm room DM18.50; singles DM28.50; doubles DM51. Buy a shower token (DM1) early to beat the crowds. Breakfast included, dinner DM8. Sheets DM5. Try to make reservations 7:30-10am.

Jugendgästehaus Thalkirchen, Miesingstr. 4 (tel. 723 65 50; fax 724 25 67). U-Bahn #1 or 2: "Sendlinger Tor," then #3 (direction: "Fürstenrieder West"): "Thalkirchen" (Zoo). From Thalkirchnerpl., follow Schäftlarnstr. toward Innsbruck and bear right around the curve, then follow Frauenbergstr. and go immediately left on Münch-nerstr; take the street as it curves left. Crowded and distant, but the rooms are immaculate. Check in 2-6pm, or call if you'll arrive later. Reception open 7am-1am. Curfew 1am. 8- to 15-bed rooms DM27.50; singles DM35.50; doubles DM63; triples DM88.50; quads DM118. Sheets and breakfast included. Bike rental DM22 per day.

4 you münchen *(ökologisches Jugendgästehaus),* Hirtenstr. 18 (tel. 55 21 660; fax 55 21 66 66), 200m from the *Hauptbahnhof.* Exit at Arnulfstr., go left, quickly turn right onto Pfefferstr., then hang a left onto Hirtenstr. Beautiful ecological youth hostel with restaurant/bar, hang-out areas, a playroom for families—everything goes "crunch." Over 27 15% surcharge. 10-bed dorms DM24; 4-, 6-, or 8-bed dorms DM29; singles DM54; doubles DM76. Key deposit DM20. Breakfast buffet DM7.50. Sheets DM5. In their adjoining hotel, singles with bath DM69; doubles with bath DM99, extra bed DM49. Breakfast included. Reception open daily 7am-noon, 3-7, and 7:30-10pm. Handicap accessible. Reserve be4 you arrive—unless you have good 4tune, acquiring a bed will be a 4midable task, and don't you 4get it.

Jugendhotel Marienberge, Goethestr. 9, 80336 München (tel. 55 58 05), less than a block from the train station, staffed by merry nuns. The rooms in this Catholic hostel are comfortable and spotless. Kitchen and laundry facilities. Wash DM2, dry DM2. Reception open 8am-midnight. Curfew midnight, before you turn into a pumpkin. *Open only to women under 26.* (No dirty old men.) Six-bed dorms DM30; singles DM40; doubles DM70; triples DM105. Breakfast included.

CVJM (YMCA) Jugendgästehaus, Landwehrstr. 13, 80336 München (tel. 552 14 10; fax 550 42 82; email muenchen@cvjm.org). Take the Bayerstr. exit from the station, head straight down Goethestr. or Schillerstr., and take the 2nd left onto Landwehr-str.; it's on the right. Central location with spic 'n' span rooms and showers in the hall. Reception open 8am-12:30am. Curfew 12:30am. Co-ed rooms for married couples only. Over 27 15% surcharge. Singles DM50; doubles DM86; triples DM120. Breakfast included. Reservations by mail, phone, fax, or email must arrive before 4pm. Nifty 50s-decorated restaurant offers dinner (DM6-10), soups, and salads Tues.-Fri. 6:30-10pm. Closed during Easter and Dec. 20-Jan. 7.

Haus International, Elisabethstr. 87, 80797 München (tel. 12 00 60; fax 12 00 62 51). U-Bahn #2 (direction: "Feldmoching"): "Hohenzollernpl.," then streetcar #12 (direction: "Romanpl.") or bus #33 (direction: "Aidenbachstr."): "Barbarastr." It's the 5-story beige building behind the BP gas station. Interior reminiscent of dorm life except that everything is delightfully clean. Free indoor pool, small beer garden, TV room, and newly renovated disco. Reception open 24hr. Singles DM55, with bath DM85; doubles DM104, with shower DM144; triples DM138; quads DM170; quints DM200. Lunch and dinner available (DM10-14). Reservations recommended in summer; depending on room availability, groups of 10 or more may be required to reserve with half-pension (add DM14 per person for dinner).

Jump In, Hochstr. 51 (tel. 48 95 34 37), a new, small, private place founded by a brother/sister team tired of big impersonal hostels. S-Bahn #1-8: "Rosenheimerpl.," then take the Gasteig exit to the left and walk left on Hochstr. (10min.). Or streetcar #27 or bus #51: "Ostfriedhof." A little disorganized, but supremely amicable and Brady-like. Spartan rooms—a funky mattress, futon, or bunkbed, and that's about it. Bunkbeds and mattresses DM29; futons DM35. Free kitchen facilities. Try to bargain for longer-term arrangements.

CAMPING

All three Munich campgrounds are open from mid-March to late October.

Campingplatz Thalkirchen, Zentralländstr. 49, 81379 München (tel. 723 17 07; fax 724 31 77), is in the Isar River Valley Conservation Area. U-Bahn #1 or 2: "Sendlinger Tor," then 3: "Thalkirchen," and change to bus #57 (20min.). Large grounds are well-run but crowded. Good hiking and cycling paths. Laundry facilities, TV lounge, billiards, and a cheap restaurant (meals DM3-8). Curfew 11pm. Adults DM7.80. Under 14 DM2.50. Small tent DM5.50. Tent for 2 or more DM7. Motorcycle DM4. Car DM9. Trailer DM19. Showers DM2.

Obermenzing, Lochhausenerstr. 59, 81247 München (tel. 811 22 35; fax 814 48 07). S-Bahn #3-6 or 8: "Passing," then bus #76: "Lochhausenerstr." Head up the street (5min.); it's on the left. Adults DM7.50. Ages 2-14 DM4. Tent DM7.50. Car DM5. Trailer DM12. Showers DM2. Dishwashing DM3.

Langwieder See, Eschenriederstr. 119, 81249 München (tel. 864 15 66; fax 863 23 42), located near a nice lake, is accessible by car. Go right off the Augsburg *Autobahn* A8, and exit at Lochhausen/Eschenried. The nearest train station is München-Lochhausen, but it's a 2km schlepp towards Eschenried.

HOTELS AND PENSIONEN

While Munich, reputedly a city of 80,000 guest beds, has a surplus of dirt-cheap (and often dirty!) accommodations, it is much safer to crash in a hostel. A clean room in a safe area costs at least DM55-65 for a single or DM80-100 for a double. Always call ahead. For *Oktoberfest* rooms you should call a few *months* in advance, as some hotels are booked for the entire two weeks by early summer. The tourist office charges DM0.50 for a hotel list and a DM5 fee to find lodgings. The EurAide staff (at the train station) may better suit your English-speaking needs and will help you for a DM6 fee. Carefully consider the location of the hotels/*Pensionen.* Since transportation is ridiculously expensive in Munich, a hasty decision may end up costing you big bucks. A final word: calling hotels and *Pensionen* to get a price quote before arriving is an absolute *must*, as prices fluctuate with the months of the year, the time of the day, and (sometimes) even your race or nationality.

Near the Hauptbahnhof

Hotel Helvetia, Schillerstr. 6, 80336 München (tel. 55 47 45; fax 55 02 381), at the corner of Bahnhofspl., next to the Vereinsbank, to the right as you exit the station. Recently renovated and delicately redecorated. Most rooms have phones. Singles DM53-62; doubles DM68-90, with shower DM115; triples DM99-120. Breakfast included. Also caters to backpackers with new hostel-like dorms: 10-bed DM19, 4 to 6-bed DM24. Breakfast DM7, sheets DM4. Laundry service (17 lb. per 8kg) DM8.50.

Pension Locarno, Bahnhofpl. 5 (tel. 55 51 64; fax 59 50 45), under the AGFA sign at the intersection with Arnulfstr. right outside the train station. Plain rooms, all with TV and phone. Helpful, homey owners. Reception open 7:30am-midnight; locked up after 10pm but your key opens the outside door 24hr. Singles DM55-75; doubles DM90; triples DM135; quads DM160. Breakfast included. DM5 less if you arrange for no breakfast. AmEx, Eurocard, MC, Visa.

Hotel Kurpfalz, Schwanthalerstr. 121, 80339 München (tel. 540 98 60; fax 54 09 88 11; email hotel-kurpfalz@munich-online.de). Exit on Bayerstr. from the station, turn right and walk 5 to 6 blocks down Bayerstr., veer left onto Holzapfelstr., and make a right onto Schwanthalerstr. (10min.). Or streetcar #18 or 19: "Holzapfelstr." (3 stops) and walk from there. The hotel's Sevdas Brothers add a dash of Bayern to their proficiency in Americana. Satellite TVs, phones, and hardwood furniture embellish all rooms. Reception open 24hr. Singles with bath DM89; doubles DM129; triples (doubles with cots) DM165. Supertasty all-you-can-eat breakfast buffet included. Free **Internet access.** Major credit cards accepted.

Hotel Central, Bayerstr. 55 (tel. 453 98 46; fax 543 98 470), 5min. from the Bayerstr. exit of the train station on the right. The unattractive exterior belies the qualities within—just like Quasimodo. While unadorned and plain, the rooms are clean and spacious. Reception open 24hr. Singles DM50-60; doubles DM85-95, with bath DM100-120. AmEx, Eurocard, Visa.

Pension Schillerhof, Schillerstr. 21, 80336 München (tel. 59 42 70; fax 550 18 35). From the "Bahnhofspl." train station exit, turn right and walk two blocks. Nondescript rooms floating around in a sea of neighborhood sex shops and *Kinos*. In-room TVs. Singles DM60-65, with shower DM70-75; doubles DM80-95, with shower DM95-110. Extra bed DM20. *Oktoberfest* surcharge DM25-40 per person. Breakfast included. Eurocard, MC, Visa.

Pension Hungaria, Briennerstr. 42, 80333 München (tel. 52 15 58). From *Hauptbahnhof*, go left onto Dachauerstr., right on Augustenstr., and right onto Briennerstr. (10min.). Or U-Bahn #1: "Stiglmaierpl.," and take the Briennerstr./Volkstheater exit; it's on the next corner at Augustenstr. Reception (2 floors up) open 8am-10pm. Oriental rugs, comfortable furnishings, and small travel library. Singles DM50-55; doubles DM80-85; triples DM105. Showers DM3. Lovely breakfasts included. *Oktoberfest* surcharge DM10-20 per room.

Pension Utzelmann, Pettenkoferstr. 6, 80336 München (tel. 59 48 89; fax 59 62 28). From the *Bahnhof* walk 4 blocks down Schillerstr. and go left on Pettenkofer; it's at the end on the left (10min.). Clean, occasionally quite elegant rooms. Reception open 7am-10pm. Singles DM48-65, with bath DM125; doubles DM90, with shower DM110, with bath DM145; triples DM125, with bath DM175. DM5 for hall showers. Breakfast included. No credit cards.

Schwabing/University/City Center

Pension Frank, Schellingstr. 24, 80799 München (tel. 28 14 51; fax 280 09 10). From the *Hauptbahnhof*, U-Bahn #4 or 5: "Odeonspl.," then U-Bahn #3 or 6: "Universität." Take the Schellingstr. exit, then the first right onto Schellingstr.; it's 2 blocks down on the right. Curious combination of scruffy backpackers, student groups, and dolled-up (second-rate) fashion models. Dig into a hearty breakfast with the rest of Kool and the Gang. Fabulous location for cafe and bookstore aficionados. Reception open 7:30am-10pm. 3- to 6-bed rooms DM35 per person. Singles DM55-65; doubles DM78-85. Single beds in shared rooms almost always available. *Oktoberfest* prices no more than DM5 higher. Breakfast and fridge access included.

Pension am Kaiserplatz, Kaiserpl. 12, 80803 München (tel. 34 91 90), is located a few blocks from nightlife central—good location if you doubt your own sense of direction after a couple bubbling brewskis. U-Bahn #3 or 6: "Münchener Freiheit." Take the escalator to Herzogstr., then left onto Viktoriastr. Walk down Viktoriastr. past the church; it's at the end of the street on the right (10min.). Sweet owner offers elegantly decorated, high-ceilinged rooms. Reception open 7am-9pm. Singles DM49-59; doubles DM82, with shower DM89; triples DM105; quads DM120-130; quints DM150-160; 6-bed rooms DM160-170. Breakfast (room service) included. DM3 to shower more than once per day—hygiene comes at a price!

Pension Geiger, Steinheilstr. 1, 80333 München (tel. 52 15 56; fax 52 31 54 71). U-Bahn #2: "Theresienstr." From Theresienstr., take a right onto Enhuberstr. and a left onto Steinheilstr.; enter through the double doors on the right. Reception (2 floors up) open 8am-10pm. Family-run *Pension* decorated like Midwestern living-room, brimming with bric-a-brac and soft sofas. Fargo before the brothers Coen; Sioux City before Mick Sweet. Singles DM45-60, with shower DM65-70; doubles DM88, DM98. Hall showers DM2. Arrive by 6pm or call. Closed Dec. 24-Jan. 31.

Pension Theresia, Luisenstr. 51, 80333 München (tel. 52 12 50; fax 542 06 33). U-Bahn #2: "Theresienstr.," take the Augustenstr./Technische Univ. exit, head straight down Theresienstr., and take the second right onto Luisenstr.; the entrance in the passageway left of the DAHLKE store. Reception (2nd floor) open 6:30am-10pm. Cheery red carpets and an elegant dining room complement the well-maintained rooms. Singles DM52-69; doubles DM88-115, with shower DM95-125; triples DM123-150; quads DM144-184. Breakfast included. Hall showers DM3. Reservations by phone or fax. AmEx, MC, Visa.

Hotel-Pension am Markt, Heiliggeiststr. 6, 80331 München (tel. 22 50 14; fax 22 40 17), smack dab in the city center. S-Bahn #1-8: "Marienpl.," walk through the *Altes Rathaus,* and turn right behind the Heiliggeist Church. Aging photographs recall celebrities who graced the hotel's small but shipshape rooms—recognize anyone?

Singles DM62-64, with shower DM110; doubles DM110-116, DM150-160; triples DM165, DM205. Breakfast included. Reserve rooms at least 3-4 weeks in advance.

■ Food

The vibrant **Viktualienmarkt,** two minutes south of Marienpl., is Munich's gastronomic center, rumbling with an endless open-air feast of bread, fruit, meat, pastries, cheese, honey, wine, vegetables, sausage, and sandwiches—lots of fun to browse through, but don't plan to do budget grocery shopping in these picturesque Bavarian shops (open Mon.-Fri. 9am-6:30pm, Sat. 9am-2pm). Located on every corner, the ubiquitous **beer gardens** (see **Beer, Beer, and More Beer,** p. 484) serve savory snacks along with the booze, yet skinflints can bring their own picnic to the assigned "self-service" areas. To stick your fangs into an authentic Bavarian lunch, grab a *Brez'n* (pretzel; pronounced "Braaayzin" by the *Müncheners*) and spread it with *Leberwurst* or cheese (DM4-5). *Weißwürste* (white veal sausages) are another native bargain, served in a pot of hot water with sweet mustard and a soft pretzel on the side. Don't eat the skin off the sausage; instead, slice it open and devour the tender meat. Traditionally, *Weißwürste* is consumed before noon during *Frühschoppen,* the merry moments of the morning, but you can find it any time. *Leberkäs,* also a *Müncbener* lunch, is a slice of a pinkish, meatloaf-like compound of ground beef and bacon which, despite its name and dubious appearance, contains neither liver nor cheese. *Leberknödel* are liver dumplings, usually served in soup or with *Kraut; Kartoffelknödel* (potato dumplings) and *Semmelknödel* (made from white bread, egg, and parsely) are eaten along with a hearty chunk of German meat. Those not interested in chowing down on all things meaty may have a tough time; vegetarians might want to head for Italian, Indian, Chinese, or other ethnic specialties.

Tengelmann, Schützenstr. 7, straight ahead from the main station, is most convenient for grocery needs (open Mon.-Wed. and Fri. 8:30am-6:30pm, Thurs. 8:30am-8:30pm, Sat. 9am-2pm). The **supermarket HL Markt,** at Rotkreuzpl. is larger and provides a little more variety. U-Bahn #1: "Rotkreuzpl." *Munich Found* (DM4) lists a few restaurants (editors' choice, of course), while *Prinz* (DM5) proffers a fairly complete listing of restaurant/cafes/bars in Munich. Countless fruit and vegetable **markets** are held throughout the city.

University Mensas

Serves large portions of cheap food (DM3-5.50), and offers at least one vegetarian dish. Student ID required. Buy your token from booths in the lobby *before* getting your meal. Open year-round.

Technical University, Arcisstr. 17, to the left of the Pinakothek Museums just below Gabelsbregstr. on Arcisstr. U-Bahn #2: "Königspl." Open Mon.-Thurs. 8:30am-4:15pm, Fri. 8:30am-2:30pm. During vacations open 8am-4pm.

Ludwig Maximilian University, Leopoldstr. 13, behind the large pink building. U-Bahn #3 or 6: "Giselastr." Open Dec.-July Mon.-Thurs. 9am-4:30pm, Fri. 9am-3pm; Aug.-Nov. Mon.-Thurs. 9am-3:45pm, Fri. 9am-3pm.

Near the University

The university district off **Ludwigstraße** is by far the best place in Munich to look for filling meals in a lively, unpretentious (but hip) atmosphere. Many restaurants and cafes cluster on Schellingstr., Amalienstr., and Türkenstr.; the nightlife scene trickles away from the city center down Leopoldstr. Unless otherwise noted, use U-Bahn #3 or 6: "Universität" to reach these restaurants. **Plus supermarket,** Schellingstr. 38, provides cheap groceries (open Mon.-Fri. 8:30am-7pm, Sat. 7:30am-2pm).

Türkenhof, Türkenstr. 78 (tel. 280 02 35), has a menu that's pseudo-Turkish, but the low-key crowd isn't pseudo-anything. Smoky and buzzing at night. Variable daily menu. Creative entrees (*Schnitzel,* omelettes, soups) DM7-14. Open Sun.-Thurs. 11am-1am, Fri.-Sat. 11am-3am.

Café Puck, Türkenstr. 33 (tel. 280 22 80). Spacious, handsome cafe and bar that exudes a hip, young, and energetic attitude. The *Milchkaffee* (DM4.80) is as smooth and rich as mother's milk. Breakfast served 9am-6pm (DM5-16); veggie specials (DM11.50-16). Open daily 9am-1am.

La Bohème, Türkenstr. 79 (tel. 272 08 33), just across from Türkenhof, is not a Jonathan Larson creation. Waiter, there's an antique trinket in my Italian food. Lunch pastas DM7-11, pizzas DM7-11, salads DM5-13. At dinner add DM1 to all dishes. Beer DM3.50 (0.4L).

Schelling Salon, Schellingstr. 54 (tel. 272 07 88). Bavarian *Knödel* and billiard balls. Founded in 1872 on the philosophy that billiards is the game *"der schweigenden Männer"* (of silent men), this pool joint has racked the balls of Lenin, Rilke, and Hitler; Franz Josef Strauss used to drop by for a snack. Breakfast DM5-9; *Wurst* DM6-7; *Russ'n Maß* DM9.40. A **billiard museum** displays a 200-year-old Polish noble's table and the history of pool back to the Pharaohs. Restaurant/museum open Thurs.-Mon. 6:30am-1pm.

News Bar, Amalienstr. 55 (tel. 28 17 87), at the corner of Schellingstr. Bustling, trendy new cafe, teeming with younger folks. Crepes DM6-11, granola with yogurt DM6.80, sandwiches DM7.50-10.50. Open daily 7:30am-2am.

In the Center

Munich's touristy interior suffers from an overabundance of high-priced eateries, but there are some good options, even for the budget traveler.

Shoya, Orlandostr. 5 (tel. 29 27 72), across from the Hofbräuhaus. The most reasonable Japanese restaurant/take-out joint in town. Fill up on rice dishes (DM13-19), *teriyaki* (DM8-16), sushi (DM5-30), and meat and veggie dishes (DM4-16) before blowing your wad at the Hofbräuhaus. Open daily 10:30am-midnight.

buxs, Frauenstr. 9 (tel. 22 94 82), on the southern edge of the Viktualienmarkt on the corner of Westernederstr. Vegetarian cafe/restaurant with tasty, artful pastas, salads (100g DM3), and other non-meaty alternatives—something green in a Munich restaurant! Open Mon.-Fri. 11am-8:30pm, Sat. 11am-3:30pm.

Beim Sendlmayr, Westenriederstr. 6 (tel. 22 62 19), off the Viktualienmarkt. Anyone craving a *Weißwurst* will crave this slice of Little Bayern. Specials DM7-25. Beer DM5.30 for 0.5L. Open daily 11am-11pm.

Elsewhere in Munich

Internet-Café, Nymphenburgerstr. 145 (tel. 129 11 20; http://www.icafe.spacenet.de), on the corner of Landshuter Allee. U-Bahn #1: "Rotkreuzpl." With the addition of 12 terminals, this is an average Italian joint *cum* hopping, glowing electronic haven—a Neuromancer's paradise. Unlimited and free Internet access as long as you order pasta (DM9.50), pizza (DM7.50-10), or beer (DM4.90 for 0.5L). Amaze your friends with emails from abroad. Cyberspace fiend? Open daily 11am-4am. **Another location,** Altheimer Eck 12 (tel. 260 78 15), sits in the center of the city between Marienpl. and Karlspl. in the pedestrian zone through "Arcade-Passage." Same stuff, different hours—daily 11am-1am.

Schwimmkrabbe, Ickstattstr. 13 (tel. 201 00 80). U-Bahn #1 or 2: "Fraunhoferstr.," then walk 1 block down Baaderstr. to Ickstattstr. Locals flock to this family-run Turkish restaurant. Try the delicious *Etli Pide* (lamb and veggies wrapped in a footlong bread with salad; DM16). Hearty dishes DM15-20. Belly-dancing darlings on Fri. and Sat. nights add some *exotica* to your trip. Adore those rippling bellies and dream away. Open daily 5pm-1am. Reserve on weekends.

Gollier, Gollierstr. 83 (tel. 50 16 73). U-Bahn #4 or 5 or S-Bahn #7 or 27: "Heimeranpl." A vegetarian cafe serving delicious homemade pizzas, crepes, and stews for DM6-19. Lunch buffet DM13. Mon.-Fri. noon-3pm and 5pm-midnight, Sat. 5pm-midnight, Sun. noon-midnight.

■ Sights

Munich's Catholic past has left many marks on the city's architecture. Numerous, often mightily impressive, sacred stone edifices prickle the area around the **Marienplatz.** The name of this square, a major S-Bahn and U-Bahn junction as well as the social nexus of the city, originates in the **Mariensäule,** an ornate 17th-century monument dedicated to the Virgin Mary. It was built to commemorate the fact that the amazing and powerful Swedes did not destroy the city during the Thirty Years War. Thanks, Thor. The onion-domed towers of the 15th-century **Frauenkirche** are one (well, maybe two) of Munich's most notable landmarks (towers open April-Oct. Mon.-Sat. 10am-5pm; DM4, students DM2, under 6 free). At the neo-Gothic **Neues Rathaus,** the **Glockenspiel** chimes with a display of jousting knights and dancing coopers. According to legend, the barrel-makers coaxed townspeople out of their homes, singing and dancing, to prove that the Great Plague had passed (daily 11am, noon, 5, and 9pm). At bedtime (9pm), a mechanical watchman marches out and the Guardian Angel escorts the *Münchner Kindl* ("Munich Child," the town's symbol) to bed. (Tower open Mon.-Fri. 9am-7pm, Sat.-Sun. 10am-7pm. DM3, under 15 DM1.50). On the face of the **Altes Rathaus** tower, to the right of the *Neues Rathaus,* are all (with one glaring exception) Munich's different coats of arms since its inception as a city. When the tower was rebuilt following its destruction in World War II, the local government refused to include the swastika-bearing coat of arms from the Nazi era.

Munich's ritual past is represented by the 11th-century **Peterskirche** at Rindermarkt and Peterspl.; its interior was baroquified in the 18th century. Over 300 steps scale the tower, christened *Alter Peter* (Old Peter) by locals (open Mon.-Sat. 9am-6pm, Sun. 10am-6pm; DM2.50, students DM1.50, children DM0.50). Ludwig II of Bayern (of crazy castle fame) rests peacefully with 40-odd other Wittelsbachs entombed in the crypt of the 16th-century Jesuit **Michaelskirche,** on Neuhauserstr. The construction of the church, designed to emphasize the city's loyalty to Catholicism during the Reformation, almost bankrupted the state treasury. Father Rupert Mayer, one of the few German clerics who spoke out against Hitler, preached here (crypt DM0.50). A Bavarian Rococo masterpiece, the **Asamkirche,** Sendlingerstr. 32, is named after its creators, the Asam brothers, who promised God that they would build a church if they survived the wreckage of their ship. The rocks at the bottom of the facade represent the rapids which serve as the reason for the church's existence.

The richly decorated rooms built from the 14th to the 19th centuries in the magnificent **Residenz,** Max-Joseph-Platz 3 (tel. 29 06 71), form the material vestiges of the Wittelsbach dynasty. The grounds now house several museums. The beautifully landscaped *Hofgarten* behind the *Residenz* houses the lovely temple of Diana. U-Bahn #3-6: "Odeonspl." The **Schatzkammer** (treasury) contains jeweled baubles, crowns, swords, china, ivorywork, and other trinkets from the 10th century on. (Open Tues.-Sun. 10am-4:30pm. DM5, students and group members DM2.50, children under 15 with adult free.) The **Residenzmuseum** comprises the former Wittelsbach apartments and State Rooms, a collection of European porcelain, and a 17th-century court chapel. The walls of the **Ahnengalerie** (Gallery of Ancestors), hung with 120 "family portraits," portray an utter loss of perspective. Charlemagne would be surprised to find himself being held accountable for the genesis of the Wittelsbach family (hours and admission same as *Schatzkammer*).

After 10 years of trying for an heir, Ludwig I celebrated the birth of his son Maximilian in 1662 by erecting an elaborate summer playroom; **Schloß Nymphenburg,** in the northwest of town, was another desperate (albeit beautiful) attempt to copy King Louis XIV of France. Streetcar #17 (direction: "Alienburgstr."): "Schloß Nymphenburg." A Baroque wonder set in a winsome park, the palace hides a number of treasures, including a two-story granite marble hall seasoned with stucco, frescoes, and a Chinese lacquer cabinet. Check out King Ludwig's "Gallery of Beauties"—whenever a woman caught his fancy, he would have her portrait painted (a scandalous hobby, considering that many of the women were commoners; a touching one, given that Ludwig grappled with an affection for men throughout his life). The palace contains a wonderful collection of antique porcelain and a modern porcelain studio's manufacturing gallery *(Schönheitgalerie),* as well as the strange **Marstallmuseum** (Carriage Museum). **Schloß** open Tues.-Sun. 9am-noon and 1-5pm; Oct.-March 10am-12:30pm and 1:30-4pm; **Amalienburg** open daily 9am-12:30pm and 1:30-5pm; **Badenburg, Pagodenburg,** and **Magdalenen hermitage** open Tues.-Sun. 10am-12:30pm and 1:30-

5pm. (Main palace DM6, students DM4; entire complex DM8, students DM5, kids under 15 with adult free. Grounds open until 9:30pm; free.)

Just next door expands the immense **Botanischer Garten,** whose greenhouses shelter rare and wonderful growths from around the world (tel. 17 86 13 10). Check out the water lily room and the unassuming moss room, with an exquisitely **romantic alcove** in the back. (Open daily 9am-7pm. Greenhouses open 9-11:45am and 1-6:30pm. DM3, students DM1.50, under 15 DM0.50). Abutting the city center is the vast **Englischer Garten,** one of Europe's oldest landscaped public parks. On sunny days, all of Munich turns out to bike, play badminton, ride horseback, or sunbathe. Nude sunbathing areas are designated "FKK" *(Freikörperkultur)* on signs and park maps. Consider yourself warned. *Müncheners* with aquatic daring-do (and a surfboard) ride the *Eisbach,* which flows artificially through the park.

Mixed with Munich's Baroque elegance are visible traces of Germany's Nazi past. Buildings erected by Hitler and his cronies that survived the bombings of 1945 stand as grim memorials. The **Haus der Kunst,** built to enshrine Nazi principles of art, serves as a modern art museum; swastika patterns have been left on its porch as reminders of its origins (see **Museums,** below). The gloomy limestone building now housing the **Music School** was built under Hitler's auspices and functioned as his Munich headquarters. From its balcony, he viewed the city's military parades; it was also here that Chamberlain signed away the Sudetenland in 1938.

■ Museums

Munich is a supreme museum city, and many of the city's offerings would independently require days for exhaustive perusal. Several museums inhabit the gilded grounds of the *Residenz* and Schloß Nymphenburg (see **Sights,** p. 479). The *Münchner Volkschule* (tel. 48 00 63 30) offers tours of many city museums for DM8.

Museumsinsel-Isartor
Deutsches Museum, on the *Museumsinsel* (Museum Island) in the Isar River (tel. 217 91 or for recording in German 217 94 33; fax 217 93 24). S-Bahn #1-8: "Isartor." One of the world's largest and best museums of science and technology. Particularly well-conceived are the displays on aerospace, photography, and astronomy. Don't miss the mining exhibit, which winds through a labyrinth of recreated subterranean mining tunnels. The hall of keyboard instruments ain't shabby either. Pick up an English guide to the exhibits (DM10). The planetarium (DM3) and daily electrical show will warm the cockles of any physicist's heart. DM10, students DM4. Open daily 9am-5pm.

Königsplatz
Alte Pinakothek, Barerstr. 27 (tel. 23 80 52 15; fax 23 80 52 21), contains Munich's most precious artistic jewels. U-Bahn #2: "Theresienstr." Thirteenth- to 17th-century Wittelsbacher family storage covers works by Giotto, Titian, da Vinci, Raphael, Dürer, Rembrandt, and Rubens. To be reopened following renovations in June/July 1998; until then, the Neue Pinakothek will house its major works in rooms 1-12.
Neue Pinakothek, Barerstr. 29 (tel. 23 80 51 95; fax 23 80 52 21), next to Alte Pinakothek. Sleek space for the 18th to 20th centuries: Van Gogh, Klimt, etc. DM7, students DM4. Open Tues. and Thurs. 10am-8pm, Wed. and Fri.-Sun. 10am-5pm.
Lenbachhaus, Luisenstr. 33 (tel. 23 33 20 00; recorded German info tel. 23 33 20 02; fax 23 33 20 03). U-Bahn #2: "Königspl." Munich cityscapes (useful if it's raining), along with works by Kandinsky, Klee, and the *Blaue Reiter* school (Münter, Marc, Macke, etc.), which disdained perfumed Impressionism, forging the aesthetic of abstraction. DM8, students DM4. Open Tues.-Sun. 10am-6pm.
Glyptothek, Königspl. 3 (tel. 28 61 00; fax 550 38 51), around the corner from the Lenbachhaus. U-Bahn #2: "Königspl." Assembled by Ludwig I, the collection features Greek, Etruscan, and Roman sculptures. DM6, students DM3.50. Joint admission with Antikensammlung DM10, students DM5. Open Tues.-Wed. and Fri.-Sun. 10am-5pm, Thurs. 10am-8pm.
Antikensammlung, Königspl. 1 (tel. 59 83 59; fax 550 38 51), across Königspl. from Glyptothek. U-Bahn #2: "Königspl." Flaunts a first-rate flock of vases and the other

half of Munich's finest collection of ancient art; features Ancient Greek and Etruscan pottery and jewelry. DM6, students DM3.50. Joint admission with Glyptothek DM10, students DM5. Open Tues. and Thurs.-Sun. 10am-5pm, Wed. 10am-8pm.

Elsewhere in Munich

Staatsgalerie moderner Kunst, Prinzregentenstr. 1 (tel. 21 12 71 37; fax 23 80 52 21), in the **Haus der Kunst** (tel. 21 12 70; fax 21 12 71 57) at the southern tip of the Englischer Garten. U-Bahn #4 or 5: "Lehel," then streetcar #20, or bus #53. A sterling 20th-century collection showcases Beckmann, Kandinsky, Klee, Picasso, Dalí, and friends. Constructed by the Nazis as the Museum of German Art, it opened with the famous *Entartete Kunst* (degenerate art) exhibit that included works of the Expressionists and Dadaists. DM6, students DM3.50. Visiting exhibitions extra. Open Tues.-Wed. and Fri.-Sun. 10am-5pm, Thurs. 10am-8pm.

Münchener Stadtmuseum, St.-Jakobs-Platz 1 (tel. 23 32 23 70 or for exhibition announcements 233 55 86; fax 233 50 33). U-Bahn #3 or 6 or S-Bahn #1-8: "Marienpl." A collection of museums, all with a Bavarian touch: photography, film, musical instruments, weapons, and more. The Puppet and Marionette museum offers the opportunity to let those creative juices flow and build your own sweet *Ding—das Ding an sich?* **Classic films** (DM8) roll every evening at 8pm. Foreign films shown with subtitles; call 233 55 86 for a program. Museum DM5, students, seniors, and children DM2.50, under 6 free. Open Tues. and Thurs.-Sun. 10am-5pm, Wed. 10am-8:30pm. Open Mon. 5pm-midnight, Tues.-Sun. 11am-midnight.

ZAM: Zentrum für außergewöhnliche Museen (Center for Unusual Museums), Westenriederstr. 26 (tel. 290 41 21). S-Bahn #1-8: "Isartor" or streetcar #17 or 18. A brilliant place which brazenly corrals under one roof such treasures as the Corkscrew Museum, the Museum of Easter Rabbits, and the Chamberpot Museum. Fan of Empress Elizabeth of Austria? Your paradise is the Sisi Museum. DM8, students, seniors, and children DM5. Open daily 10am-6pm.

Museum für erotische Kunst (Museum of Erotic Art), Odeonspl. 8 (tel. 228 35 44), in same building as the Filmcasino. U-Bahn #3-6: "Odeonspl." or bus #53. For those lonely days when you're 5000km away from your beloved (or those uninspired days when you're right next to your beloved), this museum covers all 4 bases around the world and through time. Features a French book of sex-gags entitled *The Circus,* hot and heavy chess pieces, and a set of juicy Japanese illustrations. DM8, students DM6. Open Tues.-Sun. 11am-7pm.

BMW Museum, Petuelring 130 (tel. 38 22 33 07; fax 38 22 36 22). U-Bahn #3: "Olympiazentrum." The ultimate driving museum features a fetching display of Bavaria's second-favorite export. Baby, you can drive my car. DM5.50, students DM4. Open daily 9am-5pm. Last entry 4pm.

Valentin Musäum, Isartorturm (tel. 22 32 66). S-Bahn #1-8 or streetcar #18 or 20: "Isartor." Decidedly esoteric peek at the comical life of Karl Valentin, the German counterpart of Charlie Chaplin, and his partner Liesl Karlstadt; Valentin was one of Bavaria's most absurd funny men. Curiosities include sham skeletons encased in the stone wall and a photograph of a Karl Valentin snowman. Admission 299*Pfennig,* students 149*Pfennig.* Open Mon.-Tues. and Fri.-Sat. 11:01am-5:29pm, Sun. 10:01am-5:29pm. Wacky Bavarians.

Spielzeugmuseum, Altes Rathaus, Marienpl. (tel 29 40 01). Two centuries of European and American toys—compare the "futuristic" World War I figurines to the slick, slim Barbie. DM5, children DM1, families DM10. Open daily 10am-5:30pm.

■ Entertainment

THEATER AND OPERA

Munich's cultural cachet rivals the world's best. The Müncheners are great funlovers and hedonists, yet they reserve a place for folksy kitsch, cultivating a supreme and diverse *Szene* with something for everyone. Eleven large theaters and countless smaller stages are scattered throughout the city. Styles range from dramatic classics at the **Residenztheater** and **Volkstheater** to comic opera at the **Staatstheater am Gärtnerplatz** to experimental works at the **Theater im Marstall** in Nymphenburg.

Leftovers tickets run around DM10. Munich's **Opera Festival** (in July) is held in the Bayerische Staatsoper (below) accompanied by a concert series in the Nymphenburg and Schleissheim palaces. Write for tickets, or call early that night (tel. 26 46 20) for leftover tickets (around DM15). The *Monatsprogramm* (DM2.50) lists schedules for all of Munich's stages, museums, and festivals.

In the **Schwabing district,** Munich shows its more bohemian face with scores of little fringe theaters, art cinemas, and artsy pubs. The **Leopoldstraße,** its main avenue leading up from the university, can be magical on a warm summer night in its own gaudy way—milling youthful crowds, art students hawking their work, and terrace-cafes create an exciting swarm. At the turn of the century this area was a distinguished center of European cultural and intellectual life, housing luminaries like Brecht, Mann, Klee, Kandinsky, Spengler and Trotsky. Today, however, the true avant-garde scene has moved to the humbler quarters of **Haidhausen** across the Isar.

Gasteig Kulturzentrum, Rosenheimerstr. 5 (tel. 48 09 80). S-Bahn #1-8: "Rosenheimerpl." or streetcar #18: "Am Gasteig." A thriving cultural center with a long history, the *Kulturzentrum* hosts musical performances ranging from classical to non-Western in its three concert halls and visual arts center. The hall rests on the former site of the *Bürgerbräukeller* where Adolf Hitler launched his abortive Beer Hall Putsch. Features the **Munich Philharmonic** and a wide range of events such as public readings and ballet. Box office in the Glashalle (tel. 54 89 89) open Mon.-Fri. 10:30am-2pm and 3-6pm, Sat. 10:30am-2pm, and 1hr. before showtime.

Bayerische Staatsoper (Bavarian State Opera), Max-Joseph-Platz (tickets tel. 21 85 19 20; recorded info tel. 21 85 19 19). U-Bahn #3-6: "Odeonspl." or streetcar #19: "National Theater." Standing-room and reduced-rate student tickets (DM15-20) to the numerous operas and ballets are sold at Maximilianstr. 11 (tel. 21 85 19 20), behind the Opera House, or 1hr. before the performance at the side entrance on Maximilianstr. Box office open Mon.-Fri. 10am-6pm, Sat. 10am-1pm. No performances Aug. to mid-Sept.

Staatstheater, Gärtnerpl. 3 (tel. 32 01 67 67). U-Bahn #1 or 2: "Fraunhoferstr." and then follow Reichenbachstr. to Gärtnerpl.; or bus #52 or 56: "Gärtnerpl." Stages comic opera and musicals. Tickets available 4 weeks before each performance at the Staatstheater box office (tel. 20 24 11). Open Mon.-Fri. 10am-6pm, Sat. 10am-1pm, and 1hr. before performance at the night counter; or at the Bavarian State Opera counter (see above). Standing room tickets start at DM14.

Drehleier, Balanstr. 23 (tel. 48 43 37). S-Bahn #1-8 or bus #51: "Rosenheimerpl." A mixture of theater, cabaret, and performance art romps across this offbeat stage. One of the best cabaret scenes in Munich. Kitchen serves inexpensive salads and noodle dishes (DM6-15) until 10pm. Tickets DM20-30. Reservations required. Open Tues.-Sat. 6:30pm-1am. Performances Tues.-Sat. 10:30pm.

Münchner Kammerspiele, Maximilianstr. 26-28 (tickets tel. 23 72 13 28; recorded info tel. 23 72 13 26). Streetcar #19: "Maxmonument." Exceptional modern theater and classics grace its two stages. **Schauspielhaus,** Maximilianstr. 26, shows Goethe and Shakespeare (DM9-46). Buy advance tickets at Münchner Kammerspiele. The **Werkraum,** at Hildegardstr. 1, features avant-garde and critical leftist pieces. Standing room tickets DM1. Tickets available one week in advance. Box office open Mon.-Fri. 10am-6pm, Sat. 10am-1pm.

FILM

Newspapers and magazines like *in München* (free) list **movie** showings. English films are often dubbed; search for the initials "OF" (original language) or "OmU" (subtitled) on the poster before buying your popcorn. Munich's **film festival** generally runs for a week in late June or early July. For schedules and information, contact **Internationale Filmwoche,** Türkenstr. 93, 80799 Munich (tel. 381 90 40).

Museum Lichtspiele, Lilienstr. 2 (tel. 48 24 03), by the Ludwigsbrücke and part of the Deutsches Museum (S-Bahn #1-6 or streetcar #18: "Isator") holds the world's record for most consecutive daily screenings of the Rocky Horror Picture Show (daily at midnight). Non-dubbed English-language films screened daily (DM11-13).

Türkencloich, Türkenstr. 74, (tel. 271 88 44), in the middle of the student district, has mini-film festivals dedicated to a particular director or theme.

Forum der Technik, Museumsinsel 1 (tel. 29 12 51 80), next to the Deutsches Museum, maxes out on magnificent **IMAX** movies (DM11.90, students DM8.90). Subtitled foreign films (DM9).

Cinema, Nymphenburgerstr. 31 (tel. 55 52 55) screens non-dubbed, English-language flicks daily. U-Bahn #1: "Stiglmaierpl."

FLEA MARKETS AND ANTIQUES

Fleamarket: Arnulfstr., to the left of the Hackerbrücke, in a former train station. S-Bahn #1-8: "Hackerbrücke." Knick-knacks, clothing, and stuff you'll never use but have been searching for forever. Open Fri.-Sat. 7am-6pm.

Antikmarkt (tel. 49 91 87 87), in Kunstpark Ost at the Ostbahnhof. Auction block, antiques, and regular flea markets. Check a Kunstpark Ost program (see **Nightlife,** p. 486, for details). Open Wed.-Thurs. 1pm-8pm, Fri. 8am-8pm, Sat. 7am-6pm.

Auer Dult: Mariahilfpl. U-Bahn #1 or 2: "Fraunhoferstr.," then streetcar #27: "Mariahilfpl." Munich's most famous fleamarket. Since 1799, all the pots, pans, china, second-hand clothes, and antiques you can mail home. Three times per year for 9 days (April 25-May 3, July 25-Aug. 2, and Oct. 17-25 in 1998).

Christkindlmarkt: Christmas comes to Munich four weeks before Christmas Eve for this annual market. Open Mon.-Wed. and Fri. 9am-7:30pm, Thurs. 9am-8:30pm, Sat. 10am-7:30pm.

If you play Schlager, I'll go home.

Not a pricey designer liquor, but rather a virulent strain of pop, Schlager music only exists in Europe—mainly in Germanic countries—where it has remained a dominant form of pop for the past 30 years. Trying to describe what Schlager sounds like without resorting to profanity proves difficult, as there are few conventions within this pseudo-musical genre. Unlike rock 'n' roll, which prescribes one drummer, one bassist, one singer, and a couple of guitars, Schlager can be produced with a melange of keyboards, guitars, and horns. The only common denominator of all Schlager songs is silliness. A classic, often recycled riff, would be *"Ich liebe dich, willst du mich lieben?"* (I love you, do you want to love me?), accompanied by a massive *Akkordeon* (accordion) solo, or "I'm a little pony! I'm a little pony! Won't you ride me, please?" An all-time German Schlager star is Rainer Pietsch, but neophytes might be more familiar with his female counterpart, Nena Hagen, whose smashing "99 Luftballons" launched Schlager into the international arena. The high point of the year for any Schlager devotee is the Eurovision contest when all *Schlagermeister*s gather. In 1998 this event will be held in Birmingham, U.K. Schlager on, baby!

BEER, BEER, AND MORE BEER

The official coat-of-arms of Munich depicts a monk holding a bible in his right hand. Unofficially, the monk's left hand firmly clenches a large, frothy brewski, raising it high and, with a twinkle in the eye, saying *"Prost."* Sacrilege? Not at all. In 1328, the Augustiner monks introduced *Bier* to unsuspecting *Müncheners,* who have since continued the 600-year-old trend. Bayern proudly holds the title as the largest producer *and* consumer of beer in Germany—in a mighty big way. Local breweries produce 123 million gallons of "liquid bread" per annum, 150,000 seats in Munich **beer gardens** beckon the thirsty, and every year, the average local imbibes over 220 liters of this amber dew of gods, more than twice the average drunk in the rest of Germany (though the figure does include the mighty *Oktoberfest,* during which locals and visitors together swig six million liters). Proudly honoring the Beer Purity Law (*Reinheitsgebot*) of 1516 (see p. 85), Bavarians reaffirm their exalted and earned reputation as the ultimate, tried-and-true beer connoisseurs. The six great Munich labels are *Augustiner, Hacker-Pschorr, Hofbräu, Löwenbräu, Paulaner,* and *Spaten-Franziskaner,* yet most restaurants and *Gaststätte* will pick a side by only serving one brewery's beer. *"Ein Bier, bitte"* will get you a liter, known to those in the know as a *Maß* (DM8-11). If you want a half-*Maß* (DM4-6), you must specify it, though many establishments will only serve *Weißbier* in 0.5L sizes.

The biggest keg party in the world, Munich's **Oktoberfest** finishes on the first Sunday of October and starts 16 days before (Sept. 19-Oct. 4 in 1998). The site of this uncontrolled revelry is known as **Theresienwiese** (Therese's meadow)—or *"Wies'n"* (shortened perhaps after one *Maß* too many). U-Bahn #4 or 5: "Theresienwiese." The festivities began in 1810 when Prince Ludwig married Princess Therese von Sachsen-Hildburghausen; ironically, no alcohol was served at the original reception. The party was so much fun that *Müncheners* repeated the revelry the next year, and every year following that, since they couldn't resist a revival. The party kicks off with speeches, a parade of horse-drawn beer wagons, and the mayor's tapping of the ceremonial first keg. The Hofbräu tent is the rowdiest and most touristy; fights break out more often than in other tents (for more on beer-tents, see the tourist office web site). Arrive early (by 4:30pm) to get a table—you must be seated to be served at *Oktoberfest*.

There are four main types of beer served in Munich: **Helles** and **Dunkles,** standard but delicious light and dark beers; **Weißbier,** a cloudy blond beer made from wheat instead of barley; and **Radler** (literally "cyclist's brew"), which is half beer and half lemon soda. Munich's beer typically has an alcohol content of 3.5%, though in *Starkbierzeit* (which runs 2 weeks, beginning with Lent), *Müncheners* traditionally drink *Salvator,* a strong, dark beer that is 5.5% alcohol. In May, art folk clean their palates with *Marbock,* a blond Bockbeer. *Frühschoppen* is drinking beer (and wolfing down *Weißwurst*) before mid-day. *Prost!*

Within Munich

Augustiner Keller, Arnulfstr. 52 (tel. 59 43 93), at Zirkus-Krone-Str. S-Bahn #1-8: "Hackerbrücke." Founded in 1824, Augustiner is viewed by most *Müncheners* as the finest beer garden in town. The lush grounds and dim lighting beneath 100-year-old chestnut trees and tasty, enormous *Brez'n* (pretzels; DM5) argue the case powerfully. The real attraction is the delicious, sharp Augustiner beer (*Maß* DM9-10) which entices locals, smart tourists, and scads of students. Food DM7-15. Open daily 10am-1am; warm food until 10pm. Beer garden open daily 10:30am-midnight.

Hofbräuhaus, Am Platzl 9 (tel. 22 16 76), 2 blocks from Marienpl. Established in 1589, Munich's world-famous beer hall was originally reserved for royalty and its invited guests (the name means "court brewery house"). The Hofbräuhaus has been tapping barrels for the commoners since 1897 and now seems reserved for drunken tourists. 15,000-30,000L of beer are sold per day. God bless all frat boys. But hey, it's a rite of passage—a stepping stone, if you will, to introduce backpackers from around the world to the joys of the Munich beer world. It was in the *Festsaal* that Hitler was proclaimed the first Nazi party chair. Small beer garden out back under chestnut trees. *Maß* DM10.40. Two *Weißwurst* sausages DM7.50. *Leberkäs* with spinach and potatoes DM9.90. Open daily 10am-midnight.

Augustiner Bräustuben, Landsbergerstr. 19 (tel. 50 70 47). S-Bahn #1-8: "Hackerbrücke." A relatively new beer hall in the Augustiner Brewery's former horse stalls. Shh, it's a local secret. Beer DM4 for 0.5L. For the hungry horse, try the *Bräustüberl* (duck, two types of pork, *Kraut,* and two types of dumplings) for DM14.60. Other delicious heaps of Bavarian food at excellent prices (DM6-20). Especially popular in winter. Open daily until 11pm.

Chinesischer Turm, in the *Englischer Garten* next to the pagoda (tel. 39 50 28). U-Bahn #3 or 6: "Giselastr." or bus #54 from *Südbahnhof:* "Chinesischer Turm." A fair-weather tourist favorite; lots of kids. *Maß* (*Weißbier*) DM9.50. Salads DM7-13.50. Pretzels DM5. Open daily in balmy weather 10:30am-11pm.

Augustiner, Neuhauserstr. 16 (tel. 55 19 92 57). Smaller manifestation of the eponymous *Keller.* Beer hall and sidewalk tables on the pedestrian zone between the station and Marienpl. The restaurant (on the right) is pricier than the beer hall. Bavarian meals in either run DM9-28. Beer hall *Maß* DM9.30; restaurant *Maß* DM10.40. Beer hall open Mon.-Sat. 9am-1am; restaurant open daily 9am-1am. Hot meals until 10:30pm.

Am Seehaus, Kleinhesselohe 3 (tel. 381 61 30). U-Bahn #6: "Dietlindenstr.," then bus #44: "Osterwaldgarten." Directly on the lovely Kleinhesseloher See in the

Englischer Garten, and beloved by locals for the lack of tourists. So don't go. *Maß* DM9.80. Open daily 10am-1am. Beer garden closes at 11pm.

Hirschgarten, Hirschgartenallee 1 (tel. 17 25 91). U-Bahn #1: "Rotkreuzpl.," then streetcar #12: "Romanpl." Walk straight to the end of Guntherstr. and enter the Hirschgarten—literally, "deer garden." The largest beer garden in Europe is boisterous and verdant, but somewhat remote (in the vicinity of Schloß Nymphenburg). Families head here for the grassy park and carousel. *Maß* DM8.60. Open daily 11am-11pm. Restaurant open Nov.-Feb. only Tues.-Sun.; entrees DM7-25.

Taxisgarten, Taxisstr. 12 (tel. 15 68 27). U-Bahn #1: "Rotkreuzpl.," then bus #83 or 177: "Klugstr." This beer garden is a gem—its small size has hidden it from tourists and kept it a favorite of locals and students. Almost always full. Saucy spare ribs, jumbo pretzels DM4.50. *Maß* DM9.50, *Weißbier* DM5. Open daily 10am-10pm.

Hofbräukeller, Innere Wienerstr. 19 (tel. 448 73 76). U-Bahn #4 or 5: "Max-Weber-Platz"—albeit no iron-cage. Pours the same brew as the Hofbräuhaus, only this time with Germans. It also has a beer garden. *Maß* DM9.50. Open daily 9am-midnight. Live jazz upstairs Tues.-Sat. 8:30pm-12:30am, cover DM10-20.

Löwenbräukeller, Nymphenburgerstr. 2 (tel. 52 60 21). U-Bahn #1: "Stiglmaierpl." Castle-like entrance, festive and loud cellar. Come here to taste the real *Löwenbräu,* if you dare: the bitter taste has a loyal core of local followers, despite general disapproval—it's considered by some to be the Budweiser of Munich beers. Ribs DM15, *Maß* DM7.80. Hot meals 11am-midnight. Open daily 9am-1am.

Pschorr-Keller, Theresienhöhe 7 (tel. 50 10 88). U-Bahn #4 or 5: "Theresienwiese." Along with the Hackerkeller down the street, an outpost of the Hacker-Pschorr brewery. Good stuff. Come here for your breakfast beer, mostly with locals. *Maß* DM9.90. Meals DM13-27. Open daily 8am-midnight.

Parkrestaurant Tarock, Sophienstr. 7, in the Alter Botanischer Garten, a block to the left from the train station (part of the **Park Café** nightclub). This peaceful outdoor beer garden, secluded from the cars and trains by oodles of greenery, is good for a train layover. *Löwenbrau* DM8.50 for *Maß*. Most meals DM6-12.

Just Outside Munich

Waldwirtschaft Großhesselohe, Georg-Kalb-Str. 3 (tel. 79 50 88). S-Bahn #7: "Großhesselohe Isartalbahnhof." From the station, go down the stairs and turn right; head down Sollnerstr. after passing Kreuzeckstr., then follow the signs; a 15-minute walk from the station. Relaxed beer garden with live music (daily from noon, no cover) and the site of Munich's recent "Beer Garden Revolution." Classic and international jazz starts on Sun. at noon. On a sunny day, schedule a *Frühschoppen* session for 11am or so. *Maß* DM9.80. Open daily 11am-10pm.

Paulaner Keller, Hochstr. 77 (tel. 459 91 30). Also known as Salvator Keller and Nockherberg. It's big, old, and has strong beer. U-Bahn #1 or 2: "Silberhornstr.," then bus #51: "Ostfriedhof." Walk back down Bonifaziusstr. over the bridge and to the right. Famous for its March *Starkbierzeit,* when extra strong brew gets consumed in vast quantities; as you swill, thank founding Monk Pater Barnabas. Remotely located on Nockherberg Hill, which is part of its charm; crowd mostly comprised of older folks. *Maß* DM10.60, "Salvator" (0.5L) DM6. *Brez'n* and *Knödel* DM11.80. Open daily 9am-11pm.

Forschungsbräuerei, Unterhachingerstr. 76 (tel. 670 11 69). Serves up some very strange brew—the name means "research brewery." Pleasant atmosphere and varieties of beer you can't find anywhere else. *Maß* DM9-10. Open Tues.-Sat. 11am-11pm, Sun. 10am-10pm.

■ Nightlife

Munich's nightlife is a curious collusion of Bavarian *Gemütlichkeit* and trendy cliquishness. Possessors of the latter trait are often referred to as *"Schicki-Mickis,"* loosely defined as a club-going German yuppies (expensively dressed, coiffed and sprayed, beautiful, shapely, blonde specimens of both sexes). With a healthy mix of students and other less pretentious, bopping locals, the streets bustle with raucous beer halls, loud discos, and exclusive cafes every night of the week; some places are as likely to be packed on a weeknight as on a Saturday. The locals tend to tackle their nightlife as an epic voyage. The odyssey begins at one of Munich's beer gardens or beer halls (see **Beer, Beer, and More Beer,** above; see beer everywhere), which generally close before midnight and are most crowded in the early evening. The alcohol keeps flowing at cafes and bars, which, except for Friday and Saturday nights, shut off their taps at 1am. Then the discos and dance clubs, sedate before midnight, suddenly spark and throb relentlessly until 4am. The trendy bars, cafes, cabarets, and discos plugged into Leopoldstr. in **Schwabing** attract tourists from all over Europe (see **Entertainment,** p. 482). Notorious are **Türsteher** (door standers)—neurotic bouncers with orders to protect the clientele from un-chic *personae non gratae.* Single men will have a harder time than single women. The best strategy is feigned *ennui*—look bored, avoid eye contact with the bouncer, and try to walk in. Dig the jaded hipster-wear out of your pack, or at least leave the white baseball hat and college T-shirt at home. A few more tips: no tennis shoes, no shorts, and no sandals (no, not even Birkenstocks—or haven't you noticed yet that you're the only person in Germany wearing them?). Oh, and no backpacks. If all else fails in the fashion department, return to the trusty standby—black. Early in the evening (before 9-11pm), bouncers aren't as picky. On weekends, on the other hand, you'll have to look like more money than your railpass cost.

The **Muffathalle,** Zellerstr. 4 (tel. 45 87 50 00) in Haidhausen, is a former power plant that generates hip student energy with ethno, hip-hop, jazz, and dance performances (cover up to DM30; open Mon.-Sat. 6pm-4am, Sun. 4pm-1am). S-Bahn #1-8: "Rosenheimerpl." or streetcar #18: "Deutsches Museum." Munich's alternative concert scene goes on at **Feierwerk,** Hansastr. 39-41 (tel. 769 36 00; fax 769 60 32), which has seven stages and huge tents. S-Bahn #7 or U-Bahn #4 or 5: "Heimeranpl.," then walk left down Hansastr. (10min.). In summer, there's lots of independent music, comedy, beer gardens, *Imbiß* stands, blues, and rock. Beer gardens open at 6pm; usually doors open at 8:30pm and concerts begin at 9pm. Check out http://db.allmusic.de/live/feierwerk for the skinny on impending shows. **Münchener Freiheit** is the most famous (and the most touristy) bar/cafe district; more low-key is the southwestern section of Schwabing, directly behind the university on Amalienstr. and Türkenstr. (see **Food,** p. 478). When they close, hangers-on head for the late-night/early-morning cafes to nurse a last beer or first cup of coffee.

Scads of culture and nightlife guides are available to help you sort out Munich's scene. Pick up *Munich Found* (DM4), *in München* (free), or *Prinz* (monthly for DM5; the hippest) at any newsstand to find out what's up. For smaller rock clubs, scope bulletin boards around the university. Big-name pop artists often perform at the **Olympia Halle,** while the **Olympia Stadion** on the northern edge of town hosts mega-concerts. Check listings for dates and ticket information or call 30 67 24 24.

BARS

Many of the charming cafes (see **Food,** p. 478) double as hip nightly haunts of *Müncheners.* A few stalwarts only open the doors for drink after 5pm, and by 1am many places squeeze revelers out into more late-night joints. Also see **Beer, Beer, and More Beer,** p. 484.

Günther Murphy's, Nikolaistr. 9a (tel. 39 89 11). U-Bahn #3 or 6: "Giselastr." Cozy yourself up in the bathtub, bed, or "snuggle-box" with a Guinness (DM6). Good ol' Irish cheer accompanies each serving of scrumptious U.K./American food (DM8-15). You won't be able to find a seat, but it's more fun to mingle with the English-speaking crowd. Open Mon.-Fri. 5pm-1am, Sat.-Sun. 11am-1am.

Reitschule, Konigstr. 34. U-Bahn #3 or 6: "Giselastr." Above a club, with windows overlooking a horseback-riding school. Marble tables and a sleek bar. Also a restaurant/cafe with a beer garden out back—very relaxed. Rumor has it this is where Boris Becker met his wife ("Mrs. Becker"). Breakfast served all day; *Weißbier* DM6.

Master's Home, Frauenstr. 11 (tel. 22 99 09). U-Bahn #3 or 6 or S-Bahn #1-8: "Marienpl." A tremendous stuffed peacock greets visitors as they descend the gold wall-papered staircase to the subterranean bar/*faux* private house. Lounge in the elegant living room with books and dusty velvet furniture, relax in the bedroom, or chill in the tub with a beer in hand. Eat gourmet Italian with the *Schicki Mickis* in the restaurant, or chill with the more relaxed crowd in the bar. Mixed drinks DM11.50, other drinks similarly high-brow in price. Weekdays comfortable; weekends mobbed. Open daily 6pm-3am.

Treznjewski, Theresienstr. 72 (tel. 22 23 49). U-Bahn #2: "Theresienstr." Handsome dark-wooded bar with stylish frescoes. Good cocktails and chatty crowds until way late. Near the university. Breakfast DM7.50-13.50. Entrees DM11-14.50. Beer DM5. Open Sun.-Thurs. 8pm-3am, Fri.-Sat. 8pm-4am.

MUSIC BARS

Shamrock, Trautenwolfstr. 6 (tel. 33 10 81). U-Bahn #3 or 6: "Giselastr." Live music runs the gamut from blues and soul to Irish fiddling to rock in this cozy Irish pub. You can pick up a comprehensive music program for all the city's Irish pubs at any one of them. Irish soccer highlights on Sundays. Guinness DM6.20. Open Mon.-Thurs. 5pm-1am, Fri.-Sat. 5pm-3am, Sun. 2pm-1am.

Nachtcafé, Maximilianspl. 5 (tel. 59 59 00). U-Bahn #4 or 5 or S-Bahn #1-8: "Karlspl." Live jazz, funk, soul, and blues until the wee hours. The chic and the wannabees rub shoulders in this modern jet-black bar. Things don't get rolling until 2am. Very *Schicki-Micki*. Breakfast served after 2am. No cover, just a bouncer—easy-going weekdays, very picky on weekends when you'll have to look the part. Karaoke on Sun. Beer DM8 (0.3L). *Melchkaffee* DM6.50.

Schwabinger Podium, Wagnerstr. 1 (tel. 39 94 82), in Old Schwabing. U-Bahn #3: "Münchener Freiheit." Live jazz and "Bluesrock" for a young crowd. Sat. excellent rhythm and blues. Beer DM6.80. Cover DM5-10. Music starts at 9pm; show up then to get a table. Open 8pm-1am.

Unterfahrt, Kirchenstr. 96 (tel. 448 27 94). S-Bahn #1-8 or U-Bahn #5: "Ostbahnhof." For the serious jazz lover. Usually the crowd is a little older. Groovy rhythms (DM5). Jam session starts every Sun. at 9pm; arrive early for a table. Professional performances from DM10. Open Tues.-Sun. 8pm-1am.

DANCE CLUBS

Kunstpark Ost, Grafingerstr. 6 (tel. 490 43 50; fax 49 04 35 35; http://www.kunstpark.de). U-Bahn #5 or S-Bahn #1-8: "Ostbahnhof." The newest and biggest addition to the Munich nightlife scene. A huge complex with 27 different venues swarms with young people hitting clubs, concerts, and bars—but most of all, dancing the night away. Try the psychedelic **Natray Temple** (open Wed. and Fri.-Sat.), the alternative cocktail and disco joint **K41** (open Tues.-Sun.), the stage/club **Babylon** (open Wed. and Fri.-Sun.), or concert hall **Incognito** (open Mon.-Sat.). Hours, cover, and themes vary—call 49 00 29 28 for info and tickets, or pick up a program in other nightlife spots.

Nachtwerk and Club, Landesbergerstr. 185 (tel. 578 38 00). Streetcar #18 or 19 or bus #83: "Lautensackstr." The older, larger **Nachtwerk** spins mainstream dance tunes for sweaty mainstream crowds in a packed warehouse. Sat. is the beloved "Best of the 50s to the 90s" night. Its little sister **Club** offers a bi-level dance floor, just as tight and swinging as its next-door neighbor. Fri. "cosmic"; Sat. acid jazz and rare grooves. Avoid Sun. night rehashing of German oldies-but-crappies. Beer DM6 at both places. Cover DM10 for both. Open daily 10pm-4am.

Reactor, Domagkstr. 33 (tel. 324 44 23), in the Alabamahalle. U-Bahn #6: "Alte Heide." Situated along with **Alabama** next door on a former military base in Schwabing. Techno, house, and German oldies. Open daily 10:30pm-4am.

Park Café, Sophienstr. 7 (tel. 59 83 13), is located at the fringe of the small *Alter Botanischer Garten*. U-Bahn #2: "Königspl." or walk north from the *Hauptbahnhof*. A pleasant beer garden by day (open daily 10am-1am; *Maß* DM8.80), it becomes a *Schicki-Micki* bumping disco come nightfall. Baroque dance floor with red curtains, chandeliers, and high ceiling with columns. Wed. funk and rap; Thurs. 80s-90s; Fri. hip-hop and house; Sat. disco and hip-hop. Cover DM10. Super exclusive—

if you dress like a backpacker, take a hike. Open Wed.-Thurs. 10:30pm-4am, Fri.-Sat. 10:30pm-5am.

Backstage, Helmholtzstr. 18 (tel. 18 33 30). S-Bahn #1-8: "Donnersbergerbrücke." Wide range of music, but lots of "little Seattle" and techno-type nights. Fri. "Gathering of the Tribes"; Sat. "Freak Out." Open Wed.-Thurs. 9pm-3am, Fri. 10pm-5am, Sat. 9pm-5am.

Pulverturm, Harthof-Schleißheimer-Str. 393 (tel. 351 99 99). U-Bahn #2: "Harthof"; it's 15min. from the stop. A bit far out, this dance club *avec* beer garden lacks the pretension of Munich's other venues. Anything from psychedelic to grunge; Fri. is indie rock and Sun. kicks back with reggae. Cover DM10. Open daily 10pm-4am.

Tilt, Helmholtzstr. 12 (tel. 129 79 69). S-Bahn #1-8 or 27: "Donnersbergerbrücke." A wacky warehouse disco. Sat. fun acid jazz (cover DM7); Mon. "spicy sounds from the swamps"—swampy Spice Girls? Tell me what you want. Bring ID if you look young. Open Wed. 9pm-1am, Thurs. 9:30pm-1am, Fri.-Sat. 10pm-3am.

■ Gay and Lesbian Munich

Although Bayern has the reputation of being intolerant of homosexuality, Munich sustains a respectably vibrant gay nightlife. The center of Munich's homosexual scene lies within the **"Golden Triangle"** defined by Sendlinger Tor, the Viktualienmarkt/Gärtnerpl. area, and Isartor. Bars, cafes, and clubs of all atmospheres abound. Pick up the free, extensive booklet *Rosa Seiten* (pink pages) at **Max und Milian Bookstore,** Ickstattstr. 2 (tel. 260 33 20; fax 26 30 59; open Mon.-Fri. 10:30am-2pm, Sat. 11am-4pm), or at any other gay locale for extensive listings of gay nightlife hotspots and services. The **Zentrum schwuler Männer** (gay men's center) offers an array of telephone services (for general information tel. 260 30 56; for violence hotline tel. 192 28; for counseling tel. 194 46; fax 260 87 90; http://www.altmann.de/sub); some English spoken, depending on the staff (open Sun.-Thurs. 7-11pm, Fri.-Sat. 7pm-midnight). For lesbian information, call **Lesbentelefon** (tel. 725 42 72; open Tues. 10:30am-1pm, Wed. 2:30-5pm, Thurs. 7-10pm). **Sapphovision,** a lesbian film center at the **Frauenzentrum Treibhaus,** Güllstr. 3 (tel. 77 40 41), shows films every second Friday of the month. **Lillemor's Frauenbuchladen** (see **Bookstores,** p. 472) provides information for lesbians.

Club Morizz, Klenzestr. 43 (tel. 201 67 76). U-Bahn #1 or 2: "Fraunhoferstr." Reminiscent of select Casablanca scenes, this relaxed cafe and bar is frequented by mostly gay men and a few lesbians. European and Thai dishes available until 12:30am; Thai curry DM19, pasta and other entrees DM15-27. Open Sun.-Thurs. 7pm-2am, Fri.-Sat. 7pm-3am.

New York, Sonnenstr. 25 (tel. 59 10 56). U-Bahn #1-3 or 6: "Sendlinger Tor." Fashionable gay men dance this disco into the ground. Laser shows Fri.-Sun. 11:30pm and 7am; cover DM10 (includes drinks). No cover other nights, but no "free" drinks. Beer DM6.50. Open daily 11pm-4am.

Café Nil, Hans-Sach-Str. 2 (tel. 26 55 45). U-Bahn #1 or 2: "Fraunhoferstr." Cozy, sleek cafe that's a day- and nighttime meeting place for gay men of all ages. Beer DM5 (0.4L), pasta DM13.50. Open Mon.-Fri. 5pm-4am, Sat.-Sun. 3pm-4am.

Soul City, Maximilianspl. 5 (tel. 59 52 72), at the intersection with Max-Joseph-Str. Purportedly the biggest gay disco in Bayern. Beer DM7.50 (0.3L), coffee DM6. Open Sun.-Thurs. 10pm-4am, Fri.-Sat. 10pm-late.

Club 9 (tel. 49 91 86 60), in Kunstpark Ost's **Incognito** (p. 488) in the Ostbahnhof. Bayern's largest *Frauen-Discothek* on the 2nd Friday of every month 9pm-4am. Live music, live comedienne, or music mix. Ladies only ordinarily, but gays welcome March, June, Sept., and Dec., or when otherwise specified by the fashion police in the gay/lesbian **"Bongo Bar,"** also in the complex. Check monthly schedules for themes and dress code.

Fortuna Musikbar, Maximilianspl. 5, Reginahaus (tel. 55 40 70). U-Bahn #4 or 5 or S-Bahn #1-8: "Karlspl.," then walk northeast along the Ring until you hit Maximilianspl. A hip and popular disco for lesbians. *The* place on Thursday evenings with shakin' salsa parties. Open Wed.-Mon. 10pm-4am.

■ Near Munich

DACHAU

"Once they burn books, they will end up burning people," wrote Heinrich Heine. This eerie statement is posted at the **Konzentrations-Lager-Gedenkstätte**, the Dachau concentration camp, next to a photograph of a Nazi book burning. The walls, gates, and crematorium have been restored since 1962 in a chillingly sparse memorial to the victims of Dachau, the first German concentration camp. Once tightly packed barracks are now for the most part only foundations; survivors ensured, however, that at least two barracks would be reconstructed to teach future generations. German school groups are increasingly coming to visit the memorial, learning about the atrocities of the Holocaust. German schoolchildren, as well as residents of the city of Dachau—and it is important to remember that there *is* a town here, which lives in the shadow of the camp every day and with every tourist who brushes by the town on his or her way to the memorial—watch visitors with uncertainty, and even insecurity. Visitors should realize that while the *KZ-Gedenkstätte* is treated as a tourist attraction by many, it is first and foremost a memorial; Jews and gentiles alike come here for personal reasons, to grieve over the horrors of the former Nazi concentration camp. Take a moment to read the sign-in log at the end of the exhibit; you'll find that visitors from all over the world come here to remember lost relatives or to pay respects to those who perished. Interwoven with the multitude of names and addresses from different countries are statements of resilience and hope. Respectful behavior by those with only a historical interest is in order.

The museum, located in the former administrative buildings, examines pre-1930 anti-Semitism, the rise of Nazism, the establishment of the concentration camp system, and the lives of prisoners through photographs, documents, and artifacts. The thick guide (DM25; available in English) translates the propaganda posters, SS files, documents, and letters; most exhibits are accompanied by short captions in English. A display copy of the English guide is available for perusal in the center of the exhibit. Also on display are texts of the letters from prisoners to their families as well as internal SS memos. A small, annotated map is available for DM0.30. A short film (22min.) is screened in English at 11:30am and 3:30pm (and on some days at 2pm).

The state offers free 2hr. **tours** in English leaving from the museum daily at 12:30pm. Call (08131) 17 41 for more info. The wrought-iron gate at the *Jourhaus*, formerly the only entrance to the camp, reads *"Arbeit Macht Frei"* ("Work Makes One Free"). It was the first sight as prisoners entered the camp. There is also a Jewish memorial, a Protestant commemorative chapel, and the Catholic *Todesangst Christ-Kapelle* (Christ in Agony Church) on the grounds. (For more discussion about the issues surrounding concentration camps, see **History: The Holocaust,** p. 68.) To get there from Munich, S-Bahn #2 (direction: "Petershausen"): "Dachau" (20min.; DM13.60 round-trip), then bus #724 (direction: "Kraütgarten") or 726 (direction: "Kopernikusstr.") from in front of the station to *KZ-Gedenkstätte* (20min.; DM2; grounds open Tues.-Sun. 9am-5pm). Free tours are given Saturday and Sunday at 12:30pm; meet in front of the museum or call (08131) 17 41 for more information.

In the mid-19th century, painters such as Carl Spitzweg and Max Liebermann traveled to Dachau. A 16th-century castle tops the *Altstadt*. The **tourist office,** Konrad Adenauer-Str. 3 (tel. 845 66), has plenty of information on the city of Dachau and sells maps for DM1. Dachau's **telephone code** is 08131.

LAKE REGION

Müncheners frequently get away to the nearby glacial lakes, particularly the beloved **Starnbergersee** and the **Ammersee.** Called the **Five Seas** *(Fünf Seen),* this region comprises an aquatic complex of Starnbergersee, Ammersee, Pilsensee, Wörthsee, and Wesslingersee. S-Bahn #6 (direction: "Tutzing") out to the beautiful lakeside promenade of **Starnberg,** an old resort town (DM6.80 one way, or 4 strips on the *Streifenkarte*). The castle where Mad King Ludwig II was confined after he was deposed is just around the tip of the lake in **Berg.** His body was found shortly thereafter, mysteriously drowned in the Starnbergersee—a cross in the water now marks the spot. For more information inquire at the main **"Five Sea" tourist office** in Starnberg, Wittelsbacherstr. 9 (tel. (08151) 130 07; fax 132 89), at Am Kirchpl. The **Starnberg tourist office** (tel. 130 08) offers a central room finding service (open June-Sept. Mon.-Fri. 8am-6pm, Sat. 9am-1pm).

HERRSCHING AND AMMERSEE

Herrsching is the start of one of the many *Wanderwege* (hiking paths) established by the transit system in connection with the S-Bahn. Munich S-Bahn #5: **"Herrsching"** (last stop; DM10.20 each way, or 6 strips) on the Ammersee (every 20min., 40min.). To get to the Ammersee from the Herrsching train station, follow Zum Landungssteg right and make a right at the end; continue until you come to the touristy beach area. If you don't mind pebbly beaches, the Ammersee is for you; ducks, kids, and sailboats seem not to. You can grab a *Maß* from the beergarden (DM8).

Down the path along the sea on the right is a whimsical red-tiled villa with pagoda toppings. It's the **Kurpark Schlößchen** built by Ludwig Scheuermann in 1888 as a summer escape from a Munich infested with beer-drinking tourists (the more things change…). Bear right through the Kurpark to cross a tiny bridge. Here you'll find **Strandbad Seewinkel** (tel. 405 71), Herrsching's public beach (no sand, but lots of grass). In its pleasant terrace beer garden, a *Bier* is DM4.20 and a meal is around DM10. Hop off the dock for a swim, but wait at least an hour after packing away that food lest you should suffer Ludwig's ignominious fate (beach area open May-Sept. daily 9am-10pm). The restaurant inside the Seewinkel is separate from the self-service beer garden (open Wed.-Mon. 5-10pm). The **Bayerische Schiffahrt,** a steamship-like tugboat, travels the northern Ammersee route to Holzhausen and Stegen for DM17 one way (50min.). Southward, chug by Riederau and Diessen for DM15 (30min.). Round-trips cost DM22, under 15 50% off, under 6 free (boats leave almost once per hr. 9am-6pm). Play **miniature golf** (DM5, under 14 DM4) back up Zum Landungssteg. (Open Mon.-Fri. 11am-9:45pm, Sat.-Sun. 10am-9:45pm. Last entrance 9pm.)

The **tourist office,** Bahnhofpl. 2 (tel. 52 27; fax 405 19), across from the train station, can help you find a room in Herrsching. They provide information on the 11 paths that leave town for the forest and sea areas, and can also find rooms in the region (open Mon.-Fri. 8:30am-noon and 2-5pm, Sat. 10am-12:30pm). Most hotel singles run DM100-150; doubles DM140-200; private rooms DM30-45, plus a DM1.50 *Kurtaxe* for everyone over 18. The nearest **Campingplatz** (tel 12 06) is in Herrsching-Mühlfeld. (DM6, under 6 DM3. Tent DM4-8. Car DM3. Caravan DM7. DM1 *Kurtaxe* if over 18. Open April-Sept.) Five other camping sites serve the area: one on the Wörthsee, one on Pilsensee, and three on the Starnberger See. **Norma supermarket** is at 11 Zum Landungssteg (open Mon.-Fri. 8am-6pm, Sat. 8am-2pm). The **post office,** 82211 Herrsching, is open Mon.-Thurs. 8am-noon and 3-6pm; Fri. 8am-noon and 3-7:30pm, Sat. 8am-noon. The **telephone code** is 08152.

ANDECHS

The monastery at **Andechs** fuses Bayern's two most acclaimed attributes—Catholicism and beer—on a gorgeous mountaintop. The monks here brew up a pale beer and a rocking **Bockbier** that is piously not served on Sundays or Saturdays from Easter to October—young firebrands used to come up the mountain for weekend debauchery, swilling *Bock* and causing too much ruckus for the monk-waiters. The beer garden, **Klosterbrauerei** (tel. (08152) 37 60; fax 37 62 60), now serves *Bockbier* on weekdays, and other beers every day, even holy ones. The secular brewing industry is currently up in arms over what they consider an unfair competitive advantage: as a religious institution, the monastery is exempt from the beer tax. (*Maß* Doppelbock Dunkel DM9, Spezial Hell DM7.60, *Weißbier* DM8.60. Open 10am-9pm.)

Pagan thoughts aside, you can tour the monastery and church to admire its ornate gold altar. Its framework and interior were originally built in 1430 under the direction of Duke Ernst of Bayern, but the church was redone in the Rococo style to celebrate its 300th anniversary (completed in 1451). The mortal remains of composer **Carl Orff** rest in the building—Carmina Burana! To reach the monastery, S-Bahn #5: "Herrsching," then switch to the private bus line **Omnibusverkehr Rauner** (6-12 per day) or to a public **MVV** bus (Mon.-Fri. 7:55 and 11:15am only, return at 10:57am or 12:37pm) for the 10-minute trip to Andechs. Bus schedules are erratic; check with the tourist office in Herrsching for departure times. The last return times (at least through early 1998, but double check) are Mon.-Fri. 5:50pm, Sat. 5:30pm, Sun. 6:45pm. Alternatively, huff and puff for a slowly sloping 3km and earn your *Bockbier*. Follow the signs marked *Fußweg nach Andechs,* which start on Kreutalstr. To get there, head straight down Bahnhofstr. as it turns into Luitpoldstr.; Kreutalstr. will be on the right (50min. to Andechs). Be sure to stick to the trail; 11 people recently have died short-cutting down the precipitous slope. The trail is clearly marked except for two three-way intersections. Whether you are headed toward Herrsching or Andechs, hang a left on the first and a right on the second.

■ Bayerische Alpen (Bavarian Alps)

South of Munich, the land buckles into a series of dramatic peaks and valleys stretching across Austria and into Italy. Throughout this magical terrain Ludwig II of Bavaria, the assertively batty "Fairy Tale King," chose to build his theatrical palaces. Mountain villages, glacial lakes, icy waterfalls, and world-class ski resorts fill the forested slopes. The rhythmic beat of cowbells ceases only at dusk, and, after a few days, cowdung no longer smells pungent and foul, but rather, fresh and springy (well, almost). This is also the region where people authentically, even nonchalantly, wear *Lederhosen*. Rail lines are sparse; buses cover the gaps (bus drivers sell timetables for DM0.50). For regional info, contact the *Fremdenverkehrsverband Oberbayern*, Bodenseestr. 113 (tel. (089) 829 21 80), in Munich (open Mon.-Fri. 9am-4:30pm, Sat. 9am-noon).

GARMISCH-PARTENKIRCHEN

Once upon a time, the 1100-year-old Garmisch and Partenkirchen were beautiful but rather unassuming Bavarian villages whose location at the foot of the **Zugspitze**—Germany's highest peak—kept them in tranquil isolation. But as the 19th century nature movement discovered the mountains, the two towns quickly became Germany's most famous mountain resort area. In 1935, it took Hitler only 48 hours to persuade the mayors of the two villages to unite them in anticipation of the 1936 Winter Olympics. To this day, however, the regions remain geographically distinct, Garmisch in the west and Partenkirchen in the east; and their inhabitants assert their individuality; both sides of the 30,000-person town staunchly maintain that they even speak in different dialects, and they don't share their neighbors' *Lederhosen*.

Practical Information Garmisch-Partenkirchen can be reached easily from Füssen by **bus** (2hr.; DM13; no railpasses valid), or from Innsbruck in Austria by train (1½hr.; DM15.40). Pick up maps of hiking trails (DM8) and city maps (free) at the **tourist office** *(Verkehrsamt der Kurverwaltung)*, on Richard-Strauss-Platz (tel. 18 06; fax 18 07 55). From the station, turn left on Bahnhofstr. and after 200m turn left again onto Von-Brug-Str.; it faces the fountain on the square. An information board in front will help you locate a room even if the office is closed, or call 194 12 (open Mon.-Sat. 8am-6pm, Sun. 10am-noon). **Public transportation** costs DM2, but is free with a *Kurkarte* (see below). Rent **bikes** at **Werdenfelser Sportagentur,** Marienpl. 18 (tel. 14 25; open Mon.-Fri. 9am-noon and 1-5pm; DM30 per day), or **Mountain-Bike Center Stefan Leiner,** Ludwigstr. 42 (tel. 795 28; fax 548 44; open Mon.-Fri. 10am-8pm, Sat. 9am-1pm). For a **snow** and **weather report** for the Zugspitze or Alpspitze call 79 79 79; for the Wank area, call 75 33 33. The **post office**, 82467 Garmisch-Partenkirchen, is across the street from the station (open Mon.-Fri. 8am-7pm, Sat. 8am-1pm). The **telephone code** is 08821.

Accommodations Reasonable rooms exist in Garmisch-Partenkirchen, but you'll have to do a bit of detective work to find one. The tourist office will help you find *Gasthäuser* and *Pensionen* (DM35-45). Alternatively, request a list of private rooms and start making calls yourself from the free hotel phone; most rooms require a three-night minimum stay (DM30 per night). No matter where you wind up, there's a DM3 **Kurtax** levied on tourists. The compensation for paying is a green card entitling you to free rides on the bus system and one free admission to the *Alpspitz-Wellenbad,* the casino, the *Kurpark,* and concerts (see below). At the **Jugendherberge (HI),** Jochstr. 10 (tel. 29 80; fax 585 36), you awake to the tolling of church bells. Cross the street from the train station and walk 25m to your left to bus #3 (direction: "Burgain") or 4 or 5 (direction: "Farchant"): "Burgrain." Walk straight down Am Lahne Wiesgraben, then turn right after two blocks onto Jochstr. Clean, somewhat institutional six- to 10-bed rooms. (Reception open 7-9am and 5-midnight. Lockout 9am-3:30pm. Curfew 11:30pm. Ages 18-27 only. DM21. Sheets DM5.50. Open Jan.-Oct.) The **Naturfreundehaus,** Schalmeiweg 21 (tel 43 22), is a friendly, independent hostel, more intimate than the *Jugendherberge,* on the edge of the forest at the east end of Partenkirchen. From the station, walk straight on Bahnhofstr. as it becomes Ludwigstr., follow the rightward bend in Ludwigstr., and turn left on Sonnenbergstr. Continue straight as this first becomes Prof.-Michael-Sachs-Str. and then Schalmeiweg. (20min. Quiet after 10pm, but no curfew. Small, so call ahead. DM15.50, breakfast DM8.) **Camping Zugspitze,** Griesenerstr. 4 in the village of Grainau (tel. 31 80), is on highway B24 at the base of the Zugspitze; take the blue-and-white bus from the station: "Schmölzabzweigung" (1 person with tent DM19, two people DM31).

Food Garmisch's restaurants cater to a range of tastes and wallet thicknesses. The best value in town is probably the friendly Italian **La Baita,** at Zugspitzstr. 16 (tel. 787 77), 100m from Marienpl. Delightful pasta dishes (DM8-16), omelettes (DM9), and pizza (DM8-14; open Thurs.-Tues. 11:30am-2:30pm and 5:30-11:30pm). In the heart of Partenkirchen, grab a giant *Schnitzel* (DM9-11) at **Gasthof Fraudorfer,** Ludwigstr. 24 (tel. 21 76; fax 710 73), where traditional Bavarian dishes are supplemented with traditional Bavarian folk dances and songs after 6:30pm. The cheapest **supermarket** is **Aldi,** at the corner of Enzianstr. and Bahnhofstr. (open Mon.-Fri. 8:30am-6:30pm, Sat. 8am-1pm). Fruits and meats are lined up in little cute rows at the **HL Markt,** at the intersection of Bahnhofstr. and Von-Brug-Str. (tel. 500 70; open Mon.-Fri. 8am-8pm, Sat. 7:30am-4pm).

Sights The mountains are the main attraction in town—marvelous views in the summer, and wild snow sports in the winter. Ride up to the Zugspitze only if it's sunny. There are three ways to conquer the Zugspitze, the highest peak in Germany. **Option 1:** Take the cog railway from the *Zugspitzbahnhof* (50m behind the Garmisch main station) via Grainau to Hotel Schneefernerhaus, then a cable car, the *Gipfelseilbahn,* to the outlook, the *Zugspitzplatt* (75min.; 60min. to the ski area; round-trip DM72 in summer, DM60 in winter). Continue with the *Gletscherbahn* cable car. **Option 2:** Get off the railway at Eibsee and take the *Eibseeseilbahn,* one of the steepest cable car runs in the world, all the way to the top (80min.; 10min. to Zugspitze; round-trip in summer DM74, in winter DM60). A **combo ticket** including the train from Munich/Augsburg and the *Zugspitze* tour costs DM89. **Option 3:** Hike it—the cheapest way to get atop the 2964m monster is to climb for about 10hr., usually as part of a two-day trip. Get a good map from the tourist office and triple check the weather report.

For other Alpine views at lower prices, take the **Alpspitzbahn** to Osterfelderkopf peak (2050m; 9min.; round-trip DM37), the **Kreuzeck** cable car to Kreuzeck (1650m; 8min.; round-trip DM26), or the **Wankbahn** (1780m; 18min.; round-trip DM26). Most trips depart hourly (May-June 8:30am-5pm; July-Sept. 8am-5pm; Oct.-Nov. 8:30am-4:30pm). A neat daytrip includes biking to the **Eibsee,** about 10km from Garmisch. The calm, crystal waters of a mountain lake against the soaring, snow-capped monumentality of the *Zugspitze* will remind you of a movie backdrop. To avoid the 14% uphill of the last 300m, take the blue and white Eibsee bus from Garmisch (round-trip DM5). One of the most popular trails leads to the dramatic, 100m deep **Partnach-klamm** gorge (DM3). Walk up to the gorge from behind the Olympic ski stadium (35min.) and then meander for another 35min. in the narrow darkish tunnels dug in the rocks, dangerously close to the foaming water. The ski season runs from October to mid-May in all its Alpine glory. Of the six area ski schools, the cheapest **equipment rental** is at **Ski-Schule,** Am Hausberg 8 (tel. 49 31 or 742 60), next to the *Hausbergbahn*. **Ski passes** in the *Zugspitzgebiet* cost DM58 per day, DM44 with railpass. More advanced leg-breakers ski in the **Verbundgebiet,** home of the World Cup Kandehar run, for DM47 per day. A week pass costs DM277, two weeks DM439. If the weather is not inclement, soak your weary feet in hot water or display your athletic prowess from the 5m high jumpboard at the **Alpspitz-Wellenbad,** Klammstr. 47, next to the Olympic stadium (tel. 75 33 13). The six-pool complex features artificial waves, saunas, restaurants, and paragliders hovering overhead. (Open Mon.-Fri. 9am-9pm, Sat.-Sun. 9am-7pm. DM7.50 for 3hr., DM10 for unlimited time; first entry free with *Kurkarte,* then DM7, DM9.)

BERCHTESGADEN

Poised at the easternmost point of the Bavarian Alps, Berchtesgaden profits from a sinister and overtouristed attraction: Hitler's **Kehlsteinhaus**—a mountaintop retreat christened "Eagle's Nest" by occupying American troops. A disconcerting horde of tourists, many of them American soldiers, besieges this Bavarian town every year to catch a glimpse of this small slice of World War II history. Historically and geographically, Berchtesgaden belongs more properly to Austria and the Archbishopic of Salzburg than to Germany, but Bavaria snatched it up in 1809 for its salt deposits. Just over those mountaintops in the northeast, *The Sound of Music*'s Julie Andrews, her arms outstreched, turned round and round in alpine ecstasy, and so could you.

Orientation and Practical Information Crouching in the southeastern corner of Germany, Berchtesgaden is a German peninsula in a sea of Austrian mountains. The Berchtesgaden **tourist office,** Königsseerstr. 2 (tel. 96 70; fax 633 00), is opposite the train station in an off-white building with blue shutters. Ask the *Lederhosen*-wearing staff—without giggling—for the *Berchtesgadener Land: General Information* pamphlet, which lists sights, concerts, and other activities. Most materials are available in English. Their hiking pass (DM5) includes tips on walking trails and climbs and comes free with the *Kurkarte,* a tourist card given to overnighters who pay the obligatory *Kurtax* (DM3). There's no room-finding service, but they have extensive lists of rooms and an automatic hotel finder in front of the office (open June-Oct. Mon.-Fri. 8am-6pm, Sat. 9am-5pm, Sun. 9am-3pm; Nov.-May Mon.-Fri. 8am-5pm, Sat. 9am-noon). Call 194 12 for a recording on **hotels.**

For **train**-related questions call the *Bahnhof* (tel. 50 74; open Mon.-Sat. 6:05am-7:35pm, Sun. 7am-7:35pm). Hourly trains run to Munich (2½hr.; change at Freilassing), Salzburg (1hr.; change at Freilassing; DM11.80), and Bad Reichenhall (45min.; DM5.60). The fare for a **bus** ride ranges from DM2 for **public transportation** in Berchtesgaden proper to DM4-6 for trips in the region (Bad Reichenhall DM5.70, Königssee DM3.20, Salzburg DM6.90). For questions about buses call the bus office in the train station (tel. 54 73; open Mon-Fri. 8am-noon and 2-4pm). Rent **bikes** at the train station (DM12-17) or **motorbikes** from **Horst Wagner,** Am Zellerbach 6 (tel. 621 01; DM34-59 per day). You can also grab a **rowboat** at the Königssee dock or a **heart-rate tester** (for hiking) at the tourist office. For the daily **pollen report** call 50 11. The **post office,** Bahnhofspl. 4, 83471 Berchtesgaden (tel. 95 60 23), is adjacent to the train station (open Mon.-Fri. 8am-noon and 2-5:30pm, Sat. 8am-noon). Most establishments also accept Austrian *Schillings;* you can **exchange currency** at the Salzburg train station post office before departing. The **telephone code** is 08652.

Accommodations and Food The **Jugendherberge (HI)**, Gebirgsjägerstr. 52, 83489 Strub (tel. 943 70; fax 94 37 37), is an uphill 30-minute walk from the station. Turn right from the station and follow the highly trafficked Ransauerstr. on the left for 15 minutes, then take the first right, and follow the signs up the steep (unnamed) gravel path on the left. Or bus #9539 (direction: "Strub Kaserne"): "Jugendherberge" (DM2.40). (Reception open 8am-noon and 5-7pm, but you can check in until 10pm. Curfew midnight. 10-bed dorm DM20, plus DM3 *Kurtax*. Breakfast included. Sheets DM5.50. Open Dec. 27-Oct.) Most private rooms and *Pensionen* cost DM28-35, with shower DM35-50; hotels run DM80-100. **Gästehaus Hansererhäusl**, Hansererweg 8 (tel. 25 23), is just behind the tourist office. Follow Rossötzweg and bear left onto Hansererweg (DM40 per person; breakfast included). The campsite **Campingplatz Allweglehen**, at Untersalzberg (tel. 23 96), is more than an hour's walk downstream from the station (DM34 with tent, children 6-16 years DM6.50). Berchtesgaden is rife with restaurants for wealthy tourists. Pick up a *Wurst* sandwich from a vendor or groceries at the **Edeka Markt**, on Dr.-Imhof-Str., in town near Griesstätterstr. (open Mon.-Fri. 8am-12:30pm and 1:30-6pm, Sat. 8am-2pm). The relaxed **Martinklause**, Ludwig-Ganghoferstr. 20, offers inexpensive soups and *Wurst* (DM5-9), beer, and pinball (open daily 10am-2pm and 5pm-midnight).

Sights The **Kehlsteinhaus** (also called "Eagle's Nest") was built for the *Führer*'s 50th birthday as a refuge of entertainment—even Adolf needed a respite from the harsh reality of politics and warfare. While Hitler merely visited the mountaintop retreat 14 times, tourists bombard it regularly with their Hawaiian-shirt presence. The stone resort house is now a pricey restaurant (tel. 29 69; meals DM9-20) with no museum in sight. In fact, the best reason for visiting the Kehlsteinhaus is on the way to the spectacular 360° view from the 1834m mountain peak. The road is something of an engineering marvel, hewn into solid rock by an army of 3000 men excused from conscription for health reasons—health reasons?! (Open daily May-Oct. except on days of heavy snow.) On the way back down, inspect what little remains of another Nazi retreat: bombed by the Allies on April 25, 1945, the **Berghof** in Obersalzberg was used by Hitler to entertain foreign dignitaries. On February 12, 1938, it was here that he browbeat Austrian Chancellor Kurt von Schuschnigg into relinquishing control of the Austrian police to the Nazis, paving the way for the *Anschluß*. Seven months later, British Prime Minister Neville Chamberlain visited Hitler to hammer out the "Munich Agreement" that Chamberlain claimed would guarantee "peace in our time"—so much for Appeasement.

To get to the Kehlsteinhaus first take the "Obersalzburg, Kehlstein" bus (#9548 or 9538) from the covered platform to the right as you exit the station: "Obersalzburg, Hintereck." (June-Oct. roughly every hr.; off-season *much* less regularly, if at all. Check with the tourist office for schedules. Round-trip DM6.80). At Hintereck, while you're waiting for bus #9549: "Kehlstein Parkpl., Eagle's Nest," buy your dual ticket for both the second leg of the bus ride and the elevator ride you'll take at the *Kasse* on the other end (DM20, with *Kurkarte* DM19; children DM13, DM12; every 30min. 9:30am-4pm). At Kehlstein, reserve your spot on a return bus (we mean it) at the booth when you get off. Reserving a place on a bus leaving one hour after the time of your Kehlstein arrival will give you enough time to explore the mountaintop if you don't plan to stop for lunch at the top (buses return to Hintereck every 30min., last one at 5:05pm). From Kehlstein Parkpl., go through the tunnel and up with the elevator to the Kehlsteinhaus; the elevator's golden mirrors are original, installed to quell Hitler's claustrophobia. Alternatively, climb up the serpentine footpath on the right as you face the mountain (20min.). You will probably want to pack a jacket for the cool weather on the peak. A short English-language **tour** of the Eagle's Nest is available daily at 10:30 and 11:30am (35min.; DM6, children free; meet at the tunnel entrance to the elevator). To catch the 10:30 tour, take the 9am bus to Hinterteck, which departs from the main post office, then the 9:40am connection to Kehlstein; for the 11:30 tour, hop the 10 and 10:40am buses, respectively. A 3½-hour English-language tour must be reserved one day in advance from **Berchtesgaden Mini Bus Tours** (tel.

BAYERN (BAVARIA)

649 71 or 648 63) in the tourist office. (DM47, under 13 DM25, under 6 free; includes second bus and elevator. Meet at the tourist office Mon.-Sat. 1:30pm.)

The Berchtesgaden Royal **Schloß** (tel. 20 85) was a monastic priory until Bavarian rulers usurped the area and appropriated the property. It now houses a collection of art and weaponry (open Sun.-Fri. 10am-1pm and 2-5pm; Oct.-Easter Mon.-Fri. 10am-1pm and 2-5pm; last entry 4pm; DM7, with *Kurkarte* DM6, students DM3.50, under 16 DM3). To reach the castle and the rest of the *Altstadt*, cross over the train tracks on the footbridge (follow the "zum Markt" signs) behind the station and continue to Bahnhofweg until you hit Maximillianstr.; then continue straight ahead.

Wedged into extraordinary Alpine cliffs, the **Königssee** calmly mirrors the landscape on its blue-green surface (whither Narcissus?); a bus from Brechtesgaden costs DM6.40 round-trip. Ships run by **Schiffahrt Königssee** (tel. 96 36 13) glide across the lake irregularly (round-trip to St. Bartholomä DM17.50, to Obersee DM21.50; children 50% off). In summer, boats leave roughly every 10 to 20 minutes starting at 7:15am; in the winter, boats go to St. Barthelomä only, and much less frequently. The best lake view is at the **Malerwinkel** (Painter's Outlook), around to the left of the lake, and the best aerial view is serviced by the Jenner cable car—1170m above sea-level. Bus #9541 (direction: "Königssee") from the main train station to the end of the line (1 per hr.; DM3.30). At the **Salzbergwerke** (salt mines) near town (tel. 600 20), you can dress up in an old salt miner's outfit, toboggan down snaking passages in the dark, and go on a raft ride on a salt lake. From the station, bus #9548: "Salzbergwerke" (1-2 per hour; 8:37am-7:40pm; DM2) or a 30-minute walk. (Open daily 9am-5pm; mid-Oct. to April Mon.-Sat. 12:30-3:30pm. DM20, children 10 and under DM9.) To go **moonlight-rafting,** call the Outdoor Club (tel. 50 01; fax 664 54).

OBERAMMERGAU AND ETTAL ABBEY

Since 1634, the tiny Alpine town of Oberammergau has been the site of the world-famous **Passion Plays.** After the town was spared from a plague that swept through Europe, the inhabitants promised to re-enact the crucifixion and resurrection of Christ every 10 years. The cast is composed of about 1000 locals who begin rehearsing long in advance, often growing long hair and beards. The plays last all day, with a short lunch break. The next Passion Plays will be presented in 2000. Reserve tickets and accommodations for the plays a good two years in advance. While the plays are not being performed, the most exciting things to do in Oberammergau are watching the beards grow and visiting nearby Ettal Abbey (see below).

Information and tickets can be obtained from the **tourist office,** Eugen-Papst-Str. 9a (tel. 923 10; fax 92 331 90), which finds rooms for a DM1 fee (rooms DM20-30 per person, DM30-40 with bath) and provides maps (open Mon.-Fri. 8:30am-4pm, Sat. 8:30am-noon; mid-June to mid-Sept. also open Sat.-Sun. 2-6pm). Turn left from the station and right at the town center onto Eugen-Papststr. For Oberammergau's **Jugendherberge (HI),** Malensteinweg 10 (tel. 41 14; fax 16 95), follow the right bank of the Ammer upstream from the station (7min.). (Reception open 7-11:30am, 4-10pm. Curfew 10pm. DM22.50. Sheets DM5.50. Closed Nov.12-Dec.25.) The **telephone code** is 08822.

In 1330, Ludwig I of Bavaria—not to be confused with *the* crazy Ludwig of Walt Disney castle fame—founded the enormous, domed **Abbey Church** in the tiny village of **Ettal,** about 4km south of Oberammergau (a 45min. hike). Since then, the abbey has conducted a brisk business in house-fermented beer and spirits. The **Klosterladen,** to the right as you face the church, sells divine six-packs of *Kloster*-brewed beer (DM14-50); there are multiple other "licensed" *Kloster Ettal* pushers in the vicinity. Beautifully stuccoed and gilded in typical Baroque over-ornateness, this rectangular sanctuary assumed its present shape after 18th-century renovations. Be careful not to drown in the human flood of visitors (open 7:45am-7:45pm; winter 7:45am-noon and 1pm-dusk). The **tourist office,** Ammergauerstr. 8 (tel.088 22 or 35 34; fax 63 99), gives out free info, including accommodations listings (rooms DM42-70) and a map of *Wanderwege* in the surrounding area (open Mon.-Fri. 8am-noon). Buses to Ettal from Oberammergau leave hourly from the train station (round-trip DM4.40).

FÜSSEN

Curled up at the toes of the Alpine foothills and at the southern end of the Romantic Road, the sedate town of Füssen is a renowned small resort for ordinary Germans and the rather extraordinary Mad King Ludwig. The town's proximity to Ludwig's famed *Königsschlösser* (Royal Castles; see p. 498) lures legions here each year. Füssen's meandering paths, mountain lakes, and old imperial Roman road deserve a few hours of aimless wandering. Under Henry VII, this town found itself a reluctant player in the game of European intrigue and politics. To help finance his Italian campaign, Henry put up the town as collateral against a loan of 400 silver *Marks* from the prince-bishop of Augsburg. Henry died indebted, so the town was forfeited to the prince-bishop from 1313 until the great German Secularization of 1802.

Reminders of the prince-bishop's medieval reign linger in architectural astonishments. The inner walls of the **Hohes Schloß** courtyard scream royalty with their arresting *trompe l'oeil* windows and towers. Along with a bevy of bureaucratic offices, the **Staatsgalerie's** (tel. 90 31 64; fax 90 32 01) collection of regional late-Gothic and Renaissance art resides in what were once the work- and love-dens of late-medieval bishops and knights (open Tues.-Sun. 11am-5pm; Nov.-March Tues.-Sun. 2-4pm; DM3, students and seniors DM2). Just below the castle rests the 8th-century Baroque basilica **St. Mangkirche** and its abbey. An ancient fresco discovered during 1950 renovations lights up the church's 10th-century subterranean crypt (tours Sat. 10:30am; call 48 44 for more info). Also in the abbey is the gaudy 18th-century Baroque library. The **Museum of Füssen** in the monastery (tel. 90 31 45; fax 90 32 01) details the history, art, and culture of the Füssen region in four Jeopardy! category installments. I'll take "Baroque Rooms" for US$500, please (tours Tues. and Thurs. 2:30pm). Inside the **Chapel of St. Anne**, macabre skeleton-decked panels depict the *Totentanz* (death dance), a public frenzy of despair which overtook Europe during the plague (open Tues.-Sun. 11am-4pm; Nov.-March Tues.-Sun. 2-4pm; chapel free, library DM3, students DM2). Not only can you send the folks a postcard of the most photographed castles in Germany, but you can also bike across the Austrian border 3km away to drop them a line from Tirol.

The **tourist office**, Kaiser-Maximilian-Platz 1 (tel. 70 77 or 70 78; fax 391 81). From the *Bahnhof*, walk the length of Bahnhofstr., then straight on Luitpoldstr. to the big yellow building. The staff finds rooms for free and proffers bike maps (DM5), hiking maps (DM7.80), and city maps (free). They organize guided hikes of the area (DM4; ask about times) and expeditions to the *Königsschlösser* (open Mon.-Fri. 8am-noon and 1:30-7pm, Sat. 9am-noon, Sun. 10am-noon). **Trains** run to Munich (every 2hr., 2hr.) and Augsburg (every 2hr., 2hr.). **Rent bikes** at the *Bahnhof* (tel. 63 13), or at **Radsport Zacherl,** Rupprechtstr. 8½ (tel. 32 92; 3-5 gear bike DM14 per day, 7-gear bike DM16). From the station, turn left on Rupprechtstr.; it's 100m down on the right (open Mon.-Fri. 9am-noon and 2-6pm, Sat. 9am-noon). The **Bahnhof Apotheke,** Bahnhofstr. 8 (tel. 918 10), has a bell for night pharmacy service (open Mon.-Fri. 8:30am-1pm and 2-6:30pm, Sat. 8:30am-12:30pm). The **post office,** 87629 Füssen, at the corner of Bahnhofstr. and Rupprechtstr. exchanges money and cashes traveler's checks (open Mon.-Fri. 8am-5:30pm, Sat. 8am-noon). The **telephone code** is 08362.

Budget singles in *Gasthäuser* run DM35-40; in *Pensionen*, DM45 and up. During high season, don't expect to find a cheap room. If worse comes to worst, head to the information pavilion in front of the *Kurverwaltung*, where you can buy an information pamphlet (DM1) or peruse a computerized database of hotels (free; open 7am-12:30am). Keep your eyes open for *"Zimmer frei"* signs in private homes; prices fall dramatically as you walk away from the pedestrian zones. Füssen's **Jugendherberge (HI),** Mariahilferstr. 5 (tel. 77 54; fax 27 70), is blessed by a lovely location and friendly staff. Turn right from the station and follow the railroad tracks (10min.). It's often packed, so make a reservation at least one day in advance; if you've made a reservation, they're obligated to find a spot for you. Remember to show up before 7pm, or your precious reservation will suddenly turn into a pumpkin and then, zimzallabim, disappear. (Reception open 7-9am, 5-7pm, and 8-10pm. Curfew 10pm, but you can get the access code. DM20.50, plus DM1.40 resort tax. Meals DM8.50. Basement lockers, DM1 deposit. Sheets DM5.50. Wash DM3, dry DM3, soap DM1. Call at least 1 day before you arrive. Open Dec.-Oct.) Eleven kilometers away in Hopfensee is **Campingplatz Bauernhof J. Guggemos,** Uferstr. 42 (tel. 33 34). **Pizza Blitz,** Luitpoldstr. 14 (tel. 383 54), offers lip-smacking gargantuan pizzas and calzones (DM6-13), making it a favorite local hangout (open Mon.-Thurs. 11am-11pm, Fri.-Sat. 11am-midnight, Sun. noon-11pm). **Plus,** on the corner of Bahnhofstr. and Luitpoldstr. is the cheapest **grocery store** around (open Mon.-Fri. 8:30am-6:30pm, Sat. 8am-1pm).

Near Füssen: Wieskirche (Church of the Meadow)

Any daytrip from Füssen (45-75min.) or Oberammergau (45-55min.) to the Ammergau Alps ought to include the **Wieskirche** (Church of the Meadows; tel. (08861) 81 73), a splendid Rococo pilgrimage church surrounded by forests, farmland, and camera-clicking tourists. The church sports two characteristic quirks. Most striking at first glance is the light pastel color scheme which dominates the rich stucco interior. Torrents of light bathe the church in astonishing brightness, and the effect is particularly riveting in the morning and evening when the sun shines directly through the arching windows. The second wonder in is the central dome's fresco, a glowing "Gate to Paradise." To fully appreciate the painter's exploitation of the dome's concavity to trick the eye, stand directly beneath the dome, then observe it again from the gallery next to the choir. The best way there is by **bus** from the Füssen station (Mon.-Sat. 1:05 and 3:05pm, Sun. 1:05pm); return on the daily 3:50 or 4:40pm bus from the church (1hr. each way, round-trip DM13).

■ Königsschlösser (The Royal Castles)

After Queen Marie bore Maximilian II two healthy sons, there was no reason to expect the fall the Bavarian royal family—but it was soon to come. Otto, the younger son, developed schizophrenia as a young adult, leaving Ludwig to carry on the family name. In 1864, he assumed the throne at the tender age of 18 as a shockingly handsome lad who was extremely naive about politics. A zany visionary and a fervent Wagner fan, Ludwig used his cash to craft his dreams into reality. He spent his private fortune creating fantastic castles that soar into the Alpine skies, hoping to realize his fantasyland in an ugly and evil world. In 1886, a band of upstart nobles and bureaucrats deposed of Ludwig in a coup d'état and imprisoned him in Schloß Berg on the Starnbergersee. Three days later, the King and a loyal advisor were discovered dead in the lake under mysterious circumstances—possibly a failed escape attempt, some hypothesize, even though Ludwig was a first-class swimmer. Even today, the enigma of Ludwig's life and dreamworld linger, captivating the imagination.

HOHENSCHWANGAU & NEUSCHWANSTEIN

These *Königsschlösser* lie 5km across the Lech River in the village of Hohenschwangau. Ludwig II grew up in **Schloß Hohenschwangau,** the buttercup-yellow neo-Gothic castle rebuilt by his father. It was here no doubt that he acquired his taste for the romantic German mythologies of the Middle Ages. Atop a humble hill and forest, this palace is a bit less touristed than its cousin, but also more authentic—the rooms actually appear to be lived in. Come here to see Wagner's maple-wood piano and a loaf of bread from 1832-36. German tours run frequently; English-speakers need to herd 20 people for a 30-minute tour in their native tongue.

Ludwig's desperate building spree across Upper Bavaria peaked with the construction of the glitzy **Schloß Neuschwanstein,** now Germany's most cliched tourist attraction and the inspiration for Disney World's "Fantasyland" castle. The first sketches of the castle were reportedly drawn by a set designer, not an architect, which explains a lot. During its construction, Ludwig kept an eagle eye on his masterpiece, using a telescope. The young Ludwig II lived a mere 173 days within the extravagant edifice, in which 63 rooms remained unfinished. The completed chambers include a Byzantine throne-room, a small artificial grotto, and an immense *Sängersaal* (Singer's Hall)—an acoustic masterpiece, built expressly for Wagner opera performances, but never used. A wood carving of a familiar but unidentifiable city skyline tops the king's bed; it depicts most of the famous towers of the world. The lines for the brisk **tours** (30min.) may seem endless, but they are the only way to get in; the best time to arrive is early in the morning. Tourists? Yes—more tourists than you can possibly imagine. (Both castles open daily 8:30am-5:30pm; Oct.-March 10am-4pm. Each castle DM10, students and disabled persons DM7.)

Consider spending the rest of the day hiking around the spectacular environs. For the fairy godmother of all views, hike up to the **Marienbrücke,** spanning the **Pöllat Gorge** behind the castle (10min.). Those with stout hearts and legs can continue uphill from here (about 1hr.) for a knockout overview of the castle and nearby lake. Sane people and insane hang-gliders ride the **Tegelbergbahn** cable car (tel. 983 60) for a glimpse of—or a dive into—the same panorama. (One-way DM15, students and disabled persons DM14.50; round-trip DM25, DM24. Open daily 8:30am-5pm; in winter 8:45am-4:30pm.)

From Füssen, hop the bus marked "Königsschlösser," which departs from the train station more or less hourly (DM2.40). It will dump you at the base of a number of surrounding hills in front of the **tourist office.** Separate paths lead up to both Hohenschwangau and Neuschwanstein. The quickest way to Hohenschwangau is *Waldweg* (#18) which runs near the info office (about 10min.; many steps). To Neuschwanstein, take path #32, from Car Park D ("Parkpl. Königsschlösser," across the street from the bus stop); it's the shortest but steepest trail to the top (25min.). Alternately, clip-clop your way to the near-tippy-top in a horse-drawn carriage (uphill DM8, downhill DM4; daily 9am-5pm) from Car Park D or Hotel Müller. Consider trekking path #33 from Neuschwanstein back to the base of the hill (20min.; open only in summer). Virtually untouristed, this route winds its way down through the dramatic **Pöllat Gorge.** Private buses run from Hotel Lisl to a beautiful vantage point 650 steep meters uphill from Neuschwanstein (DM3.50 uphill, DM2 downhill). For maps or more information on trails, check out the **information booth** (*Schlossverwaltung Hohenschwangau;* tel. 811 27) where the bus to the castles (direction: Hohenschwangau Village) stops. **Buses** depart from the Garmisch-Partenkirchen train station and stop directly in the Hohenschwangau village (daily at 8:05am, 1:05, 4:15, and 5:05pm and Mon.-Fri. at 9:35 and 11:15am; return daily at 8:50, 9:51am, 2:35, 4:40, and 6:41pm; round-trip with *Tagesticket* DM13; 2hr.). From Munich, take a **train** to Buchloe and transfer for the regional train to Füssen (2hr.; DM30).

SCHLOß LINDERHOF

Halfway between Garmisch-Partenkirchen and Oberammergau lies the exquisite **Schloß Linderhof,** Ludwig II's compact hunting palace, surrounded by a meticulously manicured park. With this edifice Ludwig paid homage to the French Bourbon kings, in particular Louis XIV (the Sun King), just as he did with his *Herrenchiemsee* palace. Though it lacks Neuschwanstein's pristine exterior, the palace bathes in gold, creating a remarkable image of decadence. The royal bedchamber, the largest room in the castle, is unbelievably lush, with gold leaf and a colossal crystal chandelier weighing half a ton. Dark blue velvet (the king's favorite color) encases the king-size bed; though he topped 195cm (6'5"), Ludwig had no trouble fitting in between the hand-carved head and foot boards—and perhaps a few mistresses fit in there as well. Across the ceiling stretches the affirmation *"Nec pluribus impar,"* which roughly translates as "I am the MackDaddy of the DaddyMacks." The two malachite tables were gifts from Russian Czarina Marie Alexandrovna, who tried to match Ludwig (a bachelor to his death) with one of her daughters. Ludwig just kept the tables.

More impressive than the palace itself is the magnificent **park.** The sheer force of water cascading down steps behind the palace powers the fountain in front. Every hour on the hour, the dam is opened and water shoots higher than the top of the palace. Paths weave through the ornately landscaped grounds. To the right of the palace and up the slope is an enormous, campy, artificial **grotto,** complete with a "subterranean" lake and floating shell-boat as in Wagner's *Tannhäuser.* The tour dramatically stages two different lighting schemes of the grotto: red and blue. Tacky, tacky, tacky. But at least it's refreshingly cool inside. Farther along, brilliant red and blue stained-glass windows richly illuminate the **Maurischer Kiosk** (Moorish Pavilion), an elaborate, mosque-shaped building, and the only sight on the grounds not built expressly for Ludwig. He saw it at the 1867 World Exposition in Paris and liked it so much that he brought it home. Within these walls, Ludwig would smoke his water pipe and implore his servants to dress up in period costumes and read him tales from *1001 Nights.* Following the path down the hill to the left (20min.) is the newly reconstructed **Hunding-Hütte,** another of Ludwig's flights of fancy, modeled after a scene in Wagner's *Die Walküre* from *The Ring of the Nibelung.* Bearskin-covered log benches surround an artificial tree. (Linderhof open April-Sept. daily 9am-12:15pm and 12:45-5:30pm; Oct.-March 10am-12:15pm and 12:45-4pm. April-Sept. DM9, students and seniors DM6; Oct.-March DM7 and DM4.)

Buses run between Oberammergau and the park somewhat hourly (9:55am-4:55pm; last bus leaves Linderhof at 5:35pm; 20min.; DM8.80 round-trip). Reach Oberammergau by bus from Schongau (50min.), Füssen (90min.), or Garmisch-Partenkirchen (40min.). A *Tagesticket* (DM13) entitles castle-hoppers to unlimited bus travel on the regional Alps buses (including the ride to Linderhof); purchase it from the bus driver. **Trains** run from Munich to Oberammergau, switching at Murnau (1¾hr.; 10 per day; DM24).

HYPERTRAVEL TO THE CASTLES

Seeing all three of the **royal castles** (*Königsschlösser*) during a daytrip from Munich requires some fancy footwork and luck with connections (and can only be done Mon.-Fri.). Take the 6:50am train from Munich to Buchloe, and transfer here onto the 7:46am to Füssen. Arriving in Füssen at 8:57am, hop on the 9:35am bus to the *Königsschlösser.* Arriving at 9:43am, you'll have three and a half hours to fight through the lines at Hohenschwangau and Neuschwanstein before you catch bus #9651 at 1:13pm to Schloß Linderhof (changing in Steingaden and Oberammergau). Until 5:40pm you can indulge in the surrounding opulence, but then it'll be time to mount bus #9606 to Oberammergau Post/Bahnhof (direction: "Füssen"). At 6pm you'll get to the Oberammergau train station with time to catch the 6:07pm train to Murnau, where you'll change trains at 6:58pm and hopefully grab a *Löwenbräu* at 7:54pm back in Munich. Double check your schedule with a timetable before departing. A simpler and more advisable option, particularly if you don't have a railpass, is to sign on with **EurAide** for a charter bus ride to Neuschwanstein, Linderhof, and Wieskirche. Tours leave on Wednesdays at 7:30am from early-June to late-July. Round-trip bus not including castle entrance fees DM70, with railpass DM55. Reserve a day ahead at the EurAide office (see p. 467).

■ Allgäu Alps

MEMMINGEN

A former imperial town and the gateway to the Allgäu region, Memmingen is generally stolid. But every four years in late July and early August, Memmingen's citizens take to the streets in a 10-day celebration of the summer of 1630, when Commander-General Albrecht von Wallenstein brought his camp to Memmingen and with it a respite from the ravages of the Thirty Years War. The next "Wallenstein-Sommer" will take place in 2000. For more information and advance tickets, contact *Sonderbüro Zollergarten* (tel. 495 065 or 495 067; fax 495 015).

Memmingen's modest Marktplatz and pedestrian zone sparkle with painted and molded facades. From the station, cross Bahnhofstr. and walk down Maximilianstr. After four blocks, take a right at the pedestrian zone of Kramerstr. and follow it to the Marktplatz. The Rococo **Rathaus**, topped by three onion domes, overlooks the market. Two blocks south of the Marktplatz, **St. Martinskirche** (St. Martin's church; the symbol of Memmingen) rises in Gothic grandeur. Of particular interest are the carved

16th-century choir stalls (open May-Sept. daily 2:30-5pm; Oct. Sun.-Fri. 2-4pm, Sat. 10am-noon; closed Nov.-April; German tours of the tower leave March-Oct. daily at 3pm; DM2). South on Frauenkirchpl. stands the eponymous **Frauenkirche** (Church of Our Lady), a 14th- and 15th-century church with an exquisite fresco cycle and dramatic vaulting over the apse. Call 22 53 for info on how to get in.

Memmingen's **tourist office,** Marktplatz 3 (tel. 85 01 72; fax 85 01 78), is across from the *Rathaus.* They have information on accommodations (DM35-65) and book rooms for free (open Mon.-Fri. 8am-noon and 2-5pm, Sat. 9:30am-12:30pm). Memmingen is connected by **train** to Augsburg (1hr.; DM20.60) and Ulm (45min.; DM14.60). The **Jugendherberge (HI),** Kempterstr. 42 (tel./fax 49 40 87), is easily reached from the train station (10min.). Follow Bahnhofstr. left from the station until you reach the park. Turn right into the park to walk the length of it (continue as it curves through the playground), then cross the street; the building is next to the gate with the tower, recessed from the street. Plain 6- to 10-bed rooms in a quasi-medieval building. (Reception open 8-10am and 5-10pm. Curfew 10pm. Lockout 9am-5pm. DM18. Breakfast included. Sheets DM5.50. Open March-Nov.) **Gästehaus Lindenbad,** Lindenbadstr. 18 (tel. 32 78), offers clean, spacious rooms near the station. (Singles with sink DM35, with shower DM50; doubles with bath DM90.) **Camping am See International,** Am Weiherhaus 7 (tel. 718 00), is close in Buxheim. Take the bus (direction: "Buxheim"): "Oben am Weiher" (DM7 per person, DM6 per tent, DM11 per car). The **telephone code** is 08331.

OTTOBEUREN

A little town with a big church, Ottobeuren lolls lazily in the rolling foothills of the Allgäu. The **Benedictine Abbey Church,** on a grassy rise in the middle of town, is about as inconspicuous as an American tourist. The **largest Baroque church in Germany,** its towers are 82m high, the nave 90m long, and the transept 60m wide. The facade is phenomenal—from afar. As you approach, the marvelous stonework flattens out into a moderately skillful painting job. The interior, however, is dazzling even up close. Intricately molded relief-work, gilded scrolling, creamy pastel marbles, and a line of frescoed domes lead mere mortals to a high altar that takes Baroque fantasy to its insanely gaudy pinnacle. The four altars under the central dome each contain the complete skeleton of a saint associated with the abbey; every one is neatly dressed in ecclesiastical garments (including embroidered slippers) and artfully arranged atop velvet pillows. (Open daily 9am-5pm; library and museum open March-Nov. daily 10am-noon and 2-5pm; Dec.-Feb. 2-5pm; admission to library DM3.) Organ performances are Saturdays at 4pm. Contact the tourist office for an up-to-date schedule of **concerts** taking place in the church from late-May to September—Herbert von Karajan and Leonard Bernstein conducted here.

The **tourist office** (tel. 92 19 50; fax 92 19 92), on the Marktplatz across from the abbey, provides free maps, finds rooms (DM20-30) for no fee, and sells tickets for abbey concerts (open Mon.-Thurs. 9am-noon and 3-5pm, Fri. 9am-noon and 2-4pm; May-Sept. also open Sat. 10am-noon). To reach Ottobeuren's **Jugendherberge (HI),** Kaltenbrunnweg 11 (tel. 368), from the end of the Marktplatz opposite the church, walk down the paved path ("Silachweg") along the church compound's wall until it ends in a road. Follow this road to the intersection at the other end of the mill. Veer left onto Faichtmayerstr.; the hostel is four blocks down to the right (20min.). Clean, comfy 8-bed rooms. The hostel would be cramped if full, but it rarely is. (Reception open 8am-noon, 5-7pm. DM11.50. Breakfast DM5. Sheets DM5.50. Open March-Oct.) Private **buses** (DM8.60 round-trip; railpasses not valid) run the 11km between Ottobeuren and Memmingen's train station. Ask at the tourist office for a map of **hiking** trails (DM6) to nearby sights and resorts. The **telephone code** is 08332.

KEMPTEN

A surprisingly urban little city in a decidedly rural area of Germany, Kempten ain't much to look at. Its several *Altstadt* treasures have long been overpowered by department stores, *Döner* stands, and the route from the station into town. Kempten feels more like American suburbia than old Germania. However, the town's manifold amenities make it an ideal base for excursions into the neighboring mountains. The elegant baroque **Fürstäbtliche Residenz** (Prince Abbot's Residence) is a sizable former Benedictine cloister with colorful portals. The building has served the town as everything from a barracks to law courts. Behind the *Residenz* stretches the terraced **Hofgarten,** webbed by paths leading to the 18th-century **Orangerie** that houses a library. (Guided tours Tues.-Sun. 10, 11am, 2, and 3pm; Oct.-April Sat. 2pm). To reach the town center from the distant train station, bus #4, 6, 8, or 9: "Residenz" (DM2.10), or walk along Bahnhofstr. until you reach the pedestrian zone. Keep on trucking until you see the trees in the park. Klostersteige leads from the *Residenz* to the cobbled pedestrian zone.

Across from the basilica on Residenzpl., the **Römische Sammlung Cambodunum** (Roman Museum of Kempten) and the **Naturkunde Museum** (Museum of the Natural History of the Allgäu) dwell in the elegant patrician **Zumsteinhaus,** Residenzpl. 31 (tel. 450; both open Tues.-Sun. 10am-4pm; DM4, students and seniors DM2). Along Burgstr., a forested park contains the **Burghalde.** The oldest part of the city, the park boasts a late Roman fortification with a Gothic tower, as well as an amphitheater that features German disco stars in the summer months.

Kempten's **tourist office** (tel. 252 52 37), Rathauspl. 24 in the city center, a few blocks from Residenzpl., provides city and hiking maps (DM3-11), accommodation listings, and 1½- to 2-hour city **tours** for free. (Open May-Oct. Mon.-Fri. 8am-noon and 1:30-5pm, Sat. 10am-1pm; Nov.-April Mon.-Fri. 8:30am-noon and 1:30-5pm. Tours in German every Sat. at 11am.) Built at a bend in the Iller River, Kempten can be reached by **train** from Lindau and Ulm, and from Munich (3 per hr.; 70min.). The noisy **Jugendherberge (HI),** Saarlandstr. 1 (tel. 736 63; fax 77 03 81), is usually packed with school groups, but opens out onto a sweeping view of the Alps beyond the Allgäu. You'll have plenty of time to enjoy the scenery on your way there by choosing from a number of unattractive options. From the station, bus #4, 6, 8, or 9: "Parktheater," and then switch to bus #32 (one per hr.): "Unzfriederstr./Altersheim." Take a left at the intersection; the gray structure surrounded by a wire fence on top of the hill is the hostel. Alternatively, tighten your backpack for a 45-minute trek. Take the small Wiesstr. behind the post office by the station to Schumacherring, then turn right and follow this never-ending street until you ascend a set of stairs to the right after the intersection with Lenzfriedenstr. Follow the signs to the *Jugendherberge.* Or split a cab ride (DM15-20). (Reception open 5-11pm. Curfew 11pm. DM18. Breakfast included. Sheets DM5.50. Open mid-Dec. to Oct.) To reach **Camping Oeschlesee** (tel. (08376) 621 or 82 62), take the bus from the *Altbahnhof* at Sulzberg (20min.; DM6) and walk to the lake (person DM5, tent DM4-7). The **telephone code** is 0831.

IMMENSTADT AND BÜHL AM ALPSEE

The small town of **Immenstadt** and the even smaller hamlet of **Bühl am Alpsee** huddle deep in the gorgeous mountains of the Allgäu south of Kempten, a world away from the resorts to the south. Streams flowing down from the Alps feed two lakes, the **Größer Alpsee** and the **Kleiner Alpsee** (Large and Small Alpine Lakes), whose cool, clear waters are unimaginably refreshing after a hike into the surrounding hills.

The Kleiner Alpsee, a 15-minute walk down Badeweg towards Bühl, offers an extensive park speckled with small, unofficial swimming holes. The Großer Alpsee has *größer* wet and wild opportunities, but certain stretches are off-limits to swimmers. Boat and windsurf-board rental on the Großer Alpsee is possible but rather expensive. Go for a dip at the **Freibad Kleiner Alpsee,** Am Kleiner Alpsee, on the other side of the lake (open daily 9am-7pm, in case of bad weather 9:30-1pm; DM5 students DM2.80). Immenstadt is also close to two huge skiing areas: **Alpsee Skizirkus** and **Mittag Ski-Center.** The season runs roughly from December to March Day passes cost about DM25 in each area, while week-long passes are DM130. Chair lifts and cable cars run summer-long for the dedicated wanderers.

The friendly Immenstadt **tourist office,** Marienpl. 3 (tel. 91 41 77; fax 91 41 95; mascot: Immi), has loads of hiking maps (DM6.80-9.90) and suggested routes, many of which will land you happily at a mountain *Gaststätte* around lunchtime (open Mon.-Fri. 8:30am-noon and 2-5:30pm, Sat. 10am-noon; Nov.-May Mon.-Fri. 8:30am-noon and 2-5:30pm). From the station, turn right on Bahnhofstr. and follow it around the corner to the town square. Immenstadt can be reached by **train** from Kempten along the Munich-Zürich route, or from Ulm along the Stuttgart-Oberstdorf route.

From Immenstadt, either grab a bus or walk along the pleasant Badeweg path (30-40min.) next door to **Bühl.** Bühl's **tourist office,** Seestr. 5 (tel. 914 78), has many of the same maps and brochures as its Immenstadt sibling, but no "Immi loves you all!" stickers (open Mon.-Fri. 8:30am-noon and 2-5pm, Sat. 10am-noon; Nov.-May Mon.-Fri. 8:30am-noon and 2-5pm). Both tourist offices find accommodations (private rooms DM18-32). Camp on the Großer Alpsee at **Bucher's Camping,** Seestr. 25 (tel. 77 26 or 48 28), in Bühl. (Person DM7. Tent DM5-6.50. Car DM2.50. DM1.50 *Kurtaxe* per person. Open Easter-early Oct.) The **telephone code** for both towns is 08323.

■ Wasserburg am Inn

Wasserburg floats dramatically atop a promontory on a bend in the Inn River between Munich and Salzburg. Four hundred years ago, the city prospered from salt-trade and shipping, yet little of the riches remain. Medieval cobblestoned paths, starting at the Innbrücke bridge, curl around the ancient half-island, snaking their way around crooked old houses. From the *Stadt Bahnhof* train station, make a left up Im Hag and then a right on Hoffstatt down Salzsenderzeile to penetrate the *Altstadt.* If your train doesn't go as far as the city train station, you'll need to take a bus from the *Hauptbahnhof,* which lies outside of the town itself. (Though it's only 4km, walking is not advisable, as it involves tangling with, if not lions and tigers and bears, then at least scary high-speed interchanges, oh my.) The buses run regularly and cost DM1. Once you finally get to the *Altstadt,* turn right down Herrengasse to reach the **Heimat Museum,** Herrengasse 15 (tel. 155 42). This late Gothic *Bürgerhaus* shows off Wasserburg rarities, including one of the oldest postal sleds in Bayern (open May-Sept. Tues.-Fri. 10am-noon and 1-4pm, Sat.-Sun. 11am-4pm; Oct.-April Tues.-Fri. 1-4pm, Sat.-Sun. 1-3pm; DM3, students DM2, children DM1). The late-Gothic **Rathaus,** built in 1250, is back at Salzsenderzeile; inside, the **Kleiner Rathaussaal** and the **Tanzhaus** host many Wasserburg weddings (tours Tues.-Fri. 10, 11am, 2, 3, and 4pm, Sat.-Sun. 10 and 11am; DM1.50, children DM0.50). The **Erstes Imaginäres Museum** (First Imaginary Museum), Bruckgasse 2 (tel. 43 58) on Marienpl., around the corner from the *Rathaus* at the foot of the bridge, is a private and eclectic collection of German Old Masters, French Impressionists, as well as primitive and pop art. Recognize them? Every single one of these famous works is a painstakingly produced copy. (Open May-Sept. Tues.-Sun. 11am-5pm; Oct.-April Tues.-Sun. 1-5pm. DM3, students and seniors DM2, under 16 DM1. Combined ticket for the Heimat Museum, the *Rathaus,* and the Erstes Imaginäres Museum DM5, students DM4, children DM2.)

Wasserburg can be reached by **train** from Munich (8 per day, 1¼hr.). The **tourist office** in the *Rathaus* (tel. 105 22) offers free maps and lists of rooms (DM20-30) for rent (open May-Sept. 9am-12:30pm and 3:30-5:30pm; Oct.-April 9am-12:30pm). Daily **boat trips** paddle around starting at the Innbrücke. (40min. trip 2pm, DM10; 1½hr. trip 11am and 3pm, DM16; 2hr. trip Tues. and Fri. 7pm, DM20; children under 15 50% off, under 6 free.) Rent a **bike** from the tourist office or a **boat** to navigate to Soyen. **Badria,** Alkorstr. 14 (tel. 81 33), Wasserburg's amazing recreation center, comes complete with outdoor and indoor swimming pools, and the **largest water slide in Germany,** miniature golf, saunas, solariums, and bowling. To get there from the train station, take the Wasserburg city bus: "Badria." (Open Mon.-Fri. 10am-9pm, Sat.-Sun. 8:30am-7pm. Admission to pool only for 4hr. DM8, unlimited time DM12, students DM5.50, DM7.50. Admission to pool and sauna for 4hr. DM16, unlimited time DM20, students DM13, DM14.) The **telephone code** is 08071.

The nearest **Jugendherberge,** Schillingerstr. 1 (tel. (08092) 225 23), in Ebersberg, is 30 minutes away by train or bus (DM16.50; breakfast included; sheets DM5.50). **Gasthof Huberwirt,** Salzburgerstr. 25 (tel. 74 33), across the Innbrücke, is a simple but affordable motel on the hill overlooking the town. Cross the Innbrücke from Marienpl. and take the steps up to Kellerbergweg on the left just before the gas station. Follow this footpath up the hill to the motel. (Singles DM34-54; doubles DM63, with shower DM90; triples DM90-111. Breakfast included.) The closest **camping** is 6km away in Soyen at **Werner Huthm,** Soyen am See (tel. 38 60), a manageable walk (open April to mid-Oct.). The **Brasserie im Stechl Keller,** Marienpl. 6 (tel. 56 53), serves a delicious *gulasch* soup (DM5) as well as beer (DM4.20 for 0.5L) and other tasty meals (DM9-18; open daily 10am-1am; kitchen open 10am-11pm).

■ Bad Reichenhall

In Bad Reichenhall, it is considered normal to sit in front of a salt water fountain daily, cover oneself in mud, and then inhale oxygen from an intimidating apparatus. Whether or not you're here for a massage and some mud, Bad Reichenhall ("rich in salt"), famous for its "White Gold" salt deposits, is a sight. Because of its proximity to Austria, the Viennese and Salzburger influences are strong in the architecture, dialect, and gastronomy. The **Salz Museum,** Alte Saline (tel. 70 02 51), travels into the 16th-century salty underworld, peppered with exhibits on the history and process of salt-making in the area. The obligatory tour in German winds through the damp underground passageways where brine (salt water) is pumped out of the mountain (tours April-Oct. daily 10am-11:30am and 2-4pm; Nov.-March Tues. and Thurs. 2-4pm; last tour at 3pm; DM8, with *Kurkarte* DM7, students DM5). At the associated **Glashütte** (tel. 697 38; fax 697 39), in the museum, you can experience the beauty of glass-making and glass-buying (tours Mon.-Fri. 9:30am-6pm, Sat. 9am-1pm). The **Glasofenwirtshaus** hosts a musical *Weißwurstfrühschoppen* (a Bavarian practice of getting plastered in the morning) every Saturday 9am-1pm (restaurant open Mon.-Fri. 9:30am-6pm, Sat. 9am-1pm; live music Wed.-Fri. 2:30-5pm).

Walk right from the Alte Saline on Salinenstr. until it becomes Ludwigstr. On the left, in the palatial 1870 **Kurgarten,** the *Altes Kurhaus* offers a therapeutic blue theater, a restful music pavilion, and a rejuvenating chess set. At the salt spring fountain, buy a *Becher* (cup) to drink from the *Trinksole* fountain (DM0.30; open Mon.-Sat. 8am-12:30pm and 3-5pm, Sun. 10am-12:30pm). The 170m **Gradierwerk** out front is a bizarre wall known as an "open air inhalatorium." Built in 1912, it's covered with *"Dornbündel"* (branches, briars, and thorns) through which mist trickles from April to October. For best results, those visiting the wall should supposedly sit and inhale for 30 minutes. Didn't do much for us, but obviously someone thinks it works, because the city spends DM100,000 on its annual upkeep—there's your *Kurtaxe* at work. (Garden open April-Oct. 7am-10pm; Nov.-March 7am-6pm. Free except for 1-1½hr. long concerts. Concerts April-Oct. Tues. 4 and 8pm, Wed. 4pm, Thurs. 8pm, Fri. and Sat. 4pm, Sun. 10:45am and 4pm; concerts DM5.10, children DM3.)

The **Predigstuhl,** the oldest cable car of its kind in the world (1928), runs up 1614m of skier's paradise. In the summer you can hike the *Höhenkurweg* trail to the *Almhütte* resthouse. (Cable car runs 1 per hr. May-Sept. 9am-9pm; Oct.-April 9am-5pm. Round-trip DM24, under 16 DM16, under 6 free. One-way DM15, under 16 DM10. Dogs DM8-10. Family cards available. For info call 21 27 or fax 43 84; weather info tel. 17 19.) The **tourist office,** Wittelsbacherstr. 15 (tel. 30 03; fax 24 27), is to the right on the same road as the station, across from the Sparkasse. They provide maps, hiking advice (mountain tours and hikes up to 500km), guest information, and tips on discounts with the *Kurkarte* (open Mon.-Fri. 8am-5:30pm, Sat. 9am-noon). From the tourist office, cross Wittelsbacherstr. over to Kurstr. to the main pedestrian zone (leading up on the right) or to the lush *Kurgarten* and *Kurhaus* on the left. **Trains** run hourly to Munich (2hr.) and Salzburg (40min.) with a change in Freilassing; both trains and buses run to and from Brechtesgaden (40-45min.). Rent a **bike** at **Sport Müller,** Spitalgasse 3 (tel. 37 76; fax 69 511), for DM12 for half a day, DM15 for a whole day (open Mon.-Fri. 9am-1pm and 2:30-6pm; Sat. 9am-12:30pm). Call **Club Aktiv** (tel. 67 238) to go **rafting** or **canyoning**. The **post office,** Bahnhofstr. 35, 83435 Bad Reichenhall (tel. 77 80), is to the right as you exit the station (open Mon.-Fri. 8am-5:30pm, Sat. 8am-noon). The **telephone code** is 08651.

There is no *Jugendherberge* in Bad Reichenhall and hotels are expensive (DM40-150). **Private rooms** usually go for DM25-40 per person (breakfast included). Along the pedestrian zones of Salzburger and Ludwigstr., you'll find endless cafes where you can try delectable *Mozart Kugeln* (marzipan/chocolate balls) and *Torte mit Sahne* (cake with cream). At **Gasthof Bürgerbräu,** Waaggasse 2 (tel. 60 89), on Rathauspl., traditionally dressed waiters serve the local beer direct from the in-house brewery (DM4.40 for 0.5L). Bavarian dishes run DM11-17 (open daily 11am-11pm, Fri.-Sun. dancing after 7pm). **Restaurant Fuchsbau,** Innsbruckerstr. 19, serves pizza and Bavarian meals (DM12-20), including *Weißwürste* (DM11.20; open Tues.-Sun. 7pm-3am). For basics, head to the **grocery store HL Markt,** Bahnhofstr. 20, to the right of the station (open Mon.-Fri. 8am-6pm, Sat. 7:30am-1pm).

■ The Chiemsee

For almost 2000 years, artists, architects, and musicians have chosen the Chiemsee as the setting for their artistic masterpieces. With its picturesque islands, meadows, pastures, forests, marshland, and dramatic crescent of mountains, the region first lured the 9th-century builders of the cloisters on **Fraueninsel**. Later, the wobbly King Ludwig II arrived to build **Herrenchiemsee,** his third and last "fairy-tale castle," on the Herreninsel. The poet Maximilian Haushofer lived and died on the Chiemsee shores in **Prien,** and 11-year-old Mozart composed a mass in Seeon while on holiday. Most modern visitors to "The Bavarian Ocean" are artists of leisure, and today the area has been overrun by resorts and prices have risen. But don't expect to find very many foreigners—Chiemsee is where the *nouveaux riches* of Munich and Northern Germany vacation. Summer weekends are sheer madness. Prien, the largest lake town, offers easy access to ski areas in the **Kampenwand,** the surrounding curtain of mountains, and resort paradises in **Aschau** and **Sachrang**. For information on white-water **rafting,** call (08649) 243. The **Trachtenfest,** with parades, folklore, and pilgrimages, takes place each year in a different town on the last Sunday in July.

■ PRIEN AM CHIEMSEE

Without question, the best thing about Prien is its idyllic Chiemsee coast and its highly frequented train station, which facilitates the use of the town as a base for the real sights elsewhere on the lake. If lugging around heavy packs wears you down, wade in the cold water of Prien's *Kneipp Water Cure* and then jump into a 90°F (32°C) thermal bath—it works wonders for some famous German soccer, err...football, players.

The train station is a few blocks from the city center and a 20-minute walk north of the lake. To reach the *Altstadt,* turn right as you exit the station and then turn left on Seestr., which becomes Alte Rathausstr. The large, modern **tourist office,** Alte Rathausstr. 11 (tel. 690 50 or 69 05 55; fax 69 05 40), five minutes away on the left, is full of free maps and English brochures. The tourist office finds rooms (DM20-40 with breakfast) in private houses for free (open Mon.-Fri. 8:30am-6pm, Sat. 9am-noon). If the **information booth** (tel. 690 50) at the train station is closed (open July-Sept. Mon.-Fri. 12:45-5:45pm), head out the main exit to find a city map 10 paces to your right. Located on the northwestern corner of the Chiemsee, Prien has a convenient and direct **train** link to Munich (1 per hr., 1hr.; DM21.30) and Salzburg, Austria (1-2 per hr., 1hr.; DM15.60). Call 28 74 for train information. You can rent a **bike** (tel. 28 74) at the train station for DM13-17; otherwise, try **Radsport Reischonböck,** Hochriesstr. 7 (tel. 46 31). To paddle the Chiemsee, rent a **boat** from **Schaber,** Harrasser Str. 143 (tel. 45 75 or 18 95). Phone 10 37 to find out which **pharmacy** is open on any single night. The **telephone code** is 08051.

The cheapest bed in town is at the raucous **Jugendherberge (HI),** Carl-Braun-Str. 66 (tel. 687 70; fax 68 77 15), a 15-minute walk from the station and 10 minutes from the

lake. From the station, go right on Seestr. and under the train overpass. After tv
blocks, take a left on Staudenstr., which curves right and turns into Carl-Braun-S
(Reception open 8-9am, 5-7, and 9:30-10pm. 6-bed rooms. Lockout 9am-1pm. Curfe
10pm. DM22 plus DM0.80 resort tax. Showers, lockers, and breakfast include
Sheets DM5.50. Open Jan.-Oct.) There is a campground, **Campingplatz Hofbauer,**
Bernauerstr. 110 (tel. 41 36; fax 626 57), just outside of town. Walk right from the s
tion, turn left at Seestr., and left again at the next intersection, and follow Bernauers
out of town (DM8.20 per person, DM9 per tent and car; open late March-Oct.). M
of the restaurants in Prien cater to the vacationing bourgeoisie. Try **Scherer SB Re
taurant,** Alte Rathausstr. 1 (tel. 45 91), on the corner of Alte Rathausstr. and Bernau
str. This self-serve restaurant cooks up hearty meals and filling salads (DM9-20; op
Mon.-Fri. 8am-8pm, Sat. 8am-3pm). Gather groceries from **HL Markt,** Seestr. 11, clc
to the station (open Mon.-Fri. 8am-6pm, Sat. 8am-4pm).

HERRENINSEL AND FRAUENINSEL

Ferries float across the waters of the Chiemsee from the port in Prien to the **Herre
insel** (Gentlemen's Island), the **Fraueninsel** (Ladies' Island), and towns on the oth
side of the lake. Both islands are co-ed, although this wasn't always the case—a mc
astery on Herreninsel once complemented the still-extant nunnery on Fraueninsel
religious chastity and isolation. Supposedly, mischievous members of the cloth (
both sexes) met up on *Krautinsel* (Vegetable Island) and practiced the eyebrow-ra
ing act of gardening; nowadays, the island remains uninhabited and unferrie
(Round-trip to Herreninsel DM14, to Fraueninsel or to both islands DM16; you c
hop on and off various round-trips to visit the islands.) To get to the dock, hang a rig
from the Prien train station's main entrance and follow Seestr. (the major thorou{
fare on the right) for about 20 minutes. Alternatively, a slow 19th-century **gre
steam train** takes visitors from the train station to the dock roughly hourly, departi
from 9:25am-6:15pm (8min.). "I think I can, I think I can." To get there, follow t
Chiemseebahn sign (one way DM3.50, round-trip DM5.50). Total package, includi
train shuttle and ship passage, DM16. The train station **information booth,** thou{
central, has very limited hours (open July to mid-Sept. Mon.-Fri.12:45-5:45pm).
sure to read the schedules to avoid getting stranded.

Schloß Herrenchiemsee on the Herreninsel

"Never can as unsuitable a location have been chosen for something as tasteless
this unfortunate copy of the palace at Versailles," Bavarian poet Ludwig Thom
pouted. Once on Herreninsel, either walk along the paved footpath to the pala
(20min.) or take one of the horse-drawn carriages that run every 15 minutes (DM
children DM2.50). The architecture of **Königsschloß Herrenchiemsee** (Herrenchie
see Royal Palace; tel. 30 69) is fabulously overwrought as only King Ludwig II cou
manage. Ludwig bankrupted Bayern while building the palace, thus leaving barr
rooms with naked white walls in stark contrast to the overadorned 20 chambe
which were completed. The entire U-shaped palace is a shameless attempt to
larger, better, and more expensive than Versailles. Ludwig II was so obsessed with t
"Sun King" that he commissioned exact replicas of Versailles originals to grace t
walls of his palace. Surprisingly, not a single image of Ludwig is to be found insi
though a tiny bust of him cowers in the far back of the grounds. There's even a **H
of Mirrors,** only Ludwig's is longer than Louis's; it took 25 people half an hour just
light all the candles in this room alone when Ludwig decided to tour his palace. C
dle-lit concerts are hosted here throughout the summer. While lacking Neuschwa
stein's pristine exterior and Linderhof's almost completely gold-laden interic
Herrenchiemsee perhaps provides a better glimpse into Ludwig's mind—no oth
Königschloß so well reflects Ludwig's obsessive qualities or his relentless insisten
upon creating a world he could never have. (Open April-Sept. daily 9am-5pm; Oc
March 10am-4pm. Admission and obligatory tour DM7, seniors, students, and disabl
persons DM4, under 16 free with adult. German tours every 10min.; English tou
10:30, 11:30am, 3, and 4pm.) A **museum** documenting Ludwig's life lies just insi

the castle entrance (DM9, students DM5). If you get caught waiting for an English tour, the cafeteria in the lobby serves up *Leberkäse mit Kartoffelsalat* (DM8.50) as well as coffee or hot chocolate (DM5). If you have time for a more relaxed meal, the only **restaurant** on the island, near the dock, has a **beer garden** (*Maß* DM9-10.40). For Herrenchiemsee **tourist information,** call (08051) 30 69.

Fraueninsel

Despite living next to Ludwig's material world, Fraueninsel is no material girl. It's a small realm with no room for cars; only footpaths wind through this village of fishermen and nuns. From the boat dock, a marked path curls toward the island cloister passing its medicinal herb garden. The nuns also make their own *Marzipan* and liqueurs, for sale in the convent shop (DM8.50 for 0.2L *Klosterlikör*). The abbey dates back to at least 866. St. Irmengard, the great-granddaughter of Charlemagne and earliest known abbess of the cloister, has a **memorial chapel** in her honor behind the main altar of the church. Her sarcophagus was exhumed in the 17th century, and in 1928 her remains were encased in glass within the altar. They're not very interesting—that's what 1000 years will do to you. More interesting are the countless messages written to Irmengard on the opposite wall in thanks for deliverance after prayer. The **Torhalle** (gate) is the oldest surviving part of the cloister. Various artifacts, including the 8th-century Merovingian **Cross of Bischofhofen,** are displayed in the room above the gate (open Mon.-Sat. 11am-6pm; mid-June to Sept. daily 11am-6pm; DM4, students DM1.50). The entire island can be circumnavigated on foot in 45 minutes. There are quite a few *Gaststätte* scattered all over the island, but prices are high because owners know they have hungry tourists trapped. Bring some food or be prepared to splurge. For **tourist information** call (08054) 511 or 603; fax 12 72.

ELSEWHERE NEAR THE CHIEMSEE

While Prien is considered the "metropolis of the Bavarian sea," endless idyllic towns melt into the landscape, offering resort luxuries, nature rambles, and historical attractions galore. **Übersee,** a haven for biking, sailing, and windsurfing, lies on the Chiemsee just past Prien on the Munich-Salzburg train line. Contact their **tourist office** (tel. (08642) 89 89 50; fax 621 14). Just northwest of Chiemsee lies **Bad Endorf,** famed for its thermal baths; call its *Kurverwaltung* for more info (tel. (08053) 30 08 22; fax 30 08 30). Bad Endorf also has a **hostel (HI),** Rankhamer Weg 11 (tel. (08053) 509; fax 32 92), that's super cheap (DM16.50; open early-Feb. to Nov.). Little villages curl up at the foothills of the mountains: **Grassau Verkehrsamt** (tel. (08641) 23 40; fax 40 08 41), **Rimsting Verkehrsamt** (tel. (08051) 44 61; fax 616 94), and **Riedering Verkehrsamt** (tel. (08036) 34 48; fax 37 58) can supply more info. **Rottau,** just south of the Chiemsee, nestles in a mountain ridge; call its **Verkehrsamt,** at Grassauerstr. 9 (tel. (08641) 27 73; fax 14 19).

Sachrang is an exquisite Alpine village on the Tyrolean border. For excellent skiing, mountain climbing, and walking tours, call **Sachrang Verkehrsamt,** Dorfstr. 20 (tel. (08057) 378; fax 10 51; open Mon.-Tues., and Thurs.-Fri. 8am-noon and 2-5pm, Wed. 8am-noon, Sat. 9am-noon). **Aschau** lies near Sachrang, with skiing and hiking trails connecting the two. The panorama is perfect, and the town touts solariums, tobogganing, sailing, and skiing. The **tourist office** is located at Kampenwandstr. 38 (tel. (08052) 90 49 37; fax 47 17; open May-Sept. Mon.-Fri. 8am-noon and 2-6pm, Sat. 9am-noon; Oct.-Dec. Mon.-Fri. 8am-noon and 2-5pm; Jan.-April Mon.-Fri. 8am-noon and 2-5pm, Sat. 9am-noon). Aschau and Sachrang are easily reached by **train** from the Munich-Salzburg route; at Prien, switch to trains headed for your destination (2hr.). **Buses** link Aschau to Munich. Affordable **accommodations,** like bungalows and vacation homes, run DM20-40 per person. The tourist office in Prien distributes information about a number of neighboring towns; drop by to browse through brochures if you're interested in exploring the region.

BAYERN (BAVARIA)

▓ Burghausen

The proverbial castle-on-the-hill, like a vicious dragon, laughingly overshadows everything else in Burghausen, a tiny town separated from Austria by the Salzach Rive Built in the 13th century, the 1034m **Schloß** (the longest medieval fortress in Europ was considered impregnable—and indeed, it was only breached once. In 1742, t Habsburg Empire, eager to extend its borders into Bayern, fell upon the border tov of Burghausen. Cowed by the Austrian show of arms and lacking outside reinforc ments, Burghausen opened its gates without a fight. Days later, on October 16, 174 Burghausen's moment of glory came: the brash 26-year-old *Hofkaminkehrermeist* (Master Chimney Sweep) Karl Franz Cura recruited 40 grenadiers for the seeming impossible task of breaking through the castle walls. In one fell swoop, Cura br liantly freed the castle and the city. Until the Habsburgs return, Burghausen w remain a medieval gem akin to Heidelberg and Rothenburg, but much less trafficke

Stepping off the train, you'll find yourself smack in the middle of Hanif's suburb Don't panic. Walk directly to your left through the parking lot (100m) to reach Ma tlerstr. Follow it to the right (taking the left fork 400m from the station to remain (Marktlerstr.); it's a 30-minute hike to the *Altstadt* at Stadtpl. Or take the bus on Ma tlerstr. around the corner of the train station (every 30min. 8:12am-7:12pm; fewer (weekends). It's four stops to "Stadtpl." (DM2).

These days, the **castle** ramparts can be walked without violent reprisals, and t upper halls contain the town's **historical museum** (tel. 651 98). For the price of punishing climb up the steep footpath, the castle also offers a ravishing view of t *Altstadt*'s roofs of red tiles and colorful gables. The footpath starts near the **St. Jakob Kirche,** dating back to 1140, across from the *Rathaus.* (Castle open Mon.-Fri. 9a noon and 1-5pm; Oct.-March 9am-noon and 1-4pm. DM4, students DM2. Museu open May-Sept. daily 9am-6:30pm; mid-March to April and Oct.-Nov. 10am-4:30p DM2.50, children DM1.) The *Burg* also houses the town's **Photo Museum** (tel. 34), tracing the historical development of the camera (open April-Oct. Wed.-Su 10am-6pm; admission DM2.50). The castle's old **torture chamber** (tel. 615 34) w used until 1918 (open mid-March to Oct. daily 9am-6pm; Nov. to mid-March Sat.-Su 9am-6pm). The **Hexenturm** across the way imprisoned many accused witches un the last trial in 1751. Below the castle, the **Stadtplatz** shimmers with such glos medieval splendor you half expect a film crew to emerge from the rows of pas facades. At the far end of the Stadtpl. looms the magnificent Baroque **Studienkirch St. Joseph,** a 1630 Jesuit convent.

The **tourist office** *(Fremdenverkehrsamt),* Stadtpl. 112-114 (tel. 24 35; fax 88 55), is located in the peppermint green **Rathaus** at the far end of the Stadtpl. On t ground floor are free maps, brochures, and information on tours of the town ar (open Mon.-Wed. and Fri. 7:30am-noon and 1:30-4pm, Thurs. 7:30am-noon and 1:3 6pm, Sat. 10am-1pm). Burghausen is most easily reached by **train** from Munich (1 p hr. via Mühldorf until 7:30pm; 2hr.), though **buses** run from Mühldorf, the transpor tion hub for eastern Bayern. For a **taxi** call 22 33. To your left as you exit the *Rathai* is an archway that opens onto a narrow cobblestone street called In den Grüben; t **post office,** 162 In den Grüben, 84489 Burghausen (tel. 45 80), is one block down (the left (open Mon.-Fri. 2:30-5pm). To **exchange currency,** try the other post office (R.-Koch-Str. (same hours). The **telephone code** is 08677.

The **Jugendherberge Burghausen (HI),** Kapuzinergasse 235 (tel. 41 87; fax 91 18) is a schlepp from the train station but close to the cafe-heavy In den Grüben. Fro the station, take the city bus at Marktlerstr. through Stadtpl.: "Hl.-Geist-Spital," wa ahead, and turn left onto Kapuzinergasse. Or follow the above directions to Stadtp and continue through the arch at the far side of the square onto In den Grüben. At t end, cross the intersection to the left of the church onto Spitalgasse and turn rig onto Kapuzinergasse. (45min. from the station. Reception open Mon.-Fri. 8-10am a 5-7pm, Sat.-Sun. 8-9am and 5-7pm. DM20. Breakfast included. Sheets DM5.50.) T tourist office finds quieter accommodations for no fee; *Pensionen* and *Gasthöfe* Burghausen start at DM30, breakfast included. If you're after Bavarian dishes, t

Hotel Post, Stadtpl. 39 (tel. 30 43). After 450 years, it knows its *Würstchen* (most meals DM13.50-18, beer DM4). Head to Austria for a *Mozart Kugel* and *Torte.* Follow Bruckgasse from the middle of Stadtpl. over the Alte Brücke spanning the Salzach River (2min.). Buy supplies at the **Edeka Markt,** In den Grüben, across from the post office (open Mon.-Fri. 8am-6pm, Sat. 7am-noon).

Passau

Napoleon Bonaparte once remarked of this "Bavarian Venice": "I have not seen a city as beautiful as Passau in all of Germany." Serenely located between two peninsulas forged by the confluence of the Danube, Inn, and Ilz Rivers, two millenia-old Passau—the *"Dreiflüssestadt"* (3-river city)—embodies the Old World city ideal. As early as 80AD, Roman generals fancied the powerful bluff overlooking the modern Austrian-German border, and the church followed suit in 739 by establishing Passau as the seat of a diocese. A few centuries later local merchants monopolized the central European salt trade—an impressive feat, considering that Passau lacked any natural resources. The castle, palaces, and monasteries all bear witness to Passau's past as a center of administrative, commercial, and religious power. Its Baroque cathedral, the *Stephansdom,* was the mother church that founded the cathedral of the same name in Vienna. In the 12th century, Wolfger, the bishop of Passau, supervised the recording of the epic *Nibelungenlied* on parchment, immediately inspiring the tourist office to coin its city the *Nibelungenstadt.* Today the great hall of Passau's *Rathaus* contains extravagant frescoes depicting scenes from the epic.

ORIENTATION AND PRACTICAL INFORMATION

Close to the Austrian border, Passau is directly accessible by rail from both Munich (every 2 hr., 2hr.) and Vienna (6 per day). Buses duplicate most rail routes and are often less expensive, but they almost double travel time. Passau proper is located almost entirely on the peninsula formed by the Danube and the Inn. The adjacent peninsula between the Danube and the Ilz is home to the local *Schloß.* Together they contain most places of interest to the *Altstadt*-minded traveler. The train station reposes on the western and more inland side of the main peninsula. To reach the city center, follow Bahnhofstr. to the right until you reach Ludwigspl. Walk downhill across Ludwigspl. to Ludwigstr., the beginning of the pedestrian zone, which becomes Rindermarkt, Steinweg, and finally Große Messergasse. If you continue straight onto Schustergasse when the street ends, you will soon reach the *Altstadt;* if you hang a left on Schrottgasse, you will stumble upon the **Rathausplatz,** where the tourist office will be on the left by the riverbank. From there, a glance up from your map yields a picturesque view of the Danube and the steep hill, beyond which lies the **Schloß.** Heading further east on the tip of the peninsula leads to the point where the three rivers converge. A little blue **City-Bus** can also escort you around town (DM0.50); one stop is directly to the right of the station as you exit.

   Tourist Office: Tourist Information, Rathauspl. 3 (tel. 95 59 80; fax 351 07). On the banks of the Danube next to the *Rathaus* (see directions above). Healthy assortment of free maps, brochures, schedules, and tour information. Room-finding for a DM5 fee; also provides information on cheaper hotels and *Pensionen* in the surrounding area. Ask for *Aktuell,* a free monthly guide to everything going down in Passau. An **Automat** in front of the tourist office gives maps and a brochure for DM1. Open April-Oct. Mon.-Fri. 8:30am-6pm, Sat.-Sun. 10am-2pm; Nov.-March Mon.-Thurs. 8:30am-5pm, Fri. 8:30am-4pm. A smaller **branch,** directly across from the train station, Bahnhofstr. 36 (tel. 955 80; fax 572 98), has free maps and brochures stocked outside in case you get into town after hours. Open mid-Oct. to Easter Mon.-Thurs. 9am-5pm, Fri. 9am-4pm. Sat.-Sun. 10am-2pm.
   Tours: German-language walking tours of the city meet at the *Königsdenkmal* (monument) in front of the church at Dompl. April-Oct. Mon.-Fri. 10:30am and 2:30pm, Sat.-Sun. 2:30pm (1hr.; DM4.50, children DM2).

Budget Travel: ITO Reisebüro, Bahnhofstr. 28 (tel. 540 48), across the street from the train station in the *Donau Passage,* a mall-type establishment. Open Mon.-Fri. 8am-6pm, Sat. 9am-1pm.

Currency Exchange: At the **post office** next to the train station. Or try **Deutsche Bank** on Ludwigspl. Open Mon. and Wed. 8:30am-noon and 1:30-3:30pm, Tues. and Fri. 8:30am-noon and 1:30-4pm, Thurs. 8:30am-noon and 1:30-6pm.

Trains: Station located west of downtown on Bahnhofstr. (tel. 194 19). Trains to Regensburg (every hr., 1-2hr.), Nürnberg (every 2hr., 2hr.), Munich (every 2 hr., 2hr.) and Vienna (6 per day, 3¼hr.).

Buses: To various towns on the outskirts of Passau and a number of stops within the city (DM4-7). For schedules call 56 02 72. The little **City-Bus** runs from the train station to the *Rathaus* (Mon.-Fri. 6:30am-10:10pm, Sat. 7:30am-4:15pm; every 10-30min.; DM0.50).

Ferries: Donau Schiffahrt (tel. 92 92 92; fax 355 18) steamers chug along the Danube to **Linz,** Austria, from late-April to mid-Oct. daily at 9am (5hrs). To daytrip it, take the morning steamer to Linz and return to Passau by bus or train in the afternoon (round-trip bus DM44; train DM46). Or stay overnight in Linz and return with the steamer the next day at 2:15pm (returns to Passau at 8:40pm; round-trip DM40). The "Three Rivers" Tour of the city runs daily from March to early Nov. (10am-5pm; every 30min.; 45min.; DM10, under 15 DM5). All ships depart from the docks along the Fritz-Schäffer-Promenade by the *Rathaus.*

Bike Rental: At the *Hauptbahnhof,* DM12.90 per day if you take the train into Passau, DM25.10 if you don't. The stunning **Donau Radweg** (bike path) begins in Donaueschingen and continues into Austria, passing through Passau; ask at the tourist office for information.

Laundromat: Rent-Wash, Neuburgerstr. 19. From Ludwigspl., walk up Dr.-Hans-Kapfinger-Str. and bear left on Neuburgerstr. Wash DM6, soap DM1. Dry DM3. Fabric softener DM0.30. Open daily 7am-midnight.

Pharmacy: 24hr. service rotates among the city's pharmacies; check the listings in the notices section of the daily newspapers, either the *Tagespresse* or the *Passauer Neue Presse,* or in the window of **Bahnhof Apotheke,** on Bahnhofstr., just to the right of the station. Open Mon.-Fri. 8am-6pm, Sat. 8am-1pm.

Hospital: Klinikum Passau, Bischof-Pilgrim-Str. 1 (tel. 530 00).

Emergency: tel. 110. **Police,** Nibelungenstr. 17 (tel. 112).

Post Office: On Bahnhofstr., 94032 Passau (tel. 50 50), to the right of the train station as you exit. Also offers **banking** services: changes money and cashes traveler's checks for DM6 per check. Open Mon.-Fri. 8am-6pm, Sat. 8am-noon. Extra window open Mon.-Fri. 7am-6:30pm.

Telephone Code: 0851.

ACCOMMODATIONS AND CAMPING

Most pensions run DM30-60, while vacation houses (2-6 beds) run DM30-75. The only youth hostel in town is usually swarming with German schoolchildren (especially during June and July).

Jugendherberge (HI), Veste Oberhaus 125, 94034 Passau (tel. 413 51; fax 437 09), in the castle on the mountain across the Danube (but no view of the city), 35-45min. from the train station and 20-30min. from the *Rathaus.* Cross the suspension bridge downstream from the *Rathaus* then **ignore** the misplaced sign pointing up the steps straight ahead, instead continuing right along the curve, through the lefthand tunnel. (Skeptics who follow the signs will get there, too—they'll just pay an extra 20min. of steep hell for their disbelief.) On your left will be a steep (but more direct) cobblestone driveway leading up to the hostel. Or you can hop the shuttle *(Pendelbus)* from Rathauspl. bound for the museum adjacent to the hostel (runs Easter to mid.-Oct. every 30min. Mon.-Fri. 10:30am-5pm, Sat.-Sun. 11:30am-6pm; DM3, round-trip DM4). Cramped 8-bed rooms. Reception open 7-11:30am and 4-11:30pm. New arrivals after 6pm only. Curfew 11:30pm. DM16.50. Breakfast included. Sheets DM5.50. Reservations recommended.

Rotel Inn, 94012 Passau (tel. 951 60; fax 951 61 00). From the train station, head straight ahead down the steps and through the tunnel toward the blue head of this strangely bright hotel. Built in the shape of a sleeping man and bedecked in primary-colored plastics, this self-proclaimed "Hotel of the Future" packs travelers into tight accommodations reminiscent of a cruise ship from the late 80s. For these prices, it's hard to complain about the Star Trek-esque blinking lights above the doorway. Everyone gets a porthole view of a rather bland section of the Danube. Reception open 24hr. Singles DM30; doubles DM50. Breakfast DM8.

Pension Rößner, Bräugasse 19 (tel. 93 13 50; fax 931 35 55). Right on the Danube, these homey rooms are among the cheapest in the *Altstadt*. From the *Rathaus,* walk downstream along the Danube. Call upstairs if no one's at reception. Singles DM60-85; doubles DM80-100. All rooms come with bath. Breakfast included.

Gästhof Blauer Bock, Höllgasse 20 (tel. 346 37; fax 323 91), on the Fritz-Schäffer-Promenade. Drab hallways but light, pastel interiors. Buzzing restaurant downstairs overlooks the Danube and serves traditional *Bayerische* de(not-so)lights. Ask for reception at the bar. Singles DM49, with bath and TV DM70; doubles DM98, DM135.

Camping: Zeltplatz Ilzstadt, Halserstr. 34, 94034 Passau (tel. 414 57). Downhill from the youth hostel, 10min. from the *Rathaus.* Cross the Luitpold bridge to the castle side, follow Angerstr. to the right, walk left through the tunnel onto F.-Wagner-Str., veer left up the hill, and take the right fork at the "Kahn/Camping" sign. Or bus #1-4 from Exerzierpl. Reception open 8-10am and 3-10pm. DM9. Under 18 DM7. Under 6 free. Showers included. No camping vehicles. Open May-Oct.

FOOD AND NIGHTLIFE

If you're searching out the student scene, you should head to **Innstraße** near the university. From Ludwigspl., head down Nikolastr. and turn right on Innstr., which runs parallel to the Inn River. The street is lined with good, cheap places to eat and, more importantly, drink—the night-time action kicks off as early as 7pm. **Tengelmann,** on Ludwigstr. at Grabengasse, provides cheap **supermarket** eats (open Mon.-Fri. 8am-8pm, Sat. 7:30am-4pm). Another supermarket option is **Spar,** Residenzpl. 13 (open Mon. 7:30am-6:30pm, Tues.-Fri. 7:30am-6pm, Sat. 7:30am-1pm).

Mensa, Innstr. 29, offers cafeteria meals (DM2.40-4.50). Any student ID will do. From Ludwigspl., follow Nikolastr., turn right onto Innstr., head under the bridge, and at #29 take the stairs up and turn right. Then head for the farthest entrance on the left (15min.). Or bus #3: "Universität" (every 20min. from Exerzierpl.). The *Mensa* (downstairs) is open Mon.-Thurs. 8am-4pm, Fri. 8am-3pm; July-Aug. Mon.-Thurs. 8am-3:30pm, Fri. 8am-3pm. A smaller **cafeteria** upstairs with snacks (no ID required) is open similar hours.

Innsteg, Innstr. 13 (tel. 355 03), one block from Nikolastr. and popular with students from morning 'til nite. Black-painted interior, yet as inviting to non-revolutionaries as to Marlyn Manson devotees. Nurse a beer (*Maß* DM7.80) on the balcony over the riverbank. Daily menu DM5-21. Salads DM5-17. Open daily 10am-1am.

Café Duft, Theresienstr. 22. Folky indoor and outdoor cafe with little lighted trees and an aquatic theme. Lip-smackin' good fruit-topped mueslix DM4.50; breakfast combos DM9-19. Soups DM5-6. Salads DM10-16. Entrees DM9-14. Open Mon.-Fri. 9am-1am, Sat.-Sun. 10am-1am. Kitchen open until 11pm.

Ratskeller, Rathauspl. 2 (tel. 26 30; fax 368 98). A bustling restaurant in the back of the *Rathaus* with picturesque outdoor seating overlooking the Danube. Salads DM4. Daily "local cuisine" specials DM8-17. Open daily 10am-11pm.

Wirtshaus Bayersche Löwe, Dr.-Hans-Kapfinger-Str. 3 (tel. 958 01 11). Authentic—or at least that's what the waves of tourists seem to think. For big German food and appetites, try either *Knödel* or *Rostbrat Würstel,* both with *Kraut* (DM8.50). Wolf your meal down with a *Brezn* (DM1.50), or soup or salad (DM6-10). Beer DM3.60-4. Open daily 9am-1am.

Camera, on Frauengasse, right around the corner from the McDonald's on Ludwigspl., is the city center's grooviest student dance lair. Its stark black exterior foreshadows an underground pit of student angst and inebriation. Open 10pm-2am.

Passau's beautiful Baroque architecture achieves its zenith in the sublime **Stephans-dom.** Hundreds of cherubs, sprawled across the ceiling, purse their lips as the **world's largest church organ** stands erect above the choir. Its 17,774 pipes can accommodate five organists at once. (Open Mon.-Sat. 8-11am and 12:30-6pm. Free. Organ concerts May-Oct. Mon.-Sat. noon, DM4, students and seniors DM2; Thurs. at 7:30pm, DM10, students and seniors DM5; no concerts on holidays.) Behind the cathedral is the **Residenzplatz,** lined with former patrician dwellings, as well as the **Residenz,** erstwhile home of Passau's bishops. The **Domschatz** (cathedral treasury) within the *Residenz* houses an extravagant collection of gold and tapestries purchased by the bishops with the wealth they tithed from their flocks (May-Oct. Mon.-Fri. 10am-4pm; DM2, children DM1). Hour-long tours (in German) meet at the Dompl. daily (April-Oct. Mon.-Sat. 10:30am and 2:30pm, Sun. 2:30pm; DM4.50).

Nearby stands the Baroque church of **St. Michael,** built and gilded by the Jesuits (open Tues.-Sun. 9am-5pm; Nov.-Jan. and March 10am-4pm; DM3, students DM1.50). The less opulent, 13th-century Gothic **Rathaus** was appropriated from a wealthy merchant in 1298 to house the city government. The *Rathaus Trunksaal* (Great Hall) is a masterpiece showcasing rich, wooden paneling and dark marble (open Easter-May 15 10am-4pm; May 16-Sept. 30 10am-5pm; Oct. Mon.-Fri. 10am-4pm; DM2, students DM1). The renowned **Passauer Glasmuseum** (tel. 350 71; fax 317 12), next to the *Rathaus* in the Wilder Mann hotel houses 30,000 examples of glasswork documenting the last 300 years of glass-making (open daily 10am-4pm; DM5, students DM3, children under 16 accompanied by parents free).

Over the *Luitpoldbrücke,* across the river and up the footpath, is the **Veste Oberhaus,** former palace of the bishopric (open early April-Oct. Tues.-Sun. 11:30am-5pm). Once a place of refuge for the bishop and a prison for various enemies of the cloth, the stronghold now contains the magnificently placed and proud-looking **Cultural History Museum** (tel. 39 63 12), in which 54 rooms of art and artifacts span the last 2000 years; the museum's second-floor restrooms offer an incredible city-wide lookout point (open March-Jan. Tues.-Thurs. and Sat.-Sun. 9am-5pm, Fri. 9am-7pm; DM6, students DM3). The same bus that goes to the hostel also stops in front of the Veste Oberhaus (every 30min. from the Rathauspl.; last bus leaves the Oberhaus at 5:15pm). In the heart of the *Altstadt,* bright, arched skylights shelter the **Museum Moderner Kunst,** Braugasse 17 (tel. 340 91; fax 340 93). The rotating art exhibitions are excellent (DM8, students and children DM5; open Tues.-Sun. 10am-6pm).

■ Landshut

Though the Wittelsbachs are perhaps better remembered for some of their more recent family members, residents of Landshut are quick to point out that the House of Wittelsbach did not always call Munich or any of the *Königsschlößer* home. Landshut served as the main seat of government for Max and Ludwig's ancestors until 1255, and even after that remained the capital of Lower Bayern. The city, just half an hour by train from Munich, frolics with style during the **Landshuter Hochzeit,** a three-week medieval orgy with authentic (read: excessive) feasting, jousting, dancing, and period plays. First celebrated in 1475 and resurrected in 1903, the festival, re-enacting the magnificent *Hochzeit* (wedding) that Duke Ludwig arranged for his son Georg and his bride Hedwig, takes place every four years. Modern-day knights and ladies will put on their best boots and wedding dresses, respectively, from June 28 to July 20 in 2001; information and tickets are available from the tourist office.

The Landshut *Altstadt* features rows of colorful gabled Gothic and Baroque houses filled with glitzy shops and cafes. The proud, light greenish-beige **Rathaus** (tel. 88 12 16) stands at the center bearing Renaissance and neo-Gothic architectural facades. Murals inside the *Prunksaal* (main hall) upstairs capture the original wedding (open Mon.-Fri. 2-3pm; free). Across from the *Rathaus* stands the **Stadtresidenz,** the first Renaissance-style palace to be built in Germany (1533-37). Its gleaming white classical facade conceals a spacious courtyard with arcades of distinct Italian influence. The **Stadtresidenz Museum** (tel. 226 38) upstairs grants peeks at gloriously decadent palace rooms from the 16th to the 18th century and also houses a regional collection of art with works from the 16th and 17th centuries. (Tours April-Sept. daily 9am-noon and 1-5pm, last tour 4:30pm; Oct.-March daily 10am-noon and 1-4pm, last tour 3:30pm; 45min; DM3, students DM2.) Geometrically intriguing bricks zig-zag the 130m spire of **St. Martin's Kirche.** Inside you can see the tasteful features, including 16th-century choir stalls and the late Gothic **Madonna and Child** elaborately carved by Hans Leinberger in 1518 (open April-Sept. daily 7am-6:30pm; Oct.-March 7am-5pm). Further up the main street a sign points to **Burg Trausnitz** (tel. 226 38). To the left and up the crooked brick stairway (5-10min.) sits a hefty brick and red-tiled fortress built in 1204. The hard, seemingly impenetrable exterior conceals a soft yellow courtyard with tiers of delicate arches. The castle was the luxurious abode of the Wittelsbacher Princes of Bavaria-Landshut until 1503. The highly amusing "Narrentreppe" (Fool's staircase) inside displays frescoed scenes from the famous Italian folk plays, the **Commedia dell'Arte.** The castle interior can only be seen with a German-language tour, but you can borrow an English translation of the guide's words. (Same times and tours as *Stadtresidenz* Museum. DM4, students and seniors DM3.) A free shuttle runs from the *Burg* to the *Altstadt* (Sat.-Sun. 1:20-6:50pm, every 30min.).

Landshut is best reached by **train** from Munich (2-3 per hr.; 45min.-1hr.) or Regensburg (2 per hr.; 45min.). From the station, it's a 25-minute walk into town. Walk straight on Luitpoldstr.; follow the curve left and cross the bridge. Go through the town gates to your left, then continue straight ahead on Theaterstr. to Altstadtstr. and turn left at the end, and the *Rathaus* will be ahead on the right. Or use **public transportation;** all buses that stop at the station run to the center of town (one-way DM2; day card DM2.70). The **tourist office** *(Verkehrsrein),* Altstadtstr. 315 (tel. 92 20 50; fax 892 75), in the *Rathaus,* has primitive city maps for free or better ones for DM2. There's no private room finding service, but they will provide a list of available rooms; prices plummet beyond the magical "20-minute radius" from the city center. Pick up a pamphlet on the history of the wedding procession (open Mon.-Fri. 9am-noon and 1:30-5pm, Sat. 9am-noon). **St. Michael's Apotheke,** Luitpoldstr. 58, lists on-call **pharmacies** (Mon.-Tues. 8:30am-1pm and 2-6:30pm, Thurs. 8:30am-1pm and 2-7pm, Wed. and Fri. 8:30am-1pm and 2-6pm, Sat. 8:30am-12:30pm). The **post office,** 84028 Landshut, is just to the left of the train station as you exit (open Mon.-Fri. 7:30am-6pm, Sat. 8am-noon). The **telephone code** is 0871.

The **Jugendherberge (HI)** is at Richard-Schirrmann-Weg 6 (tel. 234 49; fax 27 49 47). From the tourist office, go up Altstadtstr. and follow the signs starting to the left of the "Burg Trausnitz" sign. Pass the stairs leading to the *Burg,* and a few steps farther on your right follow Richard-Schirrmann-Weg to the end. The elegant modern villa sits on quiet, green grounds overlooking town. (Reception open Mon.-Fri. 9am-noon and 5-8pm, Sat.-Sun. 5-8pm. DM20-29. Breakfast included. Sheets DM5.50. Closed Dec. 23-Jan. 7.) One of the more affordable places in town is the **Pfälzer Weinstube Heigl,** Herrngasse 385 (tel. 891 32; fax 67 01 56), in the city center. Walk right from the *Rathaus* and take the fourth right onto Herrngasse. The rooms are drab, but after an exceedingly cheery day in the colorful *Altstadt,* maybe you'll even be thankful (singles DM58, with bath DM67;·doubles DM92, with bath DM102). Halfway between the *Hauptbahnhof* and the *Altstadt,* **Hotel Park Café,** Papierstr. 36 (tel. 693 39; fax 63 03 07), offers the bare necessities of a room. From the station, walk straight on Luitpoldstr., take a left on Stethaimerstr., and a right onto Papierstr. (15min.; singles DM55-95; doubles DM95-160; breakfast included). **Café Cappuccino,** Altstadtstr. 337 (tel. 270 92), back through the passageway, has tasty daily specials, hearty *Schweineschitzel* (DM10.90), as well as salads (DM7-14), pasta (DM12-13), and, of course, cappuccino (DM3.90; open Mon.-Thurs. 9am-midnight, Fri.-Sat. 9am-1am, Sun. 2-11pm). A fruit and vegetable **market** appears Monday through Thursday and Saturday (7am-noon) in the *Altstadt,* and Friday on Am alten Viehmarkt (6am-1pm). **HL Markt,** Dreisaltigkeitspl. 177, provides **groceries** (open Mon.-Fri. 8am-8pm, Sat. 7am-4pm).

BAYERN (BAVARIA)

■ Straubing

Perched on the fringe of the Bayerischer Wald near the Danube, Straubing lets down its medieval hair for the annual 10-day **Gäubodenvolksfest** (Aug 7-17 in 1998). The festival, which started as an agricultural fair in 1812 under King Max, has since evolved into a massive beer-guzzling phenomenon second in size only to *Oktoberfest.* Seven enormous beer tents welcome over a million revelers, who, after imbibing a few liters of the local brews, blow their wad on a bevy of amusement park rides. Adjoining the *Volksfest* is the **Ostbayernschau** (East Bavarian Show), a regional trade and industry exhibition (read: more beer; Aug. 8-16 in 1998). Both are held in "Am Hagen," the *Fest* area 10 minutes north of the Markt. During the rest of the year, Straubing serves as a convenient entrance to the Bayerischer Wald.

Orientation and Practical Information Straubing is easily reached by train from Regensburg (DM11.80) or Passau (DM18.80). The *Altstadt* lies northwest of the train station, five minutes away on foot. Cross the street in front of the station, and follow it straight past the post office as it curves right and turns into Bahnhofstr. Cross the foot bridge and continue down Steinergasse to the pastel green turreted tower. On your left after you pass through the clock tower arch is the **tourist office,** Theresienpl. 20 (tel. 94 43 07; fax 94 41 03), which has free maps and extensive brochures on Straubing and neighboring towns. It finds rooms (DM25-30 per person) for a DM3 fee (open Mon.-Wed. 9am-5pm, Thurs. 9am-6pm; May-Sept. also Sat. 9am-noon). German **tours** of the town leave from the tourist office (June to mid-Sept. Wed. 2pm and Sat. 10:30am; DM3, students and seniors DM1, under 6 free; English tours by appointment DM60). For **train** info, call 194 19. **Rent bikes** at **Bund Naturschutz,** Ludwigspl. 14, first floor (tel. 25 12), for DM8 with a DM50 deposit (open Mon.-Fri. 9am-noon and 1-5pm). For the **weather,** call 011 64. Lists of available **pharmacies** are posted at **Agnes Bernauer Apotheke,** Bahnhofstr. 16 (tel. 806 75; open Mon-Fri. 8am-6pm, Sat. 8am-noon). The **post office,** Bahnhofspl. 1, 94315 Straubing (tel. 86 10), sits across from the train station (open Mon.-Fri. 7:30am-12:30pm and 2-7pm, Sat. 9am-12:30pm). The **telephone code** is 09421.

Accommodations The **Jugendherberge (HI),** Friedhofstr. 12 (tel. 804 36; fax 120 94), is 10 minutes from the train station (within earshot). Turn right from the front entrance of the station and follow the curve of the main road left. Turn immediately right onto Schildhauerstr. as it curves into Äußere-Passauer-Str., by the "Passau" sign. A crosswalk and a *Jugendherberge* sign pointing left up Friedhofstr. follows; the hostel is on your right. Though the building is old and some rooms are cramped, this is a family place where cleanliness is king. Doubles are available if you're lucky, but most rooms are 4-, 6-, or 8-beds. (Reception open 7-9am and 5-10pm. Lockout 9am-5pm. 10pm curfew, but keys available with DM10 deposit. DM16.50. Showers between 6-8am and 5-10pm. Breakfast included. Sheets DM5.50. Open April-Oct.)

The cheapest and most convenient beds can be found at **Pension Fürst,** Theresienpl. 32 (tel. 107 92). Follow the directions to the *Altstadt,* turning left at the tourist office; it's on the left just past the gold figure. Not the most aesthetically pleasing locale, but central and cheap (singles DM30; doubles DM60; no breakfast). A bit further down is the **Weißes Rößl,** Landshuterstr. 65 (tel. 325 81), on the left. It's sweet staff runs a pacific ship (singles DM35; doubles DM65; breakfast included).

Food Fresh fruits and vegetables are sold at the **market** on Ludwigspl. (open Mon.-Thurs. and Sat. 7am-noon, Fri. 7am-5pm). A **farmer's market** is also held on Saturdays at Theresienpl. The restaurant in the **Hotel Bischershof,** Frauenhofer 16, just past the main pedestrian area, serves salads (DM3-9), grill specialties (DM13-21), and super cheap beer (*Maß* DM5.80). There's a beer garden out back (open Mon.-Sat. 11am-2:30pm and 5:30pm-1am, Sun. 11am-1am). **Metzgerei Königsbauer,** Ludwigspl. 6 (tel. 815 94), near the *Stadtturm,* serves a hefty lunch crowd at its *Stehcafé* (standing cafe); every entree is also available *zum Mitnehmen* (take-out), including *Wiener-schnitzel, Wurst, Knödel,* and every other German meat specialty (DM2-10; open Mon.-Fri. 7:30am-6pm, Sat. 7:30am-4pm). **Norma,** Bahnhofstr. 14, on the left as you walk into town, has cheap groceries (open Mon.-Fri. 8:30am-6pm, Sat. 8am-1pm).

Sights The five-turreted gothic **watchtower** in the middle of the market square is the city symbol. Erected in the 14th century, the teal-green structure with an inset gold figure of Mary splits the Marktplatz. (Tours in German April-Oct. Thurs. 2pm, Sat.-Sun. 10:30am; DM5, students DM3.) To the right, Ludwigspl. hosts the daily fruit and vegetable market (see above). The **St. Peter's** complex houses a medieval grave-yard with wrought-iron crosses and gravestones from as far back as the 13th century, a Romanesque basilica from roughly 1180, and three Gothic chapels, including one with a red marble epitaph devoted to the memory of Agnes Bernauer (see below). Tours depart from the tourist office (1½hr.; Wed. and Sat. 2pm; DM5, students DM3). The **Gäubodenmuseum,** Fraunhoferstr. 9 (tel. 818 11), off the main square, houses exhibits from the Early Bronze Age and from the "Roman Find" of 1950, as well as a collection of regional art and folklore (open Tues.-Sun. 10am-4pm; DM4, under 19 DM3). At the end of the street, turn right down Zollergasse and around to the late-Gothic **Karmelitenkirche,** Albrechtsgasse 21, with a stunning Baroque interior. Angels and disciples peer down from the lavish gold altar and stolid white columns.

One block down on Burggasse, the **Ursulinenkirche** suffers behind an off-putting white stone facade. Built from 1736-1741 by the renowned Asam Brothers as their last joint endeavor, the interior exhibits all the opulent, overbearing kitsch of Rococo. Peach marble columns snake up to the ceiling, lavishly covered in flashy gold and fanatic frescoes. Back down across Fürstenstr. on the banks of the Danube, parts of the **Herzogsschloß** date from 1356. Most of the palace interior is closed to the public, its innards clogged with bureaucracy. A few renovated floors house a new state museum (tel. 211 14) with a rather bland exhibition of images of worship from the 17th to the 20th century (open Tues.-Sun. 10am-4pm; DM4, under 19 DM3). Joint entrance to both the state and Gäuboden museums DM6, students DM4.50.

Entertainment and Nightlife For complete concert, live music, and club information, pick up the free magazine *in'said* at the tourist office and local bars. Noc-turnal activity oscillates between bad and disco. **Max,** Hebbelstr. 14 (tel. 34 31), hid-den in the shopping complex Gläuboden Park, is the place to trot to techno, trance, rap, and funk (cover DM10; beer DM4.50; open Wed., Fri.-Sat. 10pm-3am).

Straubing recently opened an enormous outdoor swimming pool complex, **AQUA-therm,** Wittelbacherhöhe 50-52 (tel. 86 41 78), with an 80m waterslide, mas-sage parlors, an indoor pool, a steam sauna, and a warm salt-water pool. Follow the tunnel to the left of the *Bahnhof* down Landshuterstr. and turn right onto Dr.-Otto-Höchtl-Str., which becomes Wittelsbacherhöhestr.; it's on the right. Or bus #2 from Ludwigspl.: "Aquatherm." (Open May and mid.-Aug. to mid-Sept. daily 8am-8pm; June to mid.-Aug. 8am-9pm. Closes 1hr. earlier Sat.-Sun. DM5 (after 5:30pm DM3), stu-dents, seniors, and under 16 DM2, under 6 free.) You can go **bowling** at **Keglerhalle am Sportzentrum Peterswöhrd** (tel. 802 48), 20 minutes from the center of town (open daily 10am-midnight).

Every four years in July, Straubing commemorates the 1435 death of Agnes Ber-nauer, the daughter of an Augsburg barber and wife of Duke Albrecht III of Straubing. Albrecht's father, Duke Ernst of Bavaria, was furious when he learned of his son's secret marriage to Agnes, a mere commoner. The senior duke condemned Agnes as a witch and sentenced to drown in the Danube while his son was away. The people of Straubing passionately re-enact the tragic love story during the **Agnes Bernauer Festspiele** (next performance July 1999).

BAYERN (BAVARIA)

■ Regensburg

Located at the northernmost point of the Danube's (long) passage to the Black Sea, Regensburg's *Altstadt* spills onto the numerous islands dodged by the sinuous river as it converges with the Regen. An enchanting city of patrician homes and Imperial administrative houses, Regensburg lies close to two extraordinary sights: **Walhalla,** a tribute from King Ludwig I to German heroes, and the **Donaudurchbruch,** where the Danube has carved a deep gorge between the high, church-dotted, grassy banks. What began as a fortress built by Marcus Aurelius in 179AD became the first capital of Bayern, then the seat of the Perpetual Imperial Diet (the parliament of the Holy Roman Empire, not an eating regimen for chubby monarchs; see **Worms,** p. 392), and finally the site of the first German parliament. But when the government opened the fourth Bavarian university here in 1967, the steady flow of students through town saturated the *Altstadt* with cafes, bars, and shops and creating a hipness that mixes well with Regensburg's Old World aura.

ORIENTATION AND PRACTICAL INFORMATION

Regensburg has easy train and bus connections to both Nürnberg and Passau. The historic *Altstadt* sprawls over a square-shaped cobblestone mecca; the Danube is to the north, the *Hauptbahnhof* and Bahnhofstr. to the south, Kumpfmühlerstr. to the west, and Maximilianstr. to the east. Maximilianstr. leads straight from the train station into the heart of the city.

Tourist Office: Altes Rathaus, on Rathauspl. (tel. 507 44 10; fax 507 44 19). From the train station, walk down Maximilianstr. to Grasgasse and take a left. Follow it as it turns into Obermünsterstr., then turn right at the end to Obere Bachgasse and follow it five blocks down Untere Bachgasse to Rathauspl. The tourist office, to your left across the square, provides a free map, finds rooms (DM1.50), and sells tickets to local sights and events. They also have a 24hr. **private room** information number (tel. 194 14). Open April-Oct. Mon.-Fri. 8:30am-6pm, Sat. 9am-4pm, Sun. 9:30am-4pm; Nov.-March Mon.-Fri. 8:30am-6pm, Sat. 9am-4pm, Sun. 9:30am-2:30pm. Pick up info on the Bayerischer Wald at the **Tourismusverband Ostbayern,** Luitpoldstr. 20 (tel. 58 53 90; fax 585 39 39).

Trains: Station at Bahnhofspl. (tel. 194 19). To Munich (every hr.., 1½hr.), Nürnberg (every 30min.-1hr., 1hr.), and Passau (every 1-2hr., 1-1½hr.). Ticket office open Mon.-Fri. 7:30am-8pm, Sat. 7:30am-6:10pm, Sun. 8am-7pm.

Public Transportation: Routes and schedules of Regensburg's new bus system are available at the service desk in the train station. The transport hub is "Albertstr.," one short block from the station on the right. Single rides cost DM2.50. No night buses. Ask the driver for a **Tages-Ticket** (all-day ticket), which costs DM6 (Mon.-Fri.) or DM4 (Sat.-Sun.). On weekends, groups can buy one **Tages-Ticket** for **2** people (DM4). People on a more extended visit traveling Mon.-Fri. make out best by getting a **12-Streifenkarte** from the kiosk in the station *before* heading for the bus (DM10; punch 3 stripes each way per person). RVV bus #5 leaves from the train station to Walhalla ("Donaustauf Walhallastr."; 25min.) Mon.-Fri. every 20min.-1hr. 5:40am-11:20pm; buses return on a similar schedule 5:25am-10:53pm. On Sat. buses leave every 20min.-1hr. 6:20am-11:20pm; they return 5:40am-10:53pm; on Sun. every hr. 6:20am-11:20pm and return 6:53am-10:53pm (one way DM3.30, children under 15 DM1.70).

Ferries: Boats leave daily from the Steinerne bridge for **Kelheim** at 9am (3½hr. DM15, round-trip DM20), or you can continue on to **Riederburg** up the Altmühl river (Regensburg-Riederburg total 5hr., DM20, round-trip DM28). There is also a boat to **Walhalla** (fancy a visit to Thor?) daily April.-Oct. at 10:30am and 2pm with another departure May-Sept. Tues.-Sun. at noon (45min; one way DM10, children DM5, families DM27; round-trip DM15, children DM7, families DM40). Call **Regensburger Personen Schiffahrt,** Werststr. 8 (tel. 553 59; fax 56 56 68) for more information.

Taxi: tel. 194 10 or 570 00.

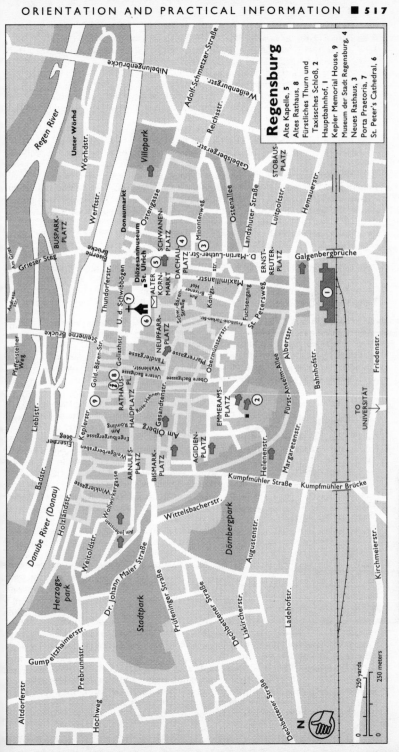

Regensburg

Alte Kapelle, 5
Altes Rathaus, 8
Fürstliches Thurn und
  Taxissches Schloß, 2
Hauptbahnhof, 1
Kepler Memorial House, 9
Museum der Stadt Regensburg, 4
Neues Rathaus, 3
Porta Praetoria, 7
St. Peter's Cathedral, 6

BAYERN (BAVARIA)

Bike Rental: Fahrradverleih PARK and BIKE, am Donaumarktpl. (tel. (0177) 831 12 34; fax (0941) 56 62 64), right on the Danube by the *Altstadt.* Rental 10am-1pm, bike return 7-8pm. DM14-17 per day, children DM10 per day.

Lost and Found: At the *Altes Rathaus* (tel. 507 21 05).

Bookstore: Booox, Goldene Bärenstr. 12, but entrance is on Brückstr. near the Steinerne Brücke (tel. 56 70 14; fax 56 70 84). Tons of discounted art booox, as well as disheveled cartooons of English language quick-reads (DM5). Ooopen Mon.-Fri. 9am-8pm, Sat. 9am-4pm.

Women's Center: Frauen Gesundheits Zentrum, Badstr. 6 (back building). Information on women's rights and health. **Lesbian cafe** (tel. 816 44). Open Tues.-10am-1pm, 2-5pm; Wed. 10am-1pm; Thurs. 2-5pm. In case of emergency, call 242 59 or 240 00.

Crisis Hotline: In case of rape or other trauma, contact **Caritas** (tel. 78 20).

Pharmacy: 24hr. service rotates among the city's pharmacies. To find out which pharmacy is on duty, visit **Maximilian Apotheke,** Maximilianstr. 29, two blocks from the train station. Open Mon.-Tues. and Thurs. 8am-6:30pm, Wed. and Fri. 8am-1:30pm, Sat. 8:30am-1pm.

Hospital: Evangelische Krankenhaus, Obere Bachgasse (tel. 504 00), near the Thurn and Taxis *Schloß,* is the most centrally located.

Emergency: tel. 110. **Police,** Minoritenweg (tel. 192 22).

Post Office: on Bahnhofstr., 93047 Regensburg, next door to the train station. The best place to **exchange money** in Regensburg. Open Mon.-Wed. and Fri. 8am-6pm, Thurs. 8am-7:30pm, Sat. 8am-noon, Sun. 10am-noon.

Telephone Code: 0941.

ACCOMMODATIONS AND CAMPING

Most of Regensburg's cheap lodgings are centrally located, but they fill up in the summer. Reserve, reserve, reserve. If the hotels and *Pensionen* are full, the tourist office might find you a room in a private home. Otherwise, try the hotels in outlying parts of town—all are linked to the center by reliable bus service.

Jugendherberge (HI), Wöhrdstr. 60, 93059 Regensburg (tel. 574 02; fax 524 11), on an island in the Danube. From the station, walk straight ahead on Maximilianstr. all the way to the end. Then turn right at the Apotheke onto Pfluggasse and immediately left at the Optik sign into the tiny Erhardigasse. At the end, take the steps down and walk left over the Eiserne Brücke (iron bridge), which becomes Wöhrdstr. on the other side. The hostel is 5min. away on the right (25min. total). Or bus #3, 8, or 9 from Albertstr. by the station: "Eisstadion." The hostel is a step ahead on the right. Renovated into pleasant though sterile modernity. Reception open 7am-11:30pm. Curfew 1am. DM22. Big breakfast included. Dinner DM9. Sheets DM5.50. Key deposit DM5.50. Reservations encouraged. Partial wheelchair access. Closed mid-Nov. to mid-Jan.

Spitalgarten, St.-Katharinen-Platz 1 (tel. 847 74), inside the walls of the old hospital built by Bishop Konrad IV in the 13th century. Cross the Danube at the Steinerne Bridge and go inside the gate to St. Katherine's on the left. Pass through another gate and go past the left side of the church. Or bus #12 from the station: "Stadtamhof." Head into the lively *Biergarten* and inquire about the *Pension* with the people behind the counter. Reception open until midnight. Singles DM40; doubles DM80. Breakfast included. Call or write well ahead.

Gaststätte Schildbräu, Stadtamhof 24 (tel. 857 24), is over the Steinerne Brücke; follow the street for about 5min. and it's on the right. Or bus #12 from the station: "Stadtamhof." Clean and orderly rooms, each with bath and geraniums spilling from every window. Reception open 7:30am-midnight. Singles DM65; doubles DM120. Breakfast included. Call ahead.

Hotel Peterhof, Fröhliche-Türken-Str. 12 (tel. 575 14; fax 575 61), 5min. from the train station. Walk straight ahead on Maximilianstr. and take the second left onto St.-Peters-Weg, which becomes Fröhliche-Türken-Str. around the corner. Rooms are neat, simple, and definitively wallpapered. The opulent dining hall is covered in butterflies, ribbons, and artificial roses. Singles DM48, with shower DM60, with bath DM80; doubles DM86, with shower DM96, with bath DM114; triples with shower DM135, with bath DM145. Breakfast included.

Hotel Apollo, Neuprüll 17 (tel. 910 50; fax 91 05 70). From Albertstr. by the station, bus #6 (direction: "Klinikum"): "Neuprüll" (15min.; DM2.50) or walk 45min. Proximity to the university and modern furnishings make it worth the trip. Rooms have TVs and telephones. Hotel has a pool, sauna, steam bath, and solarium. Singles DM55, with shower DM65, with bath DM75; doubles DM99, with shower DM110, with bath DM140. Breakfast included.

Camping: Azur-Camping, Am Weinweg 40 (tel. 27 00 25). From Albertstr. (one block in front of the station) bus #11 (direction: "West Bad"): "Westheim." DM10 per adult, DM7 per child under 12, DM7 per tent, with car DM13. Prices lower in the off-season (mid-Jan. to March and Sept. to mid-Dec.).

FOOD

The 17th-century English dramatist and diplomat Sir George Etherege commented that Regensburg's "noble, serene air makes us hungry as hawks"—a laudable attempt to blame his swelling belly on the atmosphere rather than the heavy Bavarian fare and beer typical of the city. A tantalizing number of cafes, bars, and beer gardens await to tempt the Imperial Diet. A plethora of supermarkets in the city, however, will mend the proverbial holes in your pockets: **Tengelmann,** Ernst-Reuter-Platz, up Maximilianstr. from the train station on the right, is a good starting point for the makings of a lazy picnic (open Mon.-Fri. 8:30am-6:30pm, Sat. 7:30am-2pm). To stock up on fruit, vegetables, and other basics, head to the **market** on Dompl. (open March-Oct. Mon.-Sat. 7am-6pm, Sun. 10:30am-6pm). Otherwise, join the rest of Regensburg at a beer garden for a meal of *Würstchen,* pretzels, and of course, *Pils vom Faß* (on tap).

University Mensa, on Albertus-Magnus-Str., in the park, on the university campus. Turn right from the train station and take the bridge over the tracks onto Galgenbergstr. Follow this street for about 20min. and take a right onto Albertus-Magnus-Str. As you emerge from underneath the parking structure, the stairs on the left will lead you up to the *Mensa.* Or bus #6 or #11 (directions: "Klinikum" or "Burgweinting"): "Universität Mensa" from the *Altes Rathaus* or Albertstr. (DM2.50). The cheapest meal in Regensburg, with a lively student crowd. Any student ID will do. Meals DM3.50-6. Open May-July and Nov.-Feb. Mon.-Thurs. 11:15am-1:45pm and 5-7pm, Fri. 11:15am-1:45pm and 5-6:30pm; March-April and Aug.-Oct. Mon.-Thurs. 11:15am-1:30pm and 5-6:30pm, Fri. 11:15am-1:30pm and 5-6pm.

Ambrosius, Brückstr. 5 (tel. 545 40), on the *Altstadt* end of the Steinerne Brucke. Closely knit tables in an odd yellow setting draw wicked diversity. Baguettes, sandwiches, and salads (DM5-14). Breakfast DM4-11. Open daily 10am-1am.

Bistro Rosarium, Hoppestr. 3a (tel. 268 85). At the edge of the superbly landscaped Dörnbergpark. A Bavarian wood-framed restaurant with rose garden, umbrella-covered tables around a fountain, students, beer, and green trees. Pasta dishes (DM11-12), *Schnitzel* (DM13), fresh salads (DM7-13), and beer (DM4.60). Breakfasts start at DM7. Open daily 11am-1am.

Café Orphée, Untere Bachgasse 8 (tel. 529 77), off Rathauspl. A Parisian salon with dark wooden walls, mirrors, candle-lit tables, and alabaster busts. I'm sorry, but are you going to order *that* wine with your entree? Chocolate crepes DM7.80. Baguettes DM7.80. Salads DM7-16. Open daily 9am-1am.

Hinterhaus, Rote-Hahnen-Gasse 2 (tel. 546 61), off Haidpl., down from Rathauspl. A politically grooving grove of left-leaning tables. Excellent vegetarian dishes and salads (DM5-14). Outdoor seating. Open Mon.-Fri. 11am-1am, Sat.-Sun. 6pm-1am.

Beer Gardens

Goldene Ente, Badstr. 32 (tel. 854 55). Under magnificent chestnut trees on the banks of the Danube just across the Eiserner Steg footbridge upstream from the Steinerne Brücke. The oldest inn in Regensburg; during the summer the beer garden is packed with pleasantly pilsnered students. More complex menu inside. Steaks, *Würstchen,* and *Schnitzel* grill for student-friendly prices (DM9-14). Salads

DM5-11.50. Beer starts at DM3.90 for 0.5L. Open Mon.-Sat. 11am-2pm and 5pm-1am, Sun. 10am-1am, though on a nice day, the beer garden is open all afternoon.

Kneitinger Keller, Galgenbergstr. 18 (tel. 766 80), to the right from the station and over the tracks (10min.). Regensburg's largest and most democratic beer garden (1200 seats). Devoted locals, large thirsty tourists, and self-loathing students alike can follow their noses: the smell of beer extends for blocks. *Maß* DM7, six *Würstchen* with bread DM8.20, big pretzels DM3. Open daily 9am-midnight.

Einhorn, Wöhrdstr. 31 (tel. 527 90), down the street from the hostel. A small outdoor garden surrounded by an old graying fence with relaxed folk discussing daily odds and ends. Pasta, meats, and salads (DM7-13). Open daily 6pm-1am.

Wurstküche, Thundorferstr. (tel. 590 98), next to the Steinerne bridge with views of the river. The oldest operating fast food joint in Europe—the 12th-century workers who built the bridge broke for lunch here. Very busy and touristy, even though it looks like a wood shack with tables. Six small, delicious *Würste* from the smoky kitchen come with sauerkraut and bread (DM7.80). Open daily 8am-7pm; Nov.-April Sun. daily 8am-2pm.

SIGHTS

Past eras are present in Regensburg. Behold the monuments built during the last centuries of the Roman Empire, as well as Gothic, Baroque, and Rococo legacies of later empires. The **Porta Praetoria** (a Roman gateway) and ruins from its accompanying wall sketch a hazy outline of the city's original fortifications. They have been incorporated into a house located on Unter-den-Schwibbögen between the *Dom* and the Danube. One block from the river on Niedermünstergasse lies the Dompl., providing a stable foundation for the soaring high-Gothic **St. Peter's Cathedral** and, adjacent to the church, the **Diocese Museum** (tel. 516 88; open April-Nov. Tues.-Sun. 10am-5pm; DM3, students DM1.50). Begun in 1276, the cathedral was finished in 1486, not counting the delicately carved twin 159m spires, which King Ludwig II added in typical grandiose style between 1859 and 1869. Once your eyes adjust to the dim lighting, the collection of richly colored stained glass windows will dazzle you. Also inside the cathedral is the **Domschatz** (treasury; tel. 576 45), a priceless collection of gold and jewels purchased by the Regensburg bishops back in the good old days of indulgences and economic exploitation by the clergy. (Cathedral open April-Oct. daily 6:30am-6pm; Nov.-March 6:30am-4pm. DM4, students DM2. Tours lasting 1¼hr. May-Oct. Mon.-Sat. 10, 11am, and 2pm, Sun. noon and 2pm; Nov.-April Mon.-Sat. 11am, Sun. noon. *Domschatz* open April-Nov. Tues.-Sat. 10am-5pm, Sun. noon-5pm; Dec.-March Fri.-Sat. 10am-4pm, Sun. noon-4pm. DM3, students DM1.50.)

A few blocks away from the cathedral, the Gothic **Altes Rathaus** served as capitol of the Holy Roman Empire until 1803. The sycophantic and impotent Imperial Parliament (the first of many similar bodies in German history) lives on in the **Reichstag Museum,** housed in the *Altes Rathaus.* The differing heights of the chairs reflect the political hierarchy of the legislators. (Tours in German April-Oct. daily every 30min. Mon.-Sat. 9:30am-4pm, Sun. 10am-4pm; Nov.-March 1 per hr.; English tour May-Sept. Mon.-Sat. at 3:15pm. DM5, students and seniors DM2.50, families DM10.)

Reclining in the western portion of the park across from the *Hauptbahnhof,* the **Fürstliches Thurn und Taxissches Schloß** (tel. 504 81 33), originally a Benedictine cloister, was the residence of the Duke of Thurn und Taxis after 1812. Little remains of the Gothic cloister beneath later Baroque additions. The Thurn und Taxis family built a franchise, granted by Kaiser Maximilian in 1490, into a feudal postal empire that had a tight grip over much of Central Europe until the Prussian Post, backed by Bismarck's armies, cancelled it in 1867. This conflict was the proximate cause for a legacy of disgruntled postal workers the world over—it sure upset Oedippa Maas. (Tours April-Oct. daily at 11am, 2, 3, and 4pm; Sat.-Sun. an additional tour at 10am; Nov.-March Sat.-Sun. at 10 and 11am, 2 and 3pm; joint admission to *Schloß* and *Kreuzgang* DM12, students DM10.) The Dukes' beer-brewing namesake, the **Fürstliches Brauerei Thurn und Taxis,** next door to the Kneitinger Keller at Galgenbergstr. 14 (tel. 134), guides visitors through a demonstration of the brewer's art and hands out free samples at the end (reservations requested several weeks in advance; free).

The iconoclastic astronomer and physicist Johannes Kepler died of meningitis in 1630 at the site of the **Kepler Memorial House,** Keplerstr. 5 (tel. 507 34 42). Period furniture, portraits, and facsimiles of Kepler's work are on display. (Open Tues.-Sat. 10am-noon and 2-4pm, tours at 10 and 11am, 2 and 3pm; DM4, students and seniors DM2, families DM8, tour free.) Up the street at Keplerstr. 2 is **Kepler's Wohnhaus,** a colorful house where he hung his hat and spent time with his family. **All-day museum cards** (DM10, students and seniors DM5, families DM20) admit bearers to the Reichstag Museum, Kepler Memorial House, Regensburg Stadt Museum, and the town's modern art gallery; purchase them at the tourist office.

Down the river from Regensburg is **Walhalla** (tel. 96 16 80; fax 96 16 82), an imitation Greek temple poised dramatically on the steep northern bank of the Danube. Ludwig I of Bavaria built the monument between 1830 and 1842 to honor Germans past and present whom he admired. Modeled after the Parthenon in Athens and named after the legendary resting place of Norse heroes, Walhalla stares imposingly down on the river as the boat from Regensburg approaches the dock (see **Practical Information,** p. 516, for ferry information). Ludwig called Walhalla "the child of my love." What a nut. The climb up the steep steps to the monument itself is tough going, but the view of the river and the opposite bank is a golden photo opportunity. In the summer, these hallowed steps provide a lively evening hangout for students who venture here by bikes and car; probably not what poor Ludwig envisioned. Inside the monument are a series of busts of German leaders and military heroes, most of whom history left in oblivion (open April-Sept. daily 9am-5:45pm; Oct. 9am-4:45pm; Nov.-March 10-11:45am and 1-3:45pm; DM3, students DM2). RVV bus #5 leaves from the train station to "Donaustauf Walhallastr." in Walhalla (Mon.-Sat. every 20min. and 1 per hr. on Sun.; 25min.; tickets DM3.30 one way, under 16 DM1.70). See **Public Transportation,** p. 516, for info on special passes.

NIGHTLIFE

Many of the cafes and beer gardens listed above (see **Food,** p. 519) double as local nighttime haunts. And good bars raise inebriation to Walhallian heights. Pick up the free *Logo*—it lists all events and addresses of more worthwhile bars and cafes.

Alte Mälzerei, Galgenbergerstr. 20 (tel. 730 33 or for tickets 757 49; fax 777 34). Regensburg's official cultural center in an old malt factory that is home not only to theater and musical events, but a ramshackle bar with pop, jazz, funk, "ethno," soul, reggae, and blues. Somehow it manages to stay "cool" despite its institutionalism. Check outside on the board for a schedule. Student crowd opts for the outdoor beer garden on summer days; there's an awesome aerial view of the massive Kneitinger Keller. Beer DM4.20-4.80. Open daily 6pm-1am. The Mälzerei is also home to a new little bar, **Cartoon,** just around the corner in the back entrance on Bischof-Werner-Str. (cover DM5-20). Postered with funny old illustrations, it serves pasta, chili, and *Schnitzel* (DM8-12). Open Mon.-Fri. 11am-1am, Sat.-Sun. 2pm-1am. For concert info call 757 38.

Wunderbar, Keplerstr. 11 (tel. 531 30). Young late-nighters pack into one of the only bars open after 1am, just a few staggers from the Steinerne Bridge. Beer starts at DM4.20, but they specialize in extravagant mixed drinks like a "Flying Kangaroo" and "Scorpion" (DM13.50-15). Cocktails DM3, cheaper Sun.-Thurs. 10pm-midnight. Open Mon.-Thurs. and Sun. 10pm-3am, Fri.-Sat. 9pm-3am.

Filmbühne, Hinter der Grieb 8 (tel. 520 51). Keep an eye out for the staircase leading down just within a green gate. Regensburg's funkiest scene attracts a diverse and bizarre crowd. Old film posters, old fans, light bulbs, and strange art scattered everywhere. Open daily 9pm-1am.

Südhaus, Untere Bachgasse 8 (tel. 519 33). One of Regensburg's best discos. Just behind Café Orphée through the little tunnel, past a gargoyled fountain and a huge stone angel with the "Südhaus" sign. Tuesday is "ultimate" alternative night. Thursday is gay night. Beer DM5.50 for 0.3L. Open Mon.-Thurs. 11pm-3am, Fri.-Sat. 11pm-4am. Cover Mon. DM3, Tues.-Thurs. DM5, Fri.-Sat. DM6.

Scala, Gesandtenstr. 6 (522 93), located in the Pustet Passage between Rote-Hahnen-Gasse and Gesandtenstr. Sandwiched by three bars, hipsters bump and grind in this disco club. Open Wed.-Thurs. and Sun. 11pm-3am, Fri.-Sat. 11pm-4am.

■ Near Regensburg: Donaudurchbruch and Kloster Weltenburg

About 35km south of Regensburg, the **Donaudurchbruch** (Danube Passage) winds 5km through magnificent stretch of nature to *Kloster Weltenburg* (Weltenburg Monastery). The lush green slopes lining this sheltered length of the Danube River are dramatically interrupted every few hundred meters by gargantuan white cliffs, which have all been given names by the river captains of the past. (The phallic, free-standing rock has been paradoxically named *Jungfrau*—the virgin.) Gurgling ferries shuttle the oohs and aahs of visitors through the *Donaudurchbruch* from the docks at Kelheim to Europe's oldest Benedictine monastery, **Kloster Weltenburg** (founded 620AD). Squatting on a jut of land at a sharp bend in the Danube, the simple, red-roofed monastery encloses a surprisingly ornate church featuring a powerful, back-lit statue of St. George spearing the last life out of a screeching dragon. A huge fresco on the right shows Christopher Columbus (and the Virgin Mary) discovering America, while high above a playful statue of the church's builder, Cosma Damian Asam (in the red coat), smiles down on all good tourists. The first 400 years of daily prayers in the monastery must have been a little, well, dull, for it wasn't until in 1050AD that the good brothers decided to found the world's first monastery brewery. Taste the product of their labor in the monastery's own beer garden—by far the most popular attraction for visitors (DM4.90 for 0.5L of the holy brew).

A visit to *Kloster Weltenburg* makes an excellent daytrip from Regensburg, but plan ahead. To do the trip in a day, take the daily RBO bus to Kelheim from platform 11 in front of the Regensburg train station at 11:45am; get off at the last stop 40 minutes later. Walk across the parking lot to the Danube riverbank, and buy a round-trip ticket for the ferry (DM9.50, under 17 DM8, under 13 DM6.50, under 5 free, families DM25) which runs every 30-45 minutes daily from mid-March to October. The boat trip to the *Kloster* takes about 50 minutes; allow 35 to 40 minutes for the return (RBO buses return to Regensburg Mon.-Fri. at 4:20 and 5:30pm, Sat. at 6pm, and Sun. at 6:25 and 8:30pm. Round-trip DM14.20; Eurailpass, Interail, German Railpass and Bahncards all valid for the bus trip.) Pack a picnic lunch, and be sure to check schedules at the tourist office before you hop on the bus.

Ess-terminate with Ess-treme Prejudice!

The story of the ess-tset ("ß") begins hundreds of years ago with the Goths, who devised a letter that efficiently did the work of a cumbersome double S with only one stroke, freeing more time for rape and plunder. As time passed, the letter gained fame and renown, featuring prominently in the works of Goethe and Schiller. But once a lovable "letter" as *echt*-ly Germanic as *Gemütlichkeit* and morbid obesity, the ß may soon be a fugitive in its own lands. It is only the most visible victim of a recent series of planned language and spelling reforms concocted by representatives of all of the German-speaking lands of Europe as "a systematic dismantling of anomalies." Thus far, opposition in Germany has been most vocal, with legal challenges cropping up from Weimar to Wiesbaden, and it is increasingly dubious that the reforms will become German law. In Austria and Switzerland, however, all systems still appear to be go for the switch, and *Kinder* are already learning to spell ketchup *"ketschup."* (Other reforms standardize and Germanize the spelling of assimilated foreign words and other eclectically spelled words.) If the ess-tset is exterminated as planned, there will be no way of knowing whether somebody is drinking within limits *(in Maßen)* or excessively *(in Massen)*—so why not opt for the latter?

■ Bayerischer Wald (Bavarian Forest)

A coddled national treasure, the Bayerischer Wald is the largest range of wooded mountains in Central Europe. These 6000kmsq. of peaks (60 of which are over 1000m high) and countless rivers and creeks stretch from the Danube and the Austrian and Czech borders to form a vast hook that lures hikers, campers, and cross-country skiers all through the year. The **Bayerischer Wald National Park,** the first national park in Germany, strictly prohibits any activities that might alter the forest ecosystem. Clearly marked trails lace 8000 hectares (20,000 acres) of forest. You can trek it alone or sign up for guided hiking tours, botanical tours, natural history tours, or tours of virgin woodlands. For information and schedules, contact either the **Nationalparkverwaltung Bayerischer Wald,** Freyunstr., 94481 Grafenau (tel. (08552) 427 43; fax 46 90); the **Dr. Hans Eisenmann Haus,** Böhmstr., 94556 Neuschönau (tel. (08558) 13 00); or the **Landratsamt,** Wolfkerstr., 94078 Freyung (tel. (08551) 571 22; fax 572 44). For news of the rest of the forest, contact the **Tourismusverband Ostbayern,** Luitpoldstr. (tel. 58 53 90; fax 585 39 39), in Regensburg. Pick up a free **encyclopedia** of the Bayerischer Wald at any tourist office in the forest—it's filled to the brim with phone numbers, maps, and listings.

The Bayerischer Wald is much more than just a verdant paradise; palaces, churches, and castle ruins are tucked away in tiny villages throughout the region. **Burgruine Hals,** an extensive castle ruin high on a woody cliff north of Passau, dates from the 12th century. The 18th-century **Wiesenfelden** (lush gardens) surround the ruins. For information contact **Herr Hubert Weinzierl** (tel. (09966) 777) or the **tourist office,** 94344 Wiesenfelden (tel. (09966) 94 00 17). **Frauenzell's** 15th-century Benedictine church is lavishly *barockisiert* (Baroquified), and parts of the **Annunciation Church** in **Chammünster** date from the 12th century.

The Bavarian region is famous for its crafts, particularly **glass-blowing,** associated with the forest for the past 700 years. The glass produced here is prized throughout the world, particularly the dark green *Waldglas* (forest glass). Every little forest village seems to have its own *Glashütte*. For more information, contact the **Bergglashütte Weinfurter,** Ferienpark Geyersberg (tel. (08551) 60 66), in Freyung; the **Freiherr von Poschinger Kristallglasfabrik,** Moosauhütte (tel. (09926) 940 10), in Frauenau; or **Joska Waldglashütte** (tel. (09924) 77 90) in Bodenmais.

The remoteness of Bayerischer Wald towns attract few English-speaking visitors, but the park maintains a heavy flow of Germans seeking healthy, sedate vacations. Use the towns below as springboards from which to explore the nooks and crannies of this mountain region. An impressive 17 **HI youth hostels** dot the forest; Regensburg's tourist office (see p. 516) has a helpful brochure as well as current addresses and phone numbers of the hostels. The towns of **Cham** and **Regen** can be reached by **train** (Cham from Regensburg or Nürnberg via Schwanndorf; Regen from Regensburg, Munich, or Passau via Platting). **Buses** run from Regensburg and Straubing to Cham and from Passau and Straubing to Regen. **Igel Buses** encompass four different regions of the national park proper; they run out of Grafenau, just outside the park.

ZWIESEL

Zwiesel makes an excellent hub for scouting the heart of the Bayerischer Wald, because of the abundance of train connections running through it. A skier's haven in the winter, in summer its focus flips to producing postmodern wine glasses. Zwiesel prides itself on an 800-year history of glass-making. Just north of town lies **Glas Park,** a village of glass-blowing houses that demonstrate how delicate fancies are created to awed spectators. Six buses per day shuttle to the Glas Park from the Stadtpl. (Mon.-Fri. beginning at 9:27am; last return at 6:37pm; check the tourist office). The **Waldmuseum** (forest museum), Am Stadtpl. 29 (tel. 608 88), behind the *Rathaus,* tells the tinkly tale of glass-making in the region. (Open May 15-Oct. 15 Mon.-Fri. 9am-5pm, Sat.-Sun. 10am-noon and 2-4pm; Oct. 16-May 14 Mon.-Fri. 10am-noon and 2-5pm, Sat.-Sun. 10am-noon; DM3, with *Kurkarte* DM2.50, students DM1.) The **tourist office,** Stadtpl. 27 (tel. 13 08; fax 56 55), in the *Rathaus,* provides maps and finds **private rooms** for free (DM20-30). From the station, turn right and walk downhill on Dr.-Schott-Str. After a few blocks, veer left onto Innenriederstr. and cross the bridge, then take the gentle left onto Stadtpl.; the *Rathaus* signs pointing to the acute left lead to the *Rathaus* parking lot (open Mon.-Fri. 8:30am-5:30pm, Sat. 10am-noon; Nov.-Dec. 8:30am-5:30pm). **Trains** run hourly from Plattling on the Nürnberg-Passau line (1hr., DM14.20). The **post office**, Dr.-Schott-Str. 55, 94227 Zwiesel, **changes money** (open Mon.-Fri. 8am-noon and 2-5:30pm, Sat. 8-11am). The **telephone code** is 09922.

The **Jugendherberge**, Hindenburgstr. 26 (tel. 10 61; fax 601 91), is a 30-minute walk from the station. Follow the directions to Stadtpl., continue past the *Rathaus*, and turn right onto Frauenauerstr. Continue straight for 10 minutes and turn left on Hindenburgstr. (one block after the "AOK" sign); the hostel is just over the hill. Or bus #1 from the station: "Jugendherberge." (DM2; 1 per hr.). This clean hostel is the choicest accommodation in the Bayerischer Wald. "*Klein aber fein*" (tiny but shiny), repeats the proud hostel mother. (Reception open 5-7pm. Curfew 10pm, but they'll give you a key. DM20. Breakfast included. Sheets DM5.50.) The **Eiscafé-Pizzeria Rialto,** Stadtpl. 23, has a sweet bar and outdoor seating on a busy street; feed the hungry beast with pizza, pasta, or an ice cream confection (DM6-11). **Lidl**, up the street from the tourist office at the intersection of Stadtpl. and Oberzwieselanerstr., is a convenient and cheap supermarket (open Mon.-Fri. 8:30am-6pm, Sat. 8am-1pm).

BODENMAIS

Bodenmais, at the heart of the forest amidst hills of velvet moss, is reachable by a miniature train ride from Zwiesel past cows, trees, and tiny red tile-roofed houses. The tourist-luring **Austen Glashütte**, on Bahnhofstr. (tel. 70 06), across from the *Rathaus*, showcases and sells wineglasses, jewelry, and cheaper fragile trinkets. You can view the glass being blown (Mon.-Fri. 9am-1pm and 2-6pm, Sat. 10am-2pm; mid-May to mid-Oct. also Sun. 10am-noon and 1-4pm), then enjoy a local brew in a personally-monogrammed souvenir *Stein* (DM3.90). **Hans und Hans'l,** two endearing Bavarians (complete with *Lederhosen*), sing and play the accordion on Fridays (1-5pm). (*Glashütte* open Mon.-Fri. 9am-6pm, Sat. 9am-2pm.)

The **Waldbahn** (adorable, no?) will drop you off literally at the doorstep of the **tourist office,** Bahnhofstr. 56 (tel. 778 35; fax 778 50), in the modern *Rathaus*. They'll give you a free book of accommodations and hiking trails, and offer a *Wanderpaß* (DM3) with tips and trails for hiking (open Mon.-Fri. 8am-6pm, Sat.-Sun. 9am-noon). Outside the tourist office is a rather impressive info center with computerized room-finding service and a weather station. **Trains** make the 20-minute journey between Zwiesel and Bodenmais roughly every hour (daily 6:25am-11:20pm to Bodenmais, 6am-10:50pm from Bodenmais). For a **taxi** call 484. Rent mountain **bikes** (DM20 per day) or **skis** at **Sport Weinberger,** Jahnstr. 20 (tel. 90 22 73), 10 minutes from the station down Bahnhofstr. The **telephone code** is 09924.

Bodenmais has 3600 inhabitants and almost twice that many hotel beds. Even so, this spa town fills quickly in summer and winter; call ahead. The **Jugendherberge,** Am Kleinen Arber (tel. 281; fax 850), is 8km from town in the mountains, a whopping 1½-hour hike (DM20; breakfast included). A right on Bahnhofstr. and then a right up Scharebenstr. will lead you to the trail. Unless you intend to visit every *Jugendherberge* in Germany, the trek to the hostel is probably not worth it; many of the private rooms and *Pensionen* are inexpensive (DM20-35). Try the computerized room-finding service (24hr.), or attack the tourist office's accommodations booklet with gusto. The **Schmanterl Metzgerei Grillstube,** Bahnhofstr. 21, on the corner of Bergknapp-str., serves *Leberkäs* with potato salad (DM8.90), *Curry-Wurst,* and fries (open Mon.-Fri. 8:30am-8pm). Grab a string of sausage, hop into the bakery up the street for *Brötchen,* and disappear into the forest—leave a trail of bread crumbs (bakery open Mon.-Fri. 7am-6pm, Sat. 7am-12:30pm; forest open daily 24hr.).

FRAUENAU

Travel on a toy train to the "glassy heart of the Bayerischer Wald," to the fragile town of Frauenau. Majestic wooded mountains circumscribe the town, and the idyllic lake to the north reflects the pristine scenery. Near the borders of the Czech Republic and away from the busier regions of Bayern, Frauenau remains virgin land, virtually untouched by tourists, with plenty of space for private exploration. To reach the **lake** (*Trinkwasser Talsperre*), take Hauptstr. up as it curves left, then right on Wasserhäuslweg (45min.). A hiking trail on the left of Wasserhäuslweg leads to Zwiesel.

The **Glasmuseum**, Am Museumspark 1 (tel. 718), sprawled across a beautiful green landscape, holds 2500 years of glass treasures (open May 15-Oct. 31 daily 9am-5pm; Dec. 20-May 14 10am-4pm; DM2.50, under 15 DM1, under 6 free). The friendly **tourist office**, Hauptstr. 12, 94258 Frauenau (tel. 710; fax 17 99), provides information on hiking trails, hotels, holiday farms, and *Pensionen*. Turn left from the station and then right up Hauptstr. For DM1 they will find **private rooms** (DM20-25) or set up farm holidays, a bargain at DM15-19 (open Mon.-Fri. 8am-noon and 1:30-5pm; May 15-Oct. 15 also Sat. 9:30-11:30am). The tourist office also rents **bikes** (DM10 per day). You can reach Frauenau by regular **train** from Zwiesel along the Zwiesel-Grafenau line (9 per day; to Frauenau 6:40am-8:12pm; from Frauenau 6:05pm-9:25pm). The **Jugendherberge**, Hauptstr. 29a (tel. 735), is in the same building as the post office, just uphill from the tourist office. The green hospital-like building is not so hospitable—stay in Zwiesel instead (DM16.50; breakfast included; sheets DM5.50). Every Thursday there's a farmer's **market** from 7am to noon at the foot of the *Rathaus* on Hauptstr. The **telephone code** is 09926.

SLEEPING AROUND IN THE BAYERISCHER WALD

Jugendherberge Neuschönau (HI), Herbergsweg 2, 94556 Neuschönau (tel. (08553) 60 00; fax 829), nestles in the heart of the forest, a 17km bus ride from the train station at Grafenau on the bus from Spiegelau or Neuschönau. (DM22. Breakfast included. Sheets DM5.50.) **Jugendherberge Mauth (HI)**, Jugendherbergestr. 11, 94151 Mauth (tel. (08557) 289; fax 15 81), is accessible from Passau (DM20; breakfast included; sheets DM5.50). Most Bayerischer Wald towns offer several *Pensionen* and *Gasthöfe* that cost DM18-30 per person (breakfast included; prices slightly higher in summer and around Christmas). The **Nationalparkverwaltung Bayerischer Wald** offers a big brochure on **camping** in the Bayerischer Wald. Drop by their offices in Regensburg or write for it. For further info, contact the **Verkehrsamt Cham**, Propsteistr. 46 (tel. (09971) 49 33), or the **Haus des Gastes** in Regen (tel. (09921) 29 29).

▉ Eichstätt

Sheltered in the valley of the Altmühl river and surrounded by the **Naturpark Altmühltal** (the largest nature preserve in Germany), the small university and episcopal town of Eichstätt flaunts its moments of lavish architecture with a self-proclaimed Mediterranean flair.

Orientation and Practical Information The Eichstätt **train station** is a 15- to 30-minute ride from Ingolstadt (DM9.60). A little train shuttles the 5km between Eichstätt *Bahnhof* and Eichstätt *Stadt*, leaving from track 1 (6am-11:30pm every 30min.-1hr., 9min., DM2.40). The **tourist office**, Kardinal-Preysing-Platz 14 (tel. 988 00; fax 98 80 30), has free maps and helps find private rooms (DM25-30) for free. From the train station, walk right and follow the information sign across the bridge (Spitalbrücke). Turn right on Residenzpl. and follow the bend left to Leonrodpl., then bear right past the church until you reach Kardinal-Preysing-Platz on the left; the tourist office is up the street on the right. (Open April-Oct. Mon.-Sat. 9am-6:30pm, Sun. 4:30-6:30pm; Nov.-March Mon.-Thurs. 9am-noon and 2-4 pm, Fri. 9am-noon.) When they're closed, go next door to the tourist information office for **Naturpark Altmühltal**, Notre Dame 1 (tel. 987 60; fax 98 76 54). Cloistered in a former monastery, they provide information on trails and paths in the nature reserve (open Easter-Oct. Mon.-Sat. 9am-5pm, Sun. 10am-5pm). **Exchange money** at **Volksbank,** on the Marktplatz (open Mon.-Wed. 8am-4:30pm, Thurs. 8am-5:30pm, Fri. 8am-2pm). Rent **bikes** at the **Fahrradgarage,** Herzoggasse 3 (tel. 21 10 or 899 87), in the tiny alley that leads from Marktplatz to the footbridge (DM12 per day). **Heinz Glas,** Industrie 18 (tel. 30 55), will rent you a **canoe** for a cruise down the Altmühl River (DM20 per day Mon.-Fri., DM25 Sat.-Sun.; under 12 50% off). A convenient **pharmacy** is **Dom Apotheke,** Dompl. 16 (tel. 15 20; open Mon.-Fri. 8am-12:30pm and 2-6pm, Sun. 8am-noon). The **post office,** 85072 Eichstätt, awaits at Dompl. 7 (open Mon.-Fri. 8:30am-5:30pm, Sat. 9am-noon). The **telephone code** is 08421.

Accommodations and Food Eichstätt's **Jugendherberge (HI),** Reichenaustr. 15 (tel. 980 40; fax 98 04 15), is clean, modern, spacious, and comfortable. Follow directions to Willibaldsburg (see **Sights,** below), but turn right halfway up Burgstr. onto Reichenaustr at the *Jugendherberge* sign. (Reception open 8-9am and 5-7pm. Lockout 10am. Curfew 10pm, but they'll give you a key if you want to party the night away. Bed in 6-bed dorm DM22. Breakfast included. Sheets DM5.50. Closed Dec.-Jan.) To get to the university **Mensa,** Universitätsallee 2 (tel. 93 14 60), walk down toward the end of Ostenstr. and hang a right onto Universitätsallee; it's on the right. Buy a card (DM3) from the cashier on the first floor. (Cashier open noon-1:30pm. Student ID required. Meals DM2-4.40. *Mensa* open Mon.-Fri. 11:30am-2pm during term; summer 11:30am-1:30pm; open mid-Sept.-Aug. 5.) A relaxed **cafeteria** on the first floor has an outdoor garden (open Mon.-Thurs. 8:15am-7pm, Fri. 8:15am-3pm; summer Mon.-Fri. 8:15am-2:45pm). In town there's **Ammonit,** Luitpoldstr. 19 (tel. 29 29), a student hangout with beer (DM4-8) and other cafe snacks (DM7-15; open Mon.-Fri. 9:30am-1am, Sat.-Sun. 9:30am-2am). **La Grotta,** Marktplatz 13 (tel. 72 80), has affordable pizzas and pasta (DM8-15; open Wed.-Mon. 10:30am-11pm).

Sights The **Willibaldsburg** conspicuously watches over the town from its high perch across the river. To reach the castle from the train station, take a right; at the main intersection, turn right and follow the main street one block to turn left onto Burgstr. The 14th-century castle now houses the **Jura-Museum** (Jurassic Museum; tel. 29 56), filled with fossils from the Jurassic period found in the Altmühltal Valley, once covered by the a vast prehistoric sea. Dinosaur movies (no Spielberg) are screened daily at 10:15am and 2:30pm. The **Museum für Ur- und Frühgeschichte** (tel. 60 01 74), also in the Willibaldsburg, picks up the story at the debut of *Homo sapiens* and continues it through the era of the Roman presence in the area. (Both museums open Tues.-Sun. 9am-noon and 1-5pm; Oct.-March Tues.-Sun. 10am-noon and 1-4pm. Each DM5, students DM4, children under 15 free.)

Across the river, Eichstätt proper is built around the extravagant **Residenzplatz,** surrounded by the Rococo episcopal palaces. The west wing has a particularly magnificent portal, and the interior is just as richly decorated. Tours of the **Residenz** (tel. 702 20) begin here if there are at least five people (Easter-Oct. Mon.-Thurs. at 11am and 3pm, Fri at 11am; Sat.-Sun every 30min. 10-11:30am and 2-3:30pm). In a corner of the Residenzpl. in the middle of a fountain stands the **Mariensäule** (Madonna Column). Behind the *Residenz* is the 14th-century **Hohe Dom** (High Cathedral), the miscegenational of the Romanesque, Gothic, and Baroque eras. The east apse features richly colored stained glass, and the north aisle shelters the intricate 15th-century stone **Pappenheim Altar.** On the other side of the high altar is the entrance to the **Mortuarium** (Mortuary), resting place of Eichstätt's bishops, in which the carved **Schöne Säule** (Beautiful Column) rises to meet the vault. (Cathedral open to tourists Mon.-Thurs. 9:45am-1pm and 2:30-4:30pm, Fri. 9:45am-1pm and 2:30-3:30pm, Sat. 9:45am-3pm, Sun. 12:30-5pm.)

Also in the cathedral complex, the **Diözesan-Museum,** Residenzpl. 7 (tel. 507 42) examines the history of the diocese since its founding in 741 by St. Willibald (open April-Oct. Tues.-Sat. 9:30am-1pm and 2-5pm, Sun. 11am-5pm; DM2.50, under 18 free). Two blocks further on Leonrodpl. is the Baroque **Schutzengelkirche** (Church of the Guardian Angel), built during the Thirty Years War, containing richly carved wooden altars and a striking golden sunburst above the high altar. Fivehundred-and-sixtyseven culpted angels—including two black angels—fly about the church's interior. Start counting.

■ Ingolstadt

Ingolstadt possesses all the elements of a good *Bayerischer Altstadt*—half-timbered houses and Renaissance facades—with fewer f tourists. Site of the first Bavarian university from 1472 to 1800, the old Danube city is now best known as the home of the Audi. The name of this luxury car company was originally *Horch,* German for "eavesdrop," and the last name of auto innovator and entrepreneur August Horch. After World War II it was changed to the Latin *Audi* (listen) to help exports in an international market resistant to German-sounding products. It would take much more than a name change, however, to shake the traditional look of this old town. The *Stadtmitte* remains a condensed chunk of history, enveloped by lush greenery with no evidence of factory production in sight. Narrow, cobbled streets wind from the main thoroughfares, intricately integrating the modern and traditional portions of the city.

Orientation and Practical Information Ingolstadt's **tourist office,** in the *Altes Rathaus,* Rathauspl. 4, 85049 Ingolstadt (tel. 305 10 98; fax 305 10 99), hands out free maps, English-language brochures, and a list of hotels and pensions in the area but does not provide a room-finding service (open Mon.-Fri. 8am-5pm, Sat. 9am-noon). They offer free German-language city tour on Saturdays at 2pm. To reach the tourist office and the rest of the old city from the distant train station, bus #10, 15, 16, or 44 (DM2.70), from the station: "Rathauspl." (5 stops; every 10-20min.). You can also follow Bahnhofstr. on the right-hand side to Münchenerstr. and head straight over the bridge down Danubestr. to the Rathauspl. (2.5km; 20min.). **Exchange money** at **Volksbank,** Theresienstr. 32 (open Mon.-Wed. 8am-4:30pm, Thurs. 8am-5:30pm).**Trains** roll between Ingolstadt and Munich (2-3 per hour.; 1 hr.). Public transportation **bus** routes center around the **Omnibusbahnhof,** located in the middle of the city (single fare DM2.70; *4-Farhten-karte* DM10). For a **taxi,** call 877 88. **Radverleih Fahrradinsel,** Münchnerstr. 2, rents **bikes** for DM19 per day (tel. 730 27; open Mon.-Fri. 9am-12:30pm and 1:30-7pm, Sat. 9am-4pm). In an **emergency,** call 192 22. The **telephone code** is 0841.

Accommodations Ingolstadt's superb **Jugendherberge (HI),** Friedhofstr. 4½ (tel. 341 77; fax 91 01 78), is located in a renovated section of the old town fortifications. From the tourist office, take Moritzstr. and make a left on Theresienstr. Follow it all the way to *Kreuztor,* then walk through the *Kreuztor* and cross Auf-der-Schanz (10min.). Large echoing rooms and cavernous hallways, with private sinks and (massage) showers, not to mention a great location and a scrumptious breakfast—hosteling life rarely gets this good. (Reception open 3-9pm. Curfew 11:15pm, but visitors have been known to climb through the large ground-floor windows. DM20. Sheets DM5.50. Open Feb. to mid-Dec., but closed every 2nd and 4th weekend from Nov. 11-Dec. 15 and Feb. 1-March 15.) **Pension Lipp,** on Feldkirchenerstr. (tel. 587 36), down Schloßländestr. along the Danube and left up Frühlingstr., is pleasant if out-of-the-way. But it's the closest remotely affordable *Pension.* (Singles DM30-40, with bath DM45; doubles DM75, with shower DM85.) Campers can head out to **Campingplatz am Auwaldsee** (tel. 68 911), but *a car is a must.* The site is off the E45/Autobahn A9, five minutes by car from the town center. (DM7.10 per person, under 12 DM4.90. DM5.10 per tent. DM9.90 per car. Open April-Sept.)

Food and Nightlife The *Kreuztor* might represent the old, traditional *Ingolstadter Altstadt,* but it's also the epicenter of all that's hip and new in town. The local nightlife centers around Kreuzstr. (which turns into Theresienstr. towards the center of town). While the local nightlife joints cater to students (and their wallets), **supermarkets** are even more budget-friendly. **Norma,** Danubestr. 16, is on the *Altstadt* side of the Konrad-Adenauer-Brücke (open Mon.-Fri. 8:30am-6pm, Sat. 8am-1pm).

Glock'n am Kreuztor, Oberer Graben 1 (tel. 349 90), is the really loud cafe abutting the *Kreuztor.* Especially popular in the summer when the benches and the kegs move outside. Daily dishes from pasta to pork DM5-15. Save DM0.50 and buy a *Maß* (DM8.50 for 1L). Grill specialties in the beer garden. (Open daily 6pm-2am.) **Sigi's Café and Bistro,** Kreuzstr. 6 (tel. 329 52), a few steps down from Glock'n, is small, chic, and light green. Nice outdoor seating. *Wieners,* mozzarella sandwiches, and salads for DM7-11. (Open daily 10am-2am.) **Restaurant Delphe,** Ludwigstr. 9. Greek delights with a bit of a Bavarian tint—it has a beer garden out back. Dinners are pricey, but lunches are affordable and tasty. From the lunch menu: omelettes DM7, Greek specialities DM9-14. (Open Mon.-Sat. 11:30am-3pm, 5pm-midnight.) **Neue Welt,** Griesbadgasse 7 (tel. 324 70). Right off Kreuzstr., this bar is home to the local artist and musician crowd, with its own stage, the **Kleinkunstbühne.** Musical cabarets and concerts premier regularly on Thurs. Try the chili, a *Tsatsiki* (DM5), or a Greek salad (DM7). (Open daily 7pm-2am.) **Goldener Stern,** Griesbadgasse 2 (tel. 354 19). Just down a step from Neue Welt, in a light yellow house with big wooden tables. Self-proclaimed student-friendly prices, and an amicable staff, too. Beer starts at DM3. Show up for the smoky crowds or relax in the beer garden. (Open daily 7pm-1am.)

Sights and Entertainment

The old city wall is magnificently represented by the turreted **Kreuztor,** topped by dainty caps and stone ornamentation. Other remnants of the city's medieval fortifications (including numerous ponds as moat relics) are scattered around the city. Just beyond the *Kreuztor* outside the city wall is the **Stadtmuseum,** Auf der Schanz 45 (im Kavalier Hepp; tel. 305 19 05), a city museum which explores the archaeological and cultural history of the area (open Tues.-Sat. 9am-5pm, Sun. 10am-5pm; DM4, Students and seniors DM2, free Sun.). Two blocks east of the *Kreuztor* stands the late Gothic **Liebfrauenmünster** (Minister of our Dear Lady), full of ornate altars and dramatic, even inspiring, vaulting. A few blocks south on Anatomiestr. is the **Alte Anatomie,** an 18th-century university building which now houses the **Deutsches Medizinhistorisches Museum** (German Museum of Medical History), Anatomiestr. 18/20 (tel. 305 18 60). It features an 18th-century "do-it-yourself" enema stool complete with a hand-operated water pump and a padded seat with a small protruding 3-inch-long pipe. That was a little more information than anyone needed to know. The "skeleton room" displays skinned human corpses with some of the dried-up muscles still attached, and an eerie collection of shrivelled guts and limbs. The fun never ends. A very detailed English brochure describing Ingolstadt's six main museums is available for free at all museum entrances, and the Medicine History museum will cheerfully lend you an even thicker English guidebook to interpret the German-only exhibits (open Tues.-Sun. 10am-noon and 2-5pm; DM4, students and seniors DM2, free on Sun.). North of the *Münster* at the corner of Jesuiten and Neubaustr. is the "Rococo jewel," the **Maria-de-Victoria-Kirche** (Church of Our Lady of Victories; tel. 175 18). This once spare chapel for students of the nearby Catholic school was rococoed with a vengeance in 1732, and an awe-inspiring frescoco now adorns the ceiling. (Open Tues.-Sun. 9am-noon and 1-5pm. Ring for the caretaker. DM1.) Across town on Paradepl. is the 15th-century **Neues Schloß,** Paradepl. 4, a red-tiled castle which now houses the **Bayerisches Armee-Museum** (Bavarian Military Museum; tel. 937 70), collected under King Ludwig "If-I-weren't-crazy-I'd-be-dangerous" II. The display of old firearms and suits of armor is notable for its size rather than its particular interest. Size matters not to a Jedi. (Open Tues.-Sun. 8:45am-4:30pm. DM5.50, students and seniors DM4, under 10 free. Joint admission to the main exhibit and to the special exhibit of armor and weapons used in WWI DM7.50, students and seniors DM5.50.) Right off of Donaustr. near the Konrad-Adenauer-Brücke is the brand new **Museum für Konkrete Kunst** (Museum for Concrete Art), Tränktorstr. 6-8 (tel. 305 18 06). Stare at bold geometric designs in primary colors until your eyes get screwy (open Tues. and Thurs.-Sun. 10am-6pm, Wed. 10am-2pm and 5-9pm; DM4, students DM2).

If afflicted by an automobile fetish, call **Audi** for information on tours (tel. 89 12 41). Ingolstadt also has a fabulous outdoor **swimming pool,** Johnstr. 29 (tel. 802 77), just to the left beyond the *Kreuztor* (open May-Sept. Mon.-Sun. 8am-8pm). There's also a **flea market** in Ingolstadt every first and fourth Sunday of the month at Manchingerstr. 125, every second Sunday in the Donauhalle, and every third Sunday in the Herrenschwaige—buy bric-a-brac for a buck.

■ Augsburg

Augsburg, founded by Caesar Augustus in 15BC, was the financial center of the Holy Roman Empire and a major commercial city by the end of the 15th century. The town owed its success and prestige mainly to the Fuggers, an Augsburger family that virtually monopolized the banking industry; Jakob Fugger "the Rich" was personal financier to the Habsburg Emperors. The third largest Bavarian city also went down in history as a focal point of the Reformation and the birthplace of Bertolt Brecht. In 1945, after years in exile, Brecht addressed the angry, haunting poem "Epistle to the Augsburgers" to the residents of the town. Today, Augsburg radiates an air of erudition, housing a sizeable university and catering to travelers zig-zagging Bayern with its semi-intact town wall and convenient "stop-over" location.

Orientation and Practical Information The resourceful **tourist office,** Bahnhofstr. 7 (tel. 50 20 70; fax 502 07 45), off Königspl. about 300m from the train station down Bahnhofstr., finds rooms for a DM3 fee (open Mon.-Fri. 9am-6pm). There's also a **branch** office at Rathauspl. (tel. 502 07 24) with longer hours. Free brochures and maps in English (open Mon.-Fri. 9am-6pm, Sat.-Sun. 10am-4pm). Walk straight from the station to the end of Bahnhofstr. and take a left at Königspl. onto Annastr. Take the third right and you'll see Rathauspl. on the left; the tourist office is on the right. The **Mitfahrzentrale,** Barthof 3 (tel. 15 70 19), arranges ride-shares for a small fee (open daily noon-9pm). **Rent bikes** at **Travel Enquires,** at the *Hauptbahnhof,* counter 6 (tel. 32 64 93; open daily 6am-8pm). Augsburg is connected by **train** to Munich (3-4 per hr., 40min.), Nürnberg (1-2 per hr., 1-1½hr.), Würzburg (change at Treuchtlingen; 1-2 per hr., 2½hr.), and Stuttgart (2-3 per hr., 1½-2hr.). The infamous **Europabus** line, canvassing the Romantische Straße route, stops at the Augsburg train station (northbound 10:30am; southbound 6:20pm). For medicinal wares, head to the **Rathaus Apotheke** on Rathauspl., to your left as you face the *Rathaus* (open Mon.-Fri. 8:30am-6pm, Sat. 8:30am-noon). Augsburg's **post office,** Halderstr. 29, 86150 Augsburg, is on your left as you face the station (open Mon.-Fri. 7am-8pm, Sat. 8am-2pm). The **telephone code** is 0821.

Accommodations Augsburg has a dearth of inexpensive, centrally located rooms, but don't panic—there are a few. To reach Augsburg's **Jugendherberge (HI),** Beim Pfaffenkeller 3 (tel. 339 09; fax 15 11 49), walk straight up Bahnhofstr. from the station to Königspl., bear left on Annastr., then right on Karlstr. Turn left on Hoherweg, then right after the church onto Inneres Pfaffengäßchen; follow the left side as it turns into Beim Pfaffenkeller. Bland, worn rooms feel like converted second-grade classrooms, but the hostel is central and the price is right. (Reception open 7-9am and 5-10pm. Curfew 1am. DM20. Sheets DM5.50. Key deposit DM20 or an ID. Excellent breakfast included. Call ahead. Open late-Jan. to early-Dec.) Or try **Gasthof Lenzhalde,** Theolottstr. 2 (tel. 52 07 45; fax 52 87 61). From the *Bahnhof,* bear right onto Halderstr., take a sharp right onto Hermannstr., and cross the Gögginger bridge. Take the first right onto Rosenaustr. and follow it for several blocks directly to the hotel, located 0.75km from the station (singles DM40, with shower DM50; doubles DM75). More central but a tad more expensive is the **Jakoberhof,** Jakoberstr. 39-41 (tel. 510 30; fax 15 08 44). Room furnishings that haven't quite made it to the 90s yet, but it's the cheapest you'll find in a central location (singles DM50, with bath DM75; doubles DM75, DM105). Or have the tourist office find you a room in the suburbs (DM30-40). To camp at **Campingplatz Augusta,** ABA Augsburg Ost, am Autobahnsee (tel. 70 75 75), take the bus (direction: "Neuburg"): "Autobahnsee" and follow the signs; the camp is about 400m away (DM7 per person, DM6 per tent).

Food Don't miss the **Stadtmarkt** (farmer's market) between Fuggerstr. and Annastr., right past the St. Anna Kirche on Fuggerstr. (open Mon.-Fri. 7am-6pm, Sat. 7am-1pm). For hot and meaty items, check the **Fleischmarkt** in the middle of the Stadtmarkt. Most corner joints sell the local beer, *Riegele Augsburg*. To stock up on basics, visit the **Penny Markt** at Maximilianstr. 71, to the right from the *Rathaus* (open Mon.-Fri. 8:30am-7pm, Sat. 8am-2pm); **Tengelmann supermarket,** at the corner of Alte Gasse and Jesuitengasse, offers a little more variety (open Mon.-Thurs. 8:30am-6:30pm, Fri. 8am-6:30pm, Sat. 8am-1pm). Restaurants in town tend to be a little pricey, so those who live in constant fear that each ATM withdrawal will be their last should probably stick to *Imbiß* fare; in the summer, a myriad of food stands line Maximilianstr., which is where all the locals go to eat.

Sights Old, rich Jakob Fugger founded the **Fuggerei** quarter in 1519 as the first welfare housing project in the world, long before Medicare was even conceived of. The narrow cobblestone streets and little gabled houses are a haven for the elderly, who earn their keep by praying for the departed souls of the Fuggers and pay only DM1.72 (the equivalent of a "Rhine Guilder") rent annually. Budget travelers need not apply, but good Catholic families and widows with total yearly earnings of less than DM250 have the chance at simple, three-room accommodations with kitchens. To reach the Fuggerei from the *Rathaus,* walk behind the Perlachturm tower on Perlachberg, which becomes Barfüßerstr. and finally Jakoberstr, and turn right under the archway. The gates close at 10pm. The **Fuggerei Museum** documents this classic piece of urban planning, as well as the financial adventures of its patrons (open March-Oct. daily 9am-6pm; DM1, students and seniors DM0.70). Fugger was also responsible for building the town palace, Maximilianstr. 36/38, where the 1518 dispute between Martin Luther and Cardinal Cafetar ensured church schism. During that time, Luther stayed in the **St.-Anna-Kirche,** on Annastr. near Königspl., which served as the center of the Protestant revolutionary movement in Augsburg.

Augsburg's medieval past unfolds at the brightly frescoed **Guildhaus,** down Burgermeister-Fischer-Str., now part of the Marktplatz area. It lies down Bahnhofstr. from the train station along the edge of the park, past the streetcars. From the Guildhaus, a left down Maximilianstr. leads to the huge Renaissance **Rathaus** (open daily 10am-6pm; free). The brightly painted ceiling of the **Goldener Saal** depicts tradesmen and women, recalling the importance of commerce in Augsburg's history (DM2). Down Hoher Weg to the left sits the **Hoher Dom,** the regional bishop's seat. The cathedral, built in the 9th century, was renovated in the Gothic style in the 14th century, and damaged in World War II. The chancel and high altar are intelligent examples of *Bauhaus*-inspired design, prevalent in German churches since the war (open Mon.-Sat. 6am-5pm; closed holidays). If you go to the left of the Perlachturm down Perlachberg and left onto Auf dem Rain, you'll arrive at the **Bertolt Brecht Haus,** currently being renovated and scheduled to reopen on February 10, 1998, the 100th anniversary of Brecht's birth there. It chronicles the life of one of the most influential 20th-century playwrights and poets through photographs, letters, and his poetry. (Open Tues.-Sun. 10am-5pm; Oct.-April Tues.-Sun. 10am-4pm. DM2.50, students and children DM1.50.) The city offers a **walking tour,** in German or English, that departs from the *Rathaus* (May-Oct. daily 2pm; DM9, students DM6).

■ Romantische Straße (Romantic Road)

Between Würzburg and Füssen, in the Lechtal at the foothills of the Alps, expands a beautiful countryside of walled cities, castles, elaborate churches, and dense forest. Sensing opportunity, the German tourist industry in 1950 christened these ancient, bucolic, and chivalrous backwaters the **Romantische Straße** and set about exploiting them. Be warned—this is **the most heavily touristed area in Germany;** although the region is beautiful, it will be a group experience. Deutsche Bahn's **Europabus** transports lots of families and elderly tourists daily from Frankfurt to Munich (April 1-Oct. 31, 12hr., change at Dinkelsbühl for Füssen) and back. Though this is the most popular way to travel the Romantische Straße, it is also one of the slower—there is only one bus in each direction per day. Buses on the Frankfurt-Munich route leave from Frankfurt (southbound 8am/northbound terminus 8:30pm), with stops in Würzburg (southbound 10am/northbound 6:45pm), Rothenburg (2:30pm/4:15pm), Dinkels-bühl (4:15pm/2pm), Augsburg (6:20pm/10:25am), Munich (7:50pm/9am), and Nördlingen (northbound only 12:15pm). On the Dinkelsbühl-Füssen route buses stop at Dinkelsbühl (southbound 4:15pm/northbound terminus 1:05pm), Augsburg (southbound 6pm/northbound 10:50am), Wieskirche (northbound only, 8:35am—with a 20min. stop for sightseeing, leaves at 8:55), Hohenschwangau (Neuschwan-stein Castle; 8:33pm/8:07am), and Füssen (8:40pm/8am)—this last bus does not stop in Munich. Check schedules with a tourist office before heading to the bus. The Eur-opabus is also relatively expensive. (Frankfurt to Rothenburg DM58, to Dinkelsbühl DM69, to Munich DM113. Dinkelsbühl to Hohenschwangau or Füssen DM60, stu-dents and under 26 10% off, under 12 and over 60 50% off, under 4 free. Eurail or Ger-man Rail Pass holders ride free, but each traveling vagrant must pay a ridiculous one-time "registration" fee of DM7 in addition to a DM3 fee for the backpack.) A more eco-nomical way to see the Romantische Straße for those without railpasses is to use the faster and much more frequent **trains,** which run to every town except Dinkelsbühl (take a tourist-free bus from Nördlingen or Dombühl). Those traveling the Roman-tische Straße by **car** may find themselves parking in large, specially built lots outside the old city walls of some towns, but will have easy access to many suburban budget hotels, *Privatzimmer,* and campgrounds that lie outside the reach of foot travelers. Tourist offices can provide maps and information to the travelers who **bike** the route. While the Romantische Straße makes a satisfying bike journey, plan carefully—most campgrounds are 10 to 20km apart. Some travelers reportedly hitch the route suc-cessfully; *Let's Go* does not recommend hitchhiking as a safe mode of transportation. For information or reservations call **Deutsche Touring** in Frankfurt, Am Römerhof 17 (tel. (069) 790 32 81; fax 790 32 19). For general information, contact the **Roman-tische Straße Arbeitsgemeinschaft,** Marktplatz, 91550 Dinkelsbühl (tel. (09851) 902 71; fax 902 79). Most of their brochures are available in English.

ROTHENBURG OB DER TAUBER

Rothenburg ob der Tauber is *the* Romantic Roadstop, touched by everyone. Expect a camera-clicking family of four from Livingston, New Jersey or Kyoto, Japan on every corner, and watch closely as they clear out of town on the afternoon bus, headed south with bagfuls of Christmas ornaments, stomachs full of Christmas pastries, and heads reeling with happy Christmas thoughts. While Rothenburg is busy enjoying the same commercialized fate as its favorite December holiday, don't knock all the touris-tic pomp; this small town is probably your only chance to see a nearly intact medieval walled city in Bayern that doesn't contain a single modern building.

Rothenburg became a first-class mecca of tourism by making a virtue out of a neces-sity. It was an opulent and free imperial city prior to the Thirty Years War, which, cou-pled with the Black Plague some years later, killed about half of the population and left Rothenburg destitute. At the end of the 19th century, locals blessed with kitschy foresight set up strict preservation laws in order to preserve their 16th century town; if only they could see it now. Rothenburg narrowly escaped complete devastation in World War II, when 40% of the town was reduced to rubble by bombs. Amazingly, the 14th-century fortified walls and towers endured and today can be toured in their entirety. To see the main sights, however, you'll have do battle with the competition, as throngs of tourists, brandishing their cameras, might make you wax nostalgic for the plundering legions.

Orientation and Practical Information Rothenburg's **tourist office,** Marktplatz 1 (tel. 404 92; fax 868 07), generously supplies handy maps in English and books rooms (DM35-60), usually for free (a DM2 fee during peak times). Walk left from the station, bear right on Ansbacherstr., and follow this street straight into the city to the Marktplatz (10-15min.). The tourist office is on your right, across the square (open Mon.-Fri. 9am-12:30pm and 2-6pm, Sat. 9am-noon and 2-4pm). **Tours in German** depart from the steps of the *Rathaus* (90min.; April-Oct. and Dec. daily at 11am and 2pm; DM5). **English-language tours** meet at the Riemenschneider Hotel, Georgengasse 11, to the left of the tourist office (daily at 1:30pm; DM6). The "night watchman" leads a special tour that is more entertaining than educating; it leaves from the town hall steps in the Marktplatz (English at 8pm; German at 9:30pm; DM6). **Trains** run every hour from major cities to Steinach, where you can transfer for a quick trip to Rothenburg (15min.). **Buses** also serve the route, sometimes in place of the train in the evening (see Europabus info, p. 536). The last bus leaves the train station for Steinach at 8:05pm. For a **taxi** call 20 00 or 72 27.

You can **exchange money** at the travel agency in the *Bahnhof* (tel. 46 11; fax 868 07), or at the post office. Rent **bikes** at the **Herrmann Kat's,** Galgengasse 33 (tel. 61 11; open daily 8am-7pm; half-day DM 10, full day DM15), or at **Rad und Tat,** Bensenstr. 17 (tel. 879 84; DM20 per day; ID required; open daily 9am-6pm). The **Wäscherei Then,** a **laundromat** located at Johannitergasse 9 (tel. 27 75; wash DM6.50, soap included; dry DM3 per 25min.; open Mon.-Fri. 8am-6pm, Sat. 8am-2pm). The laundromat and Pension Then (see below) are owned by a father-son tandem; they *love* tourists; in a pinch, you can stop by until 8pm and buy a token for DM9 (soap not included). **Toppler-Apotheke,** Ansbacherstr. 15 (tel. 36 56), has a list in its window of opening times and addresses of all other **pharmacies** (open Mon.-Tues. and Thurs.-Fri. 8am-12:30pm and 1:30-6pm, Sat. 8am-12:30pm). **Schlecker,** Wengasse 44, services your drug-store needs (open Mon.-Fri. 9am-6pm, Sat. 8am-1pm). The main **post office,** 91541 Rothenburg, is at Bahnhofstr. 7 (tel. 941 50; open Mon.-Fri. 8:15am-noon and 2-5:30pm, Sat. 8:15am-noon); a smaller branch sits at Milchmarktstr. 5 (tel. 922 92; open Mon.-Fri. 9am-6pm, Sat. 8am-1pm). The **telephone code** is 09861.

Accommodations An incredible number of **private rooms** (DM20-45) not registered with the tourist office are available—they're marked by *"Zimmer frei"* signs. Just knock on the doors with the signs to inquire. Housed in medieval buildings, Rothenburg's two youth hostels share common management. "Wonder Twin powers...activate!" Check in at the **Jugendherberge Rossmühle (HI),** on Mühlacker 1 (tel. 941 60; fax 94 16 20; email jhrothen@aol.com), at Rossmühleweg, a former horse-powered mill that shelters a modern set of carpeted rooms and a groovy staff. Amenities include ping-pong tables, a TV room where you can borrow movies, free storage lockers (DM5 deposit required), train schedules, and a weather board—this is what all hostels should be like. Follow the directions to the tourist office, take a left down Obere Schmiedgasse, and go straight until you see the *Jugendherberge* sign to the right. (Reception open 7-9am, 5-7pm, and 8-10pm. Curfew 11:30pm, but they'll give you an access code to the door. DM22. Tasty breakfast included. Sheets DM5.50.) The **Jugendherberge Spitalhof (HI)** exists as extra housing for Rossmühle; a mere stone's throw down the street (same reception, curfew, and hours).

Rothenburg has an unbelievable number of *Pensionen* for a town of its size, but most of them are expensive. For an exception, check out **Pension Raidel,** Wenggasse 3 (tel. 31 15), on the way to the hostel. Head down Obere Schmiedgasse and make a left on Wenggasse. Bright rooms and fluffy featherbeds, each one built, carved, painted, and restored by the mellow, do-it-yourself owner, make this the most charming and authentic of the affordable *Pensionen* in the *Altstadt*. (Singles DM35, with bath DM69; doubles DM69, with shower DM89. Breakfast included. Call ahead.) Included in the price of a room or apartment at **Pension Then,** Johannitergasse 8a (tel. 51 77; fax 860 14), in the proximity of the train station, is an insider's advice on the ins and outs of Rothenburg, an optional trip to the Wednesday night meeting of the local English conversation club (of which the owner Willy Then is vice president), and a chance to go fishing on the Tauber with Willy. (Singles DM40; doubles DM70. Apartment with kitchen DM25 per person, 3-day minimum.) From train station, turn left and then right on Ansbacherstr., then right on Johannitergasse.

Food With a cozy Christmas theme all year-round, it's not surprising that Rothenburg is famous for its delicious *Schneeballen* (snowballs): large balls of sweet dough dipped in a melange of chocolate, nuts, and powdered sugar; sometimes with a sweet center (often marzipan). **Dillers,** Hofbronner-Gasse 16 or Hafengasse 4 (tel. 866 23), offers these doughy concoctions at industrially-produced rates (DM2.40-5); you can also watch the bizarre snowball-making process there (open daily 10am-6pm). The **Roter Hahn,** Obere Schmiedgasse 21 (tel. 50 88; fax. 515 40) is the right place for meat-loving Germans and tourists alike. Hearty dishes go for around DM10-12. Those with a sweet tooth try the *Apfelkuchen* (DM2.50) at the **Bäckerei-Café,** Golgengasse 6 (tel 33 59). The **Fränkisches Haus,** Golgengasse 13 (tel 34 39), offers regional food in a modern setting (DM10-17); they also proffer salads (DM7), and other vegetarian dishes (open Mon.-Fri. 8am-6pm, Sat. 8:30am-6pm, Sun 9am-6pm). **Pizzeria Roma,** Galgengasse 19 (tel. 45 40), serves hefty pasta dishes (DM8-13) and pizzas (DM9-12) long after the rest of town goes to bed (open daily 11:30am-midnight). Pick up fresh goods from vendors at **Marktplatz** (open Wed. and Sat. 7am-noon). **Kapsch supermarket** is on the Rödergassen, inside the city wall as you enter the town (open Mon.-Tues. and Thurs.-Fri. 8:30am-6:30pm, Sat. 8am-1pm).

Sights On Marktplatz stands the Renaissance **Rathaus** (open daily 8am-6pm; free), from whose tower you can scope out the town (open daily 9:30am-12:30pm and 1-5pm; Nov.-March Mon.-Fri. 9:30am-12:30pm, Sat.-Sun. noon-3pm; DM1, children DM0.50). On this site in 1631, the conquering Catholic general Johann Tilly offered to spare the town from devastation if any local resident could chug a wine keg containing almost a gallon of wine. *Bürgermeister* Georg Nusch successfully met the challenge, and then passed out for several days. His saving **Meistertrunk** (master drink) is reenacted with great fanfare each year—live. Bring a jug of Rossi. The town clock acts out a watered-down version of the episode over the Marktplatz (hourly 11am-3pm and 8-10pm). Inside the courtyard behind the *Rathaus* are the **Historien-Gewölbe** (Historical Archways), which articulate the history of the Thirty Years War. Three gloomy stone cells lurk in the dungeon, where Mayor Heinrich Toppler and his son were once imprisoned by King Ruprecht (open daily 9am-6pm; Oct.-Nov. and Jan.-April 10am-5pm; Dec. 1-4pm; DM2.50, students DM1.50, children DM1). **Herrngasse,** the town's widest street, and **Schmiedgasse** are lined with old patrician homes. **Burggasse,** thought to be the oldest lane in town, was once affectionately referred to as "Hell" because of its darkness. **St. Jacob's Church,** Klostergasse 15, houses the Holy Blood Altar by Tilman Riemenschreider, a 5500-pipe organ, and 14th-century stained glass windows, which allow rivets of harlequin light into the church. (Open April-Oct. Mon.-Fri. 9am-5:30pm, Sun. 10:30am-5:30pm; Dec. noon-2pm and 4-5pm; closed Nov. and Jan.-March; DM2.50, students DM1.) The **Reichsstadtmuseum,** Klosterhof 5 (tel. 404 58), housed in a former 13th-century Dominican convent, displays numerous rooms whose contents are preserved from the Middle Ages. Adore the famous 15th-century 12-panel painting of Christ's passion and the original wine *Krug* from the *Meistertrunk* (open daily 9:30am-5:30pm; Nov.-March 1-4pm; DM4, students DM3, children DM2).

The town's **Medieval Crime Museum,** Burggasse 3 (tel. 53 59), is definitely worth the entrance fee for anyone who can stomach the thought of iron-maiden justice. Take a picture of yourself in the stocks outside before heading into the dim, creepy basement for the **torture exhibits.** *Feel* the pain. The large rooms upstairs continue the fun, with exhibits on "eye for an eye" jurisprudence and the special punishments once reserved for bad musicians, dishonest bakers, and frivolous gossips. All displays are labeled in English for foreign Natural Born Killers (open daily 9:30am-5:30pm; Dec. and March 10am-3:30pm; Nov. and Jan.-Feb. 2-3:30pm; DM5, students DM4, children DM3). The **Doll and Toy Museum,** Hofbronnengasse 13, off the Marktplatz (tel. 73 30), offers lots of old toys displayed in neat little rows and glass cases (open daily 9:30am-6pm; Jan.-Feb. 11am-5pm; DM5, students DM3.50, families DM12).

Camp holds brazen sway at Käthe Wohlfahrt's **Christkindlmarkt** (Christ Child Market), Herrngasse 2, and the more extensive **Weihnachtsdorf** (Christmas Village), Herrngasse 1 (tel. 40 90; fax 40 94 10). They're a must-see even if you *aren't* looking for 4m-long nutcracker or a pea-sized porcupine. As your eyes glaze over like *Schnee ballen,* head to the second floor of the *Weihnachtsdorf* for damaged items at 20-50% off; the cash registers never stop jingling, as more nutcrackers get sold than there ar nuts on the planet to crack (stores open Mon.-Fri. 9am-6:30pm, Sat. 8am-2pm; als Easter-Nov. Sun. 10am-6pm). If you manage to escape without puking pink and pu ple, **Toyland,** Marktplatz 9, provides further amusement. Toy along to Rothenburg townhall, standing proud and unblemished, and enjoy the view on a 2.5km wal along the wall from **Klingen Bastion** to **Kobolzeller Gate.**

Entertainment The **Figurentheater,** am Burgtor at Herrngasse 38 (tel. 73 54 o 33 33; fax. 39 41), is Rothenburg's fantastically nonsensical puppet theatre—bette than the Von Trapp kid show. The guest book proudly displays Pablo Picasso's simpl but elegant word of applause, *"Merveilleux."* (Shows June-Sept. Mon.-Sat. at 3 an 9pm; Nov.-May Mon.-Sat. at 8:30pm; 90min. evening shows DM15, students DM1(45min. matinees DM10, students DM8.) To go **fishing** in the Tauber River, call Her Schmidt (the town tour guide and grave digger) at tel. 58 39.

Rothenburg prides itself on a tourist-friendly array of annual festivals. On Easter Su day, the famed **Hans-Sachs-Spiele** (Hans Sachs play) and the **Schäfertanz** (Shep herd's Dance) are performed on the Marktplatz. The two displays celebrate respectively, the shoemaker-cum-*Meistersinger* Hans Sachs, who wrote 208 plays and the banishment of the plague from Rothenburg by dancing shepherds. The his toric **Meistertrunk** is re-enacted almost constantly during Easter weekend. The **Reich sstadt-Festtage** (City Festival) is held in the second week of September with marche and festivals, as cattle traders, knights, and mutinous peasants all gather. Tickets for a events can be purchased at the *Reisebüro* (DM12-25). At Christmas, Rothenbur; becomes a giant gingerbread house filled with mulled wine, Franconian *Bratwürs* organ and brass band concerts, and nightly torchlight processions through the snow A ski jump has been incorporated as part of the re-enactment of the *Meistertrunk.* Bu remember, the Rothenburgers are professionals who've been doing this for centuries *Let's Go* does not recommend drinking and skiing.

DINKELSBÜHL

Forty kilometers south of Rothenburg, Dinkelsbühl boasts an impressive bevy o medieval half-timbered houses, a climbable 16th-century churchtower, and a naviga ble town wall. Sound familiar? It is, though locals claim their town's superiority lie with Dinkelsbühl's authenticity; it houses the largest collection of original, unrestore(structures on the Romantische Straße (repainting, of course, doesn't count). Th Gothic **St. Georgskirche,** which dominates the Weinmarkt at the center of town sprouts a Romanesque tower and striking fan vaulting. A tale for tourists explains wh the houses along **Nördlingerstraße** are oddly-shaped—medieval superstition hel(that homes with right angles housed demons. Since every little hamlet needs a cut(little festival, Dinkelsbühl's got **Kinderzeche** (children's weeping), which celebrate the town's salvation during the Thirty Years War, and the **100 Years Children's festi val,** an even larger bash that occurs in the summer (July 17-26 in 1998) commemorat ing a century of this infantile partying. The town tots' tears reputedly persuaded th(invading field commander of Swedish King Gustavus Adolphus II to spare Dinkels bühl. A recreation of the event accompanies parades, fireworks, dances, and, o course, crying kids—a strangely satisfying experience for hosteling travelers (DM4 fo the required "festival badge"; seats at the various performances DM3-16). The **Par** **Ring** around the *Altstadt* separates the old and newer parts of town. New to the ol(town is the spiffy **3-Dimensional Museum** (tel. 63 36), housed in the Nördlinger To of the town wall (entrance through the gate and to the left). The only such museun in the world, it encompasses all the different ways (since the Middle Ages) that peopl(have represented thick stuff in thin ways (open daily 10am-6pm; Nov.-March Sat.-Sun 11am-4pm; DM10, DM9 with tourist office coupon).

The **tourist office** (tel. 902 40; fax 902 79), on the Marktplatz, finds rooms for a DM3 fee and distributes free maps and schedules to the *Kinderzeche* festival. The office also **rents bikes** (DM7 per day). To get there, walk right from the *Bahnhof* and take the first left. Follow the footpath over tow bridges and into the city, then take the first right onto Nördlingerstr., which empties into the Marktplatz; the tourist office is in the rust-colored building on your right. (Open Mon.-Fri. 9am-noon and 2-6pm, Sat. 10am-noon and 2-5pm, Sun. 10am-1pm; Nov.-March Mon.-Fri. 9am-noon and 2-6pm, Sat. 10am-1pm.) The town's defunct **train station** now serves as a **bus station.** When traveling by bus to and from Dinkelsbühl, plan ahead. Regional buses go to Rothenburg two times a week (DM22.50), and to Nördlingen (5-6 per day, 2-4 per day on weekends; DM7.90). Schedules are posted at the tourist office and at the station. If you plan poorly, you might get stuck with the crowded and expensive **Europabus,** which takes tourists along the Romantische Straße (see p. 530). **St. Paul's Apotheke,** Nördlingerstr. 7 (tel. 34 35), is the most convenient **pharmacy** (open Mon.-Fri. 8am-12:30pm and 2-6pm, Sat. 8am-noon). For the **police,** call 888. The **post office,** 91550 Dinkelsbühl, is 100m to the right of the station (open Mon.-Fri. 9am-5pm, Sat. 9am-noon). The **telephone code** is 09851.

Built in 1508 as a grain store, the **Jugendherberge (HI),** Koppengasse 10 (tel. 95 09; fax 48 74), is a huge, half-timbered house with an awesome interior, three blocks from the town center. (Reception open 5-10pm. DM18. Breakfast included. Sheets DM5.50. Open March-Oct.) **Pension Gerda,** Nestleinsberggasse 22 (tel. 18 60), is a 10-minute walk away from the Marktplatz (DM35 per person; breakfast included). Following the directions to the tourist office, take a left onto Turmgasse, and then a right onto Nestleinberggasse by the city wall. A more friendly option closer to the hustle and bustle of the Markt, **Gasthof Zur Sonne,** Weinmarkt 11 (tel. 57 670; fax 75 48), has airy rooms to which you can stumble after visiting their *Biergarten.* (Singles DM45; doubles DM75; triples DM102. Breakfast included. No showers.) Check the tourist office for **private accommodations** (doubles from DM45). Over the river, north of the city on Dürrwangerstr., is the **DCC Campingpark Romantische Straße** (tel. 78 17; DM6.50 per person, DM15 per tent and car; reservations accepted).

Budget food is hard to find in touristy Dinkelsbühl. Head to **City Grill,** Nördlingerstr. 8, for burgers and *Würste* (DM3.50-8; open Mon.-Sat. 11am-1am, Sun. noon-1am). **Café Lechler,** Nördlingerstr. 17 (tel. 73 70), is a favorite of locals and tourists alike, serving beer (DM3.40), elaborate ice cream concoctions (DM8-12), and portions of local cuisine (open Mon.-Sat. 9am-midnight, Sun. 1pm-midnight). **Tengelmann,** Nördlingerstr. 13 (tel. 35 09), conveniently fulfills **supermarket** needs (open Mon.-Wed. 8:30am-6:30pm, Thurs. 8:30am-7pm, Fri. 8am-6:30pm, Sat. 8am-1pm).

▚ Würzburg

Surrounded by vineyard slopes and bisected by the Main River, Würzburg is the bustling center of the Franconian wine region and home to one of Germany's greatest palaces, the magnificent Baroque "Residenz." The imposing 13th-century Marienburg Fortress across the river provides a formidable backdrop for the palace, all but overshadowing it. The fortress is a testament to the immense secular power of Würzburg's *Fürstbischöfe* (prince-bishops), whose forerunners first established themselves when Würzburg became a bishopric in 742. Despite its origins as a religious center, Würzburg is now largely a *Uni*-town. It was at Würzburg's university that Wilhelm Conrad Röntgen discovered X-rays and their medical applications in 1895, for which he was awarded the first Nobel Prize six years later. Though wartime bombing destroyed much of the town's 18th-century magnificence—in 1945 all that remained intact was the spire of Marienkapelle, pointing like an admonishing finger to heaven—its older giants remain unchanged, making Würzburg a scenic portal for Germany's great tourist trail, the Romantische Straße.

ORIENTATION AND PRACTICAL INFORMATION

With its three separate tourist information offices (one situated right outside the trai
station), Würzburg is a traveler's dream come true. To get to the city's center at th
Markt, follow Kaiserstr. straight ahead from the station, then take a right on Juliu
promenade, and hang a left onto Schönbornstr., the main pedestrian and streetca
road; the Markt is a few blocks down and to your right. The Main River separates th
rest of the city from the green, steep hills on which the fortress stands.

Tourist Office: Main Office, in the **Palais am Congress Centrum** (tel. 373 35), nea
the Friedensbrücke, where Röntgenring intersects the Main. Open Mon.-Thurs
8:30am-5pm, Fri. 8:30am-noon. Another branch in front of the **train station** (te
374 36) provides a packet with a free map and a hotel list for DM0.50; they also fin
rooms for DM5. Open Mon.-Sat. 10am-6pm. If it's past hours, grab a hotel list fro
the machine outside (DM0.50). A 3rd office is located in the **Haus zum Falken** (te
373 98), an ornamental yellow building on the Marktplatz that's reminiscent of
wedding cake. Open Mon.-Fri. 10am-6pm, Sat.-Sun. 10am-2pm. There's also a **24h
accommodations hotline** at 194 14.

Trains: Bahnhofpl. (tel. 344 25). Trains run to Frankfurt (1 per hr.; 1hr.), Nürnberg (
per hr.; 1-1½hr.), Munich (1 per hr.; 2½hr.), Hamburg (1 per hr.; 3½hr.), and Rot
enburg (13 per day; 1hr.; change at Steinach).

American Express: Haugerpfarrgasse 1 (tel. 35 56 90; fax 355 69 69), between Ka
serstr. and Bahnhofstr., a block from the station. The usual array of services fo
those who don't leave home without it; commission-free money exchange even fo
those who did. Open Mon.-Fri. 9:30am-6pm, Sat. 10am-1pm.

Buses: Europabuses trace the Romantische Straße to Rothenburg (DM26) an
Munich (DM82) daily at 10am, departing from bus platform #13 right of the station
Eurail and German Rail Passes valid (except the *BahnCard*). Students and yout
under 26 get 10% off. The return bus to Frankfurt stops at Würzburg daily a
6:45pm. Reservations can be made 3 days in advance with the **Deutsche Tourin
Büro,** Am Römerhof 17 (tel. (069) 790 32 81; fax (069) 790 32 19).

Public Transportation: For information, call 36 13 52. **Streetcars** are the fastest an
most convenient way around, but large sections of the city are not covered. Th
bus network is comprehensive, though most routes do not run nights and wee
ends. Ask for **night bus** schedules at the WSB kiosk in front of the train station. Sin
gle fare DM2, 24hr. ticket DM6.50.

Ferries: Schiffstouristik Kurth & Schiebe (tel. 46 29 82; dock kiosk tel. 585 73; fa
513 13) or **Veitshöchheimer Personenschiffahrt GMBH** (tel. 915 53; dock kios
tel. 556 33; fax 632 99) depart from the Alter Kranen wharf near the Congress Cen
trum to the Veitschöchheim Castle (40min.; DM8, round-trip DM13).

Bike Rental: Fahrrad Station, Bahnhofpl. 4 (tel. 574 45; fax 574 65). DM12-13 pe
day. When exiting the station turn left around the corner. Open Tues. and Sat.-Su
9am-1pm, Wed.-Fri. 9am-6pm.

Mitfahrzentrale: Kiosk to the left of station's exit (tel. 194 48 or 140 85). Arrange
ride shares. Open Mon.-Fri. 10am-6pm, Sat. 10am-1pm, Sun. 11am-1pm.

Bookstore: Buchladen Neuer Weg, Sanderstr. 23/25 (tel. 35 59 10). Has a small bu
adequate selection of novels. Open Mon.-Fri. 9am-8pm, Sat. 9am-4pm.

Pharmacy: Engel-Apotheke, Marktplatz 36 (tel. 32 13 40; fax 321 34 12), lists nigh
pharmacies on the door. Open Mon.-Fri. 8:30am-6pm, Sat. 8:30am-1pm.

Rape Crisis Line: Contact **Frauenhaus** (tel. 45 00 70).

Emergency: Medical Aid, tel. 192 22. **Police,** tel. 110. **Fire,** tel. 112.

Post Office: Bahnhofpl. 2, 97070 Würzburg (tel. 330). Exchange money, cash trav
eler's checks. Open Mon.-Fri. 6am-7pm, Sat. 6am-4pm, Sun. 10am-2pm.

Telephone Code: 0931.

ACCOMMODATIONS AND CAMPING

The one drawback to this otherwise excellent city is the lack of budget accommoda
tions. Aside from the youth hostel, rooms for under DM45 are rare—they're about a
hard to find as Waldo. Würzburg's least expensive beds are around the train station
on (or just off) Kaiserstr. and Bahnhofstr.

Jugendgästehaus (HI), Bukarderstr. 44 (tel. 425 90; fax 41 68 62), near St. Burkard's Basilica, across the river from downtown. Streetcar #3 (direction: "Heidingsfeld") or 5 (direction: "Heuchelhof"): "Löwenbrücke," then backtrack; go down the stairs marked by the "Jugendherberge/Kappele" sign, turn right, walk all the way past 2 streets and a Sparkasse on the left, go through the tunnel, and it's immediately on your left. A modern, enormous villa, with views of the fortress from the carpeted, spacious rooms. Reception open 8am-10pm. Check-in 2-5:15pm and 6:30-10pm. Curfew 1am. Dorm DM25, others DM29. Full breakfast and sheets included.

Pension Spehnkuch, Röntgenring 7 (tel. 547 52; fax 547 60), to the right of the *Bahnhof* down Röntgenringstr. Newly redone by the laid-back owner, very white, and very bright. Singles DM50; doubles DM90. Breakfast included.

Pension Siegel, Reisgrubengasse 7 (tel. 529 41), a block down Kaiserstr. from the train station, on your left. Amateur murals of tropical isles lead up cramped stairs to small but comfortable-and-clean rooms. Reception open before 2pm and 5-10:30pm. Nice singles DM46; doubles DM89. Breakfast included. Call ahead.

Gasthof Goldener Hahn, Marktgasse 7 (tel. 519 41; fax 519 61), in a little golden building with green-checkered stained glass windows directly off the Markt. Clean rooms have phones and TVs; some have partial views of the Markt. Singles DM40-50 (hall shower DM3), with bath DM80; doubles with bath DM140.

Camping Kanu-Club, Mergentheimerstr. 13b (tel. 725 36). Streetcar #3 or 5 (direction: "Heidingsfeld"): "Judenbühlweg." Right on the river. Reception open noon-10pm. Person DM4, tent DM3, shower DM1.50.

OOD AND ENTERTAINMENT

o sample some of the Würzburg region's distinctive wines, try **Haus des Frankenveins Fränkischer Weinverband,** Krankenkai 1 (tel. 120 93). The city's answer to Munich's *Oktoberfest,* the lively **Kiliani Festival,** is held during the first two weeks in uly. The huge annual **Wine Festival** takes place in early June and late September to arly October. Adventurous souls should snoop around the bohemian back alleys of he city's south side, especially on Sandestr., the heart of the university subculture, vhere idiosyncratic people and curious food abound in smoky dens and grottoes. here is a **farmer's market** on the Markt (open Tues. 6am-6pm, Wed. 6am-4pm, Fri. am-6pm, Sat. 6am-2pm). For inexpensive foodstuffs, hit **Kapsch supermarket,** at the nd of Kaiserstr. away from the station (open Mon.-Fri. 8:30-6:30pm, Sat. 8am-2pm).

University Mensa, in the *Studentenhaus* on Am Exerzierpl., at Münzstr.; through the doors to your left. Assembly-line eating. Würzburg University ID technically required for discounts, but even without one, it's cheap. Buy meal tickets at the machines outside of the dining room. Meals run DM2.25 (with ID) to DM4.50 (without ID). Open mid-Oct. to mid-July Mon.-Fri. 11am-1:30pm, Sat. 11:30am-1:30pm; evening meals Mon.-Thurs. 5:30-7:30pm. Feb.-March closed Sat. Look for job offers, roommates, and musical/cultural happenings.

Kult, Landwehrstr. 10 (tel. 531 43), right off Sanderstr., is one of the more visible barcafe-*Kneipen* for hip local alternatives. Mustard yellow interior, staff clad all in black, and revolutions brewing in the corner—we are angry, very angry. Mexican peanuts and corn kernels in hot chili oil, with bread (DM5.80). Mellow, but crowded at night. Open Mon.-Fri. 9am-1am (if too hot outside, open 9am-2pm and 6pm-1am), Sat. 6pm-1am, Sun. 11am-1am.

Uni Café, Neubaustr. 2 (tel. 156 72), on the corner of Sanderstr. Relaxed student atmosphere and outdoor sidewalk seating. *Very* popular. Cakes, baguettes, salads, breakfasts (DM3.50-9.50). Open Mon.-Sat. 8am-1am, Sun. 9am-1pm.

Cafehaus Brückenbäck, An der Alten Mainbrücke (tel. 41 45 45). From the hostel, turn left on Saalgasse and walk 2 blocks. A view of Marienburg fortress, a view of the Main, a view of all the interesting folks crossing the main pedestrian bridge too. Tasty *Apfelstrudel* (DM3.50), salads (DM 6-13), and an unending list of liquid refreshments. Open Mon.-Fri. 8am-1am, Sat.-Sun. 8:30am-1am.

La Clochard, Neubaustr. 20 (tel. 129 07). Crepes (DM5-8), sandwiches (DM7-11), and vegetarian dishes like *Jogurt-Kartoffeln* (potatoes topped with yogurt, cucum-

BAYERN (BAVARIA)

bers, and tomatoes; DM10.90) by a cozy corner fireplace. Old-World decor clash
with alternative music in this student hangout.

Till Eulenspiegel, Sanderstr. 1a (tel. 134 73). Ivy-covered building with a beer gard
out back. Big Würzburger bar scene, named after medieval Germany's merry jest
Beer and cocktails (DM3.50 and up). Entrees served Mon.-Thurs. until 9:30pm, F
Sat. until 11:30pm (DM4-16). Open daily 6pm-1am.

Pepper La Pub, on Bahnhofstr., down and left as you exit the station. "House of 1
beers"—from the Czech Republic, Russia, Nigeria, Tahiti, and more. Also serv
plain ol' Guinness on tap (DM3.20), sandwiches, soups, and pastas (DM5-13). C
rectly match six mystery beers with their labels on Mondays at 6pm, and you c
walk on the clouds of inebriation without paying a single *pfennig*—test your pro
ess. Open Mon.-Sat. 11am-1am, Sun. 2pm-1am.

SIGHTS

Marienburg Fortress, the striking symbol of the city, keeps its vigil high on a hillsi
over the Main. The footpath to the fortress starts a short distance from the **Alte Mai
brücke,** more than 500 years old and lined with statues of saints. German painting
furniture, and *objets d'art* cluster in the **Fürstenbau Museum** (tel. 438 38; op
Tues.-Sun. 9am-12:30pm and 1-5pm; Oct.-March Tues.-Sun. 10am-12:30 and 1-4p
DM4, students DM3, under 15 free if accompanied by adult). The fortress also hous
the **Mainfränkisches Museum** (tel. 430 16), an extensive collection of works by T
polo and statues by Würzburg's native son, Tilman Riemenschneider, the **Master
Würzburg.** A genius of Gothic styling, Riemenschneider sided with the peasants
their 16th-century revolts against Luther and the powers-that-were. When the ins
rection was suppressed, the sculptor's fingers were broken as punishment, and
could never work again. (Open Tues.-Sun. 10am-5pm; Nov.-March Tues.-Sun. 10a
4pm; DM3.50, students DM2; pass to both museums DM6.) Masochists can make t
climb to the fortress in less than 30 minutes. Or bus #9 from the "Spitäle" bus stop
the western end of the bridge (May to mid-Oct. every 30min. 9:43am-5:43pm; DM:
Weekend tours of the fortress depart from the Rundkirchekasse in the Fürsterb
(Sat.-Sun. hourly 10-11am and 1-4pm). On the next hill stands the **Käppele,** a grace
18th-century church designed by Würzburg architect Balthasar Neumann.

In 1168, 12 years after he married in Würzburg, Friedrich Barbarossa raised t
local bishop to the rank of "Prince." The **Residenz** palace (tel. 355 17 12), Neumann
masterpiece, was the base camp for Würzburg's prince-bishops during the Enlighte
ment. It stands over the sweeping Residenzpl. (a 15min. walk down Kaiserstr. a
Theaterstr. from the station). The vibrant ceiling fresco by Johannes Zick in the fir
floor garden room has never been restored; in fact, his use of extravagant colors g
Zick fired. The Italian painter Giovanni Tiepolo was hired to finish the job in a mo
sedate style. His ceiling fresco in the grand staircase is the largest in the world, a
certainly among the most ostentatious. (Open Tues.-Sun. 9am-5pm; Nov.-March Tue
Sun. 10am-4pm. DM5, students and seniors DM3.50. Last admission 30min. befo
closing.) The **Residenzhofkirche** is astounding—the gilded moldings, pink marb
and frescoes make this little church the apex of Baroque fantasy (open Tues.-Su
9am-noon and 1-5pm; Nov.-March Tues.-Sun. 10am-noon and 1-4pm; free).

Behind the *Residenz* complex is the **Hofgarten,** a studiously laid-out park with
large rose garden (open dawn-dusk). In front of the *Residenz* down Hofstr. stands t
900-year-old **Dom of St. Killian,** Domstr. (tel. 536 91). It was rebuilt in the mid-196
after being obliterated in 1945. St. Killian, an Irish missionary bishop who became t
city's patron saint, was killed with two other missionaries in the ducal court in t
year 689. The *Dom* is supposed to hold his remains. Tilman Riemenschneider (s
above) is responsible for the Gothic highlights of this large Romanesque cathedr
(Open Mon.-Fri. 10am-5pm, Sun. 1-6pm; Nov.-Easter Mon.-Fri. 10am-noon and 2-5p
Sun. 12:30-1:30pm and 2:30-6pm. Tours April-Oct. Mon.-Sat. at noon, Sun.
12:30pm. DM4, children DM2.) The **Stift Haug,** at the end of Bahnhofstr., is a gr
find with its moving altarpiece, Tintoretto's *Crucifixion.* Two different operators r
cruises (see **Ferries,** p. 536) to the **Veitshöchheim Castle** (tel. 915 82). The pala

grounds are a public park (open April-Sept. Tues.-Sun. 9am-noon and 1-5pm; DM3, students DM2). Two-hour English-language **tours** around the city are given mid-April to October, Tues.-Sun. at 11am. Tour fees (DM12, students DM9) includes entrance to the *Residenz;* meet at the *Haus zum Falken* tourist office. A German-language tour without the *Residenz* (1½hr.) is given daily at 10:30 am (April-Oct. DM9, students DM7). Free **Rathaus tours** (1½hr.) in German are given every Saturday at 10am and 4:30pm (Nov.-Dec. and Feb.-April 10am only). Two-hour **bus tours** depart from the *Busbahnhof* (Mon.-Sat. 2:30pm, Sun. 10:30am; DM13, students DM11).

■ Nürnberg (Nuremberg)

While few visible scars remain and the city's historical landmarks impress, Nürnberg is a city inextricably bound to a darker past. The city still conjures up totalitarian images of the sort immortalized in Leni Riefenstahl's film *Triumph des Willens.* Nürnberg played host to the massive Nazi party rallies held between 1933 and 1938, and lent its name to the 1935 Racial Purity Laws. Because of Nürnberg's close ties to Nazi power, the Allies chose this city as the site for the war-crimes tribunals.

Nürnberg's long association with the imperial traditions of the Holy Roman Empire originally attracted Hitler to the city. After Kaiser Ludwig the Bavarian proclaimed Nürnberg a "free city" in 1332, its local government answered to no authority lower than the Emperor. The imperial *Reichstag* met here until 1543, the imperial jewels were locked in a tower over the *Spital,* and each of the Holy Roman Emperors paid an obligatory visit to the city's Kaiserburg. Nürnberg's happy days in the 15th and 16th centuries came to an end as trade-routes shifted westward following the discovery of the Americas; furthermre the Thirty Years War destroyed large parts of the city. The dark years of Nürnberg lasted until the *Geld* started rolling in as the Nazis build up the armament industry. World War II took its toll, and in 1945, 90% of the city was reduced to rubble. Roughly half of that damage was a result of the bombings of January 2. Now, Nürnberg's old homes, shops, and churches are reconstructed.

Today, Nürnberg, the second largest city in Bayern after Munich, jives with a steady German beat. Best known for its toy fair and *Christmasmarkt,* its sausages and gingerbread, and its association with artists and former resident Albrecht Dürer, the city persists in the historical and contemporary consciousness of the German landscape.

ORIENTATION AND PRACTICAL INFORMATION

The old city wall neatly circumscribes Nürnberg's thriving central district. From the train station, the main shopping district is across the street on Königstr. **Lorenzerplatz** and the **Hauptmarkt** lie just beyond the shopping district in the heart of the city. Much of the *Altstadt* lies within a pedestrian zone. The **Burg** perches on a hill, overlooking the town from the northernmost part of the *Altstadt.*

Tourist Offices: Verkehrsverein, (tel. 233 61 32; fax 233 61 66), is in the central hall of the *Hauptbahnhof.* Mailing address: Congress und Tourismus Zentrale, Frauentorgraben 3, 90443 Nürnberg. They will provide you with English-language city maps (DM0.50), free brochures, schedules of events, and, by request, *Die Club-Seite* (a list of nightlife hot spots). They also find rooms for a DM5 fee. Open Mon.-Sat. 9am-7pm. The **branch office** lies on the northern side of the Hauptmarkt. Open Mon.-Sat. 9am-6pm, Sun. 10am-1 and 2-4pm; Oct.-April Mon.-Sat. 9am-6pm.
Tours: 2½hr. tours depart from the main tourist office daily at 2pm May-Oct. and during *Christkindlesmarkt* (DM14).
Budget Travel: abr Reisebüro, across from the tourist office in the train station (tel. 201 00), deciphers timetables. Open Mon.-Fri. 9:30am-6pm, Sat. 10am-2pm.
Currency Exchange: The AmEx office is the cheapest option for those with or without The Card; the post office is another good bet. Beware the often absurd fees and rates at *Wechsel* stands.
American Express: Adlerstr. 2 (tel. 23 23 97; fax 22 49 26), off Königstr., near Lorenzerpl. Great rates and no service charges for changing cash and traveler's checks.

All AmEx services for cardholders or possessors of traveler's checks. Open Mor Fri. 9:30am-5:30pm (cashier closed noon-2pm), Sat. 9:30am-12:30pm.

Flights: Located north of the city on Flughafenstr. (tel. 350 62 00). **City-Airpor Express** runs shuttles from the train station (5:30am-11:30pm, every 20-30mir 20min.; DM6). Follow signs at the train station to the traffic island in front.

Trains: Hauptbahnhof, Bahnhofpl. 9 (tel. 194 19). To Munich (2-3 per hr., 1½-2hr Berlin (every 1-2hr., 5½-6hr.), Regensburg (1-2 per hr., 1hr.), Würzburg (2-3 per hr 1hr.). A computer outside the *Reisezentrum* helps decipher the pesky details.

Public Transportation: The multitude of possibilities consist of subway, streetca bus, regional train (known as *R-Bahn*), or S-Bahn. Single-ride tickets within the ci DM3.30 (1½hr. with transfers). *Kurzstrecke* (short distance) DM2.50. 10 *Streife karte* (multi-use cards) DM12.90. Day or weekend card DM7.80. Pick up a map the tourist office.

Bike Rental: Fahrradkiste, Knauerstr. 9 (tel. 287 90 64; fax 287 90 65), outside th southwest corner of the walled *Altstadt*. Basic wheels DM9 per day (DM2(deposit required). Mountain bikes DM15 per day (DM400 deposit). Foreign cu rency accepted as deposit. Open Mon.-Fri. 11am-6pm, Sat. 10am-1pm.

Mitfahrzentrale: Strauchstr. 1 (tel. 194 44). A safer alternative to hitching. Ope Mon.-Fri. 10am-6:30pm, Sat. 11am-2pm.

Hitchhiking: *Let's Go* does not recommend hitchhiking as a safe means of transpor tion. Hitchers headed to Munich and Austria: U-Bahn #1 or 11: "Bauernfeindstr. then bus #59: "Am Zollhaus" and the *Autobahn* interchange. To Würzburg ar Frankfurt: U-Bahn #1: "Stadtgrenze" and walk to the A-3 interchange.

Lost and Found: Fundbüro, Allesbergerstr. 17-19 (tel. 431 76 24). Open Mon.-We 9:30am-4pm, Thurs. 9:30am-6pm, Fri. 9:30am-12:30pm.

Laundromat: SB Waschsalon, Spitzenbergstr. 2, near the University Mensa. Take load off for DM6; suds run DM1. Open daily 6am-11pm.

Rape Crisis: tel. 28 44 00. Counseling Mon. 10am-noon, Tues. 7-8pm, Thurs. 4-6pm

Pharmacy: City Apotheke, Königstr. 29. Open Mon.-Fri. 8:30am-6:30pm, Sat. 9ar 4pm. Check the notices in *Nürnberger Zeitung* for 24hr. pharmacies.

Hospital: Städtisches Klinikum, Flurstr. 17 (tel. 39 80). **Medical Assistance,** tel. 5 32 11 or 53 37 71.

Emergency: tel. 110 or 192 22. **Police,** Jakobspl. 5, Nürnberg Mitte 1.

Internet access: In Internetcafé Falkens Maze (see **Food,** p. 542).

Post Office: Bahnhofpl. 1, 90402 Nürnberg. Cashes traveler's checks, exchange money, and holds mail. Open Mon.-Fri. 8am-7pm, Sat. 9am-2pm, Sun. 11am-2pm.

Telephone Code: 0911.

ACCOMMODATIONS AND CAMPING

You don't have to trek outside the *Altstadt* walls to hang your hat in an inexpensiv *Pension,* but during the warmer months, you'd best phone first. If all else fails, th tourist office places dazed travelers into dazzling accommodations for a DM5 fe Nearby Erlangen also offers an infrequently filled hostel/guest house (see p. 546).

Jugendgästehaus (HI), Burg 2, 90403 Nürnberg (tel. 230 93 60; fax 23 09 36 11 From the main hall of the train station, take the escalator down into the tunnel pa sage and walk straight ahead, then left up to the sloping exit. Follow this mai shopping street (Königstr.) through Lorenzerpl. over the bridge to the Hauptmarl (10min.). Head in the direction of the golden fountain on the far left and bear rig on Burgstr., then huff and puff up to the top of the hill (in the direction of the sig pointing to the *Schulmuseum;* 20min.). Once a stable and grain storage house fc the imperial castle, it's now a summer *Treffpunkt* (meeting place) for the town high school hipsters. The hostel's Romanesque arches, dizzying panorama over th city, and friendly desk staff (prone to playing with the loudspeakers) make for goo traveler storage. Reception open 7am-1am. Curfew 1am. Theoretical quiet tim 10pm-7am. Frequently booked solid; reservations strongly recommended.

Jugend-Hotel Nürnberg, Rathsbergstr. 300, 90411 Nürnberg (tel. 521 60 92; fax 52 69 54). Streetcar #3: "Ziegelstein," or bus #41: "Felsenkeller" (25min.). Rustic an cheerful, but far from the action. Nice surrounding grounds complement the dor

Nürnberg (Nuremberg)

Albrecht Dürer Haus, **9**
Altstadthof, **8**
Frauenkirche, **4**
Germanisches National
  Museum, **2**
Hauptbahnhof, **I**
Lorenzkirche, **3**
Rathaus, **7**
Schöner Brunnen, **5**
Sebalduskirche, **6**
Stadtmuseum Fembohaus, **10**

rooms, all with bath. 3-bed dorms DM25 (DM22 for stays of for more than 2 nights); singles DM35; doubles DM70. Breakfast DM7.50. Call ahead.

Bahnhofsmission, Bahnhofspl. 9 (tel. 22 99). Located in the basement of the train station; take the escalator down from the main hall into the passage and swing left. If you lack the luck, money, or energy to go anywhere else, you can sleep in one of their rooms, separated by curtains into primitive singles, doubles, and triples. If you're looking for comfort, this is not the place. 24hr. guards. DM17 per person, breakfast included. You must arrive after 8pm.

Hotel Garni Probst, Luitpoldstr. 9 (tel. 20 34 33; fax 205 93 36), is 5min. from the train station. Follow the underground passage from the train station to Königspl. past Burger King on the left. Though the block is seedy, the location is central. It's a jolly family establishment with raspberry halls and spruce rooms. Lucky attic singles DM35, other singles DM62, with shower DM70, with bath DM75-85; doubles DM90, with shower DM100, with bath DM110-125.

Gasthof Schwänlein, Hintere Sterngasse 11 (tel. 22 51 62; fax 241 90 08). Five minutes from the train station. Take the underground passage from the main hall of the train station up to Königstr. Back on your left is Frauentor Mauerstr., which runs into Hintere Sterngasse. The hotel is up on the left. Because the *Pension* borders the red light district, solo packsters might feel more comfortable taking the left at Luipoldstr. Two more lefts onto Vordere Sterngasse and Hintere Sterngasse will bring you to the door. The quiet hallways of the *Pension* are soothing, although rooms are slightly cramped. There is a small garden out back. Singles DM35-40, with shower DM50; doubles DM60-70, with shower DM80. Mail reservations only.

Pension Vater Jahn, Jahnstr. 13 (tel./fax 44 45 07). From the west exit of the station, head straight on Eilgutstr. for three blocks (under the pedestrian underpass), then left under the heavily trafficked Tafelfeld Tunnel (8min.). "*Vater Jahn*" is written on the side of the tall *Pension.* Comfortable, tidy rooms. Singles DM43, with bath DM63; doubles DM75, with shower DM85, with bath DM95. Breakfast included.

Pension Brendel, Blumenstr. 1 (tel./fax 22 56 18). From Königspl. veer right or Königstorgraben, which turns into Marientorgraben; Blumenstr. will glare at you from the right. Five minutes from Lorenzerpl. Paint-chipped exterior, tacky furniture, and spacious rooms. Most rooms equipped with TVs. Singles DM38-42, with bath DM48-55; doubles DM76-84, with bath DM90-98. Reception open 7am-8pm.

Camping: Campingplatz im Volkspark Dutzendteich, Hans-Kalb-Str. 56 (tel. 81 11 22), behind the soccer stadium. U-Bahn South: "Messe Zentrum." Person DM8. Tent DM5. Car DM5. Call ahead. Open May-Sept.

FOOD

Nürnberg titillates the palate of any gourmet or brutally hungry pig. The city is famous for its speciality foods: *Rostbratwurst* (rough but delectable grilled sausage), boiled *Sauerwurst,* and *Lebkuchen,* a candied variant of gingerbread (traditionally devoured at Christmas, but always available at an *Imbiß* stand near you). For a super food, film and beer extravaganza, bust a move to Cince Citta (see **Entertainment and Nightlife** p. 545). If your wallet squeaks, reprimanding you for spending your *Geld* lavishly **Aldi,** on Königstr. near the train station, fulfills the longing for cheap grocery options (open Mon.-Fri. 8:30am-6pm, Sat. 8am-2pm).

Bratwurst Häusle, Rathauspl. 1, next to St. Sebald's Church, is the most famous and crowded *Bratwurst* spot in Nürnberg for a reason. As one local put it, "No one from Nürnberg comes here without his tourist." Six *Rostbratwürste* with *Sauerkraut* or spiced potato salad DM9-15.50. Open Mon.-Sat. 10am-9:30pm.

Internetcafé Falkens Maze, Färberstr. 11 (tel. 23 23 84; fax 23 23 92), at the corner of Frauengasse. Head up to the third floor of the *Maximum* complex to grab a soda or cup of coffee (DM3), then email or surf your night and sorrows away. An amateur DJ mixes hardcore tunes as crazy cyber-punks fight over electronic machines—it's crowded here. Open Mon.-Sat. noon-midnight, Sun. 4pm-midnight 30min. connection DM5, 1hr. DM8 (noon-4pm 1hr. DM5).

Cafe Mohr, Färberstr. 3 (tel. 24 31 39), at the intersection with Karolinenstr. With an Art Deco-ish atmosphere overlooking a lively square, it's a fun place to meet and eat. Crepes (DM4.50-8.50), healthy salads (DM6.50-11.50), and cappuccino lovelies (DM3.50). Open Mon.-Thurs. 9am-midnight, Fri.-Sat. 9am-1am, Sun. 2pm-midnight

Al Castello, Burgstr. 12, sits just below the youth hostel. This rather dingy-looking building conceals some excellent pizza (DM9-15) and pasta dishes (DM9-14), as well as an extensive CD collection and amusing wall decoration. Don't be fooled—*Pizza Brot* means garlic bread (DM5.80). Open daily 6pm-1am.

SIGHTS

Allied bombing left little of old Nürnberg for posterity. The churches, castle, and buildings were all reconstructed from the original stone between 1945 and 1966 most churches display post-war photos and feature empty pedestals where exterior statues were lost in the bombing. From the station, the closest part of the *Altstadt* is walled-in area filled with cottages and shops; this is the **Handwerkhof,** a tourist trap masquerading as an historical attraction. The real sights lie farther up **Königstraße.**

Around the Altstadt and Castle

Nürnberg flaunts its opulence in the *Altstadt*'s three churches. The **Lorenzkirche** on Lorenzerpl., originally Catholic like the town's other churches, later converted to Protestantism (after Nürnberg became Lutheran in 1525). In World War II, all the transportable artwork was stashed in the cellar, while the church itself was completely destroyed except for the towers. The beautiful Gothic structure has been completely restored and once again displays priceless works of art. Of particular interest is the 20m high **tabernacle,** with delicate stone tendrils curling up into the roof vaulting. The large wooden carving hanging in front of the altar is Veit Stoß's 1517 masterpiece *Engelsgruß* (Angel's Greeting; open Mon.-Sat. 9am-5pm, Sun. 1-4pm).

Across the river on Hauptmarktpl., the **Frauenkirche** (Church of Our Lady) rests, constructed in 1352-61 (open Mon.-Sat. 9am-6pm, Sun. and holidays 12:30-6pm; summer tours Mon. 12:10pm and Wed. 6pm). The clock in the center of the facade is the site of the *Männleinlaufen* every day at noon: seven little **Kurfürsten** (nobles) circle three times around the seated figure of (Krazy) Kaiser Karl IV, the emperor who had the Frauenkirche built in 1350. Also on the Hauptmarkt is the **Schöner Brunnen** (Beautiful Fountain), which resembles nothing so much as the steeple of a Gothic church. Check out the 40 imaginatively carved figures, with Moses and the prophets way up top. On the side of the fountain facing into the market, a petite golden ring has been incorporated into the wrought-iron railing. The trick is that there is no seam or joint in either ring or rail. Legend has it that a young metal-worker fell in love with the king's daughter and fashioned the seamless ring-rail in tribute; her father was so impressed that he allowed them to marry. Nürnberg superstition says that if you turn it three times, your wish will come true. According to legend, turning a ring elsewhere on the fountain brings bad, bad, bad luck.

Uphill and on the right from the Schöner Brunnen resides the **Rathaus.** Built between 1616 and 1622 in early Baroque style, sprinkled with a little Renaissance classicism, Nürnberg's *Rathaus* once held the largest council chamber in central Europe, until it was destroyed by fire in 1945—we don't need no water. Beneath the building caves the **Lochgefängnisse** (dungeons; tel. 231 26 90), exhibiting juicy medieval torture instruments. (Obligatory 30min. German tour every 30min.; English translation sheet available upon request. Open April to mid-Oct. and during *Christkindlesmarkt* Mon.-Fri. 10am-4:30pm, Sat.-Sun. 10am-1pm. DM4, students and children DM2.) To continue your tour of the Nürnberg Underground and rat playground, meet at the nearby Albrecht-Dürer-Platz for a one-hour guided walk through the **Felsengänge,** Bergstr. 19 (tel. 22 70 66; fax 89 93 61), in the *Altstadthof,* a web of passageways and cellars four to 25m below the *Altstadt* streets dating back over 100 years. Bring a jacket; it's cold enough down there to store large barrels of beer. (Tours descend daily from the Dürer statue at 11am, 1, 3, and 5pm. DM7, students DM5, kids under 11 free.) Across from the *Rathaus* stands the **Sebalduskirche.** The Catholic congregation maliciously celebrates the annual feast-day of St. Sebaldus by parading through town with his relics (that is, his corpse). During the other 364 days, he rests in his gilded cast bronze tomb in front of the altar (open March-May daily 9:30am-6pm; June-Aug. 9:30am-8pm; Jan.-Feb. and Nov. 9:30am-4pm). Up Burgstr. from the church is the fabulous **Fembo-Haus,** Burgstr. 15 (tel. 231 25 95), a lavishly ornamented patrician house which now contains the **Stadtmuseum,** scheduled to reopen in March 1998 following serious renovations. (Open March-Oct. and during *Christkindlesmarkt* Tues.-Sun. 10am-5pm; Nov.-Feb. except *Christkindlesmarkt* Tues.-Fri. 1-5pm, Sat.-Sun. 10am-5pm. DM4, students and kids DM2.)

Up the hill is the three-part castle: the **Kaiserburg** (Emperor's fortress), the **Burggrafenburg** (the fortress count's fortress), and the **Stadtburg** (the city fortress; tel. 22 57 26). Kaiser Konrad III in the 13th century originally erected the Kaiserburg and the next emperor, Friedrich Barbarossa, expanded it significantly. The spartan chambers of the Kaiserburg housed every Holy Roman Emperor after Konrad III—it was law that every German *Kaiser* spend at least his first day in office here. Since the castle had no heating, however, the *Kaiser*s usually spent their nights in the warm patrician homes of the *Altstadt.* Beyond the stone wall on the way up to the *Burg,* mysterious hoofprints are left by the steed of a German Robin Hood who escaped an execution Inside lurk the Romanesque **Emperor's Chapel** and the imperial living quarters. A 45 minute tour in German covers all parts of the Kaiserburg; the English-language tour offered by the tourist office also covers the castle (see p. 539). Maps in English cost DM2.50. (Open April-Sept. daily 9am-noon and 12:45-5pm; Oct.-March 9:30am-noon and 12:45-4pm. Last morning tour noon, last afternoon tour April-Sept. 4:30pm; Oct.-March 3:30pm. DM5, children DM3.50.)

Ruins of the Third Reich

The ruins of **Dutzendteich Park,** site of the Nazi *Parteitage* (Party Convention) rallies in the 1930s, ring with a deserted disquiet and an unsettling non-presence, reminding visitors of a darker time in German history. The annual rallies drew over 500,000 citizens of the *Reich.* S-Bahn #2: "Dutzendteich," then left as you exit the station until a long building appears on your right; the museum is in the middle of the building. **Zeppelin Field** sits on the far side of the lake near the massive marble platform from which Hitler addressed the throngs. The faint remains of a swastika, stained into the marble, is visible on the central promontory despite attempts to efface it, evidence that the past still haunts the fields.

The poles spaced intermittently along the desolate field once waved enormous banners, and were made infamous by Leni Riefenstahl's film **Triumph des Willens** (Triumph of the Will), which immortalized the 1935 Party rally in one of the most terrifying, enduring depictions of the "Fascist aesthetic." The overwhelming emotional power of Nazi events—injecting Wagnerian theater and Catholic ritual into Fascist grandiosity—can be seen in the exhibit *"Faszination und Gewalt"* (Fascination and Terror), located inside the **Zeppelin Tribüne** in the **Golden Hall** (entrance in rear tel. 86 98 97). The exhibits cover the rise of the Third Reich, Nürnberg's role in the growth of National Socialism, and the *Nürnberg Prozesse* (Nürnberg War Trials of 1946). The photographs, depicting columns of uniformed Nazi troopers marching next to rows of concentration camp prisoners, are as frightful as they are moving. The gold mosaic swastika on the ceiling of the tribune is still uncannily intact (open mid. May to Oct. Tues.-Sun. 10am-6pm; DM2, students DM1). The rest of the park envelops the Nazi-era **New Congress Hall** and the broad, untrafficked **Great Road.** The predominant building style represents the apogee of Nazi architecture—massive and harsh, mixing modernist straight lines with Neoclassical pretension. The litter strewn about and the overgrowth on the paths and buildings define the mood today.

On the other side of town, Nazi leaders faced Allied military judges during the infamous war-crimes trials held in room 600 of the **Justizgebäude,** Fürtherstr. 22. Soon after the trials, in October 1946, 12 men were hanged for their crimes against humanity. The building still serves as a courthouse. U-Bahn #1:"Barenschanze," and continue on Furtherstr., walking away from the old town.

MUSEUMS

The **Albrecht Dürer Haus,** Albrecht-Dürer-Str. 29 (tel. 231 25 68), uphill from the Sebalduskirche entrance, was the last residence of Nürnberg's favorite son during his final years (1509-1528). The *Fachwerk* contains period furniture along with Dürer's etchings and copies of his paintings (most originals are on display in Vienna, Munich and Berlin), as well as an exhibit of Dürer-derived works by modern artists alongside the originals (open Tues.-Sun. 10am-5pm; DM5, students DM3).

The **Altstadthof,** Bergstr. 19 (tel. 22 43 27; fax 40 61 58), features an historic brewery. No free samples, but tempting liter bottles of house brew cost a mere DM6.80 including a DM2 deposit. (Hourly tours Mon.-Fri. 2-7pm, Sat.-Sun. 11am-5pm; during *Christkindlesmarkt* daily 11am-7pm. DM4.50, children DM2.50.) Across the river is the **Germanisches Nationalmuseum,** Kartäusergasse 1 (tel. 133 10; fax 133 12 00). From the Königstr. exit of the tunnel from the station, turn left through the archway onto Frauentormauer and right on Kartäusergasse. This huge, gleaming, modern building chronicles the last millennium of German art, with huge displays of medieval sculpture and painting and scientific instruments from Baroque and Renaissance Ger many, as well as wholesome offerings of rural farm costumes and furnishings. There is also a small floor devoted to toys and dollhouses (open Tues.-Sun. 10am-5pm, Wed. 10am-9pm; DM6, students DM3, seniors DM3).

ENTERTAINMENT AND NIGHTLIFE

Nürnberg's nightspots run the gamut from ultra-traditional to hyper-modern—it takes the fun-loving freak on a roller-coaster ride of sweet, diverse entertainment of all kinds. The *Altstadt* is packed with bars and clubs, and the teeny-bopper crowd hangs out at **Albrecht-Dürer-Platz** (uphill from Sebalduskirche). Pick up the weekly *Plärrer* (DM4), the region's best magazine, listing musical events, cultural happenings, and addresses of bars, discos, and cafes. The tourist office's publication *Club-Seite* offers an amazing and hip overview of clubs in town and their programs. The free regional cultural guide *Doppelpunkt* is doled out at many bars and discos.

   Cine Citta, Gewerbemuseumspl. 3 (tel. 20 66 60), pronounced "Chinnay-Cheeta," packs seven cafes, 12 cinemas, and a disco into its eight-story, river-view, eating-out-and-getting-drunk multimedia mega-complex. The Italian joint, cappuccino bar, Tex-Mex place, and *crêperie* offer never-ending affordable options. Although most movies are in German, the weekly *Filmtips* provides a schedule of original language films (open Sun.-Thurs. until 3am, Fri.-Sat. until 4am). The **Roxy,** Julius-Loßman-Str. 16 (tel. 488 40), shows more current English-language flicks about ass-kicking presidents. The **Planetarium,** Regiomontarsweg 1 (tel. 959 35 38; fax 929 65 54), puts on old, new, and crazy shows. (Shows Wed. 4 and 7:30pm, Thurs. 7:30pm, and 2 weekends per month Sat. 2:30pm, Sun. 11:30pm. Call for schedules. DM5, students DM3.50.)

Bars

   Starclub, Maxtorgraben 33 (tel. 55 16 82), entrance is in the back—follow the graffiti. No papparazzi, but a relaxed ramshackle garden house with rooms bathed in cool blue lights. Classy, diverse young crew creates a pocket of mischief in a residential area. Pinball, *Fußball,* TVs, and packed tables. Beer from DM3.90. Baguette DM5. Open Mon.-Fri. 9:30am-1am, Sat.-Sun. 2:30pm-1am.

   Saigon, Lammsgasse 8 (tel. 244 86 57), off Albrecht-Dürer-Str., across from the Burghotel. *The* trendy *Kneipe* at the moment, arguably the hippest place in town. Faddish, yet relaxing. Espresso DM3, cocktails DM9.50-10. Open daily 9pm-3am.

   Treibhaus, Karl-Grillenberger-Str. 28 (tel. 22 30 41), in the west part of the *Altstadt,* a bit south of Westtor. Metal tables and dim lighting draw a slightly older crowd (i.e., no high-schoolers) to this bistro-bar. As the candlelight softens the look of your tablemate's skin, so do the killer cocktails soften your selectivity. Snacks, salads, pastas, and breakfast (DM5-16.50). Their speciality *Milchkaffee*s give "foam" a new meaning—be initiated. Open Mon.-Wed 8am-1am, Thurs.-Fri. 8am-2am, Sat. 9am-2am, Sun. 9am-1am. Kitchen open daily until 10pm.

   Ruhestörung, Tetzelgasse 21 (tel. 22 19 21), is a 5min. walk from the *Rathaus;* head right on Theresienstr., then left on Tetzelgasse. Relaxed atmosphere, though something of a scene—people-watch with a vengeance. Outdoor seating with patio furniture; the inside is black. Breakfast, sandwiches, warm meals like chili, pasta, and hamburgers (DM8.50-13.50). Beer on tap from DM4.50; Guinness DM6.50. Open Mon.-Fri. 7:30am-1am, Sat. 9:30am-1am.

   Cartoon, An der Sparkasse 6 (tel. 22 71 70), is a central, popular gay bar just off Theatergasse, near Lorenzpl. Smallish, but stylishly awash in mahogany. Baguettes DM7. Beer DM4.30-4.50. Open Mon.-Sat. 11am-1am, Sun. 2pm-1am.

Dance Clubs

   Mach I, Kaiserstr. 1-9 (tel. 20 30 30), in the center of the *Altstadt* near Karlsbrücke. Grooving patrons change size, shape, and drapery depending on the day. Thurs. attracts the mellower "Best of the 70s to 90s" crowd; Fri. swings with soul and hip-hop; Sat. signifies house. Cover DM10. Open Thurs.-Fri. 10pm-4am, Sat. 10pm-5am.

   Forum, Regensburgerstr. 334. S-Bahn #2: "Frankenstadion." Two dance floors assuage the musical needs of the cool. Fri. is the night of nights—choose between hip-hop, hardcore, and experimental in the big hall, or progressive and trip-hop in the smaller hall. Techno parties and live music on Sat. Some of the best bands around play at this joint. Open Fri.-Sat. and every second Thurs. 9pm-4am.

Tolerant, Königstr. 39, Eingweikertsgäßchen. A mixed club, frequented by gays, lesbians, and heteros, centrally located. Mon. plays Schlager—we warned you (see p. 484); Wed. women only; Thurs. 60s and 70s dance tracks; Sat. "Saturgay night"; Sun. delicious dance mix. Cover DM10. Open Fri.-Sat. 9pm-5am, Sun.-Tues. and Thurs. 9pm-4am, Wed. 8pm-4am.

■ Near Nürnberg: Erlangen

Once packed with the Huguenots, today Nürnberg's little neighborhood buddy is an academic and industrial powerhouse. It's here that the elegant **Friedrich-Alexander-University** (founded 1743) boasts eleven distinguished faculties educating 28,000 students. Here, too, the German electronics giant **Siemens AG** conducts its most secretive research. Walk one block straight ahead from the train station to reach the city's center, **Hugenottenplatz,** and its pedestrian artery (called **Hauptstraße** to your left and **Nürnbergerstraße** a few blocks to your right).

One block left up Hauptstr. from Hugenottenpl. is a large square whose left part is the Marktplatz, and whose right portion is the Schloßpl. Entering the square, the **Palais Stutterheim** (tel. 86 27 35), built in 1728, looms behind you. Once the town hall, it now shelves the town's books as official library and art gallery (library open Mon.-Fri. 10am-6:30pm, Sat. 9am-noon; gallery open Tues.-Fri. 10am-6:30pm, Sat.-Sun. 10am-5pm). The huge **Schloß** commands the right part of the square. Built in 1700 by Ludwig I, king of Bayern, it's now home to the university administration. In front of the *Schloß* is a statue of the Margrave Friedrich, a former occupant of the *Schloß* and founder of the university. Years of rough weather have bleached his face, leaving the eye-sockets black, as if the poor man's eyes had been gouged out. The *Schloß*'s gray facade hides the vast 18th-century **Schloßgarten,** which begins in back of the building. The beautifully manicured landscape and peaceful fountain attract many summer picnickers and other vacationers. Jazz and classical concerts are given in the garden during the summer (open daily 6:30am-8pm; free). Around the left of the *Schloß* and past the semi-circular Orangerie lies the exotic **Botanical Garden,** cared for by the scholars at the Institute of Botany. (Open Mon.-Sat. 8am-4pm; Oct.-March Mon.-Fri. 8am-4pm, Sat. 8am-noon; greenhouse open Tues.-Sun. 9:30-11:30am and 1:30-3pm; Oct.-March Tues.-Sun. 9:30-11:30am. Free.)

Erlangen's **tourist office,** Rathauspl. 1 (tel. 895 10; fax 89 51 51), cheerfully draws you into a sea of free brochures. They also find private rooms (DM20-45) for free. Walk one block straight ahead from the station, right at McDonald's, and continue until you see the ugly, ugly *Rathaus* high-rise on the left; the tourist office is just up the open-air stairs. (Open Mon. 8am-6pm, Tues.-Thurs. 8am-4:30pm, Fri. 8am-12:30pm. 24hr. computer info screen outside the office.) Rent **bikes** at **Fahrradkiste** (tel. 20 99 40) at the corner of Werner-von-Siemens-Str. and Henkestr. (Tour bike DM9 per day; mountain bike DM15 per day; ID and DM200 deposit required. Open Mon.-Fri. 11am-6pm, Sat. 10am-1pm.) For a **pharmacy,** try **Kaiser Drogerie** on Hauptstr. (open Mon.-Fri. 8:30am-6pm, Sat. 8am-2pm). The **post office,** Güterhallenstr. 1, 91058 Erlangen, sits two blocks to the right of the station (open Mon.-Fri. 8am-6:30pm, Sat. 8am-2pm). The **telephone code** is 09131.

The **Jugendherberge,** Südliche Stadtmauerstr. 35 (tel. 86 25 55; fax 86 21 19), is centrally convenient. Walk one block straight ahead from the station, turn right at the McDonald's, and take the second left onto Südl.-Stadtmauer-Str. The hostel is 10 minutes away in a stolid, square building. The sign reads *"Freizeitzentrum Frankenhof,"* and it's a central site for Erlangen's *Kinderkultur*—clubs, playing rooms, etc. (Reception open Mon.-Fri. 5-10pm, Sat.-Sun. 7-11am and 4-10pm. Curfew 10pm, key available. DM18. Great breakfast included. Sheets DM5.50.) Inside the *Freizeitzentrum* you'll also find the **Gästehaus** (address and tel. as above) for those 18 and over. (Singles with toilet DM37, with bath DM 46; doubles with toilet DM50, with bath DM72; triples with toilet DM75.) **Camp** at **Naturfreunde Erlangen,** Wohrmühle 6 (tel. 253 03), on an island in the Regnitz river behind the station. Walk under the tracks from the station, right onto Münchenerstr., left on Gerbereistr., and left just after the overpass onto Wohrmühlsteg (person DM6.50, tent DM5; open year round).

This lively student town is packed with good cafes and restaurants with affordable prices. One source of listings is Nürnberg's weekly magazine *Plärrer*. The Italian restaurant **Spago,** Hauptstr. 91 (tel. 20 30 81), flaunts a stylish decor, and serves inexpensive, finger-lickin' good pizza (DM8.50-12). Connect to the ubiquitous internet at the **Café Online** (tel. 89 76 32; fax 89 76 31; http://www.c-online.de). Be careful not to spill your coffee (DM3), bits of your crepe (DM6-9), or your pasta (DM8-10) as you have electronic intercourse with friends back home (30min. connection DM6, 1hr. DM10; open Mon.-Sat. 10am-1am, Sun. 10am-10pm). A fresh produce **market** conquers the Marktplatz (Mon.-Fri. 7am-6pm, Sat. 7am-2pm). **Aldi supermarket** on the Marktplatz is cheap and convenient (open Mon.-Fri. 8:30am-6pm, Sat. 8am-2pm).

Groove, and we mean groove, at **E-Werk,** Fuchsenwiese 1 (tel. 80 05 12), a funked-up industrial building. Walk up Hauptstr. and left at Engelstr.—the building is straight ahead. Erlangen's *Kommunikationszentrum* leans left with musically and artistically hip folk. Inside the *E-Werk,* the **Tanz-Werk** (dance factory) cranks out indy on Tuesdays, while Wednesdays feature either *Frauendisco* (4th Wed. each month), *Männerdisco* (2nd Wed. each month), or R&B (1st and 3rd Wed. each month), and Thursdays challenge you to "all you can groove." Friday is hip-hop and pop, and Saturdays are straight rock. On Sundays, oldies play. They also have films and jazz as well as weekly gallery exhibits. (Ticket office open Tues.-Fri. noon-6pm; dance parties Tues. and Thurs. 10pm-2am, 1st and 3rd Wed. 9:30pm-2am, 2nd Wed. 8:30pm-2am, 4th Wed. 9pm-2am, Fri. 9pm-2am, Sat. 10pm-4am, Sun. 9pm-2am.)

■ Bayreuth

Once you've turned off of Tristanstr. onto Isoldenstr., walked past Walküregasse, and finally headed into the Parsifal Pharmacy, there will be little doubt that you're in Bayreuth, the adopted home of Richard Wagner and the site of the annual *Festspiele*—an *en masse* pilgrimage of BMW-driving devotees coming to bask in his operatic masterpieces. Full of himself in all respects, Wagner retreated to Bayreuth in 1872 to escape his creditors and other folks he had burned. King Ludwig II conveniently paid off Wagner's debts and kept him out of jail. The remote town promised privacy, an 18th-century opera house, and an enchanting ego-fluffing concept—fans would now have to journey long distances to experience a true Wagner performance. As with most "sacred" cities, the grandiosity has left Bayreuth a treasure trove of gorgeous buildings. An affection for pomp (or a need to mock Wagner groupies) makes Bayreuth worthwhile even for those less-than-enthralled with the man and his music.

Orientation and Practical Information Bayreuth is pronounced "Buy Royt," *not* "Bay Ruth"; you will be scorched by lightning should you speak otherwise. The *Altstadt* lies five minutes south of the train station; exit to the left and walk down Bahnhofstr. The **tourist office,** Luitpoldpl. 9 (tel. 885 88; fax 885 55), to the left and about four blocks from the station, provides city maps, hotel listings, a monthly calendar of events, and city **walking tours** in German (DM8, students DM5; tours May-Oct. Tues.-Sat. 10am; Nov.-April Sat. only). **Private rooms** are only available during the *Festspiele* (DM3 fee); at other times, they will help you find a room in a hotel or *Pension* for the same fee (open Mon.-Fri. 9am-6pm, Sat. 9:30am-12:30). Outside the office, an automat dispenses maps, city info, and a hostel list (DM1). A **branch office** is located at Jean-Paul-Platz 1 (tel. 69 01; fax. 885 55; same hours as main office). They find accommodations for a DM3 fee and sell tickets to Bayreuth's lively year-round theater, opera, and musical performances. **Exchange money** at **Citibank,** Opernstr. 2, beneath Hotel Anker, which offers 24hr. bankcard service (open Mon. and Thurs. 8:45am-1pm and 2-6pm, Tues. and Fri. 8:45am-1pm and 2-4pm, Wed. 8:45am-1pm and 1:30-4pm). The town is an easy daytrip by hourly **trains** from Nürnberg (1hr.; DM23.20); travelers from the north have to change in Lichtenfels. The **post office,**

Bürgerreutherrstr. 1, 95444 Bayreuth (tel. 78 00), is across from the train station and to the right (open Mon.-Fri. 8am-7pm, Sat. 8am-1pm). The **telephone code** is 0921.

Accommodations If you visit during the *Festspiele* and forgot to book your room last year, don't even try to stay in Bayreuth. Almost any other time, though, prices are reasonable and beds available. Bayreuth's brand-new **Jugendherberge (HI)**, Universitätsstr. 28, 95447 Bayreuth (tel. 252 62; fax 51 28 05), lies outside the city center beyond the *Hofgarten* near the university. Bus #4 (DM2.30) from the Marktplatz: "Mensa." If the sun is shining, walk down Ludwigstr. from the city center, take a left onto Friedrichstr., then veer left onto Jean-Paul-Str., which merges with Universitätsstr. Or bus #11 (direction: "Wolfsbach") or 8 (direction: "Bodenseering-Markt-Universität"): "Kreuzsteinbad" (bus #11 leaves Mon.-Fri. 9am-6pm on the every hr., Sat.-Sun. less frequently; bus #18 Mon.-Fri. 7am-6:40pm every 20min.). Follow the sidewalk up ahead (5min.) to the large square *Jugendherberge* on your right. It's friendly but a tad regimented: at 10pm, *everything* locks up. (Reception open 7am-12pm. Lockout 9-11:30am. Curfew 10pm. DM20. Breakfast included. Sheets DM5.50. Open March to mid-Dec.)

Gasthof Hirsch, St. Georgen 26 (tel. 267 14), is a 10-minute walk behind the train station, on a corner with a rainbow of geraniums spilling out the windows. Exit the train station in the back, just beyond track 5; take a left as you exit, then right onto Brandenburgerstr., and left onto St. Georgen. It's clean and crisp with 18 beds (singles DM35-40; doubles DM70-80). At **Gasthof zum Brandenburger**, St. Georgen 9 (tel. 78 90 60; fax 78 90 62 40), the rooms are nice and sunny, as is the beer garden, and spiffy ivy wallpaper adorns the third floor. (Singles DM35, with shower DM60; doubles DM60, with shower DM130. AmEx, Diners, MC, Visa.) **Gasthof Schindler**, Bahnhofstr. 9 (tel. 262 49), is close to the station. Clean rooms complement the restaurant with yellow tables in the basement (singles DM60; doubles DM95).

Food Fill 'er up at the **University Mensa** (tel. 60 81) for DM3-6; any student ID should do. Bus #4 (DM2.30) from the bus stations at the end of Luitpoldpl. on the right: "Mensa," then walk past the buildings straight ahead. The *Mensa* is to the right up the steps. It's an enormous, low-roofed building (open Oct.-July Mon.-Thurs. 8am-6pm, Fri. 8am-2pm; Aug.-Sept. Mon.-Thurs. 11:15am-1:30pm, Fri. 11:15am-1:15pm). **Braunbierhaus**, Kanzleistr. 15 (tel. 696 77), beyond Bayreuth's *Stadtkirche*, is an authentic delight nearly 900 years old. Share the authenticity with other authentic tourists while munching on a *Ritterbratwurst* with hashbrowns (DM9), *Schnitzel* (DM15-17), or small veggie dishes (DM5-9; open Mon.-Sat. 11:30am-2pm and 5:30-10:30pm; Sun. 11:30am-2pm). **Gastätte Porsch**, Maximilianstr. 63 (tel. 649 49), serves pile-icious portions at great prices. *Schnitzels* and steak meals run DM11-17 (open Mon.-Sat. 7am-8:30pm). Across the road rests **Brauereischänke am Markt**, Maximilianstr. 56 (tel. 649 19), serving *Bratwurst* with potato salad or *Kraut* (DM8.80; open Mon.-Sat. 11am-10pm). **Künstlerkneipe Eule**, Kirchgasse 8 (tel. 575 54), is tucked in a small alley to the left off Maximilianstr. *Wiener Schnitzel* with fries and salad runs DM12.80 (open daily 11am-11pm).

Café Wundertüte, Richard-Wagner-Str. 33 (tel. 51 47 48), has a cup of coffee and a slice of raspberry *Torte* with your name on it (DM5.30), served in a wood-paneled atmosphere rounded out by small salads, noodles, *Wieners*, and cheeses (DM5-9.50; open Mon.-Tues. and Thurs.-Fri. 8am-6pm, Sat. 9am-6pm). Fill up your basket at the **market** in the Rotmainhal near Hindenburgstr. (Wed. and Sat. 7am-5pm). **Norma**, Richard-Wagner-Str. 11, is the local **supermarket** with the fixings for a perfect picnic (open Mon.-Fri. 8:30am-7pm, Sat. 8am-4pm).

The Wagner Festspiele For Wagnerians, a devotional visit to Bayreuth is like a pious pilgrimage to Mecca. Every summer from July 25 to August 28 (the dates are the same every year), thousands of visitors pour in for the **Bayreuth Festspiele**, a vast and bombastic—in a word, Wagnerian—celebration of the composer's works. The music fills the **Festspielhaus** theater that Wagner built for his "music of the future."

The world's operatic darlings, directors, and conductors have been taking on *The Ring of the Nibelung, Tannhäuser, Parsifal,* and *Tristan and Isolde* here since 1876. Judging by the number of German Wagner Societies and Clubs, the spectacle will probably continue for as long as the Holy Grail is old. Tickets (DM80-300, obstructed view DM40-50) for the festival go on sale several years in advance and sell out almost immediately. Write to Bayreuther Festspiele, 95402 Bayreuth, well before the September *three years* before you wish to attend. Your request will be processed when it is received; you'll be notified some time after mid-November. Reserve a room in town as soon as you get tickets—Wagnerophiles just write **every year** and hope for the best.

Sights If you're not a Wagner fan, feign appreciation for a day in this devoted opera-town. Wagner devotees visiting Bayreuth when the *Festspiele* is over console themselves with a **Festspielhaus** tour (tel. 787 80); go right at the station and up at the end of Siegfried-Wagner-Allee. To fund the 1872 construction, the composer hit up sugar daddy Ludwig II, who was in the midst of his own egocentric building spree. Ludwig responded with modest amounts of cash, resulting in a semi-spartan structure—Wagner fans must endure cushionless seats and precious little leg room to catch a show. (Tours April-Sept. Tues.-Sun. 10, 10:45am, 2:15, 3pm, Oct. and Dec.-March Tues.-Sun. 10 and 10:45am. No tours during rehearsal or *Festspiele*. DM3, students DM2.)

The composer's house, *Haus Wahnfried,* is now the **Richard Wagner Museum,** Richard-Wagner-Str. 48 (tel. 757 28 16; fax 757 28 22). It houses an inexhaustible and kitschy—yet valuable—collection of scores, costumes, and stage sets. See Wagner playing cards, stamps, and coins, as well as his spoons, mirror, and little *Wotan* and *Sieglinde* dolls (the Wagnerian Barbie and Ken). Three death masks provide morbid pleasure: Wagner's, composer Carl Maria von Weber's, and that of his friend and patsy, Ludwig II. The thousands of exhibits are in German only—it might behoove you to pick up the melodramatic English guide-booklet (DM3). Wagner's compositions are played in the drawing room daily at 10am, noon, and 2pm; videos shown at 11am and 3pm. Those who fail to appreciate his "Total Works of Art" (as he modestly referred to them) should recall Mark Twain's fiendishly accurate assessment of Wagner's music: "It's better than it sounds." (Open Mon., Wed., and Fri. 10am-5pm, Tues. and Thurs. 10am-8:30pm. July-Aug. DM5, students DM2; Sept.-June DM4, students DM2. 3-day passes for the Wagner Museum, the Jean Paul Museum, and Franz Liszt Museum available for DM6.) Behind the house lie the graves of Wagner, his wife Cosima, and Russ, his big black dog.

Farther behind the house is the **Hofgarten,** an English-style park. Turn right as you enter and be led to the **German Freemason Museum,** Hofgarten 1 (tel. 698 24; fax 512 850; ring the bell). If you've wondered what's inside those windowless temples or what the strange symbols mean (or have your suspicions after reading *Foucault's Pendulum*), this is the place for you, complete with floor plans and pink roses. The bizarre rituals have transpired in Bayreuth for 225 years (open Tues.-Fri. 10am-noon and 2-4pm, Sat. 10am-noon; DM2, students DM1). In the shadow of the haughty Wagner Museum, the **Franz Liszt Museum,** Wahnfriedstr. 9 (tel. 757 28 18), exhibits the composer's pianos and music sheets and morbidly displays the room where he died (again, complete with death mask). In Bayreuth, Liszt is probably best known for fathering Wagner's wife—indeed, musical virtuosos also inbreed (open daily 9am-noon and 2-5pm; DM3, students and seniors DM1). The **Jean Paul Museum,** Wahnfriedstr. 1 (tel. 757 28 17), celebrates the life of Bayreuth's greatest poet with an endless collection of notebooks and chairs (open July-Sept. daily 10am-5pm; Sept.-June daily 10am-noon and 2-5pm; DM3, students DM1).

Just down Wahnfriedstr., enter the lovely gardens once again to wander down the primrose path to the 18th-century Baroque **Neues Schloß** (tel. 759 69 21), former residence of Friedrich the Great's sister, Margravine Wilhelmine. Considered one of Europe's most brilliant and cultured women, she married the Margrave of Bayreuth and ended up stuck in what must have seemed a provincial cow town. After a mysterious castle fire, she redecorated and rococoed like mad King Ludwig, and when she finished gilding the home furnishings, she swept her eyes across Bayreuth and strove to cosmopolitanize it. (Castle open Tues.-Sun. 10-11:20am and 1:30-4:10pm; Oct.-March Tues.-Sun. 10-11:20am and 1:30-2:50pm; DM3, students DM1). The lavishly ornate **1748 Margravian Opera House** is the tangible result of such frustration combined with more money than is good for a person. Wagner originally thought this theater's pomp appropriate for his production, but its 500 seats and stage proved way too small for his lofty needs. (Tours in German every 30min., borrow an English text. Open Tues.-Sun. 9-11:30am and 1:30-4:30pm; Oct.-March Tues.-Sun. 10-11:30am and 1:30-3pm. DM3, students DM2.) If you're sweating from all this palatial magnificence, make a splash in Bayreuth's fabulous outdoor pool, **Kreuzsteinbad** (tel. 661 07), and see that grand Wagnerian style is not limited to 18th-century opera houses. (Open June-Aug. daily 7am-8pm; Sept.-May daily 7am-7:30pm. Last entry 30min. before closing. DM4, students DM2. Massage DM15.)

▓ Coburg

Coburg only joined Bayern in 1920 after years spent as a member of Sachsen. This move fortuitously saved the city from inclusion in the GDR. The 1947 division of Germany shifted the town's geographical location from the heartland to the margins. Today, wealthy Coburg sits at the center again, but a brief trip north across the old GDR border reveals the vast incongruities the past 45 years have created. This 11th-century town has been beautifully preserved, thanks to an arbitrary line in the woods.

From the train station, turn right on Lossaustr., left at the light onto Mohrenstr., around the large, central *Stadtcafe,* and right on Spitalgasse to reach the Renaissance **Altstadt** (15min.). The huge 16th-century structure on the Marktplatz is the frescoed **Rathaus.** The old **Stadthaus** across the square was once the abode of the Coburg *Herzog* (Duke). The proud central statue is of **Prince Albert,** the Coburger husband of Queen Victoria. To the right down Herrngasse towers the part-Renaissance, part-neo-Gothic **Schloß Ehrenburg** (Castle of Honor; tel. 808 80), the town residence of the Coburg Dukes from 1547 to 1918. When the *Herzog* built the palace, he did so without borrowing too much money and without grossly oppressing his peasantry. When the *Kaiser* toured the site, he remarked that it stood as a monument to the *Herzog*'s honor, and the name stuck. The palace later fell to the Sachsen-Coburg-Gothas, and Albert spent his childhood within its walls. Victoria's private quarters can be toured. (Tours Tues.-Sun. 10, 11am, 1:30, 2:30, 3:30, and 4:30pm; Oct.-March Tues.-Sun. 10, 11am, 1:30, 2:30, and 3:30pm. DM4, students and seniors DM3.)

Paved footpaths wind through the **Hofgarten,** a shaded, grassy expanse stretching from Schloß Ehrenburg to the 11th-century **Veste** (fortress). Allow 30 to 45 minutes to hike up the deceptively steep hill. Otherwise, bus #8 from in front of the *Rathaus:* "Veste" (DM2) and walk up about 50m. The 16th-century fortress, encircled by a double set of fortified walls, was inhabited until 1918, when Karl Eduard abdicated the dukedom. The main buildings are the **Fürstenbau** (prince's palace; tel. 920 88; open Tues.-Sun. 9:30am-noon and 2-4pm with tours every 30min.; Nov.-March tours 2 and 3pm; DM4, students DM3, under 14 DM2, under 6 free) and the **Coburg Art Museum** (tel. 87 90 or 741 80; open Tues.-Sun. 9:30am-1pm and 2-5pm; Nov.-March Tues.-Sun. 2-5pm; DM5, students DM3, under 6 with parents free). The half-timbered *Fürstenbau* contains a chapel commemorating Martin Luther's 1530 stay, as well as the beautifully furnished ducal living quarters. (Tours of the *Veste,* including the art museum, April-Oct. Sun. 10am; DM7 includes art museum admission.) Back in town to the right of Herrngasse is the minty-green **Coburger Puppen-Museum** (Doll Museum), Rückertstr. 2-3 (tel. 740 47; fax 271 16). In one of its 32 chronologically ordered rooms, following doll history from 1800 to 1955, spot Lilli, a curvy German doll from the 1950s intended for adults; the then-unknown American toy company Mattel bought the rights to her in 1958, and one year later young girls went Barbie-crazy, playing with an awkwardly shaped blonde. Contemplate the corporate toy world at the adjoining **Café Hello Dolly.** (Open April-Oct. daily 9am-5pm; Nov.-March Tues.-Sun. 10am-5pm. DM3.50, students DM3, under 14 DM2.)

Many **train** travelers need to change at Lichtenfels on the Nürnberg-Berlin line to reach Coburg. From Coburg, trains go to Bamberg (1-5 per hr., 50min; DM14.20), Nürnberg (1-2 per hr., 1½-2hr.), Würzburg (hourly, 2hr.), and Berlin (8 per day, 5hr. 40min.). Hourly **buses** travel to the Thüringer Wald (2hr.). Coburg's **tourist office,** Herrngasse 4 (tel. 741 80; fax 741 829), off the Markt, offers free maps and finds rooms (DM30-60) for free (open Mon.-Fri. 9am-6:30pm, Sat. 9am-1pm; Nov.-March Mon.-Fri. 9am-5pm, Sat. 9am-1pm). A **walking tour** in German departs from the *Denkmal* on the Markt (Sat. 3pm; DM5). The **post office,** Hindenburgstr. 6, 96450 Coburg (tel. 910), to the left off Mohrenstr. on the way to the *Altstadt,* **exchanges money** (open Mon.-Fri. 8am-6pm, Sat. 8am-noon). The **telephone code** is 09561.

Jugendherberge Schloß Ketschendorf (HI), Parkstr. 2 (tel. 153 30; fax 286 53), rests in a sublime converted palace. The sight of play-school *Jugendherberge* furniture in the grand castle is a funny sight, but the modern rooms make spotless sense. Bus #1 (from the Markt): "DJH." Parkstr. is up on the left. Or walk on Ketschengasse to Ketschendorferstr., then all the way to Parkstr. to make a left (25min.). Ketschendorf proudly displays plaques proclaiming itself the "Best Bavarian Youth Hostel." Billiard tables and a disco back up the claim. (Reception open 5-6pm and 8-9:30pm. Lockout 10am-noon. Curfew 10pm, but they'll give you a key. Hot showers available 7-9am and 3-10pm. DM22. Breakfast included. Sheets DM5.50.) The **Gasthof Goldenes Kreuz,** Herrngasse 1 (tel. 904 73; fax 905 02), on the Marktplatz, offers clean, simple rooms and a restaurant downstairs. (Singles DM45, with shower DM50; doubles DM90, DM100.) Try the bargain prices at **Zum Hohenfels,** Geleitstr. 12 (tel. 385 79). Follow Lossaustr. left from the train station under the underpass, turn right, cross the intersection, and turn left onto Geleitstr. at the far side of the park (15min.). (Doubles DM70. Call ahead.) The **Münchner Hofbräu,** Kleine Johannisgasse 8 (tel. 750 49; fax 904 34), is both a hopping restaurant and *Pension,* two blocks from the Marktplatz off Spitalgasse. (Singles with bath DM55; doubles with bath DM105.) The restaurant serves just what you would expect, given the name—beer and plates of *Klößer-* and *Rostbratwürstchen* (grilled sausages; DM8-14). Old clocks and stained glass windows add to the fun atmosphere (open daily 10am-midnight).

Two of Coburg's specialty foods are the *Thüringer Klößer* (dumplings) and *Coburger Bratwurst.* Billowing clouds of smoke and the smell of grilled *Coburger Bratwürste* hang thick in the air over the market square, in which a **farmer's market** (Wed. and Sat. 7am-5pm) and a **fruit market** (Tues. 7am-noon) take place. **Café Prinz Albert,** at the corner of Albertspl. down Ketschengasse from the market (tel. 954 20), offers ice cream (DM4-7.80) and sweet cakes (DM4), as well as small snacks (open Mon.-Sat. 8:30am-6:30pm, Sun. 10am-6pm). **Norma supermarket** lies on Hindenburgstr., across from the post office (open Mon.-Fri. 8:30am-6:30pm, Sat. 8am-2pm).

For nightlife, **Café Filou,** Bahnhofstr. 11 (tel. 900 70), offers a relaxed atmosphere with funky round chairs and sepia-toned photographs. Try to grab a sweet table in the greenhouse (pizza and pasta DM8.50-14.50; open Mon.-Sat. 9:30am-1am). **Café-Floh,** Herrngasse 12, off the Marktplatz, attracts students with its dark-wooded environment, conducive to late-night philosophizing over a beer. Fresh baguettes (DM3-7) and pizza (DM6.40; open daily 8pm-3am).

■ Near Coburg: Vierzehnheiligen

About 20 minutes south of Coburg by car is the resplendent Rococo masterpiece, **Vierzehnheiligen Kirche** (Fourteen Saints' Church; tel. (09571) 950 80), which stands on a broad grassy rise above the Main River. It was on this site in 1445-46 that local villagers saw visions of the Christ Child and the "Fourteen Saints of Intercession." The spot became an important pilgrimage destination, and the present church was erected in the 18th century. The facade is a sumptuous example of detailing, with golden, glowing stone and unusually high towers for a church its age. The Rococo interior is dominated by the *Nothelfer Altar,* which protects the square meter of holy ground on which the vision appeared. The Christ Child sits at the top of the altar surrounded by statues of all 14 saints, each interceding for a particular cause. Pray to the decapitated St. Dionysus if you have a headache, or to St. Christopher for budget travel tips (open daily 9am-6pm; free). To reach Vierzehnheiligen from Coburg, take the **train** to Lichtenfels (15min.; DM5.80). The church is about 6km from town. An infrequent **bus** runs from the Lichtenfels station to the church (Tues.-Thurs. 8:15am and 2pm; return 10:40am and 5:40pm). A **taxi** costs about DM20 from the Lichtenfels train station and the **walk** takes 1½-2 hours.

■ Bamberg

Packed with sights, but largely overlooked by travelers, this little city on the Regnitz boasts a history spanning a thousand years. Emperor Heinrich II liked Bamberg so much that he made it the center of his empire, crowning it with a colossal cathedral. The magnificent building is but one shining example of the city's beauty. Bamberg's architectural treasures owe a great deal to the city's sheer luck—it escaped two virulent wars relatively unscathed. In the Thirty Years War, Bamberg survived two sieges by the formidable Swedish King Gustavus Adolphus II, and three centuries later, the city emerged from World War II with only minor bruises. The residents of Bamberg celebrate their good fortune by drinking an astounding amount of beer—330 liters per capita every year, the highest consumption rate in the world.

ORIENTATION AND PRACTICAL INFORMATION

The heart of Bamberg lies on an island between the Rhine-Main-Danube Canal and the Regnitz river (named for its location at the confluence of the Regen and the Pegnitz Rivers). Across the Regnitz from the island lie the winding streets of the *Altstadt*. To reach the *Altstadt* from the *Bahnhof*, walk straight on Luitpoldstr., cross the canal, and straight on Willy-Lessing-Str. until it empties into Schönleinspl. Turn right onto Langestr. and left up Obere Brückestr., which leads through the archway of the *Rathaus* and across the Regnitz (25-30min.). Or grab a city bus in front of the *Hauptbahnhof* for a quick ride into town (DM1.50). The **Bamberg Card** (valid for 48hr.) is a great deal, allowing free public transportation in the city, a free walking tour, and admission to four museums (1 person DM13, 2 people DM24, 3 people DM35).

Tourist Office: Fremdenverkehrsamt, Geyerwörthstr. 3, 96047 Bamberg (tel. 87 11 61; fax 87 19 60), on an island in the Regnitz. To get there, follow the directions to the *Altstadt*. Once through the *Rathaus*, take two lefts and re-cross the Regnitz on the wooden footbridge; the tourist office is on your right under the arches. You can avoid paying DM0.50 for their map by picking up a free hotel list or monthly program, which have better maps. A vending machine outside dispenses hotel lists and city maps for DM0.50. They also find rooms in hotels or pensions by mail or in person for a DM5 fee. Open Mon.-Fri. 9am-6pm, Sat. 9am-3pm. **Walking tours** of the city meet in front of the tourist office. (April-Oct. Mon.-Sat. 10:30am and 2pm, Sun. 11am; Nov.-March Mon.-Sat. 2pm, Sun. 11am. DM8, students DM5.) Tours of the cathedral and the *Neue Residenz* meet at the *Neue Residenz* and leave when there are "enough people." (Available April-Sept. daily 9am-noon and 1:30-5pm; Oct.-March 9am-noon and 1:30-4pm. DM8, students DM6).

Currency Exchange: Citibank, on Schönleinspl., accepts nearly any card. Open Mon. and Thurs. 8:45am-1pm and 2-6pm, Tues. and Fri. 8:45am-1pm and 2-4pm, Wed. 8:45am-1pm and 1:30-4pm.

Trains: The main station is on Ludwigstr. (tel. 194 19). Trains to Nürnberg (2-4 per hr., 30min.-1hr.), Würzburg (1 per hr., 1¼hr.), Frankfurt (1 per hr., 2hr. 40min.), and Munich (1-2 per hr., 2½-4hr.).

Public Transportation: An excellent transportation net centers around the **ZOB (Zentral Omnibus Bahnhof)** on Promenadestr. off Schönleinspl. Ask at the tourist office for schedules. One-way bus fare DM1.50. Four-ride ticket DM5.

Taxi: call 150 15 or 345 45.

Bike Rental: Fahrradhaus Griesmann, Kleberstr. 25 (tel. 229 67). Walk straight on Luitpoldstr. from the train station, right on Heinrichsdamm after the bridge, left at the next bridge, and take the first right onto Kleberstr. DM12 per day. ID required.

Bookstore: Görres Bücher, Langestr. 24, stocks a small selection of contemporary novels in English on the top floor. Open Mon.-Fri. 8:30am-6pm, Sat. 8:30am-1pm.

Laundromat: SB Waschsalon, in the Atrium mall left of the train station, 2nd floor (tel. 20 29 40). Wash DM6. Dry DM1 per 10min. Open Mon.-Fri. 9am-7pm, Sat. 8am-8pm, Sun. 9am-2pm.

Women's Resources: Every Tuesday evening in **Café Jenseits,** at Promenadestr. 5 (tel. 210 94), off Schönleinspl., a *Frauencafé* pops up with discussions of contemporary issues, films, and readings.

Rape Crisis Line: tel. 582 80.

Pharmacy: Einhorn Apotheke, Grüner Markt 3, just around the corner from Langestr., has a list of 24hr. pharmacies in the window. Open Mon.-Fri. 8:15am-6pm, Sat. 8:30am-12:30pm.

Hospital: Klinikum Bamberg, Bugerstr. 80 (tel. 50 30).

Emergency: tel. 110. **Police,** Schildstr. 81 (tel. 18 50).

Post Office: Hauptpostamt, Ludwigstr. 25, 96052 Bamberg (tel. 83 62 81), across from the train station, helps you with telegrams and **currency exchange.** Also cashes traveler's checks (DM6). Open Mon.-Fri. 8am-6pm, Sat. 8am-12:30pm.

Telephone Code: 0951.

ACCOMMODATIONS AND CAMPING

Accommodations in Bamberg tend to be very expensive, largely because *Privatzimmer* are illegal to rent.

Jugendherberge Wolfsschlucht (HI), Oberer Leinritt 70, 96049 Bamberg (tel. 560 02 or 563 44; fax 552 11). Bus #18 (from *ZOB*): "Am Regnitzufer" (every 20min.; DM1.50). Far from the city center, but the rooms are tidy. Reception open 4-10pm. Curfew 10pm. Breakfast included. Sheets DM5.50. Because it's the only hostel in Bamberg, it fills up snap-crackle-pop quick; call very early for summer reservations. If full, try the hostels in Erlangen or Coburg. Open Feb. to mid-Dec.

Hospiz, Promenadestr. 3, 96047 Bamberg (tel. 98 12 60; fax 981 26 66). Large doubles, balconies, great breakfast—all in a central location, off Schönleinspl. Reception open 7am-10pm. Check-out 11am. Singles (some with TV) DM50, with bath DM66; doubles with shower DM80, with bath DM88-98; triples with shower DM100, with bath DM126. Phone, fax, or mail reservations accepted. Call ahead.

Maisel-Bräu-Stübl, Obere Königstr. 38 (tel./fax 255 03), 10 minutes from the station. Left off Luitpoldstr. Large rooms with balconies overlook a pleasant courtyard. Big fluffy pillows. Reception open 9am-midnight. Singles DM39; doubles DM70, with shower DM80. Breakfast included. Delectable dinners from DM13.

Fässla, Obere Königstr. 19-21, (tel. 265 16 or 229 98; fax 20 19 89). Go right off Luitpoldstr. Also 10 minutes from the station. Cozy and comfortable with TVs and phones. Fässla ("little keg" in Bavarian dialect) keeps its own **brewery** downstairs that's very popular with the locals. All rooms with bath. Singles DM63; doubles DM98; triples DM130. Breakfast buffet included. Parking DM5. Luggage storage available. Closed after 1pm on Sundays.

Camping: Campingplatz Insel, Am Campingpl. 1 (tel. 563 20). Bus #18 (direction: "Klinikum"): "Bug." Prime riverside locale. Showers, toilets, washing machines. Adult DM6.50. Child DM4.50. Tent DM4.50. Car DM11.

FOOD

Bamberg boasts several breweries, but its most unusual specialty is **Rauchbier** (smoke beer). The daring can try its sharp, smoky taste (DM3.20 for 0.5L) at **Schlenkerla,** Dominikanerstr. 6 (tel. 560 60), *Rauchbier*'s traditional home. The smoke brewery lies at the foot of the steps leading up to Dompl. **Der Beck,** Hauptwachstr. 16, at Hauptwacheck, offers scrumptious snacks and delicious pastries from the bakery (open Mon.-Fri. 6:30am-7:30pm, Sat. 6:30am-2pm). The **Tengelmann supermarket,** Langestr. 14 (open Mon.-Fri. 8:30am-7pm, Sat. 7:30am-4pm) sells groceries.

University Mensa, Austr. 37, off Obstmarkt, serves the cheapest edible meals in town for under DM5. Dine on yellow plastic trays (or put your meal on one). Menu

changes daily. Any student ID will do. Open daily 11:30am-2pm. **Snack hall** open
until 7pm. Check bulletin boards for jobs, rooms, and nightlife happenings.

Café Müller, Austr. 23 (tel. 20 29 43). Wallsized open windows create an illusory out-
door ambience in this student hangout with a French feel—look out for Catherine
Deneuve. Breakfast until 2pm (DM3.50-14.80). Crepes DM4.80-8. Pasta and salad
DM8-10. Open Mon.-Thurs. 9am-11pm, Fri.-Sat. 9am-1am, Sun. 11am-10pm.

Kachelofen, Obere Sandstr. 1 (tel. 571 72), in the *Fränkisches Gasthaus*. Roly-poly
families pack in like sardines at the outside tables. Try the *Leberknödel* ("liver
balls"—better than you might think) with *Kraut* (DM13), or other Bavarian specialities (DM13-26.50). Open daily 10am-1am (kitchen open until 11pm).

Polarbär, Judenstr. 7 (tel. 536 01). In the *Altstadt*, across the walking bridge and left
a block or two. Groovy beer garden with aromatic atmosphere. Baguettes DM7.30.
Salads DM4-9. Vegetarian dishes DM8-12. After 10pm you can sneak your way into
the exciting Black Bar. Polarbär open daily 11am-midnight. Kitchen open noon-
3pm and 5-10pm. Black Bar open Sun.-Fri. until 11am, Sat. until midnight.

SIGHTS

The **Altes Rathaus** guards the middle of the Regnitz River like an anchored ship. Built
in the 15th century, its strategic location belied no preference for the church nor for
the civic powers, both of which held seats on opposite banks of the river. Stand on
one of the two bridges to gaze at this half-*Fachwerk*, half-Baroque facade with a
Rococo tower in between. You'll notice a number of visual oddities in the frescoes—
painted cherubs have three-dimensional limbs and bodies that jut from the wall
where sculpted stone has been attached.

Across the river and up the hill are the **Dom** (tel. 50 23 30) and the **Neue Residenz,**
the former episcopal palace. Cathedral construction began in 1004, and the transition
from Romanesque to Gothic can be traced in the architecture of the building. The
most famous object within the *Dom* is the equestrian statue called the **Bamberger
Reiter** (the Bamberg Knight), which dates from the 13th century and depicts the
chivalric ideal of the medieval warrior-king. Many stories have grown up around the
statue over the years, including one that the statue was a prophecy of Hitler's rise to
power. People tell dumb stories. The tomb of Heinrich II and Queen Kunigunde of
the Holy Roman Empire lies near the east apse; Heinrich sponsored the construction
of the cathedral and was later canonized. The west apse claims the grave of the only
pope buried in Germany—Clement II, who died in 1047. Heinrich and Kunigunde's
crowns are also on display, each in a glass box on its own altar. (Cathedral open daily
8am-6pm; Nov.-March 8am-5pm—except during services. Also 30min. organ concerts May-Oct. Sat. noon; free. For info on tours see **Practical Information,** p. 552, or
call 50 23 30.) The **Diözesanmuseum** includes the *Domschatz* (cathedral treasures)
and *Kaisermantel* (emperor's coat); enter through the *Dom* (tours daily 11am and
3pm; DM3, students and seniors DM3.50). Across the square, the **Neue Residenz,**
Dompl. 8 (tel. 563 51), strikes baroque poses amongst roses; from its prim rose garden, the town stretches out like a sea of roofs and the air smells rosy from 40 paces
(Open daily 9am-noon and 1:30-5pm; Oct.-March 9am-noon and 1:30-4pm; last entry
30min. before morning and afternoon closing. DM4, students and seniors DM3.)

In town, the streets between the *Rathaus* and the *Dom* are lined with 18th-century
Baroque houses, many of them not yet renovated. At **Pfahlplätzchen,** at the pink
house on the corner of Judenstr., you can see the bay window out of which Hegel
used to peer while editing the proofs of the *Phenomenology of Spirit*. At the time
unable to find a university teaching position, the philosopher was serving as editor of
the Bamberg newspaper (1807-08).

Böttinger Palace, on Judenstr., displays a 1713 facade inspired by a Venetian palace and a similarly exotic courtyard. Farther down the street, the lovely **Concordia-
haus** is now the local Institute for Geochemical Research. Across the river at
Schillerpl. 26 is the **E.T.A. Hoffmann House.** Author of the nightmarish *Sandmann,*
Hoffmann wrote his uncanny stories in this rickety three-story house for five years. He
and his wife rented two little rooms directly over one another, and they often chatted
through a small opening in the floor (open May-Oct. Tues.-Fri. 4-6pm, Sat.-Sun. and

holidays 10am-noon; DM2, students DM1). Go to **Jazzclub,** Obere Sandstr. 18 (tel. 537 40). for a funky mix of goth, alternative, punk, grunge, and mystic. Fri.-Sat. hosts the local jazz scene from 9pm-1am. Crowded, diverse student joint. Cover hovers at DM10, students DM8, DM4 on Tues (Open on Tues. and Thurs. 9pm-1am.) The **Live Club,** Obere Sandstr. 7 (tel. 50 04 58), offers varied disco. Scenes change with the days, mixing everything from rhythm and blues to hip-hop to hardcore. Stop by for a schedule. (Open Mon. and Wed. 9pm-1am, Sat. 9pm-2am.)

■ Aschaffenburg

The Bavarian king Ludwig I affectionately referred to Aschaffenburg as his "Bavarian Nice." The city that served as a second residence for the Electors of Mainz still retains much of its past charm. Not even the near-total destruction of this Frankfurt suburb during World War II and its subsequent military occupation have frustrated the *Freundlichkeit* and hospitality of the locals. "Aschaffenburg Likes You!" proclaims a glossy brochure—and they're not kidding. After a cold spell in Frankfurt, don't be surprised if you're *Guten Tag*-ed frequently during your stay in *A-burg*.

After the annual winter hiatus, when *Fräulein* summer enters the stage, Aschaffenburg blossoms like a spring flower. Locals and tourists alike indulge in the city's home-brewed pride and joy, **Heylands Beer,** as they party with fireworks and merry-go-rounds for 11 days straight during the **Volksfest** in mid-June. In July, the **Kippenburg** and **Schloß wine festival** act as magnets for the city. The annual **Carillion-Fest,** held the first weekend in August, brings renowned ringers from around the globe and tin-tinnabulating tourists who come to swim in the musical swell.

Schloß-Johannisburg, the former domain of the Mainz bishops, is now an extensive museum of art by old Dutch and German masters. (*Schloß* open Tues.-Sun. 9am-noon and 1-5pm; Nov.-March Tues.-Sun. 11am-4pm. Museum open Tues.-Sun. 9-11:30am and 1-4:30pm; Nov.-March Tues.-Sun. 11am-4pm; museum DM4, students DM3.) A set of 48 chromatically tuned bronze bells rings across the landscape daily at 9:05am, 12:05, and 5:05pm. The **Schloßgarten** possesses intricate pathways, ivy-canopied benches, and old town walls, forming a secluded haven for romance (open daily until 9pm). Sweetly tucked behind the *Schloßgarten* is the **Pompejanum,** a Pompeii-style structure built for Ludwig I in the mid-19th century (open Tues.-Sun. 10am-12:30pm and 1:30-5:30pm; DM3, students DM2). Walking south on Schloßgasse, turn left at Dalbergstr. to find the famous **Stiftskirche St. Peter and Alexander.** The repository of a millennium of cultural history, the collection includes a 10th-century crucifix, Mathias Grünewald's painting *Beweinung Christi* (Mourning of Christ), and Vischer's *Magdalenenaltar* (open Wed.-Mon. 10am-1pm and 2pm-5pm. DM3, students DM2). Continuing down Dalbergstr. as it becomes Sandgasse, beautiful *Fachwerkhäuser* (half-timbered houses) pepper the path to the **Sandkirche,** a carefully preserved 1756 Rococo church—undamaged durign World War II. For acute cases of cutesy church nausea, the **Rosso Bianco Automuseum,** Obernauerstr. 125, specializes in two-seater cars; the collection includes over 200 rare and unique automobiles from all over the world, including Alfa Romeos, Porsches, and Ferraris (open April-Oct. Tues.-Sun. 10am-6pm, Nov.-March Sun. 10am-6pm; DM10, students DM6). Motor over on bus #1 (a Mercedes-Benz bus!) from the train station.

Just past the tightly packed *Altstadt* lie the famous **Schönbusch Gardens** and the newly reopened **Schloß Schönbusch,** a country house built between 1778 and 1780 for the archbishop of Mainz. The view from the second-floor **Chamber of Mirrors** (preserved from the original house and hence a bit distorted) reveals the surrounding city basking in the rich backdrop of the Spessart forests. The archbishop allowed no vegetation between his summer home and Schloß-Johannisburg (3km away), and the two castles remain in that aristocratic see-you-see-me stance today (castle open mid-March to mid-Oct. Tues.-Sun. 10am-12:30pm and 1:30-4:30pm. Admission and tour DM4, students DM3). The park itself was built by Elector Friedrich Karl Joseph in 1775 as an experiment in the novel English style of landscape architecture involving "naturalized" tree-scaping. Embellished with artificial ponds, islands, and bridges, as well as tiny buildings like the **Freundschafts tempel** (friendship temple) and the **Philosophenhaus,** the park reeks of fairy tale fallacy. If that prince on a white horse never shows up, navigate yourself to the *Schloß* after **renting a boat** at the **Unterer** (rentals daily 10am-7pm; DM6 for 30min.). The **Irrgarten,** close to the restaurant at the park's entrance, is a maze formed by trimmed bushes, planted in 1829. To hedge the fate of the minotaur, climb the wooden tower-thing to gain an overhead view before tackling the labyrinth (open daily 9am-dusk). Watch out for David Bowie in tight, tight pants. Bus #4 or 52 from the main station (DM1.50 one-way).

Built on a high bank at a bend in the Main, Aschaffenburg is accessible by **trains** (every 30min.) from Frankfurt or Würzburg. To reach the *Schloß* and the **tourist office,** Schloßpl. 1 (tel. 39 58 00; fax 39 58 02), bear right on Ludwigstr. in front of the station and walk down Duccastr.; cross the street to take a left down Friedrichstr., then the next right down Erthalstr., and a final left onto Strickergstr. Stuck in an ultra-modern library, the office has free maps and a free room-finding service (open Mon.-Fri. 9am-5pm, Sat. 10am-1pm). For a 1½-hour **tour** of the town in German (DM4, under 12 free), meet in front of the tourist office on Sunday at 2pm. **Rent bikes** at **Bazoom Bikes 'n Boards,** Ohmbachsgasse 6 (tel. 135 51; fax 157 55). From the station, veer left onto Frohsinnstr., left again on Weißenburgerstr., and then a sharp right onto Roßmarkt; Bazoom will be on your right across from the Heylands brewery (open Mon.-Fri. 11am-6pm, Sat. 11am-4pm; DM20 per day; ID required; Visa accepted). A **laundromat, SB Waschsalon,** Beckerstr. 26, is on the corner of Kneippstr. close to the hostel (open Mon.-Sat. 9am-9pm; wash DM6, dry DM6, soap DM1). The **post office,** 63739 Aschaffenburg (tel. 36 90), left of the train station, exchanges currency (open Mon.-Fri. 7am-6pm, Sat. 8am-noon). The **telephone code** is 06021.

Aschaffenburg's **Jugendherberge (HI),** Beckerstr. 47 (tel. 93 07 63; fax 97 06 94), is reached from the station by bus #40 or 41: "Schroberstr." Head left up Kneippstr. and right onto Beckerstr.; the hostel is on the left. Try your luck at a little b-ball with the kids. (Reception open 8-9am, noon-1pm, and 5-7pm. Curfew 11:30pm. DM18.50. Breakfast included. Sheets DM5.50.) Just outside the pedestrian zone, the cheerful owner of **Hotel Pape Garni,** Würzburgerstr. 16 (tel. 226 73; fax 226 22), provides a home-cooked breakfast with her rooms. From the Schloßpl., follow Schloßgasse or Pfaffengasse and turn left onto Dalbergstr., which turns into Sandgasse and then into Würzburgerstr. (singles DM48; doubles DM85). The friendly **Goldener Karpfen,** Löherstr. 30 (tel. 239 46), provides a homey ambience and a "snug as a bug in a rug" bar in their hotel. (Singles DM50, with shower DM53; doubles with shower DM96; triples DM129. Breakfast included.) Hidden just inside the city wall, **Zum Roten Kopf** has mastered hearty food—strong enough for Bavarians, but made for tourists: daily specials include soup (DM12.50). From Schloßpl., walk down Schloßberg to the right of the tourist office and left on Suicardusstr. (open Wed.-Mon. 10am-midnight). Also convenient is the **Stadtschänke,** on your left as you exit the station. Daily menu options (DM7-15) include an entree and salad (open Mon.-Sat. 9am-midnight).

APPENDIX

HOLIDAYS AND FESTIVALS

Consult the German National Tourist Offices's publication *Forthcoming Events: 1998* for the dates of major trade fairs, art exhibitions, theater and music festivals, folk fairs, and sporting events. Each town's tourist office can provide specific information. Where possible, *Let's Go* lists specific 1998 dates in individual cities. Holidays in European countries are listed daily in the International Herald Tribune. Be aware of them, as banks, restaurants, stores, and museums may all close, potentially leaving you broke and hungry.

Date	Festival	Location
January-December	Gothic Year in Köln	Köln
January-December	350th Anniversary of the Peace of Westphalia	Münster, Osnabrück
January 1	New Year's Day (*Neujahrstag*)	National
January 6	Epiphany (*Heilige Drei Könige*)	National
February 17-24	Carnival (*Karneval*)	Köln, Düsseldorf, Mainz
February 27-March 3	Carnival (*Fasching*)	Munich
February 25	Ash Wednesday (*Aschermittwoch*)	National
Late February to Early March	Film Festival	Berlin
April 10	Good Friday (*Karfreitag*)	National
April 12	Easter Sunday (*Ostersonntag*)	National
April 13	Easter Monday (*Ostermontag*)	National
Late April to Late May	Spring Cathedral Festival (*Frühlingsdom*)	Hamburg
May 1	Labor Day (*Tag der Arbeit*)	National
May 8	Ascension Day (*Christ Himmelfahrt*)	National
May 17	Whit Sunday/Pentecost (*Pfingstsonntag*)	National
May 19	Whit Monday (*Pfingstmontag*)	National
May 29	Corpus Christi (*Fronleichnam*)	National
June-July	Art and Theater Festival	Weimar
Early June	Wine Festival	Würzburg
June 27-28	Christopher Street Day	Berlin
Late June to Early July	Film Festival	Munich
July 11	Love Parade	Berlin
July-August	Bach Festival	Leipzig
July-August	Film Festival	Dresden
August	Summer Cathedral Festival (*Sommerdom*)	Hamburg
August 7-17	Agricultural Festival (*Gäubodenvolksfest*)	Straubing
August 15	Assumption Day (*Maria Himmelfahrt*)	National

September 19-October 4	Oktoberfest	Munich
Late September to Early October	Wine Festival	Würzburg
October 3	Day of German Unity (*Tag der deutschen Einheit*)	National, *natürlich*
Late October	Film Festival	Leipzig
October 31	Reformation Day (*Reformationtag*)	National
November 1	All Saint's Day (*Allerheiligen*)	National
December	Winter Cathedral Festival (*Winterdom*)	Hamburg
December 25-26	Christmas (*Weihnachtstag*)	National

TEMPERATURE IN FOUR CITIES

The following chart gives the average temperatures in degrees centigrade (Celsius) during four months of the year.

Temp in °C	January	April	July	October
Berlin	0.0	11.0	21.1	10.0
Frankfurt a. M.	2.0	11.6	22.1	9.9
Hamburg	-0.4	9.0	20.0	9.6
Munich	2.1	11.8	22.3	10.4

To convert from °C to °F, multiply by 1.8 and add 32. For an approximation, double the Celsius and add 25. To convert from °F to °C, subtract 32 and multiply by 0.55.

°C	-5	0	5	10	15	20	25	30	35	40
°F	23	32	41	50	59	68	77	86	95	104

TIME ZONES

Germany uses West European time (abbreviated MEZ in German). Add six hours to Eastern Standard Time and one hour to Greenwich Mean Time. Subtract nine hours from Eastern Australia Time and 11 hours from New Zealand Time.

BUSINESS HOURS

Store hours in Germany have traditionally been maddeningly brief as a result of the *Ladenschlußgesetz* (store-closing law), which applies to most businesses. In June 1996, however, the *Bundestag* passed a bill allowing shops to expand their hours to 8pm on weekdays and 4pm on Saturdays (see **This Year in Germany,** p. 73). Yay! **Store hours** thus frequently run Monday-Friday 9am-8pm, Saturday 9am-4pm. Most stores should have expanded their hours, but don't count on these changes—many stores in smaller cities still cling to a schedule of Monday-Friday 9am-6pm, Saturday 9am-1pm. To avoid starvation after hours and on Sunday, try shops inside train stations in larger cities, which are allowed to remain open longer. Many smaller shops take a mid-day break (*Mittagspause*), usually noon-2pm. **Bank hours** are often extremely bizarre. In all but the biggest cities, it is unwise to put off financial chores until the weekend; many towns have no banks open between Saturday morning and Monday.

APPENDIX

TELEPHONE AREA CODES

Berlin	30
Bremen	421
Bonn	228
Dresden	351
Düsseldorf	211
Erfurt	361
Essen	201
Frankfurt	69
Freiburg	761

Göttingen	551
Hamburg	40
Hannover	511
Heidelberg	6221
Kassel	561
Kiel	431
Koblenz	261
Köln	221
Leipzig	341

Magdeburg	391
Munich	89
Nürnberg	911
Regensburg	941
Rostock	381
Saarbrücken	681
Schwerin	385
Stuttgart	711
Weimar	3643

When phoning from within Germany add a 0 before the telephone area codes listed above.

COUNTRY CODES

Australia	61
Austria	43
Canada	1

France	33
Germany	49
Spain	34

S. Africa	27
U.K.	44
U.S.	1

MEASUREMENTS

Germany uses the metric system. Germans also commonly use some traditional measurements, but they have been modified to match the metric system more closely. Thus, a *Pfund* is half a kilogram and a *Meil* is two kilometers. All you really need to know to get around is that a meter is a little more than a yard, a kilometer is five-eigths of a mile, a liter is a little more than a quart, a *Maß* is one liter (about the size of a 40 oz.), a kilogram is a little more than two pounds, and 100 grams of cheese or sausage is plenty for lunch. For more exact conversion you can refer to this handy table.

1 inch = 25 millimeter (mm)	1mm = 0.04 inch (in.)
1 foot = 0.30 meter (m)	1m = 3.33 foot (ft.)
1 yard = 0.91m	1m = 1.1 yard (yd.)
1 mile = 1.61kilometer (km)	1km = 0.62 mile (mi.)
1 ounce = 25 gram (g)	1g = 0.04 ounce (oz.)
1 pound = 0.45 kilogram (kg)	1kg = 2.22 pound (lb.)
1 quart = 0.94 liter (L)	1 liter = 1.06 quart (qt.)

ELECTRICAL CURRENT

Electricity is 220 volts AC, enough to fry any 110V North American appliance. 220V electrical appliances don't like 110V current, either. Visit a hardware store for an adapter (which changes the shape of the plug) and a converter (which changes the voltage). Don't make the mistake of using only an adapter unless appliance instructions explicitly state otherwise, or you'll melt your radio.

APPENDIX

LANGUAGE

Although the majority of the post-World War II generations in Germany speak English, you'll experience many real face-to-face encounters with people who don't—especially traveling in Eastern Germany. German is a very rigidly structured language, following strict grammatical rules. However, mastering the rules is quite an accomplishment in itself—"Life," Thomas Love Peacock said, "is too short to learn German." German uses three genders (*der, die,* and *das*), and has five ways of saying the simple (but oh-so-useful) word, "the." Before asking someone a question, always preface your query with a polite *"Sprechen Sie englisch?"* (Do you speak English?).

Pronunciation

Although you cannot hope to speak correct German without studying it, you can make yourself understood by learning only a little German. The first step is to master the pronunciation system. Unlike English, German pronunciation is consistent with spelling; once you learn the rules, everything is easy. There are no silent letters.

Consonants are pronounced as in English with the following exceptions: **C:** exists in German only in borrowed foreign words, and is pronounced like a K. **J:** always pronounced as a Y. **K:** always pronounced, even before an N. **P:** always pronounced, even before an F. **QU:** pronounced KV. **S:** pronounced as Z at the beginning of a word. **V:** pronounced as F. **W:** pronounced as V. **Z:** pronounced as TS.

The hissing, aspirant German CH sound, appearing in such basic words as "Ich" (I), "nicht" (not), and "sprechen" (to speak), is quite tricky for untrained English-speaking vocal cords. After A, O, U, or AU, it is pronounced as in the Scottish "loch." After other vowels, CH sounds like the English H in "huge" or "hubris" if you draw out this sound before saying the U. If you can't hack it, use an SH sound in the south and a KH sound in the north.

German has one consonant which does not exist in English, **the "ß";** which is alternately referred to as the *"scharfes S"* (sharp S) or the *"Ess-tsett."* It is simply a shorthand symbol for a **double-S,** and is pronounced just like an English "ss." It appears in two of the most important German words for travelers: *die Straße,* "the street," which is pronounced "SHTRAH-ssuh" and abbreviated "Str."; and *das Schloß,* "the castle," simply pronounced "SCHLOSS." Note that the use of the "ß" is slowly being elimated from modern German in an effort to standardize spelling and create less confusion for German schoolchildren learning the language (see **That "ß" Thing, Plus A Few Necessary German Words,** p. 61 and **Ess-terminate with Ess-treme Prejudice!,** p. 522).

German vowel and dipthong sounds are also pronounced differently: **A:** as in "father." **E:** like the A in "hay." **I:** like the EE in "creep." **O:** as in "oh." **U:** as in "fondue." **Y:** like the OO in "boot." **AU:** as in "sauerkraut." **IE:** as in "thief." **EI:** like the I in "wine." **EU:** like the OI in "boil."

An **umlaut** over a letter (e.g., Ü) changes the pronunciation. An umlaut is often replaced by an E following the vowel, e.g., "schön" becomes "schoen." In the speech of most Germans, Ä is the equivalent of an American long A (as in "hay"). To make the Ö sound, round your lips to say "oh," freeze them in that position, and try to say "a" as in "hay." To make the Ü sound, round your lips to say "ooh," freeze them in that position, and try to say "ee" instead. Germans are very forgiving towards foreigners who butcher their mother tongue. There is, however, one important exception—place names. If you learn nothing else in German, learn to pronounce the names of cities properly. Berlin is "bare-LEEN," Köln is "KURLN," Hamburg is "HAHM-boorg," Munich (München) is "MEUWN-khen."

Once you've learned a bit of German, you can appreciate the startling differences among dialects. When both speak in the vernacular, a *Kölner* and a *Münchener* cannot understand each another. The Austrian and Swiss German dialects diverge even more strongly from the *Hochdeutsch* (High German) of the north. In general, linguistic distinctions in Germany follow the same pattern as in the U.S.; southerners speak in a more relaxed fashion, while the northern style is harsh and refined, with fully enunciated consonant sounds. For the purposes of the traveler, the crucial distinction is that southerners say *"zwo"* (TSVO) instead of *"zwei"* for the number two.

Numbers, Dates, and Times

A space or period rather than a comma is used to indicate thousands, e.g., 10,000 is written 10 000 or 10.000. Instead of a decimal point, Germans use a comma, e.g., 3.1415 is written 3,1415. Months and days are written in the reverse of the American manner, e.g., 10.11.92 is November 10, not October 11. The numeral 7 is written with a slash through the vertical line, and the numeral 1 is written with an upswing, resembling an inverted "V." Note that the number in the ones place is pronounced before the number in the tens place; thus "zweihundertfünfundsiebzig" (TSVEI-hun-duhrt-fuhnf-oont-ZEEB-tsikh) is 275, *NOT* 257. This can be very hard to keep in mind.

The months in German are *Januar, Februar, März, April, Mai, Juni, Juli, August, September, Oktober, November, Dezember.* The days of the week are *Montag, Dienstag, Mittwoch, Donnerstag, Freitag, Samstag/Sonnabend,* and *Sonntag.* Germany uses the 24hr. clock for all official purposes: 8pm equals 20.00. Thus, *vierzehn Uhr* is 2pm, *fünfzehn Uhr* is 3pm, etc. When Germans say "half eight" (halb acht), they mean 7:30; "three quarters eight" (dreiviertel acht) means 7:45 and "quarter eight" (viertel acht) means 7:15.

PHRASEBOOK

Numbers

0	null	10	zehn	20	zwanzig
1	eins	11	elf	30	dreißig
2	zwei	12	zwölf	40	vierzig
3	drei	13	dreizehn	50	fünfzig
4	vier	14	vierzehn	60	sechzig
5	fünf	15	fünfzehn	70	siebzig
6	sechs	16	sechszehn	80	achtzig
7	sieben	17	siebzehn	90	neunzig
8	acht	18	achtzehn	100	ein hundert
9	neun	19	neunzehn	1000	tausend

English	German	Pronunciation

Basic Expressions

English	German	Pronunciation
Good morning/day/evening	Guten Morgen/Tag/Abend	(GOO-ten MOHR-gen/ tahg/AH-bend)
Good day (in Bavaria)	Grüss Gott	(grews goht)
Goodbye	Auf Wiedersehen/ Auf Wiederschauen	(Auf VEE-der-zane/ Auf VEE-d-er-show-en)
Hello	Hallo	(HAH-loh)
Please	Bitte	(BIT-tuh)
Thank you	Danke	(DAHN-kuh)
You're welcome.	Bitte	(BIT-tuh)
Excuse me.	Entschuldigung	(Ent-SHOOL-dee-gung)
Yes/No	Ja/Nein	(ya/nine)
I'm sorry.	Es tut mir leid.	(es toot meer lide)
I don't speak German.	Ich spreche kein deutsch.	(ikh SPRAY-shuh kine doytch)

Does anyone here speak English?	Spricht jemand hier englisch?	(sprikht YAY-mant heer AYN-glish?)
Can you help me?	Können Sie mir helfen?	(KUR-nen zee meer HEL-fen?)
I don't understand.	Ich verstehe nicht.	(ikh fair-SHTAY-uh nikht)
Do you understand?	Verstehen Sie?	(fair-SHTAY-en zee?)
How do you say ... in German?	Wie sagt man ... auf deutsch?	(vee zahgt mahn...auf doytch?)
I would like	Ich möchte	(ikh MURSH-tuh)
How much does ... cost?	Wieviel kostet?	(vee-feel KOHS-tet...?)
Where is ...?	Wo ist?	(Vo ist?)
When is ...?	Wann ist?	(Vann ist?)
At what time. . .?	Um wieviel Uhr. . .?	(oom vee-feel oor)
What time is it, please?	Wie spät es es, bitte?	(VEE SPAYT ist es, BIT-tuh?)
yesterday	gestern	(ges-tern)
today	heute	(HOY-tuh)
tomorrow	morgen	(mor-gen)
open	geöffnet	(geh-UHRF-net)
closed	geschlossen/zu	(geh-SCHLOSS-sen / tsoo)
left	links	(links)
right	rechts	(reckts)
straight ahead	geradeaus	(geh-RAH-duh-ows)
coming to terms with the past	Vergangenheitsbewältigung	(Fair-GAHNG-en-hights-be-VAYL-tee-gung)

Travel Necessities

ticket (for travel)	die Fahrkarte	(FAHR-kar-tuh)
ticket (theater, etc.)	die Karte	(KAR-tuh)
reservation	die Reservierung/ Vorbestellung	(Reh-zehr-FEER-oong/ FOAR-beh-SHTEL-oong)
one-way	Hinfahrt	(HIN-fahrt)
round-trip	Hin- und Rückfahrt	(HIN- und RUKE-fahrt
arrival/departure	Ankunft /Abfahrt	(AHN-kunft/AHB-fahrt)
train	der Zug	(tsoog)
train station	der Bahnhof	(BON-hohf)
main train station	der Hauptbahnhof	(HOWPT-bahn-hohf)
bus station	der Busbahnhof	(BUES-bahn-hohf)
airplane	das Flugzeug	(FLOOK-tsoyg)
airport	der Flughafen	(FLOOK-half-en)
(train) track	das Gleis	(glice)
train platform	der Bahnsteig	(BAHN-shteig)
airport gate	der Flugsteig	(FLOOK-shteig)
bus	der Bus	(bues)
(bus, subway) stop	die Haltestelle	(HAHL-tuh-shtel-luh)
entrance/exit	der Eingang /Ausgang	(der EIN-gang /AUS-gang)
hospital	das Krankenhaus	(KRONK-en-hows)
police	die Polizei	(poe-lee-TSEI)
Help!	Hilfe!	(HILL-fuh!)

I am tipsy.	Ich bin beschwippst.	(ikh bin beh-SHVIPST)
I am drunk.	Ich bin betrunken.	(ikh bin BETROONKEN)
My goodness! I'm wasted.	Um Gottes Willen! Ich bin besoffen!	(oom GOET-tes VIL-len! ikh bin be-ZOF-fen!)
I am sick.	Ich bin krank.	(ikh bin kronk.)
toilet	die Toilette/W.C.	(toi-LET-tuh/vay-SAY)
shower	die Dusche	(DOO-shuh)
youth hostel	die Jugendherberge	(YOO-gend-hair-BAIR-guh)
campground	der Campingplatz	(CAMP-ing-plats)
post office	die Post	(post)
tourist office	der Verkehrsamt/	(Fair-KAYR-zahmt/
	Verkehrsverein	Fair-KAYRZ-fair-ein)
cathedral	der Dom	(dohm)
palace	das Schloß	(shloss)
church	die Kirche	(KEER-shuh)
old city	die Altstadt	(AHLT-shtahtt)
theater	das Theater	(tay-AH-ter)
waiter/waitress	der Kellner/die Kellnerin	(KELL-ner/KELL-ner-in)
beer	das Bier	(beer)
sausage	die Wurst	(voorst)
My intestines feel like jelly. I think I ate too much sausage.	Mein Gedärme sind gallertartige Masse. Ich denke, daß ich zu viel Wurst gegessen habe.	(mine ge-DAYR-muh zind gall-ler-TART-ig-guh MASS-suh. ikh DEN-kuh, dass ikh tsoo feel voorst ge-gess-en HAB-uh)
bread	das Brot	(broht)
water/ tap water	das Wasser/Leitungswasser	(VAS-ser / LEI-toongz-vas-ser)
cheese	der Käse	(KAY-zuh)
breakfast	das Frühstück	(FREW-stewk)
lunch	das Mittagsessen	(MIT-tahgs-ess-en)
supper	das Abendessen	(AH-bend-ess-en)

Making Reservations by Phone

Phone greeting:	Guten Tag!	(GU-ten tahg)
Do you speak English?	Sprechen Sie englisch?	(SPRAY-ken zee AYN-glish?)
Do you have a room free?	Haben Sie ein Zimmer frei?	(HAH-ben zee ein TSIM-mer frei?
single room/double room	Einzelsimmer/Doppelzimmer	(EIN-stel-tsim-mer/DOHP-pehl-tsim-mer)
for tonight?	für heute abend?	(fewr HOY-tuh AH-bend?)
for tomorrow?	für morgen?	(fewr MOR-gen)
for a day / for 2 days?	für einen Tag/zwei Tage	(fewr EIN-nen tahg/TSVEI tah-guh?)
from the 4th of July. . .	vom vierten Juli. . .	(vom FEER-ten YOO-lee)
until the 6th of July?	bis zum sechsten Juli?	(bis tsum ZECK-sten YOO-lee)
with bathroom/shower?	mit W.C./Dusche?	(mit vay-SAY/doo-shuh)
My name is. . .	Ich heiße. . .	(ikh HIGH-suh)
I'm coming immediately	Ich komme gleich	(ikh KUM-muh glishe)
I'm coming at 8am/8pm	Ich komme um acht Uhr am Morgen/Abend	(ikh KUM-muh uhm ackt uhr am MOR-gen/AH-bend)
No, we're booked/full.	Nein, es ist alles besetzt/voll/ komplett	(nine, es ist all-es be-zetst/foll/ kom-plett)

Index

★Let's Go 1998 Reader Questionnaire

> Please fill this out and return it to **Let's Go, St. Martin's Press,** 175 Fifth Ave., New York, NY 10010-7848. All respondents will receive a free subscription to *The Yellowjacket,* the Let's Go Newsletter.

Name: _____

Address: _____

City: _____ **State:** _____ **Zip/Postal Code:** _____

Email: _____ **Which book(s) did you use?** _____

How old are you? under 19   19-24   25-34   35-44   45-54   55 or over

Are you (circle one)   in high school   in college   in graduate school   employed   retired   between jobs

Have you used Let's Go before? yes no **Would you use it again?** yes no

How did you first hear about Let's Go? friend   store clerk   television   bookstore display   advertisement/promotion   review   other

Why did you choose Let's Go (circle up to two)? reputation budget focus   price   writing style   annual updating   other: _____

Which other guides have you used, if any? Frommer's $-a-day   Fodor's   Rough Guides   Lonely Planet   Berkeley   Rick Steves   other: _____

Is Let's Go the best guidebook? yes no

If not, which do you prefer? _____

Please rank each of the following parts of Let's Go 1 to 5 (1=needs improvement, 5=perfect). packaging/cover   practical information   accommodations   food   cultural introduction   sights   practical introduction ("Essentials")   directions   entertainment   gay/lesbian information   maps   other: _____

How would you like to see the books improved? (continue on separate page, if necessary) _____
_____

How long was your trip?   one week   two weeks   three weeks   one month   two months or more

Which countries did you visit? _____

What was your average daily budget, not including flights? _____

Have you traveled extensively before? yes no

Do you buy a separate map when you visit a foreign city? yes no

Have you seen the Let's Go Map Guides? yes no

Have you used a Let's Go Map Guide? yes no

If you have, would you recommend them to others? yes no

Did you use the Internet to plan your trip? yes no

Would you use a Let's Go: recreational (e.g. skiing) guide   gay/lesbian guide   adventure/trekking guide   phrasebook   general travel information guide

Which of the following destinations do you hope to visit in the next three to five years (circle one)? South Africa   China   South America   Russia   Caribbean   Scandinavia   other: _____

Where did you buy your guidebook?   Internet   chain bookstore   independent bookstore   college bookstore   travel store   other: _____

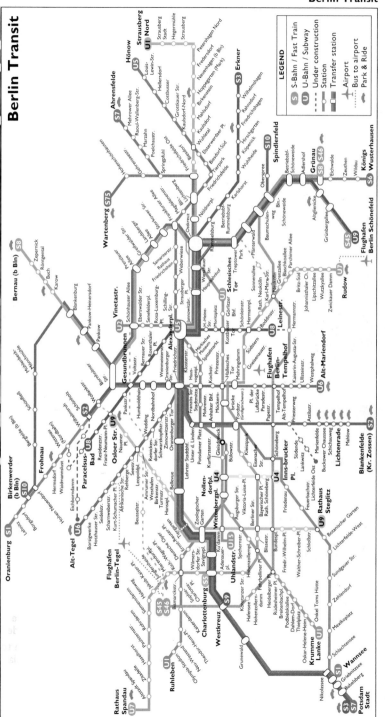

Berlin Transit

Munich Transit

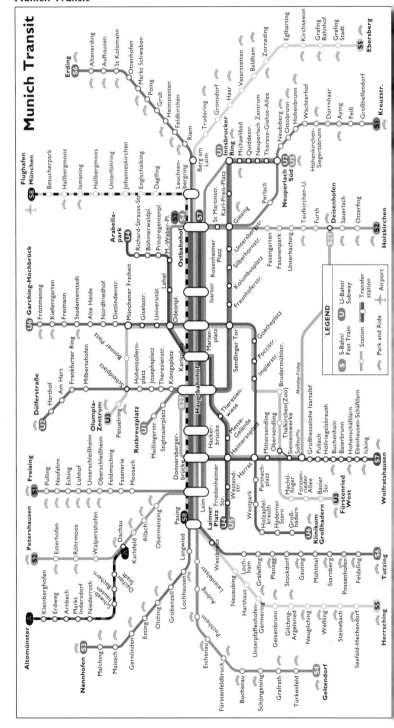

Hamburg Transit

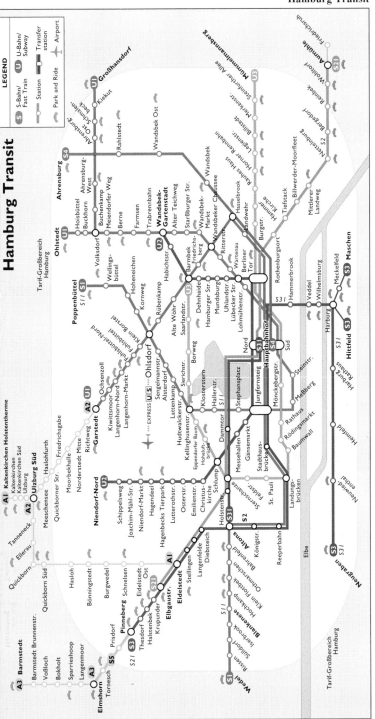

Frankfurt Transit

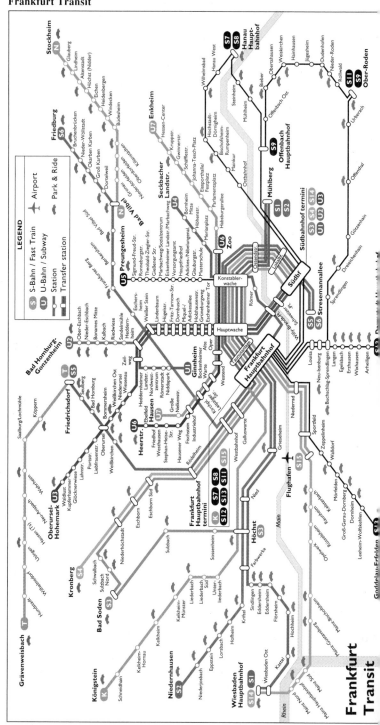

Frankfurt Transit